Understanding Psychology

EIGHTH EDITION

Understanding Psychology

Robert S. Feldman
University of Massachusetts–Amherst

Boston   Burr Ridge, IL   Dubuque, IA   New York   San Francisco   St. Louis
Bangkok   Bogotá   Caracas   Kuala Lumpur   Lisbon   London   Madrid   Mexico City
Milan   Montreal   New Delhi   Santiago   Seoul   Singapore   Sydney   Taipei   Toronto

The McGraw·Hill Companies

Mc Graw Hill Higher Education

UNDERSTANDING PSYCHOLOGY
Published by McGraw-Hill, an imprint of The McGraw-Hill Companies, Inc., 1221 Avenue of the Americas, New York, NY 10020. Copyright © 2008, 2005, 2002, 1999, 1996, 1993, 1990, 1987 by the McGraw-Hill Companies, Inc. All rights reserved. No part of this publication may be reproduced or distributed in any form or by any means, or stored in a database or retrieval system, without the prior written consent of The McGraw-Hill Companies, Inc., including, but not limited to, in any network or other electronic storage or transmission, or broadcast for distance learning. Some ancillaries, including electronic and print components, may not be available to customers outside the United States.

This book is printed on acid-free paper.

1 2 3 4 5 6 7 8 9 0 DOW/DOW 0 9 8 7 6

ISBN: 978-0-07-353193-9
MHID: 0-07-353193-6

Editor in Chief: Emily Barrosse
Publisher: Beth Mejia
Executive Editor: Suzanna Ellison
Senior Development Editor: Judith Kromm
Development Editor, Supplements: Meghan Campbell
Editorial Assistant: Charon Kraus
Executive Marketing Manager: Sarah Martin
Media Producer: Alexander Rohrs
Production Editors: Melissa Williams and Lake Lloyd, EPS Inc., NYC
Manuscript Editor: Dawn Adams
Art Director: Jeanne M. Schreiber
Cover Design: Cassandra Chu and Irene Morris
Interior Design: Ellen Pettengell
Lead Production Supervisor: Randy Hurst
Illustrators: John Waller, Judy Waller, Kara Fellows, Sally Sturman
Photo Research: Toni Michaels, PhotoFind
Cover photos: Front: © Royalty-Free/Corbis; Back (left to right): © Elizabeth Young/Stone/Getty Images, © Simon Marcus/ Corbis, © Derek Lebowski/The Image Bank/Getty Images, © Royalty-Free/ Corbis, © Royalty-Free/Corbis

Psychology Advisory Board:
Melissa Acevedo, Westchester Community College
Jennifer Brooks, Collin County Community College
Jeffrey Green, Virginia Commonwealth University
Holly Haynes, Georgia Perimeter College
Julie Bauer Morrison, Glendale Community College
Phil Pegg, Western Kentucky University
Tammy Rahhal, University of Massachusetts, Amherst
Tanya Renner, University of Hawaii
Carla Strassle, York College of Pennsylvania
Jim Stringham, University of Georgia

This book was set in 9.5/12 Palatino by Electronic Publishing Services, Inc. and printed on 45# Pub Thin Bulk by R.R. Donnelley and Sons.

Photo and text credits can be found following the References on page C-1, a continuation of the copyright page.

Library of Congress Control Number: 2006459800

www.mhhe.com

To
Jonathan, Leigh, Joshua, Sarah,
and Kathy

About the Author

ROBERT S. FELDMAN is Associate Dean of the College of Social and Behavioral Sciences and Professor of Psychology at the University of Massachusetts at Amherst. Feldman, a winner of the College Distinguished Teacher award, has also taught courses at Mount Holyoke College, Wesleyan University, and Virginia Commonwealth University.

Feldman, who initiated the Minority Mentoring Program, teaches introductory psychology to classes ranging in size from 20 to nearly 500 students. He also has served as a Hewlett Teaching Fellow and Senior Online Teaching Fellow, and he frequently gives talks on the use of technology in teaching. He initiated distance learning courses in psychology at the University of Massachusetts.

A Fellow of the American Psychological Association and the Association for Psychological Science, Feldman received a B.A. with High Honors from Wesleyan University and an M.S. and Ph.D. from the University of Wisconsin–Madison. He is a winner of a Fulbright Senior Research Scholar and Lecturer award, and has written more than 100 books, book chapters, and scientific articles. His books include *Fundamentals of Nonverbal Behavior, Development of Nonverbal Behavior in Children, Social Psychology, Development Across the Life Span,* and *P.O.W.E.R. Learning: Strategies for Success in College and Life,* and they have been translated into a number of languages, including Spanish, French, Portuguese, Dutch, Chinese, and Japanese. His research interests include honesty and deception and the use of nonverbal behavior in impression management, and his research has been supported by grants from the National Institute of Mental Health and the National Institute on Disabilities and Rehabilitation Research.

Feldman's spare time is most often devoted to serious cooking and earnest, if not entirely expert, piano playing. He also loves to travel. He has three children and lives with his wife Kathy, who is also a psychologist, overlooking the Holyoke mountain range in Amherst, Massachusetts.

Brief Contents

APPENDIX | # Going by the Numbers: Statistics in Psychology A-1

Contents

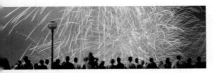

CHAPTER 5
States of Consciousness 144

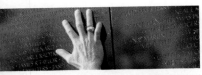

CHAPTER 11

Sexuality and Gender 354

CHAPTER 12

Development 396

CHAPTER 13

Personality 450

CHAPTER 14

Health Psychology: Stress, Coping, and Well-Being 484

CHAPTER 15

Psychological Disorders 514

CHAPTER 16

Treatment of Psychological Disorders 554

CHAPTER 17

Social Psychology 584

Preface

Students first.

If I were to use only a few words to summarize my goal for this book, as well as my teaching philosophy, that's what I would say. I believe that an effective textbook must be oriented to students—informing them, engaging them, exciting them about the field, and expanding their intellectual capabilities. When students are engaged and challenged, they understand psychology at a deep and meaningful level. Only then are they able to learn and retain the material.

Luckily, psychology is a science that is inherently interesting to students. It is a discipline that speaks with many voices, offering a personal message to each student. To some, psychology provides a better understanding of others' behavior. Some view psychology as a pathway to self-understanding. Still others see the potential for a future career, and some are drawn to psychology by the opportunity for intellectual discovery that its study provides.

No matter what brings students into the introductory course and regardless of their initial motivation, *Understanding Psychology*, Eighth Edition, is designed to draw students into the field and stimulate their thinking. This revision integrates a variety of elements that foster students' understanding of psychology and its impact on our everyday lives. It also provides instructors with a fully integrated assessment package to objectively gauge their students' mastery of psychology's key principles and concepts.

A Framework for Learning and Assessment

Understanding Psychology, Eighth Edition, is the core of a learning-centered multimedia package that comprises a complete framework for learning and assessment. Conforming to recommendations of a 2002 APA task force report on undergraduate student competencies (Board of Educational Affairs, 2002), *every* component of the package is tied to specific psychological concepts and their application in everyday life. Though the book forms the core of this framework, its power to enrich and empirically demonstrate learning is expanded through a unique library of electronic activities with concept-based quizzes, all developed to accompany this text. Instructors can create a seamless, custom set of assignments from the available resources, or they can opt for a traditional, text-based approach, depending on their specific needs. A chart indicating how the features of the textbook directly address the APA student competencies is provided in Figure 1 on the following page. Equally important, every one of the thousands of test items in the Test Banks available to instructors is keyed to its corresponding APA competency in a document that is available on the Instructor's Resource CD-ROM.

PSYCHOLOGY AND EVERYDAY LIFE

Understanding Psychology, Eighth Edition, provides broad coverage of the field of psychology, including the theories, research, and applications that permeate the discipline. Along with the traditional areas of psychology (behavioral neuroscience, sensation and

Book Feature	APA Learning Goals									
	Knowledge Base of Psychology	Research Methods in Psychology	Critical Thinking Skills in Psychology	Application of Psychology	Values in Psychology	Information and Technological Literacy	Communication Skills	Sociocultural and International Awareness	Personal Development	Career Planning and Development
Chapter Content	X	X	X	X	X	X	X	X	X	X
Prologue	X		X	X				X		
Looking Ahead	X	X	X		X					
Key Concepts	X		X	X				X		
PsychInteractive Prompts	X		X	X		X	X		X	X
Applying Psychology in the 21st Century	X	X		X				X	X	X
Exploring Diversity	X				X		X	X	X	
Running Glossary	X			X		X				
Becoming an Informed Consumer of Psychology	X	X		X	X		X		X	X
Recap/Evaluate/Rethink	X		X	X						
Looking Back	X		X	X		X	X			
Epilogue	X		X	X				X		
Mastery Reviews	X	X	X	X		X		X		

FIGURE 1 This grid shows the relationship between the broad learning goals devised by the American Psychological Association and specific types of content in *Understanding Psychology*. In addition, each of the test items in the Test Bank for the book, consisting of nearly 4,000 individual, scorable items, is keyed to specific learning outcomes.

perception, states of consciousness, learning, memory, cognition, human development, personality, abnormal behavior and treatment, and social psychology), the applied topics of gender, sexuality, and health psychology receive extensive attention.

Putting students first and teaching them the science of psychology by helping them make the connection between psychology and everyday life has been a goal of this text from its first edition. The prologues that open each chapter, together with *Becoming an Informed Consumer of Psychology* sections, *Applying Psychology in the 21st Century* boxes, and examples presented throughout the text, help students see the real benefits of psychological research. For the Eighth Edition, we have extended this theme to *PsychInteractive Online* exercises and assessments and to the Online Learning Center, allowing students to hone the ability to apply psychological concepts to everyday situations.

CHAPTER AND MODULAR FORMAT

The book contains 17 numbered chapters and an appendix covering the major areas of psychology. Each chapter is divided into 3 or more short modules, a format that was introduced in the last edition and a change that has proven highly popular. Rather than facing a long and potentially daunting chapter, students can study material in smaller chunks, which psychological research long ago found to be the optimal way to learn. Moreover, instructors can customize assignments for their students by asking them to read only those modules that fit their course outline and in the sequence that matches their syllabus. Alternatively, instructors who prefer to assign whole chapters can do so.

At the beginning of each module, one or more questions introduce the key concepts covered in the module. To reinforce key concepts, a series of online multimedia exercises and self-tests can be found on the Online Learning Center for the text (www.mhhe.com/feldmanup8), by linking to *PsychInteractive Online*. In the text, references and icons direct students to these activities.

For example, consider the key concept of communication between neurons. The text presentation of this concept includes a verbal explanation and figures plus a text reference and marginal icon prompting students to complete a *PsychInteractive Online* activity on the nature of neural communication and a follow-up quiz. Additionally, the Online Learning Center provides review exercises and links to other Web sites that offer further information relevant to the key concepts and content for that section.

PSYCHOLOGY AND EVERYDAY LIFE

Putting students first and teaching them the science of psychology by helping them make the connection between psychology and everyday life has been a goal of this text from its first edition. The prologues that open each chapter, together with *Becoming an Informed Consumer of Psychology* sections, *Applying Psychology in the 21st Century* boxes, and examples presented throughout the text, help students see the real benefits of psychological research. I have extended this theme to *PsychInteractive Online* exercises and assessments and to the Online Learning Center to encourage students to apply psychological concepts to everyday situations.

PSYCHINTERACTIVE ONLINE

Each interactive exercise in this multimedia learning tool, accessible through the Online Learning Center, includes assessment items tied to the key concepts, and instructors can elect to have the results of these concept quizzes incorporated into any of the major course management systems. Embedding assessment tools in every exercise allows both students and instructors to track progress in mastering key concepts in a way that has not been possible until now.

www.mhhe.com/feldmanup8
PsychInteractive Online

Additionally, suggestions for using the activities can be found in the Instructor's Manual, and questions based on them are included in the Test Banks. These resources, combined with other features of the book and the supplements package, comprise a complete framework for learning and assessment of key concepts.

VISUAL MASTERY REVIEWS

New to this edition are reviews of five key concepts to help students master the difficult concepts in the course. These mastery sections follow the chapters in which the concepts are presented. Their format is more visual than verbal. They include self-assessment questions so that students can assess their understanding of these important topics, which were identified as challenging by classroom instructors, reviewers, survey respondents, and students:

- Mastering the difference between dependent and independent variables in experimental research (p. 56)
- Mastering the action potential (p. 94)
- Mastering the difference between sensation and perception (p. 142)
- Mastering the difference between reinforcement and punishment (p. 214)
- Mastering attitude change (p. 620)

Content Changes in the Eighth Edition

This edition incorporates a significant amount of new and updated information, reflecting the advances in the field and the suggestions of reviewers. *Well over 1000 new citations have been added, and most of them refer to articles and books published after 2000.* For instance, studies in aggression and modeling from media and computer games, brain and behavior, human genome mapping, cognition, emotions, and cultural approaches to psychological phenomena receive expanded coverage. Additionally, this edition incorporates a wide range of new topics. The following sample of new and revised topics provides a good indication of the book's currency.

(1) Introduction to Psychology
- Historical forces (e.g., Locke and *tabula rasa*)
- Barriers faced by women
- Counseling psychology
- Functionalism
- Ebbinghaus and Wertheimer
- New Prologue on Hurricane Katrina and its aftermath
- New material on "psychology matters"
- New Rethink questions relating to careers (in every module in book)

(2) Psychological Research
- Drawbacks to case studies
- Implicit Association Test
- New prologue on bystander intervention
- Extended example of scientific method
- Scientific method and communication of results
- Statistically-significant difference
- Revised research methods summary table

(3) Neuroscience and Behavior
- TMS (Transcranial Magnetic Stimulation)
- fMRI scans
- Evolutionary psychology and behavioral genetics
- Gene therapy and genetic counseling
- Stem cell research and controversy
- Evolution, behavioral genetics, molecular genetics
- Neuroplasticity
- Oxytocin and trust
- Neuroforensics

(4) Sensation and Perception
- Individual without pain sensations
- Technologies for restoring sight and sound
- Revamped moon illusion explanation
- Gender differences in pain perception
- Genetic causes of pain sensitivity
- Umami taste
- Interaction of senses
- Synesthesia

(5) States of Consciousness
- New prologue on sleep
- Caveats on use of forensic hypnosis
- Methamphetamine use
- Expanded sleep and drug sections
- Therapy for insomnia

(6) Learning
- Positive and negative punishment
- Extended examples of negative reinforcement
- Stimulus discrimination
- PTSD and classical conditioning
- Evolved fear module in brain for learning specific associations
- Allergic reactions as a conditioned response
- Habituation
- learned taste aversion term
- "Scalloping effect" for fixed-interval schedules
- Application of conditioning in rats to discover land mines
- Table comparing classical and operant conditioning
- New prologue on helper monkey

(7) Memory
- False memory material
- Implicit memory
- Semantic memory
- Stress and working memory
- Biological aspects of memory
- Use of drugs to eliminate traumatic memories

(8) Cognition and Language
- Representativeness heuristic
- Artificial intelligence
- Neuroscientific approach to language
- New prologue on inventiveness
- Neuropsychology of creativity
- Cross-cultural evidence on linguistic relativity hypothesis

(9) Intelligence
- Fetal alcohol syndrome
- Sternberg three-part conception of intelligence
- Web-based testing and importance of reliability, validity

(10) Motivation and Emotion
- Fat cells and obesity set point
- Dialect theory of emotional expressivity
- Television viewing and obesity

(11) Sexuality and Gender
- Transgenderism and transsexualism
- Sexually transmitted infections
- Imaging studies of brain during sexual arousal
- Stereotypes regarding working mothers

(12) Development
- *In vitro* fertilization
- GIFT and ZIFT
- gene therapy
- cloning
- sensitive periods
- fetal alcohol syndrome and fetal alcohol effects
- cultural differences in children's play
- medical consensus on use of hormone therapy for menopause symptoms

(13) Personality
- Horney
- Jung
- Reconciliation of Freud and neuroscientific evidence
- Use of tests in employment decisions
- Downside of high self-esteem

(14) Health Psychology
- Health and loneliness in college students
- Hostility in Type A behavior pattern in relationship with coronary heart disease
- Stress module reorganization
- Positive illusions
- Career-related information on health psychology
- Individual differences in coping
- Emotions and immune system response

(15) Psychological Disorders
- Terrorist suicide bombers
- Definition of abnormal behavior
- Onset of schizophrenia
- Glutamate and schizophrenia
- Brain scans of depressives
- Type I and Type II schizophrenia

(16) Treatment of Psychological Disorders
- Transcranial Magnetic Stimulation (TMS)
- Gestalt therapy
- Dialectical behavior therapy
- Gene therapy and psychological disorders

(17) Social Psychology
- Collectivistic/individualistic orientation
- Thin slices of behavior and impression formation
- Stereotype threat

STUDENTS FIRST: THE BOTTOM LINE

Based on extensive student feedback, systematic research involving a wide range of instructors, and endorsements received from reviewers at a variety of schools, I am confident that this edition reflects what instructors want and need: a book that motivates students to understand and apply psychology to their own lives. *Understanding Psychology*, Eighth Edition, is designed to expose readers to the content—and promise—of psychology, and to do so in a way that will nurture students' excitement about psychology and keep their enthusiasm alive for a lifetime.

State-of-the-Art Support Materials for Students and Instructors

Resources available for use with this text support both new and veteran instructors, whether they favor traditional text-based instruction or a blend of traditional and electronic media. The eighth edition text and support materials provide complementary experiences for instructors and students. All of these components are built around the core concepts articulated in the text to promote a deeper understanding of psychology. This type of integration gives instructors the flexibility to use any of the text-specific electronic or print materials knowing they are completely compatible with one another.

FOR STUDENTS AND INSTRUCTORS

Online Learning Center. The Student Center of the companion Web site for *Understanding Psychology,* Eighth Edition (www.mhhe.com/feldmanup8), includes an array of module-by-module study aids, such as detailed outlines, flashcards, and self-quizzes (created by Dave Alfano of The Community College of Rhode Island). Here students will also find a link to *PsychInteractive Online,* a Web-based library of multi-media interactivities and assessments developed to promote mastery of key concepts. All material on the Student Center, including *PsychInteractive Online,* is accessible without a password.

The password-protected Instructor's Online Learning Center contains all materials on the Student Center, downloadable versions of the Instructor's Manual and PowerPoint presentation slides, a variety of other text-specific resources—including a gallery of more than 100 figures from the text—and access to our acclaimed course Web site creation tool, Page Out! Instructors in need of assistance with any of these offerings can contact their McGraw-Hill sales representative via e-mail through the Online Learning Center. Visit us at www.mhhe.com/feldmanup8.

All of the electronic content for *Understanding Psychology,* Eighth Edition, is available for Blackboard and WebCT course management systems. McGraw-Hill is also able to offer this material for other learning management systems. For details, contact a McGraw-Hill sales representative.

FOR STUDENTS

PsychInteractive Online. Accessible through the text's Online Learning Center (www.mhhe.com/feldmanup8), *PsychInteractive Online* features activities related to key concepts in every chapter and more than 70 conceptual self-tests. For each concept, students can also create and print a personalized study page.

Study Guide by Rachel August of California State University, Sacramento, with **ESL** component by Lisa Valentino of Seminole Community College. The printed Study Guide contains a comprehensive review of the text material. Features include text overviews plus multiple-choice, fill-in-the-blank, matching, and short answer questions for each module. An answer key provides answers to all of the exercises in a chapter, along with feedback for all multiple-choice items. Also in the study guide is material created to help speakers of other languages understand and retain course content.

FOR INSTRUCTORS

PrepCenter enables instructors to build classroom presentations whenever, wherever, and however they want. In one convenient online location, PrepCenter offers figures from the textbook, PowerPoint presentations for each key concept, dozens of video clips embedded in PowerPoint slides, and animations explaining biological and other difficult concepts. Each is ready to use or to drop into a PowerPoint slideshow or your course Web page. Individual resources can be researched by chapter, by concept, or by type of media. Access PrepCenter through the Instructor's Online Learning Center (www.mhhe.com/feldmanup8).

Instructor's Resource CD-ROM. The Instructor's Resource CD-ROM (IRCD) contains essential instructor's resources for *Understanding Psychology,* Eighth Edition, in a flexible format. An easy-to-use interface for the design and delivery of multimedia classroom presentations makes the Instructor's Manual, two Test Banks (in both Word and computerized formats), PowerPoint presentation slides, and Image Gallery very customizable. All IRCD materials, except the Test Banks, are also accessible through the Instructor's Online Learning Center.

Instructor's Manual by Susan Krauss Whitbourne, University of Massachusetts at Amherst. This comprehensive guide provides all the tools and resources instructors need to present and enhance their introductory psychology course. The Instructor's Manual contains detailed lecture launchers, learning objectives, interesting lecture and media presentation ideas, student assignments and handouts, as well as descriptions of the exciting new interactivities that have been developed for *PsychInteractive*. The many tips and activities in this manual can be used with any class, regardless of size or teaching approach.

Test Banks. Test Bank I by Jamie McMinn of Westminster College; Test Bank II by Joyce Bateman-Jones of Central Texas College. Both test banks incorporate the new content in *Understanding Psychology,* Eighth Edition. Each test bank contains more than 2000 multiple-choice items, classified by cognitive type and level of difficulty, and keyed to the appropriate key concept and page in the textbook. Fill-in-the-blank, matching, and short-answer questions are provided for all modules. Moreover, each of the thousands of test items is keyed to the APA core psychology competencies.

Computerized Test Banks. Available for Macintosh or Windows users, the computerized test banks (on the Instructor's Resource CD-ROM) make all the items from Test Bank I and II easily available to instructors who like to create their own tests. The test-generating program facilitates the selection of questions from the each test bank and the printing of tests and answer keys, and also allows instructors to import questions from other sources.

Optional Modules on Diversity and I/O Psychology. For instructors who like to incorporate lectures on diversity or industrial/organizational issues in their introductory psychology course, optional full-color modules on these topics can be packaged with students' copies of *Understanding Psychology,* Eighth Edition. The Diversity module, written by Mark H. Chae of William Paterson University, discusses the roots of diversity and addresses related issues, such as conflict and cooperation. The module on Industrial-Organizational Psychology broadly introduces this growing area of interest. Instructors may request these modules through their McGraw-Hill sales representative.

Image Gallery. More than 100 figures from the text can be found on the Instructor's Resource CD-ROM for use on the course Web site or in PowerPoint presentations. These images also can be downloaded from the Image Gallery on the Instructor's Online Learning Center.

Classroom Performance System Content by Donelson Forsyth of the University of Richmond. The Classroom Performance System (CPS) from eInstruction allows instructors to gauge immediately what students are learning during lectures. With CPS and student "clickers," available at a discount to adopters of *Understanding Psychology*, instructors can draw on the quiz and poll questions provided on the Instructor's Online Learning Center and on the Instructor's Resource CD-ROM (or craft their own), and get instant feedback, even from students who are reluctant to speak out in class. In addition, CPS facilitates taking attendance, giving and grading pop quizzes, and giving formal, printed class tests with multiple versions of the test using CPS for immediate grading.

Additional Resources for Introductory Psychology

Please see your McGraw-Hill sales representative for information on policy, price, and availability of the following supplements.

In-Class Activities Manual for Instructors of Introductory Psychology (by the Illinois State University team of Pat Jarvis, Cynthia Nordstrom, and Karen Williams). This activities manual covers every major topic in the course. Nineteen chapters include 58 separate activities, all of which have been used successfully in the authors' classes. Each activity includes a short description of the demonstration, the approximate time needed to complete the activity, the materials needed, step-by-step procedures, practical tips, and suggested readings related to the activity.

Annual Editions: Psychology 07/08 (edited by Karen Duffy, State University College—Geneseo). This annually updated reader provides convenient, inexpensive access to current articles selected from the best of the public press. Organizational features include an annotated listing of selected World Wide Web sites; an annotated table of contents; a topic guide; a general introduction; brief overviews for each section; a topical index; and an instructor's resource guide with testing materials.

Classic Edition Sources: Psychology, 4e (edited by Terry Pettijohn of Ohio State University—Marion). This reader provides more than 40 selections of enduring intellectual value—classic articles, book excerpts, and research studies—that have shaped the study of psychology and our contemporary understanding of it.

Taking Sides: Clashing Views on Controversial Psychological Issues, 14e (edited by Brent Slife of Brigham Young University). This reader presents current controversial issues in a debate-style format designed to stimulate student interest and develop critical thinking skills. Each issue is thoughtfully framed with an issue summary, an issue introduction, and a postscript. An instructor's manual with testing material is available for each volume.

COURSE MANAGEMENT SYSTEMS

WebCT and Blackboard. Populated **WebCT** and **Blackboard** course cartridges are available free upon adoption of a McGraw-Hill textbook. Contact your McGraw-Hill sales representative for details.

PageOut! Build your own course Web site in less than an hour. You don't have to be a computer whiz to create a Web site with this exclusive McGraw-Hill product. It requires no prior knowledge of HTML, no long hours of coding, and no design skills on your part. With PageOut, even the most inexperienced computer user can quickly and easily create a professional-looking course Web site. Simply fill in templates with your information and with content provided by McGraw-Hill, choose a design, and you've got a Web site specifically designed for your course. Best of all, it's free! Visit us at **www.pageout.net** to find out more.

VIDEO RESOURCES

Media Resources for Teaching Psychology (Available as a DVD + CD-ROM set or as 2 VHS Tapes + CD-ROM). This exciting set of video segments and interactivities was designed to provide instructors of introductory psychology with a set of lecture tools that will enhance student interest and involvement. Fifty video segments and 22 interactivities have been carefully edited and arranged for undergraduate instruction. Thirty-six of the video segments—more than 2½ hours of footage—are available either on DVD or on two VHS videocassettes, through an exclusive partnership McGraw-Hill has established with **The Discovery Channel Education**™. The other video segments (animations) and interactivities are available on an accompanying CD-ROM. The video segments range in length from under 5 minutes to 12 minutes. Detailed teaching notes provide a summary of the activity, suggestions on how to use it in class, and discussion questions.

McGraw-Hill Introduction to Psychology Videos. Taken from Films for Humanities & Sciences videos, each of these clips is 5 to 10 minutes in length and is designed to serve as a lecture launcher. Topics include gestalt theories, classic and operant conditioning, eyewitness testimony, language development, Piaget's preoperational stage, and schizophrenia.

Acknowledgments

One of the central features of *Understanding Psychology* is the involvement of both professionals and students in the review process. The eighth edition of *Understanding Psychology* has relied heavily—and benefited substantially—from the advice of instructors and students from a wide range of backgrounds.

I am extraordinarily grateful to the following reviewers, who provided their time and expertise to help insure that *Understanding Psychology,* Eighth Edition, reflects the best that psychology has to offer.

Bill Adler, *Collin County Community College*

Ronald Baenninger, *Temple University*

Michael Cortese, *College of Charleston*

Perry Fuchs, *University of Texas, Arlington*

Rebecca Holbrook, *Loyola Marymount University*

Julian Paul Keenan, *Montclair State University*

Mark Krause, *University of Portland*

Kim MacLin, *University of Northern Iowa*

Julie Bauer Morrison, *Glendale Community College*

Ron Mulson, *Hudson Valley Community College*

Brad Reburn, *Johnson County Community College*

Jennifer Stevens, *William & Mary*

Meral Topcu-LaCroix, *Ferris State University*

Thomas Weatherly, *Georgia Perimeter College*

Karen Yanowitz, *Arkansas State University*

Karen Yescavage, *Colorado State University, Pueblo*

Also central to this revision of *Understanding Psychology* were the recommendations of the *PsychInteractive* Advisory Board. The following Advisory Board members have provided valuable input during the development of *PsychInteractive Online* that have broadened the scope and effectiveness of the student activities.

Melissa Acevedo, *Valencia Community College*

Jennifer Brooks, *Collin County Community College*

Jeffrey Green, *Virginia Commonwealth University*

Holly Haynes, *Georgia Perimeter College*

Julie Bauer Morrison, *Glendale Community College*

Phil Pegg, *Western Kentucky University*

Tammy Rahhal, *University of Massachusetts, Amherst*

Tanya Renner, *University of Hawaii*

Carla Strassle, *York College of Pennsylvania*

Jim Stringham, *University of Georgia*

Many teachers along my educational path have shaped my thinking. I was introduced to psychology at Wesleyan University, where several committed and inspiring teachers—and in particular Karl Scheibe—conveyed their sense of excitement about the field and made its relevance clear to me. Karl epitomizes the teacher-scholar combination to which I aspire, and I continue to marvel at my good fortune in having such a role model.

By the time I left Wesleyan I could envision no other career but that of psychologist. Although the nature of the University of Wisconsin, where I did my graduate work, could not have been more different from the much smaller Wesleyan, the excitement and inspiration were similar. Once again, a cadre of excellent teachers—led, especially, by the late Vernon Allen—molded my thinking and taught me to appreciate the beauty and science of the discipline of psychology.

My colleagues and students at the University of Massachusetts at Amherst provide ongoing intellectual stimulation, and I thank them for making the university a fine place to work. Several people also provided extraordinary research and editorial help. In particular, I am grateful to my superb students, past and present, including Jim Tyler, Brent Weiss, and Chris Poirier. Finally, I am extremely grateful to John Graiff, whose hard work and dedication helped immeasurably on just about everything involving this book.

I also offer great thanks to the McGraw-Hill editorial team that participated in this edition of the book. Steve Debow's and Emily Barrosse's hands-on interest, as well as their friendship, helped the project at every critical juncture. I'm particularly grateful to Steve for appointing me Writer in Residence at McGraw-Hill's office in New York, facilitating the writing of this book while I was on sabbatical.

Publisher Beth Mejia created a creative, energetic, and supportive environment, and I am in awe of her enthusiasm, commitment, and extremely good ideas. I also thank the very able Judith Kromm, master-of-all-details-while-still-seeing-the-big-picture Developmental Editor on this edition. Judith does a fantastic job, and I'm lucky to have worked with her on this edition. I'm also pleased to welcome Executive Editor Suzanna Ellison to this edition of *Understanding Psychology*. I am very happy that someone with her motivation, intelligence, and good ideas has joined the team, and I look forward to working with her. Finally, every reader of this book owes a debt to Rhona Robbin, developmental editor on the earliest editions of *Understanding Psychology*. Her relentless pursuit of excellence helped form the core of this book, and she taught me a great deal about the craft and art of writing.

I am also grateful to the team that spent untold hours developing the teaching and learning tools that complement the book, including Art Kohn, Portland State University; Stephanie George, Media Producer; and my master-of-all-pedagogies colleague Susan Whitbourne, University of Massachusetts at Amherst. I am convinced their efforts have created an instructional framework that is boundary-breaking.

Central to the design, production, and marketing process were Manager of Publishing Services Melissa Williams, Lead Production Editor Lake Lloyd, Lead Production Supervisor Randy Hurst, and Designer Ellen Pettengell. Photo editor Toni Michaels did her usual superb job in choosing photos and, as always, was a pleasure to work with. I would also like to thank Executive Marketing Manager Sarah Martin for her enthusiasm and commitment to this project. I am proud to be a part of this world-class team.

Finally, I remain completely indebted to my family. My parents, Leah Brochstein and the late Saul D. Feldman, provided a lifetime foundation of love and support, and I continue to see their influence in every corner of my life. I am grateful, too, to Harry Brochstein, who has enriched my life and thinking in many ways.

My extended family also plays a central role in my life. They include, more or less in order of age, my nieces and nephews, my terrific brother, my brothers- and sisters-in-law, and Ethel Radler. Finally, my mother-in-law, the late Mary Evans Vorwerk, had an important influence on this book, and I remain ever grateful to her.

Ultimately, my children, Jonathan, Joshua, and Sarah; my daughter-in-law Leigh; and my wife, Katherine, remain the focal point of my life. I thank them, with immense love.

Robert S. Feldman
Amherst, Massachusetts

Using Understanding Psychology

If you're reading this page, you're probably taking an introductory psychology course. Maybe you're studying psychology because you've always been interested in what makes people tick. Or perhaps you've had a friend or family member who has sought assistance for a psychological disorder. Or maybe you have no idea what psychology is all about, but you know that taking introductory psychology would fulfill a degree requirement.

Whatever your motivation for taking the course and reading this book, here's my commitment to you: By the time you finish this text, you will have a better understanding of why people—including you—behave the way they do. You will know how, and why, psychologists conduct research and will have an understanding of the theories that guide their research. You will become acquainted with the breadth of the field and will obtain practical, useful information, as well as a wealth of knowledge that hopefully will excite your curiosity and increase your understanding of people's behavior.

To meet this commitment, *Understanding Psychology,* Eighth Edition, has been written with you, the reader, in mind. At every step in the development of the book, students and instructors have been consulted in an effort to identify the combination of learning tools that would maximize readers' ability to learn and retain the subject matter of psychology. The result is a book that contains features that will not only help you to understand psychology, but also make it a discipline that is part of your life.

Now it's your turn. You will need to take several steps to maximize the effectiveness of the learning tools in the book. These steps include familiarizing yourself with the scope and structure of the book, using the built-in learning aids, and employing a systematic study strategy.

Familiarize Yourself with the Scope and Organization of *Understanding Psychology*

Begin by reading the list of modules and skimming the detailed table of contents at the front of the book. From this exercise, you will get a sense of the topics covered and the logic behind the sequence of modules. Then take some time to flip through the book. Choose a section that looks particularly interesting to you, skim it, and see for yourself how the modules are laid out.

Each module provides logical starting and stopping points for reading and studying. You can plan your studying around the modules that cover a particular topic. For instance, if your instructor assigns a group of modules to read over the course of a week, you might plan to read and study one module each day, using later days in the week to review the material.

A Guide for Students

Use the Learning Aids Built into the Book

Once you have acquired a broad overview of *Understanding Psychology*, you are ready to begin reading and learning about psychology. Each chapter contains learning aids that will help you master the material.

KEY CONCEPTS Each module begins with the key concepts discussed in that section. The key concepts, phrased as questions, provide a framework for understanding and organizing the material that follows. They will also help you to understand what the important content is.

Key Concepts for Chapter 6

What is learning? ● How do we learn to form associations between stimuli and responses?

MODULE 17

Classical Conditioning
The Basics of Classical Conditioning
Applying Conditioning Principles to Human Behavior
Extinction
Generalization and Discrimination
Beyond Traditional Classical Conditioning: Challenging Basic Assumptions

What is the role of reward and punishment in learning? ● What are some practical methods for bringing about behavior [change] and in others?

MODULE 18

Operant Conditioning
Thorndike's Law of Effect
The Basics of Operant Conditioning
Positive Reinforcers, Negative Reinforcers, and Punishment
The Pros and Cons of Punishment: Why Reinforcement Beats Punishment

Prologue A Friend Named Minnie

The cell phone drops out of Craig Cook's lap and tumbles to the floor. The phone is his lifeline. Cook is quadriplegic—he lost the use of his legs and has only limited use of his arms after a 1996 car wreck....

But that's when Minnie springs to action. She pulls the cord to open her cage, scampers to the kitchen floor, grabs the phone, scales Cook's leg and puts it back on his lap. She climbs to his shoulder, nuzzles against his face and eagerly awaits her reward—a fingertip dab of peanut butter.

"How cool is that?" Cook says, beaming like a proud father. "My very own monkey...." An 18-year-old South American capuchin

monkey, Minnie is trained to help Cook do much of what his body won't allow him to do.

She's a 5-pound bundle of fur with big, brown, expressive eyes and tiny fingers that resemble a child's hands. She turns lights on and off, opens soda bottles and retrieves Hot Pockets from the microwave....

When Cook's left foot falls sideways on his wheelchair foot rest, he calls out, "Minnie. Foot."

She scampers over to the wheelchair, uses her strength to straighten his foot again, then climbs on his lap for her peanut butter reward.

He holds up his hand and Minnie responds with a strong high-five (Carpenter & Maciel, 2004, p. 1).

Looking Ahead

Minnie's expertise did not just happen, of course. It is the result of painstaking training procedures—the same ones that are at work in each of our lives, illustrated by our ability to read a book, drive a car, play poker, study for a test, or perform any of the numerous activities that make up our daily routine. Like Minnie, each of us must acquire and then refine our skills and abilities through learning.

Learning is a fundamental topic for psychologists and plays a central role in almost every specialty area of psychology. For example, a psychologist studying perception might ask, "How do we learn that people who look small from a distance are far away and not simply tiny?" A developmental psychologist might inquire, "How do babies learn to distinguish their mothers from other people?" A clinical psychologist might wonder, "Why do some people learn to be afraid

when they see a spider?" A social psychologist might ask, "How do we learn to believe that we've fallen in love?"

Each of these questions, although drawn from very different branches of psychology, can be answered only through an understanding of basic learning processes. In each case, a skill or a behavior is acquired, altered, or refined through experience.

Psychologists have approached the study of learning from several angles. Among the most fundamental are studies of the type of learning that is illustrated in responses ranging from a dog salivating when it hears its owner opening a can of dog food to the emotions we feel when our national anthem is played. Other theories consider how learning is a consequence of rewarding circumstances. Finally, several other approaches focus on the cognitive aspects of learning, or the thought processes that underlie learning.

PROLOGUE Each chapter begins with a Prologue and ends with an Epilogue. The Prologue sets the stage for the chapter, providing a brief account of a real-life event that is relevant to the content of the modules, and demonstrating why the material in the chapter is important.

LOOKING AHEAD The Looking Ahead sections, which follow the prologues, identify the key themes and issues addressed in the chapter.

www.mhhe.com/feldmanup8

PsychInteractive Online

Heuristics

ACTIVITY PROMPTS Throughout the book, you will find text references and marginal icons that will guide you to virtual activities that are part of a framework for learning surrounding the text. The multimedia and print components of this framework will help you fully understand the key concepts of psychology and show how psychology affects your everyday life. Go to the book's Web site (www.mhhe.com/feldmanup8), where you will find the link to *PsychInteractive Online,* which contains the visual activities and simulations, video and audio demonstrations, and mastery exercises that will enable you to achieve a richer and deeper understanding of the basic principles of the discipline.

APPLYING PSYCHOLOGY IN THE 21ST CENTURY

A box in each chapter describing psychological research that is being applied to everyday problems. Read these boxes to understand how psychology promises to improve the human condition, in ways ranging from the development of ways to reduce violence to explaining the behavior of suicide bombers.

APPLYING PSYCHOLOGY IN THE 21ST CENTURY

Virtual-Reality Therapy: Facing the Images of Fear

For therapist Hunter Hoffman and colleagues, the patient presented a particularly difficult case. For 20 years, the woman—nicknamed Miss Muffet—had suffered from an anxiety disorder in which she had profound spider phobia:

> She routinely fumigated her car with smoke and pesticides to get rid of spiders. Every night she sealed all her bedroom windows with duct tape after scanning the room for spiders. She searched for the arachnids wherever she went and avoided walkways where she might find one. After washing her clothes, she immediately sealed them inside a plastic bag to make sure they remained free of spiders (Hoffman, 2004, p. 58).

When Miss Muffet's fears began to prevent her from leaving home, she decided to seek therapy. What she found was a novel approach using virtual-reality therapy. In *virtual-reality therapy,* therapists use a computer to create a virtual-reality display of the feared object. The display projects an image of anxiety-producing situation onto the inside of a helmet visor, and the image moves according to head or hand movements (Wiederhold & Wiederhold, 2005a).

In this case, Miss Muffet saw a range of anxiety-producing images, beginning with a view of a realistic virtual tarantula in a virtual kitchen. She was asked to approach the image as close as possible using a handheld joystick. The goal of the first session was to come within a few feet of the tarantula.

In subsequent sessions, she wore a glove that created an image of her hand on the display. She was able to move her hand closer and closer to the tarantula until she (virtually) touched it, and the spider made a noise and scurried away. Still later, she was able to virtually touch the spider and later actually handle a furry toy spider.

Following the highly successful treatment, Miss Muffet allowed an actual tarantula to crawl up her arm for several minutes with only minor anxiety. Miss Muffet's results

Researcher Hunter Hoffman, holding a virtual spider near the face of a patient as part of virtual-reality phobia exposure therapy to reduce fear of spiders. In the virtual world called SpiderWorld, patients can reach out and touch a furry toy spider, adding tactile cues to the virtual image, creating the illusion that they are physically touching the virtual spider. (Photo Mary Levin, U.W., with permission from Hunter Hoffman, U.W.)

have been validated by subsequent research, which shows that virtual-reality therapy is highly effective with a variety of phobias (Garcia-Palacios, Hoffman, & Carlin, 2002; Wiederhold & Wiederhold, 2005a).

Virtual-reality therapy has been extended to treatment of posttraumatic stress disorder (PTSD). For instance, a woman who survived the World Trade Center terrorist attack first viewed virtual jets flying into the twin towers. In subsequent sessions, the level of detail increased until she was exposed to people jumping from the towers, flames, screams, and sirens. By acclimating to such stimuli, the woman was able to recall the actual events with less anxiety (Difede & Hoffman, 2002)

Virtual-reality therapy has been used in other innovative ways. For example,

engaging in a virtual-reality experience can distract burn patients from the excruciating pain that accompanies treatment. Studies show that the pain relief is quite real: Functional magnetic resonance imaging shows that brain activity related to pain actually drops when involved in virtual-reality therapy (Hoffman, 2004).

Despite its apparent success, further research is needed to confirm the effectiveness of virtual-reality therapy. For example, large-scale clinical trials must be carried out to determine if virtual-reality therapy is superior to other forms of systematic desensitization training. Still, the work is promising, and it is likely to lead to even more elaborate applications in the future (Attree, Brooks, & Rose, 2005; Cottraux, 2005).

RETHINK

Do you believe virtual-reality therapy can be more effective than traditional psychotherapy involving face-to-face interaction? Is there something unique about the curative powers of human interaction? Why or why not?

EXPLORING DIVERSITY Every chapter includes at least one section devoted to an aspect of racial, ethnic, gender, or cultural diversity. These features focus on the contributions of psychology to a better understanding of multicultural issues that are so central to our global society.

Exploring DIVERSITY

Does Culture Influence How We Learn?

When a member of the Chilcotin Indian tribe teaches her daughter to prepare salmon, at first she only allows the daughter to observe the entire process. A little later, she permits her child to try out some basic parts of the task. Her response to questions is noteworthy. For example, when the daughter asks about how to do "the backbone part," the mother's response is to repeat the entire process with another fish. The reason? The mother feels that one cannot learn the individual parts of the task apart from the context of preparing the whole fish (Tharp, 1989).

It should not be surprising that children raised in the Chilcotin tradition, which stresses instruction that starts by communicating the entire task, may have difficulty with traditional Western schooling. In the approach to teaching most characteristic of Western culture, tasks are broken down into their component parts. Only after each small step is learned is it thought possible to master the complete task.

Do the differences in teaching approaches between cultures affect how people learn? Some psychologists, taking a cognitive perspective on learning, suggest that people develop particular *learning styles*, characteristic ways of approaching material, based on their cultural background and unique pattern of abilities (Anderson & Adams, 1992; Chi-Ching & Noi, 1994; Furnham, 1995; Sternberg & Grigorenko, 1997; Barmeyer, 2004).

Learning styles differ along several dimensions. For example, one central dimension is analytical versus relational approaches to learning (Anderson, 1988; Tharp, 1989). As illustrated in Figure 2, people with a *relational learning style* master material best through exposure to a full unit or phenomenon. Parts of the unit are comprehended only when their relationship to the whole is understood.

In contrast, people with an *analytical learning style* do best when they can carry out an initial analysis of the principles and components underlying a phenomenon or situation. By developing an understanding of the fundamental principles and components, they are best able to understand the full picture.

Although research findings are mixed, some evidence suggests that particular minority groups in Western societies display characteristic learning styles. For instance, James Anderson and Maurianne Adams (1992) argue that Caucasian females

Relational Style	Analytical Style
1. Perceive information as part of total picture	1. Able to dis-embed information from total picture (focus on detail)
2. Exhibit improvisational and intuitive thinking	2. Exhibit sequential and structured thinking
3. More easily learn materials that have a human, social content and are characterized by experimental/cultural relevance	3. More easily learn materials that are inanimate and impersonal
4. Have a good memory for verbally presented ideas and information, especially if relevant	4. Have a good memory for abstract ideas and irrelevant information
5. Are more task-oriented concerning nonacademic areas	5. Are more task-oriented concerning academics
6. Are influenced by authority figures' expression of confidence or doubt in students' ability	6. Are not greatly affected by the opinions of others
7. Prefer to withdraw from unstimulating task performance	7. Show ability to persist at unstimulating tasks
8. Style conflicts with the traditional school environment	8. Style matches most school environments

...s relational approaches to learning offers one example of how learning styles differ along several dimensions.

To solve this problem, psychologists typically use a procedure in which all the participants receive a treatment, but those in the control group receive only a **placebo,** a false treatment, such as a pill, "drug," or other substance, that has no significant chemical properties or active ingredient. Because members of both groups are kept in the dark about whether they are getting a real or a false treatment, any differences in outcome can be attributed to the quality of the drug and not to the possible psychological effects of being administered a pill or other substance (Kirsch, 1999; Enserink, 1999, 2000; Kim & Holloway, 2003).

However, there is one more safeguard that a careful researcher must apply in an experiment such as this. To overcome the possibility that *experimenter* expectations will affect the participant, the person who administers the drug shouldn't know whether it is actually the true drug or the placebo. By keeping both the participant and the experimenter who interacts with the participant "blind" to the nature of the drug that is being administered, researchers can more accurately assess the effects of the drug. This method is known as the *double-blind procedure.*

Placebo: A false treatment, such as a pill, "drug," or other substance, without any significant chemical properties or active ingredient.

If you were about to purchase an automobile, it is unlikely that you would stop at the nearest car dealership and drive off with the first car a salesperson recommended. Instead, you would probably mull over the purchase, read about automobiles, consider the alternatives, talk to others about their experiences, and ultimately put in a fair amount of thought before you made such a major purchase.

BECOMING AN INFORMED CONSUMER

of Psychology

Thinking Critically About Research

In contrast, many of us are considerably less conscientious when we expend our intellectual, rather than financial, assets. People often jump to conclusions on the basis of incomplete and inaccurate information, and only rarely do they take the time to critically evaluate the research and data to which they are exposed.

Because the field of psychology is based on an accumulated body of research, it is crucial for psychologists to scrutinize thoroughly the methods, results, and claims of researchers. Yet it is not just psychologists who need to know how to evaluate research critically; all of us are constantly exposed to the claims of others. Knowing how to approach research and data can be helpful in areas far beyond the realm of psychology.

Several basic questions can help us sort through what is valid and what is not.

RUNNING GLOSSARY When a key term or concept appears in the text, it appears either in **boldface** or *italics*. Boldfaced words are of primary importance; italicized words are of secondary importance. Terms and concepts in bold are defined in the text where they are introduced and in the text margins, as well as in the glossary at the back of the book. In addition, boldfaced terms are included in the list of Key Terms at the end of every module, along with page references. You might want to highlight these terms.

BECOMING AN INFORMED CONSUMER OF PSYCHOLOGY

One of the major goals of *Understanding Psychology* is to make readers more informed, critical consumers of information relating to psychological issues. These discussions give you the tools to evaluate information concerning human behavior that you may hear or read about in the media or on the Web.

RECAP/EVALUATE/RETHINK SEGMENTS

Every module ends with a *Recap/Evaluate/Rethink* segment. *Recap* sections review the key concepts found at the beginning of each module. *Evaluate* sections provide a series of questions on the module content that ask for concrete information, in a matching, multiple choice, fill-in, or true-false format. The questions in the *Rethink* sections are designed to encourage you to think critically about a topic or issue, and they often have more than one correct answer.

Answer *Evaluate* and *Rethink* questions! Your responses will indicate both your degree of mastery of the material and the depth of your knowledge. If you have no trouble with the questions, you can be confident that you are studying effectively. Use questions with which you have difficulty as a basis for further study.

LOOKING BACK, EPILOGUE, AND VISUAL MASTERY REVIEWS

Each chapter ends with a Looking Back section that extends the chapter content to the Web. The Epilogue refers back to the Prologue at the start of the set of modules, placing it in the context of the chapter's subject matter and asking questions designed to encourage you to think critically about what you've read.

In addition, several chapters conclude with a visual mastery review that revisits a key point from the chapter in a verbal and pictorial way. Studying these reviews and answering the questions that go with them will make recall and application of the material easier.

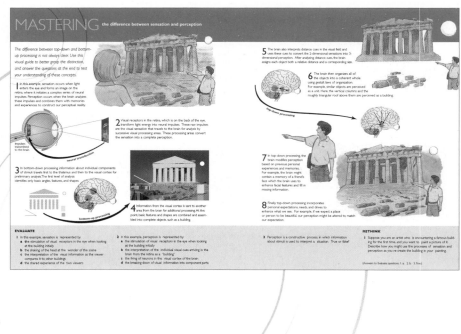

You'll find the same features in every chapter, providing familiar landmarks to help you chart your way through new material. This structure will help you organize, learn, and remember the content.

An additional note about this text: The reference citations follow the style endorsed by the American Psychological Association (APA). According to APA style, citations include a name and date, typically set off in parentheses at the end of a sentence and specifying the author of the work being cited and the year of publication, as in this example: (Angier & Chang, 2005). Each of these names and dates refers to a book or article included in the References section at the end of this book.

STRATEGIES FOR EFFECTIVE STUDY AND CRITICAL THINKING

Now that you are acquainted with the special features of *Understanding Psychology*, you should consider using a general study strategy. It is ironic that although we are expected to study and ultimately learn a wide range of material throughout our schooling, we are rarely taught any systematic strategies that permit us to study more effectively. Psychologists have devised several excellent (and proven) techniques for improving study skills, two of which are described here. By employing one of these procedures—known by the initials "P.O.W.E.R." and "SQ3R"—you can increase your ability to learn and retain information and to think critically, not just in psychology classes but also in all academic subjects.

P.O.W.E.R.   The *P.O.W.E.R.* learning strategy includes five key steps: *Prepare, Organize, Work, Evaluate,* and *Rethink. P.O.W.E.R.* systematizes the acquisition of new material by providing a learning framework. It stresses the importance of learning objectives and appropriate preparation prior to beginning to study, as well as the significance of self-evaluation and the incorporation of critical thinking into the learning process. Specifically, use of the P.O.W.E.R. learning system entails the following steps:

- **Prepare.** Before starting any journey, we need to know where we are headed. Academic journeys are no different; we need to know what our goals are. The *Prepare* stage consists of thinking about what we hope to gain from reading a particular section of the text by identifying specific goals that we seek to accomplish. In *Understanding Psychology,* Eighth Edition, these goals are presented as broad questions at the start of each chapter and again at the beginning of each module.
- **Organize.** Once we know what our goals are, we can develop a route to accomplish those goals. The *Organize* stage involves developing a mental roadmap of where we are headed. *Understanding Psychology* highlights the organization of each upcoming chapter. Read the outline to get an idea of what topics are covered and how they are organized.

- **Work.** The key to the P.O.W.E.R. learning system is actually reading and studying the material presented in the book. In some ways *Work* is the easy part, because, if you have carried out the steps in the preparation and organization stage, you'll know where you're headed and how you'll get there. Of course, you'll need the motivation to conscientiously read and think about the material presented. And remember, the main text isn't the only material that you need to read and think about. It's also important to read the boxes, the marginal glossary terms, and the special sections in order to gain a full understanding of the material, so be sure to include them as part of the *Work* of reading the chapter.

- **Evaluate.** The fourth step, *Evaluate,* provides the opportunity to determine how effectively mastered the material. In *Understanding Psychology,* a series of questions at the end of each module permits a rapid check of your understanding of the material. Quizzes on the book's Web site, or Online Learning Center, and within *PsychInteractive Online* provide additional opportunities to test yourself. Evaluating your progress is essential to assessing your degree of mastery of the material.

- **Rethink.** The final step in the P.O.W.E.R. learning system requires thinking critically about the content. Critical thinking entails re-analyzing, reviewing, questioning, and challenging assumptions. It affords the opportunity to look at the big picture by thinking about how material fits with other information that already learned. Every major section of *Understanding Psychology* ends with a *Rethink* section that contains thought-provoking questions. Answering them will help you understand the material more fully and at a deeper level.

SQ3R. The *SQ3R* method has five steps, designated by the initials *S-Q-R-R-R.* The first step is to *survey* the material by reading the outlines that open each module, the headings, figure captions, recaps, and Looking Ahead and Looking Back sections, providing yourself with an overview of the major points of the chapter. The next step—the "Q" in SQ3R—is to *question.* Formulate questions about the material—either aloud or in writing—prior to actually reading a section of text. The questions posed at the beginning of each module and the *Evaluate* and *Rethink* questions that end each part of the chapter are examples.

The next three steps in SQ3R ask you to *read, recite,* and *review* the material. *Read* carefully and, even more importantly, read actively and critically. While you are reading, answer the questions you have asked yourself. Critically evaluate material by considering the implications of what you are reading, thinking about possible exceptions and contradictions, and examining underlying assumptions. The *recite* step involves describing and explaining to yourself (or to a friend) the material you have just read and answering the questions you have posed earlier. Recite aloud; the recitation process helps to identify your degree of understanding of the material you have just read. Finally, *review* the material, looking it over, reading the Looking Back summaries, and answering the in-text review questions.

Some Final Comments. Both P.O.W.E.R. and SQ3R are proven means of increasing your study effectiveness. But you need not feel tied to a particular strategy. You might want to combine other elements to create your own study system. Additional learning tips and strategies for critical thinking are presented throughout *Understanding Psychology;* for example, in Chapter 7, the use of mnemonics (memory techniques for organizing material to help its recall) is discussed. If these tactics help you to successfully master new material, stick with them.

Whatever learning strategy you use, you will maximize your understanding of the material in this book and master techniques that will help you learn and think critically in all of your academic endeavors. More importantly, you will optimize your understanding of the field of psychology. It is worth the effort: The excitement, challenges, and promise that psychology holds for you are significant.

CHAPTER I

Introduction to Psychology

Key Concepts for Chapter 1

What is the science of psychology? ● What are the major specialties in the field of psychology? ● Where do psychologists work?

What are the origins of psychology? ● What are the major approaches in contemporary psychology?

What are psychology's key issues and controversies? ● What is the future of psychology likely to hold?

Prologue   A Calamity Called Katrina

It began with a mild disturbance in the atmosphere off the coast of Africa. At first it caused barely a ripple in the air, but the eventual result, a monster hurricane named Katrina, bore down on New Orleans, bombarding the city and surrounding coastline with winds of over 150 miles per hour and waves higher than 20 feet.

The torrents of water that lashed New Orleans in August 2005 caused levees built to keep Lake Pontchartrain from overflowing into the city's low-lying neighborhoods to give way, flooding much of the area. When the waters receded weeks after the hurricane, the devastation was unbelievable. Entire neighborhoods had been destroyed. The death toll climbed into the thousands, and more than a hundred thousand people were left homeless.

Yet the most memorable stories to come out of New Orleans in the days and weeks following Hurricane Katrina are about human kindness. More fortunate residents invited homeless strangers to share their homes. People thousands of miles away rushed to the afflicted areas to help search for victims, evacuate stranded residents, and rebuild the Big Easy. Citizens from all over the globe provided millions of dollars in aid to victims.

Looking Ahead

Although it originated as a meteorological event, Hurricane Katrina and its aftermath gave rise to a host of intriguing questions. For example,

- What internal biological changes occurred in the bodies of people fleeing for their lives from the hurricane?

- What memories did people have of the catastrophe afterward? How would the loss of loved ones during the storm affect children immediately afterward and in the future?

- What would be the long-term effects of the disaster on the health of individuals who lived through the disaster?

- What are the most effective ways to help people cope with the loss of family members and the destruction of their homes?

- Why did so many people offer help for those affected by the hurricane?

As we'll soon see, psychology addresses questions like these—and many, many more. In this chapter, we begin our examination of psychology, the different types of psychologists, and the various roles that psychologists play.

Psychologists at Work

Psychology is the scientific study of behavior and mental processes. The simplicity of this definition is in some ways deceiving, concealing ongoing debates about how broad the scope of psychology should be. Should psychologists limit themselves to the study of outward, observable behavior? Is it possible to study thinking scientifically? Should the field encompass the study of such diverse topics as physical and mental health, perception, dreaming, and motivation? Is it appropriate to focus solely on human behavior, or should the behavior of other species be included?

Most psychologists would argue that the field should be receptive to a variety of viewpoints and approaches. Consequently, the phrase *behavior and mental processes* in the definition of psychology must be understood to mean many things: It encompasses not just people's actions, but also their thoughts, emotions, perceptions, reasoning processes, memories, and even the biological activities that maintain bodily functioning.

Psychologists try to describe, predict, and explain human behavior and mental processes, as well as helping to change and improve the lives of people and the world in which they live. They use scientific methods to find answers that are far more valid and legitimate than those resulting from intuition and speculation, which are often inaccurate (see Figure 1).

Key Concepts

What is the science of psychology?

What are the major specialties in the field of psychology?

Where do psychologists work?

Psychology: The scientific study of behavior and mental processes.

FIGURE 1 The scientific method is the basis of all psychological research and is used to find valid answers. Test your knowledge of psychology by answering these questions. (Source: Lamal, 1979.)

Psychological Truths?

To test your knowledge of psychology, try answering the following questions:

1. Infants love their mothers primarily because their mothers fulfill their basic biological needs, such as providing food. True or false? _____
2. Geniuses generally have poor social adjustment. True or false? _____
3. The best way to ensure that a desired behavior will continue after training is completed is to reward that behavior every single time it occurs during training rather than rewarding it only periodically. True or false? _____
4. People with schizophrenia have at least two distinct personalities. True or false? _____
5. If you are having trouble sleeping, the best way to get to sleep is to take a sleeping pill. True or false? _____
6. Children's IQ scores have little to do with how well they do in school. True or false? _____
7. Frequent masturbation can lead to mental illness. True or false? _____
8. Once people reach old age, their leisure activities change radically. True or false? _____
9. Most people would refuse to give painful electric shocks to other people. True or false? _____
10. One of the least important factors affecting how much we like another person is that person's physical attractiveness. True or false? _____

Scoring: The truth about each of these items: They are all false. Based on psychological research, each of these "facts" has been proven untrue. You will learn the reasons why as we explore what psychologists have discovered about human behavior.

The questions in Figure 1 provide just a hint of the topics that we will encounter in the study of psychology. Our discussions will take us through the range of what is known about behavior and mental processes.

The Subfields of Psychology: Psychology's Family Tree

www.mhhe.com/feldmanup8

PsychInteractive Online

Multiple Causes of Behavior

As the study of psychology has grown, it has given rise to a number of subfields (described in Figure 2 and illustrated in the PsychInteractive exercise on multiple causes of behavior). The subfields of psychology can be likened to an extended family, with assorted nieces and nephews, aunts and uncles, and cousins who, although they may not interact on a day-to-day basis, are related to one another because they share a common goal: understanding behavior. One way to identify the key subfields is to look at some of the basic questions about behavior that they address.

WHAT ARE THE BIOLOGICAL FOUNDATIONS OF BEHAVIOR?

In the most fundamental sense, people are biological organisms. *Behavioral neuroscience* is the subfield of psychology that mainly examines how the brain and the nervous system—as well as other biological processes—determine behavior. Thus, neuroscientists consider how our bodies influence our behavior. For example, they may examine the link between specific sites in the brain and the muscular tremors of people affected by Parkinson's disease or attempt to determine how our emotions are related to physical sensations. Behavioral neuroscientists might want to know what physiological changes occurred in people who fled New Orleans as Hurricane Katrina was bearing down on the city.

HOW DO PEOPLE SENSE, PERCEIVE, LEARN, AND THINK ABOUT THE WORLD?

If you have ever wondered why you are susceptible to optical illusions, how your body registers pain, or how to make the most of your study time, an experimental psychologist can answer your questions. *Experimental psychology* is the branch of psychology that studies the processes of sensing, perceiving, learning, and thinking about the world. (The term *experimental psychologist* is somewhat misleading: Psychologists in every specialty area use experimental techniques.)

Several subspecialties of experimental psychology have become specialties in their own right. One example is *cognitive psychology,* which focuses on higher mental processes, including thinking, memory, reasoning, problem solving, judging, decision making, and language. A cognitive psychologist might be interested in what victims of Hurricane Katrinia remembered about their experience.

WHAT ARE THE SOURCES OF CHANGE AND STABILITY IN BEHAVIOR ACROSS THE LIFE SPAN?

A baby producing her first smile . . . taking her first step . . . saying her first word. These universal milestones in development are also singularly special and unique for each person. *Developmental psychology* studies how people grow and change from the moment of conception through death. *Personality psychology* focuses on the consistency in people's behavior over time and the traits that differentiate one person from another.

Subfield	Description
Behavioral genetics	*Behavioral genetics* studies the inheritance of traits related to behavior.
Behavioral neuroscience	*Behavioral neuroscience* examines the biological basis of behavior.
Clinical psychology	*Clinical psychology* deals with the study, diagnosis, and treatment of psychological disorders.
Clinical neuropsychology	*Clinical neuropsychology* unites the areas of biopsychology and clinical psychology, focusing on the relationship between biological factors and psychological disorders.
Cognitive psychology	*Cognitive psychology* focuses on the study of higher mental processes.
Counseling psychology	*Counseling psychology* focuses primarily on educational, social, and career adjustment problems.
Cross-cultural psychology	*Cross-cultural psychology* investigates the similarities and differences in psychological functioning in and across various cultures and ethnic groups.
Developmental psychology	*Developmental psychology* examines how people grow and change from the moment of conception through death.
Educational psychology	*Educational psychology* is concerned with teaching and learning processes, such as the relationship between motivation and school performance.
Environmental psychology	*Environmental psychology* considers the relationship between people and their physical environment.
Evolutionary psychology	*Evolutionary psychology* considers how behavior is influenced by our genetic inheritance from our ancestors.
Experimental psychology	*Experimental psychology* studies the processes of sensing, perceiving, learning, and thinking about the world.
Forensic psychology	*Forensic psychology* focuses on legal issues, such as determining the accuracy of witness memories.
Health psychology	*Health psychology* explores the relationship between psychological factors and physical ailments or disease.
Industrial/organizational psychology	*Industrial/organizational psychology* is concerned with the psychology of the workplace.
Personality psychology	*Personality psychology* focuses on the consistency in people's behavior over time and the traits that differentiate one person from another.
Program evaluation	*Program evaluation* focuses on assessing large-scale programs, such as the Head Start preschool program, to determine whether they are effective in meeting their goals.
Psychology of women	*Psychology of women* focuses on issues such as discrimination against women and the causes of violence against women.
School psychology	*School psychology* is devoted to counseling children in elementary and secondary schools who have academic or emotional problems.
Social psychology	*Social psychology* is the study of how people's thoughts, feelings, and actions are affected by others.
Sport psychology	*Sport psychology* applies psychology to athletic activity and exercise.

FIGURE 2 The major subfields of psychology.

HOW DO PSYCHOLOGICAL FACTORS AFFECT PHYSICAL AND MENTAL HEALTH?

Frequent depression, stress, and fears that prevent people from carrying out their normal activities are topics that would interest a health psychologist, a clinical psychologist, and a counseling psychologist. *Health psychology* explores the relationship between psychological factors and physical ailments or disease. For example, health psychologists are interested in how long-term stress (a psychological factor) can affect physical health and in identifying ways to promote behavior that brings about good health (Nelson & Simmons, 2003). The long-term health effects of stress resulting from the loss of a home and evacuation to another state in the aftermath of Hurricane Katrina would be of concern to a health psychologist.

Clinical psychology deals with the study, diagnosis, and treatment of psychological disorders. Clinical psychologists are trained to diagnose and treat problems that range from the crises of everyday life, such as unhappiness over the breakup of a relationship, to more extreme conditions, such as profound, lingering depression. Some clinical psychologists also research and investigate issues that range from identifying the early signs of psychological disturbance to studying the relationship between family communication patterns and psychological disorders. A clinical psychologist might be called on to help a New Orleans evacuee cope with the loss of a loved one and ambivalence about going back.

Like clinical psychologists, counseling psychologists deal with people's psychological problems, but the problems they deal with are more specific. *Counseling psychology* is the branch of psychology that focuses primarily on educational, social, and career adjustment problems. Almost every college has a center staffed with counseling psychologists. This is where students can get advice on the kinds of jobs they might be best suited for, methods of studying effectively, and strategies for resolving everyday difficulties, such as problems with roommates and concerns about a specific professor's grading practices. Many large business organizations also employ counseling psychologists to help employees with work-related problems.

HOW DO OUR SOCIAL NETWORKS AFFECT BEHAVIOR?

Our complex networks of social interrelationships are the focus of study for a number of subfields of psychology. For example, *social psychology* is the study of how people's thoughts, feelings, and actions are affected by others. Social psychologists focus on such diverse topics as human aggression, liking and loving, persuasion, and conformity. For a social psychologist, Hurricane Katrina raises questions about why so many people volunteered to help in the search and rescue operation and a few took advantage of the situation for their own personal gain.

Cross-cultural psychology investigates the similarities and differences in psychological functioning in and across various cultures and ethnic groups. For example, cross-cultural psychologists examine how cultures differ in their use of punishment during child rearing or why certain cultures view academic success as being determined mostly by hard work whereas others see it as being determined mostly by innate ability (Matsumoto, 2004; Schoenpflug, 2003; Shweder, 2003).

EXPANDING PSYCHOLOGY'S FRONTIERS

The boundaries of the science of psychology are constantly growing. Three newer members of the field's family tree—evolutionary psychology, behavioral genetics, and clinical neuropsychology—have sparked particular excitement, and debate, within psychology.

Evolutionary Psychology. *Evolutionary psychology* considers how behavior is influenced by our genetic inheritance from our ancestors. The evolutionary approach suggests that the chemical coding of information in our cells not only determines traits such as hair color and race but also holds the key to understanding a broad variety of behaviors that helped our ancestors survive and reproduce (Buss, 2004; Ellis & Bjorklund, 2005).

Evolutionary psychology stems from Charles Darwin's arguments in his ground-breaking 1859 book, *On the Origin of Species*. Darwin suggested that a process of natural selection leads to the survival of the fittest and the development of traits that enable a species to adapt to its environment.

Evolutionary psychologists take Darwin's arguments a step further. They argue that our genetic inheritance determines not only physical traits such as skin and eye color, but certain personality traits and social behaviors as well. For example, evolutionary psychologists suggest that behavior such as shyness, jealousy, and cross-cultural similarities in qualities desired in potential mates are at least partially determined by genetics, presumably because such behavior helped increase the survival rate of humans' ancient relatives (Buss, 2003b).

Although they are increasingly popular, evolutionary explanations of behavior have stirred controversy. By suggesting that many significant behaviors unfold automatically because they are wired into the human species, evolutionary approaches minimize the role of environmental and social forces. Still, the evolutionary approach has stimulated a significant amount of research on how our biological inheritance influences our traits and behaviors (Begley, 2005b).

Behavioral Genetics. Another rapidly growing area in psychology focuses on the biological mechanisms, such as genes and chromosomes, that enable inherited behavior to unfold. *Behavioral genetics* seeks to understand how we might inherit certain behavioral traits and how the environment influences whether we actually display such traits (Gottlieb & Lickliter, 2004; Ellis & Bjorklund, 2005; Li, 2005; Tuvblad, Eley, & Lichtenstein, 2005).

Clinical Neuropsychology. *Clinical neuropsychology* unites the areas of neuroscience and clinical psychology: It focuses on the origin of psychological disorders in biological factors. Building on advances in our understanding of the structure and chemistry of the brain, this specialty has already led to promising new treatments for psychological disorders as well as debates over the use of medication to control behavior.

Working at Psychology

Help Wanted: Assistant professor at a small liberal arts college. Teach undergraduate courses in introductory psychology and courses in specialty areas of cognitive psychology, perception, and learning. Strong commitment to quality teaching and student advising necessary. The candidate must also provide evidence of scholarship and research productivity.

* * *

Help Wanted: Industrial-organizational consulting psychologist. International firm seeks psychologists for full-time career positions as consultants to management. Candidates must have the ability to establish a rapport with senior business executives and help them find innovative, practical, and psychologically sound solutions to problems concerning people and organizations.

* * *

Help Wanted: Clinical psychologist. Ph.D., internship experience, and license required. Comprehensive clinic seeks psychologist to work with children and adults providing individual and group therapy, psychological evaluations, crisis intervention, and development of behavior treatment plans on multidisciplinary team. Broad experience with substance-abuse problems is desirable.

FIGURE 3 The breakdown of where U.S. psychologists (who have a Ph.D. or Psy.D. degree) work (APA, 2000). Why do you think so many psychologists work in college settings?

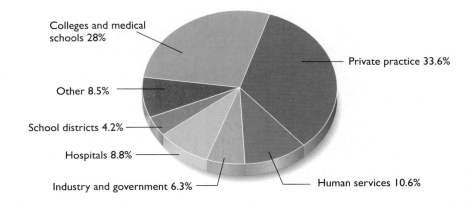

Colleges and medical schools 28%

Private practice 33.6%

Other 8.5%

School districts 4.2%

Hospitals 8.8%

Industry and government 6.3%

Human services 10.6%

As these advertisements suggest, psychologists are employed in a variety of settings. Many doctoral-level psychologists are employed by institutions of higher learning (universities and colleges) or are self-employed, usually working as private practitioners treating clients (see Figure 3). Other work sites include hospitals, clinics, mental health centers, counseling centers, government human-services organizations, and schools (APA, 2000).

Why do so many psychologists work in academic settings? Because these are effective settings for three major roles played by psychologists in society: teacher, scientist, and clinical practitioner. Many psychology professors are also actively involved in research or in serving clients. Whatever the particular job site, however, psychologists share a commitment to improving individual lives as well as society in general.

PSYCHOLOGISTS: A PORTRAIT

Is there an "average" psychologist in terms of personal characteristics? Probably not. About half of U.S. psychologists are men, and about half are women. Predictions are that by 2010 women will outnumber men in the field. Right now, around 70 percent of new psychology Ph.D. degrees are earned by women (Fowler, 2002; Harton & Lyons, 2003; Frincke & Pate, 2004).

Although most psychologists today work in the United States, about one-third of the world's 500,000 psychologists are found elsewhere (see Figure 4). Psychologists outside the United States are increasingly influential in adding to the knowledge base and practices of psychology (Mays et al., 1996; Pawlik & d'Ydewalle, 1996; Peiro & Lunt, 2002).

According to figures compiled by the American Psychological Association (APA), the vast majority of psychologists in the United States are white, limiting the diversity of the field. Only 6 percent of all psychologists are members of racial minority groups. Although the number of minority individuals entering the field is increasing—almost one-fifth of new recipients of Ph.D. degrees are people of color—this increase has not kept up with the growth of the minority population at large (Bailey, 2004; Hoffer et al., 2005).

The underrepresentation of racial and ethnic minorities among psychologists is significant for several reasons. First, the field of psychology is diminished by a lack of the diverse perspectives and talents that minority-group members can provide. Furthermore, minority-group psychologists serve as role models for members of minority communities, and their underrepresentation in the profession might deter other minority-group members from entering the field. Finally, because members of minority groups often prefer to receive psychological therapy from treatment providers of their own race or ethnic group, the rarity of minority psychologists can discourage some members of minority groups from seeking treatment (Bernal et al., 2002; Jenkins, Albee, & Paster, 2003; Bryant et al., 2005).

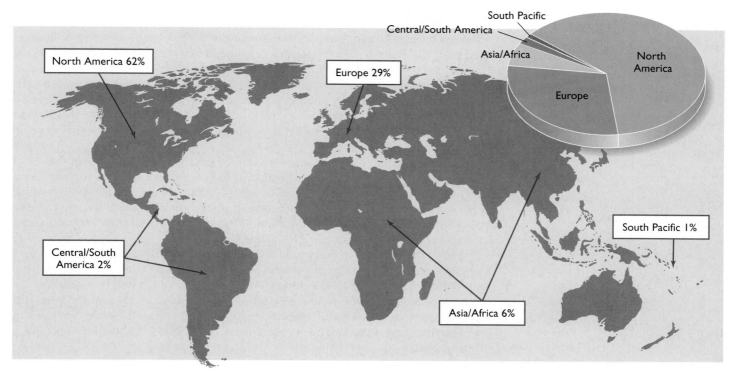

FIGURE 4 Origin of published research (APA, 2000). How do you think the heavy concentration of psychologists in North America affects the field of psychology?

THE EDUCATION OF A PSYCHOLOGIST

How do people become psychologists? The most common route is a long one. Most psychologists have a doctorate, either a *Ph.D.* (doctor of philosophy) or, less frequently, a *Psy.D.* (doctor of psychology). The Ph.D. is a research degree that requires a dissertation based on an original investigation. The Psy.D. is obtained by psychologists who wish to focus on the treatment of psychological disorders. (Psychologists are distinct from psychiatrists, who are physicians who specialize in the treatment of psychological disorders.)

Both the Ph.D. and the Psy.D. typically take four or five years of work past the bachelor's level. Some fields of psychology involve education beyond the doctorate. For instance, doctoral-level clinical psychologists, who deal with people with psychological disorders, typically spend an additional year doing an internship.

About a third of people working in the field of psychology have a master's degree as their highest degree, which is earned after two or three years of graduate work. These psychologists teach, provide therapy, conduct research, or work in specialized programs dealing with drug abuse or crisis intervention. Some work in universities, government, and business, collecting and analyzing data.

Although it takes a considerable amount of time to be trained as a psychologist, the number of psychologists continues to grow. Currently, there are close to 60,000 students enrolled in psychology graduate programs, a 10 percent increase from six years earlier. Some of these students are motivated by the desire to provide direct care to people facing psychological difficulties; others are driven by curiosity about the determinants of behavior. Some see themselves primarily as scientists, researching questions about human behavior, whereas others are more interested in providing help to specific individuals. Regardless of their specific interest, these students, along with current members of the field, share a desire to improve the human condition and believe that psychology provides a route to that goal (Chamberlin, 2000).

CAREERS FOR PSYCHOLOGY MAJORS

Although some psychology majors head for graduate school in psychology or an unrelated field, the majority join the workforce immediately after graduation. Most report that the jobs they take after graduation are related to their psychology background.

An undergraduate major in psychology provides excellent preparation for a variety of occupations. Because undergraduates who specialize in psychology develop good analytical skills, are trained to think critically, and are able to synthesize and evaluate information well, employers in business, industry, and the government value their preparation (Kuther, 2003).

The most common areas of employment for psychology majors are in the social services, including working as an administrator, serving as a counselor, and providing direct care. Some 20 percent of recipients of bachelor's degrees in psychology work in the social services or in some other form of public affairs. In addition, psychology majors often enter the fields of education or business or work for federal, state, and local governments (see Figure 5; APA, 2000; Murray, 2002).

What's the pay in psychology-related fields? In the early 2000s, starting salaries for people with a psychology major who have just graduated with a B.A. degree have ranged from $20,000 to $45,000, depending on the type of job and location, with an average starting salary of around $30,000. Business-related fields pay the best, and social service jobs in nonprofit agencies are at the low end of the scale. But even in lower-paying jobs, salaries rise as employees move into administrative positions (Murray, 2002).

FIGURE 5 Although many psychology majors pursue employment in social services, a background in psychology can prepare one for many professions outside the social services field. What is it about the science of psychology that makes it such a versatile field? (Source: Kuther, 2003.)

Positions Obtained by Psychology Majors		
Business Field	**Education/Academic**	**Social Fields**
Administrative assistant	Administration	Activities coordinator
Affirmative action officer	Child-care provider	Behavioral specialist
Advertising trainee	Child-care worker/	Career counselor
Benefits manager	supervisor	Case worker
Claims specialist	Data management	Child protection worker
Community relations officer	Laboratory assistant	Clinical coordinator
Customer relations	Parent/family education	Community outreach worker
Data management	Preschool teacher	Corrections officer
Employee recruitment	Public opinion surveyor	Counselor assistant
Employee counselor	Research assistant	Crisis intervention counselor
Human resources coordinator/	Teaching assistant	Employment counselor
manager/specialist		Group home attendant
Labor relations manager/specialist		Occupational therapist
Loan officer		Probation officer
Management trainee		Program manager
Marketing		Rehabilitation counselor
Personnel manager/officer		Residence counselor
Product and services research		Mental health assistant
Programs/events coordination		Social service assistant
Public relations		Social worker
Retail sales management		Substance abuse counselor
Sales representative		Youth counselor
Special features writing/reporting		
Staff training and development		
Trainer/training officer		

RECAP/EVALUATE/RETHINK

RECAP

What is the science of psychology?

- Psychology is the scientific study of behavior and mental processes, encompassing not just people's actions but their biological activities, feelings, perceptions, memory, reasoning, and thoughts. (p. 5)

What are the major specialties in the field of psychology?

- Behavioral neuroscientists focus on the biological basis of behavior, and experimental psychologists study the processes of sensing, perceiving, learning, and thinking about the world. (p. 6)
- Cognitive psychology, an outgrowth of experimental psychology, studies higher mental processes, including memory, knowing, thinking, reasoning, problem solving, judging, decision making, and language. (p. 6)
- Developmental psychologists study how people grow and change throughout the life span. (p. 6)
- Personality psychologists consider the consistency and change in an individual's behavior, as well as the individual differences that distinguish one person's behavior from another's. (p. 6)
- Health psychologists study psychological factors that affect physical disease, while clinical psychologists consider the study, diagnosis, and treatment of abnormal behavior. Counseling psychologists focus on educational, social, and career adjustment problems. (p. 8)
- Social psychology is the study of how people's thoughts, feelings, and actions are affected by others. (p. 8)
- Cross-cultural psychology examines the similarities and differences in psychological functioning among various cultures. (p. 8)
- Other increasingly important fields are evolutionary psychology, behavioral genetics, and clinical neuropsychology. (pp. 8–9)

Where do psychologists work?

- Psychologists are employed in a variety of settings. Although the primary sites of employment are private practice and colleges, many psychologists are found in hospitals, clinics, community mental health centers, and counseling centers. (p. 10)

EVALUATE

Match each subfield of psychology with the issues or questions posed below.

a. behavioral neuroscience
b. experimental psychology
c. cognitive psychology
d. developmental psychology
e. personality psychology
f. health psychology
g. clinical psychology
h. counseling psychology
i. educational psychology
j. school psychology
k. social psychology
l. industrial/organizational psychology

1. Joan, a college freshman, is worried about her grades. She needs to learn better organizational skills and study habits to cope with the demands of college.
2. At what age do children generally begin to acquire an emotional attachment to their fathers?
3. It is thought that pornographic films that depict violence against women may prompt aggressive behavior in some men.
4. What chemicals are released in the human body as a result of a stressful event? What are their effects on behavior?
5. Luis is unique in his manner of responding to crisis situations, with an even temperament and a positive outlook.
6. The teachers of 8-year-old Jack are concerned that he has recently begun to withdraw socially and to show little interest in schoolwork.
7. Janetta's job is demanding and stressful. She wonders if her lifestyle is making her more prone to certain illnesses, such as cancer and heart disease.
8. A psychologist is intrigued by the fact that some people are much more sensitive to painful stimuli than others are.
9. A strong fear of crowds leads a young woman to seek treatment for her problem.
10. What mental strategies are involved in solving complex word problems?
11. What teaching methods most effectively motivate elementary school students to successfully accomplish academic tasks?
12. Jessica is asked to develop a management strategy that will encourage safer work practices in an assembly plant.

RETHINK

1. Do you think intuition and common sense are sufficient for understanding why people act the way they do? In what ways is a scientific approach appropriate for studying human behavior?

2. *From an educator's perspective:* Suppose you are a teacher who has a 7-year-old child in your class who was having unusual difficulty learning to read. Imagine that you could consult as many psychologists with different specialities as you wanted. What are the different types of psychologists that you might approach to address the problem?

Answers to Evaluate Questions

1. h. counseling psychology; 2. d. developmental psychology; 3. k. social psychology; 4. a. behavioral neuroscience; 5. e. personality psychology; 6. j. school psychology; 7. f. health psychology; 8. b. experimental psychology; 9. g. clinical psychology; 10. c. cognitive psychology; 11. i. educational psychology; 12. l. industrial/organizational psychology

KEY TERM

psychology p. 5

A Science Evolves: The Past, the Present, and the Future

Seven thousand years ago, people assumed that psychological problems were caused by evil spirits. To allow those spirits to escape from a person's body, ancient healers performed an operation called *trephining*. Trephining consisted of chipping a hole in a patient's skull with crude stone instruments. Because archaeologists have found skulls with signs of healing around the opening, it's a fair guess that some patients survived the cure.

* * *

According to the seventeenth-century philosopher Descartes, nerves were hollow tubes through which "animal spirits" conducted impulses in the same way that water is transmitted through a pipe. When a person put a finger too close to a fire, heat was transmitted to the brain through the tubes.

* * *

Franz Josef Gall, an eighteenth-century physician, argued that a trained observer could discern intelligence, moral character, and other basic personality characteristics from the shape and number of bumps on a person's skull. His theory gave rise to the "science" of phrenology, employed by hundreds of devoted practitioners in the nineteenth century.

Although these explanations might sound far-fetched, in their own times they represented the most advanced thinking about what might be called the psychology of the era. Our understanding of behavior has progressed tremendously since the eighteenth century, but most of the advances have been recent. As sciences go, psychology is one of the "new kids on the block." (For highlights in the development of the field, see Figure 1, and explore psychology's timeline further in the PsychInteractive excercise on milestones in psychology.

Key Concepts

What are the origins of psychology? What are the major approaches in contemporary psychology?

www.mhhe.com/feldmanup8
PsychInteractive Online

Milestones in Psychology

The Roots of Psychology

Psychology's roots can be traced back to the ancient Greeks, who considered the mind to be a suitable topic for scholarly contemplation. Later philosophers argued for hundreds of years about some of the questions psychologists grapple with today. For example, the seventeenth-century British philosopher John Locke (1632–1704) believed that children were born into the world with minds like "blank slates" (*tabula rasa* in Latin) and that their experiences determined what kind of adults they would become. His views contrasted with those of philosophers such as Plato (427–347 B.C.E.) and French philosopher and mathematician René Descartes (1596–1650), who believed that some knowledge was inborn in humans.

However, the formal beginning of psychology as a scientific discipline is generally considered to be in the late nineteenth century, when, in Leipzig, Germany, Wilhelm Wundt established the first experimental laboratory devoted to psychological phenomena. At about the same time, William James was setting up his laboratory in Cambridge, Massachusetts.

When Wundt set up his laboratory in 1879, his aim was to study the building blocks of the mind. He considered psychology to be the study of conscious experience.

Wilhelm Wundt

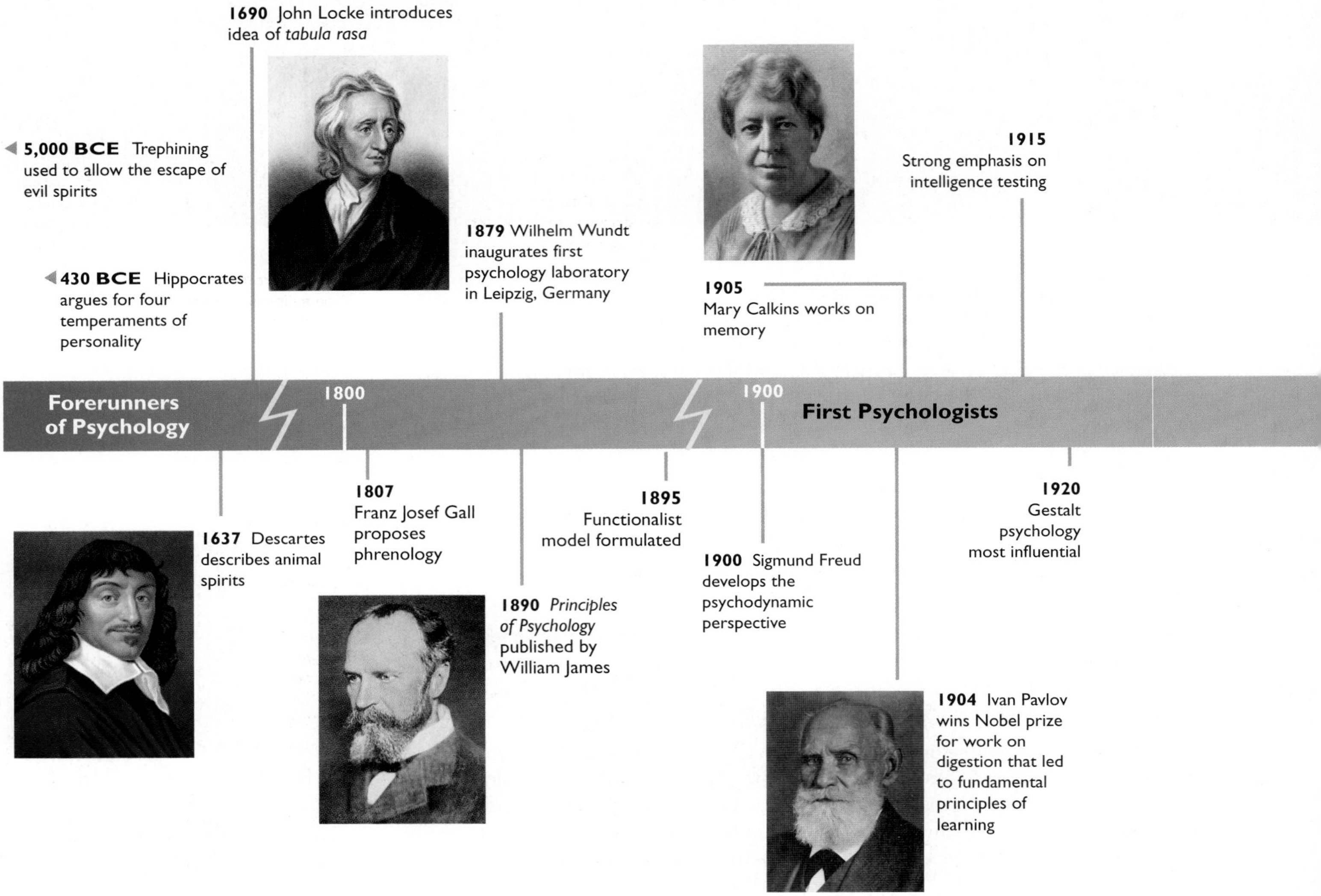

1690 John Locke introduces idea of *tabula rasa*

5,000 BCE Trephining used to allow the escape of evil spirits

430 BCE Hippocrates argues for four temperaments of personality

1879 Wilhelm Wundt inaugurates first psychology laboratory in Leipzig, Germany

1915 Strong emphasis on intelligence testing

1905 Mary Calkins works on memory

Forerunners of Psychology

1800

1900

First Psychologists

1637 Descartes describes animal spirits

1807 Franz Josef Gall proposes phrenology

1895 Functionalist model formulated

1900 Sigmund Freud develops the psychodynamic perspective

1920 Gestalt psychology most influential

1890 *Principles of Psychology* published by William James

1904 Ivan Pavlov wins Nobel prize for work on digestion that led to fundamental principles of learning

FIGURE 1 This timeline illustrates major milestones in the development of psychology.

Structuralism: Wundt's approach, which focuses on uncovering the fundamental mental components of consciousness, thinking, and other kinds of mental states and activities.

Introspection: A procedure used to study the structure of the mind in which subjects are asked to describe in detail what they are experiencing when they are exposed to a stimulus.

Functionalism: An early approach to psychology that concentrated on what the mind does—the functions of mental activity—and the role of behavior in allowing people to adapt to their environments.

His perspective, which came to be known as **structuralism,** focused on uncovering the fundamental mental components of perception, consciousness, thinking, emotions, and other kinds of mental states and activities.

To determine how basic sensory processes shape our understanding of the world, Wundt and other structuralists used a procedure called **introspection,** in which they presented people with a stimulus—such as a bright green object or a sentence printed on a card—and asked them to describe, in their own words and in as much detail as they could, what they were experiencing. Wundt argued that by analyzing their reports, psychologists could come to a better understanding of the structure of the mind.

Over time, psychologists challenged Wundt's approach. They became increasingly dissatisfied with the assumption that introspection could reveal the structure of the mind. Introspection was not a truly scientific technique, because there were few ways an outside observer could confirm the accuracy of others' introspections. Moreover, people had difficulty describing some kinds of inner experiences, such as emotional responses. Those drawbacks led to the development of new approaches, which largely supplanted structuralism.

The perspective that replaced structuralism is known as functionalism. Rather than focusing on the mind's structure, **functionalism** concentrated on what the mind

1924
John B. Watson, an early behaviorist, publishes *Behaviorism*

1980
Jean Piaget, an influential developmental psychologist, dies

2000
New subfields develop such as clinical neuropsychology and evolutionary psychology

1957 Leon Festinger publishes *A Theory of Cognitive Dissonance*, producing a major impact on social psychology

1951
Carl Rogers publishes *Client-Centered Therapy*, helping to establish the humanistic perspective

1990 Greater emphasis on multiculturalism and diversity

Modern Psychology

2000

1969
Arguments regarding the genetic basis of IQ fuel lingering controversies

1953
B. F. Skinner publishes *Science and Human Behavior*, advocating the behavioral perspective

1985 Increasing emphasis on cognitive perspective

1928
Leta Stetter Hollingworth publishes work on adolescence

1954
Abraham Maslow publishes *Motivation and Personality*, developing the concept of self-actualization

1981 David Hubel and Torsten Wiesel win Nobel prize for work on vision cells in the brain

2000
Elizabeth Loftus does pioneering work on false memory and eyewitness testimony

does and how behavior *functions*. Functionalists, whose perspective became prominent in the early 1900s, asked what role behavior plays in allowing people to adapt to their environments. For example, a functionalist might examine the function of the emotion of fear in preparing us to deal with an emergency situation.

Led by the American psychologist William James, the functionalists examined how behavior allows people to satisfy their needs and how our "stream of consciousness" permits us to adopt to our environment. The American educator John Dewey drew on functionalism to develop the field of school psychology, proposing ways to best meet students' educational needs.

Another important reaction to structuralism was the development of gestalt psychology in the early 1900s. **Gestalt psychology** emphasizes how perception is organized. Instead of considering the individual parts that make up thinking, gestalt psychologists took the opposite tack, studying how people consider individual elements together as units or wholes. Led by German scientists such as Hermann Ebbinghaus and Max Wertheimer, gestalt psychologists proposed that "The whole is different from the sum of its parts," meaning that our perception, or understanding, of objects is greater and more meaningful than the individual elements that make up our perceptions. Gestalt psychologists have made substantial contributions to our understanding of perception.

Gestalt (geh SHTALLT) psychology: An approach to psychology that focuses on the organization of perception and thinking in a "whole" sense rather than on the individual elements of perception.

WOMEN IN PSYCHOLOGY: FOUNDING MOTHERS

As in many scientific fields, social prejudices hindered women's participation in the early development of psychology. For example, many universities would not even admit women to their graduate psychology programs in the early 1900s.

Still, despite the hurdles they faced, several women made major contributions to psychology, although their impact on the field was largely overlooked until recently. For example, Margaret Floy Washburn (1871–1939) was the first woman to receive a doctorate in psychology, and she did important work on animal behavior. Leta Stetter Hollingworth (1886–1939) was one of the first psychologists to focus on child development and on women's issues. She collected data to refute the view, popular in the early 1900s, that women's abilities periodically declined during parts of the menstrual cycle (Hollingworth, 1943/1990; Denmark & Fernandez, 1993; Furumoto & Scarborough, 2002).

Mary Calkins (1863–1930), who studied memory in the early part of the twentieth century, became the first female president of the American Psychological Association. Karen Horney (pronounced "HORN-eye") (1885–1952) focused on the social and cultural factors behind personality, and June Etta Downey (1875–1932) spearheaded the study of personality traits and became the first woman to head a psychology department at a state university. Anna Freud (1895–1982), the daughter of Sigmund Freud, also made notable contributions to the treatment of abnormal behavior, and Mamie Phipps Clark (1917–1983) carried out pioneering work on how children of color grew to recognize racial differences (Horney, 1937; Stevens & Gardner, 1982; Lal, 2002).

Today's Perspectives

The women and the men who laid the foundations of psychology shared a common goal: to explain and understand behavior using scientific methods. Seeking to achieve the same goal, the tens of thousands of psychologists who followed those early pioneers embraced—and often rejected—a variety of broad perspectives.

The perspectives of psychology offer distinct outlooks and emphasize different factors. Just as we can use more than one map to find our way around a particular region—for instance, a map that shows roads and highways and another map that shows major landmarks—psychologists developed a variety of approaches to understanding behavior. When considered jointly, the different perspectives provide the means to explain behavior in its amazing variety.

Today, the field of psychology includes five major perspectives (summarized in Figure 2 and reviewed in the PsychInteractive excercise on the five perspectives of psychology). These broad perspectives emphasize different aspects of behavior and mental processes, and each takes our understanding of behavior in a somewhat different direction.

THE NEUROSCIENCE PERSPECTIVE: BLOOD, SWEAT, AND FEARS

When we get down to the basics, humans are animals made of skin and bones. The **neuroscience perspective** considers how people and nonhumans function biologically: how individual nerve cells are joined together, how the inheritance of certain characteristics from parents and other ancestors influences behavior, how the functioning of the body affects hopes and fears, which behaviors are instinctual, and so forth. Even more complex kinds of behaviors, such as a baby's response to strangers, are viewed as having critical biological components by psychologists who embrace the neuroscience perspective. This perspective includes the study of heredity and evolution, which considers how heredity may influence behavior, and behavioral neuroscience, which examines how the brain and the nervous system affect behavior.

Because every behavior can be broken down to some extent into its biological components, the neuroscience perspective has broad appeal. Psychologists who subscribe to this perspective have made major contributions to the understanding and

www.mhhe.com/feldmanup8
PsychInteractive Online

Five Perspectives of Psychology

Neuroscience perspective: The approach that views behavior from the perspective of the brain, the nervous system, and other biological functions.

Neuroscience

Views behavior from the perspective of biological functioning

Psychodynamic

Believes behavior is motivated by inner, unconscious forces over which a person has little control

Behavioral

Focuses on observable behavior

Cognitive

Examines how people understand and think about the world

Humanistic

Contends that people can control their behavior and that they naturally try to reach their full potential

FIGURE 2 The major perspectives of psychology.

betterment of human life, ranging from cures for certain types of deafness to drug treatments for people with severe mental disorders.

THE PSYCHODYNAMIC PERSPECTIVE: UNDERSTANDING THE INNER PERSON

To many people who have never taken a psychology course, psychology begins and ends with the psychodynamic perspective. Proponents of the **psychodynamic perspective** argue that behavior is motivated by inner forces and conflicts about which we have little awareness or control. Dreams and slips of the tongue are viewed as indications of what a person is truly feeling within a seething cauldron of unconscious psychic activity.

The origins of the psychodynamic view are intimately linked with one individual: Sigmund Freud. Freud was a Viennese physician in the early 1900s whose ideas about unconscious determinants of behavior had a revolutionary effect on twentieth-century thinking, not just in psychology but in related fields as well. Although some of the original Freudian principles have been roundly criticized, the contemporary psychodynamic perspective has provided a means not only to understand and treat some kinds of psychological disorders but also to understand everyday phenomena such as prejudice and aggression.

THE BEHAVIORAL PERSPECTIVE: OBSERVING THE OUTER PERSON

Whereas the neuroscience and psychodynamic approaches look inside the organism to determine the causes of its behavior, the behavioral perspective takes a very different approach. The **behavioral perspective** grew out of a rejection of psychology's early emphasis on the inner workings of the mind. Instead, behaviorists suggested that the field should focus on observable behavior that can be measured objectively.

John B. Watson was the first major American psychologist to advocate a behavioral approach. Working in the 1920s, Watson was adamant in his view that one could gain a complete understanding of behavior by studying and modifying the environment in which people operate.

In fact, Watson believed rather optimistically that it was possible to elicit any desired type of behavior by controlling a person's environment. This philosophy is clear in his own words: "Give me a dozen healthy infants, well-formed, and my own

Sigmund Freud

Psychodynamic perspective: The approach based on the view that behavior is motivated by unconscious inner forces over which the individual has little control.

Behavioral perspective: The approach that suggests that observable, measurable behavior should be the focus of study.

specified world to bring them up in and I'll guarantee to take any one at random and train him to become any type of specialist I might select—doctor, lawyer, artist, merchant-chief, and yes, even beggar-man and thief, regardless of his talents, penchants, tendencies, abilities, vocations and race of his ancestors" (Watson, 1924).

The behavioral perspective was championed by B. F. Skinner, who remains one of the best-known psychologists. Much of our understanding of how people learn new behaviors is based on the behavioral perspective.

As we will see, the behavioral perspective crops up along every byway of psychology. Along with its influence in the area of learning processes, this perspective has made contributions in such diverse areas as treating mental disorders, curbing aggression, resolving sexual problems, and ending drug addiction.

THE COGNITIVE PERSPECTIVE: IDENTIFYING THE ROOTS OF UNDERSTANDING

Cognitive perspective: The approach that focuses on how people think, understand, and know about the world.

Efforts to understand behavior lead some psychologists straight into the mind. Evolving in part from structuralism and in part as a reaction to behaviorism, which focused so heavily on observable behavior and the environment, the **cognitive perspective** focuses on how people think, understand, and know about the world. The emphasis is on learning how people comprehend and represent the outside world within themselves and how our ways of thinking about the world influence our behavior.

Many psychologists who adhere to the cognitive perspective compare human thinking to the workings of a computer, which takes in information and transforms, stores, and retrieves it. In their view, thinking is *information processing*.

Psychologists who rely on the cognitive perspective ask questions ranging from how people make decisions to whether a person can watch television and study at the same time. The common elements that link cognitive approaches are an emphasis on how people understand and think about the world and an interest in describing the patterns and irregularities in the operation of our minds.

THE HUMANISTIC PERSPECTIVE: THE UNIQUE QUALITIES OF THE HUMAN SPECIES

Humanistic perspective: The approach that suggests that all individuals naturally strive to grow, develop, and be in control of their lives and behavior.

Rejecting the view that behavior is determined largely by automatically unfolding biological forces, unconscious processes, or the environment, the **humanistic perspective** instead suggests that all individuals naturally strive to grow, develop, and be in control of their lives and behavior. Humanistic psychologists maintain that each of us has the capacity to seek and reach fulfillment.

According to Carl Rogers and Abraham Maslow, who were central figures in the development of the humanistic perspective, people will strive to reach their full potential if they are given the opportunity. The emphasis of the humanistic perspective is on *free will*, the ability to freely make decisions about one's own behavior and life. The notion of free will stands in contrast to *determinism*, which sees behavior as caused, or determined, by things beyond a person's control.

The humanistic perspective assumes that people have the ability to make their own choices about their behavior rather than relying on societal standards. More than any other approach, it stresses the role of psychology in enriching people's lives and helping them achieve self-fulfillment. By reminding psychologists of their commitment to the individual person in society, the humanistic perspective has been an important influence.

It is important not to let the abstract qualities of the broad approaches we have discussed lull you into thinking that they are purely theoretical: These perspectives underlie ongoing work of a practical nature, as we will discuss throughout this book. To start seeing how psychology can improve everyday life, read the *Applying Psychology in the 21st Century* box.

Psychology Matters

"Investigators search for clues at site of suicide bombing."

"Latest figures show AIDS epidemic kills hundreds of thousands."

"Eyewitness to killing proves unable to provide reliable clues."

A quick review of any day's news headlines reminds us that the world is beset by a variety of stubborn problems that resist easy solution. At the same time, a considerable number of psychologists are devoting their energies and expertise to addressing these problems and improving the human condition. Let's consider some of the ways in which psychology has addressed and helped work toward solutions of major societal problems (Zimbardo, 2004):

- **What are the causes of terrorism?** What motivates suicide bombers? Are they psychologically disordered, or can their behavior be seen as a rational response to a particular system of beliefs? As we'll see in Module 48 when we discuss abnormal behavior, psychologists are gaining an understanding of the factors that lead people to embrace suicide and to engage in terrorism to further a cause in which they deeply believe.
- **How can behavior associated with better physical and psychological health be encouraged?** Many psychologists seek to help people live healthier lives. For example, some have devised ways to prevent the spread of AIDS. One such approach, showing soap operas in which the characters engage in safer sex, has led viewers in Tanzania to reduce the number of sexual partners they have (Bandura, 2004).
- **Why is aggression so prevalent, and how can more humane and peaceful alternatives be promoted?** Aggression, whether it be on the playground or the battlefield, is arguably the world's greatest problem. Psychologists have sought to understand how aggression

Terrorism and its causes are among the world's most pressing issues. What can psychologists add to our understanding of the problem?

begins in children and how it may be prevented. For example, psychologists Brad Bushman and Craig Anderson have been looking at the ways in which violent video games may result in heightened violence on the part of those who play them. They have found that people who play such games have an altered view of the world, seeing it as a more violent place. In addition, they are more apt to respond to aggression even when provoked only minimally. Other psychologists are working to limit the prevalence of violent behavior, and some have designed programs to teach people how to cope with exposure to violence (Bushman & Anderson, 2001, 2002; Crawford, 2002).

- **Why do eyewitnesses to crimes often remember the events inaccurately, and how can we increase the precision of eyewitness accounts?** Psychologists' research has come to an important conclusion: Eyewitness testimony in criminal cases is often inaccurate and biased. Memories of crimes are often clouded by emotion, and the questions asked by police investigators often elicit inaccurate responses. Work by psychologists has been used to provide national guidelines for obtaining more accurate memories during criminal investigations (Bernstein & Kassin, 2005; Loftus, 2005).

These four topics represent just a few of the issues that psychologists address on a daily basis. To further explore the many ways that psychology has an impact on everyday life, check out the Psychology Matters Web site of the American Psychological Association, which features psychological applications in everyday life, at www.psychologymatters.org.

RETHINK

What do *you* think are the major problems affecting society today? What are the psychological issues involved in these problems, and how might psychologists help find solutions to them?

RECAP/EVALUATE/RETHINK

RECAP

What are the origins of psychology?

- Wilhelm Wundt laid the foundation of psychology in 1879, when he opened his laboratory in Germany. (p. 15)
- Early perspectives that guided the work of were structuralism, functionalism, and gestalt theory. (pp. 16–17)

What are the major approaches in contemporary psychology?

- The neuroscience approach focuses on the biological components of the behavior of people and animals. (p. 18)
- The psychodynamic perspective suggests that powerful, unconscious inner forces and conflicts about which people have little or no awareness are the primary determinants of behavior. (p. 19)
- The behavioral perspective deemphasizes internal processes and concentrates instead on observable, measurable behavior, suggesting that understanding and controlling a person's environment are sufficient to fully explain and modify behavior. (p. 19)
- Cognitive approaches to behavior consider how people know, understand, and think about the world. (p. 20)
- The humanistic perspective emphasizes that people are uniquely inclined toward psychological growth and higher levels of functioning and that they will strive to reach their full potential. (p. 20)

EVALUATE

1. Wundt described psychology as the study of conscious experience, a perspective he called _____.
2. Early psychologists studied the mind by asking people to describe what they were experiencing when exposed to various stimuli. This procedure was known as

_____.

3. The statement "In order to study human behavior, we must consider the whole of perception rather than its component parts" might be made by a person subscribing to which perspective of psychology?
4. Jeanne's therapist asks her to recount a violent dream she recently experienced in order to gain insight into the unconscious forces affecting her behavior. Jeanne's therapist is working from a _____ perspective.
5. "It is behavior that can be observed that should be studied, not the suspected inner workings of the mind." This statement was most likely made by someone with which perspective?
   a. cognitive perspective
   b. neuroscience perspective
   c. humanistic perspective
   d. behavioral perspective
6. "My therapist is wonderful! She always points out my positive traits. She dwells on my uniqueness and strength as an individual. I feel much more confident about myself—as if I'm really growing and reaching my potential." The therapist being described most likely follows a _____ perspective.

RETHINK

1. Focusing on one of the five major perspectives in use today (i.e., neuroscience, psychodynamic, behavioral, cognitive, and humanistic), can you describe the kinds of research questions and studies that researchers using that perspective might pursue?
2. *From a journalist's perspective:* Choose a current major political controversy. What psychological approaches or perspectives can be applied to that issue?

Answers to Evaluate Questions

1. structuralism; 2. introspection; 3. gestalt; 4. psychodynamic; 5. d; 6. humanistic.

KEY TERMS

structuralism p. 16
introspection p. 16
functionalism p. 16

gestalt psychology p. 17
neuroscience perspective
   p. 18

psychodynamic perspective
   p. 19
behavioral perspective p. 19

cognitive perspective p. 20
humanistic perspective p. 20

Psychology's Key Issues and Controversies

As you consider the many topics and perspectives that make up psychology, ranging from a narrow focus on minute biochemical influences on behavior to a broad focus on social behaviors, you might find yourself thinking that the discipline lacks cohesion. However, the field is more unified than a first glimpse might suggest. For one thing, no matter what topical area a psychologist specializes in, he or she will rely primarily on one of the five major perspectives. For example, a developmental psychologist who specializes in the study of children could make use of the cognitive perspective or the psychodynamic perspective or any of the other major perspectives.

Psychologists also agree on what the key issues of the field are. (Figure 1 and the PsychInteractive excercise on key issues in psychology summarize those issues.) Although there are major arguments regarding how best to address and resolve the key issues, psychology is a unified science because psychologists of all perspectives agree that the issues must be addressed if the field is going to advance. As you contemplate these key issues, try not to think of them in "either/or" terms. Instead, consider the opposing viewpoints on each issue as the opposite ends of a continuum, with the positions of individual psychologists typically falling somewhere between the two ends.

Nature (heredity) versus nurture (environment) is one of the major issues that psychologists address. How much of people's behavior is due to their genetically determined nature (heredity), and how much is due to nurture, the influences of the physical and social environment in which a child is raised? Furthermore, what is the

Key Concepts

What are psychology's key issues and controversies?

What is the future of psychology likely to hold?

www.mhhe.com/feldmanup8
PsychInteractive Online

Key Issues in Psychology

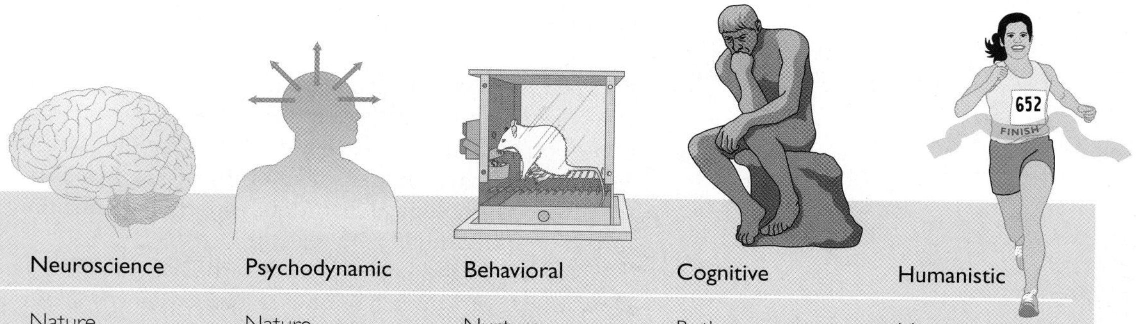

Issue	Neuroscience	Psychodynamic	Behavioral	Cognitive	Humanistic
Nature (heredity) vs. nurture (environment)	Nature (heredity)	Nature (heredity)	Nurture (environment)	Both	Nurture (environment)
Conscious vs. unconscious determinants of behavior	Unconscious	Unconscious	Conscious	Both	Conscious
Observable behavior vs. internal mental processes	Internal emphasis	Internal emphasis	Observable emphasis	Internal emphasis	Internal emphasis
Free will vs. determinism	Determinism	Determinism	Determinism	Free will	Free will
Individual differences vs. universal principles	Universal emphasis	Universal emphasis	Both	Individual emphasis	Individual emphasis

FIGURE 1 Key issues in psychology and the positions taken by psychologists subscribing to the five major perspectives of psychology.

interplay between heredity and environment? These questions have deep philosophical and historical roots, and it is a factor in many topics in psychology.

A psychologist's take on this issue depends partly on which major perspective she or he subscribes to. For example, developmental psychologists, whose focus is on how people grow and change throughout the course of their lives, may be most interested in learning more about hereditary influences if they follow a neuroscience perspective. In contrast, developmental psychologists who are proponents of the behavioral perspective would be more likely to focus on environment (Rutter, 2002).

However, every psychologist would agree that neither nature nor nurture alone is the sole determinant of behavior; rather, it is a combination of the two. In a sense, then, the real controversy involves how much of our behavior is caused by heredity and how much is caused by environmental influences.

A second major question addressed by psychologists concerns *conscious versus unconscious causes of behavior.* How much of our behavior is produced by forces of which we are fully aware, and how much is due to unconscious activity—mental processes that are not accessible to the conscious mind? This question represents one of the great controversies in the field of psychology. For example, clinical psychologists adopting a psychodynamic perspective argue that psychological disorders are brought about by unconscious factors, whereas psychologists employing the cognitive perspective suggest that psychological disorders largely are the result of faulty thinking processes. The specific approach taken has a clear impact on how psychological disorders are diagnosed and treated.

The next issue is *observable behavior versus internal mental processes.* Should psychology concentrate solely on behavior that can be seen by outside observers, or should it focus on unseen thinking processes? Some psychologists, particularly those relying on the behavioral perspective, contend that the only legitimate source of information for psychologists is behavior that can be observed directly. Other psychologists, building on the cognitive perspective, argue that what goes on inside a person's mind is critical to understanding behavior, and so we must concern ourselves with mental processes.

Free will versus determinism is another key issue. How much of our behavior is a matter of **free will** (choices made freely by an individual), and how much is subject to **determinism,** the notion that behavior is largely produced by factors beyond people's willful control? An issue long debated by philosophers, the free-will/determinism argument is also central to the field of psychology (Dennett, 2003).

For example, some psychologists who specialize in psychological disorders argue that people make intentional choices and that those who display so-called abnormal behavior should be considered responsible for their actions. Other psychologists disagree and contend that such individuals are the victims of forces beyond their control. The position psychologists take on this issue has important implications for the way they treat psychological disorders, especially in deciding whether treatment should be forced on individuals who reject it.

The last of the key issues concerns *individual differences versus universal principles.* How much of our behavior is a consequence of our unique and special qualities, and how much reflects the culture and society in which we live? How much of our behavior is universally human? Psychologists who rely on the neuroscience perspective tend to look for universal principles of behavior, such as how the nervous system operates or the way certain hormones automatically prime us for sexual activity. Such psychologists concentrate on the similarities in our behavioral destinies despite vast differences in our upbringing. In contrast, psychologists who employ the humanistic perspective focus more on the uniqueness of every individual. They consider every person's behavior a reflection of distinct and special individual qualities.

The question of the degree to which psychologists can identify universal principles that apply to all people has taken on new significance in light of the tremendous demographic changes now occurring in the United States. For instance, the proportion of people of Hispanic descent in the United States in 2050 is projected to be more than twice what it is today. Soon after that, non-Hispanic whites will be a numerical

Free will: The idea that behavior is caused primarily by choices that are made freely by the individual.

Determinism: The idea that people's behavior is produced primarily by factors outside of their willful control.

minority in the United States. Similar demographic changes are under way around the world. As we discuss next, these and other changes raise new and critical issues for the discipline of psychology in the twenty-first century.

Exploring DIVERSITY
Understanding How Culture, Ethnicity, and Race Influence Behavior

A mother in Burr Ridge, Illinois, helps her son with his math assignment. After he complains that he is "terrible at math," she tries to cheer him up by saying, "Don't feel bad; some people are born to do well in math, and others have a lot of trouble with it. It's just the way things are." At the same time, on the other side of the world in Taipei, Taiwan, a mother is helping her daughter with her math homework. When the daughter complains that she's no good at math, the mother tells her to keep at it because everyone has pretty much the same ability in math, and it is hard work that guarantees success.

These two apparently simple parent-child exchanges reveal a deep difference in perspectives on the world. People in Europe and North America are far more likely to attribute success to unchanging causes, such as intelligence, than are people in Asia, who are more likely to attribute school performance to temporary, situational factors such as the amount of effort expended.

These different perspectives may help explain the fact that Asian students often outperform U.S. students in international comparisons of student achievement. Asian students are taught that hard work and increased effort lead to academic success, and so they may be more willing to put in more effort to achieve success. In contrast, North American students tend to believe that their ability is fixed at birth and largely determines their success, and so they may be less willing to work hard (Chen & Stevenson, 1995; Chao, 2000; Leung, 2002).

Our knowledge that people in different cultures can have very different views of the world underlines the importance of moving beyond North America and studying other cultural groups in order to identify universal principles of behavior. Furthermore, broad cultural differences are not the only ones taken into account by psychologists in their attempts to identify general principles of behavior. Subcultural, ethnic, racial, and socioeconomic differences are increasingly important targets of study by psychologists (Tucker & Herman, 2002; Cardemil, Pinedo, & Miller, 2005).

Although the discipline is growing more aware of the importance of taking cultural and subcultural factors into account, progress has not been rapid in actual practice.

Members of different cultures attribute academic success to different factors. How might different cultural perspectives affect the performance of Asian versus North American students?

For example, the amount of research conducted in the United States on groups other than white middle-class college students is woefully small. Furthermore, progress has been slowed by disagreement about what constitutes a culture or subculture. There isn't even universal agreement on the use of terms such as *race* and *ethnic group,* which sometimes have been used inappropriately. Race, for instance, is a biological concept that, technically, should be used only to refer to classifications based on the physical characteristics of an organism or species. In contrast, *ethnic group* and *ethnicity* are broader terms that refer to cultural background, nationality, religion, and language.

The notion of race has been particularly difficult to address. Despite the formal, biological meaning, *race* has been used to denote anything from skin color to culture. As a concept, it has remained quite imprecise. For example, depending on one's definition, anywhere from 3 to 300 races exist. In addition, no race is "pure" in a biological sense (Betancourt & Lopez, 1993; Winkler, 1997; Pääbo, 2001).

To compound the difficulty, there are no universally acceptable names for races and ethnic groups. Psychologists—like other members of U.S. society—are divided on whether they should use the label *African American* (which focuses on geographical origins) or *black* (which focuses on skin color), just as they disagree about whether to use *Caucasian* or *white, Hispanic* or *Latino,* and *Native American* or *American Indian* (CNPAAEMI, 2000; Phinney, 2003; Wang & Sue, 2005).

Psychologists also know that the consequences of race as a biological factor cannot be understood without taking into account environmental and cultural factors. Whatever aspects of people's behavior are based on race are a joint product of their race and of the treatment they receive from others because of it. In sum, only by examining behavior across ethnic, cultural, and racial lines can psychologists differentiate principles that are universal from those which are culture-bound.

Psychology's Future

We have examined psychology's foundations, but what does the future hold for the discipline? Although the course of scientific development is notoriously difficult to predict, several trends seem likely:

- As its knowledge base grows, psychology will become increasingly specialized and new perspectives will evolve. For example, with our growing understanding of the brain and the nervous system and as scientific advances such as gene therapy become common, more psychologists will find it possible to focus on the *prevention* of psychological disorders rather than on their treatment.
- Psychological treatments will become more available and socially acceptable as the number of psychologists increases.
- The evolving sophistication of neuroscientific approaches is likely have an increasing influence over other branches of psychology. For instance, social psychologists already are increasing their understanding of behavior such as attitude change by examining brain scans (Cacioppo & Berntson, 2004).
- Technological advances also are likely to change the face of psychology. For example, Web-based psychological interventions may become possible. New technologies for repairing damaged nerve cells and even the brain are likely to evolve. Advances in our ability to examine internal changes in the nervous system will lead to greater understanding of its operation
- Psychology's influence on issues of public interest also will grow. The major problems of our time—such as violence, racial and ethnic prejudice, poverty, and environmental and technological disasters—have important psychological aspects, and it is likely that psychologists will make important practical contributions toward their resolution (Lerner, Fisher, & Weinberg, 2000; Zimbardo, 2004).
- Finally, as the population of the United States becomes more diverse, issues of diversity—embodied in the study of racial, ethnic, linguistic, and cultural fac-

tors—will become more important to psychologists providing services and doing research. The result will be a field that can provide an understanding of *human* behavior in its broadest sense (Leung & Blustein, 2000; Wang & Sue, 2005).

- An advertisement in a national magazine proclaims a cure for a major psychological problem: "The 8-week Phobia Treatment: A Complete Home-Treatment Guide to Phobia and Stress Relief." For only $29.95 (plus $3.05 for postage), a reader can obtain an "amazing" book covering topics such as "why pills and medication won't help," "your own tests," and "much, much more."
- An advertisement selling computer software proclaims in bold type, "Announcing the new hi-tech program that gives you a short-cut to success."
- A Web site invites visitors to submit by e-mail confidential questions regarding their relationships, which will be answered by "cybershrinks."
- "Expand Your Mind Beyond Virtual Reality . . . & Learn at the Speed of Light!" declares the sales pitch that arrives in the day's spam. "I have an astounding technology I'm going to share with you. Something so profound it will launch your brain beyond Virtual Reality . . . and transform your mind and soul forever."

BECOMING AN INFORMED CONSUMER of Psychology

Thinking Critically About Psychology: Distinguishing Legitimate Psychology from Pseudo-Psychology

From advertisements to television and radio talk shows to the Internet, we are subjected to a barrage of information about psychology. We are told that we can become better adjusted, smarter, more insightful, and happier individuals by learning the secrets that psychologists have revealed.

However, such promises are usually empty. If self-improvement were this easy, we would live in a country of happy-go-lucky, fully satisfied, fulfilled individuals. Obviously life is not quite so simple, and the quality of advice provided by self-styled experts—and even, on occasion, by some less-than-reputable psychologists—varies widely.

How can we separate accurate information, which is backed by science and objective research, from pseudo-psychology based on anecdotes, opinions, and even outright fraud? The best approach is to employ critical thinking techniques. Developed by psychologists who specialize in learning, memory, cognition, intelligence, and education, critical thinking procedures provide the tools to scrutinize assumptions, evaluate assertions, and think with greater precision (Halpern & Riggio, 2002; Lilienfeld, Lynn, & Lohr, 2003).

We'll be considering ways to boost critical thinking skills in *Becoming an Informed Consumer of Psychology* sections throughout the book. To get started, let's consider what you need in order to evaluate information of a psychological nature, whether the source is an advertisement, a television show, a magazine article, or even a book as seemingly reliable as a college textbook.

- For starters, know who is offering the information and advice. Are the providers of the information trained psychologists? What kinds of degrees do they have? Are they licensed? Are they affiliated with a particular institution? Before seriously relying on experts' advice, check out their credentials.
- Keep in mind that there is no free ride. If it is possible to solve major psychological ills by buying a $29.95 book, why do many people who suffer from such problems typically expend a considerable amount of time and money before they can be helped? If you could buy a computer program that would really "unlock the hidden truths" about others, wouldn't it be in widespread use? Be wary of simple, glib responses to major difficulties.
- Be aware that few universal cures exist for humankind's ills. No method or technique works for everyone. The range of difficulties attached to the human

condition is so broad that any procedure that purports to resolve all problems is certain to disappoint.

- Finally, remember that no source of information or advice is definitive. The notion of infallibility is best left to the realm of religion, and you should approach psychological information and advice from a critical and thoughtful perspective.

Despite these cautions, you should remember that the field of psychology has provided a wealth of information that people can draw upon for suggestions about every phase of life. One of the major goals of this book is to make you an informed consumer of psychological knowledge by enhancing your ability to evaluate what psychologists have to offer. Ultimately, this book will provide you with the tools you need to analyze critically the theories, research, and applications that psychologists have developed. As a result, you will be able to appreciate the real contributions that the field of psychology has made to improving human life.

RECAP/EVALUATE/RETHINK

RECAP

What are psychology's key issues and controversies?

- Psychology's key issues and controversies center on how much of human behavior is a product of nature or nurture, conscious or unconscious thoughts, observable actions or internal mental processes, free will or determinism, and individual differences or universal principles. (pp. 23–24)

What is the future of psychology likely to hold?

- Psychology will become increasingly specialized, will pay increasing attention to prevention instead of just treatment, will become increasingly concerned with the public interest, and will take the growing diversity of the country's population into account more fully. (pp. 26–27)

EVALUATE

1. The view that behavior is largely produced by factors beyond people's willful control is known as _____.

2. In the nature-nurture issue, nature refers to heredity, and nurture refers to the _____.
3. Race is a biological concept, rather than a psychological one. True or false?

RETHINK

1. "The fact that some businesses now promote their ability to help people 'expand their minds beyond virtual reality' shows the great progress psychology has made lately." Criticize this statement in light of what you know about professional psychology and pseudo-psychology.
2. *From a social worker's perspective:* Imagine that you have a caseload of clients who come from diverse cultures, ethnicities, and races. How might you consider their diverse backgrounds when interacting with them and when assisting them with identifying and obtaining social services?

Answers to Evaluate Questions

1. determinism; 2. environment; 3. true

KEY TERMS

free will p. 24   determinism p. 24

Psychology on the Web

1. Practice using several search strategies to find information on the Web about one of the key issues in psychology (e.g., free will versus determinism, nature versus nurture, or conscious versus unconscious determinants of behavior), using (a) a general-purpose search engine (such as Google at www.google.com) and (b) a more specialized search engine (such as Yahoo!'s Psychology section, under the "Social Science" heading, at www.yahoo.com). Summarize and then compare the kinds of information you have found through each strategy.

2. Search the Web for discussions of youth violence and try to find (a) an article in the general news media, (b) information from a psychological point of view (e.g., experimental information or recommendations for parents from a professional organization), and (c) political opinion or debate about how to address the issue of youth violence.

3. After completing the PyschInteractive exercise on multiple causes of behavior, identify a current news item (either from an online source or a daily newspaper) relating to human behavior. How would the different subfields of psychology be useful in explaining the behavior described in the news item? Which subfields are the most relevant, and which have the least relevance to the topic of the news item?ß

Epilogue

The field of psychology, as we have seen, is broad and diverse. It encompasses many different subfields and specialties practiced in a variety of settings, with new subfields continually arising. We have also seen that even within the various subfields of the field, it is possible to adopt several different approaches, including the neuroscience, psychodynamic, behavioral, cognitive, and humanistic perspectives.

For all its diversity, though, psychology focuses on certain key issues that serve to unify the field along common lines and shared findings. These issues will reappear as themes throughout this book as we discuss the work and accomplishments of psychologists in the many subfields of the discipline.

In light of what you've already learned about the field of psychology, reconsider the questions raised regarding the hurricane that struck New Orleans in 2005 and answer the following questions:

1. If they were using the neuroscience perspective, on what kinds of factors might psychologists focus to explain people's reactions to the hurricane?

2. Assume that two developmental psychologists are considering the effects of watching television news reports of the disaster on a child's later development. How would the questions of interest to the psychologists differ if one employed the psychodynamic perspective and the other employed the behavioral perspective?

3. What aspects of the disaster would a clinical psychologist likely focus on?

4. How might social psychologists explore the helpfulness and generosity of people in providing aid to the victims of the hurricane?

CHAPTER 2

Psychological Research

Key Concepts for Chapter 2

What is the scientific method? ● What role do theory and hypotheses play in psychological research?

What research methods do psychologists use? ● How do psychologists establish cause-and-effect relationships in research studies?

What major issues confront psychologists conducting research?

Prologue   Why Did No One Help?

Mike Petre wasn't thrilled about getting punched by six thugs aboard a light-rail train. But what really hurt was the fact that none of the other passengers lifted a finger to help him. "It's a fact of life," Mike said. "Most people are afraid to get involved."

Mike, 19, is a college student. He was riding home one night when the attack occurred on the Rancho Cordova line of Sacramento Regional Transit. "This sort of behavior is reality," he said. "For the people who attacked me, that's their way of life. They go around intimidating people, but they won't shut me up." Mike said the six were harassing two young women. He asked them to stop. They began harassing him. "One guy asked if I was gay and started to grab my backpack. That's when it started," Mike said. . . . Mike still rides light rail, but he would like to see passengers band together against thugs (Graswich, 2004, p. B1).

Looking Ahead

If Mike Petre's experience were an isolated incident, we might be able to attribute the bystanders' inaction to something specific about the situation. However, events such as this one are all too common.

In one infamous case, a woman named Kitty Genovese was attacked by a man near an apartment building in Queens, New York. At one point during the assault, which lasted thirty minutes, she managed to free herself and screamed, "Oh, my God, he stabbed me. Please help me!" In the stillness of the night, no fewer than thirty-eight neighbors heard her screams. Windows opened, and lights went on. One couple pulled chairs up to the window and turned off the lights so that they could see better. Someone called out, "Let that girl alone." But shouts were not enough to scare off the killer. He chased Genovese, stabbing her eight more times, and sexually molested her before leaving her to die. And how many of those thirty-eight witnesses came to her aid? As in Petre's case, not one person helped (Rogers & Eftimiades, 1995).

Such incidents remain dismaying—and puzzling. Why don't bystanders intervene in such situations, particularly when there are many of them who could potentially offer help? At the time of the Kitty Genovese murder, editorial writers suggested that the incidents could be attributed to the basic shortcomings of "human nature," but such an assumption is woefully inadequate. Many people have risked their own lives to help others in dangerous situations, and so "human nature" encompasses a wide range of both negative and positive responses.

Psychologists puzzled over the problem for many years. After much research they reached an unexpected conclusion: Kitty Genovese probably would have been better off if only a few people, rather than many, had heard her cries for help. In fact, if only one bystander had been present, the chances of that person intervening might have been fairly high. It turns out that the fewer the witnesses to an assault, the better the victim's chances of getting help.

How did psychologists come to such a curious conclusion? After all, logic and common sense clearly suggest that more bystanders would produce a greater likelihood that someone would help a person in need. This seeming contradiction—and the way psychologists resolved it—illustrates a central challenge for the field of psychology: asking useful questions about the unknown and getting valid answers.

Like professionals in any science, psychologists are vitally concerned with refining and expanding knowledge within their field. In the following modules we'll see how psychologists pose questions of interest and answer them through scientific research. We'll find that the answers psychologists obtain from their research not only advance our understanding of behavior, but also offer the potential to improve the human condition.

The Scientific Method

"Birds of a feather flock together" . . . or "opposites attract"? "Two heads are better than one" . . . or "if you want a thing done well, do it yourself"? "The more the merrier" . . . or "two's company, three's a crowd"?

If we were to rely on common sense to understand behavior, we'd have considerable difficulty—especially because commonsense views are often contradictory. In fact, one of the major undertakings for the field of psychology is to develop suppositions about behavior and to determine which of those suppositions are accurate.

Psychologists—as well as scientists in other disciplines—meet the challenge of posing appropriate questions and properly answering them by relying on the scientific method. The **scientific method** is the approach used by psychologists to systematically acquire knowledge and understanding about behavior and other phenomena of interest. As illustrated in Figure 1, it consists of three main steps: (1) identifying questions of interest, (2) formulating an explanation, and (3) carrying out research designed to support or refute the explanation.

Key Concepts

What is the scientific method?

What role do theory and hypotheses play in psychological research?

Scientific method: The approach through which psychologists systematically acquire knowledge and understanding about behavior and other phenomena of interest.

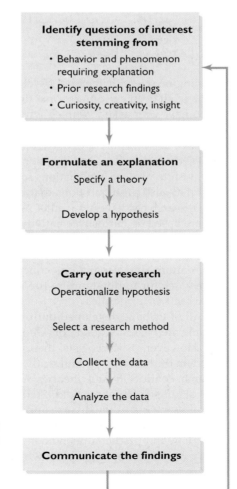

Identify questions of interest stemming from
- Behavior and phenomenon requiring explanation
- Prior research findings
- Curiosity, creativity, insight

Formulate an explanation
Specify a theory
Develop a hypothesis

Carry out research
Operationalize hypothesis
Select a research method
Collect the data
Analyze the data

Communicate the findings

FIGURE 1 The scientific method, which encompasses the process of identifying, asking, and answering questions, is used by psychologists, and by researchers from every other scientific discipline, to come to an understanding about the world. What do you think are the advantages of this method?

33

Theories: Specifying Broad Explanations

In using the scientific method, psychologists start by identifying questions of interest. We have all been curious at some time about our observations of everyday behavior. If you have ever asked yourself why a particular teacher is so easily annoyed, why a friend is always late for appointments, or how your dog understands your commands, you have been formulating questions about behavior.

Psychologists, too, ask questions about the nature and causes of behavior. They may wish to explore explanations for everyday behaviors or for various phenomena. They may also pose questions that build on findings from their previous research or from research carried out by other psychologists. Or they may produce new questions that are based on curiosity, creativity, or insight.

Once a question has been identified, the next step in the scientific method is to develop a theory to explain the observed phenomenon. **Theories** are broad explanations and predictions concerning phenomena of interest. They provide a framework for understanding the relationships among a set of otherwise unorganized facts or principles.

All of us have developed our own informal theories of human behavior, such as "People are basically good" or "People's behavior is usually motivated by self-interest." However, psychologists' theories are more formal and focused. They are established on the basis of a careful study of the psychological literature to identify relevant research conducted and theories formulated previously, as well as psychologists' general knowledge of the field (Sternberg & Beall, 1991; McGuire, 1997).

Growing out of the diverse approaches employed by psychologists, theories vary both in their breadth and in their level of detail. For example, one theory might seek to explain and predict a phenomenon as broad as emotional experience. A narrower theory might attempt to explain why people display the emotion of fear nonverbally after receiving a threat.

Theories: Broad explanations and predictions concerning phenomena of interest.

Psychologists Bibb Latané and John Darley, responding to the failure of bystanders to intervene when Kitty Genovese was murdered in New York, developed what they called a theory of *diffusion of responsibility* (Latané & Darley, 1970). According to their theory, the greater the number of bystanders or witnesses to an event that calls for helping behavior, the more the responsibility for helping is perceived to be shared by all the bystanders. Thus, the greater the number of bystanders in an emergency situation, the smaller the share of the responsibility each person feels—and the less likely it is that any single person will come forward to help.

Hypotheses: Crafting Testable Predictions

Although the diffusion of responsibility theory seems to make sense, it represented only the beginning phase of Latané and Darley's investigative process. Their next step was to devise a way to test their theory. To do this, they needed to create a hypothesis. A **hypothesis** is a prediction stated in a way that allows it to be tested. Hypotheses stem from theories; they help test the underlying validity of theories.

> **Hypothesis:** A prediction, stemming from a theory, stated in a way that allows it to be tested.

In the same way that we develop our own broad theories about the world, we also construct hypotheses about events and behavior. Those hypotheses can range from trivialities (such as why our English instructor wears those weird shirts) to more meaningful matters (such as what is the best way to study for a test). Although we rarely test these hypotheses systematically, we do try to determine whether they are right. Perhaps we try comparing two strategies: cramming the night before an exam versus spreading out our study over several nights. By assessing which approach yields better test performance, we have created a way to compare the two strategies.

Latané and Darley's hypothesis was a straightforward prediction from their more general theory of diffusion of responsibility: The more people who witness an emergency situation, the less likely it is that help will be given to a victim. They could, of course, have chosen another hypothesis (for instance, that people with more first-aid skills will be less affected by the presence of others and more likely to help than will those with fewer first-aid skills), but their initial formulation seemed to offer the most direct test of the theory.

Psychologists rely on formal theories and hypotheses for many reasons. For one thing, theories and hypotheses allow them to make sense of unorganized, separate observations and bits of information by permitting them to place the pieces within a structured and coherent framework. In addition, theories and hypotheses offer psychologists the opportunity to move beyond already known facts and principles and make deductions about unexplained phenomena. In this way, theories and hypotheses provide a reasoned guide to the direction that future investigation ought to take (Howitt & Cramer, 2000; Cohen, 2003).

In short, the scientific method, with its emphasis on theories and hypotheses, helps psychologists pose appropriate questions. With properly stated questions in hand, psychologists then can choose from a variety of research methods to find answers. (To get a better understanding of the scientific method used by psychologists, try the PsychInteractive exercise on the scientific method.)

www.mhhe.com/feldmanup8
PsychInteractive Online

The Scientific Method

RECAP/EVALUATE/RETHINK

RECAP

What is the scientific method?

- The scientific method is the approach psychologists use to understand behavior. It consists of three steps: identifying questions of interest, formulating an explanation, and carrying out research that is designed to support or refute the explanation. (p. 33)

What role do theory and hypotheses play in psychological research?

- Research in psychology is guided by theories (broad explanations and predictions regarding phenomena of interest) and hypotheses (theory-based predictions stated in a way that allows them to be tested). (pp. 33–34)

EVALUATE

1. An explanation for a phenomenon of interest is known as a _____.
2. To test this explanation, it must be stated in terms of a testable question known as a _____.

RETHINK

1. Starting with the theory that diffusion of responsibility causes responsibility for helping to be shared among bystanders, Latané and Darley derived the hypothesis that the more people who witness an emergency situation, the less likely it is that help will be given to a victim. How many other hypotheses can you think of that are based on the same theory of diffusion of responsibility?
2. *From a lawyer's perspective:* Imagine that you are assigned to a case similar to the one of Kitty Genovese. Your supervisor, who is unfamiliar with psychological research, asks you to provide information (e.g., characteristics) about the eyewitnesses to explain why they did not help her. What would you include in your report?

Answers to Evaluate Questions

1. theory; 2. hypothesis

KEY TERMS

scientific method p. 33   theories p. 34   hypothesis p. 35

Conducting Psychological Research

Research—systematic inquiry aimed at the discovery of new knowledge—is a central ingredient of the scientific method in psychology. It provides the key to understanding the degree to which hypotheses (and the theories behind them) are accurate.

Just as we can apply different theories and hypotheses to explain the same phenomena, we can use a number of alternative methods to conduct research (Ray, 2000). First, though, the hypothesis must be restated in a way that will allow it to be tested, which involves creating an operational definition. An **operational definition** is the translation of a hypothesis into specific, testable procedures that can be measured and observed.

There is no single way to go about devising an operational definition for a hypothesis; it depends on logic, the equipment and facilities available, the psychological perspective being employed, and ultimately the creativity of the researcher. For example, one researcher might develop a hypothesis in which she uses as an operational definition of "fear" an increase in heart rate. In contrast, another psychologist might use as an operational definition of "fear" a written response to the question "How much fear are you experiencing at this moment?"

In our discussion of research methods, we will consider several major tools in the psychologist's research kit. Keep in mind that their relevance extends beyond testing and evaluating hypotheses in psychology. Even people who do not have degrees in psychology often carry out elementary forms of research on their own. For instance, a supervisor might need to evaluate an employee's performance; a physician might systematically test the effects of different doses of a drug on a patient; a salesperson might compare different persuasive strategies. Each of these situations draws on the research practices we are about to discuss.

Furthermore, knowledge of the research methods used by psychologists permits us to better evaluate the research that others conduct. The media constantly bombard us with claims about research studies and findings. Knowledge of research methods allows us to sort out what is credible from what should be ignored. Finally, there is evidence that by studying some kinds of research methods in depth, people learn to reason more critically and effectively. Understanding the methods by which psychologists conduct research can enhance our ability to analyze and evaluate the situations we encounter in our everyday lives (Shaughnessy, Zechmeister, & Zechmeister, 2000; Shadish, Cook, & Campbell, 2002; Tryon & Bernstein, 2003).

Descriptive Research

Let's begin by considering several types of **descriptive research** designed to systematically investigate a person, group, or patterns of behavior. These methods include archival research, naturalistic observation, survey research, and case studies.

ARCHIVAL RESEARCH

Suppose that, like the psychologists Latané and Darley (1970), you were interested in finding out more about emergency situations in which bystanders did not provide help. One of the first places you might turn to would be historical accounts. By search-

Key Concepts

What research methods do psychologists use?

How do psychologists establish cause-and-effect relationships in research studies?

Operational definition: The translation of a hypothesis into specific, testable procedures that can be measured and observed.

Descriptive research: An approach to research designed to systematically investigate a person, group, or patterns of behavior.

Archival research: Research in which existing data, such as census documents, college records, and newspaper clippings, are examined to test a hypothesis.

Naturalistic observation: Research in which an investigator simply observes some naturally occurring behavior and does not make a change in the situation.

Dian Fossey, a pioneer in the study of endangered mountain gorillas in their native habitat, relied on naturalistic observation for her research. What are the advantages of this approach?

www.mhhe.com/feldmanup8

PsychInteractive Online

Naturalistic Observation

Survey research: Research in which people chosen to represent a larger population are asked a series of questions about their behavior, thoughts, or attitudes.

ing newspaper records, for example, you might find support for the notion that a decrease in helping behavior historically has accompanied an increase in the number of bystanders.

Using newspaper articles is an example of archival research. In **archival research,** existing data, such as census documents, college records, and newspaper clippings, are examined to test a hypothesis. For example, college records may be used to determine if there are gender differences in academic performance.

Archival research is a relatively inexpensive means of testing a hypothesis because someone else has already collected the basic data. Of course, the use of existing data has several drawbacks. For one thing, the data may not be in a form that allows the researcher to test a hypothesis fully. The information could also be incomplete, or it could have been collected haphazardly (Simonton, 2000a; Riniolo et al., 2003).

Most attempts at archival research are hampered by the simple fact that records with the necessary information often do not exist. In these instances, researchers often turn to another research method: naturalistic observation.

NATURALISTIC OBSERVATION

In **naturalistic observation,** the investigator observes some naturally occurring behavior and does not make a change in the situation. For example, a researcher investigating helping behavior might observe the kind of help given to victims in a high-crime area of a city. The important point to remember about naturalistic observation is that the researcher simply records what occurs, making no modification in the situation that is being observed (Schutt, 2001; Moore, 2002).

Although the advantage of naturalistic observation is obvious—we get a sample of what people do in their "natural habitat"—there is also an important drawback: the inability to control any of the factors of interest. For example, we might find so few naturally occurring instances of helping behavior that we would be unable to draw any conclusions. Because naturalistic observation prevents researchers from making changes in a situation, they must wait until the appropriate conditions occur. Furthermore, if people know they are being watched, they may alter their reactions, producing behavior that is not truly representative. (To get more information on research using naturalistic observation, try the PsychInteractive exercise on naturalistic observation.)

SURVEY RESEARCH

There is no more straightforward way of finding out what people think, feel, and do than asking them directly. For this reason, surveys are an important research method. In **survey research,** a *sample* of people chosen to represent a larger group of interest (a *population*) is asked a series of questions about their behavior, thoughts, or attitudes. Survey methods have become so sophisticated that even with a very small sample researchers are able to infer with great accuracy how a larger group would respond. For instance, a sample of just a few thousand voters is sufficient to predict within one or two percentage points who will win a presidential election—if the representative sample is chosen with care (Sommer & Sommer, 2001; Groves et al., 2004).

Researchers investigating helping behavior might conduct a survey by asking people to complete a questionnaire in which they indicate their reasons for not wanting to come forward to help another individual. Similarly, researchers interested in learning about sexual practices have carried out surveys to learn which practices are common and which are not and to chart changing notions of sexual morality over the last several decades.

However, survey research has several potential pitfalls. For one thing, if the sample of people who are surveyed is not representative of the broader population of interest, the results of the survey will have little meaning. For instance, if a sample of voters in a town only included Republicans, it would hardly be useful for predict-

Secret Bias: Using the Implicit Association Test to Measure Hidden Prejudice

A 34-year-old white woman sat down in her Washington office to take a psychological test. Her office decor attested to her passion for civil rights—as a senior activist at a national gay rights organization, and as a lesbian herself, fighting bias and discrimination is what gets her out of bed every morning. A rainbow flag rested in a mug on her desk....

All [the test] asked her to do was distinguish between a series of black and white faces. When she saw a black face she was to hit a key on the left, when she saw a white face she was to hit a key on the right. Next, she was asked to distinguish between a series of positive and negative words. Words such as "glorious" and "wonderful" required a left key, words such as "nasty" and "awful" required a right key. The test remained simple when two categories were combined: The activist hit the left key if she saw either a white face or a positive word, and hit the right key if she saw either a black face or a negative word.

Then the groupings were reversed. The woman's index fingers hovered over her keyboard. The test now required her to group black faces with positive words, and white faces with negative words. She leaned forward intently. She made no mistakes, but it took her longer to correctly sort the words and images.

Her result appeared on the screen, and the activist became very silent. The test found she had a bias for whites over blacks (Vedatam, 2005, p. W12).

Could you, like this woman, be prejudiced and not even know it? The answer, according to the researchers who developed the *Implicit Association Test,* is probably yes. People often fool themselves, and they are very careful about revealing their true attitudes about members of various groups, not only to others but to themselves. However, even though they may truly believe that they are unprejudiced, the reality is that they actually routinely differentiate between people on the basis of race, ethnicity, and sexual orientation.

The Implicit Association Test, or IAT, is an ingenious measure of prejudice that permits a more accurate assessment of people's discrimination among members of different groups. It was developed, in part, as a reaction to the difficulty in finding a questionnaire that would reveal prejudice. Direct questions such as, "Would you prefer interacting with a member of Group X rather than Group Y?" typically identify only the most blatant prejudices, because people try to censor their responses.

In contrast, the IAT makes use of the fact that people's automatic reactions often provide the most valid indicator of what they actually believe. Having grown up in a culture that teaches us to think about members of particular groups in specific ways, we tend to absorb associations about those groups that are reflective of the culture.

The results of the IAT show that almost 90 percent of test-takers have a pro-white implicit bias, and more than two-thirds of non-Arab, non-Muslim volunteers display implicit biases against Arab Muslims. Moreover, more than 80 percent of heterosexuals display an implicit bias against gays and lesbians.

Of course, having an implicit bias does not mean that people will overtly discriminate, a criticism that has been made of the test. Yet it does mean that the cultural lessons to which we are exposed have a considerable unconscious influence on us.

Interested in how you would perform on the IAT? Go to this Web site to take the test: implicit.harvard.edu/implicit.

RETHINK

Why do you think it is so difficult to get people to reveal their true feelings about prejudice using traditional questionnaires? If a person who is revealed by the IAT to be biased truly does not believe that he or she is prejudiced, does that mean the IAT is not a valid measure?

---

ing the results of an election in which both Republicans and Democrats were voting (Daley et al., 2003).

People may also respond inaccurately if the survey includes *loaded questions,* questions that represent only one side of an issue or lead to biased responses. For example, someone who answers the question "Do you support reducing welfare benefits in order to reduce the budget deficit?" positively may actually be against a reduction in welfare benefits but agree with the question because it is placed in the context of deficit reduction.

Finally, survey respondents may not want to admit to holding socially undesirable attitudes. To overcome participants' reluctance to be truthful, researchers are developing alternative, and often ingenious, research techniques, as we consider in the *Applying Psychology in the 21st Century* box. (See also the PsychInteractive exercise on self-report bias in surveys for information on self-report bias in surveys.)

www.mhhe.com/feldmanup8
PsychInteractive Online

Self-Report Bias in Surveys

"This is the New York 'Times'
Business Poll again, Mr. Landau.
Do you feel better or worse about the economy
than you did twenty minutes ago?"

Case study: An in-depth, intensive investigation of an individual or small group of people.

Variables: Behaviors, events, or other characteristics that can change, or vary, in some way.

Correlational research: Research in which the relationship between two sets of variables is examined to determine whether they are associated, or "correlated."

THE CASE STUDY

When a coordinated group of terrorists bombed the London subway system in 2005, many people wondered what it was about the bombers' personalities or backgrounds that might have led to their behavior. To answer this question, psychologists might conduct a case study. In contrast to a survey, in which many people are studied, a **case study** is an in-depth, intensive investigation of a single individual or a small group. Case studies often include *psychological testing,* a procedure in which a carefully designed set of questions is used to gain some insight into the personality of the individual or group (Breakwell, Hammond, & Fife-Schaw, 2000; Gass et al., 2000).

When case studies are used as a research technique, the goal is often not only to learn about the few individuals being examined but also to use the insights gained from the study to improve our understanding of people in general. Sigmund Freud developed his theories through case studies of individual patients. Similarly, case studies of the London bombers might help identify others who are prone to violence.

The drawback to case studies? If the individuals examined are too unique, it is impossible to make valid generalizations to a larger population. Still, they sometimes lead the way to new theories and treatments.

CORRELATIONAL RESEARCH

In using the descriptive research methods we have discussed, researchers often wish to determine the relationship between two variables. **Variables** are behaviors, events, or other characteristics that can change, or vary, in some way. For example, in a study to determine whether the amount of studying makes a difference in test scores, the variables would be study time and test scores.

In **correlational research,** two sets of variables are examined to determine whether they are associated, or "correlated." The strength and direction of the relationship between the two variables are represented by a mathematical statistic known as a *correlation* (or, more formally, a *correlation coefficient*), which can range from +1.0 to −1.0.

A *positive correlation* indicates that as the value of one variable increases, we can predict that the value of the other variable will also increase. For example, if we predict that the more time students spend studying for a test, the higher their grades on the test will be, and that the less they study, the lower their test scores will be, we are expecting to find a positive correlation. (Higher values of the variable "amount of study time" would be associated with higher values of the variable "test score," and lower values of "amount of study time" would be associated with lower values of "test score.") The correlation, then, would be indicated by a positive number, and the stronger the association was between studying and test scores, the closer the number would be to +1.0. For example, we might find a correlation of +.85 between test scores and amount of study time, indicating a strong positive association.

In contrast, a *negative correlation* tells us that as the value of one variable increases, the value of the other decreases. For instance, we might predict that as the number of hours spent studying increases, the number of hours spent in partying decreases. Here we are expecting a negative correlation, ranging between 0 and −1.0. More studying is associated with less partying, and less studying is associated with more partying. The stronger the association between studying and partying is, the closer the correlation will be to −1.0. For instance, a correlation of −.85 would indicate a strong negative association between partying and studying.

Of course, it's quite possible that little or no relationship exists between two variables. For instance, we would probably not expect to find a relationship between number of study hours and height. Lack of a relationship would be indicated by a correlation close to 0. For example, if we found a correlation of −.02 or +.03, it would indicate that there is virtually no association between the two variables; knowing how much someone studies does not tell us anything about how tall he or she is.

When two variables are strongly correlated with each other, it is tempting to assume that one variable causes the other. For example, if we find that more study time is associated with higher grades, we might guess that more studying *causes* higher grades. Although this is not a bad guess, it remains just a guess—because finding that two variables are correlated does not mean that there is a causal relationship between them. The strong correlation suggests that knowing how much a person studies can help us predict how that person will do on a test, but it does not mean that the studying causes the test performance. It might be, for instance, that people who are more interested in the subject matter tend to study more than do those who are less interested, and that the amount of interest, not the number of hours spent studying, predicts test performance. The mere fact that two variables occur together does not mean that one causes the other. (To better understand this principle, use the PsychInteractive exercise on correlation to participate in a demonstration of how correlation is unrelated to causation.)

Another example illustrates the critical point that correlations tell us nothing about cause and effect but merely provide a measure of the strength of a relationship between two variables. We might find that children who watch a lot of television programs featuring high levels of aggression are likely to demonstrate a relatively high degree of aggressive behavior and that those who watch few television shows that portray aggression are apt to exhibit a relatively low degree of such behavior (see Figure 1). But we cannot say that the aggression is *caused* by the TV viewing, because several other explanations are possible.

For instance, it could be that children who have an unusually high level of energy seek out programs with aggressive content *and* are more aggressive. The children's energy level, then, could be the true cause of the children's higher incidence of aggression. Finally, it is also possible that people who are already highly aggressive choose to watch shows with a high aggressive content *because* they are aggressive. Clearly, then, any number of causal sequences are possible—none of which can be ruled out by correlational research.

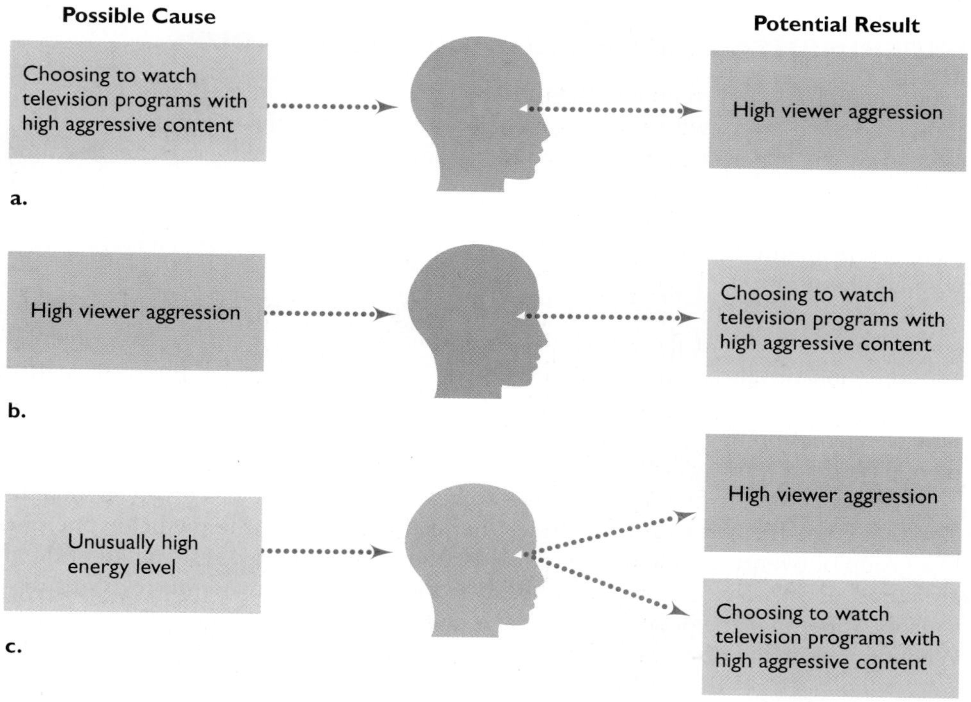

www.mhhe.com/feldmanup8
PsychInteractive Online

Correlation

Possible Cause

a.
Choosing to watch television programs with high aggressive content → → High viewer aggression

Potential Result

b.
High viewer aggression → → Choosing to watch television programs with high aggressive content

c.
Unusually high energy level → → High viewer aggression / Choosing to watch television programs with high aggressive content

FIGURE 1 If we find that frequent viewing of television programs with aggressive content is associated with high levels of aggressive behavior, we might cite several plausible causes, as suggested in this figure. For example, choosing to watch shows with aggressive content could produce aggression (a); or being a highly aggressive person might cause one to choose to watch televised aggression (b); or having a high energy level might cause a person to both choose to watch aggressive shows and act aggressively (c). Correlational findings, then, do not permit us to determine causality. Can you think of a way to study the effects of televised aggression on aggressive behavior that is not correlational?

Many studies show that the observation of violence in the media is associated with aggression in viewers. Can we conclude that the observation of violence causes aggression?

Experiment: The investigation of the relationship between two (or more) variables by deliberately producing a change in one variable in a situation and observing the effects of that change on other aspects of the situation.

Experimental manipulation: The change that an experimenter deliberately produces in a situation.

Treatment: The manipulation implemented by the experimenter.

Experimental group: Any group participating in an experiment that receives a treatment.

Control group: A group participating in an experiment that receives no treatment.

The inability of correlational research to demonstrate cause-and-effect relationships is a crucial drawback to its use. There is, however, an alternative technique that does establish causality: the experiment.

Experimental Research

The *only* way psychologists can establish cause-and-effect relationships through research is by carrying out an experiment. In a formal **experiment,** the relationship between two (or more) variables is investigated by deliberately changing one variable in a controlled situation and observing the effects of that change on other aspects of the situation. In an experiment, then, the conditions are created and controlled by the researcher, who deliberately makes a change in those conditions in order to observe the effects of that change.

The change that the researcher deliberately makes in an experiment is called the **experimental manipulation.** Experimental manipulations are used to detect relationships between different variables.

Several steps are involved in carrying out an experiment, but the process typically begins with the development of one or more hypotheses for the experiment to test. For example, Latané and Darley, in testing their theory of the diffusion of responsibility in bystander behavior, developed this hypothesis: The higher the number of people who witness an emergency situation is, the less likely it is that any of them will help the victim. They then designed an experiment to test this hypothesis.

Their first step was to formulate an operational definition of the hypothesis by conceptualizing it in a way that could be tested. Latané and Darley had to take into account the fundamental principle of experimental research mentioned earlier: Experimenters must manipulate at least one variable in order to observe the effects of the manipulation on another variable while keeping other factors in the situation constant. However, the manipulation cannot be viewed by itself, in isolation; if a cause-and-effect relationship is to be established, the effects of the manipulation must be compared with the effects of no manipulation or a different kind of manipulation.

EXPERIMENTAL GROUPS AND CONTROL GROUPS

Experimental research requires, then, that the responses of at least two groups be compared. One group will receive some special **treatment**—the manipulation implemented by the experimenter—and another group will receive either no treatment or a different treatment. Any group that receives a treatment is called an **experimental group;** a group that receives no treatment is called a **control group.** (In some experiments there are multiple experimental and control groups, each of which is compared with another group.)

By employing both experimental and control groups in an experiment, researchers are able to rule out the possibility that something other than the experimental manipulation produced the results observed in the experiment. Without a control group, we couldn't be sure that some other variable, such as the temperature at the time we were running the experiment, the color of the experimenter's hair, or even the mere passage of time, wasn't causing the changes observed.

For example, consider a medical researcher who thinks she has invented a medicine that cures the common cold. To test her claim, she gives the medicine one day to a group of twenty people who have colds, and finds that ten days later all of them are cured. Eureka? Not so fast. An observer viewing this flawed study might reasonably argue that the people would have gotten better even without the medicine. What the researcher obviously needed was a control group consisting of people with colds who *don't* get the medicine and whose health is also checked ten days later.

Only if there is a significant difference between experimental and control groups can the effectiveness of the medicine be assessed. Through the use of control groups, then, researchers can isolate specific causes for their findings—and draw cause-and-effect inferences.

Returning to Latané and Darley's experiment, we see that the researchers needed to translate their hypothesis into something testable. To do this, they decided to create a false emergency situation that would appear to require the aid of a bystander. As their experimental manipulation, they decided to vary the number of bystanders present. They could have had just one experimental group with, say, two people present, and a control group for comparison purposes with just one person present. Instead, they settled on a more complex procedure involving the creation of groups of three sizes—consisting of two, three, and six people—that could be compared with one another.

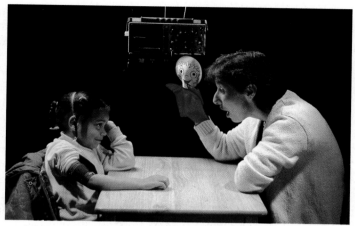

In this experiment, preschoolers' reactions to the puppet are monitored. Can you think of a hypothesis that might be tested in this way?

INDEPENDENT AND DEPENDENT VARIABLES

Latané and Darley's experimental design now included an operational definition of what is called the **independent variable.** The independent variable is the condition that is manipulated by an experimenter. (You can think of the independent variable as being independent of the actions of those taking part in an experiment; it is controlled by the experimenter.) In the case of the Latané and Darley experiment, the independent variable was the number of people present, which was manipulated by the experimenters.

Independent variable: The variable that is manipulated by an experimenter.

The next step was to decide how they were going to determine the effect that varying the number of bystanders had on behavior of those in the experiment. Crucial to every experiment is the **dependent variable,** the variable that is measured and is expected to change as a result of changes caused by the experimenter's manipulation of the independent variable. The dependent variable is dependent on the actions of the *participants* or *subjects*—the people taking part in the experiment.

Dependent variable: The variable that is measured and is expected to change as a result of changes caused by the experimenter's manipulation of the independent variable.

Latané and Darley had several possible choices for their dependent measure. One might have been a simple yes/no measure of the participants' helping behavior. But the

"What if these guys in white coats who bring us food are, like, studying us and we're part of some kind of big experiment?"

www.mhhe.com/feldmanup8

PsychInteractive Online

Experimental Design

investigators also wanted a more precise analysis of helping behavior. Consequently, they also measured the amount of time it took for a participant to provide help.

Latané and Darley now had all the necessary components of an experiment. The independent variable, manipulated by them, was the number of bystanders present in an emergency situation. The dependent variable was the measure of whether bystanders in each of the groups provided help and the amount of time it took them to do so. Consequently, like all experiments, this one had both an independent variable and a dependent variable. (To remember the difference, recall that a hypothesis predicts how a dependent variable *depends* on the manipulation of the independent variable.) *All* true experiments in psychology fit this straightforward model. (For more information try the PsychInteractive exercise on experimental design.)

RANDOM ASSIGNMENT OF PARTICIPANTS

To make the experiment a valid test of the hypothesis, Latané and Darley needed to add a final step to the design: properly assigning participants to a particular experimental group.

The significance of this step becomes clear when we examine various alternative procedures. For example, the experimenters might have assigned just males to the group with two bystanders, just females to the group with three bystanders, and both males and females to the group with six bystanders. If they had done this, however, any differences they found in helping behavior could not be attributed with any certainty solely to group size, because the differences might just as well have been due to the composition of the group. A more reasonable procedure would be to ensure that each group had the same composition in terms of gender; then the researchers would be able to make comparisons across groups with considerably more accuracy.

Participants in each of the experimental groups ought to be comparable, and it is easy enough to create groups that are similar in terms of gender. The problem becomes a bit more tricky, though, when we consider other participant characteristics. How can we ensure that participants in each experimental group will be equally intelligent, extroverted, cooperative, and so forth, when the list of characteristics—any one of which could be important—is potentially endless?

Random assignment to condition:
A procedure in which participants are assigned to different experimental groups or "conditions" on the basis of chance and chance alone.

The solution is a simple but elegant procedure called **random assignment to condition:** Participants are assigned to different experimental groups or "conditions" on the basis of chance and chance alone. The experimenter might, for instance, flip a coin for each participant and assign a participant to one group when "heads" came up, and to the other group when "tails" came up. The advantage of this technique is that participant characteristics have an equal chance of being distributed across the various groups. When a researcher uses random assignment—which in practice is usually carried out using computer-generated random numbers—chances are that each of the groups will have approximately the same proportion of intelligent people, cooperative people, extroverted people, males and females, and so on.

Figure 2 provides another example of an experiment. Like all experiments, it includes the following set of key elements, which are important to keep in mind as you consider whether a research study is truly an experiment:

- An independent variable, the variable that is manipulated by the experimenter;
- A dependent variable, the variable that is measured by the experimenter and that is expected to change as a result of the manipulation of the independent variable;
- A procedure that randomly assigns participants to different experimental groups or "conditions" of the independent variable; and
- A hypothesis that predicts the effect the independent variable will have on the dependent variable.

Only if each of these elements is present can a research study be considered a true experiment in which cause-and-effect relationships can be determined. (For a summary of the different types of research that we've discussed, see Figure 3 on page 46.)

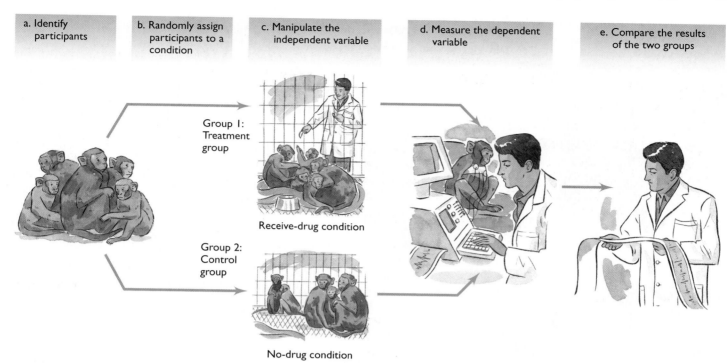

a. Identify participants

b. Randomly assign participants to a condition

c. Manipulate the independent variable

d. Measure the dependent variable

e. Compare the results of the two groups

Group 1: Treatment group

Receive-drug condition

Group 2: Control group

No-drug condition

FIGURE 2 In this depiction of a study investigating the effects of the drug propranolol on stress, we can see the basic elements of all true experiments. The participants in the experiment were monkeys, who were randomly assigned to one of two groups. Monkeys assigned to the treatment group were given a drug, propranolol, hypothesized to prevent heart disease, whereas those in the control group were not given the drug. Administration of the drugs, then, was the independent variable.

All the monkeys were given a high-fat diet that was the human equivalent of two eggs with bacon every morning, and they occasionally were reassigned to different cages to provide a source of stress. To determine the effects of the drug, the monkeys' heart rates and other measures of heart disease were assessed after twenty-six months. These measures constituted the dependent variable. (The results? As hypothesized, monkeys that received the drug showed lower heart rates and fewer symptoms of heart disease than those who did not.) (Based on a study by Kaplan & Manuck, 1989.)

WERE LATANÉ AND DARLEY RIGHT?

To test their hypothesis that increasing the number of bystanders in an emergency situation would lower the degree of helping behavior, Latané and Darley placed the participants in a room and told them that the purpose of the experiment was to talk about personal problems associated with college. The discussion was to be held over an intercom, supposedly to avoid the potential embarrassment of face-to-face contact. Chatting about personal problems was not, of course, the true purpose of the experiment, but telling the participants that it was was a way of keeping their expectations from biasing their behavior. (Consider how they would have been affected if they had been told that their helping behavior in emergencies was being tested. The experimenters could never have gotten an accurate assessment of what the participants would actually do in an emergency. By definition, emergencies are rarely announced in advance.)

The sizes of the discussion groups were two, three, and six people, which constituted the manipulation of the independent variable of group size. Participants were randomly assigned to these groups upon their arrival at the laboratory. Each group included a trained *confederate*, or employee, of the experimenters. In each two-person group, then, there was only one real "bystander."

As the participants in each group were holding their discussion, they suddenly heard through the intercom one of the other participants—the confederate—having what sounded like an epileptic seizure and calling for help.

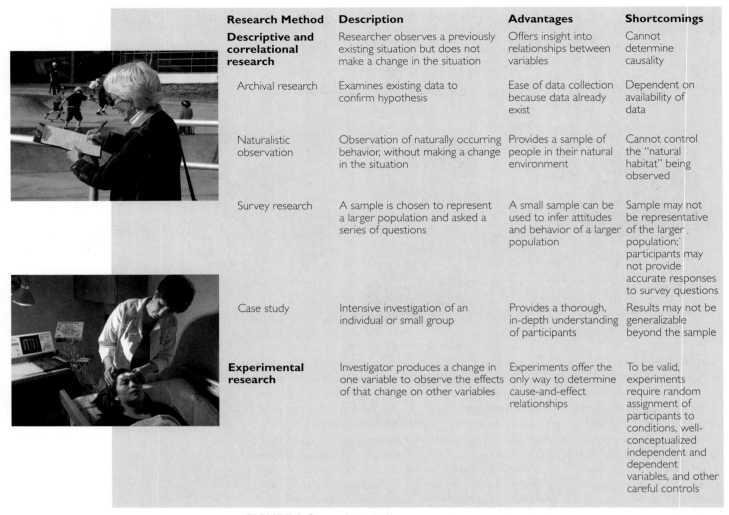

Research Method	Description	Advantages	Shortcomings
Descriptive and correlational research	Researcher observes a previously existing situation but does not make a change in the situation	Offers insight into relationships between variables	Cannot determine causality
Archival research	Examines existing data to confirm hypothesis	Ease of data collection because data already exist	Dependent on availability of data
Naturalistic observation	Observation of naturally occurring behavior, without making a change in the situation	Provides a sample of people in their natural environment	Cannot control the "natural habitat" being observed
Survey research	A sample is chosen to represent a larger population and asked a series of questions	A small sample can be used to infer attitudes and behavior of a larger population	Sample may not be representative of the larger population; participants may not provide accurate responses to survey questions
Case study	Intensive investigation of an individual or small group	Provides a thorough, in-depth understanding of participants	Results may not be generalizable beyond the sample
Experimental research	Investigator produces a change in one variable to observe the effects of that change on other variables	Experiments offer the only way to determine cause-and-effect relationships	To be valid, experiments require random assignment of participants to conditions, well-conceptualized independent and dependent variables, and other careful controls

FIGURE 3 Research strategies.

The participants' behavior was now what counted. The dependent variable was the time that elapsed from the start of the "seizure" to the time a participant began trying to help the "victim." If six minutes went by without a participant's offering help, the experiment was ended.

As predicted by the hypothesis, the size of the group had a significant effect on whether a participant provided help. The more people who were present, the less likely it was that someone would supply help, as you can see in Figure 4 (Latané & Darley, 1970).

Because these results are so straightforward, it seems clear that the experiment confirmed the original hypothesis. However, Latané and Darley could not be sure that the results were truly meaningful until they determined whether the results represented a **significant outcome.** Using statistical analysis, researchers can determine whether a numeric difference is a real difference or is due merely to chance. Only when differences between groups are large enough that statistical tests show them to be significant is it possible for researchers to confirm a hypothesis (Cwikel, Behar, & Rabson-Hare, 2000; Cohen, 2002).

Significant outcome: Meaningful results that make it possible for researchers to feel confident that they have confirmed their hypotheses.

MOVING BEYOND THE STUDY

The Latané and Darley study contains all the elements of an experiment: an independent variable, a dependent variable, random assignment to conditions, and multiple

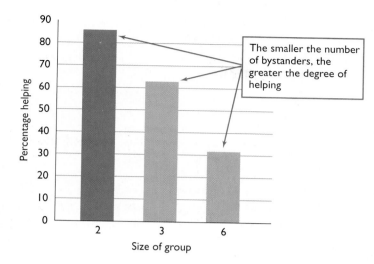

The smaller the number of bystanders, the greater the degree of helping

FIGURE 4 The Latané and Darley experiment showed that as the size of the group witnessing an emergency increased, helping behavior decreased. (Source: Darley & Latané, 1968.)

experimental groups. Consequently, we can say with some confidence that group size *caused* changes in the degree of helping behavior.

Of course, one experiment alone does not forever resolve the question of bystander intervention in emergencies. Psychologists require that findings be **replicated,** or repeated, sometimes using other procedures, in other settings, with other groups of participants, before full confidence can be placed in the validity of any single experiment. A procedure called *meta-analysis* permits psychologists to combine the results of many separate studies into one overall conclusion (Peterson & Brown, 2005).

Replication: The repetition of research, sometimes using other procedures, settings, and groups of participants, to increase confidence in prior findings.

In addition to replicating experimental results, psychologists need to test the limitations of their theories and hypotheses to determine under which specific circumstances they do and do not apply. It seems unlikely, for instance, that increasing the number of bystanders *always* results in less helping. Therefore, it is critical to continue carrying out experiments to understand the conditions in which exceptions to this general rule occur and other circumstances in which the rule holds (Garcia et al., 2002).

Before leaving the Latané and Darley study, it's important to note that it represents a good illustration of the basic principles of the scientific method that we considered earlier (as outlined in Figure 1 in Module 4). The two psychologists began with a *question of interest,* in this case stemming from a real-world incident in which bystanders in an emergency did not offer help. They then *formulated an explanation* by specifying a theory of diffusion of responsibility, and from that formulated the specific hypothesis that increasing the number of bystanders in an emergency situation would lower the degree of helping behavior. Finally, they *carried out research* to confirm their hypothesis. This three-step process embodied in the scientific method underlies all scientific inquiry, allowing us to develop a valid understanding of others'—and our own—behavior.

RECAP/EVALUATE/RETHINK

RECAP

What research methods do psychologists use?

- Archival research uses existing records, such as old newspapers or other documents, to test a hypothesis. In naturalistic observation, the investigator acts mainly as an observer, making no change in a naturally occurring situation. In survey research, people are asked a series of questions about their behavior, thoughts, or attitudes. The case study is an in-depth interview and examination of one person or group. (pp. 36–39)

- These descriptive research methods rely on correlational techniques, which describe associations between variables but cannot determine cause-and-effect relationships. (pp. 39–41)

How do psychologists establish cause-and-effect relationships in research studies?

- In a formal experiment, the relationship between variables is investigated by deliberately producing a change—called the experimental manipulation—in one variable and observing changes in the other variable. (p. 41)

- To test a hypothesis, researchers must formulate an operational definition, which translates the abstract concepts of the hypothesis into the actual procedures used in the study. (p. 41)
- In an experiment, at least two groups must be compared to assess cause-and-effect relationships. The group receiving the treatment (the special procedure devised by the experimenter) is the experimental group; the second group (which receives no treatment) is the control group. There also may be multiple experimental groups, each of which is subjected to a different procedure and then compared with the others. (p. 41)
- The variable that experimenters manipulate is the independent variable. The variable that they measure and expect to change as a result of manipulation of the independent variable is called the dependent variable. (p. 42)
- In a formal experiment, participants must be assigned randomly to treatment conditions, so that participant characteristics are distributed evenly across the different conditions. (p. 43)
- Psychologists use statistical tests to determine whether research findings are significant. (p. 45)

EVALUATE

1. An experimenter is interested in studying the relationship between hunger and aggression. She decides that she will measure aggression by counting the number of times a participant will hit a punching bag. In this case, her _____ definition of aggression is the number of times the participant hits the bag.
2. Match the following forms of research to their definition:
   1. Archival research
   2. Naturalistic observation
   3. Survey research
   4. Case study
   a. Directly asking a sample of people questions about their behavior
   b. Examining existing records to test a hypothesis
   c. Looking at behavior in its true setting without intervening in the setting
   d. Doing an in-depth investigation of a person or small group

3. Match each of the following research methods with its primary disadvantage:
   1. Archival research
   2. Naturalistic observation
   3. Survey research
   4. Case study
   a. This method may not be able to generalize to the population at large.
   b. People's behavior can change if they know they are being watched.
   c. The data may not exist or may be unusable.
   d. People may lie in order to present a good image.
4. A friend tells you, "Anxiety about speaking in public and performance are negatively correlated. Therefore, high anxiety must cause low performance." Is this statement true or false, and why?
5. A psychologist wants to study the effect of attractiveness on willingness to help a person with a math problem. Attractiveness would be the _____ variable, and the amount of helping would be the _____ variable.
6. The group in an experiment that receives no treatment is called the _____ group.

RETHINK

1. Can you describe how a researcher might use naturalistic observation, case studies, and survey research to investigate gender differences in aggressive behavior at the workplace? First state a hypothesis and then describe your research approaches. What positive and negative features does each method have?
2. *From a health care worker's perspective:* Tobacco companies have asserted that no experiment has ever proved that tobacco use causes cancer. Can you explain this claim in terms of the research procedures and designs discussed in this module? What sort of research would establish a cause-and-effect relationship between tobacco use and cancer? Is such a research study possible?

Answers to Evaluate Questions

1. operational; 2. 1-b, 2-c, 3-a, 4-d; 3. 1-c, 2-b, 3-d, 4-a; 4. False. Correlation does not imply causation. Just because two variables are related does not mean that one causes the other. Poor performance may cause people to become more anxious, or a third variable may cause both of these effects; 5. independent, dependent; 6. control

KEY TERMS

operational definition p. 37
descriptive research p. 37
archival research p. 38
naturalistic observation p. 38
survey research p. 38
case study p. 40

variable p. 40
correlational research p. 40
experiment p. 42
experimental
   manipulation p. 42
treatment p. 42

experimental group p. 42
control group p. 42
independent variable p. 43
dependent variable p. 43
random assignment to
   condition p. 44

significant outcome: p. 46
replication p. 47

Critical Research Issues

You probably realize by now that there are few simple formulas for psychological research. Psychologists must make choices about the type of study to conduct, the measures to take, and the most effective way to analyze the results. Even after they have made these essential decisions, they must still consider several critical issues. We turn first to the most fundamental of these issues: ethics.

Key Concept

What major issues confront psychologists conducting research?

The Ethics of Research

Put yourself in the place of one of the participants in the experiment conducted by Latané and Darley to examine the helping behavior of bystanders, in which another "bystander" simulating a seizure turned out to be a confederate of the experimenters (Latané & Darley, 1970). How would you feel when you learned that the supposed victim was in reality a paid accomplice?

Although you might at first experience relief that there had been no real emergency, you might also feel some resentment that you had been deceived by the experimenter. You might also experience concern that you had been placed in an embarrassing or compromising situation—one that might have dealt a blow to your self-esteem, depending on how you had behaved.

Most psychologists argue that deception is sometimes necessary to prevent participants from being influenced by what they think a study's true purpose is. (If you knew that Latané and Darley were actually studying your helping behavior, wouldn't you automatically have been tempted to intervene in the emergency?) To avoid such outcomes, a small proportion of research involves deception.

Nonetheless, because research has the potential to violate the rights of participants, psychologists are expected to adhere to a strict set of ethical guidelines aimed at protecting participants (APA, 2002). As the Interactivity on ethical dilemmas illustrates, those guidelines involve the following safeguards:

- Protection of participants from physical and mental harm
- The right of participants to privacy regarding their behavior
- The assurance that participation in research is completely voluntary
- The necessity of informing participants about the nature of procedures before their participation in the experiment

All experiments that use humans as participants must be reviewed by an independent panel before being conducted, including the minority of studies that involve deception (Fisher et al., 2002; Fisher, 2003; Smith, 2003). (Also try the PsychInteractive exercise on ethical dilemmas).

One of psychologists' key ethical principles is **informed consent.** Before participating in an experiment, the participants must sign a document affirming that they have been told the basic outlines of the study and are aware of what their participation will involve, what risks the experiment may hold, and the fact that their participation is purely voluntary and they may terminate it at any time. Furthermore, after participation in a study, they must be given a debriefing in which they receive an explanation of the study and the procedures involved. The only time informed

www.mhhe.com/feldmanup8
PsychInteractive Online

Ethical Dilemmas

Informed consent: A document signed by participants affirming that they have been told the basic outlines of the study and are aware of what their participation will involve.

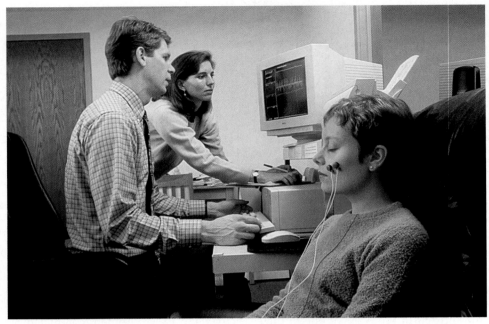

Although readily available and widely used as research subjects, college students may not represent the population at large. What are some advantages and drawbacks of using college students as subjects?

consent and a debriefing can be eliminated is in experiments in which the risks are minimal, as in a purely observational study in a public place (Chastain & Landrum, 1999; DuBois, 2002; Koocher, Norcross, & Hill, 2005).

Exploring DIVERSITY

Choosing Participants Who Represent the Scope of Human Behavior

When Latané and Darley, both college professors, decided who would participate in their experiment, they turned to the most available people: college students. In fact, college students are used so frequently in experiments that psychology has been called—somewhat contemptuously—the "science of the behavior of the college sophomore" (Rubenstein, 1982).

Using college students as participants has both advantages and drawbacks. The big benefit is that because most research occurs in university settings, college students are readily available. Typically, they cost the researcher very little: They participate for either extra course credit or a relatively small payment.

The problem is that college students may not represent the general population adequately. They tend to be younger and better educated than a significant percentage of the rest of the population of the United States. Compared with older adults, their attitudes are likely to be less well formed, and they are more apt to be influenced by authority figures and peers (Sears, 1986).

College students are also disproportionately white and middle class. However, even in research that does not involve college students, participants tend to be white, middle-class participants; the use of African Americans, Latinos, Asians, and other minorities as participants is low (Graham, 1992; Guthrie, 1998). Because psychology is a science that purports to explain human behavior in general, something is therefore amiss. Consequently, psychological researchers have become increasingly sensitive to the importance of using participants who are fully representative of the general population. Furthermore, the National Institute of Mental Health and the National Science Foundation—the primary U.S. funding sources for psychological research—now require that experiments address issues of diverse populations (Rogler, 1999; Carpenter, 2002).

Research involving animals is controversial but, when conducted within ethical guidelines, yields significant benefits for humans.

Should Animals Be Used in Research?

Like those who work with humans, researchers who use nonhuman animals in experiments have their own set of exacting guidelines to ensure that the animals do not suffer. Specifically, researchers must make every effort to minimize discomfort, illness, and pain. Procedures that subject animals to distress are permitted only when an alternative procedure is unavailable and when the research is justified by its prospective value. Moreover, there are federal regulations specifying how animals are to be housed, fed, and maintained. Not only must researchers strive to avoid causing physical discomfort, but they are also required to promote the *psychological* well-being of some species of research animals, such as primates (Novak & Petto, 1991; APA, 1993).

Why should animals be used for research in the first place? Is it really possible to learn about human behavior from the results of research employing rats, gerbils, and pigeons? The answer is that psychological research that does employ animals has a different focus and is designed to answer different questions than is research with humans. For example, the shorter life span of animals (rats live an average of two years) allows researchers to learn about the effects of aging in a much shorter time frame than they could by using human participants. It is also possible to provide greater experimental control over nonhumans and to carry out procedures that might not be possible with people. For example, some studies require large numbers of participants that share similar backgrounds or have been exposed to particular environments—conditions that could not practically be met with human beings (Gallagher & Rapp, 1997; Mukerjee, 1997).

Research with animals has provided psychologists with information that has profoundly benefited humans. For instance, it furnished the keys to detecting eye disorders in children early enough to prevent permanent damage, to communicating more effectively with severely retarded children, and to reducing chronic pain in people, to name just a few results (APA, 1988; Botting & Morrison, 1997).

Despite the value of research with animal participants, the use of animals in psychological research is highly controversial. For example, some critics believe that animals have rights no less significant than those of humans, and that the use of animals in studies is unethical because they are unable to give their consent. Others object to animal research on methodological grounds, saying it is impossible to generalize from findings on nonhuman species to humans (Plous & Herzog, 2000).

Because the issues surrounding animal research involve complex moral and philosophical concerns, they are not easily resolved. As a consequence, review panels, which must approve all research before it is carried out, are particularly careful to ensure that research involving animals is conducted ethically (Plous, 1996a, 1996b; Barnard & Kaufman, 1997; Herzog, 2005).

Threats to Experiment Validity: Experimenter and Participant Expectations

Experimental bias: Factors that distort how the independent variable affects the dependent variable in an experiment.

Even the best-laid experimental plans are susceptible to **experimental bias**—factors that distort the way the independent variable affects the dependent variable in an experiment. One of the most common forms of experimental bias is *experimenter expectations:* An experimenter unintentionally transmits cues to participants about the way they are expected to behave in a given experimental condition. The danger is that those expectations will bring about an "appropriate" behavior—one that otherwise might not have occurred (Rosenthal, 2002, 2003).

A related problem is *participant expectations* about appropriate behavior. If you have ever been a participant in an experiment, you know that you quickly develop guesses about what is expected of you. In fact, it is typical for people to develop their own hypotheses about what the experimenter hopes to learn from the study. If participants form their own hypotheses, it may the participant's expectations, rather than the experimental manipulation, that produce an effect.

To guard against participant expectations biasing the results of an experiment, the experimenter may try to disguise the true purpose of the experiment. Participants who do not know that helping behavior is being studied, for example, are more apt to act in a "natural" way than they would if they knew.

Sometimes it is impossible to hide the actual purpose of research; when that is the case, other techniques are available to prevent bias. Suppose you were interested in testing the ability of a new drug to alleviate the symptoms of severe depression. If you simply gave the drug to half your participants and not to the other half, the participants who were given the drug might report feeling less depressed merely because they knew they were getting a drug. Similarly, the participants who got nothing might report feeling no better because they knew that they were in a no-treatment control group.

To solve this problem, psychologists typically use a procedure in which all the participants receive a treatment, but those in the control group receive only a **placebo,** a false treatment, such as a pill, "drug," or other substance, that has no significant chemical properties or active ingredient. Because members of both groups are kept in the dark about whether they are getting a real or a false treatment, any differences in outcome can be attributed to the quality of the drug and not to the possible psychological effects of being administered a pill or other substance (Kirsch, 1999; Enserink, 1999, 2000; Kim & Holloway, 2003).

However, there is one more safeguard that a careful researcher must apply in an experiment such as this. To overcome the possibility that *experimenter* expectations will affect the participant, the person who administers the drug shouldn't know whether it is actually the true drug or the placebo. By keeping both the participant and the experimenter who interacts with the participant "blind" to the nature of the drug that is being administered, researchers can more accurately assess the effects of the drug. This method is known as the *double-blind procedure.*

Placebo: A false treatment, such as a pill, "drug," or other substance, without any significant chemical properties or active ingredient.

BECOMING AN INFORMED CONSUMER of Psychology
Thinking Critically About Research

If you were about to purchase an automobile, it is unlikely that you would stop at the nearest car dealership and drive off with the first car a salesperson recommended. Instead, you would probably mull over the purchase, read about automobiles, consider the alternatives, talk to others about their experiences, and ultimately put in a fair amount of thought before you made such a major purchase.

In contrast, many of us are considerably less conscientious when we expend our intellectual, rather than financial, assets. People often jump to conclusions on the basis of incomplete and inaccurate information, and only rarely do they take the time to critically evaluate the research and data to which they are exposed.

Because the field of psychology is based on an accumulated body of research, it is crucial for psychologists to scrutinize thoroughly the methods, results, and claims of researchers. Yet it is not just psychologists who need to know how to evaluate research critically; all of us are constantly exposed to the claims of others. Knowing how to approach research and data can be helpful in areas far beyond the realm of psychology.

Several basic questions can help us sort through what is valid and what is not. Among the most important questions to ask are the following:

- *What was the purpose of the research?* Research studies should evolve from a clearly specified theory. Furthermore, we must take into account the specific hypothesis that is being tested. Unless we know what hypothesis is being examined, it is not possible to judge how successful a study has been.
- *How well was the study conducted?* Consider who the participants were, how many were involved, what methods were employed, and what problems the researcher encountered in collecting the data. There are important differences, for example, between a case study that reports the anecdotes of a handful of respondents and a survey that collects data from several thousand people.
- *Are the results presented fairly?* It is necessary to assess statements on the basis of the actual data they reflect and their logic. For instance, when the manufacturer of car X boasts that "no other car a has a better safety record than car X," this does not mean that car X is safer than every other car. It just means that no other car has been proved safer, though many other cars could be just as safe as car X. Expressed in the latter fashion, the finding doesn't seem worth bragging about.

These three basic questions can help you assess the validity of research findings you come across—both within and outside the field of psychology. The more you know how to evaluate research in general, the better you will be able to assess what the field of psychology has to offer.

RECAP/EVALUATE/RETHINK

RECAP

What major issues confront psychologists conducting research?

- One of the key ethical principles followed by psychologists is that of informed consent. Participants must be informed, before participation, about the basic outline of the experiment and the risks and potential benefits of their participation. (p. 48)
- Although the use of college students as participants has the advantage of easy availability, there are drawbacks too. For instance, students do not necessarily represent the population as a whole. The use of animals as participants may also have costs in terms of generalizability, although the benefits of using animals in research have been profound. (pp. 49–50)
- Experiments are subject to a number of threats, or biases. Experimenter expectations can produce bias when an experimenter unintentionally transmits cues to participants about her or his expectations regarding their behavior in a given experimental condition. Participant expectations can also bias an experiment. Among the tools experimenters use to help eliminate bias are placebos and double-blind procedures. (pp. 50–51)

EVALUATE

1. Ethical research begins with the concept of informed consent. Before signing up to participate in an experiment, participants should be informed of
   a. The procedure of the study, stated generally.
   b. The risks that may be involved.
   c. Their right to withdraw at any time.
   d. All of the above.
2. List three benefits of using animals in psychological research.
3. Deception is one means experimenters can use to try to eliminate participants' expectations. True or false?

KEY TERMS

informed consent p. 49   experimental bias p. 52   placebo p. 53

4. A false treatment, such as a pill, that has no significant chemical properties or active ingredient, is known as a
   _____.
5. According to a report, a study has shown that men differ from women in their preference for ice cream flavors. This study was based on a sample of two men and three women. What might be wrong with this study?

RETHINK

1. A researcher strongly believes that college professors tend to show female students less attention and respect in the classroom than they show male students. She sets up an experimental study involving observations of classrooms in different conditions. In explaining the study to the professors and students who will participate, what steps should the researcher take to eliminate experimental bias based on both experimenter expectations and participant expectations?
2. Imagine that you pick up the newspaper and read an article about a new drug that claims to significantly prolong the life of terminally ill cancer patients. The article states: "Our study shows that patients who took the drug once a day lived longer than patients who did not take the drug." Based on the knowledge you learned in this module, are the results of this study valid? Why or why not?
3. *From a research analyst's perspective:* You are hired to study people's attitudes toward welfare programs by developing and circulating a questionnaire via the Internet. Is this study likely to accurately reflect the views of the general population? Why or why not?

Answers to Evaluate Questions

1. d.; 2. (1) We can study some phenomena in animals more easily than we can in people, because with animal subjects we have greater control over environmental and genetic factors. (2) Large numbers of similar participants can be easily obtained. (3) We can look at generational effects much more easily in animals, because of their shorter life span, than we can with people; 3. true; 4. placebo; 5. There are far too few participants. Without a larger sample, no valid conclusions can be drawn about ice cream preferences based on gender.

Looking Back

Psychology on the Web

1. Identify a product or service that is advertised on the Internet using broad, unspecific claims, such as a weight-loss formula or body-building method. Find at least two advertisements on the Internet for that product or service and evaluate the claims they make according to the principles discussed in this group of modules. Summarize the evidence that is presented for those claims, and describe a method by which you might confirm the claims by using actual research.

2. Find a Web site that focuses on an important social issue (e.g., urban violence, gender differences in hiring or promotion, poverty) and locate descriptions of a research study about the issue. Evaluate the study by identifying the hypotheses that were tested, the methods used to test them, and the validity of the results reported.

3. After completing the online PsychInteractive exercise on ethical issues in psychology, consult the most recent revision of the American Psychological Association ethical guidelines (found online at www.apa.org/ethics/code2002.html). If ethical standards for psychologists are based on enduring ethical principles, why do you think it is necessary to periodically revise the ethical standards?

Epilogue

We have been discussing the ways in which psychologists seek to understand phenomena and answer questions of interest. We've examined the scientific method and its reliance on posing good questions, creating productive theories, and crafting testable hypotheses. We have also looked at the basic methods psychologists use to conduct research studies and compared correlational methods and experimental methods. Finally, we've explored some of the major challenges that psychologists have to deal with when conducting research, including ethical considerations, the use of animals in research, and potential bias.

Before leaving this topic, reconsider the lack of bystander help in the case of Mike Petre, who was beaten while riding a train. Reflect on the following questions in light of what you now know about conducting psychological research.

1. Suppose you were interested in studying aggressive behavior among criminals such as the ones who beat Mike Petre. Can you formulate a theory that might explain why criminals behave violently?

2. What hypotheses (testable predictions) can you construct to test your theory?

3. Can you design a correlational study to test one of your hypotheses? Which correlational method(s) (archival research, naturalistic observation, survey research, case study) would you use in your study?

4. Can you design an experimental study to test the same or another hypothesis? Describe the experiment, including the participants, the experimental manipulation, the treatment, and the independent and dependent variables.

MASTERING the difference between dependent and independent variables

Experiments are used to establish a cause-and-effect relationship between two variables. Use this visual guide to better understand how experiments can help researchers draw conclusions by using experimental and control groups and random assignment. Then answer the questions below to test your understanding of the concepts.

1 Researchers develop *theories* to explain behavior. As an example, they might theorize that children who are exposed to violence in the media behave more aggressively than other children. Based on this theory they develop a *hypothesis* to test the prediction that playing violent video games causes children to behave aggressively.

2 An experiment in a controlled setting is the most powerful method of establishing a cause-and-effect relationship. Participants in an experiment are randomly assigned to either the *experimental group* (the group that receives a treatment) or the *control group* (the group that receives no special treatment).

EVALUATE

1 In this example, the independent variable is _____ and the dependent variable is _____.
 a aggressive behavior; exposure to violent video games
 b the experimenter; who wins the card games
 c exposure to violent video games; aggression displayed by the children
 d the card games; the violent video games

2 In this example, the experimental group _____ and the control group _____.
 a plays cards; plays violent video games
 b plays violent video games; does not play violent video games
 c is randomly assigned to condition; is not randomly assigned
 d does not play violent video games; plays violent video games

3 In this example, the *independent variable,* the variable that researchers manipulate, is exposure to violent video games. The experimental group is given a violent video game to play, while the control group is not given the violent game.

4 Afterwards, the experimental group and control group are brought together to play card games. A researcher who doesn't know which children are in the experimental group or the control group watches through a two-way mirror and records signs of aggressive behavior (the *dependent variable*).

5 If the results show that the children in the experimental group (who had played the violent video games) were significantly more aggressive than the children in the control group (who hadn't played the game), the hypothesis is confirmed. The results would then support the researcher's theory that exposure to media violence *causes* aggression in children. Of course, no single experiment is sufficient to confirm a theory; additional research is needed.

3 Because the control group receives no treatment in this example, we cannot use it to draw conclusions about cause and effect. True or False?

RETHINK

1 Suppose you believe that listening to music while studying can improve test scores. Design an experiment that could be used to test your hypothesis. Be sure to include an experimental group and a control group.

CHAPTER 3

Neuroscience and Behavior

Key Concepts for Chapter 3

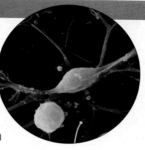
Why do psychologists study the brain and nervous system? ● What are the basic elements of the nervous system? ● How does the nervous system communicate electrical and chemical messages from one part to another?

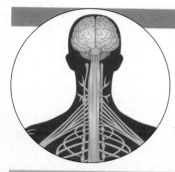

How are the structures of the nervous system linked together? ● How does the endocrine system affect behavior?

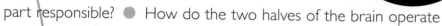

How do researchers identify the major parts and functions of the brain? ● What are the major parts of the brain, and for what behaviors is each part responsible? ● How do the two halves of the brain operate interdependently? ● How can an understanding of the nervous system help us find ways to alleviate disease and pain?

Prologue   Out of Jail

For Ray Farkas, the first signs of Parkinson's disease came on the tennis court, when he began to lose to opponents he had previously beaten. Later, when his legs began to shake and he had balance problems, his doctors informed him he had Parkinson's—a disorder marked by varying degrees of muscular rigidity and shaking.

Farkas was willing to try anything to prevent the spread of the disease, which had killed his father. When he learned he was a candidate for a new procedure called deep brain stimulation (DBS), he decided to take a chance on it. In DBS, surgeons implant a battery-operated neurostimulator that delivers tiny electric pulses to specific areas of the brain that control movement.

The electrical stimulation blocks abnormal nerve signals that produce the symptoms of Parkinson's.

Because DBS requires patients to be awake during the operation, Farkas was well aware of the procedure:

"The surgeons numbed my skull and began drilling. When the anesthesia wore off, they were already in my head and I didn't even know it! . . . Next, the doctors inserted a high-tech microrecorder and began listening to brain waves to locate the part of my brain, the subthalamic nucleus, that had been affected by Parkinson's. When they detected that part of my brain—it sounds like rain on a tin roof—they knew they had the right spot and stimulated it with an electrical charge. Suddenly, I could feel my legs quieting down— and my doctor could see it. It was a cool, peaceful feeling. I urgently whispered, 'More alternating current, more alternating current!' For the first time in years, I was lying still. I felt like I had gotten out of jail." (Farkas, 2004, p. 100).

Looking Ahead

The ability of surgeons to identify damaged portions of the brain and carry out repairs is little short of miraculous. The greater miracle is the brain itself. An organ roughly half the size of a loaf of bread, the brain controls our behavior through every waking and sleeping moment. Our movements, thoughts, hopes, aspirations, dreams—our very awareness that we are human—all depend on the brain and the nerves that extend throughout the body, constituting the nervous system.

Because of the importance of the nervous system in controlling behavior, and because humans at their most basic level are biological beings, many researchers in psychology and other fields as diverse as computer science, zoology, and medicine have made the biological underpinnings of behavior their specialty. These experts collectively are called *neuroscientists* (Beatty, 2000; Posner & DiGiorlamo, 2000; Gazzaniga, Ivry, & Mangun, 2002).

Psychologists who specialize in considering the ways in which the biological structures and functions of the body affect behavior are known as **behavioral neuroscientists** (or *biopsychologists*). They

seek to answer several key questions: How does the brain control the voluntary and involuntary functioning of the body? How does the brain communicate with other parts of the body? What is the physical structure of the brain, and how does this structure affect behavior? Are psychological disorders caused by biological factors, and how can such disorders be treated?

As you consider the biological processes that we'll discuss in this chapter, it is important to keep in mind why behavioral neuroscience is an essential part of psychology: Our understanding of human behavior requires knowledge of the brain and other parts of the nervous system. Biological factors are central to our sensory experiences, states of consciousness, motivation and emotion, development throughout the life span, and physical and psychological health. Furthermore, advances in behavioral neuroscience have led to the creation of drugs and other treatments for psychological and physical disorders. In short, we cannot understand behavior without understanding our biological makeup (Kosslyn et al., 2002; Plomin, 2003a).

Neurons: The Basic Elements of Behavior

Watching Serena Williams hit a stinging backhand, Dario Vaccaro carry out a complex ballet routine, or Derek Jeter swing at a baseball, you may have marveled at the complexity—and wondrous abilities—of the human body. But even the most everyday tasks, such as picking up a pencil, writing, and speaking, depend on a sophisticated sequence of events in the body that is itself truly impressive. For instance, the difference between saying the words *dime* and *time* rests primarily on whether the vocal cords are relaxed or tense during a period lasting no more than one one-hundredth of a second, yet it is a distinction that most of us can make with ease.

The nervous system is the pathway for the instructions that permit our bodies to carry out such precise activities. Here we will look at the structure and function of neurons, the cells that make up the nervous system, including the brain.

The Structure of the Neuron

Playing the piano, driving a car, or hitting a tennis ball depends, at one level, on exact muscle coordination. But if we consider *how* the muscles can be activated so precisely, we see that there are more fundamental processes involved. For the muscles to produce the complex movements that make up any meaningful physical activity, the brain has to provide the right messages to them and coordinate those messages.

Such messages—as well as those which enable us to think, remember, and experience emotion—are passed through specialized cells called neurons. **Neurons,** or nerve cells, are the basic elements of the nervous system. Their quantity is staggering—perhaps as many as 1 *trillion* neurons throughout the body are involved in the control of behavior (Boahen, 2005).

Although there are several types of neurons, they all have a similar structure, as illustrated in Figure 1. Like most cells in the body, neurons have a cell body that contains a nucleus. The nucleus incorporates the hereditary material that determines how a cell will function. Neurons are physically held in place by *glial cells.* Glial cells provide nourishment to neurons, insulate them, help repair damage, and generally support neural functioning (Uylings & Vrije, 2002; Fields, 2004; Kettenmann & Ransom, 2005).

In contrast to most other cells, however, neurons have a distinctive feature: the ability to communicate with other cells and transmit information across relatively long distances. Many of the body's neurons receive signals from the environment or relay the nervous system's messages to muscles and other target cells, but the vast majority of neurons communicate only with other neurons in the elaborate information system that regulates behavior.

As you can see in Figure 1, a neuron has a cell body with a cluster of fibers called **dendrites** at one end. Those fibers, which look like the twisted branches of a tree, receive messages from other neurons. On the opposite end of the cell body is a long, slim, tubelike extension called an **axon.** The axon carries messages received by the dendrites to other neurons. The axon is considerably longer than the rest of the neuron. Although most axons are several millimeters in length, some are as long as three feet. Axons end in small bulges called **terminal buttons,** which send messages to other neurons.

Key Concepts

Why do psychologists study the brain and nervous system?

What are the basic elements of the nervous system?

How does the nervous system communicate electrical and chemical messages from one part to another?

Behavioral neuroscientists: Psychologists who specialize in considering the ways in which the biological structures and functions of the body affect behavior.

Neurons: Nerve cells, the basic elements of the nervous system.

Dendrite: A cluster of fibers at one end of a neuron that receive messages from other neurons.

Axon: The part of the neuron that carries messages destined for other neurons.

Terminal buttons: Small bulges at the end of axons that send messages to other neurons.

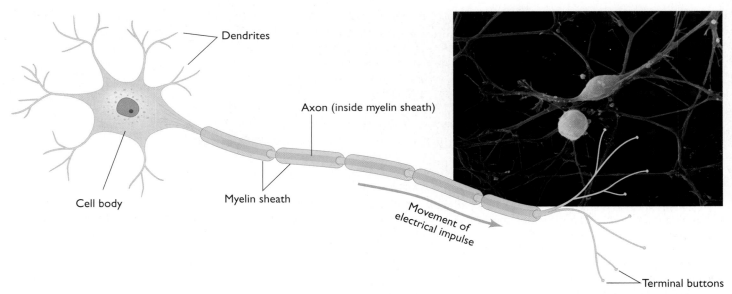

Dendrites

Axon (inside myelin sheath)

Cell body

Myelin sheath

Movement of electrical impulse

Terminal buttons

FIGURE I The primary components of the specialized cell called the neuron, the basic element of the nervous system (Van de Graaff, 2000). A neuron, like most types of cells in the body, has a cell body and a nucleus, but it also contains structures that carry messages: the dendrites, which receive messages from other neurons, and the axon, which carries messages to other neurons or body cells. In this neuron, as in most neurons, the axon is protected by the sausagelike myelin sheath. What advantages does the treelike structure of the neuron provide?

The messages that travel through a neuron are electrical in nature. Although there are exceptions, those electrical messages, or *impulses*, generally move across neurons in one direction only, as if they were traveling on a one-way street. Impulses follow a route that begins with the dendrites, continues into the cell body, and leads ultimately along the tubelike extension, the axon, to adjacent neurons. *D*endrites, then, *d*etect messages from other neurons; *a*xons carry signals *a*way from the cell body.

To prevent messages from short-circuiting one another, axons must be insulated in some fashion (just as electrical wires must be insulated). Most axons are insulated by a **myelin sheath,** a protective coating of fat and protein that wraps around the axon like links of sausage.

The myelin sheath also serves to increase the velocity with which electrical impulses travel through axons. Those axons that carry the most important and most urgently required information have the greatest concentrations of myelin. If your hand touches a painfully hot stove, for example, the information regarding the pain is passed through axons in the hand and arm that have a relatively thick coating of myelin, speeding the message of pain to the brain so that you can react instantly. In certain diseases, such as multiple sclerosis, the myelin sheath surrounding the axon deteriorates, exposing parts of the axon that are normally covered. This short-circuits messages between the brain and muscles and results in symptoms such as the inability to walk, difficulties with vision, and general muscle impairment. (To review, try the PsychInteractive exercise on the structure of neurons.)

Myelin sheath: A protective coat of fat and protein that wraps around the axon.

www.mhhe.com/feldmanup8
PsychInteractive Online

Structure of Neurons

How Neurons Fire

Like a gun, neurons either fire—that is, transmit an electrical impulse along the axon—or don't fire. There is no in-between stage, just as pulling harder on a gun trigger doesn't make the bullet travel faster. Similarly, neurons follow an **all-or-none law:** They are either on or off, with nothing in between the on state and the off state. Once there is enough force to pull the trigger, a neuron fires.

All-or-none law: The rule that neurons are either on or off.

Before a neuron is triggered—that is, when it is in a **resting state**—it has a negative electrical charge of about 270 millivolts (a millivolt is one one-thousandth of a volt). This charge is caused by the presence of more negatively charged ions within the neuron than outside it. (An ion is an atom that is electrically charged.) You might think of the neuron as a miniature battery in which the inside of the neuron represents the negative pole and the outside represents the positive pole.

When a message arrives at a neuron, its cell membrane opens briefly to allow positively charged ions to rush in at rates as high as 100 million ions per second. The sudden arrival of these positive ions causes the charge within the nearby part of the cell to change momentarily from negative to positive. When the positive charge reaches a critical level, the "trigger" is pulled, and an electrical impulse, known as an action potential, travels along the axon of the neuron (see Figure 2).

The **action potential** moves from one end of the axon to the other like a flame moving along a fuse. As the impulse travels along the axon, the movement of ions causes a change in charge from negative to positive in successive sections of the axon (see Figure 3). After the impulse has passed through a particular section of the axon, positive ions are pumped out of that section, and its charge returns to negative while the action potential continues to move along the axon.

Just after an action potential has passed through a section of the axon, the cell membrane in that region cannot admit positive ions again for a few milliseconds, and so a neuron cannot fire again immediately no matter how much stimulation it receives. It is as if the gun has to be reloaded after each shot. There then follows a period in which, though it is possible for the neuron to fire, a stronger stimulus is needed than would be needed if the neuron had reached its normal resting state. Eventually, though, the neuron is ready to fire once again.

These complex events can occur at dizzying speeds, although there is great variation among different neurons. The particular speed at which an action potential travels along an axon is determined by the axon's size and the thickness of its myelin sheath. Axons with small diameters carry impulses at about 2 miles per hour; longer and thicker ones can average speeds of more than 225 miles per hour.

Neurons differ not only in terms of how quickly an impulse moves along the axon but also in their potential rate of firing. Some neurons are capable of firing as many as a thousand times per second; others fire at much slower rates. The intensity of a stimulus determines how much of a neuron's potential firing rate is reached. A strong

Resting state: The state in which there is a negative electrical charge of about 270 millivolts within a neuron.

Action potential: An electric nerve impulse that travels through a neuron when it is set off by a "trigger," changing the neuron's charge from negative to positive.

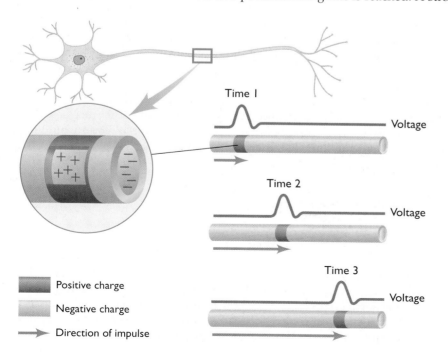

Time 1

Voltage

Time 2

Voltage

Time 3

Voltage

Positive charge

Negative charge

Direction of impulse

FIGURE 2 Movement of an action potential across an axon. Just before Time 1, positively charged ions enter the cell membrane, changing the charge in the nearby part of the neuron from negative to positive and triggering an action potential. The action potential travels along the axon, as illustrated in the changes occurring from Time 1 to Time 3 (from top to bottom in this drawing). Immediately after the action potential has passed through a section of the axon, positive ions are pumped out, restoring the charge in that section to negative. The change in voltage illustrated at the top of the axon can be seen in greater detail in Figure 3 on page 64 (Stevens, 1979).

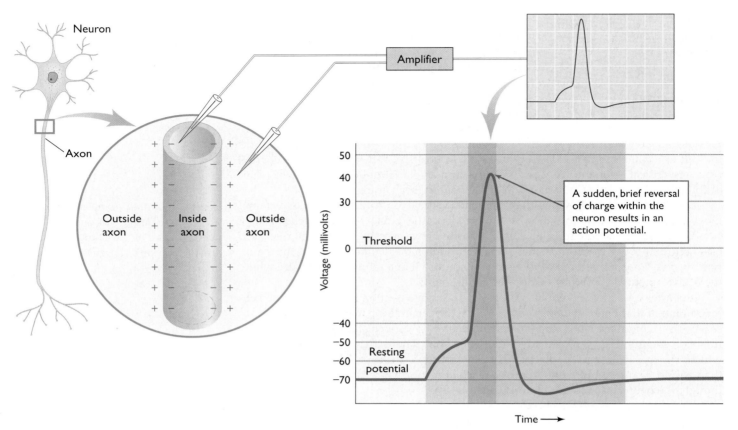

FIGURE 3 Changes in the electrical charge in a neuron during the passage of an action potential. In its normal resting state, a neuron has a negative charge. When an action potential is triggered, however, the charge becomes positive, increasing from around −70 millivolts to about +40 millivolts. Following the passage of the action potential, the charge becomes even more negative than it is in its typical state. It is not until the charge returns to its resting state that the neuron will be fully ready to be triggered once again. (Source: Mader, 2000.)

stimulus, such as a bright light or a loud sound, leads to a higher rate of firing than a less intense stimulus does. Thus, even though all impulses move at the same strength or speed through a particular axon—because of the all-or-none law—there is variation in the frequency of impulses, providing a mechanism by which we can distinguish the tickle of a feather from the weight of someone standing on our toes.

The structure, operation, and functions of the neuron are fundamental biological aspects of the body that underlie several primary psychological processes. Our understanding of the way we sense, perceive, and learn about the world would be greatly restricted without the knowledge about the neuron that behavioral neuroscientists and other researchers have acquired.

Where Neurons Meet: Bridging the Gap

Synapse: The space between two neurons where the axon of a sending neuron communicates with the dendrites of a receiving neuron by using chemical messages.

If you have ever looked inside a computer, you've seen that each part is physically connected to another part. In contrast, evolution has produced a neural transmission system that at some points has no need for a structural connection between its components. Instead, a chemical connection bridges the gap, known as a synapse, between two neurons (see Figure 4). The **synapse** is the space between two neurons where the

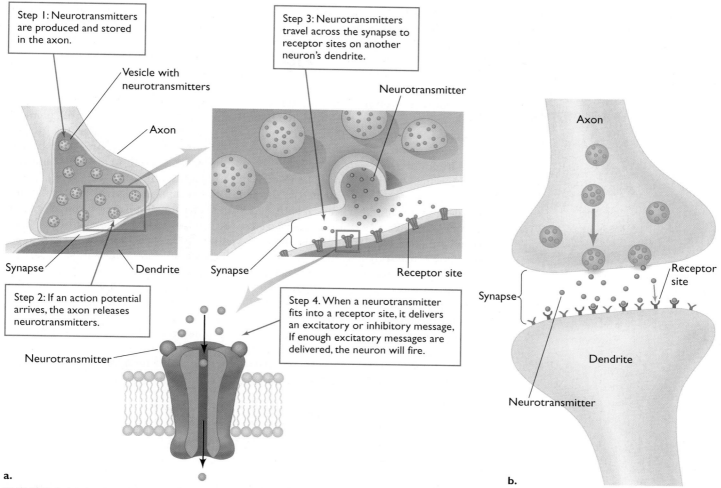

Step 1: Neurotransmitters are produced and stored in the axon.

Vesicle with neurotransmitters

Axon

Synapse

Dendrite

Step 2: If an action potential arrives, the axon releases neurotransmitters.

Neurotransmitter

Step 3: Neurotransmitters travel across the synapse to receptor sites on another neuron's dendrite.

Neurotransmitter

Synapse

Receptor site

Step 4. When a neurotransmitter fits into a receptor site, it delivers an excitatory or inhibitory message, If enough excitatory messages are delivered, the neuron will fire.

a.

Axon

Receptor site

Synapse

Dendrite

Neurotransmitter

b.

FIGURE 4 (a) A synapse is the junction between an axon and a dendrite. The gap between the axon and the dendrite is bridged by chemicals called neurotransmitters (Mader, 2000). (b) Just as the pieces of a jigsaw puzzle can fit in only one specific location in a puzzle, each kind of neurotransmitter has a distinctive configuration that allows it to fit into a specific type of receptor cell (Johnson, 2000). Why is it advantageous for axons and dendrites to be linked by temporary chemical bridges rather than by the hard wiring typical of a radio connection or telephone hookup?

axon of a sending neuron communicates with the dendrites of a receiving neuron by using chemical messages (Holt & Jahn, 2004; Fanselow & Poulos, 2005).

When a nerve impulse comes to the end of the axon and reaches a terminal button, the terminal button releases a chemical courier called a neurotransmitter. **Neurotransmitters** are chemicals that carry messages across the synapse to a dendrite (and sometimes the cell body) of a receiving neuron. Like a boat that ferries passengers across a river, these chemical messengers move toward the shorelines of other neurons. The chemical mode of message transmission that occurs between neurons is strikingly different from the means by which communication occurs inside neurons: Although messages travel in electrical form *within* a neuron, they move *between* neurons through a chemical transmission system.

There are several types of neurotransmitters, and not all neurons are capable of receiving the chemical message carried by a particular neurotransmitter. In the same way that a jigsaw puzzle piece can fit in only one specific location in a puzzle, each kind of neurotransmitter has a distinctive configuration that allows it to fit into a specific type of receptor site on the receiving neuron (see Figure 4b). It is only when a neurotransmitter fits precisely into a receptor site that successful chemical communication is possible.

Neurotransmitters: Chemicals that carry messages across the synapse to the dendrite (and sometimes the cell body) of a receiver neuron.

Excitatory message: A chemical message that makes it more likely that a receiving neuron will fire and an action potential will travel down its axon.

Inhibitory message: A chemical message that prevents or decreases the likelihood that a receiving neuron will fire.

Reuptake: The reabsorption of neurotransmitters by a terminal button.

If a neurotransmitter does fit into a site on the receiving neuron, the chemical message it delivers is basically one of two types: excitatory or inhibitory. **Excitatory messages** make it more likely that a receiving neuron will fire and an action potential will travel down its axon. **Inhibitory messages,** in contrast, do just the opposite; they provide chemical information that prevents or decreases the likelihood that the receiving neuron will fire.

Because the dendrites of a neuron receive both excitatory and inhibitory messages simultaneously, the neuron must integrate the messages by using a kind of chemical calculator. Put simply, if the concentration of excitatory messages ("fire") is greater than the concentration of inhibitory ones ("don't fire"), the neuron fires. In contrast, if the inhibitory messages outnumber the excitatory ones, nothing happens, and the neuron remains in its resting state (Mel, 2002; Rapport, 2005).

If neurotransmitters remained at the site of the synapse, receiving neurons would be awash in a continual chemical bath, producing constant stimulation of the receiving neurons—and effective communication across the synapse would no longer be possible. To solve this problem, neurotransmitters are either deactivated by enzymes or—more commonly—reabsorbed by the terminal button in an example of chemical recycling called **reuptake.** Like a vacuum cleaner sucking up dust, neurons reabsorb the neurotransmitters that are now clogging the synapse. All this activity occurs at lightning speed, with the process taking just several milliseconds (Helmuth, 2000; Holt & Jahn, 2004).

Our understanding of the process of reuptake has permitted the development of a number of drugs used in the treatment of psychological disorders. As we'll discuss later in the book, some antidepressant drugs, called *SSRIs* or *selective serotonin reuptake inhibitors,* permit certain neurotransmitters to remain active for a longer period at certain synapses in the brain, thereby reducing the symptoms of depression.

Neurotransmitters: Multitalented Chemical Couriers

Neurotransmitters are a particularly important link between the nervous system and behavior. Not only are they important for maintaining vital brain and body functions, a deficiency or an excess of a neurotransmitter can produce severe behavior disorders. More than a hundred chemicals have been found to act as neurotransmitters, and neuroscientists believe that more may ultimately be identified (Purves et al., 1997; Penney, 2000).

Neurotransmitters vary significantly in terms of how strong their concentration must be to trigger a neuron to fire. Furthermore, the effects of a particular neurotransmitter vary, depending on the area of the nervous system in which it is produced. The same neurotransmitter, then, can act as an excitatory message to a neuron located in one part of the brain and can inhibit firing in neurons located in another part. (The major neurotransmitters and their effects are described in Figure 5.)

One of the most common neurotransmitters is *acetylcholine* (or *ACh,* its chemical symbol), which is found throughout the nervous system. ACh is involved in our every move, because—among other things—it transmits messages relating to our skeletal muscles. ACh is also involved in memory capabilities, and diminished production of ACh may be related to Alzheimer's disease (Selkoe, 1997; Mohapel et al., 2005).

Another common excitatory neurotransmitter, *glutamate,* plays a role in memory. Memories appear to be produced by specific biochemical changes at particular synapses, and glutamate, along with other neurotransmitters, plays an important role in this process (Bennett, 2000; Riedel, Platt, & Micheau, 2003; Winters & Bussey, 2005).

Gamma-amino butyric acid (GABA), which is found in both the brain and the spinal cord, appears to be the nervous system's primary inhibitory neurotransmitter. It moderates a variety of behaviors, ranging from eating to aggression. Several common substances, such as the tranquilizer Valium and alcohol, are effective because they permit GABA to operate more efficiently (Tabakoff & Hoffman, 1996; Ball, 2004).

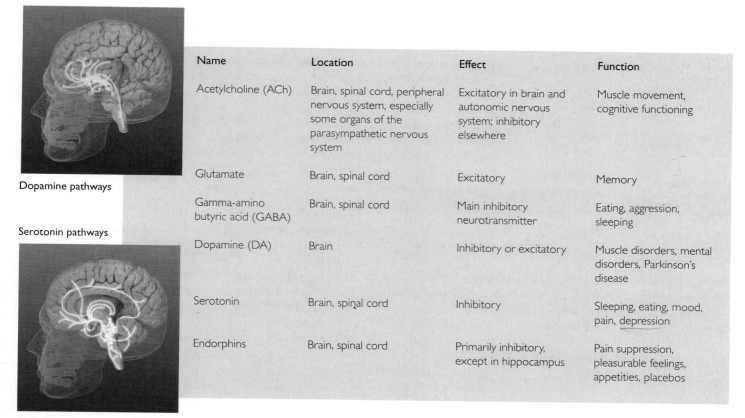

Dopamine pathways

Serotonin pathways

Name	Location	Effect	Function
Acetylcholine (ACh)	Brain, spinal cord, peripheral nervous system, especially some organs of the parasympathetic nervous system	Excitatory in brain and autonomic nervous system; inhibitory elsewhere	Muscle movement, cognitive functioning
Glutamate	Brain, spinal cord	Excitatory	Memory
Gamma-amino butyric acid (GABA)	Brain, spinal cord	Main inhibitory neurotransmitter	Eating, aggression, sleeping
Dopamine (DA)	Brain	Inhibitory or excitatory	Muscle disorders, mental disorders, Parkinson's disease
Serotonin	Brain, spinal cord	Inhibitory	Sleeping, eating, mood, pain, depression
Endorphins	Brain, spinal cord	Primarily inhibitory, except in hippocampus	Pain suppression, pleasurable feelings, appetites, placebos

FIGURE 5 Some major neurotransmitters.

Another major neurotransmitter is *dopamine (DA),* which is involved in movement, attention, and learning. The discovery that certain drugs can have a significant effect on dopamine release has led to the development of effective treatments for a wide variety of physical and mental ailments. For instance, Parkinson's disease, from which actor Michael J. Fox suffers, is caused by a deficiency of dopamine in the brain. Techniques for increasing the production of dopamine in Parkinson's patients are proving effective (Schapira, 1999; Heikkinen, Nutt, & LeWitt, 2001; Kaasinen & Rinne, 2002; Willis, 2005).

In other instances, *over*production of dopamine produces negative consequences. For example, researchers have hypothesized that schizophrenia and some other severe mental disturbances are affected or perhaps even caused by the presence of unusually high levels of dopamine. Drugs that block the reception of dopamine reduce the symptoms displayed by some people diagnosed with schizophrenia (Baumeister & Francis, 2002; Bolonna & Kerwin, 2005).

Another neurotransmitter, *serotonin,* is associated with the regulation of sleep, eating, mood, and pain. A growing body of research points toward a broader role for serotonin, suggesting its involvement in such diverse behaviors as alcoholism, depression, suicide, impulsivity, aggression, and coping with stress (Zalsman & Apter, 2002; Addolorato et al., 2005).

Endorphins, another class of neurotransmitters, are a family of chemicals produced by the brain that are similar in structure to painkilling drugs such as morphine. The production of endorphins seems to reflect the brain's effort to deal with pain as well as to elevate mood. People who are afflicted with diseases that produce long-term, severe pain often develop large concentrations of endorphins in their brains.

Michael J. Fox, who suffers from Parkinson's disease, has become a strong advocate for research into the disorder.

Endorphins also may produce the euphoric feelings that runners sometimes experience after long runs. Although the research evidence is not firm, the exertion and perhaps the pain involved in a long run stimulate the production of endorphins, ultimately resulting in what has been called "runner's high" (Kremer & Scully, 1994; Kolata, 2002b; Pert, 2002).

Endorphin release might also explain other phenomena that have long puzzled psychologists. For example, the act of taking placebos (pills or other substances that contain no actual drugs but that patients *believe* will make them better) may induce the release of endorphins, leading to the reduction of pain. In support of such reasoning, increasing evidence shows that people who are given placebos actually exhibit changes in brain functioning (Leuchter et al., 2002; Stewart-Williams & Podd, 2004).

RECAP/EVALUATE/RETHINK

RECAP

Why do psychologists study the brain and nervous system?

- A full understanding of human behavior requires knowledge of the biological influences underlying that behavior, especially those originating in the nervous system. Psychologists who specialize in studying the effects of biological structures and functions on behavior are known as behavioral neuroscientists. (p. 60)

What are the basic elements of the nervous system?

- Neurons, the most basic elements of the nervous system, carry nerve impulses from one part of the body to another. Information in a neuron generally follows a route that begins with the dendrites, continues into the cell body, and leads ultimately down the tubelike extension, the axon. (p. 61)

How does the nervous system communicate electrical and chemical messages from one part to another?

- Most axons are insulated by a coating called the myelin sheath. When a neuron receives a message to fire, it releases an action potential, an electric charge that travels through the axon. Neurons operate according to an all-or-none law: Either they are at rest, or an action potential is moving through them. There is no in-between state. (p. 62)
- Once a neuron fires, nerve impulses are carried to other neurons through the production of chemical substances, neurotransmitters, that actually bridge the gaps—known as synapses—between neurons. Neurotransmitters may be either excitatory, telling other neurons to fire, or inhibitory, preventing or decreasing the likelihood of other neurons firing. Among the major neurotransmitters are acetylcholine (ACh), which produces contractions of skeletal muscles, and dopamine, which is

involved in movement, attention, and learning and has been linked to Parkinson's disease and certain mental disorders, such as schizophrenia. (pp. 64–67)

- Endorphins, another type of neurotransmitter, are related to the reduction of pain. Endorphins aid in the production of a natural painkiller and are probably responsible for creating the kind of euphoria that joggers sometimes experience after running. (pp. 67–68)

EVALUATE

1. The _____ is the fundamental element of the nervous system.
2. Neurons receive information through their _____ and send messages through their _____.
3. Just as electrical wires have an outer coating, axons are insulated by a coating called the _____.
4. The gap between two neurons is bridged by a chemical connection called a _____.
5. Endorphins are one kind of _____, the chemical "messengers" between neurons.

RETHINK

1. How might psychologists use drugs that mimic the effects of neurotransmitters to treat psychological disorders?
2. *From the perspective of a healthcare provider:* How would you explain the placebo effect and the role of endorphins to patients who wish to try unproven treatment methods that they find on the Web?

Answers to Evaluate Questions

1. neuron; 2. dendrites, axons; 3. myelin sheath; 4. synapse; 5. neurotransmitter

KEY TERMS

behavioral neuroscientists (or biopsychologists) p. 61	dendrite p. 61	all-or-none law p. 62	neurotransmitters p. 65
	axon p. 61	resting state p. 63	excitatory message p. 66
	terminal buttons p. 61	action potential p. 63	inhibitory message p. 66
neurons p. 61	myelin sheath p. 62	synapse p. 64	reuptake p. 66

The Nervous System and the Endocrine System: Communicating Within the Body

In light of the complexity of individual neurons and the neurotransmission process, it should come as no surprise that the connections and structures formed by the neurons are complicated. Because each neuron can be connected to 80,000 other neurons, the total number of possible connections is astonishing. For instance, estimates of the number of neural connections within the brain fall in the neighborhood of 10 quadrillion—a 1 followed by 16 zeros—and some experts put the number even higher. However, connections among neurons are not the only means of communication within the body; as we'll see, the endocrine system, which secretes chemical messages that circulate through the blood, also communicates messages that influence behavior and many aspects of biological functioning (Kandel, Schwartz, & Jessell, 2000; Forlenza & Baum, 2004; Boahen, 2005).

The Nervous System

Whatever the actual number of neural connections, the human nervous system has both logic and elegance. We turn now to a discussion of its basic structures.

CENTRAL AND PERIPHERAL NERVOUS SYSTEMS

As you can see from the schematic representation in Figure 1, the nervous system is divided into two main parts: the central nervous system and the peripheral nervous system. The **central nervous system (CNS)** is composed of the brain and spinal cord. The **spinal cord,** which is about the thickness of a pencil, contains a bundle of neurons that leaves the brain and runs down the length of the back (see Figure 2 on page 71). As you can see in Figure 1 and in the PsychInteractive exercise on the organization of the nervous system, the spinal cord is the primary means for transmitting messages between the brain and the rest of the body.

However, the spinal cord is not just a communication channel. It also controls some simple behaviors on its own, without any help from the brain. An example is the way the knee jerks forward when it is tapped with a rubber hammer. This behavior is a type of **reflex,** an automatic, involuntary response to an incoming stimulus. A reflex is also at work when you touch a hot stove and immediately withdraw your hand. Although the brain eventually analyzes and reacts to the situation ("Ouch—hot stove—pull away!"), the initial withdrawal is directed only by neurons in the spinal cord.

Three kinds of neurons are involved in reflexes. **Sensory (afferent) neurons** transmit information from the perimeter of the body to the central nervous system. **Motor (efferent) neurons** communicate information from the nervous system to muscles and glands. **Interneurons** connect sensory and motor neurons, carrying messages between the two.

The importance of the spinal cord and reflexes is illustrated by the outcome of accidents in which the cord is injured or severed. In some cases, injury results in *quad-*

Key Concepts

How are the structures of the nervous system linked together?

How does the endocrine system affect behavior?

www.mhhe.com/feldmanup8
PsychInteractive Online

Organization of the Nervous System

Central nervous system (CNS): The part of the nervous system that includes the brain and spinal cord.

Spinal cord: A bundle of neurons that leaves the brain and runs down the length of the back and is the main means for transmitting messages between the brain and the body.

Reflex: An automatic, involuntary response to an incoming stimulus.

Sensory (afferent) neurons: Neurons that transmit information from the perimeter of the body to the central nervous system.

Motor (efferent) neurons: Neurons that communicate information from the nervous system to muscles and glands.

Interneurons: Neurons that connect sensory and motor neurons, carrying messages between the two.

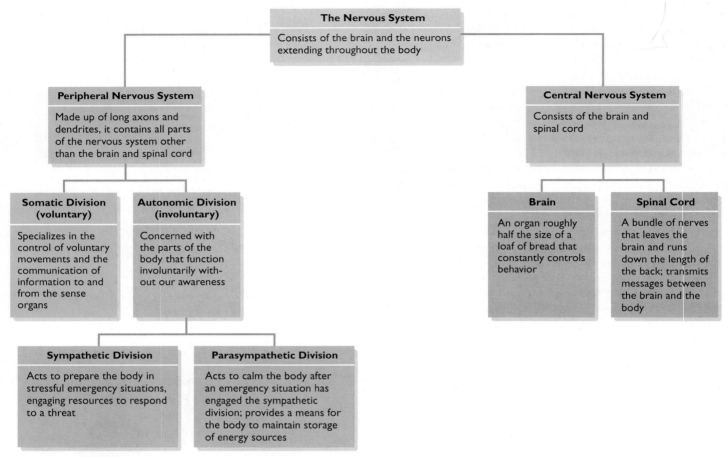

The Nervous System

Consists of the brain and the neurons extending throughout the body

Peripheral Nervous System

Made up of long axons and dendrites, it contains all parts of the nervous system other than the brain and spinal cord

Central Nervous System

Consists of the brain and spinal cord

Somatic Division (voluntary)

Specializes in the control of voluntary movements and the communication of information to and from the sense organs

Autonomic Division (involuntary)

Concerned with the parts of the body that function involuntarily without our awareness

Brain

An organ roughly half the size of a loaf of bread that constantly controls behavior

Spinal Cord

A bundle of nerves that leaves the brain and runs down the length of the back; transmits messages between the brain and the body

Sympathetic Division

Acts to prepare the body in stressful emergency situations, engaging resources to respond to a threat

Parasympathetic Division

Acts to calm the body after an emergency situation has engaged the sympathetic division; provides a means for the body to maintain storage of energy sources

FIGURE 1 A schematic diagram of the relationship of the parts of the nervous system.

riplegia, a condition in which voluntary muscle movement below the neck is lost. In a less severe but still debilitating condition, *paraplegia,* people are unable to voluntarily move any muscles in the lower half of the body.

As suggested by its name, the **peripheral nervous system** branches out from the spinal cord and brain and reaches the extremities of the body. Made up of neurons with long axons and dendrites, the peripheral nervous system encompasses all the parts of the nervous system other than the brain and spinal cord. There are two major divisions—the somatic division and the autonomic division—both of which connect the central nervous system with the sense organs, muscles, glands, and other organs. The **somatic division** specializes in the control of voluntary movements—such as the motion of the eyes to read this sentence or those of the hand to turn this page—and the communication of information to and from the sense organs. On the other hand, the **autonomic division** controls the parts of the body that keep us alive—the heart, blood vessels, glands, lungs, and other organs that function involuntarily without our awareness. As you are reading at this moment, the autonomic division of the peripheral nervous system is pumping blood through your body, pushing your lungs in and out, overseeing the digestion of the meal you had a few hours ago, and so on—all without a thought or care on your part.

Activating the Divisions of the Autonomic Nervous System. The autonomic division plays a particularly crucial role during emergencies. Suppose that as you are reading you suddenly sense that a stranger is watching you through the window.

Peripheral nervous system: The part of the nervous system that includes the autonomic and somatic subdivisions; made up of neurons with long axons and dendrites, it branches out from the spinal cord and brain and reaches the extremities of the body.

Somatic division: The part of the peripheral nervous system that specializes in the control of voluntary movements and the communication of information to and from the sense organs.

Autonomic division: The part of the peripheral nervous system that controls involuntary movement of the heart, glands, lungs, and other organs.

As you look up, you see the glint of something that might be a knife. As confusion clouds your mind and fear overcomes your attempts to think rationally, what happens to your body? If you are like most people, you react immediately on a physiological level. Your heart rate increases, you begin to sweat, and you develop goose bumps all over your body.

The physiological changes that occur during a crisis result from the activation of one of the two parts of the autonomic nervous system: the **sympathetic division.** The sympathetic division acts to prepare the body for action in stressful situations by engaging all of the organism's resources to run away or confront the threat. This response is often called the "fight or flight" response. In contrast, the **parasympathetic division** acts to calm the body after the emergency has ended. When you find, for instance, that the stranger at the window is actually your roommate, who has lost his keys and is climbing in the window to avoid waking you, your parasympathetic division begins to predominate, lowering your heart rate, stopping your sweating, and returning your body to the state it was in before you became alarmed. The parasympathetic division also directs the body to store energy for use in emergencies. The sympathetic and parasympathetic divisions work together to regulate many functions of the body (see Figure 3). For instance, sexual arousal is controlled by the parasympathetic division but sexual orgasm is a function of the sympathetic division.

THE EVOLUTIONARY FOUNDATIONS OF THE NERVOUS SYSTEM

The complexities of the nervous system can be better understood if we take the course of evolution into consideration. The forerunner of the human nervous system is found in the earliest simple organisms to have a spinal cord. Basically, those organisms were simple input-output devices: When the upper side of the spinal cord was stimulated by, for instance, being touched, the organism reacted with a simple response, such as jerking away. Such responses were completely a consequence of the organism's genetic makeup.

Over millions of years, the front end of the spinal cord became more specialized, and organisms became capable of distinguishing between different kinds of stimuli and responding appropriately to them. Ultimately, the front end of the spinal cord evolved into what we would consider a primitive brain. At first, it had just three parts, devoted to close stimuli (such as smell), more distant stimuli (such as sights and sounds), and the ability to maintain balance and bodily coordination. In fact, many animals, such as fish, still have a nervous system that is structured in roughly similar fashion today. In contrast, the human brain evolved from this three-part configuration into an organ that is far more complex and differentiated (Merlin, 1993).

Furthermore, the nervous system is *hierarchically organized,* meaning that relatively newer (from an evolutionary point of view) and more sophisticated regions of the brain regulate the older, and more primitive, parts of the nervous system. As we move up along the spinal cord and continue upward into the brain, then, the functions controlled by the various regions become progressively more advanced.

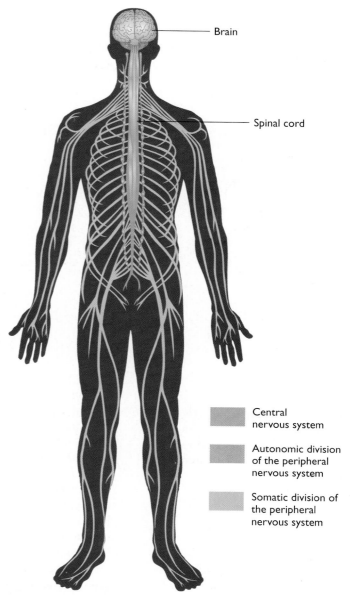

FIGURE 2 The central nervous system, consisting of the brain and spinal cord, and the peripheral nervous system. (Source: Loftus & Wortmann, 1989)

Brain

Spinal cord

Central nervous system

Autonomic division of the peripheral nervous system

Somatic division of the peripheral nervous system

Sympathetic division: The part of the autonomic division of the nervous system that acts to prepare the body for action in stressful situations, engaging all the organism's resources to respond to a threat.

Parasympathetic division: The part of the autonomic division of the nervous system that acts to calm the body after an emergency or stressful situation has ended.

FIGURE 3 The major functions of the autonomic nervous system. The sympathetic division acts to prepare certain organs of the body for stressful situations, and the parasympathetic division acts to calm the body after the emergency has been passed. Can you explain why each response of the sympathetic division might be useful in an emergency?

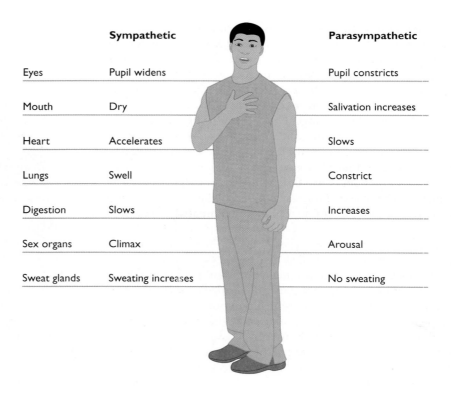

	Sympathetic		Parasympathetic
Eyes	Pupil widens		Pupil constricts
Mouth	Dry		Salivation increases
Heart	Accelerates		Slows
Lungs	Swell		Constrict
Digestion	Slows		Increases
Sex organs	Climax		Arousal
Sweat glands	Sweating increases		No sweating

Evolutionary psychology: The branch of psychology that seeks to identify behavior patterns that are a result of our genetic inheritance from our ancestors.

Why should we care about the evolutionary background of the human nervous system? The answer comes from researchers working in the area of **evolutionary psychology,** the branch of psychology that seeks to identify how behavior is influenced and produced by our genetic inheritance from our ancestors.

Evolutionary psychologists argue that the course of evolution is reflected in the structure and functioning of the nervous system and that evolutionary factors consequently have a significant influence on our everyday behavior. Their work, in conjunction with the research of scientists studying genetics, biochemistry, and medicine, has led to an understanding of how our behavior is affected by heredity, our genetically determined heritage. In fact, evolutionary psychologists have spawned a new and increasingly influential field: behavioral genetics.

BEHAVIORAL GENETICS

Behavioral genetics: The study of the effects of heredity on behavior.

Our evolutionary heritage manifests itself not only through the structure and functioning of the nervous system but through our behavior as well. In the view of a growing area of study, people's personality and behavioral habits are affected in part by their genetic heritage. **Behavioral genetics** studies the effects of heredity on behavior. Behavioral genetics researchers are finding increasing evidence that cognitive abilities, personality traits, sexual orientation, and psychological disorders are determined to some extent by genetic factors (Reif & Lesch, 2003; Viding et al., 2005).

Behavioral genetics lies at the heart of the nature-nurture question, one of the key issues in the study of psychology. Although no one would argue that our behavior is determined *solely* by inherited factors, evidence collected by behavioral geneticists does suggest that our genetic inheritance predisposes us to respond in particular ways to our environment, and even to seek out particular kinds of environments. For instance, research indicates that genetic factors may be related to such diverse behaviors as level of family conflict, schizophrenia, learning disabilities, and general sociability (Berrettini, 2000; McGuire, 2003; Harlaar et al., 2005).

Furthermore, important human characteristics and behaviors are related to the presence (or absence) of particular *genes,* the inherited material that controls the transmission of traits. For example, researchers have found evidence that novelty-seeking behavior is determined, at least in part, by a certain gene.

As we will consider later in the book when we discuss human development, researchers have identified some 25,000 individual genes, each of which appears in a specific sequence on a particular *chromosome,* a rod-shaped structure that transmits genetic information across generations. In 2003, after a decade of effort, researchers identified the sequence of the 3 billion chemical pairs that make up human *DNA,* the basic component of genes. Understanding the basic structure of the human *genome*— the "map" of humans' total genetic makeup—brings scientists a giant step closer to understanding the contributions of individual genes to specific human structures and functioning (Plomin & McGuffin, 2003; Plomin et al., 2003; Andreasen, 2005).

Molecular Genetics and Psychological Disorders. Despite its relative infancy, the field of behavioral genetics has already made substantial contributions to our understanding of behavior. One branch of behavioral genetics, *molecular genetics,* seeks to identify specific genes that are associated with behavior and, in particular, psychological disorders. Genes that are physically close to one another on a particular chromosome tend to be linked and inherited together. By finding *genetic markers*—genes with a known location—that are linked to a disorder, scientists are beginning to learn how disorders such as schizophrenia and depression develop and can potentially be treated.

Molecular geneticists have already found that the risk of developing autism (a severe disorder that influences the development of language and effective social functioning) is increased in the presence of a gene related to early brain development. Children with this gene, a variation of the gene called *HOXA1,* are twice as likely to develop the disorder as children who do not have this variant (Hyman, 2003).

Yet having the variant gene does not always lead to autism. More than 99.5 percent of people with the variant do not develop the disorder, and 60 percent of those with autism do not have the variant. It is probable that autism, like other disorders with a genetic basis, is not triggered by the presence or absence of a single, particular gene. More likely, it is produced by several genes in combination, as well as perhaps requiring the presence of certain environmental influences, such as infection or brain injury. The challenge for behavior geneticists, then, is not only to determine what genes are responsible for particular behaviors, but also to identify the environmental triggers that activate those genes.

In examining the genetic roots of various behaviors, the study of behavioral genetics has stirred controversy. For instance, questions about the existence of genetic influences on criminality, intelligence, and homosexuality raise considerable emotion. Furthermore, it is unclear what the social and political consequences of discoveries in behavioral genetics would be. Might the discovery of a set of genes that cause homosexuality lead to greater or less prejudice against gays and lesbians? Would finding a strong genetic basis for criminal behavior lead to genetic screening and restricted civil rights for individuals having "criminal" genes? Clearly, behavioral genetic discoveries could have an impact on a number of important social issues.

Behavioral Genetics, Gene Therapy, and Genetic Counseling. Behavioral genetics also holds the promise of developing new diagnostic and treatment techniques for genetic deficiencies that can lead to physical and psychological difficulties. In *gene therapy,* scientists inject genes meant to cure a particular disease into a patient's bloodstream. When the genes arrive at the site of defective genes that are producing the illness, they trigger the production of chemicals that can treat the disease (Grady & Kolata, 2003; Lymberis et al., 2004; Rattazzi, LaFuci, & Brown, 2004).

The number of diseases that can be treated through gene therapy is growing, as we will see when we discuss human development. For example, gene therapy is now being used with patients suffering from cancer, leukemia, and Hodgkin's disease (Nakamura, 2004; Wagner et al., 2004).

Advances in behavioral genetics also have led to the development of a profession that did not exist several decades ago: genetic counseling. Genetic counselors help people deal with issues related to inherited disorders. For example, genetic counselors provide advice to prospective parents about the potential risks in a future pregnancy, based on their family history of birth defects and hereditary illnesses. In addition, the counselor will consider the parents' age and problems with children they already have. They also can take blood, skin, and urine samples to examine specific chromosomes.

Scientists have already developed genetic tests to determine whether someone is susceptible to certain types of cancer or heart disease, and it may not be long before analysis of a drop of blood can indicate whether a child—or potentially an unborn fetus—is susceptible to certain psychological disorders. How such knowledge will be used is a source of considerable speculation and controversy, controversy that is certain to grow as genetic testing becomes more common (Etchegary, 2004).

The Endocrine System: Of Chemicals and Glands

Endocrine system: A chemical communication network that sends messages throughout the body via the bloodstream.

Hormones: Chemicals that circulate through the blood and regulate the functioning or growth of the body.

Another of the body's communication systems, the **endocrine system** is a chemical communication network that sends messages throughout the body via the bloodstream. Its job is to secrete **hormones,** chemicals that circulate through the blood and regulate the functioning or growth of the body. It also influences—and is influenced by—the functioning of the nervous system. Although the endocrine system is not part of the brain, it is closely linked to the hypothalamus.

As chemical messengers, hormones are like neurotransmitters, although their speed and mode of transmission are quite different. Whereas neural messages are measured in thousandths of a second, hormonal communications may take minutes to reach their destination. Furthermore, neural messages move through neurons in specific lines (like a signal carried by wires strung along telephone poles), whereas hormones travel throughout the body, similar to the way radio waves are transmitted across the entire landscape. Just as radio waves evoke a response only when a radio is tuned to the correct station, hormones flowing through the bloodstream activate only those cells which are receptive and "tuned" to the appropriate hormonal message.

Pituitary gland: The major component of the endocrine system, or "master gland," which secretes hormones that control growth and other parts of the endocrine system.

A key component of the endocrine system is the tiny **pituitary gland,** which is found near—and regulated by—the hypothalamus. The pituitary gland has sometimes been called the "master gland" because it controls the functioning of the rest of the endocrine system. But the pituitary gland is more than just the taskmaster of other glands; it has important functions in its own right. For instance, hormones secreted by the pituitary gland control growth. Extremely short people and unusually tall ones usually have pituitary gland abnormalities. Other endocrine glands, shown in Figure 4, affect emotional reactions, sexual urges, and energy levels.

Despite its designation as the "master gland," the pituitary is actually a servant of the brain, because the brain is ultimately responsible for the endocrine system's functioning. The brain regulates the internal balance of the body, ensuring that homeostasis is maintained through the hypothalamus.

Structure

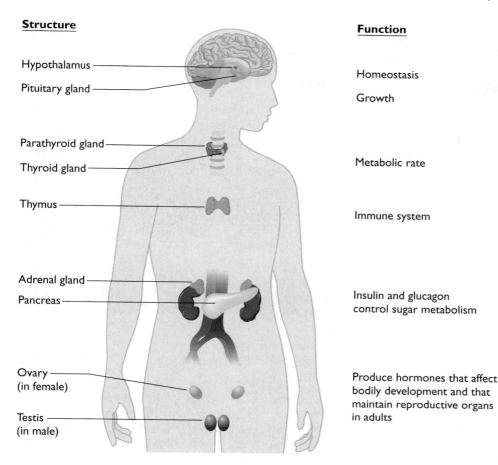

- Hypothalamus
- Pituitary gland
- Parathyroid gland
- Thyroid gland
- Thymus
- Adrenal gland
- Pancreas
- Ovary (in female)
- Testis (in male)

Function

Homeostasis

Growth

Metabolic rate

Immune system

Insulin and glucagon control sugar metabolism

Produce hormones that affect bodily development and that maintain reproductive organs in adults

FIGURE 4 Location and function of the major endocrine glands (Mader, 2000). The pituitary gland controls the functioning of the other endocrine glands and in turn is regulated by the hypothalamus. Steroids, drugs which act like testosterone, can provide added muscle and strength, but they have dangerous side effects.

Individual hormones can wear many hats, depending on circumstances. For example, the hormone oxytocin is at the root of many of life's satisfactions and pleasures. In new mothers, oxytocin produces an urge to nurse newborn offspring. The same hormone also seems to stimulate cuddling between species members. And—at least in rats—it encourages sexually active males to seek out females more passionately, and females to be more receptive to males' sexual advances. There's even evidence that oxytocin is related to the development of trust in others, helping to grease the wheels of effective social interaction (Angier, 1991; Quadros et al., 2000; Kosfeld et al., 2005).

Although hormones are produced naturally by the endocrine system, the ingestion of artificial hormones has proved to be both beneficial and potentially dangerous. For example, before the early 2000s, physicians frequently prescribed hormone replacement therapy (HRT) to treat symptoms of menopause in older women. However, because recent research suggests that the treatment has potentially dangerous side effects, health experts now warn that the dangers outweigh the benefits (Herrington & Howard, 2003).

The use of testosterone, a male hormone, and drugs known as *steroids*, which act like testosterone, is increasingly common. For athletes and others who want to bulk up their appearance, steroids provide a way to add muscle weight and increase strength. However, these drugs can lead to heart attacks, strokes, cancer, and even violent behavior, making them extremely dangerous (Kolata, 2002a; Arangure, 2005).

Steroids can provide added muscle and strength, but they have dangerous side effects. A number of well-known athletes have been accused of using the drugs illegally.

RECAP/EVALUATE/RETHINK

RECAP

How are the structures of the nervous system linked together?

- The nervous system is made up of the central nervous system (the brain and spinal cord) and the peripheral nervous system. The peripheral nervous system is made up of the somatic division, which controls voluntary movements and the communication of information to and from the sense organs, and the autonomic division, which controls involuntary functions such as those of the heart, blood vessels, and lungs. (pp. 69–70)
- The autonomic division of the peripheral nervous system is further subdivided into the sympathetic and parasympathetic divisions. The sympathetic division prepares the body in emergency situations, and the parasympathetic division helps the body return to its typical resting state. (p. 71)
- Evolutionary psychology, the branch of psychology that seeks to identify behavior patterns that are a result of our genetic inheritance, has led to increased understanding of the evolutionary basis of the structure and organization of the human nervous system. Behavioral genetics extends this study to include the evolutionary and hereditary basis of human personality traits and behavior. (pp. 71–72)

How does the endocrine system affect behavior?

- The endocrine system secretes hormones, chemicals that regulate the functioning of the body, via the bloodstream. The pituitary gland secretes growth hormones and influences the release of hormones by other endocrine glands, and in turn is regulated by the hypothalamus. (pp. 74–75)

EVALUATE

1. If you put your hand on a red-hot piece of metal, the immediate response of pulling it away would be an example of a(n) _____.
2. The central nervous system is composed of the _____ and _____.
3. In the peripheral nervous system, the _____ division controls voluntary movements, whereas the _____ division controls organs that keep us alive and functioning without our awareness.
4. Maria saw a young boy run into the street and get hit by a car. When she got to the fallen child, she was in a state of panic. She was sweating, and her heart was racing. Her biological state resulted from the activation of what division of the nervous system?
   a. Parasympathetic
   b. Central
   c. Sympathetic
5. The increasing complexity and hierarchy of the nervous system over millions of years is the subject of study for researchers working in the field of _____.
6. The emerging field of _____ studies ways in which our genetic inheritance predisposes us to behave in certain ways.

RETHINK

1. In what ways is the fight-or-flight response helpful to humans in emergency situations?
2. *From the perspective of a genetic counselor:* How would you explain the pros and cons of genetic counseling to someone who was interested in receiving genetic screening for various diseases and disorders?

Answers to Evaluate Questions

1. reflex; 2. brain, spinal cord; 3. somatic, autonomic; 4. sympathetic; 5. evolutionary psychology; 6. behavioral genetics

KEY TERMS

central nervous system (CNS) p. 69
spinal cord p. 69
reflex p. 69
sensory (afferent) neurons p. 69

motor (efferent) neurons p. 69
interneurons p. 69
peripheral nervous system p. 70
somatic division p. 70

autonomic division p. 70
sympathetic division p. 71
parasympathetic division p. 71
evolutionary psychology p. 72

behavioral genetics p. 72
endocrine system p. 74
hormones p. 74
pituitary gland p. 74

The Brain

It is not much to look at. Soft, spongy, mottled, and pinkish-gray in color, it hardly can be said to possess much in the way of physical beauty. Despite its physical appearance, however, it ranks as the greatest natural marvel that we know and has a beauty and sophistication all its own.

The object to which this description applies: the brain. The brain is responsible for our loftiest thoughts—and our most primitive urges. It is the overseer of the intricate workings of the human body. If one were to attempt to design a computer to mimic the range of capabilities of the brain, the task would be nearly impossible; in fact, it has proved difficult even to come close. The sheer quantity of nerve cells in the brain is enough to daunt even the most ambitious computer engineer. Many billions of neurons make up a structure weighing just 3 pounds in the average adult. However, it is not the number of cells that is the most astounding thing about the brain but its ability to allow the human intellect to flourish by guiding our behavior and thoughts.

We turn now to a consideration of the particular structures of the brain and the primary functions to which they are related. However, a caution is in order. Although we'll discuss specific areas of the brain in relation to specific behaviors, this approach is an oversimplification. No simple one-to-one correspondence exists between a distinct part of the brain and a particular behavior. Instead, behavior is produced by complex interconnections among sets of neurons in many areas of the brain: Our behavior, emotions, thoughts, hopes, and dreams are produced by a variety of neurons throughout the nervous system working in concert.

Key Concepts

How do researchers identify the major parts and functions of the brain?

What are the major parts of the brain, and for what behaviors is each part responsible?

How do the two halves of the brain operate interdependently?

How can an understanding of the nervous system help us find ways to alleviate disease and pain?

Studying the Brain's Structure and Functions: Spying on the Brain

The brain has posed a continual challenge to those who would study it. For most of history, its examination was possible only after an individual had died. Only then could the skull be opened and the brain cut into without serious injury. Although informative, this procedure could hardly tell us much about the functioning of the healthy brain.

Today, however, brain-scanning techniques provide a window into the living brain. Using these techniques, investigators can take a "snapshot" of the internal workings of the brain without having to cut open a person's skull. The most important scanning techniques, illustrated in Figure 1, are the electroencephalogram (EEG), positron emission tomography (PET), functional magnetic resonance imaging (fMRI), and transcranial magnetic stimulation imaging (TMS) .

The *electroencephalogram (EEG)* records electrical activity in the brain through electrodes placed on the outside of the skull. Although traditionally the EEG could produce only a graph of

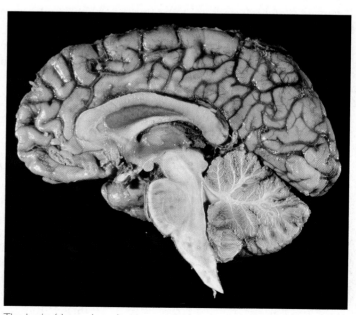

The brain (shown here in cross section) may not be much to look at, but it represents one of the great marvels of human development. Why do most scientists believe that it will be difficult, if not impossible, to duplicate the brain's abilities?

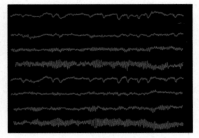

a. EEG

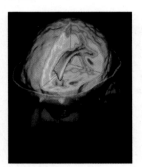

b. fMRI scan

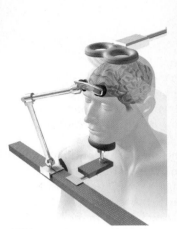

c. TMS apparatus

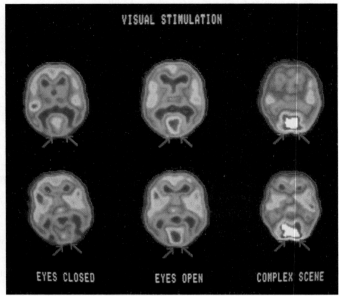

d. PET scan

FIGURE 1 Brain scanning techniques. (a) A computer-produced EEG image. (b) The fMRI scan uses a magnetic field to provide a detailed view of brain activity on a moment-by-moment basis. (c) Transcranial Magnetic Stimulation (TMS), the newest type of scan, produces a momentary disruption in an area of the brain, allowing researchers to see what activities are controlled by that area. TMS also has the potential to treat some psychological disorders. (d) The PET scan displays the functioning of the brain at a given moment.

electrical wave patterns, new techniques are now used to transform the brain's electrical activity into a pictorial representation of the brain that, as a result of their greater detail, allows more precise diagnosis of disorders such as epilepsy and learning disabilities.

Positron emission tomography (PET) scans show biochemical activity within the brain at a given moment. PET scans begin with the injection of a radioactive (but safe) liquid into the bloodstream, which makes its way to the brain. By locating radiation within the brain, a computer can determine which are the more active regions, providing a striking picture of the brain at work. For example, PET scans may be used in cases of memory problems, seeking to identify the presence of brain tumors (Gronholm et al., 2005).

Functional magnetic resonance imaging (fMRI) scans provide a detailed, three-dimensional computer-generated image of brain structures and activity by aiming a powerful magnetic field at the body. With fMRI scanning, it is possible to produce vivid, detailed images of the functioning of the brain.

Using fMRI scans, researchers are able to view features of less than a millimeter in size and view changes occurring in intervals of one-tenth of a second. For example, fMRI scans can show the operation of individual bundles of nerves by tracing the flow of blood, opening the way for improved diagnosis of ailments ranging from chronic back pain to nervous system disorders such as strokes, multiple sclerosis, and Alzheimer's. Scans using fMRI are routinely used in planning brain surgery, because they can help surgeons distinguish areas of the brain involved in normal and disturbed functioning. In addition, fMRI scans have become a valuable research tool in a variety of areas of psychology, ranging from better understanding thinking and memory to learning about the development of language (Knops et al., 2005; Mazard et al., 2005; Quenot et al., 2005).

Transcranial magnetic stimulation (TMS) is one of the newest types of scans. By exposing a tiny region of the brain to a strong magnetic field, TMS causes a momentary interruption of electrical activity. Researchers then are able to note the effects of this interruption on normal brain functioning. The procedure is sometimes called a "virtual lesion" because it

Mind Reading: Harnessing Brainpower to Improve Lives

A baggage screener at the Atlanta Hartsfield Airport is looking at his nine-hundredth bag of the day. Just as his attention begins to wander, an alarm sounds, reminding him that he needs to focus more carefully. While this is happening, an air controller in the control tower, working an overtime shift, begins to feel sleepy. At that very moment, a buzzer sounds, jolting her to full attention.

Although for the moment this scenario remains the stuff of fiction, it may soon become a reality. According to researchers working in a new field called *neuroergonomics,* innovative brain imaging technologies will soon allow employers to anticipate when wandering attention or fatigue may impair workers' performance. Neuroergonomics combines neuroscience and ergonomics, a field that examines how objects and environments can best be designed to make use of human capabilities (Parasuraman & Rizzo, 2005).

The main stumbling block to applying neuroergonomics to job situations is the awkward nature of brain scanning devices. Most now require that scans be carried out in large, body-encompassing equipment. However, more sophisticated devices are on the horizon, such as near infrared spectroscopy (NIRS), which makes use of laser optics and requires only a headpiece during a scan (Huff, 2004).

Neuroscientists are also developing techniques whereby brain waves can be harnessed to activities outside the mind. Even now, it is possible for people to control computers by using only their thoughts. For example, using EEG scanning techniques that react to the pattern of brain waves originating in the brain, one patient who suffered from paralysis learned to boost and curtail certain types of brain waves. After hundreds of hours of practice, he was able to select letters that appeared on a video screen. By stringing letters together, he could spell out messages. The process, which makes use of brain waves called slow cortical potentials, permitted the patient to communicate effectively for the first time in years. Although the method is slow and tedious—the patient can produce only about two characters per minute—it holds great promise (Mitchener, 2001; Hinterberger, Birbaumer, & Flor, 2005).

As our understanding of the meaning of brain wave patterns becomes more sophisticated, significant privacy issues are likely to emerge. Conceivably, the military could screen soldiers for homosexuality, or prison authorities could screen for potential violence in prisoners up for parole. Police could use "brain profiling" to search suspects for brain wave patterns indicative of an inclination to violence. Employers might use brain scans to weed out job applicants who are dishonest. Such possibilities, once seen as merely theoretical, may need to be addressed within the next few years (Goldberg, 2003; Ross, 2003; Grezes, Frith, & Passingham, 2004; Rosen, 2005).

After extensive practice, people can learn to control a computer using only their thoughts.

RETHINK

Should the technology become available, do you think it would be appropriate to observe brain wave patterns of students in classes to make sure that they were paying attention to an instructor? Would it be ethical to require convicted sex offenders to have their brains monitored constantly to ensure that they don't sexually assault a child?

produces effects analogous to what would occur if areas of the brain were physically cut. The enormous advantage of TMS, of course, is that the virtual cut is only temporary.

In addition to identifying areas of the brain that are responsible for particular functions, TMS has the potential to treat certain kinds of psychological disorders, such as depression and schizophrenia, by shooting brief magnetic pulses through the brain. Also, TMS might be used on patients who have suffered brain damage due to a stroke. TMS has the potential to activate undamaged areas of the brain to take over the functions of the damaged areas (George, 2003; Doumas, Praamstra, & Wing, 2005; Simons & Dierick, 2005).

Each of these imaging techniques offers exciting possibilities not only for the diagnosis and treatment of brain disease and injuries, but also for an increased understanding of the normal functioning of the brain. Advances in brain imaging also have given rise to *neuroforensics,* the application of brain science, behavioral genetics, and neural imaging to legal questions. For example, brain scanning has the potential to determine if suspects are telling the truth or lying. In addition, specialists in behavioral genetics and molecular genetics have helped develop procedures to match suspects with crime scene evidence (Grezes, Frith, & Passingham, 2004; Saks & Koehler, 2005).

Advances in our understanding of the brain also are paving the way for the development of new methods for harnessing the brain's neural signals. We consider some of these intriguing findings in the *Applying Psychology in the 21st Century* box.

The Central Core: Our "Old Brain"

Although the capabilities of the human brain far exceed those of the brain of any other species, humans share some basic functions, such as breathing, eating, and sleeping, with more primitive animals. Not surprisingly, those activities are directed by a relatively primitive part of the brain. A portion of the brain known as the **central core** (see Figure 2) is quite similar in all vertebrates (species with backbones). The central core is sometimes referred to as the "old brain" because its evolution can be traced back some 500 million years to primitive structures found in nonhuman species.

If we were to move up the spinal cord from the base of the skull to locate the structures of the central core of the brain, the first part we would come to would be the *hindbrain,* which contains the *medulla,* pons, and cerebellum (see Figure 3). The medulla controls a number of critical body functions, the most important of which are breathing and heartbeat. The *pons* comes next, joining the two halves of the cerebellum, which lies adjacent to it. Containing large bundles of nerves, the pons acts as a transmitter of motor information, coordinating muscles and integrating movement between the right and left halves of the body. It is also involved in regulating sleep.

The **cerebellum** is found just above the medulla and behind the pons. Without the help of the cerebellum we would be unable to walk a straight line without staggering and lurching forward, for it is the job of the cerebellum to control bodily balance. It constantly monitors feedback from the muscles to coordinate their placement, movement, and tension. In fact, drinking too much alcohol seems to depress the activity of the cerebellum, leading to the unsteady gait and movement characteristic of drunkenness. The cerebellum is also involved in several intellectual functions, ranging from the analysis and coordination of sensory information to problem solving (Saab & Willis, 2003; Bower & Parsons, 2003; Paquier & Mariën, 2005).

The **reticular formation** extends from the medulla through the pons, passing through the middle section of the brain—or *midbrain*—and into the front-most part of the brain, called the *forebrain.* Like an ever-vigilant guard, the reticular formation is made up of groups of nerve cells that can activate other parts of the brain immediately

Central core: The "old brain," which controls basic functions such as eating and sleeping and is common to all vertebrates.

Cerebellum (ser uh BELL um): The part of the brain that controls bodily balance.

Reticular formation: The part of the brain extending from the medulla through the pons and made up of groups of nerve cells that can immediately activate other parts of the brain to produce general bodily arousal.

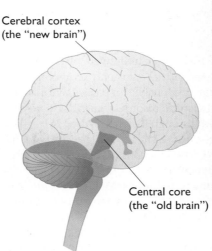

Cerebral cortex
(the "new brain")

Central core
(the "old brain")

FIGURE 2 The major divisions of the brain: the cerebral cortex and the central core. (Source: Seeley, Stephens, & Tate, 2000.)

Although the cerebellum is involved in several intellectual functions, its main duty is to control balance, constantly monitoring feedback from the muscles to coordinate their placement, movement, and tension. Do you think the cerebellum is under conscious or automatic control as people negotiate difficult balancing tasks?

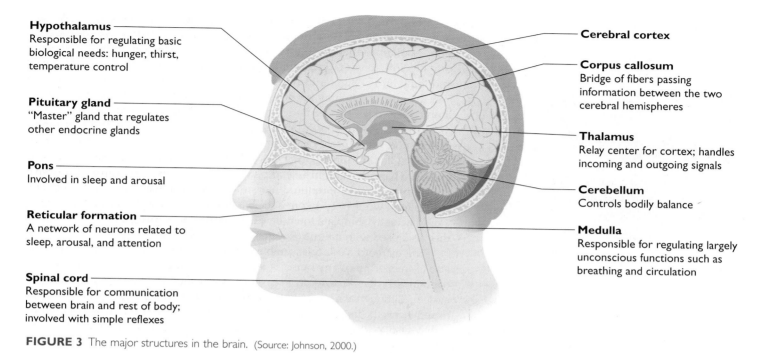

Hypothalamus
Responsible for regulating basic biological needs: hunger, thirst, temperature control

Pituitary gland
"Master" gland that regulates other endocrine glands

Pons
Involved in sleep and arousal

Reticular formation
A network of neurons related to sleep, arousal, and attention

Spinal cord
Responsible for communication between brain and rest of body; involved with simple reflexes

Cerebral cortex

Corpus callosum
Bridge of fibers passing information between the two cerebral hemispheres

Thalamus
Relay center for cortex; handles incoming and outgoing signals

Cerebellum
Controls bodily balance

Medulla
Responsible for regulating largely unconscious functions such as breathing and circulation

FIGURE 3 The major structures in the brain. (Source: Johnson, 2000.)

to produce general bodily arousal. If, for example, we are startled by a loud noise, the reticular formation can prompt a heightened state of awareness to determine whether a response is necessary. The reticular formation serves a different function when we are sleeping, seeming to filter out background stimuli to allow us to sleep undisturbed.

Hidden within the forebrain, the **thalamus** acts primarily as a relay station for information about the senses. Messages from the eyes, ears, and skin travel to the thalamus to be communicated upward to higher parts of the brain. The thalamus also integrates information from higher parts of the brain, sorting it out so that it can be sent to the cerebellum and medulla.

The **hypothalamus** is located just below the thalamus. Although tiny—about the size of a fingertip—the hypothalamus plays an extremely important role. One of its major functions is to maintain *homeostasis*, a steady internal environment for the body. The hypothalamus helps provide a constant body temperature and monitors the amount of nutrients stored in the cells. A second major function is equally important: The hypothalamus produces and regulates behavior that is critical to the basic survival of the species, such as eating, self-protection, and sex.

The Limbic System: Beyond the Central Core

In an eerie view of the future, some science fiction writers have suggested that people someday will routinely have electrodes implanted in their brains. Those electrodes will permit them to receive tiny shocks that will produce the sensation of pleasure by stimulating certain centers of the brain. When they feel upset, people will simply activate their electrodes to achieve an immediate high.

Although far-fetched—and ultimately improbable—such a futuristic fantasy is based on fact. The brain does have pleasure centers in several areas, including some in the **limbic system.** Consisting of a series of doughnut-shaped structures that include the *amygdala, hippocampus,* and *fornix,* the limbic system borders the top of the central core and has connections with the cerebral cortex (see Figure 4).

Thalamus: The part of the brain located in the middle of the central core that acts primarily to relay information about the senses.

Hypothalamus: A tiny part of the brain, located below the thalamus, that maintains homeostasis and produces and regulates vital behavior, such as eating, drinking, and sexual behavior.

Limbic system: The part of the brain that controls eating, aggression, and reproduction.

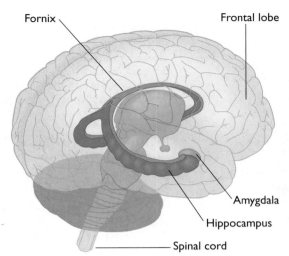

FIGURE 4 The limbic system consists of a series of doughnut-shaped structures that are involved in self-preservation, learning, memory, and the experience of pleasure.

The structures of the limbic system jointly control a variety of basic functions relating to emotions and self-preservation, such as eating, aggression, and reproduction. Injury to the limbic system can produce striking changes in behavior. Such injuries can turn animals that are usually docile and tame into belligerent savages. Conversely, animals that are usually wild and uncontrollable may become meek and obedient following injury to the limbic system (Bedard & Persinger, 1995; Gontkovsky, 2005).

Research examining the effects of mild electric shocks to parts of the limbic system and other parts of the brain has produced some thought-provoking findings (Olds & Milner, 1954; Olds & Fobes, 1981). In one experiment, rats that pressed a bar received mild electric stimulation through an electrode implanted in their brains, which produced pleasurable feelings. Even starving rats on their way to food would stop to press the bar as many times as they could. Some rats would actually stimulate themselves literally thousands of times an hour—until they collapsed with fatigue (Routtenberg & Lindy, 1965).

The extraordinarily pleasurable quality of certain kinds of stimulation has also been experienced by humans, who, as part of the treatment for certain kinds of brain disorders, have received electrical stimulation to certain areas of the limbic system. Although at a loss to describe just what it feels like, these people report the experience to be intensely pleasurable, similar in some respects to sexual orgasm.

The limbic system also plays an important role in learning and memory, a finding demonstrated in patients with epilepsy. In an attempt to stop their seizures, such patients have had portions of the limbic system removed. One unintended consequence of the surgery is that individuals sometimes have difficulty learning and remembering new information. In one case, a patient who had undergone surgery was unable to remember where he lived, although he had resided at the same address for eight years. Further, even though the patient was able to carry on animated conversations, he was unable, a few minutes later, to recall what had been discussed (Milner, 1966).

The limbic system, then, is involved in several important functions, including self-preservation, learning, memory, and the experience of pleasure. These functions are hardly unique to humans; in fact, the limbic system is sometimes referred to as the "animal brain" because its structures and functions are so similar to those of other mammals. To identify the part of the brain that provides the complex and subtle capabilities that are uniquely human, we need to turn to another structure—the cerebral cortex.

The Cerebral Cortex: Our "New Brain"

As we have proceeded up the spinal cord and into the brain, our discussion has centered on areas of the brain that control functions similar to those found in less sophisticated organisms. But where, you may be asking, are the portions of the brain that enable humans to do what they do best and that distinguish humans from all other animals? Those unique features of the human brain—indeed, the very capabilities that allow you to come up with such a question in the first place—are embodied in the ability to think, evaluate, and make complex judgments. The principal location of these abilities, along with many others, is the **cerebral cortex.**

The cerebral cortex is referred to as the "new brain" because of its relatively recent evolution. It consists of a mass of deeply folded, rippled, convoluted tissue. Although only about one-twelfth of an inch thick, it would, if flattened out, cover an area more than two feet square. This configuration allows the surface area of the cortex to be considerably greater than it would be if it were smoother and more uniformly packed into the skull. The uneven shape also permits a high level of integration of neurons, allowing sophisticated information processing.

The cortex has four major sections called **lobes.** If we take a side view of the brain, the *frontal lobes* lie at the front center of the cortex and the *parietal lobes* lie behind them.

Cerebral cortex: The "new brain," responsible for the most sophisticated information processing in the brain; contains four lobes.

Lobes: The four major sections of the cerebral cortex: frontal, parietal, temporal, and occipital.

The *temporal lobes* are found in the lower center portion of the cortex, with the *occipital lobes* lying behind them. These four sets of lobes are physically separated by deep grooves called sulci. Figure 5 shows the four areas. To further review the parts of the cortex, try the Interactivity on areas and functions of the brain.

Another way to describe the brain is in terms of the functions associated with a particular area. Figure 5 also shows the specialized regions within the lobes related to specific functions and areas of the body. Three major areas are known: the motor areas, the sensory areas, and the association areas. Although we will discuss these areas as though they were separate and independent, keep in mind that this is an oversimplification. In most instances, behavior is influenced simultaneously by several structures and areas within the brain, operating interdependently. Furthermore, even within a given area, additional subdivisions exist. Finally, when people suffer certain kinds of brain injury, uninjured portions of the brain can sometimes take over the functions that were previously handled by the damaged area. In short, the brain is extraordinarily adaptable (Sharma, Angelucci, & Sur, 2000; Sacks, 2003; Boller, 2004).

www.mhhe.com/feldmanup8
PsychInteractive Online

Areas and Functions of the Brain

THE MOTOR AREA OF THE CORTEX

If you look at the frontal lobe in Figure 5, you will see a shaded portion labeled **motor area.** This part of the cortex is largely responsible for the body's voluntary movement. Every portion of the motor area corresponds to a specific locale within the body. If we were to insert an electrode into a particular part of the motor area of the cortex and apply mild electrical stimulation, there would be involuntary movement in the corresponding part of the body. If we moved to another part of the motor area and stimulated it, a different part of the body would move.

Motor area: The part of the cortex that is largely responsible for the body's voluntary movement.

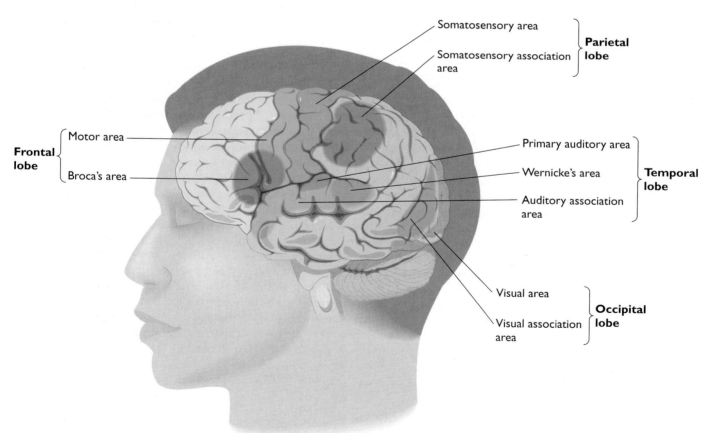

FIGURE 5 The cerebral cortex of the brain. The major physical structures of the cerebral cortex are called lobes. This figure also illustrates the functions associated with particular areas of the cerebral cortex. Are any areas of the cerebral cortex present in nonhuman animals?

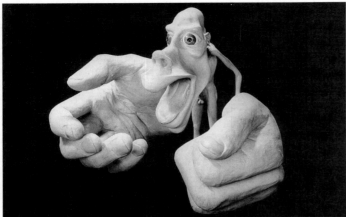

FIGURE 6 The greater the amount of tissue in the somatosensory area of the brain that is related to a specific body part, the more sensitive is that body part. If the size of our body parts reflected the corresponding amount of brain tissue, we would look like this strange creature.

Sensory area: The site in the brain of the tissue that corresponds to each of the senses, with the degree of sensitivity related to the amount of tissue allocated to that sense.

The motor area is so well mapped that researchers have identified the amount and relative location of cortical tissue used to produce movement in specific parts of the human body. For example, the control of movements that are relatively large scale and require little precision, such as the movement of a knee or a hip, is centered in a very small space in the motor area. In contrast, movements that must be precise and delicate, such as facial expressions and finger movements, are controlled by a considerably larger portion of the motor area.

In short, the motor area of the cortex provides a guide to the degree of complexity and the importance of the motor capabilities of specific parts of the body. It may do even more, in fact: Increasing evidence shows that not only does the motor cortex control different parts of the body, but it may also direct body parts into complex postures, such as the stance of a football center just before the ball is snapped to the quarterback or a swimmer standing at the edge of a diving board (Graziano, Taylor, & Moore, 2002; Dessing et al., 2005).

Ultimately, movement, like other behavior, is produced through the coordinated firing of a complex variety of neurons in the nervous system. The neurons that produce movement are linked in elaborate ways and work closely together.

THE SENSORY AREA OF THE CORTEX

Given the one-to-one correspondence between the motor area and body location, it is not surprising to find a similar relationship between specific portions of the cortex and the senses. The **sensory area** of the cortex includes three regions: one that corresponds primarily to body sensations (including touch and pressure), one relating to sight, and a third relating to sound. For instance, the *somatosensory area* encompasses specific locations associated with the ability to perceive touch and pressure in a particular area of the body. As with the motor area, the amount of brain tissue related to a particular location on the body determines the degree of sensitivity of that location: the greater the area devoted to a specific area of the body within the cortex, the more sensitive that area of the body. As you can see from the weird-looking individual in Figure 6, parts such as the fingers are related to proportionally more area in the somatosensory area and are the most sensitive.

The senses of sound and sight are also represented in specific areas of the cerebral cortex. An *auditory area* located in the temporal lobe is responsible for the sense of hearing. If the auditory area is stimulated electrically, a person will hear sounds such as clicks or hums. It also appears that particular locations within the auditory area respond to specific pitches (deCharms, Blake, & Merzenich, 1998; Klinke et al., 1999; Hudspeth, 2000).

The visual area in the cortex, located in the occipital lobe, responds in the same way to electrical stimulation. Stimulation by electrodes produces the experience of flashes of light or colors, suggesting that the raw sensory input of images from the eyes is received in this area of the brain and transformed into meaningful stimuli. The visual area provides another example of how areas of the brain are intimately related to specific areas of the body: Specific structures in the eye are related to a particular part of the cortex—with, as you might guess, more area of the brain given to the most sensitive portions of the retina (Wurtz & Kandel, 2000).

THE ASSOCIATION AREAS OF THE CORTEX

Twenty-five-year-old Phineas Gage, a railroad employee, was blasting rock one day in 1848 when an accidental explosion punched a 3-foot-long spike, about an inch in diameter, completely through his skull. The spike entered just under his left cheek, came out the top of his head, and flew into the air. Gage immediately suffered a series of convulsions, yet a few minutes later was talking with rescuers. In fact, he was able to walk up a long flight of stairs before receiving any medical attention. Amazingly, after a few weeks his wound healed, and he was physically close to his old self again. Mentally, however, there was a difference: Once a careful and hard-working person, Phineas now became enamored with wild schemes and was flighty and often irresponsible. As one of his physicians put it, "Previous to his injury, though untrained in the schools, he possessed a well-balanced mind, and was looked upon by those who knew him as a shrewd, smart businessman, very energetic and persistent in executing all his plans of operation. In this regard his mind was radically changed, so decidedly that his friends and acquaintances said he was 'no longer Gage'" (Harlow, 1869, p. 14).

What had happened to the old Gage? Although there is no way of knowing for sure—science being what it was in the 1800s—we can speculate that the accident may have injured the region of Gage's cerebral cortex known as the **association areas,** which generally are considered to be the site of higher mental processes such as thinking, language, memory, and speech (Rowe et al., 2000).

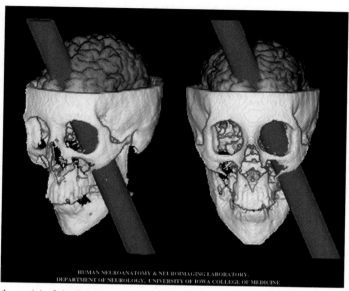

HUMAN NEUROANATOMY & NEUROIMAGING LABORATORY. DEPARTMENT OF NEUROLOGY, UNIVERSITY OF IOWA COLLEGE OF MEDICINE

A model of the injury sustained by Phineas Gage.

The association areas make up a large portion of the cerebral cortex and consist of the sections that are not directly involved in either sensory processing or directing movement. Most of our understanding of the association areas comes from patients who, like Phineas Gage, have suffered some type of brain injury. In some cases, the injury stemmed from natural causes, such as a tumor or a stroke, either of which would block certain blood vessels in the cerebral cortex. In other cases, accidental causes were the culprits, as was true of Gage. In any event, damage to these areas can result in unusual behavioral changes, indicating the importance of the association areas to normal functioning (Gannon et al., 1998; Macmillan, 2000).

Association areas: One of the major regions of the cerebral cortex; the site of the higher mental processes, such as thought, language, memory, and speech.

Gage's case provides evidence that there are specialized areas for making rational decisions. When those areas are damaged, people undergo personality changes that affect their ability to make moral judgments and process emotions. At the same time, people with damage in those areas can still be capable of reasoning logically, performing calculations, and recalling information (Damasio, 1999).

Injuries to other parts of the association areas can produce a condition known as *apraxia.* Apraxia occurs when an individual is unable to integrate activities in a rational or logical manner. The disorder is most evident when people are asked to carry out a sequence of behaviors requiring a degree of planning and foresight, suggesting that the association areas act as "master planners," that is, organizers of actions.

Injuries to the association areas of the brain can also produce *aphasia,* problems with language. In *Broca's aphasia* (caused by damage to the part of the brain first identified by a French physician, Paul Broca, in 1861), speech becomes halting, laborious, and often ungrammatical. The speaker is unable to find the right words in a kind of tip-of-the-tongue phenomenon that we all experience from time to time. People with aphasia, though, grope for words almost constantly, eventually blurting out a kind of "verbal telegram." A phrase like "I put the book on the table" comes out as "I . . . put . . . book . . . table" (Faroqui-Shah & Thompson, 2003; Kearns, 2005).

Wernicke's aphasia is a disorder named for Carl Wernicke, who identified it in the 1870s. Wernicke's aphasia produces difficulties both in understanding others' speech and in the production of language. The disorder is characterized by speech that sounds fluent but makes no sense. For instance, one patient, asked what brought him to a hospital, gave this rambling reply: "Boy, I'm sweating, I'm awful nervous, you know, once in a while I get caught up, I can't mention the tarripoi, a month ago, quite a little, I've done a lot well, I impose a lot, while, on the other hand, you know what I mean, I have to run around, look it over, trebbin and all that sort of stuff" (Gardner, 1975, p. 68).

Mending the Brain

Shortly after he was born, Jacob Stark's arms and legs started jerking every 20 minutes. Weeks later he could not focus his eyes on his mother's face. The diagnosis: uncontrollable epileptic seizures involving his entire brain.

His mother, Sally Stark, recalled: "When Jacob was two and a half months old, they said he would never learn to sit up, would never be able to feed himself. Nothing could be done to prevent profound retardation. They told us to take him home, love him and find an institution" (Blakeslee, 1992, p. C3).

Instead, the Starks brought Jacob to the University of California at Los Angeles for brain surgery when he was five months old. Surgeons removed 20 percent of his brain. The operation was a complete success. Three years later Jacob seemed normal in every way, with no sign of seizures.

Jacob's surgery is representative of increasingly daring approaches in the treatment of brain disorders. It also illustrates how our growing understanding of the processes that underlie brain functioning can be translated into solutions to difficult problems.

The surgery that helped Jacob was based on the premise that the diseased part of his brain was producing seizures throughout the brain. Surgeons reasoned that if they removed the misfiring portion, the remaining parts of the brain, which appeared intact in PET scans, would take over. They bet that Jacob could still lead a normal life after surgery, particularly because the surgery was being done at so young an age. Clearly, the gamble paid off.

The success of Jacob's surgery illustrates something that has been known for some time: The brain has the ability to shift functions to different locations after injury to a specific area or in cases of surgery. But equally encouraging are some new findings about the *regenerative* powers of the brain and nervous system. Scientists had assumed for decades that the neurons of the spinal cord and brain could never be replaced. However, new evidence is beginning to suggest otherwise. For instance, researchers have found that the cells from the brains of adult mice can produce new neurons, at least in a test-tube environment.

Similarly, researchers have reported partial restoration of movement in rats who had a one-fifth-inch-long gap in their spinal cords and, as a result, were unable to move their hind limbs. The researchers transplanted neurons from the peripheral nervous system into the gap, and subsequently the rats were able to flex their legs. One year after the operation, they were able to support themselves and move their legs, and examination of the neurons in the spinal cord showed significant regeneration around the area of the transplantation (Cheng, Cao, & Olson, 1996; McDonald, 1999; Blakeslee, 2000).

The future also holds promise for people who suffer from the tremors and loss of motor control produced by Parkinson's disease, although the research is mired in controversy. Because Parkinson's disease is caused by a gradual loss of cells that stimulate the production of dopamine in the brain, many investigators have reasoned that a procedure that would increase the supply of dopamine might be effective. They seem to be on the right track. When stem cells from human fetuses are injected directly into the brains of Parkinson's sufferers, they seem to take root, stimulating dopamine production. For most of those who have undergone this procedure, the preliminary results have been promising, with some patients showing great improvement (Pollack, 2000; Siderowf & Stearn, 2003; Levy et al., 2004).

The technique of implanting stem cells raises some thorny ethical issues. *Stem cells* are immature cells that have the potential to develop into a variety of more specialized, different cell types, depending on where they are implanted. When a stem cell divides, each newly created cell has the potential to be transformed into more specialized cells. In the process, they could—at least theoretically—repair damaged cells. Because many of the most disabling diseases, ranging from cancer to stroke, result from damage to cells, the potential of stem cells to revolutionize medicine is significant.

However, the source of the implanted stem cells is aborted fetuses, making the use of such cells quite controversial. Some have argued that the use of stem cells in research and treatment should be prohibited, while others argue that the potential benefits of the research are so great that stem cell research should be unrestricted. The issue has been politicized, and whether and how stem cell research should be regulated remains a source of argument (Rosen, 2005).

NEUROPLASTICITY AND THE BRAIN

Regardless of the outcome of the continuing debate over the use of stem cells, it is clear that the brain continually reorganizes itself in a process termed **neuroplasticity.** Although for many years conventional wisdom held that no new brain cells are created after childhood, new research finds otherwise. Not only do the interconnections between neurons become more complex throughout life, but recent findings suggest that new neurons are also created in certain areas of the brain during adulthood. In fact, new neurons may become integrated with existing neural connections after some kinds of brain injury during adulthood (Lichtenwalner & Parent, 2005).

The ability of neurons to renew themselves during adulthood has significant implications for the potential treatment of disorders of the nervous system. For example, drugs that trigger the development of new neurons might be used to counter diseases like Alzheimer's that are produced when neurons die (Stix, 2003; Lie et al., 2004).

Furthermore, specific experiences can modify the way in which information is processed. For example, if you learn to read Braille, the amount of tissue in your cortex related to sensation in the fingertips will expand. Similarly, if you take up the violin, the area of the brain that receives messages from your fingers will grow—but only relating to the fingers that actually move across the violin's strings (Schwartz & Begley, 2002; Kolb, Gibb, & Robinson, 2003).

> **Neuroplasticity:** Changes in the brain that occur throughout the life span relating to the addition of new neurons, new interconnections between neurons, and the reorganization of information-processing areas.

The Specialization of the Hemispheres: Two Brains or One?

The most recent development, at least in evolutionary terms, in the organization and operation of the human brain probably occurred in the last million years: a specialization of the functions controlled by the left and right sides of the brain (McManus, 2004; Sun et al., 2005).

The brain is divided into two roughly mirror-image halves. Just as we have two arms, two legs, and two lungs, we have a left brain and a right brain. Because of the way nerves in the brain are connected to the rest of the body, these symmetrical left and right halves, called **hemispheres,** control motion in—and receive sensation from—the side of the body opposite their location. The left hemisphere of the brain, then, generally controls the right side of the body, and the right hemisphere controls the left side of the body. Thus, damage to the right side of the brain is typically indicated by functional difficulties in the left side of the body.

Despite the appearance of similarity between the two hemispheres of the brain, they are somewhat different in the functions they control and in the ways they control them. Certain behaviors are more likely to reflect activity in one hemisphere than in the other. Early evidence for the functional differences between the halves of the brain came from studies of people with aphasia. Researchers found that people with the speech difficulties characteristic of aphasia tended to have physical damage to the left hemisphere of the brain. In contrast, physical abnormalities in the right hemisphere tended to produce far fewer problems with language. This finding led researchers to conclude that for most people, language is **lateralized,** or located more in one hemisphere than in the other—in this case, in the left side of the brain (Grossi et al., 1996; Ansaldo, Arguin, & Roch 2002).

> **Hemispheres:** Symmetrical left and right halves of the brain that control the side of the body opposite to their location.

> **Lateralization:** The dominance of one hemisphere of the brain in specific functions, such as language.

It now seems clear that the two hemispheres of the brain are somewhat specialized in the functions they carry out. The left hemisphere concentrates more on tasks that require verbal competence, such as speaking, reading, thinking, and reasoning. The right hemisphere has its own strengths, particularly in nonverbal areas such as the understanding of spatial relationships, recognition of patterns and drawings, music, and emotional expression. Cerebral specialization starts at a very early age. For example, even before infants under the age of one year have developed real language skills, their babbling involves left hemisphere specialization (Holowka & Petitto, 2002).

In addition, information is processed somewhat differently in each hemisphere. The left hemisphere tends to consider information sequentially, one bit at a time, whereas the right hemisphere tends to process information globally, considering it as a whole (Turkewitz, 1993; Banich & Heller, 1998; Hines, 2004).

However, it is important to keep in mind that the differences in specialization between the hemispheres are not great and that the degree and nature of lateralization vary from one person to another. If, like most people, you are right-handed, the control of language is probably concentrated more in your left hemisphere. By contrast, if you are among the 10 percent of people who are left-handed or are ambidextrous (you use both hands interchangeably), it is much more likely that the language centers of your brain are located more in the right hemisphere or are divided equally between the left and right hemispheres.

Researchers have also unearthed evidence that there may be subtle differences in brain lateralization patterns between males and females. In fact, some scientists have suggested that there are slight differences in the structure of the brain according to gender and culture. As we see next, such findings have led to a lively debate in the scientific community.

Exploring DIVERSITY

Human Diversity and the Brain

The interplay of biology and environment in behavior is particularly clear when we consider evidence suggesting that even in brain structure and function there are both sex and cultural differences. Let's consider sex first. Accumulating evidence seems to show intriguing differences in males' and females' brain lateralization and weight, although the nature of those differences—and even their existence—is the source of considerable controversy (Kimura, 1992; Dorion, 2000; Hugdahl & Davidson, 2002; Boles, 2005).

Some statements can be made with reasonable confidence. For instance, most males tend to show greater lateralization of language in the left hemisphere. For them, language is clearly relegated largely to the left side of the brain. In contrast, women display less lateralization, with language abilities apt to be more evenly divided between the two hemispheres (Gur et al., 1982; Kulynych et al., 1994; Shaywitz et al., 1995). Such differences in brain lateralization may account, in part, for the superiority often displayed by females on certain measures of verbal skills, such as the onset and fluency of speech, and the fact that far more boys than girls have reading problems in elementary school (Kitterle, 1991).

Other research suggests that men's brains are somewhat bigger than women's brains even after taking differences in body size into account. In contrast, part of the *corpus callosum*, a bundle of fibers that connects the hemispheres of the brain, is proportionally larger in women than in men. Furthermore, some research suggests that in women, a higher proportion of brain neurons are actually involved in thinking compared with men (Falk et al., 1999; Gur et al., 1999; Cahill, 2005).

Men and women also may process information differently. For example, in one study, fMRI brain scans of men making judgements discriminating real from false words showed activation of the left hemisphere of the brain, whereas women used areas on both sides of the brain (Rossell et al., 2002; see Figure 7). Similarly, PET brain scans of men and women while they are not engaged in mental activity show differences in the use of glucose (Gur et al., 1995; Gur, 1996).

The meaning of such sex differences is far from clear. Consider one possibility related to differences in the proportional size of the corpus callosum. Its greater size in women may permit stronger connections to develop between the parts of the brain that control speech. In turn, this would explain why speech tends to emerge slightly earlier in girls than in boys.

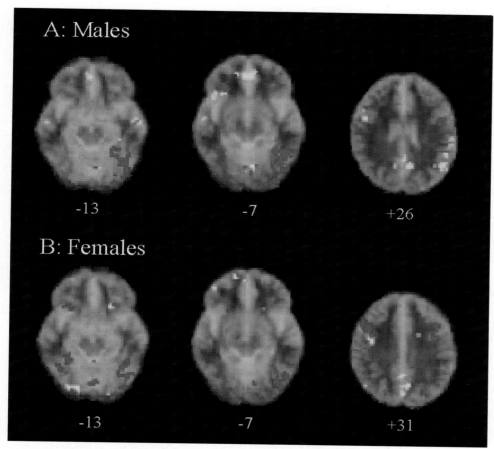

FIGURE 7 These composite fMRI brain scans show the distribution of active areas in the brains of males (top) and females (bottom) during a verbal task involving judgments of whether words were real or were nonwords. In males, activation is more lateralized, or confined, to the left hemisphere, whereas in females, activation is bilateralized, that is, occurring in both hemispheres of the brain. (Source: Rossell et al., 2002.)

Before we rush to such a conclusion, though, it is important to consider an alternative hypothesis: The reason verbal abilities emerge earlier in girls may be that infant girls receive greater encouragement to talk than do infant boys. In turn, this greater early experience may foster the growth of certain parts of the brain. Hence, physical brain differences may be a *reflection* of social and environmental influences rather than a *cause* of the differences in men's and women's behavior. At this point, it is impossible to confirm which of these two alternative hypotheses is correct.

The culture in which people are raised also may give rise to differences in brain lateralization. Native speakers of Japanese seem to process information regarding vowel sounds primarily in the brain's left hemisphere. In contrast, North and South Americans, Europeans, and individuals of Japanese ancestry who learn Japanese later in life handle vowel sounds principally in the right hemisphere.

The reason for this cultural difference in lateralization? One explanation is that certain characteristics of the Japanese language, such as the ability to express complex ideas by using only vowel sounds, result in the development of a specific type of brain lateralization in native speakers. Differences in lateralization may account for other dissimilarities between the ways in which native Japanese speakers and Westerners think about the world (Tsunoda, 1985; Kess & Miyamoto, 1994).

Scientists are just beginning to understand the extent, nature, and meaning of sex and cultural differences in lateralization and brain structure. In evaluating research on brain lateralization, keep in mind also that the two hemispheres of the brain function

www.mhhe.com/feldmanup8

PsychInteractive Online

Brain Lateralization

in tandem. It is a mistake to think of particular kinds of information as being processed solely in the right or the left hemisphere. The hemispheres work interdependently in deciphering, interpreting, and reacting to the world.

In addition, people who suffer injury to the left side of the brain and lose linguistic capabilities often recover the ability to speak: The right side of the brain often takes over some of the functions of the left side, especially in young children; the extent of recovery increases the earlier the injury occurs (Gould et al., 1999; Kempermann & Gage, 1999; Johnston, 2004). (For first-hand experience, complete the PsychInteractive exercise on brain lateralization)

The Split Brain: Exploring the Two Hemispheres

The patient, V.J., had suffered severe seizures. By cutting her corpus callosum, the fibrous portion of the brain that carries messages between the hemispheres, surgeons hoped to create a firebreak to prevent the seizures from spreading. The operation did decrease the frequency and severity of V.J.'s attacks. But V.J. developed an unexpected side effect: She lost the ability to write at will, although she could read and spell words aloud (Strauss, 1998, p. 287).

People like V.J., whose corpus callosum has been surgically cut to stop seizures and who are called *split-brain patients,* offer a rare opportunity for researchers investigating the independent functioning of the two hemispheres of the brain. For example, psychologist Roger Sperry—who won the Nobel Prize for his work—developed a number of ingenious techniques for studying how each hemisphere operates (Sperry, 1982; Baynes et al., 1998; Gazzaniga, 1998).

In one experimental procedure, blindfolded patients touched an object with their right hand and were asked to name it. Because the right side of the body corresponds to the language-oriented left side of the brain, split-brain patients were able to name it. However, if blindfolded patients touched the object with their left hand, they were unable to name it aloud, even though the information had registered in their brains: When the blindfold was removed, patients could identify the object they had touched. Information can be learned and remembered, then, using only the right side of the brain. (By the way, unless you've had a split-brain operation, this experiment won't work with you, because the bundle of fibers connecting the two hemispheres of a normal brain immediately transfers the information from one hemisphere to the other.)

It is clear from experiments like this one that the right and left hemispheres of the brain specialize in handling different sorts of information. At the same time, it is important to realize that both hemispheres are capable of understanding, knowing, and being aware of the world, in somewhat different ways. The two hemispheres, then, should be regarded as different in terms of the efficiency with which they process certain kinds of information, rather than as two entirely separate brains. Moreover, in people with normal, nonsplit brains, the hemispheres work interdependently to allow the full range and richness of thought of which humans are capable.

BECOMING AN INFORMED CONSUMER of Psychology

Learning to Control Your Heart—and Mind—Through Biofeedback

Tammy DeMichael was cruising along the New York State Thruway with her fiancé when he fell asleep at the wheel. The car slammed into the guardrail and flipped, leaving DeMichael with what the doctors called a "splattered C-6, 7"—a broken neck and crushed spinal cord.

After a year of exhaustive medical treatment, she still had no function or feeling in her arms and legs. "The experts said I'd be a quadriplegic for the rest of my life, able to move only from the neck up," she recalls.... But DeMichael proved the experts wrong. Today, feeling has returned to her limbs, her arm strength is normal or better, and she no longer uses a wheelchair. "I can walk about 60 feet with just a cane, and I can go almost anywhere with crutches," she says (Morrow & Wolf, 1991, p. 64).

The key to DeMichael's astounding recovery: biofeedback. **Biofeedback** is a procedure in which a person learns to control through conscious thought internal physiological processes such as blood pressure, heart and respiration rate, skin temperature, sweating, and the constriction of particular muscles. Although it traditionally had been thought that the heart rate, respiration rate, blood pressure, and other bodily functions are under the control of parts of the brain over which we have no influence, psychologists have discovered that these responses are actually susceptible to voluntary control (Bazell, 1998; Martin, 2002; Violani & Lombardo, 2003; Nagai et al., 2004).

In biofeedback, a person is hooked up to electronic devices that provide continuous feedback relating to the physiological response in question. For instance, a person interested in controlling headaches through biofeedback might have electronic sensors placed on certain muscles on her head and learn to control the constriction and relaxation of those muscles. Later, when she felt a headache starting, she could relax the relevant muscles and abort the pain.

In DeMichael's case, biofeedback was effective because not all of the nervous system's connections between the brain and her legs were severed. Through biofeedback, she learned how to send messages to specific muscles, "ordering" them to move. Although it took more than a year, DeMichael was successful in restoring a large degree of her mobility.

Although the control of physiological processes through the use of biofeedback is not easy to learn, it has been employed with success in a variety of ailments, including emotional problems (such as anxiety, depression, phobias, tension headaches, insomnia, and hyperactivity), physical illnesses with a psychological component (such as asthma, high blood pressure, ulcers, muscle spasms, and migraine headaches), and physical problems (such as DeMichael's injuries, strokes, cerebral palsy, and curvature of the spine).

Biofeedback: A procedure in which a person learns to control through conscious thought internal physiological processes such as blood pressure, heart and respiration rate, skin temperature, sweating, and the constriction of particular muscles.

RECAP/EVALUATE/RETHINK

RECAP

How do researchers identify the major parts and functions of the brain?

- Brain scans take a "snapshot" of the internal workings of the brain without having to cut surgically into a person's skull. Major brain-scanning techniques include the electroencephalogram (EEG), positron emission tomography (PET), functional magnetic resonance imaging (fMRI), and transcranial magnetic stimulation imaging (TMS). (pp. 77–78)

What are the major parts of the brain, and for what behaviors is each part responsible?

- The central core of the brain is made up of the medulla (which controls functions such as breathing and the heartbeat), the pons (which coordinates the muscles and the two sides of the body), the cerebellum (which controls balance), the reticular formation (which acts to heighten awareness in emergencies), the thalamus (which communicates sensory messages to and from the brain), and the hypothalamus (which maintains homeostasis, or body equilibrium, and regulates behavior related to basic survival). The functions of the central core structures are similar to those found in other vertebrates. This central core is sometimes referred to as the "old brain." Increasing evidence also suggests that male and female brains may differ in structure in minor ways. (pp. 80–81)

- The cerebral cortex—the "new brain"—has areas that control voluntary movement (the motor area); the senses (the sensory area); and thinking, reasoning, speech, and memory (the association areas). The limbic system, found on the border of the "old" and "new" brains, is associated with eating, aggression, reproduction, and the experiences of pleasure and pain. (pp. 82–84)

How do the two halves of the brain operate interdependently?

- The brain is divided into left and right halves, or hemispheres, each of which generally controls the opposite side of the body. Each hemisphere can be thought of as being specialized in the functions it carries out: The left is best at verbal tasks, such as logical reasoning, speaking, and reading; the right is best at nonverbal tasks, such as spatial perception, pattern recognition, and emotional expression. (p. 87)

How can an understanding of the nervous system help us find ways to alleviate disease and pain?

- Biofeedback is a procedure by which a person learns to control internal physiological processes. By controlling what were once considered involuntary responses, people are able to relieve anxiety, tension, migraine headaches, and a wide range of other psychological and physical problems. (pp. 90–91)

EVALUATE

1. Match the name of each brain scan with the appropriate description:
   a. EEG
   b. fMRI
   c. PET
   1. By locating radiation within the brain, a computer can provide a striking picture of brain activity.
   2. Electrodes placed around the skull record the electrical signals transmitted through the brain.
   3. Provides a three-dimensional view of the brain by aiming a magnetic field at the body
2. Match the portion of the brain with its function:
   a. medulla
   b. pons
   c. cerebellum
   d. reticular formation
   1. Maintains breathing and heartbeat
   2. Controls bodily balance

3. Coordinates and integrates muscle movements
4. Activates other parts of the brain to produce general bodily arousal

3. A surgeon places an electrode on a portion of your brain and stimulates it. Immediately, your right wrist involuntarily twitches. The doctor has most likely stimulated a portion of the _____ area of your brain.
4. Each hemisphere controls the _____ side of the body.
5. Nonverbal realms, such as emotions and music, are controlled primarily by the _____ hemisphere of the brain, whereas the _____ hemisphere is more responsible for speaking and reading.
6. The left hemisphere tends to consider information _____, whereas the right hemisphere tends to process information _____.

RETHINK

1. Before sophisticated brain-scanning techniques were developed, behavioral neuroscientists' understanding of the brain was based largely on the brains of people who had died. What limitations would this pose, and in what areas would you expect the most significant advances once brain-scanning techniques became possible?
2. Could personal differences in people's specialization of right and left hemispheres be related to occupational success? For example, might an architect who relies on spatial skills have a different pattern of hemispheric specialization than a writer?
3. *From the perspective of an educator:* How might you use different techniques to teach reading to boys and girls based on research showing difference in male and female brains?

Answers to Evaluate Questions

1. a-2, b-3, c-1; 2. a-1, b-3, c-2, d-4; 3. motor; 4. opposite; 5. right, left; 6. sequentially, globally

KEY TERMS

central core p. 80
cerebellum (ser uh BELL um) p. 80
reticular formation p. 80

thalamus p. 81
hypothalamus p. 81
limbic system p. 81
cerebral cortex p. 82

lobes p. 82
motor area p. 83
sensory area p. 84
association areas p. 85

neuroplasticity p. 87
hemispheres p. 87
lateralization p. 87
biofeedback p. 91

Looking Back

Psychology on the Web

1. Biofeedback research is continuously changing and being applied to new areas of human functioning. Find at least two Web sites that discuss recent research on biofeedback and summarize the research and any findings it has produced. Include in your summary your best estimate of future applications of this technique.
2. Find one or more Web sites on Parkinson's disease and learn more about this topic. Specifically, find reports of new treatments for Parkinson's disease that do not involve the use of fetal tissue. Write a summary of your findings.
3. After completing the PsychInteractive exercise on areas and functions of the brain, choose one of the structures of the brain that is discussed and Enter it in one of the major search engines. After consulting at least three reputable Web sites, write a brief summary of recent findings about the particular structure in which you are interested.

 In our examination of neuroscience, we've traced the ways in which biological structures and functions of the body affect behavior. Starting with neurons, we considered each of the components of the nervous system, culminating in an examination of how the brain permits us to think, reason, speak, recall, and experience emotions—the hallmarks of being human.

Before proceeding, turn back for a moment to the chapter prologue about Ray Farkas, whose symptoms of Parkinson's disease were relieved by a daring medical procedure. Consider the following questions.

1. Using what you now know about brain structures and functioning, can you explain what might have produced Farkas's Parkinson's disease in the first place?
2. The operation used to treat Farkas's disorder disrupted the functioning of certain neurons in his brain. What part of the brain might the operation have affected?
3. Do you think biofeedback techniques could be used to control the symptoms of Parkinson's disease? Why or why not?

MASTERING the action potential

The action potential is an electrical impulse that travels along the axon of a neuron. Use this visual guide to understand the process by which the impulse travels through a neuron and on to other neurons. Then answer the questions below to test your understanding of the concepts.

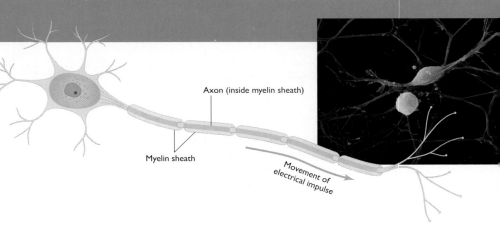

Axon (inside myelin sheath)

Myelin sheath

Movement of electrical impulse

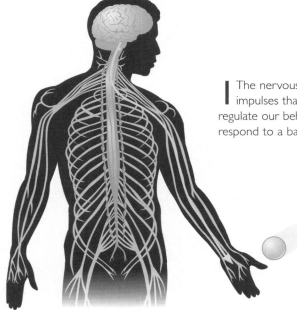

I The nervous system communicates by means of electrical signals or impulses that travel from one neuron to another. These impulses regulate our behavior, instructing our muscles, for example, how to respond to a ball moving toward us through the air.

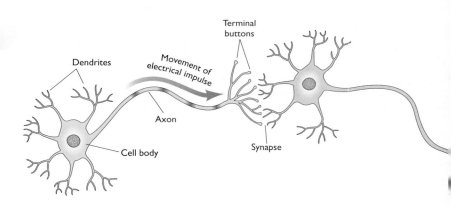

Dendrites

Movement of electrical impulse

Terminal buttons

Axon

Synapse

Cell body

2 Impulses travel from the neuron's dendrites, through the cell body and the axon to the terminal buttons. The terminal buttons release chemicals called neurotransmitters into the synapse, where they are sent to the dendrites of the adjacent neuron to transmit the impulse to the next neuron.

EVALUATE

I An action potential travels across an axon
 a in a chemical form
 b as an electrical impulse
 c as a sound wave
 d in a corkscrew pattern

2 The _____ is the space between neurons that is bridged by chemicals released from the terminal buttons.

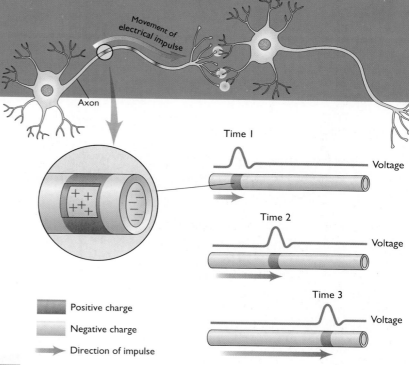

Movement of electrical impulse

Axon

3 In its normal, resting state, a neuron has a negative internal electrical charge. When the neuron is activated, its internal charge briefly becomes positive as an electrical impulse, called an *action potential,* moves through the neuron. An action potential travels through the neuron like a flame along a fuse. After it has passed, the negative charge is restored.

Time 1 — Voltage

Time 2 — Voltage

Positive charge

Negative charge

Direction of impulse

Time 3 — Voltage

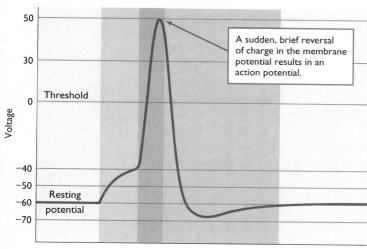

A sudden, brief reversal of charge in the membrane potential results in an action potential.

Threshold

Resting potential

Time ⟶

4 An action potential is generated only if the charge of the incoming impulse is sufficiently strong to cross the neuron's cell membrane and raise the neuron's charge to a level of +40 millivolts. Equally important, the impulse does not travel faster, nor is it stronger, if the voltage exceeds the threshold. Neurons operate according to an *all-or-none law:* Either a neuron is at rest, or an action potential is moving through it. There is no in-between state.

5 Most impulses move in one direction, either away from or toward the brain or spinal cord. When we catch a ball, neurons in the hand send a signal to the brain for interpretation; the brain, in turn, sends a signal telling the hand what to do next. Due to the speed at which nerve impulses travel—some move as quickly as 225 miles per hour—the whole process occurs with amazing rapidity and coordination.

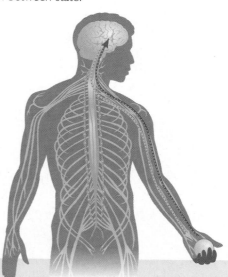

RETHINK

1 What is the process by which one neuron sends a message to another neuron?

3 The all-or-none law says that all neurons must fire at the same time for an impulse to be transmitted. True or False?

Answers to Evaluate questions: 1. b; 2. synapse; 3. false

95

CHAPTER 4

Sensation and Perception

Key Concepts for Chapter 4

What is sensation, and how do psychologists study it? ● What is the relationship between a physical stimulus and the kinds of sensory responses that result from it?

What basic processes underlie the sense of vision? ● How do we see colors?

What role does the ear play in the senses of sound, motion, and balance? ● How do smell and taste function? ● What are the skin senses, and how do they relate to the experience of pain?

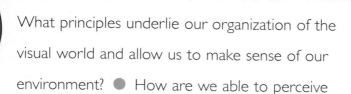

What principles underlie our organization of the visual world and allow us to make sense of our environment? ● How are we able to perceive the world in three dimensions when our retinas are capable of sensing only two-dimensional images? ● What clues do visual illusions give us about our understanding of general perceptual mechanisms?

Prologue Feeling No Pain

How lucky can you get? That's what John and Tara Blocker figured when their then two-week-old baby daughter Ashlyn developed a diaper rash so terrible it hurt just to look at it. Miraculously, here she was with an awful inflammation, and still this sweet child—who always slept through the night and never cried—was acting like nothing was wrong. Recalls Tara, 33: "We took her to the doctor and we were like, 'Wow, we have the happiest baby in the world because she's not even affected by this.'"

It wasn't until a few months later, when Ashlyn's left eye became bloodshot, that the Blockers began to worry. "We gave her eyedrops, but she wasn't getting better," says Tara, a homemaker. "My mommy instincts just kept saying, 'Something's not right.'" Sure enough, an ophthalmologist discovered a massive corneal abrasion, a condition normally so painful that even an adult would be howling. But not Ashlyn (Tresniowski, 2005, p. 99).

Looking Ahead

It was only then that physicians diagnosed the problem: Ashlyn suffered from an extremely rare and untreatable condition that made her completely insensitive to pain or extreme temperatures.

Although at first a condition like Ashlyn's would seem to be an advantage, in fact it is typically a death sentence. Few of those afflicted with it live past young adulthood because they accidentally injure themselves so frequently.

Pain, like our other senses, provides a window to the world, providing us with not only an awareness, understanding, and appreciation of the world's beauty, but alerting us to its dangers. Our senses enable us to feel the gentlest of breezes, see flickering lights miles away, and hear the soft murmuring of distant songbirds.

In the next four modules, we focus on the field of psychology that is concerned with the ways our bodies take in information through the senses and the ways we interpret that information. We will explore both sensation and perception. Sensation encompasses the processes by which our sense organs receive information from the environment. Perception is the brain's and the sense organs' sorting out, interpretation, analysis, and integration of stimuli.

Although perception clearly represents a step beyond sensation, in practice it is sometimes difficult to find the precise boundary between the two. Indeed, psychologists—and philosophers as well—have argued for years over the distinction. The primary difference is that sensation can be thought of as an organism's first encounter with a raw sensory stimulus, whereas perception is the process by which that stimulus is interpreted, analyzed, and integrated with other sensory information.

For example, if we were considering sensation, we might ask about the loudness of a ringing fire alarm. If we were considering perception, we might ask whether someone recognizes the ringing sound as an alarm and identifies its meaning. Similarly, when baseball batters are judging whether they should swing the bat after a ball is pitched, they first make use of sensation in noting the moment when the ball is released from the pitcher's hand. But because a baseball is pitched at speeds faster than the eye can follow (it turns out that the old advice to keep your eye on the ball is impossible to follow), batters must depend on perception to anticipate when, and where, the ball is likely to arrive. Clearly, both sensation and perception are necessary for transforming the physical world into our psychological reality (Bahill & Karnavas, 1993; Gray, 2002).

To a psychologist interested in understanding the causes of behavior, sensation and perception are fundamental topics because so much of our behavior is a reflection of how we react to and interpret stimuli from the world around us. The areas of sensation and perception deal with a wide range of questions—among them, how we respond to the characteristics of physical stimuli; what processes enable us to see, hear, and experience pain; why visual illusions fool us; and how we distinguish one person from another. As we explore these issues, we'll see how the senses work together to provide us with an integrated view and understanding of the world.

Sensing the World Around Us

As Isabel sat down to Thanksgiving dinner, her father carried the turkey in on a tray and placed it squarely in the center of the table. The noise level, already high from the talking and laughter of family members, grew louder still. As Isabel picked up her fork, the smell of the turkey reached her and she felt her stomach growl hungrily. The sight and sound of her family around the table, along with the smells and tastes of the holiday meal, made Isabel feel more relaxed than she had since starting school in the fall.

Put yourself in this setting and consider how different it might be if any one of your senses was not functioning. What if you were blind and unable to see the faces of your family members or the welcome shape of the golden-brown turkey? What if you had no sense of hearing and could not listen to the conversations of family members or were unable to feel your stomach growl, smell the dinner, or taste the food? Clearly, you would experience the dinner very differently than would someone whose sensory apparatus was intact.

Moreover, the sensations mentioned above barely scratch the surface of sensory experience. Although perhaps you were taught, as I was, that there are just five senses—sight, sound, taste, smell, and touch—that enumeration is too modest. Human sensory capabilities go well beyond the basic five senses. For example, we are sensitive not merely to touch but to a considerably wider set of stimuli—pain, pressure, temperature, and vibration, to name a few. In addition, vision has two subsystems—relating to day and night vision—and the ear is responsive to information that allows us not only to hear but also to keep our balance.

To consider how psychologists understand the senses and, more broadly, sensation and perception, we first need a basic working vocabulary. In formal terms, **sensation** is the activation of the sense organs by a source of physical energy. **Perception** is the sorting out, interpretation, analysis, and integration of stimuli carried out by the sense organs and brain. A **stimulus** is any passing source of physical energy that produces a response in a sense organ.

Stimuli vary in both type and intensity. Different types of stimuli activate different sense organs. For instance, we can differentiate light stimuli (which activate the sense of sight and allow us to see the colors of a tree in autumn) from sound stimuli (which, through the sense of hearing, permit us to hear the sounds of an orchestra).

How intense a light stimulus needs to be before it can be detected and how much perfume a person must wear before it is noticed by others are questions related to stimulus intensity.

The issue of how the intensity of a stimulus influences our sensory responses is considered in a branch of psychology known as psychophysics. **Psychophysics** is the study of the relationship between the physical aspects of stimuli and our psychological experience of them. Psychophysics played a central role in the development of the field of psychology, and many of the first psychologists studied issues related to psychophysics (Chechile, 2003; Gardner, 2005).

Key Concepts

What is sensation, and how do psychologists study it?

What is the relationship between a physical stimulus and the kinds of sensory responses that result from it?

Sensation: The activation of the sense organs by a source of physical energy.

Perception: The sorting out, interpretation, analysis, and integration of stimuli by the sense organs and brain.

Stimulus: Energy that produces a response in a sense organ.

Psychophysics: The study of the relationship between the physical aspects of stimuli and our psychological experience of them.

Absolute Thresholds: Detecting What's Out There

Absolute threshold: The smallest intensity of a stimulus that must be present for the stimulus to be detected.

Just when does a stimulus become strong enough to be detected by our sense organs? The answer to this question requires an understanding of the concept of absolute threshold. An **absolute threshold** is the smallest intensity of a stimulus that must be present for it to be detected.

Our senses are extremely responsive to stimuli. For example, the sense of touch is so sensitive that we can feel a bee's wing falling on our cheeks when it is dropped from a distance of one centimeter. Test your knowledge of the absolute thresholds of other senses by completing the questionnaire in Figure 1.

In fact, our senses are so fine-tuned that we might have problems if they were any more sensitive. For instance, if our ears were slightly more acute, we would be able to hear the sound of air molecules in our ears knocking into the eardrum—a phenomenon that would surely prove distracting and might even prevent us from hearing sounds outside our bodies.

Of course, the absolute thresholds we have been discussing are measured under ideal conditions. Normally our senses cannot detect stimulation quite as well because of the presence of noise. *Noise*, as defined by psychophysicists, is background stimulation that interferes with the perception of other stimuli. Hence, noise refers not just to auditory stimuli, as the word suggests, but also to unwanted stimuli that interfere with other senses. Picture a talkative group of people crammed into a small, crowded, smoke-filled room at a party. The din of the crowd makes it hard to hear individual voices, and the smoke makes it difficult to see, or even taste, the food. In this case, the smoke and the crowded conditions would both be considered "noise" because they are preventing sensation at more discriminating levels.

Difference Thresholds: Noticing Distinctions Between Stimuli

Suppose you wanted to choose the six best apples from a supermarket display—the biggest, reddest, and sweetest apples. One approach would be to compare one apple with

Crowded conditions, sounds, and sights can all be considered as noise that interferes with sensation. Can you think of other examples of noise that is not auditory in nature?

FIGURE 1 This test can shed some light on how sensitive the human senses are. (Source: Galanter, 1962.)

How Sensitive Are You?

To test your awareness of the capabilities of your senses, answer the following questions:

1. How far can a candle flame be seen on a clear, dark night:
   a. From a distance of 10 miles _____
   b. From a distance of 30 miles _____
2. How far can the ticking of a watch be heard under quiet conditions?
   a. From 5 feet away _____
   b. From 20 feet away _____
3. How much sugar is needed to allow it to be detected when dissolved in 2 gallons of water?
   a. 2 tablespoons _____
   b. 1 teaspoon _____
4. Over what area can a drop of perfume be detected?
   a. A 5-foot by 5-foot area _____
   b. A 3-room apartment _____

Scoring: In each case, the answer is b, illustrating the tremendous sensitivity of our senses.

another systematically until you were left with a few so similar that you could not tell the difference between them. At that point, it wouldn't matter which ones you chose.

Psychologists have discussed this comparison problem in terms of the **difference threshold,** the smallest level of added (or reduced) stimulation required to sense that a *change* in stimulation has occurred. Thus, the difference threshold is the minimum change in stimulation required to detect the difference between two stimuli, and so it also is called a **just noticeable difference.**

The stimulus value that constitutes a just noticeable difference depends on the initial intensity of the stimulus. The relationship between changes in the original value of a stimulus and the degree to which a change will be noticed forms one of the basic laws of psychophysics: Weber's law. **Weber's law** (with *Weber* pronounced "vay-ber") states that a just noticeable difference is a *constant proportion* of the intensity of an initial stimulus.

For example, Weber found that the just noticeable difference for weight is 1:50. Consequently, it takes a 1-ounce increase in a 50-ounce weight to produce a noticeable difference, and it would take a 10-ounce increase to produce a noticeable difference if the initial weight were 500 ounces. In both cases, the same proportional increase is necessary to produce a just noticeable difference—1:5=10:500. Similarly, the just noticeable difference distinguishing changes in loudness between sounds is larger for sounds that are initially loud than it is for sounds that are initially soft, but the *proportional* increase remains the same.

Weber's law helps explain why a person in a quiet room is more apt to be startled by the ringing of a telephone than is a person in an already noisy room. To produce the same amount of reaction in a noisy room, a telephone ring might have to approximate the loudness of cathedral bells. Similarly, when the moon is visible during the late afternoon, it appears relatively dim—yet against a dark night sky, it seems quite bright. By trying the PsychInteractive exercise, in which you can conduct an experiment on your ability to discern differences in sound levels, you can see for yourself how Weber's law operates.

Difference threshold (just noticeable difference): The smallest level of added or reduced stimulation required to sense that a change in stimulation has occurred.

Weber's law: A basic law of psychophysics stating that a just noticeable difference is in constant proportion to the intensity of an initial stimulus.

www.mhhe.com/feldmanup8
PsychInteractive Online

Weber's Law

Sensory Adaptation: Turning Down Our Responses

You enter a movie theater, and the smell of popcorn is everywhere. A few minutes later, though, you barely notice the smell. The reason you acclimate to the odor is sensory adaptation. **Adaptation** is an adjustment in sensory capacity after prolonged exposure to unchanging stimuli. Adaptation occurs as people become accustomed to a stimulus and change their frame of reference. In a sense, our brain mentally turns down the volume of the stimulation it's experiencing.

One example of adaptation is the decrease in sensitivity that occurs after repeated exposure to a strong stimulus. If you were to hear a loud tone over and over again, eventually it would begin to sound softer. Similarly, although jumping into a cold lake may be temporarily unpleasant, eventually we probably will get used to the temperature.

This apparent decline in sensitivity to sensory stimuli is due to the inability of the sensory nerve receptors to fire off messages to the brain indefinitely. Because these receptor cells are most responsive to *changes* in stimulation, constant stimulation is not effective in producing a sustained reaction.

Judgments of sensory stimuli are also affected by the context in which the judgments are made. This is the case because judgments are made not in isolation from other stimuli but in terms of preceding sensory experience. You can demonstrate this for yourself by trying a simple experiment:

Take two envelopes, one large and one small, and put fifteen nickels in each one. Now lift the large envelope, put it down, and lift the small one. Which seems to weigh more? Most people report that the small one is heavier, although, as you know,

Adaptation: An adjustment in sensory capacity after prolonged exposure to unchanging stimuli.

the weights are nearly identical. The reason for this misconception is that the visual context of the envelope interferes with the sensory experience of weight. Adaptation to the context of one stimulus (the size of the envelope) alters responses to another stimulus (the weight of the envelope) (Coren & Ward, 2004).

RECAP/EVALUATE/RETHINK

RECAP

What is sensation, and how do psychologists study it?

- Sensation is the activation of the sense organs by any source of physical energy. In contrast, perception is the process by which we sort out, interpret, analyze, and integrate stimuli to which our senses are exposed. (p. 99)

What is the relationship between a physical stimulus and the kinds of sensory responses that result from it?

- Psychophysics studies the relationship between the physical nature of stimuli and the sensory responses they evoke. (p. 99)
- The absolute threshold is the smallest amount of physical intensity at which a stimulus can be detected. Under ideal conditions absolute thresholds are extraordinarily sensitive, but the presence of noise (background stimuli that interfere with other stimuli) reduces detection capabilities. (p. 100)
- The difference threshold, or just noticeable difference, is the smallest change in the level of stimulation required to sense that a change has occurred. According to Weber's law, a just noticeable difference is a constant proportion of the intensity of an initial stimulus. (pp. 100–101)
- Sensory adaptation occurs when we become accustomed to a constant stimulus and change our evaluation of it. Repeated exposure to a stimulus results in an apparent decline in sensitivity to it. (p. 101)

EVALUATE

1. _____ is the stimulation of the sense organs; _____ is the sorting out, interpretation, analysis, and integration of stimuli by the sense organs and the brain.
2. The term *absolute threshold* refers to the _____ intensity of a stimulus that must be present for the stimulus to be detected.
3. Weber discovered that for a difference between two stimuli to be perceptible, the stimuli must differ by at least a _____ proportion.
4. After completing a very difficult rock climb in the morning, Carmella found the afternoon climb unexpectedly easy. This case illustrates the phenomenon of _____.

RETHINK

1. Do you think it is possible to have sensation without perception? Is it possible to have perception without sensation?
2. *From the perspective of a manufacturer:* How might you need to take psychophysics into account when developing new products or modifying existing ones?

Answers to Evaluate Questions

1. sensation, perception; 2. smallest; 3. constant; 4. adaptation

KEY TERMS

sensation p. 99
perception p. 99
stimulus p. 99
psychophysics p. 99

absolute threshold p. 100
difference threshold (just noticeable difference) p. 101

Weber's law p. 101
adaptation p. 101

Vision: Shedding Light on the Eye

If, as poets say, the eyes provide a window to the soul, they also provide us with a window to the world. Our visual capabilities permit us to admire and react to scenes ranging from the beauty of a sunset, to the configuration of a lover's face, to the words written on the pages of a book.

Vision starts with light, the physical energy that stimulates the eye. Light is a form of electromagnetic radiation waves, which, as shown in Figure 1, are measured in wavelengths. The sizes of wavelengths correspond to different types of energy. The range of wavelengths that humans are sensitive to—called the *visual spectrum*—is relatively small. Many nonhuman species have different capabilities. For instance, some reptiles and fish sense energies of longer wavelengths than humans do, and certain insects sense energies of shorter wavelengths than humans do.

Light waves coming from some object outside the body (such as the tree in Figure 2) are sensed by the only organ that is capable of responding to the visible spectrum: the eye. Our eyes convert light to a form that can be used by the neurons that serve as messengers to the brain. The neurons themselves take up a relatively small percentage of the total eye. Most of the eye is a mechanical device that is similar in many respects to a camera without film, as you can see in Figure 2.

Despite the similarities between the eye and a camera, vision involves processes that are far more complex and sophisticated than those of any camera. Furthermore, once an image reaches the neuronal receptors of the eye, the eye/camera analogy ends, for the processing of the visual image in the brain is more reflective of a computer than it is of a camera. The animation of the eye in the PsychInteractive exercise on how we see will help you to understand how we are able to see.

Key Concepts

What basic processes underlie the sense of vision?

How do we see colors?

www.mhhe.com/feldmanup8
PsychInteractive Online

How Do We See?

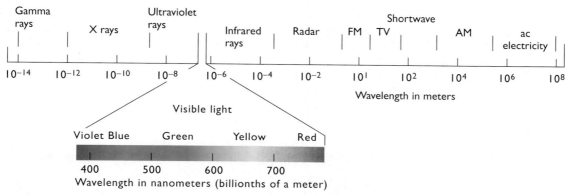

FIGURE I The visible spectrum—the range of wavelengths to which people are sensitive—is only a small part of the kinds of wavelengths present in our environment. Is it a benefit or disadvantage to our everyday lives that we aren't more sensitive to a broader range of visual stimuli? Why?

A camera's lens focuses the inverted image on the film in the same way the eye's lens focuses images on the retina.

Fovea

Cornea

Iris

Pupil

Lens

Optic nerve

Blind spot

Retina

Nonsensor cells of retina

FIGURE 2 Although human vision is far more complicated than the most sophisticated camera, in some ways basic visual processes are analogous to those used in photography.

Illuminating the Structure of the Eye

The ray of light being reflected off the tree in Figure 2 first travels through the *cornea*, a transparent, protective window. The cornea, because of its curvature, bends (or *refracts*) light as it passes through to focus it more sharply. After moving through the cornea, the light traverses the pupil. The *pupil* is a dark hole in the center of the *iris*, the colored part of the eye, which in humans ranges from a light blue to a dark brown. The size of the pupil opening depends on the amount of light in the environment. The dimmer the surroundings are, the more the pupil opens to allow more light to enter.

Why shouldn't the pupil be open completely all the time, allowing the greatest amount of light into the eye? The answer relates to the basic physics of light. A small pupil greatly increases the range of distances at which objects are in focus. With a wide-open pupil, the range is relatively small, and details are harder to discern. The eye takes advantage of bright light by decreasing the size of the pupil and thereby becoming more discerning. In dim light the pupil expands to enable us to view the

Like the automatic lighting system on a camera, the pupil in the human eye expands to let in more light (left) and contracts to block out light (right). Can humans adjust their ears to let in more or less sound in similar manner?

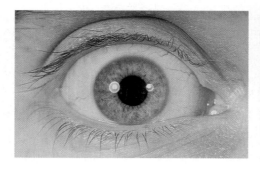
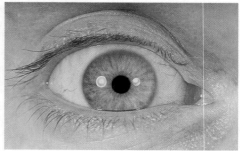

situation better—but at the expense of visual detail. (Perhaps one reason candlelight dinners are thought of as romantic is that the dim light prevents one from seeing a partner's physical flaws.)

Once light passes through the pupil, it enters the *lens,* which is directly behind the pupil. The lens acts to bend the rays of light so that they are properly focused on the rear of the eye. The lens focuses light by changing its own thickness, a process called *accommodation:* It becomes flatter when viewing distant objects and rounder when looking at closer objects.

REACHING THE RETINA

Having traveled through the pupil and lens, our image of the tree finally reaches its ultimate destination in the eye—the **retina.** Here the electromagnetic energy of light is converted to electrical impulses for transmission to the brain. It is important to note that because of the physical properties of light, the image has reversed itself in traveling through the lens, and it reaches the retina upside down (relative to its original position). Although it might seem that this reversal would cause difficulties in understanding and moving about the world, this is not the case. The brain interprets the image in terms of its original position.

The retina consists of a thin layer of nerve cells at the back of the eyeball (see Figure 3). There are two kinds of light-sensitive receptor cells in the retina. The names they have been given describe their shapes: rods and cones. **Rods** are thin, cylindrical receptor cells that are highly sensitive to light. **Cones** are cone-shaped, light-sensitive receptor cells that are responsible for sharp focus and color perception, particularly in bright light. The rods and cones are distributed unevenly throughout the retina. Cones are concentrated on the part of the retina called the *fovea.* The fovea is a particularly sensitive region of the retina. If you want to focus on something of particular interest, you will automatically try to center the image on the fovea to see it more sharply.

The density of cones declines just outside the fovea, although cones are found throughout the retina in lower concentrations. In contrast, there are no rods in the fovea. The density of rods is greatest just outside the fovea and then gradually declines toward the edges of the retina. Because the fovea covers only a small portion of the eye, we have fewer cones (between 5 million and 7 million) than rods (between 100 million and 125 million).

The rods and cones are not only structurally dissimilar but they also play distinctly different roles in vision. Cones are primarily responsible for the sharply focused perception of color, particularly in brightly lit situations; rods are related to vision in dimly lit situations and are largely insensitive to color and to details as sharp as those the cones are capable of recognizing. The rods play a key role in *peripheral vision*—seeing objects that are outside the main center of focus—and in night vision.

Rods and cones also are involved in *dark adaptation,* the phenomenon of adjusting to dim light after being in brighter light. (Think of the experience of walking into a dark movie theater and groping your way to a seat but a few minutes later seeing the seats quite clearly.) The speed at which dark adaptation occurs is a result of the rate of change in the chemical composition of the rods and cones. Although the cones reach their greatest level of adaptation in just a few minutes, the rods take 20 to 30 minutes to reach the maximum level. The opposite phenomenon—*light adaptation,* or the process of adjusting to bright light after exposure to dim light—occurs much faster, taking only a minute or so.

The distinctive abilities of rods and cones make the eye analogous to a camera that is loaded with two kinds of film. One type is a highly sensitive black-and-white film (the rods). The other type is a somewhat less sensitive color film (the cones).

SENDING THE MESSAGE FROM THE EYE TO THE BRAIN

When light energy strikes the rods and cones, it starts a chain of events that transforms light into neural impulses that can be communicated to the brain. Even before the

Retina: The part of the eye that converts the electromagnetic energy of light to electrical impulses for transmission to the brain.

Rods: Thin, cylindrical receptor cells in the retina that are highly sensitive to light.

Cones: Cone-shaped, light-sensitive receptor cells in the retina that are responsible for sharp focus and color perception, particularly in bright light.

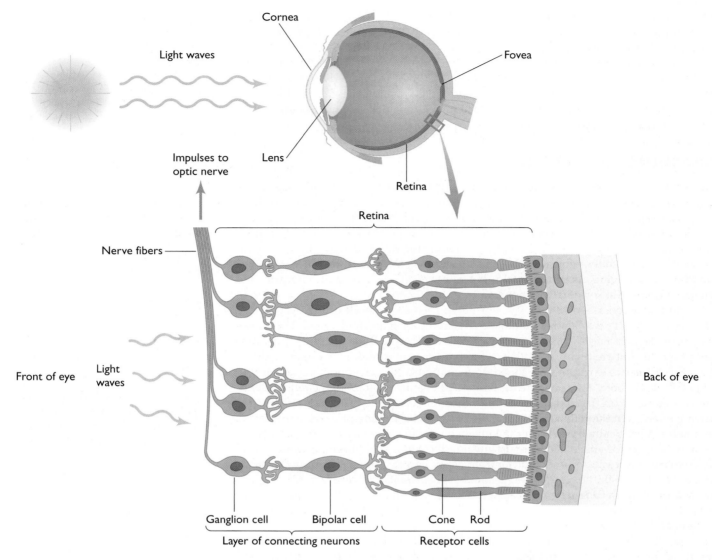

FIGURE 3 The basic cells of the eye. Light entering the eye travels through the ganglion and bipolar cells and strikes the light-sensitive rods and cones located at the back of the eye. The rods and cones then transmit nerve impulses to the brain via the bipolar and ganglion cells. (Source: Shier, Butler, & Lewis, 2000.)

neural message reaches the brain, however, some initial coding of the visual information takes place.

What happens when light energy strikes the retina depends in part on whether it encounters a rod or a cone. Rods contain *rhodopsin,* a complex reddish-purple substance whose composition changes chemically when energized by light. The substance in cone receptors is different, but the principles are similar. Stimulation of the nerve cells in the eye triggers a neural response that is transmitted to other nerve cells in the retina called *bipolar cells* and *ganglion cells.*

Bipolar cells receive information directly from the rods and cones and communicate that information to the ganglion cells. The ganglion cells collect and summarize visual information, which is then moved out of the back of the eyeball and sent to the brain through a bundle of ganglion axons called the **optic nerve.**

Because the opening for the optic nerve passes through the retina, there are no rods or cones in the area, and that creates a blind spot. Normally, however, this

Optic nerve: A bundle of ganglion axons that carry visual information to the brain.

FIGURE 4 To find your blind spot, close your right eye and look at the haunted house with your left eye. You will see the ghost on the periphery of your vision. Now, while staring at the house, move the page toward you. When the book is about a foot from your eye, the ghost will disappear. At this moment, the image of the ghost is falling on your blind spot.

But also notice how, when the page is at that distance, not only does the ghost seem to disappear, but the line seems to run continuously through the area where the ghost used to be. This shows how we automatically compensate for missing information by using nearby material to complete what is unseen. That's the reason you never notice the blind spot. What is missing is replaced by what is seen next to the blind spot. Can you think of any advantages that this tendency to provide missing information gives humans as a species?

absence of nerve cells does not interfere with vision because you automatically compensate for the missing part of your field of vision (Ramachandran, 1995). To find your blind spot, see Figure 4.

Once beyond the eye itself, the neural impulses relating to the image move through the optic nerve. As the optic nerve leaves the eyeball, its path does not take the most direct route to the part of the brain right behind the eye. Instead, the optic nerves from each eye meet at a point roughly between the two eyes—called the optic chiasm (pronounced "ki-asm")—where each optic nerve then splits.

When the optic nerves split, the nerve impulses coming from the right half of each retina are sent to the right side of the brain, and the impulses arriving from the left half of each retina are sent to the left side of the brain. Because the image on the retinas is reversed and upside down, however, those images coming from the right half of each retina actually originated in the field of vision to the person's left, and the images coming from the left half of each retina originated in the field of vision to the person's right (see Figure 5).

PROCESSING THE VISUAL MESSAGE

By the time a visual message reaches the brain, it has passed through several stages of processing. One of the initial sites is the ganglion cells. Each ganglion cell gathers information from a group of rods and cones in a particular area of the eye and compares the amount of light entering the center of that area with the amount of light in the area around it. Some ganglion cells are activated by light in the center (and darkness in the surrounding area). Other ganglion cells are activated when there is darkness in the center and light in the surrounding areas. The ultimate effect of this process is to maximize the detection of variations in light and darkness. The image that is passed on to the brain, then, is an enhanced version of the actual visual stimulus outside the body (Kubovy, Epstein, & Gepshtein, 2003; Pearson & Clifford, 2005).

The ultimate processing of visual images takes place in the visual cortex of the brain, and it is here that the most complex kinds of processing occur. Psychologists David Hubel and Torsten Wiesel won the Nobel Prize in 1981 for their discovery that many neurons in the cortex are extraordinarily specialized, being activated only by visual stimuli of a particular shape or pattern—a process known as **feature detection.** They found that some cells are activated only by lines of a particular width, shape, or orientation. Other cells are activated only by moving, as opposed to stationary, stimuli (Hubel & Wiesel, 2004).

More recent work has added to our knowledge of the complex ways in which visual information coming from individual neurons is combined and processed.

Feature detection: The activation of neurons in the cortex by visual stimuli of specific shapes or patterns.

FIGURE 5 Because the optic nerve coming from each eye splits at the optic chiasm, the image to a person's right is sent to the left side of the brain and the image to the person's left is transmitted to the right side of the brain. (Source: Mader, 2000.)

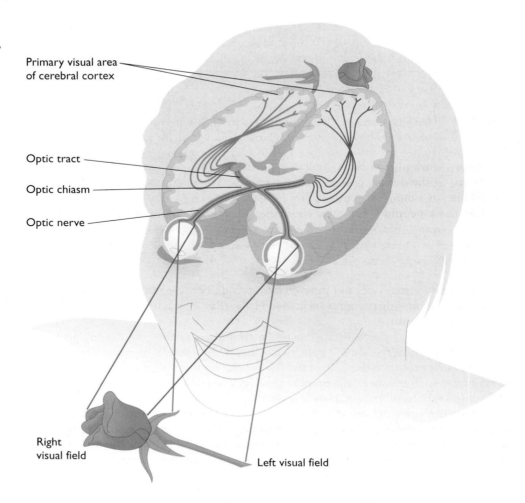

Primary visual area of cerebral cortex

Optic tract

Optic chiasm

Optic nerve

Right visual field

Left visual field

Different parts of the brain process nerve impulses in several individual systems simultaneously. For instance, one system relates to shapes, one to colors, and others to movement, location, and depth. Furthermore, different parts of the brain appear to be involved in the perception of specific *kinds* of stimuli, showing distinctions between the perception of faces, cats, and inanimate stimuli (Haxby et al., 2001; Hasson et al., 2004; Brady, Campbell, & Flaherty, 2005).

If separate neural systems exist for processing information about specific aspects of the visual world, how are all these data integrated by the brain? Although the exact process is not well understood, it seems likely that the brain makes use of information regarding the frequency, rhythm, and timing of the firing of particular sets of neural cells. Furthermore, it appears that the brain's integration of visual information does not occur in any single step or location in the brain but instead is a process that occurs on several levels simultaneously. The ultimate outcome, though, is indisputable: a vision of the world around us (deGelder, 2000; Macaluso, Frith, & Driver, 2000).

Color Vision and Color Blindness: The Seven-Million-Color Spectrum

Although the range of wavelengths to which humans are sensitive is relatively narrow, at least in comparison with the entire electromagnetic spectrum, the portion to which we are capable of responding allows us great flexibility in sensing the world. Nowhere is this clearer than in terms of the number of colors we can discern. A person with normal color vision is capable of distinguishing no less than 7 million different colors (Bruce, Green, & Georgeson, 1997; Rabin, 2004).

Although the variety of colors that people are generally able to distinguish is vast, there are certain individuals whose ability to perceive color is quite limited—the color-blind. Interestingly, the condition of these individuals has provided some of the most important clues to understanding how color vision operates (Neitz, Neitz, & Kainz, 1996).

Before continuing, though, look at the photos shown in Figure 6. If you have difficulty seeing the differences among the series of photos, you may well be one of the 1 in 50 men or 1 in 5,000 women who are color-blind.

For most people with color-blindness, the world looks quite dull. Red fire engines appear yellow, green grass seems yellow, and the three colors of a traffic light all look yellow. In fact, in the most common form of color-blindness, all red and green objects are seen as yellow. There are other forms of color-blindness as well, but they are quite rare. In yellow-blue blindness, people are unable to tell the difference between yellow and blue, and in the most extreme case an individual perceives no color at all. To such a person the world looks something like the picture on a black-and-white television set.

EXPLAINING COLOR VISION

To understand why some people are color-blind, we need to consider the basics of color vision. There are two processes involved. The first process is explained by the **trichromatic theory of color vision.** This theory suggests that there are three kinds of cones in the retina, each of which responds primarily to a specific range of wavelengths. One is most responsive to blue-violet colors, one to green, and the third to yellow-red (Brown & Wald, 1964). According to trichromatic theory, perception of

Trichromatic theory of color vision: The theory that there are three kinds of cones in the retina, each of which responds primarily to a specific range of wavelengths.

a. b. c.

FIGURE 6 (a) To someone with normal vision, the hot-air balloon in the foreground appears with regions of very pure red, orange, yellow, green, blue, and violet, as well as off-white; and the balloon in the rear is a bright shade of red-orange. (b) A person with red-green color blindness would see the scene in part (a) like this, in hues of blue and yellow. (c) A person who is blue-yellow blind, conversely, would see it in hues of red and green.

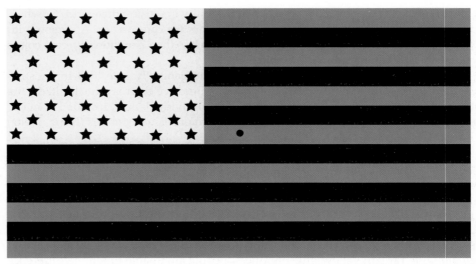

FIGURE 7 Stare at the dot in this flag for about a minute and then look at a piece of plain white paper. What do you see? Most people see an afterimage that converts the colors in the figure into the traditional red, white, and blue U.S. flag. If you have trouble seeing it the first time, blink once and try again.

color is influenced by the relative strength with which each of the three kinds of cones is activated. If we see a blue sky, the blue-violet cones are primarily triggered, and the others show less activity. The trichromatic theory provides a straightforward explanation of color-blindness. It suggests that one of the three cone systems malfunctions, and thus colors covered by that range are perceived improperly (Nathans et al., 1989).

However, there are aspects of color vision that the trichromatic theory is less successful at explaining. For example, the theory does not explain what happens after you stare at something like the flag shown in Figure 7 for about a minute. Try this yourself and then look at a blank white page: You'll see an image of the traditional red, white, and blue U.S. flag. Where there was yellow, you'll see blue, and where there were green and black, you'll see red and white.

The phenomenon you have just experienced is called an *afterimage*. It occurs because activity in the retina continues even when you are no longer staring at the original picture. However, it also demonstrates that the trichromatic theory does not explain color vision completely. Why should the colors in the afterimage be different from those in the original?

Because trichromatic processes do not provide a full explanation of color vision, alternative explanations have been proposed. According to the **opponent-process theory of color vision,** receptor cells are linked in pairs, working in opposition to each other. Specifically, there is a blue-yellow pairing, a red-green pairing, and a black-white pairing. If an object reflects light that contains more blue than yellow, it will stimulate the firing of the cells sensitive to blue, simultaneously discouraging or inhibiting the firing of receptor cells sensitive to yellow—and the object will appear blue. If, in contrast, a light contains more yellow than blue, the cells that respond to yellow will be stimulated to fire while the blue ones are inhibited, and the object will appear yellow.

The opponent-process theory provides a good explanation for afterimages. When we stare at the yellow in the figure, for instance, our receptor cells for the yellow component of the yellow-blue pairing become fatigued and are less able to respond to yellow stimuli. In contrast, the receptor cells for the blue part of the pair are not

Opponent-process theory of color vision: The theory that receptor cells for color are linked in pairs, working in opposition to each other.

tired, because they are not being stimulated. When we look at a white surface, the light reflected off it would normally stimulate both the yellow and the blue receptors equally. But the fatigue of the yellow receptors prevents this from happening. They temporarily do not respond to the yellow, which makes the white light appear to be blue. Because the other colors in the figure do the same thing relative to their specific opponents, the afterimage produces the opponent colors—for a while. The afterimage lasts only a short time, because the fatigue of the yellow receptors is soon overcome, and the white light begins to be perceived more accurately.

Both opponent processes and trichromatic mechanisms are at work in allowing us to see color. However, they operate in different parts of the visual sensing system. Trichromatic processes work within the retina itself, whereas opponent mechanisms operate both in the retina and at later stages of neuronal processing (de Valois & de Valois, 1993; Lee, Wachtler, & Sejnowski, 2002; Gegenfurtner, 2003; Chen, Zhou, & Gong, 2004).

RECAP/EVALUATE/RETHINK

RECAP

What basic processes underlie the sense of vision?

- Vision depends on sensitivity to light, electromagnetic waves in the visible part of the spectrum (wavelengths of roughly 390 to 770 nm) that are either reflected off objects or produced by an energy source. The eye shapes the light into an image that is transformed into nerve impulses and interpreted by the brain. (p. 103)
- As light enters the eye, it passes through the cornea, pupil, and lens and ultimately reaches the retina, where the electromagnetic energy of light is converted to nerve impulses for transmission to the brain. These impulses leave the eye via the optic nerve. (pp. 104–106)
- The visual information gathered by the rods and cones is transferred via bipolar and ganglion cells through the optic nerve, which leads to the optic chiasm—the point where the optic nerve splits. (pp. 106–107)

How do we see colors?

- Color vision seems to be based on two processes described by the trichromatic theory and the opponent-process theory. (pp. 109–110)
- The trichromatic theory suggests that there are three kinds of cones in the retina, each of which is responsive to a certain range of colors. The opponent-process theory presumes pairs of different types of cells in the eye that work in opposition to each other. (pp. 109–111)

EVALUATE

1. Light entering the eye first passes through the _____, a protective window.
2. The structure that converts light into usable neural messages is called the _____.
3. A woman with blue eyes could be described as having blue pigment in her _____.
4. What is the process by which the thickness of the lens is changed in order to focus light properly?
5. The proper sequence of structures that light passes through in the eye is the _____, _____, _____, and _____.
6. Match each type of visual receptor with its function.
   - a. Rods 1. Used for dim light, largely insensitive to color
   - b. Cones 2. Detect color, good in bright light
7. Paco was to meet his girlfriend in the movie theater. As was typical, he was late and the movie had begun. He stumbled down the aisle, barely able to see. Unfortunately, the woman he sat down beside and attempted to put his arm around was not his girlfriend. He sorely wished he had given his eyes a chance and waited for _____ adaptation to occur.
8. _____ theory states that there are three types of cones in the retina, each of which responds primarily to a different color.

RETHINK

1. If the eye had a second lens that "unreversed" the image hitting the retina, do you think there would be changes in the way people perceive the world?
2. *From the perspective of an advertising specialist:* How might you market your products similarly or differently to

those who are color-blind versus those who have normal color vision?

Answers to Evaluate Questions

1. cornea; 2. retina; 3. iris; 4. accommodation; 5. cornea, pupil, lens, retina; 6. a-1, b-2; 7. dark; 8. trichromatic

KEY TERMS

retina p. 105
rods p. 105
cones p. 105

optic nerve p. 106
feature detection p. 107

trichromatic theory of color
    vision p. 109

opponent-process theory of
    color vision p. 110

Hearing and the Other Senses

The blast-off was easy compared with what the astronaut was experiencing now: space sickness. The constant nausea and vomiting were enough to make him wonder why he had worked so hard to become an astronaut. Even though he had been warned that there was a two-thirds chance that his first experience in space would cause these symptoms, he wasn't prepared for how terribly sick he really felt.

Whether or not the astronaut wishes he could head right back to earth, his experience, a major problem for space travelers, is related to a basic sensory process: the sense of motion and balance. This sense allows people to navigate their bodies through the world and keep themselves upright without falling. Along with hearing—the process by which sound waves are translated into understandable and meaningful forms—the sense of motion and balance resides in the ear.

Key Concepts

What role does the ear play in the senses of sound, motion, and balance?

How do smell and taste function?

What are the skin senses, and how do they relate to the experience of pain?

Sensing Sound

Although many of us think primarily of the outer ear when we speak of the ear, that structure is only one simple part of the whole. The outer ear acts as a reverse megaphone, designed to collect and bring sounds into the internal portions of the ear (see Figure 1). The location of the outer ears on different sides of the head helps with *sound localization,* the process by which we identify the direction from which a sound is coming. Wave patterns in the air enter each ear at a slightly different time, and the brain uses the discrepancy as a clue to the sound's point of origin. In addition, the two outer ears delay or amplify sounds of particular frequencies to different degrees (Yost, 2000).

Sound is the movement of air molecules brought about by a source of vibration. Sounds travel through the air in wave patterns similar in shape to those made in water when a stone is thrown into a still pond. Sounds, arriving at the outer ear in the form of wavelike vibrations, are funneled into the *auditory canal,* a tubelike passage that leads to the eardrum. The **eardrum** is aptly named because it operates like a miniature drum, vibrating when sound waves hit it. The more intense the sound, the more the eardrum vibrates. These vibrations are then transferred into the *middle ear,* a tiny chamber containing three bones (the *hammer,* the *anvil,* and the *stirrup*) that transmit vibrations to the oval window, a thin membrane leading to the inner ear. Because the hammer, anvil, and stirrup act as a set of levers, they not only transmit vibrations but increase their strength. Moreover, because the opening into the middle ear (the eardrum) is considerably larger than the opening out of it (the *oval window*), the force of sound waves on the oval window becomes amplified. The middle ear, then, acts as a tiny mechanical amplifier.

The *inner ear* is the portion of the ear that changes the sound vibrations into a form in which they can be transmitted to the brain. (As you will see, it also contains the organs that allow us to locate our position and determine how we are moving through space.) When sound enters the inner ear through the oval window, it moves into the **cochlea,** a coiled tube that looks something like a snail and is filled with fluid that vibrates in response to sound. Inside the cochlea is the **basilar membrane,** a structure that runs through the center of the cochlea, dividing it into an upper chamber and a lower chamber. The basilar membrane is

Sound: The movement of air molecules brought about by a source of vibration.

Eardrum: The part of the ear that vibrates when sound hits it.

Cochlea (KOKE lee uh): A coiled tube in the ear filled with fluid that vibrates in response to sound.

Basilar membrane: A vibrating structure that runs through the center of the cochlea, dividing it into an upper chamber and a lower chamber and containing sense receptors for sound.

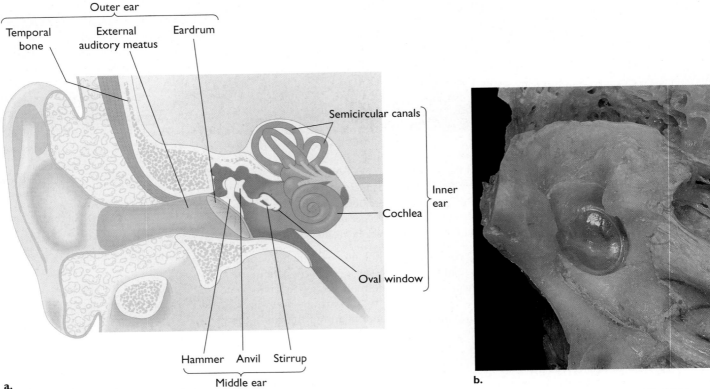

FIGURE 1 (a) The major regions and parts of the ear (Seeley, Stephens, & Tate, 2000). (b) The eardrum. This structure is aptly named because it operates like a miniature drum, vibrating when sound waves hit it.

Hair cells: Tiny cells covering the basilar membrane that, when bent by vibrations entering the cochlea, transmit neural messages to the brain.

covered with **hair cells.** When the hair cells are bent by the vibrations entering the cochlea, the cells send a neural message to the brain (Cho, 2000; Zhou, Liu, & Davis, 2005).

Although sound typically enters the cochlea via the oval window, there is an additional method of entry: bone conduction. Because the ear rests on a maze of bones in the skull, the cochlea is able to pick up subtle vibrations that travel across the bones from other parts of the head. For instance, one of the ways you hear your own voice is through bone conduction. This explains why you sound different to yourself than to other people who hear your voice. (Listen to a recording of your voice to hear what you *really* sound like!) The sound of your voice reaches you both through the air and via bone conduction and therefore sounds richer to you than to everyone else.

THE PHYSICAL ASPECTS OF SOUND

As we mentioned earlier, what we refer to as sound is actually the physical movement of air molecules in regular, wavelike patterns caused by a vibrating source. Sometimes it is even possible to see these vibrations: If you have ever seen an audio speaker that has no enclosure, you know that, at least when the lowest notes are playing, you can see the speaker moving in and out. What is less obvious is what happens next: The speaker pushes air molecules into waves with the same pattern as its movement. Those wave patterns soon reach your ear, although their strength has been weakened considerably during their travels. All other sources that produce sound work in essentially the same fashion, setting off wave patterns that move through the air to the ear. Air—or some other medium, such as water—is necessary to make the vibrations of objects reach us. This explains why there can be no sound in a vacuum.

We are able to see the audio speaker moving when low notes are played because of a primary characteristic of sound called frequency. *Frequency* is the number of wave

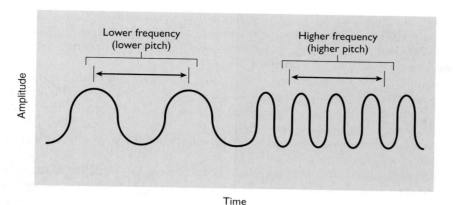

FIGURE 2 The waves produced by different stimuli are transmitted—usually through the air—in different patterns, with lower frequencies indicated by fewer peaks and valleys per second. (Source: Seeley, Stephens, & Tate, 2000.)

cycles that occur in a second. At very low frequencies there are relatively few wave cycles per second (see Figure 2). These cycles are visible to the naked eye as vibrations in the speaker. Low frequencies are translated into a sound that is very low in pitch. (*Pitch* is the characteristic that makes sound seem "high" or "low.") For example, the lowest frequency that humans are capable of hearing is 20 cycles per second. Higher frequencies are heard as sounds of higher pitch. At the upper end of the sound spectrum, people can detect sounds with frequencies as high as 20,000 cycles per second.

Amplitude is a feature of wave patterns that allows us to distinguish between loud and soft sounds. Amplitude is the spread between the up-and-down peaks and valleys of air pressure in a sound wave as it travels through the air. Waves with small peaks and valleys produce soft sounds; those with relatively large peaks and valleys produce loud sounds (see Figure 2).

We are sensitive to broad variations in sound amplitudes. The strongest sounds we are capable of hearing are over a trillion times as intense as the very weakest sound we can hear. This range is measured in *decibels*. When sounds get higher than 120 decibels, they become painful to the human ear. (For a review, try the PsychInteractive exercise on hearing.)

www.mhhe.com/feldmanup8
PsychInteractive Online

Hearing

HEARING LOSS AND DEAF CULTURE

Kathy Peck has some great memories of her days playing bass and singing with The Contractions, an all-female punk band. The San Francisco group developed a loyal following as it played hundreds of shows, and released two singles and an album between 1979 and 1985. Their music was fun, fast, and loud. Too loud, as it turned out. After The Contractions opened for Duran Duran in front of thousands of screaming teeny-boppers at the Oakland Coliseum in 1984, Peck's ears were ringing for days. Then her hearing gradually deteriorated. "It got to the point where I couldn't hear conversations," says Peck, now in her 50s. "People's lips would move and there was no sound. I was totally freaked out." (Noonan, 2005, p. 42).

The delicacy of the organs involved in hearing makes the ear vulnerable to damage.

Former punk rocker Kathy Peck suffered severe hearing loss that cut short her music career.

Exposure to intense levels of sound—coming from events ranging from rock concerts to overly loud earphones—eventually can result in hearing loss, as the hair cells of the basilar membrane lose their elasticity (see Figure 3). Such hearing loss is often permanent.

Some 28 million people in the United States have some degree of hearing impairment, and the number is predicted to climb to 78 million by 2030. Although minor hearing impairment can be treated with hearing aids that increase the volume of sounds reaching the ear, in some cases they are ineffective. In such situations, technological advances have provided some amazing innovations, as we consider in the *Applying Psychology in the 21st Century* box.

Although the restoration of hearing to a deaf person may seem like an unquestionably positive achievement, some advocates for the deaf suggest otherwise, especially when it comes to deaf children who are not old enough to provide informed consent. These critics suggest that deafness represents a legitimate culture—no better or worse than the hearing culture—and that providing even limited hearing to deaf children robs them of their natural cultural heritage. It is, without doubt, a controversial position.

SORTING OUT THEORIES OF SOUND

How are our brains able to sort out wavelengths of different frequencies and intensities? One clue comes from studies of the basilar membrane, the area in the cochlea that translates physical vibrations into neural impulses. It turns out that sounds affect different areas of the basilar membrane, depending on the frequency of the sound wave. The part of the basilar membrane nearest to the oval window is most sensitive to high-

Sound	Decibel Level	Exposure Time Leading to Damage	
Whispering	25 dB		
Library	30 dB		
Average home	50 dB		
Normal conversation	60 dB		
Washing machine	65 dB		
Car	70 dB		
Vacuum cleaner	70 dB		
Busy traffic	75 dB		
Alarm clock	80 dB		
Noisy restaurant	80 dB		
Average factory	85 dB	16	hours
Live rock music (moderately loud)	90 dB	8	hours
Screaming child	90 dB	8	hours
Subway train	100 dB	2	hours
Jackhammer	100 dB	2	hours
Loud song played through earphones	100 dB	30	minutes
Helicopter	105 dB	1	hour
Sandblasting	110 dB	30	minutes
Auto horn	120 dB	7.5	minutes
Live rock music (loud)	130 dB	3.75	minutes
Air raid siren	130 dB	3.75	minutes
THRESHOLD OF PAIN	140 dB	Immediate damage	
Jet engine	140 dB	Immediate damage	
Rocket launching	180 dB	Immediate damage	

FIGURE 3 Various sounds, their decibel levels, and the amount of exposure that results in hearing damage. Source: © 1998 Better Hearing Institute, Washington, DC. All rights reserved.

Making Senses: New Technologies for Restoring Sound and Sight

You'd almost think Amy Ecklund is a contestant on a game show called *Guess That Sound*. "That's a glass!" she proudly exclaims as she hears a clinking noise in the New Haven pub where she's having lunch. "Silverware!" she cries at the clang of a fork. When a hammer bangs, Ecklund gets really excited. "Wow!" she says, "that is loud!" (Ecklund, 1999, p. 68.)

Ecklund's ability to hear is the result of a dramatic operation in which she received a cochlear implant. Hearing-impaired from the age of six, Ecklund, a television soap opera star, can now hear nearly normally.

Ecklund is one of the 90,000 people worldwide who have cochlear implants, which treat certain forms of deafness produced by damage to the ear's hair cells. A *cochlear implant* consists of a tiny receiver inside the ear and an electrode that stimulates hair cells, controlled by a small external sound processor worn behind the ear. The electrodes stimulate nerve endings, thereby relaying the information to the brain, where it can be interpreted as meaningful sound.

The cochlear implant is just one of a new generation of technological devices that offer the promise of restored hearing to the tens of thousands of people with hearing impairments. For example, the *bone anchored hearing appliance* (BAHA) is a device for people with deafness in one ear or damage to the middle or outer ear. A BAHA transports vibrations from the damaged ear to the good ear, helping people to hear sounds originating from both sides of their ears. Similarly, the *penetrating auditory brainstem implant* (PABI) is an experimental technology that sidesteps the auditory nerve and sends sound stimuli directly to the auditory area of the brain stem. By

Amy Ecklund's life changed when she received a cochlear implant.

working directly at the brain stem, the new device bypasses the auditory nerves and nerve endings that often degenerate soon after people lose their hearing (Murugasu, 2005; Rauschecker & Shannon, 2002).

It's not just individuals with hearing impairments who are benefiting from technologies designed to overcome physical limitations. For example, scientists are developing new technologies to help restore vision to blind people. In one advance, eye specialists have invented tiny silicon chips containing thousands of receptors that can help people suffering from retinitis pigmentosa, a disease that slowly damages light-sensitive cells in the eye. The chips, which surgeons surgically implant underneath people's retinas, convert light into electrical energy that stimulates the damaged cells (Chow et al., 2004; Palanker et al., 2005).

Taking a more direct route, another experimental technique for restoring vision involves wiring a small digital camera directly into the brain. Mounted on a pair of sunglasses, the camera connects to the brain's surface through a small opening in the skull behind the person's ear. The camera, equipped with an ultrasonic range finder, transmits information to a small computer, which in turn stimulates an area on the brain associated with vision. Although much research remains before techniques like this will recreate the vision provided by normal eyesight, initial results are promising (Dobelle, 2000; Boahen, 2005).

Once they have been perfected, these technologies will drastically change the way users perceive the world. By enhancing people's perceptual abilities, they present the opportunity of experiencing everyday life in an exciting new way.

RETHINK

What psychological reactions might be expected in people who can newly hear or see and never experienced these senses previously? How might psychologists help people adjust to these new experiences?

Place theory of hearing: The theory that different areas of the basilar membrane respond to different frequencies.

Frequency theory of hearing: The theory that the entire basilar membrane acts like a microphone, vibrating as a whole in response to sound.

frequency sounds, and the part nearest to the cochlea's inner end is most sensitive to low-frequency sounds. This finding has led to the **place theory of hearing,** which states that different areas of the basilar membrane respond to different frequencies.

However, place theory does not tell the full story of hearing, because very low frequency sounds trigger neurons across such a wide area of the basilar membrane that no single site is involved. Consequently, an additional explanation for hearing has been proposed: frequency theory. The **frequency theory of hearing** suggests that the entire basilar membrane acts like a microphone, vibrating as a whole in response to a sound. According to this explanation, the nerve receptors send out signals that are tied directly to the frequency (the number of wave crests per second) of the sounds to which we are exposed, with the number of nerve impulses being a direct function of a sound's frequency. Thus, the higher the pitch of a sound (and therefore the greater the frequency of its wave crests), the greater the number of nerve impulses that are transmitted up the auditory nerve to the brain.

Neither place theory nor frequency theory provides the full explanation for hearing (Hirsh & Watson, 1996; Hudspeth, 2000). Place theory provides a better explanation for the sensing of high-frequency sounds, whereas frequency theory explains what happens when low-frequency sounds are encountered. Medium-frequency sounds incorporate both processes.

After an auditory message leaves the ear, it is transmitted to the auditory cortex of the brain through a complex series of neural interconnections. As the message is transmitted, it is communicated through neurons that respond to specific types of sounds. Within the auditory cortex itself, there are neurons that respond selectively to very specific sorts of sound features, such as clicks and whistles. Some neurons respond only to a specific pattern of sounds, such as a steady tone but not an intermittent one. Furthermore, specific neurons transfer information about a sound's location through their particular pattern of firing (Hackett & Kass, 2003; Polyakov & Pratt, 2003; Middlebrooks et al., 2005; Wang et al., 2005).

If we were to analyze the configuration of the cells in the auditory cortex, we would find that neighboring cells are responsive to similar frequencies. The auditory cortex, then, provides us with a "map" of sound frequencies, just as the visual cortex furnishes a representation of the visual field.

BALANCE: THE UPS AND DOWNS OF LIFE

Semicircular canals: Three tubelike structures of the inner ear containing fluid that sloshes through them when the head moves, signaling rotational or angular movement to the brain.

Otoliths: Tiny, motion-sensitive crystals within the semicircular canals that sense body acceleration.

Several structures of the ear are related more to our sense of balance than to our hearing. The **semicircular canals** of the inner ear (refer to Figure 1) consist of three tubes containing fluid that sloshes through them when the head moves, signaling rotational or angular movement to the brain. The pull on our bodies caused by the acceleration of forward, backward, or up-and-down motion, as well as the constant pull of gravity, is sensed by the **otoliths,** tiny, motion-sensitive crystals in the semicircular canals. When we move, these crystals shift like sands on a windy beach. The brain's inexperience in interpreting messages from the weightless otoliths is the cause of the space sickness commonly experienced by two-thirds of all space travelers (Flam, 1991; Stern & Koch, 1996).

Smell and Taste

Until he bit into a piece of raw cabbage on that February evening . . . , Raymond Fowler had not thought much about the sense of taste.

The cabbage, part of a pasta dish he was preparing for his family's dinner, had an odd, burning taste, but he did not pay it much attention. Then a few minutes later, his daughter handed him a glass of cola, and he took a swallow. "It was like sulfuric acid," he said. "It was like the hottest thing you could imagine boring into your mouth" (Goode, 1999, pp. D1–D2).

The weightlessness of the ear's otoliths produces space sickness in most astronauts.

It was evident that something was very wrong with Fowler's sense of taste. After extensive testing, it became clear that he had damaged the nerves involved in his sense of taste, probably because of a viral infection or a medicine he was taking. (Luckily for him, a few months later his sense of taste returned to normal.)

Even without disruptions in our ability to perceive the world such as those experienced by Fowler, we all know the important roles that taste and smell play. We'll consider these two senses next.

SMELL

Although many animals have keener abilities to detect odors than we do, the human sense of smell *(olfaction)* permits us to detect more than 10,000 separate smells. We also have a good memory for smells, and long-forgotten events and memories can be brought back with the mere whiff of an odor associated with a memory (Gillyatt, 1997; Schiffman et al., 2002; DiLorenzo & Youngentob, 2003; Stevenson & Case, 2005).

Results of "sniff tests" have shown that women generally have a better sense of smell than men do (Engen, 1987). People also seem to have the ability to distinguish males from females on the basis of smell alone. In one experiment, blindfolded students who were asked to sniff the breath of a female or male volunteer who was hidden from view were able to distinguish the sex of the donor at better than chance levels. People can also distinguish happy from sad emotions by sniffing underarm smells, and women are able to identify their babies solely on the basis of smell just a few hours after birth (Doty et al., 1982; Haviland-Jones & Chen, 1999).

Our understanding of the mechanisms that underlie the sense of smell is just beginning to emerge. We do know that the sense of smell is sparked when the molecules of a substance enter the nasal passages and meet *olfactory cells,* the receptor neurons of the nose, which are spread across the nasal cavity. More than 1,000 separate types of receptors have been identified on those cells so far. Each of these receptors is so specialized that it responds only to a small band of different odors. The responses of the separate olfactory cells are then transmitted to the brain, where they are combined into recognition of a particular smell (Rubin & Katz, 1999; Murphy et al., 2004).

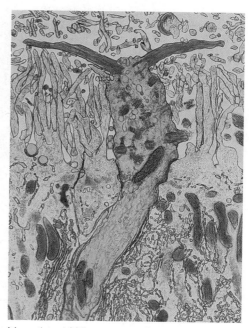

More than 1,000 receptor cells, known as olfactory cells, are spread across the nasal cavity. The cells are specialized to react to particular odors. Do you think it is possible to "train" the nose to pick up a greater number of odors?

There is increasing evidence that smell can also act as a hidden means of communication for humans. It has long been known that nonhumans release *pheromones,* chemicals secreted into the environment by individuals that produce a reaction in other members of the same species, permitting the transmission of messages such as sexual availability. For instance, the vaginal secretions of female monkeys contain pheromones that stimulate sexual interest in male monkeys (Holy, Dulac, & Meister, 2000).

Although it seems reasonable that humans might also communicate through the release of pheromones, the evidence is still scanty. Women's vaginal secretions contain chemicals similar to those found in monkeys, but in humans the smells do not seem to be related to sexual activity. However, the presence of these substances may explain why women who live together for long periods of time tend to start their menstrual cycles on the same day (McClintock et al., 2001; McCoy & Pitino, 2002).

TASTE

The sense of taste (*gustation*) involves receptor cells that respond to four basic stimulus qualities: sweet, sour, salty, and bitter. A fifth category also exists, a flavor called *umami,* although there is controversy about whether it qualifies as a fundamental taste. Umami is a hard-to-translate Japanese word, although the English "meaty" or "savory" comes close. Chemically, umami involves food stimuli that contain amino acids (the substances that make up proteins) (Smith & Margolskee, 2001; de Araujo, Kringelbach, & Rolls, 2003; Shi, Huang, & Zhang, 2005).

Although the specialization of the receptor cells leads them to respond most strongly to a particular type of taste, they also seem capable of responding to other tastes as well. Ultimately, every taste is simply a combination of the basic flavor qualities, in the same way that the primary colors blend into a vast variety of shades and hues (Gilberson, Damak, & Margolskee, 2000; DiLorenzo & Youngentob, 2003).

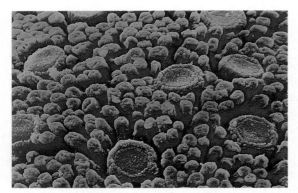

There are 10,000 taste buds on the tongue and other parts of the mouth. Taste buds wear out and are replaced every ten days. What would happen if taste buds were not regenerated?

The receptor cells for taste are located in roughly 10,000 *taste buds,* which are distributed across the tongue and other parts of the mouth and throat. The taste buds wear out and are replaced every ten days or so. That's a good thing, because if our taste buds weren't constantly reproducing, we'd lose the ability to taste after we'd accidentally burned our tongues.

The sense of taste differs significantly from one person to another, largely as a result of genetic factors. Some people, dubbed "supertasters," are highly sensitive to taste; they have twice as many taste receptors as "nontasters," who are relatively insensitive to taste. Supertasters (who, for unknown reasons, are more likely to be female than male) find sweets sweeter, cream creamier, and spicy dishes spicier, and weaker concentrations of flavor are enough to satisfy any cravings they may have. In contrast, because they aren't so sensitive to taste, nontasters may seek out relatively sweeter and fattier foods in order to maximize the taste. As a consequence, they may be prone to obesity (Bartoshuk & Drewnowski, 1997; Bartoshuk, 2000; Snyder, Fast, & Bartoshuk, 2004).

Are you a supertaster? To find out, complete the questionnaire in Figure 4.

The Skin Senses: Touch, Pressure, Temperature, and Pain

It started innocently when Jennifer Darling hurt her right wrist during gym class. At first it seemed like a simple sprain. But even though the initial injury healed, the excruciating, burning pain accompanying it did not go away. Instead, it spread to her other arm and

Take a Taste Test

1. Taste Bud Count
   Punch a hole with a standard hole punch in a square of wax paper. Paint the front of your tongue with a cotton swab dipped in blue food coloring. Put wax paper on the tip of your tongue, just to the right of center. With a flashlight and magnifying glass, count the number of pink, unstained circles. They contain taste buds.
2. Sweet Taste
   Rinse your mouth with water before tasting each sample. Put 1/2 cup sugar in a measuring cup, and then add enough water to make 1 cup. Mix. Coat front half of your tongue, including the tip, with a cotton swab dipped in the solution. Wait a few moments. Rate the sweetness according to the scale shown below.
3. Salt Taste
   Put 2 teaspoons of salt in a measuring cup and add enough water to make 1 cup. Repeat the steps listed above, rating how salty the solution is.
4. Spicy Taste
   Add 1 teaspoon of Tabasco sauce to 1 cup of water. Apply with a cotton swab to first half inch of the tongue, including the tip. Keep your tongue out of your mouth until the burn reaches a peak, then rate the burn according to the scale.

TASTE SCALE

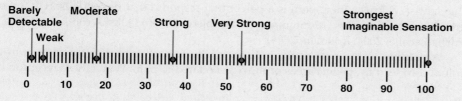

	SUPERTASTERS	NONTASTERS
No. of taste buds	25 on Average	10
Sweet rating	56 on Average	32
Tabasco	64 on Average	31

Average tasters lie in between supertasters and nontasters. Bartoshuk and Lucchina lack the data at this time to rate salt reliably, but you can compare your results with others taking the test.

FIGURE 4 All tongues are not created equal, according to taste researchers Linda Bartoshuk and Laurie Lucchina. Instead, they suggest that the intensity of a flavor experienced by a given person is determined by that person's genetic background. This taste test can help determine if you are a nontaster, average taster, or supertaster. (Source: Bartoshuk & Lucchina, 1997.)

then to her legs. The pain, which Jennifer described as similar to "a hot iron on your arm," was unbearable—and never stopped.

The source of Darling's pain turned out to be a rare condition known as "reflex sympathetic dystrophy syndrome," or RSDS for short. For a victim of RSDS, a stimulus as mild as a gentle breeze or the touch of a feather can produce agony. Even bright sunlight or a loud noise can trigger intense pain.

Pain like Darling's can be devastating, yet a lack of pain can be equally bad. If—like Ashlyn Blocker, whose case was described in the chapter-opening Prologue—you never experienced pain, for instance, you might not notice that your arm had brushed against a hot pan, and you would suffer a severe burn. Similarly, without the warning sign of abdominal pain that typically accompanies an inflamed appendix, your appendix might eventually rupture, spreading a fatal infection throughout your body.

In fact, all our **skin senses**—touch, pressure, temperature, and pain—play a critical role in survival, making us aware of potential danger to our bodies. Most of these senses operate through nerve receptor cells located at various depths throughout the skin, distributed unevenly throughout the body. For example, some areas, such as the fingertips, have many more receptor cells sensitive to touch and as a consequence

Skin senses: The senses of touch, pressure, temperature, and pain.

are notably more sensitive than other areas of the body (Gardner & Kandel, 2000; see Figure 5).

Probably the most extensively researched skin sense is pain, and with good reason: People consult physicians and take medication for pain more than for any other symptom or condition. Pain costs $100 billion a year in the United States alone (Price, 2000; Kalb, 2001a; Kalb, 2003).

Pain is a response to a great variety of different kinds of stimuli. A light that is too bright can produce pain, and sound that is too loud can be painful. One explanation is that pain is an outcome of cell injury; when a cell is damaged, regardless of the source of damage, it releases a chemical called *substance P* that transmits pain messages to the brain.

Some people are more susceptible to pain than others. For example, women experience painful stimuli more intensely than men. These gender differences are associated with the production of hormones related to menstrual cycles. In addition, certain genes are linked to the experience of pain, so that we may inherit our sensitivity to pain (Zubieta et al., 2003; Frot, Feine, & Bushnell, 2004; Apkarian et al., 2005).

But the experience of pain is not determined by biological factors alone. For example, women report that the pain experienced in childbirth is moderated to some degree by the joyful nature of the situation. In contrast, even a minor stimulus can produce the perception of strong pain if it is accompanied by anxiety (like a visit to the dentist). Clearly, then, pain is a perceptual response that depends heavily on our emotions and thoughts (Montgomery & Bovbjerg, 2003; Hadjistavropoulos, Craig, & Fuchs-Lacelle, 2004; Rollman, 2004).

According to the **gate-control theory of pain,** particular nerve receptors in the spinal cord lead to specific areas of the brain related to pain. When these receptors are

Gate-control theory of pain: The theory that particular nerve receptors lead to specific areas of the brain related to pain.

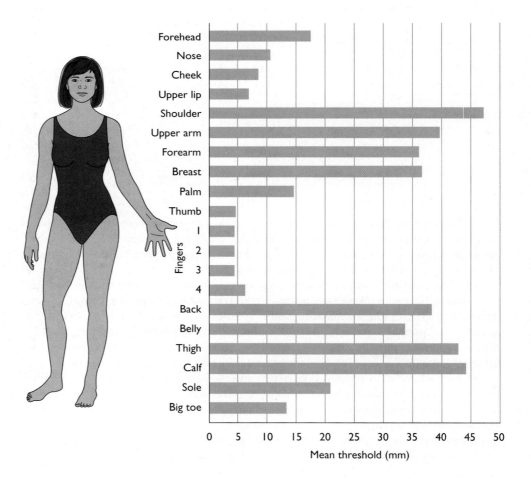

FIGURE 5 Skin sensitivity in various areas of the body. The lower the mean threshold is, the more sensitive a body part is. The fingers and thumb, lips, nose, cheeks, and big toe are the most sensitive. Why do you think certain areas are more sensitive than others? (Source: Kenshalo, *The Skin Senses.* 1968. Courtesy of Charles C. Thomas, Publisher, Ltd., Springfield, Illinois.)

activated because of an injury or problem with a part of the body, a "gate" to the brain is opened, allowing us to experience the sensation of pain (Melzack & Katz, 2004).

However, another set of neural receptors can, when stimulated, close the "gate" to the brain, thereby reducing the experience of pain. The gate can be shut in two different ways. First, other impulses can overwhelm the nerve pathways relating to pain, which are spread throughout the brain. In this case, nonpainful stimuli compete with and sometimes displace the neural message of pain, thereby shutting off the painful stimulus. This explains why rubbing the skin around an injury (or even listening to distracting music) helps reduce pain. The competing stimuli can overpower the painful ones (Villemure, Slotnick, & Bushnell, 2003).

Psychological factors account for the second way a gate can be shut. Depending on an individual's current emotions, interpretation of events, and previous experience, the brain can close a gate by sending a message down the spinal cord to an injured area, producing a reduction in or relief from pain. Thus, soldiers who are injured in battle may experience no pain—the surprising situation in more than half of all combat injuries. The lack of pain probably occurs because a soldier experiences such relief at still being alive that the brain sends a signal to the injury site to shut down the pain gate (Turk, 1994; Gatchel & Weisberg, 2000; Pincus & Morley, 2001).

Gate-control theory also may explain cultural differences in the experience of pain. Some of these variations are astounding. For example, in India people who participate in the "hook-swinging" ritual to celebrate the power of the gods have steel hooks embedded under the skin and muscles of their backs. During the ritual, they swing from a pole, suspended by the hooks. What would seem likely to induce excruciating pain instead produces a state of celebration and near euphoria. In fact, when the hooks are later removed, the wounds heal quickly, and after two weeks almost no visible marks remain (Kosambi, 1967; Melzack & Wall, 2001).

Gate-control theory suggests that the lack of pain is due to a message from the participant's brain, which shuts down the pain pathways. Gate-control theory also may explain the effectiveness of *acupuncture,* an ancient Chinese technique in which sharp needles are inserted into various parts of the body. The sensation from the needles may close the gateway to the brain, reducing the experience of pain. It is also possible that the body's own painkillers—called endorphins—as well as positive and negative emotions, play a role in opening and closing the gate (Daitz, 2002; Fee et al., 2002).

For some people, pain is an everyday part of life, sometimes so much so that it interferes with the most simple tasks. Chronic, lingering pain may start when someone experiences an injury that damages neurons involved in the transmission of pain. These injured neurons send out endless false alarms to the brain and cause the brain to experience pain. For many people, pain is unceasing: According to the American Pain Foundation, some 50 million people in the United States suffer from chronic pain (Clay, 2002; Marx, 2004).

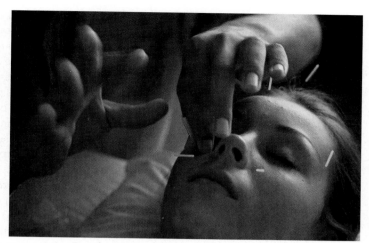

The ancient practice of acupuncture is still used in the twenty-first century. How does the gate-control theory of pain explain how acupuncture works?

Psychologists and medical specialists have devised several strategies to fight pain. Among the most important approaches are the following:

- *Medication.* Painkilling drugs are the most popular treatment in fighting pain. Drugs range from those which directly treat the source of the pain—such as reducing

BECOMING AN
INFORMED CONSUMER
of Psychology

Managing Pain

swelling in painful joints—to those which work on the symptoms. Medication can be in the form of pills, patches, injections, or liquids. In a recent innovation, drugs are pumped directly into the spinal cord (Wallace, 2002; Kalb, 2003).

- *Nerve and brain stimulation.* Pain can sometimes be relieved when a low-voltage electric current is passed through the specific part of the body that is in pain. In even more severe cases, electrodes can be implanted surgically directly into the brain, or a handheld battery pack can stimulate nerve cells to provide direct relief. This process is known as *transcutaneous electrical nerve stimulation,* or *TENS* (Ross, 2000; Campbell & Ditto, 2002).
- *Light therapy.* One of the newest forms of pain reduction involves exposure to specific wavelengths of red or infrared light. Certain kinds of light increase the production of enzymes that may promote healing (Whelan et al., 2001; Underwood, 2003).
- *Hypnosis.* For people who can be hypnotized, hypnosis can greatly relieve pain (Nash, 2001; Ketterhagen, VandeVusse, & Berner, 2002; Patterson, 2004).
- *Biofeedback and relaxation techniques.* Using *biofeedback,* people learn to control "involuntary" functions such as heartbeat and respiration. If the pain involves muscles, as in tension headaches or back pain, sufferers can be trained to relax their bodies systematically (National Institutes of Health, 1996; Middaugh & Pawlick, 2002).
- *Surgery.* In one of the most extreme methods, nerve fibers that carry pain messages to the brain can be cut surgically. Still, because of the danger that other bodily functions will be affected, surgery is a treatment of last resort, used most frequently with dying patients (Cullinane, Chu, & Mamelak, 2002).
- *Cognitive restructuring.* Cognitive treatments are effective for people who continually say to themselves, "This pain will never stop," "The pain is ruining my life," or "I can't take it anymore" and are thereby likely to make their pain even worse. By substituting more positive ways of thinking, people can increase their sense of control—and actually reduce the pain they experience. Teaching people to rewrite their pain "script" through therapy can result in significant reductions in their perception of pain (Mufson, 1999; Pincus & Morley, 2001; Bruehl & Chung, 2004).

To learn more about chronic pain, you can consult the American Pain Society (847-375-4715; www.ampainsoc.org) or the American Chronic Pain Association (916-632-0922; www.theacpa.org). Many hospitals have clinics that specialize in the treatment of pain. Any pain clinic, though, should be approved by the Commission for the Accreditation of Rehabilitative Facilities or the Joint Commission on the Accreditation of Health-Care Organizations.

How Our Senses Interact

When Matthew Blakeslee shapes hamburger patties with his hands, he experiences a vivid bitter taste in his mouth. Esmerelda Jones (a pseudonym) sees blue when she listens to the note C sharp played on the piano; other notes evoke different hues—so much so that the piano keys are actually color-coded, making it easier for her to remember and play musical scales. And when Jeff Coleman looks at printed black numbers, he sees them in color, each a different hue. (Ramachandran & Hubbard, 2004, p. 53).

The explanation? Each of these people has a rare condition known as *synesthesia,* in which exposure to one sensation (such as sound) evokes an additional one (such as vision).

We don't know why some people experience synesthesia. It is possible that they have unusually dense neural linkages between the different sensory areas of the brain. Another hypothesis is that they lack neural controls that usually inhibit con-

FIGURE 6 Try to pick out the 2s in the display in (a). Most people take several seconds to find them buried among the 5s and to see that the 2s form a triangle. For people with certain forms of synesthesia, however, it's easy, because they perceive the different numbers in contrasting colors, as in (b). (Based on Ramachandran & Hubbard, 2001.)

nections between sensory areas (Ramachandran & Hubbard, 2001; Shannon, 2003; Ramachandran, 2004).

Whatever the reason for synesthesia, it is a rare condition, and most of us do not experience it. (If you'd like to check out this phenomenon, see Figure 6.) Even so, the senses of all of us do interact and integrate in a variety of ways.

For example, the taste of food is influenced by its texture and temperature. We perceive food that is warmer as sweeter (think of the sweetness of steamy hot chocolate compared with cold chocolate milk). Spicy foods stimulate some of the same pain receptors that are also stimulated by heat—making the use of "hot" as a synonym for "spicy" quite accurate (Cruz & Green, 2000; Green & George, 2004; Balaban, McBurney, & Affeltranger, 2005).

It's important, then, to think of our senses as interacting. They work in tandem to build our complex understanding of the world around us.

RECAP/EVALUATE/RETHINK

RECAP

What role does the ear play in the senses of sound, motion, and balance?

- Sound, motion, and balance are centered in the ear. Sounds, in the form of vibrating air waves, enter through the outer ear and travel through the auditory canal until they reach the eardrum. (p. 113)
- The vibrations of the eardrum are transmitted into the middle ear, which consists of three bones: the hammer, the anvil, and the stirrup. These bones transmit vibrations to the oval window. (p. 113)
- In the inner ear, vibrations move into the cochlea, which encloses the basilar membrane. Hair cells on the basilar membrane change the mechanical energy of sound waves into nerve impulses that are transmitted to the brain. The ear is also involved in the sense of balance and motion. (pp. 113–114, 118)
- Sound has a number of physical characteristics, including frequency and amplitude. The place theory of hearing and the frequency theory of hearing explain the

processes by which we distinguish sounds of varying frequency and intensity. (pp. 114–115, 118)

How do smell and taste function?

- Smell depends on olfactory cells (the receptor cells of the nose), and taste is centered in the tongue's taste buds. (pp. 119–120)

What are the skin senses, and how do they relate to the experience of pain?

- The skin senses are responsible for the experiences of touch, pressure, temperature, and pain. Gate-control theory suggests that particular nerve receptors, when activated, open a "gate" to specific areas of the brain related to pain, and that another set of receptors closes the gate when stimulated. (pp. 121–123)
- Among the techniques used frequently to alleviate pain are medication, hypnosis, biofeedback, relaxation techniques, surgery, nerve and brain stimulation, and cognitive therapy. (p. 124–125)

EVALUATE

1. The tubelike passage leading from the outer ear to the eardrum is known as the _____ _____.
2. The purpose of the eardrum is to protect the sensitive nerves underneath it. It serves no purpose in actual hearing. True or false?
3. The three middle ear bones transmit their sound to the _____.
4. The _____ theory of hearing states that the entire basilar membrane responds to a sound, vibrating more or less, depending on the nature of the sound.
5. The three fluid-filled tubes in the inner ear that are responsible for our sense of balance are known as the _____ _____.
6. The _____–_____ theory states that when certain skin receptors are activated as a result of an injury, a "pathway" to the brain is opened, allowing pain to be experienced.

RETHINK

1. Much research is being conducted on repairing faulty sensory organs through devices such as personal guidance systems and eyeglasses, among others. Do you think that researchers should attempt to improve normal sensory capabilities beyond their "natural" range (for example, make human visual or audio capabilities more sensitive than normal)? What benefits might this ability bring? What problems might it cause?
2. *From the perspective of a social worker:* How would you handle the case of a deaf child whose hearing could be restored with a cochlear implant, but different family members had conflicting views on whether the procedure should be done?

Answers to Evaluate Questions

1. auditory canal; 2. false; it vibrates when sound waves hit it, and transmits the sound; 3. oval window; 4. frequency; 5. semicircular canals; 6. gate-control.

KEY TERMS

sound p. 113
eardrum p. 113
cochlea p. 113
basilar membrane p. 113
hair cells p. 114

place theory of hearing
  p. 118
frequency theory of hearing
  p. 118
semicircular canals p. 118

otoliths p. 118
skin senses p. 121
gate-control theory of pain
  p. 122

Perceptual Organization: Constructing Our View of the World

Consider the vase shown in Figure 1a for a moment. Or is it a vase? Take another look, and instead you may see the profiles of two people.

Now that an alternative interpretation has been pointed out, you will probably shift back and forth between the two interpretations. Similarly, if you examine the shapes in Figures 1b and 1c long enough, you will probably experience a shift in what you're seeing. The reason for these reversals is this: Because each figure is two-dimensional, the usual means we employ for distinguishing the figure (the object being perceived) from the *ground* (the background or spaces within the object) do not work.

The fact that we can look at the same figure in more than one way illustrates an important point. We do not just passively respond to visual stimuli that happen to fall on our retinas. Instead, we actively try to organize and make sense of what we see.

We turn now from a focus on the initial response to a stimulus (sensation) to what our minds make of that stimulus—perception. Perception is a constructive process by which we go beyond the stimuli that are presented to us and attempt to construct a meaningful situation.

The Gestalt Laws of Organization

Some of the most basic perceptual processes can be described by a series of principles that focus on the ways we organize bits and pieces of information into meaningful wholes. Known as **gestalt laws of organization**, these principles were set forth in

Key Concepts

What principles underlie our organization of the visual world and allow us to make sense of our environment?

How are we able to perceive the world in three dimensions when our retinas are capable of sensing only two-dimensional images?

What clues do visual illusions give us about our understanding of general perceptual mechanisms?

Gestalt laws of organization: A series of principles that describe how we organize bits and pieces of information into meaningful wholes.

a.

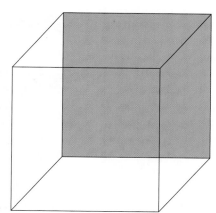

b.

c.

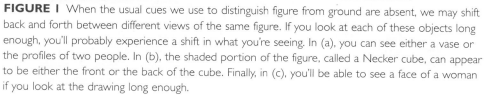

FIGURE 1 When the usual cues we use to distinguish figure from ground are absent, we may shift back and forth between different views of the same figure. If you look at each of these objects long enough, you'll probably experience a shift in what you're seeing. In (a), you can see either a vase or the profiles of two people. In (b), the shaded portion of the figure, called a Necker cube, can appear to be either the front or the back of the cube. Finally, in (c), you'll be able to see a face of a woman if you look at the drawing long enough.

| a. Closure | b. Proximity | c. Similarity | d. Simplicity |

FIGURE 2 Organizing these various bits and pieces of information into meaningful wholes constitutes some of the most basic processes of perception, which are summed up in the gestalt laws of organization. Do you think any other species share this organizational tendency? How might we find out?

the early 1900s by a group of German psychologists who studied patterns, or *gestalts* (Wertheimer, 1923). Those psychologists discovered a number of important principles that are valid for visual (as well as auditory) stimuli, illustrated in Figure 2: closure, proximity, similarity, and simplicity.

Figure 2a illustrates *closure.* We usually group elements to form enclosed or complete figures rather than open ones. We tend to ignore the breaks in Figure 2a and concentrate on the overall form. Figure 2b demonstrates the principle of *proximity:* We perceive elements that are closer together as grouped together. As a result, we tend to see pairs of dots rather than a row of single dots in Figure 2b.

Elements that are *similar* in appearance we perceive as grouped together. We see, then, horizontal rows of circles and squares in Figure 2c instead of vertical mixed columns. Finally, in a general sense, the overriding gestalt principle is *simplicity:* When we observe a pattern, we perceive it in the most basic, straightforward manner that we can. For example, most of us see Figure 2d as a square with lines on two sides, rather than as the block letter *W* on top of the letter *M.* If we have a choice of interpretations, we generally opt for the simpler one.

Although gestalt psychology no longer plays a prominent role in contemporary psychology, its legacy endures. One fundamental gestalt principle that remains influential is that two objects considered together form a whole that is different from the simple combination of the objects. Gestalt psychologists argued, quite convincingly, that the perception of stimuli in our environment goes well beyond the individual elements that we sense. Instead, it represents an active, constructive process carried out within the brain. There, bits and pieces of sensations are put together to make something more meaningful than the separate elements (Humphreys & Müller, 2000; Lehar, 2003; see Figure 3).

FIGURE 3 Although at first it is difficult to distinguish anything in this drawing, keep looking, and eventually you'll probably be able to see the figure of a dog (James, 1966). The dog represents a gestalt, or perceptual whole, which is something greater than the sum of the individual elements.

Feature Analysis: Focusing on the Parts of the Whole

A more recent approach to perception— **feature analysis**—considers how we perceive a shape, pattern, object, or scene through the reaction of specific neurons to the individual elements that make up the stimulus. We then use those individual components to understand the overall nature of what we are perceiving. Feature analysis begins with the evidence that individual neurons in the brain are sensitive to specific spatial configurations, such as angles, curves, shapes, and edges. The presence of these neurons suggests that any stimulus can be broken down into a series of component features. For example, the letter *R* is a combination of a vertical line, a diagonal line, and a half circle (see Figure 4).

According to feature analysis, when we encounter a stimulus—such as a letter— the brain's perceptual processing system initially responds to its component parts. Each of those parts is compared with information about components that is stored in memory. When the specific components we perceive match up with a particular set of components we have encountered previously, we are able to identify the stimulus (Spillmann & Werner, 1990; Ullman, 1996).

According to some research, the way we perceive complex objects is similar to the way we perceive simple letters—viewing them in terms of their component elements. For instance, just 36 fundamental components seem to be capable of producing over 150 million objects—more than enough to describe the 30,000 separate objects that the average person can recognize (see Figure 5). Ultimately, these component features are combined into a representation of the whole object in the brain. This representation is compared to existing memories, thereby permitting us to identify the object (Biederman, 1987, 1990).

Psychologist Anne Treisman has a different perspective. She suggests that the perception of objects is best understood in terms of a two-stage process. In the *preattentive stage,* we focus on the physical features of a stimulus, such as its size, shape, color, orientation, and direction of movement. This initial stage takes little or no conscious effort. In the *focused-attention stage,* we pay attention to particular features of an

Feature analysis: An approach to perception suggesting that we perceive a shape, pattern, object, or scene through the reaction of specific neurons to the individual elements that make up the stimulus.

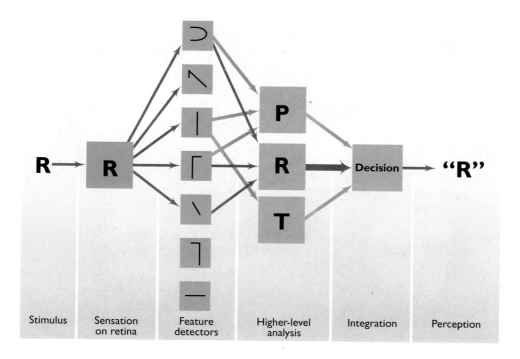

FIGURE 4 According to feature analysis approaches to perception, we break down stimuli into their component parts and then compare those parts to information that is stored in memory. When we find a match, we are able to identify the stimulus. In this example, the process by which we recognize the letter *R* is illustrated (Goldstein, 1984).

FIGURE 5 Components and simple objects created from them. (Source: Adapted from Biederman, 1990.)

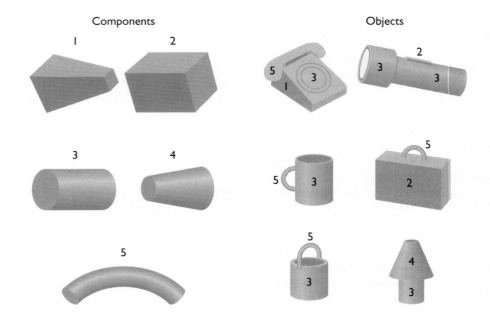

object, choosing and emphasizing features that were initially considered separately (Treisman, 1988, 1993, 2004).

For example, take a look at the two upside-down photos in Figure 6. Probably, your first impression is that you're viewing two similar photos of the Mona Lisa. But now look at them right side up, and you'll be surprised to note that one of the photos has distorted features. In Treisman's terms, your initial scanning of the photos took place at the preattentive stage. When you turned them over, however, you immediately progressed to the focused-attention stage, where you were able to consider the actual nature of the stimuli more carefully.

Treisman's perspective (and other approaches to feature analysis), compared with that of proponents of the gestaltist perspective, raises a fundamental question about the nature of perceptual processes: Is perception based mainly on consideration of the

FIGURE 6 Double Mona Lisas? These pictures appear similar at first glance because only our preattentive process is active. When the pictures are seen upright, the true detail in the two faces is revealed. (Source: Julesz, 1986.)

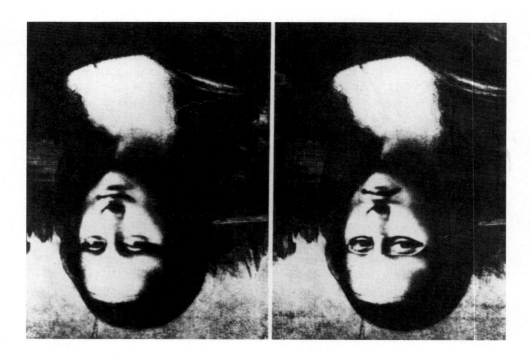

component parts of a stimulus, or is it grounded primarily in perception of the stimulus as a whole? This is the issue to which we turn next.

Top-Down and Bottom-Up Processing

Ca- yo- re-d t-is -en-en-e, w-ic- ha- ev-ry -hi-d l-tt-r m-ss-ng? It probably won't take you too long to figure out that it says, "Can you read this sentence, which has every third letter missing?"

If perception were based primarily on breaking down a stimulus into its most basic elements, understanding the sentence, as well as other ambiguous stimuli, would not be possible. The fact that you were probably able to recognize such an imprecise stimulus illustrates that perception proceeds along two different avenues, called top-down processing and bottom-up processing.

In **top-down processing,** perception is guided by higher-level knowledge, experience, expectations, and motivations. You were able to figure out the meaning of the sentence with the missing letters because of your prior reading experience, and because written English contains redundancies. Not every letter of each word is necessary to decode its meaning. Moreover, your expectations played a role in your being able to read the sentence. You were probably expecting a statement that had *something* to do with psychology, not the lyrics to an Eminem song.

Top-down processing is illustrated by the importance of context in determining how we perceive objects. Look, for example, at Figure 7. Most of us perceive that the first row consists of the letters *A* through *F,* while the second contains the numbers 10 through 14. But take a more careful look and you'll see that the "B" and the "13" are identical. Clearly, our perception is affected by our expectations about the two sequences—even though the two stimuli are exactly the same.

However, top-down processing cannot occur on its own. Even though top-down processing allows us to fill in the gaps in ambiguous and out-of-context stimuli, we would be unable to perceive the meaning of such stimuli without bottom-up processing. **Bottom-up processing** consists of the progression of recognizing and processing information from individual components of a stimuli and moving to the perception of the whole. We would make no headway in our recognition of the sentence without being able to perceive the individual shapes that make up the letters. Some perception, then, occurs at the level of the patterns and features of each of the separate letters.

It should be apparent that top-down and bottom-up processing occur simultaneously, and interact with each other, in our perception of the world around us. Bottom-up processing permits us to process the fundamental characteristics of stimuli, whereas top-down processing allows us to bring our experience to bear on perception. As we learn more about the complex processes involved in perception, we are developing a better understanding of how the brain continually interprets information from the senses and permits us to make responses appropriate to the environment.

Top-down processing: Perception that is guided by higher-level knowledge, experience, expectations, and motivations.

Bottom-up processing: Perception that consists of the progression of recognizing and processing information from individual components of a stimuli and moving to the perception of the whole.

FIGURE 7 The power of context is shown in this figure. Note how the B and the 13 are identical. (Source: Coren & Ward, 1989.)

Perceptual Constancy

Consider what happens as you finish a conversation with a friend and she begins to walk away from you. As you watch her walk down the street, the image on your retina becomes smaller and smaller. Do you wonder why she is shrinking?

Of course not. Despite the very real change in the size of the retinal image, you factor into your thinking the knowledge that your friend is moving farther away from you because of perceptual constancy. *Perceptual constancy* is a phenomenon in which physical objects are perceived as unvarying and consistent despite changes in their appearance or in the physical environment.

In some cases, though, our application of perceptual constancy can mislead us. One good example of this involves the rising moon. When the moon first appears at night, close to the horizon, it seems to be huge—much larger than when it is high in the sky later in the evening. You may have thought that the apparent change in the size of the moon was caused by the moon's being physically closer to the earth when it first appears. In fact, though, this is not the case at all: the actual image of the moon on our retina is the same, whether it is low or high in the sky.

Instead, the moon appears to be larger when it is close to the horizon primarily because of the phenomenon of perceptual constancy. When the moon is near the horizon, the perceptual cues of intervening terrain and objects such as trees on the horizon produce a misleading sense of distance. The phenomenon of perceptual constancy leads us to take that assumed distance into account when we view the moon, and it leads us to misperceive the moon as relatively large.

In contrast, when the moon is high in the sky, we see it by itself, and we don't try to compensate for its distance from us. In this case, then, perceptual constancy leads us to perceive it as relatively small. To demonstrate perceptual constancy for yourself, try looking at the moon when it is relatively low on the horizon through a paper-towel tube; the moon suddenly will appear to "shrink" back to normal size (Coren, 1992; Ross & Plug, 2002).

In addition to the phenomenon of perceptual constancy, other factors may contribute to the moon illusion. In fact, scientists have put forward a variety of pos-

When the moon is near the horizon, we do not see it by itself and perceptual constancy leads us to take into account a misleading sense of distance.

sibilities over the years and have yet to agree on the best explanation (Kaufman & Kaufman, 2000).

Although we don't fully understand the moon illusion as yet, it is clear that perceptual constancy is a primary ingredient in our susceptibility to the illusion. Furthermore, perceptual constancy applies not just to size (as with the moon illusion) but to shape and color as well. For example, despite the varying images on the retina as a plane approaches, flies overhead, and disappears, we do not perceive the plane as changing shape (Redding, 2002; Wickelgren, 2004).

Depth Perception: Translating 2-D to 3-D

As sophisticated as the retina is, the images projected onto it are flat and two-dimensional. Yet the world around us is three-dimensional, and we perceive it that way. How do we make the transformation from 2-D to 3-D?

The ability to view the world in three dimensions and to perceive distance—a skill known as **depth perception—is** due largely to the fact that we have two eyes. Because there is a certain distance between the eyes, a slightly different image reaches each retina. The brain integrates the two images into one composite view, but it also recognizes the difference in images and uses it to estimate the distance of an object from us. The difference in the images seen by the left eye and the right eye is known as *binocular disparity.*

To get a sense of binocular disparity for yourself, hold a pencil at arm's length and look at it first with one eye and then with the other. There is little difference between the two views relative to the background. Now bring the pencil just six inches away from your face, and try the same thing. This time you will perceive a greater difference between the two views.

The fact that the discrepancy between the images in the two eyes varies according to the distance of objects that we view provides us with a means of determining distance. If we view two objects and one is considerably closer to us than the other is, the retinal disparity will be relatively large and we will have a greater sense of depth between the two. However, if the two objects are a similar distance from us, the retinal disparity will be minor, and we will perceive them as being a similar distance from us.

In some cases, certain cues permit us to obtain a sense of depth and distance with just one eye. These cues are known as *monocular cues.* One monocular cue—*motion parallax*—is the change in position of an object on the retina caused by movement of your body relative to the object. For example, suppose you are a passenger in a moving car, and you focus your eye on a stable object such as a tree. Objects that are closer than the tree will appear to move backward, and the nearer the object is, the more quickly it will appear to move. In contrast, objects beyond the tree will seem to move at a slower speed, but in the same direction as you are. Your brain is able to use these cues to calculate the relative distances of the tree and other objects.

Similarly, experience has taught us that if two objects are the same size, the one that makes a smaller image on the retina is farther away than is the one that provides a larger image—an example of the monocular cue of *relative size.* But it's not just size of an object that provides information about distance; the quality of the image on the retina helps us judge distance. The monocular cue of *texture gradient* provides information about distance because the details of things that are far away are less distinct.

Finally, anyone who has ever seen railroad tracks that seem to join together in the distance knows that distant objects appear to be closer together than are nearer ones, a phenomenon called linear perspective. People use *linear perspective* as a monocular cue in estimating distance, allowing the two-dimensional image on the retina to record the three-dimensional world (Bruce, Green, & Georgeson, 1997; Dobbins et al., 1998; Shimono & Wade, 2002).

Depth perception: The ability to view the world in three dimensions and to perceive distance.

Railroad tracks that seem to join together in the distance are an example of linear perspective.

www.mhhe.com/feldmanup8

PsychInteractive Online

Depth Perception

The way in which we use cues to perceive depth is illustrated in the PsychInteractive exercise on depth perception. Try it to see how judgments about depth perception, although quite sophisticated, can also be misled by the context in which we make our judgments.

Motion Perception: As the World Turns

When a batter tries to hit a pitched ball, the most important factor is the motion of the ball. How is a batter able to judge the speed and location of a target that is moving at some 90 miles per hour?

The answer rests in part on several cues that provide us with relevant information about the perception of motion. For one thing, the movement of an object across the retina is typically perceived relative to some stable, unmoving background. Moreover, if the stimulus is heading toward us, the image on the retina will expand in size, filling more and more of the visual field. In such cases, we assume that the stimulus is approaching—not that it is an expanding stimulus viewed at a constant distance.

It is not, however, just the movement of images across the retina that brings about the perception of motion. If it were, we would perceive the world as moving every time we moved our heads. Instead, one of the critical things we learn about perception is to factor information about our own head and eye movements along with information about changes in the retinal image.

Perceptual Illusions: The Deceptions of Perceptions

If you look carefully at the Parthenon, one of the most famous buildings of ancient Greece, still standing at the top of an Athens hill, you'll see that it was built with a bulge on one side. If it didn't have that bulge—and quite a few other "tricks" like it, such

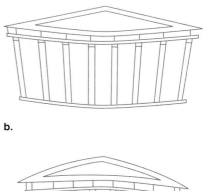

b.

c.

a.

FIGURE 8 In building the Parthenon, the Greeks constructed an architectural wonder that looks perfectly straight, with right angles at every corner, as in (a). However, if it had been built with completely true right angles, it would have looked as it does in (b). To compensate for this illusion, the Parthenon was designed to have a slight upward curvature, as shown in (c). (Source: Coren & Ward, 1989, p. 5.)

as columns that incline inward—it would look as if it were crooked and about to fall down. Instead, it appears to stand completely straight, at right angles to the ground.

The fact that the Parthenon appears to be completely upright is the result of a series of visual illusions. **Visual illusions** are physical stimuli that consistently produce errors in perception. In the case of the Parthenon, the building appears to be completely square, as illustrated in Figure 8a. However, if it had been built that way, it would look to us as it does in Figure 8b. The reason for this is an illusion that makes right angles placed above a line appear as if they were bent. To offset the illusion, the Parthenon was constructed as in Figure 8c, with a slight upward curvature.

Such perceptual insights did not stop with the Greeks. Modern-day architects and designers also take visual distortions into account in their planning. For example, the New Orleans Superdome makes use of several visual tricks. Its seats vary in color throughout the stadium to give the appearance, from a distance, that there is always a full house. The carpeting in some of the sloping halls has stripes that make people slow their pace by producing the perception that they are moving faster than they actually are. The same illusion is used at toll booths on superhighways. Stripes painted on the pavement in front of the toll booths make drivers feel that they are moving more rapidly than they actually are and cause them to decelerate quickly.

The implications of visual illusions go beyond design features. For instance, suppose you were an air traffic controller watching a radar screen like the one shown in Figure 9a. You might be tempted to sit back and relax as the two planes, whose flight paths are indicated in the figure, drew closer and closer together. If you did, however, the result might be an air disaster. Although it looks as if the two planes will miss each other, they are headed for a collision. Investigation has suggested that some 70 to 80 percent of all airplane accidents are caused by pilot errors of one sort or another (Krause, 2003; Shappell & Wiegmann, 2003).

The flight-path illustration provides an example of a well-known visual illusion called the *Poggendorf illusion*. As you can see in Figure 9b, the Poggendorf illusion, when stripped down to its basics, gives the impression that line X would pass below line Y if it were extended through the pipelike figure, instead of heading directly toward line Y as it actually does.

Visual illusions: Physical stimuli that consistently produce errors in perception.

FIGURE 9 (a) Put yourself in the shoes of a flight controller and look at the flight paths of the two planes on this radar screen. A first glance suggests that they are headed on different courses and will not hit each other. But now take a ruler and lay it along the two paths. Your career as a flight controller might well be over if you were guiding the two planes and allowed them to continue without a change in course (Coren, Porac, & Ward, 1984, p. 7). (b) The Poggendorf illusion, in which the two diagonal lines appear (incorrectly) as if they would not meet if extended toward each other.

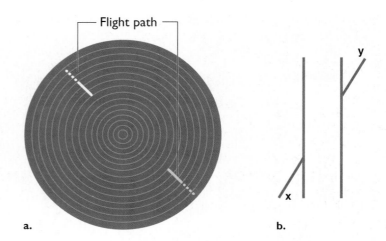

a.

b.

The Poggendorf illusion is just one of many that consistently fool the eye (Perkins, 1983; Greist-Bousquet & Schiffman, 1986). Another, illustrated in Figure 10, is called the *Müller-Lyer illusion*. Although the two lines are the same length, the one with the arrow tips pointing inward (Figure 10a, top) appears to be longer than the one with the arrow tips pointing outward (Figure 10a, bottom).

Although all kinds of explanations for visual illusions have been suggested, most concentrate either on the physical operation of the eye or on our misinterpretation of the visual stimulus. For example, one explanation for the Müller-Lyer illusion is that eye movements are greater when the arrow tips point inward, making us perceive the line as longer than it is when the arrow tips face outward. In contrast, a different expla-

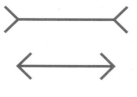

a.

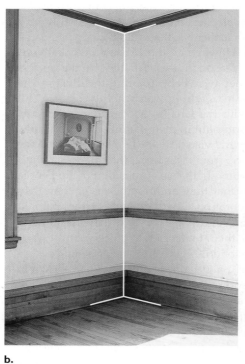

b.

c.

FIGURE 10 In the Müller-Lyer illusion (a), the upper horizontal line appears longer than the lower one. One explanation for the Müller-Lyer illusion suggests that the line with arrow points directed inward is to be interpreted as the inside corner of a rectangular room extending away from us (b), and the line with arrow points directed outward is viewed as the relatively close corner of a rectangular object, such as the building corner in (c). Our previous experience with distance cues leads us to assume that the outside corner is closer than the inside corner and that the inside corner must therefore be longer.

nation for the illusion suggests that we unconsciously attribute particular significance to each of the lines (Gregory, 1978; Redding & Hawley, 1993). When we see the top line in Figure 10a, we tend to perceive it as if it were the inside corner of a room extending away from us, as illustrated in Figure 10b. In contrast, when we view the bottom line in Figure 10a, we perceive it as the relatively close outside corner of a rectangular object such as the building corner in Figure 10c. Because previous experience leads us to assume that the outside corner is closer than the inside corner, we make the further assumption that the inside corner must therefore be larger.

Despite the complexity of the latter explanation, a good deal of evidence supports it. For instance, cross-cultural studies show that people raised in areas where there are few right angles—such as the Zulu in Africa—are much less susceptible to the illusion than are people who grow up where most structures are built using right angles and rectangles (Segall, Campbell, & Herskovits, 1966).

To better understand illusions and the reasons we're susceptible to them, try the PsychInteractive exercise on visual illusions.

www.mhhe.com/feldmanup8
PsychInteractive Online

Visual Illusions

As the example of the Zulu indicates, the culture in which we are raised has clear consequences for how we perceive the world. Consider the drawing in Figure 11. Sometimes called the "devil's tuning fork," it is likely to produce a mind-boggling effect, as the center tine of the fork alternates between appearing and disappearing.

Exploring DIVERSITY
Culture and Perception

Now try to reproduce the drawing on a piece of paper. Chances are that the task is nearly impossible for you—unless you are a member of an African tribe with little exposure to Western cultures. For such individuals, the task is simple; they have no trouble reproducing the figure. The reason seems to be that Westerners automatically interpret the drawing as something that cannot exist in three dimensions, and they therefore are inhibited from reproducing it. The African tribal members, in contrast, do not make the assumption that the figure is "impossible" and instead view it in two dimensions, a perception that enables them to copy the figure with ease (Deregowski, 1973).

Cultural differences are also reflected in depth perception. A Western viewer of Figure 12 would interpret the hunter in the drawing as aiming for the antelope in the foreground, while an elephant stands under the tree in the background. A member of an isolated African tribe, however, interprets the scene very differently by assuming that the hunter is aiming at the elephant. Westerners use the difference in sizes

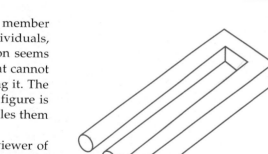

FIGURE 11 The "devil's tuning fork" has three prongs . . . or does it have two?

FIGURE 12 Is the man aiming for the elephant or the antelope? Westerners assume that the differences in size between the two animals indicate that the elephant is farther away, and therefore the man is aiming for the antelope. In contrast, members of some African tribes, not used to depth cues in two-dimensional drawings, assume that the man is aiming for the elephant. (The drawing is based on Deregowski, 1973.) Do you think Westerners, who view the picture in three dimensions, could explain what they see to someone who views the scene in two dimensions and eventually get that person to view it in three dimensions?

between the two animals as a cue that the elephant is farther away than the antelope (Hudson, 1960).

The misinterpretations created by visual illusions are ultimately due, then, to errors in both fundamental visual processing and the way the brain interprets the information it receives. But visual illusions, by illustrating something fundamental about perception, become more than mere psychological curiosities. There is a basic connection between our prior knowledge, needs, motivations, and expectations about how the world is put together and the way we perceive it. Our view of the world is very much a function, then, of fundamental psychological factors. Furthermore, each person perceives the environment in a way that is unique and special—a fact that allows each of us to make our own special contribution to the world.

Subliminal Perception

Can stimuli that we're not even aware we've been exposed to change our behavior in a significant way? Probably not.

Subliminal perception refers to the perception of messages about which we have no awareness. The stimulus could be a word, a sound, or even a smell that activates the sensory system but that is not intense enough for a person to report having experienced it. For example, in some studies people are exposed to a descriptive label—called a *prime*—about a person (such as the word *smart* or *happy*) so briefly that they cannot report seeing the label. Later, however, they form impressions that are influenced by the content of the prime. Somehow, they have been influenced by the prime that they say they couldn't see, providing some evidence for subliminal perception (Greenwald, Draine, & Abrams, 1996; Key, 2003).

Does this mean that subliminal messages can actually lead to significant changes in attitudes or behavior? Most research suggests that they cannot. Although we are able to perceive at least some kinds of information of which we are unaware, no evidence demonstrates that subliminal messages can change our attitudes or behavior in any substantial way (Greenwald et al., 1991; Greenwald et al., 2002).

EXTRASENSORY PERCEPTION (ESP)

Given the lack of evidence that subliminal perception can meaningfully affect our behavior, psychologists are even more skeptical of reports of *extrasensory perception,*

A short-lived scandal of the 2000 U.S. presidential campaign involved a George Bush political advertisement in which the word "RATS" appeared for one-thirtieth of a second while a voice-over criticized his opponent Al Gore's prescription drug plan. Critics argued that the ad sought to take advantage of subliminal perception. Based on the research evidence, do you think this use of "RATS" could have been effective in influencing voters?

or *ESP*—perception that does not involve our known senses. Although half of the general population of the United States believes it exists, most psychologists reject the existence of ESP, asserting that there is no sound documentation of the phenomenon (Swets & Bjork, 1990; Hyman, 1994; Gallup Poll, 2001).

However, debate in one of the most prestigious psychology journals, *Psychological Bulletin,* heightened interest in ESP. According to proponents of ESP, reliable evidence exists for an "anomalous process of information transfer," or *psi.* These researchers, who painstakingly reviewed considerable evidence, argued that a cumulative body of research shows reliable support for the existence of psi (Bem & Honorton, 1994; Storm & Ertel, 2001).

Their conclusion was challenged on several counts. For example, critics suggest that the research methodology was inadequate and that the experiments supporting psi are flawed (Hyman, 1994; Milton & Wiseman, 1999; Kennedy, 2004).

Because of questions about the quality of the research, as well as a lack of any credible theoretical explanation for how extrasensory perception might take place, most psychologists continue to believe that there is no reliable scientific support for ESP (Rose & Blackmore, 2002; Wiseman & Greening, 2002). Still, the exchanges in *Psychological Bulletin* are likely to heighten the debate. More important, the renewed interest in ESP among psychologists is likely to inspire more research, which is the only way the issue can be resolved.

RECAP/EVALUATE/RETHINK

RECAP

What principles underlie our organization of the visual world and allow us to make sense of our environment?

- Perception is a constructive process in which people go beyond the stimuli that are physically present and try to construct a meaningful interpretation. (p. 127)
- The gestalt laws of organization are used to describe the way in which we organize bits and pieces of information into meaningful wholes, known as gestalts, through closure, proximity, similarity, and simplicity. (pp. 127–128)
- Feature analysis pertains to how we perceive shapes, patterns, objects, or scenes through the reaction of specific neurons to the individual elements that make them up. (pp. 129–130)
- In top-down processing, perception is guided by higher-level knowledge, experience, expectations, and motivations. In bottom-up processing, perception consists of the progression of recognizing and processing information from individual components of a stimuli and moving to the perception of the whole. (p. 131)
- Perceptual constancy permits us to perceive stimuli as unvarying in size, shape, and color despite changes in the environment or the appearance of the objects being perceived. (p. 132)

How are we able to perceive the world in three dimensions when our retinas are capable of sensing only two-dimensional images?

- Depth perception is the ability to perceive distance and view the world in three dimensions even though the images projected on our retinas are two-dimensional. We are able to judge depth and distance as a result of binocular disparity and monocular cues, such as motion parallax, the relative size of images on the retina, and linear perspective. (p. 133)
- Motion perception depends on cues such as the perceived movement of an object across the retina and information about how the head and eyes are moving. (p. 134)

What clues do visual illusions give us about our understanding of general perceptual mechanisms?

- Visual illusions are physical stimuli that consistently produce errors in perception, causing judgments that do not reflect the physical reality of a stimulus accurately. Two of the best-known illusions are the Poggendorf illusion and the Müller-Lyer illusion. (pp. 135–137)
- Visual illusions are usually the result of errors in the brain's interpretation of visual stimuli. Furthermore, culture clearly affects how we perceive the world. (pp. 137–138)
- Subliminal perception refers to the perception of messages about which we have no awareness. The reality of the phenomenon, as well as of ESP, is open to question and debate. (pp. 138–139)

EVALUATE

1. Match each of the following organizational laws with its meaning:

    a. Closure

    b. Proximity

    c. Similarity

    d. Simplicity

    1. Elements close together are grouped together.
    2. Patterns are perceived in the most basic, direct manner possible.
    3. Groupings are made in terms of complete figures.
    4. Elements similar in appearance are grouped together.

2. _____ analysis deals with the way in which we break an object down into its component pieces in order to understand it.

3. Processing that involves higher functions such as expectations and motivations is known as _____, whereas processing that recognizes the individual components of a stimulus is known as _____.

4. When a car passes you on the road and appears to shrink as it gets farther away, the phenomenon of _____ permits you to realize that the car is not in fact getting smaller.

5. _____ is the ability to view the world in three dimensions instead of two.

6. The brain makes use of a phenomenon known as _____, or the difference in the images the two eyes see, to give three dimensions to sight.

7. Match the monocular cues with their definitions.

    a. Relative size

    b. Linear perspective

    c. Motion parallax

    1. Straight lines seem to join together as they become more distant.
    2. An object changes position on the retina as the head moves.
    3. If two objects are the same size, the one producing the smaller retinal image is farther away.

RETHINK

1. In what ways do painters represent three-dimensional scenes in two dimensions on a canvas? Do you think artists in non-Western cultures use the same or different principles to represent three-dimensionality? Why?

2. *From the perspective of a corporate executive:* What arguments might you make if a member of your staff proposed a subliminal advertising campaign? Do you think your explanation would be enough to convince them? Why?

Answers to Evaluate Questions

1. a-3, b-1, c-4, d-2; 2. feature; 3. top-down, bottom-up; 4. perceptual constancy; 5. depth perception; 6. binocular disparity; 7. a-3, b-1, c-2

KEY TERMS

gestalt laws of organization p. 127

feature analysis p. 129

top-down processing p. 131

bottom-up processing p. 131

depth perception p. 133

visual illusions p. 135

Looking Back

Psychology on the Web

1. Select one topic of personal interest to you that was mentioned in this set of modules (for instance, psi, cochlear implants, visual illusions). Find one "serious" or scientific Web site and one "popular" or commercial Web site with information about the chosen topic. Compare the type, level, and reliability of the information that you find on each site. Write a summary of your findings.
2. Are there more gestalt laws of organization than the four we've considered (closure, proximity, similarity, and simplicity)? Find the answer to this question on the Web and write a summary of any additional gestalt laws you find.
3. After completing the Interactivity on how we see, search the Web for a recent research finding about the eye. Summarize the findings in several paragraphs, describing why you think it is important.

Epilogue

We have noted the important distinction between sensation and perception, and we have examined the processes that underlie both of them. We've seen how external stimuli evoke sensory responses and how our different senses process the information contained in those responses. We also have focused on the physical structure and internal workings of the individual senses, including vision, hearing, balance, smell, taste, and the skin senses, and we've explored how our brains organize and process sensory information to construct a consistent, integrated picture of the world around us.

To complete our investigation of sensation and perception, let's reconsider the story of Ashlyn Blocker, the girl who couldn't feel pain. Using your knowledge of sensation and perception, answer the following questions:

1. Why is pain such an important sense? How would an evolutionary psychologist explain its value?
2. People who suffer from the same disorder as Ashlyn Blocker often develop emotional problems, showing bad judgment and taking excessive risks. Why do you think this is true?
3. How might you compensate for a lack of awareness of pain?

MASTERING

The difference between the processes of sensation and perception is not always clear. Use this visual guide to better grasp the difference between the two. Then answer the questions below to test your understanding of these concepts.

In this example, **sensation** occurs when light enters the eye and forms an image on the retina, where it initiates a complex series of neural impulses. **Perception** occurs, by means of bottom-up and top-down processing, when the brain analyzes these impulses and combines them with memories and experiences. Bottom-up and top-down processing occur simultaneously and, along with the gestalt principle and depth perception, help us to construct our perceptual reality.

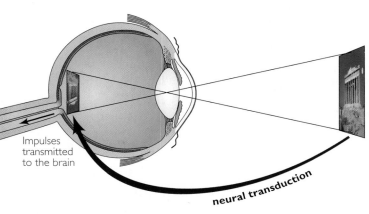

Impulses transmitted to the brain

neural transduction

2 Visual receptors in the retina, which is on the back of the eye, transform light energy into neural impulses. These raw impulses are the visual sensation that travels to the brain for analysis by successive visual processing areas. These processing areas convert the sensation into a complete perception.

3 In **bottom-up processing** information about individual components of stimuli travels first to the thalamus and then to the visual cortex for preliminary analysis. The first level of analysis identifies only basic angles, features, and shapes.

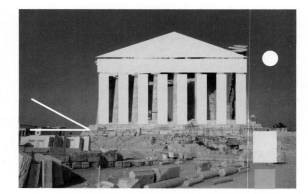

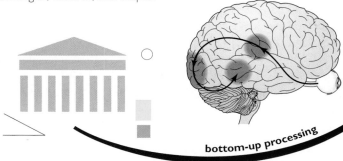

bottom-up processing

4 Next, neurons transport information about basic features and shapes from the visual cortex to another area of the brain. At this point, basic features and are combined and assembled into complete objects, such as a building.

EVALUATE

1. In this example, sensation is represented by
  a. the stimulation of visual receptors in the eye when looking at the building initially
  b. the interpretation of the individual visual cues arriving in the brain from the retina as a "building"
  c. the interpretation of the visual information as the viewer compares it to other buildings

  d. the breaking down of visual information into component parts

2. In this example, perception is represented by
  a. the stimulation of visual receptors in the eye when looking at the building initially
  b. the interpretation of the individual visual cues arriving in the brain from the retina as a "building"

5 The brain also interprets distance cues in the visual field and uses these cues to convert the 2-dimensional sensations into 3-dimensional perception. After analyzing distance cues, the brain assigns each object both a relative distance and a corresponding size, resulting in **depth perception.**

6 Using **gestalt laws of organization,** the brain then organizes all of the objects into a coherent whole. For example, similar objects are perceived as a unit. Here, the vertical columns and the roughly triangular roof above them are perceived as a building.

top-down processing

7 In **top-down processing,** the brain modifies perception based on previous personal experiences and memories. For example, the brain might contain a memory of a friend's face which the brain uses to enhance facial features and fill in missing information.

8 Finally, top-down processing incorporates personal expectations, needs, and drives to enhance what we see. For example, if we expect a place or person to be beautiful, our perception might be altered to match our expectation.

---

   c. the interpretation of the visual information as the viewer compares it to other buildings

   d. the breaking down of visual information into component parts

3. Perception is a constructive process, in which sensory information about stimuli is used to interpret a situation. True or false?

RETHINK

1 Suppose you are an artist who is encountering a famous building for the first time, and you want to paint a picture of it. Describe how you might use the processes of sensation and perception as you re-create the building in your painting.

Answers to Evaluate questions: 1. a; 2. b; 3. True

CHAPTER 5

States of Consciousness

Key Concepts for Chapter 5

Prologue   Violent Sleep

Awake, Jim Smith was an amiable and popular man.

As the director of public works in the small town of Osseo, Minnesota, he could be counted on to make house calls day or night, attending to burst pipes or broken water mains.

In fall, he hunted deer with buddies, who affectionately called him Smitty. In summer, he took his family pan-fishing for crappie.

It was only when Smith fell asleep that something changed.

Wrapped in slumber, he would shout obscenities, kick the walls, punch the pillows. Sometimes, he hit his wife, Dee, in the back or grabbed her by the hair. One night, dreaming that he was putting a wounded deer out of its misery, he came close to breaking his wife's wrist.

"I just didn't sleep real sound," Mrs. Smith recalled. "Once he started talking or swearing, I would be afraid that the next thing, he would be swinging his fists." (Goode, 2003a, p. 12A).

Looking Ahead

Smith's wife had good reason to worry. Smith was suffering from a rare condition (called *REM sleep behavior disorder*) in which the mechanism that usually shuts down bodily movement during dreams does not function properly. People with the malady have been known to hit others, smash windows, punch holes in walls—all while fast asleep.

Luckily, Smith's problem had a happy ending. With the help of clonazepam, a drug that suppresses movement during dreams, his malady vanished, permitting him (and his wife!) to sleep through the night undisturbed.

In this and the following modules we'll consider a range of topics about sleep and, more broadly, states of consciousness. What is sleep? Why do we dream, and do dreams have meaning? Can people be forced into altered states of consciousness, say by hypnosis, against their will? What leads people to use consciousness-altering drugs? In the following modules we will address these questions by considering the nature of both normal and altered states of consciousness.

Consciousness is the awareness of the sensations, thoughts, and feelings being experienced at a given moment. Consciousness is our subjective understanding of both the environment around us and our private internal world, unobservable to outsiders.

In waking consciousness, we are awake and aware of our thoughts, emotions, and perceptions. All other states of consciousness are considered altered states of consciousness. Among these, sleeping and dreaming occur naturally; drug use and hypnosis, in contrast, are methods of deliberately altering one's state of consciousness.

Because consciousness is so personal a phenomenon, psychologists sometimes have been reluctant to study it. After all, who can say that your consciousness is similar to or, for that matter, different from anyone else's? Although the earliest psychologists, including William James (1890), saw the study of consciousness as central to the field, later psychologists suggested that it was out of bounds for the discipline. They argued that consciousness could be understood only by relying "unscientifically" on what experimental participants said they were experiencing. In this view, it was philosophers—not psychologists—who should speculate on such knotty issues as whether consciousness is separate from the physical body, how people know they exist, how the body and mind are related to each other, and how we identify what state of consciousness we are in at any given moment (Rychlak, 1997; Gennaro, 2004).

Contemporary psychologists reject the view that the study of consciousness is unsuitable for the field of psychology. Instead, they argue that several approaches permit the scientific study of consciousness. For example, behavioral neuroscientists can measure brain-wave patterns under conditions of consciousness ranging from sleep to waking to hypnotic trances. And new understanding of the chemistry of drugs such as marijuana and alcohol has provided insights into the way they produce their pleasurable—as well as adverse—effects (Damasio, 1999; Sommerhof, 2000).

Whatever state of consciousness we are in—be it waking, sleeping, hypnotic, or drug-induced—the complexities of consciousness are profound.

Sleep and Dreams

Mike Trevino, 29, slept nine hours in nine days in his quest to win a 3,000-mile, cross-country bike race. For the first 38 hours and 646 miles, he skipped sleep entirely. Later he napped—with no dreams he can remember—for no more than 90 minutes a night. Soon he began to imagine that his support crew was part of a bomb plot. "It was almost like riding in a movie. I thought it was a complex dream, even though I was conscious," says Trevino, who finished second (Springen, 2004, p. 47).

Trevino's case is unusual—in part because he was able to function with so little sleep for so long—and it raises a host of questions about sleep and dreams. Can we live without sleep? What is the meaning of dreams? More generally, what is sleep?

Although sleeping is a state that we all experience, there are still many unanswered questions about sleep that remain, along with a considerable number of myths. Test your knowledge of sleep and dreams by answering the questionnaire in Figure 1.

Key Concepts

What are the different states of consciousness?

What happens when we sleep, and what are the meaning and function of dreams?

What are the major sleep disorders, and how can they be treated?

How much do we daydream?

Consciousness: The awareness of the sensations, thoughts, and feelings being experienced at a given moment.

Sleep Quiz

Although sleeping is something we all do for a significant part of our lives, myths and misconceptions about the topic abound. To test your own knowledge of sleep and dreams, try answering the following questions before reading further.

_____ 1. Some people never dream **True or false?**	_____ 6. If we lose some sleep we will eventually make up all the lost sleep the next night or another night. **True or false?**
_____ 2. Most dreams are caused by bodily sensations such as an upset stomach. **True or false?**	_____ 7. No one has been able to go for more than 48 hours without sleep. **True or false?**
_____ 3. It has been proved that people need eight hours of sleep to maintain mental health. **True or false?**	_____ 8. Everyone is able to sleep and breathe at the same time. **True or false?**
_____ 4. When people do not recall their dreams, it is probably because they are secretly trying to forget them. **True or false?**	_____ 9. Sleep enables the brain to rest because little brain activity takes place during sleep. **True or false?**
_____ 5. Depriving someone of sleep will invariably cause the individual to become mentally imbalanced. **True or false?**	_____ 10. Drugs have been proved to provide a long term cure for sleeplessness. **True or false?**

Scoring: This is an easy set of questions to score for every item is false. But don't lose any sleep if you missed them; they were chosen to represent the most common myths regarding sleep.

FIGURE 1 There are many unanswered questions about sleep. Taking this quiz can help you clear up some of the myths.

The Stages of Sleep

Most of us consider sleep a time of tranquility when we set aside the tensions of the day and spend the night in uneventful slumber. However, a closer look at sleep shows that a good deal of activity occurs throughout the night, and that what at first appears to be a unitary state is, in fact, quite diverse.

Much of our knowledge of what happens during sleep comes from the *electroencephalogram, or EEG,* a measurement of electrical activity in the brain. When probes from an EEG machine are attached to the surface of a sleeping person's scalp and face, it becomes clear that the brain is active throughout the night. It produces electrical discharges with systematic, wavelike patterns that change in height (or amplitude) and speed (or frequency) in regular sequences. Instruments that measure muscle and eye movements also reveal a good deal of physical activity.

People progress through five distinct stages of sleep during a night's rest—known as *stage 1* through *stage 4* and *REM sleep*—moving through the stages in cycles lasting about ninety minutes. Each of these sleep stages is associated with a unique pattern of brain waves, which you can see in Figure 2.

When people first go to sleep, they move from a waking state in which they are relaxed with their eyes closed into **stage 1 sleep,** which is characterized by relatively rapid, low-amplitude brain waves. This is actually a stage of transition between wakefulness and sleep and lasts only a few minutes. During stage 1, images sometimes appear, as if we were viewing still photos, although this is not true dreaming, which occurs later in the night.

As sleep becomes deeper, people enter **stage 2 sleep,** which makes up about half of the total sleep of those in their early twenties and is characterized by a slower, more regular wave pattern. However, there are also momentary interruptions of sharply pointed, spiky waves that are called, because of their configuration, *sleep spindles.* It becomes increasingly difficult to awaken a person from sleep as stage 2 progresses.

As people drift into **stage 3 sleep,** the brain waves become slower, with higher peaks and lower valleys in the wave pattern. By the time sleepers arrive at **stage 4 sleep,** the pattern is even slower and more regular, and people are least responsive to outside stimulation.

Stage 1 sleep: The state of transition between wakefulness and sleep, characterized by relatively rapid, low-amplitude brain waves.

Stage 2 sleep: A deeper sleep than that of stage 1, characterized by a slower, more regular wave pattern, along with momentary interruptions of "sleep spindles."

Stage 3 sleep: Sleep characterized by slow brain waves, with greater peaks and valleys in the wave pattern than in stage 2 sleep.

Stage 4 sleep: The deepest stage of sleep, during which we are least responsive to outside stimulation.

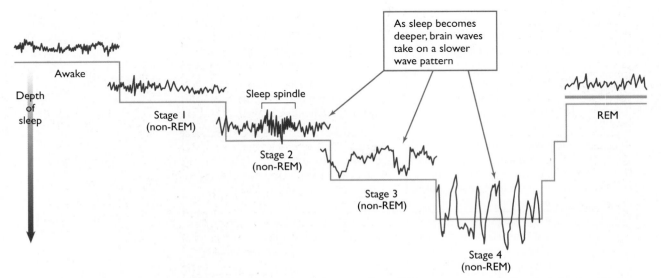

FIGURE 2 Brain-wave patterns (measured by an EEG apparatus) vary significantly during the different stages of sleep (Hobson, 1989). As sleep moves from stage 1 through stage 4, brain waves become slower.

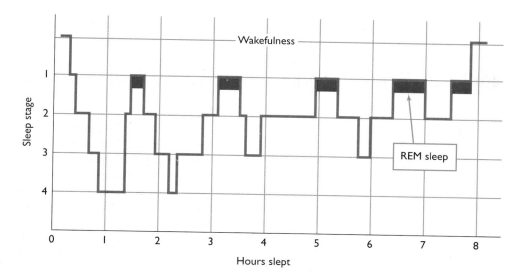

FIGURE 3 During the night, the typical sleeper passes through all four stages of sleep and several REM periods. (Source: Hartmann, 1967.)

As you can see in Figure 3, and learn more about in the PsychInteractive exercise on sleep stages, stage 4 sleep is most likely to occur during the early part of the night. In the first half of the night, sleep is dominated by stages 3 and 4. The second half is characterized by stages 1 and 2—as well as a fifth stage during which dreams occur.

www.mhhe.com/feldmanup8
PsychInteractive Online

Sleep Stages

REM Sleep: The Paradox of Sleep

Several times a night, when sleepers have cycled back to a shallower state of sleep, something curious happens. Their heart rate increases and becomes irregular, their blood pressure rises, their breathing rate increases, and males—even male infants—have erections. Most characteristic of this period is the back-and-forth movement of their eyes, as if they were watching an action-filled movie. This period of sleep is called **rapid eye movement,** or **REM sleep,** and contrasts with

Rapid eye movement (REM) sleep: Sleep occupying 20 percent of an adult's sleeping time, characterized by increased heart rate, blood pressure, and breathing rate; erections (in males); eye movements; and the experience of dreaming.

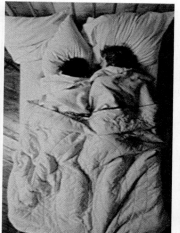

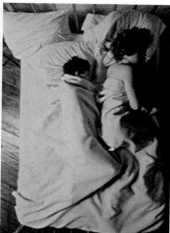

People progress through four distinct stages of sleep during a night's rest spread over cycles lasting about ninety minutes. REM sleep, which occupies only 20 percent of adults' sleeping time, occurs in stage 1 sleep. These photos, taken at different times of night, show the synchronized patterns of a couple accustomed to sleeping in the same bed.

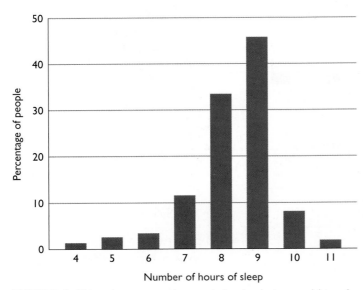

FIGURE 4 Although most people report sleeping between eight and nine hours per night, the amount varies a great deal (Borbely, 1996). Where would you place yourself on this graph, and why do you think you need more or less sleep than others?

stages 1 through 4, which are collectively labeled *non-REM* (or *NREM*) sleep. REM sleep occupies a little over 20 percent of adults' total sleeping time.

Paradoxically, while all this activity is occurring, the major muscles of the body appear to be paralyzed—except in rare cases such as Jim Smith's (described in the Prologue). In addition, and most important, REM sleep is usually accompanied by dreams, which—whether or not people remember them—are experienced by *everyone* during some part of the night. Although some dreaming occurs in non-REM stages of sleep, dreams are most likely to occur in the REM period, where they are the most vivid and easily remembered (Dement, 1999; Schwartz & Maquet, 2002; Titone, 2002; Conduit, Crewther, & Coleman, 2004).

There is good reason to believe that REM sleep plays a critical role in everyday human functioning. People deprived of REM sleep—by being awakened every time they begin to display the physiological signs of that stage—show a *rebound effect* when allowed to rest undisturbed. With this rebound effect, REM-deprived sleepers spend significantly more time in REM sleep than they normally would.

Why Do We Sleep, and How Much Sleep Is Necessary?

Sleep is a requirement for normal human functioning, although, surprisingly, we don't know exactly why. It is reasonable to expect that our bodies would require a tranquil "rest and relaxation" period to revitalize themselves, and experiments with rats show that total sleep deprivation results in death. But why?

Some researchers, using an evolutionary perspective, suggest that sleep permitted our ancestors to conserve energy at night, a time when food was relatively hard to come by. Others suggest that the reduced activity of the brain during non-REM sleep may give neurons in the brain a chance to repair themselves. Another hypothesis suggests that the onset of REM sleep stops the release of neurotransmitters called *monoamines,* and so permits receptor cells to get some necessary rest and to increase their sensitivity during periods of wakefulness. Still, these explanations remain speculative (Porkka-Heiskanen et al., 1997; Siegel, 2003; McNamara, 2004).

Scientists have also been unable to establish just how much sleep is absolutely required. Most people today sleep between seven and eight hours each night, which is three hours a night *less* than people slept a hundred years ago. In addition, there is wide variability among individuals, with some people needing as little as three hours of sleep. Sleep requirements also vary over the course of a lifetime: As they age, people generally need less and less sleep (see Figures 4 and 5).

People who participate in sleep deprivation experiments, in which they are kept awake for stretches as long as 200 hours, show no lasting effects. It's no fun—they feel weary and irritable, can't concentrate, and show a loss of creativity, even after only minor deprivation. They also show a decline in logical reasoning ability. However, after being allowed to sleep normally, they bounce back quickly and are able to perform at predeprivation levels after just a few days (Dinges et al., 1997; Veasey et al., 2002).

In short, as far as we know, most people suffer no permanent consequences of such temporary sleep deprivation. But—and this is an important but—a lack of sleep can make us feel edgy, slow our reaction time, and lower our performance on aca-

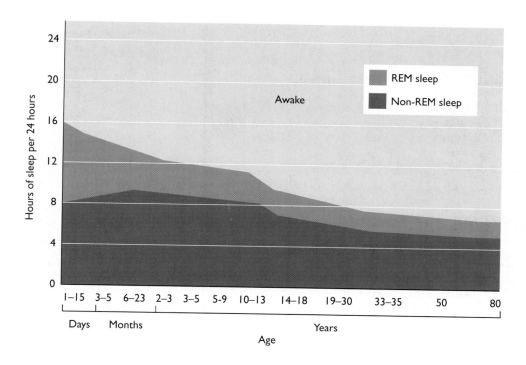

FIGURE 5 As people get older, they spend less time sleeping (Roffwarg, Muzio, & Dement, 1966). In addition, the proportion of REM sleep decreases with age.

demic and physical tasks. In addition, we put ourselves, and others, at risk when we carry out routine activities, such as driving, when we're very sleepy (Walker et al., 2002; Thiffault & Bergeron, 2003; Stickgold, Winkelman, & Wehrwein, 2004; Philip et al., 2005).

The Function and Meaning of Dreaming

I was sitting at my desk when I remembered that this was the day of my chemistry final! I was terrified, because I hadn't studied a bit for it. In fact, I had missed every lecture all semester. In a panic, I began running across campus desperately searching for the classroom, to which I'd never been. It was hopeless; I knew I was going to fail and flunk out of college.

If you have had a similar dream—a surprisingly common dream among people involved in academic pursuits—you know how utterly convincing are the panic and fear that the events in the dream can bring about. *Nightmares,* unusually frightening dreams, occur fairly often. In one survey, almost half of a group of college students who kept records of their dreams over a two-week period reported having at least one nightmare. This works out to some twenty-four nightmares per person each year, on average (Wood & Bootzin, 1990; Berquier & Ashton, 1992; Tan & Hicks, 1995; Blagrove, Farmer, & Williams, 2004).

However, most of the 150,000 dreams the average person experiences by the age of 70 are much less dramatic. They typically encompass everyday events such

THE FAR SIDE® BY GARY LARSON

"I've got it again, Larry ... an eerie feeling like there's something on top of the bed."

FIGURE 6 Although dreams tend to be subjective to the person having them, there are common elements that frequently occur in everyone's dreams. Why do you think so many common dreams are unpleasant and so few are pleasant? Do you think this tells us anything about the function of dreams?

Thematic Element	Percentage of Respondents Reporting at Least One	
	Males	Females
Aggression	47%	44%
Friendliness	38	42
Sexuality	12	4
Misfortune	36	33
Success	15	8
Failure	15	10

Source: Schneiger, A., & Domhoff, G. W. (2002).

FIGURE 6 Although dreams tend to be subjective to the person having them, there are common elements that frequently occur in everyone's dreams. Why do you think so many common dreams are unpleasant and so few are pleasant? Do you think this tells us anything about the function of dreams?

as going to the supermarket, working at the office, and preparing a meal. Students dream about going to class; professors dream about lecturing. Dental patients dream of getting their teeth drilled; dentists dream of drilling the wrong tooth. The English take tea with the queen in their dreams; in the United States, people go to a bar with the president (Webb, 1992; Potheraju & Soper, 1995; Domhoff, 1996; Schredl & Piel, 2005). See Figure 6 for the most common themes found in people's dreams.

But what, if anything, do all these dreams mean? Whether dreams have a specific significance and function is a question that scientists have considered for many years, and they have developed several alternative theories.

DO DREAMS REPRESENT UNCONSCIOUS WISH FULFILLMENT?

Unconscious wish fulfillment theory: Sigmund Freud's theory that dreams represent unconscious wishes that dreamers desire to see fulfilled.

Latent content of dreams: According to Freud, the "disguised" meanings of dreams, hidden by more obvious subjects.

Manifest content of dreams: According to Freud, the apparent story line of dreams.

Sigmund Freud viewed dreams as a guide to the unconscious (Freud, 1900). In his **unconscious wish fulfillment theory,** he proposed that dreams represent unconscious wishes that dreamers desire to see fulfilled. However, because these wishes are threatening to the dreamer's conscious awareness, the actual wishes—called the **latent content of dreams**—are disguised. The true subject and meaning of a dream, then, may have little to do with its apparent story line, which Freud called the **manifest content of dreams.**

To Freud, it was important to pierce the armor of a dream's manifest content to understand its true meaning. To do this, Freud tried to get people to discuss their dreams, associating symbols in the dreams with events in the past. He also suggested that certain common symbols with universal meanings appear in dreams. For example, to Freud, dreams in which a person is flying symbolize a wish for sexual intercourse. (See Figure 7 for other common symbols.)

Symbol (Manifest Content of Dream)	Interpretation (Latent Content)
Climbing up a stairway, crossing a bridge, riding an elevator, flying in an airplane, walking down a long hallway, entering a room, train traveling through a tunnel	Sexual intercourse
Apples, peaches, grapefruits	Breasts
Bullets, fire, snakes, sticks, umbrellas, guns, hoses, knives	Male sex organs
Ovens, boxes, tunnels, closets, caves, bottles, ships	Female sex organs

FIGURE 7 According to Freud, dreams contain common symbols with universal meanings.

Many psychologists reject Freud's view that dreams typically represent unconscious wishes and that particular objects and events in a dream are symbolic. Instead, they believe that the direct, overt action of a dream is the focal point of its meaning. For example, a dream in which we are walking down a long hallway to take an exam for which we haven't studied does not relate to unconscious, unacceptable wishes. Instead, it simply may mean that we are concerned about an impending test. Even more complex dreams can often be interpreted in terms of everyday concerns and stress (Domhoff, 1996; Nikles et al., 1998; Picchioni et al., 2002).

Moreover, some dreams reflect events occurring in the dreamer's environment as he or she is sleeping. For example, sleeping participants in one experiment were sprayed with water while they were dreaming. Those unlucky volunteers reported more dreams involving water than did a comparison group of participants who were left to sleep undisturbed (Dement & Wolpert, 1958). Similarly, it is not unusual to wake up to find that the doorbell that was heard ringing in a dream is actually an alarm clock telling us it is time to get up.

However, recent research lends some support for the wish fulfillment view. For instance, according to work by Allen Braun and colleagues, the parts of the brain associated with emotions and visual imagery are strongly activated during REM sleep. Using positron emission tomography (PET) scans that show brain activity, Braun's research team found that the limbic and paralimbic regions of the brain, which are associated with emotion and motivation, are particularly active during REM sleep. At the same time, the association areas of the prefrontal cortex, which control logical analysis and attention, are inactive during REM sleep (Braun, 1998; Occhionero, 2004; see Figure 8).

These results can be viewed as consistent with several aspects of Freudian theory. For example, the high activation of emotional and motivational centers of the brain during dreaming makes it more plausible that dreams may reflect unconscious wishes and instinctual needs, just as Freud suggested. Similarly, the fact that the areas of the brain responsible for emotions are highly active, whereas the brain regions responsible for rational thought are offline during REM sleep, suggests that conscious parts of personality (what Freud called the ego and the superego) are inactive. This inactivity permits unconscious thoughts to dominate.

DREAMS-FOR-SURVIVAL THEORY

According to the **dreams-for-survival theory,** dreams permit information that is critical for our daily survival to be reconsidered and reprocessed during sleep. Dreaming is seen as an inheritance from our animal ancestors, whose small brains were unable to sift sufficient information during waking hours. Consequently, dreaming provided a mechanism that permitted the processing of information twenty-four hours a day.

According to this theory, dreams represent concerns about our daily lives, illustrating our uncertainties, indecisions, ideas, and desires. Dreams are seen, then, as consistent with everyday living. Rather than being disguised wishes, as Freud suggested, they represent key concerns growing out of our daily experiences (Pavlides & Winson, 1989; Winson, 1990).

Research supports the dreams-for-survival theory, suggesting that certain dreams permit people to focus on and consolidate memories, particularly dreams that pertain to "how-to-do-it" memories related to motor skills. For example, rats seem to dream about mazes that they learned to run through during the day, at least according to the patterns of brain activity that appear while they are sleeping (Kenway & Wilson, 2001; Stickgold et al., 2001; Kuriyama, Stickgold, & Walker, 2004)

A similar phenomenon appears to work in humans. For instance, in one experiment, participants learned a visual memory task late in the day. They were then sent

Dreams-for-survival theory: The theory suggesting that dreams permit information that is critical for our daily survival to be reconsidered and reprocessed during sleep.

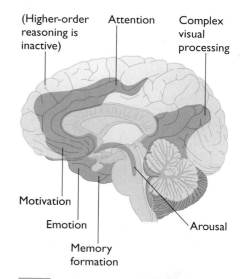

(Higher-order reasoning is inactive)   Attention   Complex visual processing

Motivation   Emotion   Arousal

Memory formation

Areas active during REM sleep

FIGURE 8 The parts of the brain that are associated with emotions and visual imagery are strongly activated during REM sleep. Why might this be the case?

to bed, but awakened at certain times during the night. When they were awakened at times that did not interrupt dreaming, their performance on the memory task typically improved the next day. But when they were awakened during rapid eye movement (REM) sleep—the stage of sleep when people dream—their performance declined. The implication is that dreaming, at least when it is uninterrupted, can play a role in helping us remember material to which we have been previously exposed (Karni et al., 1992, 1994).

ACTIVATION-SYNTHESIS THEORY

Activation-synthesis theory: Hobson's theory that the brain produces random electrical energy during REM sleep that stimulates memories lodged in various portions of the brain.

According to psychiatrist J. Allan Hobson, who proposed the **activation-synthesis theory,** the brain produces random electrical energy during REM sleep, possibly as a result of changes in the production of particular neurotransmitters. This electrical energy randomly stimulates memories lodged in various portions of the brain. Because we have a need to make sense of our world even while asleep, the brain takes these chaotic memories and weaves them into a logical story line, filling in the gaps to produce a rational scenario (Porte & Hobson, 1996; Hobson, 2005).

However, Hobson does not entirely reject the view that dreams reflect unconscious wishes. He suggests that the particular scenario a dreamer produces is not random but instead is a clue to the dreamer's fears, emotions, and concerns. Hence, what starts out as a random process culminates in something meaningful.

DREAM THEORIES IN PERSPECTIVE

The range of theories about dreaming clearly illustrates that researchers have yet to agree on the fundamental purpose of dreams. Figure 9 summarizes the three major theories. In fact, there are quite a few additional theories of dreaming, probably reflecting the fact that dream research ultimately must rely on self-reports of hidden phenomena that are not directly observable. For now, the true meaning of dreams remains a mystery (Domhoff, 2001, 2003; Stern, 2001). (For more on the significance of dreaming, see the *Applying Psychology in the 21st Century* box.)

Sleep Disturbances: Slumbering Problems

At one time or another, almost all of us have difficulty sleeping—a condition known as insomnia. It could be due to a particular situation, such as the breakup of a relationship, concern about a test score, or the loss of a job. Some cases of insomnia, however, have no obvious cause. Some people are simply unable to fall asleep easily, or they go

Theory	Basic Explanation	Meaning of Dreams	Is Meaning of Dream Disguised?
Unconscious wish fulfillment theory (Freud)	Dreams represent unconscious wishes the dreamer wants to fulfill	Latent content reveals unconscious wishes	Yes, by manifest content of dreams
Dreams-for-survival theory	Information relevant to daily survival is reconsidered and reprocessed	Clues to everyday concerns about survival	Not necessarily
Activation-synthesis theory	Dreams are the result of random activation of various memories, which are tied together in a logical story line	Dream scenario that is constructed is related to dreamer's concerns	Not necessarily

FIGURE 9 Three theories of dreams. Researchers have yet to agree on the fundamental meaning of dreams, and so several theories about dreaming have emerged.

Analyze This

At about 11 P.M. on a Wednesday, 23-year-old Yamara Coutinho, a research subject at Beth Israel Deaconess Medical Center, settled into bed. It would not be a restful night, though. Just as she drifted off, Coutinho—her face and scalp dotted with electrodes, her head covered with a caplike device used for monitoring sleep—was jolted awake by a computerized voice asking her to "please report now" (Zook, 2004, p. 7).

The voice was telling Coutinho, a volunteer participating in a study conducted by researcher Robert Stickgold, to describe any dreams she might be having. Stickgold is studying how our daytime, waking experiences are incorporated into dreams.

To figure out how our dreams may reflect our waking experiences, Stickgold asks participants to play video games such as Tetris or Alpine Racer. In one study, for example, he had a group of participants play Tetris just before going to sleep. When they were awakened during the night, more than half reported seeing falling Tetris objects in their dreams. Even more interesting, some of the participants in the study had psychological disorders that prevented them from recalling what happened during the day. But even those participants with the disorder—who couldn't remember their day's activities—dreamed of Tetris pieces (Stickgold et al., 2001; Walker & Stickgold, 2004, 2005).

Other research shows that it's not just information that we're thinking about that shows up in our dreams. Even material that we're attempting to suppress from consciousness has a way of becoming the stuff of dreams. According to studies by psychologist Daniel Wegner, when we try to *not* think about someone before we go to sleep, we're actually more likely to dream about that person than if we're not avoiding thoughts about that individual (Wegner, Wenzlaff, & Kozak, 2004).

Can we use dreams to help solve problems? Some researchers believe so. According to dream researcher Deirdre Barrett (2001), people are particularly able to solve visual problems, such as how to fit furniture from an old apartment into a new one, as a result of dreaming about the problem. She also points out that many artists, such as Jasper Johns and Salvador Dali, claim to have had their creativity inspired by their dreams.

In support of such reasoning, researchers at the University of Chicago trained college students to understand distorted speech produced by a speech synthesizer. They found that students who learned the task and then had a good night's sleep did better on the task the next day compared with students who were tested two hours after learning the task, but who had no sleep. A good night's rest, by itself, may be sufficient (and perhaps even necessary) to enhance our cognitive abilities. Getting some extra hours of shut-eye, then, may not only make college students less sleepy—it may make them do better on their schoolwork (Fenn, Nussbaum, & Margoliash, 2003; Cipolli et al., 2005; Margoliash, 2005).

RETHINK

Which of the theories of dreaming is consistent with the research findings showing that sleep improves problem solving and learning? If you wanted to use these findings to improve performance on an upcoming test, what would you do?

---

to sleep readily but wake up frequently during the night. Insomnia is a problem that afflicts as many as one-third of all people (Blais et al., 2001; Monti, 2004; American Insomnia Association, 2005).

Interestingly, some people who *think* they have sleeping problems are mistaken. For example, researchers in sleep laboratories have found that some people who report being up all night actually fall asleep in thirty minutes and stay asleep all night. Furthermore, some people with insomnia accurately recall sounds that they heard while they were asleep, which gives them the impression that they were awake during the night. In fact, some researchers suggest that future drugs for insomnia could function by changing people's *perceptions* of how much they have slept, rather than by making them sleep more (Engle-Friedman, Baker, & Bootzin, 1985; Klinkenborg, 1997; Semler & Harvey, 2005).

Other sleep problems are less common than insomnia, although they are still widespread. For instance, some 20 million people suffer from *sleep apnea,* a condition in which a person has difficulty breathing while sleeping. The result is disturbed, fitful sleep, as the person is constantly reawakened when the lack of oxygen becomes great enough to trigger a waking response. Some people with apnea wake as many as 500 times during the course of a night, although they may not even be aware that they have wakened. Not surprisingly, such disturbed sleep—which may be related to a loss of neurons in the brain stem—results in complaints of fatigue the next day. Sleep apnea also may play a role in *sudden infant death syndrome (SIDS),* a mysterious killer of seemingly normal infants who die while sleeping (Rambaud & Guilleminault, 2004; Gami et al., 2005).

Night terrors are sudden awakenings from non-REM sleep that are accompanied by extreme fear, panic, and strong physiological arousal. Usually occurring in stage 4 sleep, night terrors may be so frightening that a sleeper awakens with a shriek. Although night terrors initially produce great agitation, victims usually can get back to sleep fairly quickly. They occur most frequently in children between the ages of 3 and 8, although adults may suffer from them as well. Their cause is not known, but they are unrelated to emotional disturbance.

Narcolepsy is uncontrollable sleeping that occurs for short periods while a person is awake. No matter what the activity—holding a heated conversation, exercising, or driving—a narcoleptic will suddenly fall asleep. People with narcolepsy go directly from wakefulness to REM sleep, skipping the other stages. The causes of narcolepsy are not known, although there could be a genetic component because narcolepsy runs in families (Lockrane, Bhatia, & Gore, 2005; Mahmood & Black 2005).

We know relatively little about sleeptalking and sleepwalking, two sleep disturbances that are usually harmless. Both occur during stage 4 sleep and are more common in children than in adults. Sleeptalkers and sleepwalkers usually have a vague consciousness of the world around them, and a sleepwalker may be able to walk with agility around obstructions in a crowded room. Unless a sleepwalker wanders into a dangerous environment, sleepwalking typically poses little risk (Hobson & Silverstri, 1999; Baruss, 2003; Guilleminault et al., 2005).

Circadian Rhythms: Life Cycles

The fact that we cycle back and forth between wakefulness and sleep is one example of the body's circadian rhythms. **Circadian rhythms** (from the Latin *circa diem,* or "around the day") are biological processes that occur regularly on approximately a twenty-four-hour cycle. Sleeping and waking, for instance, occur naturally to the beat of an internal pacemaker that works on a cycle of about twenty-four hours. Several other bodily functions, such as body temperature, hormone production, and blood pressure, also follow circadian rhythms (Oren & Terman, 1998; Czeisler et al., 1999; Young, 2000; Saper et al., 2005).

Circadian cycles are complex, and they involve a variety of behaviors (see Figure 10). For instance, sleepiness occurs not just in the evening but throughout the day in regular patterns, with most of us getting drowsy in midafternoon— regardless of whether we have eaten a heavy lunch. By making an afternoon siesta part of their everyday habit, people in several cultures take advantage of the body's natural inclination to sleep at this time (Ezzel, 2002; Wright, 2002; Takahashi et al., 2004).

The brain's *suprachiasmatic nucleus (SCN)* controls circadian rhythms. However, the relative amount of light and darkness, which varies with the seasons of the year, also plays a role in regulating circadian rhythms. In fact, some people experience *seasonal affective disorder,* a form of severe depression in which feelings of despair and hopelessness increase during the winter and lift during the rest of the year. The disorder appears to be a result of the brevity and gloom of winter days. Daily exposure to bright lights is sometimes sufficient to improve the mood of those with this disorder (Roush, 1995; Oren & Terman, 1998; Young, 2000; Eagles, 2001; Golden et al., 2005).

Circadian rhythms explain the phenomenon of *jet lag,* caused by flying through multiple time zones. Pilots, as well as others who must work on constantly chang-

Circadian rhythms: Biological processes that occur regularly on approximately a twenty-four-hour cycle.

6:00 A.M.
• Onset of menstruation is most likely
• Insulin levels in the bloodstream are lowest
• Blood pressure and heart rate begin to rise
• Levels of the stress hormone cortisol increase
• Melatonin levels begin to fall

7:00 A.M.
• Hay fever symptoms are worst

8:00 A.M.
• Risk for heart attack and stroke is highest
• Symptoms of rheumatoid arthritis are worst
• Helper T lymphocytes are at their lowest daytime level

Noon
• Level of hemoglobin in the blood is at its peak

3:00 P.M.
• Grip strength, respiratory rate, and reflex sensitivity are highest

4:00 A.M.
• Asthma attacks are most likely to occur

2:00 A.M.
• Levels of growth hormone are highest

1:00 A.M.
• Pregnant women are most likely to go into labor
• Immune cells called helper T lymphocytes are at their peak

4:00 P.M.
• Body temperature, pulse rate, and blood pressure peak

6:00 P.M.
• Urinary flow is highest

9:00 P.M.
• Pain threshold is lowest

11:00 P.M.
• Allergic responses are most likely

FIGURE 10 Day times, night times: regular body changes over every 24-hour period. Over the course of the day, our circadian rhythms produce a wide variety of effects. (Source: Young, 2000.)

ing time shifts (police officers and physicians), must fight their internal clocks. The result can be fatigue, irritability, and, even worse, outright error. In fact, an analysis of major disasters caused by human error finds that many, including the *Exxon Valdez* oil spill in Alaska and the Chernobyl nuclear reactor accident, occurred late at night (Moore-Ede, 1993; Refinetti, 2005).

Daydreams: Dreams Without Sleep

It is the stuff of magic: Our past mistakes can be wiped out and the future filled with noteworthy accomplishments. Fame, happiness, and wealth can be ours. In the next moment, though, the most horrible tragedies can occur, leaving us devastated, alone, and penniless.

The source of these scenarios is **daydreams,** fantasies that people construct while awake. Unlike dreaming that occurs during sleep, daydreams are more under people's control. Therefore, their content is often more closely related to immediate events in the environment than is the content of the dreams that occur during sleep. Although they may include sexual content, daydreams also pertain to other activities or events that are relevant to a person's life.

Daydreams are a typical part of waking consciousness, even though our awareness of the environment around us declines while we are daydreaming. People vary considerably in the amount of daydreaming they do. For example, around 2 to 4 percent of the population spend at least half their free time fantasizing. Although most

Daydreams are fantasies that people construct while they are awake. What are the similarities and differences between daydreams and night dreams?

Daydreams: Fantasies that people construct while awake.

people daydream much less frequently, almost everyone fantasizes to some degree. Studies that ask people to identify what they are doing at random times during the day have shown that they are daydreaming about 10 percent of the time. As for the content of fantasies, most concern such mundane, ordinary events as paying the telephone bill, picking up the groceries, and solving a romantic problem (Singer, 1975; Lynn & Rhue, 1988; Lynn et al., 1996).

Frequent daydreaming may seem to suggest psychological difficulties, but there appears to be little relationship between psychological disturbance and daydreaming. Except in those rare cases in which a daydreamer is unable to distinguish a fantasy from reality (a mark of serious psychological problems), daydreaming seems to be a normal part of waking consciousness. Indeed, fantasy can contribute to the psychological well-being of some people by enhancing their creativity and permitting them to use their imagination to understand what other people are experiencing (Lynn & Rhue, 1988; Pihlgren, Gidycz, & Lynn, 1993; Lynn et al., 1996).

BECOMING AN INFORMED CONSUMER of Psychology

Sleeping Better

Do you have trouble sleeping? You're not alone—70 million people in the United States have sleep problems. For those of us who spend hours tossing and turning in bed, psychologists studying sleep disturbances have a number of suggestions for overcoming insomnia (Edinger et al., 2001; Benca, 2005; Finley & Cowley, 2005). Here are some ideas.

- *Exercise during the day (at least six hours before bedtime) and avoid naps.* Not surprisingly, it helps to be tired before going to sleep! Moreover, learning systematic relaxation techniques and biofeedback can help you unwind from the day's stresses and tensions.
- *Choose a regular bedtime and stick to it.* Adhering to a habitual schedule helps your internal timing mechanisms regulate your body more effectively.
- *Don't use your bed as an all-purpose area.* Leave studying, reading, eating, watching TV, and other recreational activities to some other part of your living quarters. If you follow this advice, your bed will become a cue for sleeping.
- *Avoid drinks with caffeine after lunch.* The effects of beverages such as coffee, tea, and some soft drinks can linger for as long as eight to twelve hours after they are consumed.
- *Drink a glass of warm milk at bedtime.* Your grandparents were right when they dispensed this advice: Milk contains the chemical tryptophan, which helps people fall asleep.
- *Avoid sleeping pills.* Even though 25 percent of U.S. adults report having taken medication for sleep in the previous year, in the long run sleep medications can do more harm than good because they disrupt the normal sleep cycle.
- *Try* not *to sleep.* This approach works because people often have difficulty falling asleep because they are trying so hard. A better strategy is to go to bed only when you feel tired. If you don't get to sleep within ten minutes, leave the bedroom and do something else, returning to bed only when you feel sleepy. Continue this process all night if necessary. But get up at your usual hour in the morning, and don't take any naps during the day. After three or four weeks, most people become conditioned to associate their beds with sleep—and fall asleep rapidly at night (Sloan et al., 1993; Ubell, 1993; Smith, 2001).
- *Talk yourself into sleeping.* In some cases, therapy is effective in reducing insomnia. For example, people who learn through therapy to replace negative

thoughts that keep them awake ("I'll never get back to sleep now, and I've got so much to do tomorrow") with more positive ones ("I'm probably sleeping more than I think I am") report sleeping better (Morin, 2004; Dooreen, 2005).

For long-term problems with sleep, you might consider visiting a sleep disorders center. For information on accredited clinics, consult the American Academy of Sleep Medicine at www.aasmnet.org.

RECAP/EVALUATE/RETHINK

RECAP

What are the different states of consciousness?

- Consciousness is a person's awareness of the sensations, thoughts, and feelings at a given moment. Waking consciousness can vary from more active to more passive states. (p. 146)
- Altered states of consciousness include naturally occurring sleep and dreaming, as well as hypnotic and drug-induced states. (p. 146)

What happens when we sleep, and what are the meaning and function of dreams?

- Using the electroencephalogram, or EEG, to study sleep, scientists have found that the brain is active throughout the night, and that sleep proceeds through a series of stages identified by unique patterns of brain waves. (pp. 147–148)
- REM (rapid eye movement) sleep is characterized by an increase in heart rate, a rise in blood pressure, an increase in the rate of breathing, and, in males, erections. Dreams occur during this stage. (p. 149)
- According to Freud, dreams have both a manifest content (an apparent story line) and a latent content (a true meaning). He suggested that the latent content provides a guide to a dreamer's unconscious, revealing unfulfilled wishes or desires. (p. 152)
- The dreams-for-survival theory suggests that information relevant to daily survival is reconsidered and reprocessed in dreams. The activation-synthesis theory proposes that dreams are a result of random electrical energy that stimulates different memories, which then are woven into a coherent story line. (pp. 153–154)

What are the major sleep disorders, and how can they be treated?

- Insomnia is a sleep disorder characterized by difficulty sleeping. Sleep apnea is a condition in which people have difficulty sleeping and breathing at the same time. People with narcolepsy have an uncontrollable urge to sleep. Sleepwalking and sleeptalking are relatively harmless. (pp. 155–156)

- Psychologists and sleep researchers advise people with insomnia to increase exercise during the day, avoid caffeine and sleeping pills, drink a glass of warm milk before bedtime, and try to avoid going to sleep. (p. 158)

How much do we daydream?

- Wide individual differences exist in the amount of time devoted to daydreaming. Almost everyone daydreams or fantasizes to some degree. (pp. 157–158)

EVALUATE

1. _____ is the term used to describe our understanding of the world external to us, as well as our own internal world.
2. A great deal of neural activity goes on during sleep. True or false?
3. Dreams occur in _____ sleep.
4. _____ are internal bodily processes that occur on a daily cycle.
5. Freud's theory of unconscious _____ states that the actual wishes an individual expresses in dreams are disguised because they are threatening to the person's conscious awareness.
6. Match the theory of dreaming with its definition.
   1. Activation-synthesis theory
   2. Dreams-for-survival theory
   3. Dreams as wish fulfillment
   a. Dreams permit important information to be reprocessed during sleep.
   b. The manifest content of dreams disguises the latent content of the dreams.
   c. Electrical energy stimulates random memories, which are woven together to produce dreams.
7. Match the sleep problem with its definition.
   1. Insomnia   a. Condition that makes breathing while sleeping difficult
   2. Narcolepsy   b. Difficulty sleeping
   3. Sleep apnea   c. Uncontrollable need to sleep during the day

RETHINK

1. Suppose that a new "miracle pill" will allow a person to function with only one hour of sleep per night. However, because a night's sleep is so short, a person who takes the pill will never dream again. Knowing what you do about the functions of sleep and dreaming, what would be some advantages and drawbacks of such a pill from a personal standpoint? Would you take such a pill?

2. *From the perspective of an educator:* How might you utilize the findings in sleep research to maximize student learning?

Answers to Evaluate Questions

1. consciousness; 2. true; 3. REM; 4. circadian rhythms; 5. wish fulfillment; 6. 1-c, 2-a, 3-b; 7. 1-b, 2-c, 3-a

KEY TERMS

consciousness p. 147
stage 1 sleep p. 148
stage 2 sleep p. 148
stage 3 sleep p. 148
stage 4 sleep p. 148
rapid eye movement (REM) sleep p. 149

unconscious wish fulfillment theory p. 152
latent content of dreams p. 152
manifest content of dreams p. 152

dreams-for-survival theory p. 153
activation-synthesis theory p. 154
circadian rhythms p. 156
daydreams p. 157

Hypnosis and Meditation

You are feeling relaxed and drowsy. You are getting sleepier and sleepier. Your body is becoming limp. Now you are starting to become warm, at ease, more comfortable. Your eyelids are feeling heavier and heavier. Your eyes are closing; you can't keep them open anymore. You are totally relaxed.

Now, as you listen to my voice, do exactly as I say. Place your hands above your head. You will find they are getting heavier and heavier—so heavy you can barely keep them up. In fact, although you are straining as hard as you can, you will be unable to hold them up any longer.

An observer watching the above scene would notice a curious phenomenon occurring. Many of the people listening to the voice would, one by one, drop their arms to their sides, as if they were holding heavy lead weights. The reason for this strange behavior? Those people have been hypnotized.

It is only recently that hypnotism has become an area considered worthy of scientific investigation. In part, the initial rejection of hypnosis relates to its bizarre eighteenth-century origins, in which Franz Mesmer argued that a form of "animal magnetism" could be used to influence people and cure their illnesses. After a commission headed by Benjamin Franklin discredited the phenomenon, it fell into disrepute, only to rise again to respectability in the nineteenth century. But even today, as we will see, the nature of hypnosis is controversial.

Hypnosis: A Trance-Forming Experience?

People under **hypnosis** are in a trancelike state of heightened susceptibility to the suggestions of others. In some respects, it appears that they are asleep. Yet other aspects of their behavior contradict this notion, for people are attentive to the hypnotist's suggestions and may carry out bizarre or silly suggestions.

Despite their compliance when hypnotized, people do not lose all will of their own. They will not perform antisocial behaviors, and they will not carry out self-destructive acts. People will not reveal hidden truths about themselves, and they are capable of lying. Moreover, people cannot be hypnotized against their will—despite popular misconceptions (Gwynn & Spanos, 1996).

There are wide variations in people's susceptibility to hypnosis. About 5 to 20 percent of the population cannot be hypnotized at all, and some 15 percent are very easily hypnotized. Most people fall somewhere in between. Moreover, the ease with which a person is hypnotized is related to a number of other characteristics. People who are hypnotized readily are also easily absorbed while reading books or listening to music, becoming unaware of what is happening around them, and they often spend an unusual amount of time daydreaming. In sum, then, they show a high ability to concentrate and to become completely absorbed in what they are doing (Rhue, Lynn, & Kirsch, 1993; Kirsch & Braffman, 2001; Rubichi et al., 2005). (To investigate hypnosis more, try the PsychInteractive exercise on Hypnosis.)

Key Concepts

What is hypnosis, and are hypnotized people in a different state of consciousness?

What are the effects of meditation?

Hypnosis: A trancelike state of heightened susceptibility to the suggestions of others.

www.mhhe.com/feldmanup8
PsychInteractive Online

Hypnosis

Despite common misconceptions, people cannot be hypnotized against their will, nor do they lose all will of their own. Why, then, do people sometimes behave so unusually when asked to by a hypnotist?

A DIFFERENT STATE OF CONSCIOUSNESS?

The question of whether hypnosis is a state of consciousness that is qualitatively different from normal waking consciousness is controversial. Psychologist Ernest Hilgard presented one side of the argument when he argued convincingly that hypnosis represents a state of consciousness that differs significantly from other states. He contended that particular behaviors clearly differentiate hypnosis from other states, including higher suggestibility, increased ability to recall and construct images, and acceptance of suggestions that clearly contradict reality. Moreover, changes in electrical activity in the brain are associated with hypnosis, supporting the position that hypnosis is a state of consciousness different from normal waking (Hilgard, 1975, 1992; Graffin, Ray, & Lundy, 1995; Kallio & Revonsuo, 2003).

On the other side of the controversy were theorists who rejected the notion that hypnosis is a state significantly different from normal waking consciousness. They argued that altered brain wave patterns are not sufficient to demonstrate a qualitative difference in light of the fact that no other specific physiological changes occur when a person is in a trance. Furthermore, little support exists for the contention that adults can recall memories of childhood events accurately while hypnotized. That lack of evidence suggests that there is nothing qualitatively special about the hypnotic trance (Spanos et al., 1993; Kirsch & Lynn, 1998; Lynn, Fassler, & Knox, 2005).

There is increasing agreement that the controversy over the nature of hypnosis has led to extreme positions on both sides of the issue. More recent approaches suggest that the hypnotic state may best be viewed as lying along a continuum in which hypnosis is neither a totally different state of consciousness nor totally similar to normal waking consciousness (Kirsch & Lynn, 1995; Kihlstrom, 2005).

As arguments about the true nature of hypnosis continue, though, one thing is clear: Hypnosis has been used successfully to solve practical human problems. In fact, psychologists working in many different areas have found hypnosis to be a reliable, effective tool. It has been applied to a number of areas, including the following:

- *Controlling pain.* Patients suffering from chronic pain may be given the suggestion, while hypnotized, that their pain is gone or reduced. They also may be taught to hypnotize themselves to relieve pain or gain a sense of control over their symptoms. Hypnosis has proved to be particularly useful during childbirth and dental procedures (Nash, 2001; Cosser, 2002; Ketterhagen, VandeVusse, & Berner, 2002; Mehl-Madrona, 2004).

- *Reducing smoking.* Although it hasn't been successful in stopping drug and alcohol abuse, hypnosis sometimes helps people stop smoking through hypnotic suggestions that the taste and smell of cigarettes are unpleasant (Barber, 2001; Zarren & Eimer, 2002; Elkins & Rajab, 2004).

- *Treating psychological disorders.* Hypnosis sometimes is used during treatment for psychological disorders. For example, it may be employed to heighten relaxation, reduce anxiety, increase expectations of success, or modify self-defeating thoughts (Fromm & Nash, 1992; Baker, 2001; Zarren & Eimer, 2002; Iglesias, 2005).

- *Assisting in law enforcement.* Witnesses and victims are sometimes better able to recall the details of a crime when hypnotized. In one often-cited case, a witness to the kidnapping of a group of California schoolchildren was placed under hypnosis and was able to recall all but one digit of the license number on the kidnapper's vehicle. However, hypnotic recollections may also be inaccurate, just as other recollections are often inaccurate. Consequently, the legal status of hypnosis is unresolved (Geiselman et al., 1985; Drogin, 2005; Whitehouse et al., 2005).

- *Improving athletic performance.* Athletes sometimes turn to hypnosis to improve their performance. For example, some baseball players have used hypnotism to increase their concentration when batting, with considerable success (Edgette & Rowan, 2003; Lindsay, Maynard, & Thomas, 2005).

Meditation: Regulating Our Own State of Consciousness

When traditional practitioners of the ancient Eastern religion of Zen Buddhism want to achieve greater spiritual insight, they turn to a technique that has been used for centuries to alter their state of consciousness. This technique is called meditation.

Meditation is a learned technique for refocusing attention that brings about an altered state of consciousness. Meditation typically consists of the repetition of a *mantra*—a sound, word, or syllable—over and over. In other forms of meditation, the focus is on a picture, flame, or specific part of the body. Regardless of the nature of the particular initial stimulus, the key to the procedure is concentrating on it so thoroughly that the meditator becomes unaware of any outside stimulation and reaches a different state of consciousness.

Meditation: A learned technique for refocusing attention that brings about an altered state of consciousness.

After meditation, people report feeling thoroughly relaxed. They sometimes relate that they have gained new insights into themselves and the problems they are facing. The long-term practice of meditation may even improve health because of the biological changes it produces. For example, during meditation, oxygen usage decreases, heart rate and blood pressure decline, and brain-wave patterns may change (Zamarra et al., 1996; Arambula et al., 2001; Barnes et al., 2004; see Figure 1).

Anyone can meditate by following a few simple procedures. The fundamentals include sitting in a quiet room with the eyes closed, breathing deeply and rhythmically, and repeating a word or sound—such as the word *one*—over and over. Practiced twice a day for twenty minutes, the technique is effective in

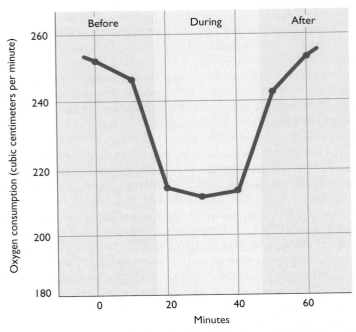

FIGURE 1 The body's use of oxygen declines significantly during meditation. (Source: Benson, 1993.)

bringing about relaxation (Benson, 1993; Benson et al., 1994; Aftanas & Golosheykin, 2005). For more information on meditation, contact the Mind/Body Medical Institute at www.mbmi.org or call (866) 509-0732.

As you may have gathered from this discussion, meditation is a means of altering consciousness that is practiced in many different cultures, though it can take different forms and serve different purposes across cultures. In fact, one impetus for the study of consciousness is the realization that people in many different cultures routinely seek ways to alter their states of consciousness.

Exploring DIVERSITY

Cross-Cultural Routes to Altered States of Consciousness

A group of Native American Sioux men sit naked in a steaming sweat lodge as a medicine man throws water on sizzling rocks to send billows of scalding steam into the air.

Aztec priests smear themselves with a mixture of crushed poisonous herbs, hairy black worms, scorpions, and lizards. Sometimes they drink the potion.

During the sixteenth century, a devout Hasidic Jew lies across the tombstone of a celebrated scholar. As he murmurs the name of God repeatedly, he seeks to be possessed by the soul of the dead wise man's spirit. If successful, he will attain a mystical state, and the deceased's words will flow out of his mouth.

Each of these rituals has a common goal: suspension from the bonds of everyday awareness and access to an altered state of consciousness. Although they may seem exotic from the vantage point of many Western cultures, these rituals represent an apparently universal effort to alter consciousness (Furst, 1977; Fine, 1994; Bartocci, 2004).

Some scholars suggest that the quest to alter consciousness represents a basic human desire (Siegel, 1989). Whether or not one accepts such an extreme view, it is clear that variations in states of consciousness share some basic characteristics across a variety of cultures. One is an alteration in thinking, which may become shallow, illogical, or otherwise different from normal. In addition, people's sense of time can become disturbed, and their perceptions of the world and of themselves may be changed. They may experience a loss of self-control, doing things that they would never otherwise do. Finally, they may feel a sense of *ineffability*—the inability to understand an experience rationally or describe it in words (Ludwig, 1969; Martindale, 1981; Finkler, 2004).

Of course, realizing that efforts to produce altered states of consciousness are widespread throughout the world's societies does not answer a fundamental question: Is the experience of unaltered states of consciousness similar across different cultures?

There are two possible responses to this question. Because humans share basic biological commonalties in the ways their brains and bodies are wired, we might assume that the fundamental experience of consciousness is similar across cultures. As a result, we could suppose that consciousness shows some basic similarities across cultures.

However, the ways in which certain aspects of consciousness are interpreted and viewed show substantial differences among different cultures. For example, people in various cultures view the experience of the passage of time in varying ways. One study found, for instance, that Mexicans view time as passing more slowly than other North Americans do (Diaz-Guerrero, 1979).

Whatever the true nature of consciousness and the reasons why people try to alter it, it is clear that people often seek the means to alter their everyday experience of the world. In some cases that need becomes overwhelming, as when people use consciousness-altering drugs, sometimes to a destructive extent.

RECAP/EVALUATE/RETHINK

RECAP

What is hypnosis, and are hypnotized people in a different state of consciousness?

- Hypnosis produces a state of heightened susceptibility to the suggestions of the hypnotist. Under hypnosis, significant behavioral changes occur, including increased concentration and suggestibility, heightened ability to recall and construct images, lack of initiative, and acceptance of suggestions that clearly contradict reality. (pp. 161–163)

What are the effects of meditation?

- Meditation is a learned technique for refocusing attention that brings about an altered state of consciousness. (p. 163)
- Different cultures have developed their own unique ways to alter states of consciousness. (p. 164)

EVALUATE

1. _____ is a state of heightened susceptibility to the suggestions of others.
2. A friend tells you, "I once heard of a person who was murdered by being hypnotized and then told to jump from the Golden Gate Bridge!" Could such a thing have happened? Why or why not?
3. _____ is a learned technique for refocusing attention to bring about an altered state of consciousness.
4. Leslie repeats a unique sound, known as a _____, when she engages in meditation.

RETHINK

1. Why do you think people in almost every culture use psychoactive drugs and search for altered states of consciousness?
2. *From the perspective of a human resources specialist:* Would you allow (or even encourage) employees to engage in meditation during the work day? Why or why not?

KEY TERMS

hypnosis p. 161   meditation p. 163

Answers to Evaluate Questions

1. hypnosis; 2. no; people who are hypnotized cannot be made to perform self-destructive acts; 3. meditation; 4. mantra

Drug Use: The Highs and Lows of Consciousness

John Brodhead's bio reads like a script for an episode of VH1's *Behind the Music*. A young rebel from the New Jersey suburbs falls in with a fast crowd, gets hooked on parties and booze, and, with intensive counseling and a bit of tough love, manages to get his life back together.

What makes his story different? Just one thing: his age. John is 13 (Rogers, 2002).

John Brodhead was lucky. Now in recovery, John had begun to drink when he was in the sixth grade. He is not alone: The number of kids who start drinking by the eighth grade has increased by almost a third since the 1970s, even though alcohol consumption overall has stayed fairly steady among the general population.

Drugs of one sort or another are a part of almost everyone's life. From infancy on, most people take vitamins, aspirin, cold-relief medicine, and the like, and surveys find that 80 percent of adults in the United States have taken an over-the-counter pain reliever in the last six months. However, these drugs rarely produce an altered state of consciousness (Dortch, 1996).

In contrast, some substances, known as psychoactive drugs, lead to an altered state of consciousness. **Psychoactive drugs** influence a person's emotions, perceptions, and behavior. Yet even this category of drugs is common in most of our lives. If you have ever had a cup of coffee or sipped a beer, you have taken a psychoactive drug. A large number of individuals have used more potent—and dangerous—psychoactive drugs than coffee and beer (see Figure 1); for instance, surveys find that 41 percent of high school seniors have used an illegal drug in the last year. In addition, 30 percent report having been drunk on alcohol. The figures for the adult population are even higher (Johnston, O'Malley, & Bachman, 2005).

Of course, drugs vary widely in the effects they have on users, in part because they affect the nervous system in very different ways. Some drugs alter the limbic system, and others affect the operation of specific neurotransmitters across the synapses of neurons. For example, some drugs block or enhance the release of neurotransmitters, others block the receipt or the removal of a neurotransmitter, and still others mimic the effects of a particular neurotransmitter (see Figure 2, and learn more by trying the PsychInteractive exercise on drug effects).

The most dangerous drugs are addictive. **Addictive drugs** produce a biological or psychological dependence in the user, and withdrawal from them leads to a craving for the drug that, in some cases, may be nearly irresistible. In *biologically based* addictions, the body becomes so accustomed to functioning in the presence of a drug that it cannot function without it. *Psychologically based* addictions are those in which people believe that they need the drug to respond to the stresses of daily living. Although we generally associate addiction with drugs such as heroin, everyday sorts of drugs, such as caffeine (found in coffee) and nicotine (found in cigarettes), have addictive aspects as well.

We know surprisingly little about the underlying causes of addiction. One of the problems in identifying those causes is that different drugs (such as alcohol and cocaine) affect the brain in very different ways—yet may be equally addicting. Furthermore, it takes longer to become addicted to some drugs than to others, even though the ultimate consequences of addiction may be equally grave (Thombs, 1999; Crombag & Robinson, 2004; Nestler & Malenka, 2004).

Key Concept

What are the major classifications of drugs, and what are their effects?

John Brodhead began to drink heavily when he was in the sixth grade.

Psychoactive drugs: Drugs that influence a person's emotions, perceptions, and behavior.

www.mhhe.com/feldmanup8
PsychInteractive Online

Drug Effects

Addictive drugs: Drugs that produce a biological or psychological dependence in the user so that withdrawal from them leads to a craving for the drug that, in some cases, may be nearly irresistible.

FIGURE 1 How many teenagers use drugs? The results of the most recent comprehensive survey of 14,000 high school seniors across the United States show the percentage of respondents who have used various substances for nonmedical purposes at least once (Johnston, O'Malley, & Bachman, 2005). Can you think of any reasons why teenagers—as opposed to older people—might be particularly likely to use drugs?

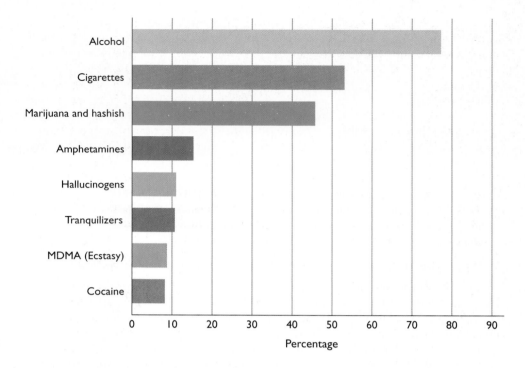

Why do people take drugs in the first place? There are many reasons, ranging from the perceived pleasure of the experience itself, to the escape that a drug-induced high affords from the everyday pressures of life, to an attempt to achieve a religious or spiritual state. However, other factors having little to do with the nature of the experience itself, also lead people to try drugs (McDowell & Spitz, 1999).

For instance, the alleged drug use of well-known role models (such as baseball player Darryl Strawberry and film star Robert Downey, Jr.), the easy availability of some illegal drugs, and peer pressure all play a role in the decision to use drugs. In some cases, the motive is simply the thrill of trying something new. Finally, the sense of helplessness experienced by unemployed individuals trapped in lives of poverty

FIGURE 2 Different drugs affect different parts of the nervous system and brain and each drug functions in one of these specific ways.

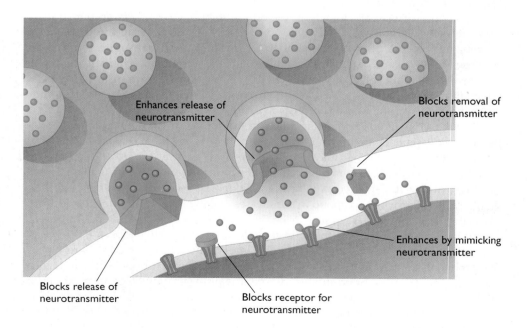

may lead them to try drugs as a way of escaping from the bleakness of their lives. Regardless of the forces that lead a person to begin using drugs, drug addiction is among the most difficult of all behaviors to modify, even with extensive treatment (Tucker, Donovan, & Marlatt, 1999; Lemonick, 2000).

Because of the difficulty in treating drug problems, there is little disagreement that the best hope for dealing with the overall societal problem of substance abuse is to prevent people from becoming involved with drugs in the first place. However, there is little accord on how to accomplish this goal. Even programs widely publicized for their effectiveness—such as D.A.R.E. (Drug Abuse Resistance Education)—are of questionable effectiveness. Used in more than 80 percent of school districts in the United States, D.A.R.E consists of a series of seventeen lessons on the dangers of drugs, alcohol, and gangs taught to fifth- and sixth-graders by a police officer. The program is highly popular with school officials, parents, and politicians. The problem is that several well-controlled evaluations have been unable to demonstrate that the D.A.R.E. program is effective in reducing drug use over the long term. In fact, one study even showed that D.A.R.E. graduates were more likely to use marijuana than was a comparison group of nongraduates (Clayton, Cattarello, & Johnstone, 1996; Lynam et al., 1999; Kalb, 2001b).

Stimulants: Drug Highs

It's one o'clock in the morning, and you still haven't finished reading the last chapter of the text on which you will be tested in the morning. Feeling exhausted, you turn to the one thing that may help you stay awake for the next two hours: a cup of strong black coffee.

If you have ever found yourself in such a position, you have resorted to a major *stimulant,* caffeine, to stay awake. *Caffeine* is one of a number of **stimulants,** drugs whose effect on the central nervous system causes a rise in heart rate, blood pressure, and muscular tension. Caffeine is present not only in coffee; it is an important ingredient in tea, soft drinks, and chocolate as well (see Figure 3).

Caffeine produces several reactions. The major behavioral effects are an increase in attentiveness and a decrease in reaction time. Caffeine can also bring about an

Stimulants: Drugs that have an arousal effect on the central nervous system, causing a rise in heart rate, blood pressure, and muscular tension.

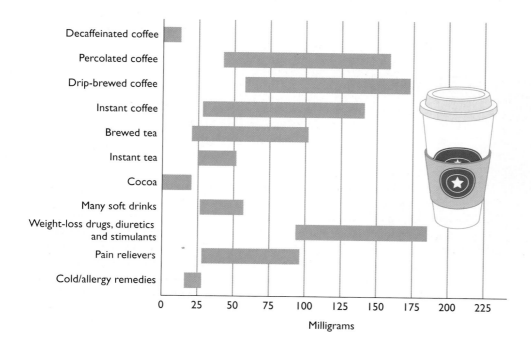

FIGURE 3 How much caffeine do you consume? This chart shows the range of caffeine found in common foods and drinks (*The New York Times*, 1991). The average person in the United States consumes about 200 milligrams of caffeine each day.

improvement in mood, most likely by mimicking the effects of a natural brain chemical, adenosine. Too much caffeine, however, can result in nervousness and insomnia. People can build up a biological dependence on the drug. Regular users who suddenly stop drinking coffee may experience headaches or depression. Many people who drink large amounts of coffee on weekdays have headaches on weekends because of the sudden drop in the amount of caffeine they are consuming (Silverman et al., 1992, 1994; James, 1997; Juliano & Griffiths, 2004).

Nicotine, found in cigarettes, is another common stimulant. The soothing effects of nicotine help explain why cigarette smoking is addictive. Smokers develop a dependence on nicotine, and those who suddenly stop smoking develop strong cravings for the drug. This is not surprising: Nicotine activates neural mechanisms similar to those activated by cocaine, which, as we see later in this section, is also highly addictive (Murray, 1990; Pich et al., 1997; Collins & Izenwasser, 2004).

AMPHETAMINES

Amphetamines are strong stimulants, such as Dexedrine and Benzedrine, popularly known as speed. In small quantities, amphetamines—which stimulate the central nervous system—bring about a sense of energy and alertness, talkativeness, heightened confidence, and a mood "high." They increase concentration and reduce fatigue. Amphetamines also cause a loss of appetite, increased anxiety, and irritability. When taken over long periods of time, amphetamines can cause feelings of being persecuted by others, as well as a general sense of suspiciousness. People taking amphetamines may lose interest in sex. If taken in too large a quantity, amphetamines overstimulate the central nervous system to such an extent that convulsions and death can occur.

Methamphetamine is a white, crystalline drug that U.S. police now say is the most dangerous street drug. "Meth" is highly addictive and relatively cheap, and it produces a strong, lingering high. It has made addicts of people across the social spectrum, ranging from soccer moms to urban professionals to poverty-stricken inner-city residents. After becoming addicted, users take it more and more frequently and in increasing doses. Long-term use of the drug can lead to brain damage (see Figure 4).

More than 1.5 million people in the United States are regular methamphetamine users. Because it can be made from nonprescription cold pills, retailers such as Wal-Mart and Target have removed these medications from their shelves. Illicit labs devoted to the manufacture of methamphetamine have sprung up in many locations around the United States (Jefferson, 2005).

FIGURE 4 This composite MRI brain scan illustrates that deficits in gray matter (indicated in red) in long-term methamphetamine abusers are particularly pronounced in an area around the corpus callosum. The volume of gray matter is more than 10 percent lower in users than non-users. (Source: Figure Id in Thompson et al., 2004, p. 6031).

COCAINE

Although its use has declined over the last decade, the stimulant cocaine and its derivative, crack, still represent a serious concern. Cocaine is inhaled or "snorted" through the nose, smoked, or injected directly into the bloodstream. It is rapidly absorbed into the body and takes effect almost immediately.

When used in relatively small quantities, cocaine produces feelings of profound psychological well-being, increased confidence, and alertness. Cocaine produces this "high" through the neurotransmitter dopamine. Dopamine is one of the chemicals that transmit between neurons messages that are related to ordinary feelings of pleasure. Normally when dopamine is released, excess amounts of the neurotransmitter are reabsorbed by the releasing neuron. However, when cocaine enters the brain, it blocks reabsorption of leftover dopamine. As a result, the brain is flooded with dopamine-produced pleasurable sensations (Landry, 1997; Bolla, Cadet, & London, 1998; Redish, 2004). Figure 5 provides a summary of the effects of cocaine and other illegal drugs.

However, there is a steep price to be paid for the pleasurable effects of cocaine. The brain may become permanently rewired, triggering a psychological and physical addiction in which users grow obsessed with obtaining the drug. Over time, users deteriorate mentally and physically. In extreme cases, cocaine can cause hallucinations—a common one is of insects crawling over one's body. Ultimately, an overdose of cocaine can lead to death (Carpenter, 2001; Nestler, 2001; George & Moselhy, 2005).

Almost 2.5 million people in the United States are occasional cocaine users, and as many as 1.8 million people use the drug regularly. Given the strength of cocaine,

Drugs	Street Name	Effects	Withdrawal Symptoms	Adverse/Overdose Reactions
Stimulants				
Cocaine	Coke, blow, snow, lady, crack	Increased confidence, mood elevation, sense of energy and alertness, decreased appetite, anxiety, irritability, insomnia, transient drowsiness, delayed orgasm	Apathy, general fatigue, prolonged sleep, depression, disorientation, suicidal thoughts, agitated motor activity, irritability, bizarre dreams	Elevated blood pressure, increase in body temperature, face picking, suspiciousness, bizarre and repetitious behavior, vivid hallucinations, convulsions, possible death
Amphetamines				
Benzedrine	Speed			
Dexedrine	Speed			
Depressants				
Alcohol	Booze	Anxiety reduction, impulsiveness, dramatic mood swings, bizarre thoughts, suicidal behavior, slurred speech, disorientation, slowed mental and physical functioning, limited attention span	Weakness, restlessness, nausea and vomiting, headaches, nightmares, irritability, depression, acute anxiety, hallucinations, seizures, possible death	Confusion, decreased response to pain, shallow respiration, dilated pupils, weak and rapid pulse, coma, possible death
Barbiturates				
Nembutal	Yellowjackets, yellows			
Seconal	Reds			
Phenobarbital				
Rohypnol	Roofies, rope, "date-rape drug"	Muscle relaxation, amnesia, sleep	Seizures	Seizures, coma, incapacitation, inability to resist sexual assault
Narcotics				
Heroin	H, hombre, junk, smack, dope, crap, horse	Anxiety and pain reduction, apathy, difficulty in concentration, slowed speech, decreased physical activity, drooling, itching, euphoria, nausea	Anxiety, vomiting, sneezing, diarrhea, lower back pain, watery eyes, runny nose, yawning, irritability, tremors, panic, chills and sweating, cramps	Depressed levels of consciousness, low blood pressure, rapid heart rate, shallow breathing, convulsions, coma, possible death
Morphine	Drugstore dope, cube, first line, mud			
Hallucinogens				
Cannabis	Bhang, kif, ganja, dope, grass, pot, hemp, joint, weed, bone, Mary Jane, reefer	Euphoria, relaxed inhibitions, increased appetite, disoriented behavior	Hyperactivity, insomnia, decreased appetite, anxiety	Severe reactions rare but include panic, paranoia, fatigue, bizarre and dangerous behavior, decreased testosterone over long-term; immune-system effects
Marijuana				
Hashish				
Hash oil				
MDMA	Ecstasy	Heightened sense of oneself and insight, feelings of peace, empathy, energy	Depression, anxiety, sleeplessness	Increase in body temperature, memory difficulties
LSD	Acid, quasey, microdot, white lightning	Heightened aesthetic responses; vision and depth distortion; heightened sensitivity to faces and gestures; magnified feelings; paranoia, panic, euphoria	Not reported	Nausea and chills; increased pulse, temperature, and blood pressure; slow, deep breathing; loss of appetite; insomnia; bizarre, dangerous behavior

FIGURE 5 Drugs and their effects. A comprehensive breakdown of effects of the most commonly used drugs.

withdrawal from the drug is difficult. Although the use of cocaine among high school students has declined in recent years, the drug still represents a major problem (Johnston et al., 2004).

Depressants: Drug Lows

Depressants: Drugs that slow down the nervous system.

In contrast to the initial effect of stimulants, which is an increase in arousal of the central nervous system, the effect of **depressants** is to impede the nervous system by causing neurons to fire more slowly. Small doses result in at least temporary feelings of *intoxication*—drunkenness—along with a sense of euphoria and joy. When large amounts are taken, however, speech becomes slurred and muscle control becomes disjointed, making motion difficult. Ultimately, heavy users may lose consciousness entirely.

ALCOHOL

The most common depressant is alcohol, which is used by more people than is any other drug. Based on liquor sales, the average person over the age of 14 drinks 2½ gallons of pure alcohol over the course of a year. This works out to more than 200 drinks per person. Although alcohol consumption has declined steadily over the last decade, surveys show that more than three-fourths of college students indicate that they have had a drink within the last thirty days (Center on Addiction and Substance Abuse, 1994; Jung, 2002).

One of the more disturbing trends is the high frequency of binge drinking among college students. For men, *binge drinking* is defined as having five or more drinks in one sitting; for women, who generally weigh less than men and whose bodies absorb alcohol less efficiently, binge drinking is defined as having four or more drinks at one sitting.

As shown in Figure 6, some 50 percent of male college students and 40 percent of female college students responding to a nationwide survey said they had engaged in binge drinking within the prior two weeks. Some 17 percent of female students and 31 percent of male students admitted drinking on ten or more occasions during the last 30 days. Furthermore, even light drinkers were affected by the high rate of alcohol use:

Although most alcohol consumers are casual users, there are more than 14 million alcoholics in the United States. The effects of alcohol vary significantly, depending on who is drinking it and the setting in which people drink. If alcohol were a newly discovered drug, do you think its sale would be legal?

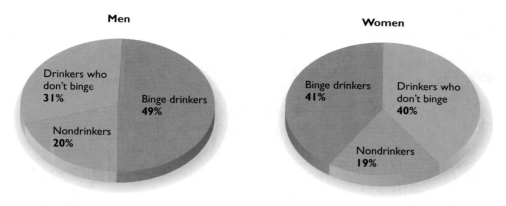

FIGURE 6 Drinking habits of college students (Wechsler et al., 2003). For men, binge drinking was defined as consuming five or more drinks in one sitting; for women, the total was four or more.

Two-thirds of lighter drinkers said that they had had their studying or sleep disturbed by drunk students, and around one-third had been insulted or humiliated by a drunk student. A quarter of the women said they had been the target of an unwanted sexual advance by a drunk classmate (Wechsler et al., 1994, 2000, 2002; Park & Grant, 2005).

Although alcohol consumption is widespread, there are significant gender and cultural variations in its use. For example, women are typically somewhat lighter drinkers than men—although the gap between the sexes is narrowing for older women and has closed completely for teenagers. In addition, not only are women usually more susceptible to the effects of alcohol, because of differences in blood volume and body fat that permit more alcohol to go directly into the bloodstream, alcohol abuse may harm the brains of women more than those of men (Blume, 1998; Wuethrich, 2001; Mann et al., 2005).

There are also ethnic differences in alcohol consumption. For example, people of East Asian backgrounds who live in the United States tend to drink significantly less than do Caucasians and African Americans, and their incidence of alcohol-related problems is lower. It may be that physical reactions to drinking, which may include sweating, a quickened heartbeat, and flushing, are more unpleasant for East Asians than for other groups (Akutsu et al., 1989; Smith & Lin, 1996; Garcia-Andrade, Wall, & Ehlers, 1997).

Although alcohol is a depressant, most people claim that it increases their sense of sociability and well-being. The discrepancy between the actual and the perceived effects of alcohol lies in the initial effects it produces in the majority of individuals who use it: release of tension and stress, feelings of happiness, and loss of inhibitions (Steele & Josephs, 1990; Sayette, 1993).

As the dose of alcohol increases, however, the depressive effects become more pronounced (see Figure 7). People may feel emotionally and physically unstable. They also show poor judgment and may act aggressively. Moreover, memory is impaired, brain processing of spatial information is diminished, and speech becomes slurred and incoherent. Eventually they may fall into a stupor and pass out. If they drink enough alcohol in a short time, they may die of alcohol poisoning (Bushman, 1993; Chin & Pisoni, 1997; Murphy et al., 1998; Zeigler et al., 2005).

Although most people fall into the category of casual users, 14 million people in the United States—one in every 13 adults—have a drinking problem. *Alcoholics,* people with alcohol-abuse problems, come to rely on alcohol and continue to drink even though it causes serious difficulties. In addition, they become increasingly immune to the effects of alcohol. Consequently, alcoholics must drink progressively more to experience the initial positive feelings that alcohol produces (Galanter & Kleber, 1999; Jung, 2002).

In some cases of alcoholism, people must drink constantly in order to feel well enough to function in their daily lives. In other cases, though, people drink inconsistently, but occasionally go on binges in which they consume large quantities of alcohol.

It is not clear why certain people become alcoholics and develop a tolerance for alcohol, whereas others do not. Some evidence suggests a genetic cause, although the question

FIGURE 7 The effects of alcohol. The quantities represent only rough benchmarks; the effects vary significantly depending on an individual's weight, height, recent food intake, genetic factors, and even psychological state.

Number of drinks consumed in two hours	Alcohol in blood (percentage)	Typical effects
2	0.05	Judgment, thought, and restraint weakened; tension released, giving carefree sensation
3	0.08	Tensions and inhibitions of everyday life lessened; cheerfulness
4	0.10	Voluntary motor action affected, making hand and arm movements, walk, and speech clumsy
7	0.20	Severe impairment—staggering, loud, incoherent, emotionally unstable, 100 times greater traffic risk; exuberance and aggressive inclinations magnified
9	0.30	Deeper areas of brain affected, with stimulus-response and understanding confused; stuporous; blurred vision
12	0.40	Incapable of voluntary action; sleepy, difficult to arouse; equivalent of surgical anesthesia
15	0.50	Comatose; centers controlling breathing and heartbeat anesthetized; death increasingly probable

Note: A drink refers to a typical 12-ounce bottle of beer, a 1.5-ounce shot of hard liquor, or a 5-ounce glass of wine.

Even legal drugs, when used improperly, can lead to addiction.

whether there is a specific inherited gene that produces alcoholism is controversial. What is clear is that the chances of becoming an alcoholic are considerably higher if alcoholics are present in earlier generations of a person's family. However, not all alcoholics have close relatives who are alcoholics. In these cases, environmental stressors are suspected of playing a larger role (Pennisi, 1997; McGue, 1999; Whitfield et al., 2004).

BARBITURATES

Barbiturates, which include drugs such as Nembutal, Seconal, and phenobarbital, are another form of depressant. Frequently prescribed by physicians to induce sleep or reduce stress, barbiturates produce a sense of relaxation. Yet they too are psychologically and physically addictive and, when combined with alcohol, can be deadly, since such a combination relaxes the muscles of the diaphragm to such an extent that the user stops breathing.

ROHYPNOL

Rohypnol is sometimes called the "date-rape drug," because when it is mixed with alcohol, it can prevent victims from resisting sexual assault. Sometimes people who are unknowingly given the drug are so incapacitated that they have no memory of the assault.

Narcotics: Relieving Pain and Anxiety

Narcotics are drugs that increase relaxation and relieve pain and anxiety. Two of the most powerful narcotics, *morphine* and *heroin,* are derived from the poppy seed pod. Although morphine is used medically to control severe pain, heroin is illegal in the United States. This has not prevented its widespread use.

Heroin users usually inject the drug directly into their veins with a hypodermic needle. The immediate effect has been described as a "rush" of positive feeling, similar in some respects to a sexual orgasm—and just as difficult to describe. After the rush, a heroin user experiences a sense of well-being and peacefulness that lasts three to five hours. When the effects of the drug wear off, however, the user feels extreme anxiety and a desperate desire to repeat the experience. Moreover, larger amounts of heroin are needed each time to produce the same pleasurable effect. These last two properties are all the ingredients necessary for biological and psychological addiction: The user is constantly either shooting up or attempting to obtain ever-increasing amounts of the drug. Eventually, the life of the addict revolves around heroin.

Because of the powerful positive feelings the drug produces, heroin addiction is particularly difficult to cure. One treatment that has shown some success is the use of methadone. *Methadone* is a synthetic chemical that satisfies a heroin user's physiological cravings for the drug without providing the "high" that accompanies heroin. When heroin users are placed on regular doses of methadone, they may be able to function relatively normally. The use of methadone has one substantial drawback, however: Although it removes the psychological dependence on heroin, it replaces the biological addiction to heroin with a biological addiction to methadone. Researchers are attempting to identify nonaddictive chemical substitutes for heroin as well as substitutes for other addictive drugs that do not replace one addiction with another (Amato et al., 2005; Verdejo, Toribio, & Orozco, 2005).

The use of heroin creates a cycle of biological and physical dependence. Combined with the strong positive feelings produced by the drug, this makes heroin addiction especially difficult to cure.

Narcotics: Drugs that increase relaxation and relieve pain and anxiety.

HALLUCINOGENS: PSYCHEDELIC DRUGS

What do mushrooms, jimsonweed, and morning glories have in common? Besides being fairly common plants, each can be a source of a powerful **hallucinogen,** a drug that is capable of producing *hallucinations*, or changes in the perceptual process.

The most common hallucinogen in widespread use today is *marijuana,* whose active ingredient—tetrahydrocannabinol (THC)—is found in a common weed, cannabis. Marijuana is typically smoked in cigarettes or pipes, although it can be cooked and eaten. Just over 34 percent of high school seniors and 12 percent of eighth-graders report having used marijuana in the last year (Johnston et al., 2004; see Figure 8).

The effects of marijuana vary from person to person, but they typically consist of feelings of euphoria and general well-being. Sensory experiences seem more vivid and intense, and a person's sense of self-importance seems to grow. Memory may be impaired, causing the user to feel pleasantly "spaced out." However, the effects are not universally

Hallucinogen: A drug that is capable of producing hallucinations, or changes in the perceptual process.

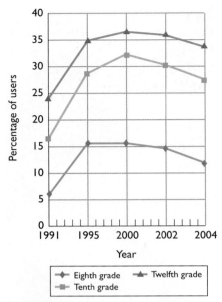

FIGURE 8 Although the level of marijuana use has declined slightly in recent years, overall the absolute number of teenagers who have used the drug in the last year remains relatively high. (Source: Johnston, O'Malley, & Bachman, 2005.)

positive. Individuals who use marijuana when they feel depressed can end up even more depressed, because the drug tends to magnify both good and bad feelings.

There are clear risks associated with long-term, heavy marijuana use. Although marijuana does not seem to produce addiction by itself, some evidence suggests that there are similarities in the way marijuana and drugs such as cocaine and heroin affect the brain. Furthermore, there is some evidence that heavy use at least temporarily decreases the production of the male sex hormone testosterone, potentially affecting sexual activity and sperm count (DiChiara & Reinhart, 1997; Block et al., 2000; Iverson, 2000).

In addition, marijuana smoked during pregnancy may have lasting effects on children who are exposed prenatally, although the results are inconsistent. Heavy use also affects the ability of the immune system to fight off germs and increases stress on the heart, although it is unclear how strong these effects are. There is one unquestionably negative consequence of smoking marijuana: The smoke damages the lungs much the way cigarette smoke does, producing an increased likelihood of developing cancer and other lung diseases (Cornelius et al., 1995; Julien, 2001).

Despite the possible dangers of marijuana use, there is little scientific evidence for the popular belief that users "graduate" from marijuana to more dangerous drugs. Furthermore, the use of marijuana is routine in certain cultures. For instance, some people in Jamaica habitually drink a marijuana-based tea related to religious practices. In addition, marijuana has several medical uses; it can be used to prevent nausea from chemotherapy, treat some AIDS symptoms, and relieve muscle spasms for people with spinal cord injuries. In a controversial move, several states have made the use of the drug legal if it is prescribed by a physician—although it remains illegal under U.S. federal law (Brookhiser, 1997; National Academy of Sciences, 1999; Iverson, 2000).

MDMA (ECSTASY) AND LSD

MDMA ("Ecstasy") and *lysergic acid diethylamide (LSD, or "acid")* fall into the category of hallucinogens. Both drugs affect the operation of the neurotransmitter serotonin in the brain, causing an alteration in brain-cell activity and perception (Aghajanian, 1994; Cloud, 2000; Buchert et al., 2004).

Ecstasy users report a sense of peacefulness and calm. People on the drug report experiencing increased empathy and connection with others, as well as feeling more relaxed, yet energetic. Although the data are not conclusive, some researchers have found declines in memory and performance on intellectual tasks, and such findings suggest that there may be long-term changes in serotonin receptors in the brain (Gowing et al., 2002; Kish, 2002; Parrott, 2002; Montgomery et al., 2005).

LSD, which is structurally similar to serotonin, produces vivid hallucinations. Perceptions of colors, sounds, and shapes are altered so much that even the most mundane experience—such as looking at the knots in a wooden table—can seem moving and exciting. Time perception is distorted, and objects and people may be viewed in a new way, with some users reporting that LSD increases their understanding of the world. For others, however, the experience brought on by LSD can be terrifying, particularly if users have had emotional difficulties in the past. Furthermore, people occasionally experience flashbacks, in which they hallucinate long after they initially used the drug (Baruss, 2003a).

What are the effects of a hallucinogen on thinking? Artists have tried to depict the hallucinogenic experience, as in this yarn painting.

In a society bombarded with commercials for drugs that are guaranteed to do everything from curing the common cold to giving new life to "tired blood," it is no wonder that drug-related problems are a major social issue. Yet many people with drug and alcohol problems deny they have them, and even close friends and family members may fail to realize when occasional social use of drugs or alcohol has turned into abuse.

BECOMING AN INFORMED CONSUMER
of Psychology
Identifying Drug and Alcohol Problems

Certain signs, however, indicate when use becomes abuse (Archambault, 1992; National Institute on Drug Abuse, 2000). Among them are the following:

- Always getting high to have a good time
- Being high more often than not
- Getting high to get oneself going
- Going to work or class while high
- Missing or being unprepared for class or work because you were high
- Feeling bad later about something you said or did while high
- Driving a car while high
- Coming in conflict with the law because of drugs
- Doing something while high that you wouldn't do otherwise
- Being high in nonsocial, solitary situations
- Being unable to stop getting high
- Feeling a need for a drink or a drug to get through the day
- Becoming physically unhealthy
- Failing at school or on the job
- Thinking about liquor or drugs all the time
- Avoiding family or friends while using liquor or drugs

Any combination of these symptoms should be sufficient to alert you to the potential of a serious drug problem. Because drug and alcohol dependence are almost impossible to cure on one's own, people who suspect that they have a problem should seek immediate attention from a psychologist, physician, or counselor.

You can also get help from national hotlines. For alcohol difficulties, call the National Council on Alcoholism at (800) 622-2255. For drug problems, call the National Institute on Drug Abuse at (800) 662-4357. You can also check your telephone book for a local listing of Alcoholics Anonymous or Narcotics Anonymous. Finally, check out the Web sites of the National Institute on Alcohol Abuse and Alcoholism (www.niaaa. nih.gov) and the National Institute on Drug Abuse (www.nida.nih.gov).

RECAP/EVALUATE/RETHINK

RECAP

What are the major classifications of drugs, and what are their effects?

- Drugs can produce an altered state of consciousness. However, they vary in how dangerous they are and in whether they are addictive. (p. 167)
- Stimulants cause arousal in the central nervous system. Two common stimulants are caffeine and nicotine. More dangerous are cocaine and amphetamines, which in large quantities can lead to convulsions and death. (pp. 169–171)
- Depressants decrease arousal in the central nervous system. They can cause intoxication along with feelings of euphoria. The most common depressants are alcohol and barbiturates. (pp. 172–174)
- Alcohol is the most frequently used depressant. Its initial effects of released tension and positive feelings yield to depressive effects as the dose of alcohol increases. Both heredity and environmental stressors can lead to alcoholism. (pp. 172–174)
- Morphine and heroin are narcotics, drugs that produce relaxation and relieve pain and anxiety. Because of their addictive qualities, morphine and heroin are particularly dangerous. (p. 175)
- Hallucinogens are drugs that produce hallucinations or other changes in perception. The most frequently used hal-

lucinogen is marijuana, which has several long-term risks. Two other hallucinogens are LSD and Ecstasy. (pp. 175–176)

- A number of signals indicate when drug use becomes drug abuse. A person who suspects that he or she has a drug problem should get professional help. People are almost never capable of solving drug problems on their own. (p. 177)

EVALUATE

1. Drugs that affect a person's consciousness are referred to as _____.
2. Match the type of drug to an example of that type.
   1. Narcotic—a pain reliever
   2. Amphetamine—a strong stimulant
   3. Hallucinogen—capable of producing hallucinations
   a. LSD
   b. Heroin
   c. Dexedrine or speed
3. Classify each drug listed as a stimulant (S), depressant (D), hallucinogen (H), or narcotic (N).
   1. Nicotine
   2. Cocaine
   3. Alcohol
   4. Morphine
   5. Marijuana
4. The effects of LSD can recur long after the drug has been taken. True or false?
5. _____ is a drug that has been used to cure people of heroin addiction.

RETHINK

1. Why have drug education campaigns largely been ineffective in stemming the use of illegal drugs? Should the use of certain now-illegal drugs be made legal? Would it be more effective to stress reduction of drug use rather than a complete prohibition of drug use?
2. *From the perspective of a substance abuse counselor:* How would you explain why people start using drugs to the family members of someone who was addicted? What types of drug prevention programs would you advocate?

Answers to Evaluate Questions

1. psychoactive; 2. 1-b, 2-c, 3-a; 3. 1-S, 2-S, 3-D, 4-N, 5-H; 4. true; 5. methadone

KEY TERMS

psychoactive drugs p. 167   stimulants p. 169   narcotics p. 175
addictive drugs p. 167   depressants p. 172   hallucinogen p. 175

Psychology on the Web

1. Find a resource on the Web that interprets dreams and another that reports the results of scientific dream research. Compare the nature and content of the two sites in terms of the topics covered, the reliability of information provided, and the promises made about the use of the site and its information. Write a summary of what you found.

2. There is considerable debate about the effectiveness of D.A.R.E., the Drug Abuse Resistance Education program. Find a discussion of both sides of the issue on the Web and summarize the arguments on each side. State your own preliminary conclusions about the D.A.R.E. program.

3. After completing the PsychInteractive exercise on drug effects, use the Web to investigate one of the illegal drugs that are described in the chapter. Consult several Web sites and summarize the way in which the drug operates on the nervous system and brain.

Epilogue

Our examination of states of consciousness has ranged widely. It focuses both on natural factors such as sleep, dreaming, and daydreaming and on more intentional modes of altering consciousness, including hypnosis, meditation, and drugs. As we consider why people seek to alter their consciousness, we need to reflect on the uses and abuses of the various consciousness-altering strategies in which people engage.

Return briefly to the case of Jim Smith, who thrashed around while sleeping because he suffered from REM sleep behavior disorder. Consider the following questions in light of your understanding of sleep and dreams:

1. What kinds of psychological consequences might REM sleep disorder produce?

2. Which of the explanations of dreaming that we discussed best explains Smith's behavior while dreaming?

3. Do you think that the suppression of movement brought about by the drug Smith was given to treat the disorder may have affected the nature of his dreams? How and why?

4. If Smith were awakened by his wife each time he showed signs of experiencing a violent dream, what consequences would there likely have been?

Key Concepts for Chapter 6

What is learning? ● How do we learn to form associations between stimuli and responses?

What is the role of reward and punishment in learning? ● What are some practical methods for bringing about behavior change, both in ourselves and in others?

What is the role of cognition and thought in learning?

Prologue   A Friend Named Minnie

The cell phone drops out of Craig Cook's lap and tumbles to the floor. The phone is his lifeline. Cook is quadriplegic—he lost the use of his legs and has only limited use of his arms after a 1996 car wreck. . . .

But that's when Minnie springs to action. She pulls the cord to open her cage, scampers to the kitchen floor, grabs the phone, scales Cook's leg and puts it back on his lap. She climbs to his shoulder, nuzzles against his face and eagerly awaits her reward—a fingertip dab of peanut butter.

"How cool is that?" Cook says, beaming like a proud father. "My very own monkey. . . ." An 18-year-old South American capuchin monkey, Minnie is trained to help Cook do much of what his body won't allow him to do.

She's a 5-pound bundle of fur with big, brown, expressive eyes and tiny fingers that resemble a child's hands. She turns lights on and off, opens soda bottles and retrieves Hot Pockets from the microwave. . . .

When Cook's left foot falls sideways on his wheelchair foot rest, he calls out, "Minnie. Foot."

She scampers over to the wheelchair, uses her strength to straighten his foot again, then climbs on his lap for her peanut butter reward.

He holds up his hand and Minnie responds with a strong high-five (Carpenter & Maciel, 2004, p. 1).

Looking Ahead

Minnie's expertise did not just happen, of course. It is the result of painstaking training procedures—the same ones that are at work in each of our lives, illustrated by our ability to read a book, drive a car, play poker, study for a test, or perform any of the numerous activities that make up our daily routine. Like Minnie, each of us must acquire and then refine our skills and abilities through learning.

Learning is a fundamental topic for psychologists and plays a central role in almost every specialty area of psychology. For example, a psychologist studying perception might ask, "How do we learn that people who look small from a distance are far away and not simply tiny?" A developmental psychologist might inquire, "How do babies learn to distinguish their mothers from other people?" A clinical psychologist might wonder, "Why do some people learn to be afraid when they see a spider?" A social psychologist might ask, "How do we learn to believe that we've fallen in love?"

Each of these questions, although drawn from very different branches of psychology, can be answered only through an understanding of basic learning processes. In each case, a skill or a behavior is acquired, altered, or refined through experience.

Psychologists have approached the study of learning from several angles. Among the most fundamental are studies of the type of learning that is illustrated in responses ranging from a dog salivating when it hears its owner opening a can of dog food to the emotions we feel when our national anthem is played. Other theories consider how learning is a consequence of rewarding circumstances. Finally, several other approaches focus on the cognitive aspects of learning, or the thought processes that underlie learning.

Classical Conditioning

Does the mere sight of the golden arches in front of McDonald's make you feel pangs of hunger and think about hamburgers? If it does, you are displaying an elementary form of learning called classical conditioning. *Classical conditioning* helps explain such diverse phenomena as crying at the sight of a bride walking down the aisle, fearing the dark, and falling in love.

Classical conditioning is one of a number of different types of learning that psychologists have identified, but a general definition encompasses them all: **Learning** is a relatively permanent change in behavior that is brought about by experience.

How do we know when a behavior has been influenced by learning—or even is a result of learning? Part of the answer relates to the nature-nurture question, one of the fundamental issues underlying the field of psychology. In the acquisition of behaviors, experience—which essential to the definition of learning—is the "nurture" part of the nature-nurture question.

However, it's not always easy to identify whether a change in behavior is due to nature or nurture. For example, some changes in behavior or performance come about through maturation alone, and don't involve experience. For instance, children become better tennis players as they grow older partly because their strength increases with their size—a maturational phenomenon. In order to understand when learning has occurred, we must differentiate maturational changes from improvements resulting from practice, which indicate that learning actually has occurred.

Similarly, short-term changes in behavior that are due to factors other than learning, such as declines in performance resulting from fatigue or lack of effort, are different from performance changes that are due to actual learning. If Serena Williams has a bad day on the tennis court because of tension or fatigue, this does not mean that she has not learned to play correctly or has "unlearned" how to play well. Because there is not always a one-to-one correspondence between learning and performance, understanding when true learning has occurred is difficult.

It is clear that we are primed for learning from the beginning of life. Infants exhibit a primitive type of learning called habituation. *Habituation* is the decrease in response to a stimulus that occurs after repeated presentations of the same stimulus. For example, young infants may initially show interest in a novel stimulus, such as a brightly colored toy, but they will soon lose interest if they see the same toy over and over. (Adults exhibit habituation, too: Newlyweds soon stop noticing that they are wearing a wedding ring.) Habituation permits us to ignore things that have stopped providing new information.

Most learning is considerably more complex than habituation, and the study of learning has been at the core of the field of psychology. Although philosophers since the time of Aristotle have speculated on the foundations of learning, the first systematic research on learning was done at the beginning of the twentieth century, when Ivan Pavlov (does the name ring a bell?) developed the framework for learning called classical conditioning.

The Basics of Classical Conditioning

Ivan Pavlov, a Russian physiologist, never intended to do psychological research. In 1904 he won the Nobel Prize for his work on digestion, testimony to his contribution

Key Concepts

What is learning?

How do we learn to form associations between stimuli and responses?

Learning: A relatively permanent change in behavior brought about by experience.

Ivan Pavlov (center) developed the principles of classical conditioning.

Classical conditioning: A type of learning in which a neutral stimulus comes to bring about a response after it is paired with a stimulus that naturally brings about that response.

Neutral stimulus: A stimulus that, before conditioning, does not naturally bring about the response of interest.

Unconditioned stimulus (UCS): A stimulus that naturally brings about a particular response without having been learned.

Unconditioned response (UCR): A response that is natural and needs no training (e.g., salivation at the smell of food).

Conditioned stimulus (CS): A once-neutral stimulus that has been paired with an unconditioned stimulus to bring about a response formerly caused only by the unconditioned stimulus.

Conditioned response (CR): A response that, after conditioning, follows a previously neutral stimulus (e.g., salivation at the ringing of a bell).

to that field. Yet Pavlov is remembered not for his physiological research, but for his experiments on basic learning processes—work that he began quite accidentally (Windholz, 1997; Marks, 2004).

Pavlov had been studying the secretion of stomach acids and salivation in dogs in response to the ingestion of varying amounts and kinds of food. While doing that, he observed a curious phenomenon: Sometimes stomach secretions and salivation would begin in the dogs when they had not yet eaten any food. The mere sight of the experimenter who normally brought the food, or even the sound of the experimenter's footsteps, was enough to produce salivation in the dogs. Pavlov's genius lay in his ability to recognize the implications of this discovery. He saw that the dogs were responding not only on the basis of a biological need (hunger), but also as a result of learning—or, as it came to be called, classical conditioning. **Classical conditioning** is a type of learning in which a neutral stimulus (such as the experimenter's footsteps) comes to elicit a response after being paired with a stimulus (such as food) that naturally brings about that response.

To demonstrate and analyze classical conditioning, Pavlov conducted a series of experiments (Pavlov, 1927). In one, he attached a tube to the salivary gland of a dog; that would allow him to measure precisely the dog's salivation. He then rang a bell and, just a few seconds later, presented the dog with meat. This pairing occurred repeatedly and was carefully planned so that each time exactly the same amount of time elapsed between the presentation of the bell and the meat. At first the dog would salivate only when the meat was presented, but soon it began to salivate at the sound of the bell. In fact, even when Pavlov stopped presenting the meat, the dog still salivated after hearing the sound. The dog had been classically conditioned to salivate to the bell.

As you can see in Figure 1, the basic processes of classical conditioning that underlie Pavlov's discovery are straightforward, although the terminology he chose is not simple. Consider first the diagram in Figure 1a. Before conditioning, there are two unrelated stimuli: the ringing of a bell and meat. We know that normally the ringing of a bell does not lead to salivation but to some irrelevant response, such as pricking up the ears or perhaps a startle reaction. The bell is therefore called the **neutral stimulus** because it is a stimulus that, before conditioning, does not naturally bring about the response in which we are interested. We also have meat, which, naturally causes a dog to salivate—the response we are interested in conditioning. The meat is considered an **unconditioned stimulus,** or **UCS,** because food placed in a dog's mouth automatically causes salivation to occur. The response that the meat elicits (salivation) is called an **unconditioned response,** or **UCR**—a natural, innate, reflexive response that is not associated with previous learning. Unconditioned responses are always brought about by the presence of unconditioned stimuli.

Figure 1b illustrates what happens during conditioning. The bell is rung just before each presentation of the meat. The goal of conditioning is for the dog to associate the bell with the unconditioned stimulus (meat) and therefore to bring about the same sort of response as the unconditioned stimulus. After a number of pairings of the bell and meat, the bell alone causes the dog to salivate.

When conditioning is complete, the bell has evolved from a neutral stimulus to what is now called a **conditioned stimulus,** or **CS.** At this time, salivation that occurs as a response to the conditioned stimulus (bell) is considered a **conditioned response,** or **CR.** This situation is depicted in Figure 1c. After conditioning, then, the conditioned stimulus evokes the conditioned response.

The sequence and timing of the presentation of the unconditioned stimulus and the conditioned stimulus are particularly important. Like a malfunctioning warning light at a railroad crossing that goes on after the train has passed by, a neutral stimulus

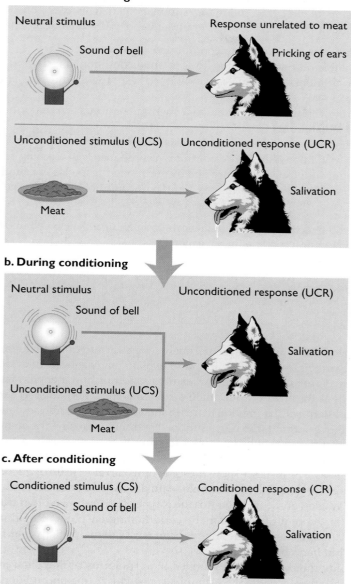

a. Before conditioning

Neutral stimulus

Sound of bell

Response unrelated to meat

Pricking of ears

Unconditioned stimulus (UCS)

Meat

Unconditioned response (UCR)

Salivation

b. During conditioning

Neutral stimulus

Sound of bell

Unconditioned response (UCR)

Salivation

Unconditioned stimulus (UCS)

Meat

c. After conditioning

Conditioned stimulus (CS)

Sound of bell

Conditioned response (CR)

Salivation

FIGURE 1 The basic process of classical conditioning. (a) Before conditioning, the ringing of a bell does not bring about salivation—making the bell a neutral stimulus. In contrast, meat naturally brings about salivation, making the meat an unconditioned stimulus and salivation an unconditioned response. (b) During conditioning, the bell is rung just before the presentation of the meat. (c) Eventually, the ringing of the bell alone brings about salivation. We now can say that conditioning has been accomplished: The previously neutral stimulus of the bell is now considered a conditioned stimulus that brings about the conditioned response of salivation.

that *follows* an unconditioned stimulus has little chance of becoming a conditioned stimulus. However, just as a warning light works best if it goes on right before a train passes, a neutral stimulus that is presented *just before* the unconditioned stimulus is most apt to result in successful conditioning. Research has shown that conditioning is most effective if the neutral stimulus (which will become a conditioned stimulus) precedes the unconditioned stimulus by between a half second and several seconds, depending on what kind of response is being conditioned (Rescorla, 1988; Wasserman & Miller, 1997).

Although the terminology Pavlov used to describe classical conditioning may seem confusing at first, the following summary can help make the relationships between stimuli and responses easier to understand and remember:

- Conditioned = learned; unconditioned = not learned.
- An *un*conditioned stimulus leads to an *un*conditioned response.
- *Un*conditioned stimulus–*un*conditioned response pairings are *un*learned and *un*trained.
- During conditioning, a previously neutral stimulus is transformed into the conditioned stimulus.
- A conditioned stimulus leads to a conditioned response, and a conditioned stimulus–conditioned response pairing is a consequence of learning and training.
- An unconditioned response and a conditioned response are similar (such as salivation in Pavlov's experiment), but the unconditioned response occurs naturally, whereas the conditioned response is learned.

The PsychInteractive exercise on classical conditioning will help you understand these principles and classical conditioning in general.

www.mhhe.com/feldmanup8

PsychInteractive Online

Classical Conditioning

Applying Conditioning Principles to Human Behavior

Although the initial conditioning experiments were carried out with animals, classical conditioning principles were soon found to explain many aspects of everyday human behavior. Recall, for instance, the earlier illustration of how people may experience hunger pangs at the sight of McDonald's golden arches. The cause of this reaction is classical conditioning: The previously neutral arches have become associated with the food inside the restaurant (the unconditioned stimulus), causing the arches to become a conditioned stimulus that brings about the conditioned response of hunger.

Emotional responses are particularly likely to be learned through classical conditioning processes. For instance, how do some of us develop fears of mice, spiders, and other creatures that are typically harmless? In a now-infamous case study, psychologist John B. Watson and colleague Rosalie Rayner (1920) showed that classical conditioning was at the root of such fears by conditioning an 11-month-old infant named Albert to be afraid of rats. "Little Albert," like most infants, initially was frightened by loud noises but had no fear of rats.

In the study, the experimenters sounded a loud noise just as they showed Little Albert a rat. The noise (the unconditioned stimulus) evoked fear (the unconditioned response). However, after just a few pairings of noise and rat, Albert began to show fear of the rat by itself, bursting into tears when he saw it. The rat, then, had become a CS that brought about the CR, fear. Furthermore, the effects of the conditioning lingered: Five days later, Albert reacted with fear not only when shown a rat, but when shown objects that looked similar to the white, furry rat, including a white rabbit, a white sealskin coat, and even a white Santa Claus mask. (By the way, we don't know what happened to the unfortunate Little Albert. It is clear that Watson, the experimenter, has been condemned for using ethically questionable procedures and that such studies would never be conducted today.)

Learning by means of classical conditioning also occurs during adulthood. For example, you may not go to a dentist as often as you should because of prior associations of dentists with pain. In more extreme cases, classical conditioning can lead to the development of *phobias,* which are intense, irrational fears that we will consider later when we discuss psychological disorders. For example, an insect phobia might develop in someone who is stung by a bee. The insect phobia might be so severe that the person refrains from leaving home. *Posttraumatic stress disorder (PTSD),* suffered by some war veterans and others who have had traumatic experiences, can also be produced by classical conditioning. Even years after their battlefield experiences, veterans may feel a rush of negative emotion at a stimulus such as a loud noise. In some cases,

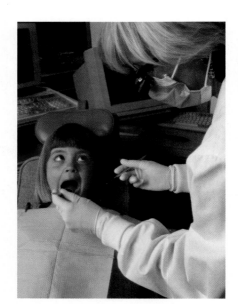

Because of a previous unpleasant experience, a person may expect a similar occurrence when faced with a comparable situation in the future, a process known as stimulus generalization. Can you think of ways this process is used in everyday life?

they may have a full-blown *panic attack,* characterized by intense fear (Jones & Friman, 1999; Frueh, Elhai, & Grubaugh, 2005; Kozaric-Kovacic & Borovecki, 2005).

On the other hand, classical conditioning also accounts for pleasant experiences. For instance, you may have a particular fondness for the smell of a certain perfume or aftershave lotion because the feelings and thoughts of an early love come rushing back whenever you encounter it. Classical conditioning, then, explains many of the reactions we have to stimuli in the world around us.

Extinction

What do you think would happen if a dog that had become classically conditioned to salivate at the ringing of a bell never again received food when the bell was rung? The answer lies in one of the basic phenomena of learning: extinction. **Extinction** occurs when a previously conditioned response decreases in frequency and eventually disappears.

To produce extinction, one needs to end the association between conditioned stimuli and unconditioned stimuli. For instance, if we had trained a dog to salivate (the conditioned response) at the ringing of a bell (the conditioned stimulus), we could produce extinction by repeatedly ringing the bell but *not* providing meat. At first the dog would continue to salivate when it heard the bell, but after a few such instances, the amount of salivation would probably decline, and the dog would eventually stop responding to the bell altogether. At that point, we could say that the response had been extinguished. In sum, extinction occurs when the conditioned stimulus is presented repeatedly without the unconditioned stimulus (see Figure 2).

We should keep in mind that extinction can be a helpful phenomenon. Consider, for instance, what it would be like if the fear you experienced while watching the shower murder scene in the classic movie *Psycho* never was extinguished. You might well tremble with fright every time you took a shower.

Once a conditioned response has been extinguished, has it vanished forever? Not necessarily. Pavlov discovered this when he returned to his dog a few days after the conditioned behavior had seemingly been extinguished. If he rang a bell, the dog once again salivated—an effect known as **spontaneous recovery,** or the reemergence of an extinguished conditioned response after a period of rest and with no further conditioning.

Spontaneous recovery helps explain why it is so hard to overcome drug addictions. For example, cocaine addicts who are thought to be "cured" can experience an irresistible impulse to use the drug again if they are subsequently confronted by a stimulus with strong connections to the drug, such as a white powder (O'Brien et al., 1992; Drummond et al., 1995; DiCano & Everitt, 2002; Rodd et al., 2004).

Extinction: A basic phenomenon of learning that occurs when a previously conditioned response decreases in frequency and eventually disappears.

Spontaneous recovery: The reemergence of an extinguished conditioned response after a period of rest and with no further conditioning.

FIGURE 2 Acquisition, extinction, and spontaneous recovery of a classically conditioned response. A conditioned response (CR) gradually increases in strength during training (a). However, if the conditioned stimulus is presented by itself enough times, the conditioned response gradually fades, and extinction occurs (b). After a pause (c) in which the conditioned stimulus is not presented, spontaneous recovery can occur (d). However, extinction typically reoccurs soon after.

Generalization and Discrimination

Despite differences in color and shape, to most of us a rose is a rose is a rose. The pleasure we experience at the beauty, smell, and grace of the flower is similar for different types of roses. Pavlov noticed a similar phenomenon. His dogs often salivated not only at the ringing of the bell that was used during their original conditioning but at the sound of a buzzer as well.

Such behavior is the result of stimulus generalization. **Stimulus generalization** occurs when a conditioned response follows a stimulus that is similar to the original conditioned stimulus. The greater the similarity between two stimuli, the greater the likelihood of stimulus generalization. Little Albert, who, as we mentioned earlier, was conditioned to be fearful of rats, grew afraid of other furry white things as well. However, according to the principle of stimulus generalization, it is unlikely that he would have been afraid of a black dog, because its color would have differentiated it sufficiently from the original fear-evoking stimulus.

The conditioned response elicited by the new stimulus is usually not as intense as the original conditioned response, although the more similar the new stimulus is to the old one, the more similar the new response will be. It is unlikely, then, that Little Albert's fear of the Santa Claus mask was as great as his learned fear of a rat. Still, stimulus generalization permits us to know, for example, that we ought to brake at all red lights, even if there are minor variations in size, shape, and shade.

On the other hand, **stimulus discrimination** occurs if two stimuli are sufficiently distinct from one another that one evokes a conditioned response but the other does not. Stimulus discrimination provides the ability to differentiate between stimuli. For example, my dog Cleo comes running into the kitchen when she hears the sound of the electric can opener, which she has learned is used to open her dog food when her dinner is about to be served. She does not bound into the kitchen at the sound of the food processor, although it sounds similar. In other words, she discriminates between the stimuli of can opener and food processor. Similarly, our ability to discriminate between the behavior of a growling dog and that of one whose tail is wagging can lead to adaptive behavior—avoiding the growling dog and petting the friendly one.

Stimulus generalization: Occurs when a conditioned response follows a stimulus that is similar to the original conditioned stimulus; the more similar the two stimuli are, the more likely generalization is to occur.

Stimulus discrimination: The process that occurs if two stimuli are sufficiently distinct from one another that one evokes a conditioned response but the other does not; the ability to differentiate between stimuli.

Beyond Traditional Classical Conditioning: Challenging Basic Assumptions

Although Pavlov hypothesized that all learning is nothing more than long strings of conditioned responses, this notion has not been supported by subsequent research. It turns out that classical conditioning provides us with only a partial explanation of how people and animals learn and that Pavlov was wrong in some of his basic assumptions (Risley & Rescorla, 1972; Hollis, 1997).

For example, according to Pavlov, the process of linking stimuli and responses occurs in a mechanistic, unthinking way. In contrast to this perspective, learning theorists influenced by cognitive psychology have argued that learners actively develop an understanding and expectancy about which particular unconditioned stimuli are matched with specific conditioned stimuli. A ringing bell, for instance, gives a dog something to think about: the impending arrival of food (Rescorla, 1988; Clark & Squire, 1998; Woodruff-Pak, 1999; Kirsch et al., 2004).

Traditional explanations of how classical conditioning operates have also been challenged by John Garcia, a learning psychologist whose research was initially concerned with the effects of exposure to nuclear radiation on laboratory animals. In the course of his experiments, he realized that rats placed in a radiation chamber drank almost no water, even though in their home cage they drank eagerly. The most obvious explanation—that it had something to do with the radiation—was soon ruled out. Garcia found that even when the radiation was not turned on, the rats still drank little or no water in the radiation chamber (Garcia, Hankins, & Rusiniak, 1974; Garcia, 1990, 2003).

Initially puzzled by the rats' behavior, Garcia eventually figured out that the drinking cups in the radiation chamber were made of plastic, giving the water an unusual, plastic-like taste. In contrast, the drinking cups in the home cage were made of glass and left no abnormal taste.

As a result, the plastic-tasting water had become repeatedly paired with illness brought on by exposure to radiation, and that had led the rats to form a classically conditioned association. The process began with the radiation acting as an unconditioned stimulus evoking the unconditioned response of sickness. With repeated pairings, the plastic-tasting water had become a conditioned stimulus that evoked the conditioned response of sickness.

The same phenomenon operates when humans learn that they are allergic to certain foods. If every time you ate peanuts you had an upset stomach several hours later, eventually you would learn to avoid peanuts, despite the time lapse between the stimulus of peanuts and response of getting ill. In fact, you might develop a *learned taste aversion*, so that peanuts no longer even tasted good to you.

Garcia's finding violated one of the basic rules of classical conditioning—that an unconditioned stimulus should *immediately* follow a conditioned stimulus for optimal conditioning to occur. Instead, Garcia showed that conditioning could occur even when the interval between exposure to the conditioned stimulus and the response of sickness was as long as eight hours. Furthermore, the conditioning persisted over very long periods and sometimes occurred after just one exposure to water that was followed later on by illness.

These findings have had important practical implications. For example, to prevent coyotes from killing their sheep, some ranchers now routinely lace a sheep carcass with a drug and leave the carcass in a place where coyotes will find it. The drug temporarily makes the coyotes quite ill, but it does not harm them permanently. After just one exposure to a drug-laden sheep carcass, coyotes avoid sheep, which are normally one of their primary natural victims (Green, Henderson, & Collinge, 2003).

The ease with which animals can be conditioned to avoid certain kinds of dangerous stimuli, such as tainted food, supports evolutionary theory. As Darwin suggested, organisms that have traits and characteristics that aid survival are more likely to thrive and have descendants. Consequently, organisms that ingest unpalatable foods (whether coyotes that eat a carcass laced with a drug or humans who suffer food poisoning after eating spoiled sushi) are likely to avoid similar foods in the future, making their survival more likely (Steinmetz, Kim, & Thompson, 2003; Cox et al., 2004).

Because of prior experience with meat that had been laced with a mild poison, this coyote does not obey its natural instincts and ignores what otherwise would be a tasty meal. What principles of classical conditioning does this phenomenon contradict?

RECAP/EVALUATE/RETHINK

RECAP

What is learning?

- Learning is a relatively permanent change in behavior resulting from experience. (p. 183)

How do we learn to form associations between stimuli and responses?

- One major form of learning is classical conditioning, which occurs when a neutral stimulus—one that normally brings about no relevant response—is repeatedly paired with a stimulus (called an unconditioned stimulus) that brings about a natural, untrained response. (pp. 183–184)
- Conditioning occurs when the neutral stimulus is repeatedly presented just before the unconditioned stimulus. After repeated pairings, the neutral stimulus elicits the same response that the unconditioned stimulus brings about. When this occurs, the neutral stimulus has become a conditioned stimulus, and the response a conditioned response. (pp. 184–185)
- Learning is not always permanent. Extinction occurs when a previously learned response decreases in frequency and eventually disappears. (p. 187)
- Stimulus generalization is the tendency for a conditioned response to follow a stimulus that is similar to, but not the same as, the original conditioned stimulus. The converse phenomenon, stimulus discrimination, occurs when an organism learns to distinguish between stimuli. (p. 188)

EVALUATE

1. _____ involves changes brought about by experience, whereas maturation describes changes resulting from biological development.
2. _____ is the name of the scientist responsible for discovering the learning phenomenon known as _____ conditioning, in which an organism learns a response to a stimulus to which it normally would not respond.

Refer to the passage below to answer questions 3 through 5:

The last three times little Theresa visited Dr. Lopez for checkups, he administered a painful preventive immunization shot that left her in tears. Today, when her mother takes her for another checkup, Theresa begins to sob as soon as she comes face to face with Dr. Lopez, even before he has had a chance to say hello.

3. The painful shot that Theresa received during each visit was a(n) _____ that elicited the _____, her tears.
4. Dr. Lopez is upset because his presence has become a _____ for Theresa's crying.
5. Fortunately, Dr. Lopez gave Theresa no more shots for quite some time. Over that period she gradually stopped crying and even came to like him. _____ had occurred.
6. _____ occurs when a stimulus that is fairly similar to the conditioned stimulus produces the same response.
7. In contrast, _____ occurs when there is no response to a stimulus that is slightly distinct from the conditioned stimulus.

RETHINK

1. How likely is it that Little Albert, Watson's experimental subject, went through life afraid of Santa Claus? Describe what could have happened to prevent his continual dread of Santa.
2. *From the perspective of an advertising executive:* How might knowledge of classical conditioning be useful in creating an advertising campaign? What, if any, ethical issues arise from this use?

Answers to Evaluate Questions

1. learning; 2. Pavlov, classical; 3. unconditioned stimulus, unconditioned response; 4. conditioned stimulus; 5. extinction; 6. stimulus generalization; 7. stimulus discrimination

KEY TERMS

learning p. 183
classical conditioning p. 184
neutral stimulus p. 184
unconditioned stimulus (UCS) p. 184

unconditioned response (UCR) p. 184
conditioned stimulus (CS) p. 184

conditioned response (CR) p. 184
extinction p. 187
spontaneous recovery p. 187

stimulus generalization p. 188
stimulus discrimination p. 188

Operant Conditioning

Very good . . . What a clever idea . . . Fantastic . . . I agree . . . Thank you . . . Excellent . . . Super . . . Right on . . . This is the best paper you've ever written; you get an A . . . You are really getting the hang of it . . . I'm impressed . . . You're getting a raise . . . Have a cookie . . . You look great . . . I love you . . .

Few of us mind being the recipient of any of the above comments. But what is especially noteworthy about them is that each of these simple statements can be used, through a process known as operant conditioning, to bring about powerful changes in behavior and to teach the most complex tasks. Operant conditioning is the basis for many of the most important kinds of human, and animal, learning.

Operant conditioning is learning in which a voluntary response is strengthened or weakened, depending on its favorable or unfavorable consequences. When we say that a response has been strengthened or weakened, we mean that it has been made more or less likely to recur regularly.

Unlike classical conditioning, in which the original behaviors are the natural, biological responses to the presence of a stimulus such as food, water, or pain, operant conditioning applies to voluntary responses, which an organism performs deliberately to produce a desirable outcome. The term *operant* emphasizes this point: The organism *operates* on its environment to produce a desirable result. Operant conditioning is at work when we learn that toiling industriously can bring about a raise or that studying hard results in good grades.

As with classical conditioning, the basis for understanding operant conditioning was laid by work with animals. We turn now to some of that early research, which began with a simple inquiry into the behavior of cats.

Key Concepts

What is the role of reward and punishment in learning?

What are some practical methods for bringing about behavior change, both in ourselves and in others?

Operant conditioning: Learning in which a voluntary response is strengthened or weakened, depending on its favorable or unfavorable consequences.

Thorndike's Law of Effect

If you placed a hungry cat in a cage and then put a small piece of food outside the cage, just beyond the cat's reach, chances are that the cat would eagerly search for a way out of the cage. The cat might first claw at the sides or push against an opening. Suppose, though, you had rigged things so that the cat could escape by stepping on a small paddle that released the latch to the door of the cage (see Figure 1). Eventually, as it moved around the cage, the cat would happen to step on the paddle, the door would open, and the cat would eat the food.

What would happen if you then returned the cat to the box? The next time, it would probably take a little less time for the cat to step on the paddle and escape. After a few trials, the cat would deliberately step on the paddle as soon as it was placed in the cage. What would have occurred, according to Edward L. Thorndike (1932), who studied this situation extensively, was that the cat would have learned that pressing the paddle was associated with the desirable consequence of getting food. Thorndike summarized that relationship by formulating the *law of effect:* Responses that lead to satisfying consequences are more likely to be repeated.

Thorndike believed that the law of effect operates as automatically as leaves fall off a tree in autumn. It was not necessary for an organism to understand that there was a link between a response and a reward. Instead, Thorndike believed, over time

FIGURE 1 Edward L. Thorndike devised this puzzle box to study the process by which a cat learns to press a paddle to escape from the box and receive food. Do you think Thorndike's work has relevance to the question of why humans voluntarily solve puzzles, such as crossword puzzles and jigsaw puzzles? Do they receive any rewards?

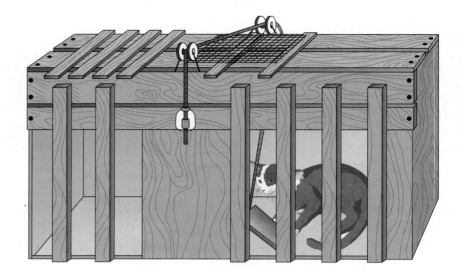

and through experience the organism would make a direct connection between the stimulus and the response without any awareness that the connection existed.

The Basics of Operant Conditioning

Thorndike's early research served as the foundation for the work of one of the twentieth century's most influential psychologists, B. F. Skinner, who died in 1990. You may have heard of the Skinner box (shown in Figure 2), a chamber with a highly controlled environment that was used to study operant conditioning processes with laboratory animals. Whereas Thorndike's goal was to get his cats to learn to obtain food by leaving the box, animals in a Skinner box learn to obtain food by operating on their environment within the box. Skinner became interested in specifying how behavior varies as a result of alterations in the environment.

FIGURE 2 B. F. Skinner with a Skinner box used to study operant conditioning. Laboratory rats learn to press the lever in order to obtain food, which is delivered in the tray.

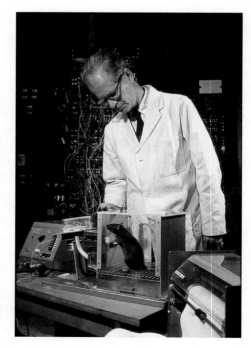

Skinner, whose work went far beyond perfecting Thorndike's earlier apparatus, is considered the inspiration for a whole generation of psychologists studying operant conditioning (Bjork, 1993; Keehn, 1996). To illustrate Skinner's contribution, let's consider what happens to a rat in the typical Skinner box.

Suppose you want to teach a hungry rat to press a lever that is in its box. At first the rat will wander around the box, exploring the environment in a relatively random fashion. At some point, however, it will probably press the lever by chance, and when it does, it will receive a food pellet. The first time this happens, the rat will not learn the connection between pressing a lever and receiving food and will continue to explore the box. Sooner or later the rat will press the lever again and receive a pellet, and in time the frequency of the pressing response will increase. Eventually, the rat will press the lever continually until it satisfies its hunger, thereby demonstrating that it has learned that the receipt of food is contingent on pressing the lever.

REINFORCEMENT: THE CENTRAL CONCEPT OF OPERANT CONDITIONING

Skinner called the process that leads the rat to continue pressing the key "reinforcement." **Reinforcement** is the process by which a stimulus increases the probability that a preceding behavior will be repeated. In other words, pressing the lever is more likely to occur again because of the stimulus of food.

In a situation such as this one, the food is called a reinforcer. A **reinforcer** is any stimulus that increases the probability that a preceding behavior will occur again. Hence, food is a reinforcer because it increases the probability that the behavior of pressing (formally referred to as the *response* of pressing) will take place.

What kind of stimuli can act as reinforcers? Bonuses, toys, and good grades can serve as reinforcers—if they strengthen the probability of the response that occurred before their introduction. What makes something a reinforcer depends on individual preferences. Although a Hershey bar can act as a reinforcer for one person, an individual who dislikes chocolate may find 75 cents more desirable. The only way we can know if a stimulus is a reinforcer for a particular organism is to observe whether the frequency of a previously occurring behavior increases after the presentation of the stimulus.

Of course, we are not born knowing that 75 cents can buy us a candy bar. Rather, through experience we learn that money is a valuable commodity because of its association with stimuli, such as food and drink, that are naturally reinforcing. This fact suggests a distinction between primary reinforcers and secondary reinforcers. A *primary reinforcer* satisfies some biological need and works naturally, regardless of a person's prior experience. Food for a hungry person, warmth for a cold person, and relief for a person in pain all would be classified as primary reinforcers. A *secondary reinforcer,* in contrast, is a stimulus that becomes reinforcing because of its association with a primary reinforcer. For instance, we know that money is valuable because we have learned that it allows us to obtain other desirable objects, including primary reinforcers such as food and shelter. Money thus becomes a secondary reinforcer. (To learn more, try the PsychInteractive exercises on operant conditioning and shaping.)

Reinforcement: The process by which a stimulus increases the probability that a preceding behavior will be repeated.

Reinforcer: Any stimulus that increases the probability that a preceding behavior will occur again.

www.mhhe.com/feldmanup8
PsychInteractive Online

Operant Conditioning
Shaping

Positive Reinforcers, Negative Reinforcers, and Punishment

In many respects, reinforcers can be thought of in terms of rewards; both a reinforcer and a reward increase the probability that a preceding response will occur again. But the term *reward* is limited to *positive* occurrences, and this is where it differs from a reinforcer—for it turns out that reinforcers can be positive or negative.

Positive reinforcer: A stimulus added to the environment that brings about an increase in a preceding response.

Negative reinforcer: An unpleasant stimulus whose removal leads to an increase in the probability that a preceding response will be repeated in the future.

Punishment: A stimulus that decreases the probability that a previous behavior will occur again.

A **positive reinforcer** is a stimulus *added* to the environment that brings about an increase in a preceding response. If food, water, money, or praise is provided after a response, it is more likely that that response will occur again in the future. The paychecks that workers get at the end of the week, for example, increase the likelihood that they will return to their jobs the following week.

In contrast, a **negative reinforcer** refers to an unpleasant stimulus whose *removal* leads to an increase in the probability that a preceding response will be repeated in the future. For example, if you have an itchy rash (an unpleasant stimulus) that is relieved when you apply a certain brand of ointment, you are more likely to use that ointment the next time you have an itchy rash. Using the ointment, then, is negatively reinforcing, because it removes the unpleasant itch. Similarly, if your iPod volume is so loud that it hurts your ears when you first turn it on, you are likely to reduce the volume level. Lowering the volume is negatively reinforcing, and you are more apt to repeat the action in the future when you first turn it on. Negative reinforcement, then, teaches the individual that taking an action removes a negative condition that exists in the environment. Like positive reinforcers, negative reinforcers increase the likelihood that preceding behaviors will be repeated.

It is important to note that negative reinforcement is not the same as punishment. **Punishment** refers to a stimulus that *decreases* the probability that a prior behavior will occur again. Unlike negative reinforcement, which produces an *increase* in behavior, punishment reduces the likelihood of a prior response. If we receive a shock that is meant to decrease a certain behavior, then, we are receiving punishment, but if we are already receiving a shock and do something to stop that shock, the behavior that stops the shock is considered to be negatively reinforced. In the first case, the specific behavior is apt to decrease because of the punishment; in the second, it is likely to increase because of the negative reinforcement.

There are two types of punishment: positive punishment and negative punishment, just as there is positive and negative reinforcement. (In both cases, "positive" means adding something, and "negative" means removing something.) *Positive punishment* weakens a response through the application of an unpleasant stimulus. For instance, spanking a child for misbehaving or spending ten years in jail for committing a crime is positive punishment. In contrast, *negative punishment* consists of the removal of something pleasant. For instance, when a teenager is told she is "grounded" and will no longer be able to use the family car because of her poor grades, or when an employee is informed that he has been demoted with a cut in pay because of poor job evaluations, negative punishment is being administered. Both positive and negative punishment result in a decrease in the likelihood that a prior behavior will be repeated.

The distinctions among positive reinforcement, negative reinforcement, positive punishment, and negative punishment may seem confusing initially, but the following rules (and the summary in Figure 3) can help you distinguish these concepts from one another:

- Reinforcement *increases* the frequency of the behavior preceding it; punishment *decreases* the frequency of the behavior preceding it.
- The *application* of a *positive* stimulus brings about an increase in the frequency of behavior and is referred to as positive reinforcement; the *application* of a *negative* stimulus decreases or reduces the frequency of behavior and is called punishment.
- The *removal* of a *negative* stimulus that results in an increase in the frequency of behavior is negative reinforcement; the *removal* of a *positive* stimulus that decreases the frequency of behavior is negative punishment.

Intended Result	When stimulus is *added*, the result is ...	When stimulus is *removed* or *terminated*, the result is ...
Increase in behavior (reinforcement)	**Positive reinforcement** Example: Giving a raise for good performance Result: *Increase* in response of good performance 	**Negative reinforcement** Example: Applying ointment to relieve an itchy rash leads to a higher future likelihood of applying the ointment Result: *Increase* in response of using ointment 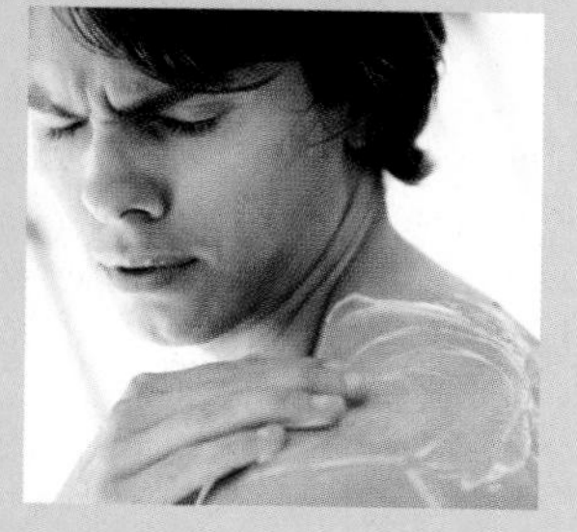
Decrease in behavior (punishment)	**Positive punishment** Example: Yelling at a teenager when she steals a bracelet Result: *Decrease* in frequency of response of stealing 	**Negative punishment** Example: Teenager's access to car restricted by parents due to teenager's breaking curfew Result: *Decrease* in response of breaking curfew 

FIGURE 3 Types of reinforcement and punishment.

The Pros and Cons of Punishment: Why Reinforcement Beats Punishment

Is punishment an effective way to modify behavior? Punishment often presents the quickest route to changing behavior that, if allowed to continue, might be dangerous to an individual. For instance, a parent may not have a second chance to warn a child not to run into a busy street, and so punishing the first incidence of this behavior may prove to be wise. Moreover, the use of punishment to suppress behavior, even temporarily, provides an opportunity to reinforce a person for subsequently behaving in a more desirable way.

There are some rare instances in which punishment can be the most humane approach to treating certain severe disorders. For example, some children suffer from *autism,* a psychological disorder that can lead them to abuse themselves by tearing at their skin or banging their heads against the wall, injuring themselves severely in the process. In such cases—and when all other treatments have failed—punishment in the form of a quick but intense electric shock has been used to prevent self-injurious behavior. Such punishment, however, is used only to keep the child safe and to buy time until positive reinforcement procedures can be initiated (Kahng, Iwata, & Lewin, 2002; Salvy, Mulick, & Butter, 2004; Toole et al., 2004).

Punishment has several disadvantages make its routine questionable. For one thing, punishment is frequently ineffective, particularly if it is not delivered shortly after the undesired behavior or if the individual is able to leave the setting in which the punishment is being given. An employee who is reprimanded by the boss may quit; a teenager who loses the use of the family car may borrow a friend's car instead. In such instances, the initial behavior that is being punished may be replaced by one that is even less desirable.

Even worse, physical punishment can convey to the recipient the idea that physical aggression is permissible and perhaps even desirable. A father who yells at and hits his son for misbehaving teaches the son that aggression is an appropriate, adult response. The son soon may copy his father's behavior by acting aggressively toward others. In addition, physical punishment is often administered by people who are themselves angry or enraged. It is unlikely that individuals in such an emotional state will be able to think through what they are doing or control carefully the degree of punishment they are inflicting. Ultimately, those who resort to physical punishment run the risk that they will grow to be feared. Punishment can also reduce the self-esteem of recipients unless they can understand the reasons for it (Baumrind, Larzelere, & Cowan, 2002; Gershoff, 2002; Holden, 2002; Parke, 2002).

Finally, punishment does not convey any information about what an alternative, more appropriate behavior might be. To be useful in bringing about more desirable behavior in the future, punishment must be accompanied by specific information about the behavior that is being punished, along with specific suggestions concerning a more desirable behavior. Punishing a child for staring out the window in school could merely lead her to stare at the floor instead. Unless we teach her appropriate ways to respond, we have merely managed to substitute one undesirable behavior for another. If punishment is not followed up with reinforcement for subsequent behavior that is more appropriate, little will be accomplished.

In short, reinforcing desired behavior is a more appropriate technique for modifying behavior than using punishment. Both in and out of the scientific arena, then, reinforcement usually beats punishment (Kahng, Iwata, & Lewin, 2002; Cicero & Pfadt, 2002; Pogarsky & Piquero, 2003; Hiby, Rooney, & Bradshaw, 2004).

Schedules of Reinforcement: Timing Life's Rewards

Schedules of reinforcement: Different patterns of frequency and timing of reinforcement following desired behavior.

Continuous reinforcement schedule: Reinforcing of a behavior every time it occurs.

Partial (or intermittent) reinforcement schedule: Reinforcing of a behavior some but not all of the time.

The world would be a different place if poker players never played cards again after the first losing hand, fishermen returned to shore as soon as they missed a catch, or telemarketers never made another phone call after their first hang-up. The fact that such unreinforced behaviors continue, often with great frequency and persistence, illustrates that reinforcement need not be received continually for behavior to be learned and maintained. In fact, behavior that is reinforced only occasionally can ultimately be learned better than can behavior that is always reinforced.

When we refer to the frequency and timing of reinforcement that follows desired behavior, we are talking about **schedules of reinforcement.** Behavior that is reinforced every time it occurs is said to be on a **continuous reinforcement schedule;** if it is reinforced some but not all of the time, it is on a **partial** (or **intermittent**) **reinforcement schedule.** Although learning occurs more rapidly under a continuous reinforcement schedule, behavior lasts longer after reinforcement stops when it is learned under a partial reinforcement schedule (Staddon & Cerutti, 2003; Gottlieb, 2004).

NEXT STIMULUS 20 MILES

WEYANT

Why should intermittent reinforcement result in stronger, longer-lasting learning than continuous reinforcement? We can answer the question by examining how we might behave when using a candy vending machine compared with a Las Vegas slot machine. When we use a vending machine, prior experience has taught us that every time we put in the appropriate amount of money, the reinforcement, a candy bar, ought to be delivered. In other words, the schedule of reinforcement is continuous. In comparison, a slot machine offers intermittent reinforcement. We have learned that after putting in our cash, most of the time we will not receive anything in return. At the same time, though, we know that we will occasionally win something.

Now suppose that, unknown to us, both the candy vending machine and the slot machine are broken, and so neither one is able to dispense anything. It would not be very long before we stopped depositing coins into the broken candy machine. Probably at most we would try only two or three times before leaving the machine in disgust. But the story would be quite different with the broken slot machine. Here, we would drop in money for a considerably longer time, even though there would be no payoff.

In formal terms, we can see the difference between the two reinforcement schedules: Partial reinforcement schedules (such as those provided by slot machines) maintain performance longer than do continuous reinforcement schedules (such as those established in candy vending machines) before *extinction*—the disappearance of the conditioned response—occurs.

Certain kinds of partial reinforcement schedules produce stronger and lengthier responding before extinction than do others. Although many different partial reinforcement schedules have been examined, they can most readily be put into two categories: schedules that consider the *number of responses* made before reinforcement is given, called fixed-ratio and variable-ratio schedules, and those which consider the *amount of time* that elapses before reinforcement is provided, called fixed-interval and variable-interval schedules (Svartdal, 2003; Pellegrini et al., 2004).

FIXED- AND VARIABLE-RATIO SCHEDULES

In a **fixed-ratio schedule,** reinforcement is given only after a specific number of responses. For instance, a rat might receive a food pellet every tenth time it pressed a lever; here, the ratio would be 1:10. Similarly, garment workers are generally paid on fixed-ratio schedules: They receive a specific number of dollars for every blouse they sew. Because a greater rate of production means more reinforcement, people on fixed-ratio schedules are apt to work as quickly as possible (see Figure 4).

In a **variable-ratio schedule,** reinforcement occurs after a varying number of responses rather than after a fixed number. Although the specific number of responses necessary to receive reinforcement varies, the number of responses usually hovers around a specific average. A good example of a variable-ratio schedule is a telephone salesperson's job. She might make a sale during the third, eighth, ninth, and twentieth calls without being successful during any call in between. Although the number of responses that must be made before making a sale varies, it averages out to a 20 percent success rate. Under these circumstances, you might expect that the salesperson would try to make as many calls as possible in as short a time as possible. This is the case with all variable-ratio schedules, which lead to a high rate of response and resistance to extinction.

FIXED- AND VARIABLE-INTERVAL SCHEDULES: THE PASSAGE OF TIME

In contrast to fixed- and variable-ratio schedules, in which the crucial factor is the number of responses, fixed-*interval* and variable-*interval* schedules focus on the

Fixed-ratio schedule: A schedule by which reinforcement is given only after a specific number of responses are made.

Variable-ratio schedule: A schedule by which reinforcement occurs after a varying number of responses rather than after a fixed number.

FIGURE 4 Typical outcomes of different reinforcement schedules. (a) In a fixed-ratio schedule, short pauses occur after each response. Because the more responses, the more reinforcement, fixed-ratio schedules produce a high rate of responding. (b) In a variable-ratio schedule, responding also occurs at a high rate. (c) A fixed-interval schedule produces lower rates of responding, especially just after reinforcement has been presented, because the organism learns that a specified time period must elapse between reinforcements. (d) A variable-interval schedule produces a fairly steady stream of responses.

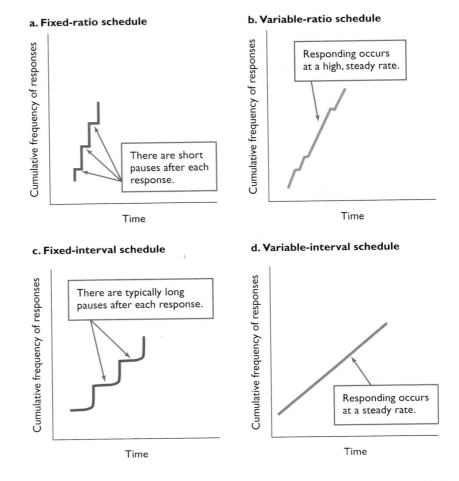

Fixed-interval schedule: A schedule that provides reinforcement for a response only if a fixed time period has elapsed, making overall rates of response relatively low.

Variable-interval schedule: A schedule by which the time between reinforcements varies around some average rather than being fixed.

amount of time that has elapsed since a person or animal was rewarded. One example of a fixed-interval schedule is a weekly paycheck. For people who receive regular, weekly paychecks, it typically makes relatively little difference exactly how much they produce in a given week.

Because a **fixed-interval schedule** provides reinforcement for a response only if a fixed time period has elapsed, overall rates of response are relatively low. This is especially true in the period just after reinforcement, when the time before another reinforcement is relatively great. Students' study habits often exemplify this reality. If the periods between exams are relatively long (meaning that the opportunity for reinforcement for good performance is given fairly infrequently), students often study minimally or not at all until the day of the exam draws near. Just before the exam, however, students begin to cram for it, signaling a rapid increase in the rate of their studying response. As you might expect, immediately after the exam there is a rapid decline in the rate of responding, with few people opening a book the day after a test. Fixed-interval schedules produce the kind of "scalloping effect" shown in Figure 4c.

One way to decrease the delay in responding that occurs just after reinforcement, and to maintain the desired behavior more consistently throughout an interval, is to use a variable-interval schedule. In a **variable-interval schedule,** the time between reinforcements varies around some average rather than being fixed. For example, a professor who gives surprise quizzes that vary from one every three days to one every three weeks, averaging one every two weeks, is using a variable-interval schedule. Compared to the study habits we observed with a fixed-interval schedule, students' study habits under such a variable-interval schedule would most likely be very different. Students would be apt to study more regularly because they would never know when the next surprise quiz was coming. Variable-interval schedules, in general, are more likely to produce relatively steady rates of responding than are fixed-interval schedules, with responses that take longer to extinguish after reinforcement ends. (To better understand schedules of reinforcement, try the PsychInteractive exercise on schedules of reinforcement.)

www.mhhe.com/feldmanup8
PsychInteractive Online

Schedules of Reinforcement

Discrimination and Generalization in Operant Conditioning

It does not take a child long to learn that a red light at an intersection means stop and a green light indicates that it is permissible to continue, in the same way that a pigeon can learn to peck a key when a green light goes on, but not when a red light appears. Just as in classical conditioning, then, operant learning involves the phenomena of discrimination and generalization.

The process by which people learn to discriminate stimuli is known as stimulus control training. In *stimulus control training,* a behavior is reinforced in the presence of a specific stimulus, but not in its absence. For example, one of the most difficult discriminations many people face is determining when someone's friendliness is not mere friendliness, but a signal of romantic interest. People learn to make the discrimination by observing the presence of certain nonverbal cues—such as increased eye contact and touching—that indicate romantic interest. When such cues are absent, people learn that no romantic interest is indicated. In this case, the nonverbal cue acts as a discriminative stimulus, one to which an organism learns to respond during stimulus control training. A *discriminative stimulus* signals the likelihood that reinforcement will follow a response. For example, if you wait until your roommate is in a good mood before you ask to borrow her favorite compact disc, your behavior can be said to be under stimulus control because you can discriminate between her moods.

Just as in classical conditioning, the phenomenon of stimulus generalization, in which an organism learns a response to one stimulus and then exhibits the same response to slightly different stimuli, occurs in operant conditioning. If you have learned that being polite helps you to get your way in a certain situation (reinforcing your politeness), you are likely to generalize your response to other situations. Sometimes, though, generalization can have unfortunate consequences, as when people behave negatively toward all members of a racial group because they have had an unpleasant experience with one member of that group.

Shaping: Reinforcing What Doesn't Come Naturally

Consider the difficulty of using operant conditioning to teach people to repair an automobile transmission. If we had to wait until they stumbled on a way to repair it correctly before providing them with reinforcement, the wait might be interminable.

There are many complex behaviors, ranging from auto repair to zoo management, that we would not expect to occur naturally as part of anyone's spontaneous behavior. For such behaviors, for which there might otherwise be no opportunity to provide reinforcement (because the behavior would never occur in the first place), a procedure

Shaping: The process of teaching a complex behavior by rewarding closer and closer approximations of the desired behavior.

known as shaping is used. **Shaping** is the process of teaching a complex behavior by rewarding closer and closer approximations of the desired behavior. In shaping, you start by reinforcing any behavior that is at all similar to the behavior you want the person to learn. Later, you reinforce only responses that are closer to the behavior you ultimately want to teach. Finally, you reinforce only the desired response. Each step in shaping, then, moves only slightly beyond the previously learned behavior, permitting the person to link the new step to the behavior learned earlier.

Shaping allows even lower animals to learn complex responses that would never occur naturally, ranging from lions jumping through hoops, dolphins rescuing divers lost at sea, or—as we consider in the *Applying Psychology in the 21st Century* box—finding hidden land mines. Shaping also underlies the learning of many complex human skills. For instance, the organization of most textbooks is based on the principles of shaping. Typically, information is presented so that new material builds on previously learned concepts or skills. Thus, the concept of shaping could not be presented until we had discussed the more basic principles of operant learning.

Biological Constraints on Learning: You Can't Teach an Old Dog Just Any Trick

Psychologists Keller and Marian Breland were pleased with their idea: As professional animal trainers, they came up with the notion of having a pig pick up a wooden disk and place it in a piggy bank. With their experience in training animals through operant conditioning, they thought the task would be easy to teach, because it was certainly well within the range of the pig's physical capabilities. Yet almost every time they tried the procedure, it failed. Rather than picking up the disk, the pigs generally pushed it along the ground, something that they appeared to be biologically programmed to do.

To remedy the problem, the Brelands substituted a raccoon. Although the procedure worked fine with one disk, when two disks were used, the raccoon refused to deposit either of them and instead rubbed the two together, as if it were washing them. Once again, it appeared that the disks evoked biologically innate behaviors that were impossible to replace through even the most exhaustive training (Breland & Breland, 1961).

The Brelands' difficulties illustrate an important point: Not all behaviors can be trained in all species equally well. Instead, there are *biological constraints,* built-in limitations in the ability of animals to learn particular behaviors. In some cases, an organism will have a special predisposition that will aid in its learning a behavior (such as pecking behaviors in pigeons); in other cases, biological constraints will act to prevent or inhibit an organism from learning a behavior.

The existence of biological constraints is consistent with evolutionary explanations of behavior. Clearly, there are adaptive benefits that promote survival for organisms that quickly learn—or avoid—certain behaviors. For example, our ability to rapidly learn to avoid touching hot surfaces increases our chances of survival. Additional support for the evolutionary interpretation of biological constraints lies in the fact the associations that animals learn most readily involve stimuli that

Biological constraints make it nearly impossible for animals to learn certain behaviors. Here, psychologist Marian Breland attempts to overcome the natural limitations that inhibit the success of conditioning this rooster.

A Nose for Danger: Saving Lives by Sniffing Out Land Mines

The Gambian giant pouched rat ... may be as good a mine detector as man or nature has yet devised. Just after sunup one dewy morning, on a football field-size patch of earth in the Mozambican countryside, Frank Weetjens and his squad of 16 giant pouched rats are proving it. Outfitted in tiny harnesses and hitched to 10-yard clotheslines, their footlong tails whipping to and fro, the rats lope up and down the lines, whiskers twitching, noses tasting the air.

Wanjiro, a sleek 2-year-old female in a bright red harness, pauses halfway down the line, sniffs, turns back, then sniffs again. She gives the red clay a decisive scratch with both forepaws. Her trainer, Kassim Mgaza, snaps a metal clicker twice, and Wanjiro waddles to him for her reward—a mouthful of banana and an affectionate pet (Wines, 2004, p. A1).

Score one for the Gambian giant pouched rat (who, weighing in at two to five pounds, is the size of an overweight gerbil). More precisely, score one for the principles of classical and operant conditioning, which are being harnessed in a process that has the potential to save a substantial number of lives.

Wanjiro is one of a group of pouched rats that are being trained to find mines that are buried below the surface of the earth. Traditional means of locating mines are not terribly effective: No mechanical device can sniff out explosives as well (they only detect metal), and other animals such as dogs have a short attention span and are so heavy that they set off the mines when they do find them. Pouched rats, on the other hand, are persistent in seeking out the odor of explosives once they are trained, and they have a highly sophisticated sense of smell that makes them quite effective. Equally important, they weigh so

A rat maneuvers a test course during training for mine-detection. Training begins at the age of five weeks.

little that they can stand on top of a buried mine and not detonate it (Wines, 2004).

The problem they are addressing is a serious one. In places like Mozambique, where they are being trained and which suffered through a civil war for 17 years, millions of mines are buried and are difficult to locate. The result is that each year thousands of people are killed and maimed by accidentally stepping on a mine.

To learn how to locate mines, trainers first teach pouched rats like Wanjiro to associate the sound of a clicker with food, in a process of classical conditioning. They then place the rats in a cage with a hole that is filled with explosive material. When the rats sniff the hole, the trainers sound the clicker and provide food. Through repeated presentations of food and explosive material, rats learn to associate the smell of explosive with food, and they begin to eagerly seek out the smell of explosives.

From there, it is only a short leap to searching the ground for buried explosive—largely because pouched rats instinctively bury food that they don't immediately eat and later hunt for it using their sense of smell. Before it can dig down to the mine, trainers give the rats food reinforcement of a peanut and banana mixture. In short, sniffing the ground for explosive becomes a reinforced behavior (Cookson, 2005; Corcoran, 2005).

Although it is too early to know how effective in the long-term the use of pouched rats will be, the initial results are promising. In fact, the project is expanding beyond Mozambique to another war-ravaged African country, Sudan. Furthermore, the procedure has the potential to be used in other ways, such as finding buried victims in earthquakes. This is the power of the classical and operant conditioning.

RETHINK

Using the terminology of classical conditioning, what is the unconditioned stimulus, the neutral stimulus, and the conditioned stimulus in the process by which the pouched rats learn to associate the sound of a clicker with food? What ethical issues might be raised in the use of trained pouched rats to identify explosives?

are most relevant to the specific environment in which they live (Barkow, Cosmides, & Tooby, 1992; Terry, 2003; Cosmides & Tooby, 2004).

Furthermore, psychologists taking an evolutionary perspective have suggested that we may be genetically predisposed to be fearful of certain stimuli, such as snakes or even threatening faces. For example, people in experiments learn associations relatively quickly between photos of faces with threatening expressions and neutral stimuli (such as an umbrella). In contrast, they are slower to learn associations between faces that have pleasant expressions and neutral stimuli. Stimuli that pose potential threats, like snakes or people with hostile facial expressions, posed a potential danger to early humans, and there may be an evolved "fear module" in the brain that is sensitized to such threats (Oehman & Mineka, 2003; Schupp et al., 2004; Georgiou et al., 2005).

COMPARING CLASSICAL AND OPERANT CONDITIONING

We've considered classical conditioning and operant conditioning as two completely different processes. And, as summarized in Figure 5, there are a number of key distinctions between the two forms of learning. For example, the key concept in classical conditioning is the association between stimuli, whereas in operant conditioning it is reinforcement. Furthermore, classical conditioning involves an involuntary, natural, innate behavior, but operant conditioning is based on voluntary responses made by an organism.

Concept	Classical Conditioning	Operant Conditioning
Basic principle	Building associations between a conditioned stimulus and conditioned response.	Reinforcement *increases* the frequency of the behavior preceding it; punishment *decreases* the frequency of the behavior preceding it.
Nature of behavior	Based on involuntary, natural, innate behavior. Behavior is elicited by the unconditioned or conditioned stimulus.	Organism voluntarily operates on its environment to produce a desirable result. After behavior occurs, the likelihood of the behavior occurring again is increased or decreased by the behavior's consequences.
Order of events	Before conditioning, an unconditioned stimulus leads to an unconditioned response. After conditioning, a conditioned stimulus leads to a conditioned response.	Reinforcement leads to an increase in behavior; punishment leads to a decrease in behavior.
Example	After a physician gives a child a series of painful injections (an unconditioned stimulus) that produce an emotional reaction (an unconditioned response), the child develops an emotional reaction (a conditioned response) whenever she sees the physician (the conditioned stimulus)	A student who, after studying hard for a test, earns an A (the positive reinforcer), is more likely to study hard in the future. A student who, after going out drinking the night before a test, fails the test (punishment) is less likely to go out drinking the night before the next test.

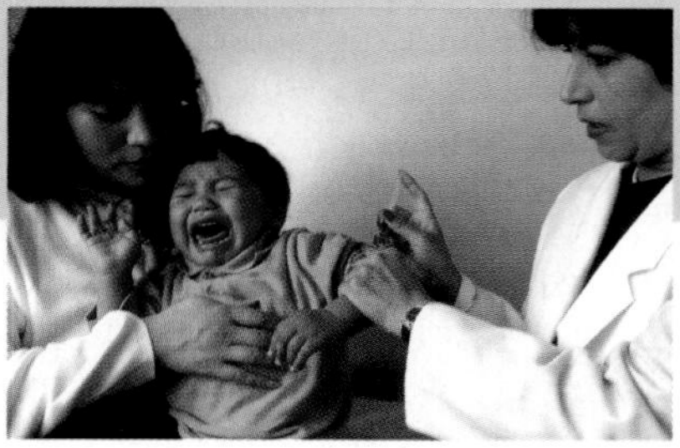

FIGURE 5 Comparing key concepts in classical conditioning and operant conditioning.

Some researchers are asking if, in fact, the two types of learning are so different after all. Learning psychologist John Donahoe and colleagues have suggested that classical and operant conditioning might share some underlying processes. Arguing from an evolutionary viewpoint, they contend that it is unlikely that two completely separate basic processes would evolve. Instead, one process—albeit with considerable complexity in the way it operates—might better explain behavior (Donahoe, 2003; Donahoe & Vegas, 2004).

It's too early to know if Donahoe's point of view will be supported. Still, it is clear that there are a number of processes that operate both in classical and operant conditioning, including extinction, stimulus generalization, and stimulus discrimination. Whether that means the distinctions between classical and operant conditioning will disappear remains to be seen.

BECOMING AN INFORMED CONSUMER
of Psychology

Using Behavior Analysis and Behavior Modification

A couple who had been living together for three years began to fight more and more frequently. The issues of disagreement ranged from the seemingly petty, such as who was going to do the dishes, to the more profound, such as the quality of their love life and whether they found each other interesting. Disturbed about this increasingly unpleasant pattern of interaction, the couple went to a behavior analyst, a psychologist who specialized in behavior-modification techniques. After interviewing each of them alone and then speaking to them together, he asked them to keep a detailed written record of their interactions over the next two weeks—focusing in particular on the events that preceded their arguments.

When they returned two weeks later, he carefully went over the records with them. In doing so, he noticed a pattern that the couple themselves had observed after they had started keeping their records: Each of their arguments had occurred just after one or the other had left a household chore undone. For instance, the woman would go into a fury when she came home from work and found that the man, a student, had left his dirty lunch dishes on the table and had not even started dinner preparations. The man would get angry when he found the woman's clothes draped on the only chair in the bedroom. He insisted it was her responsibility to pick up after herself.

Using the data the couple had collected, the behavior analyst devised a system for the couple to try out. He asked them to list all the chores that could possibly arise and assign each one a point value depending on how long it took to complete. Then he had them divide the chores equally and agree in a written contract to fulfill the ones assigned to them. If either failed to carry out one of the assigned chores, he or she would have to place $1 per point in a fund for the other to spend. They also agreed to a program of verbal praise, promising to reward each other verbally for completing a chore.

Although skeptical about the value of such a program, the couple agreed to try it for a month and to keep careful records of the number of arguments they had during that period. To their surprise, the number declined rapidly, and even the more basic issues in their relationship seemed on the way to being resolved.

This case provides an illustration of **behavior modification,** a formalized technique for promoting the frequency of desirable behaviors and decreasing the incidence of unwanted ones. Using the basic principles of learning theory, behavior-modification techniques have proved to be helpful in a variety of situations. People with severe mental retardation have learned the rudiments of language and, for the first time in their lives, have started dressing and feeding themselves. Behavior modification has

Behavior modification: A formalized technique for promoting the frequency of desirable behaviors and decreasing the incidence of unwanted ones.

also helped people lose weight, give up smoking, and behave more safely (Sulzer-Azaroff & Mayer, 1991; Lamb et al., 2004; Wadden, Crerand, & Brock, 2005).

The techniques used by behavior analysts are as varied as the list of processes that modify behavior. They include reinforcement scheduling, shaping, generalization training, discrimination training, and extinction. Participants in a behavior-change program do, however, typically follow a series of similar basic steps that include the following:

- *Identifying goals and target behaviors.* The first step is to define *desired behavior*. Is it an increase in time spent studying? A decrease in weight? An increase in the use of language? A reduction in the amount of aggression displayed by a child? The goals must be stated in observable terms and lead to specific targets. For instance, a goal might be "to increase study time," whereas the target behavior would be "to study at least two hours per day on weekdays and an hour on Saturdays."
- *Designing a data-recording system and recording preliminary data.* To determine whether behavior has changed, it is necessary to collect data before any changes are made in the situation. This information provides a baseline against which future changes can be measured.
- *Selecting a behavior-change strategy.* The most crucial step is to select an appropriate strategy. Because all the principles of learning can be employed to bring about behavior change, a "package" of treatments is normally used. This might include the systematic use of positive reinforcement for desired behavior (verbal praise or something more tangible, such as food), as well as a program of extinction for undesirable behavior (ignoring a child who throws a tantrum). Selecting the right reinforcers is critical; it may be necessary to experiment a bit to find out what is important to a particular individual. It is best for participants to avoid threats, because they are merely punishing and ultimately not very effective in bringing about long-term changes in behavior.
- *Implementing the program.* The next step is to institute the program. Probably the most important aspect of program implementation is consistency. It is also important to make sure that one is reinforcing the behavior he or she wants to reinforce. For example, suppose a mother wants her daughter to spend more time on her homework, but as soon as the child sits down to study, she asks for a snack. If the mother gets a snack for her, she is likely to be reinforcing her daughter's delaying tactic, not her studying. Instead, the mother might tell her child that she will provide her with a snack after a certain time interval has gone by during which she has studied—thereby using the snack as a reinforcement for studying.
- *Keeping careful records after the program is implemented.* Another crucial task is record keeping. If the target behaviors are not monitored, there is no way of knowing whether the program has actually been successful. Participants are advised not to rely on memory, because memory lapses are all too common.
- *Evaluating and altering the ongoing program.* Finally, the results of the program should be compared with baseline, preimplementation data to determine its effectiveness. If the program has been successful, the procedures employed can be phased out gradually. For instance, if the program called for reinforcing every instance of picking up one's clothes from the bedroom floor, the reinforcement schedule could be modified to a fixed-ratio schedule in which every third instance was reinforced. However, if the program has not been successful in bringing about the desired behavior change, consideration of other approaches might be advisable.

Behavior-change techniques based on these general principles have enjoyed wide success and have proved to be one of the most powerful means of modifying behavior (Greenwood et al., 1992). Clearly, it is possible to employ the basic notions of learning theory to improve our lives.

RECAP/EVALUATE/RETHINK

RECAP

What is the role of reward and punishment in learning?

- Operant conditioning is a form of learning in which a voluntary behavior is strengthened or weakened. According to B. F. Skinner, the major mechanism underlying learning is reinforcement, the process by which a stimulus increases the probability that a preceding behavior will be repeated. (pp. 191–193)
- Primary reinforcers are rewards that are naturally effective without prior experience because they satisfy a biological need. Secondary reinforcers begin to act as if they were primary reinforcers through association with a primary reinforcer. (p. 193)
- Positive reinforcers are stimuli that are added to the environment and lead to an increase in a preceding response. Negative reinforcers are stimuli that remove something unpleasant from the environment, also leading to an increase in the preceding response. (pp. 193–194)
- Punishment decreases the probability that a prior behavior will occur. Positive punishment weakens a response through the application of an unpleasant stimulus, whereas negative punishment weakens a response by the removal of something positive. In contrast to reinforcement, in which the goal is to increase the incidence of behavior, punishment is meant to decrease or suppress behavior. (pp. 194–196)
- Schedules and patterns of reinforcement affect the strength and duration of learning. Generally, partial reinforcement schedules—in which reinforcers are not delivered on every trial—produce stronger and longer-lasting learning than do continuous reinforcement schedules. (pp. 196–197)
- Among the major categories of reinforcement schedules are fixed- and variable-ratio schedules, which are based on the number of responses made, and fixed- and variable-interval schedules, which are based on the time interval that elapses before reinforcement is provided. (pp. 197–199)
- Stimulus control training (similar to stimulus discrimination in classical conditioning) is reinforcement of a behavior in the presence of a specific stimulus but not in its absence. In stimulus generalization, an organism learns a response to one stimulus and then exhibits the same response to slightly different stimuli. (p. 199)
- Shaping is a process for teaching complex behaviors by rewarding closer and closer approximations of the desired final behavior. (pp. 199–200)
- There are biological constraints, or built-in limitations, on the ability of an organism to learn: Certain behaviors will be relatively easy for individuals of a species to learn, whereas other behaviors will be either difficult or impossible for them to learn. (p. 200)

What are some practical methods for bringing about behavior change, both in ourselves and in others?

- Behavior modification is a method for formally using the principles of learning theory to promote the frequency of desired behaviors and to decrease or eliminate unwanted ones. (pp. 203–204)

EVALUATE

1. _____ conditioning describes learning that occurs as a result of reinforcement.
2. Match the type of operant learning with its definition:
   1. An unpleasant stimulus is presented to decrease behavior.
   2. An unpleasant stimulus is removed to increase behavior.
   3. A pleasant stimulus is presented to increase behavior.
   4. A pleasant stimulus is removed to decrease behavior.
   a. Positive reinforcement
   b. Negative reinforcement
   c. Positive punishment
   d. Negative punishment
3. Sandy had had a rough day, and his son's noisemaking was not helping him relax. Not wanting to resort to scolding, Sandy told his son in a serious manner that he was very tired and would like the boy to play quietly for an hour. This approach worked. For Sandy, the change in his son's behavior was
   a. Positively reinforcing.
   b. Negatively reinforcing.
4. In a _____ reinforcement schedule, behavior is reinforced some of the time, whereas in a _____ reinforcement schedule, behavior is reinforced all the time.
5. Match the type of reinforcement schedule with its definition.
   1. Reinforcement occurs after a set time period.
   2. Reinforcement occurs after a set number of responses.
   3. Reinforcement occurs after a varying time period.
   4. Reinforcement occurs after a varying number of responses.
   a. Fixed-ratio
   b. Variable-interval
   c. Fixed-interval
   d. Variable-ratio
6. Fixed reinforcement schedules produce greater resistance to extinction than do variable reinforcement schedules. True or false?

RETHINK

1. Using the scientific literature as a guide, what would you tell parents who wish to know if the routine use of physical punishment is a necessary and acceptable form of child rearing?
2. *From the perspective of an educator:* How would you utilize your knowledge of operant conditioning in the classroom to set up a program to increase the likelihood children will complete their homework more frequently?

Answers to Evaluate Questions

1. operant; 2. 1-c, 2-b, 3-a, 4-d; 4. partial (or intermittent), continuous; 5. 1-c, 2-a, 3-b, 4-d; 6. false; variable ratios are more resistant to extinction

KEY TERMS

operant conditioning p. 191
reinforcement p. 193
reinforcer p. 193
positive reinforcer p. 194
negative reinforcer p. 194

punishment p. 194
schedules of reinforcement p. 196
continuous reinforcement schedule p. 196

partial (or intermittent) reinforcement schedule p. 196
fixed-ratio schedule p. 197
variable-ratio schedule p. 197

fixed-interval schedule p. 198
variable-interval schedule p. 198
shaping p. 200
behavior modification p. 203

Cognitive Approaches to Learning

Consider what happens when people learn to drive a car. They don't just get behind the wheel and stumble around until they randomly put the key into the ignition, and later, after many false starts, accidentally manage to get the car to move forward, thereby receiving positive reinforcement. Instead, they already know the basic elements of driving from prior experience as passengers, when they more than likely noticed how the key was inserted into the ignition, the car was put in drive, and the gas pedal was pressed to make the car go forward.

Clearly, not all learning is due to operant and classical conditioning. In fact, activities like learning to drive a car imply that some kinds of learning must involve higher-order processes in which people's thoughts and memories and the way they process information account for their responses. Such situations argue against regarding learning as the unthinking, mechanical, and automatic acquisition of associations between stimuli and responses, as in classical conditioning, or the presentation of reinforcement, as in operant conditioning.

Some psychologists view learning in terms of the thought processes, or cognitions, that underlie it—an approach known as **cognitive learning theory.** Although psychologists working from the cognitive learning perspective do not deny the importance of classical and operant conditioning, they have developed approaches that focus on the unseen mental processes that occur during learning, rather than concentrating solely on external stimuli, responses, and reinforcements.

In its most basic formulation, cognitive learning theory suggests that it is not enough to say that people make responses because there is an assumed link between a stimulus and a response as a result of a past history of reinforcement for a response. Instead, according to this point of view, people—and even animals—develop an *expectation* that they will receive a reinforcer after making a response. Two types of learning in which no obvious prior reinforcement is present are latent learning and observational learning.

Latent Learning

Evidence for the importance of cognitive processes comes from a series of animal experiments that revealed a type of cognitive learning called latent learning. In **latent learning,** a new behavior is learned but not demonstrated until some incentive is provided for displaying it (Tolman & Honzik, 1930). In short, latent learning occurs without reinforcement.

In the studies demonstrating latent learning, psychologists examined the behavior of rats in a maze such as the one shown in Figure 1a. In one experiment, a group of rats was allowed to wander around the maze once a day for seventeen days without ever receiving a reward. Understandably, those rats made many errors and spent a relatively long time reaching the end of the maze. A second group, however, was always given food at the end of the maze. Not surprisingly, those rats learned to run quickly and directly to the food box, making few errors.

Key Concept

What is the role of cognition and thought in learning?

Cognitive learning theory: An approach to the study of learning that focuses on the thought processes that underlie learning.

Latent learning: Learning in which a new behavior is acquired but is not demonstrated until some incentive is provided for displaying it.

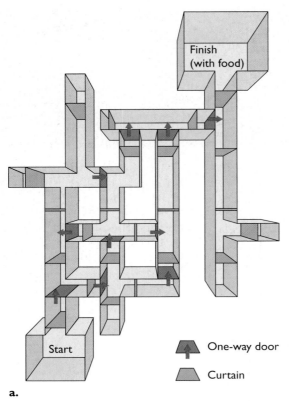

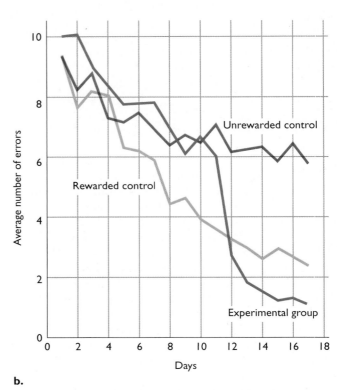

a.

b.

FIGURE I (a) In an attempt to demonstrate latent learning, rats were allowed to roam through a maze of this sort once a day for seventeen days. (b) The rats that were never rewarded (the non-rewarded control condition) consistently made the most errors, whereas those which received food at the finish every day (the rewarded control condition) consistently made far fewer errors. But the results also showed latent learning: Rats that were initially unrewarded but began to be rewarded only after the tenth day (the experimental group) showed an immediate reduction in errors and soon became similar in error rate to the rats that had been rewarded consistently. According to cognitive learning theorists, the reduction in errors indicates that the rats had developed a cognitive map—a mental representation—of the maze. Can you think of other examples of latent learning?

A third group of rats started out in the same situation as the unrewarded rats, but only for the first ten days. On the eleventh day, a critical experimental manipulation was introduced: From that point on, the rats in this group were given food for completing the maze. The results of this manipulation were dramatic, as you can see from the graph in Figure 1b. The previously unrewarded rats, which had earlier seemed to wander about aimlessly, showed such reductions in running time and declines in error rates that their performance almost immediately matched that of the group that had received rewards from the start.

To cognitive theorists, it seemed clear that the unrewarded rats had learned the layout of the maze early in their explorations; they just never displayed their latent learning until the reinforcement was offered. Instead, those rats seemed to develop a *cognitive map* of the maze—a mental representation of spatial locations and directions.

People, too, develop cognitive maps of their surroundings. For example, latent learning may permit you to know the location of a kitchenware store at a local mall you've frequently visited, even though you've never entered the store and don't even like to cook.

The possibility that we develop our cognitive maps through latent learning presents something of a problem for strict operant conditioning theorists. If we consider the results of the maze-learning experiment, for instance, it is unclear what reinforcement permitted the rats that initially

received no reward to learn the layout of the maze, because there was no obvious reinforcer present. Instead, the results support a cognitive view of learning, in which changes occurred in unobservable mental processes (Beatty, 2002; Voicu & Schmajuk, 2002; Frensch & Rünger, 2003).

Observational Learning: Learning Through Imitation

Let's return for a moment to the case of a person learning to drive. How can we account for instances in which an individual with no direct experience in carrying out a particular behavior learns the behavior and then performs it? To answer this question, psychologists have focused on another aspect of cognitive learning: observational learning.

According to psychologist Albert Bandura and colleagues, a major part of human learning consists of **observational learning,** which is learning by watching the behavior of another person, or *model*. Because of its reliance on observation of others—a social phenomenon—the perspective taken by Bandura is often referred to as a *social cognitive* approach to learning (Bandura, 1986, 1999, 2004).

Bandura dramatically demonstrated the ability of models to stimulate learning in a classic experiment. In the study, young children saw a film of an adult wildly hitting a five-foot-tall inflatable punching toy called a Bobo doll (Bandura, Ross, & Ross, 1963a, 1963b). Later the children were given the opportunity to play with the Bobo doll themselves, and, sure enough, most displayed the same kind of behavior, in some cases mimicking the aggressive behavior almost identically. (See more about how people learn aggressive behavior through the PsychInteractive exercise on observational learning.)

Not only negative behaviors are acquired through observational learning. In one experiment, for example, children who were afraid of dogs were exposed to a model—dubbed the Fearless Peer—playing with a dog (Bandura, Grusec, & Menlove, 1967). After exposure, observers were considerably more likely to approach a strange dog than were children who had not viewed the Fearless Peer.

According to Bandura, observational learning takes place in four steps: (1) paying attention and perceiving the most critical features of another person's behavior, (2) remembering the behavior, (3) reproducing the action, and (4) being motivated to learn and carry out the behavior in the future. Instead of learning occurring through trial and error, then, with successes being reinforced and failures being punished, many important skills are learned through observational processes (Bandura, 1986).

Observational learning is particularly important in acquiring skills in which the operant conditioning technique of shaping is inappropriate. Piloting an airplane and performing brain surgery, for example, are behaviors that could hardly be learned by using trial-and-error methods without grave cost—literally—to those involved in the learning process.

Not all behavior that we witness is learned or carried out, of course. One crucial factor that determines whether we later imitate a model is whether the model is rewarded for his or her behavior. If we observe a friend being rewarded for putting more time into her studies by receiving higher grades, we are more likely to imitate her behavior than we would be if her behavior resulted only in being stressed and tired. Models who are rewarded for behaving in a particular way are more apt to be mimicked than are models who receive punishment. Interestingly, though, observing the punishment of a model does not necessarily stop observers from learning the behavior. Observers can still describe the model's behavior—they are just less apt to perform it (Bandura, 1977, 1986, 1994).

Observational learning is central to a number of important issues relating to the extent to which people learn simply by watching the behavior of others. For instance, the degree to which observation of media aggression produces subsequent aggression on the part of viewers is a crucial—and controversial—question, as we discuss next.

Albert Bandura examined the principles of observational learning.

Observational learning: Learning by observing the behavior of another person, or model.

www.mhhe.com/feldmanup8
PsychInteractive Online

Observational Learning

This boy is displaying observational learning based on prior observation of his father. How does observational learning contribute to defining gender roles?

Violence in Television and Video Games: Does the Media's Message Matter?

In an episode of *The Sopranos* television series, fictional mobster Tony Soprano murdered one of his associates. To make identification of the victim's body difficult, Soprano and one of his henchmen dismembered the body and dumped the body parts.

A few months later, two real-life half brothers in Riverside, California, strangled their mother and then cut her head and hands from her body. Victor Bautista, 20, and Matthew Montejo, 15, who were caught by police after a security guard noticed that the bundle they were attempting to throw in a dumpster had a foot sticking out of it, told police that the plan to dismember their mother was inspired by *The Sopranos* episode (Martelle, Hanley, & Yoshino, 2003).

Like other "media copycat" killings, the brothers' cold-blooded brutality raises a critical issue: Does observing violent and antisocial acts in the media lead viewers to behave in similar ways? Because research on modeling shows that people frequently learn and imitate the aggression that they observe, this question is among the most important being addressed by psychologists.

Certainly, the amount of violence in the mass media is enormous. By the time of elementary school graduation, the average child in the United States will have viewed more than 8,000 murders and more than 800,000 violent acts on network television (Huston et al., 1992; Mifflin, 1998).

Most experts agree that watching high levels of media violence makes viewers more susceptible to acting aggressively, and recent research supports this claim. For example, one survey of serious and violent young male offenders incarcerated in Florida showed that one-fourth of them had attempted to commit a media-inspired copycat crime (Surette, 2002). A significant proportion of those teenage offenders noted that they paid close attention to the media.

Violent video games have also been linked with actual aggression. In one of a series of studies by psychologist Craig Anderson and his colleagues, for example, college students who frequently played violent video games, such as *Postal* or *Doom*, were more likely to have been involved in delinquent behavior and aggression. Frequent players also had lower academic achievement (Anderson & Dill, 2000; Bartholow & Anderson, 2001; Anderson et al., 2004).

Several aspects of media violence may contribute to real-life aggressive behavior (Bushman & Anderson, 2001; Johnson et al., 2002). For one thing, experiencing violent media content seems to lower inhibitions against carrying out aggression—watching television portrayals of violence or using violence to win a video game makes aggression seem a legitimate response to particular situations. Exposure to media violence also may distort our understanding of the meaning of others' behavior, predisposing us to view even nonaggressive acts by others as aggressive. Finally, a continuous diet of aggression may leave us desensitized to violence, and what previously would have repelled us now produces little emotional response. Our sense of the pain and suffering brought about by aggression may be diminished (Anderson & Bushman, 2002; Anderson, Carnagey, & Eubanks, 2003; Huesmann et al., 2003; Funk, 2005).

What about real-life exposure to *actual* violence? Does it also lead to increases in aggression? The answer is yes. Exposure to actual firearm violence (being shot or being shot at) doubles the probability that an adolescent will commit serious violence over the next two years. Whether the violence is real or fictionalized, then, observing violent behavior leads to increases in aggressive behavior (Bingenheimer, Brennan, & Earls, 2005).

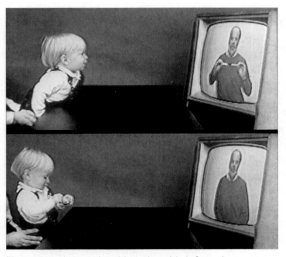

Illustrating observational learning, this infant observes an adult on the television and then is able to imitate his behavior. Learning has obviously occurred through the mere observation of the television model.

When a member of the Chilcotin Indian tribe teaches her daughter to prepare salmon, at first she only allows the daughter to observe the entire process. A little later, she permits her child to try out some basic parts of the task. Her response to questions is noteworthy. For example, when the daughter asks about how to do "the backbone part," the mother's response is to repeat the entire process with another fish. The reason? The mother feels that one cannot learn the individual parts of the task apart from the context of preparing the whole fish (Tharp, 1989).

Exploring DIVERSITY

Does Culture Influence How We Learn?

It should not be surprising that children raised in the Chilcotin tradition, which stresses instruction that starts by communicating the entire task, may have difficulty with traditional Western schooling. In the approach to teaching most characteristic of Western culture, tasks are broken down into their component parts. Only after each small step is learned is it thought possible to master the complete task.

Do the differences in teaching approaches between cultures affect how people learn? Some psychologists, taking a cognitive perspective on learning, suggest that people develop particular *learning styles,* characteristic ways of approaching material, based on their cultural background and unique pattern of abilities (Anderson & Adams, 1992; Chi-Ching & Noi, 1994; Furnham, 1995; Sternberg & Grigorenko, 1997; Barmeyer, 2004).

Learning styles differ along several dimensions. For example, one central dimension is analytical versus relational approaches to learning (Anderson, 1988; Tharp, 1989). As illustrated in Figure 2, people with a *relational learning style* master material best through exposure to a full unit or phenomenon. Parts of the unit are comprehended only when their relationship to the whole is understood.

In contrast, people with an *analytical learning style* do best when they can carry out an initial analysis of the principles and components underlying a phenomenon or situation. By developing an understanding of the fundamental principles and components, they are best able to understand the full picture.

Although research findings are mixed, some evidence suggests that particular minority groups in Western societies display characteristic learning styles. For instance, James Anderson and Maurianne Adams (1992) argue that Caucasian females

Relational Style	Analytical Style
1. Perceive information as part of total picture	1. Able to dis-embed information from total picture (focus on detail)
2. Exhibit improvisational and intuitive thinking	2. Exhibit sequential and structured thinking
3. More easily learn materials that have a human, social content and are characterized by experimental/cultural relevance	3. More easily learn materials that are inanimate and impersonal
4. Have a good memory for verbally presented ideas and information, especially if relevant	4. Have a good memory for abstract ideas and irrelevant information
5. Are more task-oriented concerning nonacademic areas	5. Are more task-oriented concerning academics
6. Are influenced by authority figures' expression of confidence or doubt in students' ability	6. Are not greatly affected by the opinions of others
7. Prefer to withdraw from unstimulating task performance	7. Show ability to persist at unstimulating tasks
8. Style conflicts with the traditional school environment	8. Style matches most school environments

FIGURE 2 A comparison of analytical versus relational approaches to learning offers one example of how learning styles differ along several dimensions.

and African American, Native American, and Hispanic American males and females are more apt to use a relational style of learning than Caucasian and Asian American males, who are more likely to employ an analytical style.

The conclusion that members of particular ethnic and gender groups have similar learning styles is controversial. Because there is so much diversity within each particular racial and ethnic group, critics argue that generalizations about learning styles cannot be used to predict the style of any single individual, regardless of group membership. Many psychologists contend that a discussion of group learning styles is a misguided undertaking. (This argument echoes an ongoing controversy about the usefulness of intelligence tests.) Instead, they suggest that it is more fruitful to concentrate on determining each individual's particular learning style and pattern of academic and social strengths.

Still, it is clear that values about learning, which are communicated through a person's family and cultural background, have an impact on how successful students are in school. One theory suggests that members of minority groups who were voluntary immigrants are more apt to be successful in school than those who are were brought into a majority culture against their will. For example, Korean children in the United States—the sons and daughters of voluntary immigrants—perform quite well, as a group, in school. In contrast, Korean children in Japan—often the sons and daughters of people who were forced to immigrate during World War II, essentially as forced laborers—tend to do poorly in school. Presumably, children in the forced immigration group are less motivated to succeed than those in the voluntary immigration group (Ogbu, 1992; Gallagher, 1994).

RECAP/EVALUATE/RETHINK

RECAP

What is the role of cognition and thought in learning?

- Cognitive approaches to learning consider learning in terms of thought processes, or cognition. Phenomena such as latent learning—in which a new behavior is learned but not performed until some incentive is provided for its performance—and the apparent development of cognitive maps support cognitive approaches. pp. 207–208)
- Learning also occurs from observing the behavior of others. The major factor that determines whether an observed behavior will actually be performed is the nature of the reinforcement or punishment a model receives. (p. 209)
- Observation of violence is linked to a greater likelihood of subsequently acting aggressively. (p. 210)
- Learning styles are characteristic ways of approaching learning, based on a person's cultural background and unique pattern of abilities. Whether an individual has an analytical or a relational style of learning, for example, may reflect family background or culture. (p. 211)

EVALUATE

1. Cognitive learning theorists are concerned only with overt behavior, not with its internal causes. True or false?

2. In cognitive learning theory, it is assumed that people develop a(n) _____ about receiving a reinforcer when they behave a certain way.
3. In _____ learning, a new behavior is learned but is not shown until appropriate reinforcement is presented.
4. Bandura's theory of _____ learning states that people learn through watching a(n) _____ —another person displaying the behavior of interest.

RETHINK

1. The relational style of learning sometimes conflicts with the traditional school environment. Could a school be created that takes advantage of the characteristics of the relational style? How? Are there types of learning for which the analytical style is clearly superior?
2. *From the perspective of a social worker:* What advice would you give to families about children's exposure to violent media and video games?

Answers to Evaluate Questions

1. false; cognitive learning theorists are primarily concerned with mental processes; 2. expectation; 3. latent; 4. observational, model

KEY TERMS

cognitive learning theory p. 207   latent learning p. 207   observational learning p. 209

Looking Back

Psychology on the Web

1. B. F. Skinner had an impact on society and on thought that is only hinted at in our discussion of learning. Find additional information on the Web about Skinner's life and influence. See what you can find out about his ideas for an ideal, utopian society based on the principles of conditioning and behaviorism. Write a summary of your findings.

2. Select a topic discussed in this set of modules that is of interest to you (reinforcement versus punishment, teaching complex behaviors by shaping, violence in video games, relational versus analytical learning styles, behavior modification, etc.). Find at least two sources of information on the Web about your topic and summarize the results of your quest. It may be most helpful to find two different approaches to your topic and compare them.

3. After completing the PsychInteractive exercise on operant conditioning, search the Web for three examples of animal training procedures that employ operant conditioning. Summarize the training techniques, identifying each use of operant conditioning.

Epilogue

Here we have discussed several kinds of learning, ranging from classical conditioning, which depends on the existence of natural stimulus–response pairings, to operant conditioning, in which reinforcement is used to increase desired behavior. These approaches to learning focus on outward, behavioral learning processes. Cognitive approaches to learning focus on mental processes that enable learning.

We have also noted that learning is affected by culture and individual differences, with individual learning styles potentially affecting the ways in which people learn most effectively. And we saw some ways in which our learning about learning can be put to practical use, through such means as behavior-modification programs designed to decrease negative behaviors and increase positive ones.

Return to the prologue of this chapter and consider the following questions in relation to Minnie, the monkey who helps quadraplegic Craig Cook:

1. Is Minnie's learning primarily an example of classical conditioning, operant conditioning, or cognitive learning? Why?

2. Do you think punishment would be an effective teaching strategy for Minnie? Why?

3. How might different schedules of reinforcement be used to train Minnie? Which schedule would likely have been most effective?

4. In what way would shaping have been used to teach Minnie some of her more complex behaviors, such as maneuvering Cook's foot into his wheelchair?

MASTERING the distinction between reinforcement and punishment

The *distinction between reinforcement and punishment is not always clear,* but the two processes have very different consequences for behavior. *Reinforcement* increases *a behavior, while punishment decreases it.* Use this visual guide to better grasp the difference, and then answer the questions below to test your understanding of the concepts.

I Alex's sloppiness bothers his roommate, Eddy, who says he can't study in a messy room. How might Eddy use reinforcement and punishment to change Alex's untidy behavior?

2 Using *positive reinforcement* to encourage Alex to keep their dorm room clean, Eddy could reward Alex after he cleans up his side of the room by helping him with calculus, something that has value to Alex. Eddy adds the tutoring to increase Alex's neat behavior.

3 Another approach would involve *negative reinforcement,* removing something Alex finds unpleasant as a reward for neat behavior. For example, Eddy could turn off his stereo when Alex is in the room so that he wouldn't have to listen to Eddy's hip-hop music, music Alex dislikes. Eddy *removes* (takes away) the hip-hop music to *increase* Alex's neat behavior.

EVALUATE

I In this example, positive reinforcement is represented by _____ _____ and negative reinforcement is represented by _____.
- **a** tutoring in calculus; refusing to lend Eddy's MP3 player to Alex
- **b** playing loud music; turning off the stereo
- **c** tutoring in calculus; turning off the stereo
- **d** playing loud music; refusing to lend Eddy's MP3 player to Alex

2 In this example, the negative punishment is _____ and the positive punishment is _____.
- **a** playing loud music; turning off the stereo
- **b** playing loud music; refusing to lend Eddy's MP3 player to Alex
- **c** refusing to lend Eddy's MP3 player to Alex; playing loud music
- **d** refusing to lend Eddy's MP3 player to Alex; tutoring in calculus

4 Of course, Eddy could discourage Alex's undesirable behavior by using *positive punishment.* In this case, he could play his hip-hop music loudly when Alex leaves the room in a messy condition. That is, Eddy *adds* the loud music to *decrease* Alex's messy behavior.

5 Or Eddy could resort to *negative punishment* and take away something Alex values when his side of the room is messy. Refusing to lend Alex his MP3 player until he cleans up the room is an example of negative punishment. Eddy *removes* (takes away) his MP3 player to *decrease* Alex's messy behavior.

---

3 Reinforcement leads to an increase in a previous response, while punishment leads to a decrease in the previous response. True or false?

RETHINK

How could the principles of reinforcement and punishment be used to explain how Alex learned to be such a sloppy person in the first place?

Answers to Evaluate questions: 1. c; 2. c; 3. True

CHAPTER 7
Memory

Key Concepts for Chapter 7

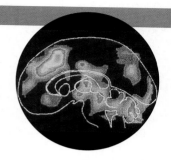

Prologue   **Who Am I? And Who Are You?**

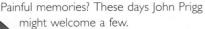

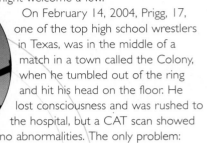

Painful memories? These days John Prigg might welcome a few.

On February 14, 2004, Prigg, 17, one of the top high school wrestlers in Texas, was in the middle of a match in a town called the Colony, when he tumbled out of the ring and hit his head on the floor. He lost consciousness and was rushed to the hospital, but a CAT scan showed no abnormalities. The only problem:

When he awoke, his memory was gone. "It was like he was in a trance," says his father, John.

Since then John has found himself marooned in a strange netherworld. He can speak and write, but he can't understand what he is reading. A former football player, he now had no idea what a football was—but when handed a ball he was able to throw a perfect spiral. He didn't know what the word *shower* meant. "So I took him in there," says his mother, Donna, who along with her husband runs a firewood business in Midlothian, Texas, near Dallas, "and said, 'This is the bar of soap; this is how you use it'" (*People Weekly*, 2004, p. 136).

Looking **Ahead**

For John Prigg, who has been diagnosed with a rare form of amnesia, the road to recovery has been a slow one. But he is making progress, and the outlook for a full recovery is good.

John's story raises several questions regarding the nature of memory loss: What was the nature of the physical trauma that devastated John's memories? Why couldn't he identify a familiar object from his past like the football, but know how to use it? Will his lost memories ever return?

Stories like John Priggs's illustrate not only the important role memory plays in our lives, but also its fragility. Memory allows us to retrieve a vast amount of information. We are able to remember

the name of a friend we haven't talked with for years and recall the details of a picture that hung in our bedroom as a child. At the same time, though, memory failures are common. We forget where we left the keys to the car and fail to answer an exam question about material we studied only a few hours earlier. Why?

We turn now to the nature of memory, considering the ways in which information is stored and retrieved. We examine the problems of retrieving information from memory, the accuracy of memories, and the reasons information is sometimes forgotten. We also consider the biological foundations of memory and discuss some practical means of increasing memory capacity.

The Foundations of Memory

You are playing a game of Trivial Pursuit, and winning the game comes down to one question: On what body of water is Bombay located? As you rack your brain for the answer, several fundamental processes relating to memory come into play. You may never, for instance, have been exposed to information regarding Bombay's location. Or if you have been exposed to it, it may simply not have registered in a meaningful way. In other words, the information might not have been recorded properly in your memory. The initial process of recording information in a form usable to memory, a process called *encoding*, is the first stage in remembering something.

Even if you had been exposed to the information and originally knew the name of the body of water, you may still be unable to recall it during the game because of a failure to retain it. Memory specialists speak of *storage*, the maintenance of material saved in memory. If the material is not stored adequately, it cannot be recalled later.

Memory also depends on one last process—*retrieval:* Material in memory storage has to be located and brought into awareness to be useful. Your failure to recall Bombay's location, then, may rest on your inability to retrieve information that you learned earlier.

In sum, psychologists consider **memory** to be the process by which we encode, store, and retrieve information (see Figure 1). Each of the three parts of this definition—encoding, storage, and retrieval—represents a different process. You can think of these processes as being analogous to a computer's keyboard (encoding), hard drive (storage), and software that accesses the information for display on the screen (retrieval). Only if all three processes have operated will you experience success and be able to recall the body of water on which Bombay is located: the Arabian Sea.

Recognizing that memory involves encoding, storage, and retrieval gives us a start in understanding the concept. But how does memory actually function? How do we explain what information is initially encoded, what gets stored, and how it is retrieved?

According to the *three-system approach to memory* that dominated memory research for several decades, there are different memory storage systems or stages through which information must travel if it is to be remembered (Atkinson & Shiffrin, 1968, 1971). Historically, the approach has been extremely influential in the development of our understanding of memory, and—although new theories have augmented it—it still provides a useful framework for understanding how information is recalled.

Key Concepts

What is memory?

Are there different kinds of memory?

What are the biological bases of memory?

Memory: The process by which we encode, store, and retrieve information.

Encoding
(Initial recording
of information)

Storage
(Information saved
for future use)

Retrieval
(Recovery of
stored information)

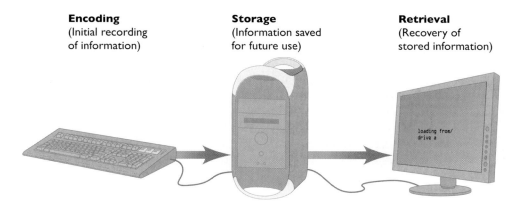

FIGURE 1 Memory is built on three basic processes—encoding, storage, and retrieval—that are analogous to a computer's keyboard, hard drive, and software that accesses the information for display on the screen. The analogy is not perfect, however, because human memory is less precise than a computer. How might you modify the analogy to make it more accurate?

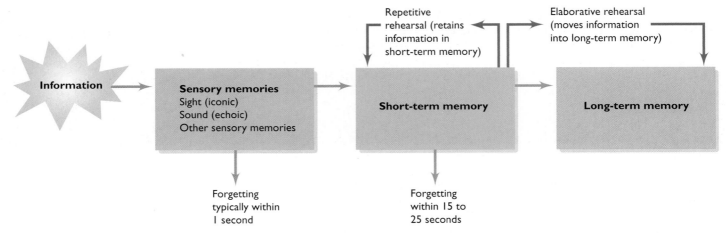

FIGURE 2 In this three-stage model of memory, information initially recorded by the person's sensory system enters sensory memory, which momentarily holds the information. The information then moves to short-term memory, which stores it for fifteen to twenty-five seconds. Finally, the information can move into long-term memory, which is relatively permanent. Whether the information moves from short-term to long-term memory depends on the kind and amount of rehearsal of the material that is carried out. (Source: Atkinson & Shifrin, 1968.)

Sensory memory: The initial, momentary storage of information, lasting only an instant.

Short-term memory: Memory that holds information for fifteen to twenty-five seconds.

Long-term memory: Memory that stores information on a relatively permanent basis, although it may be difficult to retrieve.

The three-system memory theory proposes the existence of the three separate memory stores shown in Figure 2. **Sensory memory** refers to the initial, momentary storage of information that lasts only an instant. Here an exact replica of the stimulus recorded by a person's sensory system is stored very briefly. In a second stage, **short-term memory** holds information for fifteen to twenty-five seconds and stores it according to its meaning rather than as mere sensory stimulation. The third type of storage system is **long-term memory.** Information is stored in long-term memory on a relatively permanent basis, although it may be difficult to retrieve.

Although we'll be discussing the three types of memory as separate memory stores, keep in mind that these are not mini-warehouses located in specific areas of the brain. Instead, they represent three different types of memory systems with different characteristics.

Sensory Memory

A momentary flash of lightning, the sound of a twig snapping, and the sting of a pinprick all represent stimulation of exceedingly brief duration, but they may nonetheless provide important information that can require a response. Such stimuli are initially— and fleetingly—stored in sensory memory, the first repository of the information the world presents to us. Actually, there are several types of sensory memories, each related to a different source of sensory information. For instance, *iconic memory* reflects information from the visual system. *Echoic memory* stores auditory information coming from the ears. In addition, there are corresponding memories for each of the other senses.

Sensory memory can store information for only a very short time. If information does not pass into short-term memory, it is lost for good. For instance, iconic memory seems to last less than a second, and echoic memory typically fades within two or three seconds. However, despite the brief duration of sensory memory, its precision is high: Sensory memory can store an almost exact replica of each stimulus to which it is exposed (Darwin, Turvey, & Crowder, 1972; Long & Beaton, 1982; Sams et al., 1993).

Psychologist George Sperling (1960) demonstrated the existence of sensory memory in a series of clever and now-classic studies. He briefly exposed people to a series of twelve letters arranged in the following pattern:

A momentary flash of lightning leaves a sensory visual memory, a fleeting but exact replica of the stimulus that fades rapidly.

```
F    T    Y    C
K    D    N    L
Y    W    B    M
```

When exposed to this pattern of letters for just one-twentieth of a second, most people could recall only four or five of the letters accurately. Although they knew that they had seen more, the memory of those letters had faded by the time they reported the first few letters. It was possible, then, that the information had initially been accurately stored in sensory memory, but during the time it took to verbalize the first four or five letters the memory of the other letters faded.

To test that possibility, Sperling conducted an experiment in which a high, medium, or low tone sounded just after a person had been exposed to the full pattern of letters. People were told to report the letters in the highest line if a high tone was sounded, the middle line if the medium tone occurred, or the lowest line at the sound of the low tone. Because the tone occurred after the exposure, people had to rely on their memories to report the correct row.

The results of the study clearly showed that people had been storing the complete pattern in memory. They accurately recalled the letters in the line that had been indicated by the tone regardless of whether it was the top, middle, or bottom line. Obviously, *all* the lines they had seen had been stored in sensory memory. Despite its rapid loss, then, the information in sensory memory was an accurate representation of what people had seen.

By gradually lengthening the time between the presentation of the visual pattern and the tone, Sperling was able to determine with some accuracy the length of time that information was stored in sensory memory. The ability to recall a particular row of the pattern when a tone was sounded declined progressively as the period between the visual exposure and the tone increased. This decline continued until the period reached about one second in duration, at which point the row could not be recalled accurately at all. Sperling concluded that the entire visual image was stored in sensory memory for less than a second. Go to the PsychInteractive exercise on sensory memory to convince yourself of Sperling's results.

In sum, sensory memory operates as a kind of snapshot that stores information—which may be of a visual, auditory, or other sensory nature—for a brief moment in time. But it is as if each snapshot, immediately after being taken, is destroyed and replaced with a new one. Unless the information in the snapshot is transferred to some other type of memory, it is lost.

www.mhhe.com/feldmanup8
PsychInteractive Online

Sensory Memory

Short-Term Memory

Because the information that is stored briefly in sensory memory consists of representations of raw sensory stimuli, it is not meaningful to us. If we are to make sense of it and possibly retain it, the information must be transferred to the next stage of memory: short-term memory. Short-term memory is the memory store in which information first has meaning, although the maximum length of retention there is relatively short.

The specific process by which sensory memories are transformed into short-term memories is not clear. Some theorists suggest that the information is first translated into graphical representations or images, and others hypothesize that the transfer occurs when the sensory stimuli are changed to words (Baddeley & Wilson, 1985). What is clear, however, is that unlike sensory memory, which holds a relatively full and detailed—if short-lived—representation of the world, short-term memory has incomplete representational capabilities.

In fact, the specific amount of information that can be held in short-term memory has been identified as seven items, or "chunks," of information, with variations up to plus or minus two chunks. A **chunk** is a meaningful grouping of stimuli that can be stored as a unit in short-term memory. According to George Miller (1956), a chunk can be individual letters or numbers, permitting us to hold a seven-digit phone number (like 226-4610) in short-term memory.

But a chunk also may consist of larger categories, such as words or other meaningful units. For example, consider the following list of twenty-one letters:

P B S F O X C N N A B C C B S M T V N B C

Because the list exceeds seven chunks, it is difficult to recall the letters after one exposure. But suppose they were presented as follows:

PBS FOX CNN ABC CBS MTV NBC

Chunk: A meaningful grouping of stimuli that can be stored as a unit in short-term memory.

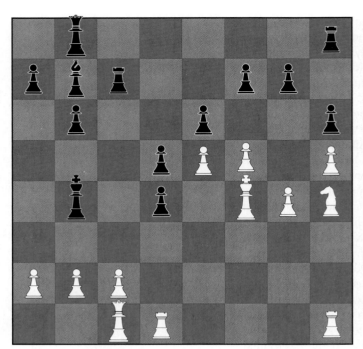

FIGURE 3 Examine the chessboard containing the chess pieces for about five seconds, and then, after covering up the board, try to draw the position of the pieces on the blank chessboard. (You could also use a chessboard of your own and place the pieces in the same positions.) Unless you are an experienced chess player, you are likely to have great difficulty carrying out such a task. Yet chess masters—the kind who win tournaments—do this quite well (deGroot, 1966). They are able to reproduce correctly 90 percent of the pieces on the board. In comparison, inexperienced chess players are typically able to reproduce only 40 percent of the board properly. The chess masters do not have superior memories in other respects; they generally test normally on other measures of memory. What they can do better than others is see the board in terms of chunks or meaningful units and reproduce the position of the chess pieces by using those units.

In this case, even though there are still twenty-one letters, you'd be able to store them in short-term memory, since they represent only seven chunks.

Chunks can vary in size from single letters or numbers to categories that are far more complicated. The specific nature of what constitutes a chunk varies according to one's past experience. You can see this for yourself by trying an experiment that was first carried out as a comparison between expert and inexperienced chess players and is illustrated in Figure 3 (deGroot, 1966; Huffman, Matthews, & Gagne, 2001; Saariluoma et al., 2004).

Although it is possible to remember seven or so relatively complicated sets of information entering short-term memory, the information cannot be held there very long. Just how brief is short-term memory? If you've ever looked up a telephone number in a phone directory, repeated the number to yourself, put away the directory, and then forgotten the number after you've tapped the first three numbers into your phone, you know that information does not remain in short-term memory very long. Most psychologists believe that information in short-term memory is lost after fifteen to twenty-five seconds—unless it is transferred to long-term memory.

REHEARSAL

Rehearsal: The repetition of information that has entered short-term memory.

The transfer of material from short- to long-term memory proceeds largely on the basis of **rehearsal,** the repetition of information that has entered short-term memory. Rehearsal accomplishes two things. First, as long as the information is repeated, it is maintained in short-term memory. More important, however, rehearsal allows us to transfer the information into long-term memory, as you can see for yourself in the PsychInteractive exercise on short term memory.

Whether the transfer is made from short- to long-term memory seems to depend largely on the kind of rehearsal that is carried out. If the information is simply repeated over and over again—as we might do with a telephone number while we rush from the phone book to the phone—it is kept current in short-term memory, but it will not necessarily be placed in long-term memory. Instead, as soon as we stop punching in the phone numbers, the number is likely to be replaced by other information and will be completely forgotten.

In contrast, if the information in short-term memory is rehearsed using a process called elaborative rehearsal, it is much more likely to be transferred into long-term memory (Craik & Lockhart, 1972). *Elaborative rehearsal* occurs when the information is considered and organized in some fashion. The organization might include expanding the information to make it fit into a logical framework, linking it to another memory, turning it into an image, or transforming it in some other way. For example, a list of vegetables to be purchased at a store could be woven together in memory as items being used to prepare an elaborate salad, could be linked to the items bought on an earlier shopping trip, or could be thought of in terms of the image of a farm with rows of each item.

By using organizational strategies such as these—called *mnemonics*—we can vastly improve our retention of information. Mnemonics (pronounced "neh MON ix") are formal techniques for organizing information in a way that makes it more likely to be remembered. For instance, when a beginning musician learns that the spaces on the music staff spell the word *FACE,* or when we learn the rhyme "Thirty days hath September, April, June, and November . . . ," we are using mnemonics (Goldstein et al., 1996; Schoen, 1996; Bellezza, 2000; Scruggs & Mastropieri, 2000; Carney & Levin, 2003).

WORKING MEMORY

Rather than seeing short-term memory as an independent way station into which memories arrive, either to fade or to be passed on to long-term memory, many contemporary memory theorists conceive of short-term memory as far more active. In this view, short-term memory is like an information processing system that manages both new material gathered from sensory memory and older material that has been pulled from long-term storage. In this increasingly influential view, short-term memory is referred to as **working memory** and defined as a set of temporary memory stores that actively manipulate and rehearse information (Bayliss et al., 2005a, 2005b; Unsworth & Engle, 2005).

Working memory is thought to contain a *central executive* processor that is involved in reasoning and decision making. The central executive coordinates three distinct storage-and-rehearsal systems: the *visual store,* the *verbal store,* and the *episodic buffer.* The visual store specializes in visual and spatial information, whereas the verbal store holds and manipulates material relating to speech, words, and numbers. The episodic buffer contains information that represents episodes or events (Baddeley, Chincotta, & Adlam, 2001; see Figure 4).

Working memory permits us to keep information in an active state briefly so that we can do something with the information. For instance, we use working memory when we're doing a multistep arithmetic problem in our heads, storing the result of one calculation while getting ready to move to the next stage. (I make use of my working memory when I figure a 20 percent tip in a restaurant by first calculating 10 percent of the total bill and then doubling it.)

Although working memory aids in the recall of information, it uses a significant amount of cognitive resources during its operation. In turn, this can make us less aware of our surroundings—something that has implications for the debate about the use of cellular telephones in automobiles. If a phone conversation requires thinking, it will burden working memory, leaving people less aware of their surroundings, an obviously dangerous state of affairs for the driver (de Fockert et al., 2001; Wickelgren, 2001; Berhaeghen, Cerella, & Basak, 2004).

www.mhhe.com/feldmanup8
PsychInteractive Online

Short-term Memory

Working memory: A set of temporary memory stores that actively manipulate and rehearse information.

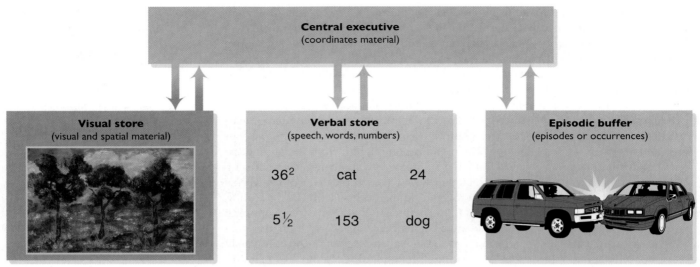

FIGURE 4 Working memory is an active "workspace" in which information is retrieved and manipulated, and in which information is held through rehearsal (Gathercole & Baddeley, 1993). It consists of a "central executive" that coordinates the visual store (which concentrates on visual and spatial information), the verbal store (which concentraes on speech, words, and numbers), and the episodic buffer (which represents episodes or occurrences that are encountered). (Source: Adapted from Baddeley, Chincotta, & Adlam, 2001.)

Furthermore, stress can reduce the effectiveness of working memory by reducing its capacity. In fact, one study found that students with the highest working memory capacity and greatest math ability were the ones who were most vulnerable to pressure to perform well. Those who should have performed best, then, were the ones most apt to choke on the test because their working memory capacities were reduced by the stress (Carey, 2004; Beilock & Carr, 2005). (To learn more, try the PsychInteractive exercise on working memory.)

Long-Term Memory

Material that makes its way from short-term memory to long-term memory enters a storehouse of almost unlimited capacity. Like a new file we save on a hard drive, the information in long-term memory is filed and coded so that we can retrieve it when we need it.

Evidence of the existence of long-term memory, as distinct from short-term memory, comes from a number of sources. For example, people with certain kinds of brain damage have no lasting recall of new information received after the damage occurred, although people and events stored in memory before the injury remain intact (Milner, 1966). Because information that was encoded and stored before the injury can be recalled and because short-term memory after the injury appears to be operational—new material can be recalled for a very brief period—we can infer that there are two distinct types of memory: one for short-term and one for long-term storage.

Results from laboratory experiments are also consistent with the notion of separate short-term and long-term memory. For example, in one set of studies people were asked to recall a relatively small amount of information (such as a set of three letters). Then, to prevent practice of the initial information, participants were required to recite some extraneous material aloud, such as counting backward by threes (Brown, 1958; Peterson & Peterson, 1959). By varying the amount of time between the presentation of the initial material and the need for its recall, investigators found that recall was quite good when the interval was very short but declined rapidly thereafter. After fifteen seconds had gone by, recall hovered at around 10 percent of the material initially presented.

Apparently, the distraction of counting backward prevented almost all the initial material from reaching long-term memory. Initial recall was good because it was coming from short-term memory, but those memories were lost at a rapid rate. Eventually, all that could be recalled was the small amount of material that had made its way into long-term storage despite the distraction of counting backward.

The distinction between short- and long-term memory is also supported by the *serial position effect,* in which the ability to recall information in a list depends on where in the list an item appears. For instance, often a *primacy effect* occurs, in which items presented early in a list are remembered better. There is also a *recency effect,* in which items presented late in a list are remembered best.

LONG-TERM MEMORY MODULES

Just as short-term memory is often conceptualized in terms of working memory, many contemporary researchers now regard long-term memory as having several different components, or *memory modules.* Each of these modules represents a separate memory system in the brain.

One major distinction within long-term memory is between declarative memory and procedural memory. **Declarative memory** is memory for factual information: names, faces, dates, and facts, such as "a bike has two wheels." In contrast, **procedural memory** (or *nondeclarative memory)* refers to memory for skills and habits, such as how to ride a bike or hit a baseball. Information about *things* is stored in declarative memory; information about *how to do things* is stored in procedural memory (Schacter, Wagner, & Buckner, 2000; Eichenbaum, 2004).

Declarative memory can be subdivided into semantic memory and episodic memory (Nyberg & Tulving, 1996; Tulving, 2002). **Semantic memory** is memory for general knowledge and facts about the world, as well as memory for the rules of logic that are used to deduce other facts. Because of semantic memory, we remember that the ZIP code for Beverly Hills is 90210, that Bombay is on the Arabian Sea, and that *memoree* is the incorrect spelling of *memory.* Thus, semantic memory is somewhat like a mental almanac of facts.

In contrast, **episodic memory** is memory for events that occur in a particular time, place, or context. For example, recall of learning to ride a bike, our first kiss, or arranging a surprise 21st birthday party for our brother is based on episodic memories. Episodic memories relate to particular contexts. For example, remembering *when* and *how* we learned that $2 \times 2 = 4$ would be an episodic memory; the fact itself (that $2 \times 2 = 4$) is a semantic memory. (To help your long-term memory keep the distinctions between the different types of long-term memory straight, study Figure 5 on page 226.)

Episodic memories can be surprisingly detailed. Consider, for instance, how you'd respond if you were asked to identify what you were doing on a specific day two years ago. Impossible? You may think otherwise as you read the following exchange between a researcher and a participant in a study who was asked, in a memory experiment, what he was doing "on Monday afternoon in the third week of September two years ago."

PARTICIPANT: Come on. How should I know?

EXPERIMENTER: Just try it anyhow.

PARTICIPANT: OK. Let's see: Two years ago . . . I would be in high school in Pittsburgh . . . That would be my senior year. Third week in September—that's just after summer—that would be the fall term . . . . Let me see. I think I had chemistry lab on Mondays. I don't know. I was probably in chemistry lab. Wait a minute—that would be the second week of school. I remember he started off with the atomic table—a big fancy chart. I thought he was crazy trying to make us memorize that thing. You know, I think I can remember sitting . . . (Lindsay & Norman, 1977).

Episodic memory, then, can provide information about events that happened long in the past (Reynolds & Takooshian, 1988). But semantic memory is no less impressive,

The ability to remember specific skills and the order in which they are used is known as procedural memory. If driving involves procedural memory, is it safe to use a cell phone while driving?

Declarative memory: Memory for factual information: names, faces, dates, and the like.

Procedural memory: Memory for skills and habits, such as riding a bike or hitting a baseball, sometimes referred to as nondeclarative memory.

Semantic memory: Memory for general knowledge and facts about the world, as well as memory for the rules of logic that are used to deduce other facts.

Episodic memory: Memory for events that occur in a particular time, place, or context.

In addition to procedural memory, driving a car involves what is known as declarative or explicit memory, which permits us to remember how to get to our destination.

FIGURE 5 Long-term memory can be subdivided into several different types. What type of long-term memory is involved in your recollection of the moment you first arrived on your campus at the start of college? What type of long-term memory is involved in remembering the lyrics to a song, compared with the tune of a song?

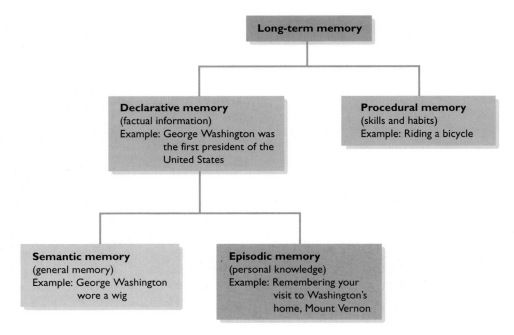

permitting us to dredge up tens of thousands of facts ranging from the date of our birthday to the knowledge that $1 is less than $5.

SEMANTIC NETWORKS

Try to recall, for a moment, as many things as you can think of that are the color red.

Now pull from your memory the names of as many fruits as you can recall.

Did the same item appear on both tasks? For many people, an apple comes to mind in both cases, since it fits equally well in each category. And the fact that you might have thought of an apple on the first task makes it even more likely that you'll think of it when doing the second task.

It's actually quite amazing that we're able to retrieve specific material from the vast store of information in our long-term memories. According to some memory researchers, one key organizational tool that allows us to recall detailed information from long-term memory is the associations that we build between different pieces of information. In this view, knowledge is stored in **semantic networks,** mental representations of clusters of interconnected information (Collins & Quillian, 1969; Collins & Loftus, 1975).

Consider, for example, Figure 6, which shows some of the relationships in memory relating to fire engines, the color red, and a variety of other semantic concepts. Thinking about a particular concept leads to recall of related concepts. For example, seeing a fire engine may activate our recollections of other kinds of emergency vehicles, such as an ambulance, which in turn may activate recall of the related concept of a vehicle. And thinking of a vehicle may lead us to think about a bus that we've seen in the past. Activating one memory triggers the activation of related memories in a process known as *spreading activation.*

THE NEUROSCIENCE OF MEMORY

Can we pinpoint a location in the brain where long-term memories reside? Is there a single site that corresponds to a particular memory, or is memory distributed in different regions across the brain? Do memories leave an actual physical trace that scientists can view?

The search for the *engram,* the term for the physical memory trace that corresponds to a memory, has proved to be a major puzzle to psychologists and other neuroscientists interested in memory. Using advanced brain scanning procedures in their efforts to determine the neuroscientific basis of memory formation, investigators have learned that certain areas and structures of the brain specialize in different types of memory-related activities. The *hippocampus,* a part of the brain's limbic system (see Figure 7),

Semantic networks: Mental representations of clusters of interconnected information.

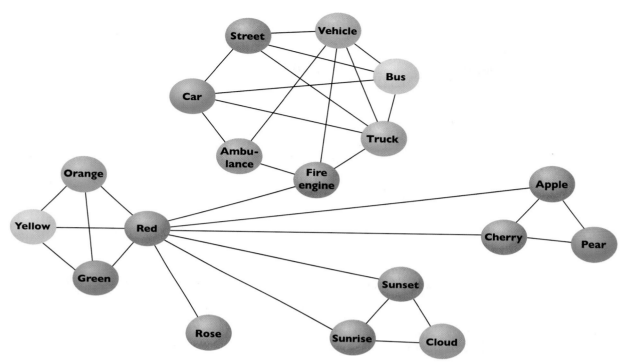

FIGURE 6 Semantic networks in memory consist of relationships between pieces of information, such as those relating to the concept of a fire engine. The lines suggest the connections that indicate how the information is organized within memory. The closer two concepts are together, the greater the strength of the association. (Source: Collins & Loftus, 1975.)

plays a central role in the consolidation of memories. Located within the brain's *medial temporal lobes,* just behind the eyes, the hippocampus aids in the initial encoding of information, acting as a kind of neurological e-mail system. That information is subsequently passed along to the cerebral cortex of the brain, where it is actually stored (Smith, 2000; Wheeler, Petersen, & Buckner, 2000; Wilson, 2002).

The *amygdala,* another part of the limbic system, also plays a role in memory. The amygdala is especially involved with memories involving emotion (Hamann, 2001; Buchanan & Adolphs, 2004). For example, if you are frightened by a large Doberman, you're likely to remember the event vividly—an outcome related to the functioning of the amygdala. Encountering the Doberman, or any large dog, in the future is likely to reactivate the amygdala and bring back the unpleasant memory.

THE BIOCHEMISTRY OF MEMORY

Although it is clear that the hippocampus and amygdala play a central role in memory formation, how is the transformation of information into a memory reflected at the level of neurons?

One answer comes from work on *long-term potentiation,* which shows that certain neural pathways become easily excited while a new response is being learned. At the same time, the number of synapses between neurons increase as the dendrites branch out to receive messages. These changes reflect a process called *consolidation,* in which memories become fixed and stable in long-term memory. Long-term memories take some time to stabilize; this explains why events and other stimuli are not suddenly fixed in memory. Instead, consolidation may continue for days and even years (Rioult-Pedotti, Friedman, & Donoghue, 2000; McGaugh, 2003; Meeter & Murre, 2004).

"The matters about which I'm being questioned, Your Honor, are all things I should have included in my long-term memory but which I mistakenly inserted in my short-term memory."

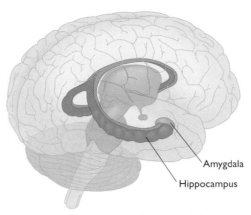

Amygdala

Hippocampus

FIGURE 7 The hippocampus and amygdala, parts of the brain's limbic system, play a central role in the consolidation of memories. (Source: Van De Graff, 2000.)

Because a stimulus may contain different sensory aspects, visual, auditory, and other areas of the brain may be simultaneously processing information about that stimulus. Information storage appears to be linked to the sites where this processing occurs, and is therefore located in the particular areas that initially processed the information in terms of its visual, auditory, and other sensory stimuli. For this reason, memory traces are distributed throughout the brain. For example, when you recall a beautiful beach sunset, your recollection draws on memory stores located in visual areas of the brain (the view of the sunset), auditory areas (the sounds of the ocean), and tactile areas (the feel of the wind) (Desimone, 1992; Brewer et al., 1998; Squire, Clark, & Bayley, 2004).

Investigators using positron emission tomography (PET) scans, which measure biological activity in the brain, have found that neural memory traces are highly specialized. For instance, the participants in one experiment were given a list of nouns to read aloud. After reading each noun, they were asked to suggest a related verb. After reading the noun *dog*, for example, they might have proposed the verb *bark*.

Several distinct areas of the brain showed increased neural activity as the participants first did the task (see Figure 8). However, if they repeated the task with the same nouns several times, the activity in the brain shifted to another area. Most interestingly, if they were given a new list of nouns, the activity returned to the areas in the brain that were initially activated.

These results suggest that a particular part of the brain is involved in the production of words, but another part takes over when the process becomes routine—in other words, when memory comes into play. It also suggests that memory is distributed in the brain not just in terms of its content, but also in terms of its function (Horgan, 1993; Petersen & Fiez, 1993; Corbetta, Kincade, & Shulman, 2002).

In short, the physical stuff of memory—the engram—is produced by a complex of biochemical and neural processes. Although memory researchers have made considerable strides in understanding the neuroscience behind memory, more remains to be learned—and remembered. (For more on the biological basis of memory, see the *Applying Psychology in the 21st Century* box.)

FIGURE 8 PET scans of a participant in an experiment who was first asked to read a list of nouns and produce a related verb (left scan). When the participant was asked to carry out the task repeatedly with the same list of nouns, different areas of the brain became active (center). However, when the participant was given a new list of nouns, the regions of the brain that were initially involved became reactivated (right). (Source: Peterson, 1993.)

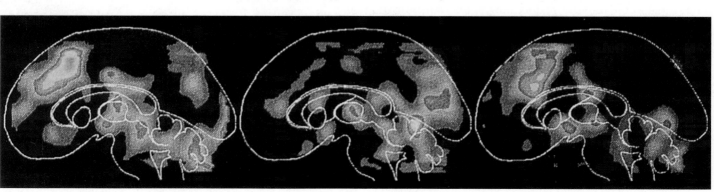

Enhancing Memory: Are We on the Road to "Cosmetic Neurology"?

Will our future trips down memory lane begin in the aisles of a drugstore?

That possibility may become reality one day as researchers find growing evidence that certain drugs help to improve memory. This research is leading to the possibility that drugs may be designed to enhance our memory capabilities or even, perhaps, to suppress unwanted ones, such as memories of traumatic events. Such "cosmetic neurology"—the use of drugs to improve our mental functioning (equivalent to the use of Botox to improve physical appearance)—may bring us closer to the day when healthy, normal individuals pop a pill to sharpen their memories prior to taking the SATs or heading out to a job interview (Begley, 2004; Chatterjee, 2004; Fields, 2005).

Scientists are developing several types of memory-enhancing drugs. For example, certain drugs, known as cholinesterase inhibitors, increase the ability of neurons to communicate with one another. One example is *donepezil* (which is sold as Aricept). Although it was developed to treat memory loss in patients with Alzheimer's disease, it turns out that even healthy individuals show enhanced memory after taking the drug. For example, in one study, researchers gave middle-aged airplane pilots doses of donepezil and placed them in a flight simulator. Compared with a control group of pilots who took a placebo pill, the pilots taking donepezil learned and remembered emergency maneuvers significantly better. Other research has confirmed the memory-enhancing effects of the drug on verbal and visual recall (Hall, 2003; Mumenthaler et al., 2003; Gron et al., 2005).

Also on the horizon is a class of drugs that allows neurons to be more responsive to incoming messages. These drugs, known as calcium channel modulators, counteract the reduction of neuronal activ-

Although memory researchers are optimistic about the potential of memory-enhancing drugs, routine use of such drugs raises important ethical issues.

ity that is associated with disorders such as Alzheimer's disease and other types of cognitive impairment associated with aging (Carmichael, 2004; Choudhary et al., 2005).

Other researchers are examining drugs that would *inhibit* certain memories. CREB inhibitors, drugs that affect the production of CREB—a protein responsible for establishment of memories—may eventually be used to prevent recurring, intrusive, unpleasant memories following a traumatic event. A person might even take such a drug *before* being exposed to a grim situation. For instance, rescue workers (such as those who pulled victims from floodwaters surrounding New Orleans) might be given a drug before reaching the scene in order to reduce future emotion-

laden, grisly memories (Chatterjee, 2004; Warburton et al., 2005).

Memory researchers are increasingly optimistic about the possibilities of developing drugs that affect how we remember. At the same time, such drugs raise important ethical issues. Is it moral for people to pop a pill to learn material with less effort than those who use only their unenhanced natural capabilities? Will those who can afford artificial enhancements have an unfair advantage over those who are unable to afford "cosmetic neurology"? Would the eradication of unpleasant memories also rob people of their identity? The answers to these questions are likely to be nothing short of memorable (Stein, 2003; Miller, 2004; Begley, 2005b).

RETHINK

Should memory enhancement drugs be limited only to clear-cut cases of disease, or should they be available to enhance memory beyond normal limits? What kind of restrictions, if any, should be put on the distribution of such drugs, and why?

RECAP/EVALUATE/RETHINK

RECAP

What is memory?

- Memory is the process by which we encode, store, and retrieve information. (p. 219)

Are there different kinds of memory?

- Sensory memory, corresponding to each of the sensory systems, is the first place where information is saved. Sensory memories are very brief, but they are precise, storing a nearly exact replica of a stimulus. (pp. 220-221)
- Roughly seven (plus or minus two) chunks of information can be transferred and held in short-term memory. Information in short-term memory is held from fifteen to twenty-five seconds and, if not transferred to long-term memory, is lost. (pp. 221-222)
- Some theorists view short-term memory as a working memory, in which information is retrieved and manipulated, and held through rehearsal. In this view, it is a central executive processor involved in reasoning and decision making; it coordinates a visual store, a verbal store, and an episodic buffer. (pp. 223-224)
- Memories are transferred into long-term storage through rehearsal. If memories are transferred into long-term memory, they become relatively permanent. (pp. 222-223)
- Long-term memory can be viewed in terms of memory modules, each of which is related to separate memory systems in the brain. For instance, we can distinguish between declarative memory and procedural memory. Declarative memory is further divided into episodic memory and semantic memory. (pp. 225-226)
- Semantic networks suggest that knowledge is stored in long-term memory as mental representations of clusters of interconnected information. (p. 226)

What are the biological bases of memory?

- The hippocampus and amygdala are particularly important in the establishment of memory. (pp. 227-228)

- Memories are distributed across the brain, relating to the different sensory information-processing systems involved during the initial exposure to a stimulus. (p. 228)

EVALUATE

1. Match the type of memory with its definition:
   1. Long-term memory
   2. Short-term memory
   3. Sensory memory
   a. Holds information fifteen to twenty-five seconds.
   b. Stores information on a relatively permanent basis.
   c. Direct representation of a stimulus.
2. A(n) _____ is a meaningful group of stimuli that can be stored together in short-term memory.
3. There appear to be two types of declarative memory: _____ memory, for knowledge and facts, and _____ memory, for personal experiences.
4. Some memory researchers believe that long-term memory is stored as associations between pieces of information in _____ networks.

RETHINK

1. It is a truism that "you never forget how to ride a bicycle." Why might this be so? In what type of memory is is information about bicycle riding stored?
2. *From a marketing specialist's perspective:* How might ways of enhancing memory be used by advertisers and others to promote their products? What ethical principles are involved? Can you think of a way to protect yourself from unethical advertising?

Answers to Evaluate Questions

1. 1-b, 2-a, 3-c; 2. chunk; 3. semantic, episodic; 4. semantic

KEY TERMS

memory p. 219
sensory memory p. 220
short-term memory p. 220

long-term memory p. 220
chunk p. 221
rehearsal p. 222

working memory p. 223
declarative memory p. 225
procedural memory p. 225

semantic memory p. 225
episodic memory p. 225
semantic networks p. 226

Recalling Long-Term Memories

An hour after his job interview, Ricardo was sitting in a coffee shop, telling his friend Laura how well it had gone, when the woman who had interviewed him walked in. "Well, hello, Ricardo. How are you doing?" Trying to make a good impression, Ricardo began to make introductions, but suddenly realized he could not remember the name of the interviewer. Stammering, he desperately searched his memory, but to no avail. "I *know* her name," he thought to himself, "but here I am, looking like a fool. I can kiss this job good-bye."

Have you ever tried to remember someone's name, convinced that you knew it, but unable to recall it no matter how hard you tried? This common occurrence—known as the **tip-of-the-tongue phenomenon**—exemplifies how difficult it can be to retrieve information stored in long-term memory (Schwartz et al., 2000; Schwartz, 2001, 2002).

Retrieval Cues

Perhaps recall of names and other memories is not perfect because there is so much information stored in long-term memory. Many psychologists have suggested that the material that makes its way to long-term memory is relatively permanent (Tulving & Psotka, 1971). If they are correct, given the broad range of people's experiences and educational backgrounds, the capacity of long-term memory is vast. For instance, if you are like the average college student, your vocabulary includes some 50,000 words, you know hundreds of mathematical "facts," and you are able to conjure up images—such as the way your childhood home looked—with no trouble at all. In fact, simply cataloging all your memories would probably take years of work.

How do we sort through this vast array of material and retrieve specific information at the appropriate time? One way is through retrieval cues. A *retrieval cue* is a stimulus that allows us to recall more easily information that is in long-term memory (Tulving & Thompson, 1983; Ratcliff & McKoon, 1989). It may be a word, an emotion, or a sound; whatever the specific cue, a memory will suddenly come to mind when the retrieval cue is present. For example, the smell of roasting turkey may evoke memories of Thanksgiving or family gatherings (Schab & Crowder, 1995).

Retrieval cues guide people through the information stored in long-term memory in much the same way that the cards in an old-fashioned card catalog guided people through a library and a search engine such as Google guides people through the World Wide Web. They are particularly important when we are making an effort to *recall* information, as opposed to being asked to *recognize* material stored in memory. In **recall,** a specific piece of information must be retrieved—such as that needed to answer a fill-in-the-blank question or write an essay on a test. In contrast, **recognition** occurs when people are presented with a stimulus

Key Concepts

What causes difficulties and failures in remembering?

Tip-of-the-tongue phenomenon: The inability to recall information that one realizes one knows—a result of the difficulty of retrieving information from long-term memory.

Recall: Memory task in which specific information must be retrieved.

Recognition: Memory task in which individuals are presented with a stimulus and asked whether they have been exposed to it in the past or to identify it from a list of alternatives.

FIGURE I Try to recall the names of these characters. Because this is a recall task, it is relatively difficult.

Answer this recognition question:
Which of the following are the names of the seven dwarves in the Disney movie *Snow White and the Seven Dwarfs*?

Goofy	Bashful
Sleepy	Meanie
Smarty	Doc
Scaredy	Happy
Dopey	Angry
Grumpy	Sneezy
Wheezy	Crazy

(The correct answers are Bashful, Doc, Dopey, Grumpy, Happy, Sleepy, and Sneezy.)

and asked whether they have been exposed to it previously, or are asked to identify it from a list of alternatives.

As you might guess, recognition is generally a much easier task than recall (see Figures 1 and 2). Recall is more difficult because it consists of a series of processes: a search through memory, retrieval of potentially relevant information, and then a decision regarding whether the information you have found is accurate. If the information appears to be correct, the search is over, but if it does not, the search must continue. In contrast, recognition is simpler because it involves fewer steps (Anderson & Bower, 1972; Miserando, 1991).

Levels of Processing

Levels-of-processing theory: The theory of memory that emphasizes the degree to which new material is mentally analyzed.

One determinant of how well memories are recalled is the way in which material is first perceived, processed, and understood. The **levels-of-processing theory** emphasizes the degree to which new material is mentally analyzed (Craik & Lockhart, 1972; Craik, 1990). It suggests that the amount of information processing that occurs when material is initially encountered is central in determining how much of the information is ultimately remembered. According to this approach, the depth of information processing during exposure to material—meaning the degree to which it is analyzed and considered—is critical; the greater the intensity of its initial processing is, the more likely we are to remember it.

Because we do not pay close attention to much of the information to which we are exposed, very little mental processing typically takes place, and we forget new material almost immediately. However, information to which we pay greater attention is processed more thoroughly. Therefore, it enters memory at a deeper level—and is less apt to be forgotten than is information processed at shallower levels.

The theory goes on to suggest that there are considerable differences in the ways in which information is processed at various levels of memory. At shallow levels, information is processed merely in terms of its physical and sensory aspects. For example, we may pay attention only to the shapes that make up the letters in the word *dog.* At an intermediate level of processing, the shapes are translated into meaningful units—in this case, letters of the alphabet. Those letters are considered in the context of words, and specific phonetic sounds may be attached to the letters.

At the deepest level of processing, information is analyzed in terms of its meaning. We may see it in a wider context and draw associations between the meaning of the information and broader networks of knowledge. For instance, we may think of dogs not merely as animals with four legs and a tail, but also in terms of their relationship to cats and other mammals. We may form an image of our own dog, thereby relating the concept to our own lives. According to the levels-of-processing approach, the deeper the initial level of processing of specific information is, the longer the information will be retained.

Although the concept of depth of processing has proved difficult to test experimentally and the levels-of-processing theory has its critics (e.g., Baddeley, 1990), it is clear that there are considerable practical implications to the notion that recall depends on the degree to which information is initially processed. For example, the depth of information processing is critical when learning and studying course material. Rote memorization of a list of key terms for a test is unlikely to produce long-term recollection of information, because processing occurs at a shallow level. In contrast, thinking about the meaning of the terms and reflecting on how they relate to information that one currently knows is a far more effective route to long-term retention. The experiment in the PsychInteractive exercise will help you understand levels-of-processing theory.

www.mhhe.com/feldmanup8
PsychInteractive Online

Levels of Processing

Explicit and Implicit Memory

If you've ever had surgery, you probably hoped that the surgeons were focused completely on the surgery and gave you their undivided attention while slicing into your body. The reality in most operating rooms is quite different, though. Surgeons may be chatting with nurses about a new restaurant as soon as they sew you up.

If you are like most patients, you are left with no recollection of the conversation that occurred while you were under anesthesia. However, it is very possible that although you had no conscious memories of the discussions on the merits of the restaurant, on some level, you probably did recall at least some information. In fact, careful studies have found that people who are anesthetized during surgery can sometimes recall snippets of conversations they heard during surgery—even though they have no conscious recollection of the information (Kihlstrom et al., 1990; Sebel, Bonke, & Winograd, 1993).

The discovery that people have memories about which they are unaware has been an important one. It has led to speculation that two forms of memory, explicit and implicit, may exist side by side. **Explicit memory** refers to intentional or conscious recollection of information. When we try to remember a name or date we have encountered or learned about previously, we are searching our explicit memory.

In contrast, **implicit memory** refers to memories of which people are not consciously aware, but which can affect subsequent performance and behavior. Skills that operate automatically and without thinking, such as jumping out of the path of an automobile coming toward us as we walk down the side of a road, are stored in implicit memory. Similarly, a feeling of vague dislike for an acquaintance, without knowing why we have that feeling, may be a reflection of implicit memories. Perhaps the person reminds us of someone else in our past that we didn't like, even though we are not aware of the memory of that other individual (Schacter & Scarry, 2000; Tulving, 2000; Uttl, Graf, & Consentino, 2003).

Implicit memory is closely related to the prejudice and discrimination people exhibit toward members of minority groups. Even though people may say and even believe they harbor no prejudice, assessment of their implicit memories may reveal that they have negative associations about members of minority groups. Such associations can influence behavior without people being aware of their underlying beliefs (Greenwald, Nosek, & Banaji, 2003; Greenwald, Nosek, & Sriram, 2006).

One way that memory specialists study implicit memory is through experiments that use priming. **Priming** is a phenomenon in which exposure to a word or concept (called a *prime*) later makes it easier to recall related information. Priming effects occur even when people have no conscious memory of the original word or concept (Schacter & Badgaiyan, 2001; Toth & Daniels, 2002; Schacter et al., 2004).

The typical experiment designed to illustrate priming helps clarify the phenomenon. In priming experiments, participants are rapidly exposed to a stimulus such as a word, an object, or perhaps a drawing of a face. The second phase of the experiment is done after an interval ranging from several seconds to several months. At that

Explicit memory: Intentional or conscious recollection of information.

Implicit memory: Memories of which people are not consciously aware, but which can affect subsequent performance and behavior.

Priming: A phenomenon in which exposure to a word or concept (called a *prime*) later makes it easier to recall related information, even when there is no conscious memory of the word or concept.

point, participants are exposed to incomplete perceptual information that is related to the first stimulus, and they are asked whether they recognize it. For example, the new material may consist of the first letter of a word that had been presented earlier, or a part of a face that had been shown earlier. If participants are able to identify the stimulus more readily than they identify stimuli that have not been presented earlier, priming has taken place. Clearly, the earlier stimulus has been remembered—although the material resides in implicit memory, not explicit memory.

The same thing happens to us in our everyday lives. Suppose several months ago you watched a documentary on the planets, and the narrator described the moons of Mars, focusing on its moon named Phobos. You promptly forget the name of the moon, at least consciously. Then, several months later, you're completing a crossword puzzle that is partially completed, and it includes the letters *obos*. As soon as you look at the set of letters, you think of Phobos, and suddenly recall for the first time since your initial exposure to the information that it is one of the moons of Mars. The sudden recollection occurred because your memory was primed by the letters *obos*.

In short, when information that we are unable to consciously recall affects our behavior, implicit memory is at work. Our behavior may be influenced by experiences of which we are unaware—an example of what has been called "retention without remembering" (Roediger, 1990; Horton et al., 2005).

Flashbulb Memories

Where were you on February 1, 2003? You will most likely draw a blank until this piece of information is added: February 1, 2003, was the date the Space Shuttle *Columbia* broke up in space and fell to Earth.

You probably have little trouble recalling your exact location and a variety of other trivial details that occurred when you heard about the shuttle disaster, even though the incident happened a few years ago. Your ability to remember details about this fatal event illustrates a phenomenon known as flashbulb memory. **Flashbulb memories** are memories related to a specific, important, or surprising event that are so vivid they represent a virtual snapshot of the event.

Several types of flashbulb memories are common among college students. For example, involvement in a car accident, meeting one's roommate for the first time, and the night of high school graduation are all typical flashbulb memories (Tekcan, 2001; Davidson & Glisky, 2002; Talarico & Rubin, 2003; see Figure 3).

Of course, flashbulb memories do not contain every detail of an original scene. I remember vividly that some four decades ago I was sitting in Mr. Sharp's tenth-grade geometry class when I heard that President John Kennedy had been shot. However, although I recall where I was sitting and how my classmates reacted to the news, I do not recollect what I was wearing or what I had for lunch that day.

Furthermore, the details recalled in flashbulb memories are often inaccurate. For example, think back to the tragic day when the World Trade Center in New York was attacked by terrorists. Do you remember watching television that morning and seeing images of the first plane, and then the second plane, striking the towers?

If you do, you are among the 73 percent of Americans who recall viewing the initial television images of both planes on September 11. However, that recollection is wrong: In fact, television broadcasts showed images only of the second plane on September 11. No video of the first plane was available until early the following morning, September 12, when it was shown on television (Begley, 2002b).

Flashbulb memories illustrate a more general phenomenon about memory: Memories that are exceptional are more easily retrieved (although not necessarily accurately) than are those relating to events that are commonplace. The more distinctive a stimulus is, and the more personal relevance the event has, the more likely we are to recall it later (von Restorff, 1933; Winningham, Hyman, & Dinnel, 2000; Berntsen & Thomsen, 2005).

Flashbulb memories: Memories centered on a specific, important, or surprising event that are so vivid it is as if they represented a snapshot of the event.

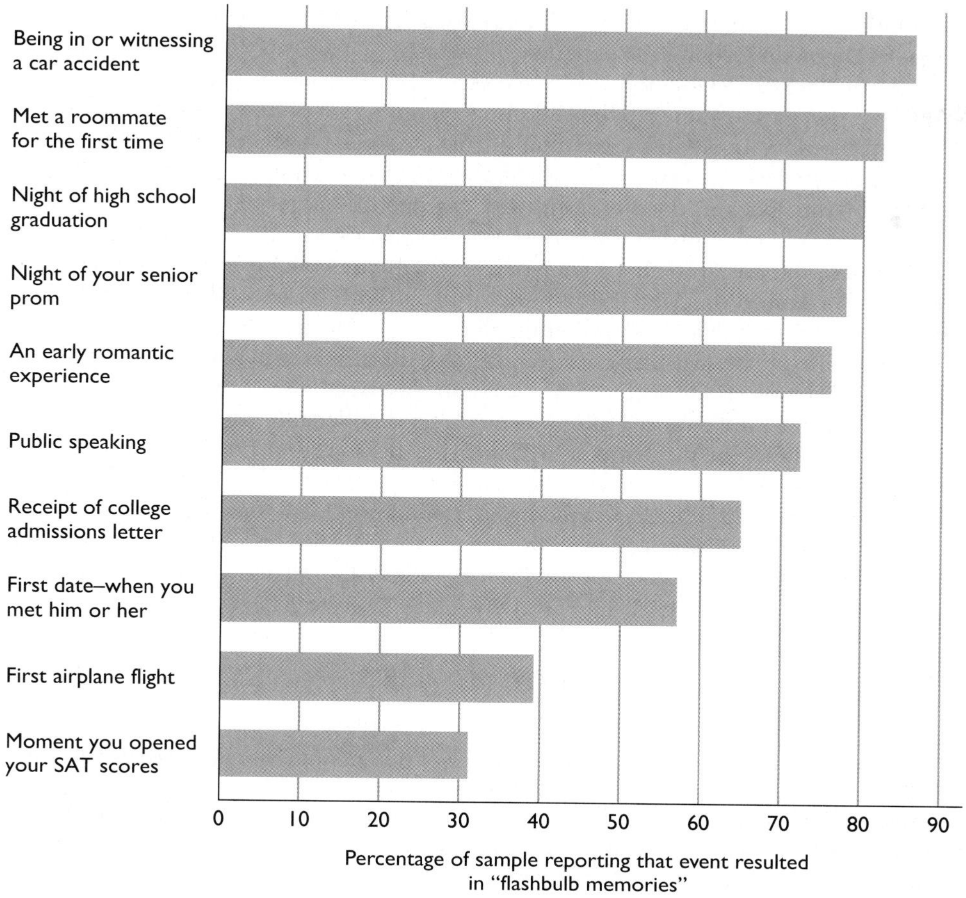
Being in or witnessing a car accident
Met a roommate for the first time
Night of high school graduation
Night of your senior prom
An early romantic experience
Public speaking
Receipt of college admissions letter
First date–when you met him or her
First airplane flight
Moment you opened your SAT scores
0
10
20
30
40
50
60
70
80
90
Percentage of sample reporting that event resulted in "flashbulb memories"

FIGURE 3 These are the most common flashbulb memory events, based on a survey of college students (Rubin, 1985). What are some of your flashbulb memories?

Even with a distinctive stimulus, however, we may not remember where the information came from. *Source amnesia* occurs when an individual has a memory for some material but cannot recall where he or she encountered it before. For example, you may have experienced source amnesia when you met someone you knew and you just couldn't remember where you'd met that person initially.

Constructive Processes in Memory: Rebuilding the Past

As we have seen, although it is clear that we can have detailed recollections of significant and distinctive events, it is difficult to gauge the accuracy of such memories. In fact, it is apparent that our memories reflect, at least in part, **constructive processes,** processes in which memories are influenced by the meaning we give to events. When we retrieve information, then, the memory that is produced is affected not just by the direct prior experience we have had with the stimulus, but also by our guesses and inferences about its meaning.

Constructive processes: Processes in which memories are influenced by the meaning we give to events.

The notion that memory is based on constructive processes was first put forward by Sir Frederic Bartlett, a British psychologist. He suggested that people tend to remember information in terms of **schemas,** organized bodies of information stored in memory that bias the way new information is interpreted, stored, and recalled (Bartlett, 1932). Our reliance on schemas means that memories often consist of a general reconstruction of previous experience. Bartlett argued that schemas are based not only on the specific material to which people are exposed, but also on their under-

Schemas: Organized bodies of information stored in memory that bias the way new information is interpreted, stored, and recalled.

standing of the situation, their expectations about the situation, and their awareness of the motivations underlying the behavior of others.

One of the earliest demonstrations of schemas came from a classic study that involved a procedure similar to the children's game of "telephone," in which information from memory is passed sequentially from one person to another. In the study, a participant viewed a drawing in which there were a variety of people of differing racial and ethnic backgrounds on a subway car, one of whom—a white person—was shown with a razor in his hand (Allport & Postman, 1958). The first participant was asked to describe the drawing to someone else without looking back at it. Then that person was asked to describe it to another person (without looking at the drawing), and then the process was repeated with still one more participant.

The report of the last person differed in significant, yet systematic, ways from the initial drawing. Specifically, many people described the drawing as depicting an African American with a knife—an incorrect recollection, given that the drawing showed a razor in the hand of a Caucasian person. The transformation of the Caucasian's razor into an African American's knife clearly indicates that the participants held a schema that included the unwarranted prejudice that African Americans are more violent than Caucasians and thus more apt to be holding a knife. In short, our expectations and knowledge—and prejudices—affect the reliability of our memories (Katz, 1989; McDonald & Hirt, 1997; Newby-Clark & Ross, 2003).

MEMORY IN THE COURTROOM: THE EYEWITNESS ON TRIAL

For William Jackson, the inadequate memories of two people cost him five years of his life. Jackson was the victim of mistaken identity when two witnesses picked him out of a lineup as the perpetrator of a crime. On that basis, he was tried, convicted, and sentenced to serve fourteen to fifty years in jail.

Five years later, the actual criminal was identified and Jackson was released. For Jackson, though, it was too late. In his words, "They took away part of my life, part of my youth. I spend five years down there, and all they said was 'we're sorry'" (*Time*, 1982).

Unfortunately, Jackson is not the only victim to whom apologies have had to be made; there have been many cases of mistaken identity that have led to unjustified legal actions. Research on eyewitness identification of suspects, as well as on memory for other details of crimes, has shown that eyewitnesses are apt to make significant errors when they try to recall details of criminal activity—even if they are highly confident about their recollections. To find out just how unreliable memory can be, try the PsychInteractive exercise on eyewitness fallibility (Miller, 2000; Thompson, 2000; Wells, Olson, & Charman, 2002).

One reason is the impact of the weapons used in crimes. When a criminal perpetrator displays a gun or knife, it acts like a perceptual magnet, attracting the eyes of the witnesses. As a consequence, witnesses pay less attention to other details of the crime and are less able to recall what actually occurred (Belli & Loftus, 1996; Steblay et al., 2003).

Even when weapons are not involved, eyewitnesses are prone to errors relating to memory. For instance, viewers of a twelve-second film of a mugging that was shown on a New York City television news program were later given the opportunity to pick out the assailant from a six-person lineup (Buckhout, 1974). Of some 2,000 viewers who called the station after the program, only 15 percent were able to pick out the right person—a percentage similar to random guessing.

One reason eyewitnesses are prone to memory-related errors is that the specific wording of questions posed to them by police officers or attorneys can affect the way they recall information, as a number of experiments illustrate. For example, in one experiment the participants were shown a film of two cars crashing into each other. Some were then asked the question, "About how fast were the cars going when they *smashed* into each other?" On average, they estimated the speed to be 40.8 miles per hour. In contrast, when another group of participants was asked, "About how fast were the cars going when they *contacted* each other?" the average estimated speed was only 31.8 miles per hour (Loftus & Palmer, 1974; see Figure 4).

www.mhhe.com/feldmanup8

PsychInteractive Online

Eyewitness Fallibility

About how fast were the cars going when they_____ each other?

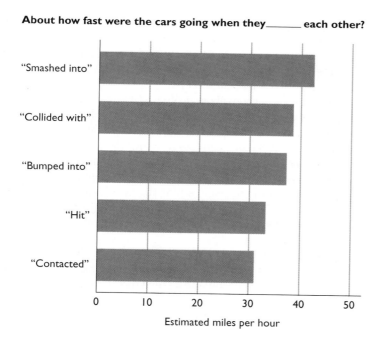

FIGURE 4 After viewing an accident involving two cars, the participants in a study were asked to estimate the speed of the two cars involved in the collision. Estimates varied substantially, depending on the way the question was worded. (Source: Loftus & Palmer, 1974.)

The problem of memory reliability becomes even more acute when children are witnesses, because increasing evidence suggests that children's memories are highly vulnerable to the influence of others (Loftus, 1993; Douglas, Brown, Goldstein, & Bjorklund, 2000). For instance, in one experiment, 5- to 7-year-old girls who had just had a routine physical examination were shown an anatomically explicit doll. The girls were shown the doll's genital area and asked, "Did the doctor touch you here?" Three of the girls who did not have a vaginal or anal exam said that the doctor had in fact touched them in the genital area, and one of those three made up the detail "The doctor did it with a stick" (Saywitz & Goodman, 1990).

Children's memories are especially susceptible to influence when the situation is highly emotional or stressful. For example, in trials in which there is significant pretrial publicity or in which alleged victims are questioned repeatedly, often by untrained interviewers, the memories of the alleged victims may be influenced by the types of questions they are asked (Scullin, Kanaya, & Ceci, 2002; Lamb & Garretson, 2003).

In short, the memories of witnesses are far from infallible, and this is especially true when children are involved. The question of the accuracy of memories becomes even more complex, however, when we consider the possibility of triggering memories of events that people at first don't even recall happening (Goodman et al., 2002, 2003; Schaaf et al., 2002; Pipe, Lamb, & Orbach, 2004).

REPRESSED AND FALSE MEMORIES: SEPARATING TRUTH FROM FICTION

Guilty of murder in the first degree.

That was the jury's verdict in the case of George Franklin, Sr., who was charged with murdering his daughter's playmate. But this case was different from most other murder cases: It was based on memories that had been repressed for twenty years. Franklin's daughter claimed that she had forgotten everything she had once known about her father's crime until two years earlier, when she began to have flashbacks of the event. Gradually, though, the memories became clearer in her mind, until she recalled her father lifting a rock over his head and then seeing her friend lying on the ground, covered with blood. On the basis of her memories, her father was convicted— and later cleared of the crime after an appeal of the conviction.

Although the prosecutor and jury clearly believed Franklin's daughter, there is good reason to question the validity of *repressed memories,* recollections of events that

As the result of testimony from Eileen Franklin, based on repressed memory, her father was found guilty of murder. His conviction was overturned six years later. The validity of repressed memory, especially in investigating crimes, remains controversial. Can you think of a test to tell whether a recovered memory is accurate?

are initially so shocking that the mind responds by pushing them into the unconscious. Supporters of the notion of repressed memory (based on Freud's psychoanalytic theory) suggest that such memories may remain hidden, possibly throughout a person's lifetime, unless they are triggered by some current circumstance, such as the probing that occurs during psychological therapy.

However, memory researcher Elizabeth Loftus (1998, 2003) maintains that so-called repressed memories may well be inaccurate or even wholly false—representing *false memory.* For example, false memories develop when people are unable to recall the source of a memory of a particular event about which they have only vague recollections. When the source of the memory becomes unclear or ambiguous, people may become confused about whether they actually experienced the event or whether it was imagined. Ultimately, people come to believe that the event actually occurred. Such memories may be so vivid that they produce strong emotional responses when they are "recalled," even though they never happened (Clancy et al., 2000; Loftus, 2004; Lewandowsky, Stritzke, & Oberauer, 2005).

It's certainly not all that difficult to create false memories. In laboratory experiments, for example, participants asked to study a list of related words (*tired, nap, snooze,* and *awake,* for example) readily come to believe that a related word like "sleep" was in the initial list, even if it wasn't. In fact, in some cases, 80 percent of participants are confident that they have seen the word earlier (Roediger & McDermott, 1995; Watson et al., 2003).

To add to the controversy about false memory, some therapists have been accused of accidentally encouraging people who come to them with psychological difficulties to re-create false chronicles of childhood sexual experiences. Furthermore, the publicity surrounding well-publicized declarations of supposed repressed memories, such as those of people who claim to be the victims of satanic rituals, makes the possibility of repressed memories seem more legitimate and ultimately may prime people to recall memories of events that never happened (Loftus, 1997).

The controversy regarding the legitimacy of repressed memories is unlikely to be resolved soon. Many psychologists, particularly those who provide therapy, give great weight to authenticity of repressed memories. Their views are supported by brain scan research showing that there are specific regions of the brain that help keep unwanted memories out of awareness (Anderson et al., 2004).

On the other side of the issue are researchers who maintain that there is insufficient scientific support for the existence of such memories. There is also a middle ground: memory researchers who suggest that false memories are a result of normal information processing. The challenge for those on all sides of the issue is to distinguish truth from fiction (Brown & Pope, 1996; Roediger & McDermott, 2000; Walcott, 2000; Leavitt, 2002; McNally, 2003).

AUTOBIOGRAPHICAL MEMORY: WHERE PAST MEETS PRESENT

Your memory of experiences in your own past may well be a fiction—or at least a distortion of what actually occurred. The same constructive processes that make us inaccurately recall the behavior of others also reduce the accuracy of autobiographical memories. **Autobiographical memories** are our recollections of circumstances and episodes from our own lives. Autobiographical memories encompass the episodic memories we hold about ourselves (Stein et al., 1997; Rubin, 1999).

For example, we tend to forget information about our past that is incompatible with the way in which we currently see ourselves. One study found that adults who were well adjusted but who had been treated for emotional problems during the early years of their lives tended to forget important but troubling childhood events, such as being in foster care. College students misremember their bad grades—but remember their good ones (Bahrick, 1998; Christensen, Wood, & Barrett, 2003; D'Argembeau, Comblain, & Van der Linden, 2003; Walker, Skowronski, & Whompson, 2003; see Figure 5).

Autobiographical memories: Our recollections of circumstances and episodes from our own lives.

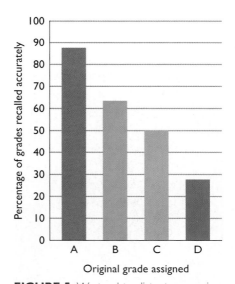

FIGURE 5 We tend to distort memories of unpleasant events. For example, college students are much more likely to accurately recall their good grades, while inaccurately recalling their poor ones (Bahrick, Hall, & Berger, 1996). Now that you know this, how well do you think you can recall your high school grades?

Similarly, when a group of 48-year-olds were asked to recall how they had responded on a questionnaire they had completed when they were high school freshman, their accuracy was no better than chance. For example, although 61 percent of the questionnaire respondents said that playing sports and other physical activities was their favorite pastime, only 23 percent of the adults recalled it accurately (Offer et al., 2000).

It is not just certain kinds of events that are distorted; particular periods of life are remembered more easily than others are. For example, when people reach late adulthood, they remember periods of life in which they experienced major transitions, such as attending college and working at their first job, better than they remember their middle-age years. Similarly, although most adults' earliest memories of their own lives are of events that occurred when they were toddlers, toddlers show evidence of recall of events that occurred when they were as young as 6 months old (Rubin, 1985; Newcombe et al., 2000; Simcock & Hayne, 2002; Wang, 2003).

Exploring DIVERSITY

Are There Cross-Cultural Differences in Memory?

Travelers who have visited areas of the world in which there is no written language often have returned with tales of people with phenomenal memories. For instance, storytellers in some preliterate cultures can recount long chronicles that recall the names and activities of people over many generations. Those feats led experts to argue initially that people in preliterate societies develop a different, and perhaps better, type of memory than do those in cultures that employ a written language. They suggested that in a society that lacks writing, people are motivated to recall information with accuracy, particularly information relating to tribal histories and traditions that would be lost if they were not passed down orally from one generation to another (Bartlett, 1932; Daftary & Meri, 2002; Berntsen & Rubin, 2004).

More recent approaches to cultural differences suggest a different conclusion. For one thing, preliterate peoples don't have an exclusive claim to amazing memory feats. Some Hebrew scholars memorize thousands of pages of text and can recall the locations of particular words on the page. Similarly, poetry singers in the Balkans can recall thousands of lines of poetry. Even in cultures in which written language exists, then, astounding feats of memory are possible (Neisser, 1982; Strathern & Stewart, 2003).

Storytellers in many cultures can recount hundreds of years of history in vivid detail. Research has found that this amazing ability is due less to basic memory processes than to the ways in which they acquire and retain information.

Memory researchers now suggest that there are both similarities and differences in memory across cultures. Basic memory processes such as short-term memory capacity and the structure of long-term memory—the "hardware" of memory—are universal and operate similarly in people in all cultures. In contrast, cultural differences can be seen in the way information is acquired and rehearsed—the "software" of memory. Culture determines how people frame information initially, how much they practice learning and recalling it, and the strategies they use to try to recall it (Wagner, 1982; Mack, 2003).

RECAP/EVALUATE/RETHINK

RECAP

What causes difficulties and failures in remembering?

- The tip-of-the-tongue phenomenon is the temporary inability to remember information that one is certain one knows. Retrieval cues are a major strategy for recalling information successfully. (p. 231)
- The levels-of-processing approach to memory suggests that the way in which information is initially perceived and analyzed determines the success with which it is recalled. The deeper the initial processing, the greater the recall. (pp. 232-233)
- Explicit memory refers to intentional or conscious recollection of information. In contrast, implicit memory refers to memories of which people are not consciously aware, but which can affect subsequent performance and behavior. (p. 233)
- Flashbulb memories are memories centered on a specific, important event. The more distinctive a memory is, the more easily it can be retrieved. (p. 234)
- Memory is a constructive process: We relate memories to the meaning, guesses, and expectations we give to events. Specific information is recalled in terms of schemas, organized bodies of information stored in memory that bias the way new information is interpreted, stored, and recalled. (pp. 235-236)
- Eyewitnesses are apt to make substantial errors when they try to recall the details of crimes. The problem of memory reliability becomes even more acute when the witnesses are children. (pp. 236-237)
- Autobiographical memory is influenced by constructive processes. (pp. 238-239)

EVALUATE

1. While with a group of friends at a dance, Eva bumps into a man she dated last month, but when she tries to introduce him to her friends, she cannot remember his name. What is the term for this occurrence?
2. _____ is the process of retrieving a specific item from memory.
3. A friend of your mother's tells you, "I know exactly where I was and what I was doing when I heard that John Lennon died." What is this type of memory phenomenon called?
4. The same person could probably also accurately describe in detail what she was wearing when she heard about John Lennon's death, right down to the color of her shoes. True or false?
5. _____ are organized bodies of information stored in memory that bias the way new information is interpreted, stored, and recalled.
6. _____ theory states that the more a person analyzes a statement, the more likely he or she is to remember it later.

RETHINK

1. Research shows that an eyewitness's memory for details of crimes can contain significant errors. How might a lawyer use this information when evaluating an eyewitness's testimony? Should eyewitness accounts be permissible in a court of law?
2. *From a social worker's perspective:* Should a child victim of sexual abuse be allowed to testify in court, based on what you've learned about children's memories under stress?

Answers to Evaluate Questions

1. tip-of-the-tongue phenomenon; 2. recall; 3. flashbulb memory; 4. false, small details probably won't be remembered through flashbulb memory; 5. schemas; 6. levels-of-processing

KEY TERMS

tip-of-the-tongue phenomenon p. 231
recall p. 231
recognition p. 231

levels-of-processing theory p. 232
explicit memory p. 233
implicit memory p. 233

priming p. 233
flashbulb memories p. 234
constructive processes p. 235

schemas p. 235
autobiographical memories p. 238

Forgetting: When Memory Fails

Known in the scientific literature by the pseudonym H. M., he could remember, quite literally, nothing—nothing, that is, that had happened since the loss of his brain's temporal lobes and hippocampus during experimental surgery to reduce epileptic seizures. Until that time, H. M.'s memory had been quite normal. But after the operation he was unable to recall anything for more than a few minutes, and then the memory was seemingly lost forever. He did not remember his address, or the name of the person to whom he was talking. H. M. would read the same magazine over and over again. According to his own description, his life was like waking from a dream and being unable to know where he was or how he got there (Milner, 1966, 2005).

As the case of H. M. illustrates, a person without a normal memory faces severe difficulties. All of us who have experienced even routine instances of forgetting—such as not remembering an acquaintance's name or a fact on a test—understand the very real consequences of memory failure.

Of course, memory failure is also essential to remembering important information. The ability to forget inconsequential details about experiences, people, and objects helps us avoid being burdened and distracted by trivial stores of meaningless data. Forgetting permits us to form general impressions and recollections. For example, the reason our friends consistently look familiar to us is because we're able to forget their clothing, facial blemishes, and other transient features that change from one occasion to the next. Instead, our memories are based on a summary of various critical features—a far more economical use of our memory capabilities.

Forgetting unnecessary information, then, is as essential to the proper functioning of memory as is remembering more important material. If you're uneasy about your own forgetfulness, try the quiz in Figure 1.

The first attempts to study forgetting were made by German psychologist Hermann Ebbinghaus about a hundred years ago. Using himself as the only participant in his study, Ebbinghaus memorized lists of three-letter nonsense syllables—meaningless sets of two consonants with a vowel in between, such as *FIW* and *BOZ*. By measuring how easy it was to relearn a given list of words after varying periods of time had passed since the initial learning, he found that forgetting occurred systematically, as shown in Figure 2 on page 243. As the figure indicates, the most rapid forgetting occurs in the first nine hours, particularly in the first hour. After nine hours, the rate of forgetting slows and declines little, even after the passage of many days.

Despite his primitive methods, Ebbinghaus's study had an important influence on subsequent research, and his basic conclusions have been upheld (Wixted & Ebbesen, 1991). There is almost always a strong initial decline in memory, followed by a more gradual drop over time. Furthermore, relearning of previously mastered material is almost always faster than starting from scratch, whether the material is academic information or a motor skill such as serving a tennis ball.

Why We Forget

Why do we forget? One reason is that we may not have paid attention to the material in the first place—a failure of *encoding*. For example, if you live in the United States, you probably

Key Concepts

Why do we forget information?

What are the major memory impairments?

FIGURE 1 If you feel that your memory isn't what it used to be, try this quiz. Based on similar tests, it is used to determine serious loss of memory, from which you as a college student are quite unlikely to suffer. (Source: Adapted from Devi, 2002.)

Take a Measure of Your Memory

If you are concerned your memory is not what it should be (or used to be), try this quiz.

1. Remember these words: *orange, telephone, lamp*
2. Remember this address: *Mary Smith, 650 Park Street, Athens, NY*
3. Who were the past five U.S. presidents?
4. Who were the last three mayors of your city?
5. What were the names of the last two movies you saw?
6. What were the names of the last two restaurants in which you ate?
7. Have you had more difficulty than usual recalling events from the previous two weeks?
   _____ Yes _____ No
8. Have you noticed a decline in your ability to remember lists, such as shopping lists?
   _____ Yes _____ No
9. Have you noticed a decline in your ability to perform mental math, like calculating change? _____ Yes _____ No
10. Have you been more forgetful about paying bills? _____ Yes _____ No
11. Have you had more trouble remembering peoples' names?
    _____ Yes _____ No
12. Have you had more trouble recognizing faces? _____ Yes _____ No
13. Do you find it harder to find the right words you want to use?
    _____ Yes _____ No
14. Have you been having more trouble remembering how to perform simple physical tasks such a operating the microwave or the remote control? _____ Yes _____ No
15. Does your memory interfere with your ability to function:
    At work? _____ Yes _____ No
    At home? _____ Yes _____ No
    In social situations? _____ Yes _____ No
16. Do you recall the three words you were given earlier?
17. Do you recall the name and address you were given earlier?

SCORING
Questions 3–6: 1 point for each correct answer (total of 12 points); **Questions 7–15:** 1 point for each "No" answer (total of 11 points); **Questions 16–17:** 1 point for each correct answer (total of 9 points).

Interpretation
Note that poor scores may be due to factors such as anxiety and inattention and not just from memory difficulties. Doing well on this simple quiz also does not ensure that you have no memory or cognitive difficulties.

The best indicator of your memory is your own assessment of your abilities. A perceived consistent change in your mental capacity is a far more sensitive indicator of cognitive difficulties that most tests, including this one. You should seek further help if this is the case.

If you scored between **28–32 points,** Congratulations!

If you scored between **22–27 points,** you may have some memory difficulties that, if persistent and interfering with everyday functioning, may need to be evaluated.

If you scored **21 or below,** and you have noticed that you have difficulty with your memory or thinking abilities of sufficient severity to interfere with functioning, you probably would benefit from a good evaluation.

have been exposed to thousands of pennies during your life. Despite this experience, you probably don't have a clear sense of the details of the coin. (See this for yourself by looking at Figure 3.) Consequently, the reason for your memory failure is that you probably never encoded the information into long-term memory initially. Obviously, if information was not placed in memory to start with, there is no way the information can be recalled.

But what about material that has been encoded into memory and that can't later be remembered? Several processes account for memory failures, including decay, interference, and cue-dependent forgetting.

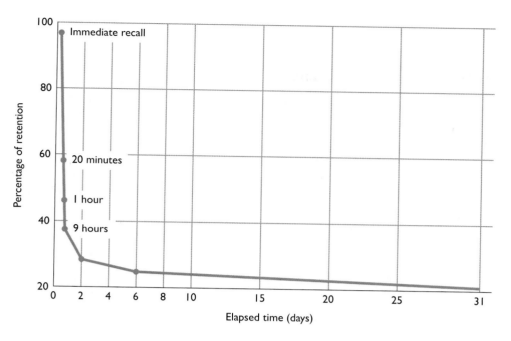

FIGURE 2 In his classic work, Ebbinghaus found that the most rapid forgetting occurs in the first nine hours after exposure to new material. However, the rate of forgetting then slows down and declines very little even after many days have passed (Ebbinghaus, 1885, 1913). Check your own memory: What were you doing exactly two hours ago? What were you doing last Tuesday at 5 P.M.? Which information is easier to retrieve?

Decay is the loss of information through nonuse. This explanation for forgetting assumes that **memory traces,** the physical changes that take place in the brain when new material is learned, simply fade away over time.

Although there is evidence that decay does occur, this does not seem to be the complete explanation for forgetting. Often there is no relationship between how long ago a person was exposed to information and how well that information is recalled. If decay explained all forgetting, we would expect that the more time that has elapsed between the initial learning of information and our attempt to recall it, the harder it would be to remember it, because there would be more time for the memory trace to decay. Yet people who take several consecutive tests on the same material often recall more of the initial information when taking later tests than they did on earlier tests. If decay were operating, we would expect the opposite to occur (Payne, 1986).

Decay: The loss of information in memory through its nonuse.

Memory trace: A physical change in the brain that occurs when new material is learned.

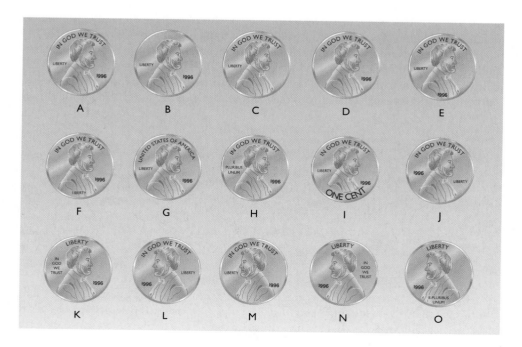

FIGURE 3 One of these pennies is the real thing. Can you find it? Why is this task harder than it seems at first? (Source: Nickerson & Adams, 1979.)

If you don't have a penny handy, the correct answer is "A."

Because decay does not fully account for forgetting, memory specialists have proposed an additional mechanism: **interference.** In interference, information in memory disrupts the recall of other information.

To distinguish between decay and interference, think of the two processes in terms of a row of books on a library shelf. In decay, the old books are constantly crumbling and rotting away, leaving room for new arrivals. Interference processes suggest that new books knock the old ones off the shelf, where they become inaccessible.

Finally, forgetting may occur because of **cue-dependent forgetting,** forgetting that occurs when there are insufficient retrieval cues to rekindle information that is in memory (Tulving & Thompson, 1983). For example, you may not be able to remember where you lost a set of keys until you mentally walk through your day, thinking of each place you visited. When you think of the place where you lost the keys—say, the library—the retrieval cue of the library may be sufficient to help you recall that you left them on the desk in the library. Without that retrieval cue, you may be unable to recall the location of the keys.

Most research suggests that interference and cue-dependent forgetting are key processes in forgetting (Mel'nikov, 1993; Bower, Thompson, & Tulving, 1994). We forget things mainly because new memories interfere with the retrieval of old ones or because appropriate retrieval cues are unavailable, not because the memory trace has decayed.

Interference: The phenomenon by which information in memory disrupts the recall of other information.

Cue-dependent forgetting: Forgetting that occurs when there are insufficient retrieval cues to rekindle information that is in memory.

Proactive and Retroactive Interference: The Before and After of Forgetting

There are actually two types of interference that influence forgetting: proactive and retroactive. In **proactive interference,** information learned earlier disrupts the recall of newer material. Suppose, as a student of foreign languages, you first learned French in the tenth grade, and then in the eleventh grade you took Spanish. When in the twelfth grade you take a college achievement test in Spanish, you may find you have difficulty recalling the Spanish translation of a word because all you can think of is its French equivalent.

In contrast, **retroactive interference** refers to difficulty in the recall of information because of later exposure to different material. If, for example, you have difficulty on a French achievement test because of your more recent exposure to Spanish, retroactive interference is the culprit (see Figure 4). One way to remember the differ-

Proactive interference: Interference in which information learned earlier disrupts the recall of newer material.

Retroactive interference: Interference in which there is difficulty in the recall of information learned earlier because of later exposure to different material.

FIGURE 4 Proactive interference occurs when material learned earlier interferes with the recall of newer material. In this example, studying French before studying Spanish interferes with performance on a Spanish test. In contrast, retroactive interference exists when material learned after initial exposure to other material interferes with the recall of the earlier material. In this case, retroactive interference occurs when recall of French is impaired because of later exposure to Spanish.

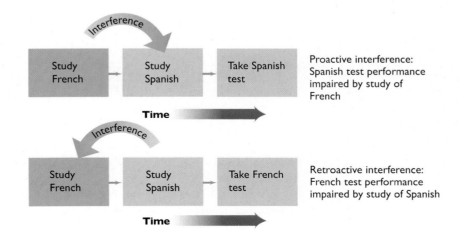

ence between proactive and retroactive interference is to keep in mind that *proactive interference* progresses in time—the past interferes with the present—whereas *retroactive* interference retrogresses in time, working backward as the present interferes with the past.

Although the concepts of proactive and retroactive interference illustrate how material may be forgotten, they still do not explain whether forgetting is caused by the actual loss or modification of information or by problems in the retrieval of information. Most research suggests that material that has apparently been lost because of interference can eventually be recalled if appropriate stimuli are presented (Tulving & Psotka, 1971; Anderson, 1981), but the question has not been fully answered.

Memory Dysfunctions: Afflictions of Forgetting

First you notice that you're always misplacing things, or that common nouns are evading you as stubbornly as the names of new acquaintances. Pretty soon you're forgetting appointments and getting flustered when you drive in traffic. On bad days you find you can't hold numbers in your mind long enough to dial the phone. You try valiantly to conceal your lapses, but they become ever more glaring. You crash your car. You spend whole mornings struggling to dress yourself properly. And even as you lose the ability to read or play the piano, you're painfully aware of what's happening to you (Cowley, 2000).

These memory problems are symptomatic of **Alzheimer's disease,** an illness characterized in part by severe memory problems. Alzheimer's is the fourth leading cause of death among adults in the United States. One in five people between the ages of 75 and 84, and almost half of those 85 and older, have Alzheimer's disease.

In the beginning, Alzheimer's symptoms appear as simple forgetfulness of things such as appointments and birthdays. As the disease progresses, memory loss becomes more profound, and even the simplest tasks—such as using a telephone—are forgotten. Ultimately, victims may lose their ability to speak or comprehend language, and physical deterioration sets in, leading to death.

Some researchers argue that a breakdown in working memory's central executive may result in the memory losses that are characteristic of Alzheimer's disease, the progressively degenerative disorder that produces loss of memory and confusion (Cherry, Buckwalter, & Henderson, 2002). The causes of Alzheimer's disease are not fully understood, however. Increasing evidence suggests that Alzheimer's results from an inherited susceptibility to a defect in the production of the protein beta amyloid, which is necessary for the maintenance of nerve cell connections. When the synthesis of beta amyloid goes awry, large clumps of cells form, triggering inflammation and the deterioration of nerve cells in the brain (Cooper et al., 2000; Hardy & Selkoe, 2002; Selkoe, 2002; see Figure 5).

Alzheimer's disease: An illness characterized in part by severe memory problems.

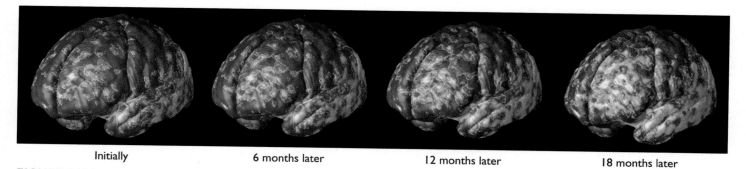

| Initially | 6 months later | 12 months later | 18 months later |

FIGURE 5 This series of brain images clearly show the changes caused by the spread of Alzheimer's disease over eighteen months, with the normal tissue (signified by the purple color) retreating over the period.

www.mhhe.com/feldmanup8
PsychInteractive Online

Alzheimer's Disease

Amnesia: Memory loss that occurs without other mental difficulties.

Retrograde amnesia: Amnesia in which memory is lost for occurrences prior to a certain event.

Anterograde amnesia: Amnesia in which memory is lost for events that follow an injury.

Korsakoff's syndrome: A disease that afflicts long-term alcoholics, leaving some abilities intact, but including hallucinations and a tendency to repeat the same story.

Alzheimer's disease (about which you can learn more in the PsychInteractive exercise) is one of a number of memory dysfunctions. Another is **amnesia,** memory loss that occurs without other mental difficulties. The type of amnesia immortalized in countless Hollywood films involves a victim who receives a blow to the head and is unable to remember anything from his or her past. In reality, amnesia of this type, known as retrograde amnesia, is quite rare. In **retrograde amnesia,** memory is lost for occurrences prior to a certain event. Usually, lost memories gradually reappear, although full restoration may take as long as several years. In certain cases, some memories are lost forever. But even in cases of severe memory loss, the loss is generally selective. For example, although people suffering from retrograde amnesia may be unable to recall friends and family members, they still may be able to play complicated card games or knit a sweater quite well (Markowitsch, 2000; Verfaellie & Keane, 2002).

A second type of amnesia is exemplified by people who remember nothing of their current activities. In **anterograde amnesia,** loss of memory occurs for events that follow an injury. Information cannot be transferred from short-term to long-term memory, resulting in the inability to remember anything other than what was in long-term storage before the accident.

Amnesia is also a consequence of **Korsakoff's syndrome,** a disease that afflicts long-term alcoholics. Although many of their intellectual abilities may be intact, Korsakoff's sufferers display a strange array of symptoms, including hallucinations and a tendency to repeat the same story over and over.

Fortunately, most of us have intact memory, and the occasional failures we suffer may actually be preferable to having a perfect memory. Consider, for instance, the case of a man who had total recall. After reading passages of the *Divine Comedy* in Italian—a language he did not speak—he was able to repeat them from memory some fifteen years later. He could memorize lists of fifty unrelated words and recall them at will more than a decade later. He could even repeat the same list of words backward, if asked (Luria, 1968).

Such a skill at first may seem to be enviable, but it actually presented quite a problem. The man's memory became a jumble of lists of words, numbers, and names, and when he tried to relax, his mind was filled with images. Even reading was difficult, since every word evoked a flood of thoughts from the past that interfered with his ability to understand the meaning of what he was reading. Partially as a consequence of the man's unusual memory, psychologist A. R. Luria, who studied his case, found him to be a "disorganized and rather dull-witted person" (Luria, 1968, p. 65).

We might be grateful, then, that forgetfulness plays a role in our lives.

BECOMING AN INFORMED CONSUMER of Psychology

Improving Your Memory

Apart from the advantages of forgetting, say, a bad date, most of us would like to find ways to improve our memories. Is it possible to find practical ways to increase our recall of information? Most definitely. Research has revealed a number of strategies for developing a better memory (VanLehn, 1996; Hermann, Raybeck, & Gruneberg, 2002; West, Thorn, & Bagwell, 2003). Let's look at some of the best.

- *The keyword technique.* Suppose you are taking a foreign language class and need to learn vocabulary words. You can try the *keyword technique* of pairing a foreign word with a common English word that has a similar sound. This English word is known as the *keyword*. For example, to learn the Spanish word for duck (*pato,* pronounced *pot-o*), you might choose the keyword *pot;* for the Spanish word for horse (*caballo,* pronounced *cob-eye-yo*), the keyword might be *eye.*

  Once you have thought of a keyword, imagine the Spanish word "interacting" with the English keyword. You might envision a duck taking a bath in a pot to remember the word *pato,* or a horse with a large, bulging eye in the center of its head to recall *caballo.* This technique has produced considerably superior results in learning foreign language vocabulary compared with more traditional techniques involving memorization of the words themselves (Pressley, 1987; Gruneberg & Pascoe, 1996; Carney & Levin, 1998).

- *Encoding specificity.* Some research suggests that we remember information best in an environment that is the same as or similar to the one where we initially learned it—a phenomenon known as *encoding specificity.* You may do better on a test, then, if you study in the classroom where the test will be given. However, if you must take a test in a room different from the one in which you studied, don't despair: The features of the test itself, such as the wording of the test questions, are sometimes so powerful that they overwhelm the subtler cues relating to the original encoding of the material (Bjork & Richardson-Klarehn, 1989).

- *Organization cues.* Many of life's important recall tasks involve texts that you have read. One proven technique for improving recall of written material is to organize the material in memory as you read it for the first time. Organize your reading on the basis of any advance information you have about the content and about its organization. You will then be able to make connections and see relationships among the various facts and process the material at a deeper level, which in turn will later aid recall.

- *Effective note taking.* "Less is more" is perhaps the best advice for taking lecture notes that facilitate recall. Rather than trying to jot down every detail of a lecture, it is better to listen and think about the material, and take down the main points. In effective note taking, thinking about the material initially is more important than writing it down. This is one reason that borrowing someone else's notes is a bad idea; you will have no framework in memory that you can use to understand them (Feldman, 2006).

- *Practice and rehearse.* Although practice does not necessarily make perfect, it helps. By studying and rehearsing material past initial mastery—a process called *overlearning*—people are able to show better long-term recall than they show if they stop practicing after their initial learning of the material. Keep in mind that as research clearly demonstrates, fatigue and other factors prevent long practice sessions from being as effective as distributed practice.

- *Don't believe claims about drugs that improve memory.* Advertisements for One-A-Day vitamins with ginkgo biloba or Quanterra Mental Sharpness Product would have you believe that taking a drug can improve your memory. Not so, according to the results of studies. No research has shown that commercial memory enhancers are effective (Gold, Cahill, & Wenk, 2002; McDaniel, Maier, & Einstein, 2002). So save your money!

RECAP/EVALUATE/RETHINK

RECAP

Why do we forget information?

- Several processes account for memory failure, including decay, interference (both proactive and retroactive), and cue-dependent forgetting. (pp. 241-245)

What are the major memory impairments?

- Among the memory dysfunctions are Alzheimer's disease, which leads to a progressive loss of memory, and amnesia, a memory loss that occurs without other mental difficulties and that can take two forms: retrograde amnesia and anterograde amnesia. Korsakoff's syndrome is a disease that afflicts long-term alcoholics, resulting in memory impairment. (pp. 245-246)

- Among the techniques for improving memory are the keyword technique to memorize foreign language vocabulary; using the encoding specificity phenomenon; organizing text material and lecture notes; and practice and rehearsal, leading to overlearning. (pp. 246-247)

EVALUATE

1. If, after learning the history of the Middle East for a class two years ago, you now find yourself unable to recall what you learned, you are experiencing memory _____, caused by nonuse.

2. Difficulty in accessing a memory because of the presence of other information is known as _____.

3. _____ interference occurs when material is difficult to retrieve because of subsequent exposure to other material; _____ interference refers to difficulty in retrieving material as a result of the interference of previously learned material.

4. Match the following memory disorders with the correct information:
   1. Affects alcoholics; may result in hallucinations.
   2. Memory loss occurring without other mental problems.
   3. Beta amyloid defect; progressive forgetting and physical deterioration.
   a. Alzheimer's disease
   b. Korsakoff's syndrome
   c. Amnesia

KEY TERMS

decay p. 243
memory trace p. 243
interference p. 244
cue-dependent forgetting
   p. 244

proactive interference p. 244
retroactive interference
   p. 244
Alzheimer's disease p. 245
amnesia p. 246

retrograde amnesia p. 246
anterograde amnesia p. 246
Korsakoff's syndrome p. 246

RETHINK

1. What are the implications of proactive and retroactive inhibition for learning multiple foreign languages? Would previous language training help or hinder learning a new language?

2. *From a healthcare provider's perspective:* Alzheimer's disease and amnesia are two of the most pervasive memory dysfunctions that threaten many individuals. What sorts of activities might healthcare providers offer their patients to help them combat their memory loss?

Answers to Evaluate Questions

1. decay; 2. interference; 3. retroactive, proactive; 4. 1-b, 2-c, 3-a

Looking Back

Psychology on the Web

1. The study of repressed memories can lead down unusual pathways—even more unusual than the criminal investigation pathway. Two other areas in which repressed memories play a large part are alien abduction and reincarnation. Find two sources on the Web that deal with one of these issues—one supportive and one skeptical. Read what they say and relate it to your knowledge of memory. Summarize your findings and indicate which side of the controversy your study of memory leads you to favor.

2. Memory is a topic of serious interest to psychologists, but it is also a source of amusement. Find a Web site that focuses on the amusing side of memory (such as memory games, tests of recall, or lists of mnemonics; hint: there's even a mnemonics generator out there!). Write down the addresses of any interesting sites that you encounter and summarize what you found.

3. After completing the PsychInteractive exercise on eyewitness fallibility, find two actual cases of failures of eyewitness memory in a courtroom situation. Summarize each case briefly.

Epilogue

Our examination of memory has highlighted the processes of encoding, storage, and retrieval and theories about how these processes occur. We also encountered several phenomena relating to memory, including the tip-of-the-tongue phenomenon and flashbulb memories. Above all, we observed that memory is a constructive process by which interpretations, expectations, and guesses contribute to the nature of our memories.

Before moving on to the next chapter, return to the prologue on John Prigg's accident and lost memories. Consider the following questions in light of what you now know about memory.

1. John Prigg's memory loss is called "retrograde amnesia." What does this mean?
2. What would have been the effects on John's life if his accident had caused anterograde amnesia?
3. If John suddenly announced that he has recovered his memory, how would psychologists know that he is really recalling the past rather than simply accepting as his own memories the stories that others have told him?
4. How might investigators examine John during his recovery to answer questions about the biological bases of memory? Assuming John gave his consent to PET scans and other means of looking inside his cerebral cortex, what sorts of questions might be explored?

CHAPTER 8

Cognition and Language

Key Concepts for Chapter 8

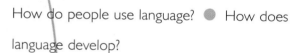

Prologue The Sky's the Limit

When the first American flew into space in 1961, Burt Rutan was a 17-year-old college freshman. Listening to news of Alan Shepard's groundbreaking suborbital flight on the radio, Rutan was euphoric. He too hoped to go into space one day. . . .

SpaceShipOne [the rocket he designed to accomplish his dream] is a shell of woven graphite glued onto a rocket motor that runs on laughing gas and rubber. The nose is punctuated by portholes, like an ocean liner. Inside, the critical instrument is a Ping-Pong ball decorated with a smiley face and attached to the cabin with a piece of string, which goes slack when the pilot reaches the zero-gravity of suborbital space.

Despite its Flash Gordon looks and unorthodox design . . . it became the first privately funded spacecraft. In October it clinched the $10 million Ansari X Prize as the first such craft to travel to space twice in two weeks. Thanks to the backing of two starry-eyed billionaires, SpaceShipOne is set to become the first in a new line of space-tourism craft coming in 2007. "It's a spaceship that fits in your two-car garage, and you can take it to space every other day," says X Prize founder Peter Diamandis. "That's pretty cool" (Taylor, 2004).

Looking Ahead

Burt Rutan has big plans for his invention. But whether or not SpaceShipOne revolutionizes space travel, it is clear that Rutan has the elusive quality that marks successful inventors: creativity.

Where did Rutan's creativity come from? More generally, how do people use information to devise innovative solutions to problems? And how do people think about, understand, and, through language, describe the world?

Answers to these questions come from **cognitive psychology,** the branch of psychology that focuses on the study of higher mental processes, including thinking, language, memory, problem solving, knowing, reasoning, judging, and decision making. Clearly, the realm of cognitive psychology is broad.

Cognitive psychology centers on three major topics: thinking and reasoning, problem solving and creativity, and language. The first topic we consider in this chapter is thinking and reasoning. Then we examine different strategies for approaching problems, means of generating solutions, and ways of making judgments about the usefulness and accuracy of solutions. Finally, we discuss how language is developed and acquired, its basic characteristics, and the relationship between language and thought.

Thinking and Reasoning

What are you thinking about at this moment?

The mere ability to pose such a question underscores the distinctive nature of the human ability to think. No other species contemplates, analyzes, recollects, or plans the way humans do. Understanding what thinking is, however, goes beyond knowing that we think. Philosophers, for example, have argued for generations about the meaning of thinking, with some placing it at the core of human beings' understanding of their own existence.

Psychologists define **thinking** as the manipulation of mental representations of information. A representation may take the form of a word, a visual image, a sound, or data in any other sensory modality stored in memory. Thinking transforms a particular representation of information into new and different forms in order to answer questions, solve problems, or reach goals.

Although a clear sense of what specifically occurs when we think remains elusive, our understanding of the nature of the fundamental elements involved in thinking is growing. We begin by considering our use of mental images and concepts, the building blocks of thought.

Mental Images: Examining the Mind's Eye

Think of your best friend.

Chances are that you "see" some kind of visual image when asked to think of her or him, or any other person or object, for that matter. To some cognitive psychologists, such mental images constitute a major part of thinking.

Mental images are representations in the mind of an object or event. They are not just visual representations; our ability to "hear" a tune in our heads also relies on a mental image. In fact, every sensory modality may produce corresponding mental images (Paivio, 1971, 1975; Kosslyn & Shin, 1994; Kosslyn, 2005).

Research has found that our mental images have many of the properties of the actual stimuli they represent. For example, it takes the mind longer to scan mental images of large objects than of small ones, just as the eye takes longer to scan an actual large object than an actual small one. Similarly, we are able to manipulate and rotate mental images of objects, just as we are able to manipulate and rotate them in the real world (Shepard et al., 2000; Mast & Kosslyn, 2002; Iachini & Giusberti, 2004; see Figure 1).

Some experts see the production of mental images as a way to improve various skills. For instance, many athletes use mental imagery in their training. Basketball

Key Concepts

What is thinking?

What processes underlie reasoning and decision making?

"What do you think I think about what you think I think you've been thinking about?"

Cognitive psychology: The branch of psychology that focuses on the study of higher mental processes, including thinking, language, memory, problem solving, knowing, reasoning, judging, and decision making.

Thinking: The manipulation of mental representations of information.

Mental images: Representations in the mind that resemble the object or event being represented.

FIGURE 1 Try to mentally rotate one of each pair of patterns to see if it is the same as the other member of that pair. It's likely that the farther you have to mentally rotate a pattern, the longer it will take to decide if the patterns match one another. (Source: Based on Shepard & Metzler, 1971.) Does this mean that it will take you longer to visualize a map of the world than a map of the United States? Why or why not?

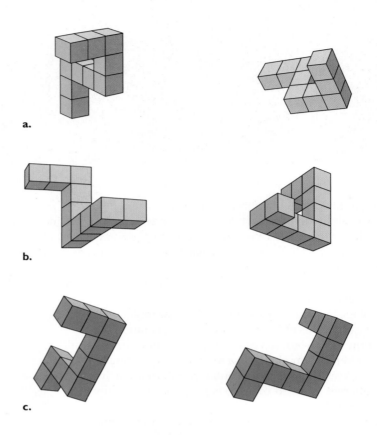

a.

b.

c.

Many athletes use mental imagery to focus on a task, a process they call "getting in the zone." What are some other occupations that require the use of strong mental imagery?

players may try to produce vivid and detailed images of the court, the basket, the ball, and the noisy crowd. They may visualize themselves taking a foul shot, watching the ball, and hearing the swish as it goes through the net. And it works: The use of mental imagery can lead to improved performance in sports (Druckman & Bjork, 1991; Cummings & Hall, 2002; MacIntyre, Moran, & Jennings, 2002; Mamassis & Doganis, 2004).

Using mental imagery may improve other types of skills as well. In music, for example, researcher Alvaro Pascual-Leone taught groups of people to play a five-finger exercise on the piano. One group practiced the exercise every day for five days, while a control group played daily without any training, just hitting the keys at random. Finally, the members of a third group were taught the exercise but were not allowed to try it out on the piano. Instead, they rehearsed it mentally, sitting at the piano every day and looking at the keys, but not actually touching them.

Comparing brain scans of people in the groups, researchers found a distinct difference between those who manually practiced the exercise and those who just randomly hit keys. However, the most surprising finding came from the group that mentally rehearsed: Their brain scans were virtually identical to those of the people who had actually practiced the exercise manually (see Figure 2). Apparently, carrying out the task involved the same network of brain cells as the network used in mentally rehearsing it (Chase, 1993; Pascual-Leone et al., 1995; Cisek & Kalaska, 2004).

Such research suggests that children whose parents nag them about practicing an instrument, a dance routine, or some other skill can now employ a new excuse: They *are* practicing—mentally.

Concepts: Categorizing the World

If someone asks you what was in your kitchen cabinet, you might answer with a detailed list of items ("a jar of peanut butter, three boxes of macaroni and cheese, six

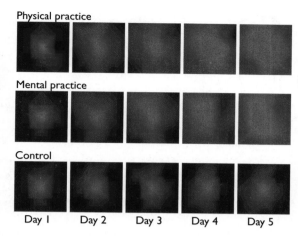

Physical practice

Mental practice

Control

Day 1   Day 2   Day 3   Day 4   Day 5

FIGURE 2 Compared with the brain scans of people who actually practiced a piano finger exercise, the brain scans of those who only used mental rehearsal but did not touch the piano were nearly identical. The results of the experiment clearly show the value of mental imagery. (Source: Pascual-Leone et al., 1995.)

unmatched dinner plates," and so forth). More likely, though, you would respond by naming some broader categories, such as "food" and "dishes."

Using such categories reflects the operation of concepts. **Concepts** are categorizations of objects, events, or people that share common properties. Concepts enable us to organize complex phenomena into simpler, and therefore more easily usable, cognitive categories (Margolis & Laurence, 1999; Goldstone & Kersten, 2003; Murphy, 2005).

Concepts help us classify newly encountered objects on the basis of our past experience. For example, we can surmise that someone tapping a handheld screen is probably using some kind of computer or PDA, even if we have never encountered that specific model before. Ultimately, concepts influence behavior; we would assume, for instance, that it might be appropriate to pet an animal after determining that it is a dog, whereas we would behave differently after classifying the animal as a wolf.

When cognitive psychologists first studied concepts, they focused on those which were clearly defined by a unique set of properties or features. For example, an equilateral triangle is a closed shape that has three sides of equal length. If an object has these characteristics, it is an equilateral triangle; if it does not, it is not an equilateral triangle.

Other concepts—often those with the most relevance to our everyday lives—are more ambiguous and difficult to define. For instance, broader concepts such as "table" and "bird" have a set of general, relatively loose characteristic features, rather than unique, clearly defined properties that distinguish an example of the concept from a nonexample. When we consider these more ambiguous concepts, we usually think in terms of examples called **prototypes.** Prototypes are typical, highly representative examples of a concept that correspond to our mental image or best example of the concept. For instance, although a robin and an ostrich are both examples of birds, the robin is an example that comes to most people's minds far more readily. Consequently, robin is a prototype of the concept "bird." Similarly, when we think of the concept of a table, we're likely to think of a coffee table before we think of a drafting table, making a coffee table closer to our prototype of a table.

Relatively high agreement exists among people in a particular culture about which examples of a concept are prototypes, as well as which examples are not. For instance, most people in Western cultures consider cars and trucks good examples of vehicles, whereas elevators and wheelbarrows are not considered very good examples. Consequently, cars and trucks are prototypes of the concept of a vehicle (see Figure 3).

Concepts: Categorizations of objects, events, or people that share common properties.

Prototypes: Typical, highly representative examples of a concept.

FIGURE 3 Prototypes are typical, highly representative examples of a concept. For instance, a highly typical prototype of the concept "furniture" is a chair, whereas a stove is not a good prototype. High agreement exists within a culture about which examples of a concept are prototypes. (Source: Adapted from Rosch & Mervis, 1975.)

Ranking of Prototype from Most to Least Typical	Concept Category			
	Furniture	Vehicle	Weapon	Vegetable
1—Most Typical	Chair	Car	Gun	Peas
2	Sofa	Truck	Knife	Carrots
3	Table	Bus	Sword	String beans
4	Dresser	Motorcycle	Bomb	Spinach
5	Desk	Train	Hand grenade	Broccoli
6	Bed	Trolley car	Spear	Asparagus
7	Bookcase	Bicycle	Cannon	Corn
8	Footstool	Airplane	Bow and arrow	Cauliflower
9	Lamp	Boat	Club	Brussels sprouts
10	Piano	Tractor	Tank	Lettuce
11	Cushion	Cart	Tear gas	Beets
12	Mirror	Wheelchair	Whip	Tomato
13	Rug	Tank	Ice pick	Lima beans
14	Radio	Raft	Fists	Eggplant
15—Least Typical	Stove	Sled	Rocket	Onion

Concepts enable us to think about and understand more readily the complex world in which we live. For example, the suppositions we make about the reasons for other people's behavior are based on the ways in which we classify behavior. Hence, our conclusion that a person who washes her hands twenty times a day could vary, depending on whether we place her behavior within the conceptual framework of a health care worker or a mental patient. Similarly, physicians make diagnoses by drawing on concepts and prototypes of symptoms that they learned about in medical school. Finally, concepts and prototypes facilitate our efforts to draw suitable conclusions through the cognitive process we turn to next: reasoning.

How do you view these structures? Whether you categorize them as two houses of worship (left & middle), as two similar examples of architecture (middle & right), or simply as three buildings, you are using concepts.

Reasoning: Making Up Your Mind

Professors deciding when students' assignments are due.
An employer determining who to hire out of a pool of job applicants.
The president concluding that it is necessary to send troops to a foreign nation.

What do these three situations have in common? Each requires *reasoning*, the process by which information is used to draw conclusions and make decisions.

Although philosophers and logicians have considered the foundations of reasoning for centuries, it is only relatively recently that cognitive psychologists have begun to investigate how people reason and make decisions. Their efforts have contributed to our understanding of formal reasoning processes as well as the cognitive shortcuts we routinely use—shortcuts that sometimes may lead our reasoning capabilities astray.

SYLLOGISTIC REASONING: THE FORMAL RULES OF LOGIC

If you've ever played a card game like poker and tried to figure out what cards your opponent was holding, you probably used **syllogistic reasoning,** a kind of formal reasoning in which a person draws a conclusion from a set of assumptions. In using syllogistic reasoning, we begin with a general assumption that we believe is true and then derive specific implications from that assumption. If the assumption is true, the conclusions must also be true (Fisk & Sharp, 2002; Marrero & Gamez, 2004).

A major technique for studying syllogistic reasoning involves asking people to evaluate a series of statements that present two assumptions, or premises, that are used to derive a conclusion. For example, consider the following syllogism:

Premise 1   All professors are mortal.
Premise 2   Dr. Rivera is a professor.
Conclusion   Therefore, Dr. Rivera is mortal.

Because both premises are true, by applying logic appropriately we come to an accurate conclusion. More abstractly, we can state the syllogism as the following:

Premise 1   All A's are B.
Premise 2   C is an A.
Conclusion   Therefore, C is a B.

However, even if the premises are correct, people may apply logic incorrectly. For example, consider the following syllogism:

Premise 1   All A's are B.
Premise 2   C is an A.
Conclusion   Therefore, all A's are C.

Although it may not be immediately apparent, the conclusion is illogical—something seen more readily if we make the syllogism more concrete:

Premise 1   All professors are mortal.
Premise 2   Professor Rivera is a professor.
Conclusion   Therefore, all professors are Dr. Rivera.

In short, syllogistic reasoning is only as accurate as the premises and the validity of the logic applied to the premises.

Syllogistic reasoning: Formal reasoning in which a person draws a conclusion from a set of assumptions.

ALGORITHMS AND HEURISTICS

Algorithm: A rule that, if applied appropriately, guarantees a solution to a problem.

Heuristic: A cognitive shortcut that may lead to a solution.

www.mhhe.com/feldmanup8

PsychInteractive Online

Heuristics

When faced with making a decision, we often turn to various kinds of cognitive shortcuts, known as algorithms and heuristics, to help us. An **algorithm** is a rule that, if applied appropriately, guarantees a solution to a problem. We can use an algorithm even if we cannot understand why it works. For example, you may know that the length of the third side of a right triangle can be found by using the formula $a^2 + b^2 = c^2$, although you may not have the foggiest notion of the mathematical principles behind the formula.

For many problems and decisions, however, no algorithm is available. In those instances, we may be able to use heuristics to help us. A **heuristic** is a cognitive shortcut that may lead to a solution. Heuristics enhance the likelihood of success in coming to a solution, but, unlike algorithms, they cannot ensure it. For example, when I play tic-tac-toe, I follow the heuristic of placing an X in the center square when I start the game. This tactic doesn't guarantee that I will win, but experience has taught me that it will increase my chances of success. Similarly, some students follow the heuristic of preparing for a test by ignoring the assigned textbook reading and only studying their lecture notes—a strategy that may or may not pay off. Practice using heuristics in the PsychInteractive exercise.

Although heuristics often help people solve problems and make decisions, certain kinds of heuristics may lead to inaccurate conclusions. For example, we sometimes use the *representativeness heuristic,* a rule we apply when we judge people by the degree to which they represent a certain category or group of people. Suppose, for instance, you are the owner of a fast-food store that has been robbed many times by teenagers. The representativeness heuristic would lead you to raise your guard each time someone of this age group enters your store (even though, statistically, it is unlikely that any given teenager will rob the store).

The *availability heuristic* involves judging the probability of an event on the basis of how easily the event can be recalled from memory. According to this heuristic, we assume that events we remember easily are likely to have occurred more frequently in the past—and are more likely to occur in the future—than events that are harder to remember.

For instance, people are usually more afraid of dying in a plane crash than in an auto accident, despite statistics clearly showing that airplane travel is much safer than auto travel. The reason is that plane crashes receive far more publicity than car crashes do, and they are therefore more easily remembered. The *availability heuristic* leads people to conclude that they are in greater jeopardy in an airplane than in a car (Schwarz et al., 1991; Vaughn & Weary, 2002; Oppenheimer, 2004).

Are algorithms and heuristics confined to human thinking, or can computers be programmed to use them to mimic human thinking and problem solving? As we discuss next, scientists are certainly trying.

Computers and Problem Solving: Searching for Artificial Intelligence

To the listening music experts, there was no mistaking who had written the piano piece: Johann Sebastian Bach, the prolific German composer who was born in the fifteenth century.

But the experts were wrong. The piece they all thought was a Bach composition was actually created by a computer named "EMI" by David Cope of the University of California. After a variety of actual Bach pieces had been scanned into its memory, EMI was able to produce music that was so similar to Bach's actual music that it fooled knowledgeable listeners (Johnson, 1997; Cope, 2001).

Such computer mimicry is possible because composers have a particular "signature" that reflects patterns, sequences, and combinations of notes. By employing those "signatures," computers can create compositions that have the full scope and emotional appeal of actual works—and show just as much creativity as those written by the actual composer (Cope, 2001, 2003).

But does EMI's success in fooling experts mean that the computer has reached the level of accomplishment shown by the actual composer? Critics say "no," suggesting that there is something unique and special about human thought and the creative process. They argue that although computers can be programmed to be sensitive to specific, rapid patterns characteristic of a particular composer, they are unable to get the broad, sweeping, "bigger picture" that characterizes the works of great composers.

We don't know whether the critics are correct. However, it is clear that computers are making significant inroads in terms of the ability to solve problems and carry out some forms of intellectual activities. In fact, the success of computers has led some researchers to consider not only whether computers can compose music, but whether they can also be said to actually think in a way that is similar to humans (Fellous & Arbib, 2005; Sabater & Sierra, 2005).

According to experts who study *artificial intelligence,* the field that examines how to use technology to imitate the outcome of human thinking, problem solving, and creative activities, computers show rudiments of humanlike thinking because of their knowledge of where to look—and where not to look—for an answer to a problem. They suggest that the capacity of computer programs (such as those that play chess) to evaluate potential moves and to ignore unimportant possibilities gives them thinking ability (Byrne, 2005; Embretson, 2005).

Many of the questions surrounding the ability of computers to think and behave creatively have not been answered. Still, it is clear that computers are becoming increasingly sophisticated, ever more closely approximating human thought processes.

RECAP/EVALUATE/RETHINK

RECAP

What is thinking?

- Cognitive psychology encompasses the higher mental processes, including the way people know and understand the world, process information, make decisions and judgments, and describe their knowledge and understanding to others. (p. 252)
- Thinking is the manipulation of mental representations of information. Thinking transforms such representations into novel and different forms, permitting people to answer questions, solve problems, and reach goals. (p. 253)
- Mental images are representations in the mind of an object or event. (p. 253)
- Concepts are categorizations of objects, events, or people that share common properties. Prototypes are representative examples of concepts. (pp. 254-255)

What processes underlie reasoning and decision making?

- In syllogistic reasoning, people derive implications from a set of assumptions that they know to be true. (pp. 256-257)

- Decisions sometimes (but not always) may be improved through the use of algorithms and heuristics. An algorithm is a rule that, if applied appropriately, guarantees a solution; a heuristic is a cognitive shortcut that may lead to a solution but is not guaranteed to do so. (pp. 257-258)

EVALUATE

1. _____ are representations in the mind of an object or event.
2. _____ are categorizations of objects that share common properties.
3. When you think of the concept "chair," you immediately think of a comfortable easy chair. A chair of this type could be thought of as a _____ of the category "chair."
4. When you ask your friend how best to study for your psychology final, he tells you, "I've always found it best to skim over the notes once, then read the book, then go over the notes again." What decision-making tool might this be an example of?

RETHINK

1. How might the availability heuristic contribute to prejudices based on race, age, and gender? Can awareness of this heuristic prevent this from happening?
2. *From the perspective of a human resources specialist:* How might you use the research on mental imagery to improve employees' performance?

KEY TERMS

cognitive psychology p. 253
thinking p. 253

mental images p. 253
concepts p. 255

prototypes p. 255
syllogistic reasoning p. 257

algorithm p. 258
heuristic p. 258

Problem Solving

According to an old legend, a group of Vietnamese monks guard three towers on which sit sixty-four golden rings. The monks believe that if they succeed in moving the rings from the first tower to the third according to a series of rigid rules, the world as we know it will come to an end. (Should you prefer that the world remain in its present state, there's no need for immediate concern: The puzzle is so complex that it will take the monks about a trillion years to solve it.)

In the Tower of Hanoi puzzle, a simpler version of the task facing the monks, three disks are placed on three posts in the order shown in Figure 1. The goal of the puzzle is to move all three disks to the third post, arranged in the same order, by using as few moves as possible. There are two restrictions: Only one disk can be moved at a time, and no disk can ever cover a smaller one during a move.

Why are cognitive psychologists interested in the Tower of Hanoi problem? Because the way people go about solving such puzzles helps illuminate how people solve complex, real-life problems. Psychologists have found that problem solving typically involves the three steps illustrated in Figure 2: preparing to create solutions, producing solutions, and evaluating the solutions that have been generated.

Key Concepts

How do people approach and solve problems?

What are the major obstacles to problem solving?

What is creativity?

Preparation: Understanding and Diagnosing Problems

When approaching a problem like the Tower of Hanoi, most people begin by trying to understand the problem thoroughly. If the problem is a novel one, they probably will pay particular attention to any restrictions placed on coming up with a solution—such as the rule for moving only one disk at a time in the Tower of Hanoi problem. If, by contrast, the problem is a familiar one, they are apt to spend considerably less time in this preparation stage.

Problems vary from well defined to ill-defined (Reitman, 1965; Arlin, 1989; Evans, 2004). In a *well-defined problem*—such as a mathematical equation or the solution to a jigsaw puzzle—both the nature of the problem itself and the information needed to solve it are available and clear. Thus, we can make straightforward judgments about whether a potential solution is appropriate. With an *ill-defined problem,* such as how to increase morale on an assembly line or bring peace to the Middle East, not only may the specific nature of the problem be unclear, the information required to solve the problem may be even less obvious.

"I don't know about hair care, Rapunzel, but I'm thinking a good cream rinse plus protein conditioner might just solve both our problems."

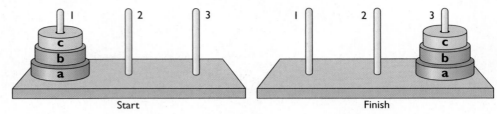

FIGURE I The goal of the Tower of Hanoi puzzle is to move all three disks from the first post to the third and still preserve the original order of the disks, using the fewest number of moves possible while following the rules that only one disk at a time can be moved and no disk can cover a smaller one during a move. Try it yourself before you look at the solution, which is listed according to the sequence of moves. (Solution: Move C to 3, B to 3, C to 2, A to 3, C to 2, A to 3, C to 1, B to 1, B to 3, and C to 3.)

Preparation

Understanding and diagnosing problems

↓

Production

Generating solutions

↓

Judgment

Evaluating solutions

FIGURE 2 Steps in problem solving.

KINDS OF PROBLEMS

Typically, a problem falls into one of the three categories shown in Figure 3: arrangement, inducing structure, and transformation. Solving each type requires somewhat different kinds of psychological skills and knowledge (Spitz, 1987; Chronicle, MacGregor, & Ormerod, 2004).

Arrangement problems require the problem solver to rearrange or recombine elements in a way that will satisfy a certain criterion. Usually, several different arrangements can be made, but only one or a few of the arrangements will produce a solution. Anagram problems and jigsaw puzzles are examples of arrangement problems (Coventry et al., 2003).

In *problems of inducing structure*, a person must identify the existing relationships among the elements presented and then construct a new relationship among them. In such a problem, the problem solver must determine not only the relationships among the elements but also the structure and size of the elements involved. In the example shown in Figure 3, a person must first determine that the solution requires the numbers to be considered in pairs (14-24-34-44-54-64). Only after identifying that part of the problem can a person determine the solution rule (the first number of each pair increases by one, while the second number remains the same).

The Tower of Hanoi puzzle represents the third kind of problem—*transformation problems*—which consist of an initial state, a goal state, and a method for changing the initial state into the goal state. In the Tower of Hanoi problem, the initial state is the original configuration, the goal state is to have the three disks on the third peg, and the method is the rules for moving the disks (Mataix-Cols & Bartres-Faz, 2002; Emick & Welsh, 2005).

Whether the problem is one of arrangement, inducing structure, or transformation, the preparation stage of understanding and diagnosing is critical in problem solving because it allows us to develop our own cognitive representation of the problem and to place it within a personal framework. We may divide the problem into subparts or ignore some information as we try to simplify the task. Winnowing out nonessential information is often a critical step in the preparation stage of problem solving.

REPRESENTING AND ORGANIZING THE PROBLEM

A crucial aspect of the initial encounter with a problem is the way in which we represent it to ourselves and organize the information presented to us (Brown & Walter, 1993; Davidson, Deuser, & Sternberg, 1994). Consider the following problem:

> A man climbs a mountain on Saturday, leaving at daybreak and arriving at the top near sundown. He spends the night at the top. The next day, Sunday, he leaves at daybreak and heads down the mountain, following the same path that he climbed the day before. The question is this: Will there be any time during the second day when he will be at exactly the same point on the mountain as he was at exactly that time on the first day?

a. Arrangement problems

1. Anagrams: Rearrange the letters in each set to make an English word:

2. Two strings hang from a ceiling but are too far apart to allow a person to hold one and walk to the other. On the floor are a book of matches, a screwdriver, and a few pieces of cotton. How could the strings be tied together?

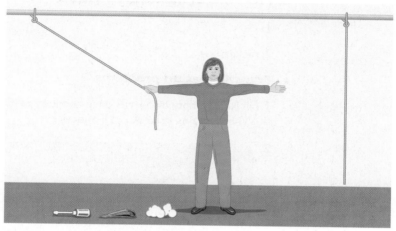

b. Problems of inducing structure

1. What number comes next in the series?

   1 4 2 4 3 4 4 4 5 4 6 4

2. Complete these analogies:

   baseball is to bat as tennis is to _____

   merchant is to sell as customer is to _____

c. Transformation problems

1. Water jars: A person has three jars with the following capacities:

   Jar A:
   28 ounces

   Jar B:
   7 ounces

   Jar C:
   5 ounces

   How can the person measure exactly 11 ounces of water?

2. Ten coins are arranged in the following way. By moving only *two* of the coins, make two rows that each contains six coins.

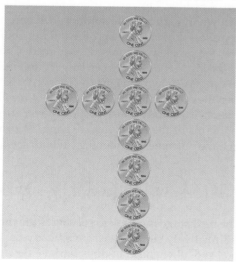

FIGURE 3 The three major categories of problems: (a) arrangement, (b) inducing structure, and (c) transformation. Solutions appear in Figure 4 on p. 264. (Sources: Bourne et al., 1986; water jar problem Aschcraft, 1994.)

FIGURE 4 Solutions to the problems in Figure 3.

a. Arrangement problems

1. FACET, DOUBT, THICK, NAIVE, ANVIL

2. The screwdriver is tied to one of the strings. This makes a pendulum that can be swung to reach the other string.

b. Problems of inducing structure

1. 7

2. racket; buy

c. Transformation problems

1. Fill jar A; empty into jar B once and into jar C twice. What remains in jar A is 11 ounces

2.

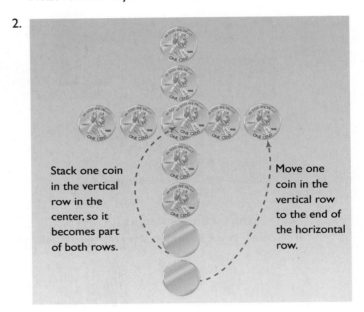

Stack one coin in the vertical row in the center, so it becomes part of both rows.
Move one coin in the vertical row to the end of the horizontal row.

Top
Sunday
Saturday
Altitude on mountain
Bottom
Sunrise
Sunset
Time of day

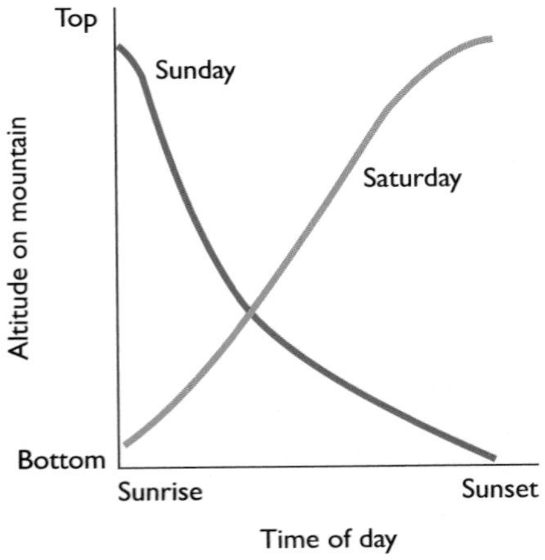

FIGURE 5 You can solve the mountain-climbing problem by using a graph. Keep in mind that the goal is not to determine the time, but just to indicate whether an exact time exists. Consequently, the speed at which the traveler is moving is unimportant (Anderson, 1980). Can you think of other approaches that might lead to a solution?

If you try to solve this problem by using algebraic or verbal representations, you will have a good deal of trouble. However, if you represent the problem with the kind of simple diagram shown in Figure 5, the solution will become apparent.

Our ability to represent a problem—and the kind of solution we eventually come to—depends on the way a problem is phrased, or framed. Consider, for example, if you were a cancer patient having to choose between surgery and radiation and were given the two sets of treatment options shown in Figure 6 (Tversky & Kahneman, 1987; Chandran & Menon, 2004). When the options are framed in terms of the likelihood of survival, only 18 percent of participants in a study chose radiation over surgery. However, when the choice was framed in terms of the likelihood of dying, 44 percent chose radiation over surgery—even though the outcomes are identical in both sets of framing conditions.

Production: Generating Solutions

After preparation, the next stage in problem solving is the production of possible solutions. If a problem is relatively simple, we may already have a direct solution stored in long-term memory, and all we need to do is retrieve the appropriate information. If

Problem: Surgery or radiation?

Survival Frame

Surgery: Of 100 people having surgery, 90 live through the post-operative period, 68 are alive at the end of the first year, and 34 are alive at the end of five years.

Radiation: Of 100 people having radiation therapy, all live through the treatment, 77 are alive at the end of one year, and 22 are alive at the end of five years.

Mortality Frame

Surgery: Of 100 people having surgery, 10 die during surgery, 32 die by the end of the first year, and 66 die by the end of five years.

Radiation: Of 100 people having radiation therapy, none die during the treatment, 23 die by the end of one year, and 78 die by the end of five years.

Far more patients choose surgery

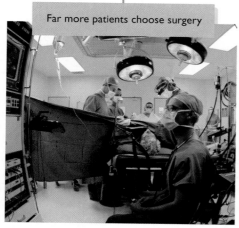

Far more patients choose radiation

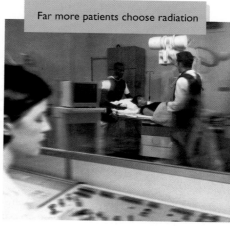

FIGURE 6 A decision often is affected by the way a problem is framed. Most people would choose surgery over radiation when the issue is framed in terms of how many survive. In contrast, most choose radiation over surgery when the issue is framed in terms of likelihood of dying.

we cannot retrieve or do not know the solution, we must generate possible solutions and compare them with information in long- and short-term memory.

At the most basic level, we can solve problems through trial and error. Thomas Edison invented the light bulb only because he tried thousands of different kinds of materials for a filament before he found one that worked (carbon). The difficulty with trial and error, of course, is that some problems are so complicated that it would take a lifetime to try out every possibility. For example, according to some estimates, there are some 10^{120} possible sequences of chess moves (Fine & Fine, 2003).

In place of trial and error, complex problem solving often involves the use of heuristics, cognitive shortcuts that can generate solutions. Probably the most frequently applied heuristic in problem solving is a **means-ends analysis,** which involves repeated tests for differences between the desired outcome and what currently exists. Consider this simple example (Newell & Simon, 1972; Huber, Beckmann, & Herrmann, 2004):

> I want to take my son to nursery school. What's the difference between what I have and what I want? One of distance. What changes distance? My automobile. My automobile won't work. What is needed to make it work? A new battery. What has new batteries? An auto repair shop . . .

In a means-end analysis, each step brings the problem solver closer to a resolution. Although this approach is often effective, if the problem requires indirect steps that temporarily *increase* the discrepancy between a current state and the solution, means-ends analysis can be counterproductive. For example, sometimes the fastest route to the summit of a mountain requires a mountain climber to backtrack temporarily; a

Means-ends analysis: Repeated testing for differences between the desired outcome and what currently exists.

means-ends approach—which implies that the mountain climber should always forge ahead and upward—will be ineffective in such instances.

For other problems, the best approach is to work backward by focusing on the goal, rather than the starting point, of the problem. Consider, for example, the water lily problem:

> Water lilies are growing on Blue Lake. The water lilies grow rapidly, so that the amount of water surface covered by lilies doubles every 24 hours.

> On the first day of summer, there was just one water lily. On the 90th day of the summer, the lake was entirely covered. On what day was the lake half covered? (Reisberg, 1997).

If you start searching for a solution to the problem by thinking about the initial state on day 1 (one water lily) and move forward from there, you're facing a daunting task of trial-and-error estimation. But try taking a different approach: Start with day 90, when the entire lake was covered with lilies. Given that the lilies double their coverage daily, on the prior day only half the lake was covered. The answer, then, is day 89, a solution found by working backward (Bourne et al., 1986; Hunt, 1994).

FORMING SUBGOALS: DIVIDING PROBLEMS INTO THEIR PARTS

Another heuristic commonly used to generate solutions is to divide a problem into intermediate steps, or *subgoals,* and solve each of those steps. For instance, in our modified Tower of Hanoi problem, we could choose several obvious subgoals, such as moving the largest disk to the third post.

If solving a subgoal is a step toward the ultimate solution to a problem, identifying subgoals is an appropriate strategy. In some cases, however, forming subgoals is not all that helpful and may actually increase the time needed to find a solution. For example, some problems cannot be subdivided. Others—like some complicated mathematical problems—are so complex that it takes longer to identify the appropriate subdivisions than to solve the problem by other means (Hayes, 1966; Reed, 1996; Kaller et al., 2004).

INSIGHT: SUDDEN AWARENESS

Some approaches to generating possible solutions focus less on step-by-step heuristics than on the sudden bursts of comprehension that one may experience during efforts to solve a problem. Just after World War I, the German psychologist Wolfgang Köhler examined learning and problem-solving processes in chimpanzees (Köhler, 1927). In his studies, Köhler exposed chimps to challenging situations in which the elements of the solution were all present; all the chimps needed to do was put them together.

In one of Köhler's studies, chimps were kept in a cage in which boxes and sticks were strewn about, and a bunch of tantalizing bananas hung from the ceiling, out of reach. Initially, the chimps made trial-and-error attempts to get to the bananas: They would throw the sticks at the bananas, jump from one of the boxes, or leap wildly from the ground. Frequently, they would seem to give up in frustration, leaving the bananas dangling temptingly overhead. But then, in what seemed like a sudden revelation, they would stop whatever they were doing and stand on a box to reach the bananas with a stick. Köhler called the cognitive process underlying the chimps' new behavior **insight,** a sudden awareness of the relationships among various elements that had previously appeared to be unrelated.

Although Köhler emphasized the apparent suddenness of insightful solutions, subsequent research has shown that prior experience and trial-and-error practice in problem solving must precede "insight" (Metcalfe, 1986; Windholz & Lamal, 2002). One study demonstrated that only chimps that had experience playing with sticks could successfully solve the problem; inexperienced chimps never made the connection between standing on the box and reaching the bananas with a stick (Birch, 1945).

www.mhhe.com/feldmanup8

PsychInteractive Online

Problem Solving

Insight: A sudden awareness of the relationships among various elements that had previously appeared to be independent of one another.

In an impressive display of insight, Sultan, one of the chimpanzees in Köhler's experiments in problem solving, sees a bunch of bananas that is out of his reach (a). He then carries over several crates (b), stacks them, and stands on them to reach the bananas (c).

Some researchers have suggested that the chimps' behavior was simply chaining together previously learned responses, no different from the way a pigeon learns, by trial and error, to peck a key (Epstein, 1987, 1996). Such studies clearly show that insight depends on previous experience with the elements involved in a problem. (To check your understanding of problem solving, try the PsychInteractive exercise.)

Judgment: Evaluating the Solutions

The final stage in problem solving is judging the adequacy of a solution. Often this is a simple matter: If the solution is clear—as in the Tower of Hanoi problem—we will know immediately whether we have been successful.

If the solution is less concrete or if there is no single correct solution, evaluating solutions becomes more difficult. In such instances, we must decide which alternative solution is best. Unfortunately, we often quite inaccurately estimate the quality of our own ideas (Johnson, Parrott, & Stratton, 1968; Eizenberg & Zaslavsky, 2004). For instance, a team of drug researchers working for a particular company may consider their remedy for an illness to be superior to all others, overestimating the likelihood of their success and downplaying the approaches of competing drug companies.

Theoretically, if we rely on appropriate heuristics and valid information to make decisions, we can make accurate choices among alternative solutions. However, as we see next, several kinds of obstacles to and biases in problem solving affect the quality of the decisions and judgments we make.

THE FAR SIDE®   **By GARY LARSON**

Impediments to Solutions: Why Is Problem Solving Such a Problem?

Consider the following problem-solving test (Duncker, 1945):

> You are given a set of tacks, candles, and matches each in a small box, and told your goal is to place three candles at eye level on a nearby door, so that wax will not drip on the floor as the candles burn [see Figure 7]. How would you approach this challenge?

If you have difficulty solving the problem, you are not alone. Most people cannot solve it when it is presented in the manner illustrated in the figure, in which the objects are *inside* the boxes. However, if the objects were presented *beside* the boxes, just resting on the table, chances are that you would solve the problem much more readily—which, in case you are wondering, requires tacking the boxes to the door and then placing the candles inside them (see Figure 9).

The difficulty you probably encountered in solving this problem stems from its presentation, which misled you at the initial preparation stage. Actually, significant obstacles to problem solving can exist at each of the three major stages. Although cognitive approaches to problem solving suggest that thinking proceeds along fairly rational, logical lines as a person confronts a problem and considers various solutions, several factors can hinder the development of creative, appropriate, and accurate solutions.

FUNCTIONAL FIXEDNESS AND MENTAL SET

Functional fixedness: The tendency to think of an object only in terms of its typical use.

The difficulty most people experience with the candle problem is caused by **functional fixedness,** the tendency to think of an object only in terms of its typical use. For instance, functional fixedness probably leads you to think of this book as something to read, instead of its potential use as a doorstop or as kindling for a fire. In the candle problem, because the objects are first presented inside the boxes, functional fixedness leads most people to see the boxes simply as containers for the objects they hold rather than as a potential part of the solution. They cannot envision another function for the boxes.

Mental set: The tendency for old patterns of problem solving to persist.

Functional fixedness is an example of a broader phenomenon known as **mental set,** the tendency for old patterns of problem solving to persist. A classic experiment (Luchins, 1946) demonstrated this phenomenon. As you can see in Figure 8, the object of the task is to use the jars in each row to measure out the designated amount of liquid. (Try it yourself to get a sense of the power of mental set before moving on.)

If you have tried to solve the problem, you know that the first five rows are all solved in the same way: First fill the largest jar (B) and then from it fill the middle-size jar (A) once and the smallest jar (C) two times. What is left in B is the designated amount. (Stated as a formula, the designated amount is B – A – 2C.) The demonstration of mental set comes in the sixth row of the problem, a point at which you prob-

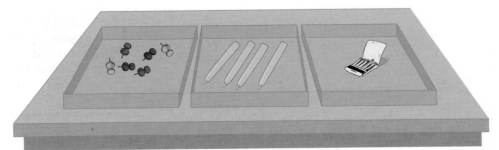

FIGURE 7 The problem here is to place three candles at eye level on a nearby door so that the wax will not drip on the floor as the candles burn—using only the objects in the figure. For a solution turn to Figure 9 on p. 270.

Given jars with these capacities (in ounces):

	A	B	C	Obtain:
1.	21	127	3	100
2.	14	163	25	99
3.	18	43	10	5
4.	9	42	6	21
5.	20	59	4	31
6.	28	76	3	25

FIGURE 8 Try this classic demonstration, which illustrates the importance of mental set in problem solving. The object is to use the jars in each row to measure out the designated amount of liquid. After you figure out the solution for the first five rows, you'll probably have trouble with the sixth row—even though the solution is actually easier. In fact, if you had tried to solve the problem in the sixth row first, you probably would have had no difficulty at all.

ably encountered some difficulty. If you are like most people, you tried the formula and were perplexed when it failed. Chances are, in fact, that you missed the simple (but different) solution to the problem, which involves merely subtracting C from A. Interestingly, people who were given the problem in row 6 *first* had no difficulty with it at all.

Mental set can affect perceptions, as well as patterns of problem solving. It can prevent you from seeing beyond the apparent constraints of a problem. For example, try to draw four straight lines so that they pass through all nine dots in the grid below—without lifting your pencil from the page.

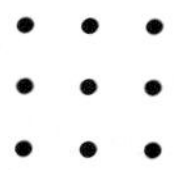

If you had difficulty with the problem, it was probably because you felt compelled to keep your lines within the grid. If you had gone outside the boundaries, however, you would have succeeded by using the solution shown in Figure 10. (The phrase "thinking outside the box"—a term commonly used in business today to encourage creativity—stems from research on overcoming the constraining effects of mental set.)

INACCURATE EVALUATION OF SOLUTIONS

When the nuclear power plant at Three Mile Island in Pennsylvania suffered its initial malfunction in 1979, a disaster that almost led to a nuclear meltdown, the plant operators immediately had to solve a problem of the most serious kind. Several monitors gave contradictory information about the source of the problem: One suggested that the pressure was too high, leading to the danger of an explosion; others indicated that the pressure was too low, which could lead to a meltdown. Although the pressure was, in fact, too low, the supervisors on duty relied on the one monitor—which turned out to be faulty—that suggested that the pressure was too high. Once they had made their decision and acted on it, they ignored the contradictory evidence from the other monitors (Wickens, 1984).

The operators' mistake exemplifies **confirmation bias,** in which problem solvers favor initial hypotheses and ignore contradictory information that supports alterna-

Confirmation bias: The tendency to favor information that supports one's initial hypotheses and ignore contradictory information that supports alternative hypotheses or solutions.

FIGURE 9 A solution to the problem in Figure 7 involves tacking the boxes to the door and placing the candles in the boxes.

tive hypotheses or solutions. Even when we find evidence that contradicts a solution we have chosen, we are apt to stick with our original hypothesis.

Confirmation bias occurs for several reasons. For one thing, rethinking a problem that appears to be solved already takes extra cognitive effort, and so we are apt to stick with our first solution. For another, we give greater weight to subsequent information that supports our initial position than to information that is not supportive of it (Gilovich, Griffin, & Kahneman, 2002; Evans & Feeney, 2004).

Creativity and Problem Solving

Creativity: The ability to generate original ideas or solve problems in novel ways.

Despite obstacles to problem solving, many people adeptly discover creative solutions to problems. One enduring question that cognitive psychologists have sought to answer is what factors underlie **creativity,** the ability to generate original ideas or solve problems in novel ways.

Although identifying the stages of problem solving helps us understand how people approach and solve problems, it does little to explain why some people come up with better solutions than others do. For instance, even the possible solutions to a simple problem often show wide discrepancies. Consider, for example, how you might respond to the question "How many uses can you think of for a newspaper?"

Now compare your solution with this one proposed by a 10-year-old boy:

You can read it, write on it, lay it down and paint a picture on it . . . You could put it in your door for decoration, put it in the garbage can, put it on a chair if the chair is messy. If you have a puppy, you put newspaper in its box or put it in your backyard for the dog to play with. When you build something and you don't want anyone to see it, put newspaper around it. Put newspaper on the floor if you have no mattress, use it to pick up something hot, use it to stop bleeding, or to catch the drips from drying clothes. You can use a newspaper for curtains, put it in your shoe to cover what is hurting your foot, make a kite out of it, shade a light that is too bright. You can wrap fish in it, wipe windows, or wrap money

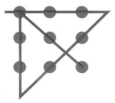

FIGURE 10 A solution to the nine-dot problem requires the use of lines drawn beyond the boundaries of the figure—something that our mental set may prevent us from seeing easily.

Pablo Picasso is considered one of the greatest artists of the twentieth century. Do you think he relied more on convergent or divergent thinking in his art?

in it . . . You put washed shoes in newspaper, wipe eyeglasses with it, put it under a dripping sink, put a plant on it, make a paper bowl out of it, use it for a hat if it is raining, tie it on your feet for slippers. You can put it on the sand if you had no towel, use it for bases in baseball, make paper airplanes with it, use it as a dustpan when you sweep, ball it up for the cat to play with, wrap your hands in it if it is cold (Ward, Kogan, & Pankove, 1972).

This list shows extraordinary creativity. Unfortunately, it is much easier to identify *examples* of creativity than to determine its causes. Several factors, however, seem to be associated with creativity (Csikszentmihalyi, 1997; Niu & Sternberg, 2003; Simonton, 2003; Kaufman & Baer, 2005).

One of these factors is **divergent thinking,** the ability to generate unusual, yet appropriate, responses to problems or questions. This type of thinking contrasts with **convergent thinking,** which produces responses that are based primarily on knowledge and logic. For instance, someone relying on convergent thinking would answer "You read it" to the query "What can you do with a newspaper?" In contrast, "You use it as a dustpan" is a more divergent—and creative—response (Baer, 1993; Runco & Sakamoto, 1993; Finke, 1995; Sternberg, 2001; Ho, 2004).

Another aspect of creativity is its *cognitive complexity,* or preference for elaborate, intricate, and complex stimuli and thinking patterns. For instance, creative people often have a wider range of interests and are more independent and more interested in philosophical or abstract problems than are less creative individuals (Barron, 1990). In addition, there may be differences in how the brain processes information in more creative people, as we discuss in the *Applying Psychology in the 21st Century* box.

One factor that is *not* closely related to creativity is intelligence. Traditional intelligence tests, which ask focused questions that have only one acceptable answer, tap convergent thinking skills. Highly creative people may therefore find that such tests penalize their divergent thinking. This may explain why researchers consistently find that creativity is only slightly related to school grades and intelligence when intelligence is measured using traditional intelligence tests (Hong, Milgram, & Gorsky, 1995; Sternberg & O'Hara, 2000).

Divergent thinking: The ability to generate unusual, yet nonetheless appropriate, responses to problems or questions.

Convergent thinking: The ability to produce responses that are based primarily on knowledge and logic.

Eureka! Understanding the Underpinnings of Creativity

The volunteers looked like electronic Medusas, with wires snaking from 30 electrodes glued to their scalps and recording their brain activity.

As they peered at a computer screen, a brainteaser flashed: Turn the incorrect Roman-numeral equation XI + I = X, made out of 10 sticks, into a correct one by moving as few sticks as possible. As soon as the volunteers figured it out, they hit a key, and another puzzle appeared. None could be solved by a plug-and-chug approach; all required insight and creativity (Begley, 2004, p. B1).

If you were one of the participants in this experiment, designed to examine the neuroscience of creativity, you might come to a quick answer. Many people arrive at a solution quite soon, saying that only one stick needs to be moved. They reason that by moving the "I" stick on the left-hand side of the equation to the right side, the equation becomes XI = XI.

Not bad—but not the most creative solution. The more creative response is that you need to move *no* sticks in order to make the equation correct. To make the equation correct, all you need to do is turn it upside down, making the equation X = I + IX.

To the excitement of neuroscientists seeking to understand the biology underlying creativity, it turns out the more creative response also produces a different pattern of brain activity than more common responses. According to neuroscientist Bhavin Sheth and colleagues, problem solvers who found the more creative solution tended to do so in a kind of "Eureka!" moment, in which the solution suddenly came to them. At that moment, a sudden decrease occurred in lower-frequency brain waves, waves that usually signify brain activity involving memory and other types of coordinated mental activity. However, the decrease in lower-frequency brain waves was followed by an increase in higher-frequency *theta brain waves* at the moment that the creative solution came to mind (Begley, 2004; Sheth, Bhattacharya, & Wu, 2004).

Because theta waves are associated with the encoding of novel information, their appearance at the "Eureka!" moment suggests that there may have been a shift in the way the problem was viewed. Specifically, problem solvers may have suddenly seen the problem in spatial terms rather than viewing it as a numeric problem.

Other researchers, taking a different approach, have looked at the link between creativity and brain disorders. For example, some research has found a link between psychological problems and creativity, although the relationship is inconsistent. Despite some conspicuous examples of well-known and highly creative individuals who appear to have suffered from psychological disorders (such as writer Sylvia Plath and artist Vincent Van Gogh), there are also many creative people who appear quite psychologically healthy (Kaufman & Baer, 2005).

Still, according to psychologist James Kaufman, the incidence of mental illness is greater in certain types of creative artists. For example, poets are more likely to suffer from mental illness than are other kinds of writers (Kaufman, 2005).

Clearly, it's still too early for psychologists to claim they have unlocked the genius of highly creative people such as a musician like Bach or a painter like Picasso. However, they are beginning to understand the basis of creativity in more everyday sorts of people.

RETHINK

What are the difficulties that psychologists face in defining creativity in an objective way? What are some of the strategies you use to devise creative solutions to problems?

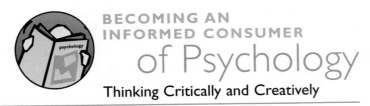

BECOMING AN INFORMED CONSUMER
of Psychology
Thinking Critically and Creatively

Can we learn to be better thinkers?

Cognitive researchers have found that people can learn the abstract rules of logic and reasoning and that such knowledge can improve our reasoning about the underlying causes of everyday events in our lives.

In short, research suggests that critical and creative thinkers are made, not born. Consider, for instance, some of these suggestions for increasing critical thinking and creativity (Feldman, Coats, & Schwartzberg, 1994; Levy, 1997; Halpern, 1998; Burbach, Matkin, & Fritz, 2004):

- *Redefine problems.* We can modify boundaries and assumptions by rephrasing a problem at either a more abstract or a more concrete level.
- *Use fractionation.* Fractionation breaks down an idea or concept into its component parts. Through fractionation, we can examine each part for new possibilities and approaches, leading to a novel solution for the problem as a whole.

The use of analogies is a characteristic of creativity. Frank Lloyd Wright incorporated into his architecture many analogies to nature, as you can see in this building he designed. How are analogies used by other creative artists?

- *Adopt a critical perspective.* Rather than passively accepting assumptions or arguments, we can evaluate material critically, consider its implications, and think about possible exceptions and contradictions.
- *Consider the opposite.* By considering the opposite of a concept we're seeking to understand, we can sometimes make progress. For example, to define "good mental health," it may be useful to consider what "bad mental health" means.
- *Use analogies.* Analogies provide alternative frameworks for the interpretation of facts and help us uncover new understanding. One particularly effective means of coming up with analogies is to look for examples in the animal world. For instance, architects discovered how to construct the earliest skyscrapers by noting how lily pads on a pond could support the weight of a person (Shouler, 1992; Getner & Holyoak, 1997; Reisberg, 1997).
- *Think divergently.* Instead of the most logical or common use for an object, consider how you might use the object if you were forbidden to use it in the usual way.
- *Take the perspective of another person.* By temporarily adopting another person's point of view, you may gain a fresh view of the situation.
- *Use heuristics.* Heuristics are cognitive shortcuts that can help bring about a solution to a problem. If the problem has a single correct answer and you can use or construct a heuristic, you can often find the solution more rapidly and effectively.
- *Experiment with various solutions.* Don't be afraid to use different routes to find solutions for problems (verbal, mathematical, graphic, even dramatic). For instance, try to come up with every conceivable idea you can, no matter how wild or bizarre it may seem at first. After you've come up with a list of solutions, review each one and try to think of ways to make what at first appeared impractical seem more feasible.

RECAP/EVALUATE/RETHINK

RECAP

How do people approach and solve problems?

- Problem solving typically involves three major stages: preparation, production of solutions, and evaluation of solutions that have been generated. (p. 261)
- Preparation involves placing the problem in one of three categories. In arrangement problems, a group of elements must be rearranged or recombined in a way that will satisfy a certain criterion. In problems of inducing structure, a person first must identify the existing relationships among the elements presented and then construct a new relationship among them. Finally, transformation problems consist of an initial state, a goal state, and a method for changing the initial state into the goal state. (pp. 261-263)
- A crucial aspect of the preparation stage is the representation and organization of the problem. (pp. 264-265)
- In the production stage, people try to generate solutions. They may find solutions to some problems in long-term memory. Alternatively, they may solve some problems through simple trial and error and use algorithms and heuristics to solve more complex problems. (p. 265)
- Using the heuristic of a means-ends analysis, a person will repeatedly test for differences between the desired outcome and what currently exists, trying each time to come closer to the goal. (pp. 265-266)
- Köhler's research with chimpanzees illustrates insight, a sudden awareness of the relationships among elements that had previously seemed unrelated. (pp. 266-267)

What are the major obstacles to problem solving?

- Several factors hinder effective problem solving. Mental set, of which functional fixedness is an example, is the tendency for old patterns of problem solving to persist. Inappropriate use of algorithms and heuristics can also act as an obstacle to the production of solutions. Confirmation bias, in which initial hypotheses are favored, can hinder the accurate evaluation of solutions to problems. (p. 269)

What is creativity?

- Creativity is the ability to combine responses or ideas in novel ways. Creativity is related to divergent thinking (the ability to generate unusual, but still appropriate, responses to problems or questions) and cognitive complexity. (pp. 270-271)

EVALUATE

1. Solving a problem by trying to reduce the difference between the current state and the goal state is known as a _____.
2. _____ is the term used to describe the sudden "flash" of revelation that often accompanies the solution to a problem.
3. Thinking of an object only in terms of its typical use is known as _____ _____. A broader, related tendency for old problem-solving patterns to persist is known as a _____.
4. _____ _____ describes the phenomenon of favoring an initial hypothesis and ignoring subsequent competing hypotheses.
5. Generating unusual but appropriate approaches to a question is known as _____.

RETHINK

1. Is the reasoning in the following syllogism correct or incorrect? Why?
   Creative people often have trouble with traditional intelligence tests.
   I have trouble with traditional intelligence tests.
   Therefore, I am a creative person.
2. *From the perspective of a manufacturer:* How might you encourage your employees to develop creative ways to improve the products that you produce?

Answers to Evaluate Questions

1. transformation; 2. insight; 3. functional fixedness, mental set; 4. confirmation bias; 5. divergent thinking

KEY TERMS

means-ends analysis p. 265
insight p. 266
functional fixedness p. 268
mental set p. 268
confirmation bias p. 269
creativity p. 270
divergent thinking p. 271
convergent thinking p. 271

Language

'Twas brillig, and the slithy toves

Did gyre and gimble in the wabe:

All mimsy were the borogoves,

And the mome raths outgrabe.

Although few of us have ever come face to face with a tove, we have little difficulty in discerning that in Lewis Carroll's (1872) poem "Jabberwocky," the expression *slithy toves* contains an adjective, *slithy*, and the noun it modifies, *toves*.

Our ability to make sense out of nonsense, if the nonsense follows typical rules of language, illustrates the complexity of both human language and the cognitive processes that underlie its development and use. The use of **language**—the communication of information through symbols arranged according to systematic rules—is an important cognitive ability, one that is indispensable for communicating with others. Not only is language central to communication, it is also closely tied to the very way in which we think about and understand the world. No wonder psychologists have devoted considerable attention to studying language (Barrett, 1999; Owens, 2001; Hoff, 2003; Saffran & Schwartz, 2003; Fitch & Sanders, 2005).

Grammar: Language's Language

To understand how language develops and relates to thought, we first need to review some of the formal elements of language. The basic structure of language rests on **grammar,** the system of rules that determine how our thoughts can be expressed.

Grammar deals with three major components of language: phonology, syntax, and semantics. **Phonology** is the study of the smallest basic units of speech, called **phonemes,** that affect meaning, and of the way we use those sounds to form words and produce meaning. For instance, the *a* sound in *fat* and the *a* sound in *fate* represent two different phonemes in English (Vihman, 1996; Baddeley, Gathercole, & Papagano, 1998).

Linguists have identified more than 800 different phonemes among all the world's languages. Although English speakers use just 52 phonemes to produce words, other languages use from as few as 15 to as many as 141. Differences in phonemes are one reason people have difficulty learning other languages. For example, to a Japanese speaker, whose native language does not have an *r* phoneme, English words such as *roar* present some difficulty (Gibbs, 2002; Iverson et al., 2002).

Syntax refers to the rules that indicate how words and phrases can be combined to form sentences. Every language has intricate rules that guide the order in which words may be strung together to communicate meaning. English speakers have no difficulty recognizing that "Radio down the turn" is not a meaningful sequence, whereas "Turn down the radio" is. To understand the effect of syntax in English, consider the changes in meaning caused by the different word orders in the following three utterances: "John kidnapped the boy," "John, the kidnapped boy," and "The boy kidnapped John" (Lasnik, 1990; Eberhard, Cutting, & Bock, 2005).

Key Concepts

How do people use language?

How does language develop?

Language: The communication of information through symbols arranged according to systematic rules.

Grammar: The system of rules that determine how our thoughts can be expressed.

Phonology: The study of the smallest units of speech, called phonemes.

Phonemes: The smallest units of speech that affect meaning.

Syntax: Ways in which words and phrases can be combined to form sentences.

Semantics: The rules governing the meaning of words and sentences.

The third major component of language is **semantics,** the meanings of words and sentences (Larson, 1990; Hipkiss, 1995; O'Grady & Dobrovolsky, 1996; Richgels, 2004). Semantic rules allow us to use words to convey the subtlest nuances. For instance, we are able to make the distinction between "The truck hit Laura" (which we would be likely to say if we had just seen the vehicle hitting Laura) and "Laura was hit by a truck" (which we would probably say if someone asked why Laura was missing class while she recuperated).

Despite the complexities of language, most of us acquire the basics of grammar without even being aware that we have learned its rules (Pinker, 1994; Plunkett & Wood, 2004). Moreover, even though we may have difficulty explicitly stating the rules of grammar, our linguistic abilities are so sophisticated that we can utter an infinite number of different statements. How do we acquire such abilities?

Language Development: Developing a Way with Words

To parents, the sounds of their infant babbling and cooing are music to their ears (except, perhaps, at three o'clock in the morning). These sounds also serve an important function. They mark the first step on the road to the development of language.

BABBLING

Babble: Meaningless speechlike sounds made by children from around the age of 3 months through 1 year.

Children **babble**—make speechlike but meaningless sounds—from around the age of 3 months through 1 year. While babbling, they may produce, at one time or another, any of the sounds found in all languages, not just the one to which they are exposed. Even deaf children display their own form of babbling, for infants who are unable to hear yet who are exposed to sign language from birth "babble" with their hands (Pettito & Marentette, 1991; Pettito, 1993; Meier & Willerman, 1995).

An infant's babbling increasingly reflects the specific language being spoken in the infant's environment, initially in terms of pitch and tone and eventually in terms of specific sounds. Young infants can distinguish among all 869 phonemes that have been identified across the world's languages. However, after the age of 6 to 8 months, that ability begins to decline. Infants begin to "specialize" in the language to which they are exposed as neurons in their brains reorganize to respond to the particular phonemes infants routinely hear.

Some theorists argue that a *critical period* exists for language development early in life, in which a child is particularly sensitive to language cues and most easily acquires language. In fact, if children are not exposed to language during this critical period, later they will have great difficulty overcoming this deficit (Bortfeld & Whitehurst, 2001; Bruer, 2001; Newport, Bavelier, & Neville, 2001; Bates, 2005).

Cases in which abused children have been isolated from contact with others support the theory of such critical periods. In one case, for example, a girl named Genie was exposed to virtually no language from the age of 20 months until she was rescued at age 13 years. She was unable to speak at all. Despite intensive instruction, she learned only some words and was never able to master the complexities of language (Rymer, 1994; Veltman & Browne, 2001).

A syllable in signed language, similar to the ones seen in the manual babbling of deaf infants and in the spoken babbling of hearing infants. The similarities in language structure suggest that language has biological roots.

PRODUCTION OF LANGUAGE

By the time children are approximately 1 year old, they stop producing sounds that are not in the language to which they have been exposed. It is then a short step to the production of actual words. In English, these are typically short words that start with a consonant sound such as *b, d, m, p,* and *t*—this helps explain why *mama* and *dada* are so often among babies' first words. Of course, even before they produce their first words, children can understand a fair amount of the language they hear. Language comprehension precedes language production.

After the age of 1 year, children begin to learn more complicated forms of language. They produce two-word combinations, the building blocks of sentences, and sharply increase the number of different words they are able to use. By age 2, the average child has a vocabulary of more than fifty words. Just six months later, that vocabulary has grown to several hundred words. At that time, children can produce short sentences, although they use **telegraphic speech**—sentences that sound as if they were part of a telegram, in which words not critical to the message are left out. Rather than saying, "I showed you the book," a child using telegraphic speech may say, "I show book," and "I am drawing a dog" may become "Drawing dog." As children get older, of course, they use less telegraphic speech and produce increasingly complex sentences (Volterra et al., 2003).

By age 3, children learn to make plurals by adding *s* to nouns and to form the past tense by adding *-ed* to verbs. This also leads to errors, since children tend to apply rules inflexibly. In such **overgeneralization**, children employ rules even when doing so results in an error. Thus, although it is correct to say "he walked" for the past tense of *walk*, the *-ed* rule doesn't work quite so well when children say "he runned" for the past tense of *run* (Marcus, 1996; Howe, 2002; Rice et al., 2004).

By age 5, children have acquired the basic rules of language. However, they do not attain a full vocabulary and the ability to comprehend and use subtle grammatical rules until later. For example, a 5-year-old boy who sees a blindfolded doll and is asked, "Is the doll easy or hard to see?" would have great trouble answering the question. In fact, if he were asked to make the doll easier to see, he would probably try to remove the doll's blindfold. By the time they are 8 years old, however, children have little difficulty understanding this question, because they realize that the doll's blindfold has nothing to do with an observer's ability to see the doll (Chomsky, 1969; Hoff, 2003).

Understanding Language Acquisition: Identifying the Roots of Language

Anyone who spends even a little time with children will notice the enormous strides that they make in language development throughout childhood. However, the reasons for this rapid growth are far from obvious. Psychologists have offered two major explanations, one based on learning theory and the other based on innate processes.

The **learning-theory approach** suggests that language acquisition follows the principles of reinforcement and conditioning discovered by psychologists who study learning. For example, a child who says "mama" receives hugs and praise from her mother, which reinforces the behavior of saying "mama" and makes its repetition more likely. This view suggests that children first learn to speak by being rewarded for making sounds that approximate speech. Ultimately, through a process of shaping, language becomes more and more like adult speech (Skinner, 1957; Ornat & Gallo, 2004).

To support the learning-theory approach to language acquisition, research shows that the more parents speak to their young children, the more proficient the children become in language use (see Figure 1). In addition, by the time they are 3 years old, children who hear higher levels of linguistic sophistication in their parents' speech show a greater rate of vocabulary growth, vocabulary use, and even general intellectual achievement than do children whose parents' speech is more simple (Hart & Risley, 1997).

Telegraphic speech: Sentences in which words not critical to the message are left out.

Overgeneralization: The phenomenon by which children apply language rules even when the application results in an error.

Learning-theory approach to language development: The theory suggesting that language acquisition follows the principles of reinforcement and conditioning.

FIGURE 1 The more words parents say to their children before the age of 3, the larger the children's vocabulary. (Source: Courtesy of Drs. Betty Hart and Todd Risley, 1997.)

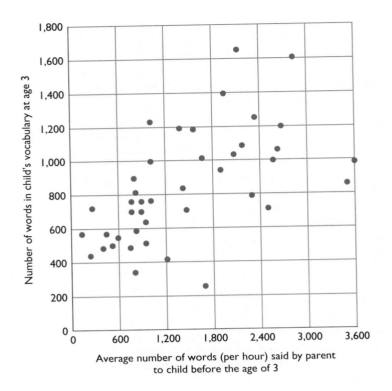

The learning-theory approach is less successful in explaining how children acquire language rules. Children are reinforced not only when they use language correctly, but also when they use it incorrectly. For example, parents answer a child's "Why the dog won't eat?" as readily as they do the correctly phrased question, "Why won't the dog eat?" Listeners understand both sentences equally well. Learning theory, then, has difficulty fully explaining language acquisition.

Pointing to such problems with learning-theory approaches to language acquisition, linguist Noam Chomsky (1968, 1978, 1991) provided a groundbreaking alternative. Chomsky argued that humans are born with an innate linguistic

Noam Chomsky argues that all languages share a universal grammar.

capability that emerges primarily as a function of maturation. According to his analysis, all the world's languages share a common underlying structure called a **universal grammar.** Chomsky suggested that the human brain has a neural system, the **language-acquisition device,** that not only lets us understand the structure language provides but also gives us strategies and techniques for learning the unique characteristics of our native language (Lidz & Gleitman, 2004; McGilvray, 2004).

Chomsky used the concept of the language-acquisition device as a metaphor, and he did not identify a specific area of the brain in which it resides. However, evidence collected by neuroscientists suggests that the ability to use language, which was a significant evolutionary advance in human beings, is tied to specific neurological developments.

For example, scientists have discovered a gene related to the development of language abilities that may have emerged as recently—in evolutionary terms—as 100,000 years ago. Furthermore, it is clear that there are specific sites within the brain that are closely tied to language, and the shape of the human mouth and throat are tailored to the production of speech (Enard et al., 2002; Hauser, Chomsky, & Fitch, 2002; Vargha-Khadem et al., 2005).

Still, Chomsky's view has its critics. For instance, learning theorists contend that the apparent ability of certain animals, such as chimpanzees, to learn the fundamentals of human language (as we discuss later in this module) contradicts the innate linguistic capability view. To reconcile such data, some theorists suggest that the brain's hardwired language-acquisition device that Chomsky and geneticists posit provides the hardware for our acquisition of language, whereas the exposure to language in our environment that learning theorists observe allows us to develop the appropriate software. But the issue of how language is acquired remains hotly contested (Pinker, 1994, 2002; Fromkin, 2000; Lana, 2002). Go to the PsychInteractive exercise to further investigate language development.

Universal grammar: Noam Chomsky's theory that all the world's languages share a common underlying structure.

Language-acquisition device: A neural system of the brain hypothesized by Noam Chomsky to permit understanding of language.

www.mhhe.com/feldmanup8
PsychInteractive Online

Language Development

The Influence of Language on Thinking: Do Eskimos Have More Words for Snow Than Texans Do?

Do Eskimos living in the frigid Arctic have a more expansive vocabulary for discussing snow than people living in warmer climates?

It makes sense, and arguments that the Eskimo language has many more words than English for snow have been made since the early 1900s. At that time, linguist Benjamin Lee Whorf contended that because snow is so relevant to Eskimos' lives, their language provides a particularly rich vocabulary to describe it—considerably larger than what we find in other languages, such as English (Martin & Pullum, 1991; Pinker, 1994).

The contention that the Eskimo language is particularly abundant in snow-related terms led to the **linguistic-relativity hypothesis,** the notion that language shapes and, in fact, may determine the way people in a particular culture perceive and understand the world. According to this view, language provides us with categories that we use to construct our view of people and events in the world around us. Consequently, language shapes and produces thought (Whorf, 1956; Smith, 1996; Oezgen & Davies, 2002; Pilling & Davies, 2004).

Let's consider another possibility, however. Suppose that instead of language being the *cause* of certain ways of thinking, thought *produces* language. The only rea-

Linguistic-relativity hypothesis: The notion that language shapes and may determine the way people in a particular culture perceive and understand the world.

He's pretty good at rote categorization and single-object relational tasks, but he's not so hot at differentiating between representational and associational signs, and he's very weak on syntax.

son to expect that Eskimo language might have more words for snow than English does is that snow is considerably more relevant to Eskimos than it is to people in other cultures.

Which view is correct? Most recent research refutes the linguistic-relativity hypothesis and suggests, instead, that thinking produces language. In fact, new analyses of the Eskimo language suggest that Eskimos have no more words for snow than English speakers, for if one examines the English language closely, one sees that it is hardly impoverished when it comes to describing snow (consider, for example, *sleet, slush, blizzard, dusting,* and *avalanche*).

Still, the linguistic-relativity hypothesis has not been entirely discarded. A newer version of the hypothesis suggests that speech patterns may influence certain aspects of thinking. For example, in some languages, such as English, speakers distinguish between nouns that can be counted (such as "five chairs") and nouns that require a measurement unit to be quantified (such as "a liter of water"). In some other languages, such as the Mayan language called Yucatec, however, all nouns require a measurement unit. In such cultures, people appear to think more closely about what things are made of than do people in cultures in which languages such as English are spoken. In contrast, English speakers focus more on the shape of objects (Gentner, Goldin, & Goldin-Meadow, 2003; Tsukasaki & Ishii, 2004).

Further support for the point of view that language helps mold thinking comes from discoveries about language used by the Piraha, a tiny hunter-gatherer tribe in the Amazon. The tribe has no words for numbers higher than two, and even these represent approximations. When asked to carry out even very simple tasks involving higher numbers (such as duplicating a row of 10 items), the Piraha tribespeople had great difficulty. Their performance suggests that their lack of language for higher numbers may place limits on their thinking about mathematical concepts (Gordon, 2004).

In short, although research does not support the linguistic-relativity hypothesis that language *causes* thought, it is clear that language influences how we think. And, of course, it certainly is the case that thought influences language, suggesting that language and thinking interact in complex ways (Heyman & Diesendruck, 2002; Kim, 2002; Ross, 2004).

Do Animals Use Language?

One question that has long puzzled psychologists is whether language is uniquely human or if other animals are able to acquire it as well. Many animals communicate with one another in rudimentary forms. For instance, fiddler crabs wave their claws to signal, bees dance to indicate the direction in which food will be found, and certain birds call "zick, zick" during courtship and "kia" when they are about to fly away. However, researchers have yet to demonstrate conclusively that these animals use true language, which is characterized in part by the ability to produce and communicate new and unique meanings by following a formal grammar.

Psychologists have, however, been able to teach chimps to communicate at surprisingly high levels. For instance, after four years of training, a chimp named Washoe learned to make signs for 132 words and combine those signs into simple sentences. Even more impressively, Kanzi, a pygmy chimpanzee, has linguistic skills that some psychologists claim are close to those of a 2-year-old human being. Kanzi's trainers suggest that he can create grammatically sophisticated sentences and can even invent new rules of syntax (Gardner & Gardner, 1969; Savage-Rumbaugh et al., 1993).

Sue Savage-Rumbaugh with a primate friend, Panbanisha. Does the use of sign language by primates indicate true mastery of language?

Despite the skills displayed by primates such as Kanzi, critics contend that the language such animals use still lacks the grammar and the complex and novel constructions of human language. Instead, they maintain that the chimps are displaying a skill no different from that of a dog that learns to lie down on command to get a reward. Furthermore, we lack firm evidence that animals can recognize and respond to the mental states of others of their species, an important aspect of human communication (Seyfarth & Cheney, 1992, 1996; Tattersall, 2002; Povinelli & Vonk, 2004).

Most evidence supports the contention that humans are better equipped than other animals to produce and organize language in the form of meaningful sentences. But the issue of whether other animals can be taught to communicate in a way that resembles human language remains controversial (Gilbert, 1996; Savage-Rumbaugh & Brakke, 1996; Wynne, 2004).

Exploring DIVERSITY

Teaching with Linguistic Variety: Bilingual Education

In New York City, one in six of the city's 1.1 million students is enrolled in some form of bilingual or English as a Second Language (ESL) instruction. And New York City is far from the only school district with a significant population of non-native English speakers. From the biggest cities to the most rural areas, the face—and voice—of education in the United States is changing. More and more schoolchildren today have last names like Kim, Valdez, and Karachnicoff. In seven states, including Texas and Colorado, more than one-quarter of the students are not native English speakers. For some 47 million Americans, English is their second language (Holloway, 2000; see Figure 2).

How to appropriately and effectively teach the increasing number of children who do not speak English is not always clear. Many educators maintain that *bilingual education* is best. With a bilingual approach, students learn some subjects in their native language while simultaneously learning English. Proponents of bilingualism believe that students must develop a sound footing in basic subject areas and that, initially at least, teaching those subjects in their native language is the only way to provide them

FIGURE 2 The language of diversity. Some 22 percent of the people in the United States speak a language other than English at home. Most of them speak Spanish; the rest speak an astounding variety of different languages. Where are the largest clusters of non-English speakers in the United States, and what do you think explains these concentrations? (Source: MLA Language Map, 2005, based on 2000 Census).

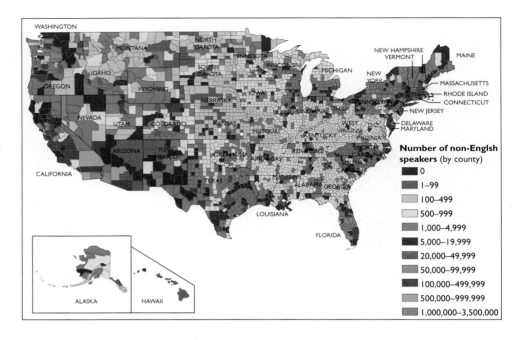

with that foundation. During the same period, they learn English, with the eventual goal of shifting all instruction into English.

In contrast, other educators insist that all instruction ought to be in English from the moment students, including those who speak no English at all, enroll in school. In *immersion programs,* students are immediately plunged into English instruction in all subjects. The reasoning—endorsed by voters in California in a referendum designed to end bilingual education—is that teaching students in a language other than English simply hinders nonnative English speakers' integration into society and ultimately does them a disservice. Proponents of English immersion programs point as evidence to improvements in standardized test scores that followed the end of bilingual education programs (Wildavsky, 2000).

Although the controversial issue of bilingual education versus immersion has strong political undercurrents, evidence shows that the ability to speak two languages provides significant cognitive benefits over speaking only one language. For example, bilingual speakers show more cognitive flexibility and may understand concepts more easily than those who speak only one language. They have more linguistic tools for thinking because of their multiple-language abilities. In turn, this makes them more creative and flexible in solving problems (Hong et al., 2000; Sanz, 2000; Heyman & Diesendruck, 2002; Bialystok & Martin, 2004).

Research also suggests that speaking several languages changes the organization of the brain, as does the timing of the acquisition of a second language. For example, one study compared bilingual speakers on linguistic tasks in their native and second languages. The study found that those who had learned their second language as adults showed different areas of brain activation compared with those who had learned their second language in childhood (Kim et al., 1997; see Figure 3).

Related to questions about bilingual education is the matter of *biculturalism,* that is, being a member of two cultures and its psychological impact. Some psychologists argue that society should promote an *alternation model* of bicultural competence. Such a model supports members of a culture in their efforts to maintain their original cultural identity, as well as in their integration into the adopted culture. In this view, a person can belong to two cultures and have two cultural identities without having to choose between them. Whether society will adopt the alternation model remains to be seen (LaFromboise, Coleman, & Gerton, 1995; Calderon & Minaya-Rowe, 2003; Carter, 2003).

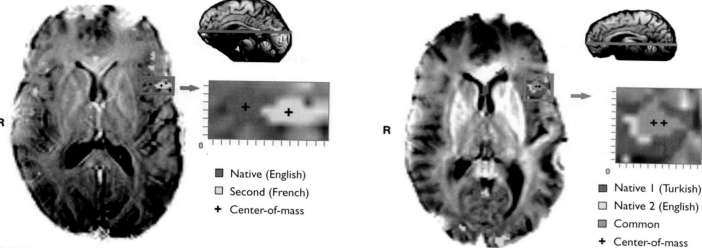

FIGURE 3 Brain functioning in bilingual speakers. When bilingual speakers carried out language tasks in their native and second languages, brain activity differed depending on when in life each speaker learned the second language. For example, the brain scan in (a), which shows two separate areas of the brain activated, is from a native English speaker who learned French in adulthood. In contrast, the brain scan in (b) is from a speaker who learned both English and Turkish in infancy. For that person, substantial overlap exists between the areas of the brain that are activated. (Source: Kim et al., 1997).

RECAP/EVALUATE/RETHINK

RECAP

How do people use language?

- Language is the communication of information through symbols arranged according to systematic rules. All languages have a grammar—a system of rules that determines how thoughts can be expressed—that encompasses the three major components of language: phonology, syntax, and semantics. (pp. 275-276)

How does language develop?

- Language production, which follows language comprehension, develops out of babbling, which then leads to the production of actual words. After 1 year of age, children use two-word combinations, increase their vocabulary, and use telegraphic speech, which drops words not critical to the message. By age 5, acquisition of language rules is relatively complete. (pp. 276-277)
- Learning theorists suggest that language is acquired through reinforcement and conditioning. In contrast, Chomsky and other linguists suggest that an innate language-acquisition device guides the development of language. (pp. 277-279)
- The linguistic-relativity hypothesis suggests that language shapes and may determine the way people think about the world. Most evidence suggests that although language does not determine thought, it does affect the

way people store information in memory and how well they can retrieve it. (pp. 279-280)
- The degree to which language is a uniquely human skill remains an open question. Some psychologists contend that even though certain primates communicate at a high level, those animals do not use language; other psychologists suggest that those primates truly understand and produce language in much the same way as humans. (p. 281)
- People who speak more than one language may have a cognitive advantage over those who speak only one. (pp. 281-282)

EVALUATE

1. Match the component of grammar with its definition:
   1. Syntax
   2. Phonology
   3. Semantics
   a. Rules showing how words can be combined into sentences
   b. Rules governing the meaning of words and sentences
   c. The study of the sound units that affect speech

2. Language production and language comprehension develop in infants at about the same time. True or false?

3. _____ _____ refers to the phenomenon in which young children omit nonessential portions of sentences.
4. A child knows that adding *-ed* to certain words puts them in the past tense. As a result, instead of saying "He came," the child says "He comed." This is an example of _____.
5. _____ theory assumes that language acquisition is based on principles of operant conditioning and shaping.
6. In his theory of language acquisition, Chomsky argues that language acquisition is an innate ability tied to the structure of the brain. True or false?

RETHINK

1. Do people who use two languages, one at home and one at school, automatically have two cultures? Why might people who speak two languages have cognitive advantages over those who speak only one?
2. *From the perspective of a child care provider:* How would you encourage children's language abilities at the different stages of development?

Answers to Evaluate Questions

1. 1-a, 2-c, 3-b; 2. false, language comprehension precedes language production; 3. telegraphic speech; 4. overgeneralization; 5. learning; 6. true

KEY TERMS

language p. 275
grammar p. 275
phonology p. 275
phonemes p. 275
syntax p. 275

semantics p. 276
babble p. 276
telegraphic speech p. 277
overgeneralization p. 277

learning-theory approach to language development p. 277
universal grammar p. 279

language-acquisition device p. 279
linguistic-relativity hypothesis p. 279

Psychology on the Web

1. In addition to mental images of sights and sounds, are there mental representations that correspond to the other senses? See whether you can answer this question by searching the Web. Summarize your findings in writing.
2. Do animals think? What evidence is there on either side of this question? Search the Web for at least one example of research and/or argument on each side of this question. Summarize your findings and use your knowledge of cognitive psychology to state your own position on this question.
3. After completing the PsychInteractive exercise on heuristics, which illustrates how the use of heuristics can sometimes lead to the wrong conclusion, consider how employing heuristics can also be helpful. Describe at least two ways in which the use of heuristics helps us in everyday life.

Epilogue

The study of cognition occupies a central place in the field of psychology, encompassing a variety of areas—including thinking, problem solving, decision making, creativity, language, memory, and intelligence. Specialists in cognitive psychology have made significant advances in the last decade that have influenced the entire field of psychology.

Before proceeding, turn back to the Prologue about Burt Rutan's SpaceShipOne, designed to bring space travel to the masses. Answer the following questions in light of what you have learned about reasoning, problem solving, and creativity:

1. What factors led up to Rutan's development of SpaceShipOne?
2. How do the concepts of functional fixedness and mental set relate to Rutan's inventiveness? Are they related to the notion of prototypes?
3. How do you think insight is involved in Rutan's inventiveness?
4. In what ways do you think divergent and convergent thinking are involved in the processes of invention? Do they play different roles in the various stages of the act of invention, including identifying the need for an invention, devising possible solutions, and creating a practical invention?

Intelligence

Key Concepts for Chapter 9

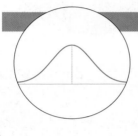

Prologue   Chris Burke and Sho Yano

When Chris Burke was born, physicians suggested to his parents that he immediately be institutionalized. He had Down syndrome, a common birth defect that produces mental retardation, and the physicians predicted that the chances of his leading anything like a normal life were slim. Chris's parents ignored the advice, and raised Chris like their other children.

It was a decision that led to an extraordinary life, in which Chris has made significant contributions to society. He speaks regularly on behalf of people with developmental disabilities, has co-authored book chapters, and has appeared regularly in a variety of television shows, including starring roles on *Life Goes On* and *Touched by an Angel* (Hassold & Patterson, 1999; McDaniel & Burke, 2001).

Sho Yano's résumé reads like the personal ad of every Mensa member's dreams: 200-plus IQ, recent honors graduate of Loyola University, about to start a dual M.D.-Ph.D. program at the University of Chicago. Reads epic poetry; plays piano works by Mozart, Beethoven, and Chopin. Black belt in tae kwon do. Life goal: to be a cancer geneticist.

One minor problem: He's 12.

In 2003 Yano became the youngest person ever to attend graduate or professional school at Chicago, one of the nation's most selective universities. This real-life Doogie Howser is also a master of understatement. "It's just fun learning," Yano says (*People Weekly,* 2003, p. 125).

Looking Ahead

Two very different people, with widely different intellectual capabilities and strengths—and yet, at their core, Chris Burke and Sho Yano share basic aspects of humanity and even, one could argue, intelligence that ultimately make them more similar than different.

In the following modules, we consider intelligence in all its many varieties. Intelligence represents a focal point for psychologists intent on understanding how people are able to adapt their behavior to the environment in which they live. It also represents a key aspect of how individuals differ from one another in the way in which they learn about and understand the world.

We begin by considering the challenges involved in defining and measuring intelligence. If you are like most people, you have probably wondered how smart you are compared with others. Psychologists, too, have pondered the nature of intelligence. We examine some of their conceptions of intelligence as well as efforts to develop and use standardized tests as a means of measuring intelligence. We also consider the two extremes of individual differences in intelligence: mental retardation and giftedness.

Finally, we explore what are probably the two most controversial issues surrounding intelligence: the degree to which intelligence is influenced by heredity and by the environment, and whether traditional tests of intelligence are biased toward the dominant cultural groups in society—difficult issues that have both psychological and social significance.

What Is Intelligence?

It is typical for the Trukese, people of a small tribe in the South Pacific, to sail a hundred miles in open ocean waters. Although their destination may be just a small dot of land less than a mile wide, the Trukese are able to sail unerringly toward it without the aid of a compass, chronometer, sextant, or any of the other sailing tools that are indispensable to modern Western navigation. They are able to sail accurately, even when prevailing winds do not allow a direct approach to the island and they must take a zigzag course (Gladwin, 1964; Mytinger, 2001).

How are the Trukese able to navigate so effectively? If you asked them, they could not explain it. They might tell you that they use a process that takes into account the rising and setting of the stars and the appearance, sound, and feel of the waves against the side of the boat. But at any given moment as they are sailing along, they could not identify their position or say why they are doing what they are doing. Nor could they explain the navigational theory underlying their sailing technique.

Some might say that the inability of the Trukese to explain in Western terms how their sailing technique works is a sign of primitive or even unintelligent behavior. In fact, if we gave Trukese sailors a Western standardized test of navigational knowledge and theory or, for that matter, a traditional test of intelligence, they might do poorly on it. Yet, as a practical matter, it is not possible to accuse the Trukese of being unintelligent: Despite their inability to explain how they do it, they are able to navigate successfully through the open ocean waters.

Trukese navigation points out the difficulty in coming to grips with what is meant by intelligence. To a Westerner, traveling in a straight line along the most direct and quickest route by using a sextant and other navigational tools is likely to represent the most "intelligent" kind of behavior; in contrast, a zigzag course, based on the "feel" of the waves, would not seem very reasonable. To the Trukese, who are used to their own system of navigation, however, the use of complicated navigational tools might seem so overly complex and unnecessary that they might think of Western navigators as lacking in intelligence.

It is clear from this example that the term *intelligence* can take on many different meanings. If, for instance, you lived in a remote part of the Australian outback, the way you would differentiate between more intelligent and less intelligent people might have to do with successfully mastering hunting skills, whereas to someone living in the heart of urban Miami, intelligence might be exemplified by being streetwise or by business success.

Each of these conceptions of intelligence is reasonable. Each represents an instance in which more intelligent people are better able to use the resources of their environment than are less intelligent people, a distinction that is presumably basic to any definition of intelligence. Yet it is also clear that these conceptions represent very different views of intelligence.

That two such different sets of behavior can exemplify the same psychological concept has long posed a challenge to psychologists. For years they have grappled with the issue of devising a general defini-

Key Concepts

What are the different definitions and conceptions of intelligence?

What are the major approaches to measuring intelligence, and what do intelligence tests measure?

What does the Trukese people's method of navigation—which is done without maps or instruments—tell us about the nature of intelligence?

tion of intelligence. Interestingly, laypersons have fairly clear ideas of what intelligence is, although the nature of their ideas is related to their culture. Westerners view intelligence as the ability to form categories and debate rationally. In contrast, people in Eastern cultures view intelligence more in terms of understanding and relating to one another. And members of some African communities are more likely to view intelligence and social competence as similar (Serpell, 2000; Nisbett, 2003; Sternberg & Grigorenko, 2005).

The definition of intelligence that psychologists employ contains some of the same elements found in the layperson's conception. To psychologists, **intelligence** is the capacity to understand the world, think rationally, and use resources effectively when faced with challenges.

This definition does not lay to rest a key question asked by psychologists: Is intelligence a unitary attribute, or are there different kinds of intelligence? We turn now to various theories of intelligence that address the issue.

Theories of Intelligence: Are There Different Kinds of Intelligence?

Perhaps you see yourself as a good writer but as someone who lacks ability in math. Or maybe you view yourself as a "science" person who easily masters physics but has few strengths in literature. Perhaps you view yourself as generally fairly smart, with intelligence that permits you to excel across domains.

The different ways in which people view their own talents mirrors a question that psychologists have grappled with: Is intelligence a single, general ability, or is it multifaceted and related to specific abilities? Early psychologists interested in intelligence assumed that there was a single, general factor for mental ability, which they called **g**, or the **g-factor.** This general intelligence factor was thought to underlie performance in every aspect of intelligence, and it was the g-factor that was presumably being measured on tests of intelligence (Spearman, 1927; Gottfredson, 2004).

More recent theories see intelligence in a different light. Rather than viewing intelligence as a unitary entity, they consider it to be a multidimensional concept that includes different types of intelligence (Tenopyr, 2002; Stankov, 2003; Sternberg & Pretz, 2005).

FLUID AND CRYSTALLIZED INTELLIGENCE

Some psychologists suggest that there are two different kinds of intelligence: fluid intelligence and crystallized intelligence. **Fluid intelligence** reflects information-processing capabilities, reasoning, and memory. If we were asked to solve an analogy, group a series of letters according to some criterion, or remember a set of numbers, we would be using fluid intelligence. We use fluid intelligence when we're trying to rapidly solve a puzzle (Cattell, 1998; Kane & Engle, 2002).

In contrast, **crystallized intelligence** is the accumulation of information, skills, and strategies that people have learned through experience and that they can apply in problem-solving situations. It reflects our ability to call up information from long-term memory. We would be likely to rely on crystallized intelligence, for instance, if we were asked to participate in a discussion about the solution to the causes of poverty, a task that allows us to draw on our own past experiences and knowledge of the world. In contrast to fluid intelligence, which reflects a more general kind of intelligence, crystallized intelligence is more a reflection of the culture in which a person is raised. The differences between fluid intelligence and crystallized intelligence become particularly evident in the elderly, who show declines in fluid, but not crystallized, intelligence (Schaie, 1994, 1996; Schretlen et al., 2000; Aartsen, Martin, & Zimprich, 2004).

Intelligence: The capacity to understand the world, think rationally, and use resources effectively when faced with challenges.

g or g-factor: The single, general factor for mental ability assumed to underlie intelligence in some early theories of intelligence.

Fluid intelligence: Intelligence that reflects information-processing capabilities, reasoning, and memory.

Crystallized intelligence: The accumulation of information, skills, and strategies that are learned through experience and can be applied in problem-solving situations.

Piloting a helicopter requires the use of both fluid intelligence and crystallized intelligence. Which of the two kinds of intelligence do you believe is more important for such a task?

Other theoreticians conceive of intelligence as encompassing even more components. For example, Louis Thurstone (1938) suggested there are seven factors, which he called primary mental abilities, and J. P. Guilford (1982) said there are 150!

GARDNER'S MULTIPLE INTELLIGENCES: THE MANY WAYS OF SHOWING INTELLIGENCE

In his consideration of intelligence, psychologist Howard Gardner has taken an approach very different from traditional thinking about the topic. Gardner argues that rather than asking "How smart are you?" we should be asking a different question: "How are you smart?" In answering the latter question, Gardner has developed a **theory of multiple intelligences** that has become quite influential (Gardner, 2000).

"*To be perfectly frank, I'm not nearly as smart as you seem to think I am.*"

Gardner argues that we have at a minimum eight different forms of intelligence, each relatively independent of the others: musical, bodily kinesthetic, logical-mathematical, linguistic, spatial, interpersonal, intrapersonal, and naturalist. (Figure 1 describes the eight types of intelligence, with some of Gardner's examples of people who excel in each type.) In Gardner's view, each of the multiple intelligences is linked to an independent system in the brain. Furthermore, he suggests that there may be even more types of intelligence, such as *existential intelligence,* which involves identifying and thinking about the fundamental questions of human existence. For example, the Dalai Lama might exemplify this type of intelligence (Gardner, 2000).

Although Gardner illustrates his conception of the specific types of intelligence with descriptions of well-known people, each person has the same eight kinds of intelligence, although in different degrees. Moreover, although the eight basic types of intelligence are presented individually, Gardner suggests that these separate intelligences do not operate in isolation. Normally, any activity encompasses several kinds of intelligence working together.

The concept of multiple intelligences has led to the development of intelligence tests that include questions in which more than one answer can be correct, providing an opportunity for test takers to demonstrate creative thinking. In addition, many educators have embraced the concept of multiple intelligences, designing classroom curricula that are meant to draw on different aspects of intelligence (Armstrong, 2000, 2003).

Theory of multiple intelligences: Gardner's intelligence theory that proposes that there are eight distinct spheres of intelligence.

IS INFORMATION PROCESSING INTELLIGENCE?

One of the newer contributions to understanding intelligence comes from the work of cognitive psychologists who take an *information-processing approach.* They assert that the way people store material in memory and use that material to solve intellectual tasks provides the most accurate measure of intelligence. Consequently, rather than focusing on the structure of intelligence or its underlying content or dimensions, information-processing approaches examine the *processes* involved in producing intelligent behavior (Embretson, 2005; Hunt, 2005; Neubauer & Fink, 2005).

For example, research shows that people with high scores on intelligence tests spend more time on the initial encoding stages of problems, identifying the parts of a problem and retrieving relevant information from long-term memory, than do people with lower scores. This initial emphasis on recalling relevant information pays off in the end; those who use this approach are more successful in finding solutions than are those who spend relatively less time on the initial stages (Sternberg, 1990; Deary & Der, 2005; Hunt, 2005).

1. Musical intelligence (skills in tasks involving music). Case example:

When he was 3, Yehudi Menuhin was smuggled into San Francisco Orchestra concerts by his parents. By the time he was 10 years old, Menuhin was an international performer.

2. Bodily kinesthetic intelligence (skills in using the whole body or various portions of it in the solution of problems or in the construction of products or displays, exemplified by dancers, athletes, actors, and surgeons). Case example:

Fifteen-year-old Babe Ruth played third base. During one game, his team's pitcher was doing very poorly and Babe loudly criticized him from third base. Brother Matthias, the coach, called out, "Ruth, if you know so much about it, *you* pitch!" Ruth said later that at the very moment he took the pitcher's mound, he *knew* he was supposed to be a pitcher.

3. Logical-mathematical intelligence (skills in problem solving and scientific thinking). Case example:

Barbara McClintock, who won the Nobel Prize in medicine, describes one of her breakthroughs, which came after thinking about a problem for half an hour . . . : "Suddenly I jumped and ran back to the (corn) field. At the top of the field (the others were still at the bottom) I shouted, 'Eureka, I have it!'"

4. Linguistic intelligence (skills involved in the production and use of language). Case example:

At the age of 10, T. S. Eliot created a magazine called *Fireside*, to which he was the sole contributor.

5. Spatial intelligence (skills involving spatial configurations, such as those used by artists and architects). Case example:

Natives of the Truk Islands navigate at sea without instruments. During the actual trip, the navigator must envision mentally a reference island as it passes under a particular star and from that he computes the number of segments completed, the proportion of the trip remaining, and any corrections in heading.

6. Interpersonal intelligence (skills in interacting with others, such as sensitivity to the moods, temperaments, motivations, and intentions of others). Case example:

When Anne Sullivan began instructing the deaf and blind Helen Keller, her task was one that had eluded others for years. Yet, just two weeks after beginning her work with Keller, Sullivan achieved great success.

7. Intrapersonal intelligence (knowledge of the internal aspects of oneself; access to one's own feelings and emotions). Case example:

In her essay "A Sketch of the Past," Virginia Woolf displays deep insight into her own inner life through these lines, describing her reaction to several specific memories from her childhood that still, in adulthood, shock her: "Though I still have the peculiarity that I receive these sudden shocks, they are now always welcome; after the first surprise, I always feel instantly that they are particularly valuable. And so I go on to suppose that the shock-receiving capacity is what makes me a writer."

8. Naturalist intelligence (ability to identify and classify patterns in nature). Case example:

During prehistoric times, hunter/gatherers would rely on naturalist intelligence to identify what flora and fauna were edible. People who are adept at distinguishing nuances between large numbers of similar objects may be expressing naturalist intelligence abilities.

FIGURE 1 According to Howard Gardner, there are eight major kinds of intelligences, corresponding to abilities in different domains. In what area does your greatest intelligence reside, and why do you think you have particular strengths in that area? (Source: Adapted from Gardner, 2000.)

Other information-processing approaches examine the sheer speed of processing. For example, research shows that the speed with which people are able to retrieve information from memory is related to verbal intelligence. In general, people with high scores on measures of intelligence react more quickly on a variety of information-processing tasks, ranging from reactions to flashing lights to distinguishing between letters. The speed of information processing, then, may underlie differences in intelligence (Siegler, 1998; Deary & Der, 2005; Jensen, 2005).

The Biological Basis of Intelligence

Using brain-scanning methods, researchers have identified several areas of the brain that relate to the intelligence. For example, according to the findings of cognitive scientist John Duncan and colleagues, the brains of people completing intelligence test questions in both verbal and spatial domains show activation in a similar location: the lateral prefrontal cortex (see Figure 2). That area is above the outer edge of the eyebrow, about where people rest their heads in the palms of their hands if they are thinking hard about a problem. This area of the brain is critical to juggling many pieces of information simultaneously and solving new problems (Bourke & Duncan, 2005; Duncan, 2005).

These findings suggest that there is a global "workspace" in the brain that organizes and coordinates information, helping to transfer material to other parts of the brain. In this view, the activity in the workspace represents general intelligence (Gray, Chabris, & Braver, 2003).

Research using nonhumans has also begun to help us better understand the biological underpinnings of intelligence. For example, rats raised in enriched environments (meaning an environment containing more toys, tunnels, and so on) develop more complex connections between neurons, along with more rapid learning and better memory. Other studies show differences in metabolism (the rate at which food is converted to energy and expended by the body) that seem to be related to intelligence (Rampon et al., 2000; Haier, 2003).

Ultimately, the search for the biological underpinnings of intelligence will not lead in a single direction. Instead, the most plausible scenario is that there are multiple areas of the brain, as well as multiple kinds of functioning, that are related to intelligent behavior.

Spatial domains

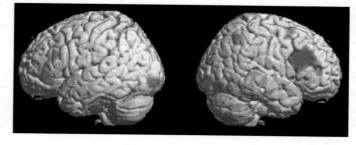

Verbal domains

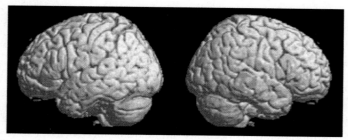

FIGURE 2 The lateral prefrontal cortex is activated when the brain is confronted with problems that involve both verbal and spatial domains. These results suggest that there is a specific area of the brain that serves as the brain's center for organizing and coordinating information. (Source: Duncan et al., 2000.)

Practical Intelligence and Emotional Intelligence: Toward a More Intelligent View of Intelligence

Consider the following situation:

> An employee who reports to one of your subordinates has asked to talk with you about waste, poor management practices, and possible violations of both company policy and the law on the part of your subordinate. You have been in your present position only a year, but in that time you have had no indications of trouble about the subordinate in question. Neither you nor your company has an "open door" policy, so it is expected that employees should take their concerns to their immediate supervisors before bringing a matter to the attention of anyone else. The employee who wishes to meet with you has not discussed this matter with her supervisors because of its delicate nature (Sternberg, 1998, p. 17).

Practical intelligence: According to Sternberg, intelligence relates to overall success in living.

Your response to this situation has a lot to do with your future success in a business career, according to its author, psychologist Robert Sternberg. The question is one of a series designed to help give an indication of your intelligence. However, it is not traditional intelligence that the question is designed to tap, but rather intelligence of a particular kind: practical intelligence. **Practical intelligence** is intelligence related to overall success in living (Sternberg, 2000, 2002a; Sternberg & Hedlund, 2002; Wagner, 2002).

Noting that traditional tests were designed to relate to academic success, Sternberg points to evidence showing that most traditional measures of intelligence do not relate particularly well to *career* success (McClelland, 1993). Specifically, although successful business executives usually score at least moderately well on intelligence tests, the rate at which they advance and their ultimate business achievements are only minimally associated with traditional measures of their intelligence.

Sternberg argues that career success requires a very different type of intelligence from that required for academic success. Whereas academic success is based on knowledge of a particular information base obtained from reading and listening, practical intelligence is learned mainly through observation of others' behavior. People who are high in practical intelligence are able to learn general norms and principles and apply them appropriately. Consequently, practical intelligence tests, like the one shown in Figure 3, measure the ability to employ broad principles in solving everyday problems (Polk, 1997; Sternberg & Pretz, 2005).

In addition to practical intelligence, Sternberg argues there are other two other basic, interrelated types of successful intelligence: analytical and creative. Analytical intelligence focuses on abstract but traditional types of problems measured on IQ tests, while creative intelligence involves the generation of novel ideas and products (Benderly, 2004; Sternberg et al., 2004; Sternberg et al., 2005).

Emotional intelligence: The set of skills that underlie the accurate assessment, evaluation, expression, and regulation of emotions.

Some psychologists broaden the concept of intelligence even further beyond the intellectual realm to include emotions. **Emotional intelligence** is the set of skills that underlie the accurate assessment, evaluation, expression, and regulation of emotions (Mayer, Salovey, & Caruso, 2004; Zeidner, Matthews, & Roberts, 2004).

According to psychologist Daniel Goleman (1995), emotional intelligence underlies the ability to get along well with others. It provides us with an understanding of what other people are feeling and experiencing and permits us to respond appropriately to others' needs. Emotional intelligence is the basis of empathy for others, self-awareness, and social skills.

Abilities in emotional intelligence may help explain why people with only modest scores on traditional intelligence tests can be quite successful, despite their lack of traditional intelligence. High emotional intelligence may enable an individual to tune into others' feelings, permitting a high degree of responsiveness to others.

Although the notion of emotional intelligence makes sense, it has yet to be quantified in a rigorous manner. Furthermore, the view that emotional intelligence is so

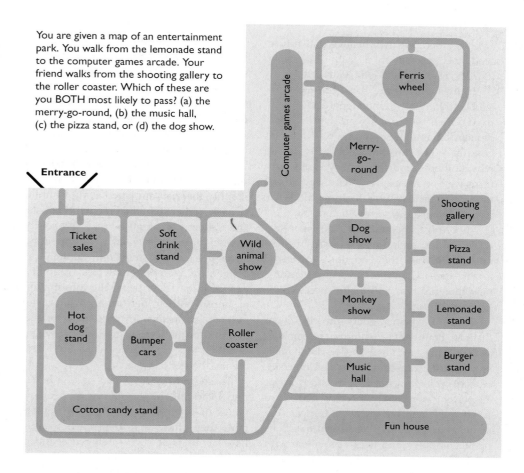

You are given a map of an entertainment park. You walk from the lemonade stand to the computer games arcade. Your friend walks from the shooting gallery to the roller coaster. Which of these are you BOTH most likely to pass? (a) the merry-go-round, (b) the music hall, (c) the pizza stand, or (d) the dog show.

FIGURE 3 Most standard tests of intelligence primarily measure analytical skills; more comprehensive tests measure creative and practical abilities as well. (Source: Sternberg, 2000, p. 389.)

important that skills related to it should be taught in school has raised concerns among some educators. They suggest that the nurturance of emotional intelligence is best left to students' families, especially because there is no well-specified set of criteria for what constitutes emotional intelligence (Sleek, 1997; Becker, 2003).

Still, the notion of emotional intelligence reminds us that there are many ways to demonstrate intelligent behavior—just as there are multiple views of the nature of intelligence (Fox & Spector, 2000; Barrett & Salovey, 2002). Figure 4 presents a summary of the different approaches used by psychologists, and the *Applying Psychology in the 21st Century* box illustrates how our own views of intelligence affect our test performance.

Major Approaches to Intelligence	
Approach	**Characteristics**
Fluid and crystallized intelligence	Fluid intelligence relates to reasoning, memory, and information-processing capabilities; crystallized intelligence relates to information, skills, and strategies learned through experience.
Gardner's multiple intelligences	Eight independent forms of intelligence.
Information-processing approaches	Intelligence is reflected in the ways people store and use material to solve intellectual tasks.
Practical intelligence	Intelligence in terms of nonacademic, career, and personal success.
Emotional intelligence	Intelligence that provides an understanding of what other people are feeling and experiencing and permits us to respond appropriately to others' needs.

FIGURE 4 Just as there are many views of the nature of intelligence, there are also numerous ways to demonstrate intelligent behavior. This summary provides an overview of the various approaches used by psychologists.

How You Think About Intelligence Helps Determine Your Success

What is your thinking on intelligence? Is it your view that what you're born with is what you've got and that your intelligence is largely fixed for life? Or do you believe intelligence is flexible and malleable, and through effort and practice, it can increase?

Think hard before you answer, because your response might well have an effect on your intellectual performance and on how your brain works. According to the research findings of cognitive neuroscientist Jennifer Mangels, people who believe that intelligence is fixed show specific brain wave patterns after finding out they answered a question wrong. Furthermore, they are less likely to show that they learned from their errors on subsequent questions, performing less well than do people who consider intelligence a flexible trait (Mangels, 2004; Mangels, Dweck, & Good, 2005).

Mangels' research expands the findings of educational psychologist Carol Dweck, who discovered that people's beliefs about intelligence basically fall into two categories. *Entity theorists* believe that intelligence is primarily fixed at birth. In their view, no amount of life experience or hard work can change the intelligence we have at birth. In contrast, *incremental theorists* see intelligence as flexible and variable, potentially changing over the course of life. In contrast to entity theorists, incremental theorists are more resilient when they fail at a task, because they believe that future academic success on a task is possible (Dweck, Mangels, & Good, 2004).

Entity theorists are sometimes victimized by their view of intelligence as largely fixed. Often they don't work hard in academic domains they assume they are not good at—"I'm not that smart at math, so why bother"—and when they don't perform well on a task, they tend to give up relatively quickly. They don't readily learn from their mistakes.

In contrast, incremental theorists often work harder, seeking to learn from their mistakes. When they do not succeed at a task, they put more effort into learning new material that will make success likelier in the future.

To learn whether entity theorists have distinct brain-wave patterns, researchers assessed college students' beliefs about intelligence. In the sample of Columbia University students who participated in the study, about 40 percent were entity theorists, half were incremental, and the rest were unclear. The students in the study were asked questions on a computer and were provided with feedback about whether they were right or wrong. They also indicated their degree of confidence in their answers.

The study found that participants showed a *metamemory mismatch P3 wave* pattern each time they received feedback. The strength of the wave was particularly pronounced when the feedback was unexpected, as indicated by participants' confidence levels. Most interesting was the difference between entity and incremental theorists: When participants learned that their response was wrong, the P3 waves of entity theorists appeared about 50 milliseconds earlier than incremental theorists. The difference suggests that the entity theorists were particularly disappointed by their erroneous response, taking it as a signal of their inherent lack of ability. In fact, rather than using the information to improve their performance later, the participants in the entity group were less likely to do better on questions in which they had low confidence than were incremental theorists.

These findings help lead us to a better understanding of the nature of people's views of intelligence. Even more important, they show that the beliefs people hold about their own intelligence affects their performance and the processing of information that goes on in their brain (Glenn, 2004).

RETHINK

Do you think of yourself as primarily an entity or incremental theorist in terms of intelligence? How do you think your view might have affected your performance on academic tasks? Do you think we should train students to think more incrementally about intelligence in order to improve their test performance?

Assessing Intelligence

Intelligence tests: Tests devised to quantify a person's level of intelligence.

Given the variety of approaches to the components of intelligence, it is not surprising that measuring intelligence has proved challenging. Psychologists who study intelligence have focused much of their attention on the development of **intelligence tests** and have relied on such tests to quantify a person's level of intelligence. These tests have proved to be of great benefit in identifying students in need of special attention in school, diagnosing cognitive difficulties, and helping people make optimal educational and vocational choices. At the same time, their use has proved quite controversial, raising important social and educational issues.

Historically, the first effort at intelligence testing was based on an uncomplicated, but completely wrong, assumption: that the size and shape of a person's head could be used as an objective measure of intelligence. The idea was put forward by Sir Francis Galton (1822–1911), an eminent English scientist whose ideas in other domains proved to be considerably better than his notions about intelligence.

Galton's motivation to identify people of high intelligence stemmed from personal prejudices. He sought to demonstrate the natural superiority of people of high social class (including himself) by showing that intelligence is inherited. He hypothesized that head configuration, being genetically determined, is related to brain size, and therefore is related to intelligence.

Galton's theories proved wrong on virtually every count. Head size and shape are not related to intellectual performance, and subsequent research has found little relationship between brain size and intelligence. However, Galton's work did have at least one desirable result: He was the first person to suggest that intelligence could be quantified and measured in an objective manner (Jensen, 2002).

Alfred Binet

BINET AND THE DEVELOPMENT OF IQ TESTS

The first real intelligence tests were developed by the French psychologist Alfred Binet (1857–1911). His tests followed from a simple premise: If performance on certain tasks or test items improved with *chronological,* or physical, age, performance could be used to distinguish more intelligent people from less intelligent ones within a particular age group. On the basis of this principle, Binet devised the first formal intelligence test, which was designed to identify the "dullest" students in the Paris school system in order to provide them with remedial aid.

Binet began by presenting tasks to same-age students who had been labeled "bright" or "dull" by their teachers. If a task could be completed by the bright students but not by the dull ones, he retained that task as a proper test item; otherwise it was discarded. In the end he came up with a test that distinguished between the bright and dull groups, and—with further work—one that distinguished among children in different age groups (Binet & Simon, 1916; Sternberg & Jarvin, 2003).

On the basis of the Binet test, children were assigned a score relating to their **mental age,** the average age of individuals who achieve a particular level of performance on a test. For example, if the average 8-year-old answered, say, 45 items correctly on a test, anyone who answered 45 items correctly would be assigned a mental age of 8 years. Consequently, whether the person taking the test was 20 years old or 5 years old, he or she would have the same mental age of 8 years.

Assigning a mental age to students provided an indication of their general level of performance. However, it did not allow for adequate comparisons among people of different chronological ages. By using mental age alone, for instance, we might assume that a 20-year-old responding at a 18-year-old's level would be as bright as a 5-year-old answering at a 3-year-old's level, when actually the 5-year-old would be displaying a much greater *relative* degree of slowness.

A solution to the problem came in the form of the **intelligence quotient,** or **IQ,** a score that takes into account an individual's mental *and* chronological ages. Historically, the first IQ scores employed the following formula, in which *MA* stands for mental age and *CA* for chronological age:

Mental age: The average age of individuals who achieve a particular level of performance on a test.

Intelligence quotient (IQ): A score that takes into account an individual's mental and chronological ages.

$$\text{IQ score} = \frac{\text{MA}}{\text{CA}} \times 100$$

Using this formula, we can return to the earlier example of a 20-year-old performing at a mental age of 18 and calculate an IQ score of (18/20) × 100 = 90. In contrast, the 5-year-old performing at a mental age of 3 comes out with a considerably lower IQ score: (3/5) × 100 = 60.

FIGURE 5 The average and most common IQ score is 100, and 68 percent of all people are within a 30-point range centered on 100. Some 95 percent of the population have scores that are within 30 points above or below 100, and 99.8 percent have scores that are between 55 and 145.

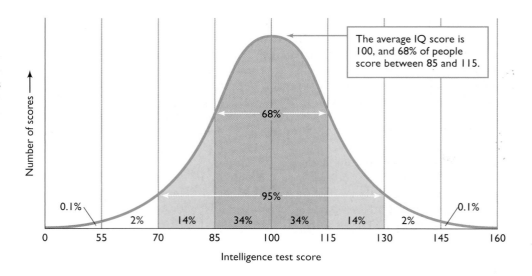

The average IQ score is 100, and 68% of people score between 85 and 115.

68%

95%

0.1%   2%   14%   34%   34%   14%   2%   0.1%

Number of scores →

0   55   70   85   100   115   130   145   160

Intelligence test score

As a bit of trial and error with the formula will show you, anyone who has a mental age equal to his or her chronological age will have an IQ equal to 100. Moreover, people with a mental age that is greater than their chronological age will have IQs that exceed 100.

Although the basic principles behind the calculation of an IQ score still hold, today IQ scores are figured in a different manner and are known as *deviation IQ scores.* First, the average test score for everyone of the same age who takes the test is determined, and that average score is assigned an IQ of 100. Then, with the aid of statistical techniques that calculate the differences (or "deviations") between each score and the average, IQ scores are assigned.

As you can see in Figure 5, when IQ scores from large numbers of people are plotted on a graph, they form a *bell-shaped distribution* (called *bell-shaped* because it looks like a bell when plotted). Approximately two-thirds of all individuals fall within 15 IQ points of the average score of 100. As scores increase or fall beyond that range, the percentage of people in a category falls considerably.

Now in its fifth edition, the Stanford-Binet test consists of a series of items that vary in nature according to the age of the person being tested. What can we learn about a person from a test of this type?

CONTEMPORARY IQ TESTS: GAUGING INTELLIGENCE

Remnants of Binet's original intelligence test are still with us, although the test has been revised in significant ways. Now in its fifth edition and called the *Stanford-Binet Intelligence Scale,* the test consists of a series of items that vary in nature according to the age of the person being tested. For example, young children are asked to copy figures or answer questions about everyday activities. Older people are asked to solve analogies, explain proverbs, and describe similarities that underlie sets of words.

The test is administered orally. An examiner begins by finding a mental age level at which a person is able to answer all the questions correctly, and then moves on to successively more difficult problems. When a mental age level is reached at which no items can be answered, the test is over. By examining the pattern of correct and incorrect responses, the examiner is able to compute an IQ score for the person being tested. In addition, the Stanford-Binet

NAME	GOAL OF ITEM	EXAMPLE
WAIS III		
VERBAL SCALE		
Information	Assess general information	Who wrote *Tom Sawyer?*
Comprehension	Assess understanding and evaluation of social norms and past experience	Why is copper often used for electrical wires?
Arithmetic	Assess math reasoning through verbal problems	Three women divided eighteen golf balls equally among themselves. How many golf balls did each person receive?
Similarities	Test understanding of how objects or concepts are alike, tapping abstract reasoning	In what way are a circle and a triangle alike?
PERFORMANCE SCALE		
Digit symbol	Assess speed of learning	Test-taker must learn what symbols correspond to what digits, and then must replace a multidigit number with the appropriate symbols. 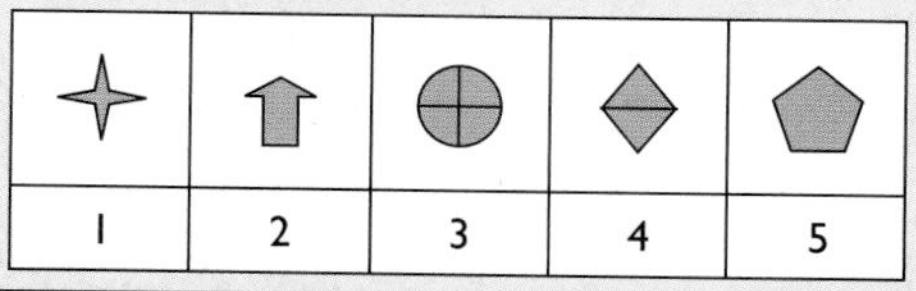
Matrix reasoning	Test spatial reasoning	Test-taker must decide which of the five possibilities replaces the question mark and completes the sequence. 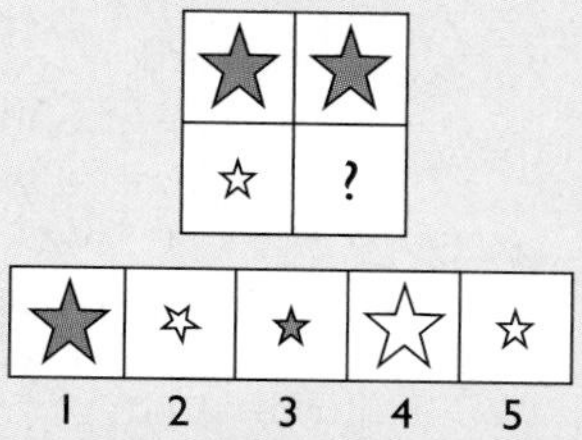
Block design item	Test understanding of relationship of parts to whole	Problems require test-takers to reproduce a design in fixed amount of time. 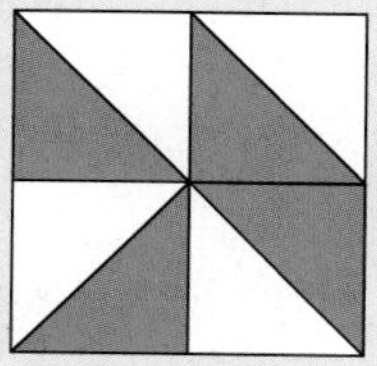

FIGURE 6 Typical kinds of items found on the verbal and performance (nonverbal) scales of the Wechsler Adult Intelligene Scale (*WAIS–III*) and the Wechsler Intelligence Scale for Children (*WISC–IV*). (continues)

test yields separate subscores that provide clues to a test-taker's particular strengths and weaknesses.

The IQ test most frequently used in the United States was devised by psychologist David Wechsler and is known as the *Wechsler Adult Intelligence Scale–III,* or, more commonly, the *WAIS–III.* There is also a children's version, the *Wechsler Intelligence Scale for Children–IV,* or *WISC–IV.* Both the WAIS–III and the WISC–IV have two major parts: a verbal scale and a performance (or nonverbal) scale.

As you can see from the sample questions in Figure 6, the verbal and performance scales include questions of very different types. Verbal tasks consist of more traditional

WISC IV		
NAME	**GOAL OF ITEM**	**EXAMPLE**
VERBAL SCALE		
Information	Assess general information	How many nickels make a dime?
Comprehension	Assess understanding and evaluation of social norms and past experience	What is the advantage of keeping money in the bank?
Arithmetic	Assess math reasoning through verbal problems	If two buttons cost 15 cents, what will be the cost of a dozen buttons?
Similarities	Test understanding of how objects or concepts are alike, tapping abstract reasoning	In what way are an hour and a week alike?
PERFORMANCE SCALE		
Digit symbol	Assess speed of learning	Match symbols to numbers using key.
Picture completion	Visual memory and attention	Identify what is missing.
Object assembly	Test understanding of relationship of parts to wholes	Put pieces together to form a whole.

FIGURE 6 concluded

kinds of problems, including vocabulary definition and comprehension of various concepts. In contrast, the performance (nonverbal) part involves the timed assembly of small objects and the arrangement of pictures in a logical order. Although an individual's scores on the verbal and performance sections of the test are generally within close range of each other, the scores of a person with a language deficiency or a background of severe environmental deprivation may show a relatively large discrepancy between the two sections. By providing separate scores, the WAIS–III and WISC–IV give a more precise picture of a person's specific abilities compared with other IQ tests (Kaufman & Lichtenberger, 1999, 2000).

Because the Stanford-Binet, WAIS–III, and WISC–IV all require individualized, one-on-one administration, it is relatively difficult and time-consuming to administer and score them on a large-scale basis. Consequently, there are now a number of IQ tests that allow group administration. Rather than having one examiner ask one person at a time to respond to individual items, group IQ tests are strictly paper-and-pencil tests. The primary advantage of group tests is their ease of administration (Anastasi & Urbina, 1997).

However, sacrifices are made in group testing that in some cases may outweigh the benefits. For instance, group tests generally offer fewer kinds of questions than do tests administered individually. Furthermore, people may be more motivated to perform at their highest ability level when working on a one-to-one basis with a test administrator than they are in a group. Finally, in some cases, it is simply impossible to employ group tests, particularly with young children or people with unusually low IQs (Aiken, 1996).

ACHIEVEMENT AND APTITUDE TESTS

IQ tests are not the only kind of tests that you might have taken during the course of your schooling. Two other kinds of tests, related to intelligence but intended to measure somewhat different phenomena, are achievement tests and aptitude tests. An **achievement test** is a test designed to determine a person's level of knowledge in a specific subject area. Rather than measuring general ability, as an intelligence test does, an achievement test concentrates on the specific material a person has learned. High school students sometimes take specialized achievement tests in particular areas such as world history and chemistry as a college entrance requirement; lawyers must pass an achievement test (in the form of the bar exam) in order to practice law.

An **aptitude test** is designed to predict a person's ability in a particular area or line of work. Most of us take one or the other of the best-known aptitude tests in the process of pursuing admission to college: the SAT and the ACT. The SAT and ACT are meant to predict how well people will do in college, and the scores have proved over the years to be moderately correlated with college grades (Hoffman, 2001).

Although in theory the distinction between aptitude tests and achievement tests is precise, it is difficult to develop an aptitude test that does not rely at least in part on past achievement. For example, the SAT has been strongly criticized for being less

Achievement test: A test designed to determine a person's level of knowledge in a given subject area.

Aptitude test: A test designed to predict a person's ability in a particular area or line of work.

Test Preparation Program Guide

SAT & PSAT ACT

Real expertise. Real strategies. Real results.

Thousands of students enroll in courses in an effort to boost their standardized test scores.

Reliability: The property by which tests measure consistently what they are trying to measure.

Validity: The property by which tests actually measure what they are supposed to measure.

Norms: Standards of test performance that permit the comparison of one person's score on a test with the scores of other individuals who have taken the same test.

an aptitude test (predicting college success) than an achievement test (assessing prior performance).

RELIABILITY AND VALIDITY: TAKING THE MEASURE OF TESTS

When we use a ruler, we expect to find that it measures an inch in the same way it did the last time we used it. When we weigh ourselves on the bathroom scale, we hope that the variations we see on the scale are due to changes in our weight and not to errors on the part of the scale (unless the change in weight is in an unwanted direction!).

In the same way, we hope that psychological tests have **reliability**—that they measure consistently what they are trying to measure. We need to be sure that each time we administer the test, a test-taker will achieve the same results—assuming that nothing about the person has changed relevant to what is being measured.

Suppose, for instance, that when you first took the SAT exams, you scored 400 on the verbal section of the test. Then, after taking the test again a few months later, you scored 700. Upon receiving your new score, you might well stop celebrating for a moment to question whether the test is reliable, for it is unlikely that your abilities could have changed enough to raise your score by 300 points.

But suppose your score changed hardly at all, and both times you received a score of about 400. You couldn't complain about a lack of reliability. However, if you knew your verbal skills were above average, you might be concerned that the test did not adequately measure what it was supposed to measure. In sum, the question has now become one of validity rather than reliability. A test has **validity** when it actually measures what it is supposed to measure.

Knowing that a test is reliable is no guarantee that it is also valid. For instance, Sir Francis Galton assumed that skull size is related to intelligence, and he was able to measure skull size with great reliability. However, the measure of skull size was not valid—it had nothing to do with intelligence. In this case, then, we have reliability without validity.

However, if a test is unreliable, it cannot be valid. Assuming that all other factors—motivation to score well, knowledge of the material, health, and so forth—are similar, if a person scores high the first time he or she takes a specific test and low the second time, the test cannot be measuring what it is supposed to measure. Therefore, the test is both unreliable and not valid.

Test validity and reliability are prerequisites for accurate assessment of intelligence—as well as for any other measurement task carried out by psychologists. Consequently, the measures of personality carried out by personality psychologists, clinical psychologists' assessments of psychological disorders, and social psychologists' measures of attitudes must meet the tests of validity and reliability for the results to be meaningful (Thompson, 2002; Phelps, 2005).

Assuming that a test is both valid and reliable, one further step is necessary in order to interpret the meaning of a particular test-taker's score: the establishment of norms. **Norms** are standards of test performance that permit the comparison of one person's score on a test to the scores of others who have taken the same test. For example, a norm permits test-takers to know that they have scored, say, in the top 15 percent of those who have taken the test previously. Tests for which norms have been developed are known as *standardized tests*.

Test designers develop norms by calculating the average score achieved by a particular group of people for whom the test has been designed. Then the test designers can determine the extent to which each person's score differs from the scores of the other individuals who have taken the test in the past and provide future test-takers with a qualitative sense of their performance.

Obviously, the samples of test-takers who are employed in the establishment of norms are critical to the norming process. The people used to determine norms must be representative of the individuals to whom the test is directed.

ADAPTIVE TESTING: USING COMPUTERS TO ASSESS PERFORMANCE

Ensuring that tests are reliable and valid, and are based on appropriate norms, has become more critical with the introduction of computers to administer standardized tests. The Educational Testing Service (ETS)—the company that devises the SAT and the Graduate Record Examination (GRE), used for college and graduate school admission—is moving to computer administration of all its standardized tests.

In computerized versions, not only are test questions viewed and answered on a computer, the test itself is individualized. Under *adaptive testing*, students do not necessarily receive identical sets of test questions. Instead, the computer first presents a randomly selected question of moderate difficulty. If the test-taker answers it correctly, the computer will then present a randomly chosen item of slightly greater difficulty. If the answer is wrong, the computer will present a slightly easier item. Each question becomes slightly harder or easier than the question preceding it, depending on whether the previous response is correct. Ultimately, the greater the number of difficult questions answered correctly, the higher the score (Wainer et al., 2000; Chang & Ansley, 2003; see Figure 7).

Because computerized adaptive testing pinpoints a test-taker's level of proficiency fairly quickly, the total time spent taking the exam is shorter than it is with a traditional exam. Test-takers are not forced to spend a great deal of time answering questions that are either much easier or much harder than they can handle.

Critics of computerized adaptive testing suggest that it may discriminate against test-takers who have limited access to computers and thus may have less practice with them or may be more intimidated by the testing medium. ETS disputes this claim, although some of its own research shows that women and older test-takers display greater anxiety at the beginning of the test. Despite this anxiety, however, their performance ultimately is not affected, and most research suggests that computerized adaptive testing provides scores equivalent to those of traditional paper-and-pencil measures for most types of testing (Tonidandel, Quinones, & Adams, 2002).

WEB-BASED TESTING: TEST-TAKER BEWARE

Although ETS and other legitimate test developers are conscientious and meticulous in developing their tests, many tests you may encounter while surfing the Web have neither reliability nor validity. Although professional organizations that regulate testing such as the American Psychological Association require that Web-based tests be held to the same high ethical principles that underlie traditional published tests, test producers often do not. For example, ethical rules require that test-makers deliver results in a sensitive way, taking into account the impact the test results will have on test-takers. But online tests on the Web often allow anyone to take a test, as long as they pay a given fee, and the results are delivered in a standardized, nonindividualized format. Similarly, procedures that lead to reliability and validity need to be followed, and sometimes online test-makers cut corners.

Consequently, because online tests are not well-regulated, their reliability and validity may be minimal. Users of Web-based tests need to be extremely cautious in making use of the feedback they receive (Kersting, 2004).

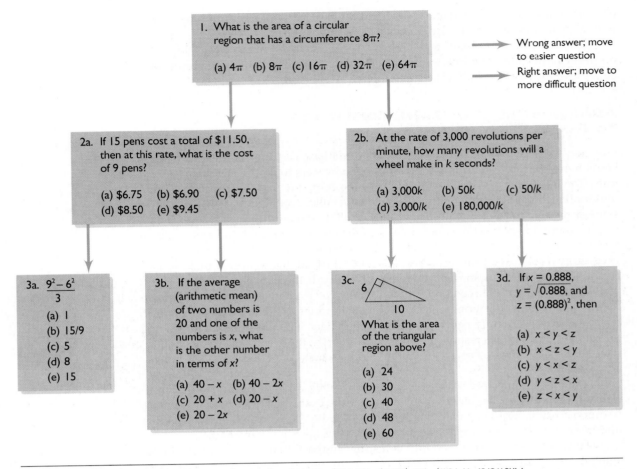

FIGURE 7 Adaptive testing. In the Graduate Record Examination (GRE), the computer randomly selects a first question of medium difficulty. If the test-taker answers the question correctly, the computer poses a more difficult question. Once the test-taker gives an incorrect answer, he or she is given a question at the next easiest level, as illustrated in this example (*The New York Times*, 1993, p. B9). Test-takers are graded based on the level of difficulty of the questions they answer correctly, meaning that two test-takers who answer the same number of questions correctly can end up with very different scores. What do you think are the drawbacks of adaptive testing of this sort? Do you think such tests may discriminate against test-takers who are less familiar with computers compared with those who have easy access to them?

BECOMING AN INFORMED CONSUMER
of Psychology

Scoring Better on Standardized Tests

Even though psychologists disagree about the nature of intelligence, intelligence tests—as well as many other kinds of tests—are widely used in a variety of situations. For example, if you are thinking about becoming a physician, a lawyer, or almost any other kind of professional in a field that requires advanced training, you will have to take a formal exam in order to be accepted for post-undergraduate training.

If you do have to take such an exam, you can do several things to maximize your score, including the following (Holmes & Keffer, 1995; Bronner, 1998; Lurie, Robinson, & Pecsenye, 2005):

- *Learn as much as you can about the test before you take it.* Know what sections will be on the test and how much each section is worth.

- *Practice.* Try as many practice tests as you can find. The more practice you have, the easier it will be when you actually take the test.
- *If the test is administered on a computer, as it probably will be, take practice tests on a computer.* The more familiar you are with computers, the more at ease you will feel when you sit down to take the test.
- *Time yourself carefully.* Don't spend too much time on early items at the expense of later ones. Your goal should be not perfection, but maximizing the number of correct responses you get.
- *Be aware of the scoring policy.* If you are not penalized for wrong answers, guess. If there are penalties, be more conservative about guessing.
- *If it is a paper-and-pencil test, complete answer sheets accurately.* Check and check again. If the test is on a computer, check your answer thoroughly before going on to the next question, because you won't be able to go back and change your answer once you've submitted it.

RECAP/EVALUATE/RETHINK

RECAP

What are the different definitions and conceptions of intelligence?

- Because intelligence can take many forms, defining it is challenging. One commonly accepted view is that intelligence is the capacity to understand the world, think rationally, and use resources effectively when faced with challenges. (pp. 289-290)
- The earliest psychologists assumed that there is a general factor for mental ability called *g*. However, later psychologists disputed the view that intelligence is unidimensional. (p. 290)
- Some researchers suggest that intelligence can be broken down into fluid intelligence and crystallized intelligence. Gardner's theory of multiple intelligences proposes that there are eight spheres of intelligence. (pp. 290-291)
- Information-processing approaches examine the processes underlying intelligent behavior rather than focusing on the structure of intelligence. (pp. 291-292)
- Practical intelligence is intelligence related to overall success in living; emotional intelligence is the set of skills that underlie the accurate assessment, evaluation, expression, and regulation of emotions. (p. 294)

What are the major approaches to measuring intelligence, and what do intelligence tests measure?

- Intelligence tests have traditionally compared a person's mental age and chronological age to yield an IQ, or intelligence quotient, score. (p. 297)
- Specific tests of intelligence include the Stanford-Binet test, the Wechsler Adult Intelligence Scale–III (WAIS–III), and the Wechsler Intelligence Scale for Children–IV (WISC–IV). Achievement tests and aptitude tests are other types of standardized tests. (pp. 298-301)

- Tests are expected to be both reliable and valid. Reliability refers to the consistency with which a test measures what it is trying to measure. A test has validity when it actually measures what it is supposed to measure. (p. 302)

EVALUATE

1. _____ is a measure of intelligence that takes into account a person's chronological and mental ages.
2. _____ tests predict a person's ability in a specific area; _____ tests determine the specific level of knowledge in an area.
3. Some psychologists make the distinction between _____ intelligence, which reflects reasoning, memory, and information-processing capabilities, and _____ intelligence, which is the information, skills, and strategies that people have learned through experience.
4. Cognitive psychologists use a(n) _____ - _____ approach to measure intelligence.

RETHINK

1. What is the role of emotional intelligence in the classroom? How might emotional intelligence be tested? Should emotional intelligence be a factor in determining academic promotion to the next grade?
2. *From the human resource specialist's perspective:* Job interviews are really a kind of test. In what ways does a job interview resemble an aptitude test? An achievement test? Do you think job interviews can be made to have validity and reliability?

Answers to Evaluate Questions

1. IQ. 2. aptitude, achievement; 3. fluid, crystallized; 4. information-processing

KEY TERMS

intelligence p. 290
g or g-factor p. 290
fluid intelligence p. 290
crystallized intelligence
    p. 290

theory of multiple
    intelligences p. 291
practical intelligence p. 294
emotional intelligence
    p. 294

intelligence tests p. 296
mental age p. 297
intelligence quotient (IQ)
    p. 297
achievement test p. 301

aptitude test p. 301
reliability p. 302
validity p. 302
norms p. 302

Variations in Intellectual Ability

"Hey, hey, hey, Fact Track!" The 11-year-old speaker chose one of his favorite programs. . . .

"What is your name?" appeared on the monitor.

"Daniel Skandera," he typed. A menu scrolled up listing the program's possibilities. Daniel chose multiplication facts, Level 1. . . .

Randomly generated multiplication facts flashed on the screen: "4 × 6," "2 × 9," "3 × 3," "7 × 6." Daniel responded, deftly punching in his answers on the computer's numeric keypad. . . .

The computer tallied the results. "You completed 20 problems in 66 seconds. You beat your goal. Problems correct = 20. Congratulations Daniel!" And with that the 11-year-old retreated hastily to the TV room. The Lakers and 76ers were about to tip off for an NBA championship game, and Daniel wanted to see the first half before bedtime (Heward & Orlansky, 1988, p. 100).

If you view people with mental retardation as inept and dull, it is time to revise your perceptions. As in the case of Daniel Skandera, described above, individuals with deficits of intellectual abilities can lead full, rounded lives and in some cases perform well in certain kinds of academic endeavors.

More than 7 million people in the United States have been identified as far enough below average in intelligence that they can be regarded as having a serious deficit. Individuals with low IQs—people with mental retardation—as well as those with unusually high IQs, or the intellectually gifted, require special attention if they are to reach their full potential.

Mental Retardation

Although sometimes thought of as a rare phenomenon, mental retardation occurs in 1 to 3 percent of the population. There is wide variation among those labeled as mentally retarded, in large part because of the inclusiveness of the definition developed by the American Association on Mental Retardation (AAMR). The association suggests that **mental retardation** is a disability characterized by significant limitations both in intellectual functioning and in conceptual, social, and practical adaptive skills (AAMR, 2002).

Although below-average intellectual functioning can be measured in a relatively straightforward manner—using standard IQ tests—it is more difficult to determine how to gauge limitations in adaptive behavior. Ultimately, this imprecision leads to a lack of uniformity in how experts apply the label *mental retardation*. Furthermore, it has resulted in significant variation in the abilities of people who are categorized as mentally retarded, ranging from those who can be taught to work and function with little special attention to those who virtually cannot be trained and must receive institutional treatment throughout their lives (Accardo & Capute, 1998; Detterman, Gabriel, & Ruthsatz, 2000).

Key Concepts

How can the extremes of intelligence be characterized?

How can we help people reach their full potential?

Mental retardation: A condition characterized by significant limitations both in intellectual functioning and in conceptual, social, and practical adaptive skills.

Most people with mental retardation have relatively minor deficits and are classified as having *mild retardation*. These individuals, who have IQ scores ranging from 55 to 69, constitute some 90 percent of all people with mental retardation. Although their development is typically slower than that of their peers, they can function quite independently by adulthood and are able to hold jobs and have families of their own (Bates et al., 2001).

At greater levels of retardation—*moderate retardation* (IQs of 40 to 54), *severe retardation* (IQs of 25 to 39), and *profound retardation* (IQs below 25)—the difficulties are more pronounced. For people with moderate retardation, deficits are obvious early, with language and motor skills lagging behind those of peers. Although these individuals can hold simple jobs, they need to have a moderate degree of supervision throughout their lives. Individuals with severe and profound mental retardation are generally unable to function independently and typically require care for their entire lives.

IDENTIFYING THE ROOTS OF MENTAL RETARDATION

What are the causes of mental retardation? In nearly one-third of the cases there is an identifiable biological reason. The most common biological cause is **fetal alcohol syndrome,** caused by a mother's use of alcohol while pregnant. Increasing evidence shows that even small amounts of alcohol intake can produce intellectual deficits (Coles, Platzman, & Lynch, 2003; Burd et al., 2003; West & Blake, 2005).

Down syndrome, the type of mental retardation experienced by actor Chris Burke, discussed in the Prologue, represents another major biological cause of mental retardation. **Down syndrome** results from the presence of an extra chromosome. In other cases of mental retardation, an abnormality occurs in the structure of a chromosome. Birth complications, such as a temporary lack of oxygen, may also cause retardation. In some cases, mental retardation occurs after birth, following a head injury, a stroke, or infections such as meningitis (Gualtiere, 2003; Selikowitz, 2003; Plomin & Kovas, 2005).

The majority of cases of mental retardation are classified as **familial retardation,** however, in which no apparent biological defect exists but there is a history of retardation in the family. Whether the family background of retardation is caused by environmental factors, such as extreme continuous poverty leading to malnutrition, or by some underlying genetic factor is usually impossible to determine (Zigler et al., 2002). Learn more about the causes of mental retardation the PsychInteractive exercise.

INTEGRATING INDIVIDUALS WITH MENTAL RETARDATION

Regardless of the cause of mental retardation, important advances in the care and treatment of those with retardation have been made in the last several decades. Much of this change was instigated by the Education for All Handicapped Children Act of 1975 (Public Law 94-142). In this federal law, Congress stipulated that people with retardation are entitled to a full education and that they must be educated and trained in the *least restrictive environment*. The law increased the educational opportunities for individuals with mental retardation, facilitating their integration into regular classrooms as much as possible—a process known as *mainstreaming* (Simmons, Kameenui, & Chard, 1998; Katsiyannis, Zhang, & Woodruff, 2005).

The philosophy behind mainstreaming suggests that the interaction of students with and without mental retardation in regular classrooms will improve educational opportunities for those with retardation, increase their social acceptance, and facilitate their integration into society as a whole. Of course, special education classes still exist; some individuals with retardation function at too low a level to benefit from placement in regular classrooms. Moreover, children with mental retardation who are mainstreamed into regular classes typically attend special classes for at least part of the day (Guralnick et al., 1996; Hastings & Oakford, 2003).

Fetal alcohol syndrome: The most common cause of mental retardation in newborns, occurring when the mother uses alcohol during pregnancy.

Down syndrome: A cause of mental retardation resulting from the presence of an extra chromosome.

Familial retardation: Mental retardation in which no apparent biological defect exists but there is a history of retardation in the family.

www.mhhe.com/feldmanup8

PsychInteractive Online

Mental Retardation

Some educators argue that an alternative to mainstreaming, called *full inclusion*, might be more effective. Full inclusion is the integration of all students, even those with the most severe educational disabilities, into regular classes and an avoidance of special, segregated special education classes. Teacher aides are assigned to help the children with special needs progress. Schools with full inclusion have no separate special education classes. However, full inclusion is a controversial practice, and it is not widely applied (Kavale, 2002; Hastings & Oakford, 2003; Praisner, 2003).

The Intellectually Gifted

Another group of people—the intellectually gifted—differ from those with average intelligence as much as do individuals with mental retardation, although in a different manner. Accounting for 2 to 4 percent of the population, the **intellectually gifted** have IQ scores greater than 130. Sho Yano, the 12-year-old described in the chapter prologue who was about to start graduate school, exemplifies a case of someone who is particularly intellectually gifted.

Intellectually gifted: The 2 to 4 percent of the population who have IQ scores greater than 130.

Although the stereotype associated with the gifted suggests that they are awkward, shy social misfits who are unable to get along well with peers, most research indicates that just the opposite is true. The intellectually gifted are most often outgoing, well-adjusted, healthy, popular people who are able to do most things better than the average person can (Harden, 2000; Winner, 2000, 2003; Rizza & Morrison, 2003; Gottfredson & Deary, 2004).

For example, in a long-term study by psychologist Lewis Terman that started in the early 1920s and is still going on, 1,500 children who had IQ scores above 140 were followed and examined periodically over the next sixty years (Terman & Oden, 1947; Sears, 1977). From the start, the members of this group were more physically, academically, and socially capable than their nongifted peers. They were generally healthier, taller, heavier, and stronger than average. Not surprisingly, they did better in school as well. They also showed better social adjustment than average. All these advantages paid off in terms of career success: As a group, the gifted received more awards and distinctions, earned higher incomes, and made more contributions in art and literature than typical individuals. For example, by the time the members of the group were 40 years old, they had collectively written more than 90 books, 375 plays and short stories, and 2,000 articles, and had registered more than 200 patents. Perhaps most important, they reported greater satisfaction in life than the nongifted.

Of course, not every member of the group Terman studied was successful. Furthermore, high intelligence is not a homogeneous quality; a person with a high overall IQ is not necessarily gifted in every academic subject, but may excel in just one or two. A high IQ is not a universal guarantee of success (Shurkin, 1992; Winner, 2003).

Although special programs attempting to overcome the deficits of people with mental retardation abound, programs targeted at the intellectually gifted are more rare. One reason for this lack of attention is that although there are as many gifted individuals as there are those with mental retardation, the definition of *gifted* is vague, especially compared with definitions of mental retardation. Furthermore, there is a persistent view that the gifted ought to be able to "make it on their own"; if they can't, they really weren't gifted in the first place (Parke, 2003; Robinson, 2003).

More enlightened approaches, however, have acknowledged that without some form of special attention, the gifted become bored and frustrated with the pace of their schooling and may never reach their potential. Consequently, programs for the gifted are designed to provide enrichment that allows participants' talents to flourish (Winner, 2000; Neber & Heller, 2002; Adams-Byers et al., 2004).

RECAP/EVALUATE/RETHINK

RECAP

How can the extremes of intelligence be characterized?

- The levels of mental retardation include mild, moderate, severe, and profound retardation. (pp. 307-308)
- About one-third of the cases of retardation have a known biological cause; fetal alcohol syndrome is the most common. Most cases, however, are classified as familial retardation, for which there is no known biological cause. (p. 308)
- The intellectually gifted are people with IQ scores greater than 130. Intellectually gifted people tend to be healthier and more successful than are the nongifted. (p. 309)

How can we help people reach their full potential?

- Advances in the treatment of people with mental retardation include mainstreaming, or the integration of individuals with mental retardation into regular education classrooms as much as possible (along with some participation in segregated special education classes), and full inclusion, in which all students, even those with the most severe educational disabilities, are fully integrated into regular classes (and separate classes are avoided). (pp. 308-309)

EVALUATE

1. The term *mental retardation* is applied specifically to people with an IQ below 60. True or false?

KEY TERMS

mental retardation p.307
fetal alcohol syndrome
  p. 308

Down syndrome p. 308
familial retardation p. 308
intellectually gifted p. 309

2. _____ is a disorder caused by an extra chromosome that is responsible for some cases of mental retardation.
3. _____ is the process by which students with mental retardation are placed in normal classrooms to facilitate learning and reduce isolation.
4. Most forms of retardation have no identifiable biological cause. True or false?
5. People with high intelligence are generally shy and socially withdrawn. True or false?

RETHINK

1. Why do you think negative stereotypes of gifted individuals and people with mental retardation persist, even in the face of contrary evidence? How can these stereotypes be changed?
2. *From a school administrator's perspective:* What advantages and disadvantages do you think full inclusion programs would present for students with mental retardation? For students without mental retardation?

Answers to Evaluate Questions

1. false; the term is used to describe a wide range of people with various degrees of mental impairment; 2. Down syndrome; 3. mainstreaming; 4. true; 5. false; the gifted are generally more socially adept than those with a lower IQ

Group Differences in Intelligence: Genetic and Environmental Determinants

Kwang is often washed with a pleck tied to a:

(a) rundel
(b) flink
(c) pove
(d) quirj

If you found this kind of item on an intelligence test, you would probably complain that the test was totally absurd and had nothing to do with your intelligence or anyone else's—and rightly so. How could anyone be expected to respond to items presented in a language that was so unfamiliar?

Yet to some people, even more reasonable questions may appear just as nonsensical. Consider the example of a child raised in a city who is asked about procedures for milking cows, or someone raised in a rural area who is asked about subway ticketing procedures. Obviously, the previous experience of the test-takers would affect their ability to answer correctly. And if such types of questions were included on an IQ test, a critic could rightly contend that the test had more to do with prior experience than with intelligence.

Although IQ tests do not include questions that are so clearly dependent on prior knowledge as questions about cows and subways, the background and experiences of test-takers do have the potential to affect results. In fact, the issue of devising fair intelligence tests that measure knowledge unrelated to culture and family background and experience is central to explaining an important and persistent finding: Members of certain racial and cultural groups consistently score lower on traditional intelligence tests than do members of other groups. For example, as a group, blacks tend to average 10 to 15 IQ points lower than whites. Does this reflect a true difference in intelligence, or are the questions biased in regard to the kinds of knowledge they test? Clearly, if whites perform better because of their greater familiarity with the kind of information that is being tested, their higher IQ scores are not necessarily an indication that they are more intelligent than members of other groups (Kamieniecki & Lynd-Stevenson, 2002; Miele, 2002; Jensen, 2003)

There is good reason to believe that some standardized IQ tests contain elements that discriminate against minority-group members whose experiences differ from those of the white majority. Consider the question "What should you do if another child grabbed your hat and ran off with it?" Most white middle-class children answer that they would tell an adult, and this response is scored as correct. However, a reasonable response might be to chase the person and fight to get the hat back, the answer that is chosen by many urban black children—but one that is scored as incorrect (Miller-Jones, 1991; Aiken, 1997; Reynolds & Ramsay, 2003).

Furthermore, tests may include even subtler forms of bias against minority groups. For example, psychologist Janet Helms (1992) argues that assessments of cognitive ability developed in the United States are sometimes constructed to favor

Key Concepts

Are traditional IQ tests culturally biased?

Are there racial differences in intelligence?

To what degree is intelligence influenced by the environment, and to what degree by heredity?

responses that implicitly reflect North American or European values, customs, or traditions. At the same time, such tests are biased against African and other cultural value systems (Byrne & Watkins, 2003).

More specifically, Helms suggests that the traditional Western value of "rugged individualism" means that correct answers to test items may require a test-taker to reason independently of a particular social context. In contrast, the African cultural value of communalism, in which one's group is valued more than individuals are, may leave test-takers from that tradition unable to answer a question that provides no information about the social context (Greenfield, 1997).

Exploring DIVERSITY
The Relative Influence of Genetics and Environment: Nature, Nurture, and IQ

Culture-fair IQ test: A test that does not discriminate against the members of any minority group.

In an attempt to produce a **culture-fair IQ test,** one that does not discriminate against the members of any minority group, psychologists have tried to devise test items that assess experiences common to all cultures or emphasize questions that do not require language usage. However, test makers have found this difficult to do, because past experiences, attitudes, and values almost always have an impact on respondents' answers. For example, children raised in Western cultures group things on the basis of what they *are* (such as putting *dog* and *fish* into the category of *animal*). In contrast, members of the Kpelle tribe in Africa see intelligence demonstrated by grouping things according to what they *do* (grouping *fish* with *swim*). Similarly, children in the United States asked to memorize the position of objects on a chess board perform better than do African children living in remote villages if household objects familiar to the U.S. children are used. But if rocks are used instead of household objects, the African children do better. In short, it is difficult to produce a test that is truly culture-fair (Sandoval et al., 1998; Samuda, & Lewis 1999; Serpell, 2000; Valencia & Suzuki, 2003).

The efforts of psychologists to produce culture-fair measures of intelligence relate to a lingering controversy over differences in intelligence between members of minority and majority groups. In attempting to identify whether there are differences between such groups, psychologists have had to confront the broader issue of determining the relative contribution to intelligence of genetic factors (heredity) and experience (environment)—the nature-nurture issue that is one of the basic issues of psychology.

Richard Herrnstein, a psychologist, and Charles Murray, a sociologist, fanned the flames of the debate with the publication of their book *The Bell Curve* in the mid-1990s (Herrnstein & Murray, 1994). They argued that an analysis of IQ differences between whites and blacks demonstrated that although environmental factors played a role, there were also basic genetic differences between the two races. They based their argument on a number of findings. For instance, on average, whites score 15 points higher than do blacks on traditional IQ tests even when socioeconomic status (SES) is taken into account. According to Herrnstein and Murray, middle- and upper-SES blacks score lower than do middle- and upper-SES whites, just as lower-SES blacks score lower on average than do lower-SES whites. Intelligence differences between blacks and whites, they concluded, could not be attributed to environmental differences alone.

Heritability: A measure of the degree to which a characteristic is related to genetic, inherited factors.

Moreover, intelligence in general shows a high degree of **heritability,** a measure of the degree to which a characteristic can be attributed to genetic, inherited factors (e.g., Grigorenko, 2000; Plomin, 2003b; Petrill, 2005). As can be seen in Figure 1, the closer the genetic link between two related people, the greater the correspondence of IQ scores. Using data such as these, Herrnstein and Murray argued that differences between races in IQ scores were largely caused by genetically based differences in intelligence.

Relationship	Genetic overlap	Rearing	Correlation
Monozygotic (identical) twins	100%	Together	.86
Dizygotic (fraternal) twins	50%	Together	.62
Siblings	50%	Together	.41
Siblings	50%	Apart	.24
Parent-child	50%	Together	.35
Parent-child	50%	Apart	.31
Adoptive parent-child	0%	Together	.16
Unrelated children	0%	Together	.25
Spouses	0%	Apart	.29

The difference between these two correlations shows the impact of the environment

The relatively low correlation for unrelated children raised together shows the importance of genetic factors

FIGURE 1 The relationship between IQ and closeness of genetic relationship. In general, the more similar the genetic and environmental background of two people, the greater the correlation. Note, for example, that the correlation for spouses, who are genetically unrelated and have been reared apart, is relatively low, whereas the correlation for identical twins reared together is substantial. (Source: Adapted from Henderson, 1982.)

However, many psychologists reacted strongly to the arguments laid out in *The Bell Curve*, refuting several of the book's basic arguments (e.g., Nisbett, 1994; American Psychological Association Task Force on Intelligence, 1996; Fish, 2002; Hall, 2002; Horn, 2002). One criticism is that even when attempts are made to hold socioeconomic conditions constant, wide variations remain among individual households. Furthermore, no one can convincingly assert that the living conditions of blacks and whites are identical even when their socioeconomic status is similar. In addition, as we discussed earlier, there is reason to believe that traditional IQ tests may discriminate against lower-SES urban blacks by asking for information pertaining to experiences they are unlikely to have had.

Moreover, blacks who are raised in economically enriched environments have similar IQ scores to whites in comparable environments. For example, a study by Sandra Scarr and Richard Weinberg (1976) examined black children who had been adopted at an early age by white middle-class families of above-average intelligence. The IQ scores of those children averaged 106—about 15 points above the average IQ scores of unadopted black children in the study. Other research shows that the racial gap in IQ narrows considerably after a college education, and cross-cultural data demonstrate that when racial gaps exist in other cultures, it is the economically disadvantaged groups that typically have lower scores. In short, the evidence that genetic factors play the major role in determining racial differences in IQ is not compelling, although the question still evokes considerable controversy (Neisser et al., 1996; Fish, 2002; Winston, 2004).

It is also crucial to remember that IQ scores and intelligence have the greatest relevance in terms of individuals, not groups. In fact, considering group *racial* differences presents some conceptually troublesome distinctions. *Race* was originally meant to be a biological concept, referring to classifications based on the physical and structural characteristics of a species. Despite its biological origins, however, the term *race* has taken on additional meanings and is used in a variety of ways, ranging from skin color to culture. In short, race is an extraordinarily inexact concept (Betancourt & Lopez, 1993; Yee et al., 1993; Beutler et al., 1996).

www.mhhe.com/feldmanup8
PsychInteractive Online

IQ Issues

Consequently, drawing comparisons between different races on any dimension, including IQ scores, is an imprecise, potentially misleading, and often fruitless venture. By far, the greatest discrepancies in IQ scores occur when comparing *individuals*, not when comparing mean IQ scores of different *groups*. There are blacks who score high on IQ tests and whites who score low, just as there are whites who score high and blacks who score low. For the concept of intelligence to aid in the betterment of society, we must examine how *individuals* perform, not the groups to which they belong. We need to focus on the degree to which intelligence can be enhanced in an individual person, not in members of a particular group (Angoff, 1988; Fagan & Holland, 2002). (For more study on the issues surrounding group IQ differences, complete the PsychInteractive exercise on IQ issues.)

Other issues make the heredity-versus-environment debate somewhat irrelevant to practical concerns. For example, there are multiple kinds of intelligence, and traditional IQ tests do not measure many of them. Furthermore, IQ scores are often inadequate predictors of ultimate occupational success.

It also appears that intelligence is more flexible and modifiable than originally envisioned. For instance, researchers have been puzzled by data showing a long-term increase in IQ scores since the early 1900s. Because the average person today gets more items correct than did the average person several generations ago on IQ tests, scores have risen significantly—a phenomenon known as the *Flynn effect* after its discoverer, psychologist James Flynn. The Flynn effect is not trivial, with the the average 20-year-old today scoring some 15 points higher than the average 20-year-old in 1940 (Flynn, 1999, 2000; see Figure 2).

The explanation for the Flynn effect is not clear. Flynn and a colleague, economist William Dickens, argue that the higher scores have resulted as people have matched their genetic gifts with their environment. Because society is increasingly complex and driven by technology, it is increasingly making demands that people with high intelligence are particularly good at meeting. Consequently, society provides greater opportunities for people with high IQs to excel, and that environment pushes them intellectually, creating an increase overall in IQ scores (Dickens & Flynn, 2001).

Other explanations for the Flynn effect suggest that it may due to better nutrition, better parenting, or improvements in the general social environment, including education. Whatever the cause, the change in IQ scores over the century is not due to evolutionary changes in human genetics: The period over which the Flynn effect has occurred is far too short for people to have evolved into a more intelligent species (Neisser, 1996; Loehlin, 2002).

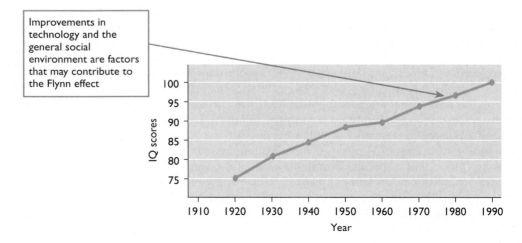

FIGURE 2 Although average IQ scores increased steadily during the 1900s—a phenomenon known as the Flynn effect—the reason for the rise is not at all clear. Do you think this trend is likely to continue in the twenty-first century? (Source: Horgan, 1995, p. 12.)

Placing the Heredity–Environment Question in Perspective

Ultimately, there is no absolute answer to the question of the degree to which intelligence is influenced by heredity and by the environment. We are dealing with an issue for which experiments to unambiguously determine cause and effect cannot be devised. (A moment's thought about how we might assign infants to enriched or deprived environments will reveal the impossibility of devising ethically reasonable experiments!)

The more critical question to ask, then, is not whether hereditary or environmental factors primarily underlie intelligence, but whether there is anything we can do to maximize the intellectual development of each individual. If we can find ways to do this, we will be able to make changes in the environment—which may take the form of enriched home and school environments—that can lead each person to reach his or her potential.

Social and economic inequality, as well as heredity and other environmental factors, are associated with differences in intelligence. People who have greater educational opportunities and who suffer fewer economic constraints are able to maximize their intelligence.

RECAP/EVALUATE/RETHINK

RECAP

Are traditional IQ tests culturally biased?

- Traditional intelligence tests have frequently been criticized for being biased in favor of the white middle-class population. This controversy has led to attempts to devise culture-fair tests, IQ measures that avoid questions that depend on a particular cultural background. (pp. 311-312)

Are there racial differences in intelligence?

- Issues of racial differences in intelligence are very controversial, in part because of the difficulty of defining the concept of race scientifically and disagreement over what constitutes an unbiased measure of race. (pp. 312-314)

To what degree is intelligence influenced by the environment, and to what degree by heredity?

- Attempting to distinguish environmental from hereditary factors in intelligence is probably futile and certainly misguided. Because individual IQ scores vary far more than do group IQ scores, it is more critical to ask what can be done to maximize the intellectual development of each individual. (pp. 314-315)

EVALUATE

1. Intelligence tests may be biased toward the prevailing culture in such a way that minorities are put at a disadvantage when taking these tests. True or false?
2. A(n) _____ – _____ test tries to use only questions appropriate to all the people taking the test.
3. IQ tests can accurately determine the intelligence of entire groups of people. True or false?
4. Intelligence can be seen as a combination of _____ and _____ factors.

RETHINK

1. What ideas do you have for explaining the Flynn effect, the steady rise in IQ scores over several decades? How would you test your ideas?
2. *From a college admissions officer's perspective:* Imagine that you notice that students who are members of minority groups systematically receive lower scores on standardized college entrance exams. What suggestions do you have for helping these students improve their

scores? What advice about their college applications would you give these students to help them be competitive applicants?

Answers to Evaluate Questions

1. true; 2. culture-fair; 3. false; IQ tests are used to measure individual intelligence; within any group there are wide variations in individual intelligence; 4. hereditary, environmental

KEY TERMS

culture-fair IQ test p. 312   heritability p. 312

Looking Back

Psychology on the Web

1. Many sites on the Web permit you to assess your IQ. Take at least two such tests and (a) compare your results, (b) indicate what mental qualities seemed to be tested on the tests, and (c) discuss your impression of the reliability and validity of the tests. Write up your conclusions.
2. Find a way to assess at least one other of your multiple intelligences (that is, one not tested by the IQ tests you took) on the Web. What sort of intelligence was the test supposed to be testing? What sorts of items were included? How valid and reliable do you think it was, both in and of itself and compared with the IQ tests you took?
3. After completing the PsychInteractive exercise on mental retardation, search the Web for further information on the causes of mental retardation. Summarize the most recent evidence you find.

Epilogue

We've just examined one of the most controversial areas of psychology—intelligence. Some of the most heated discussions in all of psychology focus on this topic, engaging educators, policymakers, politicians, and psychologists. The issues include the very meaning of intelligence, its measurement, individual extremes of intelligence, and, finally, the heredity–environment question. We saw that the quest to partition intelligence into hereditary factors versus environmental factors is generally pointless. In the area of intelligence, the focus of our efforts should be on making sure that every individual has the opportunity to achieve his or her potential.

Before we leave the topic of intelligence, return to the stories of the two persons of widely different intellectual capabilities discussed in the Prologue, Chris Burke and Sho Yano. Consider the following questions on the basis of what you have learned about intelligence.

1. Chris Burke's physicians concluded in his infancy that he would never be able to function effectively in society and should be immediately institutionalized. How do you think the physicians came to their conclusions, and why do you think they were proven wrong?
2. In what ways would placing Burke in a separate educational program have helped or hurt his chances of reaching his full potential?
3. How might the educational acceleration of Sho Yano help and hinder his later development? Do you think slowing down his educational progress might be beneficial? How?
4. Based on research relating to individuals who have unusually high IQ scores, what do you think Sho's emotional intelligence is like?

CHAPTER 10

Motivation and Emotion

Key Concepts for Chapter 10

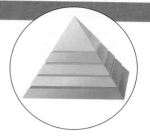

Prologue   **Tour de Lance**

Nine years before he crossed the finish line to win the Tour de France for the seventh time, no one had given Lance Armstrong much of a chance to live, yet alone race again.

Armstrong had been diagnosed with testicular cancer that had spread to his lungs and brain. Told his chances for survival were less than 50 percent, Armstrong set about fighting the disease with same motivation that led him to become the world's best cyclist. He endured surgery and intense chemotherapy. At the same time, he refused to give up cycling, riding 20 to 50 miles a day even after enduring week-long rounds of chemotherapy.

Armstrong beat the odds, in the same way he would go on to beat every challenger in the Tour de France after returning to racing. When he retired after winning his seventh and final race, he left the sport not only as an example of an athlete at the top of his game but as a testament to willpower, drive, and the undauntability of the human spirit (Abt, 1999; Coyle, 2005; Wyatt, 2005).

Looking Ahead

What motivation lay behind Armstrong's determination to overcome his cancer and participate in the Tour de France? Was it the anticipation of the emotional thrill of winning the biking's most prestigious race? The potential rewards that would follow if he succeeded? The excitement of participating? The satisfaction of achieving a long-sought goal?

In this chapter, we consider the issues that can help to answer such questions, as we address the topic of motivation and the related area of emotion. The topics of motivation and emotion are central in attempting to explain Armstrong's extraordinary courage and determination. Psychologists who study motivation seek to discover the particular desired goals—the motives—that underlie behavior. Behaviors as basic as drinking to satisfy thirst and as inconsequential as taking a stroll to get exercise exemplify motives. Psychologists specializing in the study of motivation assume that such underlying motives steer our choices of activities.

While motivation concerns the forces that direct future behavior, emotion pertains to the feelings we experience throughout our lives. The study of emotions focuses on our internal experiences at any given moment. All of us feel a variety of emotions: happiness at succeeding at a difficult task, sadness over the death of a loved one, anger at being treated unfairly. Because emotions not only play a role in motivating our behavior but also act as a reflection of our underlying motivation, they play an important role in our lives.

We begin this set of modules by focusing on the major conceptions of motivation, discussing how different motives and needs jointly affect behavior. We consider motives that are biologically based and universal in the animal kingdom, such as hunger, as well as motives that are unique to humans, such as the need for achievement.

We then turn to emotions. We consider the roles and functions that emotions play in people's lives and discuss several approaches that explain how people understand their emotions. Finally, we look at how nonverbal behavior communicates emotions.

Explaining Motivation

In just a moment, 27-year-old Aron Ralston's life changed. An 800-pound boulder dislodged in a narrow canyon where Ralston was hiking in an isolated Utah canyon, pinning his lower arm to the ground.

For the next five days, Ralston lay in the dense, lonely forest, unable to escape. An experienced climber who had search-and-rescue training, he had ample time to consider his options. He tried unsuccessfully to chip away at the rock, and he rigged up ropes and pulleys around the boulder in a vain effort to move it.

Finally, out of water and nearly dehydrated, Ralston reasoned there was only one option left short of dying. In acts of incredible bravery, Ralston broke two bones in his wrist, applied a tourniquet, and used a dull pen knife to amputate his arm beneath the elbow.

Freed from his entrapment, Ralston climbed down from where he had been pinned, and then hiked five miles to safety (Cox, 2003; Lofholm, 2003).

Ralston, who now has a prosthetic arm, recovered from his ordeal. He remains an active outdoorsman and hiker.

What lies behind Ralston's incredible determination and will to live? To answer such questions, psychologists employ the concept of **motivation,** the factors that direct and energize the behavior of humans and other organisms. Motivation has biological, cognitive, and social aspects, and the complexity of the concept has led psychologists to develop a variety of approaches. All seek to explain the energy that guides people's behavior in particular directions.

Motivation: The factors that direct and energize the behavior of humans and other organisms.

Instinct Approaches: Born to Be Motivated

When psychologists first tried to explain motivation, they turned to **instincts,** inborn patterns of behavior that are biologically determined rather than learned. According to instinct approaches to motivation, people and animals are born preprogrammed with sets of behaviors essential to their survival. Those instincts provide the energy that channels behavior in appropriate directions. Hence, sexual behavior may be a response to an instinct to reproduce, and exploratory behavior may be motivated by an instinct to examine one's territory.

This conception presents several difficulties, however. For one thing, psychologists do not agree on what, or even how many, primary instincts exist. One early psychologist, William McDougall (1908), suggested that there are eighteen instincts. Other theorists came up with even more—with one sociologist (Bernard, 1924) claiming that there are exactly 5,759 distinct instincts!

Furthermore, explanations based on the concept of instincts do not go very far toward explaining why one specific pattern of behavior, and not others, has appeared in a given species. In addition, although it is clear that much animal behavior is based on instincts, because much of the variety and complexity of human behavior is learned, that behavior cannot be seen as instinctual.

Instincts: Inborn patterns of behavior that are biologically determined rather than learned.

As a result of these shortcomings, newer explanations have replaced conceptions of motivation based on instincts. However, instinct approaches still play a role in certain theories, particularly those based on evolutionary approaches that focus on our genetic inheritance. Furthermore, Freud's work suggests that instinctual drives of sex and aggression motivate behavior (Katz, 2001).

Drive-Reduction Approaches: Satisfying Our Needs

Drive-reduction approaches to motivation: Theories suggesting that a lack of a basic biological requirement such as water produces a drive to obtain that requirement (in this case, the thirst drive).

Drive: Motivational tension, or arousal, that energizes behavior to fulfill a need.

After rejecting instinct theory, psychologists first proposed simple drive-reduction theories of motivation to take its place (Hull, 1943). **Drive-reduction approaches** suggest that a lack of some basic biological requirement such as water produces a drive to obtain that requirement (in this case, the thirst drive).

To understand this approach, we begin with the concept of drive. A **drive** is motivational tension, or arousal, that energizes behavior to fulfill a need. Many basic drives, such as hunger, thirst, sleep, and sex, are related to biological needs of the body or of the species as a whole. These are called *primary drives.* Primary drives contrast with secondary drives, in which behavior fulfills no obvious biological need. In *secondary drives,* prior experience and learning bring about needs. For instance, some people have strong needs to achieve academically and professionally. We can say that their achievement need is reflected in a secondary drive that motivates their behavior (McMillan & Katz, 2002; McKinley et al., 2004).

We usually try to satisfy a primary drive by reducing the need underlying it. For example, we become hungry after not eating for a few hours and may raid the refrigerator, especially if the next scheduled meal is not imminent. If the weather turns cold, we put on extra clothing or raise the setting on the thermostat to keep warm. If our bodies need liquids to function properly, we experience thirst and seek out water.

HOMEOSTASIS

Homeostasis: The body's tendency to maintain a steady internal state.

Homeostasis, the body's tendency to maintain a steady internal state, underlies primary drives. Using feedback loops, homeostasis brings deviations in body functioning back to an optimal state, similar to the way a thermostat and a furnace work in a home heating system to maintain a steady temperature (see Figure 1). Receptor cells throughout the body constantly monitor factors such as temperature and nutrient levels, and when deviations from the ideal state occur, the body adjusts in an effort to return to an optimal state. Many fundamental needs, including the needs for food, water, stable body temperature, and sleep, operate via homeostasis (Canteras, 2002; Machado, Suchecki, & Tufik, 2005).

Although drive-reduction theories provide a good explanation of how primary drives motivate behavior, they cannot fully explain a behavior in which the goal is not to reduce a drive, but rather to maintain or even increase the level of excitement or arousal. For instance, some behaviors seem to be motivated by nothing more than curiosity, such as rushing to check e-mail messages. Similarly, many people pursue thrilling activities such as riding a roller coaster and steering a raft down the rapids of a river. Such behaviors certainly don't suggest that people seek to reduce all drives, as drive-reduction approaches would indicate (Loewenstein, 1994; Begg & Langley, 2001; Rosenbloom & Wolf, 2002).

Both curiosity and thrill-seeking behavior, then, shed doubt on drive-reduction approaches as a complete explanation for motivation. In both cases, rather than seeking to reduce an underlying drive, people and animals appear to be motivated to increase their overall level of stimulation and activity. To explain this phenomenon, psychologists have devised an alternative: arousal approaches to motivation.

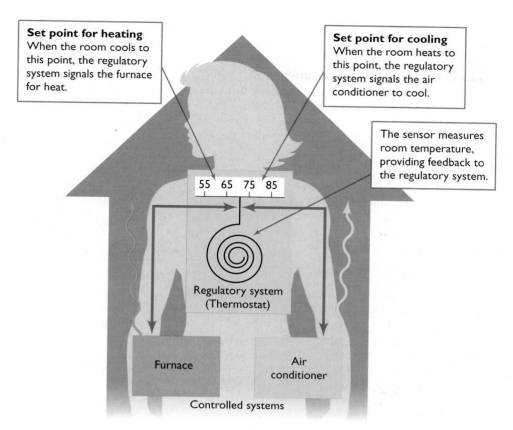

FIGURE 1 With homeostasis, a series
of feedback loops is used to regulate body
functions, similar to the way a thermostat
turns on the furnace when a room's air
temperature becomes too cool and turns it
off when the air temperature becomes too
warm. Similarly, when body temperature
becomes too low, the blood vessels con-
strict, causing shivering and making us seek
warmth. When body temperature becomes
too high, the blood vessels expand, and we
sweat as our bodies try to lower the temperature. Can you think of other internal
systems that operate via homeostasis?

Arousal Approaches: Beyond Drive Reduction

Arousal approaches seek to explain behavior in which the goal is to maintain or increase excitement (Berlyne, 1967; Brehm & Self, 1989). According to **arousal approaches to motivation,** each person tries to maintain a certain level of stimulation and activity. As with the drive-reduction model, this model suggests that if our stimulation and activity levels become too high, we try to reduce them. But in contrast to the drive-reduction model, the arousal model also suggests that if levels of stimulation and activity are too low, we will try to increase them by seeking stimulation.

People vary widely in the optimal level of arousal they seek out, with some people looking for especially high levels of arousal. For example, people who participate in daredevil sports, high-stakes gamblers, and criminals who pull off high-risk robber-ies may be exhibiting a particularly high need for arousal (Farley, 1986; Zuckerman & Kuhlman, 2000; Zuckerman, 2002; see Figure 2 and try the PsychInteractive exercise on sensation-seeking behavior.

Arousal approaches to motivation: The belief that we try to maintain certain lev-els of stimulation and activity, increasing or reducing them as necessary.

www.mhhe.com/feldmanup8
PsychInteractive Online

Sensation-seeking Behavior

Incentive Approaches: Motivation's Pull

When a luscious dessert appears on the table after a filling meal, its appeal has little or nothing to do with internal drives or the maintenance of arousal. Rather, if we

FIGURE 2 Some people seek high levels of arousal, while others are more easygoing. You can get a sense of your own preferred level of stimulation by completing this questionnaire. (Source: Zuckerman, 1978, 1994.)

Do You Seek Out Sensation?

How much stimulation do you crave in your everyday life? You will have an idea after you complete the following questionnaire, which lists some items from a scale designed to assess your sensation-seeking tendencies. Circle either A or B in each pair or statements.

1. A I would like a job that requires a lot of travelling.
   B I would prefer a job in one location.
2. A I am invigorated by a brisk, cold day.
   B I can't wait to get indoors on a cold day.
3. A I get bored seeing the same old faces.
   B I like the comfortable familiarity of everyday friends.
4. A I would prefer living in an ideal society in which everyone was safe, secure, and happy.
   B I would have preferred living in the unsettled days of our history.
5. A I sometimes like to do things that are a little frightening.
   B A sensible person avoids activities that are dangerous.
6. A I would not like to be hypnotized.
   B I would like to have the experience of being hypnotized.
7. A The most important goal of life is to live it to the fullest and to experience as much as possible.
   B The most important goal of life is to find peace and happiness.
8. A I would like to try parachute jumping.
   B I would never want to try jumping out of a plane, with or without a parachute.
9. A I enter cold water gradually, giving myself time to get used to it.
   B I like to dive or jump right into the ocean or a cold pool.
10. A When I go on a vacation, I prefer the comfort of a good room and bed.
    B When I go on a vacation, I prefer the change of camping out.
11. A I prefer people who are emotionally expressive, even if they are a bit unstable.
    B I prefer people who are calm and even-tempered.
12. A A good painting should shock or jolt the senses.
    B A good painting should give one a feeling of peace and security.
13. A People who ride motorcycles must have some kind of unconscious need to hurt themselves.
    B I would like to drive or ride a motorcycle.

Scoring: Give yourself one point for each of the following responses: 1A, 2A, 3A, 4B, 5A, 6B, 7A, 8A, 9B, 10B, 11A, 12A, 13B. Find your total score by adding up the number of points and then use the following scoring key.

0–3 very low sensation seeking

4–5 low

6–9 average

10–11 high

12–13 very high

Keep in mind, of course, that this short questionnaire, for which the scoring is based on the results of college students who have taken it, provides only a rough estimate of your sensation-seeking tendencies. Moreover, as people get older, their sensation-seeking scores tend to decrease. Still, the questionnaire will at least give you an indication of how your sensation-seeking tendencies compare with those of others.

choose to eat the dessert, such behavior is motivated by the external stimulus of the dessert itself, which acts as an anticipated reward. This reward, in motivational terms, is an *incentive*.

Incentive approaches to motivation:
Theories suggesting that motivation stems from the desire to obtain valued external goals, or incentives.

Incentive approaches to motivation suggest that motivation stems from the desire to obtain valued external goals, or incentives. In this view, the desirable properties of external stimuli—whether grades, money, affection, food, or sex—account for a person's motivation.

Although the theory explains why we may succumb to an incentive (such as a mouthwatering dessert) even though we lack internal cues (such as hunger), it does not provide a complete explanation of motivation, because organisms sometimes seek to fulfill needs even when incentives are not apparent. Consequently, many psychologists believe that the internal drives proposed by drive-reduction theory work in tandem with the external incentives of incentive theory to "push" and "pull" behavior, respectively. Thus, at the same time that we seek to satisfy our underlying hunger needs (the push of drive-reduction theory), we are drawn to food that appears particularly appetizing (the pull of incentive theory). Rather than contradicting each other, then, drives and incentives may work together in motivating behavior (Petri, 1996; Pinel, Assanand, & Lehman, 2000; Lowery, Fillingim, & Wright, 2003; Berridge, 2004).

Cognitive Approaches: The Thoughts Behind Motivation

Cognitive approaches to motivation suggest that motivation is a product of people's thoughts, expectations, and goals—their cognitions. For instance, the degree to which people are motivated to study for a test is based on their expectation of how well studying will pay off in terms of a good grade (Wigfield & Eccles, 2000).

Cognitive theories of motivation draw a key distinction between intrinsic and extrinsic motivation. *Intrinsic motivation* causes us to participate in an activity for our own enjoyment rather than for any concrete, tangible reward that it will bring us. In contrast, *extrinsic motivation* causes us to do something for money, a grade, or some other concrete, tangible reward. For example, when a physician works long hours because she loves medicine, intrinsic motivation is prompting her; if she works hard to make a lot of money, extrinsic motivation underlies her efforts (Rawsthorne & Elliot, 1999; Ryan & Deci, 2000; Pedersen, 2002; Lepper, Corpus, & Iyengar, 2005).

We are more apt to persevere, work harder, and produce work of higher quality when motivation for a task is intrinsic rather than extrinsic. In fact, in some cases providing rewards for desirable behavior (thereby increasing extrinsic motivation) actually may decrease intrinsic motivation (Sansone & Haracklewicz, 2000; Deci, Koestner, & Ryan, 2001; Henderlong & Lepper, 2002; James, 2005).

> **Cognitive approaches to motivation:** Theories suggesting that motivation is a product of people's thoughts and expectations—their cognitions.

Maslow's Hierarchy: Ordering Motivational Needs

What do Eleanor Roosevelt, Abraham Lincoln, and Albert Einstein have in common? The common thread, according to a model of motivation devised by psychologist Abraham Maslow, is that each of them fulfilled the highest levels of motivational needs underlying human behavior.

Maslow's model places motivational needs in a hierarchy and suggests that before more sophisticated, higher-order needs can be met, certain primary needs must be satisfied (Maslow, 1987). A pyramid can represent the model, with the more basic needs at the bottom and the higher-level needs at the top (see Figure 3). To activate a particular higher-order need, thereby guiding behavior, a person must first fulfill the more basic needs in the hierarchy.

The basic needs are primary drives: needs for water, food, sleep, sex, and the like. To move up the hierarchy, a person must first meet these basic physiological needs.

FIGURE 3 Maslow's hierarchy shows how our motivation progresses up the pyramid from the broadest, most fundamental biological needs to higher-order ones. (After Maslow, 1987.) Do you agree that lower-order needs must be satisfied before higher-order needs? Do hermits and monks who attempt to fulfill spiritual needs while denying basic physical needs contradict Maslow's hierarchy?

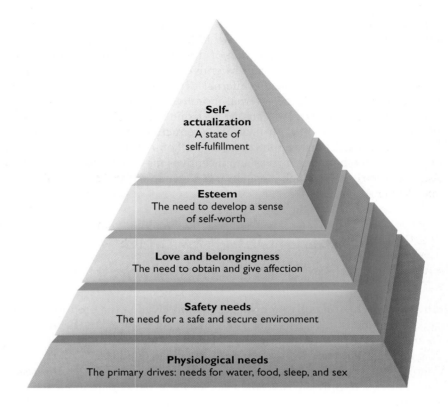

Self-
actualization
A state of
self-fulfillment

Esteem
The need to develop a sense
of self-worth

Love and belongingness
The need to obtain and give affection

Safety needs
The need for a safe and secure environment

Physiological needs
The primary drives: needs for water, food, sleep, and sex

Self-actualization: A state of self-fulfillment in which people realize their highest potential, each in his or her own unique way.

Safety needs come next in the hierarchy; Maslow suggests that people need a safe, secure environment in order to function effectively. Physiological and safety needs compose the lower-order needs.

Only after meeting the basic lower-order needs can a person consider fulfilling higher-order needs, such as the needs for love and a sense of belonging, esteem, and self-actualization. Love and belongingness needs include the need to obtain and give affection and to be a contributing member of some group or society. After fulfilling these needs, a person strives for esteem. In Maslow's thinking, esteem relates to the need to develop a sense of self-worth by knowing that others know and value one's competence.

Once these four sets of needs are fulfilled—no easy task—a person is able to strive for the highest-level need, self-actualization. **Self-actualization** is a state of self-fulfillment in which people realize their highest potentials, each in his or her own unique way. Although Maslow first suggested that self-actualization occurred in only a few, famous individuals, he later expanded the concept to encompass everyday people. For example, a parent with excellent nurturing skills who raises a family, a teacher who year after year creates an environment that maximizes students' opportunities for success, and an artist who realizes his creative potential all may be self-actualized. The important thing is that people feel at ease with themselves and satisfied that they are using their talents to the fullest. In a sense, achieving self-actualization reduces the striving and yearning for greater fulfillment that mark most people's lives and instead provides a sense of satisfaction with the current state of affairs (Jones & Crandall, 1991; Hamel, Leclerc, & Lefrancois, 2003; Piechowski, 2003; Reiss & Havercamp, 2005).

Although research has been unable to validate the specific ordering of Maslow's stages, and although it is difficult to measure self-actualization objectively, Maslow's model is important for two reasons: It highlights the complexity of human needs, and it emphasizes the idea that until more basic biological needs are met, people will be relatively unconcerned with higher-order needs. For example, if people are hungry, their first interest will be in obtaining food; they will not be concerned with needs such as love and self-esteem (Hanley & Abell, 2002; Samantaray, Srivastava, & Mishra, 2002).

Applying the Different Approaches to Motivation

The various theories of motivation (summarized in Figure 4) give several different perspectives on motivation. Which provides the fullest account of motivation? Actually, many of the approaches are complementary, rather than contradictory. In fact, employing more than one approach can help us understand motivation in a particular instance.

Consider, for example, Aron Ralston's accident while hiking (described earlier in the chapter). His interest in climbing in an isolated and potentially dangerous area may be explained by arousal approaches to motivation. From the perspective of instinct approaches, we see that Aron had an overwhelming instinct to preserve his life at all costs. From a cognitive perspective, we see his careful consideration of various strategies to extricate himself from the boulder.

In short, applying multiple approaches to motivation in a given situation provides a broader understanding than we might obtain by employing only a single approach. We'll see this again when we consider specific motives—such as the needs for food, achievement, affiliation, and power—and draw on several of the theories for the fullest account of what motivates our behavior.

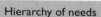

Instinct

People and animals are born with preprogrammed sets of behaviors essential to their survival.

Drive reduction

When some basic biological requirement is lacking, a drive is produced.

Arousal

People seek an optimal level of stimulation. If the level of stimulation is too high, they act to reduce it; if it is too low, they act to increase it.

Incentive

External stimuli direct and energize behavior.

Cognitive

Thoughts, expectations, and understanding of the world direct motivation.

Hierarchy of needs

Needs form a hierarchy; before higher-order needs are met, lower-order needs must be fulfilled.

FIGURE 4 The major approaches to motivation.

RECAP/EVALUATE/RETHINK

RECAP

How does motivation direct and energize behavior?

- Motivation relates to the factors that direct and energize behavior. (p. 321)
- Drive is the motivational tension that energizes behavior to fulfill a need. (p. 322)
- Homeostasis, the maintenance of a steady internal state, often underlies motivational drives. (p. 322)
- Arousal approaches suggest that we try to maintain a particular level of stimulation and activity. (p. 323)
- Incentive approaches focus on the positive aspects of the environment that direct and energize behavior. (pp. 323-325)
- Cognitive approaches focus on the role of thoughts, expectations, and understanding of the world in producing motivation. (p. 325)
- Maslow's hierarchy suggests that there are five basic needs: physiological, safety, love and belongingness, esteem, and self-actualization. Only after the more basic needs are fulfilled can a person move toward meeting higher-order needs. (pp. 325-326)

EVALUATE

1. _____ are forces that guide a person's behavior in a certain direction.
2. Biologically determined, inborn patterns of behavior are known as _____.
3. Your psychology professor tells you, "Explaining behavior is easy! When we lack something, we are motivated to get it." Which approach to motivation does your professor subscribe to?
4. By drinking water after running a marathon, a runner tries to keep his or her body at an optimal level of functioning. This process is called _____.
5. I help an elderly person cross the street because doing a good deed makes me feel good. What type of motivation is at work here? What type of motivation would be at work if I were to help an elderly man across the street because he paid me $20?
6. According to Maslow, a person with no job, no home, and no friends can become self-actualized. True or false?

RETHINK

1. Which approaches to motivation are more commonly used in the workplace? How might each approach be used to design employment policies that can sustain or increase motivation?
2. *From the perspective of an educator:* Do you think that giving students grades serves as an external reward that would decrease intrinsic motivation for the subject matter? Why or why not?

Answers to Evaluate Questions

1. motives; 2. instincts; 3. drive reduction; 4. homeostasis; 5. intrinsic, extrinsic; 6. false; lower-order needs must be fulfilled before self-actualization can occur.

KEY TERMS

motivation p. 321	drive p. 322	incentive approaches to	self-actualization p. 326
instincts p. 321	homeostasis p. 322	motivation p. 324	
drive-reduction approaches	arousal approaches to moti-	cognitive approaches to	
to motivation p. 322	vation p. 323	motivation p. 325	

Human Needs and Motivation: Eat, Drink, and Be Daring

As a sophomore at the University of California, Santa Cruz, Lisa Arndt followed a menu of her own making: For breakfast she ate cereal or fruit, with 10 diet pills and 50 chocolate-flavored laxatives. Lunch was a salad or sandwich; dinner: chicken and rice. But it was the feast that followed that Arndt relished most. Almost every night at about 9 P.M., she would retreat to her room and eat an entire small pizza and a whole batch of cookies. Then she'd wait for the day's laxatives to take effect. "It was extremely painful," says Arndt of those days.... "But I was that desperate to make up for my bingeing. I was terrified of fat the way other people are afraid of lions or guns" (Hubbard, O'Neill, & Cheakalos, 1999, p. 59).

Lisa was one of the 10 million women (and 1 million men) who are estimated to suffer from an eating disorder. These disorders, which usually appear during adolescence, can bring about extraordinary weight loss and other forms of physical deterioration. Extremely dangerous, they sometimes result in death.

Why are Lisa and others like her subject to such disordered eating, which revolves around the motivation to avoid weight gain at all costs? And why do so many other people engage in overeating, which leads to obesity?

To answer these questions, we must consider some of the specific needs that underlie behavior. In this module, we examine several of the most important human needs. We begin with hunger, the primary drive that has received the most attention from researchers, and then turn to secondary drives—those uniquely human endeavors, based on learned needs and past experience, that help explain why people strive to achieve, to affiliate with others, and to seek power over others.

Key Concepts

What biological and social factors underlie hunger?

How are needs relating to achievement, affiliation, and power motivation exhibited?

The Motivation Behind Hunger and Eating

Two-thirds of the people in the United States are overweight, and almost a quarter are so heavy that they have **obesity,** body weight that is more than 20 percent above the average weight for a person of a particular height. And the rest of the world is not far behind: A billion people around the globe are overweight or obese. The World Health Organization has said that worldwide obesity has reached epidemic proportions, producing increases in heart disease, diabetes, cancer, and premature deaths (Grady, 2002; Calle & Kaaks, 2004; McNeil, 2005; Hill, Catenacci, & Wyatt, 2005).

The most widely used measure of obesity is *body mass index (BMI),* which is based on a ratio of weight to height. People with a BMI greater than 30 are considered obese, whereas those with a BMI between 25 and 30 are overweight. (Use the formulas in Figure 1 to determine your own BMI.)

Although the definition of obesity is clear from a scientific point of view, people's perceptions of what an ideal body looks like vary significantly across different cultures and, within Western cultures, from one time period to another. For instance, many contemporary Western cultures stress the importance of slimness in women—a relatively recent view. In nineteenth-century Hawaii, the most attractive women were

Obesity: Body weight that is more than 20 percent above the average weight for a person of a particular height.

FIGURE I Use this procedure to find your body mass index.

To calculate your body mass index, follow these steps:

1. Indicate your weight in pounds: _____ pounds
2. Indicate your height in inches: _____ inches
3. Divide your weight (item I) by your height (item 2), and write the outcome here:

   _____

4. Divide the result above (item 3) by your height (item 2), and write the outcome here:

   _____

5. Multiply the number above by 703, and write the product here: _____. This is your body mass index.

Example:
   For a person who weights 210 pounds and who is 6 feet tall, divide 210 pounds by 72 inches, which equals 2.917. Then divide 2.917 by 72 inches (item 3), which yields .041. Multiplying .041 (from item 4) by 703 yields a BMI of 28.5.

Interpretation:
- Underweight = less than 18.5
- Normal weight = 18.5–24.9
- Overweight = 25–29.9
- Obesity = BMI of 30 or greater

Keep in mind that a BMI greater than 25 may or may not be due to excess body fat. For example, professional athletes may have little fat but weigh more than the average person because they have greater muscle mass.

those who were the heaviest. Furthermore, for most of the twentieth century—except for periods in the 1920s and the most recent decades—the ideal female figure was relatively full. Even today, weight standards differ among different cultural groups. For instance, African Americans generally judge heavier women more positively than whites do. In some traditional Arab cultures, obese women are so prized as wives that parents force-feed their female children to make them more desirable (Mills et al., 2002; Naik, 2003; Pettijohn & Jungesberg, 2004).

Regardless of cultural standards for appearance and weight, no one doubts that being overweight represents a major health risk. However, controlling weight is complicated, because eating behavior involves a variety of mechanisms. In our discussion of what motivates people to eat, we'll start with the biological aspects of eating.

BIOLOGICAL FACTORS IN THE REGULATION OF HUNGER

In contrast to human beings, other species are unlikely to become obese. Internal mechanisms regulate not only the quantity of food they take in but also the kind of food they desire. For example, rats that have been deprived of particular foods seek out alternatives that contain the specific nutrients their diet is lacking, and many species, given the choice of a wide variety of foods, select a well-balanced diet (Bouchard & Bray, 1996; Woods et al., 2000; Jones & Corp, 2003).

Complex mechanisms tell organisms whether they require food or should stop eating. It's not just a matter of an empty stomach causing hunger pangs and a full one alleviating those pangs. (Even individuals who have had their stomachs

"Gee, I had no idea you were married to a supermodel."

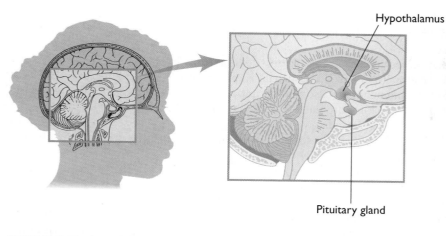

Hypothalamus

Pituitary gland

FIGURE 2 The hypothalamus acts as the brain's "feeding center," being primarily responsible for the monitoring of food intake.

removed still experience the sensation of hunger.) One important factor is changes in the chemical composition of the blood. In particular, changes in levels of glucose, a kind of sugar, regulate feelings of hunger (Campfield et al., 1996; Mulligan et al., 2002; Bergh et al., 2003; Chapelot et al., 2004).

The brain's *hypothalamus* (see Figure 2) monitors glucose levels. Increasing evidence suggests that the hypothalamus carries the primary responsibility for monitoring food intake. Injury to the hypothalamus has radical consequences for eating behavior, depending on the site of the injury. For example, rats whose *lateral hypothalamus* is damaged may literally starve to death. They refuse food when it is offered, and unless they are force-fed, they eventually die. Rats with an injury to the *ventromedial hypothalamus* display the opposite problem: extreme overeating. Rats with this injury can increase in weight by as much as 400 percent. Similar phenomena occur in humans who have tumors of the hypothalamus (Woods et al., 1998; Woods & Seeley, 2002).

Although the important role the hypothalamus plays in regulating food intake is clear, the exact way this organ operates is still unclear. One hypothesis suggests that injury to the hypothalamus affects the **weight set point,** or the particular level of weight that the body strives to maintain, which in turn regulates food intake. Acting as a kind of internal weight thermostat, the hypothalamus calls for either greater or less food intake (Capaldi, 1996; Woods et al., 2000; Berthoud, 2002).

In most cases, the hypothalamus does a good job. Even people who are not deliberately monitoring their weight show only minor weight fluctuations in spite of substantial day-to-day variations in how much they eat and exercise. However, injury to the hypothalamus can alter the weight set point, and a person then struggles to meet the internal goal by increasing or decreasing food consumption. Even temporary exposure to certain drugs can alter the weight set point (Cabanac & Frankhan, 2002; Hallschmid et al., 2004).

Genetic factors determine the weight set point, at least in part. People seem destined, through heredity, to have a particular **metabolism,** the rate at which food is converted to energy and expended by the body. People with a high metabolic rate can eat virtually as much as they want without gaining weight, whereas others, with low metabolism, may eat literally half as much yet gain weight readily (Woods et al., 1998; Jequier, 2002).

Weight set point: The particular level of weight that the body strives to maintain.

Metabolism: The rate at which food is converted to energy and expended by the body.

SOCIAL FACTORS IN EATING

You've just finished a full meal and feel completely stuffed. Suddenly your host announces with great fanfare that he will be serving his "house specialty" dessert, bananas flambé, and that he has spent the better part of the afternoon preparing it. Even though you are full and don't even like bananas, you accept a serving of his dessert and eat it all.

Clearly, internal biological factors do not fully explain our eating behavior. External social factors, based on societal rules and on what we have learned about appropriate eating behavior, also play an important role. Take, for example, the simple fact that people customarily eat breakfast, lunch, and dinner at approximately the same times every day. Because we tend to eat on schedule every day, we feel hungry as the usual hour approaches, sometimes quite independently of what our internal cues are telling us.

Similarly, we put roughly the same amount of food on our plates every day, even though the amount of exercise we may have had, and consequently our need for energy replenishment, varies from day to day. We also tend to prefer particular foods over others. Rats and dogs may be a delicacy in certain Asian cultures, but few people in Western cultures find them appealing despite their potentially high nutritional value. Even the amount of food we eat varies according to cultural norms. For instance, people in the United States eat bigger portions than people in France. In sum, cultural influences and our individual habits play important roles in determining when, what, and how much we eat (Capaldi, 1996; Miller & Pumariega, 2001; Rozin et al., 2003).

Other social factors relate to our eating behavior as well. Some of us head toward the refrigerator after a difficult day, seeking solace in a pint of Heath Bar Crunch ice cream. Why? Perhaps when we were children, our parents gave us food when we were upset. Eventually, we may have learned, through the basic mechanisms of classical and operant conditioning, to associate food with comfort and consolation. Similarly, we may learn that eating, which focuses our attention on immediate pleasures, provides an escape from unpleasant thoughts. Consequently, we may eat when we feel distressed (McManus & Waller, 1995; Hill & Peters, 1998; Bulik et al., 2003; O'Connor & O'Connor, 2004).

THE ROOTS OF OBESITY

Given that both biological and social factors influence eating behavior, determining the causes of obesity has proved to be a challenging task. Researchers have followed several paths.

Some psychologists suggest that oversensitivity to external eating cues based on social factors, coupled with insensitivity to internal hunger cues, produces obesity. Others argue that overweight people have higher weight set points than other people do. Because their set points are unusually high, their attempts to lose weight by eating less may make them especially sensitive to external, food-related cues and therefore more apt to overeat, perpetuating their obesity (Hill & Peters, 1998; Tremblay, 2004; West, Harvey-Berino, & Raczynski, 2004).

But why may some people's weight set points be higher than those of others? One biological explanation is that obese individuals have a higher level of the hormone *leptin,* which appears to be designed, from an evolutionary standpoint, to "protect" the body against weight loss. The body's weight-regulation system thus appears to be designed more to protect against losing weight than to protect against gaining it, meaning that it's easier to gain weight than to lose it (Friedman, 2003; Ahiima & Osei, 2004; Zhang et al., 2005).

Another biologically based explanation for obesity relates to fat cells in the body. Starting at birth, the body stores fat either by increasing the number of fat cells or by increasing the size of existing fat cells. Furthermore, any loss of weight past infancy does not decrease the number of fat cells; it only affects their size. Consequently, people are stuck with the number of fat cells they inherit from an early age, and the rate of weight gain during the first four months of life is related to being overweight during later childhood (Stettler et al., 2005).

According to the weight-set-point hypothesis, the presence of too many fat cells from earlier weight gain may result in the set point becoming "stuck" at a higher level than is desirable. In such circumstances, losing weight becomes a difficult proposition, because one is constantly at odds with one's own internal set point when dieting (Freedman, 1995; Leibel, Rosenbaum, & Hirsch, 1995).

Not everyone agrees with the set-point explanation for obesity. Pointing to the rapid rise in obesity over the last several decades in the United States, some researchers suggest that the body does not try to maintain a fixed weight set point. Instead, they suggest, the body has a *settling point*, determined by a combination of our genetic heritage and the nature of the environment in which we live. If high-fat foods are prevalent in our environment and we are genetically predisposed to obesity, we settle into an equilibrium that maintains relatively high weight. In contrast, if our environment is nutritionally healthier, a genetic predisposition to obesity will not be triggered, and we will settle into an equilibrium in which our weight is lower (Comuzzie & Allison, 1998; Pi-Sunyer, 2003).

Eating Disorders

One devastating weight-related disorder is **anorexia nervosa.** In this severe eating disorder, people may refuse to eat while denying that their behavior and appearance—which can become skeletonlike—are unusual. Some 10 percent of people with anorexia literally starve themselves to death.

Anorexia nervosa mainly afflicts females between the ages of 12 and 40, although both men and women of any age may develop it. People with the disorder typically come from stable homes, and they are often successful, attractive, and relatively affluent. The disorder often occurs after serious dieting, which somehow gets out of control. Life begins to revolve around food: Although people with the disorder eat little, they may cook for others, go shopping for food frequently, or collect cookbooks (Rosen, 1999; Reijonen et al., 2003; Polivy, Herman, & Boivin, 2005).

A related problem, **bulimia,** from which Lisa Arndt (described earlier) suffered, is a disorder in which people binge on large quantities of food. For instance, they may consume an entire gallon of ice cream and a whole pie in a single sitting. After such a binge, sufferers feel guilt and depression and often induce vomiting or take laxatives to rid themselves of the food—behavior known as purging. Constant bingeing-and-purging cycles and the use of drugs to induce vomiting or diarrhea can lead to heart failure. Often, though, the weight of a person with bulimia remains normal (Phillips et al., 2003; Mora-Giral et al., 2004).

Eating disorders represent a growing problem: Estimates show that between 1 and 4 percent of high school-age and college-age women have either anorexia nervosa or bulimia. As many as 10 percent of women suffer from bulimia at some point in their lives. Furthermore, an increasing number of men are diagnosed with eating disorders; an estimated 10 to 13 percent of all cases occur in males (NIMH, 2000; DeAngelis, 2002; Morgan, 2002; Kaminski et al., 2005).

What are the causes of anorexia nervosa and bulimia? Some researchers suspect a biological cause such as a chemical imbalance in the hypothalamus or pituitary gland, perhaps brought on by genetic factors. Others believe that the cause has roots in society's valuation of slenderness and the parallel notion that obesity is undesirable. These researchers maintain that people with anorexia nervosa and bulimia become preoccupied with their weight and take to heart the cliché that one can never be too thin. This may explain why, as countries become more developed and Westernized, and dieting becomes more popular, eating disorders increase. Finally, some psychologists suggest that the disorders result from overly demanding parents or other family problems (Goldner, Cockell, & Srikameswaran, 2002; Polivy & Herman, 2002; Grilo et al., 2003).

The complete explanations for anorexia nervosa and bulimia remain elusive. These disorders probably stem from both biological and social causes, and successful

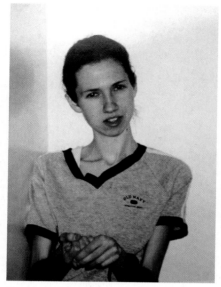

Despite looking skeletonlike to others, people with the weight disorder anorexia nervosa see themselves as overweight.

Anorexia nervosa: A severe eating disorder in which people may refuse to eat while denying that their behavior and appearance—which can become skeletonlike—are unusual.

Bulimia: A disorder in which a person binges on incredibly large quantities of food and later may attempt to purge the food through vomiting or the use of laxatives.

treatment probably encompasses several strategies, including therapy and dietary changes (Striegel-Moore & Smolak, 2001; Wilson & Fairburn, 2002; Patel, Pratt, & Greydanus, 2003; Richard, 2005). If you or a family member needs advice or help with an eating problem, contact the American Anorexia Bulimia Association at www.aabainc.org or call 212-575-6200. You can get more information at www.nlm.nih.gov/medlineplus/eatingdisorders.html.

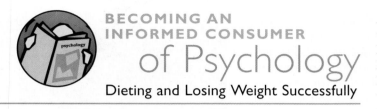

BECOMING AN INFORMED CONSUMER
of Psychology
Dieting and Losing Weight Successfully

Although 60 percent of the people in the United States say they want to lose weight, it's a losing battle for most of them. Most people who diet eventually regain the weight they have lost, and so they try again and get caught in a seemingly endless cycle of weight loss and gain. Given what we know about the causes of obesity, this is not entirely surprising, because so many factors affect eating behavior and weight (Lowe, 1993; Newport & Carroll, 2002; Parker-Pope, 2003).

According to diet experts, you should keep several things in mind when trying to lose weight (CR, 1993; Gatchel & Oordt, 2003; Heshka et al., 2003):

- *There is no easy route to weight control.* You will have to make permanent changes in your life to lose weight without gaining it back. The most obvious strategy—cutting down on the amount of food you eat—is just the first step toward a lifetime commitment to changing your eating habits. You must consider the nutrient content, as well as the overall quantity, of the food you consume.
- *Keep track of what you eat and what you weigh.* Unless you keep careful records, you won't really know how much you are eating and whether any diet is working.
- *Eat "big" foods.* Eat foods that are bulky and heavy but low in calories, such as grapes and soup. Such foods trick your body into thinking you've eaten more, decreasing hunger.
- *Cut out television.* One reason for the epidemic of obesity is the number of hours spent viewing television by people in the United States. Not only does watching television preclude other activities that burn calories (even walking around the house is helpful), people often gorge on junk food while watching. One study found that after researchers took into account the effects of exercise, smoking, age, and diet, each 2-hour increase in daily TV-viewing led to a 23 percent increase in obesity (Hu et al., 2003).
- *Exercise.* When you exercise, you use up fat stored in your body as fuel for muscles, which is measured in calories. As you use up this fat, you will probably lose weight. Almost any activity helps burn calories (see Figure 3). The weight-set-point hypothesis suggests another advantage to moderate exercise: It may lower your set point. Although just how much exercise is sufficient to lower weight is disputed, most experts recommend at least thirty consecutive minutes of moderate exercise at least three times a week. (If nothing else, the release of endorphins, neurotransmitters involved in pain reduction, after exercise will make you feel better even if you don't lose weight.)
- *Decrease the influence of external, social stimuli on your eating behavior.* For instance, serve yourself smaller portions of food, and leave the table before you see what is being served for dessert. Don't even buy snack foods such as nachos and potato chips; if they're not readily available in the kitchen cupboard, you're not apt to eat them. Wrap refrigerated foods in aluminum foil so that you cannot see the contents and be tempted every time you open the refrigerator.
- *Avoid fad diets.* No matter how popular they are at a particular time, extreme diets, including liquid diets, usually don't work in the long run and can be dangerous to your health.
- *Maintain good eating habits.* When you have reached your desired weight, maintain the new habits you learned while dieting to avoid gaining back the weight you have lost.

More vigorous/
less time

Stair walking for 15 minutes

Shoveling snow for 15 minutes

Running 1½ miles in 15 minutes (10 min./mile)

Jumping Rope for 15 minutes

Bicycling 4 miles in 15 minutes

Basketball (playing a game) for 15–20 minutes

Wheelchair basketball for 20 minutes

Swimming laps for 20 minutes

Water aerobics for 30 minutes

Walking 2 miles in 30 minutes (15 min./mile)

Raking leaves for 30 minutes

Pushing a stroller 1½ miles in 30 minutes

Dancing fast (social) for 30 minutes

Bicycling 5 miles in 30 minutes

Basketball (shooting baskets) for 30 minutes

Walking 1¾ miles in 35 minutes (20 min./mile)

Wheeling self in wheelchair for 30-45 minutes

Gardening for 35–45 minutes

Playing touch football for 30–45 minutes

Playing volleyball for 45 minutes

Washing windows or floors for 45–60 minutes

Washing and waxing a car for 45–60 minutes

Less vigorous/
more time

FIGURE 3 Ways to burn 150 calories: People can expend 150 calories by spending more time at a less vigorous activity or spending less time at a more vigorous activity. (Source: Adapted from Lertola, 1997.)

- *Set reasonable goals.* Know how much weight you want to lose before you start to diet. Don't try to lose too much weight too quickly or you may doom yourself to failure. Even small changes in behavior—such as walking fifteen minutes a day or eating a few less bites at each meal—can prevent weight gain (Hill et al., 2003).
- *Don't feel guilty!* Above all, don't blame yourself if you don't succeed in losing weight. Given the evidence that obesity may be genetically determined, the inability to lose weight should not be seen as a moral failing. Indeed, you are in good company, for some 90 to 95 percent of dieters regain the weight they have lost (Fritsch, 1999; Friedman, 2003).

In light of the difficulty of losing weight, psychologists Janet Polivy and C. Peter Herman suggest—paradoxically—that the best approach may be to avoid dieting in the first place. They recommend that people eat what they really want to eat, even if this means indulging in candy or ice cream every so often. This freedom to eat anything may reduce binge eating, which is more likely to occur when dieters feel that bingeing represents their only opportunity to eat what they really wish to eat. Although such an approach may not produce major weight loss, even a relatively small weight loss is better than none: Just a ten- to fifteen-pound drop in body weight may lower the major health risks that are associated with obesity (Bruce & Wilfley, 1996; *HealthNews,* 1999; Polivy & Herman, 2002; Avenell et al., 2004).

The Need for Achievement: Striving for Success

Although hunger may be one of the more potent primary drives in our day-to-day lives, powerful secondary drives that have no clear biological basis also motivate us. Among the more prominent of these is the need for achievement.

Need for achievement: A stable, learned characteristic in which a person obtains satisfaction by striving for and attaining a level of excellence.

The **need for achievement** is a stable, learned characteristic in which a person obtains satisfaction by striving for and attaining a level of excellence (McClelland et al., 1953). People with a high need for achievement seek out situations in which they can compete against some standard—be it grades, money, or winning at a game—and prove themselves successful. But they are not indiscriminate when it comes to picking their challenges: They tend to avoid situations in which success will come too easily (which would be unchallenging) and situations in which success is unlikely. Instead, people high in achievement motivation generally choose tasks that are of intermediate difficulty.

In contrast, people with low achievement motivation tend to be motivated primarily by a desire to avoid failure. As a result, they seek out easy tasks, being sure to avoid failure, or seek out very difficult tasks for which failure has no negative implications, because almost anyone would fail at them. People with a high fear of failure will stay away from tasks of intermediate difficulty, because they may fail where others have been successful (Atkinson & Feather, 1966; Martin & Marsh, 2002; Puca, 2005).

A high need for achievement generally produces positive outcomes, at least in a success-oriented society such as ours. For instance, people motivated by a high need for achievement are more likely to attend college than are their low-achievement counterparts, and once they are in college, they tend to receive higher grades in classes that are related to their future careers. Furthermore, high achievement motivation indicates future economic and occupational success (McClelland, 1985; Thrash & Elliot, 2002). (To learn more, try the PsychInteractive exercise on the need for achievement.)

www.mhhe.com/feldmanup8
PsychInteractive Online

Need for Achievement

MEASURING ACHIEVEMENT MOTIVATION

How can we measure a person's need for achievement? The measuring instrument used most frequently is the *Thematic Apperception Test (TAT)* (Spangler, 1992). In the TAT, an examiner shows a series of ambiguous pictures, such as the one in Figure 4. The examiner tells participants to write a story that describes what is happening, who the people are, what led to the situation, what the people are thinking or wanting, and what will happen next. Researchers then use a standard scoring system to determine the amount of achievement imagery in people's stories. For example, someone who writes a story in which the main character strives to beat an opponent, studies in order to do well at some task, or works hard in order to get a promotion shows clear signs of an achievement orientation. The inclusion of such achievement-related imagery in the participants' stories is assumed to indicate an unusually high degree of concern with—and therefore a relatively strong need for—achievement (Tuerlinckx, DeBoeck, & Lens, 2002).

FIGURE 4 This ambiguous picture is similar to those used in the Thematic Apperception Test to determine people's underlying motivation (© 1943 by the President and Fellows of Harvard College; 1971 by Henry A. Murray.) What do *you* see? Do you think your response is related to your motivation?

Need for affiliation: An interest in establishing and maintaining relationships with other people.

The Need for Affiliation: Striving for Friendship

Few of us choose to lead our lives as hermits. Why?

One main reason is that most people have a **need for affiliation,** an interest in establishing and maintaining relationships with other people. Individuals with a high need for affiliation write TAT stories that emphasize the desire to maintain or reinstate friendships and show concern over being rejected by friends.

People who have higher affiliation needs are particularly sensitive to relationships with others. They desire to be with their friends more of the time, and alone less often, compared with people who are lower in the need for affiliation. However, gender is a greater determinant of how much time is actually spent with friends: Regardless of their affiliative orientation, female students spend significantly more time with their friends and less time alone than male students do (Wong & Csikszentmihalyi, 1991; O'Connor & Rosenblood, 1996; Cantwell & Andrews, 2002; Johnson, 2004).

The Need for Power: Striving for Impact on Others

If your fantasies include becoming president of the United States or running Microsoft, your dreams may reflect a high need for power. The **need for power,** a tendency to seek impact, control, or influence over others and to be seen as a powerful individual, is an additional type of motivation (Winter, 1973, 1987; Lee-Chai & Bargh, 2001).

As you might expect, people with strong needs for power are more apt to belong to organizations and seek office than are those low in the need for power. They also tend to work in professions in which their power needs may be fulfilled, such as business management and—you may or may not be surprised—teaching (Jenkins, 1994). In addition, they seek to display the trappings of power. Even in college, they are more likely to collect prestigious possessions, such as electronic equipment and sports cars.

Some significant gender differences exist in the display of need for power. Men with high power needs tend to show unusually high levels of aggression, drink heavily, act in a sexually exploitative manner, and participate more frequently in competitive sports—behaviors that collectively represent somewhat extravagant, flamboyant behavior. In contrast, women display their power needs with more restraint; this is congruent with traditional societal constraints on women's behavior. Women with high power needs are more apt than men are to channel those needs in a socially responsible manner, such as by showing concern for others or displaying highly nurturing behavior (Winter, 1988, 1995; Maroda, 2004).

> **Need for power:** A tendency to seek impact, control, or influence over others, and to be seen as a powerful individual.

RECAP/EVALUATE/RETHINK

RECAP

What biological and social factors underlie hunger?

- Eating behavior is subject to homeostasis, as most people's weight stays within a relatively stable range. The hypothalamus in the brain is central to the regulation of food intake. (pp. 329-332)
- Social factors, such as mealtimes, cultural food preferences, and other learned habits, also play a role in the regulation of eating, determining when, what, and how much one eats. An oversensitivity to social cues and an insensitivity to internal cues may also be related to obesity. In addition, obesity may be caused by an unusually high weight set point—the weight the body attempts to maintain—and genetic factors. (pp. 332-333)

How are needs relating to achievement, affiliation, and power motivation exhibited?

- Need for achievement refers to the stable, learned characteristic in which a person strives to attain a level of excellence. Need for achievement is usually measured through the Thematic Apperception Test (TAT), a series of pictures about which a person writes a story. (pp. 335-336)

- The need for affiliation is a concern with establishing and maintaining relationships with others, whereas the need for power is a tendency to seek to exert an impact on others. (pp. 336-337)

EVALUATE

1. Match the following terms with their definitions:
   1. Hypothalamus
   2. Lateral hypothalamic damage
   3. Ventromedial hypothalamic damage
   a. Leads to refusal of food and starvation
   b. Responsible for monitoring food intake
   c. Causes extreme overeating
2. The _____ _____ _____ is the particular level of weight the body strives to maintain.
3. _____ is the rate at which energy is produced and expended by the body.
4. Julio is the type of person who constantly strives for excellence. He feels intense satisfaction when he is able to master a new task. Julio most likely has a high need for _____.
5. Debbie's *Thematic Apperception Test (TAT)* story depicts a young girl who is rejected by one of her peers and seeks

to regain her friendship. What major type of motivation is Debbie displaying in her story?

a. Need for achievement
b. Need for motivation
c. Need for affiliation
d. Need for power

RETHINK

1. In what ways do societal expectations, expressed by television shows and commercials, contribute to both obesity and excessive concern about weight loss? How could television contribute to better eating habits and attitudes toward weight? Should it be required to do so?

2. *From the perspective of a human resources specialist:* How might you use characteristics such as need for achievement, need for power, and need for affiliation to select workers for jobs? What additional criteria would you have to consider?

Answers to Evaluate Questions

1. 1-b, 2-a, 3-c; 2. weight set point; 3. metabolism; 4. achievement; 5. c.

KEY TERMS

obesity p. 329
weight set point p. 331

metabolism p. 331
anorexia nervosa p. 333

bulimia p. 333
need for achievement p. 336

need for affiliation p. 336
need for power p. 337

Understanding Emotional Experiences

Karl Andrews held in his hands the envelope he had been waiting for. It could be the ticket to his future: an offer of admission to his first-choice college. But what was it going to say? He knew it could go either way; his grades were pretty good and he had been involved in some extracurricular activities, but his SAT scores had been not so terrific. He felt so nervous that his hands shook as he opened the thin envelope (not a good sign, he thought). Here it comes. "Dear Mr. Andrews," it read. "The Trustees of the University are pleased to admit you. . . ." That was all he needed to see. With a whoop of excitement, Karl found himself jumping up and down gleefully. A rush of emotion overcame him as it sank in that he had, in fact, been accepted. He was on his way.

At one time or another, all of us have experienced the strong feelings that accompany both very pleasant and very negative experiences. Perhaps we have felt the thrill of getting a sought-after job, the joy of being in love, sorrow over someone's death, or the anguish of inadvertently hurting someone. Moreover, we experience such reactions on a less intense level throughout our daily lives: the pleasure of a friendship, the enjoyment of a movie, and the embarrassment of breaking a borrowed item.

Despite the varied nature of these feelings, they all represent emotions. Although everyone has an idea of what an emotion is, formally defining the concept has proved to be an elusive task. We'll use a general definition: **Emotions** are feelings that generally have both physiological and cognitive elements and that influence behavior.

Think, for example, about how it feels to be happy. First, we obviously experience a feeling that we can differentiate from other emotions. It is likely that we also experience some identifiable physical changes in our bodies: Perhaps the heart rate increases, or—as in the example of Karl Andrews—we find ourselves "jumping for joy." Finally, the emotion probably encompasses cognitive elements: Our understanding and evaluation of the meaning of what is happening prompts our feelings of happiness.

It is also possible, however, to experience an emotion without the presence of cognitive elements. For instance, we may react with fear to an unusual or novel situation (such as coming into contact with an erratic, unpredictable individual), or we may experience pleasure over sexual excitation without having cognitive awareness or understanding of just what it is about the situation that is exciting.

Some psychologists argue that entirely separate systems govern cognitive responses and emotional responses. A current controversy focuses on whether the emotional response predominates over the cognitive response or vice versa. Some theorists suggest that we first respond to a situation with an emotional reaction and later try to understand it (Zajonc, 1985; Zajonc & McIntosh, 1992; Murphy & Zajonc, 1993). For example, we may enjoy a complex modern symphony without at first understanding it or knowing why we like it.

In contrast, other theorists propose that people first develop cognitions about a situation and then react emotionally. This school of thought suggests that we must think about and understand a stimulus or situation, relating it to what we already know, before we can react on an emotional level (Lazarus, 1991a, 1991b, 1994, 1995).

Proponents of both sides of this debate can cite research to support their viewpoints, and so the question is far from resolved. Perhaps the sequence varies from situation to situation, with emotions predominating in some instances and cognitive

Key Concepts

What are emotions, and how do we experience them?

What are the functions of emotions?

What are the explanations for emotions?

Emotions: Feelings that generally have both physiological and cognitive elements and that influence behavior.

processes occurring first in others. Both sides agree that we can experience emotions that involve little or no conscious thought. We may not know why we're afraid of mice, understanding objectively that they represent no danger, but we may still be frightened out of our wits when we see them (Lewis & Haviland-Jones, 2000).

The Functions of Emotions

Imagine what it would be like if we didn't experience emotion—no depths of despair, no depression, no remorse, but at the same time no happiness, joy, or love. Obviously, life would be considerably less satisfying, and even dull, if we lacked the capacity to sense and express emotion.

But do emotions serve any purpose beyond making life interesting? Indeed they do. Psychologists have identified several important functions that emotions play in our daily lives (Averill, 1994; Scherer, 1994; Frederickson & Branigan, 2005; Frijda, 2005). Among the most important of those functions are the following:

- *Preparing us for action.* Emotions act as a link between events in our environment and our responses. For example, if we saw an angry dog charging toward us, the emotional reaction (fear) would be associated with physiological arousal of the sympathetic division of the autonomic nervous system, the activation of the fight-or-flight response. The role of the sympathetic division is to prepare us for emergency action, which presumably would get us moving out of the dog's way—quickly.
- *Shaping our future behavior.* Emotions promote learning that will help us make appropriate responses in the future. For example, the emotional response that occurs when we experience something unpleasant—such as a threatening dog—teaches us to avoid similar circumstances in the future. In the same way, pleasant emotions act as positive reinforcement for prior behavior and therefore may lead an individual to seek out similar situations in the future.
- *Helping us interact more effectively with others.* We often communicate the emotions we experience through our verbal and nonverbal behaviors, making our emotions obvious to observers. These behaviors can act as a signal to observers, allowing them to understand better what we are experiencing and to predict our future behavior. In turn, this promotes more effective and appropriate social interaction.

Determining the Range of Emotions: Labeling Our Feelings

If we were to list the words in the English language that have been used to describe emotions, we would end up with at least 500 examples (Averill, 1975). The list would range from such obvious emotions as *happiness* and *fear* to less common ones, such as *adventurousness* and *pensiveness.*

One challenge for psychologists has been to sort through this list to identify the most important, fundamental emotions. Theorists have hotly contested the issue of cataloging emotions and have come up with different lists, depending on how they define the concept of emotion. In fact, some reject the question entirely, saying that *no* set of emotions should be singled out as most basic, and that emotions are best understood by breaking them down into their component parts. Other researchers argue for looking at emotions in terms of a hierarchy, dividing them into positive and negative categories, and then organizing them into increasingly narrower subcategories (Carroll & Russell, 1997; Manstead, Frijda, & Fischer, 2003; see Figure 1).

Still, most researchers suggest that a list of basic emotions would include, at a minimum, happiness, anger, fear, sadness, and disgust. Other lists are broader, includ-

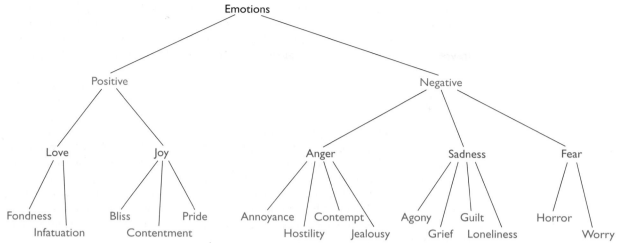

FIGURE 1 One approach to organizing emotions is to use a hierarchy, which divides emotions into increasingly narrow subcategories. (Source: Adapted from Fischer, Shaver, & Carnochan, 1990.)

ing emotions such as surprise, contempt, guilt, and joy (Plutchik, 1980; Ortony & Turner, 1990; Russell, 1991; Ekman, 1994a; Shweder, 1994; Tracy & Robins, 2004).

One difficulty in defining a basic set of emotions is that substantial differences exist in descriptions of emotions among various cultures. For instance, Germans report experiencing *schadenfreude,* a feeling of pleasure over another person's difficulties, and the Japanese experience *hagaii,* a mood of vulnerable heartache colored by frustration. In Tahiti, people experience *musu,* a feeling of reluctance to yield to unreasonable demands made by one's parents.

Finding *schadenfreude, hagaii,* or *musu* in a particular culture doesn't mean that the members of other cultures are incapable of experiencing such emotions, of course. It does suggest, though, that fitting a particular emotion into a linguistic category to describe that emotion may make it easier to discuss, contemplate, and perhaps experience (Russell, 1991; Mesquita & Frijda, 1992; Russell & Sato, 1995; Li, Wang, & Fischer, 2004).

The Roots of Emotions

I've never been so angry before; I feel my heart pounding, and I'm trembling all over . . . I don't know how I'll get through the performance. I feel like my stomach is filled with butterflies . . . That was quite a mistake I made! My face must be incredibly red . . . When I heard the footsteps in the night, I was so frightened that I couldn't catch my breath.

If you examine our language, you will find that there are literally dozens of ways to describe how we feel when we experience an emotion, and that the language we use to describe emotions is, for the most part, based on the physical symptoms that are associated with a particular emotional experience (Koveces, 1987; Kobayashi, Schallert, & Ogren, 2003; Manstead & Wagner, 2004).

Consider, for instance, the experience of fear. Pretend that it is late on New Year's Eve. You are walking down a dark road, and you hear a stranger approaching behind you. It is clear that he is not trying to hurry by but is coming directly toward you. You think about what you will do if the stranger attempts to rob you or, worse, hurt you in some way.

While these thoughts are running through your head, something rather dramatic will be happening to your body. The most likely reactions, which are associated with activation of the autonomic nervous system, include an increase in your rate of breathing, an acceleration of your heart rate, a widening of your pupils (to increase visual sensitivity), and a dryness in your mouth as the functioning of your salivary glands, and in fact of your entire digestive system, ceases. At the same time, though, your sweat glands probably will increase their activity, because increased sweating will help you rid yourself of the excess heat developed by any emergency activity in which you engage.

Of course, all these physiological changes are likely to occur without your awareness. At the same time, though, the emotional experience accompanying them will be obvious to you: You most surely would report being fearful.

Although it is easy to describe the general physical reactions that accompany emotions, defining the specific role that those physiological responses play in the experience of emotions has proved to be a major puzzle for psychologists. As we shall see, some theorists suggest that specific bodily reactions *cause* us to experience a particular emotion—we experience fear, for instance, *because* the heart is pounding and we are breathing deeply. In contrast, other theorists suggest that the physiological reaction results from the experience of an emotion. In this view, we experience fear, and as a result the heart pounds and our breathing deepens.

THE JAMES-LANGE THEORY: DO GUT REACTIONS EQUAL EMOTIONS?

To William James and Carl Lange, who were among the first researchers to explore the nature of emotions, emotional experience is, very simply, a reaction to instinctive bodily events that occur as a response to some situation or event in the environment. This view is summarized in James's statement, "we feel sorry because we cry, angry because we strike, afraid because we tremble" (James, 1890).

James and Lange took the view that the instinctive response of crying at a loss leads us to feel sorrow, that striking out at someone who frustrates us results in our feeling anger, that trembling at a menacing threat causes us to feel fear. They suggested that for every major emotion there is an accompanying physiological or "gut" reaction of internal organs—called a *visceral experience.* It is this specific pattern of visceral response that leads us to label the emotional experience.

In sum, James and Lange proposed that we experience emotions as a result of physiological changes that produce specific sensations. The brain interprets these sensations as particular kinds of emotional experiences (see Figure 2). This view has come to be called the **James-Lange theory of emotion** (Laird & Bresler, 1990; Cobos et al., 2002).

James-Lange theory of emotion: The belief that emotional experience is a reaction to bodily events occurring as a result of an external situation ("I feel sad because I am crying").

The James-Lange theory has some serious drawbacks, however. For the theory to be valid, visceral changes would have to occur relatively quickly, because we experience some emotions—such as fear upon hearing a stranger rapidly approaching on a dark night—almost instantaneously. Yet emotional experiences frequently occur even before there is time for certain physiological changes to be set into motion. Because of the slowness with which some visceral changes take place, it is hard to see how they could be the source of immediate emotional experience.

The James-Lange theory poses another difficulty: Physiological arousal does not invariably produce emotional experience. For example, a person who is jogging has an increased heartbeat and respiration rate, as well as many of the other physiological changes associated with certain emotions. Yet joggers typically do not think of such changes in terms of emotions. There cannot be a one-to-one correspondence, then, between visceral changes and emotional experience. Visceral changes by themselves may not be sufficient to produce emotion.

Finally, our internal organs produce a relatively limited range of sensations. Although some types of physiological changes are associated with specific emotional experiences, it is difficult to imagine how each of the myriad emotions that people are capable of experiencing could be the result of a unique visceral change. Many emotions actually are associated with relatively similar sorts of visceral changes, a fact that contradicts the James-Lange theory (Davidson et al., 1994; Cameron, 2002).

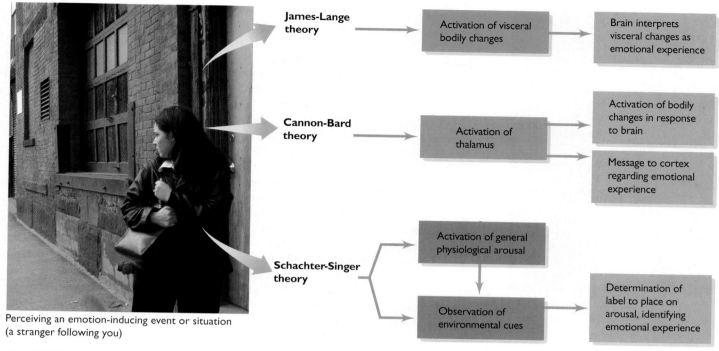

Perceiving an emotion-inducing event or situation (a stranger following you)

FIGURE 2 A comparison of three models of emotion.

THE CANNON-BARD THEORY: PHYSIOLOGICAL REACTIONS AS THE RESULT OF EMOTIONS

In response to the difficulties inherent in the James-Lange theory, Walter Cannon, and later Philip Bard, suggested an alternative view. In what has come to be known as the **Cannon-Bard theory of emotion,** they proposed the model illustrated in the second part of Figure 2 (Cannon, 1929). This theory rejects the view that physiological arousal alone leads to the perception of emotion. Instead, the theory assumes that both physiological arousal *and* the emotional experience are produced simultaneously by the same nerve stimulus, which Cannon and Bard suggested emanates from the thalamus in the brain.

The theory states that after we perceive an emotion-producing stimulus, the thalamus is the initial site of the emotional response. Next, the thalamus sends a signal to the autonomic nervous system, thereby producing a visceral response. At the same time, the thalamus also communicates a message to the cerebral cortex regarding the nature of the emotion being experienced. Hence, it is not necessary for different emotions to have unique physiological patterns associated with them—as long as the message sent to the cerebral cortex differs according to the specific emotion.

The Cannon-Bard theory seems to have been accurate in rejecting the view that physiological arousal alone accounts for emotions. However, more recent research has led to some important modifications of the theory. For one thing, we now understand that the hypothalamus and the limbic system, not the thalamus, play a major role in emotional experience. In addition, the simultaneous occurrence of the physiological and emotional responses, which is a fundamental assumption of the Cannon-Bard theory, has yet to be demonstrated conclusively. This ambiguity has allowed room for yet another theory of emotions: the Schachter-Singer theory.

THE SCHACHTER-SINGER THEORY: EMOTIONS AS LABELS

Suppose that, as you are being followed down a dark street on New Year's Eve, you notice a man being followed by another shady figure on the other side of the street.

Cannon-Bard theory of emotion: The belief that both physiological arousal and emotional experience are produced simultaneously by the same nerve stimulus.

This is the high, swaying suspension bridge that was used to increase the physiological arousal of male subjects. What other types of behavior can be explained by the Schachter-Singer theory of emotion?

Schachter-Singer theory of emotion: The belief that emotions are determined jointly by a nonspecific kind of physiological arousal and its interpretation, based on environmental cues.

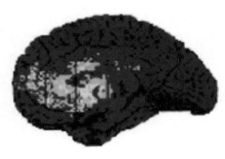

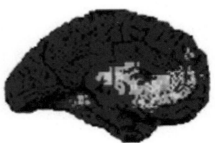

FIGURE 3 Experiencing different emotions activates particular areas of the brain, as these scans illustrate. (Source: Mark George, NIMH.)

Now assume that instead of reacting with fear, the man begins to laugh and act gleeful. Would the reactions of this other individual be sufficient to lay your fears to rest? Might you, in fact, decide there is nothing to fear, and get into the spirit of the evening by beginning to feel happiness and glee yourself?

According to an explanation that focuses on the role of cognition, the **Schachter-Singer theory of emotion,** this might very well happen. This approach to explaining emotions emphasizes that we identify the emotion we are experiencing by observing our environment and comparing ourselves with others (Schachter & Singer, 1962).

Schachter and Singer's classic experiment found evidence for this hypothesis. In the study, participants were told that they would receive an injection of a vitamin. In reality, they were given epinephrine, a drug that causes an increase in physiological arousal, including higher heart and respiration rates and a reddening of the face, responses that typically occur during strong emotional reactions. The members of both groups were then placed individually in a situation where a confederate of the experimenter acted in one of two ways. In one condition he acted angry and hostile, and in the other condition he behaved as if he were exuberantly happy.

The purpose of the experiment was to determine how the participants would react emotionally to the confederate's behavior. When they were asked to describe their own emotional state at the end of the experiment, the participants exposed to the angry confederate reported that they felt angry, while those exposed to the happy confederate reported feeling happy. In sum, the results suggest that participants turned to the environment and the behavior of others for an explanation of the physiological arousal they were experiencing.

The results of the Schachter-Singer experiment, then, supported a cognitive view of emotions, in which emotions are determined jointly by a relatively nonspecific kind of physiological arousal *and* the labeling of that arousal on the basis of cues from the environment (refer to the third part of Figure 2).

Although later research has found that arousal is not as nonspecific as Schachter and Singer assumed, it is clear that arousal can magnify, and be mistaken for, many emotions. For example, in one experiment, men who crossed a swaying 450-foot suspension bridge spanning a deep canyon were more attracted to a woman they encountered at the other end than were those who crossed a stable bridge spanning a shallow stream. Apparently, the men who crossed the frightening bridge attributed their subsequent high arousal to the woman, rather than to the swaying bridge (Dutton & Aron, 1974; Schorr, 2001).

In short, the Schachter-Singer theory of emotions is important because it suggests that, at least under some circumstances, emotional experiences are a joint function of physiological arousal and the labeling of that arousal. When the source of physiological arousal is unclear, we may look to our surroundings to determine just what we are experiencing.

CONTEMPORARY PERSPECTIVES ON THE NEUROSCIENCE OF EMOTIONS

When Schachter and Singer carried out their groundbreaking experiment in the early 1960s, the ways in which they could evaluate the physiology that accompanies emotion were relatively limited. However, advances in the measurement of the nervous system and other parts of the body have allowed researchers to examine more closely the biological responses involved in emotion. As a result, contemporary research on emotion points to a revision of earlier views that physiological responses associated with emotions are undifferentiated. Instead, evidence is growing that specific patterns of biological arousal are associated with individual emotions (Levenson, 1994; Franks & Smith, 1999; Vaitl, Schienle, & Stark, 2005).

For instance, researchers have found that specific emotions produce activation of very different portions of the brain. In one study, participants undergoing positron

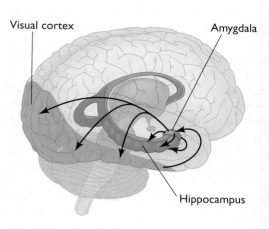

Visual cortex

Amygdala

Hippocampus

FIGURE 4 Connections from the amygdala, seen here in red, allow it to mediate many of the autonomic expressions of emotional states through the hippocampus (blue) and visual cortex (orange). (Source: Dolan, 2002.)

emission tomography (PET) brain scans were asked to recall events, such as deaths and funerals, that made them feel sad, or events that made them feel happy, such as weddings and births. They also looked at photos of faces that appeared to be happy or sad. The results of the PET scans were clear: Happiness was related to a decrease in activity in certain areas of the cerebral cortex, whereas sadness was associated with increases in activity in particular portions of the cortex (see Figure 3). Ultimately, it may be possible to map each particular emotion to specific a site in the brain (George et al., 1995; Hamann et al., 2002; Prohovnik et al., 2004).

The *amygdala,* in the brain's temporal lobe, also is important in the experience of emotions, for it provides a link between the perception of an emotion-producing stimulus and the recall of that stimulus later. For example, if we've once been attacked by a vicious pit bull, the amygdala processes that information and leads us to react with fear when we see a pit bull later—an example of a classically conditioned fear response (Adolphs, 2002; Miller et al., 2005).

Because neural pathways connect the amygdala, the visual cortex, and the *hippocampus* (which plays an important role in the consolidation of memories), some scientists speculate that emotion-related stimuli can be processed and responded to almost instantaneously (see Figure 4). This immediate response occurs so rapidly that higher-order, more rational thinking, which takes more time, seems not to be involved initially. In a slower, but more thoughtful, response to emotion-evoking stimuli, emotion-related sensory information is first evaluated and then sent on to the amygdala. It appears that the quicker system offers an immediate response to emotion-evoking stimuli, whereas the slower system helps confirm a threat and prepare a more thoughtful response (Dolan, 2002).

MAKING SENSE OF THE MULTIPLE PERSPECTIVES ON EMOTION

As new approaches to emotion continue to develop, it is reasonable to ask why so many theories of emotion exist and, perhaps more important, which one provides the most complete explanation. Actually, we have only scratched the surface. There are almost as many explanatory theories of emotion as there are individual emotions (e.g., Mayne & Bonanno, 2001; DeCoster, 2003; Manstead, Frijda, & Fischer, 2003; Frijda, 2005).

Why are theories of emotion so plentiful? For one thing, emotions are not a simple phenomenon but are intertwined closely with motivation, cognition, neuroscience,

The Truth About Lies: Detecting Deception in Terrorists and Your Next-Door Neighbor

John Yarbrough was working patrol for the Los Angeles Country Sheriff's Department. It was about two in the morning. He and his partner were in the Willowbrook section of South Central Los Angeles, and they pulled over a sports car.... [Yarbrough] opened the door and stepped out onto the street, walking toward the vehicle with his weapon drawn. Suddenly, a man jumped out of the passenger side and pointed a gun directly at him. The two of them froze, separated by no more than a few yards. "There was a tree behind him, to his right," Yarbrough recalls. "He was about seventeen. He had the gun in his right hand. He was on the curb side. I was on the other side, facing him. It was just a matter of who was going to shoot first.... If you looked at it logically, I should have shot him. But logic had nothing to do with it. Something just didn't feel right. It was a gut reaction not to shoot—a hunch that at that exact moment he was not an imminent threat to me." (Gladwell, 2002, p. 38).

Yarbrough's hunch was right: The man with the gun backed down. That hunch was based on the officer's reading of the man's nonverbal behavior—the gunman's facial expressions, his body movements, his gestures. And that reading was, fortunately for the suspect, an accurate one.

For most people, though, accuracy at reading others' deceptive intent is not so good. Although people generally are able to decode basic emotions from the facial expressions of others, they are not very good at determining when others are being deceptive. In fact, most of the time, we only perform at slightly above chance levels when evaluating whether we are being lied to (DePaulo & Morris, 2005).

Why are we so bad at determining when others are deceptive? One hypothesis is that deception is so rare in everyday life that we don't get much practice or feedback in lie detection. But it turns out that everyday folks are actually quite often deceptive, something I found in my own research.

In one study, my students and I asked pairs of previously unacquainted undergraduates to get to know one another during a ten-minute meeting that was secretly videotaped. Then we showed the tape to the participants, who were asked to indicate each time they said something that was not accurate. The results were startling. Around 60 percent of the participants lied at least once during the ten minutes, and the average number of lies was about three. There was also an interesting gender difference: Although men and women created the same number of lies, they lied differently. Women lied more to make their partner feel better ("You look great in that sweater"). In contrast, men lied more to make *themselves* look better ("I aced the test") (Feldman, Forrest, & Happ, 2002; Feldman & Tyler, 2005).

Clearly, the explanation for why people are not good at detecting lies is not because they are rarely exposed to lies, for lying is a frequent occurrence in everyday life. A better explanation may be that skilled liars can control their nonverbal behavior, thereby making detection difficult or impossible. In fact, a careful analysis of the nonverbal behavior of people who lie shows that few cues consistently reveal deception. Even *polygraphs*, electronic lie detectors that measure physiological arousal, can be inaccurate, because there is no foolproof technique for assessing the extent of the physiological changes that may indicate a lie (Committee to Review the Scientific Evidence on the Polygraph, 2003; DePaulo et al., 2003).

Because of the failure of traditional means of identifying liars, and spurred on by government efforts to identify terrorists, researchers are seeking to develop automated equipment that can instantly analyze the nonverbal behaviors of large numbers of people with the goal of identifying suspects who can then be further investigated. For instance, one research group has developed a high-definition thermal-imaging technique able to detect deceit by examining the thermal patterns on people's faces. Soon, airports and other high-traffic public areas will be able to use imaging techniques like this in conjunction with other technologies, such as voice analysis equipment, surveillance video analysis software, and instantaneous background checks, to quickly screen large crowds for criminals or terrorists. At security checkpoints, people may eventually pass through nonverbal behavior detectors just as they pass through metal detectors today (Pavlidis, Eberhardt, & Levine, 2002; Cooper, 2004; Kevenaar et al., 2005).

RETHINK

In addition to their security and law enforcement uses, how might nonverbal behavior analysis technologies be used in other contexts? How might such technologies be misused?

and a host of related branches of psychology. For example, evidence from brain imaging studies shows that even when people come to supposedly rational, nonemotional decisions—such as making moral, philosophical judgments—emotions come into play (Greene et al., 2001).

In short, emotions are such complex phenomena, encompassing both biological and cognitive aspects, that no single theory has been able to explain fully all the facets of emotional experience. Furthermore, contradictory evidence of one sort or another challenges each approach, and therefore no theory has proved invariably accurate in its predictions.

This abundance of perspectives on emotion is not a cause for despair—or unhappiness, fear, or any other negative emotion. It simply reflects the fact that psychology is an evolving, developing science. As we gather more evidence, the specific answers to questions about the nature of emotions will become clearer. Furthermore, even as our understanding of emotions continues to grow, ongoing efforts are applying our knowledge of emotions to practical problems, as we consider in the *Applying Psychology in the 21st Century* box and the PsychInteractive exercise on the detection of deception.

www.mhhe.com/feldmanup8
PsychInteractive Online

Detection of Deception

RECAP/EVALUATE/RETHINK

RECAP

What are emotions, and how do we experience them?

- Emotions are broadly defined as feelings that may affect behavior and generally have both a physiological component and a cognitive component. Debate continues over whether separate systems govern cognitive and emotional responses and whether one has primacy over the other. (pp. 339-340)

What are the functions of emotions?

- Emotions prepare us for action, shape future behavior through learning, and help us interact more effectively with others. (p. 340)

What are the explanations for emotions?

- Several theories explain emotions. The James-Lange theory suggests that emotional experience is a reaction to bodily, or visceral, changes that occur as a response to an environmental event and are interpreted as an emotional response. (p. 342)
- In contrast, the Cannon-Bard theory contends that both physiological arousal and an emotional experience are produced simultaneously by the same nerve stimulus and that the visceral experience does not necessarily differ among differing emotions. (p. 343)
- The Schachter-Singer theory suggests that emotions are determined jointly by a relatively nonspecific physiological arousal and the subsequent labeling of that arousal, using cues from the environment to determine how others are behaving in the same situation. (pp. 343-344)
- The most recent approaches to emotions focus on their biological origins. For instance, it now seems that specific patterns of biological arousal are associated with individual emotions. Furthermore, new scanning techniques have identified the specific parts of the brain that are activated during the experience of particular emotions. (p. 344-345)

EVALUATE

1. Emotions are always accompanied by a cognitive response. True or false?
2. The _____ - _____ theory of emotions states that emotions are a response to instinctive bodily events.
3. According to the _____ - _____ theory of emotion, both an emotional response and physiological arousal are produced simultaneously by the same nerve stimulus.
4. Your friend—a psychology major—tells you, "I was at a party last night. During the course of the evening, my general level of arousal increased. Since I was at a party where people were enjoying themselves, I assume I must have felt happy." What theory of emotion does your friend subscribe to?
5. The _____, or "lie detector," is an instrument used to measure physiological responses associated with answers to questions.

RETHINK

1. If researchers learned how to control emotional responses so that targeted emotions could be caused or prevented, what ethical concerns might arise? Under what circumstances, if any, should such techniques be used?

2. *From the perspective of an advertising executive:* How might you use the findings by Schachter and Singer on the labeling of arousal to create interest in a product? Can you think of other examples whereby people's arousal could be manipulated, which would lead to different emotional responses?

KEY TERMS

emotions p. 339
James-Lange theory of emotion p. 342

Cannon-Bard theory of emotion p. 343

Schachter-Singer theory of emotion p. 344

Nonverbal Behavior and the Expression of Emotions

Ancient Sanskrit writings speak of someone who, on giving an evasive answer, "rubs the great toe along the ground, and shivers." Shakespeare describes Macbeth's face as "a place where men may read strange matters." An old love song claims that "your eyes are the eyes of a woman in love." Such examples demonstrate how nonverbal behavior has long had the reputation of revealing people's emotions. Only recently, though, have psychologists demonstrated the validity of such claims, finding that nonverbal behavior is an important way in which we communicate our emotions.

Nonverbal behavior communicates messages simultaneously across several channels, or paths. For example, facial expressions, eye contact, body movements, tone of voice, and even less obvious behaviors such as the positioning of the eyebrows are separate nonverbal channels of communication. Furthermore, each channel can carry a particular message—which may or may not be related to the messages being carried by the other channels. Because facial expressions represent the primary means of communicating emotional states, we will examine their role in the experience of emotions.

Key Concept

How does nonverbal behavior relate to the expression of emotions?

Consider, for a moment, the six photos displayed in Figure 1. Can you identify the emotions being expressed by the person in each of the photos?

If you are a good judge of facial expressions, you will conclude that these expressions display six of the basic emotions: happiness, anger, sadness, surprise, disgust, and fear. Hundreds of studies of nonverbal behavior show that these emotions are consistently distinct and identifiable, even by untrained observers (Ekman & O'Sullivan, 1991).

Exploring DIVERSITY

Do People in All Cultures Express Emotion Similarly?

It is particularly interesting that these six emotions are not unique to members of Western cultures; rather, they constitute the basic emotions expressed universally by members of the human race, regardless of where individuals have been raised and what learning experiences they have had. Psychologist Paul Ekman convincingly demonstrated this point when he studied the members of an isolated New Guinea jungle tribe who had had almost no contact with Westerners (Ekman, 1972). The people of the tribe did not speak or understand English, had never seen a movie, and had had very limited experience with Caucasians before Ekman's arrival. Yet their nonverbal responses to emotion-evoking stories, as well as their ability to identify basic emotions, were quite similar to those of Westerners.

Being so isolated, the New Guineans could not have learned from Westerners to recognize or produce similar facial expressions. Instead, their similar abilities and manner of responding emotionally appear to have been present innately. Although one could argue that similar experiences in both cultures led the members of each one to learn similar types of nonverbal behavior, this appears unlikely, because the two cultures are so very different. The expression of basic emotions, then, seems to be universal (Ekman, 1994b; Izard, 1994; Matsumoto, 2002). (Try the PsychInteractive exercise about the expression of emotions and nonverbal behavior).

Why do people across cultures express emotions similarly? A hypothesis known as the **facial-affect program** gives one explanation (Ekman, 1972, 2003).

The facial-affect program—which is assumed to be universally present at birth—is analogous to a computer program that is turned on when a particular emotion is

www.mhhe.com/feldmanup8
PsychInteractive Online

Emotions and Nonverbal Behavior

Facial-affect program: Activation of a set of nerve impulses that make the face display the appropriate expression.

FIGURE 1 These photos demonstrate six of the primary emotions: happiness, anger, sadness, surprise, disgust, and fear.

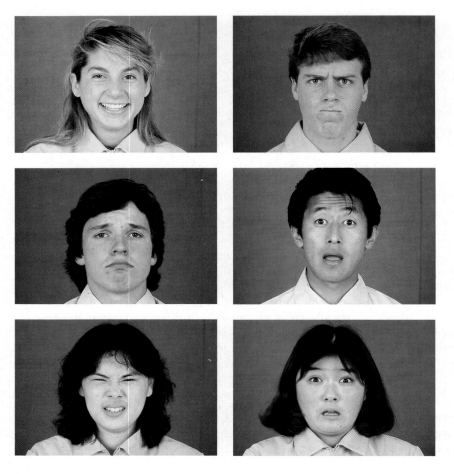

experienced. When set in motion, the "program" activates a set of nerve impulses that make the face display an appropriate expression. Each primary emotion produces a unique set of muscular movements, forming the kinds of expressions shown in Figure 1. For example, the emotion of happiness is universally displayed by movement of the zygomatic major, a muscle that raises the corners of the mouth—forming what we would call a smile (Ekman, Davidson, & Friesen, 1990; Ekman, 2003; Kohler et al., 2004).

Display Rules

If you've ever traveled in another culture, you've probably encountered people whose nonverbal behavior is quite different from what you are accustomed to. For instance, perhaps you've been to Japan or other Asian countries, where effusive emotional displays tend to be rarer than they are in Western countries. How do such differences correspond with the evidence showing that the expression of basic emotions is similar across cultures?

Some cultural differences in emotional expression are analogous to the way in which spoken languages show regional differences. For example, even though English is spoken in both the United States and Australia, speakers in the two countries show clear differences in accent. Similarly, people in different cultures may display basic emotions in slightly different ways; for this reason, we recognize emotions more accurately when

"And just exactly what is that expression intended to convey?"

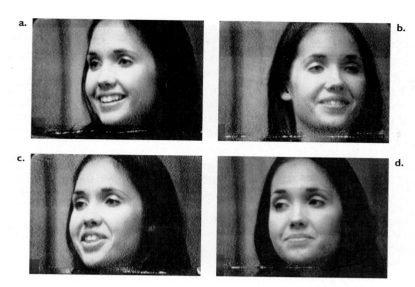

FIGURE 2 Which is the real smile? In comparison to a true happy smile—the smile in (a)—the smiles in the other photos are false. In (b) and (c) the person is actually experiencing disgust; in (d), the person is actually feeling sad. (Source: Ekman, Friesen, & O'Sullivan, 1988.)

the emotion is displayed by a member of our own national, ethnic, or regional group (Elfenbein & Ambady, 2002; Elfenbein, 2005).

The use of different display rules provides another reason for these cultural differences. **Display rules** are the guidelines that govern the appropriateness of showing emotion nonverbally. Display rules, which are learned during childhood, act to exaggerate, minimize, or mask emotional expressions (Feldman, 1993; Diefendorff & Richard, 2003; Matsumoto et al., 2005).

People use display rules fairly well, because we all have plenty of practice. For instance, people who receive an unwanted gift learn to paste a smile on their faces, at least in the presence of the gift giver. Similarly, card players learn to avoid gloating when they have a good hand (instead displaying a "poker face").

However, we do not always successfully mask our true feeling, and subtle indications may give away our actual emotions. For instance, you may observe slight differences in true and sham smiles when you compare the photos in Figure 2.

The nature of display rules varies considerably from one culture to another. For instance, Asians, by and large, consider it less desirable to express emotions than do people in Mediterranean and Latin cultures. Although the evidence is sketchy, some research also suggests that differences in display rules exist between whites and African Americans within the United States. For instance, one study suggests that whites display more restrained emotional than African Americans do. Still, research has not fully established the scope and reliability of such within-culture findings (Hanna, 1984; Manstead, 1991; Matsumoto, 2001).

One explanation that accounts for subtle cross-cultural differences in emotional expressivity is *dialect theory*, proposed by psychologists Hillary Elfenbein and Nalini Ambady. In the same way that a particular language can be spoken with different dialects or different accents, yet still be the same basic language, nonverbal expressivity may take on slightly different forms in different cultures (Elfenbein & Ambady, 2003; Elfenbein et al., 2004).

Dialect theory accounts for findings that an in-group advantage exists in decoding emotional expressions. This in-group advantage is shown when members of a given culture are somewhat more accurate at understanding the meaning of the facial expressions of members of their own culture than of other cultures (Elfenbein, 2005).

Display rules: Guidelines that govern the appropriateness of showing emotion nonverbally.

The Facial-Feedback Hypothesis: Smile, Though You're Feeling Blue

If you want to feel happy, try smiling. That is the implication of an intriguing notion known as the **facial-feedback hypothesis.** According to this hypothesis, facial expressions

Facial-feedback hypothesis: The hypothesis that facial expressions not only reflect emotional experience but also help determine how people experience and label emotions.

not only *reflect* emotional experience, they also help *determine* how people experience and label emotions (Izard, 1990). Basically put, "wearing" an emotional expression provides muscular feedback to the brain that helps produce an emotion congruent with that expression. For instance, the muscles activated when we smile may send a message to the brain indicating the experience of happiness—even if there is nothing in the environment that would produce that particular emotion. Some theoreticians have gone further, suggesting that facial expressions are *necessary* for an emotion to be experienced (Rinn, 1984, 1991). According to this view, if no facial expression is present, the emotion cannot be felt.

Support for the facial-feedback hypothesis comes from a classic experiment carried out by psychologist Paul Ekman and colleagues (Ekman, Levenson, & Friesen, 1983). In the study, professional actors were asked to follow very explicit instructions regarding the movements of muscles in their faces. You might try this example yourself:

- Raise your brows and pull them together.
- Raise your upper eyelids.
- Now stretch your lips horizontally back toward your ears.

After carrying out these directions—which, as you may have guessed, are meant to produce an expression of fear—the actors' heart rates rose and their body temperatures declined, physiological reactions that characterize fear. Overall, facial expressions representing the primary emotions produced physiological effects similar to those accompanying the genuine emotions in other circumstances (Keillor et al., 2002; Soussignan, 2002).

RECAP/EVALUATE/RETHINK

RECAP

How does nonverbal behavior relate to the expression of emotions?

- A person's facial expressions can reveal emotions. In fact, members of different cultures understand the emotional expressions of others in similar ways. One explanation for this similarity is that an innate facial-affect program activates a set of muscle movements representing the emotion being experienced. (pp. 349-350)
- The facial-feedback hypothesis suggests that facial expressions not only reflect, but also produce, emotional experiences. (pp. 351-352)

EVALUATE

1. What are the six primary emotions that can be identified from facial expressions?
2. Viewed as similar to a computer program, the _____ – _____ program provides a possible explanation for the universality in the expression of emotions.

3. According to the _____ – _____ hypothesis, an emotion cannot be felt without an accompanying facial response.

RETHINK

1. What might be the biological reasons for the fact that the six basic emotions are associated with universal facial expressions? The facial-affect program is said to be "universally present at birth"; how can this be confirmed through experimentation?
2. *From the perspective of a business executive:* How could you use your knowledge of display rules when negotiating? How might your strategies vary depending on the cultural background of the person with whom you were negotiating?

Answers to Evaluate Questions

1. surprise, sadness, happiness, anger, disgust, and fear; 2. facial-affect; 3. facial-feedback

KEY TERMS

facial-affect program p. 349
display rules p. 351

facial-feedback hypothesis p. 351

Looking Back

Psychology on the Web

1. Find two different Web sites that deal with nonverbal behavior. One site should present a fairly "academic" discussion of the topic, and the other should be more informal. (Hint: The terms nonverbal behavior and nonverbal communication may lead you to more formal discussions of the topic, whereas body language may lead you to less formal discussions.) Compare and contrast your findings from the two sites.

2. Find one or more Web sites that offer information on polygraphs (lie detectors). The sites should be intended either to advertise (i.e., sell) lie detectors or lie detection services or to debunk lie detector tests (e.g., by showing how to cheat on them). Evaluate the information on the Web site(s), using your understanding of the lie detection techniques discussed earlier. Summarize your findings and conclusions.

3. After completing the PsychInteractive exercise on detection of deception, use the Web to find two examples of attempts to identify potential terrorists via their nonverbal behavior. Summarize what you find and consider the feasibility of these efforts based on what you have learned about nonverbal behavior and deception detection.

Epilogue

Motivation and emotions are two interrelated aspects of psychology. In these modules, we first considered the topic of motivation, which has spawned a great deal of theory and research examining primary and secondary drives. We then turned to a discussion of emotions, beginning with their functions and proceeding to a review of three major theories that seek to explain what emotions are and how they, and their associated physiological symptoms, emerge in the individual. Finally, we looked at cultural differences in the expression and display of emotions and discussed the facial-affect program, which seems to be innate and to regulate the nonverbal expression of the basic emotions.

Before proceeding to the next group of modules, return to the opening scenario of this group of modules, which describes how cyclist Lance Armstrong overcame cancer and won the Tour de France. Using your knowledge of motivation and emotion, consider the following questions:

1. Which approach or approaches to motivation—instinctual, drive reduction, arousal, incentive, or cognitive—most effectively explain why an athlete like Armstrong will work exceptionally hard over many years to become a competitive cyclist?

2. How might the need for achievement have contributed to Armstrong's decision to continue competitive cycling after his cancer treatment? Would the need for affiliation have played a role? How?

3. What function might Armstrong's emotions have served in helping him to overcome his cancer and continue racing competitively?

4. After he won the Tour de France, Armstrong said, "I think it's a miracle." How can this statement be interpreted in terms of your understanding of motivation and emotion?

CHAPTER II

Sexuality and Gender

Key Concepts for Chapter 11

Prologue One Event, Two Perspectives

Bob: Patty and I were in the same statistics class together. She usually sat near me and was always very friendly. I liked her and thought maybe she liked me, too. Last Thursday I decided to find out. After class I suggested that she come to my place to study for midterms together. She agreed immediately, which was a good sign. That night everything seemed to go perfectly. We studied for a while and then took a break. I could tell that she liked me, and I was attracted to her. I was getting excited. I started kissing her. I could tell that she really liked it. We started touching each other and it felt really good. All of a sudden she pulled away and said "Stop." I figured she didn't want me to think that she was "easy" or "loose." A lot of girls think they have to say "no" at first. I knew once I showed her what a good time she could have, and that I would respect her in the morning, it would be OK.

***

Patty: I knew Bob from my statistics class. He's cute and we are both good at statistics, so when a tough midterm was scheduled, I was glad that he suggested we study together. It never occurred to me that it was anything except a study date. That night everything went fine at first, we got a lot of studying done in a short amount of time, so when he suggested we take a break I thought we deserved it. Well, all of a sudden he started acting really romantic and started kissing me. I liked the kissing but then he started touching me below the waist. I pulled away and tried to stop him but he didn't listen. After a while I stopped struggling; he was hurting me and I was scared. He was so much bigger and stronger than me. I couldn't believe it was happening to me. I didn't know what to do. He actually forced me to have sex with him. (Hughes & Sandler, 1987, p. 1).

Looking Ahead

Bob and Patty's perceptions of the same evening's events could hardly have been more different. Yet this example of date rape illustrates the emotion, confusion, and downright ignorance that often characterizes one of the most universal of behaviors: sexuality.

Exemplifying major personal, as well as societal, concerns, sex and the interrelated-topic of gender are also key topics for psychologists in a variety of specialties. For instance, psychologists interested in motivation view sexuality in terms of sexual needs, drives, and gratification. Neuroscientists consider sexuality from the perspective of the relationship of the brain and nervous system to the functioning of the sexual organs. Social psychologists and psychologists who

specialize in the study of women focus on society's rules of sexual conduct and the role sexual behavior plays in interpersonal behavior.

In this set of modules, we consider human sexuality from several of these vantage points. We begin by examining gender, discussing differences in societal expectations about how men and women should behave and the impact of those expectations on behavior and attitudes. Next we turn to sexual behavior. We describe the biological aspects of sexual excitement and arousal and then examine the variety of sexual activities in which people engage. We conclude with a discussion of nonconsenting sex, sexually transmitted infections, and the psychological aspects of sexual difficulties.

Gender and Sex

"It's a girl!" "It's a boy!"

One of these exclamations, or some variant, is typically the first sentence uttered upon the birth of a child. However, the consequences of whether we are born with male or female sex organs extend well beyond the moment of birth. Throughout our lives, the ways that others think of us, and even the ways in which we view ourselves, are based to a large extent on whether we are labeled as a woman or a man by society—our gender.

Gender is the perception of being male or female. Although there is a good deal of overlap between the concepts of sex and gender, they are not the same: *Sex* typically refers to sexual anatomy and sexual behavior, whereas *gender* refers to the sense of maleness or femaleness related to our membership in a given society.

Gender Roles: Society's Expectations for Women and Men

Our conclusions about what is or is not "appropriate" behavior for others and ourselves are based on **gender roles.** Gender roles are the set of expectations, defined by a particular society, that indicate what is appropriate behavior for men and women.

If men's and women's gender roles were equivalent, they would have only a minor impact on our lives. However, expectations about men and women differ significantly, and this may result in favoritism toward members of one of the sexes. Gender roles also may produce *stereotyping,* judgments about individual members of a group on the basis of their membership in that group. Stereotypes about gender roles

Key Concept

What are the major differences between male and female gender roles?

Gender: The perception of being male or female.

Gender roles: The set of expectations, defined by a particular society, that indicate what is appropriate behavior for men and women.

From the moment of birth, gender differences are defined by outside influences. Is it possible for a family to block these influences completely? Would it be desirable to do so?

FIGURE 1 In spite of numerous differences among cultures, research has found strong similarities in the content of gender stereotypes. (Source: Williams & Best, 1990).

Words Used to Describe Males		Words Used to Describe Females
Active	Initiative	Affected
Adventurous	Inventive	Affectionate
Aggressive	Lazy	Attractive
Ambitious	Logical	Charming
Arrogant	Loud	Curious
Assertive	Masculine	Dependent
Autocratic	Opportunistic	Dreamy
Clear-thinking	Progressive	Emotional
Coarse	Rational	Fearful
Courageous	Realistic	Feminine
Cruel	Reckless	Gentle
Daring	Robust	Mild
Determined	Rude	Sensitive
Disorderly	Self-confident	Sentimental
Dominant	Serious	Sexy
Egotistical	Severe	Softhearted
Energetic	Stern	Submissive
Enterprising	Stolid	Superstitious
Forceful	Strong	Talkative
Hardheaded	Unemotional	Weak
Hardhearted	Wise	
Independent		

Sexism: Negative attitudes and behavior toward a person based on that person's gender.

www.mhhe.com/feldmanup8

PsychInteractive Online

Gender Stereotypes

are reflected in **sexism,** negative attitudes ánd behavior toward a person that are based on that person's gender.

People in Western societies like ours generally hold well-defined stereotypes about men and women, which prevail regardless of age, economic status, and social and educational background. Men are more apt to be viewed as having traits involving competence, such as independence, objectivity, and competitiveness. In contrast, women tend to be seen as having traits involving warmth and expressiveness, such as gentleness and awareness of others' feelings. Because Western society traditionally values competence more than warmth and expressiveness, the perceived differences between men and women are biased in favor of men (Eagly & Wood, 2003; Hyde, 2004).

What's more, cross-cultural research finds remarkable similarity in the content of gender stereotypes in different societies. For example, a twenty-five–nation study identified a core set of descriptors that were consistently used to describe men and women (Williams & Best, 1990). Women were seen as sentimental, submissive, and superstitious, whereas men were seen as adventurous, forceful, and independent (see Figure 1). These stereotypical similarities across cultures may be due to similarities in status between men and women across the cultures; in most, men receive somewhat higher status than women (Lips, 2003).

Such stereotypes matter. By shaping beliefs about how men and women should behave, they potentially keep inequalities between the genders alive. Stereotypes put pressure on people to fulfill the stereotypes, and they may lead people to perform in accordance with the stereotypes rather than in accordance with their own abilities (Lips, 2003). To learn more about gender stereotypes, try the PsychInteractive exercise on gender stereotypes.

SEXISM ON THE JOB

Differences still exist regarding which occupations are deemed appropriate for men and for women. Women continue to be viewed as best suited for traditionally female jobs: "pink-collar" jobs such as secretary, nurse, cashier, and other female-

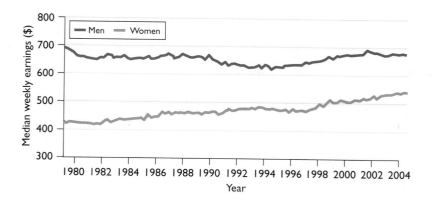

FIGURE 2 Men's wages have stagnated since 2001, while women's pay has moved up. Still, women earn an average of 80 cents for every dollar that men earn. The disparity is even worse for women who are members of minority groups. What factors account for the continuing gap between men and women's wages? (Source: U.S. Bureau of Labor Statistics, 2005.)

dominated professions that often feature low pay and low status. Men and women alike still report that they expect greater success when they enter a profession viewed as appropriate for their gender. Furthermore, women hold lower expectations than do men about their entering and peak salaries. (MacPherson, 2002; Crawford & Unger, 2004).

Those expectations reflect the reality that women, on average, earn less than men. Although the gap has been decreasing, women overall earn an average of 80 cents for every dollar that men earn. (Women who are members of minority groups are even worse off: Black women earn 71 cents for every dollar men make, and Hispanic and Latino women earn just 58 cents for every dollar men earn.) Furthermore, even when they are in the same professions as men, women generally make less than men in comparable positions earn (Crosby, Williams, & Biernat, 2004; U.S. Bureau of Labor Statistics, 2004; see Figure 2).

On the other hand, attitudes are shifting. Most people endorse gender equality in the workplace, and they believe that women should be given the same opportunities as men. For example, just about as many men as women endorse the idea that jobs should be family-friendly by offering flexible work schedules. In addition, polls today find that most men no longer believe that a woman's most appropriate role is to care for her home and children while men should be earning money—a shift from the 1970s, when the majority of men did endorse that traditional view (Bond et al., 2003; Barnett, 2004).

Still, even when women are successful on the job and are promoted into upper-level, high-status positions, they may face significant hurdles in their efforts to move up the corporate ladder. This is especially true for professional women who become mothers, who tend to be newly perceived viewed as warm, but less competent than they were prior to motherhood. The same thing doesn't happen to men who become fathers; they are most likely to be viewed as warm *and* competent (Cuddy, Fiske, & Glick, 2004).

Because of such stereotypic views, many women eventually hit what has come to be called the glass ceiling. The *glass ceiling* is an invisible barrier within an organization that, because of gender discrimination, may prevent women from being promoted beyond a certain level. The glass ceiling is even found in colleges and universities. For example, although women fill 29 percent of science and engineering jobs at U.S. educational institutions, they occupy only 15 percent of those positions at the top 50 research universities (Austin, 2000; Rudman & Glick, 2001; Whisenant, Pedersen, & Obenour, 2002; Ripley, 2005).

As phenomena such as the glass ceiling make clear, male gender stereotypes are typically more positive than female stereotypes. Although such stereotypes reflect

Sexual harassment consists of unwanted sexual attention. How is it possible for men and women to perceive this issue so differently?

people's perceptions and not necessarily the reality of the world, people often act as if they were real and modify their behavior to conform to the stereotypes. As a result, gender stereotypes limit both women's and men's behavior and ultimately lead to the unfortunate consequence of preferential treatment of men.

SEXUAL HARASSMENT

In addition to pay inequity and limited job advancement, women—even those in high-status professions—may face workplace sexism in the form of *sexual harassment,* defined as unwanted sexual attention, the creation of a hostile or abusive environment, or explicit coercion to engage in unwanted sexual activity. Sexual harassment is not a minor problem. One-fifth of women surveyed in polls say that they have been sexually harassed at work. And it is not just women who encounter harassment: Some 10 percent of men report experiencing sexual harassment on the job (Burgess & Borgida, 1997; Fineran, 2002; DeSouza & Fansler, 2003).

Sexual harassment is not just a workplace issue. Thirty percent of the female graduates of one large California university reported being the recipients of some form of harassment. Such harassment begins earlier in life: In one survey, 81 percent of middle and high school students reported receiving some form of sexual harassment in school, and six in ten experienced physical sexual harassment at some point in their school lives (see Figure 3). A third of students were afraid of being sexually harassed, with girls more than twice as likely as boys to report concern. Overall, estimates suggest that one of every two women will be harassed at some point during her academic or working life (AAUW, 2001; Fitzgerald, 2003).

FIGURE 3 Sexual harassment in school. The number of students who report experiencing unwelcomed sexual attention often or occasionally at school is significant. (Source: American Association of University Women, 2001.)

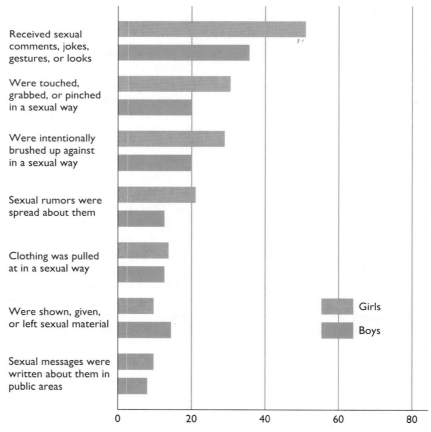

Percentage of students experiencing each kind of behavior

Sexual harassment often has less to do with sex than with power (similar to the motivation behind many cases of rape, as we'll discuss later). In this view, higher-status persons who engage in harassment may be less interested in receiving sexual favors than in demonstrating their power over the victim (Paludi, 1996; O'Donohue, 1997).

In some cases, harassment stems from *benevolent sexism,* stereotyped and restrictive attitudes that appear, on the surface, to be beneficial to women. For example, a male employer may compliment a woman on her attractiveness or offer her an easy job so that she won't have to "work so hard." The reality, however, is that such comments or "favors" may undermine the employee's sense of competence, and she may feel that she is not being taken seriously (Munson, Hulin, & Drasgow, 2000; Glick & Fiske, 2001; Glick et al., 2004).

Regardless of the motivation that lies behind sexual harassment, the consequences for the victim are clear. Feelings of shame and embarrassment are standard. Because targets of harassment are typically in lower-status positions, such feelings may be compounded by a sense of helplessness and powerlessness. People in these situations often suffer emotional and physical consequences, and the quality of their work may decline (Gutek, Cohen, & Tsui, 1996; Jorgenson & Wahl, 2000; Magley, 2002).

Gender Differences: More Similar Than Dissimilar

Not surprisingly, gender stereotyping, combined with other factors, results in actual behavior differences between men and women. Before we consider the nature of gender differences, however, it is important to keep in mind that in most respects men and women are more similar to one another than they are different. Furthermore, the differences that have been found reflect *average* male and female *group* differences, and this tells us little or nothing about any *individual* male or female (Tavris, 1992; Deaux, 1995).

For example, even if we find that males, on the whole, generally tend to be more talkative than females—as they do, according to research findings (Matlin, 2000)—an individual man can be less talkative than most women. Similarly, an individual woman may be more talkative than most men. When we consider any single person, our focus should be on the individual rather than on his or her gender group. It is important to take this into account as we examine the findings on gender differences.

PERSONALITY FACTORS

One of the most pronounced differences between men and women lies in their degree of aggressive behavior. By the time they are 2 years old, boys tend to display more aggression than girls do, and this higher level of aggression persists throughout the life span. Furthermore, compared with men, women experience greater anxiety and guilt about their aggressiveness and are more concerned about its effects on their victims (Feingold, 1994; Munroe et al., 2000; Hyde, DeLamater, & Byers 2006).

Men generally seem to have higher self-esteem than women do, although the size of the difference is not great and is based on different factors. Women's self-esteem is influenced to a large extent by their perception of their sense of interdependence and connection with others. In contrast, men's self-esteem stems from their assessment of their unique characteristics and abilities, traits that help them distinguish themselves from other people (Feingold, 1994; Stetsenko et al., 2000; Kling, Ryff, & Love 2003).

Men and women differ in how positively they view their own abilities and how they estimate the probability of their future success. In general, women evaluate themselves more harshly than do men. For example, a survey of first-year college students compared men's and women's views of whether they were above or below average. As you can see in Figure 4, more men than women considered themselves

FIGURE 4 Male first-year college students are much more likely than female first-year college students to rate themselves as above average in academic ability, mathematical ability, and emotional health. (Source: Dey, Astin, Korn, & Berz, 2004.)

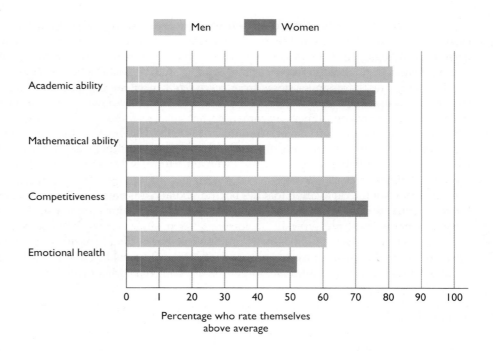

above average in overall academic and mathematical ability, competitiveness, and emotional health. Such self-perceptions matter, because they influence motivation, as well as academic and career choices. They even influence performance. For example, when women experience *stereotype threat*—the perception that a performance measure is sensitive to gender differences—their performance declines (Orenstein, 2001; Nosek, Banaji, & Greenwald, 2002; Steele, Spencer, & Aronson, 2002).

The content of men's and women's speech also differs, with women's speech being more precise. However, women's speech patterns lead others to view them as more tentative and less assertive. Women more often raise their pitch at the end of a sentence, and add "tags" at the end of an opinion, rather than stating the opinion outright. For example, instead of saying "It's awfully warm today," a female speaker might say instead "It's awfully warm today, *isn't it?*" thereby appearing less certain of her opinion. When females use such tentative language, they are judged to be less competent and knowledgeable than they are when they speak assertively (Carli & Bukatko, 2000; Matlin, 2000; Popp, Donovan, & Crawford, 2003).

Research has shown that boys from age 2 tend to be more aggressive than girls, a pattern that continues throughout the life span.

Women's and men's nonverbal behavior differs as well in several significant respects. In conversations with people of the other sex, women look at their partner significantly more while listening than while speaking, whereas men's levels of looking while speaking and listening are about the same. The effect of the male's pattern is to communicate power and dominance, whereas the woman's pattern is associated more with cooperation. Women, however, are generally better than men at decoding the facial expressions of others (Coats & Feldman, 1996; Burgoon & Bacue, 2003; LaFrance & Harris, 2004).

COGNITIVE ABILITIES

No general differences exist between men and women in overall IQ scores, learning, memory, problem solving, and concept-formation tasks. A few differences in more specific cognitive areas have been identified, although the true nature of those differences—and even their existence—has been called into question by more recent research (Halpern, 2000).

When Eleanor Maccoby and Carol Jacklin carried out a pioneering study of sex differences in 1974, they concluded that girls outperformed boys in verbal abilities and that boys had superior quantitative and spatial abilities. That conclusion was accepted widely as one of the truisms of the psychological literature.

However, recent and more sophisticated analyses have questioned the specific nature and magnitude of those differences. Psychologist Janet Hyde and colleagues, for instance, examined the mathematical performance of males and females in 100 studies encompassing some 4 million subjects. Contrary to traditional wisdom, females slightly outperformed males in math in elementary and middle school. The finding was reversed in high school, where males scored higher in mathematical problem solving. This difference is reflected in SAT scores, where girls score about 7 percent lower than boys (Hyde, Fennema, & Lamon, 1990; Ripley, 2005).

Yet the apparent male superiority in math is not universal. In some parts of the world, the sexes are on a par. For example, Japanese boys and girls perform quite similarly on math tests except for the single math area of probability—and Japanese girls routinely outperform both boys and girls in the United States on comparable tests of mathematical ability. Furthermore, in some places, girls outshine boys in math. In Iceland, for instance, female high school students score significantly better on standardized math tests than boys. Overall, the differences between males and females in math are inconsistent, and generally those differences are insignificant and, if anything, appear to be declining (Benbow, Lubinski, & Hyde, 1997; Nosek, Banaji, & Greenwald, 2002; Angier & Chang, 2005; Walt, 2005).

Psychologists have drawn a similar conclusion about the extent of gender differences in verbal skills. Despite the earlier view that women show greater verbal abilities than men, a more careful analysis of 165 studies of gender differences in verbal ability, representing the testing of close to 1.5 million subjects, has led to the conclusion that verbal gender differences are insignificant. Furthermore, verbal SAT scores are quite similar for boys and girls (Hyde & Linn, 1988; Hedges & Nowell, 1995; Angier & Chang, 2005).

Current evidence suggests, then, that gender differences in cognitive skills are minimal. On the other hand, particular tests of mathematical and verbal skills do elicit differences in performance, as in the example of the mathematics part of the SAT, where very high scorers are predominantly male. Differences such as these illustrate the fact that we still do not have the full story on gender differences in cognitive abilities (Halpern, 2000; Lippa, 2005; Ripley, 2005).

Sources of Gender Differences: Where Biology and Society Meet

If the identification of gender differences has presented a difficult challenge for researchers, the search for their causes has proved even more daunting. Given the indisputable fact that sex is a biological variable, it would seem reasonable to look at factors involving biological differences between men and women. It is also true that, from the time they are born, people are treated differently on the basis of their sex. Consequently, we must take into account both biological and social factors when we try to understand the source of gender differences.

Although we'll consider biological and environmental variables separately, neither alone can provide a full explanation for gender differences. Some combination of the two, interacting with each other, will ultimately provide us with an understanding of why men and women may behave differently.

BIOLOGICAL AND EVOLUTIONARY FACTORS

Do differences between male and female brains underlie sex and gender differences? This intriguing hypothesis has been put forward by some psychologists studying brain structure and functioning. For instance, girls who were exposed before birth to unusually high levels of *androgen,* a male hormone, because their mothers accidentally took a drug containing that hormone while pregnant, preferred different toys from those preferred by girls not exposed to androgens. Specifically, they were more likely to play with toys that are stereotypically preferred by boys (such as cars) and less likely to play with toys stereotypically associated with girls (such as dolls). Although you can probably think of several alternative explanations for these results, one possibility is that exposure to the male hormone may have affected the development of the girls' brains, making them favor toys that involve certain kinds of skills, such as those related to spatial abilities (Levine et al., 1999; Mealey, 2000; Hines et al., 2002).

Similarly, some evidence suggests that women perform better on tasks involving verbal skill and muscular coordination during periods when their production of the female sex hormone *estrogen* is relatively high, compared with periods when it is low. In contrast, they perform better on tasks involving spatial relationships when the estrogen level is relatively low (Kimura, 1999; Rosenberg & Park, 2002).

Some psychologists argue that evolutionary forces lead to certain differences between men's and women's behavior. For example, David Buss and colleagues point to differences in the nature of jealousy between men and women. Men are more jealous in cases of sexual infidelity than in cases of emotional infidelity; women are more jealous in cases of emotional infidelity than in cases of sexual infidelity (Buss et al., 1992; Buss, 2003c).

According to Buss's controversial explanation, the root cause for the differences in jealousy lies in the evolutionary implications of sexual, versus emotional, infidelity for men and women. He argues that for males, sexual infidelity represents a threat to their ability to ensure that their children are actually their own (and are the ones who have inherited their genes). In contrast, females have no doubt that a child that they carry through pregnancy is their own. However, their major concern is ensuring the male's protection and support during child rearing. Thus, to females, maintaining males' emotional attachment is crucial.

Psychologists relying on the evolutionary approach also argue that similarities in the division of labor between men and women across different cultures suggest that sex differences are due to evolutionary factors. Their argument is that even in very different types of cultures, men tend to be more aggressive, competitive, and prone to taking risks than women are—traits that had an evolutionary advantage (Mealey, 2000; Buss, 2003c).

However, many critics question the assumptions of the evolutionary approach. Rather than assuming that the differences are due to evolutionary forces, some psychologists suggest that differences in males' and females' beliefs about the meaning of infidelity are the actual cause of their jealousy differences. For instance, men may believe that women have sex only when they are in love. Consequently, sexual infidelity may be seen as a sign that a woman is in love with another man and may produce more jealousy than emotional infidelity alone would. In contrast, women may believe that men are capable of having sex without being in love, and consequently they may find a man's sexual infidelity less bothersome because it does not necessarily mean that he is in love with someone else (Harris & Christenfeld, 1996; DeSteno, Bartlett, & Braverman, 2002).

Psychologists Alice Eagly and Wendy Wood criticize evolutionary explanations for gender differences on different grounds. They argue, in their *biosocial approach*, that one important source of gender differences is the difference in the physical capabilities of men and women. Consistently across cultures, the division of labor between men and women is based largely on men's size, strength, and speed and women's capacity for pregnancy and caring for children. However, the specific nature of activities in which men and women specialize varies from one culture to another, depending on the specifics of a culture (Wood & Eagly, 2002).

The extent to which biological and evolutionary factors may underlie gender differences is an unanswered, and highly controversial, question. One thing is clear, however: Biological factors and evolutionary factors alone do not explain the complete range of differences between male and female behavior. To fully understand the source of gender differences, we also must consider the social environment, as we do next.

THE SOCIAL ENVIRONMENT

Starting from the moment of birth, with blue blankets for boys and pink ones for girls, most parents and other adults provide environments that differ in important respects according to gender. For example, boys and girls are given different kinds of toys, and—until protests recently brought the practice to an end—items in the largest toy store chain in the United States were laid out according to the gender appropriateness of particular toys (Bannon, 2000; Wood, Desmarais, & Gugula, 2002; see Figure 5).

Parents interact with their children differently, depending on their sex. Fathers play more roughly with their infant sons than with their infant daughters. Middle-class mothers tend to talk more to their daughters than to their sons. It is clear that adults frequently treat children differently on the basis of gender (McHale, Crouter, & Tucker, 1999; Tenenbaum & Leaper, 2002).

Such differences in behavior, and there are many more, produce different socialization experiences for men and women. *Socialization* is the process by which an individual learns the rules and norms of appropriate behavior. In this case, it refers to learning what society considers appropriate behavior for men and women. According to the processes of social learning theory, boys and girls are taught, and rewarded for performing, the socially perceived appropriate behaviors for men and for women, respectively (Archer & Lloyd, 2002; Liben & Bigler, 2002).

Boy's World
- Action figures
- Sports collectibles
- Radio remote-control cars
- Tonka trucks
- Boy's role play
- Walkie-talkies

Girl's World
- Barbie
- Baby dolls
- Doll houses
- Collectible horses
- Play kitchens
- Housekeeping toys
- Girl's dress-up
- Jewelry
- Cosmetics
- Bath and body

FIGURE 5 The placement of toys in toy stores according to gender was commonplace until protests forced a nationwide chain to discontinue the practice.

Children's reading books have traditionally portrayed girls in stereotypically nurturing roles using photos such as this, whereas boys have been given more physical and action-oriented roles. Do you think there are cultures in which this is not the case?

Gender schema: A mental framework that organizes and guides a child's understanding of information relevant to gender.

Androgynous: Characterized by gender roles that encompass psychological and behavioral traits thought typical of both sexes.

It is not just parents, of course, who provide socialization experiences for children. Society as a whole communicates clear messages to children as they are growing up. Children's reading books traditionally have portrayed girls in stereotypically nurturing roles, whereas boys have been given more physical and action-oriented roles. Television, too, acts as a particularly influential source of socialization. Men outnumber women on television, and women are often cast in such stereotypical roles as housewife, secretary, and mother. The potency of television as an agent of socialization is underscored by data indicating that the more television children watch, the more sexist they become (Furnham, Pallangyo, & Gunter, 2001; Turkel, 2002; Ogletree, Martinez, & Turner, 2004).

Our educational system also treats boys and girls differently. For example, in elementary school, boys are five times more likely to receive attention from classroom teachers than girls. Boys receive significantly more praise, criticism, and remedial help than girls do. They are also more likely to be praised for the intelligence shown in their work, whereas girls are more apt to be commended for their neatness. Even in college classes, male students receive more eye contact from their professors than female students, men are called upon more frequently in class, and men are more apt to receive extra help from their professors (AAUW, 1992; Sadker & Sadker, 1994; Einarsson & Granstroem, 2002; Koch, 2003).

According to Sandra Bem (1998), socialization produces a **gender schema,** a mental framework that organizes and guides a child's understanding of information relevant to gender. On the basis of their schemas for appropriate and inappropriate behavior for males and females, children begin to behave in ways that reflect society's gender roles. Hence, a child who goes to summer camp and is offered the opportunity to sew a costume may evaluate the activity not in terms of the intrinsic components of the process (such as the mechanics of using a needle and thread), but in terms of whether the activity is compatible with his or her gender schema (Bem, 1993, 1998; Martin, Ruble, & Szkrybalo, 2002).

Bem suggests that one way to decrease the likelihood that children will develop gender schemas is to encourage them to be androgynous. **Androgynous** individuals combine the psychological and behavioral characteristics thought typical of both sexes. Specifically, an androgynous individual may be forceful, assertive, and self-reliant (characteristics typically viewed by society as masculine) in certain circumstances and compassionate, gentle, and soft-spoken (characteristics typically thought of as feminine) when the situation calls for such behavior.

"Sometimes it would be helpful if you were a bit more androgynous."

Androgynous individuals tend to defy stereotypes by combining the psychological and behavioral characteristics thought typical of both sexes.

The concept of androgyny does not suggest that there should be no differences between men and women. Far from it: Androgyny proposes that differences should be based on choices, freely made, of the best *human* characteristics, not on an artificially restricted inventory of characteristics deemed by society to be appropriate only for men or only for women.

RECAP/EVALUATE/RETHINK

RECAP

What are the major differences between male and female gender roles?

- Gender is the perception of being male or female. Gender roles are the expectations, defined by society, of what is appropriate behavior for men and women. When gender roles reflect favoritism toward one sex, they lead to stereotyping and produce sexism. (pp. 357–358)
- The gender-role stereotype for men suggests that they are endowed with competence-related traits, whereas women are seen in terms of their capacity for warmth and expressiveness. Actual sex differences are much less clear, and of smaller magnitude, than the stereotypes would suggest. The differences that do exist are produced by a combination of biological and environmental factors. (p. 358)

- Biological causes of sex difference are reflected by evidence suggesting a possible difference in brain structure and functioning between men and women and may be associated with differential exposure to hormones before birth. (p. 364)
- An evolutionary approach explains gender differences in terms of different male-female concerns regarding the inheritance of genes and the need for child rearing, but this approach is highly controversial. (pp. 364–365)
- Socialization experiences produce gender schemas, mental frameworks that organize and guide a child's understanding of information relevant to gender. (p. 366)

EVALUATE

1. _____ are sets of societal expectations about what is appropriate behavior for men and women.
2. Gender stereotypes seem to be much less prevalent today than they were several decades ago. True or false?

3. Which of the following statements about male-female differences in aggression is true?
   a. Males are physically more aggressive than females only during childhood.
   b. Male-female differences in aggression first become evident during adolescence.
   c. Males are more aggressive than females throughout the life span.
   d. Females and males feel equally anxious about their aggressive acts.

4. _____ are frameworks that organize understanding of gender-specific information.

RETHINK

1. The U.S. Congress has enacted laws prohibiting women in the armed forces from participating directly in combat in the interest of keeping them safe. Do you think such laws are protective or sexist? How might this be an an example of "benevolent sexism"?

2. *From the perspective of a business executive:* Evidence shows that sexism in the workplace is widespread. If you wanted to end sexism in organizational settings, can you think of ways to narrow the gap between men and women in terms of occupations and salary?

Answers to Evaluate Questions

1. gender roles; 2. false; they are still prevalent; 3. c; 4. gender schemas

KEY TERMS

gender p. 357
gender roles p. 357

sexism p. 358

gender schema p. 366

androgynous p. 366

Understanding Human Sexual Response: The Facts of Life

When I started "tuning out," teachers thought I was sick—physically sick that is. They kept sending me to the school nurse to have my temperature taken. If I'd told them I was carrying on with Jennifer Lopez in their classes, while supposedly learning my Caesar and my Latin vocabulary, they'd have thought I was—well, delirious. I was! (based on Coles & Stokes, 1985, pp. 18–19).

Not everyone's sexual fantasies are as consuming as those reported by this teenage boy. Yet sex is an important consideration in most people's lives, for although the physical aspects of human sex are not all that different from those of other species, the meaning, values, and feelings that humans place on sexual behavior elevate it to a special plane. To fully appreciate this difference, however, it is necessary to understand the basic biology underlying sexual responses.

The Basic Biology of Sexual Behavior

Anyone who has seen two dogs mating knows that sexual behavior has a biological basis. Their sexual behavior appears to occur naturally, without much prompting on the part of others. A number of genetically controlled factors influence the sexual behavior of nonhuman animals. For instance, animal behavior is affected by the presence of certain hormones in the blood. Moreover, female animals are receptive to sexual advances only during certain relatively limited periods of the year.

Human sexual behavior, by comparison, is more complicated, although the underlying biology is not all that different from that of related species. In males, for example, the *testes* begin to secrete **androgens,** male sex hormones, at puberty. (See Figure 1 for the basic anatomy of the male and female **genitals,** or sex organs.) Not only do androgens produce secondary sex characteristics, such as the growth of body hair and a deepening of the voice, they also increase the sex drive. Because the level of androgen production by the testes is fairly constant, men are capable of (and interested in) sexual activities without any regard to biological cycles. Given the proper stimuli leading to arousal, male sexual behavior can occur (Goldstein, 2000).

Women show a different pattern. When they reach maturity at puberty, the two *ovaries* begin to produce **estrogens** and **progesterone,** female sex hormones. However, those hormones are not produced consistently; instead, their production follows a cyclical pattern. The greatest output occurs during **ovulation,** when an egg is released from the ovaries, making the chances of fertilization by a sperm cell highest. While in nonhumans the period around ovulation is the only time the female is receptive to sex, people are different. Although there are variations in reported sex drive, women are receptive to sex throughout their cycles.

In addition, some evidence suggests that males have a stronger sex drive than females, although the difference may be the result of society's discouragement of female sexuality rather than of innate differences between men and women. It is clear that men think about sex more than women: while 54 percent of men report thinking about sex every day, only 19 percent of women report thinking about it on a daily basis (Baumeister & Twenge, 2002; Peplau, 2003; Mendelsohn & Rosano, 2003; Gangestad et al., 2004).

Key Concept

Why, and under what circumstances, do we become sexually aroused?

Androgens: Male sex hormones secreted by the testes.

Genitals: The male and female sex organs.

Estrogens: Class of female sex hormones.

Progesterone: A female sex hormone secreted by the ovaries.

Ovulation: The point at which an egg is released from the ovaries.

FIGURE 1 Cutaway side views of the female and male sex organs.

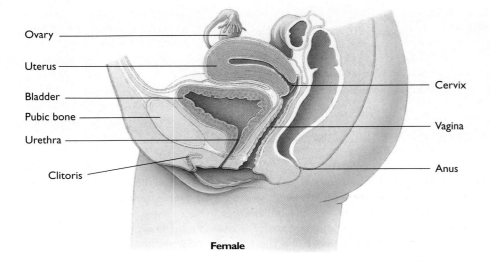

Female

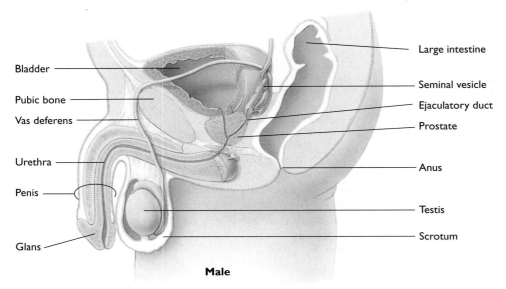

Male

Though biological factors "prime" people for sex, it takes more than hormones to motivate and produce sexual behavior (McClintock & Herdt, 1996). In animals the presence of a partner who provides arousing stimuli leads to sexual activity. Humans are considerably more versatile; not only other people but nearly any object, sight, smell, sound, or other stimulus can lead to sexual excitement. Because of prior associations, then, people may be turned on sexually by the smell of Chanel No. 5 or Brut or the sound of a favorite song hummed softly in their ears. The reaction to a specific, potentially arousing stimulus, as we shall see, is highly individual—what turns one person on may do just the opposite for another (Benson, 2003).

Psychological Aspects of Sexual Excitement: What Turns People On?

If you were to argue that the major human sex organ is the brain, in a sense you would be right. Much of what is considered sexually arousing in our society has little or nothing to do with our genitals, but instead is related to external stimuli that, through a process of learning, have come to be labeled as erotic, or sexually stimulating.

For example, there are no areas of the body that *automatically* produce sexual arousal when touched. Areas of the body, called **erogenous zones,** that have an unusually rich array of nerve receptors are particularly sensitive not just to sexual touch but to any kind of touch. When a physician touches a breast or a penis, the information sent to the brain by the nerve cells is essentially the same as that sent when a sexual partner touches that spot. What differs is the interpretation given to the touch. Sexual arousal is likely only when a certain part of the body is touched in what people define as a sexual manner and when a person is receptive to sexual activity (Gagnon, 1977; Goldstein, 2000).

Although people can learn to respond sexually to almost any stimulus, there is a good deal of agreement within a society or culture about what usually represents an erotic stimulus. In many Western societies breast size is often the standard by which female appeal is measured, but in many other cultures breast size is irrelevant (Rothblum, 1990).

Sexual fantasies also play an important role in producing sexual arousal. Not only do people have fantasies of a sexual nature during their everyday activities, about 60 percent of all people have fantasies during sexual intercourse. Interestingly, such fantasies often include having sex with someone other than one's partner of the moment (Hicks & Leitenberg, 2001; Trudel, 2002).

Men's and women's fantasies differ little from each other in terms of content or quantity, although men seem to fantasize about sex more than women do (Jones & Barlow, 1990; Hsu et al., 1994). As you can see in Figure 2 , thoughts of being sexually irresistible and of engaging in oral-genital sex are most common for both sexes. It is important to note that fantasies do not represent an actual desire for their fulfillment in the real world. Thus, we should not assume from data about female fantasies that women want to be sexually overpowered or assume from data about male fantasies that every male is desirous of forcing sexual overtures on a submissive victim. (Try the PsychInteractive exercise to get a deeper understanding of sexual arousal.)

The Phases of Sexual Response: The Ups and Downs of Sex

Although the kinds of stimuli that produce sexual arousal are to some degree unique to each individual, there are some basic aspects of sexual responsiveness that we all share. According to pioneering work done by William Masters and Virginia Johnson (1966), who studied sexual behavior in carefully controlled laboratory settings, sexual responses follow a regular pattern consisting of four phases: excitement, plateau, orgasm, and resolution. Although other researchers argue that sexual responses proceed somewhat differently (e.g., Kaplan, 1974; Zilbergeld & Ellison, 1980), Masters and Johnson's research is the most widely accepted account of what happens when people become sexually excited (Masters & Johnson, 1994).

In the *excitement phase,* which can last from just a few minutes to over an hour, an arousing stimulus begins a sequence that prepares the genitals for sexual intercourse. In the male, the *penis* becomes erect when blood flows into it; in the female, the *clitoris* swells because of an increase in the blood supply to that area, and the *vagina* becomes lubricated. Women may also experience a "sex flush," a red rash that typically spreads over the chest and throat.

Next comes the **plateau phase,** the body's preparation for orgasm. During this stage, the maximum level of sexual arousal is attained as the penis and clitoris swell with blood. Women's breasts and vaginas expand, heartbeat and blood pressure rise, and breathing rate increases. Muscle tension becomes greater as the body prepares itself for the next stage, orgasm. Although it is difficult to explain the sensation of **orgasm** beyond saying that it is an intense, highly pleasurable experience, the biological events that accompany the feeling are fairly straightforward. When the orgasm

Erogenous zones: Areas of the body that are particularly sensitive because of the presence of an unusually rich array of nerve receptors.

www.mhhe.com/feldmanup8
PsychInteractive Online

Sexual Response

Plateau phase: The period in which the maximum level of arousal is attained, the penis and clitoris swell with blood, and the body prepares for orgasm.

Orgasm: The peak of sexual excitement, during which rhythmic muscular contractions occur in the genitals.

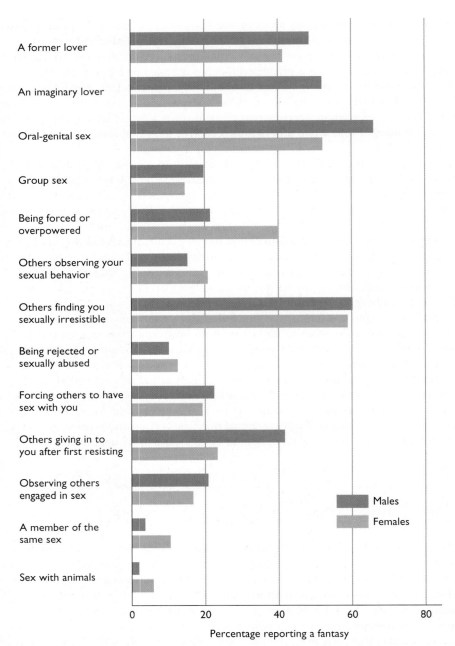

A former lover

An imaginary lover

Oral-genital sex

Group sex

Being forced or overpowered

Others observing your sexual behavior

Others finding you sexually irresistible

Being rejected or sexually abused

Forcing others to have sex with you

Others giving in to you after first resisting

Observing others engaged in sex

A member of the same sex

Sex with animals

Males
Females

0   20   40   60   80

Percentage reporting a fantasy

FIGURE 2 The kinds of fantasies that men and women have during sexual intercourse are relatively similar (Sue, 1979). Why do you think this is true, and do you think the fantasies are similar in non-Western cultures?

stage is reached, rhythmic muscular contractions occur in the genitals every eight-tenths of a second. In the male, the contractions expel *semen*, a fluid containing sperm, from the penis—a process known as *ejaculation*. For women and men, breathing and heart rates reach their maximum.

Although we can't be sure, the subjective experience of orgasm seems identical for males and females despite the differences in the organs that are involved. In one experiment, a group of men and women wrote down their descriptions of how an orgasm felt to them. Those descriptions were given to a group of experts, who were asked to identify the sex of each writer. The results showed that the experts were correct at

What does it feel like to have an orgasm? The following ten descriptions were written by men and women in an introductory psychology class. As you read through them, see if you can tell which were written by men and which by women.

1. Your heart pounds more than 100 miles per hour, your body tenses up, you feel an overwhelming sensation of pleasure and joy.

2. An orgasm feels like blood pulsating through my body, rushing essentially to the genital area, a surge of contraction-like waves paired with a rapidly beating heart and strong pulse; my heart feels like someone is squeezing it, painful, and I have trouble breathing deeply.

3. Feels like being plugged into an electrical socket, but pleasurable rather than painful. Nearly indescribable!

4. It's as if every muscle in your body is being charged with intense electricity; your mind is incapable of thinking about anything, and you become totally incoherent. All the nerves in your body tremble, and you have trouble breathing, and get the urge to scream, or yell, or do something wild.

5. An orgasm to me is like the sensations of hot and cold coming together in one throbbing, thrusting, prolonged moment. It is the ultimate excitement of my passion.

6. Like exquisite torture. The sudden release of all the primal urges in the body. The gladness and yet the sadness that the fun is over.

7. An orgasm is that point when you don't care if anyone hears you screaming out your pleasures of ecstasy.

8. It's like all the cells in my brain popping at once and whirling around, while all the muscles in my body heave upward till I reach ultimate sensory bliss.

9. Tingling, throbbing, pleasurable feeling. Breathing is very fast and not rhythmic. Tend to hold my breath at peak. Possible shaking afterward and tightening/contraction of muscles.

10. An orgasm is a heavenly experience. It can be compared to nothing.

If you thought that men and women experience orgasm differently, you may be surprised at how hard it is to tell the difference from these descriptions. The correct answers: 1. Male 2. Female 3. Male 4. Female 5. Female 6. Male 7. Female 8. Male 9. Female 10. Male

FIGURE 3 There appears to be little difference between men and women when it comes to their subjective experience of orgasm. The photo, from the movie *When Harry Met Sally,* illustrates the actress Meg Ryan's portrayal of an orgasm.

no better than chance levels, suggesting that there was little means to distinguish the descriptions of orgasms on the basis of gender (Vance & Wagner, 1976). To get a sense of how people describe orgasms, see Figure 3.

After orgasm, people move into the last stage of sexual arousal, the **resolution stage.** The body returns to its resting state, reversing the changes brought about by arousal. The genitals resume their unaroused size and shape, and blood pressure, breathing, and heart rate return to normal.

Male and female responses differ significantly during the resolution stage; these differences are depicted in Figure 4. Women are able to cycle back to the orgasm phase and experience repeated orgasms. Ultimately, of course, females enter the final resolution stage, and then they return to their prestimulation state. In contrast, it generally is thought that men enter a refractory period during the resolution stage. During the **refractory period,** men are unable to develop an erection and therefore are unable to have another orgasm and ejaculate. The refractory period may last from a few minutes to several hours, although in the elderly it may continue for several days (Goldstein, 2000).

It's not only women's and men's genitals that behave differently during sex—so do their brains. Imaging studies are beginning to show that the brains of women and men react quite distinctly during sexual arousal. For instance, in one experiment,

Resolution stage: The interval after orgasm in which the body returns to its unaroused state, reversing the changes brought about by arousal.

Refractory period: A temporary period that follows the resolution stage and during which the male cannot develop an erection again.

a. Male pattern

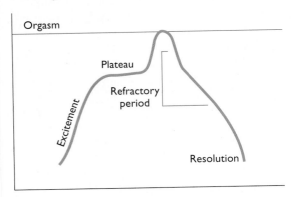

b. Female patterns

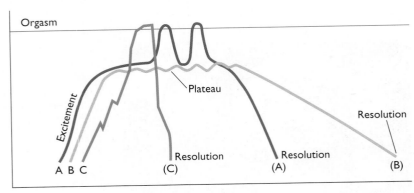

FIGURE 4 A four-stage model of the sexual response cycle for males and females based on the findings of Masters and Johnson (1966). Note how the male pattern (a) includes a refractory period. Part (b) shows three possible female patterns. In A, the pattern is closest to the male cycle, except that the woman has two orgasms in a row. In B, there is no orgasm, whereas in C orgasm is reached quickly and the woman rapidly returns to an unaroused state. (Source: After Masters & Johnson, 1966.)

heterosexual men and women watched arousing erotic photos of the other sex while having an fMRI (functional Magnetic Resonance Image) made of the brain (admittedly not the most romantic set of circumstances). Although both men and women reported similar amounts of arousal, their brain told a different story. The amygdala, the seat of emotions in the brain, reacted much more vigorously in the men than women (Hamann, Hermann, & Nolan, 2004; see Figure 5).

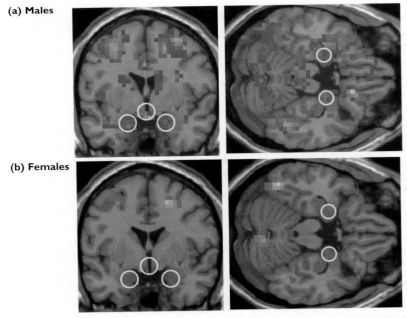

FIGURE 5 As shown in these two views of the brain, men (a) showed greater brain activity in the amygdala while viewing sexually exciting photos than women (b) viewing the same photos, even though men and women reported the same level of sexual arousal. The white circles indicate primary regions of interest hypothesized to show the greatest male-female activation differences. (Source: Hamann, Hermann, & Nolan, 2004, Figure 2e, f.)

Waris Dirie was just an innocent, unknowing child of 5 when she begged her mother to let her be circumcised like virtually all females in Somalia. "When you've been told over and over that, until this happens, you're filthy and no man would ever marry you, you believe what everybody says," Dirie explains. "I just wanted to be like the other girls."

Exploring DIVERSITY

Female Circumcision: A Celebration of Culture—or Genital Mutilation?

Months later her awful wish came true. As her mother held down the crying, blindfolded Diri, a gypsy performed the circumcision using a dirty, dull razor and no anesthetic. She sewed the ragged wound with thorns and thread. "It's not a pain you forget," says Dirie, in a whisper. She was left with only a tiny opening, and urinating became torture. Later, menstruation was so unbearable that Dirie routinely fainted (Cheakalos & Heyn, 1998, p. 149).

The operation in question—female circumcision—represents one of the most controversial procedures relating to sex throughout the world. In such an operation, the clitoris is removed, resulting in permanent inability to experience sexual pleasure.

Some 80 million women, living mostly in Africa and Asia, have undergone female circumcision. More than 90 percent of Nigerian women have been circumcised during childhood, and more than 90 percent intend to circumcise their daughters. Furthermore, in some cases, more extensive surgery is carried out, in which additional parts of the female genitals are removed or are sewn together with catgut or thorns (French, 1997; Obermeyer, 2001; Lacey, 2002).

Those who practice female circumcision say it upholds an ancient societal tradition and is no different from other cultural customs. Its purpose, they say, is to preserve virginity before marriage, keep women faithful to their husbands after marriage, and enhance a woman's beauty. Furthermore, proponents believe that it differs little from the common Western practice of male circumcision, in which the foreskin of the penis is surgically removed soon after birth.

Critics, in contrast, argue that female circumcision is nothing less than female mutilation. Not only does the practice permanently eliminate sexual pleasure, it can also lead to constant pain and infection, depending on the nature of the surgery. In fact, because the procedure is traditionally conducted in a ritualistic fashion without an anesthetic, using a razor blade, sawtooth knife, or glass, the circumcision itself can be physically traumatic (Dugger, 1996).

The procedure raises some difficult issues, which have been brought to light in various court cases. For instance, a Nigerian immigrant, living temporarily in the United States, went to court to argue that she should be allowed to remain permanently. Her plea: If she and her young daughters were sent back to Nigeria, her daughters would face circumcision upon their return. The court agreed and permitted her to stay indefinitely (Gregory, 1994; Dugger, 1996).

In reaction to the controversy about female circumcision, Congress recently passed laws that make the practice illegal in the United States. Still, some argue that female circumcision is a valued cultural custom, and that no one, particularly someone judging from the perspective of another culture, should prevent people from carrying out the customs they think are important. In addition, critics point to the practice of *male* circumcision, in which the foreskin of the penis is surgically removed. They suggest that male circumcision provides few significant health benefits, and that the decision to have male infants circumcised—an accepted practice in U.S. society—rests on religious, social, and cultural traditions (American Academy of Pediatrics, 1999b; Boyle et al., 2002).

RECAP/EVALUATE/RETHINK

RECAP

Why, and under what circumstances, do we become sexually aroused?

- Although biological factors, such as the presence of androgens (male sex hormones) and estrogens and progesterone (female sex hormones), prime people for sex, almost any kind of stimulus can produce sexual arousal, depending on a person's prior experience. (pp. 369-370)
- People's sexual responses follow a regular pattern consisting of four phases: excitement, plateau, orgasm, and resolution. (pp. 371-373)

EVALUATE

1. Match the phase of sexual arousal with its characteristics
   1. Excitement phase
   2. Plateau phase
   3. Orgasm phase
   4. Resolution phase
   a. Maximum level of sexual arousal
   b. Erection and lubrication
   c. Rhythmic muscular contractions and ejaculation
   d. Return of body to resting state
2. Men are generally thought to enter a _____ period after sex, in which orgasm is impossible for a period of time.

3. Whereas men are interested in sexual activity regardless of their biological cycles, women are truly receptive to sex only during ovulation, when the production of their sex hormones is greatest. True or false?
4. Men's and women's sexual fantasies are essentially similar to each other. True or false?

RETHINK

1. Why do you think humans differ from other species in their year-round receptivity to sex and in the number and variety of stimuli they perceive as sexual? What evolutionary purpose might this difference serve in humans?
2. *From the perspective of a sex counselor:* How do people learn to be aroused by the stimuli that their society considers erotic? When do they learn this, and where does the message come from?

Answers to Evaluate Questions

1. 1-b, 2-a, 3-c, 4-d; 2. refractory; 3. false; women are receptive through-out their cycle; 4. true

KEY TERMS

androgens p. 369
genitals p. 369
estrogens p. 369

progesterone p. 369
ovulation p. 369
erogenous zones p. 371

plateau phase p. 371
orgasm p. 371
resolution stage p. 373

refractory period p. 373

The Diversity of Sexual Behavior

A boy who practices this habit can never be the best that Nature intended him to be. His wits are not so sharp. His memory is not so good. His power of fixing his attention on whatever he is doing is lessened. . . . A boy like this is a poor thing to look at. . . . [He is] untrustworthy, unreliable, untruthful, and probably even dishonest (Schofield & Vaughan-Jackson, 1913, pp. 30–42).

The cause of this condition: masturbation—at least according to the authors of the early 1900s sex manual *What Every Boy Should Know*. The consequences of masturbation for women were considered no less severe. In the words of one nineteenth-century physician, "There is hardly an end to the diseases caused by masturbation: dyspepsia, spinal disease, headache, epilepsy, various kinds of fits . . . impaired eyesight, palpitation of the heart, pain in the side and bleeding at the lungs, spasm of the heart, and sometimes sudden death" (Gregory, 1856).

Such views may seem bizarre and far-fetched to you, as they do to contemporary experts on human sexual behavior. At one time, however, they were considered perfectly sound by quite reasonable people. Indeed, trivia buffs might be interested to learn that corn flakes owe their invention to a nineteenth-century physician, J. W. Kellogg, who believed that because the enjoyment of tasty food provoked sexual excitation, an alternative of "unstimulating" grains was needed.

Clearly, sex and sex-related behavior are influenced by expectations, attitudes, beliefs, and the state of medical and biological knowledge in a given period. Today we know that sexual behavior may take diverse forms, and much of what was once seen as "unnatural" and "lewd" is often more likely to be accepted in contemporary society. Similarly, sexual behavior that is commonplace in one culture is seen as appalling in others. For instance, seven societies are known in which kissing never occurs (Ford & Beach, 1951; Mason, 1995). In sum, distinctions between normal and abnormal sexual behavior are not easy to draw. That certainly hasn't prevented people from trying to draw them, however.

Key Concepts

What is "normal" sexual behavior?

How do most people behave sexually?

Times change: The veiled sexuality of Victorian-era paintings has given way to a more frank acknowledgment of sexual behavior.

Approaches to Sexual Normality

One approach is to define abnormal sexual behavior in terms of deviation from the average, or typical, behavior. To determine abnormality, we simply observe what behaviors are rare and uncommon in a society and label those deviations from the norm as abnormal.

The difficulty with such an approach, however, is that some behaviors that are statistically unusual hardly seem worthy of concern. Even though most people have sexual intercourse in the bedroom, does the fact that someone prefers sex in the dining room imply abnormality? If some people prefer portly sexual partners, are they abnormal in a society that holds slimness in high regard? Clearly, the answer to both of these questions is no, and so an approach that defines sexual abnormality in terms of deviation from the average is inappropriate. (The same difficulties are encountered in considering definitions of psychological abnormality.)

An alternative approach would be to compare sexual behavior against some standard or ideal. But here, again, there is a problem: What standard should we use? Some might suggest philosophy, some might turn to the Bible, and some might even consider psychology the ultimate determinant. The trouble is that none of these potential sources of standards is universally acceptable. Furthermore, since standards change radically with shifts in societal attitudes and new knowledge, such an approach is undesirable. For instance, forty years ago, the American Psychiatric Association labeled homosexuality a mental illness. However, as evidence to the contrary accumulated, in 1973 the organization determined that homosexuality should no longer be considered a mental disorder. Obviously the behavior had not changed. Only the label placed on it by the psychiatric profession had been modified.

In light of the difficulties with other approaches, probably the most reasonable definition of sexual normality is one that considers the psychological consequences of the behavior. In this approach, sexual behavior is considered abnormal if it produces a sense of distress, anxiety, or guilt—or if it is harmful to some other person. According to this view, then, sexual behaviors can be viewed as abnormal only when they have a negative impact on a person's sense of well-being or if they hurt someone else.

It is important to recognize that what is seen as normal and what is seen as abnormal sexual behavior are dictated primarily by societal values, and that there have

Same-sex marriages, already legal in some countries, represent a significant social issue dividing people in the United States.

been dramatic shifts from one generation to another in definitions of what constitutes appropriate sexual behavior. People can and should make their own personal value judgments about what is appropriate in their own sex lives, but there are few universally accepted absolute rights and wrongs.

Surveying Sexual Behavior: What's Happening Behind Closed Doors?

For most of recorded history, the vast variety of sexual practices remained shrouded in ignorance. However, in the late 1930s, biologist Alfred Kinsey launched a series of surveys on the sexual behavior of people in the United States. The result was the first comprehensive attempt to see what people were actually doing sexually, highlighted by the publication of Kinsey's landmark volumes *Sexual Behavior in the Human Male* (Kinsey, Pomeroy, & Martin, 1948) and *Sexual Behavior in the Human Female* (Kinsey et al., 1953).

Kinsey's efforts represented the first major systematic approach to learning about human sexual behavior. Kinsey and his colleagues interviewed tens of thousands of individuals, and the interview techniques they devised are still regarded as exemplary because of their ability to elicit sensitive information without causing embarrassment.

On the other hand, Kinsey's samples reflected an overrepresentation of college students, young people, well-educated individuals, urban dwellers, and people living in Indiana and the northeast (Kirby, 1977). Furthermore, as with all surveys involving volunteer participants, it is unclear how representative his data are of people who refused to participate in the study. Similarly, because no survey observes behavior directly, it is difficult to assess how accurately people's descriptions of what they do in private match their actual sexual practices.

Kinsey's work set the stage for later surveys, although because of political reasons (the use of government funding for sex surveys is controversial), surprisingly few comprehensive large-scale, representative surveys—either in the United States or in other countries—have been carried out since Kinsey did his initial work (Pinkerton et al., 2003). However, by examining the common results gleaned from different samples of subjects, we now have a reasonably complete picture of contemporary sexual practices—to which we turn next.

Masturbation: Solitary Sex

If you listened to physicians seventy-five years ago, you would have been told that **masturbation,** sexual self-stimulation, often using the hand to rub the genitals, would lead to a wide variety of physical and mental disorders, ranging from hairy palms to insanity. If those physicians had been correct, however, most of us would be wearing gloves to hide the sight of our hair-covered palms—for masturbation is one of the most frequently practiced sexual activities. Some 94 percent of all males and 63 percent of all females have masturbated at least once, and among college students, the frequency ranges from "never" to "several times a day" (Hunt, 1974; Michael et al., 1994; Laqueur, 2003).

Men and women typically begin to masturbate for the first time at different ages, as you can see in Figure 1. Furthermore, men masturbate considerably more often than women, although there are differences in frequency according to age. Male masturbation is most common in the early teens and then declines, whereas females both begin and reach a maximum frequency later. There are also some racial differences: African American men and women masturbate less than whites do (Oliver & Hyde, 1993; Pinkerton et al., 2002).

Although masturbation is often considered an activity to engage in only if no other sexual outlets are available, this view bears little relationship to reality. Close

Masturbation: Sexual self-stimulation.

FIGURE 1 The age at which a sample of college students first masturbated. The percentages are based on only those people who had experience with masturbation. (Source: Arafat & Cotton, 1974.)

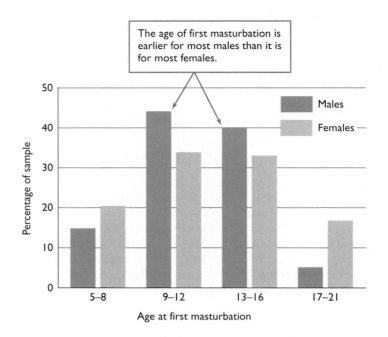

The age of first masturbation is earlier for most males than it is for most females.

to three-quarters of married men (age 20 to 40) report masturbating an average of twenty-four times a year, and 68 percent of the married women in the same age group masturbate an average of ten times a year (Hunt, 1974; Michael et al., 1994).

Despite the high incidence of masturbation, attitudes toward it still reflect some of the negative views of yesteryear. For instance, one survey found that around 10 percent of people who masturbated experienced feelings of guilt, and 5 percent of the males and 1 percent of the females considered their behavior perverted (Arafat & Cotton, 1974). Despite these negative attitudes, however, most experts on sex view masturbation as a healthy and legitimate—and harmless—sexual activity. In addition, masturbation is seen as providing a means of learning about one's own sexuality and a way of discovering changes in one's body such as the emergence of precancerous lumps (Coleman, 2002).

Heterosexuality

People often believe that the first time they have sexual intercourse they have achieved one of life's major milestones. However, **heterosexuality,** sexual attraction and behavior directed to the other sex, consists of far more than male-female intercourse. Kissing, petting, caressing, massaging, and other forms of sex play are all components of heterosexual behavior. Still, the focus of sex researchers has been on the act of intercourse, particularly in terms of its first occurrence and its frequency.

Heterosexuality: Sexual attraction and behavior directed to the other sex.

PREMARITAL SEX

Until fairly recently, premarital sexual intercourse, at least for women, was considered one of the major taboos in our society. Traditionally, women have been warned by society that "nice girls don't do it"; men have been told that although premarital sex is okay for them, they should make sure they marry virgins. This view that premarital sex is permissible for males but not for females is called the **double standard.**

Although as recently as the 1960s the majority of adult Americans believed that premarital sex was always wrong, since that time there has been a dramatic change in public opinion. For example, as you can see in Figure 2, the percentage of middle-age people who say sex before marriage is "not wrong at all" has increased considerably,

Double standard: The view that premarital sex is permissible for males but not for females.

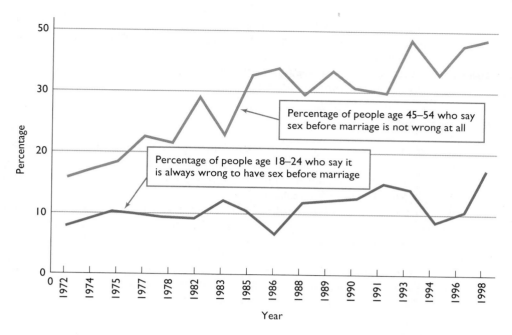

and overall 60 percent of Americans say premarital sex is okay. More than half say that living together before marriage is morally acceptable (C&F Report, 2001; Thornton & Young-DeMarco, 2001).

Changes in attitudes toward premarital sex were matched by changes in actual rates of premarital sexual activity. For instance, the most recent figures show that just over one-half of women between the ages of 15 and 19 have had premarital sexual intercourse. These figures are close to double the number of women in the same age range who reported having intercourse in 1970. Clearly, the trend over the last several decades has been toward more women engaging in premarital sexual activity (Jones, Darroch, & Singh, 2005).

Males, too, have shown an increase in the incidence of premarital sexual intercourse, although the increase has not been as dramatic as it has been for females—probably because the rates for males were higher to begin with. For instance, the first surveys of premarital intercourse carried out in the 1940s showed an incidence of 84 percent across males of all ages; recent figures put the figure at closer to 95 percent. Moreover, the average age of males' first sexual experience has been declining steadily. Almost half of males have had sexual intercourse by the age of 18, and by the time they reach age 20, 88 percent have had intercourse. There also are race and ethnicity differences: African Americans tend to have sex for the first time earlier than do Puerto Ricans, who have sex earlier than whites do. Racial and ethnic differences probably reflect differences in socioeconomic opportunities and family structure (Arena, 1984; CDC, 1992; Singh et al., 2000; Hyde, DeLamater, & Byers 2006).

What may be most interesting about the patterns of premarital sex is that they show a convergence of male and female attitudes and behavior. But is the change sufficient to signal an end to the double standard?

Probably. For many people, particularly younger individuals, the double standard has been succeeded by a new view: *permissiveness with affection*. According to those holding this view, premarital intercourse is permissible for both men and women if it occurs within a long-term, committed, or loving relationship (DeGaton, Weed, & Jensen, 1996; Hyde, 2006).

Still, the double standard has not disappeared completely. Where differing standards remain, the attitudes are almost always more lenient toward the male than toward the female (Sprecher & Hatfield, 1996).

Furthermore, there are substantial cultural differences regarding the incidence and acceptability of premarital intercourse. For instance, the proportions of male teen-

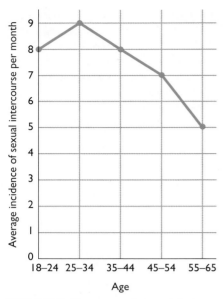

FIGURE 3 Once a couple is past their midthirties, the average number of times per month they have sexual intercourse declines (Clements, 1994). Why do older couples have intercourse less frequently than do younger ones?

Extramarital sex: Sexual activity between a married person and someone who is not his or her spouse.

Homosexuals: Persons who are sexually attracted to members of their own sex.

Bisexuals: Persons who are sexually attracted to people of the same sex and the other sex.

agers who have intercourse before the seventeenth birthday in Jamaica, the United States, and Brazil are about 10 times the level reported in the Philippines. And in some cultures, such as those in sub-Saharan Africa, women become sexually active at an earlier age than do men—although this may be due to the fact that they marry at a younger age than men do (Singh et al., 2000).

MARITAL SEX

To judge by the number of articles about sex in marriage, one would think that sexual behavior was the number one standard by which marital bliss is measured. Married couples are often concerned that they are having too little sex, too much sex, or the wrong kind of sex (Harvey & Wenzel, 2004).

Although there are many different dimensions along which sex in marriage is measured, one is certainly the frequency of sexual intercourse. What is typical? As with most other types of sexual activities, there is no easy answer to the question, because there are such wide variations in patterns between individuals. We do know that 43 percent of married couples have sexual intercourse a few times a month and 36 percent of couples have it two or three times a week. With increasing age and length of marriage, the frequency of intercourse declines. Still, sex continues into late adulthood, with almost half of people reporting that they engage in sexual activity at least once a month and that its quality is high (Michael et al., 1994; see Figure 3).

Although early research found **extramarital sex** to be widespread, the current reality appears to be otherwise. According to surveys, 85 percent of married women and more than 75 percent of married men are faithful to their spouses. Furthermore, the median number of sex partners, inside and outside of marriage, since the age of 18 for men was six, and for women two. Accompanying these numbers is a high, consistent degree of disapproval of extramarital sex, with nine of ten people saying that it is "always" or "almost always" wrong (Michael et al., 1994; Calmes, 1998; Duncombe et al., 2004).

Homosexuality and Bisexuality

Homosexuals are sexually attracted to members of their own sex, whereas **bisexuals** are sexually attracted to people of the same sex and the other sex. Many male homosexuals prefer the term *gay* and female homosexuals the label *lesbian,* because they refer to a broader array of attitudes and lifestyles than the term *homosexual,* which focuses on the sexual act.

The number of people who choose same-sex sexual partners at one time or another is considerable. Estimates suggest that around 20 to 25 percent of males and about 15 percent of females have had at least one gay or lesbian experience during adulthood. The exact number of people who identify themselves as exclusively homosexual has proved difficult to gauge, with some estimates as low as 1.1 percent and some as high as 10 percent. Most experts suggest that between 5 and 10 percent of both men and women are exclusively gay or lesbian during extended periods of their lives (Hunt, 1974; Sells, 1994; Firestein, 1996).

Although people often view homosexuality and heterosexuality as two completely distinct sexual orientations, the issue is not that simple. Pioneering sex researcher Alfred Kinsey acknowledged this when he considered sexual orientation along a scale or continuum, with "exclusively homosexual" at one end and "exclusively heterosexual" at the other. In the middle were people who showed both homosexual and heterosexual behavior (see Figure 4). Kinsey's approach suggests that sexual orientation is dependent on a person's sexual feelings and behaviors and romantic feelings (Weinberg, Williams, & Pryor, 1991).

What determines whether people become homosexual or heterosexual? Although there are a number of theories, none has proved completely satisfactory.

0	1	2	3	4	5	6
Exclusive heterosexual behavior	Primarily heterosexual, but incidents of homosexual behavior	Primarily heterosexual, but more than incidental homosexual behavior	Equal amounts of heterosexual and homo-sexual behavior	Primarily homosexual, but more than incidental heterosexual behavior	Primarily homosexual, but incidents of heterosexual behavior	Exclusively homosexual behavior

FIGURE 4 The Kinsey scale is designed to define the degree to which sexual orientation is heterosexual, homosexual, or bisexual. Although Kinsey saw people as falling along a continuum, most people believe that they belonged to a specific category. (Source: After Kinsey, Pomeroy, & Martin, 1948.)

Some explanations for sexual orientation are biological in nature, suggesting that there are genetic causes. Evidence for a genetic origin of sexual orientation comes from studies of identical twins, which have found that when one twin identified himself or herself as homosexual, the occurrence of homosexuality in the other twin was higher than it was in the general population. Such results occur even for twins who have been separated early in life and who therefore are not necessarily raised in similar social environments (Hamer et al., 1993; Turner, 1995; Kirk, Bailey, & Martin, 2000).

Hormones also may play a role in determining sexual orientation. For example, research shows that women exposed to DES, or diethylstilbestrol, before birth (their mothers took the drug to avoid miscarriage) were more likely to be homosexual or bisexual (Meyer-Bahlburg, 1997).

Some evidence suggests that differences in brain structures may be related to sexual orientation. For instance, the structure of the anterior hypothalamus, an area of the brain that governs sexual behavior, differs in male homosexuals and heterosexuals. Similarly, other research shows that, compared with heterosexual men or women, gay men have a larger anterior commissure, which is a bundle of neurons connecting the right and left hemispheres of the brain (LeVay, 1993; Byne, 1996).

However, research suggesting that biological causes are at the root of homosexuality is not conclusive because most findings are based on only small samples of individuals. Still, the possibility is real that some inherited or biological factor exists that predisposes people toward homosexuality, if certain environmental conditions are met (Veniegas, 2000; Teodorov et al., 2002; Rahman, Kumari, & Wilson, 2003). (For more on the possible genetic roots of sexual orientation, see the *Applying Psychology in the 21st Century* box.)

Extensive research has found that bisexuals and homosexuals enjoy the same overall degree of mental and physical health as heterosexuals.

Sexual Orientation: How Genes Matter

When the genetically altered fruit fly was released into the observation chamber, it did what these breeders par excellence tend to do. It pursued a waiting virgin female. It gently tapped the girl with its leg, played her a song (using wings as instruments) and, only then, dared to lick her—all part of standard fruit fly seduction (Rosenthal, 2005, p. A1).

Nothing surprising in all this—except for the fact that the fruit fly was a female, displaying the equivalent of insect homosexuality. To scientists watching the behavior of the genetically altered female fruit fly, her behavior was nothing short of astounding.

To arrive at these results, scientists inserted a singe male-type gene into female fruit flies. The introduction of the one gene was enough to alter a range of complex behaviors, all related to sexual orientation, in which the female flies displayed behavior similar to courting males (Demir & Dickson, 2005).

Analogously, insertion of the female variant of the gene into male fruit flies made them avidly pursue other males. The findings suggest that, at least in fruit flies, there is a single gene—which is called *fru*—operating as a kind of master sexual control over a complex range of behaviors relating to sexual orientation and mating behavior.

The existence of *fru* has been known for some time. *Fru* controls several dozen neurons that, if damaged, were known to disrupt sexual behavior. However, until this most recent research, investigators had no idea that inserting a variation of *fru* into a fly would result in the courtship behavior displayed by the other sex. According to researcher Barry Dickson, who conducted the research, "We have shown that a single gene in the fruit fly is sufficient to determine all aspects of the flies' sexual orientation and behavior. It's very surprising. What it tells us is that instinctive behaviors can be specified by genetic programs" (Rosenthal, 2005, p. A1).

What implications do the findings have for the determinants of sexual orientation in humans? Although the results are consistent with genetic explanations of homosexuality, humans are far more complex than fruit flies. Certainly, it is unlikely that a single gene is responsible for triggering sexual behavior or orientation in humans. Still, the results are intriguing, and they illustrate the importance of gaining a full understanding the neuroscience behind sexuality.

RETHINK

What relevance do you think this research has to our understanding of human gender differences in nonsexual behaviors such as academic performance? How might environmental influences interact with genetic factors to produce homosexuality in humans?

Little evidence suggests that sexual orientation is brought about by child-rearing practices or family dynamics. Although classic psychoanalytic theories argued that the nature of the parent-child relationship can produce homosexuality (e.g., Freud, 1922/1959), research evidence does not support such explanations (Isay, 1994; Roughton, 2002).

Another explanation for sexual orientation rests on learning theory (Masters & Johnson, 1979). According to this view, sexual orientation is learned through rewards and punishments in much the same way that we may learn to prefer swimming over tennis. For example, a young adolescent who had an unpleasant heterosexual experience might develop disagreeable associations with the other sex. If the same person had a rewarding, pleasant gay or lesbian experience, homosexuality might be incorporated into his or her sexual fantasies. If such fantasies are used during later sexual activities—such as masturbation—they may be positively reinforced through orgasm, and the association of homosexual behavior and sexual pleasure eventually may cause homosexuality to become the preferred form of sexual behavior.

Although the learning-theory explanation is plausible, several difficulties rule it out as a definitive explanation. Because our society tends to hold homosexuality in low esteem, one ought to expect that the punishments involved in homosexual behavior would outweigh the rewards attached to it. Furthermore, children growing up with a gay or lesbian parent are statistically unlikely to become homosexual, thus contradicting the notion that homosexual behavior may be learned from others (Victor & Fish, 1995; Golombok & Tasker, 1996; Tasker, 2005).

Because of the difficulty in finding a consistent explanation, we can't answer the question of what determines sexual orientation. It does seem unlikely that that any single factor orients a person toward homosexuality or heterosexuality. Instead, it seems reasonable to assume that a combination of biological and environmental factors is involved (Greene & Herek, 1994; Bem, 1996; Hyde, DeLamater & Byers 2006).

Although we don't know at this point exactly why people develop a particular sexual orientation, one thing is clear: There is no relationship between sexual orientation and psychological adjustment. Gays, lesbians, and bisexuals generally enjoy the same quality of mental and physical health that heterosexuals do, although the discrimination they experience may produce higher rates of some disorders, such as depression. Bisexuals and homosexuals also hold equivalent ranges and types of attitudes about themselves, independent of sexual orientation. For such reasons, the American Psychological Association and most other mental health organizations have endorsed efforts to reduce discrimination against gays and lesbians, such as revoking the ban against homosexuals in the military (Cochran, 2000; Perez, DeBord, & Bieschke, 2000; Morris, Waldo, & Rothblum, 2001). (Try the PsychInteractive exercise for more on attitudes regarding sexuality.)

"Frankly, I've repressed my sexuality so long I've actually forgotten what my orientation is."

Transsexualism

From the first day of kindergarten, Alyn Libman felt different. The other girls played with Barbies and dress-up games; Alyn wanted to climb trees. The big problem came at potty break, when Alyn headed for the boys' room—and the teacher stepped in the way. "I just said, 'Why?'" recalls Libman. "I didn't understand" (Fields-Meyer & Wihlborg, 2003, p. 109.)

Although born a female, Libman never felt like one. Now considering reconstructive surgery, Libman represents a category of sexuality not encompassed by heterosexuality, homosexuality, or bisexuality: transsexualism.

Transsexuals are people who believe they were born with the body of the other gender. In fundamental ways, transsexualism represents less a sexual difficulty than a gender issue involving one's sexual identity (Meyerowitz, 2004).

Transsexuals may seek sex-change operations in which their existing genitals are surgically removed and the genitals of the desired sex are fashioned. Several steps, including intensive counseling and hormone injections, along with living as a member of the desired sex for several years, precede surgery, which is, not surprisingly, highly complicated. The outcome, though, can be quite positive (Fields-Meyer & Wihlborg, 2003; O'Keefe & Fox, 2003; Stegerwald & Janson, 2003).

Transsexualism is part of a broader category known as transgenderism. The term *transgenderism* encompasses not only transsexuals but also people who view themselves as a third gender, transvestites (who dress in the clothes of the other gender), or others who believe that traditional male-female gender classifications inadequately characterize themselves (Prince, 2005; Hyde, DeLamater, & Byers, 2006).

www.mhhe.com/feldmanup8

PsychInteractive Online

Attitudes Toward Sexuality

RECAP/EVALUATE/RETHINK

RECAP

What is "normal" sexual behavior?

- There are a number of approaches to determining normality: deviation from the average, comparison of sexual behavior with some standard or ideal, and consideration of the psychological and physical consequences of the behavior to the person and to others. (p. 378)

How do most people behave sexually?

- The frequency of masturbation is high, particularly for males. Although increasingly liberal, attitudes toward masturbation have traditionally been negative even though no negative consequences have been detected. (pp. 379-380)
- Heterosexuality, or sexual attraction to members of the other sex, is the most common sexual orientation. (p. 380)
- The double standard by which premarital sex is thought to be more permissible for men than for women has

declined, particularly among young people. For many people, the double standard has been replaced by endorsement of "permissiveness with affection," the view that premarital intercourse is permissible if it occurs in the context of a loving and committed relationship. (pp. 380-381)

• The frequency of marital sex varies widely. However, younger couples tend to have sexual intercourse more frequently than older ones. In addition, most men and women do not engage in extramarital sex. (p. 382)

• Homosexuals are sexually attracted to members of their own sex; bisexuals are sexually attracted to people of the same sex and the other sex. No explanation for why people become homosexual has been confirmed; among the possibilities are genetic or biological factors, childhood and family influences, and prior learning experiences and conditioning. However, no relationship exists between sexual orientation and psychological adjustment. (p. 382-384)

EVALUATE

1. The work carried out by _____ in the 1930s was the first systematic study of sexual behavior ever undertaken.

KEY TERMS

masturbation p. 379	double standard p. 380	homosexuals p. 382
heterosexuality p. 380	extramarital sex p. 382	bisexuals p. 382

2. Although the incidence of masturbation among young adults is high, once men and women become involved in intimate relationships, they typically cease masturbating. True or false?

3. The increase in premarital sex in recent years has been greater for women than for men. True or false?

4. _____ refers to the view that premarital sex is acceptable within a loving, long-term relationship.

5. Research comparing homosexuals and heterosexuals clearly demonstrates that there is no difference in the level of adjustment or psychological functioning between the two groups. True or false?

RETHINK

1. What societal factors have led to a reduction in the double standard by which sexuality in men and women is regarded differently? Do you think the double standard has completely vanished?

2. *From the perspective of a public opinion surveyor:* In what ways might a sample of respondents to a survey about sexual practices be biased? How might bias in such a survey be reduced?

Answers to Evaluate Questions

1. Kinsey; 2. false; even people in married relationships show a continued incidence of masturbation; 3. true; 4. permissiveness with affection; 5. true

Sexual Difficulties: When Sex Goes Wrong

It was a warm Friday evening in autumn, the kind of night that makes a college campus seem a magical place, full of excitement and promise. Exhilarated by her new independence, Casey Letvin, like hundreds of other recently arrived University of Colorado freshmen, was looking for a party. The students milling about the streets of Boulder seemed convivial, and Casey and her roommate thought nothing of stopping four upperclassmen to ask where the parties were. . . . The four young men offered to take them to a nearby off-campus house where about twenty students were gathered. But approximately four hours later, the evening ended in a brutal breach of trust. At 12:30 A.M., Casey Letvin was taken back to her dormitory and raped on her own narrow bed by a man she might never have spoken to had he not been a fellow student (Freeman, 1990, p. 94).

What happened to Casey Letvin unfortunately is not rare. Rapes occur among women of all ages, from all economic levels, and from all ethnic groups. Female college students, who enjoy newfound freedoms while living in a community of strangers, have a particular vulnerability to rape.

When sex—an activity that should be pleasurable, joyful, and intimate—is forced on someone, it becomes one of the ultimate acts of aggression and brutality, and few crimes produce such profound and long-lasting consequences. But sexual crimes are not the only category of serious problems related to sex. Few personal difficulties produce as much anxiety, embarrassment, and even shame as do sexually transmitted infections and sexual dysfunctions. We now turn to the major types of problems related to sex.

Key Concepts

How prevalent are rape and other forms of nonconsenting sex, and what are their causes?

What are the major sexually transmitted infections?

What sexual difficulties do people most frequently encounter?

Rape

Rape occurs when one person forces another person to submit to sexual activity such as intercourse or oral-genital sex. Although it usually applies to a male forcing a female, rape can be said to occur when members of either sex are forced into sexual activities without their consent.

Most people think of rape as a rare crime committed by strangers. Unfortunately, they are wrong on both counts. In fact, rape occurs far more frequently than is commonly thought, and rapists are typically acquaintances of their victims. Although it is hard to obtain reliable estimates, most research suggests that there is a 14 to 25 percent chance that a woman will be the victim of a rape during her lifetime. Furthermore, more than half a million sexual assaults are directed against women each year in the United States (Kilpatrick, Edmunds, & Seymour, 1992; Wiehe & Richards, 1995).

Furthermore, a national survey conducted at thirty-five universities revealed the startling finding that one out of eight female college students reported having been raped. Among the women who had been raped, about half said the rapists were first dates, casual dates, or romantic acquaintances—a phenomenon called **date rape.** Girls in high school also suffer both sexual and physical abuse: In one survey, 9 percent of 14- to 18-year-old girls said they had been forced into sexual activity

Rape: The act by which one person forces another person to submit to sexual activity.

Date rape: Rape in which the rapist is either a date or a romantic acquaintance.

by a date, and in more than half of those cases the incident had been accompanied by hitting, slapping, or shoving (Koss, 1993; Silverman, 2001; Ackard & Neumark-Sztainer, 2002).

Women in some segments of society are more at risk for rape than are others. Although the likelihood of sexual assault is considerably lower among Latino women in comparison to non-Latino white women, the rate for black women is slightly higher in comparison to white women. Such racial differences may stem from differing cultural views of women and male dominance (Wyatt, 1992; Koss, 1993; Black & Weisz, 2004).

Although on the surface it might appear that rape is primarily a crime of sex, other types of motivation also underlie the behavior. In many cases, the rapist uses sex as a means of demonstrating power and control over the victim. In such cases, there is little that is sexually satisfying about rape to the rapist; instead, the pleasure comes from forcing someone else to be submissive (Zurbriggen, 2000; Gowaty, 2003).

In other cases of rape, the primary motivation is anger. Sexual behavior is used to show the male rapist's rage at women in general, usually because of some perceived rejection or hurt that he has suffered in the past. Such rapes are likely to include physical violence and degrading acts against the victim.

Some rapes are based on a desire for sexual gratification. Some men hold the attitude that it is appropriate and desirable for them to actively seek out sex. To them, sexual encounters represent a form of "war" between the sexes—with winners and losers—and violence is sometimes considered an appropriate way to obtain what they want. According to their reasoning, using force to obtain sexual gratification is permissible (Malamuth et al., 1995; Hall, 1996).

Finally, there is a common, although unfounded, societal belief that many women offer token resistance to sex, saying no to sex when they mean yes. If a man holds such a view, he may ignore a woman's protestations that she doesn't want sex (Muehlenhard & Hollabaugh, 1988; Anderson, Cooper, & Okamura, 1997).

The repercussions of rape are devastating for the victims. During a rape, women experience fear, terror, and physical pain. Later, victims report shock, disbelief, panic, extreme anxiety, and suspiciousness—reactions that are sometimes intensified by implications that somehow the victim was to blame because of her style of dress or her presence in the wrong neighborhood.

The psychological reactions to rape are no different whether it is date rape or rape by a stranger. These feelings may continue for years, even though the victim outwardly appears to have recovered. However, immediate psychological intervention, such as that provided by rape crisis centers, may be helpful in diminishing the long-term reactions to rape (Monnier et al., 2002; Zaslow, 2003).

Childhood Sexual Abuse

One form of sexual behavior that is surprisingly common, yet little understood, is the sexual abuse of children. Each year a half million children are sexually abused. In fact, between 5 and 10 percent of boys and 20 percent of girls will be abused (Villarosa, 2002; see Figure 1).

Who commits child sexual abuse? In most cases it is a relative or acquaintance; in only about one-quarter of the cases is the abuse carried out by a stranger. The most vulnerable age for being molested is between 7 and 13 years old, and the abusers tend to be about twenty years older than their victims. In most instances, the abuser is a male heterosexual (Wolfe, 1999, Finkelhor, Ormrod, & Turner, 2005).

The short- and longer-term consequences of childhood sexual abuse can be extremely damaging. In terms of initial effects, victims report fear, anxiety, depression, anger, and hostility. Long-term effects may include depression, self-destruc-

VICTIMS
Every year, 500,000 children in the United States are sexually abused. The peak age of vulnerability is 7 to 13.

1 or 2 of every 20 boys will be abused during childhood.

4 of every 20 girls will be abused.

ABUSERS
70 to 90 percent of abuse is committed by a person who knows the child.

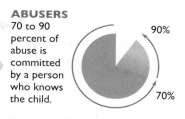

Family members make up one-third to one-half of abusers of girls, and 10 to 20 percent of abusers of boys.

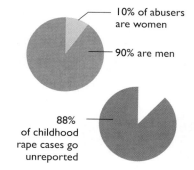

10% of abusers are women

90% are men

88% of childhood rape cases go unreported

FIGURE 1 Studies have found that the sexual abuse of children often is committed by a person who knows the child, with almost a third of the abusers being family members. (Source: Dr. David Finkelhor, University of New Hampshire.)

tive behavior, feelings of isolation, poor self-esteem, and substance abuse. Although they may experience sexual difficulties later in life, the victims are not more likely to become sexual abusers themselves. Ultimately, the consequences of childhood sexual abuse are related to the specific nature of the abuse. Experiences involving fathers, genital contact, and the use of force are the most damaging (Berkowitz, 2000; Hawke, Jainchill, & De Leon, 2000; Berliner & Elliott, 2002).

Sexually Transmitted Infections (STIs)

Millions of people suffer the discomfort—not to mention the psychological distress—of a **sexually transmitted infection (STI),** a medical condition acquired through sexual contact. Estimates suggest that one of five people in the United States is infected with some form of STI, and at least one of four will probably contract a STI during their lifetimes. The United States has the highest rate of sexually transmitted infections of all the economically developed countries in the world, in part because people in the United States don't talk about sex as frankly or provide as much sex education as people in other developed nations do (Centers for Disease Control and Prevention, 2000; see Figure 2).

These are the major STIs:

- *Chlamydia.* The most widespread STI is *chlamydia,* a disease that in women initially produces no symptoms and in men causes a burning sensation during urination and a discharge from the penis. If it is left untreated, chlamydia can lead to pelvic inflammation, urethral damage, arthritis, and even sterility. There are almost 3 million new cases each year in the United States. Because it usually produces no symptoms in females, the Center for Disease Control recommends that sexually active women under age 26 be tested for the disease every year. Once diagnosed, chlamydia can be cured with antibiotics, most often azithromycin or doxycycline (Ku et al., 2002; CDC, 2004a).

- *Genital herpes. Genital herpes* is a virus related to the cold sores that sometimes appear around the mouth. Herpes first appears as small blisters or sores around the genitals that later break open, causing severe pain. These sores heal after a few weeks, but the disease usually reappears, typically four or five times in the year following infection. Later outbreaks are less frequent, but the infection, which cannot be cured, often causes psychological distress for those who know they are infected. During the active phases of the disease

Sexually transmitted infection (STI): A disease transmitted through sexual contact.

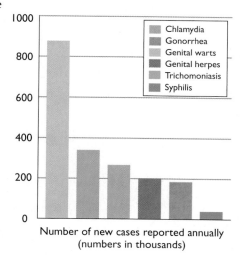

Number of new cases reported annually (numbers in thousands)

FIGURE 2 Estimates of the numbers of new cases annually of sexually transmitted infections in the United States. There are many more new cases of chlamydia each year than any other sexually transmitted infection. (Source: Centers for Disease Control and Prevention, 2003.)

it can be transmitted to sexual partners. Genital herpes is common among college-age students: around 17 percent of 20- to 29-year-olds have the infection (Farrell, 2005).

- *Trichomoniasis.* *Trichomoniasis* is an infection occurring in the vagina or penis. Caused by a parasite, it is often without symptoms, especially in men. Eventually, it can cause painful urination and intercourse, a discharge from the vagina, and an unpleasant odor. The 5 million cases reported each year can be treated with antibiotics.
- *Gonorrhea.* *Gonorrhea* is one of the STIs that has been recognized the longest by scientists. Gonorrhea often has no symptoms but can produce a burning sensation when urinating or a discharge from the penis or vagina. The infection can lead to fertility problems and, in women, pelvic inflammatory disease. Although antibiotics usually can cure gonorrhea, a number of drug-resistant strains of the disease are growing, making treatment more difficult.
- *Syphilis.* If untreated, *syphilis* may affect the brain, the heart, and a developing fetus, and can even be fatal. Syphilis first reveals itself through a small sore at the point of sexual contact. In its secondary stage, it may include a rash. Syphilis can be treated successfully with antibiotics if it is diagnosed early enough.
- *Genital warts.* Another common STI is *genital warts* (caused by *human papilloma virus*). Genital warts are small, lumpy warts that form on or near the penis or vagina. The warts are easy to diagnose because of their distinctive appearance: They look like small cauliflower bulbs. They usually form about two months after exposure and can be treated with a drug called metronidazole (Cothran & White, 2002).
- *AIDS.* In the last two decades, no sexually transmitted infection has had a greater impact on sexual behavior—and society as a whole—than **acquired immune deficiency syndrome (AIDS).** Although in the United States AIDS at first was found primarily in gay men, it has spread to other populations, such as intravenous drug users and heterosexuals. In the United States, AIDS is the leading cause of death among men 25 to 44 years of age and the third leading cause of death among women in that age range. The worldwide figures are even more daunting: Already, 25 million people have died from AIDS, and people living with the disease number 40 million worldwide (Quinn & Overbaugh, 2005; See Figure 3).

The spread of AIDS is particularly pronounced among women, who now account for almost half the cases worldwide. The annual number of AIDS cases increased 15 percent among women, compared with 1 percent among men, between 1999 and 2003. Younger women and women of color are particularly vulnerable. For instance, the rate of AIDS diagnosis was around 25 times higher for African American women than for white women, and four times higher for Hispanic women (Quinn & Overbaugh, 2005).

The extent of the AIDS epidemic has led to significant changes in sexual behavior. People are less likely to engage in "casual" sex with new acquaintances, and the use of condoms during sexual intercourse has increased. Nonetheless, the only foolproof method of avoiding AIDS is total abstinence—an alternative that many people find unrealistic. However, there are several ways to reduce the risk of contracting AIDS (as well as other sexually transmitted infections); these methods have come to be called "safer sex" practices (Carr, 2002):

- *Know your sexual partner—well.* Before having sex with someone, learn about his or her sexual history.
- *Use condoms.* For those in sexual relationships, condoms are the most reliable means of preventing transmission of the AIDS virus.

Acquired immune deficiency syndrome (AIDS): A fatal, sexually transmitted infection caused by a virus that destroys the body's immune system.

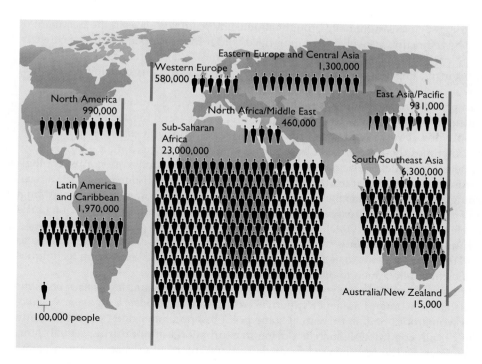

- *Avoid the exchange of bodily fluids, particularly semen.* In particular, avoid anal intercourse. The AIDS virus can spread through small tears in the rectum, making anal intercourse without condoms particularly dangerous. Oral sex, once thought relatively safe, is now viewed as potentially dangerous.
- *Stay sober.* Using alcohol and drugs impairs judgment and can lead to poor decisions—and it makes using a condom correctly more difficult.
- *Consider the benefits of monogamy.* People in long-term, monogamous relationships with partners who have been faithful are at a lower risk of contracting AIDS.

Sexual Problems

Few people would feel embarrassed by a sprained ankle or broken arm. In contrast, sexual difficulties are often a source of concern and self-consciousness because of the importance that society places on "desirable" sexual conduct. And such difficulties are surprisingly common, with 43 percent of women and 31 percent of men experiencing problems associated with sexual performance. Among the most widespread are the disorders we discuss below (Laumann, Park, & Rosen, 1999; Goldstein, 2000; Rosner, 2001).

Erectile dysfunction is the inability of a male to achieve or maintain an erection. The rare case is a male who has never been able to have an erection, and the more common case is a male who, though now unable to have an erection, has had one at least once in the past. Erectile dysfunction is not an uncommon problem, even among younger men—about 5 to 10 percent of men under 50 have erection problems. It is the rare man who has never experienced it at least once during his lifetime. This is hardly surprising, because the ability to achieve and hold an erection is sensitive to alcohol, drugs, performance fears, anxiety, and a host of other factors. Erectile dysfunction becomes a more serious problem when it occurs more than occasionally (Mendelssohn, 2003).

Erectile dysfunction: The inability of a male to achieve or maintain an erection.

Drugs such as Viagra have brought about significant advances in the treatment of erectile dysfunction, as well as bringing the disorder into the open through a constant barrage of commercials on television and magazines. Viagra treats erectile dysfunction by increasing the flow of blood through a man's penis, producing an erection relatively quickly.

Premature ejaculation: The inability of a male to delay orgasm as long as he wishes.

In **premature ejaculation,** a male is unable to delay orgasm as long as he wishes. Because "as long as he wishes" is dependent on a man's—and his partner's—attitudes and opinions about how long is appropriate, this is a difficult disorder to diagnose, and sometimes the problem can be resolved simply by having a male redefine how long he wants to delay ejaculation. Premature ejaculation is most often a psychological problem, as there are rarely physical reasons for it. One cause may be early sexual learning: Because sexual experiences during adolescence are often accompanied by a fear of being caught, some men learn early in their lives to reach orgasm as quickly as possible (Astbury-Ward, 2002).

Inhibited ejaculation: The inability of a male to ejaculate when he wants to, if at all.

Inhibited ejaculation is the opposite problem. In this case, the male is unable to ejaculate when he wants to, if at all. Sometimes learning general relaxation techniques is sufficient to allow men to overcome the difficulty.

Anorgasmia (an-or-GAZ-mee-uh): A female's lack of orgasm.

Some women experience **anorgasmia,** or a lack of orgasm. In *primary orgasmic dysfunction,* a woman has never experienced orgasm. In *secondary orgasmic dysfunction,* a woman has had an orgasm at some point but no longer does, or does so only under certain conditions—such as during masturbation but not during sexual intercourse. Because the lack of orgasm during sexual intercourse is so common (some one-third of women report they do not receive sufficient stimulation to reach orgasm during sexual intercourse), this state of affairs can be considered a normal variation of female sexuality.

Inhibited sexual desire: A sexual dysfunction in which the motivation for sexual activity is restrained or lacking entirely.

Finally, **inhibited sexual desire** occurs when the motivation for sexual activity is restrained or lacking entirely. When people with inhibited sexual desire find themselves in circumstances that typically would evoke sexual feelings, they begin to turn off sexually and may even experience a kind of "sexual anesthesia." Ultimately they may begin to avoid situations of a sexual nature, thereby forgoing intimacy with others (Meston, 2003).

It is important to note that many of the problems we have discussed turn up at one time or another in most people's sex lives. It is only when these problems persist, cause undue anxiety, and turn sex from play into work that they are cause for concern. Furthermore, treatments for common sexual problems have a good rate of success (Masters & Johnson, 1994; Rosner, 2001). (To explore sexual disorders in greater depth, complete the PsychInteractive exercise.)

www.mhhe.com/feldmanup8
PsychInteractive Online

Sexual Disorders

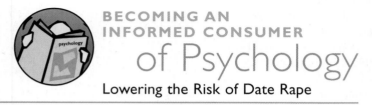

BECOMING AN INFORMED CONSUMER of Psychology

Lowering the Risk of Date Rape

As we have seen, surveys of college women make clear that the greatest danger of rape comes not from some unknown assailant but from a fellow student. There are ways, however, to reduce the likelihood of date rape. The following suggestions provide some guidance for women and men (American College Health Association, 1989; Jackson, 1996; Shultz, Scherman, & Marshall, 2000):

- Women should believe in their rights to set limits and communicate those limits clearly, firmly, and early on. They should say no when they mean no.
- Women should be assertive when someone is pressuring them to engage in an activity in which they don't want to engage. They should keep in mind that men may interpret passivity as permission.
- Women should be aware of situations in which they are at risk.

- Women should keep in mind the fact that some men interpret certain kinds of dress as sexually provocative, and that not all men subscribe to the same standards of sex as they do.
- Women should keep close tabs on what they are given to drink in social situations; victims of date rape have sometimes been given mind-altering drugs.
- Men should be aware of their dates' views on sexual behavior.
- Men should not hold the view that the goal of dating is to "score."
- The word *no* should be understood to mean no and not be interpreted as an invitation to continue. Men should know that a woman who says no is not rejecting them but is rejecting a specific act at a specific time.
- Men should not assume that certain kinds of dress or flirtatious behavior are an invitation to sex.
- Both men and women should understand that alcohol and drugs cloud judgment and hinder communication between them.

RECAP/EVALUATE/RETHINK

RECAP

How prevalent are rape and other forms of nonconsenting sex, and what are their causes?

- Rape occurs when one person forces another person to submit to sexual activity. Often the victim is acquainted with the rapist. The motivation for rape is only sometimes sexual gratification. More frequently it is power, aggression, or anger. (pp. 387-388)
- Childhood sexual abuse is surprisingly widespread. Most often the perpetrator is an acquaintance or a family member. (pp. 388-389)

What are the major sexually transmitted infections?

- Acquired immune deficiency syndrome, or AIDS, is bringing about profound changes in people's sexual practices. Other sexually transmitted infections include chlamydia, genital herpes, trichomoniasis, gonorrhea, syphilis, and genital warts. (pp. 389-390)

What sexual difficulties do people most frequently encounter?

- Among the major sexual problems reported by males are erectile dysfunction, premature ejaculation, and inhibited ejaculation. For females, the major problem is anorgasmia, or a lack of orgasm. Both men and women may suffer from inhibited sexual desire. (pp. 391-392)

EVALUATE

1. A college woman is more likely to be raped by an acquaintance than by a stranger. True or false?
2. Which of the following is unlikely to be a motivation for the act of rape?
   a. Need for power
   b. Desire for sexual intimacy
   c. Desire for sexual gratification
   d. Anger against women in general
3. Which of the following STIs is the most widespread?
   a. Genital herpes
   b. Gonorrhea
   c. Chlamydia
   d. Syphilis
4. Which of the following is not true about changes in sexual behavior as a result of the AIDS epidemic?
   a. The use of condoms has increased.
   b. People are less likely to engage in casual sex.
   c. HIV infection rates are dropping because most unmarried people have adopted abstinence.
   d. The risk of contracting AIDS may be reduced by engaging in safer sex practices.
5. Sexual dysfunctions, even if they occur only once, are cause for considerable concern and should be treated immediately. True or false?

RETHINK

1. Should women be free to dress any way they want without being concerned about "giving off the wrong signals"? Is it reasonable for men to assume that women sometimes give off signals that indicate that they really want sex even when they say they don't?
2. *From the perspective of a politician:* What responsibilities do people who learn they have a sexually transmitted infection have to their sexual partners, and what responsibilities do public health officials have? Should legislation be designed to restrict sexual behavior for those who have sexually transmitted infections?

Answers to Evaluate Questions

1. true; 2. b; 3. c; 4. c; 5. false; sexual dysfunction is experienced by almost everyone at one time or another

KEY TERMS

rape p. 387
date rape p. 387
sexually transmitted infection (STI) p. 389

acquired immune deficiency syndrome (AIDS) p. 390
erectile dysfunction p. 391
premature ejaculation p. 392

inhibited ejaculation p. 392
anorgasmia (an-or-GAZ-mee-uh) p. 392
inhibited sexual desire p. 392

Psychology on the Web

1. Find at least two recent news articles or discussions on the Web dealing with the issue of gender equality in school or the workplace, especially unequal treatment of individuals because of their gender. Summarize in writing what you found, and discuss your own attitudes toward this issue.

2. Find information on the Web about date rape, including guidelines or suggestions published by other colleges, for preventing rape among students. Summarize your findings, including recommendations for behavioral or policy changes that might be effective at your college. If your college's policies toward or publications about this topic could benefit from your findings, bring them to the attention of the appropriate office at your institution and suggest specific changes.

3. After completing the PsychInteractive exercise on sexual disorders, search the Web for the latest statistics on the spread of AIDS around the world. Where is the incidence of AIDS growing most rapidly and why is it increasing in those areas?

Epilogue

We have seen how the topics of gender and sex are dealt with by psychologists, first with regard to gender roles, gender stereotyping, gender schemas, and sexism. The expectations of society regarding male and female characteristics and behaviors lead to inequities in the treatment of men and women in school, the workplace, and the rest of society—inequities that largely favor men.

With regard to sexuality, we discussed the nature of the physical processes that surround sexuality and addressed the controversial issue of "normality" in sexual behavior. We saw the broad diversity of sexual behavior, and we discussed premarital sex and marital sex, as well as heterosexuality, homosexuality, and bisexuality. We also examined rape and other forms of nonconsenting sex, including childhood sexual abuse.

Finally, we looked at the sexual problems that people may have, including sexually transmitted infections and sexual dysfunctions. We explored the nature of these problems and discussed ways to treat and deal with them.

Before we turn to the subject of human development in the next few modules, return to the prologue of this chapter, concerning the case of date rape involving Bob and Patty. Using your knowledge of gender and sex, consider the following questions.

1. How could situations such as this be prevented?
2. What specific strategies could Patty have used to prevent the situation from escalating? What specific strategies could Bob have used to avoid such a situation?
3. Why is communication about sexual issues so difficult, especially in dating situations?
4. Why might the traditional "double standard" lead to situations such as this one?

Development

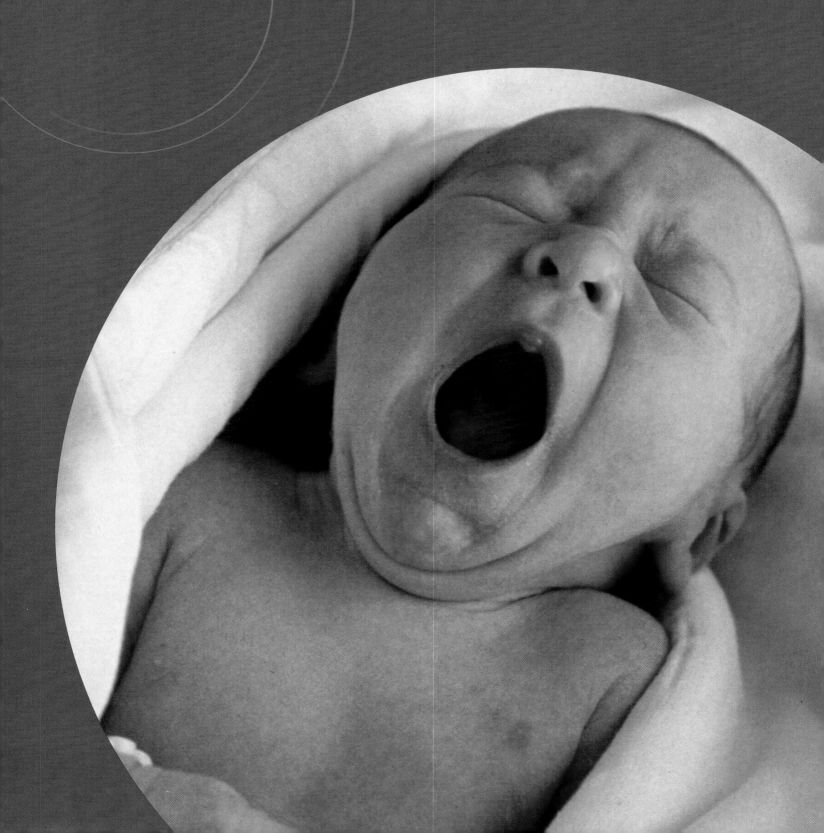

Key Concepts for Chapter 12

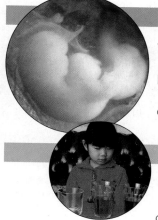
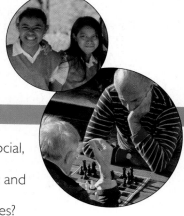

Prologue   **Test-Tube Baby Birthday**

It seems like a typical, if rather elaborate, birthday celebration. There are clowns on stilts, a falcon demonstration, artists applying henna tattoos, and an inflatable castle for the young partygoers to bounce in. A thousand guests are milling about the manicured lawns of this Jacobean estate in the English countryside, and families have traveled from Iceland, Norway, the Middle East, and the United States. Among those who made the trip are scores of twins plus several sets of triplets and quadruplets.

Amid the din, everyone gathers and sings "Happy Birthday" to a 25-year-old woman. Wearying a beige pantsuit and her hair in a ponytail, Louise Brown, the world's first test-tube baby, shyly blows out the candles and cuts into a white-frosted chocolate cake. Her guests include hundreds also conceived by *in vitro* fertilization, a tiny fraction of the 1.5 million IVF babies born since 1978 (Rohm, 2003, p. 157).

Looking **Ahead**

If Louise Brown's conception was unconventional, her life has unfolded in more traditional ways. In fact, even her conception in a laboratory used a procedure that has now become nearly routine.

Welcome to the brave new world of childhood—or rather one of the brave new worlds. From new ways of conceiving children to learning how to raise children most sensibly to dealing with the milestones of life that we all face, the issues involved in human development touch each of us.

Developmental psychology, the branch of psychology that studies the patterns of growth and change that occur throughout life, addresses these issues, along with many others. In large part, developmental psychologists study the interaction between the unfolding of biologically predetermined patterns of behavior and a constantly changing, dynamic environment. They ask how our genetic background affects our behavior throughout our lives and whether our potential is limited by heredity. Similarly, they seek to understand the way in which the environment works with—or against—our genetic capabilities, how the world we live in affects our development, and how we can be encouraged to reach our full potential.

We begin by examining the approaches developmental psychologists use to study the environmental and genetic factors: the nature-nurture issue. Then we consider the very start of development, beginning with conception and the nine months of life before birth. We describe both genetic and environmental influences on the unborn individual and the way they can affect behavior throughout the remainder of the life cycle.

Next, we examine development that occurs after birth, witnessing the enormous and rapid growth that takes place during the early stages of life, focusing on physical, social, and cognitive change throughout infancy, toddlerhood, and middle childhood. We then move on to development from adolescence through adulthood. We end with a discussion of the ways in which people prepare themselves for death.

Nature and Nurture: The Enduring Developmental Issue

How many bald, six-foot-six, 250-pound volunteer firefighters in New Jersey wear droopy mustaches, aviator-style eyeglasses, and a key ring on the right side of the belt?

The answer is two: Gerald Levey and Mark Newman. They are twins who were separated at birth. Each twin did not even know the other existed until they were reunited—in a fire station—by a fellow firefighter who knew Newman and was startled to see his double, Levey, at a firefighters' convention.

The lives of the twins, although separate, took remarkably similar paths. Levey went to college, studying forestry; Newman planned to study forestry in college but instead took a job trimming trees. Both had jobs in supermarkets. One had a job installing sprinkler systems; the other installed fire alarms.

Both men are unmarried and find the same kind of woman attractive: "tall, slender, long hair." They share similar hobbies, enjoying hunting, fishing, going to the beach, and watching old John Wayne movies and professional wrestling. Both like Chinese food and drink the same brand of beer. Their mannerisms are also similar—for example, each one throws his head back when he laughs. And, of course, there is one more thing: They share a passion for fighting fires.

The similarities we see in twins Gerald Levey and Mark Newman vividly raise one of the fundamental questions posed by **developmental psychology,** the study of the patterns of growth and change that occur throughout life. The question is this: How can we distinguish between the *environmental* causes of behavior (the influence of parents, siblings, family, friends, schooling, nutrition, and all the other experiences to which a child is exposed) and *hereditary* causes (those based on the genetic makeup of an individual that influence growth and development throughout life)? This question embodies the **nature-nurture issue.** In this context, nature refers to hereditary factors, and nurture to environmental influences.

Although the question was first posed as a nature-*versus*-nurture issue, developmental psychologists today agree that *both* nature and nurture interact to produce specific developmental patterns and outcomes. Consequently, the question has evolved into *how and to what degree* do environment and heredity both produce their effects? No one grows up free of environmental influences, nor does anyone develop without being affected by his or her inherited *genetic makeup.* However, the debate over the comparative influence of the two factors remains active, with different approaches and theories of development emphasizing the environment or heredity to a greater or lesser degree (de Waal, 1999; Pinker, 2002; Gottesman & Hanson, 2005).

For example, some developmental theories rely on basic psychological principles of learning and stress the role learning plays in producing changes in behavior in a developing child. Such theories emphasize the role of the environment in development. In contrast, other developmental theories emphasize the influence of one's physiological makeup and functioning on development. Such theories stress the role of heredity and *maturation*—the unfolding of biologically predetermined patterns of behavior—in producing developmental change. Maturation can be seen, for instance, in the development of sex characteristics (such as

Key Concept

How do psychologists study the degree to which development is an interaction of hereditary and environmental factors?

Developmental psychology: The branch of psychology that studies the patterns of growth and change that occur throughout life.

Nature-nurture issue: The issue of the degree to which environment and heredity influence behavior.

Gerald Levey and Mark Newman

breasts and body hair) that occurs at the start of adolescence. Furthermore, the work of behavioral geneticists, who study the effects of heredity on behavior, and the theories of evolutionary psychologists, who identify behavior patterns that result from our genetic inheritance, have influenced developmental psychologists. Both behavioral geneticists and evolutionary psychologists have highlighted the importance of heredity in influencing human behavior (Buss, 2003a; Reif & Lesch, 2003).

Despite their differences over theory, developmental psychologists concur on some points. They agree that genetic factors not only provide the potential for particular behaviors or traits to emerge, but also place limitations on the emergence of such behavior or traits. For instance, heredity defines people's general level of intelligence, setting an upper limit that—regardless of the quality of the environment—people cannot exceed. Heredity also places limits on physical abilities; humans simply cannot run at a speed of sixty miles an hour, nor will they grow as tall as ten feet, no matter what the quality of their environment (Plomin & McClearn, 1993; Steen, 1996; Pinker, 2002, 2004; Dodge, 2004).

Figure 1 lists some of the characteristics most affected by heredity. As you consider these items, it is important to keep in mind that these characteristics are not *entirely* determined by heredity, but that environmental factors also play a role.

Developmental psychologists also agree that in most instances environmental factors play a critical role in enabling people to reach the potential capabilities that their genetic background makes possible. If Albert Einstein had received no intellectual stimulation as a child and had not been sent to school, it is unlikely that he would have reached his genetic potential. Similarly, a great athlete such as baseball star Derek Jeter would have been unlikely to display much physical skill if he had not been raised in an environment that nurtured his innate talent and gave him the opportunity to train and perfect his natural abilities.

Clearly, the relationship between heredity and environment is far from simple. As a consequence, developmental psychologists typically take an *interactionist* position on the nature-nurture issue, suggesting that a combination of hereditary and environmental factors influences development. Developmental psychologists face the challenge of identifying the relative strength of each of these influences on the individual, as well as that of identifying the specific changes that occur over the course of development (Plomin & Neiderhiser, 1992; Wozniak & Fischer, 1993; Saudino & Plomin, 1996; McGregor & Capone, 2004).

Determining the Relative Influence of Nature and Nurture

Developmental psychologists use several approaches to determine the relative influence of genetic and environmental factors on behavior. In one approach, researchers

FIGURE 1 Characteristics influenced significantly by genetic factors. Although these characteristics have strong genetic components, they are also affected by environmental factors.

Physical Characteristics	Intellectual Characteristics	Emotional Characteristics and Disorders
Height	Memory	Shyness
Weight	Intelligence	Extraversion
Obesity	Age of language acquisition	Emotionality
Tone of voice	Reading disability	Neuroticism
Blood pressure	Mental retardation	Schizophrenia
Tooth decay		Anxiety
Athletic ability		Alcoholism
Firmness of handshake		
Age of death		
Activity level		

can experimentally control the genetic makeup of laboratory animals by carefully breeding them for specific traits. For instance, by observing animals with identical genetic backgrounds placed in varied environments, researchers can learn the effects of particular kinds of environmental stimulation. Although researchers must be careful when generalizing the findings of nonhuman research to a human population, findings from animal research provide important information that cannot be obtained, for ethical reasons, by using human participants.

Human twins serve as another important source of information about the relative effects of genetic and environmental factors. If **identical twins** (those who are genetically identical) display different patterns of development, those differences have to be attributed to variations in the environment in which the twins were raised. The most useful data come from identical twins (such as Gerald Levey and Mark Newman) who are adopted at birth by different sets of adoptive parents and raised apart in differing environments. Studies of nontwin siblings who are raised in totally different environments also shed some light on the issue. Because they have relatively similar genetic backgrounds, siblings who show similarities a as adults provide strong evidence for the importance of heredity (Gottesman, 1997; Sternberg, 2002a).

Researchers can also take the opposite tack. Instead of concentrating on people with similar genetic backgrounds who are raised in different environments, they may consider people raised in similar environments who have totally dissimilar genetic backgrounds. If they find, for example, similar courses of development in two adopted children who have different genetic backgrounds and have been raised in the same family, they have evidence for the importance of environmental influences on development. Moreover, psychologists can carry out research involving animals with dissimilar genetic backgrounds; by experimentally varying the environment in which they are raised, we can determine the influence of environmental factors (independent of heredity) on development (Segal, 1993; Vernon et al., 1997; Petrill & Deater-Deckard, 2004). (To better understand the nature-nurture issue, complete the PsychInteractive exercise.)

Identical twins: Twins who are genetically identical.

www.mhhe.com/feldmanup8
PsychInteractive Online

Nature and Nurture

Developmental Research Techniques

Because of the demands of measuring behavioral change across different ages, developmental researchers use several unique methods. The most frequently used, **cross-sectional research,** compares people of different ages at the same point in time. Cross-sectional studies provide information about differences in development between different age groups (Creasey, 2005).

Suppose, for instance, we were interested in the development of intellectual ability in adulthood. To carry out a cross-sectional study, we might compare a sample of 25-, 45-, and 65-year-olds who all take the same IQ test. We then can determine whether average IQ test scores differ in each age group.

Cross-sectional research has limitations, however. For instance, we cannot be sure that the differences in IQ scores we might find in our example are due to age differences alone. Instead, the scores may reflect differences in the educational attainment of the cohorts represented. A *cohort* is a group of people who grow up at similar times, in similar places, and in similar conditions. In the case of IQ differences, any age differences we find in a cross-sectional study may reflect educational differences among the cohorts studied: People in the older age group may belong to a cohort that was less likely to attend college than were the people in the younger groups.

A longitudinal study, the second major research strategy used by developmental psychologists, provides one way around this problem. **Longitudinal research** traces the behavior of one or more participants as the participants age. Longitudinal studies assess *change* in behavior over time, unlike cross-sectional studies, which assess *differences* among groups of people.

For instance, consider how we might investigate intellectual development during adulthood by using a longitudinal research strategy. First, we might give an IQ test to a group of 25-year-olds. We'd then come back to the same people twenty years later

Cross-sectional research: A research method that compares people of different ages at the same point in time.

Longitudinal research: A research method that investigates behavior as participants age.

and retest them at age 45. Finally, we'd return to them once more when they were 65 years old and test them again.

By examining changes at several points in time, we can clearly see how individuals develop. Unfortunately, longitudinal research requires an enormous expenditure of time (as the researcher waits for the participants to get older), and participants who begin a study at an early age may drop out, move away, or even die as the research continues. Moreover, participants who take the same test at several points in time may become "test-wise" and perform better each time they take it, having become more familiar with the test.

To make up for the limitations in both cross-sectional and longitudinal research, investigators have devised an alternative strategy. Known as **sequential research,** it combines cross-sectional and longitudinal approaches by taking a number of different age groups and examining them at several points in time. For example, investigators might use a group of 3-, 5-, and 7-year-olds, examining them every six months for a period of several years. This technique allows a developmental psychologist to tease out the specific effects of age changes from other possibly influential factors.

Sequential research: A research method that combines cross-sectional and longitudinal research by considering a number of different age groups and examining them at several points in time.

RECAP/EVALUATE/RETHINK

RECAP

How do psychologists study the degree to which development is an interaction of hereditary and environmental factors?

- Developmental psychology studies growth and change throughout life. One fundamental question is how much developmental change is due to heredity and how much is due to environment—the nature-nurture issue. Heredity seems to define the upper limits of our growth and change, whereas the environment affects the degree to which the upper limits are reached. (pp. 399–400)
- Cross-sectional research compares people of different ages with one another at the same point in time. In contrast, longitudinal research traces the behavior of one or more participants as the participants become older. Finally, sequential research combines the two methods by taking several different age groups and examining them at several points in time. (pp. 401–402)

EVALUATE

1. Developmental psychologists are interested in the effects of both _____ and _____ on development.
2. Environment and heredity both influence development, with genetic potentials generally establishing limits on environmental influences. True or false?

3. By observing genetically similar animals in differing environments, we can increase our understanding of the influences of hereditary and environmental factors in humans. True or false?
4. _____ research studies the same individuals over a period of time, whereas _____-_____ research studies people of different ages at the same time.

RETHINK

1. When researchers find similarities in development between very different cultures, what implications might such findings have for the nature-nurture issue?
2. *From the perspective of a childcare provider:* Consider what factors might determine why a child is not learning to walk at the same pace as his peers. What kinds of environmental influences might be involved? What kinds of genetic influences might be involved? What recommendations might you make to the child's parents about the situation?

Answers to Evaluate Questions

1. heredity (or nature), environment (or nurture); 2. true; 3. true; 4. longitudinal, cross-sectional

KEY TERMS

developmental psychology
  p. 399
nature-nurture issue p. 399
identical twins p. 401
cross-sectional research
  p. 401
longitudinal research p. 401
sequential research p. 402

Prenatal Development: Conception to Birth

A routine prenatal test brought Jennifer and Brian Buchkovich horrifying news: Their unborn baby, Ethan, was afflicted with spina bifida, a failure of the spine to close over the spinal cord. The birth defect, which affects 2,000 children a year, usually leads to paralysis and cognitive delays. But doctors offered the Windber, Pennsylvania, couple a glimmer of hope—an experimental operation designed to reduce the damage and to eliminate or delay the need for a surgically implanted shunt to drain excess fluid from the brain. The hitch: The surgery would have be performed while Ethan was still inside Jennifer's womb (*People Weekly*, 2000, p. 117).

The Buchkoviches took the risk, and it appears to have paid off: Although Ethan has shown some developmental delays, he's just a bit behind schedule.

Our increasing understanding of the first stirrings of life spent inside a mother's womb has permitted significant medical advances like those that helped Ethan Buchkovich. Yet our knowledge of the biology of *conception*—when a male's sperm cell penetrates a female's egg cell—and its aftermath makes the start of life no less of a miracle. Let's consider how an individual is created by looking first at the genetic endowment that a child receives at the moment of conception.

Key Concepts

What is the nature of development before birth?

What factors affect a child during the mother's pregnancy?

The Basics of Genetics

The one-cell entity established at conception contains twenty-three pairs of **chromosomes,** rod-shaped structures that contain all basic hereditary information. One member of each pair is from the mother, and the other is from the father.

Each chromosome contains thousands of **genes**—smaller units through which genetic information is transmitted (see Figure 1). Either individually or in combination,

Chromosomes: Rod-shaped structures that contain all basic hereditary information.

Genes: The parts of the chromosomes through which genetic information is transmitted.

a. Conception

b. 23 pairs of chromosomes

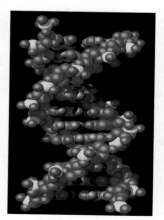
c. DNA sequence

d. Genes

FIGURE 1 Every individual's characteristics are determined by the individual's specific genetic information. At the moment of conception (a), humans receive twenty-three pairs of chromosomes (b), half from the mother and half from the father. These chromosomes are made up of coils of DNA (c). Each chromosome contains thousands of genes (d) that "program" the future development of the body.

genes produce the particular characteristics of each person. Composed of sequences of *DNA (deoxyribonucleic acid)* molecules, genes are the biological equivalent of "software" that programs the future development of all parts of the body's hardware. Humans have some 25,000 different genes.

Some genes control the development of systems common to all members of the human species—the heart, circulatory system, brain, lungs, and so forth; others shape the characteristics that make each human unique, such as facial configuration, height, and eye color. The child's sex is also determined by a particular combination of genes. Specifically, a child inherits an X or a Y chromosome from its father. When it receives an XX combination, it is a female; with an XY combination, it develops as a male. Male development is triggered by a single gene on the Y chromosome, and without the presence of that specific gene, the individual will develop as a female (see Figure 2).

As behavioral geneticists have discovered, genes are also at least partially responsible for a wide variety of personal characteristics, including cognitive abilities, personality traits, and psychological disorders. Of course, few of these characteristics are determined by a single gene. Instead, most traits result from a combination of multiple genes, which operate together with environmental influences (Funder, 1997; Plomin & McGuffin, 2003; Plomin et al., 2003; Haberstick et al., 2005).

To better understand how genes influence human characteristics and behavior, in the last few years scientists have mapped the specific location and sequence of every human gene. The *Applying Psychology in the 21st Century* box considers how our increasing understanding of genetics is likely to produce a revolution in health care, as scientists identify the particular genes responsible for genetically caused disorders.

The Earliest Development

When an egg becomes fertilized by the sperm, the resulting one-celled entity, called a **zygote,** immediately begins to develop. The zygote starts out as a microscopic speck. Three days after fertilization, though, the zygote increases to around 32 cells, and

Zygote: The new cell formed by the union of an egg and sperm.

FIGURE 2 When an egg and a sperm meet at the moment of fertilization, the egg provides an X chromosome, and the sperm provides either an X or a Y chromosome. If the sperm contributes an X chromosome, the child will have an XX pairing on the 23rd chromosome and will be a girl. If the sperm contributes a Y chromosome, the result will be an XY pairing—a boy.

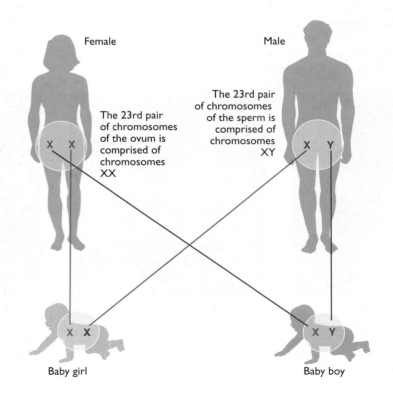

Gene Therapy and the Coming Medical Revolution

A pediatrician rubs a cotton swab across Meghan Johannsen's inside cheek in order to get a DNA sample of the month-old girl and hands it to a technician. In several hours, he has a printout on his desk which provides a complete DNA analysis. He calls Meghan's parents and gives them the good news: By and large, Meghan is quite healthy. However, there are some potential problems— a mild allergy to peanuts, and, more seriously, the likelihood that she will develop high blood pressure in middle age. The pediatrician advises the parents to consider inserting a gene that will prevent her blood pressure from rising to dangerous levels and becoming a major problem.

This futuristic view of a visit to a pediatrician's office is no longer the stuff of science fiction. In the not-so-distant future, advances in our understanding of genetics are likely to lead to not only to the identification of risk factors in children, but also to the development of new treatments for psychological disorders and physical diseases.

In *gene therapy*, health care providers inject genes to correct particular diseases directly into a patient's bloodstream. When the gene arrives at the location of a problem (or potential problem), it leads the body to produce chemicals that can allevi-

ate the danger. For instance, in Meghan's fictitious case, corrective genes could be added that act directly to reduce blood pressure by altering the operation of blood vessels. In other cases, additional genes could be inserted that replace missing or defective cells. It also may be possible to "harvest" defective cells from a child prior to birth. These cells could be treated by gene therapy and reintroduced into the unborn child, thereby repairing the defect (Levy, 2000; Grady & Kolata, 2003; Lymberis et al., 2004).

Although the promise of gene therapy is real, the number of diseases that can be treated today is actually fairly short. Furthermore, the long-term success of gene therapy remains unknown. In fact, after they initially seem to be cured, some recipients of gene therapy have relapsed, and some have suffered from unpleasant side effects (Nakamura et al., 2004; Harris, 2004; Wagner et al., 2004).

The number of uses of gene therapy is growing rapidly. For example, such disorders as AIDS, cystic fibrosis, and rheumatoid arthritis already are strong candidates for gene therapy. In addition, even more promising therapies are coming. For example, a process called germline gene therapy

can correct problems not only for unborn individuals, but for future generations as well. In germline gene therapy, scientists "harvest" defective cells soon after conception, removing them from the fertilized egg within the mother, placing them in a test-tube culture, repairing the defects in the cells, and returning them to the mother. In a more extreme possibility, cells from one parent might be altered genetically to remove any defects, and this clone could then be permitted to grow. The result would be offspring genetically identical to the parent except for the genetic defect. (Weiner, 2000; Smith, 2004; Allhoff, 2005).

Cloning advances raise significant ethical issues. In one radical possibility, cloning might be employed if both a husband and wife were infertile. In such a case, they might consider cloning one or the other of themselves in order to have at least one child who was genetically similar (in this case, genetically identical) to one of them. The ethical and moral issues of such a procedure, of course, are profound. Most Americans oppose cloning of human embryos, and laws limiting human cloning have already been enacted (Levick, 2004; McGee, Caplan, & Malhotra, 2004; Greene et al., 2005; Harris, 2005).

RETHINK

Would you choose to be genetically tested so that you could know your susceptibility to genetic diseases? Would you be tested if you might learn that you had a genetic disorder that was likely to shorten your life? Why or why not?

---

within a week it has grown to 100–150 cells. These first two weeks are known as the *germinal period.*

Two weeks after conception, the developing individual enters the *embryonic period,* which lasts from week 2 through week 8, and he or she is now called an **embryo.** As an embryo develops through an intricate, preprogrammed process of cell division, it grows 10,000 times larger by 4 weeks of age, attaining a length of about one-fifth of an inch. At this point it has developed a rudimentary beating heart, a brain, an intestinal tract, and a number of other organs. Although all these organs are at a primitive stage of development, they are clearly recognizable. Moreover, by week 8, the embryo is about an inch long, and has discernible arms and legs and a face.

From week 8 and continuing until birth, the developing individual enters the *fetal period* and is called a **fetus.** At the start of this period, it begins to be responsive to touch; it bends its fingers when touched on the hand. At 16 to 18 weeks, its movements become strong enough for the mother to sense them. At the same time, hair may begin to grow on the fetus's head, and the facial features become similar to those the child

Embryo: A developed zygote that has a heart, a brain, and other organs.

Fetus: A developing individual, from eight weeks after conception until birth.

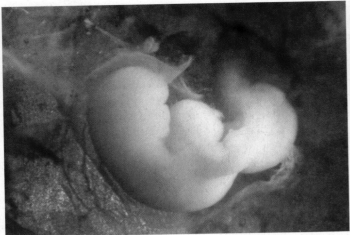
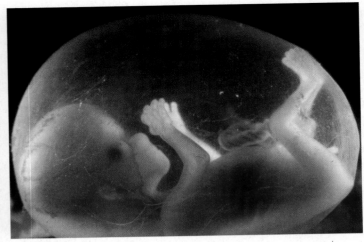

These remarkable photos of live fetuses display the degree of physical development at prenatal ages 4 and 15 weeks.

will display at birth. The major organs begin functioning, although the fetus could not be kept alive outside the mother. In addition, a lifetime's worth of brain neurons are produced—although it is unclear whether the brain is capable of thinking at this early stage.

By week 24, a fetus has many of the characteristics it will display as a newborn. In fact, when an infant is born prematurely at this age, it can open and close its eyes; suck; cry; look up, down, and around; and even grasp objects placed in its hands, although it is still unable to survive for long outside the mother.

Age of viability: The point at which a fetus can survive if born prematurely.

The fetus continues to develop before birth. It begins to grow fatty deposits under the skin, and it gains weight. The fetus reaches the **age of viability,** the point at which it can survive if born prematurely, at about prenatal age 22 weeks, although through advances in medical technology this crucial age is getting earlier. At prenatal age 28 weeks, the fetus weighs less than three pounds and is about sixteen inches long. It may be capable of learning: One study found that the infants of mothers who had repeatedly read aloud the Dr. Seuss story *The Cat in the Hat* before the infants' birth preferred the sound of that particular story to other stories after they were born (Spence & DeCasper, 1982).

Before birth, a fetus passes through several *sensitive periods* (also referred to as *critical periods*). A sensitive period is the time when organisms are particular susceptible to certain kinds of stimuli. For example, fetuses are especially affected by their mothers' use of drugs during certain sensitive periods before birth. If they are exposed to a particular drug before or after the sensitive period, it may have relatively little impact, but if exposure comes during a critical period, the impact will be significant. Sensitive periods can also occur after birth. Some language specialists suggest, for instance, that there is a period in which children are particularly receptive to developing language (deVilliers & deVilliers, 1999; Thompson & Nelson, 2001; Waters & Beauchaine, 2003; Konig, 2005; Werker & Tees, 2005).

In the final weeks of pregnancy, the fetus continues to gain weight and grow. At the end of the normal thirty-eight weeks of pregnancy the fetus typically weighs around seven pounds and is about twenty inches in length. However, the story is different for *preterm infants,* who are born before week 38. Because they have not been able to develop fully, they are at higher risk for illness, future problems, and even death. For infants who have been in the womb for more than thirty weeks, the prospects are relatively good. However, for those born before week 30, the story is often less positive. Such newborns, who may weigh as little as two pounds at birth, are in grave danger because they have immature organs; they have less than a 50–50 chance of survival. If they do survive—and it takes extraordinarily heroic (and expensive) medical intervention to assure this—they may later experience significant developmental delays.

GENETIC INFLUENCES ON THE FETUS

The process of fetal growth that we have just described reflects normal development, which occurs in 95 to 98 percent of all pregnancies. Some individuals are less fortunate, for in the remaining 2 to 5 percent of cases, children are born with serious birth defects. A major cause of such defects is faulty genes or chromosomes. Here are some of the more common genetic and chromosomal difficulties.

- *Phenylketonuria (PKU).* A child born with the inherited disease phenylketonuria cannot produce an enzyme that is required for normal development. This results in an accumulation of poisons that eventually cause profound mental retardation. The disease is treatable, however, if it is caught early. Most infants today are routinely tested for PKU, and children with the disorder can be placed on a special diet that allows them to develop normally (Walter et al., 2002; Gassio et al., 2005; Ievers-Landis et al., 2005).
- *Sickle-cell anemia.* About 10 percent of the African American population has the possibility of passing on sickle-cell anemia, a disease that gets its name from the abnormally shaped red blood cells it causes. Children with the disease may have poor appetites, swollen stomachs, yellowish eyes, and cognitive difficulties; they frequently die during childhood (Helps et al., 2003; Kral & Brown, 2004; Taras & Potts-Datema, 2005).
- *Tay-Sachs disease.* Children born with Tay-Sachs disease, a disorder most often found in Jews of eastern European ancestry, usually die by age 3 or 4 because of the body's inability to break down fat. If both parents carry the genetic defect that produces the fatal illness, their child has a one in four chance of being born with the disease (Navon & Proia, 1989; Leib et al., 2005).
- *Down syndrome.* Down syndrome, one of the causes of mental retardation, occurs when the zygote receives an extra chromosome at the moment of conception. Down syndrome is often related to the mother's age; mothers over 35 and younger than 18, in particular, stand a higher risk than other women of having a child with the syndrome (Roizen & Patterson, 2003).

PRENATAL ENVIRONMENTAL INFLUENCES

Genetic factors are not the only causes of difficulties in fetal development. Environmental influences—the *nurture* part of the nature-nurture equation—also affect the fetus. Some of the more profound consequences are brought about by **teratogens**, environmental agents such as a drug, chemical, virus, or other factor that produce a birth defect. Among the major prenatal environmental influences on the fetus are the following:

Teratogens: Environmental agents such as a drug, chemical, virus, or other factor that produce a birth defect.

- *Mother's nutrition.* What a mother eats during her pregnancy can have important implications for the health of her baby. Seriously undernourished mothers cannot provide adequate nutrition to a growing fetus, and they are likely to give birth to underweight babies. Poorly nourished babies are also more susceptible to disease, and a lack of nourishment may have an adverse impact on their mental development (Adams & Parker, 1990; Ricciuti, 1993; Sigman, 1995; Zigler, Finn-Stevenson, & Hall, 2002; Najman et al., 2004).
- *Mother's illness.* Several diseases that have a relatively minor effect on the health of a mother can have devastating consequences for a developing fetus if they are contracted during the early part of a pregnancy. For example, rubella (German measles), syphilis, diabetes, and high blood pressure may each produce a permanent effect on the fetus. The virus that causes AIDS can also be passed from mother to child before birth, as well as through breast-feeding after birth (Nesheim et al., 2004; Magoni et al., 2005).

• *Mother's emotional state.* A mother's emotional state affects her baby. Mothers who are anxious and tense during the last months of their pregnancies are more apt to have irritable infants who sleep and eat poorly. The reason? The autonomic nervous system of the fetus becomes especially sensitive as a result of chemical changes produced by the mother's emotional state (Relier, 2001).

• *Mother's use of drugs.* Mothers who take illegal, physically addictive drugs such as cocaine run the risk of giving birth to babies who are similarly addicted. Their newborns suffer painful withdrawal symptoms and sometimes show permanent physical and mental impairment as well. Even legal drugs taken by a pregnant woman (who may not know that she has become pregnant) can have a tragic effect. For example, drugs such as the acne medicine Accutane can produce abnormalities (Streissguth et al., 1999; Ikonomidou et al., 2000; Schechter, Finkelstein, & Koren, 2005).

• *Alcohol use.* Alcohol is dangerous to fetal development. For example, 1 out of every 750 infants is born with *fetal alcohol syndrome (FAS)*, a condition resulting in below-average intelligence, growth delays, and facial deformities. FAS is now the primary preventable cause of mental retardation (Steinhausen & Spohr, 1998; Burd et al., 2003; Wass, Mattson, & Riley, 2004). Even mothers who use small amounts of alcohol during pregnancy place their child at risk. *Fetal alcohol effects (FAE)* is a condition in which children display some, although not all, of the problems of FAS due to their mother's consumption of alcohol during pregnancy (Streissguth, 1997; Baer, Sampson, & Barr, 2003).

• *Nicotine use.* Pregnant mothers who smoke put their children at considerable risk. Smoking by pregnant women leads to more than 100,000 miscarriages and the deaths of 5,600 babies in the United States alone each year (Mills, 1999; Ness et al., 1999; Haslam & Lawrence, 2004).

Several other environmental factors have an impact on the child before and during birth (see Figure 3). Keep in mind, however, that although we have been discussing the influences of genetics and environment separately, neither factor works alone. (Complete the PsychInteractive exercise to gain a fuller understanding of prenatal development.) Furthermore, despite the emphasis here on some of the ways in which

www.mhhe.com/feldmanup8

PsychInteractive Online

Prenatal Development

FIGURE 3 A variety of environmental factors can play a role in prenatal development.

Environmental Factor	Possible Effect on Prenatal Development
Rubella (German measles)	Blindness, deafness, heart abnormalities, stillbirth
Syphilis	Mental retardation, physical deformities, maternal miscarriage
Addictive drugs	Low birth weight, addiction of infant to drug, with possible death after birth from withdrawal
Nicotine	Premature birth, low birth weight and length
Alcohol	Mental retardation, lower-than-average birth weight, small head, limb deformities
Radiation from X rays	Physical deformities, mental retardation
Inadequate diet	Reduction in growth of brain, smaller-than-average weight and length at birth
Mother's age—younger than 18 at birth of child	Premature birth, increased incidence of Down syndrome
Mother's age—older than 35 at birth of child	Increased incidence of Down syndrome
DES (diethylstilbestrol)	Reproductive difficulties and increased incidence of genital cancer in children of mothers who were given DES during pregnancy to prevent miscarriage
AIDS	Possible spread of AIDS virus to infant; facial deformities; growth failure
Accutane	Mental retardation and physical deformities

development can go wrong, the vast majority of births occur without difficulty. And in most instances, subsequent development also proceeds normally.

ALTERNATIVE PATHS TO CONCEPTION

For most couples, conception is routine, and pregnancy unfolds without incident. In other cases, though, conception represents a major challenge. Sometimes it is due to males producing too few sperm. In other cases, the inability to become pregnant, known as infertility, is due to the advanced age of the parents, use of drugs, or previous cases of sexually transmitted disease.

Scientists have devised several remedies to overcome infertility. One option is *in vitro fertilization (IVF),* the process used to conceive Louise Brown (discussed in the prologue). *In vitro* fertilization is a procedure in which a woman's eggs are removed from her ovaries, and a man's sperm is used to fertilize the eggs in a laboratory. A fertilized egg is then implanted in a woman's uterus. Similarly, *gamete intrafallopian transfer (GIFT)* and *zygote intrafallopian transfer (ZIFT)* are procedures in which an egg and sperm or fertilized egg are implanted in a woman's fallopian tubes. In IVF, GIFT, and ZIFT, the fertilized egg typically is implanted in the woman who provided the eggs. In some cases, eggs are implanted in a *surrogate mother,* a woman who agrees to carry the child to term.

RECAP/EVALUATE/RETHINK

RECAP

What is the nature of development before birth?

- Each chromosome contains genes, through which genetic information is transmitted. Genes, which are composed of DNA sequences, are the "software" that programs the future development of the body's hardware. (p. 403)
- Genes affect not only physical attributes but also a wide array of personal characteristics such as cognitive abilities, personality traits, and psychological disorders. (p. 403)
- At the moment of conception, a male's sperm cell and a female's egg cell unite, with each contributing to the new individual's genetic makeup. The union of sperm and egg produces a zygote, which contains 23 pairs of chromosomes—with one member of each pair coming from the father and the other coming from the mother. (pp. 403-404)
- After two weeks the zygote becomes an embryo. By week 8, the embryo is called a fetus and is responsive to touch and other stimulation. At about week 22 it reaches the age of viability, which means it may survive if born prematurely. A fetus is normally born after thirty-eight weeks of pregnancy, weighing around seven pounds and measuring about twenty inches. (pp. 405-407)

What factors affect a child during the mother's pregnancy?

- Genetic abnormalities produce birth defects such as phenylketonuria (PKU), sickle-cell anemia, Tay-Sachs disease, and Down syndrome. (p. 407)
- Among the environmental influences on fetal growth are the mother's nutrition, illnesses, and drug intake. (pp. 407-408)

EVALUATE

1. Match each of the following terms with its definition:
    1. Zygote
    2. Gene
    3. Chromosome
    a. Smallest unit through which genetic information is passed
    b. Fertilized egg
    c. Rod-shaped structure containing genetic information
2. Specific kinds of growth must take place during a _____ period if the embryo is to develop normally.
3. A _____ is an environmental agent such as a drug, chemical, virus, or other factor that produces a birth defect.

RETHINK

1. Given the possible effects of the environment on a developing fetus, do you think pregnant women should

be prosecuted for the use of alcohol and other drugs that may do serious harm to their unborn children? Defend your position.

2. *From the perspective of an educator:* How would you use your knowledge of sensitive periods in language to improve students' learning? Would you want to teach children more than one language during this time?

Answers to Evaluate Questions

1. 1-b, 2-a, 3-c; 2. sensitive or critical; 3. teratogen

KEY TERMS

chromosomes p. 403

genes p. 403

zygote p. 404

embryo p. 405

fetus p. 405

age of viability p. 406

teratogens p. 407

Infancy and Childhood

His head was molded into a long melon shape and came to a point at the back.... He was covered with a thick greasy white material known as "vernix," which made him slippery to hold, and also allowed him to slip easily through the birth canal. In addition to a shock of black hair on his head, his body was covered with dark, fine hair known as "lanugo." His ears, his back, his shoulders, and even his cheeks were furry.... His skin was wrinkled and quite loose, ready to scale in creased places such as his feet and hands.... His ears were pressed to his head in unusual positions—one ear was matted firmly forward on his cheek. His nose was flattened and pushed to one side by the squeeze as he came through the pelvis (Brazelton, 1969, p. 3).

What kind of creature is this? Although the description hardly fits that of the adorable babies seen in advertisements for baby food, we are in fact talking about a normal, completely developed child just after the moment of birth. Called a **neonate,** a newborn arrives in the world in a form that hardly meets the standards of beauty against which we typically measure babies. Yet ask any parents: Nothing is more beautiful or exciting than the first glimpse of their newborn.

Key Concepts

What are the major competencies of newborns?

What are the milestones of physical and social development during childhood?

How does cognitive development proceed during childhood?

Neonate: A newborn child.

The Extraordinary Newborn

Several factors cause a neonate's strange appearance. The trip through the mother's birth canal may have squeezed the incompletely formed bones of the skull together and squashed the nose into the head. The skin secretes *vernix,* a white, greasy covering, for protection before birth, and the baby may have *lanugo,* a soft fuzz, over the entire body for a similar purpose. The infant's eyelids may be puffy with an accumulation of fluids because of the upside-down position during birth.

Reflexes: Unlearned, involuntary responses that occur automatically in the presence of certain stimuli.

All this changes during the first two weeks of life as the neonate takes on a more familiar appearance. Even more impressive are the capabilities a neonate begins to display from the moment of birth—capabilities that grow at an astounding rate over the ensuing months.

REFLEXES

A neonate is born with a number of **reflexes**—unlearned, involuntary responses that occur automatically in the presence of certain stimuli. Critical for survival, many of those reflexes unfold naturally as part of an infant's ongoing maturation. The *rooting reflex,* for instance, causes neonates to turn their heads toward things that touch their cheeks—such as the mother's nipple or a bottle. Similarly, a *sucking reflex* prompts infants to suck at things that touch their lips. Among other reflexes are a *gag reflex* (to clear the throat), the *startle reflex* (a series of movements in which an infant flings out the arms, fans the fingers, and arches the back in response to a sudden

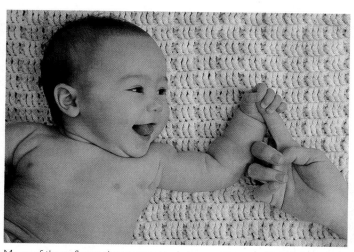

Many of the reflexes that a neonate is born with are critical for survival and unfold naturally as a part of an infant's ongoing maturation. Do you think humans have more or fewer reflexes than other animals?

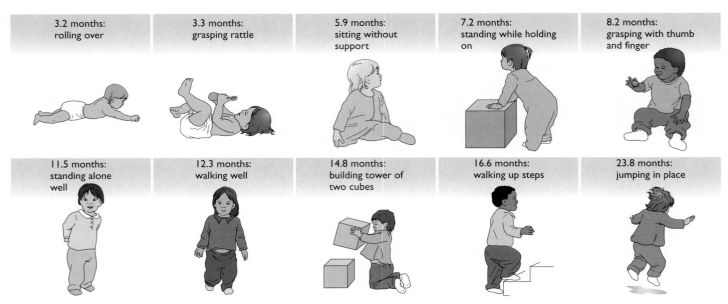

FIGURE 1 Although at birth a neonate can make only jerky, limited voluntary movements, during the first year of life the ability to move independently grows enormously. The ages indicate the time when 50 percent of children are able to perform each skill (Frankenburg et al., 1992). Remember, however, that the time when each skill appears can vary considerably. For example, 25 percent of children are able to walk well at age 11 months, and by 15 months 90 percent of children are walking well.

noise), and the *Babinski reflex* (a baby's toes fan out when the outer edge of the sole of the foot is stroked).

Infants lose these primitive reflexes after the first few months of life, replacing them with more complex and organized behaviors. Although at birth a neonate is capable of only jerky, limited voluntary movements, during the first year of life the ability to move independently grows enormously. The typical baby rolls over by the age of 3 months, sits without support at 6 months, stands alone at about 11 months, and walks at just over a year old. Not only does the ability to make large-scale movements improve during this time, fine-muscle movements become increasingly sophisticated (see Figure 1).

DEVELOPMENT OF THE SENSES: TAKING IN THE WORLD

When proud parents peer into the eyes of their neonate, is the child able to return their gaze? Although it was thought for some time that newborns can see only a hazy blur, most current findings indicate that the capabilities of neonates are far more impressive. Although their eyes have a limited capacity to focus on objects that are not within a seven- to eight-inch distance from the face, neonates can follow objects moving within their field of vision. They also show the rudiments of depth perception, as they react by raising their hands when an object appears to be moving rapidly toward the face (Gelman & Kit-Fong Au, 1996; Maurer et al., 1999).

You might think that it would be hard to figure out just how well neonates can see, because their lack of both language and reading ability clearly prevents them from saying what direction the *E* on a vision chart is facing. However, researchers have devised a number of ingenious methods, relying on the newborn's biological responses and innate reflexes, to test perceptual skills.

For instance, infants who see a novel stimulus typically pay close attention to it, and, as a consequence, their heart rates increase. But if they repeatedly see the same stimulus, their attention to it decreases, as indicated by a return to a slower heart rate. This phenomenon is known as **habituation,** the decrease in the response to a stimulus that occurs after repeated presentations of the same stimulus. By studying habituation, developmental psychologists can tell when a stimulus can be detected and discriminated by a child who is too young to speak (Grunwald et al., 2003; Hannon & Johnson, 2005).

Researchers have developed many other methods for measuring neonate and infant perception. One technique, for instance, involves babies sucking on a nipple attached to a computer. A change in the rate and vigor with which the babies suck helps researchers infer that babies can perceive variations in stimuli. Other approaches include examining babies' eye movements and observing which way babies move their heads in response to a visual stimulus (George, 1999; Franklin, Pilling, & Davies, 2005).

Through the use of such research techniques, we now know that infants' visual perception is remarkably sophisticated from the start of life. At birth, babies prefer patterns with contours and edges over less distinct patterns, indicating that they can respond to the configuration of stimuli. Furthermore, even newborns are aware of size constancy, because they are apparently sensitive to the phenomenon by which objects stay the same size even though the image on the retina may change size as the distance between the object and the retina varies (Slater, 1996; Johnson et al., 2003; Norcia et al., 2005).

In fact, neonates can discriminate facial expressions—and even imitate them. As you can see in Figure 2, newborns who see an adult with a happy, sad, or surprised facial expression can produce a good imitation of the adult's expression. Even very young infants, then, can respond to the emotions and moods that their caregivers' facial expressions reveal. This capability provides the foundation for social interaction skills in children (Meltzoff, 1996; Montague & Walker-Andrews, 2002; Lavelli & Fogel, 2005).

Other visual abilities grow rapidly after birth. By the end of their first month, babies can distinguish some colors from others, and after four months they can focus on near or far objects. By age 4 or 5 months they are able to recognize two- and three-dimensional objects, and they can perceive the gestalt organizing principles discovered by

Habituation: The decrease in the response to a stimulus that occurs after repeated presentations of the same stimulus.

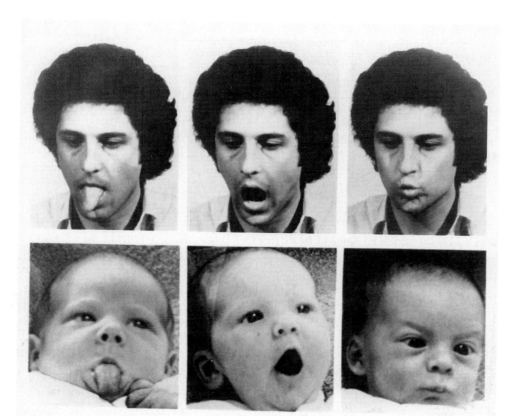

FIGURE 2 This newborn infant is clearly imitating the expressions of the adult model in these amazing photos. How does this ability contribute to social development? (Courtesy of Dr. Tiffany Field.)

psychologists who study perception. Furthermore, their perceptual abilities rapidly improve: Sensitivity to visual stimuli, for instance, becomes three to four times greater at 1 year of age than it was at birth (Slater, 1996; Vital-Durand, Atkinson, & Braddick, 1996; Johnson et al., 2003; Johnson, 2004).

In addition to vision, infants display other impressive sensory capabilities. Newborns can distinguish different sounds to the point of being able to recognize their own mothers' voices at the age of 3 days. They can also make the subtle perceptual distinctions that underlie language abilities. For example, at 2 days of age, infants can distinguish between their native tongue and foreign languages, and they can discriminate between such closely related sounds as *ba* and *pa* when they are 4 days old. By 6 months of age, they can discriminate virtually any difference in sound that is relevant to the production of language. Moreover, they can recognize different tastes and smells at a very early age. There even seems to be something of a built-in sweet tooth: Neonates prefer liquids that have been sweetened with sugar over their unsweetened counterparts (Bornstein & Arterberry, 1999; Akman et al., 2002; Cohen & Cashon, 2003; Rivera-Gaxiola et al., 2005).

The Growing Child: Infancy Through Middle Childhood

It was during the windy days of March that the problem in the day care center first arose. Its source: 10-month-old Russell Ruud. Otherwise a model of decorum, Russell had somehow learned how to unzip the Velcro chin strap to his winter hat. He would remove the hat whenever he got the urge, seemingly oblivious to the potential health problems that might follow.

But that was just the start of the real difficulty. To the chagrin of the teachers in the day care center, not to speak of the children's parents, soon other children were following his lead, removing their own caps at will. Russell's mother, made aware of the anarchy at the day care center—and the other parents' distress over Russell's behavior—pleaded innocent. "I never showed Russell how to unzip the Velcro," claimed his mother, Judith Ruud, an economist with the Congressional Budget Office in Washington, D.C. "He learned by trial and error, and the other kids saw him do it one day when they were getting dressed for an outing" (Goleman, 1993, p. C10).

At the age of 10 months, Russell asserted his personality, illustrating the tremendous growth that occurs in a variety of domains during the first year of life. Throughout the remainder of childhood, moving from infancy into middle childhood and the start of adolescence around age 11 or 12, children develop physically, socially, and cognitively in extraordinary ways. In the remainder of this module, we'll consider this development.

PHYSICAL DEVELOPMENT

Children's physical growth provides the most obvious sign of development. During the first year of life, children typically triple their birthweight, and their height increases by about half. This rapid growth slows down as the child gets older—think how gigantic adults would be if that rate of growth were constant—and from age 3 to the beginning of adolescence at around age 13, growth averages a gain of about five pounds and three inches a year (see Figure 3).

The physical changes that occur as children develop are not just a matter of increasing growth; the relationship of the size of the various body parts to one another changes dramatically as children age. As you can see in Figure 4, the head of a fetus (and a newborn) is disproportionately large. However, the head soon

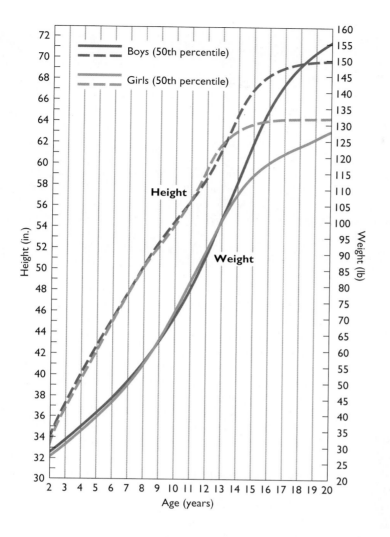

FIGURE 3 The average heights and weights of males and females in the United States from birth through age 20. At what ages are girls typically heavier and taller than boys? (Source: National Center for Health Statistics, 2000.)

becomes more proportional in size to the rest of the body as growth occurs mainly in the trunk and legs.

DEVELOPMENT OF SOCIAL BEHAVIOR: TAKING ON THE WORLD

As anyone who has seen an infant smiling at the sight of his or her mother can guess, at the same time that infants grow physically and hone their perceptual abilities, they also develop socially. The nature of a child's early social development provides the foundation for social relationships that will last a lifetime.

Attachment, the positive emotional bond that develops between a child and a particular individual, is the most important form of social development that occurs during infancy. The earliest studies of attachment were carried out by animal ethologist Konrad Lorenz (1966). Lorenz focused on newborn goslings, which under normal circumstances instinctively follow their mother, the first moving object they perceive after birth. Lorenz found that goslings whose eggs were raised in an incubator and which viewed him immediately after hatching would follow his every movement, as if he were their mother. He labeled this process *imprinting,* behavior that takes place during a critical period and involves attachment to the first moving object that is observed.

Our understanding of attachment progressed when psychologist Harry Harlow, in a classic study, gave infant monkeys the choice of cuddling a wire "monkey" that

Attachment: The positive emotional bond that develops between a child and a particular individual.

FIGURE 4 As development progresses, the size of the head relative to the rest of the body decreases until the individual reaches adulthood. Why do you think the head starts out so large?

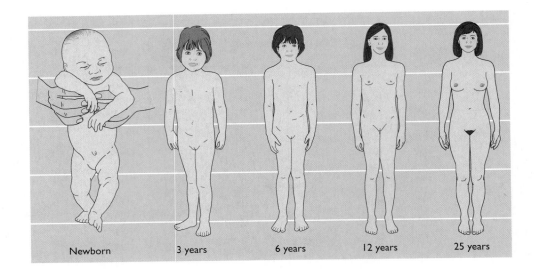

| Newborn | 3 years | 6 years | 12 years | 25 years |

FIGURE 5 Although the wire "mother" dispensed milk to the hungry infant monkey, the infant preferred the soft, terry-cloth "mother." Do you think human babies would react the same way? What does this tell us about attachment? (Source: Harry Harlow Primate Laboratory/ University of Wisconsin.)

provided milk or a soft, terry-cloth "monkey" that was warm but did not provide milk. Their choice was clear: They spent most of their time clinging to the warm cloth "monkey," although they made occasional forays to the wire monkey to nurse. Obviously, the cloth monkey provided greater comfort to the infants; milk alone was insufficient to create attachment (Harlow & Zimmerman, 1959; Blum, 2002; see Figure 5).

Building on this pioneering work with nonhumans, developmental psychologists have suggested that human attachment grows through the responsiveness of infants' caregivers to the signals the babies provide, such as crying, smiling, reaching, and clinging. The greater the responsiveness of the caregiver to the child's signals, the more likely it is that the child will become securely attached. Full attachment eventually develops as a result of the complex series of interactions between caregiver and child illustrated in Figure 6. In the course of these interactions, the infant plays as critical and active a role as the caregiver in the formation of the bond. Infants who respond positively to a caregiver produce more positive behavior on the part of the caregiver, which in turn produces an even stronger degree of attachment in the child.

Assessing Attachment. Developmental psychologists have devised a quick and direct way to measure attachment. Developed by Mary Ainsworth, the *Ainsworth strange situation* consists of a sequence of events involving a child and (typically) his or her mother. Initially, the mother and baby enter an unfamiliar room, and the mother permits the baby to explore while she sits down. An adult stranger then enters the room, after which the mother leaves. The mother returns, and the stranger leaves. The mother once again leaves the baby alone, and the stranger returns. Finally, the stranger leaves, and the mother returns (Ainsworth et al., 1978; Waters & Beauchaine, 2003; Izard & Abe, 2004).

Babies' reactions to the experimental situation vary drastically, depending, according to Ainsworth, on their degree of attachment to the mother. One-year-old children who are *securely attached* employ the mother as a kind of home base, exploring independently but returning to her occasionally. When she leaves, they exhibit distress, and they go to her when she returns. *Avoidant* children do not cry when the mother leaves, and they seem to avoid her when she returns, as if they were indifferent to her. *Ambivalent* children display anxiety before they are separated and are upset when the mother leaves, but they may show ambivalent reactions to her return, such as seeking close contact but simultaneously hitting and

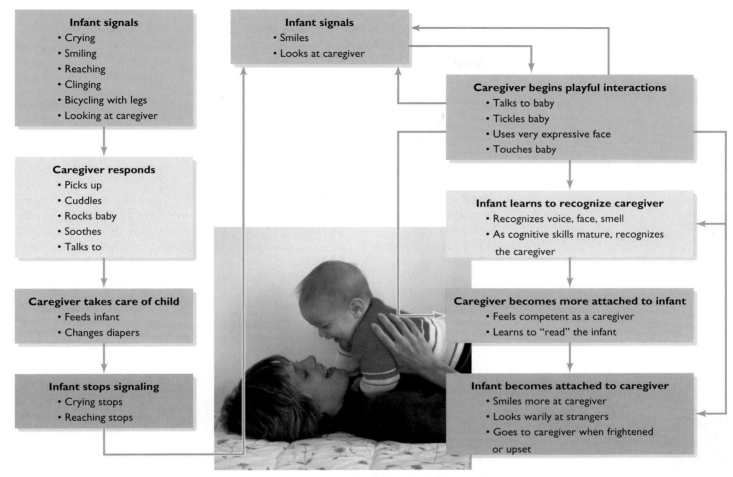

FIGURE 6 The Attachment Behavioral System shows the sequence of activities that infants employ to keep their primary caregivers physically close and bring about attachment. Early in life, crying is the most effective behavior. Later, though, infants keep the caregiver near through other, more socially appropriate behaviors such as smiling, looking, and reaching. After they are able to walk, children play a more active role in staying close to the caregiver. At the same time, the caregiver's behavior interacts with the baby's activities to promote attachment. (Source: Tomlinson-Keasey, 1985.)

kicking her. A fourth reaction is *disorganized-disoriented;* these children show inconsistent, often contradictory behavior.

The nature of attachment between children and their mothers has far-reaching consequences for later development. For example, children who are securely attached to their mothers tend to be more socially and emotionally competent than are their less securely attached peers, and others find them more cooperative, capable, and playful. Furthermore, children who are securely attached at age 1 show fewer psychological difficulties when they grow older compared with avoidant and ambivalent youngsters. As adults, children who are securely attached tend to have more successful romantic relationships. On the other hand, being securely attached at an early age does not guarantee good adjustment later, and, conversely, children who lack secure attachment do not always have difficulties later in life (Hamilton, 2000; Waters, Hamilton, & Weinfield, 2000; Bakermans-Kranenburg, van Ijzendoorn, & Juffer, 2003; Fraley & Spieker, 2003; Mikulincer & Shaver, 2005; Roisman et al., 2005).

The Father's Role. Although early developmental research focused largely on the mother-child relationship, more recent research has highlighted the father's role in parenting, and with good reason: The number of fathers who are primary caregivers for their children has grown significantly, and fathers play an increasingly important role in their children's lives. For example, in almost 20 percent of families with children, the father is the parent who stays at home to care for preschoolers (Fitzgerald et al., 2003; Parke, 2004; Day & Lamb, 2004).

When fathers interact with their children, their play often differs from that of mothers. Fathers engage in more physical, rough-and-tumble sorts of activities, whereas mothers play more verbal and traditional games, such as peekaboo. Despite such behavioral differences, the nature of attachment between fathers and children compared with that between mothers and children can be similar. In fact, children can form multiple attachments simultaneously (Genuis & Violato, 2000; Sagi et al., 2002; Paquette, Carbonneau, & Dubeau, 2003).

Social Relationships with Peers. By the time they are 2 years old, children become less dependent on their parents and more self-reliant, increasingly preferring to play with friends. Initially, play is relatively independent: Even though they may be sitting side by side, 2-year-olds pay more attention to toys than to one another when playing. Later, however, children actively interact, modifying one another's behavior and later exchanging roles during play (Bukowski, Newcomb, & Hartup, 1996; Lindsey & Colwell, 2003; Colwell & Lindsey, 2005).

Cultural factors also affect children's styles of play. For example, Korean American children engage in a higher proportion of parallel play than their Anglo-American counterparts, while Anglo-American preschoolers are involved in more pretend play (Farver, Kim, & Lee-Shin, 1995; Farver & Lee-Shin, 2000; Bai, 2005; Drewes, 2005).

As children reach school age, their social interactions begin to follow set patterns, as well as becoming more frequent. They may engage in elaborate games involving teams and rigid rules. This play serves purposes other than mere enjoyment. It allows children to become increasingly competent in their social interactions with others. Through play they learn to take the perspective of other people and to infer others' thoughts and feelings, even when those thoughts and feelings are not directly expressed (Asher & Parker, 1991; Royzman, Cassidy, & Baron, 2003).

In short, social interaction helps children interpret the meaning of others' behavior and develop the capacity to respond appropriately. Furthermore, children learn physical and emotional self-control: They learn to avoid hitting a playmate who beats them at a game, be polite, and control their emotional displays and facial expressions (e.g., smiling even when receiving a disappointing gift). Situations that provide children with opportunities for social interaction, then, may enhance their social development (Feldman, 1982, 1993; Lengua & Long, 2002).

The Consequences of Child Care Outside the Home. Research on the importance of social interaction is corroborated by work that examines the benefits of child care out of the home, which is an important part of an increasing number of children's lives. For instance, almost 20 percent of preschool children whose mothers work outside the home spend their days in child-care centers. More than 80 percent of infants are cared for by people other than their mothers for part of the day during the first year of life. Most of these infants begin child care before the age of 4 months and are cared for by people other than their mothers for almost thirty hours per week (NICHD Early Child Care Research Network, 1997; National Research Council, 2000; see Figure 7).

Do out-of-the-home child-care arrangements benefit children's development? If the programs are of high quality, they can. According to the results of a large study supported by the U.S. National Institute of Child Health and Development, children who attend high-quality child-care centers may not only do as well as children who stay at home with their parents, but in some respects may actually do better. Children in child care are generally more considerate and sociable than other children are, and they interact more positively with teachers. They may also be more compliant and regulate their own behavior more effectively, and their mothers show increased sensitivity to their children (Lamb, 1996; NICHD Early Child Care Research Network, 1997, 1998, 1999, 2001).

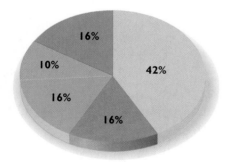

- A parent not employed outside home
- One or both parents employed outside home
- Other relatives (grandparents, siblings, etc.)
- Paid home-based care
- Paid day care centers or preschools

FIGURE 7 Almost 20 percent of children younger than 5 years of age whose mothers work outside the home spend their days in child care or preschool centers; the remainder receive care in their own or someone else's home. (Source: U.S. Bureau of the Census, 1999.)

In addition, especially for children from poor or disadvantaged homes, child care in specially enriched environments—those with many toys, books, a variety of children, and high-quality care providers—often proves to be more intellectually stimulating than the home environment. Such child care can lead to increased intellectual achievement, demonstrated in higher IQ scores and better language development. In fact, children in care centers sometimes are found to score higher on tests of cognitive abilities than those who are cared for by their mothers or by sitters or home day-care providers—effects lasting into adulthood (Wilgoren, 1999; Burchinal, Roberts, & Riggins, 2000).

However, outside-the-home child care does not have universally positive outcomes. Children may feel insecure after placement in low-quality child care or in multiple child-care settings. Furthermore, some research suggests that infants who are involved in outside care more than twenty hours a week in the first year show less secure attachment to their mothers than do those who have not been in outside-the-home child care. Finally, children who spent long hours in child care as infants and preschoolers may have a reduced ability to work independently and to manage their time effectively when they reach elementary school (Belsky & Rovine, 1988; NICHD Early Child Care Research Network, 1997, 1998, 2001; Belsky, 2002; Brooks-Gunn, Han, & Waldfogel, 2002; Vandell et al., 2005).

The key to the success of nonparental child care is its quality. High-quality child care produces benefits; low-quality child care provides little or no gain, and may even hinder children's development. In short, significant benefits result from the social interaction and intellectual stimulation provided by high-quality child-care centers—particularly for children from impoverished environments (NICHD Early Child Care Research Network, 2000, 2002; Ghazvini & Mullis, 2002; Friedman, 2004; National Association for the Education of Young Children, 2005; Papero, 2005).

Parenting Styles and Social Development. Parents' child-rearing practices are critical in shaping their children's social competence, and—according to classic research by developmental psychologist Diana Baumrind—four main categories describe different parenting styles (Figure 8). Rigid and punitive, **authoritarian parents** value unquestioning obedience from their children. They have strict standards and discourage expressions of disagreement. **Permissive parents** give their children relaxed or inconsistent

Authoritarian parents: Parents who are rigid and punitive and value unquestioning obedience from their children.

Permissive parents: Parents who give their children relaxed or inconsistent direction and, although warm, require little of them.

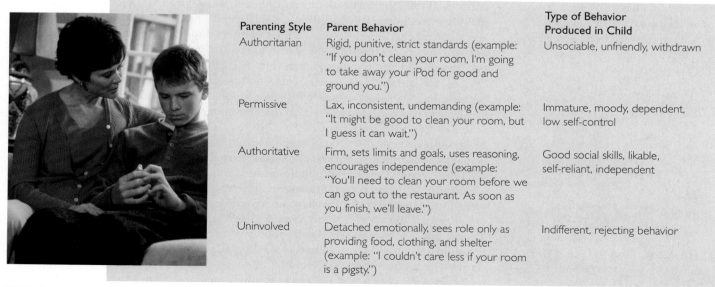

Parenting Style	Parent Behavior	Type of Behavior Produced in Child
Authoritarian	Rigid, punitive, strict standards (example: "If you don't clean your room, I'm going to take away your iPod for good and ground you.")	Unsociable, unfriendly, withdrawn
Permissive	Lax, inconsistent, undemanding (example: "It might be good to clean your room, but I guess it can wait.")	Immature, moody, dependent, low self-control
Authoritative	Firm, sets limits and goals, uses reasoning, encourages independence (example: "You'll need to clean your room before we can go out to the restaurant. As soon as you finish, we'll leave.")	Good social skills, likable, self-reliant, independent
Uninvolved	Detached emotionally, sees role only as providing food, clothing, and shelter (example: "I couldn't care less if your room is a pigsty.")	Indifferent, rejecting behavior

FIGURE 8 According to developmental psychologist Diana Baumrind (1971), four main parenting styles characterize child rearing.

Authoritative parents: Parents who are firm, set clear limits, reason with their children, and explain things to them.

Uninvolved parents: Parents who show little interest in their children and are emotionally detached.

Temperament: Basic, innate disposition.

Psychosocial development: Development of individuals' interactions and understanding of each other and of their knowledge and understanding of themselves as members of society.

direction and, although warm, require little of them. In contrast, **authoritative parents** are firm, setting limits for their children. As the children get older, these parents try to reason and explain things to them. They also set clear goals and encourage their children's independence. Finally, **uninvolved parents** show little interest in their children. Emotionally detached, they view parenting as nothing more than providing food, clothing, and shelter for children. At their most extreme, uninvolved parents are guilty of neglect, a form of child abuse (Baumrind, 1971, 1980; Maccoby & Martin, 1983; Winsler, Madigan, & Aquilino, 2005).

As you might expect, the four kinds of child-rearing styles seem to produce very different kinds of behavior in children (with many exceptions, of course). Children of authoritarian parents tend to be unsociable, unfriendly, and relatively withdrawn. In contrast, permissive parents' children show immaturity, moodiness, dependence, and low self-control. The children of authoritative parents fare best: With high social skills, they are likable, self-reliant, independent, and cooperative. Worst off are the children of uninvolved parents; they feel unloved and emotionally detached, and their physical and cognitive development is impeded (Saarni, 1999; Berk, 2005; Snyder, Cramer, & Afrank, 2005).

Before we rush to congratulate authoritative parents and condemn authoritarian, permissive, and uninvolved ones, it is important to note that in many cases nonauthoritative parents also produce perfectly well-adjusted children. Moreover, children are born with a particular **temperament**—a basic, innate disposition. Some children are naturally easygoing and cheerful, whereas others are irritable and fussy. The kind of temperament a baby is born with may in part bring about particular kinds of parental child-rearing styles (Chess, 1997; Porter & Hsu, 2003; Lengua & Kovacs, 2005).

In addition, children vary considerably in their degree of *resilience,* the ability to overcome circumstances that place them at high risk for psychological or even physical harm. Highly resilient children have temperaments that evoke positive responses from caregivers. Such children display unusual social skills: outgoingness, intelligence, and a feeling that they have control over their lives. In a sense, resilient children try to shape their own environment, rather than being victimized by it (Werner, 1995; Luthars, Cicchetti, & Becker, 2000; Deater-Deckard, Ivy, & Smith, 2005).

We also need to keep in mind that these findings regarding child-rearing styles apply primarily to U.S. society, which highly values children's growing independence and diminishing reliance on their parents. In contrast, Japanese parents encourage dependence to promote the values of cooperation and community life. These differences in cultural values result in very different philosophies of child rearing. For example, Japanese mothers believe it is a punishment to make a young child sleep alone, and so many children sleep next to their mothers throughout infancy and toddlerhood (Miyake, Chen, & Campos, 1985; Kawasaki et al., 1994; Dennis et al., 2002).

In sum, a child's upbringing results from the child-rearing philosophy parents hold, the specific practices they use, and the nature of their own and their child's personalities. As is the case with other aspects of development, then, behavior is a function of a complex interaction of environmental and genetic factors.

Erikson's Theory of Psychosocial Development. In tracing the course of social development, some theorists have considered how the challenges of society and culture change as an individual matures. Following this path, psychoanalyst Erik Erikson developed one of the more comprehensive theories of social development. Erikson (1963) viewed the developmental changes occurring throughout life as a series of eight stages of psychosocial development, of which four occur during childhood. **Psychosocial development** involves changes in our interactions and understanding of one another as well as in our knowledge and understanding of ourselves as members of society.

Erikson suggests that passage through each of the stages necessitates the resolution of a crisis or conflict. Accordingly, Erikson represents each stage as a pairing of the most positive and most negative aspects of the crisis of that period. Although

"Please Jason. Don't you want to grow up to be an autonomous person?"

each crisis is never resolved entirely—life becomes increasingly complicated as we grow older—it has to be resolved sufficiently to equip us to deal with demands made during the following stage of development.

In the first stage of psychosocial development, the **trust-versus-mistrust stage** (ages birth to 1½ years), infants develop feelings of trust if their physical requirements and psychological needs for attachment are consistently met and their interactions with the world are generally positive. In contrast, inconsistent care and unpleasant interactions with others can lead to mistrust and leave an infant unable to meet the challenges required in the next stage of development.

In the second stage, the **autonomy-versus-shame-and-doubt stage** (ages 1½ to 3 years), toddlers develop independence and autonomy if exploration and freedom are encouraged, or they experience shame, self-doubt, and unhappiness if they are overly restricted and protected. According to Erikson, the key to the development of autonomy during this period is for the child's caregivers to provide the appropriate amount of control. If parents provide too much control, children cannot assert themselves and develop their own sense of control over their environment; if parents provide too little control, the children become overly demanding and controlling.

Next, children face the crises of the **initiative-versus-guilt stage** (ages 3 to 6). In this stage, children's desire to act independently conflicts with the guilt that comes from the unintended and unexpected consequences of such behavior. Children in this period come to understand that they are persons in their own right, and they begin to make decisions about their behavior. If parents react positively to children's attempts at independence, they will help their children resolve the initiative-versus-guilt crisis positively.

The fourth and last stage of childhood is the **industry-versus-inferiority stage** (ages 6 to 12). During this period, increasing competency in all areas, whether social interactions or academic skills, characterizes successful psychosocial development. In contrast, difficulties in this stage lead to feelings of failure and inadequacy.

Erikson's theory suggests that psychosocial development continues throughout life, and he proposes four more crises that are faced after childhood. Although his theory has been criticized on several grounds—such as the imprecision of the concepts he employs and his greater emphasis on male development than female development—it remains influential and is one of the few theories that encompass the entire life span.

COGNITIVE DEVELOPMENT: CHILDREN'S THINKING ABOUT THE WORLD

Suppose you had two drinking glasses of different shapes—one short and broad and one tall and thin. Now imagine that you filled the short, broad one with soda about halfway and then poured the liquid from that glass into the tall one. The soda would appear to fill about three-quarters of the second glass. If someone asked you whether there was more soda in the second glass than there had been in the first, what would you say?

You might think that such a simple question hardly deserves an answer; of course there is no difference in the amount of soda in the two glasses. However, most 4-year-olds would be likely to say that there is more soda in the second glass. If you then poured the soda back into the short glass, they would say there is now less soda than there was in the taller glass.

Why are young children confused by this problem? The reason is not immediately obvious. Anyone who has observed preschoolers must be impressed by how far they have progressed from the early stages of development. They speak with ease, know the alphabet, count, play complex games, use tape players, tell stories, and communicate ably. Yet despite this seeming sophistication, there are deep gaps in children's understanding of the world. Some theorists have suggested that children cannot understand certain ideas and concepts until they reach a particular stage of **cognitive development**—the process by which a child's understanding of the world changes as a function of age and experience. In contrast to the theories of physical and social development discussed earlier (such as those of Erikson), theories of cognitive

Trust-versus-mistrust stage: According to Erik Erikson, the first stage of psychosocial development, occurring from birth to age 1½ years, during which time infants develop feelings of trust or lack of trust.

Autonomy-versus-shame-and-doubt stage: The period during which, according to Erikson, toddlers (ages 1½ to 3 years) develop independence and autonomy if exploration and freedom are encouraged, or shame and self-doubt if they are restricted and overprotected.

Initiative-versus-guilt stage: According to Erikson, the period during which children ages 3 to 6 years experience conflict between independence of action and the sometimes negative results of that action.

Industry-versus-inferiority stage: According to Erikson, the last stage of childhood, during which children age 6 to 12 years may develop positive social interactions with others or may feel inadequate and become less sociable.

Cognitive development: The process by which a child's understanding of the world changes as a function of age and experience.

development seek to explain the quantitative and qualitative intellectual advances that occur during development.

Piaget's Theory of Cognitive Development. No theory of cognitive development has had more impact than that of Swiss psychologist Jean Piaget. Piaget (1970) suggested that children around the world proceed through a series of four stages in a fixed order. He maintained that these stages differ not only in the *quantity* of information acquired at each stage but in the *quality* of knowledge and understanding as well. Taking an interactionist point of view, he suggested that movement from one stage to the next occurs when a child reaches an appropriate level of maturation *and* is exposed to relevant types of experiences. Piaget assumed that, without having such experiences, children cannot reach their highest level of cognitive growth.

Piaget proposed four stages: the sensorimotor, preoperational, concrete operational, and formal operational (see Figure 9). Let's examine each of them and the approximate ages that they span.

Sensorimotor Stage: Birth to 2 Years. During the **sensorimotor stage,** children base their understanding of the world primarily on touching, sucking, chewing, shaking, and manipulating objects. In the initial part of the stage, children have relatively little competence in representing the environment by using images, language, or other kinds of symbols. Consequently, infants lack what Piaget calls **object permanence,** the awareness that objects—and people—continue to exist even if they are out of sight.

How can we know that children lack object permanence? Although we cannot ask infants, we can observe their reactions when a toy they are playing with is hidden under a blanket. Until the age of about 9 months, children will make no attempt to locate the hidden toy. However, soon after that age they will begin to search actively for the missing object, indicating that they have developed a mental representation of the toy. Object permanence, then, is a critical development during the sensorimotor stage.

Preoperational Stage: 2 to 7 Years. The most important development during the **preoperational stage** is the use of language. Children develop internal representational systems that allow them to describe people, events, and feelings. They even use symbols in play, pretending, for example, that a book pushed across the floor is a car.

Although children use more advanced thinking in this stage than they did in the earlier sensorimotor stage, their thinking is still qualitatively inferior to that of adults. We see this when we observe a preoperational child using **egocentric thought,** a way of thinking in which the child views the world entirely from his or her own perspective. Preoperational children think that everyone shares their perspective and knowl-

---

Sensorimotor stage: According to Jean Piaget, the stage from birth to 2 years, during which a child has little competence in representing the environment by using images, language, or other symbols.

Object permanence: The awareness that objects—and people—continue to exist even if they are out of sight.

Preoperational stage: According to Piaget, the period from 2 to 7 years of age that is characterized by language development.

Egocentric thought: A way of thinking in which a child views the world entirely from his or her own perspective.

Cognitive Stage	Approximate Age Range	Major Characteristics
Sensorimotor	Birth–2 years	Development of object permanence, development of motor skills, little or no capacity for symbolic representation
Preoperational	2–7 years	Development of language and symbolic thinking, egocentric thinking
Concrete operational	7–12 years	Development of conservation, mastery of concept of reversibility
Formal operational	12 years–adulthood	Development of logical and abstract thinking

FIGURE 9 According to Jean Piaget, all children pass through four stages of cognitive development.

edge. Thus, children's stories and explanations to adults can be maddeningly uninformative, as they are delivered without any context. For example, a preoperational child may start a story with "He wouldn't let me go," neglecting to mention who "he" is or where the storyteller wanted to go. We also see egocentric thinking when children at the preoperational stage play hiding games. For instance, 3-year-olds frequently hide with their faces against a wall, covering their eyes—although they are still in plain view. It seems to them that if *they* cannot see, then no one else will be able to see them, because they assume that others share their view.

In addition, preoperational children have not yet developed the ability to understand the **principle of conservation,** which is the knowledge that quantity is unrelated to the arrangement and physical appearance of objects. Children who have not mastered this concept do not know that the amount, volume, or length of an object does not change when its shape or configuration changes. The question about the two glasses—one short and broad and the other tall and thin—with which we began our discussion of cognitive development illustrates this point clearly. Children who do not understand the principle of conservation invariably state that the amount of liquid changes as it is poured back and forth. They cannot comprehend that a transformation in appearance does not imply a transformation in amount. Instead, it seems as reasonable to the child that there is a change in quantity as it does to the adult that there is no change.

In a number of other ways, some quite startling, the failure to understand the principle of conservation affects children's responses. Research demonstrates that principles that are obvious to and unquestioned by adults may be completely misunderstood by children during the preoperational period, and that it is not until the next stage of cognitive development that children grasp the concept of conservation. (To get a deeper understanding of the concept of conservation, examine Figure 10 and complete the PsychInteractive exercise on conservation.)

Concrete Operational Stage: 7 to 12 Years. Mastery of the principle of conservation marks the beginning of the **concrete operational stage.** However, children do not fully understand some aspects of conservation—such as conservation of weight and volume—for a number of years.

During the concrete operational stage, children develop the ability to think in a more logical manner, and begin to overcome some of the egocentrism characteristic of the preoperational period. One of the major principles children learn during this stage is reversibility, the idea that some changes can be undone by reversing an earlier action. For example, they can understand that when someone rolls a ball of clay into a long sausage shape, that person can re-create the original ball by reversing the action. Children can even conceptualize this principle in their heads, without having to see the action performed before them.

Although children make important advances in their logical capabilities during the concrete operational stage, their thinking still displays one major limitation: They are largely bound to the concrete, physical reality of the world. For the most part, they have difficulty understanding questions of an abstract or hypothetical nature.

Formal Operational Stage: 12 Years to Adulthood. The **formal operational stage** produces a new kind of thinking that is abstract, formal, and logical. Thinking is no longer tied to events that individuals observe in the environment but makes use of logical techniques to resolve problems.

The way in which children approach the "pendulum problem" devised by Piaget (Piaget & Inhelder, 1958) illustrates the emergence of formal operational thinking. The problem solver is asked to figure out what determines how fast a pendulum swings. Is it the length of the string, the weight of the pendulum, or the force with which the pendulum is pushed? (For the record, the answer is the length of the string.)

Children in the concrete operational stage approach the problem haphazardly, without a logical or rational plan of action. For example, they may simultaneously

Children who have not mastered the principle of conservation assume that the volume of a liquid increases when it is poured from a short, wide container to a tall, thin one. What other tasks might a child under age 7 have difficulty comprehending?

www.mhhe.com/feldmanup8

PsychInteractive Online

Conservation

Principle of conservation: The knowledge that quantity is unrelated to the arrangement and physical appearance of objects.

Concrete operational stage: According to Piaget, the period from 7 to 12 years of age that is characterized by logical thought and a loss of egocentrism.

Formal operational stage: According to Piaget, the period from age 12 to adulthood that is characterized by abstract thought.

FIGURE 10 These tests are frequently used to assess whether children have learned the principle of conservation across a variety of dimensions. Do you think children in the preoperational stage can be taught to avoid conservation mistakes before the typical age of mastery?

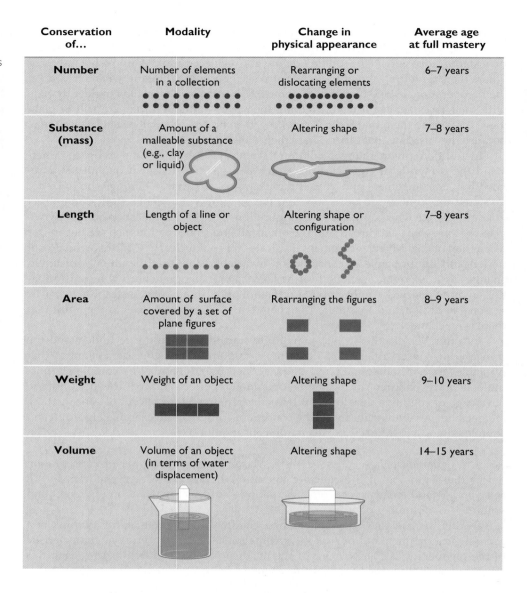

Conservation of...	Modality	Change in physical appearance	Average age at full mastery
Number	Number of elements in a collection	Rearranging or dislocating elements	6–7 years
Substance (mass)	Amount of a malleable substance (e.g., clay or liquid)	Altering shape	7–8 years
Length	Length of a line or object	Altering shape or configuration	7–8 years
Area	Amount of surface covered by a set of plane figures	Rearranging the figures	8–9 years
Weight	Weight of an object	Altering shape	9–10 years
Volume	Volume of an object (in terms of water displacement)	Altering shape	14–15 years

change the length of the string and the weight on the string and the force with which they push the pendulum. Because they are varying all the factors at once, they cannot tell which factor is the critical one. In contrast, people in the formal operational stage approach the problem systematically. Acting as if they were scientists conducting an experiment, they examine the effects of changes in one variable at a time. This ability to rule out competing possibilities characterizes formal operational thought.

Although formal operational thought emerges during the teenage years, some individuals use this type of thinking only infrequently. Moreover, it appears that many individuals never reach this stage at all; most studies show that only 40 to 60 percent of college students and adults fully reach it, with some estimates running as low as 25 percent of the general population. In addition, in certain cultures—particularly those which are less technologically sophisticated than most Western societies—almost no one reaches the formal operational stage (Chandler, 1976; Keating & Clark, 1980; Super, 1980).

Stages versus Continuous Development: Is Piaget Right? No other theorist has given us as comprehensive a theory of cognitive development as that of Piaget. Still, many contemporary theorists suggest that a better explanation of how children develop cognitively can be provided by theories that do not involve a stage approach. For instance, children are not always consistent in their performance of tasks that—if

Piaget's theory is accurate—ought to be performed equally well at a particular stage (Feldman, 2003, 2004).

Furthermore, some developmental psychologists suggest that cognitive development proceeds in a more continuous fashion than Piaget's stage theory implies. They propose that cognitive development is primarily quantitative in nature, rather than qualitative. They argue that although there are differences in when, how, and to what extent a child can use specific cognitive abilities—reflecting quantitative changes—the underlying cognitive processes change relatively little with age (Gelman & Baillargeon, 1983; Case & Okamoto, 1996).

Piaget also underestimated the age at which infants and children can understand specific concepts and principles; in fact, they seem to be more sophisticated in their cognitive abilities than Piaget believed. For instance, some evidence suggests that infants as young as 5 months have rudimentary mathematical skills (Wynn, 1995, 2000; Wynn, Bloom, & Chiang, 2002).

Despite such criticisms, most developmental psychologists agree that although the processes that underlie changes in cognitive abilities may not unfold in the manner suggested by his theory, Piaget has generally provided us with an accurate account of age-related changes in cognitive development. Moreover, his theory has had an enormous influence in education. For example, Piaget suggests that individuals cannot increase their cognitive performance unless both cognitive readiness brought about by maturation and appropriate environmental stimulation are present. This view has inspired the nature and structure of educational curricula and teaching methods. Researchers have also used Piaget's theory and methods to investigate issues surrounding animal cognition, such as whether primates show object permanence (they seem to; Funk, 1996; Hauser, 2000; Egan, 2005).

Information-Processing Approaches: Charting Children's Mental Programs. If cognitive development does not proceed as a series of stages, as Piaget suggested, what does underlie the enormous growth in children's cognitive abilities that even the most untutored eye can observe? To many developmental psychologists, changes in **information processing,** the way in which people take in, use, and store information, account for cognitive development (Siegler, 1998; Lacerda, von Hofsten, & Heimann, 2001; Cashon & Cohen, 2004).

According to this approach, quantitative changes occur in children's ability to organize and manipulate information. From this perspective, children become increasingly adept at information processing, much as a computer program may become more sophisticated as a programmer modifies it on the basis of experience. Information-processing approaches consider the kinds of "mental programs" that children invoke when approaching problems (Reyna, 1997).

Several significant changes occur in children's information-processing capabilities. For one thing, speed of processing increases with age, as some abilities become more automatic. The speed at which children can scan, recognize, and compare stimuli increases with age. As they grow older, children can pay attention to stimuli longer and discriminate between different stimuli more readily, and they are less easily distracted (Miller & Vernon, 1997; Rose, Feldman, & Jankowski, 2002; Myerson et al., 2003; Van den Wildenberg & Van der Molen, 2004).

Memory also improves dramatically with age. Preschoolers can hold only two or three chunks of information in short-term memory, 5-year-olds can hold four, and 7-year-olds can hold five. (Adults are able to keep seven, plus or minus two, chunks in short-term memory.) The size of chunks also grows with age, as does the sophistication and organization of knowledge stored in memory (see Figure 11). Still, memory capabilities are impressive at a very early age: Even before they can speak, infants can remember for months events in which they actively participated (Rovee-Collier, 1993; Bauer, 1996; Cowan et al., 2003; Bayliss et al., 2005b).

Finally, improvement in information processing relates to advances in **metacognition,** an awareness and understanding of one's own cognitive processes.

Information processing: The way in which people take in, use, and store information.

Metacognition: An awareness and understanding of one's own cognitive processes.

FIGURE 11 Memory span increases with age for both numbers and letters. (Source: Adapted from Dempster, 1981.)

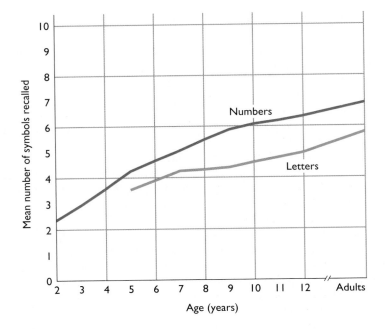

Metacognition involves the planning, monitoring, and revising of cognitive strategies. Younger children, who lack an awareness of their own cognitive processes, often do not realize their incapabilities. Thus, when they misunderstand others, they may fail to recognize their own errors. It is only later, when metacognitive abilities become more sophisticated, that children are able to know when they *don't* understand. Such increasing sophistication reflects a change in children's *theory of mind,* their knowledge and beliefs about the way the mind operates (Taylor, 1996; Flavell, 2002; McCormick, 2003; Bernstein, Loftus, & Meltzoff, 2005).

Vygotsky's View of Cognitive Development: Considering Culture. According to Russian developmental psychologist Lev Vygotsky, the culture in which we are raised significantly affects our cognitive development. In an increasingly influential view, Vygotsky suggests that the focus on individual performance of both Piagetian and information-processing approaches is misplaced. Instead, he holds that we cannot understand cognitive development without taking into account the social aspects of learning (Vygotsky, 1926/1997; Beilin, 1996; John-Steiner & Mahn, 2003; Maynard & Martini, 2005).

Vygotsky argues that cognitive development occurs as a consequence of social interactions in which children work with others to jointly solve problems. Through such interactions, children's cognitive skills increase, and they gain the ability to function intellectually on their own. More specifically, he suggests that children's cognitive abilities increase when they encounter information that falls within their zone of proximal development. The **zone of proximal development,** or **ZPD,** is the level at which a child can almost, but not fully, comprehend or perform a task on his or her own. When children receive information that falls within the ZPD, they can increase their understanding or master a new task. In contrast, if the information lies outside children's ZPD, they will not be able to master it (see Figure 12).

In short, cognitive development occurs when parents, teachers, or skilled peers assist a child by presenting information that is both new and within the ZPD. This type of assistance, called *scaffolding,* provides support for learning and problem solving that encourages independence and growth. Vygotsky claims that scaffolding not only promotes the solution of specific problems, but also aids in the development of overall cognitive abilities (Steward, 1995; Schaller & Crandall, 2004).

Zone of proximal development (ZPD): According to Lev Vygotsky, the level at which a child can almost, but not fully, comprehend or perform a task on his or her own.

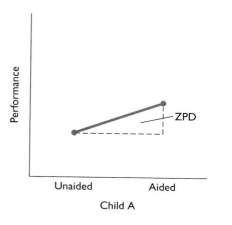
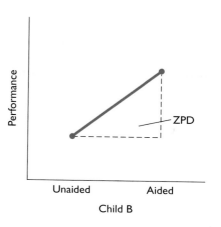

FIGURE 12 Although the performances of the two children initially working at a task without aid are similar, the second child benefits more from aid and thus has a larger zone of proximal development (ZPD).

More than other approaches to cognitive development, Vygotsky's theory considers how an individual's specific cultural and social context affects intellectual growth. The way in which children understand the world grows out of interactions with parents, peers, and other members of a specific culture (Tomasello, 2000; John-Steiner & Mahn, 2003; Kozulin et al., 2003).

RECAP/EVALUATE/RETHINK

RECAP

What are the major competencies of newborns?

- Newborns, or neonates, have reflexes that include a rooting reflex, the startle reflex, and the Babinski reflex. After birth, physical development is rapid; children typically triple their birthweight in a year. (pp. 411-412, 414)
- Sensory abilities also develop rapidly; infants can distinguish color, depth, sound, tastes, and smells relatively soon after birth. (pp. 412-414)

What are the milestones of physical and social development during childhood?

- Attachment—the positive emotional bond between a child and a particular individual—marks social development in infancy. Measured in the laboratory by means of the Ainsworth strange situation, attachment relates to later social and emotional adjustment. (pp. 415-416)
- As children become older, the nature of their social interactions with peers changes. Initially play occurs relatively independently, but it becomes increasingly cooperative. (p. 418)
- The different child-rearing styles include authoritarian, permissive, authoritative, and uninvolved. (pp. 419-420)
- According to Erikson, eight stages of psychosocial development involve people's changing interactions and understanding of themselves and others. During childhood, the four stages are trust-versus-mistrust (birth to 1½ years), autonomy-versus-shame-and-doubt (1½ to

3 years), initiative-versus-guilt (3 to 6 years), and industry-versus-inferiority (6 to 12 years). (pp. 420-421)

How does cognitive development proceed during childhood?

- Piaget's theory suggests that cognitive development proceeds through four stages in which qualitative changes occur in thinking: the sensorimotor stage (birth to 2 years), the preoperational stage (2 to 7 years), the concrete operational stage (7 to 12 years), and the formal operational stage (12 years to adulthood). (pp. 422-424)
- Information-processing approaches suggest that quantitative changes occur in children's ability to organize and manipulate information about the world, such as significant increases in speed of processing, attention span, and memory. In addition, children advance in metacognition, the awareness and understanding of one's own cognitive processes. (p. 425)
- Vygotsky argued that children's cognitive development occurs as a consequence of social interactions in which children and others work together to solve problems. (p. 426)

EVALUATE

1. Researchers studying newborns use _____, or the decrease in the response to a stimulus that occurs after repeated presentations of the same stimulus, as an indicator of a baby's interest.
2. The emotional bond that develops between a child and its caregiver is known as _____.

3. Match the parenting style with its definition:
    1. Permissive
    2. Authoritative
    3. Authoritarian
    4. Uninvolved
    a. Rigid; highly punitive; demanding obedience
    b. Gives little direction; lax on obedience
    c. Firm but fair; tries to explain parental decisions
    d. Emotionally detached and unloving

4. Erikson's theory of _____ development involves a series of eight stages, each of which must be resolved for a person to develop optimally.

5. Match the stage of development with the thinking style characteristic of that stage:
    1. Egocentric thought
    2. Object permanence
    3. Abstract reasoning
    4. Conservation; reversibility
    a. Sensorimotor
    b. Formal operational
    c. Preoperational
    d. Concrete operational

6. _____ - _____ theories of development suggest that the way in which a child handles information is critical to his or her development.

7. According to Vygotsky, information that is within a child's _____ is most likely to result in cognitive development.

RETHINK

1. Do you think the widespread use of IQ testing in the United States contributes to parents' views that their children's academic success is due largely to the children's innate intelligence? Why? Would it be possible (or desirable) to change this view?

2. *From the perspective of a child care provider:* If a parent wasn't sure whether to enroll his or her child in your program, what advice would you give about the possible positive and negative consequences about day care?

Answers to Evaluate Questions

1. habituation; 2. attachment; 3. 1-b, 2-c, 3-a, 4-d; 4. psychosocial; 5. 1-c, 2-a, 3-b, 4-d; 6. information-processing; 7. zone of proximal development

KEY TERMS

neonate p. 411
reflexes p. 411
habituation p. 413
attachment p. 415
authoritarian parents p. 419
permissive parents p. 419
authoritative parents p. 420
uninvolved parents p. 420
temperament p. 420
psychosocial development
    p. 420

trust-versus-mistrust stage
    p. 421
autonomy-versus-shame-
    and-doubt stage p. 421
initiative-versus-guilt stage
    p. 421
industry-versus-inferiority
    stage p. 421
cognitive development
    p. 421

sensorimotor stage p. 422
object permanence p. 422
preoperational stage p. 422
egocentric thought p. 422
principle of conservation
    p. 423
concrete operational stage
    p. 423
formal operational stage
    p. 423

information processing
    p. 425
metacognition p. 425
zone of proximal develop-
    ment (ZPD) p. 426

Adolescence: Becoming an Adult

Joseph Charles, Age 13: Being 13 is very hard at school. I have to be bad in order to be considered cool. I sometimes do things that aren't good. I have talked back to my teachers and been disrespectful to them. I do want to be good, but it's just too hard (Gibbs, 2005, p. 51).

* * *

Trevor Kelson, Age 15: "Keep the Hell Out of my Room!" says a sign on Trevor's bedroom wall, just above an unmade bed, a desk littered with dirty T-shirts and candy wrappers, and a floor covered with clothes. Is there a carpet? "Somewhere," he says with a grin. "I think it's gold" (Fields-Meyer, 1995, p. 53).

* * *

Lauren Barry, Age 18: "I went to a National Honor Society induction. The parents were just staring at me. I think they couldn't believe someone with pink hair could be smart. I want to be a high-school teacher, but I'm afraid that, based on my appearance, they won't hire me" (Gordon et al., 1999, p. 47).

Although Joseph, Trevor, and Lauren have never met, they share anxieties that are common to adolescence—concerns about friends, parents, appearance, independence, and their futures. **Adolescence,** the developmental stage between childhood and adulthood, is a crucial period. It is a time of profound changes and, occasionally, turmoil. Considerable biological change occurs as adolescents attain sexual and physical maturity. At the same time, and rivaling these physiological changes, important social, emotional, and cognitive changes occur as adolescents strive for independence and move toward adulthood.

Because many years of schooling precede most people's entry into the workforce in Western societies, the stage of adolescence is fairly long, beginning just before the teenage years and ending just after them. No longer children but considered by society to be not quite adults, adolescents face a period of rapid physical, cognitive, and social change that affects them for the rest of their lives.

Dramatic changes in society also affect adolescents' development. More than half of all children in the United States will spend all or some of their childhood and adolescence in single-parent families. Furthermore, adolescents spend considerably less time with their parents, and more with their peers, than they did several decades ago. Finally, the ethnic and cultural diversity of adolescents as a group is increasing dramatically. A third of all adolescents today are of non-European descent, and by the year 2050 the number of adolescents of Hispanic, African American, Native American, and Asian origin will have grown significantly (Carnegie Council on Adolescent Development, 1995; Dreman, 1997).

Physical Development: The Changing Adolescent

If you think back to the start of your own adolescence, the most dramatic changes you probably remember are physical ones. A spurt in height, the growth of breasts in girls,

Key Concept

What major physical, social, and cognitive transitions characterize adolescence?

Adolescence: The developmental stage between childhood and adulthood.

Although puberty begins around age 11 or 12 for girls and 13 or 14 for boys, there are wide variations. What are some advantages and disadvantages of early puberty?

Puberty: The period at which maturation of the sexual organs occurs, beginning at about age 11 or 12 for girls and 13 or 14 for boys.

deepening voices in boys, the development of body hair, and intense sexual feelings cause curiosity, interest, and sometimes embarrassment for individuals entering adolescence.

The physical changes that occur at the start of adolescence result largely from the secretion of various hormones, and they affect virtually every aspect of an adolescent's life. Not since infancy has development been so dramatic. Weight and height increase rapidly because of a growth spurt that typically begins around age 10 for girls and age 12 for boys. Adolescents may grow as much as five inches in one year.

Puberty, the period at which maturation of the sexual organs occurs, begins at about age 11 or 12 for girls, when menstruation starts. However, there are wide variations (see Figure 1). For example, some girls begin to menstruate as early as age 8 or 9 or as late as age 16. Furthermore, in Western cultures, the average age at which adolescents reach sexual maturity has been steadily decreasing over the last century, most likely as a result of improved nutrition and medical care. Sexual *attraction* to others begins even before the maturation of the sexual organs, at around age 10 (Tanner, 1990; Finlay, Jones, & Coleman, 2002).

For boys, the onset of puberty is marked by their first ejaculation, known as *spermarche*. Spermarche usually occurs around the age of 13 (see Figure 1). At first, relatively few sperm are produced during an ejaculation, but the amount increases significantly within a few years.

FIGURE 1 The range of ages during which major sexual changes occur during adolescence is shown by the colored bars. (Source: Based on Tanner, 1978.)

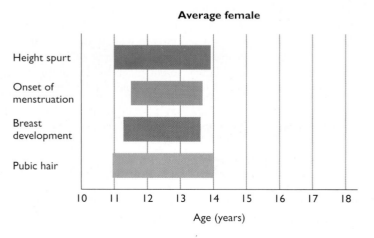

The age at which puberty begins has implications for the way adolescents feel about themselves—as well as the way others treat them. Early-maturing boys have a distinct advantage over later-maturing boys. They do better in athletics, are generally more popular with peers, and have more positive self-concepts (Duncan et al., 1985; Peterson, 1985; Anderson & Magnusson, 1990).

The picture differs for girls. Although early-maturing girls are more sought after as dates and have better self-esteem than do later-maturing girls, some consequences of early physical maturation may be less positive. For example, early breast development may set them apart from their peers and be a source of ridicule (Simmons & Blyth, 1987; Ge, Conger, & Elder, 1996; Nadeem & Graham, 2005).

Late physical maturation may produce certain psychological difficulties for both boys and girls. Boys who are smaller and less coordinated than their more mature peers tend to feel ridiculed and less attractive. Similarly, late-maturing girls are at a disadvantage in middle school and early high school. They hold relatively low social status and may be overlooked in dating (Clarke-Stewart & Friedman, 1987; Lanza & Collins, 2002).

Clearly, the rate at which physical changes occur during adolescence can affect the way in which people are viewed by others and the way they view themselves. Just as important as physical changes, however, are the psychological and social changes that unfold during adolescence.

Moral and Cognitive Development: Distinguishing Right from Wrong

In a European country, a woman is near death from a special kind of cancer. The one drug that the doctors think might save her is a medicine that a medical researcher has recently discovered. The drug is expensive to make, and the researcher is charging ten times the cost, or $5,000, for a small dose. The sick woman's husband, Henry, approaches everyone he knows in hopes of borrowing money, but he can get together only about $2,500. He tells the researcher that his wife is dying and asks him to lower the price of the drug or let him pay later. The researcher says, "No, I discovered the drug, and I'm going to make money from it." Henry is desperate and considers stealing the drug for his wife.

What would you tell Henry to do?

KOHLBERG'S THEORY OF MORAL DEVELOPMENT

In the view of psychologist Lawrence Kohlberg, the advice you give Henry reflects your level of moral development. According to Kohlberg, people pass through a series of stages in the evolution of their sense of justice and in the kind of reasoning they use to make moral judgments (Kohlberg, 1984). Largely because of the various cognitive limitations that Piaget described, preadolescent children tend to think either in terms of concrete, unvarying rules ("It is always wrong to steal" or "I'll be punished if I steal") or in terms of the rules of society ("Good people don't steal" or "What if everyone stole?").

Adolescents, however, can reason on a higher plane, having typically reached Piaget's formal operational stage of cognitive development. Because they are able to comprehend broad moral principles, they can understand that morality is not always black and white and that conflict can exist between two sets of socially accepted standards.

Kohlberg (1984) suggests that the changes in moral reasoning can be understood best as a three-level sequence (see Figure 2). His theory assumes that people move through the levels in a fixed order, and that they cannot reach the highest level until about age 13—primarily because of limitations in cognitive development before that age. However, many people never reach the highest level of moral reasoning. In fact,

	Sample Moral Reasoning of Subjects	
Level	In Favor of Stealing the Drug	Against Stealing the Drug
Level 1 Preconventional morality: At this level, the concrete interests of the individual are considered in terms of rewards and punishments.	"If you let your wife die, you will get in trouble. You'll be blamed for not spending the money to save her, and there'll be an investigation of you and the druggist for your wife's death."	"You shouldn't steal the drug because you'll be caught and sent to jail if you do. If you do get away, your conscience will bother you thinking how the police will catch up with you at any minute."
Level 2 Conventional morality: At this level, people approach moral problems as members of society. They are interested in pleasing others by acting as good members of society.	"If you let your wife die, you'll never be able to look anybody in the face again."	"After you steal the drug, you'll feel bad thinking how you've brought dishonor on your family and yourself; you won't be able to face anyone again."
Level 3 Postconventional morality: At this level, people use moral principles which are seen as broader than those of any particular society.	"If you don't steal the drug, and if you let your wife die, you'll always condemn yourself for it afterward. You won't be blamed and you'll have lived up to the outside rule of the law, but you won't have lived up to your own conscience and standards of honesty."	"If you steal the drug, you won't be blamed by other people, but you'll condemn yourself because you won't have lived up to your own conscience and standards of honesty."

FIGURE 2 Developmental psychologist Lawrence Kohlberg theorized that people move through a three-level sequence of moral reasoning in a fixed order. However, he contended that few people ever reach the highest level of moral reasoning.

Kohlberg found that only a relatively small percentage of adults rise above the second level of his model (Kohlberg & Ryncarz, 1990; Hedgepeth, 2005).

Although Kohlberg's theory has had a substantial influence on our understanding of moral development, the research support is mixed. One difficulty with the theory is that it pertains to moral *judgments,* not moral *behavior.* Knowing right from wrong does not mean that we will always act in accordance with our judgments. In addition, the theory applies primarily to Western society and its moral code; cross-cultural research conducted in cultures with different moral systems suggests that Kohlberg's theory is not necessarily applicable (Coles, 1997; Damon, 1999; Nucci, 2002).

MORAL DEVELOPMENT IN WOMEN

One glaring shortcoming of Kohlberg's research is that he primarily used male participants. Furthermore, psychologist Carol Gilligan (1996) argues that because of men's and women's distinctive socialization experiences, a fundamental difference exists in the way each gender views moral behavior. According to Gilligan, men view morality primarily in terms of broad principles, such as justice and fairness. In contrast, women see it in terms of responsibility toward individuals and willingness to make sacrifices to help a specific individual within the context of a particular relationship. Compassion for individuals is a more salient factor in moral behavior for women than it is for men.

Because Kohlberg's model defines moral behavior largely in terms of abstract principles such as justice, Gilligan finds it inadequately describes the moral development of females. She suggests that women's morality centers on individual well-being and social relationships—a morality of *caring.* In her view, compassionate concern for the welfare of others represents the highest level of morality.

The fact that Gilligan's conception of morality differs greatly from Kohlberg's suggests that gender plays an important role in determining what a person sees as moral. Although the research evidence is not definitive, it seems plausible that their differing conceptions of what constitutes moral behavior may lead men and women to regard the morality of a particular behavior in different ways (Wark & Krebs, 1996; Jaffee & Hyde, 2000; Tangney & Dearing, 2002; Weisz & Black, 2002; Lippa, 2005).

To check your understanding of moral development, complete the PsychInteractive exercise.

www.mhhe.com/feldmanup8
PsychInteractive Online

Stages of Moral Development

Social Development: Finding Oneself in a Social World

"Who am I?" "How do I fit into the world?" "What is life all about?"

Questions such as these assume particular significance during the teenage years, as adolescents seek to find their place in the broader social world. As we will see, this quest takes adolescents along several routes.

ERKISON'S THEORY OF PSYCHOSOCIAL DEVELOPMENT: THE SEARCH FOR IDENTITY

Erik Erikson's theory of psychosocial development emphasizes the search for identity during the adolescent years. As was noted earlier, psychosocial development encompasses the way people's understanding of themselves, one another, and the world around them changes during the course of development (Erikson, 1963).

The fifth stage of Erikson's theory (summarized, with the other stages, in Figure 3), the **identity-versus-role-confusion stage,** encompasses adolescence. During this stage, a time of major testing, people try to determine what is unique about themselves. They attempt to discover who they are, what their strengths are, and what kinds of roles they are best suited to play for the rest of their lives—in short, their **identity.** A person confused about the most appropriate role to play in life may lack a stable identity, adopt an unacceptable role such as that of a social deviant, or have difficulty maintaining close personal relationships later in life (Brendgen, Vitaro, & Bukowski, 2000; Updegraff et al., 2004; Vleioras & Bosma, 2005).

Identity-versus-role-confusion stage: According to Erik Erikson, a time in adolescence of major testing to determine one's unique qualities.

Identity: The distinguishing character of the individual: who each of us is, what our roles are, and what we are capable of.

Stage	Approximate Age	Positive Outcomes	Negative Outcomes
1. Trust-vs.-mistrust	Birth–1 1/2 years	Feelings of trust from environmental support	Fear and concern regarding others
2. Autonomy-vs.-shame-and-doubt	1 1/2–3 years	Self-sufficiency if exploration is encouraged	Doubts about self, lack of independence
3. Initiative-vs.-guilt	3–6 years	Discovery of ways to initiate actions	Guilt from actions and thoughts
4. Industry-vs.-inferiority	6–12 years	Development of sense of competence	Feelings of inferiority, no sense of mastery
5. Identity-vs.-role-confusion	Adolescence	Awareness of uniqueness of self, knowledge of role to be followed	Inability to identify appropriate roles in life
6. Intimacy-vs.-isolation	Early adulthood	Development of loving, sexual relationships and close friendships	Fear of relationships with others
7. Generativity-vs.-stagnation	Middle adulthood	Sense of contribution to continuity of life	Trivialization of one's activities
8. Ego-integrity-vs.-despair	Late adulthood	Sense of unity in life's accomplishments	Regret over lost opportunities of life

FIGURE 3 Erikson's stages of psychosocial development. According to Erikson, shown in the photo, people proceed through eight stages of psychosocial development across their lives. He suggested that each stage requires the resolution of a crisis or conflict and may produce both positive and negative outcomes.

THE WORLD'S FIRST GENETICALLY ENGINEERED HUMAN HITS ADOLESCENCE

Intimacy-versus-isolation stage:
According to Erikson, a period during early adulthood that focuses on developing close relationships.

Generativity-versus-stagnation stage:
According to Erikson, a period in middle adulthood during which we take stock of our contributions to family and society.

Ego-integrity-versus-despair stage:
According to Erikson, a period from late adulthood until death during which we review life's accomplishments and failures.

During the identity-versus-role-confusion period, an adolescent feels pressure to identify what to do with his or her life. Because these pressures come at a time of major physical changes as well as important changes in what society expects of them, adolescents can find the period a particularly difficult one. The identity-versus-role-confusion stage has another important characteristic: declining reliance on adults for information, with a shift toward using the peer group as a source of social judgments. The peer group becomes increasingly important, enabling adolescents to form close, adultlike relationships and helping them clarify their personal identities. According to Erikson, the identity-versus-role-confusion stage marks a pivotal point in psychosocial development, paving the way for continued growth and the future development of personal relationships.

During early adulthood, people enter the **intimacy-versus-isolation stage.** Spanning the period of early adulthood (from postadolescence to the early thirties), this stage focuses on developing close relationships with others. Difficulties during this stage result in feelings of loneliness and a fear of such relationships, whereas successful resolution of the crises of the stage results in the possibility of forming relationships that are intimate on a physical, intellectual, and emotional level.

Development continues during middle adulthood as people enter the **generativity-versus-stagnation stage.** Generativity is the ability to contribute to one's family, community, work, and society, and assist the development of the younger generation. Success in this stage results in a person feeling positive about the continuity of life, whereas difficulties lead a person to feel that his or her activities are trivial or stagnant and have done nothing for upcoming generations. In fact, if a person has not successfully resolved the identity crisis of adolescence, he or she may still be foundering as far as identifying an appropriate career is concerned.

Finally, the last stage of psychosocial development, the **ego-integrity-versus-despair** stage, spans later adulthood and continues until death. Now a sense of accomplishment signifies success in resolving the difficulties presented by this stage of life; failure to resolve the difficulties results in regret over what might have been achieved but was not.

Notably, Erikson's theory suggests that development does not stop at adolescence but continues throughout adulthood, a view that a substantial amount of research now confirms. For instance, a 22-year study by psychologist Susan Whitbourne found considerable support for the fundamentals of Erikson's theory, determining that psychosocial development continues through adolescence and adulthood. In sum, adolescence is not an end point but rather a way station on the path of psychosocial development (Whitbourne et al., 1992; McAdams et al., 1997).

Although Erikson's theory provides a broad outline of identity development, critics have pointed out that his approach is anchored in male-oriented concepts of individuality and competitiveness. In an alternative conception, psychologist Carol Gilligan suggests that women may develop identity through the establishment of relationships. In her view, a primary component of women's identity is the construction of caring networks among themselves and others (Brown & Gilligan, 1990; Gilligan, 2004).

STORMY ADOLESCENCE: MYTH OR REALITY?

Does puberty invariably foreshadow a stormy, rebellious period of adolescence?

At one time, psychologists thought most children entering adolescence were beginning a period fraught with stress and unhappiness. However, research now shows that this characterization is largely a myth, that most young people pass through adolescence without appreciable turmoil in their lives, and that parents speak easily—and fairly often—with their children about a variety of topics (Klein, 1998; van Wel, Linssen, & Abma, 2000; Granic, Hollenstein, & Dishion, 2003).

This does not mean that adolescence is completely calm. In most families with adolescents, the amount of arguing and bickering clearly rises. Most young teenagers, as part of their search for identity, experience tension between their attempts to become independent from their parents and their actual dependence on them. They may experiment with a range of behaviors, flirting with a variety of activities that their parents, and even society as a whole, find objectionable. Happily, though, for most families such tensions stabilize during middle adolescence—around age 15 or 16—and eventually decline around age 18 (Eccles, Lord, & Roeser, 1996; Gullotta, Adams, & Markstrom, 1999; Smetana, Daddis, & Chuang, 2003; Smetana, 2005).

One reason for the increase in discord during adolescence appears to be the protracted period in which children stay at home with their parents. In prior historical periods—and in some non-Western cultures today—children leave home immediately after puberty and are considered adults. Today, however, sexually mature adolescents may spend as many as seven or eight years with their parents. Current social trends even hint at an extension of the conflicts of adolescence beyond the teenage years, because a significant number of young adults—known as *boomerang children*—return to live with their parents after leaving home for some period. Although some parents welcome the return of their children, others are less sympathetic, and this opens the way to conflict (Bianchi & Casper, 2000; Lewin, 2003).

Another source of strife with parents lies in the way adolescents think. Adolescence fosters *adolescent egocentrism,* a state of self-absorption in which a teenager views the world from his or her own point of view. Egocentrism leads adolescents to be highly critical of authority figures, unwilling to accept criticism, and quick to fault others. It also makes them believe that they are the center of everyone else's attention, leading to self-consciousness. Furthermore, they develop *personal fables,* the belief that their experience is unique, exceptional, and shared by no one else. Such personal fables may make adolescents feel invulnerable to the risks that threaten others (Elkind, 1985; Goosens, et al., 2002; Frankenberger, 2004).

Adolescence also introduces a variety of stresses outside the home. Typically, adolescents change schools at least twice (from elementary to middle school or junior high, then to senior high school), and relationships with friends and peers are particularly volatile. Many adolescents hold part-time jobs, increasing the demands of school, work, and social activities on their time. Such stressors can lead to tensions at home (Steinberg & Dornbusch, 1991; Dworkin, Larson, & Hansen, 2003).

ADOLESCENT SUICIDE

Although the vast majority of teenagers pass through adolescence without major psychological difficulties, some experience unusually severe psychological problems. Sometimes those problems become so extreme that adolescents take their own lives. Suicide is the third leading cause of death for adolescents (after accidents and homicide) in the United States. More teenagers and young adults die from suicide than from cancer, heart disease, AIDS, birth defects, stroke, pneumonia and influenza, and chronic lung disease combined (CDC, 2004).

A teenager commits suicide every ninety minutes. Furthermore, the reported rate of suicide may actually be understated, because medical personnel hesitate to report suicide as a cause of death. Instead, they frequently label a death as an accident in an effort to protect the survivors. Overall, as many as 200 adolescents may attempt suicide for every one who actually takes his or her own life (Berman & Jobes, 1991; Gelman, 1994; CDC, 2000).

Male adolescents are five times more likely to commit suicide than are females, although females *attempt* suicide more often than males do. The rate of adolescent suicide is significantly greater among whites than among nonwhites. However, the suicide rate of African American males has

These students are mourning the deaths of two classmates who committed suicide. The rate of suicide among teenagers has risen significantly over the last few decades. Can you think of any reasons for this phenomenon?

increased much more rapidly than has that of white males over the last two decades. Native Americans have the highest suicide rate of any ethnic group in the United States, and Asian Americans have the lowest rate (Anderson & Smith, 2003; CDC, 2004; Gutierrez et al., 2005).

Although the rate of suicide has slowly declined, the rates are still higher for adolescents than any other age group except for the elderly. Some psychologists suggest that the sharp rise in stress that teenagers experience—in terms of academic and social pressure, alcoholism, drug abuse, and family difficulties—provokes the most troubled adolescents to take their own lives. However, that is not the whole story, for the suicide rate for other age groups has remained fairly stable in the last few decades. It is unlikely that stress has increased only for adolescents and not for the rest of the population (Lubell et al., 2004).

Although the question of why adolescent suicide rates are so high remains unanswered, several factors put adolescents at risk. One factor is depression, characterized by unhappiness, extreme fatigue, and—a variable that seems particularly important—a profound sense of hopelessness. In other cases, adolescents who commit suicide are perfectionists, inhibited socially and prone to extreme anxiety when they face any social or academic challenge (Ayyash-Abdo, 2002; Goldston, 2003; CDC, 2004; Richardson et al., 2005; see Figure 4).

Family background and adjustment difficulties are also related to suicide. A long-standing history of conflicts between parents and children may lead to adolescent behavior problems, such as delinquency, dropping out of school, and aggressive tendencies. In addition, teenage alcoholics and abusers of other drugs have a relatively high rate of suicide (Wagner, 1997; Stronski, Ireland, & Michaud, 2000; Winstead, 2005).

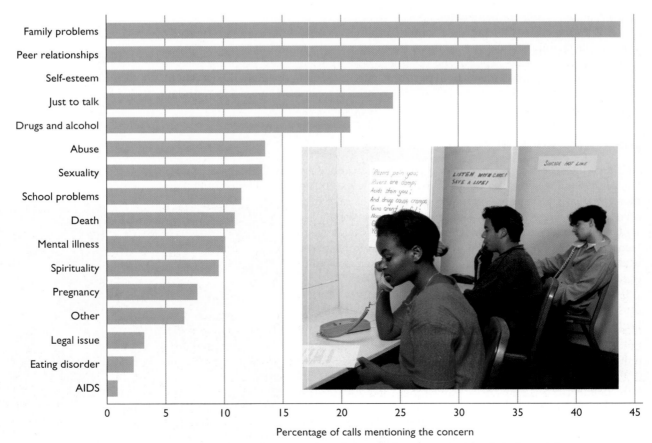

FIGURE 4 According to a review of phone calls to one telephone help line, adolescents who were considering suicide most often mentioned family, peer relationships, and self-esteem problems. (Source: Boehm & Campbell, 1995.)

Several warning signs indicate when a teenager's problems may be severe enough to warrant concern about the possibility of a suicide attempt. They include the following:

- School problems, such as missing classes, truancy, and a sudden change in grades
- Frequent incidents of self-destructive behavior, such as careless accidents
- Loss of appetite or excessive eating
- Withdrawal from friends and peers
- Sleeping problems
- Signs of depression, tearfulness, or overt indications of psychological difficulties, such as hallucinations
- A preoccupation with death, an afterlife, or what would happen "if I died"
- Putting affairs in order, such as giving away prized possessions or making arrangements for the care of a pet
- An explicit announcement of thoughts of suicide

If you know someone who shows signs that he or she is suicidal, urge that person to seek professional help. You may need to take assertive action, such as enlisting the assistance of family members or friends. Talk of suicide is a serious signal for help, not a confidence to be kept.

For immediate help with a suicide-related problem, call (800) 784-2433 or (800) 448-3000, national hotlines staffed with trained counselors.

(To more fully understand the causes of suicide, complete the PsychInteractive exercise on suicide risk factors.)

www.mhhe.com/feldmanup8
PsychInteractive Online

Suicide Risk Factors

Exploring DIVERSITY

Rites of Passage: Coming of Age Around the World

It is not easy for male members of the Awa tribe in New Guinea to make the transition from childhood to adulthood. First come whippings with sticks and prickly branches, both for the boys' own past misdeeds and in honor of those tribesmen who were killed in warfare. In the next phase of the ritual, adults jab sharpened sticks into the boys' nostrils. Then they force a five-foot length of vine into the boys' throats, until they gag and vomit. Finally, tribesmen cut the boys' genitals, causing severe bleeding.

Although the rites that mark the coming of age of boys in the Awa tribe sound horrifying to Westerners, they are comparable to those in other cultures. In some, youths must kneel on hot coals without displaying pain. In others, girls must toss wads of burning cotton from hand to hand and allow themselves to be bitten by hundreds of ants (Selsky, 1997).

Other cultures have less fearsome, although no less important, ceremonies that mark the passage from childhood to adulthood. For instance, when a girl first menstruates in traditional Apache tribes, the event is marked by dawn-to-dusk chanting. Western religions, too, have several types of celebrations, including bar and bat mitzvahs at age 13 for Jewish boys and girls and confirmation ceremonies for children in many Christian denominations (Myerhoff, 1982; Dunham et al., 1986; Rakoff, 1995).

In most societies, males, but not females, are the focus of coming-of-age ceremonies. The renowned anthropologist Margaret Mead remarked, only partly in jest, that the preponderance of male ceremonies might reflect the fact that "the worry that boys will not grow up to be men is much more widespread than that girls will not grow up to be women" (1949, p. 195). Said another way, it may be that in most cultures men traditionally have higher status than women, and therefore those cultures regard boys' transition into adulthood as more important.

However, another fact may explain why most cultures place greater emphasis on male rites than on female ones. For females, the transition from childhood is marked by a definite, biological event: menstruation. For males, in contrast, no single event can be used to pinpoint entry into adulthood. Thus, men are forced to rely on culturally determined rituals to acknowledge their arrival into adulthood.

RECAP/EVALUATE/RETHINK

RECAP

What major physical, social, and cognitive transitions characterize adolescence?

- Adolescence, the developmental stage between childhood and adulthood, is marked by the onset of puberty, the point at which sexual maturity occurs. The age at which puberty begins has implications for the way people view themselves and the way others see them. (pp. 429-431)
- Moral judgments during adolescence increase in sophistication, according to Kohlberg's three-level model. Although Kohlberg's levels provide an adequate description of males' moral judgments, Gilligan suggests that women view morality in terms of caring for individuals rather than in terms of broad, general principles of justice. (pp. 431-433)
- According to Erikson's model of psychosocial development, adolescence may be accompanied by an identity crisis. Adolescence is followed by three more stages of psychosocial development that cover the remainder of the life span. (pp. 433-434)
- Suicide is the third leading cause of death in adolescents. (p. 435)

EVALUATE

1. _____ is the period during which the sexual organs begin to mature.

2. Delayed maturation typically provides both males and females with a social advantage. True or false?

3. _____ proposed a set of three levels of moral development ranging from reasoning based on rewards and punishments to abstract thinking involving concepts of justice.

4. Erikson believed that during adolescence, people must search for _____, whereas during the early adulthood, the major task is _____.

RETHINK

1. In what ways do school cultures help or hurt teenage students who are going through adolescence? What school policies might benefit early-maturing girls and late-maturing boys? Explain how same-sex schools could help, as some have argued.

2. _From the perspective of a social worker:_ How might you determine if an adolescent was at risk for suicide? What strategies would you use to prevent the teen from committing suicide? Would you use different strategies depending on the teenager's gender?

Answers to Evaluate Questions

1. puberty; 2. false; both male and female adolescents suffer if they mature late; 3. Kohlberg; 4. identity, intimacy

KEY TERMS

adolescence p. 429
puberty p. 430
identity-versus-role-confusion stage p. 433

identity p. 433
intimacy-versus-isolation stage p. 434

generativity-versus-stagnation stage p. 434

ego-integrity-versus-despair stage p. 434

Adulthood

I thought I got better as I got older. I found out that wasn't the case in a real hurry last year. After going twelve years in professional football and twelve years before that in amateur football without ever having surgery performed on me, the last two seasons of my career I went under the knife three times. It happened very quickly and without warning, and I began to ask myself, "Is this age? Is this what's happening?" Because up until that moment, I'd never realized that I was getting older (Kotre & Hall, 1990, p. 257, 259–260).

As a former professional football player, Brian Sipes intensely felt the changes in his body brought about by aging. But the challenges he experienced are part of a normal process that affects all people as they move through adulthood.

Psychologists generally agree that early adulthood begins around age 20 and lasts until about age 40 to 45, with middle adulthood beginning then and continuing until around age 65. Despite the enormous importance of these periods of life in terms of both the accomplishments that occur in them and their overall length (together they span some forty-five years), they have been studied less than has any other stage. For one reason, the physical changes that occur during these periods are less apparent and more gradual than are those at other times during the life span. In addition, the diverse social changes that arise during this period defy simple categorization. However, developmental psychologists have recently begun to focus on the period, particularly on the social changes in the family and women's careers.

Physical Development: The Peak of Health

For most people, early adulthood marks the peak of physical health. From about 18 to 25 years of age, people's strength is greatest, their reflexes are quickest, and their chances of dying from disease are quite slim. Moreover, reproductive capabilities are at their highest level.

Around age 25, the body becomes slightly less efficient and more susceptible to disease. Overall, however, ill health remains the exception; most people stay remarkably healthy during early adulthood. (Can you think of any machine other than the body that can operate without pause for so long a period?)

During middle adulthood people gradually become aware of changes in their bodies. People often begin to put on weight (although this can be avoided through diet and exercise). Furthermore, the sense organs gradually become less sensitive, and reactions to stimuli are slower. But generally, the physical declines that occur during middle adulthood are minor and often unnoticeable (DiGiovanna, 1994; Forzanna et al., 1994).

The major biological change that does occur pertains to reproductive capabilities during middle adulthood. On average, during their late forties or early fifties, women begin **menopause,** during which they stop menstruating and are no longer fertile. Because menopause is accompanied by a significant reduction in the production of estrogen, a female hormone, women sometimes experience symptoms such as hot flashes, sudden sensations of heat. Many symptoms can be treated through *hormone therapy (HT),* in which menopausal women take the hormones estrogen and progesterone.

Key Concepts

What are the principal kinds of physical, social, and intellectual changes that occur in early and middle adulthood, and what are their causes?

How does the reality of late adulthood differ from the stereotypes about that period?

How can we adjust to death?

Menopause: The period during which women stop menstruating and are no longer fertile.

Women's reactions to menopause vary significantly across cultures, and according to one study, the more a society values old age, the less difficulty its women have during menopause. Why do you think this would be the case?

However, hormone therapy poses several dangers, such as an increase in the risk of breast cancer, blood clots, and heart disease. These uncertainties make the routine use of HT controversial. Currently, the medical consensus seems to be that younger women with severe menopausal symptoms ought to consider HT on a short-term basis. On the other hand, HT provides little benefit, and potential harm, to older women after menopause, and there is no reason for them to use it (Parker-Pope, 2003; Col & Komaroff, 2004).

Menopause was once blamed for a variety of psychological symptoms, including depression and memory loss. However, such difficulties, if they do occur, may be caused by women's expectations about reaching an "old" age in a society that highly values youth.

Furthermore, women's reactions to menopause vary significantly across cultures. According to anthropologist Yewoubdar Beyene, the more a society values old age, the less difficulty its women have during menopause. In a study of women in Mayan villages, she found that women looked forward to menopause, because they then stopped having children. In addition, they didn't experience some of the classic symptoms of menopause; hot flashes, for example, were unheard of (Beyene, 1989, 1992; Mingo, Herman, & Jasperse, 2000; Elliot, Berman, & Kim, 2002).

For men, the aging process during middle adulthood is somewhat subtler. There are no physiological signals of increasing age equivalent to the end of menstruation in women, and so no male menopause exists. In fact, men remain fertile and are capable of fathering children until well into late adulthood. However, some gradual physical decline occurs: Sperm production decreases, and the frequency of orgasm tends to decline. Once again, though, any psychological difficulties associated with these changes are usually brought about not so much by physical deterioration as by the inability of an aging individual to meet the exaggerated standards of youthfulness.

Social Development: Working at Life

Whereas physical changes during adulthood reflect development of a quantitative nature, social developmental transitions are qualitative and more profound. During this period, people typically launch themselves into careers, marriage, and families.

The entry into early adulthood is usually marked by leaving one's childhood home and entering the world of work. People envision life goals and make career choices. Their lives often center on their careers, which form an important part of their identity (Vaillant & Vaillant, 1990; Levinson, 1990, 1992).

In their early forties, however, people may begin to question their lives as they enter a period called the *midlife transition*. The idea that life will end at some point becomes increasingly influential in their thinking, and they may question their past accomplishments (Gould, 1978). Facing signs of physical aging and feeling dissatisfaction with their lives, some individuals experience what has been popularly labeled a *midlife crisis*.

In most cases, though, the passage into middle age is relatively calm. Most 40-year-olds view their lives and accomplishments positively enough to proceed relatively smoothly through midlife, and the forties and fifties are often a particularly rewarding period. Rather than looking to the future, people concentrate on the present, and their involvement with their families, friends, and other social groups takes on new importance. A major developmental thrust of this period is coming to terms with one's circumstances (Whitbourne, 2000).

Finally, during the last stages of adulthood people become more accepting of others and of their own lives and are less concerned about issues or problems that once bothered them. People come to accept the fact that death is inevitable, and they try to understand their accomplishments in terms of the broader meaning of life. Although people may begin, for the first time, to label themselves as "old," many also develop a sense of wisdom and feel freer to enjoy life (Baltes & Kunzmann, 2003; Miner-Rubino, Winter, & Stewart, 2004).

Marriage, Children, and Divorce: Family Ties

In the typical fairy tale, a dashing young man and a beautiful young woman marry, have children, and live happily ever after. However, that scenario does not match the realities of love and marriage in the twenty-first century. Today, it is just as likely that the man and woman would first live together, then get married and have children, but ultimately get divorced.

The percentage of U.S. households made up of unmarried couples has increased dramatically over the last two decades. At the same time, the average age at which marriage takes place is higher than at any time since the turn of the last century. These changes have been dramatic, and they suggest that the institution of marriage has changed considerably from earlier historical periods (see Figure 1).

When people do marry, the probability of divorce is high, particularly for younger couples. Even though divorce rates have been declining since they peaked in 1981, about half of all first marriages end in divorce. Before they are 18 years old, two-fifths of children will experience the breakup of their parents' marriages. Moreover, the rise in divorce is not just a U.S. phenomenon: The divorce rate has accelerated over the last several decades in most industrialized countries. In some countries, the increase has been enormous. In South Korea, for example, the divorce rate quadrupled from 11 percent to 47 percent in the 12-year period ending in 2002 (Schaefer, 2000; Lankov, 2004; Olson & DeFrain, 2005).

Changes in marriage and divorce trends have doubled the number of single-parent households in the United States over the last two decades. Almost a quarter of all family households are now headed by one parent, compared with 13 percent in 1970. If present trends continue, almost three-fourths of American children will spend some portion of their lives in a single-parent family before they turn 18. For children in minority households, the numbers are even higher. Almost 60 percent of all black children and more than a third of Hispanic children live in homes with only one parent. Furthermore, in most single-parent families, it is the mother, rather than the father, with whom the children reside—a phenomenon that is consistent across racial and ethnic groups throughout the industrialized world (U.S. Bureau of the Census, 2000).

What are the economic and emotional consequences for children living in homes with only one parent? Single-parent families are often economically less well off, and this has an

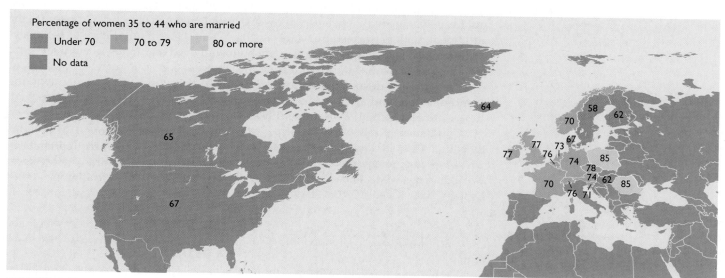

FIGURE 1 The percentage of women who are married has declined in most Western countries over previous decades. What do you think are some of the reasons for the declines, and do you think they will be permanent? (Source: Statistical Office of the European Communities, 1998.)

impact on children's opportunities. Over a third of single-mother families with children have incomes below the poverty line. In addition, good child care is often hard to find. Time is always at a premium in single-parent families. Furthermore, for children of divorce, the parents' separation is often a painful experience that may result in obstacles to establishing close relationships later in life. Children may blame themselves for the breakup or feel pressure to take sides (Hetherington, 1999; U.S. Bureau of the Census, 2000; Wallerstein et al., 2000).

Most evidence, however, suggests that children from single-parent families are no less well adjusted than are those from two-parent families. In fact, children may be more successful growing up in a harmonious single-parent family than in a two-parent family that engages in continuous conflict (Harold et al., 1997; Clarke-Stewart et al., 2000; Kelly, 2000; Olson & DeFrain, 2005).

CHANGING ROLES OF MEN AND WOMEN: THE TIME OF THEIR LIVES

One of the major changes in family life in the last two decades has been the evolution of men's and women's roles. More women than ever before act simultaneously as wives, mothers, and wage earners—in contrast to women in traditional marriages, in which the husband is the sole wage earner and the wife assumes primary responsibility for care of the home and children.

Close to 75 percent of all married women with school-age children are now employed outside the home, and 55 percent of mothers with children under age 6 are working. In the mid-1960s, only 17 percent of mothers of 1-year-olds worked full-time; now, more than half are in the labor force (Carnegie Task Force, 1994; U.S. Bureau of the Census, 2001; Halpern, 2005).

Most married working women are not free of household responsibilities. Even in marriages in which the spouses hold jobs that have similar status and require similar hours, the distribution of household tasks between husbands and wives has not changed substantially. Working wives are still more likely than husbands to feel responsible for traditional homemaking tasks such as cooking and cleaning. In contrast, husbands still view themselves as responsible primarily for household tasks such as repairing broken appliances, putting up screens in the summer, and doing yard work (Ganong & Coleman, 1999; Juster, Ono, & Stafford, 2002).

Women's "Second Shift." The number of hours put in by working mothers can be staggering. One survey, for instance, found that when you added the number of hours worked on the job and in the home, employed mothers of children under 3 years of age put in an average of ninety hours per week! Sociologist Arlie Hochschild refers to the additional work performed by women as the "second shift." According to her analysis of national statistics, women who are both employed and mothers put in an extra month of twenty-four-hour days during the course of a year. Researchers see similar patterns in many developing societies throughout the world, with women working at full-time jobs and also having primary responsibilities for child care (Hochschild, 1990, 2001; Hochschild & Machung, 1990; Jacobs & Gerson, 2004).

Consequently, rather than careers being a substitute for what women do at home, they often exist in addition to the role of homemaker. It is not surprising that some wives feel resentment toward husbands who spend less time on child care and housework than the wives had expected before the birth of their children (Stier & Lewin-Epstein, 2000; Kiecolt, 2003; Gerstel, 2005).

The Later Years of Life: Growing Old

I've always enjoyed doing things in the mountains—hiking or, more recently, active cliff-climbing. The more difficult the climb, the more absorbing it is. The climbs I really remember are the ones I had to work on. Maybe a particular section where it took two or three tries before I found the right combination of moves that got me up easily—and, preferably,

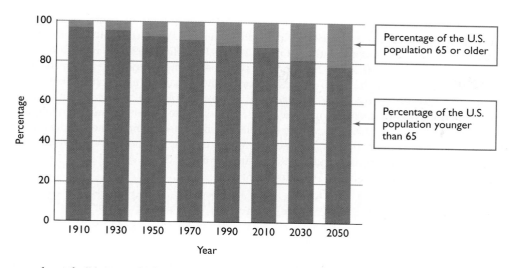

FIGURE 2 Projections suggest that by the year 2050, 20 percent of the U.S. population will be over age 65. What implications does this statistic have for U.S. society?

elegantly. It's a wonderful exhilaration to get to the top and sit down and perhaps have lunch and look out over the landscape and be so grateful that it's still possible for me to do that sort of thing (Lyman Spitzer, age 74, quoted in Kotre & Hall, 1990, pp. 358–359).

If you can't quite picture a 74-year-old rock-climbing, some rethinking of your view of late adulthood may be in order. In spite of the societal stereotype of "old age" as a time of inactivity and physical and mental decline, gerontologists, specialists who study aging, are beginning to paint a very different portrait of late adulthood.

By focusing on the period of life that starts at around age 65, gerontologists are making important contributions to clarifying the capabilities of older adults. Their work is demonstrating that significant developmental processes continue even during old age. And as life expectancy increases, the number of people who reach older adulthood will continue to grow substantially (see Figure 2). Consequently, developing an understanding of late adulthood has become a critical priority for psychologists (Birren, 1996; Moody, 2000).

Physical Changes in Late Adulthood: The Aging Body

Napping, eating, walking, conversing. It probably doesn't surprise you that these relatively nonstrenuous activities represent the typical pastimes of late adulthood. But it is striking that these activities are identical to the most common leisure activities reported in a survey of college students (Harper, 1978). Although the students cited more active pursuits—such as sailing and playing basketball—as their favorite activities, in actuality they engaged in such sports relatively infrequently, spending most of their free time napping, eating, walking, and conversing. (To learn more about age stereotypes, complete the PsychInteractive exercise.)

Although the leisure activities in which older adults engage may not differ all that much from the ones younger people pursue, many physical changes are, of course, brought about by the aging process. The most obvious are those of appearance—hair thinning and turning gray, skin wrinkling and folding, and sometimes a slight loss of height as the thickness of the disks between vertebrae in the spine decreases—but subtler changes also occur in the body's biological functioning. For example, sensory capabilities decrease as a result of aging: Vision, hearing, smell, and taste become less sensitive. Reaction time slows, and physical stamina changes (DiGiovanna, 1994; Whalley, 2003; Stenklev & Laukli, 2004).

What are the reasons for these physical declines? **Genetic preprogramming theories of aging** suggest that human cells have a built-in time limit to their reproduction. These theories suggest that after a certain time cells stop dividing or become harmful to the body—as if a kind of automatic self-destruct button had been pushed. In contrast, **wear-and-tear theories of aging** suggest that the mechanical functions of the body

www.mhhe.com/feldmanup8
PsychInteractive Online

Attitudes Toward Aging

Genetic preprogramming theories of aging: Theories that suggest that human cells have a built-in time limit to their reproduction, and that after a certain time they are no longer able to divide.

Wear-and-tear theories of aging: Theories that suggest that the mechanical functions of the body simply stop working efficiently.

simply work less efficiently as people age. Waste byproducts of energy production eventually accumulate, and mistakes are made when cells divide. Eventually the body, in effect, wears out, just as an old automobile does (Hayflick, 1994; Ly et al., 2000).

Evidence supports both the genetic preprogramming and the wear-and-tear views, and it may be that both processes contribute to natural aging. It is clear, however, that physical aging is not a disease, but a natural biological process. Many physical functions do not decline with age. For example, sex remains pleasurable well into old age (although the frequency of sexual activity decreases), and some people report that the pleasure they derive from sex increases during late adulthood (Olshansky, Carnes, & Cassel, 1990; Gelfand, 2000; DeLamater & Sill, 2005).

Cognitive Changes: Thinking About— and During—Late Adulthood

At one time, many gerontologists would have agreed with the popular view that older adults are forgetful and confused. Today, however, most research indicates that this is far from an accurate assessment of older people's capabilities.

One reason for the change in view is that more sophisticated research techniques exist for studying the cognitive changes that occur in late adulthood. For example, if we were to give a group of older adults an IQ test, we might find that the average score was lower than the score achieved by a group of younger people. We might conclude that this signifies a decline in intelligence. Yet if we looked a little more closely at the specific test, we might find that that conclusion was unwarranted. For instance, many IQ tests include portions based on physical performance (such as arranging a group of blocks) or on speed. In such cases, poorer performance on the IQ test may be due to gradual decreases in reaction time—a physical decline that accompanies late adulthood and has little or nothing to do with the intellectual capabilities of older adults (Schaie, 1991).

Other difficulties hamper research into cognitive functioning during late adulthood. For example, older people are often less healthy than younger ones; when only *healthy* older adults are compared to healthy younger adults, intellectual differences are far less evident. Furthermore, the average number of years in school is often lower in older adults (for historical reasons) than in younger ones, and older adults may be less motivated to perform well on intelligence tests than younger people. Finally, traditional IQ tests may be inappropriate measures of intelligence in late adulthood. Older adults sometimes perform better on tests of practical intelligence than do younger individuals (Kausler, 1994; Willis & Schaie, 1994; Dixon & Cohen, 2003).

Still, some declines in intellectual functioning during late adulthood do occur, although the pattern of age differences is not uniform for different types of cognitive abilities (see Figure 3). In general, skills relating to *fluid intelligence* (which involves information-processing skills such as memory, calculations, and solving analogies) show declines in late adulthood. In contrast, skills relating to *crystallized intelligence* (intelligence based on the accumulation of information, skills, and strategies learned through experience) remain steady and in some cases actually improve (Schaie, 1994; Salthouse, 1996; Stankov, 2003; Rozencwajg et al., 2005).

Even when changes in intellectual functioning occur during late adulthood, people often are able to compensate for any decline. They can still learn what they want to; it may just take more time. Furthermore, teaching older adults strategies for dealing with new problems can prevent declines in performance (Coffey, Saxton, & Ratcliff, 1999; Saczynski, Willis, & Schaie, 2002; Cavallini, Pagnin, & Vecchi, 2003).

MEMORY CHANGES IN LATE ADULTHOOD: ARE OLDER ADULTS FORGETFUL?

One of the characteristics most frequently attributed to late adulthood is forgetfulness. How accurate is this assumption?

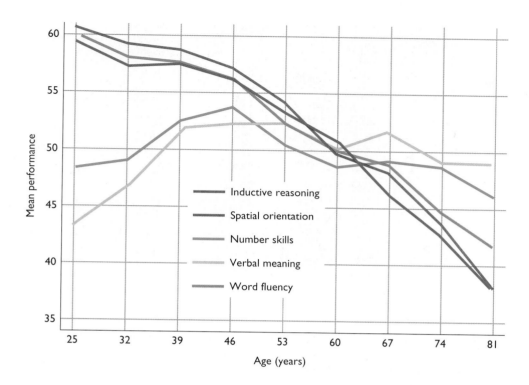

FIGURE 3 Age-related changes in intellectual skills vary according to the specific cognitive ability in question. (Source: Schaie, 1994.)

Legend for chart:
- Inductive reasoning
- Spatial orientation
- Number skills
- Verbal meaning
- Word fluency

Y-axis: Mean performance
X-axis: Age (years)

Most evidence suggests that memory change is not an inevitable part of the aging process. For instance, research shows that older people in cultures in which older adults are held in high esteem, such as mainland China, are less likely to show memory losses than are those living in cultures in which the expectation is that memory will decline. Similarly, when older people in Western societies are reminded of the advantages of age (for example, "age brings wisdom"), they tend to do better on tests of memory (Levy & Langer, 1994; Levy, 1996; Hess, Hinson, & Statham, 2004).

Even when people show memory declines during late adulthood, their deficits tend to be limited to particular types of memory. For instance, losses tend to be limited to episodic memories, which relate to specific experiences in people's lives. Other types of memories, such as semantic memories (which refer to general knowledge and facts) and implicit memories (memories of which we are not consciously aware), are largely unaffected by age (Graf, 1990; Russo & Parkin, 1993; Fleischman et al., 2004).

Declines in episodic memories can often be traced to changes in the lives of older adults. For instance, it is not surprising that a retired person, who may no longer face the same kind of consistent intellectual challenges encountered on the job, may be less practiced in using memory or even be less motivated to remember things, leading to an apparent decline in memory. Even in cases in which long-term memory declines, older adults can usually profit from compensatory efforts. Training older adults to use the mnemonic strategies developed by psychologists studying memory not only may prevent their long-term memory from deteriorating, but may actually improve it (Verhaeghen, Marcoen, & Goosens, 1992; West, 1995).

In the past, older adults with severe cases of memory decline, accompanied by other cognitive difficulties, were said to suffer from senility. *Senility* is a broad, imprecise term typically applied to older adults who experience progressive deterioration of mental abilities, including memory loss, disorientation to time and place, and general confusion. Once thought to be an inevitable state that accompanies aging, senility is now viewed by most gerontologists as a label that has outlived its usefulness. Rather than senility being the cause of certain symptoms, the symptoms are deemed to be caused by some other factor.

Some cases of memory loss, however, are produced by actual disease. For instance, **Alzheimer's disease** is a progressive brain disorder that leads to a gradual and irreversible

Alzheimer's disease: A progressive brain disorder that leads to a gradual and irreversible decline in cognitive abilities.

Although there are declines in fluid intelligence in late adulthood, skills relating to crystallized intelligence remain steady and may actually improve.

People in late adulthood usually see themselves as functioning, well-integrated members of society, and many maintain activities in which they participated earlier in life.

decline in cognitive abilities. Nineteen percent of people age 75 to 84 have Alzheimer's, and almost 50 percent of people over age 85 are affected by the disease. Unless a cure is found, some 14 million people will experience Alzheimer's by 2050—more than three times the current number (Cowley, 2000; Feinberg, 2002; Lovestone, 2002).

In other cases, cognitive declines may be caused by temporary anxiety and depression, which can be treated successfully, or may even be due to overmedication. The danger is that people with such symptoms may be labeled senile and left untreated, thereby continuing their decline—even though treatment would have been beneficial (Selkoe, 1997; Sachs-Ericsson et al., 2005).

In sum, declines in cognitive functioning in late adulthood are, for the most part, not inevitable. The key to maintaining cognitive skills may lie in intellectual stimulation. Like the rest of us, older adults need a stimulating environment in order to hone and maintain their skills (Bosma et al., 2002; Bosma et al., 2003).

The Social World of Late Adulthood: Old but Not Alone

Just as the view that old age predictably means mental decline has proved to be wrong, so has the view that late adulthood inevitably brings loneliness. People in late adulthood most often see themselves as functioning members of society, with only a small number of them reporting that loneliness is a serious problem (Binstock & George, 1996; Jylha, 2004).

Disengagement theory of aging: A theory that suggests that aging produces a gradual withdrawal from the world on physical, psychological, and social levels.

Activity theory of aging: A theory that suggests that the elderly who are most successful while aging are those who maintain the interests and activities they had during middle age.

There is no single way to age successfully. According to the **disengagement theory of aging,** aging produces a gradual withdrawal from the world on physical, psychological, and social levels (Cummings & Henry, 1961; Adams, 2004). However, such disengagement serves an important purpose, providing an opportunity for increased reflectiveness and decreased emotional investment in others at a time of life when social relationships will inevitably be ended by death.

The **activity theory of aging** presents an alternative view of aging, holding that the people who age most successfully are those who maintain the interests, activities, and level of social interaction they experienced during middle adulthood. According to activity theory, late adulthood should reflect a continuation, as much as possible, of the activities in which people participated during the earlier part of their lives (Blau, 1973; Crosnoe & Elder, 2002).

Both disengagement and activity can lead to successful aging. Not all people in late adulthood need a life filled with activities and social interaction to be happy; as in every stage of life, some older adults are just as satisfied leading a relatively inactive, solitary existence. What may be more important is how people view the aging process: Evidence shows that positive self-perceptions of aging are associated with increased longevity (Charles, Reynolds, & Gatz, 2001; Levy et al., 2002; Levy & Myers, 2004).

Regardless of whether people become disengaged or maintain their activities from earlier stages of life, most engage in a process of **life review,** in which they examine and evaluate their lives. Remembering and reconsidering what has occurred in the past, people in late adulthood often come to a better understanding of themselves, sometimes resolving lingering problems and conflicts, and facing their lives with greater wisdom and serenity.

Life review: The process by which people examine and evaluate their lives.

Clearly, people in late adulthood are not just marking time until death. Rather, old age is a time of continued growth and development, as important as any other period of life.

At some time in our lives, we all face death—certainly our own, as well as the deaths of friends, loved ones, and even strangers. Although there is nothing more inevitable in life, death remains a frightening, emotion-laden topic. Certainly, little is more stressful than the death of a loved one or the contemplation of our own imminent death, and preparing for death is one of our most crucial developmental tasks (Aiken, 2000).

BECOMING AN INFORMED CONSUMER
of Psychology

Adjusting to Death

A generation ago, talk of death was taboo. The topic was never mentioned to dying people, and gerontologists had little to say about it. That changed, however, with the pioneering work of Elisabeth Kübler-Ross (1969), who brought the subject of death into the open with her observation that those facing impending death tend to move through five broad stages:

- *Denial.* In this stage, people resist the idea that they are dying. Even if told that their chances for survival are small, they refuse to admit that they are facing death.
- *Anger.* After moving beyond the denial stage, dying people become angry— angry at people around them who are in good health, angry at medical professionals for being ineffective, angry at God.
- *Bargaining.* Anger leads to bargaining, in which the dying try to think of ways to postpone death. They may decide to dedicate their lives to religion if God saves them; they may say, "If only I can live to see my son married, I will accept death then."
- *Depression.* When dying people come to feel that bargaining is of no use, they move to the next stage: depression. They realize that their lives really are coming to an end, leading to what Kübler-Ross calls "preparatory grief" for their own deaths.
- *Acceptance.* In this stage, people accept impending death. Usually they are unemotional and uncommunicative; it is as if they have made peace with themselves and are expecting death with no bitterness.

It is important to keep in mind that not everyone experiences each of these stages in the same way. In fact, Kübler-Ross's stages pertain only to people who are fully aware that they are dying and have the time to evaluate their impending death. Furthermore, vast differences occur in the way individuals react to impending death. The specific cause and duration of dying, as well as the person's sex, age, and personality and the type of support received from family and friends, all have an impact on how people respond to death (Zautra, Reich, & Guarnaccia, 1990; Stroebe, Stroebe, & Hansson, 1993; Carver & Scheier, 2002).

Few of us enjoy the contemplation of death. Yet awareness of its psychological aspects and consequences can make its inevitable arrival less anxiety-producing and perhaps more understandable.

RECAP/EVALUATE/RETHINK

RECAP

What are the principal kinds of physical, social, and intellectual changes that occur in early and middle adulthood, and what are their causes?

- Early adulthood marks the peak of physical health. Physical changes occur relatively gradually in men and women during adulthood. (p. 439)
- One major physical change occurs at the end of middle adulthood for women: They begin menopause, after which they are no longer fertile. (p. 439)
- During middle adulthood, people typically experience a midlife transition in which the notion that life is not unending becomes more important. In some cases this may lead to a midlife crisis, although the passage into middle age is typically relatively calm. (p. 440)
- As aging continues during middle adulthood, people realize in their fifties that their lives and accomplishments are fairly well set, and they try to come to terms with them. (p. 440)
- Among the important developmental milestones during adulthood are marriage, family changes, and divorce. Another important determinant of adult development is work. (pp. 441-442)

How does the reality of late adulthood differ from the stereotypes about that period?

- Old age may bring marked physical declines caused by genetic preprogramming or physical wear and tear. Although the activities of people in late adulthood are not all that different from those of younger people, older adults experience declines in reaction time, sensory abilities, and physical stamina. (pp. 443-444)
- Intellectual declines are not an inevitable part of aging. Fluid intelligence does decline with age, and long-term memory abilities are sometimes impaired. In contrast, crystallized intelligence shows slight increases with age, and short-term memory remains at about the same level. (pp. 444-445)
- Disengagement theory sees successful aging as a process of gradual withdrawal from the physical, psychological, and social worlds. In contrast, activity theory suggests that the maintenance of interests and activities from earlier years leads to successful aging. (p. 446)

How can we adjust to death?

- According to Kübler-Ross, dying people move through five stages as they face death: denial, anger, bargaining, depression, and acceptance. (p. 447)

EVALUATE

1. Rob recently turned 40 and surveyed his goals and accomplishments to date. Although he has accomplished a lot, he realized that many of his goals will not be met in his lifetime. This stage is called a _____.
2. In households where both partners have similar jobs, the division of labor that generally occurs is the same as in "traditional" households where the husband works and the wife stays at home. True or false?
3. _____ theories suggest that there is a maximum time span in which cells are able to reproduce. This time limit explains the eventual breakdown of the body.
4. Lower IQ test scores during late adulthood do not necessarily mean a decrease in intelligence. True or false?
5. During old age, a person's _____ intelligence continues to increase, whereas _____ intelligence may decline.
6. In Kübler-Ross's _____ stage, people resist the idea of death. In the _____ stage, they attempt to make deals to avoid death, and in the _____ stage, they passively await death.

RETHINK

1. Is the possibility that life may be extended for several decades a mixed blessing? What societal consequences might an extended life span bring about?
2. *From the perspective of a health care provider:* What sorts of recommendations would you make to your older patients about how to deal with aging? How would you handle someone who believed that getting older had only negative consequences?

Answers to Evaluate Questions

1. midlife transition; 2. true; 3. genetic preprogramming; 4. true; 5. crystallized, fluid; 6. denial, bargaining, acceptance

KEY TERMS

menopause p. 439
genetic preprogramming
   theories of aging p. 443
wear-and-tear theories of
   aging p. 443

Alzheimer's disease p. 445
disengagement theory of
   aging p. 446
activity theory of aging
   p. 446

life review p. 447

Looking Back

Psychology on the Web

1. Find information on the Web about cloning. What recent advances in cloning have been made by researchers? What developments appear to be on the horizon? What ethical issues have been raised regarding the cloning of humans?

2. Find different answers to the question "Why do people die?" Search the Web for scientific, philosophical, and spiritual/religious answers. Write a summary in which you compare the different approaches to this question. Does the thinking in any one realm influence the thinking in the others? How?

3. After completing the PsychInteractive exercise on suicide risk factors, search the Web for the most recent statistics on adolescent suicide. How have the trends changed over the last ten years, and what factors explain those changes?

Epilogue

We have traced major events in the development of physical, social, and cognitive growth throughout the life span. Clearly, people change throughout their lives.

As we explored each area of development, we encountered anew the nature-nurture issue, concluding in every significant instance that both nature and nurture contribute to a person's development of skills, personality, and interactions. Specifically, our genetic inheritance—nature—lays down general boundaries within which we can advance and grow, and our environment—nurture—helps determine the extent to which we take advantage of our potential.

Before proceeding to the next set of modules, turn once again to the prologue that introduced this chapter, on Louise Brown, who was conceived using *in vitro* fertilization. Using your knowledge of childhood development, consider the following questions.

1. Do you think there is any way in which Louise Brown's birth, infancy, and development differ from those of her classmates who were not conceived through *in vitro* fertilization? Why or why not?

2. How would you design a longitudinal study of the development of individuals who were conceived through *in vitro* fertilization? What sorts of questions would this type of study help you answer?

3. What sorts of questions could you examine through a cross-sectional study? A cross-sequential study?

4. If a future Louise Brown were *cloned* from one of her parents, do you think she would turn out to be exactly like that parent, or different in some ways? Why?

CHAPTER 13

Personality

Key Concepts for Chapter 13

How do psychologists define and use the concept of personality? ● What do the theories of Freud and his successors tell us about the structure and development of personality?

What are the major aspects of trait, learning, biological and evolutionary, and humanistic approaches to personality?

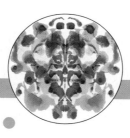

How can we most accurately assess personality? ●

What are the major types of personality measures?

Prologue A Real-Life Tony Soprano

John Gotti appeared to be an ordinary fellow. He described himself as a salesman who sold plumbing and heating supplies to builders, and zippers to dressmakers. He lived in a modest home with a satellite dish on the roof. His friends and admirers—of whom there were many—said he was just an ordinary guy.

There was another side to Gotti, though. He frequented posh, expensive restaurants, wearing custom-made $1,800 suits and designer socks. His hair was always freshly barbered, and his nails were meticulously manicured. If you met him at such a nightspot, you might guess he was a rich, successful entrepreneur.

But there were even more contradictions in the life of John Gotti. To U.S. prosecutors, he was a real-life Tony Soprano, the head of a crime family portrayed on the HBO show *The Sopranos*. Like his fictional counterpart, prosecutors said Gotti was a vicious, cold-hearted killer who was responsible for the deaths of scores of people. And they convinced a jury: Gotti was convicted for murder and was given a life sentence. He died in prison (Poniewozik, 2002; Cutler & Saporta, 2003; Smith, 2005).

Looking Ahead

Just who was John Gotti? A warm, friendly neighbor? A wealthy entrepreneur? A ruthless, greedy mobster, willing to do anything to keep control of his crime family?

Many people, like the real Gotti or the fictional Tony Soprano, have different sides to their personalities, appearing one way to some people and quite differently to others. Yet, to any one group of people who were acquainted with Gotti, his behavior was probably so consistent that (they thought) they could easily predict how he would behave, no matter what the situation.

Personality is the pattern of enduring characteristics that produce consistency and individuality in a given person. Personality encompasses the behaviors that make us unique and that differenti-

ate us from others. It is also personality that leads us to act consistently in different situations and over extended periods of time.

We will consider a number of approaches to personality. For historical reasons, we begin with psychodynamic theories of personality, which emphasize the importance of the unconscious. Next, we consider approaches that concentrate on identifying the most fundamental personality traits, theories that view personality as a set of learned behaviors, biological and evolutionary perspectives on personality, and approaches, known as humanistic theories, that highlight the uniquely human aspects of personality. We end our discussion by focusing on how personality is measured and how personality tests can be used.

Psychodynamic Approaches to Personality

The college student was intent on making a good first impression on an attractive woman he had spotted across a crowded room at a party. As he walked toward her, he mulled over a line he had heard in an old movie the night before: "I don't believe we've been properly introduced yet." To his horror, what came out was a bit different. After threading his way through the crowded room, he finally reached the woman and blurted out, "I don't believe we've been properly seduced yet."

Although this student's error may seem to be merely an embarrassing slip of the tongue, according to some personality theorists, such a mistake is not an error at all (Motley, 1987). Instead, psychodynamic personality theorists might argue that the error illustrates one way in which behavior is triggered by inner forces that are beyond our awareness. These hidden drives, shaped by childhood experiences, play an important role in energizing and directing everyday behavior.

Psychodynamic approaches to personality are based on the idea that personality is motivated by inner forces and conflicts about which people have little awareness and over which they have no control. The most important pioneer of the psychodynamic approach was Sigmund Freud. A number of Freud's followers, including Carl Jung, Karen Horney, and Alfred Adler, refined Freud's theory and developed their own psychodynamic approaches.

Freud's Psychoanalytic Theory: Mapping the Unconscious Mind

Sigmund Freud, an Austrian physician, developed **psychoanalytic theory** in the early 1900s. According to Freud's theory, conscious experience is a small part of our psychological makeup and experience. He argued that much of our behavior is motivated by the **unconscious,** a part of the personality that contains the memories, knowledge, beliefs, feelings, urges, drives, and instincts of which the individual is not aware.

Like the unseen mass of a floating iceberg, the contents of the unconscious far surpass in quantity the information in our conscious awareness. Freud maintained that to understand personality, it is necessary to expose what is in the unconscious. But because the unconscious disguises the meaning of the material it holds, the content of the unconscious cannot be observed directly. It is therefore necessary to interpret clues to the unconscious—slips of the tongue, fantasies, and dreams—to understand the unconscious processes that direct behavior. A slip of the tongue such as the one quoted earlier (sometimes termed a *Freudian slip*) may be interpreted as revealing the speaker's unconscious sexual desires.

To Freud, much of our personality is determined by our unconscious. Some of the unconscious is made up of the *preconscious,* which contains material that is not threatening and is easily brought to mind, such as the knowledge that 2 + 2 = 4. But deeper in the unconscious are instinctual drives, the wishes, desires, demands, and

Key Concepts

How do psychologists define and use the concept of personality?

What do the theories of Freud and his successors tell us about the structure and development of personality?

Personality: The pattern of enduring characteristics that produce consistency and individuality in a given person.

Psychodynamic approaches to personality: Approaches that assume that personality is motivated by inner forces and conflicts about which people have little awareness and over which they have no control.

Psychoanalytic theory: Freud's theory that unconscious forces act as determinants of personality.

Unconscious: A part of the personality that contains the memories, knowledge, beliefs, feelings, urges, drives, and instincts of which the individual is not aware.

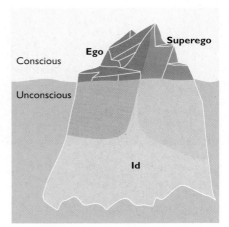

FIGURE 1 In Freud's model of personality, there are three major components: the id, the ego, and the superego. As the iceberg analogy shows, only a small portion of personality is conscious. Why do you think that only the ego and superego have conscious components?

Id: The raw, unorganized, inborn part of personality whose sole purpose is to reduce tension created by primitive drives related to hunger, sex, aggression, and irrational impulses.

Ego: The part of the personality that provides a buffer between the id and the outside world.

Superego: According to Freud, the final personality structure to develop; it represents the rights and wrongs of society as handed down by a person's parents, teachers, and other important figures.

Psychosexual stages: Developmental periods that children pass through during which they encounter conflicts between the demands of society and their own sexual urges.

Fixations: Conflicts or concerns that persist beyond the developmental period in which they first occur.

needs that are hidden from conscious awareness because of the conflicts and pain they would cause if they were part of our everyday lives. The unconscious provides a "safe haven" for our recollections of threatening events.

STRUCTURING PERSONALITY: ID, EGO, AND SUPEREGO

To describe the structure of personality, Freud developed a comprehensive theory that held that personality consists of three separate but interacting components: the id, the ego, and the superego. Freud suggested that the three structures can be diagrammed to show how they relate to the conscious and the unconscious (see Figure 1).

Although the three components of personality described by Freud may appear to be actual physical structures in the nervous system, they are not. Instead, they represent abstract conceptions of a general *model* of personality that describes the interaction of forces that motivate behavior.

If personality consisted only of primitive, instinctual cravings and longings, it would have just one component: the id. The **id** is the raw, unorganized, inborn part of personality. From the time of birth, the id attempts to reduce tension created by primitive drives related to hunger, sex, aggression, and irrational impulses. Those drives are fueled by "psychic energy," which can be thought of as a limitless energy source constantly putting pressure on the various parts of the personality.

The id operates according to the *pleasure principle,* in which the goal is the immediate reduction of tension and the maximization of satisfaction. However, reality prevents the fulfillment of the demands of the pleasure principle in most cases: We cannot always eat when we are hungry, and we can discharge our sexual drives only when the time and place are appropriate. To account for this fact of life, Freud suggested a second component of personality, which he called the ego.

The **ego,** which begins to develop soon after birth, strives to balance the desires of the id and the realities of the objective, outside world. In contrast to the pleasure-seeking id, the ego operates according to the *reality principle,* in which instinctual energy is restrained to maintain the safety of the individual and help integrate the person into society. In a sense, then, the ego is the "executive" of personality: It makes decisions, controls actions, and allows thinking and problem solving of a higher order than the id's capabilities permit.

The **superego,** the final personality structure to develop in childhood, represents the rights and wrongs of society as taught and modeled by a person's parents, teachers, and other significant individuals. The superego includes the *conscience,* which prevents us from behaving in a morally improper way by making us feel guilty if we do wrong. The superego helps us control impulses coming from the id, making our behavior less selfish and more virtuous.

According to Freud's theory, both the superego and the id are unrealistic in that they do not consider the practical realities imposed by society. The superego, if left to operate without restraint, would create perfectionists unable to make the compromises that life requires. An unrestrained id would create a primitive, pleasure-seeking, thoughtless individual seeking to fulfill every desire without delay. As a result, the ego must mediate between the demands of the superego and the demands of the id.

DEVELOPING PERSONALITY: PSYCHOSEXUAL STAGES

Freud also provided us with a view of how personality develops through a series of five **psychosexual stages,** during which individuals encounter conflicts between the demands of society and their own sexual urges (in which sexuality is more about experiencing pleasure and less about lust). According to Freud, failure to resolve the conflicts at a particular stage can result in **fixations,** conflicts or concerns that persist beyond the developmental period in which they first occur. Such conflicts may be due to having needs ignored or (conversely) being overindulged during the earlier period.

Freud suggests that the superego, the part of personality that represents the rights and wrongs of society, develops from direct teaching from parents, teachers, and other significant individuals.

The sequence Freud proposed is noteworthy because it explains how experiences and difficulties during a particular childhood stage may predict specific characteristics in the adult personality. This theory is also unique in associating each stage with a major biological function, which Freud assumed to be the focus of pleasure in a given period.

In the first psychosexual stage of development, called the **oral stage,** the baby's mouth is the focal point of pleasure (see Figure 2 for a summary of the stages). During the first 12 to 18 months of life, children suck, mouth, and bite anything that can put into their mouths. To Freud, this behavior suggested that the mouth is the primary site of a kind of sexual pleasure, and that weaning (withdrawing the breast or bottle) represents the main conflict during the oral stage. If infants are either overindulged (perhaps by being fed every time they cry) or frustrated in their search for oral gratification, they may become fixated at this stage. For example, fixation might occur if an infant's oral needs were constantly gratified immediately at the first sign of hunger,

Oral stage: According to Freud, a stage from birth to age 12 to 18 months, in which an infant's center of pleasure is the mouth.

Stage	Age	Major Characteristics
Oral	Birth to 12–18 months	Interest in oral gratification from sucking, eating, mouthing, biting
Anal	12–18 months to 3 years	Gratification from expelling and withholding feces; coming to terms with society's controls relating to toilet training
Phallic	3 to 5–6 years	Interest in the genitals, coming to term with Oedipal conflict leading to identification with same-sex parent
Latency	5–6 years to adolescence	Sexual concerns largely unimportant
Genital	Adolescence to adulthood	Reemergence of sexual interests and establishment of mature sexual relationships

FIGURE 2 Freud's theory of personality development suggests that there are several distinct stages.

According to Freud, a child goes through the anal stage from age 12 to 18 months until 3 years of age. Toilet training is a crucial event at this stage, one that psychoanalytic theory claims directly influences the formation for an individual's personality.

Anal stage: According to Freud, a stage from age 12 to 18 months to 3 years of age, in which a child's pleasure is centered on the anus.

Phallic stage: According to Freud, a period beginning around age 3 during which a child's pleasure focuses on the genitals.

Oedipal conflict: A child's sexual interest in his or her opposite-sex parent, typically resolved through identification with the same-sex parent.

Identification: The process of wanting to be like another person as much as possible, imitating that person's behavior and adopting similar beliefs and values.

Latency period: According to Freud, the period between the phallic stage and puberty during which children's sexual concerns are temporarily put aside.

Genital stage: According to Freud, the period from puberty until death, marked by mature sexual behavior (that is, sexual intercourse).

rather than the infant learning that feeding takes place on a schedule because eating whenever an infant wants to eat is not always realistic. Fixation at the oral stage might produce an adult who was unusually interested in oral activities—eating, talking, smoking—or who showed symbolic sorts of oral interests: being either "bitingly" sarcastic or very gullible ("swallowing" anything).

From around age 12 to 18 months until 3 years of age—a period when the emphasis in Western cultures is on toilet training—a child enters the **anal stage.** At this point, the major source of pleasure changes from the mouth to the anal region, and children obtain considerable pleasure from both retention and expulsion of feces. If toilet training is particularly demanding, fixation might occur. Fixation during the anal stage might result in unusual rigidity, orderliness, punctuality—or extreme disorderliness or sloppiness—in adulthood.

At about age 3, the **phallic stage** begins. At this point there is another major shift in the primary source of pleasure for the child. Now interest focuses on the genitals and the pleasures derived from fondling them. During this stage the child must also negotiate one of the most important hurdles of personality development: the **Oedipal conflict.** According to Freudian theory, as children focus attention on their genitals, the differences between male and female anatomy become more salient. Furthermore, according to Freud, at this time the male unconsciously begins to develop a sexual interest in his mother, starts to see his father as a rival, and harbors a wish to kill his father—as Oedipus did in the ancient Greek tragedy. But because he views his father as too powerful, he develops a fear that his father may retaliate drastically by removing the source of the threat: the son's penis. The fear of losing one's penis leads to *castration anxiety,* which ultimately becomes so powerful that the child represses his desires for his mother and identifies with his father. **Identification** is the process of wanting to be like another person as much as possible, imitating that person's behavior and adopting similar beliefs and values. By identifying with his father, a son seeks to obtain a woman like his unattainable mother.

For girls, the process is different. Freud reasoned that girls begin to experience sexual arousal toward their fathers and begin to experience penis envy. They wish they had the anatomical part that, at least to Freud, seemed most clearly "missing" in girls. Blaming their mothers for their lack of a penis, girls come to believe that their mothers are responsible for their "castration." (This aspect of Freud's theory later provoked accusations that he considered women to be inferior to men.) Like males, though, they find that they can resolve such unacceptable feelings by identifying with the same-sex parent, behaving like her and adopting her attitudes and values. In this way, a girl's identification with her mother is completed.

At this point, the Oedipal conflict is said to be resolved, and Freudian theory assumes that both males and females move on to the next stage of development. If difficulties arise during this period, however, all sorts of problems are thought to occur, including improper sex-role behavior and the failure to develop a conscience.

After the resolution of the Oedipal conflict, typically at around age 5 or 6, children move into the **latency period,** which lasts until puberty. During this period, sexual interests become dormant, even in the unconscious. Then, during adolescence, sexual feelings reemerge, marking the start of the final period, the **genital stage,** which extends until death. The focus during the genital stage is on mature, adult sexuality, which Freud defined as sexual intercourse.

DEFENSE MECHANISMS

Freud's efforts to describe and theorize about the underlying dynamics of personality and its development were motivated by very practical problems that his patients faced in dealing with *anxiety,* an intense, negative emotional experience. According to Freud, anxiety is a danger signal to the ego. Although anxiety can arise from realistic fears—

such as seeing a poisonous snake about to strike—it can also occur in the form of *neurotic anxiety*, in which irrational impulses emanating from the id threaten to burst through and become uncontrollable.

Because anxiety, obviously, is unpleasant, Freud believed that people develop a range of defense mechanisms to deal with it. **Defense mechanisms** are unconscious strategies that people use to reduce anxiety by concealing the source from themselves and others.

The primary defense mechanism is **repression,** in which unacceptable or unpleasant id impulses are pushed back into the unconscious. Repression is the most direct method of dealing with anxiety; instead of handling an anxiety-producing impulse on a conscious level, one simply ignores it. For example, a college student who feels hatred for her mother may repress those personally and socially unacceptable feelings. The feelings remain lodged within the unconscious, because acknowledging them would provoke anxiety. Similarly, memories of childhood abuse may be repressed. Although such memories may not be consciously recalled, according to Freud, they can affect later behavior, and they may be revealed through dreams or slips of the tongue or symbolically in some other fashion.

If repression is ineffective in keeping anxiety at bay, other defense mechanisms may be used. Freud, and later his daughter Anna Freud (who became a well-known psychoanalyst), formulated an extensive list of potential defense mechanisms. The major defense mechanisms are summarized in Figure 3 (Basch, 1996; Cramer, 2000b; Conte, Plutchik, & Draguns, 2004; Hentschel et al., 2004). To clearly understand these defense mechanisms, complete the PsychInteractive exercise.

All of us employ defense mechanisms to some degree, according to Freudian theory, and they can serve a useful purpose by protecting us from unpleasant information. Yet some people fall prey to them to such an extent that a large amount of psychic energy must constantly be directed toward hiding and rechanneling unacceptable impulses. When this occurs, everyday living becomes difficult. In such cases, the result is a mental disorder produced by anxiety—what Freud called "neurosis" (a term rarely used by psychologists today, although it endures in everyday conversation).

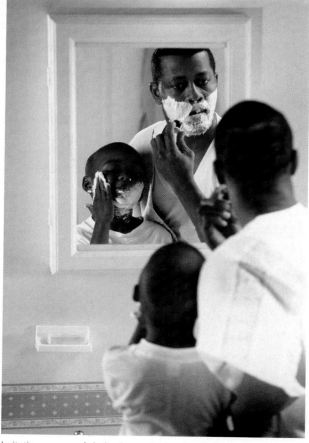

Imitating a person's behavior and adopting similar beliefs and values is part of Freud's concept of identification. How can this concept be applied to the definition of gender roles? Is identification similar in all cultures?

EVALUATING FREUD'S LEGACY

Freud's theory has had a significant impact on the field of psychology—and even more broadly on Western philosophy and literature. The ideas of the unconscious, defense mechanisms, and childhood roots of adult psychological difficulties have been accepted by many people.

However, personality psychologists have leveled significant criticisms against psychoanalytic theory. Among the most important is the lack of compelling scientific data to support it. Although individual case studies *seem* supportive, we lack conclusive evidence showing that the personality is structured and operates along the lines Freud laid out. This is due, in part, to the fact that Freud's conception of personality is built on unobservable abstract concepts. Moreover, it is not clear that the stages of personality that Freud laid out provide an accurate description of personality development. We also know now that important changes in personality can occur in adolescence and adulthood—something that Freud did not believe happened, thinking that personality largely is set by adolescence.

The vague nature of Freud's theory also makes it difficult to predict how certain developmental difficulties will be displayed in an adult. For instance, if a person is

Defense mechanisms: In Freudian theory, unconscious strategies that people use to reduce anxiety by concealing the source of the anxiety from themselves and others.

Repression: The primary defense mechanism in which unacceptable or unpleasant id impulses are pushed back into the unconscious.

www.mhhe.com/feldmanup8
PsychInteractive Online

Defense Mechanisms

Freud's Defense Mechanisms		
Defense Mechanism	**Explanation**	**Example**
Repression	Unacceptable or unpleasant impulses are pushed back into the unconscious.	A woman is unable to recall that she was raped.
Regression	People behave as if they were at an earlier stage of development.	A boss has a temper tantrum when an employee makes a mistake.
Displacement	The expression of an unwanted feeling or thought is redirected from a more threatening powerful person to a weaker one.	A brother yells at his younger sister after a teacher gives him a bad grade.
Rationalization	People provide self-justifying explanations in place of the actual, but threatening, reason for their behavior.	A student who goes out drinking the night before a big test rationalizes his behavior by saying the test isn't all that important.
Denial	People refuse to accept or acknowledge an anxiety-producing piece of information.	A student refuses to believe that he has flunked a course.
Projection	People attribute unwanted impulses and feelings to someone else.	A man who is angry at his father acts lovingly to his father but complains that his father is angry with him.
Sublimation	People divert unwanted impulses into socially approved thoughts, feelings, or behaviors.	A person with strong feelings of aggression becomes a soldier.
Reaction formation	Unconscious impulses are expressed as their opposite in consciousness.	A mother who unconsciously resents her child acts in an overly loving way toward the child.

FIGURE 3 According to Freud, people are able to use a wide range of defense mechanisms to cope with anxieties.

fixated at the anal stage, according to Freud, he or she may be unusually messy—or unusually neat. Freud's theory offers no way to predict how the difficulty will be exhibited (Crews, 1996; Macmillan, 1996). Furthermore, Freud can be faulted for seeming to view women as inferior to men, because he argued that women have weaker superegos than men do and in some ways unconsciously yearn to be men (the concept of penis envy).

Finally, Freud made his observations and derived his theory from a limited population. His theory was based almost entirely on upper-class Austrian women living in the strict, puritanical era of the early 1900s who had come to him seeking treatment for psychological and physical problems. How far one can generalize beyond this population is a matter of considerable debate. For instance, in some Pacific Island societies, the role of disciplinarian is played by the mother's oldest brother, not the father. In such a culture, it is unreasonable to argue that the Oedipal conflict will progress in the same way that it did in Austrian society, where the father typically was the major disciplinarian. In short, a cross-cultural perspective raises questions about the universality of Freud's view of personality development (Doi, 1990; Brislin, 1993; Altman, 1996).

Still, Freud generated an important method of treating psychological disturbances called *psychoanalysis.* As we will see when we discuss treatment approaches to psychological disorder, psychoanalysis remains in use today (Guterl, 2002; Messer & McWilliams, 2003; Heller, 2005).

Moreover, Freud's emphasis on the unconscious has been partially supported by current research on dreams and implicit memory. As we first noted when we discussed dreaming, advances in neuroscience are consistent with some of Freud's arguments. For example, the fact that some behavior is motivated by occurrences that have been apparently forgotten, as well as the discovery of neural pathways relating to emotional memories, support the notion of repression. Furthermore, cognitive and social psychologists have found increasing evidence that unconscious processes help us think about and evaluate our world, set goals, and choose a course of action. It remains to be seen whether future neuroscientific advances can help overcome the criticisms leveled against Freud's psychoanalytic theory (Ekstrom, 2004; Wilson, 2004; Solms, 2005).

The Neo-Freudian Psychoanalysts: Building on Freud

Freud laid the foundation for important work done by a series of successors who were trained in traditional Freudian theory but later rejected some of its major points. These theorists are known as **neo-Freudian psychoanalysts.**

The neo-Freudians placed greater emphasis than Freud had on the functions of the ego, suggesting that it has more control than does the id over day-to-day activities. They also minimized the importance of sex as a driving force in people's lives. Furthermore, they paid greater attention to social factors and the effects of society and culture on personality development.

Neo-Freudian psychoanalysts: Psychoanalysts who were trained in traditional Freudian theory but who later rejected some of its major points.

JUNG'S COLLECTIVE UNCONSCIOUS

One of the most influential neo-Freudians, Carl Jung (pronounced "yoong"), rejected the Freud's view of the primary importance of unconscious sexual urges. Instead, he looked at the primitive urges of the unconscious more positively, arguing that they represented a more general, and positive, life force that encompasses an inborn drive motivating creativity and more positive resolution of conflict (Lothane, 2005).

Jung suggested that we have a universal **collective unconscious,** a common set of ideas, feelings, images, and symbols that we inherit from our relatives, the whole human race, and even nonhuman animal ancestors from the distant past. This collective unconscious is shared by everyone and is displayed in behavior that is common across diverse cultures—such as love of mother, belief in a supreme being, and even behavior as specific as fear of snakes (Oehman & Mineka, 2003; Drob, 2005).

Jung went on to propose that the collective unconscious contains **archetypes,** universal symbolic representations of a particular person, object, or experience. For instance, a mother archetype, which contains reflections of our ancestors' relationships with mother figures, is suggested by the prevalence of mothers in art, religion, literature, and mythology. (Think of the Virgin Mary, Earth Mother, wicked stepmothers

Collective unconscious: According to Carl Jung, a common set of ideas, feelings, images, and symbols that we inherit from our ancestors, the whole human race, and even nonhuman ancestors from the distant past.

Archetypes: According to Jung, universal symbolic representations of a particular person, object, or experience (such as good and evil).

In Jungian terms, Professor Charles Xavier (left) and Magneto (right) in the film *X-Men: The Last Stand* represent the archetypes, or universally recognizable symbols, of good and evil, respectively.

in fairy tales, Mother's Day, and so forth!) Jung also suggested that men possess an unconscious feminine archetype affecting how they behave, whereas women have a male archetype that colors their behavior (Jung, 1961; Bair, 2003).

To Jung, archetypes play an important role in determining our day-to-day reactions, attitudes, and values. For example, Jung might explain the popularity of the *Star Wars* movies as being due to their use of broad archetypes of good (Luke Skywalker) and evil (Darth Vader).

Although there is no reliable research evidence confirming the existence of the collective unconscious—and even Jung acknowledged that such evidence would be difficult to produce—Jung's theory has had significant influence in areas beyond psychology. For example, personality types derived from Jung's personality approach form the basis for the Myers-Briggs personality test, which is widely used in business and industry (Gladwell, 2004; Bayne, 2005; Furnham & Crump, 2005).

HORNEY'S NEO-FREUDIAN PERSPECTIVE

Karen Horney (pronounced "HORN-eye") was one of the earliest psychologists to champion women's issues and is sometimes called the first feminist psychologist. Horney suggested that personality develops in the context of social relationships and depends particularly on the relationship between parents and child and how well the child's needs are met. She rejected Freud's suggestion that women have penis envy, asserting that what women envy most in men is not their anatomy but the independence, success, and freedom that women often are denied (Horney, 1937; Miletic, 2002).

Horney was also one of the first to stress the importance of cultural factors in the determination of personality. For example, she suggested that society's rigid gender roles for women lead them to experience ambivalence about success, fearing that they will lose their friends. Her conceptualizations, developed in the 1930s and

Karen Horney was one of the earliest proponents of women's issues.

1940s, laid the groundwork for many of the central ideas of feminism that emerged decades later (Eckardt, 2005).

ADLER AND THE OTHER NEO-FREUDIANS

Alfred Adler, another important neo-Freudian psychoanalyst, also considered Freudian theory's emphasis on sexual needs misplaced. Instead, Adler proposed that the primary human motivation is a striving for superiority, not in terms of superiority over others but in a quest for self-improvement and perfection.

Adler used the term **inferiority complex** to describe situations in which adults have not been able to overcome the feelings of inferiority they developed as children, when they were small and limited in their knowledge about the world. Early social relationships with parents have an important effect on children's ability to outgrow feelings of personal inferiority and instead orient themselves toward attaining more socially useful goals, such as improving society.

Other neo-Freudians included such figures as Erik Erikson, whose theory of psychosocial development we discussed in earlier modules, and Freud's daughter, Anna Freud. Like Adler and Horney, they focused less than Freud on inborn sexual and aggressive drives and more on the social and cultural factors behind personality.

Inferiority complex: According to Alfred Adler, a problem affecting adults who have not been able to overcome the feelings of inferiority that they developed as children, when they were small and limited in their knowledge about the world.

RECAP/EVALUATE/RETHINK

RECAP

How do psychologists define and use the concept of personality?

- Personality is the pattern of enduring characteristics that produce consistency and individuality in a given person. (p. 452)

What do the theories of Freud and his successors tell us about the structure and development of personality?

- According to psychodynamic explanations of personality, much behavior is caused by parts of personality that are found in the unconscious and of which we are unaware. (p. 453)
- Freud's psychoanalytic theory, one of the psychodynamic approaches, suggests that personality is composed of the id, the ego, and the superego. The id is the unorganized, inborn part of personality whose purpose is to immediately reduce tensions relating to hunger, sex, aggression, and other primitive impulses. The ego restrains instinctual energy to maintain the safety of the individual and help the person be a member of society. The superego represents the rights and wrongs of society and includes the conscience. (pp. 454–455)
- Freud's psychoanalytic theory suggests that personality develops through a series of psychosexual stages, each of which is associated with a primary biological function. (pp. 455–456)
- Defense mechanisms, according to Freudian theory, are unconscious strategies with which people reduce anxieties relating to impulses from the id. (pp. 456–457)

- Freud's psychoanalytic theory has provoked a number of criticisms, including a lack of supportive scientific data, the theory's inadequacy in making predictions, and its reliance on a highly restricted population. Nevertheless, recent neuroscience research provides support for the concept of unconscious processes. (pp. 457–458)
- Neo-Freudian psychoanalytic theorists built on Freud's work, although they placed greater emphasis on the role of the ego and paid more attention to the role of social factors in determining behavior. (pp. 459–461)

EVALUATE

1. _____ approaches state that behavior is motivated primarily by unconscious forces.
2. Match each section of the personality (according to Freud) with its description:
   1. Ego
   2. Id
   3. Superego
   a. Determines right from wrong on the basis of cultural standards.
   b. Operates according to the "reality principle"; energy is redirected to integrate the person into society.
   c. Seeks to reduce tension brought on by primitive drives.

3. Which of the following represents the proper order of personality development, according to Freud?
   a. Oral, phallic, latency, anal, genital
   b. Anal, oral, phallic, genital, latency
   c. Oral, anal, phallic, latency, genital
   d. Latency, phallic, anal, genital, oral
4. In the resolution of the _____ complex, Freud believed that boys learn to repress their desire for their mothers and identify with their fathers.
5. _____ is the term Freud used to describe unconscious strategies used to reduce anxiety.

KEY TERMS

personality p. 453
psychodynamic approaches
   to personality p. 453
psychoanalytic theory p. 453
unconscious p. 453
id p. 454

ego p. 454
superego p. 454
psychosexual stages p. 454
fixations p. 454
oral stage p. 455
anal stage p. 456

phallic stage p. 456
Oedipal conflict p. 456
identification p. 456
latency period p. 456
genital stage p. 456
defense mechanisms p. 457

repression p. 457
neo-Freudian
   psychoanalysts p. 459
collective unconscious p. 459
archetypes p. 459
inferiority complex p. 461

RETHINK

1. Can you think of ways in which Freud's theories of unconscious motivations are commonly used in popular culture? How accurately do you think such popular uses of Freudian theories reflect Freud's ideas?
2. *From the perspective of an advertising executive:* How might you use Jung's concept of archetypes in designing your advertisements? Which of the archetypes would you use?

Answers to Evaluate Questions

1. psychodynamic; 2. 1-b, 2-c, 3-a; 3. c; 4. Oedipal; 5. defense mechanisms

Trait, Learning, Biological, Evolutionary, and Humanistic Approaches to Personality

"Tell me about Nelson," said Johnetta.

"Oh, he's just terrific. He's the friendliest guy I know—goes out of his way to be nice to everyone. He hardly ever gets mad. He's just so even-tempered, no matter what's happening. And he's really smart, too. About the only thing I don't like is that he's always in such a hurry to get things done. He seems to have boundless energy, much more than I have."

"He sounds great to me, especially in comparison to Rico," replied Johnetta. "He is so self-centered and arrogant that it drives me crazy. I sometimes wonder why I ever started going out with him."

Friendly. Even-tempered. Smart. Energetic. Self-centered. Arrogant.

The above exchange is made up of a series of trait characterizations of speakers' friends. In fact, much of our own understanding of others' behavior is based on the premise that people possess certain traits that are consistent across different situations. For example, we generally assume that if someone is outgoing and sociable in one situation, he or she is outgoing and sociable in other situations (Gilbert et al., 1992; Gilbert, Miller, & Ross, 1998; Mischel, 2004).

Dissatisfaction with the emphasis in psychoanalytic theory on unconscious—and difficult to demonstrate—processes in explaining a person's behavior led to the development of alternative approaches to personality, including a number of trait-based approaches. Other theories reflect established psychological perspectives, such as learning theory, biological and evolutionary approaches, and the humanistic approach.

Key Concept

What are the major aspects of trait, learning, biological and evolutionary, and humanistic approaches to personality?

Trait Approaches: Placing Labels on Personality

If someone asked you to characterize another person, it is probable that—like Johnetta and her friend—you would come up with a list of that individual's personal qualities, as you see them. But how would you know which of those qualities are most important to an understanding of that person's behavior?

Personality psychologists have asked similar questions. To answer them, they have developed a model of personality known as trait theory. **Trait theory** seeks to explain, in a straightforward way, the consistencies in individuals' behavior. **Traits** are consistent personality characteristics and behaviors displayed in different situations.

Trait theorists do not assume that some people have a trait and others do not; rather, they propose that all people possess certain traits, but that the degree to which a particular trait applies to a specific person varies and can be quantified. For instance, you may be relatively friendly, whereas I may be relatively unfriendly. But we both have a "friendliness" trait, although your degree of "friendliness" is higher than mine. The major challenge for trait theorists taking this approach has been to identify the

Trait theory: A model of personality that seeks to identify the basic traits necessary to describe personality.

Traits: Consistent personality characteristics and behaviors displayed in different situations.

specific primary traits necessary to describe personality. As we shall see, different theorists have come up with surprisingly different sets of traits.

ALLPORT'S TRAIT THEORY: IDENTIFYING BASIC CHARACTERISTICS

When personality psychologist Gordon Allport systematically pored over an unabridged dictionary in the 1930s he came up with some 18,000 separate terms that could be used to describe personality. Although he was able to pare down the list to a mere 4,500 descriptors after eliminating words with the same meaning, he was left with a problem crucial to all trait approaches: Which of those traits were the most basic?

Allport eventually answered this question by suggesting that there are three fundamental categories of traits: cardinal, central, and secondary (Allport, 1961, 1966). A *cardinal trait* is a single characteristic that directs most of a person's activities. For example, a totally selfless woman may direct all her energy toward humanitarian activities; an intensely power-hungry person may be driven by an all-consuming need for control.

Most people, however, do not develop a single, comprehensive cardinal trait. Instead, they possess a handful of central traits that make up the core of personality. *Central traits,* such as honesty and sociability, are the major characteristics of an individual; they usually number from five to ten in any one person. Finally, *secondary traits* are characteristics that affect behavior in fewer situations and are less influential than central or cardinal traits. For instance, a reluctance to eat meat and a love of modern art would be considered secondary traits (Nicholson, 2003).

CATTELL AND EYSENCK: FACTORING OUT PERSONALITY

Later attempts to identify primary personality traits have centered on a statistical technique known as factor analysis. *Factor analysis* is a statistical method of identifying associations among a large number of variables to reveal more general patterns. For example, a personality researcher might administer a questionnaire to many participants, asking them to describe themselves by referring to an extensive list of traits. By statistically combining responses and computing which traits are associated with one another in the same person, a researcher can identify the most fundamental patterns or combinations of traits—called *factors*—that underlie participants' responses.

Using factor analysis, personality psychologist Raymond Cattell (1965) suggested that sixteen pairs of *source traits* represent the basic dimensions of personality. Using those source traits, he developed the Sixteen Personality Factor Questionnaire, or 16 PF, a measure that provides scores for each of the source traits. Figure 1 shows the pattern of average scores on each of the source traits for two different groups of participants—airplane pilots, and writers (Cattell, Cattell, & Cattell, 2000).

Another trait theorist, psychologist Hans Eysenck (Eysenck et al., 1992; Eysenck 1994, 1995), also used factor analysis to identify patterns of traits, but he came to a very different conclusion about the nature of personality. He found that personality could best be described in terms of just three major dimensions: *extraversion, neuroticism,* and *psychoticism.* The extraversion dimension relates to the degree of sociability, whereas the neurotic dimension encompasses emotional stability. Finally, psychoticism refers to the degree to which reality is distorted. By evaluating people along these three dimensions, Eysenck was able to predict behavior accurately in a variety of situations. Figure 2 lists specific traits associated with each of the dimensions.

THE BIG FIVE PERSONALITY TRAITS

For the last two decades, the most influential trait approach contends that five traits or factors—called the "Big Five"—lie at the core of personality. Using modern factor analytic statistical techniques, a host of researchers have identified a similar set of five factors that

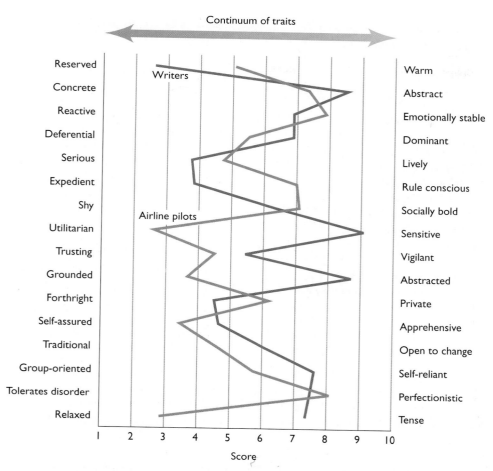

Continuum of traits

Reserved		Warm
Concrete		Abstract
Reactive		Emotionally stable
Deferential		Dominant
Serious		Lively
Expedient		Rule conscious
Shy		Socially bold
Utilitarian		Sensitive
Trusting		Vigilant
Grounded		Abstracted
Forthright		Private
Self-assured		Apprehensive
Traditional		Open to change
Group-oriented		Self-reliant
Tolerates disorder		Perfectionistic
Relaxed		Tense

Writers

Airline pilots

Score 1 2 3 4 5 6 7 8 9 10

FIGURE 1 Personality profiles for source traits developed by Cattell for two groups of subjects: writers, and airline pilots. The average score for the general population is between 4.5 and 6.5 on each scale. On what traits do airline pilots and writers differ most? How do these differences contribute to their chosen work? (Source: Data derived from Cattell, Eber, and Tatsuoka: Handbook for the 16PF, Copyright © 1970, 1988, 1992 by the Institute for Personality and Ability Testing Inc., Champaign, Illinois, USA. All rights reserved.)

Extraversion
• Sociable
• Lively
• Active
• Assertive
• Sensation-seeking

Neuroticism
• Anxious
• Depressed
• Guilt feelings
• Low self-esteem
• Tense

Psychoticism
• Aggressive
• Cold
• Egocentric
• Impersonal
• Impulsive

FIGURE 2 According to Eysenck, personality could best be described in terms of just three major dimensions: extraversion, neuroticism, and psychoticism. Eysenck was able to predict behavior accurately in a variety of types of situations by evaluating people along these three dimensions (Eysenck, 1990). How do you think an airline pilot would score on Eysenck's scale?

---

underlie personality. The five factors, described in Figure 3, are *openness to experience, conscientiousness, extraversion, agreeableness,* and *neuroticism* (emotional stability).

The Big Five emerge quite consistently across a number of domains. For example, factor analyses of major personality inventories, self-report measures made by observers of others' personality traits, and checklists of self-descriptions yield similar factors quite consistently. In addition, the Big Five emerge consistently in different populations of individuals, including children, college students, older adults, and speakers of different languages. Finally, cross-cultural research conducted in areas ranging from Europe to the Middle East to Africa also has been supportive (Paunonen, 2003; McCrae et al., 2005; Rossier, Dahourou, & McCrae, 2005).

In short, a growing consensus exists that the "Big Five" represent the best description of personality traits we have today. Still, the debate over the specific number and kinds of traits—and even the usefulness of trait approaches in general—remains remains a lively one.

EVALUATING TRAIT APPROACHES TO PERSONALITY

Trait approaches have several virtues. They provide a clear, straightforward explanation of people's behavioral consistencies. Furthermore, traits allow us to readily compare one person with another. Because of these advantages, trait approaches to personality have had an important influence on the development of several useful personality measures (Funder, 1991; Wiggins, 2003; Larsen & Buss, 2005).

However, trait approaches also have some drawbacks. For example, we have seen that various trait theories describing personality come to very different conclusions about which traits are the most fundamental and descriptive. The difficulty in deter-

FIGURE 3 Five broad trait factors, referred to as the "Big Five," are considered to be the core of personality. You can memorize these traits by using the mnemonic OCEAN, representing the first letter of each trait. (Source: Adapted from Pervin, 1990, Chapter 3, and McCrae & Costa, 1986, p. 1002.)

The Big Five Personality Factors and Dimensions of Sample Traits

Openness to experience
Independent—Conforming
Imaginative—Practical
Preference for variety—Preference for routine

Conscientiousness
Careful—Careless
Disciplined—Impulsive
Organized—Disorganized

Extraversion
Talkative—Quiet
Fun-loving—Sober
Sociable—Retiring

Agreeableness
Sympathetic—Fault-finding
Kind—Cold
Appreciative—Unfriendly

Neuroticism (Emotional Stability)
Stable—Tense
Calm—Anxious
Secure—Insecure

mining which of the theories is the most accurate has led some personality psychologists to question the validity of trait conceptions of personality in general.

Actually, there is an even more fundamental difficulty with trait approaches. Even if we are able to identify a set of primary traits, we are left with little more than a label or description of personality—rather than an explanation of behavior. If we say that someone who donates money to charity has the trait of generosity, we still do not know *why* that person became generous in the first place or the reasons for displaying generosity in a specific situation. In the view of some critics, then, traits do not provide explanations for behavior; they merely describe it.

Learning Approaches: We Are What We've Learned

The psychodynamic and trait approaches we've discussed concentrate on the "inner" person—the fury of an unobservable but powerful id or a hypothetical but critical set of traits. In contrast, learning approaches to personality focus on the "outer" person. To a strict learning theorist, personality is simply the sum of learned responses to the external environment. Internal events such as thoughts, feelings, and motivations are ignored. Although the existence of personality is not denied, learning theorists say that it is best understood by looking at features of a person's environment.

SKINNER'S BEHAVIORIST APPROACH

According to the most influential learning theorist, B. F. Skinner (who carried out pioneering work on operant conditioning), personality is a collection of learned behavior patterns (Skinner, 1975). Similarities in responses across different situations are caused by similar patterns of reinforcement that have been received in such situations in the past. If I am sociable both at parties and at meetings, it is because I have been reinforced for displaying social behaviors—not because I am fulfilling an unconscious wish based on experiences during my childhood or because I have an internal trait of sociability.

Strict learning theorists such as Skinner are less interested in the consistencies in behavior across situations than in ways of modifying behavior. Their view is that humans are infinitely changeable through the process of learning new behavior patterns. If one is able to control and modify the patterns of reinforcers in a situation, behavior that other theorists would view as stable and unyielding can be changed and ultimately improved. Learning theorists are optimistic in their attitudes about the potential for resolving personal and societal problems through treatment strategies based on learning theory.

SOCIAL COGNITIVE APPROACHES TO PERSONALITY

Not all learning theories of personality take such a strict view in rejecting the importance of what is "inside" a person by focusing solely on the "outside." Unlike other learning approaches to personality, **social cognitive approaches** emphasize the influence of cognition—thoughts, feelings, expectations, and values—as well as observation of other's behavior, on personality. According to Albert Bandura, one of the main proponents of this point of view, people can foresee the possible outcomes of certain behaviors in a particular setting without actually having to carry them out. This takes place mainly through the mechanism of *observational learning*—viewing the actions of others and observing the consequences (Bandura, 1986, 1999).

For instance, children who view a model behaving in, say, an aggressive manner tend to copy the behavior if the consequences of the model's behavior are seen to be positive. If, in contrast, the model's aggressive behavior has resulted in no consequences or negative consequences, children are considerably less likely to act aggressively. According to social cognitive approaches, then, personality develops through repeated observation of the behavior of others.

Self-Efficacy. Bandura places particular emphasis on the role played by **self-efficacy**, belief in one's personal capabilities. Self-efficacy underlies people's faith in their ability to carry out a particular behavior or produce a desired outcome. People with high self-efficacy have higher aspirations and greater persistence in working to attain goals and ultimately achieve greater success than do those with lower self-efficacy (Bandura, 1997, 1999; Pajares, 2003).

How do we develop self-efficacy? One way is by paying close attention to our prior successes and failures. If we try snowboarding and experience little success, we'll be less likely to try it again. However, if our initial efforts appear promising, we'll be more likely to attempt it again. Direct reinforcement and encouragement from others also play a role in developing self-efficacy (Bandura, 1988; Jenkins & Gortner, 1998).

Compared with other learning theories of personality, social cognitive approaches are distinctive in their emphasis on the reciprocity between individuals and their environment. Not only is the environment assumed to affect personality, but people's behavior and personalities are also assumed to "feed back" and modify the environment (Bandura, 1999, 2000).

Self-Esteem. Our behavior also reflects the view we have of ourselves and the way we value the various parts of our personalities. **Self-esteem** is the component of personality that encompasses our positive and negative self-evaluations. Although people have a general level of self-esteem, it is not unidimensional. We may see ourselves positively in one domain but negatively in others. For example, a good student may have high self-esteem in academic domains but lower self-esteem in sports (Moretti & Higgins, 1990; Baumeister, 1998; Crocker & Park, 2004).

Self-esteem has strong cultural components. For example, having high *relationship harmony*—a sense of success in forming close bonds with other people—is more important to self-esteem in Asian cultures than it is in more individualistic Western societies (Kwan, Bond, & Singelis, 1997; Twenge & Crocker, 2002; Spencer-Rodgers et al., 2004).

Although almost everyone goes through periods of low self-esteem (after, for instance, an undeniable failure), some people are chronically low in self-esteem. For them, failure seems to be an inevitable part of life. In fact, low self-esteem may lead to a cycle of failure in which past failure breeds future failure.

Consider, for example, students with low self-esteem who are studying for a test. Because of their low self-esteem, they expect to do poorly on the test. In turn, this

Social cognitive approaches to personality: Theories that emphasize the influence of a person's cognitions—thoughts, feelings, expectations, and values—as well as observation of others' behavior, in determining personality.

Self-efficacy: Belief in one's personal capabilities. Self-efficacy underlies people's faith in their ability to carry out a particular behavior or produce a desired outcome.

Self-esteem: The component of personality that encompasses our positive and negative self-evaluations.

Self-efficacy, the belief in one's own capabilities, leads to higher aspirations and greater persistence.

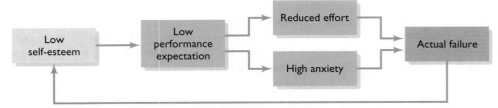

FIGURE 4 The cycle of low self-esteem begins with an individual already having low self-esteem. As a consequence, the person will have low performance expectations and expect to fail a test, thereby producing anxiety and reduced effort. As a result, the person will actually fail, and failure in turn reinforces low self-esteem.

raises their anxiety level, making it increasingly difficult to study and perhaps even leading them not to work as hard. Because of these attitudes, the ultimate outcome is that they do, in fact, perform badly on the test. Ultimately, the failure reinforces their low self-esteem, and the cycle is perpetuated, as illustrated in Figure 4. In short, low self-esteem can lead to a cycle of failure that is self-destructive.

In other cases, though, high self-esteem can have disadvantages. Consider, for example, the problems produced by high self-esteem that we discuss in the *Applying Psychology in the 21st Century* box.

EVALUATING LEARNING APPROACHES TO PERSONALITY

Because they ignore the internal processes that are uniquely human, traditional learning theorists such as Skinner have been accused of oversimplifying personality to such an extent that the concept becomes meaningless. In the eyes of their critics, reducing behavior to a series of stimuli and responses, and excluding thoughts and feelings from the realm of personality, leaves behaviorists practicing an unrealistic and inadequate form of science.

Of course, some of these criticisms are blunted by social cognitive approaches, which explicitly consider the role of cognitive processes in personality. Still, learning approaches tend to share a highly *deterministic* view of human behavior, maintaining that behavior is shaped primarily by forces beyond the control of the individual. As in psychoanalytic theory (which suggests that personality is determined by the unconscious forces) and trait approaches (which view personality in part as a mixture of genetically determined traits), learning theory's reliance on deterministic principles deemphasizes the ability of people to pilot their own course through life.

Nonetheless, learning approaches have had a major impact on the study of personality. For one thing, they have helped make personality psychology an objective, scientific venture by focusing on observable behavior and environment. In addition, they have produced important, successful means of treating a variety of psychological disorders. The degree of success of these treatments is a testimony to the merits of learning theory approaches to personality.

Biological and Evolutionary Approaches: Are We Born with Personality?

Biological and evolutionary approaches to personality: Theories that suggest that important components of personality are inherited.

Coming at the question of what determines personality from a different direction, **biological and evolutionary approaches** to personality suggest that important components of personality are inherited. Building on the work of behavioral geneticists, researchers using biological and evolutionary approaches argue that personality is determined at

The Downside of High Self-Esteem

One widely held societal belief is that we should do everything we can to nurture people's self-esteem. High self-esteem is usually viewed as a forerunner of success and accomplishment, and low self-esteem is seen as a problem to be remedied. Some people even argue that raising self-esteem will solve a variety of social ills, ranging from delinquency to general psychological problems across the nation.

But not everyone agrees. According to psychologist Roy Baumeister and his colleagues, not only can unjustified high self-esteem be psychologically damaging to the person who experiences it, but it can also lead to a variety of undesirable outcomes (Baumeister et al., 2003, 2005).

For example, Baumeister suggests that if self-esteem is unjustified by actual accomplishments, people may react negatively when they experience failure or are challenged. This is particularly true of individuals with *narcissism*, a personality disorder in which people hold unjustifiably positive views of themselves. When their unwarranted positive view of themselves is contradicted, they may feel so threatened that they lash out, sometimes violently. In short, people with unjustified high self-esteem are likely to view any challenge as highly threatening, and they may strike out against the source of the threat with violence (Baumeister, Bushman, & Campbell, 2000).

In the same way, efforts to increase self-esteem so as to improve the performance of academically challenged students may backfire. For example, in one study, students who were receiving Ds and Fs in a college psychology class were divided into two groups. One group received the message that bad grades were caused by a lack of confidence and low self-esteem. The other group received a different message; they were told that it was hard work that produced good grades. At the end of the semester, the group that received the low self-esteem message ended up with significantly lower grades than the other group (Forsyth & Kerr, 1999).

These findings have direct relevance to social programs that uncritically aim to raise self-esteem. Feel-good messages that seek to instill higher self-esteem in everyone ("we're all special" and "we applaud ourselves") may be off the target, leading people to develop unwarranted self-esteem. Instead, parents, schools, and community institutions should seek to provide opportunities for people to earn self-esteem through their actual achievements (Crocker & Park, 2004).

RETHINK

Are there specific areas of society in which the issue of self-esteem is of particular importance? For example, what might be the consequences if a politician—say, a presidential candidate—had unjustified self-esteem?

---

least in part by our genes, in much the same way that our height is largely a result of genetic contributions from our ancestors. The evolutionary perspective assumes that personality traits that led to survival and reproductive success of our ancestors are more likely to be preserved and passed on to subsequent generations (Buss, 2001).

The importance of genetic factors in personality is illustrated by studies of twins. For instance, personality psychologists Auke Tellegen and colleagues at the University

Biological and evolutionary approaches to personality seek to explain the consistencies in personality that are found in some families.

of Minnesota examined the personality traits of pairs of twins who were genetically identical but were raised apart from each other (Tellegen et al., 1988, Bouchard et al., 2004). In the study, each twin was given a battery of personality tests, including one that measured eleven key personality characteristics.

The results of the personality tests indicated that in major respects the twins were quite similar in personality, despite having separated at an early age. Moreover, certain traits were more heavily influenced by heredity than were others. For example, social potency (the degree to which a person assumes mastery and leadership roles in social situations) and traditionalism (the tendency to follow authority) had particularly strong genetic components, whereas achievement and social closeness had relatively weak genetic components (see Figure 5).

Temperament: The innate disposition that emerges early in life.

Furthermore, it is increasingly clear that the roots of adult personality emerge in the earliest periods of life. Infants are born with a particular **temperament,** an innate disposition. Temperament encompasses several dimensions, including general activity level and mood. For instance, some individuals are quite active, while others are relatively calm. Similarly, some are relatively easygoing, while others are irritable, easily upset, and difficult to soothe. Temperament is quite consistent, with significant stability from infancy well into adolescence (Clark & Watson, 1999; Molfese & Molfese, 2000; Caspi, Harrington, & Milne, 2003; Wachs et al., 2004).

Some researchers contend that specific genes are related to personality. For example, people with a longer dopamine-4 receptor gene are more likely to be thrill seekers than are those without such a gene. These thrill seekers tend to be extroverted, impulsive, quick-tempered, and always in search of excitement and novel situations (Hamer et al., 1993; Zuckerman & Kuhlman, 2000).

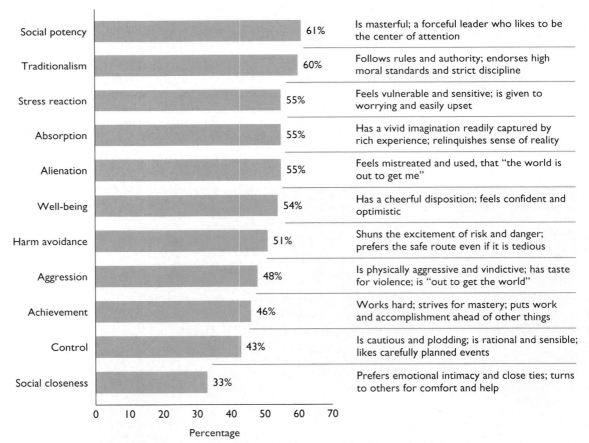

FIGURE 5 The roots of personality. The percentages indicate the degree to which eleven personality characteristics reflect the influence of heredity. (Source: Tellegen et al., 1988.)

Does the identification of specific genes linked to personality, coupled with the existence of temperaments from the time of birth, mean that we are destined to have certain types of personalities? Hardly. First, it is unlikely that any single gene is linked to a specific trait. For instance, the dopamine-4 receptor accounts for only around 10 percent of the variation in novelty seeking between different individuals. The rest of the variation is attributable to other genes and environmental factors (Angier, 1996; Keltikangas-Järvinen et al., 2004; Lahti et al., 2005).

More importantly, genes interact with the environment. As we see in discussions of the heritability of intelligence and the nature-nurture issue, it is impossible to completely divorce genetic factors from environmental factors. Although studies of identical twins raised in different environments are helpful, they are not definitive, because it is impossible to assess and control environmental factors fully. Furthermore, estimates of the influence of genetics are just that—estimates—and apply to groups, not individuals. Consequently, findings such as those shown in Figure 5 must be regarded as approximations.

Finally, even if more genes are found to be linked to specific personality characteristics, genes still cannot be viewed as the sole cause of personality. For one thing, genetically determined characteristics may not be expressed if they are not "turned on" by particular environmental experiences. Furthermore, behaviors produced by genes may help to create a particular environment. For instance, a cheerful, smiley baby may lead her parents to smile more and be more responsive, thereby creating an environment that is supportive and pleasant. In contrast, the parents of a cranky, fussy baby may be less inclined to smile at the child; in turn, the environment in which that child is raised will be a less supportive and pleasant one. In a sense, then, genes not only influence a person's behavior—they also help produce the environment in which a person develops (Scarr, 1993, 1998; Plomin & Caspi, 1999; Kim-Cohen et al., 2003, 2005).

Although an increasing number of personality theorists are taking biological and evolutionary factors into account, no comprehensive, unified theory that considers biological and evolutionary factors is widely accepted. Still, it is clear that certain personality traits have substantial genetic components, and that heredity and environment interact to determine personality (Buss, 2000; Ebstein, Benjamin, & Belmaker, 2003; Plomin et al., 2003; Bouchard, 2004).

Infants are born with particular temperaments, dispositions that are consistent throughout childhood.

Humanistic Approaches: The Uniqueness of You

Where, in all the approaches to personality that we have discussed, is an explanation for the saintliness of a Mother Teresa, the creativity of a Michelangelo, and the brilliance and perseverance of an Einstein? An understanding of such unique individuals—as well as more ordinary sorts of people who have some of the same attributes—comes from humanistic theory.

According to humanistic theorists, all the approaches to personality we have discussed share a fundamental misperception in their views of human nature. Instead of seeing people as controlled by unconscious, unseen forces (as do psychodynamic approaches), a set of stable traits (trait approaches), situational reinforcements and punishments (learning theory), or inherited factors (biological and evolutionary approaches), **humanistic approaches** emphasize people's inherent goodness and their tendency to grow to higher levels of functioning. It is this conscious, self-motivated ability to change and improve, along with people's unique creative impulses, that humanistic theorists argue make up the core of personality.

Humanistic approaches to personality: Theories that emphasize people's innate goodness and desire to achieve higher levels of functioning.

ROGERS AND THE NEED FOR SELF-ACTUALIZATION

The major proponent of the humanistic point of view is Carl Rogers (1971). Along with other humanistic theorists, such as Abraham Maslow, Rogers maintains that

"So, while extortion, racketeering, and murder may be bad acts, they don't make you a bad person."

Self-actualization: A state of self-fulfillment in which people realize their highest potential, each in his or her own unique way.

www.mhhe.com/feldmanup8

PsychInteractive Online

Your Ideal Self

Unconditional positive regard: An attitude of acceptance and respect on the part of an observer, no matter what a person says or does.

all people have a fundamental need for **self-actualization,** a state of self-fulfillment in which people realize their highest potential, each in a unique way. He further suggests that people develop a need for positive regard that reflects the desire to be loved and respected. Because others provide this positive regard, we grow dependent on them. We begin to see and judge ourselves through the eyes of other people, relying on their values and being preoccupied with what they think of us.

According to Rogers, one outgrowth of placing importance on the opinions of others is that a conflict may grow between people's experiences and their *self-concepts*, the set of beliefs they hold about what they are like as individuals. If the discrepancies are minor, so are the consequences. But if the discrepancies are great, they will lead to psychological disturbances in daily functioning, such as the experience of frequent anxiety. (To better understand this, complete the PsychInteractive exercise on your ideal self.)

Rogers suggests that one way of overcoming the discrepancy between experience and self-concept is through the receipt of unconditional positive regard from another person—a friend, a spouse, or a therapist. **Unconditional positive regard** refers to an attitude of acceptance and respect on the part of an observer, no matter what a person says or does. This acceptance, says Rogers, gives people the opportunity to evolve and grow both cognitively and emotionally and to develop more realistic self-concepts. You may have experienced the power of unconditional positive regard when you confided in someone, revealing embarrassing secrets because you knew the listener would still love and respect you, even after hearing the worst about you (Snyder, 2002).

In contrast, *conditional positive regard* depends on your behavior. In such cases, others withdraw their love and acceptance if you do something of which they don't approve. The result is a discrepancy between your true self and what others wish you would be, leading to anxiety and frustration (see Figure 6).

EVALUATING HUMANISTIC APPROACHES

Although humanistic theories suggest the value of providing unconditional positive regard toward people, unconditional positive regard toward humanistic theories has been less forthcoming. The criticisms have centered on the difficulty of verifying the basic assumptions of the approach, as well as on the question of whether unconditional positive regard does, in fact, lead to greater personality adjustment.

Humanistic approaches have also been criticized for making the assumption that people are basically "good"—a notion that is unverifiable—and, equally important, for using nonscientific values to build supposedly scientific theories. Still, humanistic theories have been important in highlighting the uniqueness of human beings and

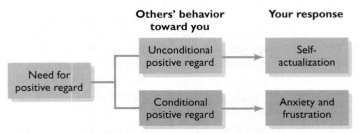

FIGURE 6 According to the humanistic view of Carl Rogers, people have a basic need to be loved and respected. If you receive unconditional positive regard from others, you will develop a more realistic self-concept, but if the response is conditional it may lead to anxiety and frustration.

Theoretical Approach and Major Theorists	Conscious Versus Unconscious Determinants of Personality	Nature (Hereditary Factors) Versus Nurture (Environmental Factors)	Free Will Versus Determinism	Stability Versus Modifiability
Psychodynamic (Freud, Jung, Horney, Adler)	Emphasizes the unconscious	Stresses innate, inherited structure of personality while emphasizing importance of childhood experience	Stresses determinism, the view that behavior is directed and caused by factors outside one's control	Emphasizes the stability of characteristics throughout a person's life
Trait (Allport, Cattell, Eysenck)	Disregards both conscious and unconscious	Approaches vary	Stresses determinism, the view that behavior is directed and caused by factors outside one's control	Emphasizes the stability of characteristics throughout a person's life
Learning (Skinner, Bandura)	Disregards both conscious and unconscious	Focuses on the environment	Stresses determinism, the view that behavior is directed and caused by factors outside one's control	Stresses that personality remains flexible and resilient throughout one's life
Biological and Evolutionary (Tellegen)	Disregards both conscious and unconscious	Stresses the innate, inherited determinants of personality	Stresses determinism, the view that behavior is directed and caused by factors outside one's control	Emphasizes the stability of characteristics throughout a person's life
Humanistic (Rogers, Maslow)	Stresses the conscious more than unconscious	Stresses the interaction between both nature and nurture	Stresses the freedom of individuals to make their own choices	Stresses that personality remains flexible and resilient throughout one's life

FIGURE 7 The multiple perspectives of personality.

guiding the development of a significant form of therapy designed to alleviate psychological difficulties (Cain, 2002).

Comparing Approaches to Personality

In light of the multiple approaches we have discussed, you may be wondering which of the theories provides the most accurate description of personality. That is a question that cannot be answered precisely. Each theory is built on different assumptions and focuses on somewhat different aspects of personality (see Figure 7). Furthermore, there is no clear way to scientifically test the various approaches and their assumptions against one another. Given the complexity of every individual, it seems reasonable that personality can be viewed from a number of perspectives simultaneously (Pervin, 2003).

RECAP/EVALUATE/RETHINK

RECAP

What are the major aspects of trait, learning, biological and evolutionary, and humanistic approaches to personality?

- Trait approaches have been used to identify relatively enduring dimensions along which people differ from one another—dimensions known as traits. (p. 463)
- Learning approaches to personality concentrate on observable behavior. To a strict learning theorist, per-

sonality is the sum of learned responses to the external environment. (p. 466)
- Social cognitive approaches concentrate on the role of cognitions in determining personality. Those approaches pay particular attention to self-efficacy and self-esteem in determining behavior. (p. 467)
- Biological and evolutionary approaches to personality focus on the way in which personality characteristics are inherited. (pp. 468–470)

- Humanistic approaches emphasize the inherent goodness of people. They consider the core of personality in terms of a person's ability to change and improve. (p. 471)
- The major personality approaches differ substantially from one another; that may reflect both their focus on different aspects of personality and the overall complexity of personality (p. 473)

EVALUATE

1. Carl's determination to succeed is the dominant force in all his activities and relationships. According to Gordon Allport's theory, this is an example of a _____ trait. In contrast, Cindy's fondness for old western movies is an example of a _____ trait.
2. A person who enjoys activities such as parties and hang gliding might be described by Eysenck as high on what trait?
3. Proponents of which approach to personality would be most likely to agree with the statement "Personality can be thought of as learned responses to a person's upbringing and environment"?
   a. Humanistic
   b. Biological and evolutionary
   c. Learning
   d. Trait
4. A person who would make the statement "I know I can't do it" would be rated by Bandura as low on _____-_____.

5. Which approach to personality emphasizes the innate goodness of people and their desire to grow?
   a. Humanistic
   b. Psychodynamic
   c. Learning
   d. Biological and evolutionary

RETHINK

1. If personality traits are merely descriptive and not explanatory, of what use are they? Can assigning a trait to a person be harmful—or helpful? Why or why not?
2. *From the perspective of a substance abuse counselor:* Many alcohol and substance abuse programs attempt to raise their clients' sense of self-worth by communicating "feel-good messages." Do you expect these messages to be beneficial or detrimental to a client? Why or why not? Can you think of alternative ways to assist and support individuals who have a drug or alcohol addiction?
3. *From the perspective of an educator:* How might you encourage your students' development of self-esteem and self-efficacy? What steps would you take to ensure that their self-esteem did not become over-inflated?

Answers to Evaluate Questions

1. cardinal, secondary; 2. extraversion; 3. c; 4. self-efficacy; 5. a

KEY TERMS

trait theory p. 463
traits p. 463
social cognitive approaches to personality p. 467
self-efficacy p. 467

self-esteem p. 467
biological and evolutionary approaches to personality p. 468
temperament p. 470

humanistic approaches to personality p. 471
self-actualization p. 472
unconditional positive regard p. 472

Assessing Personality: Determining What Makes Us Distinctive

You have a need for other people to like and admire you.

You have a tendency to be critical of yourself.

You have a great deal of unused potential that you have not turned to your advantage.

Although you have some personality weaknesses, you generally are able to compensate for them.

Relating to members of the opposite sex has presented problems to you.

Although you appear to be disciplined and self-controlled to others, you tend to be anxious and insecure inside.

At times you have serious doubts about whether you have made the right decision or done the right thing.

You prefer a certain amount of change and variety and become dissatisfied when hemmed in by restrictions and limitations.

You do not accept others' statements without satisfactory proof.

You have found it unwise to be too frank in revealing yourself to others.

If you think these statements provide a surprisingly accurate account of your personality, you are not alone: Most college students think that these descriptions are tailored just to them. In fact, the statements were designed intentionally to be so vague that they apply to just about anyone (Forer, 1949; Russo, 1981).

The ease with which we can agree with such imprecise statements underscores the difficulty in coming up with accurate and meaningful assessments of people's personalities (also see the PsychInteractive exercise on personality assessment). Psychologists interested in assessing personality must be able to define the most meaningful ways of discriminating between one person's personality and another's. To do this, they use **psychological tests,** standard measures devised to assess behavior objectively. With the results of such tests, psychologists can help people understand themselves better and make decisions about their lives. Psychological tests are also employed by researchers interested in the causes and consequences of personality (Groth-Marnat, 1996; Aiken, 2000; Kaplan & Saccuzzo, 2001).

Like the assessments that seek to measure intelligence, all psychological tests must have reliability and validity. *Reliability* refers to the measurement consistency test. If a test is reliable, it yields the same result each time it is administered to a particular person or group. In contrast, unreliable tests give different results each time they are administered.

For meaningful conclusions to be drawn, tests also must be valid. Tests have *validity* when they actually measure what they are designed to measure. If a test is constructed to measure sociability, for instance, we need to know that it actually measures sociability, not some other trait.

Finally, psychological tests are based on *norms,* standards of test performance that permit the comparison of one person's score on a test with the scores of others who

Key Concepts

How can we most accurately assess personality?

What are the major types of personality measures?

www.mhhe.com/feldmanup8
PsychInteractive Online

Personality Assessment

Psychological tests: Standard measures devised to assess behavior objectively; used by psychologists to help people make decisions about their lives and understand more about themselves.

have taken the same test. For example, a norm permits test-takers who have received a particular score on a test to know that they have scored in the top 10 percent of all those who have taken the test.

Norms are established by administering a particular test to a large number of people and determining the typical scores. It is then possible to compare a single person's score with the scores of the group, providing a comparative measure of test performance against the performance of others who have taken the test.

The establishment of appropriate norms is not a simple endeavor. For instance, the specific group that is employed to determine norms for a test has a profound effect on the way an individual's performance is evaluated. In fact, as we discuss next, the process of establishing norms can take on political overtones.

Exploring DIVERSITY
Should Race and Ethnicity Be Used to Establish Norms?

The passions of politics may confront the objectivity of science when test norms are established, at least in the realm of standardized tests that are meant to predict future job performance. In fact, a national controversy has developed around the question of whether different norms should be established for members of various racial and ethnic groups (Brown, 1994; Babkrina & Bondi, 2003; Manly, 2005).

At issue is the U.S. government's fifty-year-old General Aptitude Test Battery, a test that measures a broad range of abilities from eye-hand coordination to reading proficiency. The problem that sparked the controversy is that African Americans and Hispanics tend to score lower on the test, on average, than do members of other groups. The lower scores often are due to a lack of prior relevant experience and job opportunities, which in turn has been due to prejudice and discrimination.

To promote the employment of minority racial groups, the government developed a separate set of norms for African Americans and Hispanics. Rather than using the pool of all people who took the test, the scores of African American and Hispanic applicants were compared only with the scores of other African Americans and Hispanics. Consequently, a Hispanic who scored in the top 20 percent of the Hispanics taking the test was considered to have performed equivalently to a white job applicant who scored in the top 20 percent of the whites who took the test, even though the absolute score of the Hispanic might be lower than that of the white.

Critics of the adjusted norming system suggest that such a procedure discriminates in favor of certain racial and ethnic groups at the expense of others, thereby fanning the flames of racial bigotry. The practice was challenged legally, and with the passage of the Civil Rights Act in 1991, race norming on the General Aptitude Test Battery was discontinued (Galef, 2001).

However, proponents of race norming continue to argue that norming procedures that take race into account are an affirmative action tool that simply permits minority job seekers to be placed on an equal footing with white job seekers. Furthermore, a panel of the National Academy of Sciences concurred with the practice of adjusting test norms. It suggested that the unadjusted test norms are not terribly useful in predicting job performance, and that they would tend to screen out otherwise qualified minority-group members. And a U.S. federal court opinion ruled in 2001 that using "bands" of score ranges was not necessarily discriminatory, unless the bands were designed on the basis of race (Fleming, 2000; Seventh U.S. Circuit Court of Appeals, 2001).

Job testing is not the only area in which issues arise regarding norms and the meaning of test scores. The issue of how to treat racial differences in IQ scores is also controversial and divisive. Clearly, race norming raises profound and intense feelings that may come into conflict with scientific objectivity (APA, 1993b; Greenlaw & Jensen, 1996; Leiter & Leiter, 2003).

The issue of establishing norms for tests is further complicated by the existence of a wide array of personality measures and approaches to assessment. We consider some of these measures, which have a variety of characteristics and purposes, next.

Self-Report Measures of Personality

If someone wanted to assess your personality, one possible approach would be to carry out an extensive interview with you to determine the most important events in your childhood, your social relationships, and your successes and failures. Obviously, though, such a technique would take extraordinary time and effort.

It is also unnecessary. Just as physicians draw only a small sample of your blood to test it, psychologists can use **self-report measures** that ask people about a relatively small sample of their behavior. This sampling of self-report data is then used to infer the presence of particular personality characteristics. For example, a researcher who was interested in assessing a person's orientation to life might administer the questionnaire shown in Figure 1. Although the questionnaire consists of only a few questions, the answers can be used to generalize about personality characteristics. (Try it yourself!)

One of the best examples of a self-report measure, and one of the most frequently used personality tests, is the **Minnesota Multiphasic Personality Inventory-2 (MMPI-2).** Although the original purpose of this measure was to identify people with specific sorts of psychological difficulties, it has been found to predict a variety of other behaviors. For instance, MMPI-2 scores have been shown to be good predictors of whether college students will marry within ten years and will get an advanced

Self-report measures: A method of gathering data about people by asking them questions about a sample of their behavior.

Minnesota Multiphasic Personality Inventory-2 (MMPI-2): A widely used self-report test that identifies people with psychological difficulties and is employed to predict some everyday behaviors.

The Life Orientation Test

Use the following scale to answer the items below:

0	1	2	3	4
Strongly disagree	Disagree	Neutral	Agree	Strongly agree

1. In uncertain times, I usually expect the best.
2. It's easy for me to relax.
3. If something can go wrong for me, it will.
4. I'm always optimistic about my future.
5. I enjoy my friends a lot.
6. It's important for me to keep busy.
7. I hardly ever expect things to go my way.
8. I don't get upset too easily.
9. I rarely count on good things happening to me.
10. Overall, I expect more good things to happen to me than bad.

Scoring. First, reverse your answers to questions 3, 7, and 9. Do this by changing a 0 to a 4, a 1 to a 3, a 3 to a 1, and a 4 to a 0 (answers of 2 stay as 2). Then sum the reversed scores, and add them to the scores you gave to questions 1, 4, and 10. (Ignore questions 2, 5, 6, and 8, which are filler items.)

The total score you get is a measure of a particular orientation to life: your degree of optimism. The higher your scores, the more positive and hopeful you generally are about life. For comparison purposes the average score for college students is 14.3, according to the results of a study by Scheier, Carver, and Bridges (1994). People with a higher degree of optimism generally deal with stress better than do those with lower scores.

FIGURE 1 The Life Orientation Test. Try this scale by indicating the degree to which you agree with each of the ten statements, using the scale from 0 to 4 for each item. Try to be as accurate as possible. There are no right or wrong answers. (Source: Adapted from Scheier, Carver, & Bridges, 1994.)

degree. Police departments use the test to measure whether police officers are likely to use their weapons. Psychologists in Russia administer a modified form of the MMPI to their astronauts and Olympic athletes (Butcher, 1995, 2005; Craig, 1999; Friedman et al., 2000; Weis, Crockett, & Vieth, 2004).

The test consists of a series of 567 items to which a person responds "true," "false," or "cannot say." The questions cover a variety of issues, ranging from mood ("I feel useless at times") to opinions ("People should try to understand their dreams") to physical and psychological health ("I am bothered by an upset stomach several times a week" and "I have strange and peculiar thoughts").

There are no right or wrong answers. Instead, interpretation of the results rests on the pattern of responses. The test yields scores on ten separate scales, plus three scales meant to measure the validity of the respondent's answers. For example, there is a "lie scale" that indicates when people are falsifying their responses in order to present themselves more favorably (through items such as "I can't remember ever having a bad night's sleep") (Butcher, 1999, 2005; Graham, 1999; Stein & Graham, 2005).

How did the authors of the MMPI-2 determine what specific patterns of responses indicate? The procedure they used is typical of personality test construction—a process known as **test standardization.** To create the test, the test authors asked groups of psychiatric patients with a specific diagnosis, such as depression or schizophrenia, to complete a large number of items. They then determined which items best differentiated members of those groups from a comparison group of normal participants, and included those specific items in the final version of the test. By systematically carrying out this procedure on groups with different diagnoses, the test authors were able to devise a number of subscales that identified different forms of abnormal behavior (see Figure 2).

Test standardization: A technique used to validate questions in personality tests by studying the responses of people with known diagnoses.

FIGURE 2 A profile on the MMPI-2 of a person who suffers from obsessional anxiety, social withdrawal, and delusional thinking. (Source: Based on data from Halgin & Whitbourne, 1994, p. 72, and Minnesota Multiphasic Personality Inventory-2. Copyright © by the Regents of the University of Minnesota, 1942, 1943 (renewed 1970, 1989).)

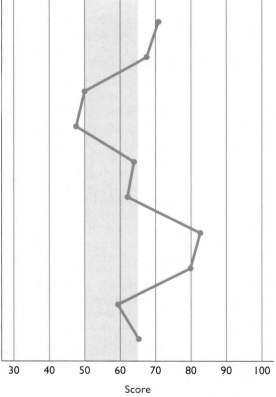

Clinical scales

Hypochondriasis: Interest in bodily symptoms

Depression: Hopeless, pessimistic attitude

Hysteria: Uses physical ailments to avoid problems

Psychopathic deviate: Antisocial behavior, disregards others

Masculinity-femininity: Interests related to gender

Paranoia: Defensiveness, suspiciousness, jealousy

Psychasthenia: obsessiveness, compulsiveness, suspiciousness

Schizophrenia: Loss of touch with reality, bizarre delusions

Hypomania: Impulsiveness, overactivity

Social introversion-extraversion: Insecure social interactions

30   40   50   60   70   80   90   100

Score

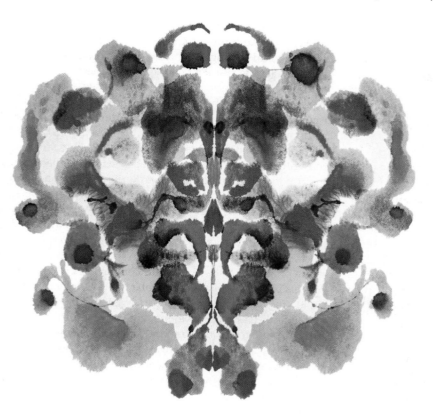

FIGURE 3 This inkblot is similar to the type used in the Rorschach personality test. (Source: Alloy, Jacobson, & Acocella, 1999.) What do you see in it?

When the MMPI-2 is used for the purpose for which it was devised—identification of personality disorders—it does a reasonably good job. However, like other personality tests, it presents an opportunity for abuse. For instance, employers who use it as a screening tool for job applicants may interpret the results improperly, relying too heavily on the results of individual scales instead of taking into account the overall patterns of results, which require skilled interpretation. Furthermore, critics point out that the individual scales overlap, making their interpretation difficult. In sum, although the MMPI-2 remains the most widely used personality test and has been translated into more than 100 different languages, it must be used with caution (Graham, 1999; Holden, 2000; Greene & Clopton, 2004; Valsiner, Diriwächter, & Sauck, 2005).

Projective Methods

If you were shown the shape presented in Figure 3 and asked what it represented to you, you might not think that your impressions would mean very much. But to a psychodynamic theoretician, your responses to such an ambiguous figure would provide valuable clues to the state of your unconscious, and ultimately to your general personality characteristics.

The shape in the figure is representative of inkblots used in **projective personality tests,** in which a person is shown an ambiguous stimulus and asked to describe it or tell a story about it. The responses are considered to be "projections" of the individual's personality.

The best-known projective test is the **Rorschach test.** Devised by Swiss psychiatrist Hermann Rorschach (1924), the test involves showing a series of symmetrical

Projective personality test: A test in which a person is shown an ambiguous stimulus and asked to describe it or tell a story about it.

Rorschach test: A test that involves showing a series of symmetrical visual stimuli to people who then are asked what the figures represent to them.

"RORSCHACH! WHAT'S TO BECOME OF YOU?"

Thematic Apperception Test (TAT):
A test consisting of a series of pictures about which a person is asked to write a story.

www.mhhe.com/feldmanup8
PsychInteractive Online

Rorschach and Projection Tests

Behavioral assessment: Direct measures of an individual's behavior used to describe personality characteristics.

stimuli, similar to the one in Figure 3, to people who are then asked what the figures represent to them. Their responses are recorded, and through a complex set of clinical judgments on the part of the examiner, people are classified by their personality type. For instance, respondents who see a bear in one inkblot are thought to have a strong degree of emotional control, according to the scoring guidelines developed by Rorschach (Aronow, Reznikoff, & Moreland, 1994; Weiner, 2004).

The **Thematic Apperception Test (TAT)** is another well-known projective test. The TAT consists of a series of pictures about which a person is asked to write a story. The stories are then used to draw inferences about the writer's personality characteristics (Kelly, 1997; Cramer, 2000a; Weiner, 2004).

Tests with stimuli as ambiguous as those used in the Rorschach and TAT require particular skill and care in their interpretation—too much, in many critics' estimation. (To see for yourself, and to learn about projective tests in general, complete the PsychInteractive exercise.) The Rorschach in particular has been criticized for requiring too much inference on the part of the examiner, and attempts to standardize scoring have frequently failed. Furthermore, many critics complain that the Rorschach does not provide much valid information about underlying personality traits. Despite such problems, both the Rorschach and the TAT are widely used, particularly in clinical settings, and their proponents suggest that their reliability and validity are great enough to provide useful inferences about personality (Meyer, 2000; Garb, 2002, 2003; Wood et al., 2003; Garb et al., 2005).

Behavioral Assessment

If you were a psychologist subscribing to a learning approach to personality, you would be likely to object to the indirect nature of projective tests. Instead, you would be more apt to use **behavioral assessment**—direct measures of an individual's behavior designed to describe characteristics indicative of personality. As with observational research, behavioral assessment may be carried out naturalistically by observing people in their own settings: in the workplace, at home, or in school. In other cases, behavioral assessment occurs in the laboratory, under controlled conditions in which a psychologist sets up a situation and observes an individual's behavior (Ramsay, Reynolds, & Kamphaus, 2002; Gladwell, 2004).

Regardless of the setting in which behavior is observed, an effort is made to ensure that behavioral assessment is carried out objectively, quantifying behavior as much as possible. For example, an observer may record the number of social contacts a person initiates, the number of questions asked, or the number of aggressive acts. Another method is to measure the duration of events: the duration of a temper tantrum in a child, the length of a conversation, the amount of time spent working, or the time spent in cooperative behavior.

Behavioral assessment is particularly appropriate for observing—and eventually remedying—specific behavioral difficulties, such as shyness in children. It provides a means of assessing the specific nature and incidence of a problem and subsequently allows psychologists to determine whether intervention techniques have been successful.

Behavioral assessment techniques based on learning theories of personality have also made important contributions to the treatment of certain kinds of psychological difficulties. Indeed, the knowledge of normal personality provided by the various personality theories has led to significant advances in our understanding and treatment of both physical and psychological disorders.

Wanted: People with "kinetic energy," "emotional maturity," and the ability to "deal with large numbers of people in a fairly chaotic situation."

BECOMING AN
INFORMED CONSUMER
of Psychology

Assessing Personality Assessments

Although this job description may seem most appropriate for the job of cohost of *Wheel of Fortune,* in actuality it is part of an advertisement for managers for American MultiCinema's (AMC) theaters. To find people with such qualities, AMC has developed a battery of personality measures for job applicants. In developing its own tests, AMC joined scores of companies, ranging from General Motors to Microsoft, that employ personality tests to help with hiring decisions (Dentzer, 1986; Hogan, Hogan, & Roberts, 1996; Poundstone, 2003; Varela et al., 2004).

For example, potential Microsoft employees have been asked brain-teasers like "If you had to remove one of the 50 U.S. states, which would it be?" (Hint: First define "remove." If you mean the death of everyone in the state, suggest a low-population state. If you mean quitting the country, then go for an outlying-state like Alaska or Hawaii.) Other employers ask questions that are even more vague ("Describe November"). With such questions, it's not always clear that the tests are formally reliable or valid (McGinn, 2003).

Before relying too heavily on the results of personality testing as a potential employee, employer, or consumer of testing services, you should keep several points in mind:

- *Understand what the test claims to measure.* Standard personality measures are accompanied by information that discusses how the test was developed, to whom it is most applicable, and how the results should be interpreted. Read any explanations of the test; they will help you understand the results.
- *Base no decision only on the results of any one test.* Test results should be interpreted in the context of other information—academic records, social interests, and home and community activities.
- *Remember that test results are not always accurate.* The results may be in error; the test may be unreliable or invalid. You may, for example, have had a "bad day" when you took the test, or the person scoring and interpreting the test may have made a mistake. You should not place too much significance on the results of a single administration of any test.

In sum, it is important to keep in mind the complexity of human behavior—particularly your own. No single test can provide an understanding of the intricacies of someone's personality without considering a good deal more information than can be provided in a single testing session (Gladwell, 2004; Paul, 2004).

RECAP/EVALUATE/RETHINK

RECAP

How can we most accurately assess personality?

- Psychological tests such as the MMPI-2 are standard assessment tools that measure behavior objectively. They must be reliable (measuring what they are trying to measure consistently) and valid (measuring what they are supposed to measure). (p. 475)

What are the major types of personality measures?

- Self-report measures ask people about a sample range of their behaviors. These reports are used to infer the presence of particular personality characteristics. (p. 477)
- Projective personality tests (such as the Rorschach and the Thematic Apperception Test) present an ambiguous stimulus; the test administrator infers information about the test-taker from his or her responses. (pp. 479–480)
- Behavioral assessment is based on the principles of learning theory. It employs direct measurement of an individual's behavior to determine characteristics related to personality. (p. 480)

EVALUATE

1. _____ is the consistency of a personality test; _____ is the ability of a test to actually measure what it is designed to measure.
2. _____ are standards used to compare scores of different people taking the same test.
3. Tests such as the MMPI-2, in which a small sample of behavior is assessed to determine larger patterns, are examples of
   a. Cross-sectional tests
   b. Projective tests
   c. Achievement tests
   d. Self-report tests
4. A person shown a picture and asked to make up a story about it would be taking a _____ personality test.

RETHINK

1. Should personality tests be used for personnel decisions? Should they be used for other social purposes, such as identifying individuals at risk for certain types of personality disorders?
2. *From the perspective of a politician:* Imagine that you had to vote on a law that would require institutions and organizations to perform race norming procedures on standardized performance tests. Would you support such a law? Why or why not? In addition to race, should norming procedures take other factors into account? Which ones and why?

Answers to Evaluate Questions

1. reliability, validity; 2. norms; 3. d; 4. projective

KEY TERMS

psychological tests p. 475
self-report measures p. 477
Minnesota Multiphasic
   Personality Inventory-2
   (MMPI-2) p. 477

test standardization p. 478
projective personality test
   p. 479
Rorschach test p. 479

Thematic Apperception Test
   (TAT) p. 480
behavioral assessment
   p. 480

Looking Back

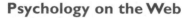

Psychology on the Web

1. Sigmund Freud is one of the towering figures in psychology. His influence extends far beyond his psychoanalytic work. Find information about Freud on the Web. Pick one aspect of his work or influence (for example, on therapy, medicine, literature, film, or culture and society) and summarize in writing what you have found, including your attitude toward your findings.

2. Find a Web site that links to personality tests and take one or two tests—remembering to take them with skepticism. For each test, summarize in writing the aspects of personality that were tested, the theoretical approach the test appeared to be based on, and your assessment of the trustworthiness of the results.

3. After completing the PsychInteractive exercise on the Rorschach and projective tests in Module 44, go to the Web to search both pro and con arguments on the use of the Rorschach. Summarize the arguments in writing.

Epilogue

We have discussed the different ways in which psychologists have interpreted the development and structure of personality. The perspectives we examined ranged from Freud's analysis of personality based primarily on internal, unconscious factors to the externally based view of personality as a learned set of traits and actions that is championed by learning theorists. We also noted that there are many ways to interpret personality, and by no means does a consensus exist on what the key traits are that are central to personality.

Return to the Prologue and consider the case of John Gotti, who was—depending on one's experience with him—either awfully nice or just awful. Use your understanding of personality to consider the following questions.

1. How might a psychoanalytic approach to personality, using the concepts of id, ego, and superego, help explain Gotti's criminal behavior?

2. Using Raymond Cattell's sixteen source traits, what sort of profile do you think Gotti would have displayed if he had been tested? Where would he fall on Hans Eysenck's major personality dimensions?

3. Would a personality profile of Gotti administered during the time he was involved in mob activities have been different from one administered when he was visiting friends? Why?

4. How would an advocate of a social cognitive approach to personality interpret and explain Gotti's seemingly contradictory behavior? How might the concepts of observational learning apply to a personality like Gotti's?

CHAPTER 14

Health Psychology: Stress, Coping, and Well-Being

Key Concepts for Chapter 14

Prologue   So Much to Do, So Little Time to Do It

Louisa Denby's day began badly: She slept through her alarm and had to skip breakfast to catch the bus to campus. Then, when she went to the library to catch up on the reading she had to do before taking a test the next day, the one article she needed was missing. The librarian told her that replacing it would take 24 hours. Feeling frustrated, she walked to the computer lab to print out the paper she had completed at home the night before.

The computer wouldn't read her disk. She searched for someone to help her, but she was unable to find anyone who knew any more about computers than she did.

It was only 9:42 A.M., and Louisa had a wracking headache. Apart from that pain, she was conscious of only one feeling: stress (Feldman, 2006, p. 384).

Looking Ahead

It's not hard to understand why Louisa Denby was experiencing stress. For people like her—and that probably includes most of us—the intensity of juggling multiple roles leads to feelings of never having sufficient time and, in some cases, takes a toll on both physical and psychological well-being.

Stress and how we cope with it have long been central topics of interest for psychologists. However, in recent years the focus has broadened as psychology has come to view stress in the broader context of one of psychology's newer subfields: health psychology. **Health psychology** investigates the psychological factors related to wellness and illness, including the prevention, diagnosis, and treatment of medical problems. Health psychologists investigate the effects of psychological factors such as stress on illness. They examine the psychological principles underlying treatments for disease and illness. They also study prevention: how more healthful behavior can help people avoid health problems such as heart disease and stress.

Health psychologists take a decisive stand on the enduring mind-body issue that philosophers, and later psychologists, have debated since the time of the ancient Greeks. In their view, the mind and the body are clearly linked, rather than representing two distinct systems (Sternberg, 2000b).

Health psychologists recognize that good health and the ability to cope with illness are affected by psychological factors such as thoughts, emotions, and the ability to manage stress. They have paid particular attention to the *immune system*, the complex of organs, glands, and cells that constitute our bodies' natural line of defense in fighting disease.

In fact, health psychologists are among the primary investigators in a growing field called **psychoneuroimmunology**, or **PNI**, the study of the relationship among psychological factors, the immune system, and the brain. PNI has led to discoveries such as the existence of an association between a person's emotional state and the success of the immune system in fighting disease (Baum, Revenson, & Singer, 2000; Ader, Felton, & Cohen, 2001; Dickerson et al., 2004; Segerstrom & Miller, 2004).

In sum, health psychologists view the mind and the body as two parts of a whole human being that cannot be considered independently. This more recent view marks a sharp departure from earlier thinking. Previously, disease was seen as a purely biological phenomenon, and psychological factors were of little interest to most health care workers. In the early twentieth century, the primary causes of death were short-term infections from which one either rapidly recovered—or died. Now, however, the major causes of death, such as heart disease, cancer, and diabetes, are chronic illnesses that often cannot be cured and may linger for years, posing significant psychological issues (Delahanty & Baum, 2000; Bishop, 2005).

Advances in health psychology have had an impact across a variety of disciplines and professions. For instance, medical professionals such as physicians and nurses, social workers, dieticians, pharmacists, occupational therapists, and even clergy are increasingly likely to receive training in health psychology.

In these modules we discuss the ways in which psychological factors affect health. We first focus on the causes and consequences of stress, as well as on the means of coping with it. Next, we explore the psychological aspects of several major health problems, including heart disease, cancer, and ailments resulting from smoking. Finally, we examine the ways in which patient-physician interactions influence our health and offer suggestions for increasing people's compliance with recommendations about behavior that will improve their well-being.

Stress and Coping

Anthony Lepre started feeling awful almost as soon as [U.S. Homeland Security Secretary] Tom Ridge put the nation on high alert for a terrorist attack. . . . He awoke in the middle of the night short of breath, his heart pounding. And the sound of his telephone seemed a sure sign of bad news. By midweek, he was rushing off to Costco to stock up on fruit juice, bottled water, peanut butter, canned tuna, "and extra food for my cats Monster, Monkey and Spike." He also picked up a first-aid kit, six rolls of duct tape, and a bulk package of plastic wrap to seal his windows. "The biggest problem was that I felt helpless," he says, "completely powerless over the situation" (Cowley, 2003, pp. 43–44).

Stress: Reacting to Threat and Challenge

Most of us need little introduction to the phenomenon of **stress**, people's response to events that threaten or challenge them. Whether it be a paper or an exam deadline, a family problem, or even the ongoing threat of a terrorist attack, life is full of circumstances and events, known as stressors, that produce threats to our well-being. Even pleasant events—such as planning a party or beginning a sought-after job—can produce stress, although negative events result in greater detrimental consequences than do positive ones.

All of us face stress in our lives. Some health psychologists believe that daily life actually involves a series of repeated sequences of perceiving a threat, considering ways to cope with it, and ultimately adapting to the threat, with greater or lesser success. Although adaptation is often minor and occurs without our awareness, adaptation requires a major effort when stress is more severe or longer lasting. Ultimately, our attempts to overcome stress may produce biological and psychological responses that result in health problems (Gatchel & Baum, 1983; Fink, 2000; Boyce & Ellis, 2005).

THE NATURE OF STRESSORS: MY STRESS IS YOUR PLEASURE

Stress is a very personal thing. Although certain kinds of events, such as the death of a loved one or participation in military combat, are universally stressful, other situations may or may not be stressful to a particular person (Affleck et al., 1994; Krohne, 1996; Robert-McComb, 2001).

Consider, for instance, bungee jumping. Some people would find jumping off a bridge while attached to a slender rubber tether extremely stressful. However, there are individuals who see such an activity as challenging and fun-filled. Whether bungee jumping is stressful depends in part, then, on a person's perception of the activity.

For people to consider an event stressful, they must perceive it as threatening and must lack the resources to deal with it effectively. Consequently, the same event may at some times be stressful and at other times provoke no stressful reaction at all. A young man may experience stress when he is turned down for a date—if he attributes the refusal to his unattractiveness or unworthiness. But if he attributes it to some factor unrelated to his self-esteem, such as a previous commitment by the woman he asked,

Key Concepts

How is health psychology a union between medicine and psychology?

What is stress, how does it affect us, and how can we best cope with it?

Health psychology: The branch of psychology that investigates the psychological factors related to wellness and illness, including the prevention, diagnosis, and treatment of medical problems.

Psychoneuroimmunology (PNI): The study of the relationship among psychological factors, the immune system, and the brain.

Stress: A person's response to events that are threatening or challenging.

the experience of being refused may create no stress at all. Hence, a person's interpretation of events plays an important role in the determination of what is stressful (Folkman & Moskowitz, 2000; Giacobbi, Jr., et al., 2004).

The severity of stress is greatest when important goals are threatened, the threat is immediate, or the anticipation of a threatening event extends over a long period. For example, members of minority groups who feel they are potentially the targets of racist behavior experience significant stress (Clark et al., 1999; Taylor & Turner, 2002; Troxel et al., 2003; Cassidy et al., 2004).

CATEGORIZING STRESSORS

What kinds of events tend to be seen as stressful? There are three general types of stressors: cataclysmic events, personal stressors, and background stressors.

Cataclysmic events are strong stressors that occur suddenly and typically affect many people simultaneously. Disasters such as tornadoes and plane crashes, as well as terrorist attacks, are examples of cataclysmic events that can affect hundreds or thousands of people simultaneously.

Although it might seem that cataclysmic events would produce potent, lingering stress, in many cases they do not. In fact, cataclysmic events involving natural disasters may produce less stress in the long run than do events that initially are not as devastating. One reason is that natural disasters have a clear resolution. Once they are over, people can look to the future knowing that the worst is behind them. Moreover, the stress induced by cataclysmic events is shared by others who also experienced the disaster. This permits people to offer one another social support and a firsthand understanding of the difficulties others are going through (Kaniasty & Norris, 1995; Hobfoll et al., 1996; Benight, 2004).

In contrast, terrorist attacks like the one on the World Trade Center in 2001 are cataclysmic events that produce considerable stress. Terrorist attacks are deliberate, and victims (and observers) know that future attacks are likely. Government warnings in the form of heightened terror alerts may further increase the stress (Graham, 2001; Pomponio, 2002; Murphy, Wismar, & Freeman, 2003).

The second major category of stressor is the personal stressor. **Personal stressors** include major life events such as the death of a parent or spouse, the loss of one's job, a major personal failure, or even something positive such as getting married. Typically, personal stressors produce an immediate major reaction that soon tapers off. For example, stress arising from the death of a loved one tends to be greatest just after the time of death, but people begin to feel less stress and are better able to cope with the loss after the passage of time.

Some victims of major catastrophes and severe personal stressors experience **posttraumatic stress disorder,** or **PTSD,** in which a person has experienced a significantly stressful event that has long-lasting effects that may include re-experiencing the event in vivid flashbacks or dreams. An episode of PTSD may be triggered by an otherwise innocent stimulus, such as the sound of a honking horn, that leads someone to re-experience a past event that produced considerable stress.

Around 16 percent of soldiers returning from Iraq have symptoms of PTSD. Furthermore, those who have experienced child abuse or rape, rescue workers facing overwhelming situations, and victims of sudden natural disaster or accidents that produce feelings of helplessness and shock may suffer from the same disorder (Hoge et al., 2004; Ozer & Weiss, 2004; Schnurr & Cozza, 2004).

Terrorist attacks produce high incidences of PTSD. For example, 11 percent of people in New York City had some form of PTSD in the months after the September 11 terrorist attacks. But the responses varied significantly with a resident's proxim-

Cataclysmic events: Strong stressors that occur suddenly, affecting many people at once (e.g., natural disasters).

Personal stressors: Major life events, such as the death of a family member, that have immediate consequences that generally fade with time.

Posttraumatic stress disorder (PTSD): A phenomenon in which victims of major catastrophes or strong personal stressors feel long-lasting effects that may include re-experiencing the event in vivid flashbacks or dreams.

Even positive events can produce significant stress.

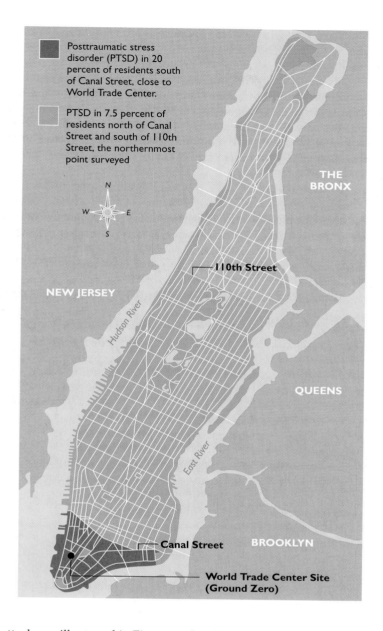

- Posttraumatic stress disorder (PTSD) in 20 percent of residents south of Canal Street, close to World Trade Center.

- PTSD in 7.5 percent of residents north of Canal Street and south of 110th Street, the northernmost point surveyed

THE BRONX

NEW JERSEY

110th Street

Hudson River

QUEENS

East River

Canal Street

BROOKLYN

World Trade Center Site (Ground Zero)

FIGURE 1 The closer people lived to the site of the World Trade Center terrorist attack, the greater the rate of posttraumatic stress disorder. (Source: Susser, Herman, & Aaron, 2002.)

ity to the attacks, as illustrated in Figure 1 ; the closer someone lived to ground zero, the greater the likelihood of PTSD (Susser, Herman, & Aaron, 2002).

Symptoms of posttraumatic stress disorder include re-experiencing the event in flashbacks or dreams, emotional numbing, sleep difficulties, problems relating to other people, alcohol and drug abuse, and—in some cases—suicide. For instance, the suicide rate for veterans of the Vietnam war is as much as 25 percent higher than it is for the general population (Wilson & Keane, 1996; Orr, Metzger, & Pitman, 2002; McKeever & Huff, 2003; Ozer et al., 2003).

Background stressors, or more informally, *daily hassles,* are the third major category of stressors. Exemplified by standing in a long line at a bank and getting stuck in a traffic jam, daily hassles are the minor irritations of life that we all face time and time again. Another type of background stressor is a long-term, chronic problem, such as experiencing dissatisfaction with school or a job, being in an unhappy relationship, or living in crowded quarters without privacy (van Eck, Nicolson, & Berkhof, 1998; Lazarus, 2000; Weinstein et al., 2004).

By themselves, daily hassles do not require much coping or even a response on the part of the individual, although they certainly produce unpleasant emotions and moods. Yet daily hassles add up—and ultimately they may take as great a toll as a single, more stressful incident does. In fact, the *number* of daily hassles people face is

Background stressors ("daily hassles"): Everyday annoyances, such as being stuck in traffic, that cause minor irritations and may have long-term ill effects if they continue or are compounded by other stressful events.

associated with psychological symptoms and health problems such as flu, sore throat, and backaches.

The flip side of hassles is *uplifts,* the minor positive events that make us feel good—even if only temporarily. As indicated in Figure 2 , uplifts range from relating well to a companion to finding one's surroundings pleasing. What is especially intriguing about uplifts is that they are associated with people's psychological health in just the opposite way that hassles are: The greater the number of uplifts experienced, the fewer the psychological symptoms people later report (Chamberlain & Zika, 1990; Roberts, 1995; Ravindran et al., 2002).

THE HIGH COST OF STRESS

Stress can produce both biological and psychological consequences. Often the most immediate reaction to stress is a biological one. Exposure to stressors generates a rise

FIGURE 2 The most common everyday hassles and uplifts (hassles: Chamberlain & Zika, 1990; uplifts: Kanner et al., 1981). How many of these are part of your life, and how do you cope with them?

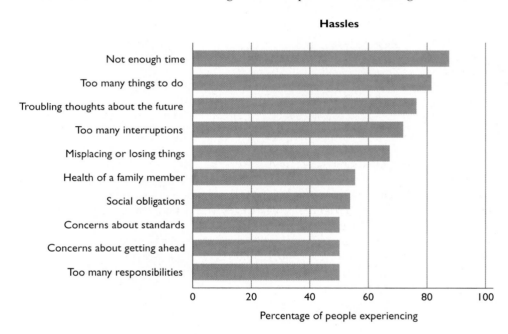

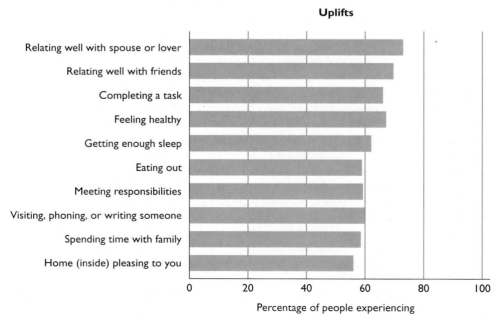

in hormone secretions by the adrenal glands, an increase in heart rate and blood pressure, and changes in how well the skin conducts electrical impulses. On a short-term basis, these responses may be adaptive because they produce an "emergency reaction" in which the body prepares to defend itself through activation of the sympathetic nervous system. Those responses may allow more effective coping with the stressful situation (Akil & Morano, 1996; McEwen, 1998).

However, continued exposure to stress results in a decline in the body's overall level of biological functioning because of the constant secretion of stress-related hormones. Over time, stressful reactions can promote deterioration of body tissues such as blood vessels and the heart. Ultimately, we become more susceptible to disease as our ability to fight off infection is lowered (Shapiro, 1996; McCabe et al., 2000; Kemeny, 2003; Brydon et al., 2004).

Furthermore, an entire class of physical problems known as **psychophysiological disorders** often result from or are worsened by stress. Once referred to as *psychosomatic disorders* (a term dropped because people assumed that the disorders were somehow unreal), psychophysiological disorders are actual medical problems that are influenced by an interaction of psychological, emotional, and physical difficulties. The more common psychophysiological disorders range from major problems such as high blood pressure to usually less serious conditions, such as headaches, backaches, skin rashes, indigestion, fatigue, and constipation. Stress has even been linked to the common cold (Cohen, 1996; Rice, 2000; Cohen et al., 2003).

On a psychological level, high levels of stress prevent people from adequately coping with life. Their view of the environment can become clouded (for example, a minor criticism made by a friend is blown out of proportion). Moreover, at the highest levels of stress, emotional responses may be so extreme that people are unable to act at all. People under a lot of stress also become less able to deal with new stressors.

In short, stress affects us in multiple ways. It may increase the risk that we will become ill, it may directly cause illness, it may make us less able to recover from a disease, and it may reduce our ability to cope with future stress. (See Figure 3 and try the PsychInteractive exercise on college stress to get a measure of your own level of stress.)

Everyone confronts daily hassles, or back-ground stressors, at some point. At what point do daily hassles become more than mere irritants?

Psychophysiological disorders: Medical problems influenced by an interaction of psychological, emotional, and physical difficulties.

www.mhhe.com/feldmanup8
PsychInteractive Online

College Stress Test

THE GENERAL ADAPTATION SYNDROME MODEL: THE COURSE OF STRESS

The effects of long-term stress are illustrated in a series of stages proposed by Hans Selye (pronounced "sell-yay"), a pioneering stress theorist (Selye, 1976, 1993). This model, the **general adaptation syndrome (GAS),** suggests that the physiological response to stress follows the same set pattern regardless of the cause of stress.

As shown in Figure 4 on page 493, the GAS has three phases. The first stage—*alarm and mobilization*—occurs when people become aware of the presence of a stressor. On a biological level, the sympathetic nervous system becomes energized, helping a person cope initially with the stressor.

However, if the stressor persists, people move into the second response stage: *resistance*. During this stage, the body prepares to fight the stressor. During resistance, people use a variety of means to cope with the stressor—sometimes successfully but at a cost of some degree of physical or psychological well-being. For example, a student who faces the stress of failing several courses might spend long hours studying, seeking to cope with the stress.

If resistance is inadequate, people enter the last stage of the GAS: *exhaustion.* During the exhaustion stage, a person's ability to adapt to the stressor declines to the point where negative consequences of stress appear: physical illness and psychological symptoms in the form of an inability to concentrate, heightened irritability, or, in

General adaptation syndrome (GAS): A theory developed by Hans Selye that suggests that a person's response to a stressor consists of three stages: alarm and mobilization, resistance, and exhaustion.

How Stressful Is Your Life?

Test your level of stress by answering these questions, and adding the score from each box. Questions apply to the last month only. A key below will help you determine the extent of your stress.

1. How often have you been upset because of something that happened unexpectedly?
   [3] 0 = never, 1 = almost never, 2 = sometimes, 3 = fairly often, 4 = very often

2. How often have you felt that you were unable to control the important things in your life?
   [1] 0 = never, 1 = almost never, 2 = sometimes, 3 = fairly often, 4 = very often

3. How often have you felt nervous and "stressed"?
   [2] 0 = never, 1 = almost never, 2 = sometimes, 3 = fairly often, 4 = very often

4. How often have you felt confident about your ability to handle your personal problems?
   [2] 4 = never, 3 = almost never, 2 = sometimes, 1 = fairly often, 0 = very often

5. How often have you felt that things were going your way?
   [3] 4 = never, 3 = almost never, 2 = sometimes, 1 = fairly often, 0 = very often

6. How often have you been able to control irritations in your life?
   [3] 4 = never, 3 = almost never, 2 = sometimes, 1 = fairly often, 0 = very often

7. How often have you found that you could not cope with all the things that you had to do?
   [1] 0 = never, 1 = almost never, 2 = sometimes, 3 = fairly often, 4 = very often

8. How often have you felt that you were on top of things?
   [2] 4 = never, 3 = almost never, 2 = sometimes, 1 = fairly often, 0 = very often

9. How often have you been angered because of things that were outside your control?
   [2] 0 = never, 1 = almost never, 2 = sometimes, 3 = fairly often, 4 = very often

10. How often have you felt difficulties were piling up so high that you could not overcome them?
    [1] 0 = never, 1 = almost never, 2 = sometimes, 3 = fairly often, 4 = very often

How You Measure Up:

Stress levels vary among individuals—compare your total score to the averages below:

AGE		GENDER	
18–29	14.2	Men	12.1
30–44	13.0	Women	13.7
45–54	12.6		
55–64	11.9		
65 & over	12.0		

MARITAL STATUS

Widowed	12.6
Married or living with a partner	12.4
Single or never wed	14.1
Divorced	14.7
Separated	16.6

FIGURE 3 To get a sense of the level of stress in your life, complete this questionnaire. (Source: Cohen, 1999.)

severe cases, disorientation and a loss of touch with reality. In a sense, people wear out, and their physical reserves are used up.

How do people move out of the third stage after they have entered it? In some cases, exhaustion allows people to avoid a stressor. For example, people who become ill from overwork may be excused from their duties for a time, giving them a temporary respite from their responsibilities. At least for a time, then, the immediate stress is reduced.

The GAS has had a substantial impact on our understanding of stress. By suggesting that the exhaustion of resources in the third stage produces biological damage, it provides a specific explanation of how stress can lead to illness. Furthermore, the GAS can be applied to both people and nonhuman species.

Selye's theory has not gone unchallenged. For example, whereas the theory suggests that regardless of the stressor, the biological reaction is similar, some health psychologists disagree. They believe that people's biological responses are specific to the way they appraise a stressful event. If a stressor is seen as unpleasant but not unusual, then the biological response may be different than if the stressor is seen as unpleasant, out of the ordinary, and unanticipated. This perspective has led to an increased focus on psychoneuroimmunology (Lazarus, 2000; Taylor et al., 2000; Gaab et al., 2005).

| | 1. Alarm and mobilization
Meeting and
resisting stressor. | 2. Resistance
Coping with stress and
resistance to stressor. | 3. Exhaustion
Negative consequences of
stress (such as illness) occur
when coping is inadequate. |

Stressor

FIGURE 4 The general adaptation syndrome (GAS) suggests that there are three major stages to stress responses. (Source: Selye, 1976.)

PSYCHONEUROIMMUNOLOGY AND STRESS

Contemporary health psychologists specializing in psychoneuroimmunology (PNI) have taken a broader approach to stress. Focusing on the outcomes of stress, they have identified three main consequences (see Figure 5).

First, stress has direct physiological results, including an increase in blood pressure, an increase in hormonal activity, and an overall decline in the functioning of the immune system. Second, stress leads people to engage in behavior that is harmful to their health, including increased nicotine, drug, and alcohol use; poor eating habits; and decreased sleep. Finally, stress produces indirect consequences that result in declines in health: a reduction in the likelihood of obtaining health care and decreased compliance with medical advice when it is sought (Gevirtz, 2000; McCabe et al., 2000; Marsland et al., 2002; Sapolsky, 2003; Broman, 2005).

Why is stress so damaging to the immune system? One reason is that stress may overstimulate the immune system. Rather than fighting invading bacteria, viruses, and other foreign invaders, it may begin to attack the body itself, damaging healthy tissue. When that happens, it can lead to disorders such as arthritis and an allergic reaction.

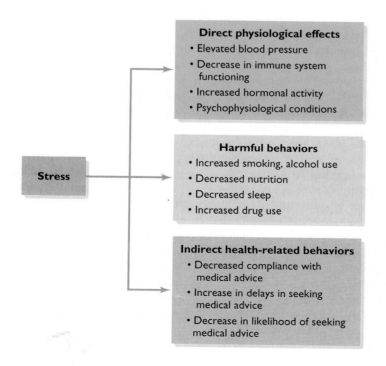

Direct physiological effects
- Elevated blood pressure
- Decrease in immune system functioning
- Increased hormonal activity
- Psychophysiological conditions

Harmful behaviors
- Increased smoking, alcohol use
- Decreased nutrition
- Decreased sleep
- Increased drug use

Indirect health-related behaviors
- Decreased compliance with medical advice
- Increase in delays in seeking medical advice
- Decrease in likelihood of seeking medical advice

Stress

FIGURE 5 Three major types of consequences result from stress: direct physiological effects, harmful behaviors, and indirect health-related behaviors. (Source: Adapted from Baum, 1994.)

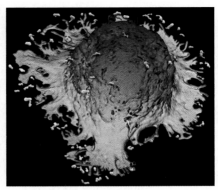

The ability to fight off disease is related to psychological factors. Here a cell from the body's immune system engulfs and destroys disease-producing bacteria.

Coping: The efforts to control, reduce, or learn to tolerate the threats that lead to stress.

Stress can also decrease the immune system response, permitting germs that produce colds to reproduce more easily or allowing cancer cells to spread more rapidly. In normal circumstances, our bodies produce *lymphocytes,* specialized white blood cells that fight disease, at an extraordinary rate—some 10 million every few seconds—and it is possible that stress can alter this level of production (Miller & Cohen, 2001; Cohen, Hamrich, & Rodriguez, 2002; Dougall & Baum, 2004; Segerstrom & Miller, 2004).

Coping with Stress

Stress is a normal part of life—and not necessarily a completely bad part. For example, without stress, we might not be sufficiently motivated to complete the activities we need to accomplish. However, it is also clear that too much stress can take a toll on physical and psychological health. How do people deal with stress? Is there a way to reduce its negative effects?

Efforts to control, reduce, or learn to tolerate the threats that lead to stress are known as **coping.** We habitually use certain coping responses to deal with stress. Most of the time, we're not aware of these responses—just as we may be unaware of the minor stressors of life until they build up to aversive levels (Snyder, 1999; Folkman & Moscowitz, 2000).

We also have other, more direct, and potentially more positive ways of coping with stress, which fall into two main categories (Folkman & Moskowitz, 2000, 2004):

- *Emotion-focused coping.* In *emotion-focused coping,* people try to manage their emotions in the face of stress, seeking to change the way they feel about or perceive a problem. Examples of emotion-focused coping include strategies such as accepting sympathy from others and looking at the bright side of a situation.
- *Problem-focused coping. Problem-focused coping* attempts to modify the stressful problem or source of stress. Problem-focused strategies lead to changes in behavior or to the development of a plan of action to deal with stress. Starting a study group to improve poor classroom performance is an example of problem-focused coping. In addition, one might take a time-out from stress by creating positive events. For example, taking a day off from caring for a relative with a serious, chronic illness to go a spa can bring significant relief from stress.

People often employ several types of coping strategies simultaneously. However, they use emotion-focused strategies more frequently when they perceive circumstances as being unchangeable and problem-focused approaches more often in situations they see as relatively modifiable (Folkman & Moskowitz, 2000; Stanton et al., 2000; Penley, Tomaka, & Wiebe, 2002).

Simply knowing about emotion-focused and problem-focused strategies can be helpful in dealing with stress. For example, in one experiment, volunteers were taken as simulated hostages in a highly stressful situation in which the terrorists were convincingly portrayed by FBI agents. Hostages who had received pre-stress training in emotion-focused coping strategies, compared to those trained in problem-focused coping strategies, were able to deal with the situation more effectively, adjusting better to the stress (Auerbach et al., 1994).

Other forms of coping are less successful. One of the least effective forms of coping is avoidant coping. In *avoidant coping,* a person may use wishful thinking to reduce stress or use more direct escape routes, such as drug use, alcohol use, and overeating. An example of wishful thinking to avoid a test would be to say to oneself, "Maybe it will snow so hard tomorrow that the test will be canceled." Alternatively, a person might get drunk to avoid a problem. Either way, avoidant coping usually results in a postponement of dealing with a stressful situation, and often makes it even worse (Appelhans & Schmeck, 2002; Roesch et al., 2005).

Another way of dealing with stress occurs unconsciously through the use of defense mechanisms. As we discussed when we considered the topic of personality, *defense mechanisms* are unconscious strategies that people use to reduce anxiety by concealing the source from themselves and others. Defense mechanisms permit people to avoid stress by acting as if the stress were not even there. For example, one study examined California college students who lived in dormitories close to a geological fault. Those who lived in dorms that were known to be unlikely to withstand an earthquake were significantly *more* likely to doubt experts' predictions of an impending earthquake than were those who lived in safer structures (Lehman & Taylor, 1988).

Another defense mechanism used to cope with stress is *emotional insulation,* in which a person stops experiencing any emotions at all, thereby remaining unaffected and unmoved by both positive and negative experiences. The problem with defense mechanisms, of course, is that they do not deal with reality but merely hide the problem.

LEARNED HELPLESSNESS

Have you ever faced an intolerable situation that you just couldn't resolve, and you finally just gave up and accepted things the way they were? This example illustrates one of the possible consequences of being in an environment in which control over a situation is not possible—a state that produces learned helplessness. According to psychologist Martin Seligman, **learned helplessness** occurs when people conclude that unpleasant or aversive stimuli cannot be controlled—a view of the world that becomes so ingrained that they cease trying to remedy the aversive circumstances, even if they actually can exert some influence on the situation (Seligman, 1975; Peterson, Maier, & Seligman, 1993). Victims of learned helplessness have concluded that there is no link between the responses they make and the outcomes that occur.

> **Learned helplessness:** A state in which people conclude that unpleasant or aversive stimuli cannot be controlled—a view of the world that becomes so ingrained that they cease trying to remedy the aversive circumstances, even if they actually can exert some influence.

Consider, for example, what often happens to elderly persons when they are placed in a nursing home or hospital. One of the most striking features of their new environment is that they are no longer independent: They do not have control over the most basic activities in their lives. They are told what and when to eat and told when they may watch TV or participate in recreational activities. In addition, their sleeping schedules are arranged by someone else. It is not hard to see how this loss of control can have negative effects on people suddenly placed, often reluctantly, in such a situation.

The results of this loss of control and the ensuing stress are frequently poorer health and even the likelihood of earlier death. These outcomes were confirmed in a classic experiment conducted in a nursing home in which elderly residents in one group were encouraged to make more choices and take greater control of their day-to-day activities (Langer & Janis, 1979). As a result, the members of that group were more active and happier than were those in a comparison group of residents who were encouraged to let the nursing home's staff take care of them. Moreover, an analysis of the residents' medical records revealed that six months after the experiment, the group encouraged to be self-sufficient showed significantly greater health improvement than did the comparison group. Even more startling was difference in the death rates of the two groups: Eighteen months after the experiment began, only 15 percent of the "independent" group had died—compared with 30 percent of the comparison group.

Other research confirms that learned helplessness has negative consequences, and not just for elderly people. People of all ages report more physical symptoms and depression when they perceive that they have little or no control than they do when they feel a sense of control over a situation (Joiner & Wagner, 1995; Shnek et al., 1995; Chou, 2005).

COPING STYLES: THE HARDY PERSONALITY

Most of us cope with stress in a characteristic manner, employing a *coping style* that represents our general tendency to deal with stress in a specific way. For example, you may know people who habitually react to even the smallest amount of stress with hysteria, and others who calmly confront even the greatest stress in an unflappable manner. These kinds of people clearly have quite different coping styles (Gallaher, 1996; Taylor & Aspinwall, 1996; Taylor, 2003; Kato & Pedersen, 2005).

Among those who cope with stress most successfully are people who are equipped with **hardiness,** a personality characteristic associated with a lower rate of stress-related illness. Hardiness consists of three components (Kobasa et al., 1994; Baumgartner, 2002):

> **Hardiness:** A personality characteristic associated with a lower rate of stress-related illness, consisting of three components: commitment, challenge, and control.

"Today, we examined our life style, we evaluated our diet and our exercise program, and we also assessed our behavioral patterns. Then we felt we needed a drink."

- *Commitment.* Commitment is a tendency to throw ourselves into whatever we are doing with a sense that our activities are important and meaningful.
- *Challenge.* Hardy people believe that change, rather than stability, is the standard condition of life. To them, the anticipation of change serves as an incentive rather than a threat to their security.
- *Control.* Hardiness is marked by a sense of control—the perception that people can influence the events in their lives.

Hardy individuals approach stress in an optimistic manner and take direct action to learn about and deal with stressors, thereby changing stressful events into less threatening ones. As a consequence, hardiness acts as a defense against stress-related illness.

For those who confront the most profound difficulties, such as the death of a loved one and a permanent injury such as paralysis after an accident, a key ingredient in their psychological recovery is their degree of resilience. *Resilience* is the ability to withstand, overcome, and actually thrive after profound adversity (Werner, 1995; Ryff & Singer, 2003; Bonanno, 2004; Norlander, Von Schedvin, & Archer, 2005).

Resilient people are generally easygoing and good-natured and have good social skills. They are usually independent, and they have a sense of control over their own destiny—even if fate has dealt them a devastating blow. In short, they work with what they have and make the best of whatever situation they find themselves in (Humphreys, 2003; Spencer, 2003; Deshields et al., 2005; Friborg et al., 2005).

SOCIAL SUPPORT: TURNING TO OTHERS

Social support: A mutual network of caring, interested others.

Our relationships with others also help us cope with stress. Researchers have found that **social support,** the knowledge that we are part of a mutual network of caring, interested others, enables us to experience lower levels of stress and be better able to cope with the stress we do undergo (Bolger, Zuckerman, & Kessler, 2000; McCabe et al., 2000; Cohen, 2004; Martin & Brantley, 2004).

The social and emotional support people provide each other helps in dealing with stress in several ways. For instance, such support demonstrates that a person is an important and valued member of a social network. Similarly, other people can provide information and advice about appropriate ways of dealing with stress (Day & Livingstone, 2003; Lindorff, 2005).

Finally, people who are part of a social support network can provide actual goods and services to help others in stressful situations. For instance, they can supply a person whose house has burned down with temporary living quarters, or they can help a student who is experiencing stress because of poor academic performance study for a test (Lepore, Ragan, & Jones, 2000; Natvig, Albrektsen, & Ovamstrom, 2003; also see the *Applying Psychology in the 21st Century* box).

Surprisingly, the benefits of social support are not limited to the comfort provided by other humans. One study found that owners of pets were less likely to require medical care after exposure to stressors than were those without pets! Dogs, in particular, helped diminish the effects of stress (Siegel, 1990, 1993).

BECOMING AN INFORMED CONSUMER
of Psychology

Effective Coping Strategies

How can we deal with the stress in our lives? Although there is no universal solution, because effective coping depends on the nature of the stressor and the degree to which it can be controlled, here are some general guidelines (Zeidner & Endler, 1996; Aspinwall & Taylor, 1997; Folkman & Moskowitz, 2000):

- *Turn threat into challenge.* When a stressful situation might be controllable, the best coping strategy is to treat the

The Value of Social Support: Sick and Lonely—Why the Two Go Together

You are a first-year college student. You haven't made many friends yet, and you're not part of an established social network. Feeling lonely is an everyday experience.

For first-year college students, loneliness, which is not uncommon, can be psychologically painful. In addition, according to the findings of a recent study on the importance of social support, it can have a negative effect on the immune system. In the study health psychologists Sheldon Cohen and colleagues traced the effectiveness of flu shots in 83 healthy first-year college students. After carefully assessing the students' health-related behaviors, including their alcohol use, physical activity, and sleep, the researchers also examined the students' internal physical state by taking saliva samples four times a day to measure the concentration of cortisol, a stress-related hormone (Pressman et al., 2005).

The participants in the study also provided frequent accounts of their perceived stress, emotions, and loneliness, by responding to the random beeps of a handheld computer four times each day. In addition, they completed loneliness questionnaires and surveys designed to gauge the extent of their social networks.

The results showed a clear relationship between loneliness and psychological stress: the greater the reported loneliness, the more negative the emotions and the greater the stress experienced. Most interestingly, participants who were the loneliest and felt most socially isolated were least responsive to the flu shot. Measures of the amount of antibodies showed that lonely, isolated students had the lowest levels of antibodies, meaning that they were the most susceptible to the flu. In contrast, flu shots were most effective in providing a defense against the flu for those students who had the largest social networks and were the least lonely.

The results of this study reinforce the importance of social support in maintaining health. It suggests that college administrators ought to encourage students to be active in community service, clubs, and sports and to develop social networks. The results also have implications for the effectiveness of flu shots for those in late adulthood—often the individuals in greatest danger from a bout of flu. During late adulthood, immune systems are often at their weakest point. Combine this weak-

Loneliness is not only psychologically painful, but also is unhealthy.

ness with the isolation that often occurs during old age, and the elderly are particularly at risk (Adelson, 2005).

RETHINK

What is it about social support that provides health benefits? Knowing the relationship between loneliness, social isolation, and responsiveness to flu shots, what interventions might you suggest for first-year college students?

---

situation as a challenge, focusing on ways to control it. For instance, if you experience stress because your car is always breaking down, you might take a course in auto mechanics and learn to deal directly with the car's problems.

- *Make a threatening situation less threatening.* When a stressful situation seems to be uncontrollable, a different approach must be taken. It is possible to change one's appraisal of the situation, view it in a different light, and modify one's attitude toward it. The old truism "Look for the silver lining in every cloud" is supported by research (Salovey et al., 2000; Smith & Lazarus, 2001; Cheng & Cheung, 2005).
- *Change your goals.* When one is faced with an uncontrollable situation, a reasonable strategy is to adopt new goals that are practical in view of the particular situation. For example, a dancer who has been in an automobile accident and has lost full use of her legs may no longer aspire to a career in dance but might modify her goals and try to become a dance instructor.
- *Take physical action.* Changing your physiological reaction to stress can help with coping. For example, biofeedback (in which a person learns to control internal physiological processes through conscious thought) can alter basic physiological processes, allowing people to reduce blood pressure, heart rate, and other consequences of heightened stress. In addition, exercise can be effective in reducing stress. Regular exercise improves overall health and may even reduce the risk of certain diseases, such as breast cancer. Finally, exercise gives people a sense

of control over their bodies, as well as a feeling of accomplishment (Tkachuk & Martin, 1999; Hong, 2000b; Langreth, 2000; Spencer, 2003).

- *Prepare for stress before it happens.* A final strategy for coping with stress is *proactive coping*, anticipating and preparing for stress *before* it is encountered. For example, if you're expecting to go through a one-week period in which you must take a number of major tests, you can try to arrange your schedule so you have more time to study. Through proactive coping, people can ready themselves for upcoming stressful events and thereby reduce their consequences (Aspinwall & Taylor, 1997).

RECAP/EVALUATE/RETHINK

RECAP

How is health psychology a union between medicine and psychology?

- The field of health psychology considers how psychology can be applied to the prevention, diagnosis, and treatment of medical problems. (p. 486)

What is stress, how does it affect us, and how can we best cope with it?

- Stress is a response to threatening or challenging environmental conditions. People encounter stressors—the circumstances that produce stress—of both a positive and a negative nature. (p. 487)
- The way an environmental circumstance is interpreted affects whether it will be considered stressful. Still, there are general classes of events that provoke stress: cataclysmic events, personal stressors, and background stressors (daily hassles). (pp. 488–489)
- Stress produces immediate physiological reactions. In the short term those reactions may be adaptive, but in the long term they may have negative consequences, including the development of psychophysiological disorders. (p. 491)
- The consequences of stress can be explained in part by Selye's general adaptation syndrome (GAS), which suggests that there are three stages in stress responses: alarm and mobilization, resistance, and exhaustion. (p. 491)
- Coping with stress can take a number of forms, including the unconscious use of defense mechanisms and the use of emotion-focused or problem-focused coping strategies. (p. 494)
- Stress can be reduced by developing a sense of control over one's circumstances. In some cases, however, people develop a state of learned helplessness. (p. 495)

EVALUATE

1. _____ is defined as a response to challenging or threatening events.
2. Match each portion of the GAS with its definition.
   1. Alarm and mobilization
   2. Exhaustion
   3. Resistance
   a. Ability to adapt to stress diminishes; symptoms appear.
   b. Activation of sympathetic nervous system.
   c. Various strategies are used to cope with a stressor.
3. Stressors that affect a single person and produce an immediate major reaction are known as
   a. Personal stressors
   b. Psychic stressors
   c. Cataclysmic stressors
   d. Daily stressors
4. People with the personality characteristic of _____ seem to be better able to successfully combat stressors.

RETHINK

1. Why are cataclysmic stressors less stressful in the long run than are other types of stressors? Does the reason relate to the coping phenomenon known as social support? How?
2. *From the perspective of a social worker:* How would you help people deal with and avoid stress in their everyday lives? How might you encourage people to create social support networks?

Answers to Evaluate Questions

1. stress; 2. 1-b; 2-a; 3-c; 3. a; 4. hardiness.

KEY TERMS

health psychology p. 487
psychoneuroimmunology (PNI) p. 487
stress p. 487
cataclysmic events p. 488

personal stressors p. 488
posttraumatic stress disorder (PTSD) p. 488
background stressors ("daily hassles") p. 489

psychophysiological disorders p. 491
general adaptation syndrome (GAS) p. 491
coping p. 494

learned helplessness p. 495
hardiness p. 495
social support p. 496

Psychological Aspects of Illness and Well-Being

Key Concept

How do psychological factors affect health-related problems such as coronary heart disease, cancer, and smoking?

Once a week they meet to talk, to cry, sometimes to laugh together. "Is the pain still worse in the mornings?" Margaret asks Kate today.

A petite, graceful woman in her late forties, Kate shakes her head no. "It's getting bad all the time," she says in a voice raw with worry and fatigue. A few weeks ago she learned that the cancer that began in her breast had spread into her bones. Since then she's hardly slept. She knows, as do the other women in the group, that her prognosis isn't good. "Sometimes I'm afraid I'm not going to do that well because it all came on so fast," she tells them. "It's like being in the ocean and the waves are just coming too fast, and you can't get your breath."

They nod in tacit understanding, eight women sitting in a loose circle of chairs here in a small, sparely furnished room at Stanford University Medical Center. They know. All of them have been diagnosed with recurrent breast cancer. . . .

They gather here each Wednesday afternoon to talk with each other and to listen. It's a chance to discuss their fears and find some small comfort, a time to feel they're not alone. And in some way that no one has been able to explain, it may be keeping them alive (Jaret, 1992, p. 87).

As recently as two decades ago, most psychologists and health care providers would have scoffed at the notion that a discussion group could improve a cancer patient's chances of survival. Today, however, such methods have gained increasing acceptance.

Growing evidence suggests that psychological factors have a substantial impact both on major health problems that were once seen in purely physiological terms and on our everyday sense of health, well-being, and happiness. We'll consider the psychological components of three major health problems—heart disease, cancer, and smoking—and then consider the nature of people's well-being and happiness.

The A's, B's, and D's of Coronary Heart Disease

Tim knew it wasn't going to be his day when he got stuck in traffic behind a slow-moving farm truck. How could the driver dawdle like that? Didn't he have anything of any importance to do? Things didn't get any better when Tim arrived on campus and discovered the library didn't have the books he needed. He could almost feel the tension rising. "I need that material to finish my paper," he thought to himself. He knew that meant he wouldn't be able to get his paper done early, and that meant he wouldn't have the time he wanted to revise the paper. He wanted it to be a first-class paper. This time Tim wanted to get a better grade than his roommate, Luis; although Luis didn't know it, Tim felt they were in direct competition and was always trying to better him, whether it was academically or just playing cards. "In fact," Tim mused to himself, "I feel like I'm in competition with everyone, no matter what I'm doing."

Type A behavior pattern: A cluster of behaviors involving hostility, competitiveness, time urgency, and feeling driven.

Type B behavior pattern: A cluster of behaviors characterized by a patient, cooperative, noncompetitive, and nonaggressive manner.

www.mhhe.com/feldmanup8

PsychInteractive Online

Type A and B Behavior

Have you, like Tim, ever seethed impatiently at being caught behind a slow-moving vehicle, felt anger and frustration at not finding material you needed at the library, or experienced a sense of competitiveness with your classmates?

Many of us experience these sorts of feelings at one time or another, but for some people they represent a pervasive, characteristic set of personality traits known as the Type A behavior pattern. The **Type A behavior pattern** is a cluster of behaviors involving hostility, competitiveness, time urgency, and feeling driven. In contrast, the **Type B behavior pattern** is characterized by a patient, cooperative, noncompetitive, and nonaggressive manner. It's important to keep in mind that Type A and Type B represent the ends of a continuum, and most people fall somewhere in between the two endpoints. Few people are purely a Type A or a Type B. (See Figure 1 and complete the PsychInteractive exercise to learn more about Type A and B tendencies.)

Type A's lead fast-paced, driven lives. They put in longer hours at work than do Type B's and are impatient with other people's performance, which they typically perceive as too slow. They also engage in "multitasking," doing several activities simultaneously, such as running on a treadmill, watching television, and reading a magazine.

The importance of the Type A behavior pattern lies in its links to coronary heart disease. Men who display the Type A pattern develop coronary heart disease twice as often and suffer significantly more fatal heart attacks than do those classified as having the Type B pattern. Moreover, the Type A pattern predicts who is going to develop heart disease at least as well as—and independently of—any other single fac-

Type Yourself

To get an idea of whether you have the characteristics of a Type A or Type B personality, answer the following questions

1. When you listen to someone talking and this person takes too long to come to the point how often do you feel like hurrying the person along?
    _____✓_____ Frequently
    _____ Occasionally
    _____ Never
2. Do you ever set deadlines of quotas for yourself at work or at home?
    _____ No
    _____✓_____ Yes, but only occasionally
    _____ Yes, once a week or more
3. Would people you know well agree that you tend to get irritated easily?
    _____ Definitely yes
    _____✓_____ Probably yes
    _____ Probably no
    _____ Definitely no
4. Would people who know you well agree that you tend to do most things in a hurry?
    _____✓_____ Definitely yes
    _____ Probably yes
    _____ Probably no
    _____ Definitely no

Scoring: The more frequently your answers reflect affirmative responses the more Type A characteristics you hold.

FIGURE 1 No one is totally a Type A or Type B personality; rather, everyone is a combination of the two types. Take this quick test to determine which type is strongest in you. (Source: Adapted from Jenkins, Zyzanski, & Rosenman, 1978.)

tor, including age, blood pressure, smoking habits, and cholesterol levels in the body (Rosenman et al., 1976, 1994; Wielgosz & Nolan, 2000).

However, it turns out that not every component of the Type A behavior pattern is bad. The key component linking the Type A behavior pattern and heart disease is hostility. Although competition, time urgency, and feeling driven may produce stress and potentially other health and emotional problems, they aren't linked to coronary heart disease in the way that hostility is. In short, hostility seems to be the lethal component of the Type A behavior pattern (Mittleman et al., 1995; McCabe et al., 2000; Williams et al., 2000a; Boyle et al., 2005).

Why is hostility so toxic? The most convincing theory is that hostility produces excessive physiological arousal in stressful situations. That arousal, in turn, results in increased production of the hormones epinephrine and norepinephrine, as well as increases in heart rate and blood pressure. Such an exaggerated physiological response ultimately produces an increased incidence of coronary heart disease (Black & Barbutt, 2002; Kahn, 2004; Eaker et al., 2004; Demaree & Everhart, 2004).

It's important to keep in mind that not everyone who displays Type A behaviors is destined to have coronary heart disease. For one thing, a firm association between Type A behaviors and coronary heart disease has not been established for women; most findings pertain to males, not to females. In addition, other types of negative emotions, besides the hostility found in Type A behavior, appear to be related to heart attacks. For example, psychologist Johan Denollet has found evidence that what he calls *Type D*—for "distressed"—behavior is linked to coronary heart disease. In his view, insecurity, anxiety, and the negative outlook displayed by Type D's puts them at risk for repeated heart attacks (Denollet & Brutsaert, 1998; Denollet, 2005; Schiffer et al., 2005).

Furthermore, the evidence relating Type A behavior (and other personality types) to coronary heart disease is correlational. Consequently, we cannot say for sure whether Type A behavior *causes* heart disease or whether, instead, some other factor causes both heart disease and Type A behavior. In fact, rather than focusing on Type A behavior as the cause of heart disease, it may make more sense to ask whether Type B behavior *prevents* heart disease (Orth-Gomér, Chesney, & Wenger, 1996; Snieder et al., 2002; Trigo, Silva, & Rocha, 2005).

Psychological Aspects of Cancer

Hardly any disease is feared more than cancer. Most people think of cancer in terms of lingering pain, and being diagnosed with the disease is typically viewed as receiving a death sentence.

Although a diagnosis of cancer is not as grim as one might at first suspect—several kinds of cancer have a high cure rate if detected early enough—cancer remains the second leading cause of death after coronary heart disease. The precise trigger for the disease is not well understood, but the process by which cancer spreads is straightforward. Certain cells in the body become altered and multiply rapidly and in an uncontrolled fashion. As those cells grow, they form tumors, which, if left unchecked, suck nutrients from healthy cells and body tissue, ultimately destroying the body's ability to function properly.

Although the processes involved in the spread of cancer are basically physiological, accumulating evidence suggests that the emotional responses of cancer patients to their disease may have a critical effect on its course. For example, one experiment found that people who adopt a fighting spirit are more likely to recover than are those who pessimistically suffer and resign themselves to death (Pettingale et al., 1985). The study analyzed the survival rates of women who had undergone the removal of a breast because of cancer.

FIGURE 2 The relationship between women's psychological response to breast cancer three months after surgery and their survival ten years after the operation (Pettingale et al., 1985). What implications do these findings have for the treatment of people with cancer?

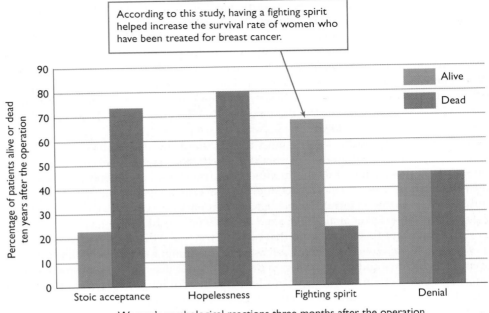

According to this study, having a fighting spirit helped increase the survival rate of women who have been treated for breast cancer.

Percentage of patients alive or dead ten years after the operation

Women's psychological reactions three months after the operation

Stoic acceptance   Hopelessness   Fighting spirit   Denial

Alive   Dead

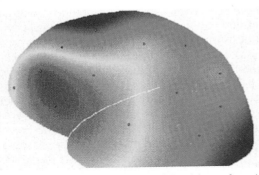

FIGURE 3 Higher activation of the right prefrontal lobes of the brain in response to negative emotions (red area) was associated with weaker immune system response. (Source: Rosenkranz et al., 2003, Figure 2.)

The results suggested that the survival rates were related to the psychological response of the women three months after surgery (see Figure 2). Women who stoically accepted their fate, trying not to complain, and those who felt the situation was hopeless and that nothing could be done showed the lowest survival rates; most of those women were dead after ten years. In comparison, the survival rates of women who showed a fighting spirit (predicting that they would overcome the disease and planning to take steps to prevent its recurrence) and the survival rates of women who (erroneously) denied that they had ever had cancer (saying that the breast removal was merely a preventive step) were significantly higher. In sum, according to this study, cancer patients with a positive attitude were more likely to survive than were those with a more negative one.

On the other hand, other research contradicts the notion that the course of cancer is affected by patients' attitudes and emotions. For example, some findings show that although a "fighting spirit" leads to better coping, the long-term survival rate is no better than it is for patients with a less positive attitude (Watson et al., 1999).

Despite the conflicting evidence, health psychologists believe that patients' emotions may at least partially determine the course of their disease. Specifically, psychologists specializing in psychoneuroimmunology (PNI) have found that a person's emotional state affects the immune system in the same way that stress affects it. For instance, in one brain imaging study, people who showed the greatest right prefrontal activation during a task involving negative emotions showed a weaker immune system response to a flu shot six months later (Rosenkranz et al., 2003; see Figure 3).

In the case of cancer, it is possible that positive emotional responses may help generate specialized "killer" cells that help control the size and spread of cancerous tumors. Conversely, negative emotions may suppress the ability of those cells to fight tumors (Andersen, Kiecolt-Glaser, & Glaser, 1994; Seligman, 1995; Schedlowski & Tewes, 1999).

Other research suggests that "joy"—referring to mental resilience and vigor—is related to the likelihood of survival of patients with recurrent breast cancer. Similarly, cancer patients who are characteristically optimistic report less distress throughout the course of their treatment (Levy et al., 1988; Carver et al., 2000; Helgeson, Snyder, & Seltman, 2004).

Is a particular personality type linked to cancer? Some findings suggest that cancer patients are less emotionally reactive, suppress anger, and lack outlets for emotional release. However, the data are too tentative and inconsistent to suggest firm conclusions about a link between personality characteristics and cancer. Certainly no conclusive evidence suggests that people who develop cancer would not have done so if their personality had been of a different sort or if their attitudes had been more positive (Smith, 1988; Zevon & Corn, 1990; Holland & Lewis, 2001).

What is increasingly clear, however, is that certain types of psychological therapy have the potential for extending the lives of cancer patients. For example, the results of one study showed that women with breast cancer who received psychological treatment lived at least a year and a half longer, and experienced less anxiety and pain, than did women who did not participate in therapy. Research on patients with other health problems, such as heart disease, also has found that therapy can be beneficial, both psychologically and medically (Spiegel, 1993, 1996b; Galavotti et al., 1997; Frasure-Smith, Lesperance, & Talajic, 2000).

Smoking

Would you walk into a convenience store and buy an item with a label warning you that its use could kill you? Although most people would probably answer no, millions make such a purchase every day: a pack of cigarettes. Furthermore, they do this despite clear, well-publicized evidence that smoking is linked to cancer, heart attacks, strokes, bronchitis, emphysema, and a host of other serious illnesses. Smoking is the greatest preventable cause of death in the United States; one in five U.S. deaths is caused by smoking. Worldwide, 3 million people die prematurely each year from the effects of smoking (Mackay & Eriksen, 2002).

WHY PEOPLE SMOKE

Why do people smoke despite all the evidence showing that it is bad for their health? It is not that they are somehow unaware of the link between smoking and disease; surveys show that most *smokers* agree with the statement "Cigarette smoking frequently causes disease and death." And almost three-quarters of the 48 million smokers in the United States say they would like to quit (CDC, 1994; Wetter et al., 1998).

Heredity seems to determine, in part, whether people will become smokers, how much they will smoke, and how easily they can quit. Genetics also influences how susceptible people are to the harmful effects of smoking. For instance, there is an almost 50 percent higher rate of lung cancer in African American smokers than in white smokers. This difference may be due to genetically produced variations in the efficiency with which enzymes are able to reduce the effects of the cancer-causing chemicals in tobacco smoke (Heath & Madden, 1995; Pomerlau, 1995; Li et al., 2003).

However, although genetics plays a role in smoking, most research suggests that environmental factors are the primary cause of the habit. Smoking at first may be seen as "cool" or sophisticated, as a rebellious act, or as facilitating calm performance in stressful situations. In addition, smoking a cigarette is sometimes viewed as a "rite of passage" for adolescents, undertaken at the urging of friends and viewed as a sign of growing up. But this may be changing: Since 1997, the percentage of U.S. teenagers who smoke has declined significantly (Koval et al., 2000; Wagner & Atkins, 2000; Johnston, O'Malley, & Bachman, 2003).

Ultimately, smoking becomes a habit. People begin to label themselves smokers, and smoking becomes part of their self-concept. Moreover, they become dependent

Although smoking is prohibited in an increasing number of places, it remains a substantial social problem.

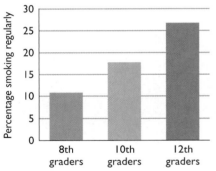

FIGURE 4 Although smoking among teenagers is lower than twenty years ago, a significant number still report smoking regularly. What factors might account for the continued high use of tobacco by teenagers, despite the increase in antismoking advertising? (Source: Monitoring the Future Study, 2005.)

physiologically as a result of smoking, because nicotine, a primary ingredient of tobacco, is highly addictive. Ultimately, a complex relationship develops among smoking, nicotine levels, and a smoker's emotional state, in which a certain nicotine level becomes associated with a positive emotional state. As a result, people smoke in an effort to regulate *both* emotional states and nicotine levels in the blood (Leventhal & Cleary, 1980; Gilbert, 1995; Kassel, Stroud, & Paronis, 2003).

QUITTING SMOKING

Because smoking has both psychological and biological components, few habits are as difficult to break. Long-term successful treatment typically occurs in just 15 percent of those who try to stop smoking, and once smoking becomes a habit, it is as hard to stop as an addiction to cocaine or heroin. In fact, some of the biochemical reactions to nicotine are similar to those to cocaine, amphetamines, and morphine. Many people try to quit and fail (Glassman & Koob, 1996; Piasecki et al., 1997; Harris Poll, 2000; Vanasse, Niyonsenga, & Courteau, 2004).

Among the most effective tools for ending the smoking habit are drugs that replace the nicotine found in cigarettes. Whether in the form of gum, patches, nasal sprays, or inhalers, these products provide a dose of nicotine that reduces dependence on cigarettes. Another approach is exemplified by the drug Zyban, which, rather than replacing nicotine, raises dopamine levels in the brain, thereby reducing the desire to smoke (Rock, 1999; Mitchell, 2000; Barringer & Weaver, 2002; Dalsgaro et al., 2004).

Behavioral strategies, which view smoking as a learned habit and concentrate on changing the smoking response, can also be effective. Initial "cure" rates of 60 percent have been reported, and one year after treatment more than half of those who quit have not resumed smoking. Counseling, either individually or in groups, also increases the rate of success in breaking the habit. The best treatment seems to be a combination of nicotine replacement and counseling. What doesn't work? Going it alone: Only 5 percent of smokers who quit cold-turkey on their own are successful (Wetter et al., 1998; Noble, 1999; Rock, 1999).

In the long term, the most effective means of reducing smoking may be changes in societal norms and attitudes toward the habit. For instance, many cities and towns have made smoking in public places illegal, and legislation banning smoking in places such as college classrooms and buildings—based on strong popular sentiment—is being passed with increasing frequency (Gibson, 1997; Jacobson, Wasserman, & Anderson, 1997).

The long-term effect of the barrage of information regarding the negative consequences of smoking on people's health has been substantial; overall, smoking has declined over the last two decades, particularly among males. Still, more than one-fourth of students enrolled in high school are active smokers by the time they graduate. Among these students, more than 10 percent become active smokers as early as the eighth grade (Johnston, O'Malley, & Bachman, 2003; see Figure 4).

Exploring DIVERSITY

Hucksters of Death: Promoting Smoking Throughout the World

In Dresden, Germany, three women in miniskirts offer passersby a pack of Lucky Strikes and a leaflet that reads: "You just got hold of a nice piece of America." Says a local doctor, "Adolescents time and again receive cigarettes at such promotions."

A Jeep decorated with the Camel logo pulls up to a high school in Buenos Aires. A woman begins handing out free cigarettes to 15- and 16-year-olds during their lunch recess. At a video arcade in Taipei, free American cigarettes are strewn atop each game. At a disco filled with high school students, free packs of Salems are on each table (Ecenbarger, 1993, p. 50).

As the number of smokers has declined in the United States, cigarette manufacturers have turned to new markets in an effort to increase the number of people who smoke. In the process, they have employed some dubious marketing techniques.

For instance, the tobacco company RJ Reynolds developed a new cigarette brand it named Uptown in the early 1990s. Because of the nature of the advertising that initiated the distribution of the cigarette, it soon became apparent that the product was targeted at African Americans (Jhally et al., 1995; Ringold, 1996; Balbach, Gasior, & Barbeau, 2003). Because of the questionable ethics of targeting a potentially life-threatening product to a minority population, the product introduction caused considerable controversy. Ultimately, the secretary of the U.S. Department of Health and Human Services condemned the tactic, and the manufacturer stopped distributing the brand soon afterward.

Because of legal constraints on smoking in the United States, manufacturers have turned their sights to other parts of the world, where they see a fertile market of non-smokers. Although they must often sell cigarettes more cheaply than they do in the United States, the number of potential smokers still makes it financially worthwhile for the tobacco companies. The United States is now the world's largest exporter of cigarettes, providing 20 percent of the world total (Bartecchi, MacKenzie, & Schrier, 1995; Brown, 2001).

Clearly, the push into worldwide markets has been successful. In some Latin American cities, as many as 50 percent of teenagers smoke. Children as young as age 7 smoke in Hong Kong, and 30 percent of children smoked their first whole cigarette before the age of 10 in India, Ghana, Jamaica, and Poland. The World Health Organization predicts that smoking will prematurely kill some 200 million of the world's children, and that ultimately 10 percent of the world's population will die as a result of smoking. Of everyone alive today, 500 million will eventually die from tobacco use. Clearly, smoking remains one of the world's greatest health problems (Mackay & Eriksen, 2002).

In some countries, children as young as 6 smoke regularly.

RECAP/EVALUATE/RETHINK

RECAP

How do psychological factors affect health-related problems such as coronary heart disease, cancer, and smoking?

- Hostility, a key component of the Type A behavior pattern, is linked to coronary heart disease. The Type A behavior pattern is a cluster of behaviors involving hostility, competitiveness, time urgency, and feeling driven. (pp. 500–501)
- Increasing evidence suggests that people's attitudes and emotional responses affect the course of cancer through links to the immune system. (pp. 501–503)
- Smoking, the leading preventable cause of health problems, has proved to be difficult for many smokers to quit, even though most smokers are aware of the dangerous consequences of the behavior. (pp. 503–504)

EVALUATE

1. Type _____ behavior is characterized by cooperativeness and by being easy going; Type _____ behavior is characterized by hostility and competitiveness.

KEY TERMS

Type A behavior pattern p. 500

Type B behavior pattern p. 500

2. The Type A behavior pattern is known to directly cause heart attacks. True or false?
3. A cancer patient's attitude and emotions may affect that person's _____ system, helping or hindering the patient's fight against the disease.
4. Smoking is used to regulate both nicotine levels and emotional states in smokers. True or false?

RETHINK

1. Is there a danger of "blaming the victim" when we argue that the course of cancer can be improved if a person with the disease holds positive attitudes or beliefs, particularly when we consider people with cancer who are not recovering? Why?
2. *From the perspective of a healthcare provider:* What type of advice would you give to your patients about the connections between personality and disease? For example, would you encourage Type A people to become "less Type A" in order to decrease their risk of heart disease?

Answers to Evaluate Questions

1. B, A; 2. false; Type A behavior is related to a higher incidence of coronary heart disease but does not necessarily cause it directly; 3. immune; 4. true

Promoting Health and Wellness

When Stuart Grinspoon first noticed the small lump in his arm, he assumed it was just a bruise from the touch football game he had played the previous week. But as he thought about it more, he considered more serious possibilities and decided that he'd better get it checked out at the university health service. But the visit was less than satisfactory. A shy person, Stuart felt embarrassed talking about his medical condition. Even worse, after answering a string of questions, he couldn't even understand the physician's diagnosis and was too embarrassed to ask for clarification.

Stuart Grinspoon's attitudes toward health care are shared by many of us. We approach physicians the same way we approach auto mechanics. When something goes wrong with the car, we want the mechanic to figure out the problem and then fix it. In the same way, when something isn't working right with our bodies, we want a diagnosis of the problem and then a (hopefully quick) repair.

Yet such an approach ignores the fact that—unlike auto repair—good health care requires taking psychological factors into account. Health psychologists have sought to determine the factors involved in the promotion of good health and, more broadly, a sense of well-being and happiness. Let's take a closer look at two areas they have tackled: producing compliance with health-related advice and identifying the determinants of well-being and happiness.

Following Medical Advice

We're not very good at taking medical advice. Consider these figures:

- As many as 85 percent of patients do not fully comply with a physician's recommendations.
- Between 14 and 21 percent of patients don't fill their drug prescriptions.
- Some 10 percent of adolescent pregnancies result from noncompliance with birth control medication.
- Sixty percent of all patients cannot identify their own medicines.
- From 30 percent to 50 percent of all patients ignore instructions or make errors in taking medication (Zuger, 1998; Christensen & Johnson, 2002; Health Pages, 2003; Colland et al., 2004).

Noncompliance with medical advice can take many forms. For example, patients may fail to show up for scheduled appointments, not follow diets or not give up smoking, or discontinue medication during treatment. In some cases, they fail to take prescribed medicine at all.

Patients also may practice *creative nonadherence,* in which they adjust a treatment prescribed by a physician, relying on their own medical judgment and experience. In many cases patients' lack of medical knowledge may be harmful (Weintraub, 1976; Taylor, 1995).

Noncompliance is sometimes a result of psychological reactance. **Reactance** is a negative emotional and cognitive reaction that results from the restriction of one's freedom. People who experience reactance feel hostility and anger. Because of such emo-

Key Concepts

How do our interactions with physicians affect our health and compliance with medical treatment?

What leads to a sense of well-being?

Reactance: A negative emotional and cognitive reaction that results from the restriction of one's freedom and that can be associated with medical regimens.

www.mhhe.com/feldmanup8

PsychInteractive Online

Compliance with Medical Advice

tions, they may seek to restore their sense of freedom, but in a self-destructive manner by refusing to accept medical advice and perhaps acting in a way that worsens their medical condition. For instance, a man who is placed on a strict diet may experience reactance and tend to eat even more than he did before his diet was restricted (Fogarty & Young, 2000; Dillard & Shen, 2004). To get a better understanding of the reasons behind compliance with medical advice, complete the PsychInteractive exercise.

FAILURE TO COMMUNICATE

> I was lying on a gurney, trying to prepare myself for a six-hour breast-reconstruction surgery. A few months earlier, I'd had a mastectomy for breast cancer. Because I'm small-boned, my doctor told me I needed to have a muscle sliced from my back and moved to my chest to create a proper foundation for an implant. I knew the operation would slow me down—bad news for someone who swims, runs, and chases three young kids. But as the surgeon diagramed incision points on my chest with a felt-tip pen, my husband asked a question: "Is it really necessary to transfer this back muscle?" (Halpert, 2003, p. 63).

The surgeon's answer shocked the patient: No, it wasn't necessary. And if she didn't have the procedure, her recovery time would be cut in half. The surgeon had simply assumed, without asking the patient, that she would prefer the more complicated procedure, because cosmetically it would be preferable. But after a hurried consultation with her husband, the patient opted for the less invasive procedure.

Lack of communication between medical care providers and patients can be a major obstacle to good medical care. Such communication failures occur for several reasons. One is that physicians make assumptions about what patients prefer, or they push a particular treatment that they prefer without consulting patients. Furthermore, the relatively high prestige of physicians may intimidate patients. Patients may also be reluctant to volunteer information that might cast them in a bad light, and physicians may have difficulties encouraging their patients to provide information. In many cases, physicians dominate an interview with questions of a technical nature, whereas patients attempt to communicate a personal sense of their illness and the impact it is having on their lives, as illustrated in Figure 1 (Graugaard, Eide, & Finset, 2003; Ihler, 2003; Schillinger et al., 2004).

Furthermore, the view held by many patients that physicians are "all-knowing" can result in serious communication problems. Many patients do not understand their treatments yet fail to ask their physicians for clearer explanations of a prescribed course of action. About half of all patients are unable to report accurately how long they are to continue taking a medication prescribed for them, and about a quarter do not even know the purpose of the drug. In fact, some patients are not even sure, as they are about to be rolled into the operating room, why they are having surgery (Svarstad, 1976; Atkinson, 1997; Halpert, 2003)!

Sometimes patient-physician communication difficulties occur because the material that must be communicated is too technical for patients, who may lack fundamental knowledge about the body and basic medical practices. In response to this problem, some health care providers routinely use baby talk (calling patients "honey" or telling them to go "night-night") and assume that patients are unable to understand even simple information (Whitbourne & Wills, 1993; DiMatteo, 1997; Basset et al., 1998).

The amount of physician-patient communication also is related to the sex of a physician. Overall, female primary care physicians provide more patient-centered communications than do male primary care physicians (Roter, Hall, & Aoki, 2002; Kiss, 2004).

"Give it to me straight, Doc. How long do I have to ignore your advice?"

A Patient Talks to Her Physician

The following excerpt from a case study used at the Harvard Medical School is an example of poor interviewing technique on the part of the physician.

Patient: I can hardly drink water.

Doctor: Um hum.

Patient: Remember when it started? . . . It was pains in my head. It must have been then.

Doctor: Um hum.

Patient: I don't know what it is. The doctor looked at it . . . said something about glands.

Doctor: Ok. Um hum, aside from this, how have you been feeling?

Patient: Terrible.

Doctor: Yeah.

Patient: Tired . . . there's pains . . . I don't know what it is.

Doctor: Ok. . . . Fever or chills?

Patient: No.

Doctor: Ok. . . . Have you been sick to your stomach or anything?

Patient: (Sniffles, crying) I don't know what's going on. I get up in the morning tired. The only time I feel good. . . . maybe like around suppertime . . . and everything (crying) and still the same thing.

Doctor: Um hum. You're getting the nausea before you eat or after? (Goleman, 1988, p. B16)

Although the frequent "um hums" suggest that the physician is listening to the patient, in fact he does not encourage the patient to disclose more pertinent details. Even more, late in the interview, the physician ignores the patient's emotional distress and coldly continues through the list of questions.

FIGURE I Effective communication between patient and physician is important, but often proves frustrating for both.

Cultural values and expectations also contribute to communication barriers between patients and their physicians. Providing medical advice to a patient whose native language is not English may be problematic. Furthermore, medical practices differ between cultures, and medical practitioners need to be familiar with a patient's culture in order to produce compliance with medical recommendations (Dressler & Oths, 1997; Whaley, 2000; Ho et al., 2004).

What can patients do to improve communication with health care providers? Here are some tips provided by physician Holly Atkinson (Atkinson, 2003):

- Make a list of health-related concerns before you visit a health care provider.
- Before a visit, write down the names and dosages of every drug you are currently taking.
- Determine if your provider will communicate with you via e-mail and the correct e-mail address.
- If you find yourself intimidated, take along an advocate—a friend or relative—who can help you communicate more effectively.
- Take notes during the visit.

INCREASING COMPLIANCE WITH ADVICE

Although compliance with medical advice does not guarantee that a patient's medical problems will go away, it does optimize the possibility that the patient's condition will improve. What, then, can health care providers do to produce greater compliance on the part of their patients? One strategy is to provide clear instructions to patients regarding drug regimens. Maintaining good, warm relations between physicians and patients also leads to increased compliance (Cramer, 1995; Cheney, 1996).

In addition, honesty helps. Patients generally prefer to be well informed—even if the news is bad—and their degree of satisfaction with their medical care is linked to how well and how accurately physicians are able to convey the nature of their medical problems and treatments (Hall, Roter, & Katz, 1988; Haley, Clair, & Saulsberry, 1992).

Positively framed messages suggest that a change in behavior will lead to a health-related gain.

The way in which a message is framed also can result in more positive responses to health-related information. *Positively framed messages* suggest that a change in behavior will lead to a gain, emphasizing the benefits of carrying out a health-related behavior. For instance, suggesting that skin cancer is curable if it is detected early, and that you can reduce your chances of getting the disease by using a sunscreen, places information in a positive frame. In contrast, *negatively framed messages* highlight what you can lose by not performing a behavior. For instance, one might say that if you don't use sunscreen, you're more likely to get skin cancer, which can kill you if it's not detected early—an example of a negative frame.

What type of message is more effective? According to psychologists Alex Rothman and Peter Salovey, it depends on the type of health behavior one is trying to bring about. Negatively framed messages are best for motivating *preventive* behavior. However, positively framed messages are most effective in producing behavior that will lead to the detection of a disease (Rothman & Salovey, 1997; Apanovitch, McCarthy, & Salovey, 2003; McCaul, Johnson, & Rothman, 2003; Lee & Aaker, 2004).

Well-Being and Happiness

What makes for a good life?

It's a question that philosophers and theologians have pondered for centuries, and now health psychologists are turning their spotlight on the question. They are doing that by investigating **subjective well-being,** people's evaluations of their lives in terms of both their thoughts and their emotions. Considered another way, subjective well-being is the measure of how happy people are (Oishi & Diener, 2001; Diener, Lucas, & Oishi, 2002; Keyes & Shapiro, 2004).

Subjective well-being: People's own evaluation of their lives in terms of both their thoughts and their emotions.

WHAT ARE THE CHARACTERISTICS OF HAPPY PEOPLE?

Research on the subject of well-being shows that happy people share several characteristics (Myers & Diener, 1996; Myers, 2000; Diener & Seligman, 2002):

- *Happy people have high self-esteem.* Particularly in Western cultures, which emphasize the importance of individuality, people who are happy like themselves. They see themselves as more intelligent and better able to get along with others than is the average person. In fact, they often hold *positive illusions* or moderately inflated views of themselves as good, competent, and desirable (Taylor et al., 2000; Boyd-Wilson, McClure, & Walkey, 2004).

- *Happy people have a firm sense of control.* They feel more in control of events in their lives, unlike those who feel they are the pawns of others and who experience learned helplessness.
- *Happy individuals are optimistic.* Their optimism permits them to persevere at tasks and ultimately to achieve more. In addition, their health is better (Peterson, 2000).
- *Happy people like to be around other people.* They tend to be extroverted and have a supportive network of close relationships.

Perhaps most important, most people are at least moderately happy most of the time. In both national and international surveys, people living in a wide variety of circumstances report being happy. Furthermore, life-altering events that one might expect would produce long-term spikes in happiness, such as winning the lottery, probably won't make you much happier than you already are, as we discuss next.

DOES MONEY BUY HAPPINESS?

If you won the lottery, would you be happier?

Probably not. At least that's the implication of health psychologists' research on subjective well-being. That research shows that although winning the lottery brings an initial surge in happiness, a year later winners' level of happiness seems to return to what it was before. The converse phenomenon occurs for people who have had serious injuries in accidents: Despite an initial decline in happiness, in most cases victims return to their prior levels of happiness after the passage of time (Srivastava, Locke, & Bartol, 2001; Diener & Biswas-Diener, 2002; Nissle & Bschor, 2002).

Why is the level of subjective well-being so stable? One explanation is that people have a general *set point* for happiness, a marker that establishes the tone for one's life. Although particular events may temporarily elevate or depress one's mood (a surprise promotion or a job loss, for example), ultimately people return to their general level of happiness.

Although it is not certain how people's happiness set points are initially established, some evidence suggests that the set point is determined at least in part by genetic factors. Specifically, identical twins who grow up in widely different circumstances turn out to have very similar levels of happiness (Lykken & Tellegen, 1996; Kahneman, Diener, & Schwarz, 1998).

Most people's well-being set point is relatively high. For example, some 30 percent of people in the United States rate themselves as "very happy," and only one in ten rates himself or herself as "not too happy." Most people declare themselves to be "pretty happy." Such feelings are graphically confirmed by people who are asked to place themselves on the measure of happiness illustrated in Figure 2. The scale clearly illustrates that most people view their lives quite positively.

Faces Scale: "Which face comes closest to expressing how you feel about your life as a whole?"

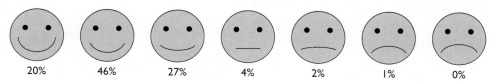

FIGURE 2 Most people in the United States rate themselves as happy, while only a small minority indicate they are "not too happy." (Source: Myers, 2000, p. 57, drawn from *Social Indicators of Well-Being: Americans' Perceptions of Life Quality* (pp. 207 and 306), by F. M. Andrews and S. B. Withey, 1976. New York, Plenum. Copyright 1976 by Plenum.)

Similar results are found when people are asked to compare themselves with others. For example, when asked, "Who of the following people do you think is the happiest?" survey respondents answered "Oprah Winfrey" (23 percent), "Bill Gates" (7 percent), "the Pope" (12 percent), "Chelsea Clinton" (3 percent), and "yourself" (49 percent), with 6 percent saying they didn't know (Black & McCafferty, 1998).

Few differences exist between members of different demographic groups. Men and women report being equally happy, and African Americans are only slightly less likely than European Americans to rate themselves as "very happy." Furthermore, happiness is hardly unique to U.S. culture. Even countries that are far from economically prosperous have, on the whole, happy residents (Myers & Diener, 1996; Diener & Clifton, 2002; Suh, 2002; Suhail & Chaudhry, 2004).

The bottom line: Money does *not* seem to buy happiness. Despite the ups and downs of life, most people tend to be reasonably happy, and they adapt to the trials and tribulations—and joys and delights—of life by returning to a steady-state level of happiness. That habitual level of happiness can have profound—perhaps life-prolonging—implications (Diener & Seligman, 2004).

RECAP/EVALUATE/RETHINK

RECAP

How do our interactions with physicians affect our health and compliance with medical treatment?

- Although patients would often like physicians to base a diagnosis only on a physical examination, communicating one's problem to the physician is equally important. (pp. 507–508)
- Patients may find it difficult to communicate openly with their physicians because of the high social prestige of physicians and the technical nature of medical information. (p. 508)

What leads to a sense of well-being?

- Subjective well-being, the measure of how happy people are, is highest in people with high self-esteem, a sense of control, optimism, and a supportive network of close relationships. (pp. 510–511)

EVALUATE

1. Health psychologists are most likely to focus on which of the following problems with health care?
   a. Incompetent health care providers
   b. Rising health care costs
   c. Ineffective communication between physician and patient
   d. Scarcity of medical research funding

2. If you want people to floss more to prevent gum disease, the best approach is to
   a. Use a negatively framed message
   b. Use a positively framed message
   c. Have a dentist deliver an encouraging message on the pleasures of flossing
   d. Provide people with free dental floss
3. Winning the lottery is likely to
   a. Produce an immediate and long-term increase in the level of well-being
   b. Produce an immediate, but not lingering, increase in the level of well-being
   c. Produce a decline in well-being over the long run
   d. Lead to an increase in greed over the long run

RETHINK

1. Do you think stress plays a role in making communication between physicians and patients difficult? Why?
2. *From the perspective of a health care provider:* How would you try to better communicate with your patients? How might your techniques vary depending upon the patient's background, gender, age, and culture?
3. If money doesn't buy happiness, what can you do to make yourself happier? As you answer, consider the research findings on stress and coping, as well as on emotions.

Answers to Evaluate Questions

1. c; 2. a; 3. b

KEY TERMS

reactance p. 507   subjective well-being p. 510

Looking Back

Psychology on the Web

1. Find three or more Web sites that deal with stress reduction. Gather at least five techniques for reducing stress and summarize them. Write a critique and evaluation of those techniques, using the information you learned about stress. Which ones seem to have a sound basis in psychological theory and/or research?

2. Are you closer to a Type A personality or a Type B? Find two Web sites offering tests that claim to provide the answer. Summarize the quality of the tests from a scientific point of view and compare the results you received from each one.

3. After completing the PsychInteractive exercise on stress, investigate reports on the Web of posttraumatic stress disorder in soldiers returning from the war in Iraq. Summarize your findings.

Epilogue

In this chapter, we have explored the intersection of psychology and biology. We saw how the emotional and psychological experience of stress can lead to physical symptoms of illness, how personality factors may be related to major health problems, and how psychological factors can interfere with effective communication between physician and patient. We also looked at the other side of the coin, noting that some relatively simple strategies can help us control stress, affect illness, and improve our interactions with physicians.

Turn back to the prologue of this set of modules, about Louisa Denby and her hectic schedule and use your understanding of health psychology and stress to consider these questions.

1. Based on the description of Denby's day, which stressors are personal and which are background stressors? What might happen to "elevate" the stress level of a background stressor to a more serious level?

2. Are there likely to be any uplifts in her day?

3. How does the general adaptation syndrome (GAS) apply to Denby's situation? How might events in her life move her along the three stages of the model?

4. What steps would you advise Denby to take to keep her level of stress under control? How might others in her life be involved in such an effort?

CHAPTER 15

Psychological Disorders

Key Concepts for Chapter 15

Prologue   Chamique Holdsclaw: In the Grip of Darkness

Nothing appeared to be outwardly wrong with Chamique Holdsclaw. But it was the middle of July, and the blackness seemed to eclipse her. Over the course of the season with the WNBA's Washington Mystics, Holdsclaw had become increasingly withdrawn, alienated from teammates and family and even her oldest confidants. "What's wrong with you?" every-

one asked. She was unable and unwilling to explain. "I was there but not there. . . ."

She slept a lot. "I was just doing my own thing, just living without all of the expectations," she said. She never turned on sports on the TV. She didn't watch when her team played, even though they went on a remarkable run to make the playoffs. She sat on the couch in her apartment just a block from the arena where they were competing, the MCI Center. "Everything was negative," she said. "Dark." (Jenkins, 2004, p. A1).

Looking Ahead

The source of Chamique Holdsclaw's journey into darkness was major depression, a psychological disorder that that afflicts as much as 10 percent of the U.S. population each year. It took her from being named "Rookie of the Year" in the WNBA to being unable to face playing a basketball game.

But Holdsclaw is one of the lucky ones. After treatment for the disorder, she made a fresh start and today is one of the best players in the WNBA.

Holdsclaw's case raises several questions. What caused her disorder? Were genetic factors involved, or were stressors in her life primarily responsible? Were there signs that others should have noticed earlier? Could her depression have been prevented?

What were the specific symptoms of her psychological disorder? And, more generally, how do we distinguish normal from abnormal behavior, and how can Holdsclaw's behavior be categorized and classified in such a way as to pinpoint the specific nature of her problem?

We address some of the issues raised by Chamique Holdsclaw's case in this and the following set of modules. We begin by discussing the difference between normal and abnormal behavior, which can be surprisingly fuzzy. We then discuss the most significant categories of psychological disorders. Finally, we consider ways of evaluating behavior—one's own and that of others—to determine whether seeking help from a mental health professional is warranted.

Normal Versus Abnormal: Making the Distinction

Universally that person's acumen is esteemed very little perceptive concerning whatsoever matters are being held as most profitable by mortals with sapience endowed to be studied who is ignorant of that which the most in doctrine erudite and certainly by reason of that in them high mind's ornament deserving of veneration constantly maintain when by general consent they affirm that other circumstances being equal by no exterior splendour is the prosperity of a nation. . . .

It would be easy to conclude that these words are the musings of a madman. To most people, the passage does not seem to make any sense at all. But literary scholars would disagree. Actually, this passage is from James Joyce's classic *Ulysses,* hailed as one of the major works of twentieth-century literature (Joyce, 1934, p. 377).

As this example illustrates, casually examining a person's writing is insufficient to determine the degree to which that person is "normal." But even when we consider more extensive samples of a person's behavior, we find that there may be only a fine line between behavior that is considered normal and that which is considered abnormal.

Defining Abnormality

Because of the difficulty in distinguishing normal from abnormal behavior, psychologists have struggled to devise a precise, scientific definition of "abnormal behavior." For instance, consider the following definitions, each of which has advantages and disadvantages:

- *Abnormality as deviation from the average.* To employ this statistically based approach, we simply observe what behaviors are rare or occur infrequently in a particular society or culture and label those deviations from the norm "abnormal."

  The difficulty with this definition is that some statistically rare behaviors clearly do not lend themselves to classification as abnormal. If most people prefer to have corn flakes for breakfast but you prefer raisin bran, this hardly makes your behavior abnormal. Similarly, such a concept of abnormality unreasonably labels a person who has an unusually high IQ as abnormal, simply because a high IQ is statistically rare. In short, a definition of abnormality that rests on deviation from the average is insufficient.

- *Abnormality as deviation from the ideal.* An alternative approach considers abnormality in relation to the standard toward which most people are striving—the ideal. This sort of definition considers behavior abnormal if it deviates enough from some kind of ideal or cultural standard. However, society has few standards on which people universally agree. (For example, we would be hard-pressed to find agreement on whether the New Testament, the Koran, the Talmud, or the Book of Mormon provided the most reasonable standards.) Furthermore, standards that do arise tend to change over time and vary across cultures, the deviation-from-the-ideal approach is inadequate.

- *Abnormality as a sense of personal discomfort.* A more useful definition concentrates on the psychological consequences of the behavior for the individual. In this approach, behavior is considered abnormal if it produces a sense of personal distress, anxiety, or guilt in an individual—or if it is harmful to others in some way.

Key Concepts

How can we distinguish normal from abnormal behavior?

What are the major perspectives on psychological disorders used by mental health professionals?

What classification system is used to categorize disorders?

Andrea Yates was sane when she drowned her five children in a bathtub, according to the first jury that heard her case. At a later trial, however, she was found not guilty by reason of insanity.

Even a definition that relies on personal discomfort has drawbacks, though, because in some particularly severe forms of mental disturbance, people report feeling wonderful, even though their behavior seems bizarre to others. In such cases, a personal state of well-being exists, yet most people would consider the behavior abnormal. For example, most of us would think that a woman who says she is hearing uplifting messages from Martians would be considered to be displaying abnormal behavior, even though she may say the messages make her feel happy.

- *Abnormality as the inability to function effectively.* Most people are able to feed themselves, hold a job, get along with others, and in general live as productive members of society. Yet there are those who are unable to adjust to the demands of society or function effectively.

  According to this view of abnormality, people who are unable to function effectively and adapt to the demands of society are considered abnormal. For example, an unemployed, homeless woman living on the street may be considered unable to function effectively. Therefore, her behavior can be viewed as abnormal, even if she has chosen to live this way. Her inability to adapt to the requirements of society is what makes her "abnormal," according to this approach.

- *Abnormality as a legal concept.* According to the first jury that heard her case, Andrea Yates was sane when she drowned her five children in a bathtub.

  Although you might question this view, it reflects the way in which the law defines abnormal behavior. To the judicial system, the distinction between normal and abnormal behavior rests on the definition of insanity, which is a legal, but not a psychological, term. The definition of insanity varies from one jurisdiction to another. It also changes over time: At a second trial, Andrea Yates was found not guilty by reason of insanity.

  In some states, insanity simply means that defendants cannot understand the difference between right and wrong at the time they commit a criminal act. Other states consider whether defendants are substantially incapable of understanding the criminality of their behavior or unable to control themselves. And in some jurisdictions pleas of insanity are not allowed at all (Weiner & Wettstein, 1993; Frost & Bonnie, 2001; Sokolove, 2003).

Clearly, none of the previous definitions is broad enough to cover all instances of abnormal behavior. Consequently, the distinction between normal and abnormal behavior often remains ambiguous even to trained professionals. Furthermore, to a large extent, cultural expectations for "normal" behavior in a particular society influence the understanding of "abnormal behavior" (Scheff, 1999; also see the *Applying Psychology in the 21st Century* box).

Given the difficulties in precisely defining the construct, psychologists typically define **abnormal behavior** broadly, considering it to be behavior that causes people to experience distress and prevents them from functioning in their daily lives (Nolen-Hoeksema, 2006). Because of the imprecision of this definition, it's best to view abnormal behavior and normal behavior as marking two ends of a continuum rather than as absolute states. Behavior should be evaluated in terms of gradations, ranging from fully normal functioning to extremely abnormal behavior. Behavior typically falls somewhere between those extremes.

Abnormal behavior: Behavior that causes people to experience distress and prevents them from functioning in their daily lives.

Perspectives on Abnormality: From Superstition to Science

Throughout much of human history, people linked abnormal behavior to superstition and witchcraft. Individuals who displayed abnormal behavior were accused of being possessed by the devil or some sort of demonic god. Authorities felt justified in "treating" abnormal behavior by attempting to drive out the source of the problem. This typically

Terrorist Suicide Bombers: Normal or Abnormal?

What kinds of people are willing to strap explosives to their bodies and blow themselves—and as many others as possible—to smithereens? Sounds crazy... but is their behavior abnormal?

According to most psychologists studying the issue, the answers to these questions are clear: Suicide bombers are *not* psychologically disordered. Almost no real-life suicide attackers are deranged, maniacal loners like the ones portrayed in movies and on television. According to psychologist Ariel Merai, who has carefully profiled many Palestinian and Lebanese suicide bombers, such attackers are usually males in their early twenties who come from a wide range of backgrounds. Some bombers are wealthy whereas others are poor, and some are highly educated whereas others are uneducated. Although suicide bombers are generally unmarried, they are otherwise similar to the average members of their societies (Merari, 1985, 2005; Goode, 2001).

Far from being loners, most suicide bombers are sociable. They have close friends and family members, and people who know them often say they are extroverted. Moreover, their psychological functioning seems generally normal: Before their attacks, they show no suicidal symptoms, and they do not express feelings of hopelessness or of having nothing to lose. In short, psychological studies of suicide bombers provide little evidence that those individuals are suffering from any type of diagnosable psychological disorder (Atran, 2003).

If they are not psychologically disordered, why do they volunteer for suicide missions? In arguing against the idea that suicide bombers are necessarily dysfunctional or pathological, psychologist Charles Ruby (2002) contends that terrorist acts differ from conventional military

Are suicide bombers psychologically disordered? Most research suggests that they are not.

operations only in terms of their methods. He suggests that because terrorists do not have access to enough weapons to attack their enemy conventionally, they use a different strategy. Terrorist leaders target innocent civilians, hoping to cultivate fear and persuade governments to change specific policies that the terrorists despise.

However, although terrorist leaders orchestrate strategy, suicide bombers are not focused only on political objectives; they are also motivated by commitment to a particular group or cause. Suicide bombers often belong to political or religious groups, and leaders of those groups work tirelessly to inspire potential bombers' loyalty to the group, to other group members, and to the leaders themselves. They feel that their goal is moral and just, and that the objective of attaining a just and fair society justifies any act. The terrorists, feeling that they have no voice in the society in which they live, come to believe that

terrorism is a legitimate response and that the dominant members of society are evil (Atran, 2003; Moghaddam, 2005).

Ultimately, situational pressures, rather than personality factors, may drive suicide bombers. Terrorists typically are part of a small, four- or five-person cell that becomes the focus of their lives. The group pressure generated by such cells may be enormously influential—strong enough to lead to the ultimate act of self-sacrifice for the good of the group (Plous & Zimbardo, 2004; Zimbardo, 2004b).

For those charged with stopping suicide bombers' attacks and other types of terrorism, it becomes quite problematic that suicide attackers are driven not by a psychological disorder, but by a complex web of emotions, loyalties, and politics. Terrorist attacks motivated by mental illness probably would be a much simpler problem to solve than are terrorist attacks inflamed by emotional, political, and religious group conflict.

RETHINK

If it were your job to combat suicide bombings, how would you do it? What kinds of psychological, political, or social interventions might help discourage potential suicide attackers from volunteering?

involved whipping, immersion in hot water, starvation, or other forms of torture in which the cure was often worse than the affliction (Howells & Osborn, 1984; Berrios, 1996).

Contemporary approaches take a more enlightened view. Today, six major perspectives are used to understand psychological disorders. These perspectives suggest not only different causes of abnormal behavior but different treatment approaches as well. Furthermore, some perspectives are more applicable to particular disorders than are others. Figure 1 summarizes the perspectives and the way in which they can be applied to the experience of Chamique Holdsclaw, described in the prologue.

Perspectives on Psychological Disorders		
Perspective	**Description**	**Possible Application of Perspective to Chamique Holdsclaw's Case**
Medical perspective	Assumes that physiological causes are at the root of psychological disorders	Examine Holdsclaw for medical problems, such as brain tumor, chemical imbalance in the brain, or disease
Psychoanalytic perspective	Argues that psychological disorders stem from childhood conflicts	Seek out information about Holdsclaw's past, considering possible childhood conflicts
Behavioral perspective	Assumes that abnormal behaviors are learned responses	Concentrate on rewards and punishments for Holdsclaw's behavior, and identify environmental stimuli that reinforce her behavior
Cognitive perspective	Assumes that cognitions (people's thoughts and beliefs) are central to psychological disorders	Focus on Holdsclaw's, perceptions of herself and her environment
Humanistic perspective	Emphasizes people's responsibility for their own behavior and the need to self-actualize	Consider Holdsclaw's behavior in terms of her choices and efforts to reach her potential
Sociocultural perspective	Assumes that behavior is shaped by family, society, and culture	Focus on how societal demands contributed to Holdsclaw's disorder

FIGURE I In considering the case of Chamique Holdsclaw, discussed in the prologue, we can employ each of the different perspectives on abnormal behavior. Note, however, that because of the nature of her psychological disorder, some of the perspectives are more applicable than others.

MEDICAL PERSPECTIVE

Medical perspective: The perspective that suggests that when an individual displays symptoms of abnormal behavior, the root cause will be found in a physical examination of the individual, which may reveal a hormonal imbalance, a chemical deficiency, or a brain injury.

When people display the symptoms of tuberculosis, medical professionals can generally find tubercular bacteria in their body tissue. Similarly, the **medical perspective** suggests that when an individual displays symptoms of abnormal behavior, the fundamental cause will be found through a physical examination of the individual, which may reveal a hormonal imbalance, a chemical deficiency, or a brain injury. Indeed, when we speak of mental "illness," "symptoms" of abnormal behavior, and mental "hospitals," we are using terminology associated with the medical perspective.

Because many abnormal behaviors have been linked to biological causes, the medical perspective is a reasonable approach, yet serious criticisms have been leveled against it. For one thing, no biological cause has been identified for many forms of abnormal behavior. In addition, some critics have argued that the use of the term *illness* implies that people who display abnormal behavior have no responsibility for their actions (Szasz, 1982, 1994, 2004).

Still, recent advances in our understanding of the biological bases of behavior underscore the importance of considering physiological factors in abnormal behavior. For instance, some of the more severe forms of psychological disturbance, such as major depression and schizophrenia, are influenced by genetic factors and malfunctions in neurotransmitter signals (Pennington, 2002; Plomin & McGuffin, 2003).

PSYCHOANALYTIC PERSPECTIVE

Psychoanalytic perspective: The perspective that suggests that abnormal behavior stems from childhood conflicts over opposing wishes regarding sex and aggression.

Whereas the medical perspective suggests that biological causes are at the root of abnormal behavior, the **psychoanalytic perspective** holds that abnormal behavior stems from childhood conflicts over opposing wishes regarding sex and aggression. According to Freud, children pass through a series of stages in which sexual and aggressive impulses take different forms and produce conflicts that require resolution. If these childhood conflicts are not dealt with successfully, they remain unresolved in the unconscious and eventually bring about abnormal behavior during adulthood.

To uncover the roots of people's disordered behavior, the psychoanalytic perspective scrutinizes their early life history. However, because there is no conclusive way to link people's childhood experiences with the abnormal behaviors they display as adults, we can never be sure that the causes suggested by psychoanalytic theory are accurate. Moreover, psychoanalytic theory paints a picture of people as having relatively little control over their behavior, because much of it is guided by unconscious impulses. In the eyes of some critics, this suggests that people have little responsibility for their own behavior.

On the other hand, the contributions of psychoanalytic theory have been significant. More than any other approach to abnormal behavior, this perspective highlights the fact that people can have a rich, involved inner life and that prior experiences can have a profound effect on current psychological functioning (Horgan, 1996; Elliott, 2002; Bornstein, 2003).

BEHAVIORAL PERSPECTIVE

Both the medical and psychoanalytic perspectives look at abnormal behaviors as *symptoms* of an underlying problem. In contrast, the **behavioral perspective** views the behavior itself as the problem. Using the basic principles of learning, behavioral theorists see both normal and abnormal behaviors as responses to various stimuli, responses that have been learned through past experience and that are guided in the present by stimuli in the individual's environment. To explain why abnormal behavior occurs, we must analyze how an individual has learned abnormal behavior and observe the circumstances in which it is displayed.

Behavioral perspective: The perspective that looks at the behavior itself as the problem.

The emphasis on observable behavior represents both the greatest strength and the greatest weakness of the behavioral approach to abnormal behavior. This perspective provides the most precise and objective approach for examining behavioral symptoms of particular disorders, such as attention-deficit hyperactivity disorder (ADHD). At the same time, though, critics charge that the perspective ignores the rich inner world of thoughts, attitudes, and emotions that may contribute to abnormal behavior.

COGNITIVE PERSPECTIVE

The medical, psychoanalytic, and behavioral perspectives view people's behavior as the result of factors largely beyond their control. To many critics of these views, however, people's thoughts cannot be ignored.

In response to such concerns, some psychologists employ a **cognitive perspective.** Rather than considering only external behavior, as in traditional behavioral approaches, the cognitive approach assumes that *cognitions* (people's thoughts and beliefs) are central to a person's abnormal behavior. A primary goal of treatment using the cognitive perspective is to explicitly teach new, more adaptive ways of thinking.

Cognitive perspective: The perspective that suggests that people's thoughts and beliefs are a central component of abnormal behavior.

For instance, suppose a student forms the erroneous belief that "doing well on this exam is crucial to my entire future" whenever he or she takes an exam. Through therapy, that person might learn to hold the more realistic, and less anxiety-producing, thought, "my entire future is not dependent on this one exam." By changing cognitions in this way, psychologists working within a cognitive framework help people free themselves from thoughts and behaviors that are potentially maladaptive (Frost & Steketee, 2002; Clark, 2004).

The cognitive perspective is not without critics. For example, it is possible that maladaptive cognitions are the symptoms or consequences of disorders, rather than their cause. Furthermore, there are circumstances in which negative beliefs may not be irrational at all, but simply reflect the unpleasant environments in which people live—after all, there are times when a single exam may be extremely important. Still, cognitive theorists would argue that one can find a more adaptive way of framing beliefs even in the most negative circumstances.

HUMANISTIC PERSPECTIVE

Psychologists who subscribe to the **humanistic perspective** emphasize the responsibility people have for their own behavior, even when their behavior is seen as abnormal. The humanistic perspective—growing out of the work of Carl Rogers and Abraham Maslow—concentrates on what is uniquely human, viewing people as basically rational,

Humanistic perspective: The perspective that emphasizes the responsibility people have for their own behavior, even when such behavior is abnormal.

"First off, you're not a nut. You're a legume."

Sociocultural perspective: The perspective that assumes that people's behavior—both normal and abnormal—is shaped by the kind of family group, society, and culture in which they live.

oriented toward a social world, and motivated to seek self-actualization (Rogers, 1995).

Humanistic approaches focus on the relationship of the individual to society, considering the ways in which people view themselves in relation to others and see their place in the world. The humanistic perspective views people as having an awareness of life and of themselves that leads them to search for meaning and self-worth. Rather than assuming that individuals require a "cure," the humanistic perspective suggests that they can, by and large, set their own limits of what is acceptable behavior. As long as they are not hurting others and do not feel personal distress, people should be free to choose the behaviors in which they engage.

Although the humanistic perspective has been criticized for its reliance on unscientific, unverifiable information and its vague, almost philosophical formulations, it offers a distinctive view of abnormal behavior. It stresses the unique aspects of being human and provides a number of important suggestions for helping those with psychological problems.

SOCIOCULTURAL PERSPECTIVE

The **sociocultural perspective** assumes that people's behavior—both normal and abnormal—is shaped by the kind of family group, society, and culture in which they live. According to this view, the nature of one's relationships with others may support abnormal behaviors and even cause them. Consequently, the kinds of stresses and conflicts people experience in their daily interactions with others can promote and maintain abnormal behavior.

This perspective finds statistical support for the position that sociocultural factors shape abnormal behavior in the fact that some kinds of abnormal behavior are far more prevalent among certain social classes than they are in others. For instance, diagnoses of schizophrenia tend to be higher among members of lower socioeconomic groups than among members of more affluent groups. Proportionally more African American individuals are hospitalized involuntarily for psychological disorders than are whites. Furthermore, poor economic times seem to be linked to general declines in psychological functioning, and social problems such as homelessness are associated with psychological disorders (Kiesler, 2000; Conger et al., 2002; López & Guarnaccia, 2005).

On the other hand, alternative explanations abound for the association between abnormal behavior and social factors. For example, people from lower socioeconomic levels may be less likely than those from higher levels to seek help, gradually reaching a point where their symptoms become severe and warrant a more serious diagnosis. Furthermore, sociocultural explanations provide relatively little specific guidance for the treatment of individuals showing mental disturbance, because the focus is on broader societal factors (Paniagua, 2000).

Classifying Abnormal Behavior: The ABCs of DSM

Crazy. Whacked. Mental. Loony. Insane. Neurotic. Psycho. Strange. Demented. Odd. Possessed.

Society has long placed labels on people who display abnormal behavior. Unfortunately, most of the time these labels have reflected intolerance and have been used with little thought to what each label signifies.

Providing appropriate and specific names and classifications for abnormal behavior has presented a major challenge to psychologists. It is not hard to understand why, given the difficulties discussed earlier in simply distinguishing normal from abnormal behavior. Yet we need to classify abnormal behavior in order to diagnose it and, ultimately, to treat it.

DSM-IV-TR: DETERMINING DIAGNOSTIC DISTINCTIONS

Over the years, mental health professionals have developed many different classification systems that vary in terms of their utility and the degree to which they have been accepted. However, one standard system, devised by the American Psychiatric Association, has emerged in the United States. Most professionals today use this classification system, known as the ***Diagnostic and Statistical Manual of Mental Disorders, Fourth Edition, Text Revision*** (*DSM-IV-TR*) to diagnose and classify abnormal behavior.

DSM-IV-TR presents comprehensive and relatively precise definitions for more than 200 disorders, divided into seventeen major categories. It also includes five types of information, known as *axes,* that have to be considered in assessing a patient. For example, Axis I relates to clinical disorders, and Axis III relates to general medical conditions that may be relevant to a psychological disorder.

By following the criteria presented in the *DSM-IV-TR* classification system, diagnosticians can identify the specific problem an individual is experiencing. (Figure 2 provides a brief outline of the major diagnostic categories, and the PsychInteractive exercise provides practice in classifying different behaviors.)

Diagnostic and Statistical Manual of Mental Disorders, Fourth Edition, Text Revision (DSM-IV-TR): A system, devised by the American Psychiatric Association, used by most professionals to diagnose and classify abnormal behavior.

www.mhhe.com/feldmanup8
PsychInteractive Online

DSM-IV-TR Classification System

Disorder	Subcategories
Anxiety (problems in which anxiety impedes daily functioning)	Generalized anxiety disorder, panic disorder, phobic disorder, obsessive-compulsive disorder, posttraumatic stress disorder
Somatoform (psychological difficulties displayed through physical problems)	Hypochondriasis, conversion disorder
Dissociative (the splitting apart of crucial parts of personality that are usually integrated)	Dissociative identity disorder (multiple personality), dissociative amnesia, dissociative fugue
Mood (emotions of depression or euphoria that are so strong they intrude on everyday living)	Major depression, bipolar disorder
Schizophrenia (declines in functioning, thought and language disturbances, perception disorders, emotional disturbances, and withdrawal from others)	Disorganized, paranoid, catatonic, undifferentiated, residual
Personality (problems that create little personal distress but that lead to an inability to function as a normal member of society)	Antisocial (sociopathic) personality disorder, narcissistic personality disorder
Sexual (problems related to sexual arousal from unusual objects or problems related to functioning)	Paraphilia, sexual dysfunction
Substance-related (problems related to drug dependence and abuse)	Alcohol, cocaine, hallucinogens, marijuana
Delirium, dementia, amnesia, and other cognitive disorders	

DIAGNOSTIC AND STATISTICAL MANUAL OF MENTAL DISORDERS

FOURTH EDITION

TEXT REVISION

DSM-IV®-TR

AMERICAN PSYCHIATRIC ASSOCIATION

FIGURE 2 This list of disorders represents the major categories from the *DSM-IV-TR.* It is only a partial list of the more than 200 disorders included there.

DSM-IV-TR is designed to be primarily descriptive and avoids suggesting an underlying cause for an individual's behavior and problems. For instance, the term *neurotic*—a label that is commonly used by people in their everyday descriptions of abnormal behavior—is not listed as a *DSM-IV-TR* category. Because the term *neurosis* refers to problems associated with a specific cause based in Freud's theory of personality, it is not included in *DSM-IV-TR*.

DSM-IV-TR has the advantage, then, of providing a descriptive system that does not specify the cause of or reason for a problem. Instead, it paints a picture of the behavior that is being displayed. Why should this be important? For one thing, it allows communication between mental health professionals of diverse backgrounds and theoretical approaches. In addition, precise classification enables researchers to explore the causes of a problem. Without reliable descriptions of abnormal behavior, researchers would be hard-pressed to find ways to investigate the disorder. Finally, *DSM-IV-TR* provides a kind of conceptual shorthand through which professionals can describe the behaviors that tend to occur together in an individual (Halling & Goldfarb, 1996; Widiger & Clark, 2000; Frances, First, & Pincus, 2002).

CONNING THE CLASSIFIERS: THE SHORTCOMINGS OF *DSM*

When clinical psychologist David Rosenhan and eight colleagues sought admission to separate mental hospitals across the United States in the 1970s, each stated that he or she was hearing voices—"unclear voices" that said "empty," "hollow," and "thud"— and each was immediately admitted to the hospital. However, the truth was that they actually were conducting a study, and none of them was really hearing voices. Aside from these misrepresentations, *everything* else they did and said represented their true behavior, including the responses they gave during extensive admission interviews and their answers to the battery of tests they were asked to complete. In fact, as soon as they were admitted, they said they no longer heard any voices. In short, each of the pseudo-patients acted in a "normal" way (Rosenhan, 1973).

We might assume that Rosenhan and his colleagues would have been quickly discovered as the impostors they were, but this was not the case. Instead, each of them was diagnosed as severely abnormal on the basis of observed behavior. Mental health professionals labeled most as suffering from schizophrenia and kept them in the hospital for three to fifty-two days, with the average stay being nineteen days. Even when they were discharged, most of the "patients" left with the label *schizophrenia—in remission*, implying that the abnormal behavior had only temporarily subsided and could recur at any time. Most disturbing, no one on the hospital staff identified any of the pseudo-patients as impostors—although some of the actual patients figured out the ruse.

The results of Rosenhan's classic study illustrate that placing labels on individuals powerfully influences the way mental health workers perceive and interpret their actions. It also points out that determining who is psychologically disordered is not always a clear-cut or accurate process.

Although *DSM-IV-TR* was developed to provide more accurate and consistent diagnoses of psychological disorders, it has not been entirely successful. For instance, critics charge that it relies too much on the medical perspective. Because it was drawn up by psychiatrists—who are physicians—some condemn it for viewing psychological disorders primarily in terms of the symptoms of an underlying physiological disorder. It also does not fully take into account the advances in behavioral neuroscience that have identified the genetic underpinnings of some psychological disorders. Moreover, critics suggest that *DSM-IV-TR* compartmentalizes people into inflexible, all-or-none categories, rather than considering the degree to which a person displays psychologically disordered behavior (Helmuth, 2003; Schmidt, Kotov, & Joiner, 2004).

Other concerns with *DSM-IV-TR* are more subtle, but equally important. For instance, some critics argue that labeling an individual as abnormal provides a dehumanizing, lifelong stigma. Furthermore, after an initial diagnosis has been made, mental health professionals, who may concentrate on the initial diagnostic category, could overlook other diagnostic possibilities (Szasz, 1994; Duffy et al., 2002; Quinn, Kahng, & Crocker, 2004).

Still, despite the drawbacks inherent in any labeling system, *DSM-IV-TR* has had an important influence on the way in which mental health professionals view psychological disorders. It has increased both the reliability and the validity of diagnostic categorization. In addition, it offers a logical way to organize our examination of the major types of mental disturbance.

RECAP/EVALUATE/RETHINK

RECAP

How can we distinguish normal from abnormal behavior?

- Definitions of abnormality include deviation from the average, deviation from the ideal, a sense of personal discomfort, the inability to function effectively, and legal conceptions. (pp. 517–518)
- Although no single definition is adequate, abnormal behavior can be considered to be behavior that causes people to experience distress and prevents them from functioning in their daily lives. Most psychologists believe that abnormal and normal behavior should be considered in terms of a continuum. (p. 518)

What are the major perspectives on psychological disorders used by mental health professionals?

- The medical perspective views abnormality as a symptom of an underlying disease. (p. 520)
- Psychoanalytic perspectives suggest that abnormal behavior stems from childhood conflicts in the unconscious. (pp. 520–521)
- Behavioral approaches view abnormal behavior not as a symptom of an underlying problem, but as the problem itself. (p. 521)
- The cognitive approach suggests that abnormal behavior is the result of faulty cognitions (thoughts and beliefs). In this view, abnormal behavior can be remedied by changing one's flawed thoughts and beliefs. (p. 521)
- Humanistic approaches emphasize the responsibility people have for their own behavior, even when such behavior is seen as abnormal. (pp. 521–522)
- Sociocultural approaches view abnormal behavior in terms of difficulties arising from family and other social relationships. (p. 522)

What classification system is used to categorize psychological disorders?

- The most widely used system for classifying psychological disorders is *DSM-IV-TR—Diagnostic and Statistical*

Manual of Mental Disorders, Fourth Edition, Text Revision. (pp. 523–524)

EVALUATE

1. One problem in defining abnormal behavior is that
   a. Statistically rare behavior may not be abnormal.
   b. Not all abnormalities are accompanied by feelings of discomfort.
   c. Cultural standards are too general to use as a measuring tool.
   d. All of the above.
2. If abnormality is defined as behavior that causes personal discomfort or harms others, which of the following people is most likely to need treatment?
   a. An executive is afraid to accept a promotion because it would require moving from his ground-floor office to the top floor of a tall office building.
   b. A woman decides to quit her job and chooses to live on the street in order to live a "simpler life."
   c. A man believes that friendly spacemen visit his house every Thursday.
   d. A photographer lives with nineteen cats in a small apartment, lovingly caring for them.
3. Virginia's mother thinks that her daughter's behavior is clearly abnormal because, despite being offered admission to medical school, Virginia decides to become a waitress. What approach is Virginia's mother using to define abnormal behavior?
4. Which of the following is a strong argument against the medical perspective on abnormality?
   a. Physiological abnormalities are almost always impossible to identify.
   b. There is no conclusive way to link past experience and behavior.
   c. The medical perspective rests too heavily on the effects of nutrition.
   d. Assigning behavior to a physical problem takes responsibility away from the individual for changing his or her behavior.

5. Cheryl is painfully shy. According to the behavioral perspective, the best way to deal with her "abnormal" behavior is to
   a. Treat the underlying physical problem
   b. Use the principles of learning theory to modify her shy behavior
   c. Express a great deal of caring
   d. Uncover her negative past experiences through hypnosis

RETHINK

1. Do you agree or disagree that the *DSM* should be updated every several years? Why? What makes abnormal behavior so variable?

2. *From the perspective of an employer:* Imagine that a well-paid employee was arrested for shoplifting a $15 sweater. What sort of explanation for this behavior would be provided by the proponents of *each* perspective on abnormality: the medical perspective, the psychoanalytic perspective, the behavioral perspective, the cognitive perspective, the humanistic perspective, and the sociocultural perspective? Based on the potential causes of the shoplifting, would you fire the employee? Why or why not?

Answers to Evaluate Questions

1. d; 2. a; 3. deviation from the ideal; 4. d; 5. b

KEY TERMS

abnormal behavior p. 518
medical perspective p. 520
psychoanalytic perspective p. 520
behavioral perspective p. 521

cognitive perspective p. 521
humanistic perspective p. 521
sociocultural perspective p. 522

Diagnostic and Statistical Manual of Mental Disorders, Fourth Edition, Text Revision (DSM-IV-TR) p. 523

The Major Psychological Disorders

Sally experienced her first panic attack out of the blue, 3 weeks after completing her senior year in college. She had just finished a job interview and was meeting some friends for dinner. In the restaurant, she began to feel dizzy. Within a few seconds, her heart was pounding, and she was feeling breathless, as though she might pass out. Her friends noticed that she did not look well and offered to drive her home. Sally suggested they stop at the hospital emergency room instead. Although she felt better by the time they arrived at the hospital, and tests indicated nothing wrong, Sally experienced a similar episode a week later while at a movie. . . .

Her attacks became more and more frequent. Before long, she was having several attacks per week. In addition, she constantly worried about having attacks. She began to avoid exercise and other activities that produced physical sensations. She also noticed the attacks were worse when she was alone. She began to avoid driving, shopping in large stores, and eating in all restaurants. Some weeks she avoided leaving the house completely (Antony, Brown, & Barlow, 1992, p. 79).

Sally suffered from panic disorder, one of the specific psychological disorders we'll consider in this module. Keep in mind that although we'll be discussing these disorders in a dispassionate manner, each represents a very human set of difficulties that influence, and in some cases considerably disrupt, people's lives.

Anxiety Disorders

All of us, at one time or another, experience *anxiety*, a feeling of apprehension or tension, in reaction to stressful situations. There is nothing "wrong" with such anxiety. It is a normal reaction to stress that often helps, rather than hinders, our daily functioning. Without some anxiety, for instance, most of us probably would not have much motivation to study hard, undergo physical exams, or spend long hours at our jobs.

But some people experience anxiety in situations in which there is no external reason or cause for such distress. When anxiety occurs without external justification and begins to affect people's daily functioning, mental health professionals consider it a psychological problem known as **anxiety disorder.** We'll discuss four types of anxiety disorders: phobic disorder, panic disorder, generalized anxiety disorder, and obsessive-compulsive disorder.

PHOBIC DISORDER

It's not easy moving through the world when you're terrified of electricity. "Donna," 45, a writer, knows that better than most. Get her in the vicinity of an appliance or a light switch or—all but unthinkable—a thunderstorm, and she is overcome by a terror so blinding she can think of nothing but fleeing. That, of course, is not always possible, so over time, Donna has come up with other answers. When she opens the refrigerator door, rubber-sole shoes are a must. If a light bulb blows, she will tolerate the dark until someone else changes it for her. Clothes shopping is done only when necessary, lest static on gar-

Anxiety disorder: The occurrence of anxiety without an obvious external cause, affecting daily functioning.

527

Phobia	Trigger	Phobia	Trigger
Acrophobia	Heights	Herpetophobia	Reptiles
Aerophobia	Flying	Hydrophobia	Water
Agoraphobia	Entering public spaces	Mikrophobia	Germs
Ailurophobia	Cats	Murophobia	Mice
Amaxophobia	Vehicles, driving	Mysophobia	Dirt or germs
Anthophobia	Flowers	Numerophobia	Numbers
Aquaphobia	Water	Nyctophobia	Darkness
Arachnophobia	Spiders	Ochlophobia	Crowds
Astraphobia	Lightning	Ophidiophobia	Snakes
Brontophobia	Thunder	Ornithophobia	Birds
Claustrophobia	Closed spaces	Phonophobia	Speaking out loud
Cynophobia	Dogs	Pyrophobia	Fire
Dementophobia	Insanity	Thanatophobia	Death
Electrophobia	Electricity	Trichophobia	Hair
Gephyrophobia	Bridges	Xenophobia	Strangers

FIGURE 1 Phobic disorders differ from generalized anxiety and panic disorders because a specific stimulus can be identified. Listed here are a number of phobias and their triggers.

Phobias: Intense, irrational fears of specific objects or situations.

www.mhhe.com/feldmanup8
PsychInteractive Online

Phobia

ments send her running from the store. And swimming at night is absolutely out of the question, lest underwater lights electrocute her (Kluger, 2001, p. 51).

Donna suffers from a **phobia,** an intense, irrational fear of a specific object or situation. For example, claustrophobia is a fear of enclosed places, acrophobia is a fear of high places, xenophobia is a fear of strangers, and—as in Donna's case—electrophobia is a fear of electricity. Although the objective danger posed by an anxiety-producing stimulus (which can be just about anything, as you can see from the list in Figure 1) is typically small or nonexistent, to the individual suffering from the phobia the danger is great, and a full-blown panic attack may follow exposure to the stimulus. Phobic disorders differ from generalized anxiety disorders and panic disorders in that there is a specific, identifiable stimulus that sets off the anxiety reaction.

Phobias may have only a minor impact on people's lives if those who suffer from them can avoid the stimuli that trigger fear. Unless one is a professional firefighter or tightrope walker, for example, a fear of heights will have little impact on one's daily life. On the other hand, a fear of strangers presents a more serious problem. In one extreme case, a Washington woman left her home just three times in thirty years—once to visit her family, once for a medical operation, and once to purchase ice cream for a dying companion (Adler, 1984). (To get a fuller understanding of phobias, complete the PsychInteractive exercise.)

PANIC DISORDER

Panic disorder: Anxiety disorder that takes the form of panic attacks lasting from a few seconds to as long as several hours.

In another type of anxiety disorder, **panic disorder,** *panic attacks* occur that last from a few seconds to several hours. Unlike phobias, which are stimulated by specific objects or situations, panic disorders do not have any identifiable stimuli. Instead, during an attack, such as the ones experienced by Sally in the case described earlier, anxiety suddenly—and often without warning—rises to a peak, and an individual feels a sense of impending, unavoidable doom. Although the physical symptoms differ from person to person, they may include heart palpitations, shortness of breath, unusual amounts of sweating, faintness and dizziness, an urge to urinate, gastric sensations, and—in extreme cases—a sense of imminent death. After such an attack, it is no wonder that people tend to feel exhausted (Pollack & Marzol, 2000; Rachman & deSilva, 2004).

Panic attacks seemingly come out of nowhere and are unconnected to any specific stimulus. Because they don't know what triggers their feelings of panic, victims of panic attacks may become fearful of going places. In fact, some people with panic disorder develop a complication called *agoraphobia,* the fear of being in a situation in which escape is difficult and in which help for a possible panic attack would not be available. In extreme cases, people with agoraphobia never leave their homes (Smith, Friedman, & Paradis, 2002; Marcaurelle, Belanger, & Marchand, 2003, 2005).

GENERALIZED ANXIETY DISORDER

People with **generalized anxiety disorder** experience long-term, persistent anxiety and worry. Sometimes their concerns are about identifiable issues involving family, money, work, or health. In other cases, though, people with the disorder feel that something dreadful is about to happen but can't identify the reason, experiencing "free-floating" anxiety.

Because of persistent anxiety, people with generalized anxiety disorder cannot concentrate, cannot set their worry and fears aside; their lives become centered on their worry. Their anxiety may eventually cause medical problems. Because of heightened muscle tension and arousal, individuals with generalized anxiety disorder may develop headaches, dizziness, heart palpitations, or insomnia. Figure 2 shows the most common symptoms of generalized anxiety disorder.

OBSESSIVE-COMPULSIVE DISORDER

In **obsessive-compulsive disorder,** people are plagued by unwanted thoughts, called obsessions, or feel that they must carry out actions, termed compulsions, against their will.

An **obsession** is a persistent, unwanted thought or idea that keeps recurring. For example, a student may be unable to stop thinking that she has neglected to put her name on a test and may think about it constantly for the two weeks it takes to get the paper back. A man may go on vacation and wonder the whole time whether he locked his house. A woman may hear the same tune running through her head over and over. In each case, the thought or idea is unwanted and difficult to put out of mind. Of course, many people suffer from mild obsessions from time to time, but usually such thoughts persist only for a short period. For people with serious obsessions, however, the thoughts persist for days or months and may consist of bizarre, troubling images (Lee & Kwon, 2003; Lee et al., 2005).

As part of an obsessive-compulsive disorder, people may also experience **compulsions,** irresistible urges to repeatedly carry out some act that seems strange and unreasonable, even to them. Whatever the compulsive behavior is, people experience extreme anxiety if they cannot carry it out, even if it is something they want to stop. The acts may be relatively trivial, such as repeatedly checking the stove to make sure all the burners are turned off, or more unusual, such as continuously washing oneself (Carter et al., 2000; Frost & Steketee, 2002).

For example, consider this case report of a 27-year-old woman with a cleaning ritual:

> Bess would first remove all of her clothing in a preestablished sequence. She would lay out each article of clothing at specific spots on her bed, and examine each one for any indications of "contamination." She would then thoroughly scrub her body, starting at her feet and working meticulously up to the top of her head, using certain washcloths for certain areas of her body. Any articles of clothing that appeared to have been "contaminated" were thrown into the laundry. Clean clothing was put in the spots that were vacant. She would then dress herself in the opposite order from which she took the clothes off (Meyer & Osborne, 1987, p. 156).

Acrophobia, the fear of heights, is not an uncommon phobia. What sort of behavior-modification approaches might be used to deal with acrophobia?

Generalized anxiety disorder: The experience of long-term, persistent anxiety and worry.

Obsessive-compulsive disorder: A disorder characterized by obsessions or compulsions.

Obsession: A persistent, unwanted thought or idea that keeps recurring.

Compulsion: An irresistible urge to repeatedly carry out some act that seems strange and unreasonable.

FIGURE 2 Frequency of symptoms in cases of generalized anxiety disorder. (Source: Adapted from Beck & Emery, 1985, pp. 87–88.)

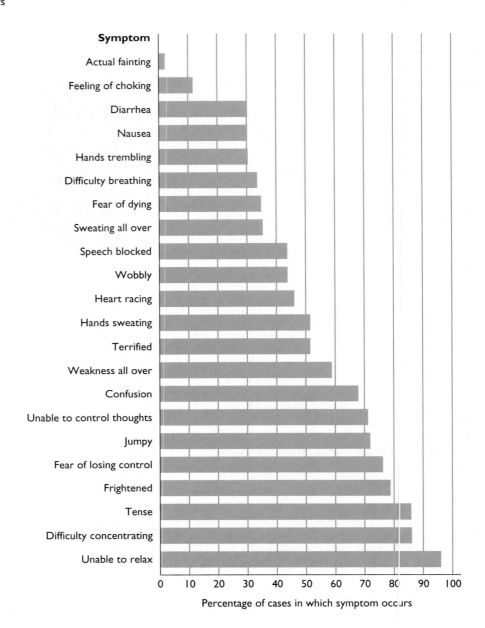

Although such compulsive rituals lead to some immediate reduction of anxiety, in the long term the anxiety returns. In fact, people with severe cases lead lives filled with unrelenting tension (Goodman, Rudorfer, & Maser, 2000; Penzel, 2000).

THE CAUSES OF ANXIETY DISORDERS

No single explanation fits all cases of anxiety disorders. Genetic factors clearly are part of the picture. For example, if one member of a pair of identical twins has panic disorder, there is a 30 percent chance that the other twin will have it also. Furthermore, a person's characteristic level of anxiety is related to a specific gene involved in the production of the neurotransmitter serotonin. This is consistent with findings indicating that certain chemical deficiencies in the brain appear to produce some kinds of anxiety disorder (Rieder, Kaufmann, & Knowles, 1996; Holmes et al., 2003).

Some researchers believe that an overactive autonomic nervous system may be at the root of panic attacks. Specifically, they suggest that poor regulation of the brain's locus ceruleus may lead to panic attacks, which cause the limbic system to become overstimulated. In turn, the overstimulated limbic system produces chronic anxiety, which ultimately leads the locus ceruleus to generate still more panic attacks (Gorman, Kent, & Sullivan, 2000; Balaban, 2002).

Psychologists who employ the behavioral perspective have taken a different approach that emphasizes environmental factors. They consider anxiety to be a learned response to stress. For instance, suppose a dog bites a young girl. When the girl next sees a dog, she is frightened and runs away—a behavior that relieves her anxiety and thereby reinforces her avoidance behavior. After repeated encounters with dogs in which she is reinforced for her avoidance behavior, she may develop a full-fledged phobia regarding dogs.

Finally, the cognitive perspective suggests that anxiety disorders grow out of inappropriate and inaccurate thoughts and beliefs about circumstances in a person's world. For example, people with anxiety disorders may view a friendly puppy as a ferocious and savage pit bull, or they may see an air disaster looming every moment they are in the vicinity of an airplane. According to the cognitive perspective, people's maladaptive thoughts about the world are at the root of an anxiety disorder (Frost & Steketee, 2002; Wang & Clark, 2002).

Somatoform Disorders

Somatoform disorders are psychological difficulties that take on a physical (somatic) form, but for which there is no medical cause. Even though an individual with a somatoform disorder reports physical symptoms, no biological cause exists, or if there is a medical problem, the person's reaction is greatly exaggerated.

One type of somatoform disorder is **hypochondriasis,** in which people have a constant fear of illness and a preoccupation with their health. These individuals believe everyday aches and pains are symptoms of a dread disease. It is not that the "symptoms" are faked; instead, it is the misinterpretation of those sensations as evidence of some serious illness—often in the face of inarguable medical evidence to the contrary—that characterizes hypochondriasis (Noyes et al., 1993, 2002, 2003; Fallon & Feinstein, 2001).

Another somatoform disorder is conversion disorder. Unlike hypochondriasis, in which there is no physical problem, **conversion disorders** involve an actual physical disturbance, such as the inability to see or hear or to move an arm or leg. The *cause* of such a physical disturbance is purely psychological; there is no biological reason for the problem. Some of Freud's classic cases involved conversion disorders. For instance, one of Freud's patients suddenly became unable to use her arm, without any apparent physiological cause. Later, just as abruptly, the problem disappeared.

Conversion disorders often begin suddenly. People wake up one morning blind or deaf, or they experience numbness that is restricted to a certain part of the body. A hand, for example, may become entirely numb, while an area above the wrist, controlled by the same nerves, remains sensitive to touch—something that is physiologically implausible. Mental health professionals refer to such a condition as "glove anesthesia," because the numb area is the part of the hand covered by a glove, not a region related to pathways of the nervous system (see Figure 3).

Surprisingly, people who experience conversion disorders frequently remain unconcerned about symptoms that most of us would expect to be highly anxiety-producing. For instance, a person in good health who wakes up blind may react in a bland, matter-of-fact way. Considering how most of us would feel if we woke up unable to see, this unemotional reaction (called *"la belle indifference,"* a French phrase meaning "a beautiful indifference") hardly seems appropriate (Brasic, 2002).

Dissociative Disorders

The classic movie *The Three Faces of Eve* and the book *Sybil* (about a girl who allegedly had sixteen personalities) represent a highly dramatic but rare class of disorders:

Somatoform disorders: Psychological difficulties that take on a physical (somatic) form, but for which there is no medical cause.

Hypochondriasis: A disorder in which people have a constant fear of illness and a preoccupation with their health.

Conversion disorder: A major somatoform disorder that involves an actual physical disturbance, such as the inability to use a sensory organ or the complete or partial inability to move an arm or leg.

FIGURE 3 Conversion disorders sometimes produce numbness in particular isolated areas of the body (indicated by the shaded areas in the figure). For instance, in glove anesthesia, the area of the body covered by a glove feels numb. However, the condition is biologically implausible because of the nerves involved, suggesting that the problem results from a psychological disorder rather than from actual nerve damage.

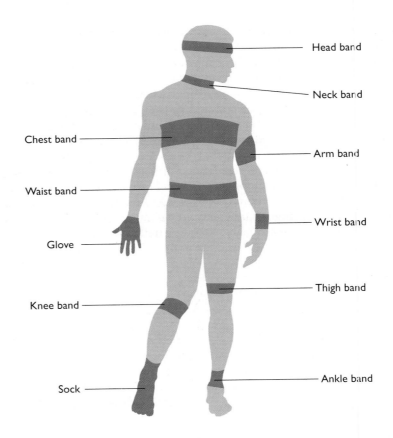

Head band

Neck band

Chest band

Arm band

Waist band

Wrist band

Glove

Thigh band

Knee band

Ankle band

Sock

Dissociative disorders: Psychological dysfunctions characterized by the separation of critical personality facets that are normally integrated, allowing stress avoidance through escape.

dissociative disorders. **Dissociative disorders** are characterized by the separation (or dissociation) of critical parts of personality that are normally integrated and work together. By dissociating key parts of the personality, people are able to keep disturbing memories or perceptions from reaching conscious awareness, thereby reducing their anxiety (Putnam, 2000; Ishikura & Tashiro, 2002; Maldonado & Spiegel, 2003).

Several dissociative disorders exist, although all of them are rare. A person with a **dissociative identity disorder** (or **multiple personality**) displays characteristics of two or more distinct personalities, identities, or personality fragments. Individual personalities often have a unique set of likes and dislikes and their own reactions to situations. Some people with multiple personalities even carry several pairs of glasses because their vision changes with each personality. Moreover, each individual personality can be well adjusted when considered on its own (Kluft, 1999; Lilienfeld & Lynn, 2003; Ellason & Ross, 2004).

Dissociative identity disorder (or multiple personality disorder): A disorder in which a person displays characteristics of two or more distinct personalities.

The problem, of course, is that the various personalities reside in only one body, forcing the personalities to take turns. Because the personalities can vary greatly from each other, the person's behavior—considered as a whole—can appear very inconsistent. For instance, in the famous case portrayed in *The Three Faces of Eve*, the meek, bland Eve White provided a stunning contrast to the dominant and carefree Eve Black (Sizemore, 1989).

Dissociative amnesia: A disorder in which a significant, selective memory loss occurs.

Dissociative amnesia is another dissociative disorder in which a significant, selective memory loss occurs. Dissociative amnesia is unlike simple amnesia, which involves an actual loss of information from memory, typically resulting from a physiological cause. In contrast, in cases of dissociative amnesia, the "forgotten" material is still present in memory—it simply cannot be recalled. The term *repressed memories* is sometimes used to describe the lost memories of people with dissociative amnesia.

In the most severe form of dissociative amnesia, individuals cannot recall their names, are unable to recognize parents and other relatives, and do not know their addresses. In other respects, though, they may appear quite normal. Apart from an inability to remember certain facts about themselves, they may be able to recall skills and abilities that they developed earlier. For instance, even though a chef may not remember where he grew up and received training, he may still be able to prepare gourmet meals.

In some cases of dissociative amnesia, the memory loss is quite profound. For example, in one dramatic case, Raymond Power Jr., an attorney, husband, father of two, and Boy Scout leader, left home to go to work one morning. Two days later he was a thousand miles away, homeless, with no memory of who he was or how he got there. Six months later he was identified, but he still had no recollection of his previous life, including his wife of 30 years and his children (Foderaro, 2006).

A more unusual form of amnesia is a condition known as **dissociative fugue.** In this state, people take sudden, impulsive trips, and sometimes assume a new identity. After a period of time—days, months, or sometimes even years—they suddenly realize that they are in a strange place and completely forget the time they have spent wandering. Their last memories are those from the time just before they entered the fugue state.

The common thread among dissociative disorders is that they allow people to escape from some anxiety-producing situation. Either the person produces a new personality to deal with stress, or the individual forgets or leaves behind the situation that caused the stress as he or she journeys to some new—and perhaps less anxiety-ridden—environment (Spiegel & Cardena, 1991; Putnam, 2000).

Dissociative fugue: A form of amnesia in which the individual leaves home and sometimes assumes a new identity.

Mood Disorders

From the time I woke up in the morning until the time I went to bed at night, I was unbearably miserable and seemingly incapable of any kind of joy or enthusiasm. Everything—every thought, word, movement—was an effort. Everything that once was sparkling now was flat. I seemed to myself to be dull, boring, inadequate, thick brained, unlit, unresponsive, chill skinned, bloodless, and sparrow drab. I doubted, completely, my ability to do anything well. It seemed as though my mind had slowed down and burned out to the point of being virtually useless (Jamison, 1995a, p. 110).

We all experience mood swings. Sometimes we are happy, perhaps even euphoric; at other times we feel upset, saddened, or depressed. Such changes in mood are a normal part of everyday life. In some people, however, moods are so pronounced and lingering—like the feelings described above by writer (and psychiatrist) Kay Jamison—that they interfere with the ability to function effectively. In extreme cases, a mood may become life-threatening, and in others it may cause the person to lose touch with reality. Situations such as these represent **mood disorders,** emotional disturbances that are strong enough to intrude on everyday living.

Mood disorder: An emotional disturbance that is strong enough to intrude on everyday living.

MAJOR DEPRESSION

President Abraham Lincoln. Queen Victoria. Newscaster Mike Wallace.

The common link among these people? Each suffered from periodic attacks of **major depression,** a severe form of depression that interferes with concentration, decision making, and sociability. Major depression is one of the more common forms of mood disorders. Some 15 million people in the United States suffer from major depression, and at any one time, 6 to 10 percent of the U.S. population is clinically depressed. Almost one in five people in the United States experiences major depression at some point in life, and 15 percent of college students have received a diagnosis of depression. The cost of depression to society approaches $50 billion a year (Dryden, 2003; Ghaemi, 2003; Hoover, 2004).

Women are twice as likely to experience major depression as men, with one-fourth of all females apt to encounter it at some point during their lives. Furthermore, although no one is sure why, the rate of depression is going up throughout the world.

Major depression: A severe form of depression that interferes with concentration, decision making, and sociability.

Results of in-depth interviews conducted in the United States, Puerto Rico, Taiwan, Lebanon, Canada, Italy, Germany, and France indicate that the incidence of depression has increased significantly over previous rates in every area. In fact, in some countries, the likelihood that individuals will have major depression at some point in their lives is three times higher than it was for earlier generations. In addition, people are developing major depression at increasingly younger ages (Beckham & Leber, 1997; Hoffman, Baldwin, & Cerbone, 2003; Miller & Gross, 2005).

When psychologists speak of major depression, they do not mean the sadness that comes from experiencing one of life's disappointments, something that we all have experienced. Some depression is normal after the breakup of a long-term relationship, the death of a loved one, or the loss of a job. It is normal even after less serious problems, such as doing badly on a test or having a romantic partner forget one's birthday.

People who suffer from major depression experience similar sorts of feelings, but the severity tends to be considerably greater. They may feel useless, worthless, and lonely and may despair over the future. Moreover, they may experience such feelings for months or even years. They may cry uncontrollably, have sleep disturbances, and be at risk for suicide. The depth of such behavior and the length of time it lasts are the hallmarks of major depression. (Figure 4 provides a self-assessment of depression.)

MANIA AND BIPOLAR DISORDER

Mania: An extended state of intense, wild elation.

While depression leads to the depths of despair, mania leads to emotional heights. **Mania** is an extended state of intense, wild elation. People experiencing mania feel intense happiness, power, invulnerability, and energy. They may become involved in wild schemes, believing they will succeed at anything they attempt. Consider, for example, the following description of an individual who experienced a manic episode:

> Mr. O'Reilly took a leave of absence from his civil service job. He purchased a large number of cuckoo clocks and then an expensive car, which he planned to use as a mobile showroom for his wares, anticipating that he would make a great deal of money. He proceeded to "tear around town" buying and selling clocks and other merchandise, and when he was not out, he was continuously on the phone making "deals." He rarely slept and, uncharacteristically, spent every evening in neighborhood bars drinking heavily and, according to him, "wheeling and dealing." . . . He was $3,000 in debt and had driven his family to exhaustion with his excessive activity and talkativeness. He said, however, that he felt "on top of the world" (Spitzer et al., 1983, p. 115).

FIGURE 4 This is a version of a test distributed by mental health organizations during the annual National Depression Screening Day, a nationwide event that seeks to identify people who are suffering from depression that is severe enough to warrant psychological intervention. (Source: National Depression Screening Day, 2003.)

A Test for Depression

To complete the questionnaire, count the number of statements with which you agree:

1. I feel downhearted, blue, and sad.
2. I don't enjoy the things that I used to.
3. I feel that others would be better off if I were dead.
4. I feel that I am not useful or needed.
5. I notice that I am losing weight.
6. I have trouble sleeping through the night.
7. I am restless and can't keep still.
8. My mind isn't as clear as it used to be.
9. I get tired for no reason.
10. I feel hopeless about the future.

Scoring: If you agree with at least five of the statements, including either item 1 or 2, and if you have had these symptoms for at least two weeks, help from a professional is strongly recommended. If you answer yes to number 3, you should get help immediately.

In many cases, people sequentially experience periods of mania and depression. This alternation of mania and depression is called **bipolar disorder** (a condition previously known as manic-depressive disorder). The swings between highs and lows may occur a few days apart or may alternate over a period of years. In addition, in bipolar disorder, periods of depression are usually longer than periods of mania. (To learn more about bipolar symptoms, complete the PsychInteractive exercise.)

Ironically, some of society's most creative individuals may have suffered from bipolar disorder. The imagination, drive, excitement, and energy that they display during manic stages allow them to make unusually creative contributions. For instance, historical analysis of the composer Robert Schumann's music shows that he was most prolific during periods of mania. In contrast, his output dropped off drastically during periods of depression (see Figure 5). On the other hand, the high output associated with mania does not necessarily lead to higher quality: Some of Schumann's greatest works were created outside his periods of mania (Ludwig, 1996; Szegedy-Maszak, 2003).

Despite the creative fires that may be lit by mania, persons who experience this disorder often show a recklessness that produces self-injury—emotionally and sometimes physically. They may alienate others with their talkativeness, inflated self-esteem, and indifference to the needs of others.

www.mhhe.com/feldmanup8
PsychInteractive Online

Bipolar Disorder

Bipolar disorder: A disorder in which a person alternates between periods of euphoric feelings of mania and periods of depression.

CAUSES OF MOOD DISORDERS

Because they represent a major mental health problem, mood disorders—and, in particular, depression—have received a good deal of study. Several approaches have been used to explain the disorder. Proponents of psychoanalytic approaches, for example, see depression as the result of feelings of loss (real or potential) or of anger directed at oneself. One psychoanalytic approach, for instance, suggests that depression is produced by the loss or threatened loss of a parent early in life. Another psychoanalytic view maintains that people feel responsible for the bad things that happen to them and direct their anger inward.

Yet compelling evidence has been found that both bipolar disorder and major depression may have genetic and biochemical roots. For example, bipolar disorder clearly runs in some families. Furthermore, several neurotransmitters appear to play a

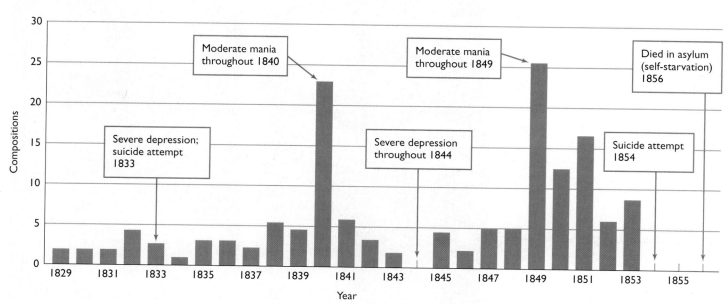

FIGURE 5 The number of musical compositions written by composer Robert Schumann in a given year is related to his periods of depression and mania (Slater & Meyer, 1959; reprinted in Jamison, 1993). Why do you think mania might be associated with creative productivity in some people?

role in depression. For instance, alterations in the functioning of serotonin and norepinephrine in the brain are related to the disorder (Vogel, Feng, & Kinney, 2000; Leonard, 2001; Plomin & McGuffin, 2003).

Behavioral theories of depression argue that the stresses of life produce a reduction in positive reinforcers. As a result, people begin to withdraw, which only serves to reduce positive reinforcers further. In addition, people receive attention for their depressive behavior, which further reinforces the depression (Lewinsohn & Essau, 2002; Lewinsohn et al., 2003).

Some explanations for mood disorders attribute them to cognitive factors. For example, psychologist Martin Seligman suggests that depression is largely a response to learned helplessness. *Learned helplessness* is a learned expectation that events in one's life are uncontrollable and that one cannot escape from the situation. As a consequence, people simply give up fighting aversive events and submit to them, thereby producing depression. Other theorists go a step further, suggesting that depression results from hopelessness, a combination of learned helplessness and an expectation that negative outcomes in one's life are inevitable (Petersen, Maier, & Seligman, 1993; Maier & Watkins, 2000; Abramson et al., 2002; Kwon & Laurenceau, 2002).

Clinical psychologist Aaron Beck has proposed that faulty cognitions underlie people's depressed feelings. Specifically, his cognitive theory of depression suggests that depressed individuals typically view themselves as life's losers, blaming themselves whenever anything goes wrong. By focusing on the negative side of situations, they feel inept and unable to act constructively to change their environment. In sum, their negative cognitions lead to feelings of depression (Newman et al., 2002).

Brain imaging studies suggest that people with depression experience a general blunting of emotional reactions. For example, one study found that the brains of people with depression showed significantly less activation when they viewed photos of human faces displaying strong emotions than those without the disorder (Gotlib et al., 2004; see Figure 6).

Other recent explanations of depression derive from evolutionary psychology, which considers how behavior is influenced by our genetic inheritance from our ancestors. In the evolutionary view, depression is an adaptive response to unattainable

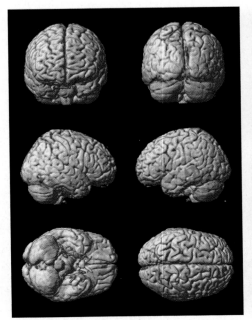
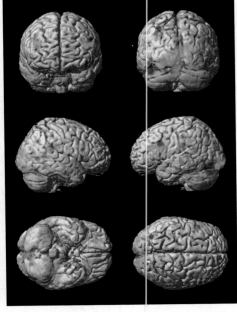

FIGURE 6 The brains of those with depression *(left)* show significantly less activation in response to photos of sad, angry, and fearful faces than those of people without the disorder *(right)*. (Source: Ian Gotlib, Stanford Mood and Anxiety Disorders Laboratory, 2005.)

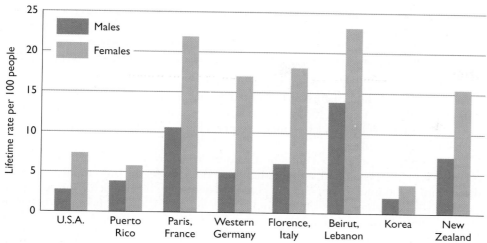

FIGURE 7 Across different places and cultures, women are diagnosed more frequently with depression than men. (Source: Weissman & Olfson, 1995.)

goals. When people fruitlessly pursue an ever-elusive goal, depression begins, ending pursuit of the goal. Ultimately, when the depression lifts, people can turn to other, more reasonable goals. In this view, depression serves a positive function, in the long run increasing the chances of survival for particular individuals, who can then pass the behavior to their offspring. Such reasoning, of course, is highly speculative (Nesse, 2000; Siegert & Ward, 2002).

The various theories of depression have not provided a complete answer to an elusive question that has dogged researchers: Why does depression occur in approximately twice as many women as men—a pattern (shown in Figure 7) that is similar across a variety of cultures?

One explanation suggests that the stress experienced by women may be greater than that experienced by men at certain points in their lives—such as when a woman must simultaneously earn a living and be the primary caregiver for her children. In addition, women have a higher risk for physical and sexual abuse, typically earn lower wages than men, report greater unhappiness with their marriages, and generally experience chronic negative circumstances (Antonucci et al., 2002; Holden, 2006; Nolen-Hoeksema, 2007).

Biological factors may also explain some women's depression. For example, because the rate of female depression begins to rise during puberty, some psychologists believe that hormones make women more vulnerable to the disorder. In addition, 25 to 50 percent of women who take oral contraceptives report symptoms of depression, and depression that occurs after the birth of a child is linked to hormonal changes. Finally, structural differences in men's and women's brains that we discussed in the neuroscience and behavior modules may be related to gender differences in depression (Strickland, 1992; Holden, 2005).

It is clear, ultimately, that researchers have discovered no definitive solutions to the puzzle of depression, and there are many alternative explanations. Most likely, a complex interaction of several factors causes mood disorders.

Schizophrenia

I'm a doctor, you know . . . I don't have a diploma, but I'm a doctor. I'm glad to be a mental patient, because it taught me how to be humble. I use Cover Girl creamy natural makeup. Oral Roberts has been here to visit me . . . This place is where *Mad* magazine is published. The Nixons make Noxon metal polish. When I was a little girl, I used to sit and tell stories to myself. When I was older, I turned off the sound on the TV set and made up dialogue to go with the shows I watched . . . I'm a week pregnant. I have schizophrenia—cancer of the nerves. My body is overcrowded with nerves. This is going to win me the Nobel Prize for medicine. I don't consider myself schizophrenic anymore. There's no such thing as schizophrenia, there's only mental telepathy. I once had a friend named Camilla Costello (Sheehan, 1982, pp. 72–73).

This excerpt illustrates the efforts of a woman with schizophrenia, one of the more severe forms of mental disturbance, to hold a conversation with a clinician. People with schizophrenia account for by far the largest percentage of those hospitalized for mental disorders. They are also in many respects the least likely to recover from their psychological difficulties.

Schizophrenia: A class of disorders in which severe distortion of reality occurs.

Schizophrenia refers to a class of disorders in which severe distortion of reality occurs. Thinking, perception, and emotion may deteriorate; the individual may withdraw from social interaction; and the person may display bizarre behavior. Although there are several types of schizophrenia (see Figure 8), the distinctions between them are not always clear-cut. Moreover, the symptoms displayed by persons with schizophrenia may vary considerably over time, and people with schizophrenia show significant differences in the pattern of their symptoms even when they are labeled with the same diagnostic category. Nonetheless, a number of characteristics reliably distinguish schizophrenia from other disorders. They include the following:

- *Decline from a previous level of functioning.* An individual can no longer carry out activities he or she was once able to do.
- *Disturbances of thought and language.* People with schizophrenia use logic and language in a peculiar way. Their thinking often does not make sense, and their information processing is frequently faulty. They also do not follow conventional linguistic rules (Penn et al., 1997). Consider, for example, the following response to the question "Why do you think people believe in God?"

> Uh, let's, I don't know why, let's see, balloon travel. He holds it up for you, the balloon. He don't let you fall out, your little legs sticking down through the clouds. He's down to the smokestack, looking through the smoke trying to get the balloon gassed up you know. Way they're flying on top that way, legs sticking out. I don't know, looking down on the ground, heck, that'd make you so dizzy you just stay and sleep you know, hold down and sleep there. I used to be sleep outdoors, you know, sleep outdoors instead of going home (Chapman & Chapman, 1973, p. 3).

As this selection illustrates, although the basic grammatical structure may be intact, the substance of thinking characteristic of schizophrenia is often illogical, garbled, and lacking in meaningful content (Holden, 2003).

FIGURE 8 The distinctions among the different types of schizophrenia are not always clear-cut, and symptoms may vary considerably over time.

Types of Schizophrenia	
Type	**Symptoms**
Disorganized (hebephrenic) schizophrenia	Innappropriate laughter and giggling, silliness, incoherent speech, infantile behavior, strange and sometimes obscene behavior
Paranoid schizophrenia	Delusions and hallucinations of persecution or of greatness, loss of judgment, erratic and unpredictable behavior
Catatonic schizophrenia	Major disturbances in movement; in some phases, loss of all motion, with patient frozen into a single position, remaining that way for hours and sometimes even days; in other phases, hyperactivity and wild, sometimes violent, movement
Undifferentiated schizophrenia	Variable mixture of major symptoms of schizophrenia; classification used for patients who cannot be typed into any of the more specific categories
Residual schizophrenia	Minor signs of schizophrenia after a more serious episode

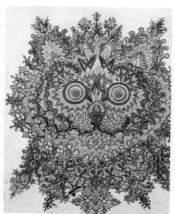

FIGURE 9 This unusual art was created by an individual with schizophrenia.

- *Delusions.* People with schizophrenia often have delusions, firmly held, unshakable beliefs with no basis in reality. Among the common delusions experienced by people with schizophrenia are the beliefs that they are being controlled by someone else, they are being persecuted by others, and their thoughts are being broadcast so that others know what they are thinking (Siddle et al., 2002; Stompe et al., 2003).

- *Hallucinations and perceptual disorders.* People with schizophrenia do not perceive the world as most other people do. They also may have *hallucinations,* the experience of perceiving things that do not actually exist. Furthermore, they may see, hear, or smell things differently from others (see Figure 9) and do not even have a sense of their bodies in the way that others do, having difficulty determining where their bodies stop and the rest of the world begins (Reichman & Rabins, 1996; Roehricht & Priebe, 2002; Copolov et al., 2003; Botvinick, 2004).

- *Emotional disturbances.* People with schizophrenia sometimes show a bland lack of emotion in which even the most dramatic events produce little or no emotional response. Conversely, they may display emotion that is inappropriate to a situation. For example, a person with schizophrenia may laugh uproariously at a funeral or react with anger when being helped by someone.

- *Withdrawal.* People with schizophrenia tend to have little interest in others. They tend not to socialize or hold real conversations with others, although they may talk at another person. In the most extreme cases they do not even acknowledge the presence of other people, appearing to be in their own isolated world.

Usually, the onset of schizophrenia occurs in early adulthood, and the symptoms follow one of two primary courses. In *process schizophrenia,* the symptoms develop slowly and subtly. There may be a gradual withdrawal from the world, excessive daydreaming, and a blunting of emotion, until eventually the disorder reaches the point where others cannot overlook it. In other cases, known as *reactive schizophrenia,* the onset of symptoms is sudden and conspicuous. The treatment outlook for reactive schizophrenia is relatively favorable, but process schizophrenia has proved more difficult to treat.

The symptoms of schizophrenia can be classified into two types. Positive-symptom schizophrenia is indicated by the presence of disordered behavior such as hallucinations, delusions, and emotional extremes. In contrast, negative-symptom schizophrenia shows an absence or loss of normal functioning, such as social withdrawal or blunted emotions. Schizophrenia researchers sometimes speak of *Type I schizophrenia,* in which positive symptoms are dominant, and *Type II schizophrenia,* in which negative symptoms are more prominent.

The distinction between Type I and Type II schizophrenia is important because it suggests that two different processes might trigger schizophrenia, the cause of which remains one of the greatest mysteries facing psychologists who deal with disordered behavior. To increase your understanding of schizophrenia, work on the PsychInteractive exercise.

SOLVING THE PUZZLE OF SCHIZOPHRENIA: BIOLOGICAL CAUSES

Although schizophrenic behavior clearly departs radically from normal behavior, its causes are less apparent. It does appear, however, that schizophrenia has both biological and environmental origins (Sawa & Snyder, 2002).

Let's first consider the evidence pointing to a biological cause. Because schizophrenia is more common in some families than in others, genetic factors seem to be involved in producing at least a susceptibility to or readiness for developing schizophrenia. For example, the closer the genetic link between a person with schizophrenia and another individual, the greater the likelihood that the other person will experience the disorder (Brzustowicz et al., 2000; Plomin & McGuffin, 2003; Gottesman & Hanson, 2005; see Figure 10).

However, if genetics alone were responsible for schizophrenia, the chance of both of two identical twins having schizophrenia would be 100 percent instead of just under 50 percent, because identical twins have the same genetic makeup. Moreover, attempts to find a link between schizophrenia and a particular gene have been only partly successful. Apparently, genetic factors alone do not produce schizophrenia (Franzek & Beckmann, 1996; Lenzenweger & Dworkin, 1998).

One intriguing biological hypothesis to explain schizophrenia is that the brains of people with the disorder may harbor either a biochemical imbalance or a structural abnormality. For example, the *dopamine hypothesis* suggests that schizophrenia occurs when there is excess activity in the areas of the brain that use dopamine as a neurotransmitter. This hypothesis came to light after the discovery that drugs that block dopamine action in brain pathways can be highly effective in reducing the symptoms of schizophrenia. Other research suggests that glutamate, another neurotransmitter, may be a major contributor to the disorder (Baumeister & Francis, 2002; Remington, 2003; Javitt & Coyle, 2004).

Some biological explanations propose that structural abnormalities exist in the brains of people with schizophrenia, perhaps as a result of exposure to a virus during prenatal development. For example, some research shows abnormalities in the neural circuits of the cortex and limbic systems of individuals with schizophrenia. Consistent with such research, people with schizophrenia and those without the disorder show different brain functioning (Brown et al., 1996; Lenzenweger & Dworkin, 1998; Bartzokis et al., 2003; see Figures 11 and 12).

FIGURE 10 The closer the genetic links between two people, the greater the likelihood that if one experiences schizophrenia, so will the other some time during his or her life. However, genetics is not the full story, because if it were, the risk of identical twins having schizophrenia would be 100 percent, not the 48 percent shown in this figure. (Source: Gottesman, 1991.)

Risk of Developing Schizophrenia, Based on Genetic Relatedness to a Person with Schizophrenia		
Relationship	**Genetic Relatedness, %**	**Risk of Developing Schizophrenia, %**
Identical twin	100	48
Child of two schizophrenic parents	100	46
Fraternal twin	50	17
Offspring of one schizophrenic parent	50	17
Sibling	50	9
Nephew or niece	25	4
Spouse	0	2
Unrelated person	0	1

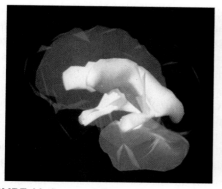
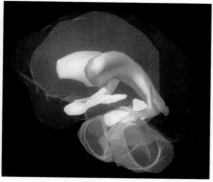

FIGURE 11 Structural changes in the brain have been found in people with schizophrenia. In the first MRI reconstruction of the brain of a patient with schizophrenia *(left)*, the hippocampus (yellow) is shrunken, and the ventricles (gray) are enlarged and fluid-filled. In contrast, the brain of a person without the disorder *(right)* appears structurally different. (Source: N.C. Andreasen, University of Iowa.)

Further evidence for the importance of biological factors shows that when people with schizophrenia hear voices during hallucinations, the parts of the brain responsible for hearing and language processing become active. When they have visual hallucinations, the parts of the brain involved in movement and color are active. At the same time, people with schizophrenia often have unusually low activity in the brain's frontal lobes—the parts of the brain involved with emotional regulation, insight, and the evaluation of sensory stimuli (Stern & Silbersweig, 2001).

ENVIRONMENTAL PERSPECTIVES ON SCHIZOPHRENIA

Although biological factors provide important pieces of the puzzle of schizophrenia, we still need to consider past and current experiences in the environments of people

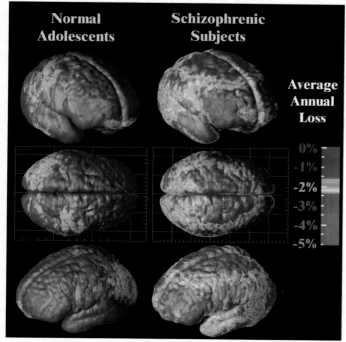

FIGURE 12 These MRI scans compare deterioration in the gray matter of the cortex of adolescent patients with one type of schizophrenia. (Source: Paul Thompson and Arthur Toga, UCLA Laboratory of Neuro Imaging, and Judith Rapoport, National Institute of Mental Health.)

who develop the disturbance. For instance, psychoanalytic approaches suggest that schizophrenia is a form of regression to earlier experiences and stages of life. Freud believed, for instance, that people with schizophrenia lack strong enough egos to cope with their unacceptable impulses. They regress to the oral stage—a time when the id and ego are not yet separated. Therefore, individuals with schizophrenia essentially lack an ego and act out impulses without concern for reality.

Although this reasoning is theoretically plausible, little evidence supports psychoanalytic explanations. Somewhat more convincing theories look toward the emotional and communication patterns of the families of people with schizophrenia. For instance, some researchers suggest that schizophrenia results from high levels of expressed emotion. *Expressed emotion* is an interaction style characterized by criticism, hostility, and emotional intrusiveness by family members. Other researchers suggest that faulty communication patterns lie at the heart of schizophrenia (Bayer, 1996; Linszen et al., 1997; Miklowitz & Tompson, 2003).

Psychologists who take a cognitive perspective on schizophrenia suggest that the problems in thinking experienced by people with the disorder point to a cognitive cause. Some suggest that schizophrenia results from *overattention* to stimuli in the environment. Rather than being able to screen out unimportant or inconsequential stimuli and focus on the most important things in the environment, people with schizophrenia may be excessively receptive to virtually everything in their environment. As a consequence, their information-processing capabilities become overloaded and eventually break down. Other cognitive experts argue that schizophrenia results from *underattention* to certain stimuli. According to this explanation, people with schizophrenia fail to focus sufficiently on important stimuli, and pay attention to other, less important information in their surroundings (Braff, 1995).

Although it is plausible that overattention and underattention are related to different forms of schizophrenia, these phenomena do not explain the origins of such information-processing disorders. Consequently, cognitive approaches—like other environmental explanations—do not provide a full explanation of the disorder.

THE MULTIPLE CAUSES OF SCHIZOPHRENIA

The predominant approach used to explain the onset of schizophrenia today, the *predisposition model of schizophrenia,* incorporates a number of biological and environmental factors. This model suggests that individuals may inherit a predisposition or an inborn sensitivity to schizophrenia that makes them particularly vulnerable to stressful factors in the environment, such as social rejection or dysfunctional family communication patterns. The stressors may vary, but if they are strong enough and are coupled with a genetic predisposition, the result will be the onset of schizophrenia. Similarly, a strong genetic predisposition may lead to the onset of schizophrenia even when the environmental stressors are relatively weak.

In short, the models used today associate schizophrenia with several kinds of biological and environmental factors. It is increasingly clear, then, that no single factor, but a combination of interrelated variables, produces schizophrenia (Lenzenweger & Dworkin, 1998; Meltzer, 2000; McDonald & Murray, 2004).

Personality Disorders

I had always wanted lots of things; as a child I can remember wanting a bullet that a friend of mine had brought in to show the class. I took it and put it into my school bag and when my friend noticed it was missing, I was the one who stayed after school with him and searched the room, and I was the one who sat with him and bitched about the other kids and how one of them took his bullet. I even went home with him to help him break the news to his uncle, who had brought it home from the war for him. But that was petty compared with the stuff I did later. I wanted a Ph.D. very badly, but I didn't want to work very hard—just enough to get by. I never did the experiments I reported; hell, I was smart enough to make up the results. I knew enough about statistics to make anything look plausible. I got my master's degree without even spending one hour in a laboratory. I mean, the professors believed anything. I'd stay out all night drinking and being with my friends, and the next day I'd get in just before them and tell 'em I'd been in the lab all night. They'd actually feel sorry for me (Duke & Nowicki, 1979, pp. 309–310).

This excerpt provides a graphic first-person account of a person with a personality disorder. A **personality disorder** is characterized by a set of inflexible, maladaptive behavior patterns that keep a person from functioning appropriately in society. Personality disorders differ from the other problems we have discussed because those affected by them often have little sense of personal distress associated with the psychological maladjustment. In fact, people with personality disorders frequently lead seemingly normal lives. However, just below the surface lies a set of inflexible, maladaptive personality traits that do not permit these individuals to function as members of society (Clarkin & Lenzenweger, 2004; Millon, Davis, & E. Millon, 1996, 2000).

The best-known type of personality disorder, illustrated by the case above, is the **antisocial personality disorder** (sometimes referred to as a sociopathic personality). Individuals with this disturbance show no regard for the moral and ethical rules of society or the rights of others. Although they can appear quite intelligent and likable (at least at first), upon closer examination they turn out to be manipulative and deceptive. Moreover, they lack any guilt or anxiety about their wrongdoing. When those with antisocial personality disorder behave in a way that injures someone else, they understand intellectually that they have caused harm but feel no remorse (Lykken, 1995; Goodwin & Hamilton, 2003).

People with antisocial personality disorder are often impulsive and lack the ability to withstand frustration. They can be extremely manipulative. They also may have excellent social skills; they can be charming, engaging, and highly persuasive. Some of the best con artists have antisocial personalities.

What causes such an unusual constellation of problem behaviors? A variety of factors have been suggested, ranging from an inability to experience emotions appropriately to problems in family relationships. For example, in many cases of antisocial behavior, the individual has come from a home in which a parent has died or left, or one in which there is a lack of affection, a lack of consistency in discipline, or outright rejection. Other explanations concentrate on sociocultural factors, because an unusually high proportion of people with antisocial personalities come from lower socioeconomic groups. Still, no one has been able to pinpoint the specific causes of antisocial personalities, and it is likely that some combination of factors is responsible (Nigg & Goldsmith, 1994; Rosenstein & Horowitz, 1996; Costa & Widiger, 2002).

People with **borderline personality disorder** have difficulty developing a secure sense of who they are. As a consequence, they tend to rely on relationships with others to define their identity. The problem with this strategy is that rejections are devastating. Furthermore, people with this disorder distrust others and have difficulty controlling their anger. Their emotional volatility leads to impulsive and self-destructive behavior. Individuals with borderline personality disorder often feel empty and alone. They may form intense, sudden, one-sided relationships, demanding the attention of another person and then feeling angry when they don't receive it. One reason for this behavior is that they may have a background in which others discounted or criticized their emotional reactions, and they may not have learned to regulate their emotions effectively (Linehan, Cochran, & Kehrer, 2001; Trull, Stepp, & Durrett, 2003). You can learn more by completing the PsychInteractive exercise on borderline personality disorders.

Personality disorder: A disorder characterized by a set of inflexible, maladaptive behavior patterns that keep a person from functioning appropriately in society.

Antisocial personality disorder: A disorder in which individuals show no regard for the moral and ethical rules of society or the rights of others.

Borderline personality disorder: A disorder in which individuals have difficulty developing a secure sense of who they are.

www.mhhe.com/feldmanup8
PsychInteractive Online

Borderline Personality Disorder

Narcissistic personality disorder:
A personality disturbance characterized by an exaggerated sense of self-importance.

Another example of a personality disturbance is the **narcissistic personality disorder,** which is characterized by an exaggerated sense of self-importance. Those with the disorder expect special treatment from others, while at the same time disregarding others' feelings. In some ways, in fact, the main attribute of the narcissistic personality is an inability to experience empathy for other people.

There are several other categories of personality disorder, ranging in severity from individuals who may simply be regarded by others as eccentric, obnoxious, or difficult to people who act in a manner that is criminal and dangerous to others. Although they are not out of touch with reality in the way that people with schizophrenia are, people with personality disorders lead lives that put them on the fringes of society (Millon, Davis, & E. Millon, 2000; Trull & Widiger, 2003).

Childhood Disorders

We typically view childhood as a time of innocence and relative freedom from stress. In reality, though, almost 20 percent of children and 40 percent of adolescents experience significant emotional or behavioral disorders (Romano et al., 2001; Broidy, Nagin, & Trembling, 2003; Nolen-Hoeksema, 2006)

For example, although major depression is more prevalent in adults, around 2.5 percent of children and more than 8 percent of adolescents suffer from the disorder. In fact, by the time they reach age 20, between 15 and 20 percent of children and adolescents will experience an episode of major depression (Garber & Horowitz, 2002).

Children do not always display depression in the same way adults do. Rather than showing profound sadness or hopelessness, childhood depression may produce the expression of exaggerated fears, clinginess, or avoidance of everyday activities. In older children, the symptoms may be sulking, school problems, and even acts of delinquency (Wenar, 1994; Koplewicz, 2002; Seroczynski, Jacquez, & Cole, 2003).

Attention-deficit hyperactivity disorder (ADHD): A disorder marked by inattention, impulsiveness, a low tolerance for frustration, and a great deal of inappropriate activity.

A considerably more common childhood disorder is **attention deficit hyperactivity disorder,** or **ADHD,** a disorder marked by inattention, impulsiveness, a low tolerance for frustration, and generally a great deal of inappropriate activity. Although all children show such behavior some of the time, it is so common in children diagnosed with ADHD that it interferes with their everyday functioning (Brown, 2000; Swanson, Harris, & Graham, 2003; Barkley, 2005).

ADHD is surprisingly widespread, with estimates ranging between 3 and 5 percent of the school-age population—or some 3.5 million children under the age of 18 in the United States. Children diagnosed with the disorder are often exhausting to parents and teachers, and even their peers find them difficult to deal with.

The cause of ADHD is not known, although most experts feel that it is produced by dysfunctions in the nervous system. For example, one theory suggests that unusually low levels of arousal in the central nervous system cause ADHD. To compensate, children with ADHD seek out stimulation to increase arousal. Still, such theories are speculative. Furthermore, because many children occasionally show behaviors characteristic of ADHD, it often is misdiagnosed. Only the frequency and persistence of the symptoms of ADHD allow for a correct diagnosis, which can be done only by a trained professional (Hinshaw et al., 1997; Barkley, 2000).

Other Disorders

It's important to keep in mind that the various forms of abnormal behavior described in *DSM-IV-TR* cover much more ground than we have been able to discuss in this module. Some relate to topics previously considered in other contexts, such as *psychoactive substance-use disorder*, in which problems arise from the abuse of drugs; *eating disorders*; and *sexual disorders*, in which one's sexual activity is unsatisfactory. Another important class of disorders is *organic mental disorders,* some of which we touched on previously. These are problems that have a purely biological basis, such as Alzheimer's disease and some types of mental retardation. There are other disorders we have not mentioned at all, and each of the classes we have discussed can be divided into several subcategories (Kopelman & Fleminger, 2002; Pratt et al., 2003; Reijonen et al., 2003).

RECAP/EVALUATE/RETHINK

RECAP

What are the major psychological disorders?

- Anxiety disorders are present when a person experiences so much anxiety that it affects daily functioning. Specific types of anxiety disorders include phobic disorder, panic disorder, generalized anxiety disorder, and obsessive-compulsive disorder. (pp. 527–530)
- Somatoform disorders are psychological difficulties that take on a physical (somatic) form, but for which there is no medical cause. Examples are hypochondriasis and conversion disorders. (p. 530)
- Dissociative disorders are marked by the separation, or dissociation, of crucial parts of personality that are usually integrated. The major kinds of dissociative disorders are dissociative identity disorder (multiple personalities), dissociative amnesia, and dissociative fugue. (pp. 531–533)
- Mood disorders are characterized by emotional states of depression or euphoria so strong that they intrude on everyday living. They include major depression and bipolar disorder. (pp. 533–535)
- Schizophrenia is one of the more severe forms of mental illness. Symptoms of schizophrenia include declines in functioning, thought and language disturbances, perceptual disorders, emotional disturbance, and withdrawal from others. (pp. 537–539)
- Strong evidence links schizophrenia to genetic, biochemical, and environmental factors. According to the predisposition model, an interaction among various factors produces the disorder. (pp. 540–542)
- People with personality disorders experience little or no personal distress, but they do suffer from an inability to function as normal members of society. These disorders include antisocial personality disorder, borderline personality disorder, and narcissistic personality disorder. (pp. 542–544)
- Childhood disorders include major depression and attention deficit hyperactivity disorder (ADHD), which is marked by inattention, impulsiveness, a low tolerance for frustration, and inappropriate activity. (p. 544)

EVALUATE

1. Kathy is terrified of elevators. She could be suffering from a(n)
   a. Obsessive-compulsive disorder
   b. Phobic disorder
   c. Panic disorder
   d. Generalized anxiety disorder
2. Carmen described an incident in which her anxiety suddenly rose to a peak and she felt a sense of impending doom. Carmen experienced a(n) _____.
3. Troubling thoughts that persist for days or months are known as
   a. Obsessions
   b. Compulsions
   c. Rituals
   d. Panic attacks
4. An overpowering urge to carry out a strange ritual is called a(n) _____.
5. In what major way does conversion disorder differ from hypochondriasis?
6. The separation of the personality, providing escape from stressful situations, is the key factor in _____ disorders.
7. States of extreme euphoria and energy paired with severe depression characterize _____ disorder.
8. _____ schizophrenia is characterized by symptoms that are sudden and of easily identifiable onset; _____ schizophrenia develops gradually over a person's life span.
9. The _____ states that schizophrenia may be caused by an excess of certain neurotransmitters in the brain.
10. Which of the following theories states that schizophrenia is caused by the combination of genetic factors and environmental stressors?
    a. Learned-inattention theory
    b. Predisposition model
    c. Dopamine hypothesis
    d. Learned-helplessness theory

RETHINK

1. What cultural factors might contribute to the rate of anxiety disorders found in a culture? How might the experience of anxiety differ among people of different cultures?

2. *From the perspective of a social worker:* Personality disorders are often not apparent to others, and many people with these problems seem to live basically normal lives and are not a threat to others. Because these people often appear from the outside to function well in society, why should they be considered psychologically disordered?

Answers to Evaluate Questions

1. b; 2. panic attack; 3. a; 4. compulsion; 5. in conversion disorder, an actual physical disturbance is present; 6. dissociative; 7. bipolar; 8. reactive, process; 9. dopamine hypothesis; 10. b

KEY TERMS

anxiety disorder p. 527
phobias p. 528
panic disorder p. 528
generalized anxiety disorder p. 529
obsessive-compulsive disorder p. 529
obsession p. 529
compulsion p. 529

somatoform disorders p. 531
hypochondriasis p. 531
conversion disorder p. 531
dissociative disorders p. 532
dissociative identity disorder (or multiple personality disorder) p. 532
dissociative amnesia p. 532

dissociative fugue p. 533
mood disorder p. 533
major depression p. 533
mania p. 534
bipolar disorder p. 535
schizophrenia p. 538
personality disorder p. 543
antisocial personality disorder p. 543

borderline personality disorder p. 543
narcissistic personality disorder p. 544
attention deficit hyperactivity disorder (ADHD) p. 544

Psychological Disorders in Perspective

The Prevalence of Psychological Disorders: The Mental State of the Union

Key Concepts

How prevalent are psychological disorders?

What indicators signal a need for the help of a mental health practitioner?

How common are the kinds of psychological disorders we've been discussing? Here's one answer: Every second person you meet in the United States is likely to suffer, at some point during his or her life, from a psychological disorder.

That's the conclusion drawn from a massive study on the prevalence of psychological disorders. In that study, researchers conducted face-to-face interviews with more than 8,000 men and women between the ages of 15 and 54 years. The sample was designed to be representative of the population of the United States. According to results of the study, 48 percent of those interviewed had experienced a disorder at some point in their lives. In addition, 30 percent experienced a disorder in any particular year, and the number of people who experienced simultaneous multiple disorders (known as *comorbidity*) was significant (Welkowitz et al., 2000; Kessler, Berglund, & Demler, 2005).

The most common disorder reported in the study was depression, with 17 percent of those surveyed reporting at least one major episode. Ten percent had suffered from depression during the current year. The next most common disorder was alcohol dependence, which occurred at a lifetime incidence rate of 14 percent. In addition, 7 percent of those interviewed had experienced alcohol dependence in the last year. Other frequently occurring psychological disorders were drug dependence, disorders involving panic (such as an overwhelming fear of talking to strangers and terror of heights), and posttraumatic stress disorder.

Although some researchers think the estimates of severe disorders may be too high (Narrow et al., 2002), the national findings are consistent with studies of college students and their psychological difficulties. For example, in one study of the problems of students who visited a college counseling center, more than 40 percent of students reported being depressed (see Figure 1). These figures include only students who sought help from the counseling center, not those who did not seek treatment. Consequently, the figures are not representative of the entire college population (Benton et al., 2003).

The significant level of psychological disorders is a problem not only in the United States; according to the World Health Organization (WHO), mental health difficulties are also a global concern. Throughout the world, psychological disorders are widespread. Furthermore, there are economic disparities in treatment, such that more affluent people with mild disorders receive more and better treatment than poor people who have more severe disorders (The WHO World Mental Health Survey Consortium, 2004; see Figure 2 on page 549).

Also, keep in mind that the incidence of specific disorders varies significantly in other cultures. For instance, cross-cultural surveys show that the incidence of major depression varies significantly from one culture to another. The probability of having at least one episode of depression is only 1.5 percent in Taiwan and 2.9 percent in Korea, compared with 11.6 percent in New Zealand and 16.4 percent in France. Such

FIGURE 1 The problems reported by students visiting a college counseling center. Would you have predicted this pattern of psychological difficulties? (Source: Benton et al., 2003.)

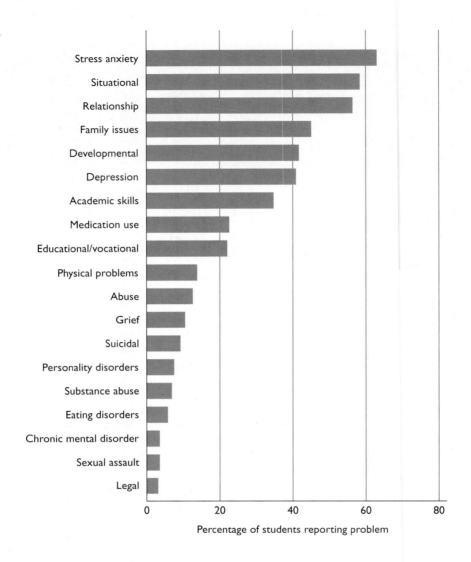

Percentage of students reporting problem

www.mhhe.com/feldmanup8
PsychInteractive Online

Prevalence of Psychological Disorders

notable differences underscore the importance of considering the cultural context of psychological disorders (Weissman et al., 1996; Horwarth & Weissman, 2000; Tseng, 2003). (You can learn more by completing the PsychInteractive exercise on prevalence of psychological disorders.)

The Social and Cultural Context of Psychological Disorders

In considering the nature of the psychological disorders described in *DSM-IV-TR*, it's important to keep in mind that the specific disorders reflect turn-of-the-twenty-first-century Western cultures. The classification system provides a snapshot of how its authors viewed mental disorders when it was published in 1994. In fact, the development of the most recent version of *DSM* was a source of great debate, in part reflecting issues that divide society.

For example, two disorders caused particular controversy during the revision process. One, known as *self-defeating personality disorder,* was ultimately removed from the appendix, where it had appeared in the previous revision. The term *self-defeating personality disorder* had been applied to cases in which people who were treated

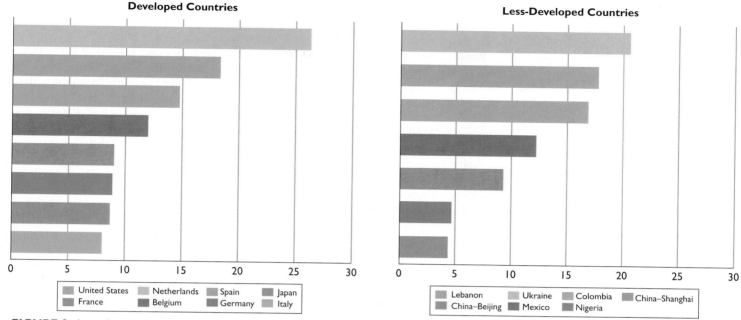

FIGURE 2 According to a global survey conducted by the World Health Organization, the prevalence of psychological disorders is widespread. These figures show the prevalence of any psychological disorder within a 12-month period. (Source: The WHO World Mental Health Survey Consortium, 2004, Table 3.)

unpleasantly or demeaningly in relationships neither left nor took other action. It was typically used to describe people who remained in abusive relationships.

Although some clinicians argued that it was a valid category, one that they observed in clinical practice, the disorder seemed to lack enough research evidence to support its designation as a disorder in *DSM*. Furthermore, some critics complained that use of the label had the effect of condemning targets of abuse for their plight—a blame-the-victim phenomenon—and as a result, the category was removed from the manual.

A second and even more controversial category was *premenstrual dysphoric disorder*. That disorder is characterized by severe, incapacitating mood changes or depression related to a woman's menstrual cycle. Some critics argued that the classification simply labels normal female behavior as a disorder. Former U.S. Surgeon General Antonia Novello suggested that what "in women is called PMS [premenstrual syndrome, a similar classification] in men is called healthy aggression and initiative" (Cotton, 1993, p. 270). Advocates for including the disorder prevailed, however, and premenstrual dysphoric disorder appears in the appendix of *DSM-IV-TR* (Hartung & Widiger, 1998).

Such controversies underline the fact that our understanding of abnormal behavior reflects the society and culture in which we live. Future revisions of *DSM* may include a different catalog of disorders. Even now, other cultures might include a list of disorders that look very different from the list that appears in the current *DSM*, as we discuss next.

In most people's estimation, a person who hears voices of the recently deceased is probably a victim of a psychological disturbance. Yet some Plains Indians routinely hear the voices of the dead calling to them from the afterlife.

This is only one example of the role of culture in labeling behavior as "abnormal." In fact, among all the major adult disorders included in the *DSM* categorization, just four are found across all cultures of

Exploring DIVERSITY

DSM and Culture—and the Culture of *DSM*

the world: schizophrenia, bipolar disorder, major depression, and anxiety disorders. *All* the rest are specific to North America and Western Europe (Kleinman, 1996; Cohen, Slomkowski, & Robins, 1999; López & Guarnaccia, 2000).

Take, for instance, anorexia nervosa, the disorder in which people develop inaccurate views of their body appearance, become obsessed with their weight, and refuse to eat, sometimes starving in the process. This disorder occurs only in cultures that hold the societal standard that slender female bodies are the most desirable. In most of the world, where such a standard does not exist, anorexia nervosa does not occur. Interestingly, there is no anorexia nervosa in all of Asia, with two exceptions: the upper and upper-middle classes of Japan and Hong Kong, where Western influence tends to be great. In fact, anorexia nervosa developed fairly recently even in Western cultures. In the 1600s and 1700s it did not occur because the ideal female body in Western cultures at that time was a full-figured one.

Similarly, dissociative identity (multiple personality) disorder makes sense as a problem only in societies in which a sense of self is fairly concrete. In India, the self is based more on external factors that are relatively independent of the person. There, when an individual displays symptoms of what people in a Western society would call dissociative identity disorder, Indians assume that that person is possessed either by demons (which they view as a malady) or by gods (which does not require treatment).

Furthermore, even though disorders such as schizophrenia are found throughout the world, cultural factors influence the particular symptoms of the disorder. Hence, catatonic schizophrenia, in which unmoving patients appear to be frozen in the same position, sometimes for days, is rare in North America and Western Europe. In contrast, in India, 80 percent of those with schizophrenia are catatonic.

Other cultures have disorders that do not appear in the West. For example, in Malaysia, a behavior called *amok* is characterized by a wild outburst in which a person, usually quiet and withdrawn, kills or severely injures another. *Koro* is a condition found in Southeast Asian males who develop an intense panic that the penis is about to withdraw into the abdomen. Some West African men develop a disorder when they first attend college that they call *brain fag;* it includes feelings of heaviness or heat in the head, as well as depression and anxiety. Finally, *ataque de nervios* is a disorder found most often among Latinos from the Caribbean. It is characterized by trembling, crying, uncontrollable screams, and incidents of verbal or physical aggression (Stix, 1996; Cohen et al., 1999; López & Guarnaccia, 2000).

In sum, we should not assume that the *DSM* provides the final word on psychological disorders. The disorders it includes are very much a creation and function of Western cultures at a particular moment in time, and its categories should not be seen as universally applicable (Tseng, 2003).

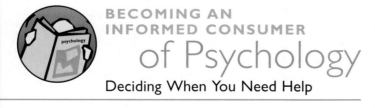

BECOMING AN INFORMED CONSUMER
of Psychology
Deciding When You Need Help

After you've considered the range and variety of psychological disturbances that can afflict people, you may begin to feel that you suffer from one (or more) of the problems we have discussed. In fact, this perception has a name: *medical student's disease.* Although in this case it might more aptly be labeled "psychology student's disease," the basic symptoms are the same: feeling that you suffer from the same sorts of problems you are studying.

Most often, of course, your concerns will be unwarranted. As we have discussed, the differences between normal and abnormal behavior are often so fuzzy that it is easy to jump to the conclusion that one has the same symptoms that are involved in serious forms of mental disturbance.

Before coming to such a conclusion, though, keep in mind that from time to time we all experience a wide range of emotions, and it is not unusual to feel deeply unhappy, fantasize about bizarre situations, or feel anxiety about life's circumstances. It is the persistence, depth, and consistency of such behavior that set normal reactions apart from abnormal ones. If you have not previously had serious doubts about the normality of your behavior, it is unlikely that reading about others' psychological disorders will prompt you to reevaluate your earlier conclusion.

On the other hand, many people do have problems that merit concern, and in such cases, it is important to consider the possibility that professional help is warranted. The following list of symptoms can serve as a guideline to help you determine whether outside intervention might be useful (Engler & Goleman, 1992):

- Long-term feelings of distress that interfere with your sense of well-being, competence, and ability to function effectively in daily activities
- Occasions in which you experience overwhelmingly high stress, accompanied by feelings of inability to cope with the situation
- Prolonged depression or feelings of hopelessness, particularly when they do not have any clear cause (such as the death of someone close)
- Withdrawal from other people
- A chronic physical problem for which no physical cause can be determined
- A fear or phobia that prevents you from engaging in everyday activities
- Feelings that other people are out to get you or are talking about and plotting against you
- Inability to interact effectively with others, preventing the development of friendships and loving relationships

This list offers a rough set of guidelines for determining when the normal problems of everyday living have escalated beyond your ability to deal with them by yourself. In such situations, the *least* reasonable approach would be to pore over the psychological disorders we have discussed in an attempt at self-diagnosis. A more reasonable strategy is to consider seeking professional help.

RECAP/EVALUATE/RETHINK

RECAP

How prevalent are psychological disorders?

- About half the people in the United States are likely to experience a psychological disorder at some point in their lives; 30 percent experience a disorder in any specific year. (p. 547)

What indicators signal a need for the help of a mental health practitioner?

- The signals that indicate a need for professional help include long-term feelings of psychological distress, feelings of inability to cope with stress, withdrawal from other people, prolonged feelings of hopelessness, chronic physical problems with no apparent causes, phobias and compulsions, paranoia, and an inability to interact with others. (p. 551)

EVALUATE

1. The latest version of *DSM* is considered to be the conclusive guideline on defining psychological disorders. True or false?
2. _____, characterized by severe, incapacitating mood changes or depression related to a woman's menstrual cycle, was eventually added to the appendix of *DSM-IV-TR* despite controversy surrounding its inclusion.
3. Match the disorder with the culture in which it is most common:
   1. amok
   2. anorexia nervosa
   3. brain fag
   4. catatonic schizophrenia
   a. India
   b. Malaysia
   c. United States
   d. West Africa

4. Recent research on the prevalence of psychological disorders has found that _____ is the most common disorder, with 17 percent of those surveyed reporting at least one major episode.

RETHINK

1. Why is inclusion in the *DSM-IV-TR* of "borderline" disorders such as self-defeating personality disorder and premenstrual dysphoric disorder so controversial and political? What disadvantages does inclusion bring? Does inclusion bring any benefits?

2. *From the perspective of a college counselor:* What indicators might be most important in determining whether a college student is experiencing a psychological disorder? Do you believe that all students who show signs of a psychological disorder should seek professional help? How might your responses change if the student was from a different culture (e.g., an African society)?

Answers to Evaluate Questions

1. false; the development of the latest version of DSM was a source of great controversy, in part reflecting issues that divide society; 2. premenstrual dysphoric disorder; 3. 1-b, 2-c, 3-d, 4-a; 4. depression

Psychology on the Web

1. On the Web, research the insanity defense as it is used in U.S. courts of law, consulting at least two sources. Summarize your findings, evaluating them against the perspectives on psychological disorders. Are there differences between legal and psychological interpretations of "sanity"? If so, what are they? Do you think such differences are appropriate?
2. Find information on the Web about the controversy surrounding dissociative (or multiple) personality disorder. Summarize both sides of the controversy. Using your knowledge of psychology, state your opinion on the matter.
3. After completing the PsychInteractivities on bipolar disorders and schizophrenia, use the Web to investigate the current status of the case of Andrea Yates, who drowned all five of her children in a bathtub. From what disorder does she suffer? In your opinion, was she legally sane at the time of the killings? Why?

Epilogue

We've discussed some of the many types of psychological disorders to which people are prone, noting the difficulty psychologists and physicians have in clearly differentiating normal from abnormal behavior and looking at some of the approaches mental health professionals have taken to explain and treat psychological disorders. We considered today's most commonly used classification scheme, categorized in *DSM-IV-TR*, and examined some of the more prevalent forms of psychological disorders. To gain a perspective on the topic of psychological disorders, we discussed the surprisingly broad incidence of psychological disorders in U.S. society and the cultural nature of such disorders.

Before we proceed to focus on treatment of such disorders, turn back to the prologue, in which the case of Chamique Holdsclaw was described. Using the knowledge you gained from this chapter, consider the following questions.

1. Holdsclaw was suffering from major depression. What elements of her behavior seem to fit the description of major depression?
2. Which perspective (i.e., medical, psychoanalytic, behavioral, cognitive, humanistic, or sociocultural) do you think would provide the best explanation for Holdsclaw's case? Would it be advisable to use several perspectives to understand her case? Why?
3. Do you think there were signs of psychological disorder in Holdsclaw's actions during adolescence? What might they have been?
4. Initially, Holdsclaw hid her disorder from her teammates and coach because she felt embarrassment and shame. Why do you think this happened? What kinds of societal changes need to occur in order to make psychological disorders be perceived less negatively?

CHAPTER 16

Treatment of Psychological Disorders

Key Concepts for Chapter 16

Prologue   **Conquering Schizophrenia**

For weeks they had practiced dance steps, shopped for formals, fretted about hairstyles and what on earth to say to their partners. Now the Big City band was pumping up the volume, and the whole ballroom was beginning to shake. Brandon Fitch, wearing a pinstripe suit and an ear-to-ear grin, shimmied with a high-stepping blond. Daphne Moss, sporting a floral dress and white corsage, delighted her dad by letting him cut in. The usually quiet Kevin Buchberger leaped onto the dance floor and flat-out boogied for the first time in his life, while Kevin Namkoong grabbed an electric guitar and jammed with the band. The prom at Case Western Reserve University had hit full tilt.

But this was a prom that almost never was. Most of the 175 participants were in their 30s; they had missed the proms of their youth—along with other adolescent rites of passage. Don't ask where they were at 18 or 21. The memories are too bleak, too fragmented to convey. They had organized this better-late-than-never prom to celebrate their remarkable "awakening" to reality after many years of being lost in the darkness of schizophrenia.

Moss, Buchberger, Fitch, and their fellow prom goers were awakened from their long nightmare of insanity by a remarkable drug called clozapine (brand name: Clozaril). The dinner dance, organized with help from psychiatrists and counselors at Case Western Reserve's affiliated University Hospitals, in Cleveland, served as a bittersweet celebration of shared loss and regained hope. (Wallis & Willwerth, 1992, p. 53).

Looking **Ahead**

The drug that has brought new life to people like Daphne Moss, Kevin Buchberger, and Brandon Fitch is just one of many that, along with other new treatment approaches, have revolutionized the treatment of psychological disorders. Although treatment can take literally hundreds of different approaches, ranging from one-meeting informal counseling sessions to long-term drug therapy, all the approaches have a common objective: the relief of psychological disorder, with the ultimate aim of enabling individuals to achieve richer, more meaningful, and more fulfilling lives.

Despite their diversity, approaches to treating psychological disorders fall into two main categories: psychologically based and biologically based therapies. Psychologically based therapy, or **psychotherapy,** is treatment in which a trained professional—a therapist—uses psychological techniques to help someone overcome psychological difficulties and disorders, resolve problems in living, or bring about personal growth. In psychotherapy, the goal is to produce psychological change in a person (called a "client" or "patient") through discussions and interactions with the therapist. In contrast, **biomedical therapy** relies on drugs and medical procedures to improve psychological functioning.

As we describe the various approaches to therapy, keep in mind that although the distinctions may seem clear-cut, the classifications and procedures overlap a good deal. In fact, many therapists today use a variety of methods with an individual patient, taking an *eclectic approach to therapy.* Assuming that both psychological and biological processes often produce psychological disorders, eclectic therapists may draw from several perspectives simultaneously to address both the psychological and the biological aspects of a person's problems (Nathan & Gorman, 1997; Wachtel & Messer, 1997; Goin, 2005).

Psychotherapy: Psychodynamic, Behavioral, and Cognitive Approaches to Treatment

Therapists use some 400 different varieties of psychotherapy, approaches to therapy that focus on psychological factors. Although diverse in many respects, all psychological approaches see treatment as a way of solving psychological problems by modifying people's behavior and helping them gain a better understanding of themselves and their past, present, and future.

In light of the variety of psychological approaches, it is not surprising that the people who provide therapy vary considerably in educational background and training (see Figure 1). Many have doctoral degrees in psychology (meaning that they have attended graduate school, learned clinical and research techniques, and held an internship). But therapy is also provided by people in fields allied with psychology, such as psychiatry and social work.

Regardless of their specific training, almost all psychotherapists employ one of four major approaches to therapy: psychodynamic, behavioral, cognitive, or humanistic treatments. These approaches are based on the models of personality and psychological disorders developed by psychologists. Here we'll consider the psychodynamic, behavioral, and cognitive approaches in turn. In the next module, we'll explore the humanistic approach, as well as interpersonal psychotherapy and group therapy, and evaluate the effectiveness of psychotherapy.

Psychodynamic Approaches to Therapy

Psychodynamic therapy seeks to bring unresolved past conflicts and unacceptable impulses from the unconscious into the conscious, where patients may deal with the problems more effectively. Psychodynamic approaches are based on Freud's psychoanalytic approach to personality, which holds that individuals employ *defense*

"Look, call it denial if you like, but I think what goes on in my personal life id none of my own damn business."

Key Concepts

What are the goals of psychologically and biologically based treatment approaches?

What are the psychodynamic, behavorial, and cognitive approaches to treatment?

Psychotherapy: Treatment in which a trained professional—a therapist—uses psychological techniques to help a person overcome psychological difficulties and disorders, resolve problems in living, or bring about personal growth.

Biomedical therapy: Therapy that relies on drugs and other medical procedures to improve psychological functioning.

Psychodynamic therapy: Therapy that seeks to bring unresolved past conflicts and unacceptable impulses from the unconscious into the conscious, where patients may deal with the problems more effectively.

FIGURE 1 A variety of professionals provide therapy and counseling. Each could be expected to give helpful advice and direction. However, the nature of the problem a person is experiencing may make one or another therapy more appropriate. For example, a person who is suffering from a severe disturbance and who has lost touch with reality will typically require some sort of biologically based drug therapy. In that case, a psychiatrist—who is a physician—would be the professional of choice. In contrast, those suffering from milder disorders, such as difficulty adjusting to the death of a family member, have a broader choice that might include any of the professionals listed at right. The decision can be made easier by initial consultations with professionals in mental health facilities in communities, colleges, and health organizations, who can provide guidance in selecting an appropriate therapist.

Getting Help from the Right Person

Clinical Psychologists

Psychologists with a Ph.D. or Psy.D. who have also completed a postgraduate internship. They specialize in assessment and treatment of psychological difficulties.

Counseling Psychologists

Psychologists with a Ph.D. or Ed.D. who typically treat day-to-day adjustment problems, often in a university mental health clinic.

Psychiatrists

M.D.s with postgraduate training in abnormal behavior. Because they can prescribe medication, they often treat the most severe disorders.

Psychoanalysts

Either M.D.s or psychologists who specialize in psychoanalysis, the treatment technique first developed by Freud.

Licensed Professional Counselors or Clinical Mental Health Counselors

Professionals with a master's degree who provide therapy to individuals, couples, and families and who hold a national or state certification.

Clinical or Psychiatric Social Workers

Professionals with a master's degree and specialized training who may provide therapy, usually regarding common family and personal problems.

---

mechanisms, psychological strategies to protect themselves from unacceptable unconscious impulses.

The most common defense mechanism is repression, which pushes threatening conflicts and impulses back into the unconscious. However, since unacceptable conflicts and impulses can never be completely buried, some of the anxiety associated with them can produce abnormal behavior in the form of what Freud called *neurotic symptoms.*

How does one rid oneself of the anxiety produced by unconscious, unwanted impulses and drives? To Freud, the answer was to confront the conflicts and impulses by bringing them out of the unconscious part of the mind and into the conscious part. Freud assumed that this technique would reduce anxiety stemming from past conflicts and that the patient could then participate in his or her daily life more effectively.

A psychodynamic therapist, then, faces the challenge of finding a way to assist patients' attempts to explore and understand the unconscious. The technique that has evolved has a number of components, but basically it consists of guiding patients to consider and discuss their past experiences, in explicit detail, from the time of their first memories. This process assumes that patients will eventually stumble upon long-hid-

Freud's psychoanalytic therapy is an intensive, lengthy process that includes techniques such as free association and dream interpretation. What are some advantages and disadvantages of psychoanalysis compared with other approaches?

den crises, traumas, and conflicts that are producing anxiety in their adult lives. They will then be able to "work through"—understand and rectify—those difficulties.

PSYCHOANALYSIS: FREUD'S THERAPY

Classic Freudian psychodynamic therapy, called psychoanalysis, tends to be a lengthy and expensive affair. **Psychoanalysis** is Freudian psychotherapy in which the goal is to release hidden unconscious thoughts and feelings in order to reduce their power in controlling behavior.

In psychoanalysis, patients typically meet with the therapist an hour a day, four to six days a week, for several years. In their sessions, they often use a technique developed by Freud called *free association.* Psychoanalysts using this technique tell patients to say aloud whatever comes to mind, regardless of its apparent irrelevance or senselessness, and the analysts attempt to recognize and label the connections between what a patient says and the patient's unconscious. Therapists also use *dream interpretation,* examining dreams to find clues to unconscious conflicts and problems. Moving beyond the surface description of a dream (called the *manifest content*), therapists seek its underlying meaning (the *latent content*), thereby revealing the true unconscious meaning of the dream (Galatzer-Levy & Cohler, 1997; Auld, Hyman, & Rudzinski, 2005).

The processes of free association and dream interpretation do not always move forward easily. The same unconscious forces that initially produced repression may keep past difficulties out of the conscious mind, producing resistance. *Resistance* is an inability or unwillingness to discuss or reveal particular memories, thoughts, or motivations. Patients can express resistance in many ways. For instance, patients may be discussing a childhood memory and suddenly forget what they were saying, or they may change the subject completely. It is the therapist's job to pick up instances of resistance and interpret their meaning, as well as to ensure that patients return to the subject—which is likely to hold difficult or painful memories for the patients.

Because of the close, almost intimate interaction between patient and psychoanalyst, the relationship between the two often becomes emotionally charged and takes on a complexity unlike most other relationships. Patients may eventually think of the analyst as a symbol of a significant other in their past, perhaps a parent or a lover, and apply some of their feelings for that person to the analyst—a phenomenon known as transference. **Transference** is the transfer of feelings to a psychoanalyst of love or anger that had been originally directed to a patient's parents or other authority figures (Mann, 1997; Gordon, 2000; Van Beekum, 2005).

A therapist can use transference to help a patient re-create past relationships that were psychologically difficult. For instance, if a patient undergoing transference views her therapist as a symbol of her father—with whom she had a difficult relationship— the patient and therapist may "redo" an earlier interaction, this time including more positive aspects. Through this process, the patient may resolve conflicts regarding her real father—something that is beginning to happen in the following therapy session:

> Sandy: My father . . . never took any interest in any of us. . . . It was my
>   mother—rest her soul—who loved us, not our father. He worked her to death.
>   Lord, I miss her. . . . I must sound angry at my father. Don't you think I have
>   a right to be angry?
> Therapist: Do you think you have a right to be angry?
> Sandy: Of course, I do! Why are you questioning me? You don't believe me, do you?
> Therapist: You want me to believe you.
> Sandy: I don't care whether you believe me or not. . . . I know what you're think-
>   ing—you think I'm crazy—you must be laughing at me—I'll probably be a case
>   in your next book! You're just sitting there—smirking—making me feel like a
>   bad person—thinking I'm wrong for being mad, that I have no right to be mad.
> Therapist: Just like your father.
> Sandy: Yes, you're just like my father.—Oh my God! Just now—I—I—thought I
>   was talking to him (Sue, Sue, & Sue, 1990, pp. 514–515).

Psychoanalysis: Freudian psychotherapy in which the goal is to release hidden unconscious thoughts and feelings in order to reduce their power in controlling behavior.

Transference: The transfer of feelings to a psychoanalyst of love or anger that had been originally directed to a patient's parents or other authority figures.

"In the mental health profession, we try to avoid negative labels, like 'a hundred and fifty bucks an hour—that's crazy!' or 'three fifty-minute sessions a week—that's insane!'"

CONTEMPORARY PSYCHODYNAMIC APPROACHES

Few people have the time, money, or patience to participate in years of traditional psychoanalysis. Moreover, no conclusive evidence shows that psychoanalysis, as originally conceived by Freud in the nineteenth century, works better than other, more recent forms of psychodynamic therapy.

Today, psychodynamic therapy tends to be of shorter duration, usually lasting no longer than three months or twenty sessions. The therapist takes a more active role than Freud would have liked, controlling the course of therapy and prodding and advising the patient with considerable directness. Finally, the therapist puts less emphasis on a patient's past history and childhood, concentrating instead on an individual's current relationships and specific complaints (Bornstein, 2001; Goode, 2003b; Charman, 2004).

EVALUATION OF PSYCHODYNAMIC THERAPY

Even with its current modifications, psychodynamic therapy has its critics. In its longer versions, it can be time-consuming and expensive, especially in comparison with other forms of psychotherapy, such as behavioral and cognitive approaches. Furthermore, less articulate patients may not do as well as more verbal ones do.

Ultimately, the most important concern about psychodynamic treatment is whether it actually works, and there is no simple answer to this question. Psychodynamic treatment techniques have been controversial since Freud introduced them. Part of the problem is the difficulty in establishing whether patients have improved after psychodynamic therapy. Determining effectiveness depends on reports from the therapist or the patients themselves, reports that are obviously open to bias and subjective interpretation.

Critics have questioned the entire theoretical basis of psychodynamic theory, maintaining that constructs such as the unconscious have not been proved to exist. Despite the criticism, though, the psychodynamic treatment approach has remained viable. To proponents, it not only provides effective treatment in many cases of psychological disturbance but also permits the potential development of an unusual degree of insight into one's life (Barber & Lane, 1995; Clay, 2000; Ablon & Jones, 2005).

Behavioral Approaches to Therapy

Perhaps, when you were a child, your parents rewarded you with an ice cream cone when you were especially good ... or sent you to your room if you misbehaved. Sound principles back up such a child-rearing strategy: Good behavior is maintained by reinforcement, and unwanted behavior can be eliminated by punishment.

These principles represent the basic underpinnings of **behavioral treatment approaches.** Building on the basic processes of learning, behavioral treatment approaches make this fundamental assumption: Both abnormal behavior and normal behavior are *learned.* People who act abnormally either have failed to learn the skills they need to cope with the problems of everyday living or have acquired faulty skills and patterns that are being maintained through some form of reinforcement. To modify abnormal behavior, then, behavioral approaches propose that people must learn new behavior to replace the faulty skills they have developed and unlearn their maladaptive behavior patterns (Bergin & Garfield, 1994; Agras & Berkowitz, 1996; Krijn et al., 2004).

Behavioral psychologists do not need to delve into people's pasts or their psyches. Rather than viewing abnormal behavior as a symptom of an underlying problem, they consider the abnormal behavior as the problem in need of modification. Changing people's behavior to allow them to function more effectively solves the problem—with no need for concern about the underlying cause. In this view, then, if you can change abnormal behavior, you've cured the problem.

Behavioral approaches to treatment would seek to modify the behavior of this couple, rather than focusing on the underlying causes of the behavior.

AVERSIVE CONDITIONING

Suppose you bite into your favorite candy bar and find that not only is it infested with ants but you've also swallowed a bunch of them. You immediately become sick to your stomach and throw up. Your long-term reaction? You never eat that kind of candy bar again, and it may be months before you eat any type of candy. You have learned to avoid candy so that you will not get sick and throw up.

This simple example illustrates how a person can be classically conditioned to modify behavior. Behavior therapists use this principle when they employ **aversive conditioning,** a form of therapy that reduces the frequency of undesired behavior by pairing an aversive, unpleasant stimulus with undesired behavior. For example, behavior therapists might use aversive conditioning by pairing alcohol with a drug that causes severe nausea and vomiting. After the two have been paired a few times, the person associates the alcohol alone with vomiting and finds alcohol less appealing.

Although aversion therapy works reasonably well in inhibiting substance-abuse problems such as alcoholism and certain kinds of sexual disorders, critics question its long-term effectiveness. Also, important ethical concerns surround aversion techniques that employ such potent stimuli as electric shock, which therapists use only in the most extreme cases, such as patient self-mutilation. Clearly, though, aversion therapy offers an important procedure for eliminating maladaptive responses for some period of time—a respite that provides, even if only temporarily, an opportunity to encourage more adaptive behavior patterns (Yuskauskas, 1992; Linscheid & Reichenbach, 2002; Bordnick et al., 2004).

SYSTEMATIC DESENSITIZATION

The most successful behavioral treatment based on classical conditioning is systematic desensitization. In **systematic desensitization,** gradual exposure to an anxiety-producing stimulus is paired with relaxation to extinguish the response of anxiety (Wolpe, 1990; St. Onge, 1995a; McGlynn, Smitherman, & Gothard, 2004).

Suppose, for instance, you were extremely afraid of flying. The very thought of being in an airplane would make you begin to sweat and shake, and you couldn't get yourself near enough to an airport to know how you'd react if you actually had to fly somewhere. Using systematic desensitization to treat your problem, you would first be trained in relaxation techniques by a behavior therapist, learning to relax your body fully—a highly pleasant state, as you might imagine (see Figure 2).

Behavioral treatment approaches: Treatment approaches that build on the basic processes of learning, such as reinforcement and extinction, and assume that normal and abnormal behavior are both learned.

Aversive conditioning: A form of therapy that reduces the frequency of undesired behavior by pairing an aversive, unpleasant stimulus with undesired behavior.

Systematic desensitization: A behavioral technique in which gradual exposure to an anxiety-producing stimulus is paired with relaxation to extinguish the response of anxiety.

Step 1. Pick a focus word or short phrase that's firmly rooted in your personal belief system. For example, a nonreligious individual might choose a neutral word like *one* or *peace* or *love*. A Christian person desiring to use a prayer could pick the opening words of Psalm 23, *The Lord is my shepherd*; a Jewish person could choose *Shalom*.

Step 2. Sit quietly in a comfortable position.

Step 3. Close your eyes.

Step 4. Relax your muscles.

Step 5. Breathe slowly and naturally, repeating your focus word or phrase silently as you exhale.

Step 6. Throughout, assume a passive attitude. Don't worry about how well you're doing. When other thoughts come to mind, simply say to yourself, "Oh, well," and gently return to the repetition.

Step 7. Continue for 10 to 20 minutes. You may open your eyes to check the time, but do not use an alarm. When you finish, sit quietly for a minute or so, at first with your eyes closed and later with your eyes open. Then do not stand for one or two minutes.

Step 8. Practice the technique once or twice a day.

FIGURE 2 Following these basic steps will help you achieve a sense of calmness by employing the relaxation response.

The next step would involve constructing a *hierarchy of fears*—a list, in order of increasing severity, of the things you associate with your fears. For instance, your hierarchy might resemble this one:

1. Watching a plane fly overhead.
2. Going to an airport.
3. Buying a ticket.
4. Stepping into the plane.
5. Seeing the plane door close.
6. Having the plane taxi down the runway.
7. Taking off.
8. Being in the air.

Once you had developed this hierarchy and had learned relaxation techniques, you would learn to associate the two sets of responses. To do this, your therapist might ask you to put yourself into a relaxed state and then imagine yourself in the first situation identified in your hierarchy. Once you could consider that first step while remaining relaxed, you would move on to the next situation, eventually moving up the hierarchy in gradual stages until you could imagine yourself being in the air without experiencing anxiety. Ultimately, you would be asked to make a visit to an airport and later to take a flight. (For some practice, complete the PsychInteractive exercise on systematic desensitization.)

Systematic desensitization has proved to be an effective treatment for a number of problems, including phobias, anxiety disorders, and even impotence and fear of sexual contact. Through this technique, we can learn to enjoy the things we once feared (Kluger, 2001; Waldrep & Waits, 2002; Tryon, 2005).

www.mhhe.com/feldmanup8
PsychInteractive Online

Systematic Desensitization

OPERANT CONDITIONING TECHNIQUES

Some behavioral approaches make use of the operant conditioning principles that we discussed earlier in the book when considering learning. These approaches are based on the notion that we should reward people for carrying out desirable behavior and extinguish undesirable behavior by either ignoring it or punishing it.

One example of the systematic application of operant conditioning principles is the *token system,* which rewards a person for desired behavior with a token such as a poker chip or some kind of play money. Although it is most frequently employed in institutional settings for individuals with relatively serious problems, and sometimes with children as a classroom management technique, the system resembles what parents do when they give children money for being well behaved—money that the children can later exchange for something they want. The desired behavior may range from simple things such as keeping one's room neat to personal grooming and interacting with other people. In institutions, patients can exchange tokens for some object or activity, such as snacks, new clothes, or, in extreme cases, being able to sleep in one's own bed rather than in a sleeping bag on the floor.

Contingency contracting, a variant of the token system, has proved quite effective in producing behavior modification. In *contingency contracting,* the therapist and client (or teacher and student, or parent and child) draw up a written agreement. The contract states a series of behavioral goals the client hopes to achieve. It also specifies the positive consequences for the client if the client reaches goals—usually an explicit reward such as money or additional privileges. Contracts frequently state negative consequences if the client does not meet the goals. For example, clients who are trying to quit smoking might write out a check to a cause they have no interest in supporting (for instance, the National Rifle Association if they are strong supporters of gun control). If the client smokes on a given day, the therapist will mail the check.

Behavior therapists also use *observational learning,* the process in which the behavior of other people is modeled, to systematically teach people new skills and ways of handling their fears and anxieties. For example, modeling helps when therapists are teaching basic social skills such as maintaining eye contact during conversation and acting assertively. Similarly, children with dog phobias have been able to overcome their fears by watching another child—called the "Fearless Peer"—repeatedly walk up to a dog, touch it, pet it, and finally play with it. Modeling, then, can play an effective role in resolving some kinds of behavior difficulties, especially if the model receives a reward for his or her behavior (Bandura, Grusec, & Menlove, 1967; St. Onge, 1995b).

These participants in a systematic desensitization program have worked to overcome their fear of flying and are about to "graduate" by taking a brief flight. In what ways is this approach based on classical conditioning?

DIALECTICAL BEHAVIOR THERAPY

In **dialectical behavior therapy,** the focus is on getting people to accept who they are, regardless of whether it matches their ideal. Even if their childhood has been dysfunctional or they have ruined relationships with others, that's in the past. What matters is who they wish to become (Linehan et al. 2001; Carey, 2005; Manning, 2005, Linehan et al., in press).

Therapists using dialectical behavior therapy seek to have patients realize that they basically have two choices: Either they remain unhappy, or they change. Once patients agree that they wish to change, it is up to them to modify their behavior. Patients are taught that even if they experience unhappiness, or anger, or any other negative emotion, it doesn't need to rule their behavior. It's their behavior that counts—not their inner life.

Dialectical behavior therapy teaches behavioral skills that help people behave more effectively and keep their emotions in check. Although it is a relatively new form of therapy, increasing evidence supports its effectiveness, particularly with certain personality disorders (McQuillan et al., 2005; Soler et al., 2005; van den Bosch et al., 2005).

Dialectical behavior therapy: A form of treatment in which the focus is on getting people to accept who they are, regardless of whether it matches their ideal.

A "Fearless Peer" who models appropriate and effective behavior can help children overcome their fears.

HOW DOES BEHAVIOR THERAPY STACK UP?

Behavior therapy works particularly well for treating phobias and compulsions, establishing control over impulses, and learning complex social skills to replace maladaptive behavior. More than any of the other therapeutic techniques, it provides methods that nonprofessionals can use to change their own behavior. Moreover, it is efficient, because it focuses on solving carefully defined problems (Wilson & Agras, 1992).

Behavior therapy does have some disadvantages. For instance, it does not treat deep depression or other severe disorders particularly successfully. In addition, because it emphasizes changing external behavior, people receiving behavior therapy do not necessarily gain insight into thoughts and expectations that may be fostering their maladaptive behavior. For these reasons, some psychologists have turned to cognitive approaches.

Cognitive Approaches to Therapy

If you assumed that illogical thoughts and beliefs lie at the heart of psychological disorders, wouldn't the most direct treatment route be to teach people new, more adaptive modes of thinking? The answer is yes, according to psychologists who take a cognitive approach to treatment.

Cognitive treatment approaches teach people to think in more adaptive ways by changing their dysfunctional cognitions about the world and themselves. Unlike behavior therapists, who focus on modifying external behavior, cognitive therapists attempt to change the way people think as well as their behavior. Because they often use basic principles of learning, the methods they employ are sometimes referred to as the **cognitive-behavioral approach** (Beck, 1991; McCullough, 1999; Frost & Steketee, 2002; Howatt, 2005).

Although cognitive treatment approaches take many forms, they all share the assumption that anxiety, depression, and negative emotions develop from maladaptive thinking. Accordingly, cognitive treatments seek to change the thought patterns that lead to getting "stuck" in dysfunctional ways of thinking. Therapists systematically teach clients to challenge their assumptions and adopt new approaches to old problems.

Cognitive therapy is relatively short-term, usually lasting a maximum of twenty sessions. Therapy tends to be highly structured and focused on concrete problems. Therapists often begin by teaching the theory behind the approach and then continue to take an active role throughout the course of therapy, acting as a combination of teacher, coach, and partner.

One good example of cognitive treatment, **rational-emotive behavior therapy,** attempts to restructure a person's belief system into a more realistic, rational, and logical set of views. According to psychologist Albert Ellis (2002, 2004), many people lead unhappy lives and suffer from psychological disorders because they harbor irrational, unrealistic ideas such as these:

- We need the love or approval of virtually every significant other person for everything we do.
- We should be thoroughly competent, adequate, and successful in all possible respects in order to consider ourselves worthwhile.
- It is horrible when things don't turn out the way we want them to.

Such irrational beliefs trigger negative emotions, which in turn support the irrational beliefs, leading to a self-defeating cycle. Ellis calls it the A-B-C model, in which negative activating conditions (A) lead to the activation of an irrational belief system (B), which in turn leads to emotional consequences (C). For example, if a person experiences the breakup of a close relationship (A) and holds the irrational belief (B) that "I'll never be loved again," this triggers negative emotions (C) that in turn feed back into support of the irrational belief (see Figure 3).

Rational-emotive behavior therapy aims to help clients eliminate maladaptive thoughts and beliefs and adopt more effective thinking. To accomplish this goal,

Cognitive treatment approaches: Treatment approaches that teach people to think in more adaptive ways by changing their dysfunctional cognitions about the world and themselves.

Cognitive-behavioral approach: A treatment approach that incorporates basic principles of learning to change the way people think.

Rational-emotive behavior therapy: A form of therapy that attempts to restructure a person's belief system into a more realistic, rational, and logical set of views by challenging dysfunctional beliefs that maintain irrational behavior.

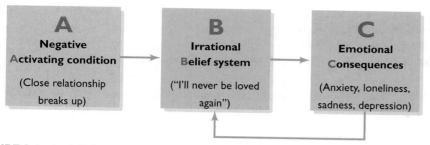

FIGURE 3 In the A-B-C model of rational-emotive behavior therapy, negative activating conditions (A) lead to the activation of an irrational belief system (B), which leads to emotional consequences (C). Those emotional consequences then feed back and support the belief system. At what steps in the model could change occur as a result of rational-emotive behavior therapy?

therapists take an active, directive role during therapy, openly challenging patterns of thought that appear to be dysfunctional. Consider this example:

> Martha: The basic problem is that I'm worried about my family. I'm worried about money. And I never seem to be able to relax.
> Therapist: Why are you worried about your family? . . . What's to be concerned about? They have certain demands which you don't want to adhere to.
> Martha: I was brought up to think that I mustn't be selfish.
> Therapist: Oh, we'll have to knock that out of your head!
> Martha: My mother feels that I shouldn't have left home—that my place is with them. There are nagging doubts about what I should—
> Therapist: Why are there doubts? Why should you?
> Martha: I think it's a feeling I was brought up with that you always have to give of yourself. If you think of yourself, you're wrong.
> Therapist: That's a belief. Why do you have to keep believing that—at your age? You believed a lot of superstitions when you were younger. Why do you have to retain them? Your parents indoctrinated you with this nonsense, because that's their belief. . . . Who needs that philosophy? All it's gotten you, so far, is guilt (Ellis, 1974, pp. 223–286).

By poking holes in Martha's reasoning, the therapist is attempting to help her adopt a more realistic view of herself and her circumstances (Dryden, 1999; Ellis, 2002).

Another form of therapy that builds on a cognitive perspective is that of Aaron Beck (1991, 1995, 2004). Like rational-emotive behavior therapy, Beck's *cognitive therapy* aims to change people's illogical thoughts about themselves and the world. However, cognitive therapy is considerably less confrontational and challenging than rational-emotive behavior therapy. Instead of the therapist actively arguing with clients about their dysfunctional cognitions, cognitive therapists more often play the role of teacher. Therapists urge clients to obtain information on their own that will lead them to discard their inaccurate thinking. During the course of treatment, therapists help clients discover ways of thinking more appropriately about themselves and others (Alford & Beck, 1997; Greenberg, 2000; Rosen, 2000; Beck, Freeman, & Davis, 2004).

Cognitive approaches to therapy have proved successful in dealing with a broad range of disorders. The willingness of cognitive therapists to incorporate additional treatment approaches (e.g., combining cognitive and behavioral techniques in cognitive behavioral therapy) has made this approach a particularly effective form of treatment (McMullin, 2000).

Check your understanding of the cognitive and other therapeutic approaches in the PsychInteractive exercise.

www.mhhe.com/feldmanup8
PsychInteractive Online

Compare and Contrast
Approaches to Therapy

"To this day, I can hear my mother's voice—harsh, accusing. 'Lost your mittens? You naughty kittens! Then you shall have no pie!'"

RECAP/EVALUATE/RETHINK

RECAP

What are the goals of psychologically and biologically based treatment approaches?

- Psychotherapy (psychologically based therapy) and bio-medical therapy (biologically based therapy) share the goal of resolving psychological problems by modifying people's thoughts, feelings, expectations, evaluations, and ultimately behavior. (p. 556)

What are the psychodynamic, behavioral, and cognitive approaches to treatment?

- Psychoanalytic approaches seek to bring unresolved past conflicts and unacceptable impulses from the unconscious into the conscious, where patients may deal with the problems more effectively. To do this, therapists use techniques such as free association and dream inter-pretation. (pp. 557–559)
- Behavioral approaches to treatment view abnormal behavior as the problem, rather than viewing that behavior as a symptom of some underlying cause. To bring about a "cure," this view suggests that the out-ward behavior must be changed by using methods such as aversive conditioning, systematic desensitization, observational learning, token systems, contingency con-tracting, and dialectical behavior therapy. (pp. 560–563)
- Cognitive approaches to treatment consider the goal of therapy to be to help a person restructure his or her faulty belief system into a more realistic, rational, and logical view of the world. Two examples of cognitive treatments are the rational-emotive behavior therapy and cognitive therapy. (pp. 564–565)

EVALUATE

1. Match the following mental health practitioners with the appropriate description.
   1. Psychiatrist
   2. Clinical psychologist
   3. Counseling psychologist
   4. Psychoanalyst
   a. Ph.D. specializing in the treatment of psychological disorders
   b. Professional specializing in Freudian therapy techniques
   c. M.D. trained in abnormal behavior
   d. Ph.D. specializing in the adjustment of day-to-day problems
2. According to Freud, people use _____ as a means of preventing unwanted impulses from intruding on conscious thought.
3. In dream interpretation, a psychoanalyst must learn to distinguish between the _____ content of a dream, which is what appears on the surface, and the _____ content, its underlying meaning.
4. Which of the following treatments deals with phobias by gradual exposure to the item producing the fear?
   a. Systematic desensitization
   b. Partial reinforcement
   c. Behavioral self-management
   d. Aversion therapy

RETHINK

1. In what ways are psychoanalysis and cognitive therapy similar, and how do they differ?
2. *From the perspective of a child-care provider:* How might you use systematic desensitization to help children over-come their fears?

Answers to Evaluate Questions

1. 1-c, 2-a, 3-d, 4-b; 2. defense mechanisms; 3. manifest, latent; 4. a

KEY TERMS

psychotherapy p. 557
biomedical therapy p. 557
psychodynamic therapy p. 557
psychoanalysis p. 559
transference p. 559

behavioral treatment approaches p. 561
aversive conditioning p. 561
systematic desensitization p. 561

dialectical behavior therapy p. 563
cognitive treatment approaches p. 564
cognitive-behavioral approach p. 564

rational-emotive behavior therapy p. 564

Psychotherapy: Humanistic, Interpersonal, and Group Approaches to Treatment

Humanistic Therapy

As you know from your own experience, a student cannot master the material covered in a course without some hard work, no matter how good the teacher and the textbook are. *You* must take the time to study, memorize the vocabulary, and learn the concepts. Nobody else can do it for you. If you choose to put in the effort, you'll succeed; if you don't, you'll fail. The responsibility is primarily yours.

Humanistic therapy draws on this philosophical perspective of self-responsibility in developing treatment techniques. The many different types of therapy that fit into this category have a similar rationale: We have control of our own behavior, we can make choices about the kinds of lives we want to live, and it is up to us to solve the difficulties we encounter in our daily lives.

Instead of being the directive figures seen in some psychodynamic and behavioral approaches, humanistic therapists view themselves as guides or facilitators. Therapists using humanistic techniques seek to help people understand themselves and find ways to come closer to the ideal they hold for themselves. In this view, psychological disorders result from the inability to find meaning in life and feeling lonely and unconnected to others (Cain, 2002).

Humanistic approaches have produced many therapeutic techniques. Among the most important is person-centered therapy.

PERSON-CENTERED THERAPY

Consider the following therapy session excerpt:

> Alice: I was thinking about this business of standards. I somehow developed a sort of a knack, I guess, of—well—habit—of trying to make people feel at ease around me, or to make things go along smoothly . . .
>
> Therapist: In other words, what you did was always in the direction of trying to keep things smooth and to make other people feel better and to smooth the situation.
>
> Alice: Yes. I think that's what it was. Now the reason why I did it probably was— I mean, not that I was a good little Samaritan going around making other people happy, but that was probably the role that felt easiest for me to play . . .
>
> Therapist: You feel that for a long time you've been playing the role of kind of smoothing out the frictions or differences or what not . . .
>
> Alice: M-hm.
>
> Therapist: Rather than having any opinion or reaction of your own in the situation. Is that it? (Rogers, 1951, pp. 152–153).

The therapist does not interpret or answer the questions the client has raised. Instead, the therapist clarifies or reflects back what the client has said (e.g., "In other words, what

Key Concepts

What are the humanistic approaches to treatment?

What is interpersonal therapy?

How does group therapy differ from individual types of therapy?

How effective is therapy, and which kind of therapy works best in a given situation?

Humanistic therapy: Therapy in which the underlying rationale is that people have control of their behavior, can make choices about their lives, and are essentially responsible for solving their own problems.

Person-centered therapy: Therapy in which the goal is to reach one's potential for self-actualization.

you did . . ."; "You feel that . . ."; "Is that it?"). This therapeutic technique, known as *non-directive counseling,* is at the heart of person-centered therapy, which was first practiced by Carl Rogers in the mid-twentieth century (Rogers, 1951, 1995, Raskin & Rogers, 1989).

Person-centered therapy (also called *client-centered therapy*) aims to enable people to reach their potential for self-actualization. By providing a warm and accepting environment, therapists hope to motivate clients to air their problems and feelings. In turn, this enables clients to make realistic and constructive choices and decisions about the things that bother them in their current lives (Bozarth, Zimring, & Tausch, 2002; Kirschenbaum, 2004).

Instead of directing the choices clients make, therapists provide what Rogers calls *unconditional positive regard*—expressing acceptance and understanding, regardless of the feelings and attitudes the client expresses. By doing this, therapists hope to create an atmosphere that enables clients to come to decisions that can improve their lives (Farber, Brink, & Raskin, 1996; Kirschenbaum & Jourdan, 2005).

Furnishing unconditional positive regard does not mean that therapists must approve of everything their clients say or do. Rather, therapists need to communicate that they are caring, nonjudgmental, and *empathetic*—understanding of a client's emotional experiences (Fearing & Clark, 2000).

Person-centered therapy is rarely used today in its purest form. Contemporary approaches tend to be somewhat more directive, with therapists nudging clients toward insights rather than merely reflecting back their statements. However, therapists still view clients' insights as central to the therapeutic process.

GESTALT THERAPY

Have you ever thought back to some childhood incident in which you were treated unfairly and again felt the rage that you had experienced at that time? To therapists working in a gestalt perspective, the healthiest thing for you to do psychologically might be to act out that rage—by hitting a pillow or yelling in frustration.

Gestalt therapy: A treatment approach in which people are led to examine their earlier experiences and complete any "unfinished business" from their past that may still affect and color present-day relationships.

The rationale for this treatment approach is the idea that people need to integrate their thoughts, feelings, and behaviors into a *gestalt,* the German term for "whole" (as we discussed in reference to perception earlier in the book). In **gestalt therapy,** people are led to examine their earlier experiences and complete any "unfinished business" from their past that may still affect and color present-day relationships. Gestalt therapy typically includes reenactments of specific conflicts that clients experienced earlier. For instance, a client might first play the part of his angry father and then play himself when his father yelled at him. Such reenactments are assumed to promote better understanding of the source of psychological disorders, as clients broaden their perspective on their situation (Perls, 1970; Perls, Hefferline, & Goodman, 1994; Serok, 2000; Woldt & Toman, 2005).

HUMANISTIC APPROACHES IN PERSPECTIVE

The notion that psychological disorders result from restricted growth potential appeals philosophically to many people. Furthermore, when humanistic therapists acknowledge that the freedom we possess can lead to psychological difficulties, clients find an unusually supportive environment for therapy. In turn, this atmosphere can help clients discover solutions to difficult psychological problems.

However, humanistic treatments lack specificity, a problem that has troubled their critics. Humanistic approaches are not very precise and are probably the least scientifically and theoretically developed type of treatment. Moreover, this form of treatment works best for the same type of highly verbal client who profits most from psychoanalytic treatment.

Interpersonal Therapy

Interpersonal therapy (IPT): Short-term therapy that focuses on the context of current social relationships.

Interpersonal therapy (IPT) considers therapy in the context of social relationships. Growing out of contemporary psychodynamic approaches, interpersonal therapy focuses more on the here and now with the goal of improving a client's current relationships.

Interpersonal therapy is more directive than traditional psychodynamic approaches. It also tends to be shorter, typically lasting a dozen weeks. Therapists make concrete suggestions on improving relations with others. Research has shown that interpersonal therapy is particularly effective in dealing with depression, anxiety, and addictions (MacKenzie & Grabovac, 2001; Ablon & Jones, 2002; Markowitz, 2003; De Mello et al., 2005).

Group Therapy and Family Therapy

Although most treatment takes place between a single individual and a therapist, some forms of therapy involve groups of people seeking treatment. In **group therapy,** several unrelated people meet with a therapist to discuss some aspect of their psychological functioning.

In group therapy, people with psychological difficulties meet with a therapist to discuss their problems.

With the group people typically discuss their problems, which often center on a common difficulty, such as alcoholism or a lack of social skills. The other members of the group provide emotional support and dispense advice on ways in which they have coped effectively with similar problems (Yalom, 1997; Free, 2000; Alonso, Alonso, & Piper, 2003; Scaturo, 2004).

Groups vary greatly in terms of the particular model they employ; one finds psychoanalytic groups, humanistic groups, and groups corresponding to the other therapeutic approaches. Furthermore, groups also differ in regard to the degree of guidance the therapist provides. In some, the therapist is quite directive, while in others, the members of the group set their own agenda and determine how the group will proceed (Spira, 1997; Earley, 1999; Beck & Lewis, 2000; Stockton, Morran, & Krieger, 2004).

Because in group therapy several people are treated simultaneously, it is a much more economical means of treatment than individual psychotherapy. On the other hand, critics argue that group settings lack the individual attention inherent in one-to-one therapy, and that especially shy and withdrawn individuals may not receive the attention they need in a group setting.

One specialized form of group therapy is family therapy. As the name implies, **family therapy** involves two or more family members, one (or more) of whose problems led to treatment. But rather than focusing simply on the members of the family who present the initial problem, family therapists consider the family as a unit, to which each member contributes. By meeting with the entire family simultaneously, family therapists try to understand how the family members interact with one another (Rolland & Walsh, 1996; Cooklin, 2000).

Family therapists view the family as a "system" and assume that individuals in the family cannot improve without understanding the conflicts found in interactions among family members. Thus, the therapist expects each member to contribute to the resolution of the problem being addressed.

Many family therapists believe that family members fall into rigid roles or set patterns of behavior, with one person acting as the scapegoat, another as a bully, and so forth. In their view, that system of roles perpetuates family disturbances. One goal of this type of therapy, then, is to get the family members to adopt new, more constructive roles and patterns of behavior (Minuchin & Nichols, 1992; Sprenkle & Moon, 1996).

Group therapy: Therapy in which people meet with a therapist to discuss problems with a group.

Family therapy: An approach that focuses on the family and its dynamics.

Evaluating Psychotherapy: Does Therapy Work?

Your best friend, Ben, comes to you because he just hasn't been feeling right about things lately. He's upset because he and his girlfriend aren't getting along, but his dif-

In family therapy, the family system as a whole—not just one family member identified as the "problem"—is treated. Why is this advantageous?

ficulties go beyond that. He can't concentrate on his studies, has a lot of trouble getting to sleep, and—this is what really bothers him—has begun to think that people are ganging up on him, talking about him behind his back. It seems that no one really cares about or understands him or makes any effort to see why he's become so miserable.

Ben knows that he ought to get *some* kind of help, but he is not sure where to turn. He is fairly skeptical of psychologists, thinking that a lot of what they say is just mumbo jumbo, but he's willing to put his doubts aside and try anything to feel better. He also knows there are many different types of therapy, and he doesn't have a clue about which would be best for him. He turns to you for advice, because he knows you are taking a psychology course. He asks, "Which kind of therapy works best?"

IS THERAPY EFFECTIVE?

This question requires a complex response. In fact, identifying the single most appropriate form of treatment is a controversial, and still unresolved, task for psychologists specializing in psychological disorders. In fact, even before considering whether one form of therapy works better than another, we need to determine whether therapy in any form effectively alleviates psychological disturbances.

Until the 1950s, most people simply assumed that therapy was effective. But in 1952 psychologist Hans Eysenck published what has become a classic article challenging that assumption. He claimed that people who received psychodynamic treatment and related therapies were no better off at the end of treatment than were people who were placed on a waiting list for treatment but never received it. According to his analysis, about two-thirds of the people who reported suffering from "neurotic" symptoms believed that those symptoms had disappeared after two years, regardless of whether they had been in therapy. Eysenck concluded that people would go into **spontaneous remission,** recovery without treatment, if they were simply left alone—certainly a cheaper and simpler process.

Spontaneous remission: Recovery without treatment.

Although others quickly challenged Eysenck's conclusions, his review stimulated a continuing stream of better controlled, more carefully crafted studies on the effectiveness of psychotherapy, and today most psychologists agree: Therapy does work. Several comprehensive reviews indicate that therapy brings about greater improvement than does no treatment at all, with the rate of spontaneous remission being fairly low. In most cases, then, the symptoms of abnormal behavior do not go away by themselves if left untreated—although the issue continues to be hotly debated (Bergin & Garfield, 1994; Seligman, 1996; Sohn, 1996). (You can explore the question of the effectiveness of therapy further in the PsychInteractive exercise.)

www.mhhe.com/feldmanup8

PsychInteractive Online

Effectiveness of Therapy

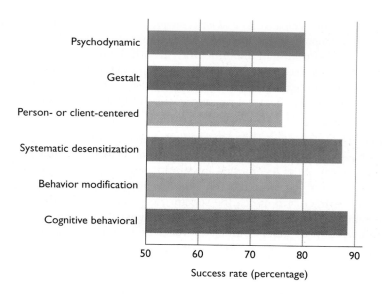

Success rate (percentage)

FIGURE 1 Estimates of the effectiveness of different types of treatment, in comparison to control groups of untreated people (Smith, Glass, & Miller, 1980). The percentile score shows how much more effective a particular type of treatment is for the average patient than is no treatment. For example, people given psychodynamic treatment score, on average, more positively on outcome measures than about three-quarters of untreated people.

WHICH KIND OF THERAPY WORKS BEST?

Although most psychologists feel confident that psychotherapeutic treatment *in general* is more effective than no treatment at all, the question of whether any specific form of treatment is superior to any other has not been answered definitively (Nathan, Stuart, & Dolan, 2000; Westen, Novotny, & Thompson-Brenner, 2004; Abboud, 2005).

For instance, one classic study comparing the effectiveness of various approaches found that although success rates vary somewhat by treatment form, most treatments show fairly equal success rates. As Figure 1 indicates, the rates ranged from about 70 to 85 percent greater success for treated compared with untreated individuals. Behavioral and cognitive approaches tended to be slightly more successful, but that result may have been due to differences in the severity of the cases treated (Smith, Glass, & Miller, 1980; Orwin & Condray, 1984).

Other research, relying on *meta-analysis,* in which data from a large number of studies are statistically combined, yields similar general conclusions. Furthermore, a large-scale survey of 186,000 individuals found that although survey respondents felt they had benefited substantially from psychotherapy (see Figure 2), there was little difference in "consumer satisfaction" on the basis of the specific type of treatment they had received (CR, 1995; Seligman, 1995; Strupp, 1996; Nielsen et al., 2004).

In short, converging evidence allows us to draw several conclusions about the effectiveness of psychotherapy (Strupp & Binder, 1992; Seligman, 1996):

- *For most people, psychotherapy is effective.* This conclusion holds over different lengths of treatment, specific kinds of psychological disorders, and various types of treatment. Thus, the question "Does psychotherapy work?" appears to have been answered convincingly: It does (Lipsey & Wilson, 1993; Seligman, 1996; Spiegel, 1999).
- *On the other hand, psychotherapy doesn't work for everyone.* As many as 10 percent of people treated show no improvement or actually deteriorate (Lambert, Shapiro, & Bergin, 1986; Luborsky, 1988; Pretzer & Beck, 2005).
- *Certain specific types of treatment are somewhat, although not invariably, better for specific types of problems.* For example, cognitive therapy works particularly well for panic disorders, and systematic desensitization relieves specific phobias effectively. However, there are many exceptions, and often the differences in success rates for different types of treatment are not substantial (Hubble, Duncan, & Miller, 1999; Miller & Magruder, 1999).

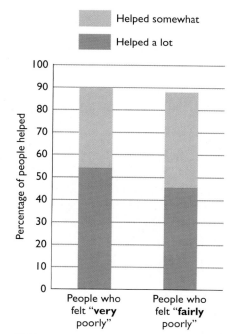

Helped somewhat

Helped a lot

Percentage of people helped

People who felt "**very** poorly"

People who felt "**fairly** poorly"

FIGURE 2 A large survey of 186,000 individuals found that while the respondents had benefited substantially from psychotherapy, there was little difference in "consumer satisfaction" based on the specific type of treatment they had received. (Source: "Mental Health: Does Therapy Help?" *Consumer Reports,* 1995.)

- *No single form of therapy works best for every problem.* Consequently, we can give no definitive answer to the question "Which therapy works best?"—nor may we find one soon—because of the difficulties in sorting out the various factors that enter into the success of therapy. Furthermore, new types of therapy continue to emerge (see, for example, the *Applying Psychology in the 21st Century* box for a discussion of virtual therapy), making it difficult to draw sweeping conclusions about treatment effectiveness.

Eclectic approach: An approach to therapy that uses techniques taken from a variety of treatment methods, rather than just one.

Because no single type of psychotherapy is invariably effective, eclectic approaches to therapy have become increasingly popular. In an **eclectic approach** to therapy, a therapist uses a variety of techniques, integrating several perspectives, to treat a person's problems. By trying more than one approach, a therapist can choose the appropriate mix of treatments to match the specific needs of the individual. Furthermore, therapists with certain personal characteristics may work better with particular individuals and types of treatments, and even racial and ethnic factors may be related to the success of treatment (Roth & Fonagy, 1996; Cheston, 2002).

Exploring DIVERSITY

Racial and Ethnic Factors in Treatment: Should Therapists be Color-Blind?

Consider the following case report, written by a school counselor about Jimmy Jones, a 12-year-old student who was referred to a counselor because of his lack of interest in schoolwork:

Jimmy does not pay attention, daydreams often, and frequently falls asleep during class. There is a strong possibility that Jimmy is harboring repressed rage that needs to be ventilated and dealt with. His inability to directly express his anger had led him to adopt passive aggressive means of expressing hostility, i.e., inattentiveness, daydreaming, falling asleep. It is recommended that Jimmy be seen for intensive counseling to discover the basis of the anger (Sue & Sue, 1990, p. 44).

The counselor was wrong, however. Rather than suffering from "repressed rage," Jimmy lived in a poverty-stricken and disorganized home. Because of overcrowding at his house, he did not get enough sleep and consequently was tired the next day. Frequently, he was also hungry. In short, the stresses arising from his environment caused his problems, not any deep-seated psychological disturbances.

This incident underscores the importance of taking people's environmental and cultural backgrounds into account during treatment for psychological disorders. In particular, members of racial and ethnic minority groups, especially those who are also poor, may behave in ways that help them deal with a society that discriminates against them. As a consequence, behavior that may signal psychological disorder in middle- and upper-class whites may simply be adaptive in people from other racial and socioeconomic groups. For instance, characteristically suspicious and distrustful people may be displaying a survival strategy to protect themselves from psychological and physical injury, rather than suffering from a psychological disturbance (Sue & Sue, 1999; Aponte & Wohl, 2000; Paniagua, 2000; Tseng, 2003).

In fact, therapists must question some basic assumptions of psychotherapy when dealing with racial, ethnic, and cultural minority-group members. For example, compared with the dominant culture, Asian and Latino cultures typically place much greater emphasis on the group, family, and society. When an Asian or Latino faces a critical decision, the family helps make it—suggesting that family members should also play a role in psychological treatment. Similarly, the traditional Chinese recommendation for dealing with depression or anxiety is to urge people who experience such problems to avoid thinking about whatever is upsetting them. Consider how this advice contrasts with treatment approaches that emphasize the value of insight (Okun, 1996; Kleinman & Cohen, 1997; Ponterotto, Gretchen, & Chauhan, 2001; McCarthy, 2005).

Clearly, therapists *cannot* be "color-blind." Instead, they must take into account the racial, ethnic, cultural, and social class backgrounds of their clients in determining the nature of a psychological disorder and the course of treatment (Sue & Sue, 1999; Aponte & Wohl, 2000; Pedersen et al., 2002).

Virtual-Reality Therapy: Facing the Images of Fear

For therapist Hunter Hoffman and colleagues, the patient presented a particularly difficult case. For 20 years, the woman—nicknamed Miss Muffet—had suffered from an anxiety disorder in which she had profound spider phobia:

> She routinely fumigated her car with smoke and pesticides to get rid of spiders. Every night she sealed all her bedroom windows with duct tape after scanning the room for spiders. She searched for the arachnids wherever she went and avoided walkways where she might find one. After washing her clothes, she immediately sealed them inside a plastic bag to make sure they remained free of spiders (Hoffman, 2004, p. 58).

When Miss Muffet's fears began to prevent her from leaving home, she decided to seek therapy. What she found was a novel approach using virtual-reality therapy. In *virtual-reality therapy,* therapists use a computer to create a virtual-reality display of the feared object. The display projects an image of anxiety-producing situation onto the inside of a helmet visor, and the image moves according to head or hand movements (Wiederhold & Wiederhold, 2005a).

In this case, Miss Muffet saw a range of anxiety-producing images, beginning with a view of a realistic virtual tarantula in a virtual kitchen. She was asked to approach the image as close as possible using a handheld joystick. The goal of the first session was to come within a few feet of the tarantula.

In subsequent sessions, she wore a glove that created an image of her hand on the display. She was able to move her hand closer and closer to the tarantula until she (virtually) touched it, and the spider made a noise and scurried away. Still later, she was able to virtually touch the spider and later actually handle a furry toy spider.

Following the highly successful treatment, Miss Muffet allowed an actual tarantula to crawl up her arm for several minutes with only minor anxiety. Miss Muffet's results

Researcher Hunter Hoffman, holding a virtual spider near the face of a patient as part of virtual-reality phobia exposure therapy to reduce fear of spiders. In the virtual world called SpiderWorld, patients can reach out and touch a furry toy spider, adding tactile cues to the virtual image, creating the illusion that they are physically touching the virtual spider. (Photo Mary Levin, U.W., with permission from Hunter Hoffman, U.W.)

have been validated by subsequent research, which shows that virtual-reality therapy is highly effective with a variety of phobias (Garcia-Palacios, Hoffman, & Carlin, 2002; Wiederhold & Wiederhold, 2005a).

Virtual-reality therapy has been extended to treatment of posttraumatic stress disorder (PTSD). For instance, a woman who survived the World Trade Center terrorist attack first viewed virtual jets flying into the twin towers. In subsequent sessions, the level of detail increased until she was exposed to people jumping from the towers, flames, screams, and sirens. By acclimating to such stimuli, the woman was able to recall the actual events with less anxiety (Difede & Hoffman, 2002)

Virtual-reality therapy has been used in other innovative ways. For example,

engaging in a virtual-reality experience can distract burn patients from the excruciating pain that accompanies treatment. Studies show that the pain relief is quite real: Functional magnetic resonance imaging shows that brain activity related to pain actually drops when involved in virtual-reality therapy (Hoffman, 2004).

Despite its apparent success, further research is needed to confirm the effectiveness of virtual-reality therapy. For example, large-scale clinical trials must be carried out to determine if virtual-reality therapy is superior to other forms of systematic desensitization training. Still, the work is promising, and it is likely to lead to even more elaborate applications in the future (Attree, Brooks, & Rose, 2005; Cottraux, 2005).

RETHINK

Do you believe virtual-reality therapy can be more effective than traditional psychotherapy involving face-to-face interaction? Is there something unique about the curative powers of human interaction? Why or why not?

RECAP/EVALUATE/RETHINK

RECAP

What are humanistic approaches to treatment?

- Humanistic therapy is based on the premise that people have control of their behavior, that they can make choices about their lives, and that it is up to them to solve their own problems. Humanistic therapies, which take a nondirective approach, include person-centered and gestalt therapy. (pp. 567–568)

What is interpersonal therapy?

- Interpersonal therapy focuses on interpersonal relationships and strives for immediate improvement during short-term therapy. (pp. 568–569)

How does group therapy differ from individual types of therapy?

- In group therapy, several unrelated people meet with a therapist to discuss some aspect of their psychological functioning, often centering on a common problem. (p. 569)

How effective is therapy, and which kind of therapy works best in a given situation?

- Most research suggests that, in general, therapy is more effective than no therapy, although how much more effective is not known. (pp. 570–571)
- The answer to the more difficult question of which therapy works best is even less clear, in part because therapies are so qualitatively different and in part because the definition of cure is so vague. Clearly, particular kinds of therapy are more appropriate for some problems than for others. (pp. 571–572)
- Because no single type of psychotherapy is invariably effective, eclectic approaches to therapy have become increasingly popular. In an eclectic approach to therapy, a therapist uses a variety of techniques, integrating several perspectives, to treat a person's problems. (p. 572)

EVALUATE

1. Match each of the following treatment strategies with the statement you might expect to hear from a therapist using that strategy.
   1. Group therapy
   2. Unconditional positive regard

3. Behavioral therapy
4. Nondirective counseling
   a. "In other words, you don't get along with your mother because she hates your girlfriend, is that right?"
   b. "I want you all to take turns talking about why you decided to come and what you hope to gain from therapy."
   c. "I can understand why you wanted to wreck your friend's car after she hurt your feelings. Now tell me more about the accident."
   d. "That's not appropriate behavior. Let's work on replacing it with something else."
2. _____ therapies assume that people should take responsibility for their lives and the decisions they make.
3. One of the major criticisms of humanistic therapies is that
   a. They are too imprecise and unstructured.
   b. They treat only the symptom of the problem.
   c. The therapist dominates the patient-therapist interaction.
   d. They work well only on clients of lower socioeconomic status.
4. In a controversial study, Eysenck found that some people go into _____, or recovery without treatment, if they are simply left alone instead of treated.
5. Treatments that combine techniques from all the theoretical perspectives are called _____ approaches.

RETHINK

1. How can people be successfully treated in group therapy when individuals with the "same" problem are so different? What advantages might group therapy offer over individual therapy?
2. *From the perspective of a social worker:* How might the types of therapies you employ vary depending on a client's cultural and socioeconomic background?

Answers to Evaluate Questions

1. 1-b, 2-c, 3-d, 4-a; 2. humanistic; 3. a; 4. spontaneous remission; 5. eclectic

KEY TERMS

humanistic therapy p. 567
person-centered therapy
  p. 568
gestalt therapy p. 568

interpersonal therapy (IPT)
  p. 568
group therapy p. 569
family therapy p. 569

spontaneous remission
  p. 570
eclectic approach p. 572

Biomedical Therapy: Biological Approaches to Treatment

If you get a kidney infection, your doctor gives you an antibiotic, and with luck, about a week later your kidney should be as good as new. If your appendix becomes inflamed, a surgeon removes it and your body functions normally once more. Could a comparable approach, focusing on the body's physiology, be effective for psychological disturbances?

According to biological approaches to treatment, the answer is yes. Therapists routinely use biomedical therapies. This approach suggests that rather than focusing on a patient's psychological conflicts or past traumas, or on environmental factors that may produce abnormal behavior, focusing treatment directly on brain chemistry and other neurological factors may be more appropriate. To do this, therapists can use drugs, electric shock, or surgery to provide treatment.

Drug Therapy

Drug therapy, the control of psychological disorders through drugs, works by altering the operation of neurotransmitters and neurons in the brain. Some drugs operate by inhibiting neurotransmitters or receptor neurons, reducing activity at particular synapses, the sites where nerve impulses travel from one neuron to another. Other drugs do just the opposite: They increase the activity of certain neurotransmitters or neurons, allowing particular neurons to fire more frequently (see Figure 1 and try the PsychInteractive exercise on drug therapy).

Key Concept

How are drug, electroconvulsive, and psychosurgical techniques used today in the treatment of psychological disorders?

Drug therapy: Control of psychological disorders through the use of drugs.

www.mhhe.com/feldmanup8
PsychInteractive Online

Drug Therapy

Drug Treatments			
Class of Drug	**Effects of Drug**	**Primary Action of Drug**	**Examples**
Antipsychotic Drugs	Reduction in loss of touch with reality, agitation	Block dopamine receptors	Chlorpromazine (Thorazine), clozapine (Clozaril), haloperidol (Haldol)
Antidepressant Drugs			
Tricyclic antidepressants	Reduction in depression	Permit rise in neurotransmitters such as norepinepherine	Trazodone (Desyrel), amitriptyline (Elavil), desipramine (Norpamin)
MAO inhibitors	Reduction in depression	Prevent MAO from breaking down neurotransmitters	Phenelzine (Nardil), tranylcypromine (Parnate)
Selective serotonin reuptake inhibitiors (SSRIs)	Reduction in depression	Inhibit reuptake of serotonin	Fluoxetine (Prozac), Luvox, Paxil, Celexa, Zoloft, nefazodone (Serzone)
Mood Stabilizers			
Lithium	Mood stabilization	Can alter transmission of impulses within neurons	Lithium (Lithonate), Depakote, Tegretol
Antianxiety Drugs	Reduction in anxiety	Increase activity of neurotrasmitter GABA	Benzodiazepines (Valium, Xanax)

FIGURE 1 The major classes of drugs used to treat psychological disorders have different effects on the brain and nervous system.

ANTIPSYCHOTIC DRUGS

Antipsychotic drugs: Drugs that temporarily reduce psychotic symptoms such as agitation, hallucinations, and delusions.

Probably no greater change has occurred in mental hospitals than the successful introduction in the mid-1950s of **antipsychotic drugs**—drugs used to reduce severe symptoms of disturbance, such as loss of touch with reality and agitation. Previously, the typical mental hospital wasn't very different from the stereotypical nineteenth-century insane asylum, giving mainly custodial care to screaming, moaning, clawing patients who displayed bizarre behaviors. Suddenly, in just a matter of days after hospital staff members administered antipsychotic drugs, the wards became considerably calmer environments in which professionals could do more than just try to get patients through the day without causing serious harm to themselves or others.

This dramatic change came about through the introduction of a drug called *chlorpromazine.* Along with other, similar drugs, chlorpromazine rapidly became the most popular and successful treatment for schizophrenia. Today drug therapy is the preferred treatment for most cases of severely abnormal behavior and, as such, is used for most patients hospitalized with psychological disorders. The drugs *clozapine* and *Zyprexa* represent the current generation of antipsychotics (Anand & Burton, 2003; Lublin, Eberhard, & Levander, 2005).

How do antipsychotic drugs work? Most block dopamine receptors at the brain's synapses. Some newer drugs, such as clozapine, increase dopamine levels in certain parts of the brain, such as those related to planning and goal-directed activity (Moghaddam & Adams, 1998; Sawa & Snyder, 2002; Advokat, 2005).

Despite the effectiveness of antipsychotic drugs, they do not produce a "cure" in the same way that, say, penicillin cures an infection. Most of the time, when the drug is withdrawn, the symptoms reappear. Furthermore, such drugs can have long-term side effects, such as dryness of the mouth and throat, dizziness, and sometimes tremors and loss of muscle control, which may continue after drug treatments are stopped (Shriqui & Annable, 1995).

ANTIDEPRESSANT DRUGS

Antidepressant drugs: Medications that improve a severely depressed patient's mood and feeling of well-being.

As you might guess from the name, **antidepressant drugs** are a class of medications used in cases of severe depression to improve the moods of patients. They were discovered by accident: Medical doctors found that patients with tuberculosis who received the drug iproniazid suddenly became happier and more optimistic. When researchers tested that drug on people with depression, a similar result occurred, and these drugs became an accepted form of treatment for depression (Shuchter, Downs, & Zisook, 1996).

Most antidepressant drugs work by changing the concentration of particular neurotransmitters in the brain. For example, *tricyclic drugs* increase the availability of norepinepherine at the synapses of neurons, whereas *MAO inhibitors* prevent the enzyme monoamine oxidase (MAO) from breaking down neurotransmitters. Newer antidepressants—such as Lexapro—are *selective serotonin reuptake inhibitors (SSRIs).* SSRIs target the neurotransmitter serotonin, permitting it to linger at the synapse. One of the latest antidepressants, nefazodone (Serzone), blocks serotonin at some receptor sites but not others (Berman, Krystal, & Charney, 1996; Williams et al., 2000; Anand, 2002; Lucki & O'Leary, 2004; see Figure 2).

Although antidepressant drugs may produce side effects such as drowsiness and faintness, their overall success rate is quite good. Unlike antipsychotic drugs, antidepressants can produce lasting, long-term recovery from depression. In many cases, even after patients stop taking the drugs, their depression does not return (Zito, 1993; Julien, 1995).

Consumers spend billions of dollars each year on antidepressant drugs, and sales are increasing more than 20 percent a year. In particular, the antidepressant *fluoxetine,* sold under the trade name *Prozac,* has been highlighted on magazine covers and has been the topic of best-sellers.

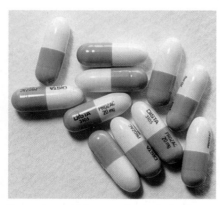

Prozac is a widely prescribed—but still controversial—antidepressant.

Does Prozac deserve its acclaim? In some respects, yes. Despite its high expense— each daily dose costs around $2—it has significantly improved the lives of thousands of depressed individuals. Compared with other antidepressants, Prozac (along with its cousins Luvox, Paxil, Celexa, and Zoloft) has relatively few side effects. Furthermore, many people who do not respond to other types of antidepressants do well on Prozac. However, like all drugs, Prozac does not agree with everyone. For example, 20 to

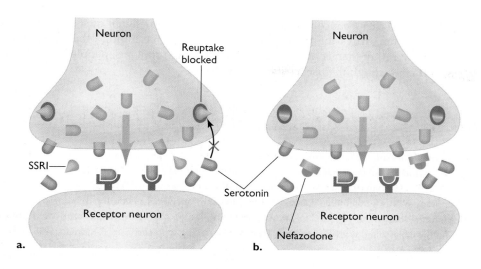

FIGURE 2 In (a), selective serotonin reuptake inhibitors (SSRIs) reduce depression by permitting the neurotransmitter serotonin to remain in the synapse. In (b), a newer antidepressant, nefazodone (Serzone), operates more selectively to block serotonin at some sites but not others, helping to reduce the side effects of the drug. (Source: Based on Mischoulon, 2000.)

30 percent of users report experiencing nausea and diarrhea, and a smaller number report sexual dysfunctions (Kramer, 1993; Glenmullen, 2000; Brambilla et al., 2005).

Another drug that has received a great deal of publicity is *St. John's wort*, an herb that some have called a "natural" antidepressant. Although it is widely used in Europe for the treatment of depression, the U.S. Food and Drug Administration considers it a dietary supplement, and therefore the substance is available here without a prescription.

Despite the popularity of St. John's wort, definitive clinical tests have found that the herb is ineffective in the treatment of depression. However, because some research shows that the herb successfully reduces certain symptoms of depression, some proponents argue that using it is reasonable. Clearly, people should not use St. John's wort to medicate themselves without consulting a mental health care professional (Maidment, 2000; Williams et al., 2000; Shelton et al., 2002).

LITHIUM

The drug **lithium,** a form of mineral salts, has been used very successfully in patients with bipolar disorders. Although no one knows definitely why, lithium and drugs such as *Depakote* and *Tegretol* effectively reduce manic episodes. However, they do not effectively treat depressive phases of bipolar disorder, so antidepressants are usually prescribed during those phases (Dubovsky, 1999; Fountoulakis et al., 2005).

Lithium and similar drugs have a quality that sets them apart from other drug treatments: They can be a *preventive* treatment, blocking future episodes of manic depression. Often, people who have had episodes of bipolar disorder can take a daily dose of lithium to prevent a recurrence of their symptoms. Most other drugs are useful only when symptoms of psychological disturbance occur.

Lithium: A drug made up of mineral salts that is used to treat and prevent manic episodes of bipolar disorder.

ANTIANXIETY DRUGS

As the name implies, **antianxiety drugs** reduce the level of anxiety a person experiences and increase feelings of well-being. They are prescribed not only to reduce general tension in people who are experiencing temporary difficulties but also to aid in the treatment of more serious anxiety disorders (Zito, 1993).

Antianxiety drugs such as Xanax and Valium are among the medications most frequently prescribed by physicians. In fact, more than half of all U.S. families have someone who has taken such a drug at one time or another.

Although the popularity of antianxiety drugs suggests that they hold few risks, they can produce a number of potentially serious side effects. For instance, they can cause fatigue, and long-term use can lead to dependence. Moreover, when taken in combination with alcohol, some antianxiety drugs can be lethal. But a more important issue concerns their use to suppress anxiety. Almost every therapeutic approach

Antianxiety drugs: Drugs that reduce the level of anxiety a person experiences, essentially by reducing excitability and increasing feelings of well-being.

to psychological disturbance views continuing anxiety as a signal of some other sort of problem. Thus, drugs that mask anxiety may simply be hiding other difficulties. Consequently, rather than confronting their underlying problems, people may be hiding from them through the use of antianxiety drugs.

Electroconvulsive Therapy (ECT)

Martha Manning had contemplated all kinds of suicide—by pills, hanging, even guns. Her depression was so deep that she lived each minute "afraid I [wouldn't] make it to the next hour." But she balked when her therapist recommended electroconvulsive therapy, commonly known as "shock treatment." Despite her training and practice as a clinical psychologist, Manning immediately flashed to scenes from *One Flew Over the Cuckoo's Nest*, "with McMurphy and the Chief jolted with electroshock, their bodies flailing with each jolt" (Guttman, 1995, p. 16).

The reality, it turned out, was quite different. Although it did produce some memory loss and temporary headaches, the procedure also brought Manning back from the brink of suicide.

First introduced in the 1930s, **electroconvulsive therapy (ECT)** is a procedure in which an electric current of 70 to 150 volts is briefly administered to a patient's head, causing a loss of consciousness and often causing seizures. Usually health professionals sedate patients and give them muscle relaxants before administering the current, and this helps reduce the intensity of muscle contractions produced during ECT. The typical patient receives about ten such treatments in the course of a month, but some patients continue with maintenance treatments for months afterward (Nierenberg, 1998; Fink, 1999; Greenberg & Kellner, 2005).

ECT is a controversial technique. Apart from the obvious distastefulness of a treatment that evokes images of electrocution, side effects occur frequently. For instance, after treatment patients often experience disorientation, confusion, and sometimes memory loss that may remain for months. Furthermore, ECT often does not produce long-term improvement; one study found that without follow-up medication, depression returned in most patients who had undergone ECT treatments. Finally, even when ECT does work, we do not know why, and some critics believe it may cause permanent brain damage (Valente, 1991; Sackeim et al., 2001; Frank, 2002).

In light of the drawbacks to ECT, why do therapists use it at all? Basically, they use it because, in many severe cases of depression, it offers the only quickly effective treatment. For instance, it may prevent depressed, suicidal individuals from committing suicide, and it can act more quickly than antidepressive medications.

The use of ECT has risen in the last decade, with more than 100,000 people undergoing it each year. Still, ECT tends to be used only when other treatments have proved ineffective, and researchers continue to search for alternative treatments (Sackheim et al., 1996; Fink, 2000; Eranti & McLoughlin, 2003).

One new and promising alternative to ECT is **transcranial magnetic stimulation (TMS).** TMS creates a precise magnetic pulse in a specific area of the brain. By activating particular neuorns, TMS has been found to be effective in relieving the symptoms of depression in a number of controlled experiments. However, the therapy can produce side effects, such as seizures and convulsions, and it is still considered experimental by the government (George, 2003; Doumas, Praamstra, & Wing, 2005; Simons, 2005).

Psychosurgery

If ECT strikes you as a questionable procedure, the use of **psychosurgery**—brain surgery in which the object is to reduce symptoms of mental disorder—probably appears even more dubious. A technique used only rarely today, psychosurgery was introduced as a "treatment of last resort" in the 1930s.

The initial form of psychosurgery, a *prefrontal lobotomy*, consisted of surgically destroying or removing parts of a patient's frontal lobes, which, surgeons thought, controlled emotion-

Electroconvulsive therapy (ECT): A procedure in which an electric current of 70 to 150 volts is briefly administered to a patient's head, causing a loss of consciousness and often causing seizures.

Transcranial magnetic stimulation (TMS): A depression treatment in which a precise magnetic pulse is directed to a specific area of the brain.

Psychosurgery: Brain surgery once used to reduce the symptoms of mental disorder but rarely used today.

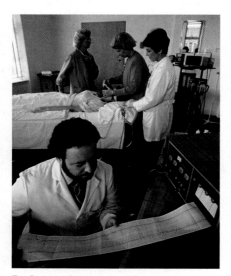

Dr. Richard B. Weiner of Duke University Medical Center reads a patient's electroencephalogram as technicians administer electroconvulsive therapy. ECT is a controversial treatment, but it does help some people whose severe depression has not responded to other approaches.

ality. In the 1930s and 1940s, surgeons performed the procedure on thousands of patients, often with little precision. For example, in one common technique, a surgeon would jab an ice pick under a patient's eyeball and swivel it back and forth (Miller, 1994; El-Hai, 2005).

Psychosurgery often did improve a patient's behavior—but not without drastic side effects. Along with remission of the symptoms of the mental disorder, patients sometimes experienced personality changes, becoming bland, colorless, and unemotional. In other cases, patients became aggressive and unable to control their impulses. In the worst cases, treatment resulted in the death of the patient.

With the introduction of effective drug treatments—and the obvious ethical questions regarding the appropriateness of forever altering someone's personality—psychosurgery became nearly obsolete. However, it is still used in very rare cases when all other procedures have failed and the patient's behavior presents a high risk to the patient and others. Today, surgeons sometimes use a more precise form of psychosurgery called a *cingulotomy* in rare cases of obsessive-compulsive disorder. Occasionally, dying patients with severe, uncontrollable pain also receive psychosurgery. Still, even these cases raise important ethical issues, and psychosurgery remains a highly controversial treatment (Miller, 1994; Baer et al., 1995; Jenike, 1998).

Biomedical Therapies in Perspective

In some respects, no greater revolution has occurred in the field of mental health than biological approaches to treatment. As previously violent, uncontrollable patients have been calmed by the use of drugs, mental hospitals have been able to concentrate more on actually helping patients and less on custodial functions. Similarly, patients whose lives have been disrupted by depression or bipolar episodes have been able to function normally, and other forms of drug therapy have also shown remarkable results.

The use of biomedical therapy for everyday problems is rising. For example, one survey of users of a college counseling service found that from 1989 to 2001, the proportion of students receiving treatment who were taking medication for psychological disorders increased from 10 percent to 25 percent (Benton et al., 2003).

Furthermore, new forms of biomedical therapy are promising. For example, the newest treatment possibility—which remains experimental at this point—is gene therapy. As we discussed when considering behavioral genetics, specific genes may be introduced to particular regions of the brain. These genes then have the potential to reverse or even prevent biochemical events that give rise to psychological disorders (Grady & Kolata, 2003; Sapolsky, 2003; Lymberis et al., 2004).

Despite their current usefulness and future promise, biomedical therapies do not represent a cure-all for psychological disorders. For one thing, critics charge that such therapies merely provide relief of the *symptoms* of mental disorder; as soon as the drugs are withdrawn, the symptoms return. Although it is considered a major step in the right direction, biomedical treatment may not solve the underlying problems that led a patient to therapy in the first place. Moreover, biomedical therapies can produce side effects, ranging from physical reactions to the development of *new* symptoms of abnormal behavior.

Still, biomedical therapies—sometimes alone and more often in conjunction with psychotherapy—have permitted millions of people to function more effectively. Furthermore, although biomedical therapy and psychotherapy appear distinct, research shows that biomedical therapies ultimately may not be as different from talk therapies as one might imagine, at least in terms of their consequences.

Specifically, measures of brain functioning as a result of drug therapy compared with psychotherapy show little difference in outcomes. For example, one study compared the reactions of patients with major depression who received either an antidepressant drug or psychotherapy. After six weeks of either therapy, activity in the portion of the brain related to the disorder—the basal ganglia—had changed in similar ways, and that area appeared to function more normally. Although such research is not definitive, it does suggest that at least for some disorders, psychotherapy may be just as effective as biomedical interventions—and vice versa. Research also makes it clear that no single treatment is effective uni-

While deinstitutionalization has had many successes, it has also contributed to the release of mental patients into the community with little or no support. As a result many have become homeless.

Community psychology: A branch of psychology that focuses on the prevention and minimization of psychological disorders in the community.

Deinstitutionalization: The transfer of former mental patients from institutions to the community.

FIGURE 3 As deinstitutionalization has become more prevalent over the last fifty years, the number of patients being treated in state mental hospitals has declined significantly, while the number of outpatient facilities has increased. (Source: National Mental Health Information Center, U.S. Department of Health and Human Services, reprinted in *Scientific American*, December, 2002, p. 38.)

versally, and that each type of treatment has both advantages and disadvantages (Brody et al., 2001; Hollon, Thase, & Markowitz, 2002; DeRubeis, Hollon, & Shelton, 2003).

Community Psychology: Focus on Prevention

Each of the treatments we have reviewed has a common element: It is a "restorative" treatment, aimed at alleviating psychological difficulties that already exist. However, an approach known as **community psychology** has a different aim: to prevent or minimize the incidence of psychological disorders.

Community psychology came of age in the 1960s, when mental health professionals developed plans for a nationwide network of community mental health centers. The hope was that those centers would provide low-cost mental health services, including short-term therapy and community educational programs. In another development, the population of mental hospitals has plunged as drug treatments made physical restraint of patients unnecessary. This transfer of former mental patients out of institutions and into the community—a process known as **deinstitutionalization**—was encouraged by the growth of the community psychology movement (see Figure 3). Proponents of deinstitutionalization wanted to ensure not only that deinstitutionalized patients received proper treatment but also that their civil rights were maintained (Melton & Garrison, 1987).

Unfortunately, the promise of deinstitutionalization has not been met, largely because insufficient resources are provided to deinstitutionalized patients. What started as a worthy attempt to move people out of mental institutions and into the community ended, in many cases, with former patients being dumped into the community without any real support. Many became homeless—between a third and a half of all homeless adults are thought to have a major psychological disorder—and some became involved in illegal acts caused by their disorders. In short, many people who need treatment do not get it, and in some cases care for people with psychological disorders has simply shifted from one type of treatment site to another (Kiesler & Simpkins, 1993; Torrey, 1997; Doyle, 2002; Lamb & Weinberger, 2005).

On the other hand, the community psychology movement has had some positive outcomes. Telephone hot lines are now common. At any time of the day or night, peo-

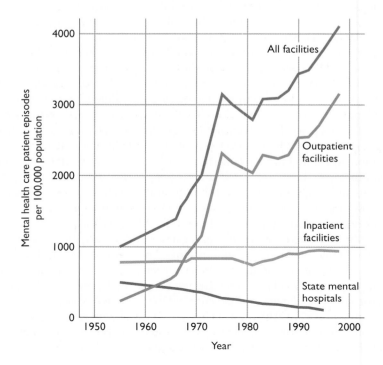

ple experiencing acute stress can call a trained, sympathetic listener who can provide immediate—although obviously limited—treatment (Blewett, 2000; Reese, Conoley, & Brossart, 2002; Paukert, Stagner, & Hope, 2004).

College and high school crisis centers are another innovation that grew out of the community psychology movement. Modeled after suicide prevention hot-line centers (services that enable potential suicide victims to call and speak to someone about their difficulties), crisis centers give callers an opportunity to discuss life crises with a sympathetic listener, who is often a volunteer.

If you decide to seek therapy, you're faced with a daunting task. Choosing a therapist is not a simple matter. One place to start the process of identifying a therapist is at the "Help Center" of the American Psychological Association at locator.apahelpcenter.org/ or 1-800-964-2000. And if you start therapy, several general guidelines can help you determine whether you've made the right choice:

BECOMING AN INFORMED CONSUMER
of Psychology
Choosing the Right Therapist

You and your therapist should agree on the goals for treatment. They should be clear, specific, and attainable.

- *You should feel comfortable with your therapist.* You should not be intimidated by, or in awe of, a therapist. Instead, you should trust the therapist and feel free to discuss even the most personal issues without fearing a negative reaction. In sum, the "personal chemistry" should be right.
- *Therapists should have appropriate training and credentials and should be licensed by appropriate state and local agencies.* Check therapists' membership in national and state professional associations. In addition, the cost of therapy, billing practices, and other business matters should be clear. It is not a breach of etiquette to put these matters on the table during an initial consultation.
- *You should feel that you are making progress after therapy has begun, despite occasional setbacks.* If you have no sense of improvement after repeated visits, you and your therapist should discuss this issue frankly. Although there is no set timetable, the most obvious changes resulting from therapy tend to occur relatively early in the course of treatment. For instance, half of patients in psychotherapy improve by the eighth session, and three-fourths by the twenty-sixth session (see Figure 4). The average number of sessions with college students is just five (Crits-Cristoph, 1992; HMHL, 1994; Lazarus, 1997).

"Looking good!"

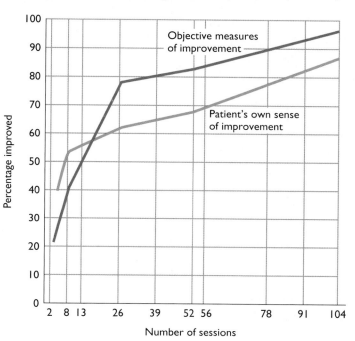

FIGURE 4 For most clients, improvements in psychological functioning occur relatively soon after therapy has begun. (Source: Howard et al., 1986.)

Be aware that you will have to put in a great deal of effort in therapy. Although our culture promises quick cures for any problem, in reality, solving difficult problems is not easy. You must be committed to making therapy work and should know that it is you, not the therapist, who must do most of the work to resolve your problems. The effort has the potential to pay off handsomely—as you experience a more positive, fulfilling, and meaningful life.

RECAP/EVALUATE/RETHINK

RECAP

How are drug, electroconvulsive, and psychosurgical techniques used today in the treatment of psychological disorders?

- Biomedical treatment approaches suggest that therapy should focus on the physiological causes of abnormal behavior, rather than considering psychological factors. Drug therapy, the best example of biomedical treatments, has brought about dramatic reductions in the symptoms of mental disturbance. (p. 575)
- Antipsychotic drugs such as chlorpromazine very effectively reduce psychotic symptoms. Antidepressant drugs such as Prozac reduce depression so successfully that they are used very widely. Antianxiety drugs, or minor tranquilizers, are among the most frequently prescribed medications of any sort. (pp. 576–577)
- In electroconvulsive therapy (ECT), used only in severe cases of depression, a patient receives a brief electric current of 70 to 150 volts. (p. 578)
- Psychosurgery typically consists of surgically destroying or removing certain parts of a patient's brain. (pp. 578–579)
- The community psychology approach encouraged deinstitutionalization, in which previously hospitalized mental patients were released into the community. (p. 580)

EVALUATE

1. Antipsychotic drugs have provided effective, long-term, and complete cures for schizophrenia. True or false?

2. One highly effective biomedical treatment for a psychological disorder, used mainly to arrest and prevent manic-depressive episodes, is
   a. Chlorpromazine
   b. Lithium
   c. Librium
   d. Valium
3. Psychosurgery has grown in popularity as a method of treatment as surgical techniques have become more precise. True or false?
4. The trend toward releasing more patients from mental hospitals and into the community is known as _____.

RETHINK

1. One of the main criticisms of biological therapies is that they treat the symptoms of mental disorder without uncovering and treating the underlying problems from which people are suffering. Do you agree with this criticism? Why?
2. *From the perspective of a politician:* How would you go about regulating the use of electroconvulsive therapy and psychosurgery? Would you restrict their use or make either one completely illegal? Why?

Answers to Evaluate Questions

1. false; schizophrenia can be controlled, but not cured, by medication; 2. b; 3. false; psychosurgery is now used only as a treatment of last resort. 4. deinstitutionalization

KEY TERMS

drug therapy p. 575	antianxiety drugs p. 577	transcranial magnetic stimulation (TMS) p. 578	community psychology p. 580
antipsychotic drugs p. 576	electroconvulsive therapy (ECT) p. 578	psychosurgery p. 578	deinstitutionalization p. 580
antidepressant drugs p. 576			
lithium p. 577			

Looking Back

Psychology on the Web

1. Investigate computer-assisted psychotherapy on the Web. Locate (a) a computerized therapy program, such as ELIZA, which offers "therapy" over the Internet, and (b) a report on "cybertherapy," in which therapists use the Web to interact with patients. Compare the two approaches, describing how each one works and relating it to the therapeutic approaches you have studied.
2. Find more information on the Web about deinstitutionalization. Try to find pro and con arguments about it and summarize the arguments, including your judgment of the effectiveness and advisability of deinstitutionalization as an approach to dealing with mental illness.
3. After completing the PsychInteractive exercise on drug therapies, investigate new drug therapies for a specific disorder of your choice, such as schizophrenia, bipolar disorder, or panic attacks. Summarize how the drugs operate, their effectiveness, and any side effects.

Epilogue

We have examined how psychological professionals treat people with psychological disorders. We considered a range of approaches, including both psychologically based and biologically based therapies. Clearly, the field has made substantial progress in recent years both in treating the symptoms of mental disorders and in understanding their underlying causes.

Before we leave the topic of treatment of psychological disorders, turn back to the prologue, in which several people who had had schizophrenia held a belated prom to celebrate their liberation from that disorder. On the basis of your understanding of the treatment of psychological disorders, consider the following questions.

1. The prom goers in the story were treated with drug therapy. How would their treatment have proceeded if they had undergone Freudian psychoanalysis? What sorts of issues might a psychoanalyst have examined?
2. Do you think any behavioral therapies would have been helpful in treating the prom goers' schizophrenia? Could behavioral therapies have helped them control the outward exhibition of symptoms?
3. Would cognitive or humanistic approaches have any effect on schizophrenia? In what ways might such approaches fall short?
4. Do you think that people who recover from schizophrenia can reenter the world quickly and calmly and take up their lives as if nothing had happened to them? What sort of adjustments might lifelong sufferers now in their thirties have to make?
5. Antipsychotic drugs sometimes have the side effect of numbing emotional responses. If it could have been known ahead of time that the prom goers would eventually experience this side effect, do you think the drug therapy would still have been advisable? Why or why not?

Social Psychology

Key Concepts for Chapter 17

Prologue Everyday Hero

Seven-year-old Joshua Pia Perez was playing near his home . . . when he was suddenly charged by two pit bulls who had broken out of a nearby yard. Kathleen Imel, 51, who was driving by, screeched to a halt. "Stop, don't run!" she yelled. But it was too late. "They started biting me," says Joshua, now 8. "I was screaming for help."

Leaping from her van, Imel, the mother of two grown sons, flung herself on top of Joshua as the larger dog, a 60-pounder name Butch, bit into the child's left ear. "I knew that either I did something or this little boy was lost," says Imel, assistant manager at a group home for people with developmental disabilities. Releasing Joshua, Butch chomped into Imel's left eyebrow instead. As the dog clamped its jaws around her elbow, a neighbor, drawn by her screams, pulled Joshua to safety. Then another neighbor beat off the dogs with an aluminum rod. . . .

Imel was left with extensive injuries to her eye area. The attack almost severed Joshua's ear and left his uninsured parents with $14,000 in bills. But their biggest debt, says father Cesar Pia, 36, a pastor and housepainter, is to Imel. "She's an angel," he says. (Fields-Meyer & Lambert, 2004b, p. 100.)

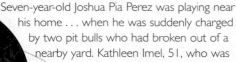

Looking Ahead

What led Kathleen Imel to behave so heroically? Was it simply the circumstances, or was it something about Imel herself? What, in general, drives some people to help others—and conversely, why do other people show no concern for the welfare of others? More broadly, how can we improve social conditions so that people can live together in harmony?

We can fully answer these questions only by taking into account findings from the field of social psychology, the branch of psychology that focuses on the aspects of human behavior that unite—and separate—us from one another. **Social psychology** is the scientific study of how people's thoughts, feelings, and actions are affected by others. Social psychologists consider the nature and causes of the behavior of the individual in social situations.

The broad scope of social psychology is conveyed by the kinds of questions social psychologists ask, such as: How can we convince people to change their attitudes or adopt new ideas and values? In what ways do we come to understand what others are like? How are we influenced by what others do and think? Why do some people display so much violence, aggression, and cruelty toward others that people throughout the world live in fear of annihilation at their hands? And why, in comparison, do some people place their own lives at risk to help others? In exploring these and other questions, we also discuss strategies for confronting and solving a variety of problems and issues that all of us face—ranging from achieving a better understanding of persuasive tactics to forming more accurate impressions of others.

We begin with a look at how our attitudes shape our behavior and how we form judgments about others. We'll discuss how we are influenced by others, and we will consider prejudice and discrimination, focusing on their roots and the ways in which we can reduce them. After examining what social psychologists have learned about the ways in which people form friendships and relationships, we'll conclude with a look at the determinants of aggression and helping.

Attitudes and Social Cognition

What do Tiger Woods, Britney Spears, and Jay Leno have in common?

Each has appeared frequently in advertisements designed to mold or change our attitudes. Such commercials are part of the barrage of messages we receive each day from sources as varied as politicians, sales staff in stores, and celebrities, all of which are meant to influence us.

Persuasion: Changing Attitudes

Persuasion is the process of changing attitudes, one of the central concepts of social psychology. **Attitudes** are evaluations of a particular person, behavior, belief, or concept. For example, you probably hold attitudes toward the U.S. president (a person), abortion (a behavior), affirmative action (a belief), or architecture (a concept) (Eagly & Chaiken, 1998; Perloff, 2003; Brock & Green, 2005).

The ease with which attitudes can be changed depends on a number of factors, including:

- *Message source.* The characteristics of a person who delivers a persuasive message, known as an *attitude communicator,* have a major impact on the effectiveness of that message. Communicators who are physically and socially attractive produce greater attitude change than those who are less attractive. Moreover, the expertise and trustworthiness of a communicator are related to the impact of a message—except in situations in which the audience believes the communicator has an ulterior motive (Hovland, Janis, & Kelly, 1953; Ziegler, Diehl, & Ruther, 2002).
- *Characteristics of the message.* It is not just *who* delivers a message but what the message is like that affects attitudes. Generally, two-sided messages—which include both the communicator's position and the one he or she is arguing against—are more effective than one-sided messages, assuming the arguments for the other side can be effectively refuted and the audience is knowledgeable about the topic. In addition, fear-producing messages ("If you don't practice safer sex, you'll get AIDS") are generally effective when they provide the audience with a means for reducing the fear. However, if the fear aroused is too strong, messages may evoke people's defense mechanisms and be ignored (Perloff, 2003).
- *Characteristics of the target.* Once a communicator has delivered a message, characteristics of the *target* of the message may determine whether the message will be accepted. For example, intelligent people are more resistant to persuasion than are those who are less intelligent. Gender differences in persuasibility also seem to exist. In public settings, women are somewhat more easily persuaded than men, particularly when they have less knowledge about the message's topic. However, they are as likely as men to change their private attitudes. In fact, the magnitude of the differences in resistance to persuasion between men and women is not large (Wood & Stagner, 1994; Wood, 2000; Guadagno & Cialdini, 2002).

Key Concepts

What are attitudes, and how are they formed, maintained, and changed?

How do we form impressions of what others are like and of the causes of their behavior?

What are the biases that influence the ways in which we view others' behavior?

Social psychology: The scientific study of how people's thoughts, feelings, and actions are affected by others.

Attitudes: Evaluations of a particular person, behavior, belief, or concept.

Companies use sports stars such as Tiger Woods to persuade consumers to buy their products. Can celebrities really affect the purchasing habits of consumers? How?

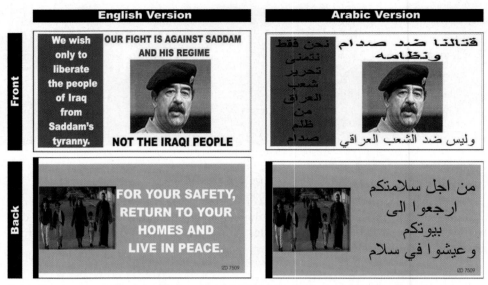

Cards like these were distributed in Iraq by U.S. Armed Forces during 2003. Do you believe they could be effective in changing the attitudes and beliefs of the Iraqi people?

ROUTES TO PERSUASION

Recipients' receptiveness to persuasive messages relates to the type of information-processing they use. Social psychologists have discovered two primary information-processing routes to persuasion: central route and peripheral route processing. **Central route processing** occurs when the recipient thoughtfully considers the issues and arguments involved in persuasion. In central route processing, people are swayed in their judgments by the logic, merit, and strength of arguments.

In contrast, **peripheral route processing** occurs when people are persuaded on the basis of factors unrelated to the nature or quality of the content of a persuasive message. Instead, factors that are irrelevant or extraneous to the issue, such as who is providing the message, how long the arguments are, or the emotional appeal of the arguments, influence them (Wegener et al., 2004; Petty et al., 2005).

In general, people who are highly involved and motivated use central route processing to comprehend a message. However, if a person is uninvolved, unmotivated, bored, or distracted, the nature of the message becomes less important, and peripheral factors become more critical (see Figure 1). Although both central route and peripheral route processing lead to attitude change, central route processing generally leads to stronger, more lasting attitude change.

Central route processing: Message interpretation characterized by thoughtful consideration of the issues and arguments used to persuade.

Peripheral route processing: Message interpretation characterized by consideration of the source and related general information rather than of the message itself.

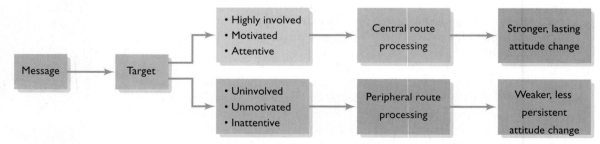

FIGURE 1 Routes to persuasion. Targets who are highly involved, motivated, and attentive use central route processing when they consider a persuasive message, which leads to a more lasting attitude change. In contrast, uninvolved, unmotivated, and inattentive targets are more likely to use peripheral route processing, and attitude change is likely to be less enduring. Can you think of particular advertisements that try to produce central route processing?

The Need for Cognition

Which of the following statements apply to you?

1. I really enjoy a task that involves coming up with new solutions to problems.
2. I would prefer a task that is intellectual, difficult, and important to one that is somewhat important but does not require much thought.
3. Learning new ways to think doesn't excite me very much.
4. The idea of relying on thought to make my way to the top does not appeal to me.
5. I think only as hard as I have to.
6. I like tasks that require little thought once I've learned them.
7. I prefer to think about small, daily projects rather than long-term ones.
8. I would rather do something that requires little thought than something that is sure to challenge my thinking abilities.
9. I find little satisfaction in deliberating hard and for long hours.
10. I don't like to be responsible for a situation that requires a lot of thinking.

Scoring: The more you agree with statements 1 and 2, and disagree with the rest, the greater the likelihood that you have a high need for cognition.

FIGURE 2 This simple questionnaire will give you a general idea of your need for cognition. (Source: Cacioppo, Berntson, & Crites, 1996.)

Are some people more likely than others to use central route processing rather than peripheral route processing? The answer is yes. People who have a high *need for cognition,* a person's habitual level of thoughtfulness and cognitive activity, are more likely to employ central route processing. Consider the statements shown in Figure 2. People who agree with the first two statements and disagree with the rest have a relatively high need for cognition (Cacioppo, Berntson, & Crites, 1996).

People who have a high need for cognition enjoy thinking, philosophizing, and reflecting on the world. Consequently, they tend to reflect more on persuasive messages by using central route processing, and are likely to be persuaded by complex, logical, and detailed messages. In contrast, those who have a low need for cognition become impatient when forced to spend too much time thinking about an issue. Consequently, they usually use peripheral route processing and are persuaded by factors other than the quality and detail of messages (Haugtvedt, Petty, & Cacioppo, 1992; Dollinger, 2003).

THE LINK BETWEEN ATTITUDES AND BEHAVIOR

Not surprisingly, attitudes influence behavior. The strength of the link between particular attitudes and behavior varies, of course, but generally people strive for consistency between their attitudes and their behavior. Furthermore, people hold fairly consistent attitudes. For instance, you would probably not hold the attitude that eating meat is immoral and still have a positive attitude toward hamburgers (Kraus, 1995; Ajzen, 2002; Conner et al., 2003).

Interestingly, the consistency that leads attitudes to influence behavior sometimes works the other way around, for in some cases it is our behavior that shapes our attitudes. Consider, for instance, the following incident:

> You've just spent what you feel is the most boring hour of your life, turning pegs for a psychology experiment. Just as you finally finish and are about to leave, the experimenter asks you to do him a favor. He tells you that he needs a helper for future experimental sessions to introduce subsequent participants to the peg-turning task. Your specific job will be to tell them that turning the pegs is an interesting, fascinating experience. Each time you tell this tale to another participant, you'll be paid $1.

If you agree to help the experimenter, you may be setting yourself up for a state of psychological tension called cognitive dissonance. According to a prominent social

Cognitive dissonance: The conflict that occurs when a person holds two contradictory attitudes or thoughts (referred to as cognitions).

psychologist, Leon Festinger (1957), **cognitive dissonance** occurs when a person holds two contradictory attitudes or thoughts (referred to as *cognitions*).

If you participate in the situation just described, you are left with two contradictory thoughts: (1) I believe the task is boring, but (2) I said it was interesting with little justification ($1). These two thoughts should arouse dissonance. How can you reduce cognitive dissonance? You cannot deny having said that the task is interesting without breaking with reality. Relatively speaking, it is easier to change your attitude toward the task—and thus the theory predicts that participants will reduce dissonance by adopting more positive attitudes toward the task (Harmon-Jones, Peterson, & Vaughn, 2003; Cooper, Mirabile, & Scher, 2005).

A classic experiment (Festinger & Carlsmith, 1959) confirmed this prediction. The experiment followed essentially the same procedure outlined earlier, in which a participant was offered $1 to describe a boring task as interesting. In addition, in a comparison condition, some participants were offered $20 to say that the task was interesting. The reasoning behind this condition was that $20 was so much money that participants in this condition had a good reason to be conveying incorrect information; dissonance would not be aroused, and less attitude change would be expected. The results supported this notion. More of the participants who were paid $1 changed their attitudes (becoming more positive toward the peg-turning task) than did participants who were paid $20.

We now know that dissonance explains many everyday events involving attitudes and behavior. For example, smokers who know that smoking leads to lung cancer hold contradictory cognitions: (1) I smoke, and (2) smoking leads to lung cancer. The theory predicts that these two thoughts will lead to a state of cognitive dissonance. More important, it predicts that—assuming that they don't change their behavior by quitting smoking—smokers will be motivated to reduce their dissonance by one of the following methods: (1) modifying one or both of the cognitions, (2) changing the perceived importance of one cognition, (3) adding cognitions, or (4) denying that the two cognitions are related to each other. Hence, a smoker may decide that he really doesn't smoke all that much or that he'll quit soon (modifying the cognition), that the evidence linking smoking to cancer is weak (changing the importance of a cognition), that the amount of exercise he gets compensates for the smoking (adding cognitions), or that there is no evidence linking smoking and cancer (denial). Whichever technique the smoker uses results in reduced dissonance (see Figure 3).

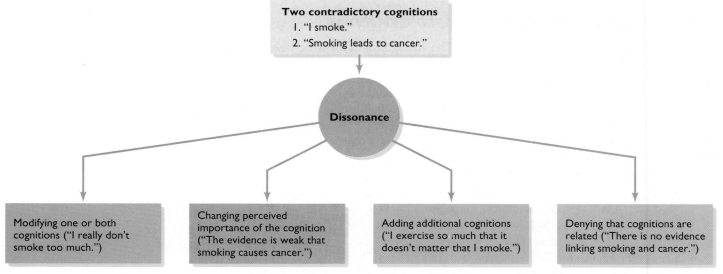

FIGURE 3 Cognitive dissonance. The simultaneous presence of two contradictory cognitions ("I smoke" and "Smoking leads to cancer") produces dissonance, which may be reduced through several methods. What are additional ways in which dissonance can be reduced?

Social Cognition: Understanding Others

Regardless of Bill Clinton's personal transgressions and impeachment trial, many Americans genuinely *liked* him when he was president, and his popularity remained high throughout his term in office. Cases like this illustrate the power of our impressions and attest to the importance of determining how people develop an understanding of others. One of the dominant areas in social psychology during the last few years has focused on learning how we come to understand what others are like and how we explain the reasons underlying others' behavior.

UNDERSTANDING WHAT OTHERS ARE LIKE

Consider for a moment the enormous amount of information about other people to which we are exposed. How can we decide what is important and what is not and make judgments about the characteristics of others? Social psychologists interested in this question study **social cognition**—the way people understand and make sense of others and themselves. Those psychologists have learned that individuals have highly developed **schemas,** sets of cognitions about people and social experiences. Those schemas organize information stored in memory, represent in our minds the way the social world operates, and give us a framework to recognize, categorize, and recall information relating to social stimuli such as people and groups (Fiske & Taylor, 1991; Brewer & Hewstone, 2003; Moskowitz, 2004).

We typically hold schemas for particular types of people. Our schema for "teacher," for instance, generally consists of a number of characteristics: knowledge of the subject matter he or she is teaching, a desire to impart that knowledge, and an awareness of the student's need to understand what is being said. Or we may hold a schema for "mother" that includes the characteristics of warmth, nurturance, and caring. Regardless of their accuracy, schemas are important because they organize the way in which we recall, recognize, and categorize information about others. Moreover, they help us predict what others are like on the basis of relatively little information, because we tend to fit people into schemas even when we do not have much concrete evidence to go on (Bargh & Chartrand, 2000; Ruscher, Fiske, & Schnake, 2000).

Social cognition: The cognitive processes by which people understand and make sense of others and themselves.

Schemas: Sets of cognitions about people and social experiences.

IMPRESSION FORMATION

How do we decide that Sayreeta is a flirt, Jacob is obnoxious, or Hector is a really nice guy? The earliest work on social cognition examined *impression formation,* the process by which an individual organizes information about another person to form an overall impression of that person. In a classic study, for instance, students learned that they were about to hear a guest lecturer (Kelley, 1950). Researchers told one group of students that the lecturer was "a rather warm person, industrious, critical, practical, and determined," and told a second group that he was "a rather cold person, industrious, critical, practical, and determined."

The simple substitution of "cold" for "warm" caused drastic differences in the way the students in each group perceived the lecturer, even though he gave the same talk in the same style in each condition. Students who had been told he was "warm" rated him considerably more positively than students who had been told he was "cold."

The findings from this experiment led to additional research on impression formation that focused on the way in which people pay particular attention to certain unusually important traits—known as **central traits**—to help them form an overall impression of others. According to this work, the presence of a central trait alters the meaning of other traits. Hence, the description of the lecturer as "industrious"

Central traits: The major traits considered in forming impressions of others.

presumably meant something different when it was associated with the central trait "warm" than it meant when it was associated with "cold" (Asch, 1946; Widmeyer & Loy, 1988).

Other work on impression formation has used information-processing approaches to develop mathematically oriented models of how individual personality traits combine to create an overall impression. Generally, the results of this research suggest that in forming an overall judgment of a person, we use a psychological "average" of the individual traits we see, just as we would find the mathematical average of several numbers (Anderson, 1996; Mignon & Mollaret, 2002).

We make such impressions remarkably quickly. In just a few seconds, using what have been called "thin slices of behavior," we are able to make judgments of people that are accurate and that match those of people who make judgments based on longer snippets of behavior (Hall & Bernieri, 2001; Choi, Gray, & Ambady, 2004).

Of course, as we gain more experience with people and see them exhibiting behavior in a variety of situations, our impressions of them become more complex. However, because our knowledge of others usually has gaps, we still tend to fit individuals into personality schemas that represent particular "types" of people. For instance, we may hold a "gregarious person" schema, made up of the traits of friendliness, aggressiveness, and openness. The presence of just one or two of those traits may be sufficient to make us assign a person to a particular schema.

However, our schemas are susceptible to error. For example, mood affects how we perceive others. Happy people form more favorable impressions and make more positive judgments than people who are in a bad mood (Forgas & Laham, 2005).

Even when schemas are not entirely accurate, they serve an important function: They allow us to develop expectations about how others will behave. Those expectations permit us to plan our interactions with others more easily and serve to simplify a complex social world.

ATTRIBUTION PROCESSES: UNDERSTANDING THE CAUSES OF BEHAVIOR

When Barbara Washington, a new employee at the Ablex Computer Company, completed a major staffing project two weeks early, her boss, Yolanda, was delighted. At the next staff meeting, she announced how pleased she was with Barbara and explained that *this* was an example of the kind of performance she was looking for in her staff. The other staff members looked on resentfully, trying to figure out why Barbara had worked night and day to finish the project not just on time but two weeks early. She must be an awfully compulsive person, they decided.

At one time or another, most of us have puzzled over the reasons behind someone's behavior. Perhaps it was in a situation similar to the one above, or it may have been in more formal circumstances, such as being a judge on a student judiciary board in a cheating case. In contrast to theories of social cognition, which describe how people develop an overall impression of others' personality traits, **attribution theory** seeks to explain how we decide, on the basis of samples of an individual's behavior, what the specific causes of that person's behavior are.

The general process we use to determine the causes of behavior and other social occurrences proceeds in several steps, as illustrated in Figure 4. After first noticing that something unusual has happened—for example, golf star Tiger Woods has played a terrible round of golf—we try to interpret the meaning of the event. This leads us to formulate an initial explanation (maybe Woods stayed up late the night before the match). Depending on the time available, the cognitive resources on hand (such as the attention we can give to the matter), and our motivation (determined in part by how important the event is), we may choose to accept our initial explanation or seek to modify it (Woods was sick, perhaps). If we have the time, cognitive resources, and motivation, the event triggers deliberate problem solving as we seek a fuller explana-

Attribution theory: The theory of personality that seeks to explain how we decide, on the basis of samples of an individual's behavior, what the specific causes of that person's behavior are.

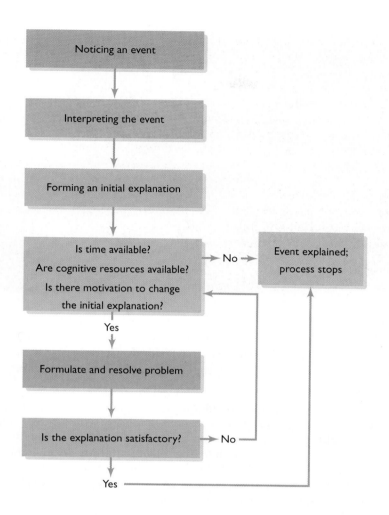

FIGURE 4 Determining why people behave the way they do. The general process we use to determine the causes of others' behavior proceeds in several steps. The kind of explanation we come up with depends on the time available to us, our cognitive resources, and our degree of motivation to come up with an accurate explanation. If time, cognitive resources, and motivation are limited, we'll make use of our first impression, which may be inaccurate. (Source: Adapted from Krull & Anderson, 1997, p. 2.)

tion. During the problem formulation and resolution stage, we may try out several possibilities before we reach a final explanation that seems satisfactory to us (Krull & Anderson, 1997; Malle, 2004).

In seeking an explanation for behavior, we must answer one central question: Is the cause situational or dispositional (Heider, 1958)? **Situational causes** are those brought about by something in the environment. For instance, someone who knocks over a quart of milk and then cleans it up probably does it not because he or she is necessarily a neat person but because the *situation* requires it. In contrast, a person who spends hours shining the kitchen floor probably does so because he or she is a neat person—hence, the behavior has a **dispositional cause**, prompted by the person's disposition (his or her internal traits or personality characteristics).

In our example involving Barbara, her fellow employees attributed her behavior to her disposition rather than to the situation. But from a logical standpoint, it is equally plausible that something about the situation caused the behavior. If asked, Barbara might attribute her accomplishment to situational factors, explaining that she had so much other work to do that she just had to get the project out of the way, or that the project was not all that difficult and so it was easy to complete ahead of schedule. To her, then, the reason for her behavior might not be dispositional at all; it could be situational.

Situational causes (of behavior): Perceived causes of behavior that are based on environmental factors.

Dispositional causes (of behavior): Perceived causes of behavior that are based on internal traits or personality factors.

ATTRIBUTION BIASES: TO ERR IS HUMAN

If we always processed information in the rational manner that attribution theory suggests, the world might run a lot more smoothly. Unfortunately, although attribution

The assumed-similarity bias leads us to believe that others hold similar attitudes, opinions, and likes and dislikes.

theory generally makes accurate predictions, people do not always process information about others in as logical a fashion as the theory seems to suggest. In fact, research reveals consistent biases in the ways people make attributions. Typical ones include the following:

- *The halo effect.* Harry is intelligent, kind, and loving. Is he also conscientious? If you were to guess, your most likely response probably would be yes. Your guess reflects the **halo effect,** a phenomenon in which an initial understanding that a person has positive traits is used to infer other uniformly positive characteristics. The opposite would also hold true. Learning that Harry was unsociable and argumentative would probably lead you to assume that he was lazy as well. However, because few people have either uniformly positive or uniformly negative traits, the halo effect leads to misperceptions of others (Feeley, 2002; Goffin, Jelley, & Wagner, 2003).

- *Assumed-similarity bias.* How similar to you—in terms of attitudes, opinions, and likes and dislikes—are your friends and acquaintances? Most people believe that their friends and acquaintances are fairly similar to themselves. But this feeling goes beyond just people we know to a general tendency—known as the **assumed-similarity bias**—to think of people as being similar to oneself, even when meeting them for the first time. Given the range of people in the world, this assumption often reduces the accuracy of our judgments (Watson, Hubbard, & Wiese, 2000).

- *The self-serving bias.* When the team wins, coaches usually feel that the team's success is due to their coaching. But when they coach a losing team, coaches may think it's due to the poor skills of their players. Similarly, if you get an A on a test, you may think it's due to your hard work, but if you get a poor grade, it's due to the professor's inadequacies. The reason is the **self-serving bias,** the tendency to attribute success to personal factors (skill, ability, or effort) and attribute failure to factors outside of oneself (Spencer et al., 2003).

- *The fundamental attribution error.* One of the more common attribution biases is the tendency to overattribute others' behavior to dispositional causes and the corresponding failure to recognize the importance of situational causes. Known as the **fundamental attribution error,** this tendency is quite prevalent in Western cultures. We tend to exaggerate the importance of personality characteristics (dispositional causes) in producing others' behavior, minimizing the influence of the environment (situational factors). For example, we are more likely to jump

Halo effect: A phenomenon in which an initial understanding that a person has positive traits is used to infer other uniformly positive characteristics.

Assumed-similarity bias: The tendency to think of people as being similar to oneself, even when meeting them for the first time.

Self-serving bias: The tendency to attribute personal success to personal factors (skill, ability, or effort) and to attribute failure to factors outside oneself.

Fundamental attribution error: A tendency to overattribute others' behavior to dispositional causes and the corresponding minimization of the importance of situational causes.

to the conclusion that someone who is often late to work is too lazy to take an earlier bus (a dispositional cause) than to assume that the lateness is due to situational factors, such as the bus always running behind schedule.

- Why is the fundamental attribution error so common? One reason pertains to the nature of information available to the people making an attribution. When we view the behavior of another person in a particular setting, the most conspicuous information is the person's behavior. Because the individual's immediate surroundings remain relatively unchanged and less attention-grabbing, we center our attention on the person whose behavior we're considering. Consequently, we are more likely to make attributions based on personal, dispositional factors and less likely to make attributions relating to the situation (Ross & Nisbett, 1991; Follett & Hess, 2002; Langdridge & Butt, 2004). To learn more, complete the PsychInteractive exercise on the fundamental attribution error.
- Despite the importance of the fundamental attribution error in shaping the perceptions of members of Western cultures, it turns out that it's not so fundamental when one looks at non-Western cultures, as we discuss next.

www.mhhe.com/feldmanup8
PsychInteractive Online

Fundamental Attribution Error

Exploring DIVERSITY

Attributions in a Cultural Context: How Fundamental Is the Fundamental Attribution Error?

Attribution biases do not affect all of us in the same way. The culture in which we are raised clearly plays a role in the way we attribute others' behavior.

Take, for example, the fundamental attribution error, the tendency to overestimate the importance of personal, dispositional factors and underattribute situational factors in determining the causes of others' behavior. The error is pervasive in Western cultures and not in Asian societies.

Specifically, social psychologist Joan Miller (1984) found that adults in India were more likely to use situational attributions than dispositional ones in explaining events. These findings are the opposite of those for the United States, and they contradict the fundamental attribution error.

Miller suggested that we can discover the reason for these results by examining the norms and values of Indian society, which emphasize social responsibility and societal obligations to a greater extent than in Western societies. She also suggested that the language spoken in a culture may lead to different sorts of attributions. For instance, a tardy person using English may say "I am late," suggesting a personal, dispositional cause ("I am a tardy person"). In contrast, users of Spanish who are late say, "The clock caused me to be late." Clearly, the statement in Spanish implies that the cause is a situational one (Zebrowitz-McArthur, 1988).

Cultural differences in attributions may have profound implications. For example, parents in Asia tend to attribute good academic performance to effort and hard work (situational factors). In contrast, parents in Western cultures tend to deemphasize the role of effort and attribute school success to innate ability (a dispositional factor). As a result, Asian students may strive harder to achieve and ultimately outperform U.S. students in school (Lee, Hallahan, & Herzog, 1996; Stevenson, Lee, & Mu, 2000).

The difference in thinking between people in Asian and Western cultures is a reflection of a broader difference in the way the world is perceived. Asian societies generally have a *collectivistic orientation,* a worldview that promotes the notion of interdependence. People with a collectivistic orientation generally see themselves as parts of a larger, interconnected social network and as responsible to others. In contrast, people in Western cultures are more likely to hold an *individualist orientation* that emphasizes personal identity and the uniqueness of the individual. They focus more on what sets them apart from others and what makes them special (Markus & Kitayama, 1991, 2003; Dennis et al., 2002; Lehman, Chiu, & Schaller, 2004; Wang, 2004).

Students in Asian societies may perform exceptionally well in school because the culture emphasizes academic success and perseverance.

RECAP/EVALUATE/RETHINK

RECAP

What are attitudes, and how are they formed, maintained, and changed?

- Social psychology is the scientific study of the ways in which people's thoughts, feelings, and actions are affected by others and the nature and causes of individual behavior in social situations. (p. 586)
- Attitudes are evaluations of a particular person, behavior, belief, or concept. (p. 587)
- Cognitive dissonance occurs when an individual simultaneously holds two cognitions—attitudes or thoughts—that contradict each other. To resolve the contradiction, the person may modify one cognition, change its importance, add a cognition, or deny a link between the two cognitions, thereby bringing about a reduction in dissonance. (p. 590)

How do we form impressions of what others are like and of the causes of their behavior?

- Social cognition involves the way people understand and make sense of others and themselves. People develop schemas that organize information about people and social experiences in memory and allow them to interpret and categorize information about others. (p. 591)
- People form impressions of others in part through the use of central traits, personality characteristics that receive unusually heavy emphasis when we form an impression. (pp. 591–592)
- Information-processing approaches have found that we tend to average together sets of traits to form an overall impression. (p. 592)
- Attribution theory tries to explain how we understand the causes of behavior, particularly with respect to situational or dispositional factors. (pp. 592–593)

What are the biases that influence the ways in which we view others' behavior?

- Even though logical processes are involved, attribution is prone to error. For instance, people are susceptible to the halo effect, assumed-similarity bias, self-serving bias, and fundamental attribution error (the tendency to over-attribute others' behavior to dispositional causes and

the corresponding failure to recognize the importance of situational causes). (pp. 594–595)

EVALUATE

1. An evaluation of a particular person, behavior, belief, or concept is called a(n) _____.
2. One brand of peanut butter advertises its product by describing its taste and nutritional value. It is hoping to persuade customers through _____ route processing. In ads for a competing brand, a popular actor happily eats the product—but does not describe it. This approach hopes to persuade customers through _____ route processing.
3. Cognitive dissonance theory suggests that we commonly change our behavior to keep it consistent with our attitudes. True or false?
4. Sopan was happy to lend his textbook to a fellow student who seemed bright and friendly. He was surprised when his classmate did not return it. His assumption that the bright and friendly student would also be responsible reflects the _____ effect.

RETHINK

1. Joan sees Annette, a new coworker, act in a way that seems abrupt and curt. Joan concludes that Annette is unkind and unsociable. The next day Joan sees Annette acting kindly toward another worker. Is Joan likely to change her impression of Annette? Why or why not? Finally, Joan sees several friends of hers laughing and joking with Annette, treating her in a very friendly fashion. Is Joan likely to change her impression of Annette? Why or why not?
2. *From the perspective of a marketing specialist:* Suppose you were assigned to develop a full advertising campaign for a product, including television, radio, and print ads. How might theories of persuasion guide your strategy to suit the different media?

Answers to Evaluate Questions

1. attitude; 2. central, peripheral; 3. false; we typically change our attitudes, not our behavior, to reduce cognitive dissonance; 4. halo

KEY TERMS

social psychology p. 587	cognitive dissonance p. 590	situational causes (of behavior) p. 593	assumed-similarity bias p. 594
attitudes p. 587	social cognition p.591	dispositional causes (of behavior) p. 593	self-serving bias p. 594
central route processing p. 588	schemas p. 591	halo effect p. 594	fundamental attribution error p. 594
peripheral route processing p. 588	central traits p. 591 attribution theory p. 592		

Social Influence

You have just transferred to a new college and are attending your first class. When the professor enters, your fellow classmates instantly rise, bow to the professor, and then stand quietly, with their hands behind their backs. You've never encountered such behavior, and it makes no sense to you. Is it more likely that you will (1) jump up to join the rest of the class or (2) remain seated?

On the basis of what research has told us about **social influence,** the process by which the actions of an individual or group affect the behavior of others, a person would almost always choose the first option. As you undoubtedly know from your own experience, pressures to conform can be painfully strong and can bring about changes in behavior that otherwise never would have occurred.

Conformity: Following What Others Do

Conformity is a change in behavior or attitudes brought about by a desire to follow the beliefs or standards of other people. Subtle or even unspoken social pressure results in conformity.

The classic demonstration of pressure to conform comes from a series of studies carried out in the 1950s by Solomon Asch (1951). In the experiments, the participants thought they were taking part in a test of perceptual skills with six other people. The experimenter showed the participants one card with three lines of varying length and a second card that had a fourth line that matched one of the first three (see Figure 1). The task was seemingly straightforward: Each of the participants had to announce aloud which of the first three lines was identical in length to the "standard" line on the second card. Because the correct answer was always obvious, the task seemed easy to the participants.

Indeed, because the participants all agreed on the first few trials, the procedure appeared to be quite simple. But then something odd began to happen. From the perspective of the participant in the group who answered last on each trial, all the answers of the first six participants seemed to be wrong—in fact, unanimously wrong. And this pattern persisted. Over and over again, the first six participants provided answers that contradicted what the last participant believed to be correct. The last participant faced the dilemma of whether to follow his or her own perceptions or follow the group by repeating the answer everyone else was giving.

As you might have guessed, this experiment was more contrived than it appeared. The first six participants were actually confederates (paid employees of the experimenter) who had been instructed to give unanimously erroneous answers in many of the trials. And the study had nothing to do with perceptual skills. Instead, the issue under investigation was conformity.

Asch found that in about one-third of the trials, the participants conformed to the unanimous but erroneous group answer, with about 75 percent of all participants conforming at least once. However, he found strong individual differences. Some participants conformed nearly all the time, whereas others never did.

Key Concept

What are the major sources and tactics of social influence?

Social influence: The process by which the actions of an individual or group affect the behavior of others.

Conformity: A change in behavior or attitudes brought about by a desire to follow the beliefs or standards of other people.

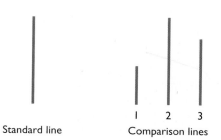

Standard line   Comparison lines

FIGURE 1 Which of the three comparison lines is the same length as the "standard" line?

597

CONFORMITY CONCLUSIONS

Since Asch's pioneering work, literally hundreds of studies have examined conformity, and we now know a great deal about the phenomenon. Significant findings focus on:

Status: The social rank held within a group.

- *The characteristics of the group.* The more attractive a group appears to its members, the greater is its ability to produce conformity (Hogg & Hains, 2001). Furthermore, a person's relative **status,** the social rank held within a group, is critical: The lower a person's status in the group, the greater the power of the group over that person's behavior.
- *The situation in which the individual is responding.* Conformity is considerably higher when people must respond publicly than it is when they can do so privately, as the founders of the United States noted when they authorized secret ballots in voting.
- *The kind of task.* People working on ambiguous tasks and questions (ones having no clear answer) are more susceptible to social pressure. Asked to give an opinion, such as what type of clothing is fashionable, a person will more likely yield to conformist pressures than he or she will if asked a question of fact. In addition, tasks at which an individual is less competent than others in the group make conformity more likely. For example, a person who is an infrequent computer user may feel pressure to conform to an opinion about computer brands when in a group of experienced computer users.

Social supporter: A group member whose dissenting views make nonconformity to the group easier.

- *Unanimity of the group.* Groups that unanimously support a position show the most pronounced conformity pressures. But what of the case in which people with dissenting views have an ally in the group, known as a **social supporter,** who agrees with them? Having just one person present who shares the minority point of view is sufficient to reduce conformity pressures (Levine, 1989; Prislin, Brewer, & Wilson, 2002).

Why can conformity pressures in groups be so strong? For one reason, groups, and other people generally, play a central role in our lives. Most of us seek social approval, and we know that groups develop and hold *norms,* expectations regarding behavior appropriate to the group. Furthermore, we understand that not adhering to group norms can result in retaliation from other group members, ranging from being ignored to being overtly derided or even being rejected or excluded by the group. Thus, people conform to meet the expectations of the group (Van Knippenberg, 1999; Baumeister, Twenge, & Nuss, 2002; Twenge, Catanese, & Baumeister, 2002).

GROUPTHINK: CAVING IN TO CONFORMITY

Although we usually think of conformity in terms of our individual relations with others, in some instances conformity pressures in organizations can lead to disastrous effects with long-term consequences. For instance, consider NASA's determination that the falling foam that hit the space shuttle *Columbia* when it took off in 2003 would pose no significant danger when it was time for the *Columbia* to land. Despite the misgivings of some engineers, a consensus formed that the foam was not dangerous to the shuttle. Ultimately, that consensus proved wrong: The shuttle came apart as it attempted to land, killing all the astronauts on board (Schwartz & Wald, 2003).

In hindsight, NASA's decision was clearly wrong. How could such a poor decision have been made?

Groupthink: A type of thinking in which group members share such a strong motivation to achieve consensus that they lose the ability to critically evaluate alternative points of view.

A phenomenon known as groupthink provides an explanation. **Groupthink** is a type of thinking in which group members share such a strong motivation to achieve consensus that they lose the ability to critically evaluate alternative points of view. Groupthink is most likely to occur when a popular or powerful leader is

The poor decisions that led to the destruction of the space shuttle *Columbia* may have been due to groupthink.

surrounded by people of lower status—obviously the case with any U.S. president and his advisers, but also true in a variety of other organizations (Janis, 1989; Kowert, 2002; Baron, 2005).

The phenomenon of groupthink is likely to happen when the following conditions exist:

- The group appears invulnerable and incapable of making major errors in judgment.
- Information contradictory to the dominant group view is ignored, discounted, or minimized.
- Group members feel pressure to conform to the majority view—although the pressure may be relatively subtle.
- The pressure to conform discourages minority viewpoints from coming before the group; consequently, the group *appears* to be unanimous, even if this is not really the case.
- The group views itself as representing something just and moral, leading members to assume that any judgment the group reaches will also be just and moral.

Groupthink almost always produces negative consequences. Groups tend to limit the list of possible solutions to just a few and spend relatively little time considering any alternatives once the leader seems to be leaning toward a particular solution. In fact, group members may completely ignore information that challenges a developing consensus. Because historical research shows that many disastrous decisions reflect groupthink, it is important for groups to be on guard (Schafer & Crichlow, 1996; Tetlock, 1997; Park, 2000; Kowert, 2002).

Compliance: Submitting to Direct Social Pressure

When we refer to conformity, we usually mean a phenomenon in which the social pressure is subtle or indirect. But in some situations social pressure is much more

Compliance: Behavior that occurs in response to direct social pressure.

obvious, with direct, explicit pressure to endorse a particular point of view or behave in a certain way. Social psychologists call the type of behavior that occurs in response to direct social pressure **compliance.**

Several specific techniques represent attempts to gain compliance. Those frequently employed include:

- *Foot-in-the-door technique.* A salesperson comes to your door and asks you to accept a small sample. You agree, thinking you have nothing to lose. A little later comes a larger request, which, because you have already agreed to the first one, you have a hard time turning down.

  The salesperson in this case is using a tried-and-true strategy that social psychologists call the foot-in-the-door technique. In the *foot-in-the-door technique,* you ask a person to agree to a small request and later ask that person to comply with a more important one. It turns out that compliance with the more important request increases significantly when the person first agrees to the smaller favor.

  Researchers first demonstrated the foot-in-the-door phenomenon in a study in which a number of experimenters went door to door asking residents to sign a petition in favor of safe driving (Freedman & Fraser, 1966). Almost everyone complied with that small, benign request. A few weeks later, different experimenters contacted the residents and made a much larger request: that the residents erect a huge sign reading "Drive Carefully" on their front lawns. The results were clear: 55 percent of those who had signed the petition agreed to the request to put up a sign, whereas only 17 percent of the people in a control group who had not been asked to sign the petition agreed to put up a sign.

  Why does the foot-in-the-door technique work? For one reason, involvement with the small request leads to an interest in an issue, and taking an action—any action—makes the individual more committed to the issue, thereby increasing the likelihood of future compliance. Another explanation revolves around people's self-perceptions. By complying with the initial request, individuals may come to see themselves as people who provide help when asked. Then, when confronted with the larger request, they agree in order to maintain the kind of consistency in attitudes and behavior that we described earlier. Although we don't know which of these two explanations is more accurate, it is clear that the foot-in-the-door strategy is effective (Guadagno et al., 2001; Guéguen, 2002; Burger & Caldwell, 2003).

- *Door-in-the-face technique.* A fund-raiser asks for a $500 contribution. You laughingly refuse, telling her that the amount is way out of your league. She then asks for a $10 contribution. What do you do? If you are like most people, you'll probably be a lot more compliant than you would be if she hadn't asked for the huge contribution first. In this tactic, called the *door-in-the-face technique,* someone makes a large request, expecting it to be refused, and follows it with a smaller one. This strategy, which is the opposite of the foot-in-the-door approach, has also proved to be effective (Millar, 2002; Pascual & Guéguen, 2005).

  In a field experiment that demonstrates the success of this approach, experimenters stopped college students on the street and asked them to agree to a substantial favor—acting as unpaid counselors for juvenile delinquents two hours a week for two years (Cialdini et al., 1975). Not surprisingly, no one agreed to make such an enormous commitment. But when they were later asked the considerably smaller favor of taking a group of delinquents on a two-hour trip to the zoo, half the people complied. In comparison, only 17 percent of a control group of participants who had not first received the larger request agreed.

The use of this technique is widespread. You may have tried it at some point yourself, perhaps by asking your parents for a large increase in your allowance and later settling for less. Similarly, television writers, by sometimes sprinkling their scripts with obscenities that they know will be cut out by network censors, hope to keep other key phrases intact (Cialdini & Sagarin, 2005).

- *That's-not-all technique.* In this technique, a salesperson offers you a deal at an inflated price. But immediately after the initial offer, the salesperson offers an incentive, discount, or bonus to clinch the deal.

  Although it sounds transparent, this practice can be quite effective. In one study, the experimenters set up a booth and sold cupcakes for 75 cents each. In one condition, the experimenters directly told customers that the price was 75 cents. But in another condition, they told customers that the price was originally $1 but had been reduced to 75 cents. As we might predict, more people bought cupcakes at the "reduced" price—even though it was identical to the price in the other experimental condition (Burger, 1986).

- *Not-so-free sample.* If you ever receive a free sample, keep in mind that it comes with a psychological cost. Although they may not couch it in these terms, salespeople who provide samples to potential customers do so to instigate the norm of reciprocity. The *norm of reciprocity* is the well-accepted societal standard dictating that we should treat other people as they treat us. Receiving a *not-so-free sample,* then, suggests the need for reciprocation—in the form of a purchase, of course (Cialdini, 1988; Spiller & Wymer, 2001).

The persuasive techniques identified by social psychologists can be seen in practice at auto dealerships.

Companies seeking to sell their products to consumers often use the techniques identified by social psychologists for promoting compliance. But employers also use them to bring about compliance and raise the productivity of employees in the workplace. In fact, a close cousin to social psychology, **industrial-organizational (I/O) psychology,** considers issues such as worker motivation, satisfaction, safety, and productivity. I/O psychologists also focus on the operation and design of organizations, asking questions such as how decision making can be improved in large organizations and how the fit between workers and their jobs can be maximized.

Industrial-organizational (I/O) psychology: The branch of psychology focusing on work and job-related issues, including worker motivation, satisfaction, safety, and productivity.

Obedience: Following Direct Orders

Compliance techniques are used to gently lead people toward agreement with a request. In some cases, however, requests aim to produce **obedience,** a change in behavior in response to the commands of others. Although obedience is considerably less common than conformity and compliance, it does occur in several specific kinds of relationships. For example, we may show obedience to our bosses, teachers, or parents merely because of the power they hold to reward or punish us.

To acquire an understanding of obedience, consider for a moment how you might respond if a stranger said to you:

> I've devised a new way of improving memory. All I need is for you to teach people a list of words and then give them a test. The test procedure requires only that you give learners a shock each time they make a mistake on the test. To administer the shocks you will use a "shock generator" that gives shocks ranging from 30 to 450 volts. You can see that the switches are labeled from "slight shock" through "danger: severe shock" at the top

Obedience: A change in behavior in response to the commands of others.

 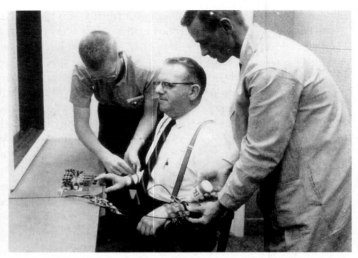

FIGURE 2 This impressive-looking "shock generator" led participants in Stanley Milgram's experiment on obedience to believe they were administering electric shocks to another person, who was connected to the generator by "electrodes" that were attached to the skin. (Source: Copyright 1965 by Stanley Milgram. From the film *Obedience*, distributed by the New York University Film Library and Pennsylvania State University, PCR.)

level, where there are three red *X*'s. But don't worry; although the shocks may be painful, they will cause no permanent damage.

Presented with this situation, you would be likely to think that neither you nor anyone else would go along with the stranger's unusual request. Clearly, it lies outside the bounds of what we consider good sense.

Or does it? Suppose the stranger asking for your help were a psychologist conducting an experiment. Or suppose the request came from your teacher, your employer, or your military commander—all people in authority with a seemingly legitimate reason for the request.

If you still believe it unlikely that you would comply—think again. The situation presented above describes a classic experiment conducted by social psychologist Stanley Milgram in the 1960s (1974). In the study, an experimenter told participants to give increasingly stronger shocks to another person as part of a study on learning (see Figure 2). In reality, the experiment had nothing to do with learning; the real issue under consideration was the degree to which participants would comply with the experimenter's requests. In fact, the "learner" supposedly receiving the shocks was a confederate who never really received any punishment.

Most people who hear a description of Milgram's experiment feel that it is unlikely that *any* participant would give the maximum level of shock—or, for that matter, any shock at all. Even a group of psychiatrists to whom the situation was described predicted that fewer than 2 percent of the participants would fully comply and administer the strongest shocks.

However, the actual results contradicted both experts' and nonexperts' predictions. Some 65 percent of the participants eventually used the highest setting on the shock generator—450 volts—to shock the learner. This obedience occurred even though the learner, who had mentioned at the start of the experiment that he had a heart condition, demanded to be released, screaming, "Let me out of here! Let me out of here! My heart's bothering me. Let me out of here!" Despite the learner's pleas, most participants continued to administer the shocks.

Why did so many individuals comply with the experimenter's demands? The participants, who were extensively interviewed after the experiment, said they obeyed primarily because they believed that the experimenter would be responsible for any potential ill effects that befell the learner. The participants accepted the experimenter's orders, then, because they thought that they personally could not be held accountable for their actions—they could always blame the experimenter (Darley, 1995; Blass, 1996).

Although most participants in the Milgram experiment said later that they felt the knowledge gained from the study outweighed the discomfort they may have felt, the experiment has been criticized for creating an extremely trying set of circumstances for the participants, thereby raising serious ethical concerns. (Undoubtedly, the experiment could not be conducted today because of ethical considerations.) Other critics have suggested that Milgram's methods were ineffective in creating a situation that actually mirrored real-world obedience. For example, how often are people placed in a situation in which someone orders them to continue hurting a victim, while the victim's protests are ignored (Miller, Collins, & Brief, 1995; Blass, 2000)?

Despite these concerns, Milgram's research remains the strongest laboratory demonstration of obedience. We need only consider actual instances of obedience to authority to witness some frightening real-life parallels. For instance, after World War II, the major defense that Nazi officers gave to excuse their participation in atrocities during the war was that they were "only following orders." Milgram's experiment, which was motivated in part by his desire to explain the behavior of everyday Germans during World War II, forces us to ask ourselves this question: Would we be able to withstand the intense power of authority? (To explore the Milgram study more thoroughly, complete the PsychInteractive exercise.)

www.mhhe.com/feldmanup8
PsychInteractive Online

Milgram Obedience Experiment

RECAP/EVALUATE/RETHINK

RECAP

What are the major sources and tactics of social influence?

- Social influence is the area of social psychology concerned with situations in which the actions of an individual or group affect the behavior of others. (p. 597)
- Conformity refers to changes in behavior or attitudes that result from a desire to follow the beliefs or standards of others. (p. 597)
- Compliance is behavior that results from direct social pressure. Among the ways of eliciting compliance are the foot-in-the-door, door-in-the-face, that's-not-all, and not-so-free-sample techniques. (pp. 599–601)
- Obedience is a change in behavior in response to the commands of others. (p. 601)

EVALUATE

1. A _____, or person who agrees with the dissenting viewpoint, is likely to reduce conformity.
2. Who pioneered the study of conformity?
   a. Skinner
   b. Asch
   c. Milgram
   d. Fiala

3. Which of the following techniques asks a person to comply with a small initial request to enhance the likelihood that the person will later comply with a larger request?
   a. Door-in-the-face
   b. Foot-in-the-door
   c. That's-not-all
   d. Not-so-free sample
4. The _____ technique begins with an outrageous request that makes a subsequent, smaller request seem reasonable.
5. _____ is a change in behavior that is due to another person's orders.

RETHINK

1. Why do you think the Milgram experiment is so controversial? What sorts of effects might the experiment have had on participants? Do you think the experiment would have had similar results if it had been conducted not in a laboratory setting, but among members of a social group (such as a fraternity or sorority) with strong pressures to conform?
2. *From the perspective of a sales representative:* Imagine that you have been trained to use the various compliance techniques described in this section. Because these compliance techniques are so powerful, should the use

of certain such techniques be forbidden? Should consumers be taught defenses against such techniques? Is the use of such techniques ethically and morally defensible? Why?

3. *From the perspective of an educator:* Student obedience in the elementary and secondary classroom is a major issue for many teachers. How might you promote student obedience in the classroom? What are some of the potentially harmful ways that teachers could use their social influence to elicit student obedience?

Answers to Evaluate Questions

1. social supporter; 2. b; 3. b; 4. door-in-the-face; 5. obedience

KEY TERMS

social influence p. 597
conformity p. 597
status p. 598

social supporter p. 598
groupthink p. 598
compliance p. 600

industrial-organizational
   (I/O) psychology p. 600
obedience p. 600

Prejudice and Discrimination

What do you think when someone says, "He's African American," "She's Chinese," or "That's a woman driver"?

If you're like most people, you'll probably automatically form some sort of impression of what each person is like. Most likely your impression is based on a **stereotype,** a set of generalized beliefs and expectations about a particular group and its members. Stereotypes, which may be negative or positive, grow out of our tendency to categorize and organize the vast amount of information we encounter in our everyday lives. All stereotypes share the common feature of oversimplifying the world: We view individuals not in terms of their unique, personal characteristics, but in terms of characteristics we attribute to all the members of a particular group.

Stereotypes can lead to **prejudice,** a negative (or positive) evaluation of a group and its members. For instance, racial prejudice occurs when a member of a racial group is evaluated in terms of race and not because of his or her own characteristics or abilities. Although prejudice can be positive ("I love the Irish"), social psychologists have focused on understanding the roots of negative prejudice ("I hate immigrants").

Common stereotypes and forms of prejudice involve racial, religious, and ethnic groups. Over the years, various groups have been called "lazy" or "shrewd" or "cruel" with varying degrees of regularity by those who are not members of that group. Even today, despite major progress toward reducing legally sanctioned forms of prejudice, such as school segregation, stereotypes remain (Madon et al., 2001; Biernat, 2003; Eberhardt et al., 2004; Pettigrew, 2004).

Even people who on the surface appear to be unprejudiced may harbor hidden prejudice. For example, when white participants in experiments are shown faces on a computer screen so rapidly that they cannot consciously perceive the faces, they react more negatively to black than to white faces—an example of what has been called *modern racism* (Greenwald et al., 2002; Dovidio, Gaertner, & Pearson, 2005).

Although usually backed by little or no evidence, stereotypes can have harmful consequences. Acting on negative stereotypes results in **discrimination**—behavior directed toward individuals on the basis of their membership in a particular group. Discrimination can lead to exclusion from jobs, neighborhoods, and educational opportunities and may result in members of particular groups receiving lower salaries and benefits. Discrimination can also result in more favorable treatment to favored groups, as when an employer hires a job applicant of his or her own racial group because of the applicant's race.

Stereotyping not only leads to overt discrimination but also can cause members of stereotyped groups to behave in ways that reflect the stereotype through a phenomenon known as the *self-fulfilling prophecy.* Self-fulfilling prophecies are expectations about the occurrence of a future event or behavior that act to increase the likelihood that the event or behavior will occur. For example, if people think that members of a particular group lack ambition, they may treat them in a way that actually brings about a lack of ambition. Furthermore, it can lead to a self-stereotyping phenomenon that we discuss in the *Applying Psychology in the 21st Century* box (Madon, Jussim, & Eccles, 1997; Oskamp, 2000; Seibt & Förster, 2004).

Key Concepts

How do stereotypes, prejudice, and discrimination differ?

How can we reduce prejudice and discrimination?

Stereotype: A set of generalized beliefs and expectations about a particular group and its members.

Prejudice: A negative (or positive) evaluation of a particular group and its members.

Discrimination: Behavior directed toward individuals on the basis of their membership in a particular group.

Fighting Stereotype Threat

"Women don't do well in math."

"African Americans don't do well academically."

"Men are inherently less socially sensitive than women."

So suggest mistaken, but persistent, stereotypes. And, according to social psychologist Claude Steele, such stereotypes have damaging and destructive effects on the performance of those who are their targets.

For example, Steele argues that many African Americans suffer from *stereotype threat*, in which members of the group fear that their behavior will confirm stereotypes about themselves. He suggests that African American students who receive instruction from teachers who may doubt their abilities and who set up special remedial programs to assist them may come to accept society's stereotypes and believe that they are prone to fail (Steele, 1992, 1997; Steele, Spencer, & Aronson, 2002).

Ultimately, such beliefs can have devastating effects. When confronted with an academic task, African American students may fear that their performance will simply confirm society's negative stereotypes. The immediate consequence of this fear is anxiety that hampers performance. But the long-term consequences may be even worse: Doubting their ability to perform successfully in academic environments, African Americans may decide that the risks of failure are so great that it is not worth the effort even to attempt to do well.

Eventually, they may disidentify with academic success by minimizing the importance of academic endeavors (Steele, 1997; Stone, 1999, 2002).

To test his hypothesis, Steele and colleagues conducted an experiment in which he gave two groups of African American and white students identical tests composed of difficult verbal skill items from the Graduate Record Examination. However, they varied the supposed purpose of the test. Some participants were told that the test measured "psychological factors involved in solving verbal problems"—information that presumably had little to do with underlying ability. In contrast, other participants were told that the test assessed various "personal factors involved in performance on problems requiring reading and verbal reasoning abilities," and that the test would be helpful in identifying personal strengths and weaknesses.

The results provided clear evidence for the stereotype threat hypothesis. When told that the test evaluated verbal abilities, African Americans scored significantly worse than whites. But when the test was described as not relating to core abilities (the "psychological factors" condition), African

Americans scored as well as whites. In contrast, white participants scored equally well, regardless of the test description. Thus, holding a negative stereotype about themselves led to poorer performance by African Americans—they were vulnerable to the stereotype threat (Steele & Aronson, 1995; Suzuki & Aronson, 2005).

In short, the evidence from this study, as well as a growing body of research, attests to the reality of stereotype threat. When we believe, even unconsciously, that society's stereotypes may have validity, our performance may suffer (Cadinu, Maass, & Rosabianca, 2005; Koenig & Eagly, 2005).

Happily, though, Steele's analysis also suggests that the targets of stereotyping may be able to overcome stereotype threat. Specifically, schools can design intervention programs to educate minority individuals about their vulnerability to stereotypes and to teach them that the stereotypes are inaccurate. Members of minority groups, convinced that they have the potential to be academically successful, may well become immune to the potentially treacherous consequences of negative stereotypes (Good, Aronson, & Inzlicht, 2003; Johns, Schmader, & Martens, 2005).

RETHINK

Have racial or gender stereotypes about academic performance affected your own academic performance? In what ways? How could we best teach young students to be less susceptible to the effects of stereotype threat?

Foundations of Prejudice

No one has ever been born disliking a particular racial, religious, or ethnic group. People learn to hate, in much the same way that they learn the alphabet.

According to *observational learning approaches* to stereotyping and prejudice, the behavior of parents, other adults, and peers shapes children's feelings about members of various groups. For instance, bigoted parents may commend their children for expressing prejudiced attitudes. Likewise, young children learn prejudice by imitating the behavior of adult models. Such learning starts at an early age: children as young as 3 years of age begin to show preferences for members of their own race (Olson & Fazio, 2001; Schneider, 2003; Nesdale, Maass, & Durkin, 2005).

The mass media also provide information about stereotypes, not just for children but for adults as well. Even today, some television shows and movies portray Italians as Mafia-like mobsters, Jews as greedy bankers, and African Americans as promiscuous or lazy. When such inaccurate portrayals are the primary source of information about minority groups, they can lead to the development and maintenance of unfavorable stereotypes (Coltraine & Messineo, 2000; Ward, 2004).

Other explanations of prejudice and discrimination focus on how being a member of a particular group helps to magnify one's sense of self-esteem. According to *social identity theory,* we use group membership as a source of pride and self-worth. Slogans such as "gay pride" and "black is beautiful" illustrate that the groups to which we belong furnish us with a sense of self-respect (Rowley et al., 1998; Tajfel & Turner, 2004).

Like father, like son: Social learning approaches to stereotyping and prejudice suggest that attitudes and behaviors toward members of minority groups are learned through the observation of parents and other individuals. How can this cycle be broken?

However, the use of group membership to provide social respect produces an unfortunate outcome. In an effort to maximize our sense of self-esteem, we may come to think that our own group (our *ingroup*) is better than groups to which we don't belong (our *outgroups*). Consequently, we inflate the positive aspects of our ingroup—and, at the same time, devalue outgroups. Ultimately, we come to view members of outgroups as inferior to members of our ingroup (Tajfel & Turner, 2004). The end result is prejudice toward members of groups of which we are not a part.

Neither the observational learning approach nor the social identity approach provides a full explanation for stereotyping and prejudice. For instance, some psychologists argue that prejudice results when there is perceived competition for scarce societal resources. Thus, when competition exists for jobs or housing, members of majority groups may believe (however unjustly or inaccurately) that minority group members are hindering their efforts to attain their goals, and this can lead to prejudice. In addition, other explanations for prejudice emphasize human cognitive limitations that lead us to categorize people on the basis of visually conspicuous physical features such as race, sex, and ethnic group. Such categorization can lead to the development of stereotypes and, ultimately, to discriminatory behavior (Dovidio, 2001; Fiske, 2002; Mullen & Rice, 2003; Weeks & Lupfer, 2004). (To learn more, complete the PsychInteractive exercise on prejudice and discrimination.)

www.mhhe.com/feldmanup8
PsychInteractive Online

Prejudice

Reducing the Consequences of Prejudice and Discrimination

How can we diminish the effects of prejudice and discrimination? Psychologists have developed several strategies that have proved effective, including these:

- *Increasing contact between the target of stereotyping and the holder of the stereotype.* Research has shown that increasing the amount of interaction between people can reduce negative stereotyping. But only certain kinds of contact are likely to reduce prejudice and discrimination. Situations in which contact is relatively intimate, the individuals are of equal status, or participants must cooperate with one another or are dependent on one another are more likely to reduce stereotyping (Oskamp, 2000; Dovidio, Gaertner, & Kawakami, 2003; Tropp & Pettigrew, 2005).

- *Making values and norms against prejudice more conspicuous.* Sometimes just reminding people about the values they already hold regarding equality and fair treatment of others is enough to reduce discrimination. Similarly, people who hear others making strong, vehement antiracist statements are subsequently more likely to strongly condemn racism (Dovidio, Kawakami, & Gaertner, 2000; Czopp & Monteith, 2003).

- *Providing information about the objects of stereotyping.* Probably the most direct means of changing stereotypical and discriminatory attitudes is education: teaching people to be more aware of the positive characteristics of targets of stereotyping. For instance, when the meaning of puzzling behavior is explained to people who hold stereotypes, they may come to appreciate the true significance of the behavior—even though it may still appear foreign and perhaps even threatening (Schaller et al., 1996; Isbell & Tyler, 2003).

RECAP/EVALUATE/RETHINK

RECAP

How do stereotypes, prejudice, and discrimination differ?

- Stereotypes are generalized beliefs and expectations about a particular group and its members. Stereotyping can lead to prejudice and self-fulfilling prophecies. (p. 605)
- Prejudice is the negative (or positive) evaluation of a particular group and its members. (p. 605)
- Stereotyping and prejudice can lead to discrimination, behavior directed toward individuals on the basis of their membership in a particular group. (p. 605)
- According to observational learning approaches, children learn stereotyping and prejudice by observing the behavior of parents, other adults, and peers. Social identity theory suggests that group membership is used as a source of pride and self-worth, and this may lead people to think of their own group as better than others. (pp. 606–607)

How can we reduce prejudice and discrimination?

- Among the ways of reducing prejudice and discrimination are increasing contact, demonstrating positive values against prejudice, and education. (pp. 607–608)

EVALUATE

1. Any expectation—positive or negative—about an individual solely on the basis of that person's membership in a group can be a stereotype. True or false?

2. The negative (or positive) evaluation of a group and its members is called
   a. Stereotyping
   b. Prejudice
   c. Self-fulfilling prophecy
   d. Discrimination
3. Paul is a store manager who does not expect women to succeed in business. He therefore offers important, high-profile responsibilities only to men. If the female employees fail to move up in the company, it could be an example of a _____-_____ prophecy.

RETHINK

1. Do you think women can be victims of stereotype vulnerability? In what topical areas might this occur? Can men be victims of stereotype vulnerability? Why?
2. *From the perspetive of a corrections officer:* How might overt forms of prejudice and discrimination toward disadvantaged groups (such as African Americans) be reduced in a state or federal prison?

Answers to Evaluate Questions

1. true; 2. b; 3. self-fulfilling

KEY TERMS

stereotype p. 605   prejudice p. 605   discrimination p. 605

Positive and Negative Social Behavior

Are people basically good or bad?

Like philosophers and theologians, social psychologists have pondered the basic nature of humanity. Is it represented mainly by the violence and cruelty we see throughout the world, or does something special about human nature permit loving, considerate, unselfish, and even noble behavior as well?

We turn to two routes that social psychologists have followed in seeking answers to these questions. We first consider what they have learned about the sources of our attraction to others, and we end with a look at two opposite sides of human behavior: aggression and helping.

Key Concepts

Why are we attracted to certain people, and what progression do social relationships follow?

What factors underlie aggression and prosocial behavior?

Liking and Loving: Interpersonal Attraction and the Development of Relationships

Nothing is more important in most people's lives than their feelings for others. Consequently, it is not surprising that liking and loving have become a major focus of interest for social psychologists. Known more formally as the study of **interpersonal attraction** or **close relationships,** this area addresses the factors that lead to positive feelings for others.

Interpersonal attraction (or close relationship): Positive feelings for others; liking and loving.

HOW DO I LIKE THEE? LET ME COUNT THE WAYS

By far the greatest amount of research has focused on liking, probably because it is easier for investigators conducting short-term experiments to produce states of liking in strangers who have just met than to instigate and observe loving relationships over long periods. Consequently, research has given us a good deal of knowledge about the factors that initially attract two people to each other (Harvey & Weber, 2002). The important factors considered by social psychologists are the following:

- *Proximity.* If you live in a dormitory or an apartment, consider the friends you made when you first moved in. Chances are, you became friendliest with those who lived geographically closest to you. In fact, this is one of the more firmly established findings in the literature on interpersonal attraction: *Proximity* leads to liking (Festinger, Schachter, & Back, 1950; Burgoon et al., 2002).
- *Mere exposure.* Repeated exposure to a person is often sufficient to produce attraction. Interestingly, repeated exposure to *any* stimulus—a person, picture, compact disc, or virtually anything—usually makes us like the stimulus more. Becoming familiar with a person can evoke positive feelings; we then transfer the positive feelings stemming from familiarity to the person himself or herself. There are excep-

"I'm attracted to you, but then I'm attracted to me, too."

tions, though. In cases of strongly negative initial interactions, repeated exposure is unlikely to cause us to like a person more. Instead, the more we are exposed to him or her, the more we may dislike the individual (Zajonc, 2001; Butler & Berry, 2004).

- *Similarity.* Folk wisdom tells us that birds of a feather flock together. However, it also maintains that opposites attract. Social psychologists have come up with a clear verdict regarding which of the two statements is correct: We tend to like those who are similar to us. Discovering that others have similar attitudes, values, or traits promotes our liking for them. Furthermore, the more similar others are, the more we like them. One reason similarity increases the likelihood of interpersonal attraction is that we assume that people with similar attitudes will evaluate us positively. Because we experience a strong **reciprocity-of-liking effect** (a tendency to like those who like us), knowing that someone evaluates us positively promotes our attraction to that person. In addition, we assume that when we like someone else, that person likes us in return (Metee & Aronson, 1974; Bates, 2002).

- *Physical attractiveness.* For most people, the equation *beautiful = good* is quite true. As a result, physically attractive people are more popular than are physically unattractive ones, if all other factors are equal. This finding, which contradicts the values that most people say they hold, is apparent even in childhood—with nursery-school-age children rating their peers' popularity on the basis of attractiveness—and continues into adulthood. Indeed, physical attractiveness may be the single most important element promoting initial liking in college dating situations, although its influence eventually decreases when people get to know each other better (Langlois, Kalakamis, & Rubenstein, 2000; van Leeuwen & Macrae, 2004; Zebrowitz & Montepare, 2005). (To learn more about how our first impressions affect liking, try the PsychInteractive exercise.)

These factors alone, of course, do not account for liking. For example, surveys have sought to identify the critical factors in friendships. In a questionnaire answered by some 40,000 respondents, people identified the qualities most valued in a friend as the ability to keep confidences, loyalty, and warmth and affection, followed closely by supportiveness, frankness, and a sense of humor (Parlee, 1979). The results are summarized in Figure 1.

Reciprocity-of-liking effect: A tendency to like those who like us.

www.mhhe.com/feldmanup8
PsychInteractive Online

First Impressions and Attraction

FIGURE 1 These are the key friendship qualities according to some 40,000 questionnaire respondents. (Source: Parlee, 1979).

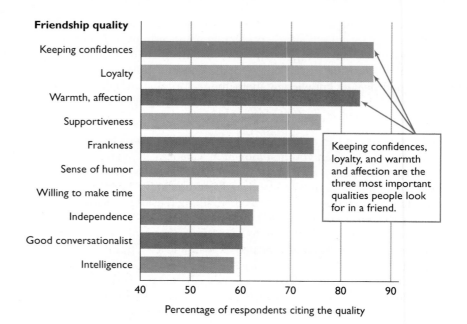

Friendship quality

Keeping confidences
Loyalty
Warmth, affection
Supportiveness
Frankness
Sense of humor
Willing to make time
Independence
Good conversationalist
Intelligence

Keeping confidences, loyalty, and warmth and affection are the three most important qualities people look for in a friend.

40   50   60   70   80   90

Percentage of respondents citing the quality

HOW DO I LOVE THEE? LET ME COUNT THE WAYS

Whereas our knowledge of what makes people like one another is extensive, our understanding of love is more limited in scope and recently acquired. For some time, many social psychologists believed that love is too difficult to observe and study in a controlled, scientific way. However, love is such a central issue in most people's lives that eventually social psychologists could not resist its allure.

As a first step, researchers tried to identify the characteristics that distinguish between mere liking and full-blown love. They discovered that love is not simply a greater quantity of liking, but a qualitatively different psychological state. For instance, at least in its early stages, love includes relatively intense physiological arousal, an all-encompassing interest in another individual, fantasizing about the other, and relatively rapid swings of emotion. Similarly, love, unlike liking, includes elements of passion, closeness, fascination, exclusiveness, sexual desire, and intense caring. We idealize partners by exaggerating their good qualities and minimizing their imperfections (Garza-Guerrero, 2000; Murray, Holmes, & Griffin, 2004).

Other researchers have theorized that there are two main types of love: passionate love and companionate love. **Passionate (or romantic) love** represents a state of intense absorption in someone. It includes intense physiological arousal, psychological interest, and caring for the needs of another. In contrast, **companionate love** is the strong affection we have for those with whom our lives are deeply involved. The love we feel for our parents, other family members, and even some close friends falls into the category of companionate love (Hendrick & Hendrick, 2003; Masuda, 2003).

Psychologist Robert Sternberg makes an even finer differentiation between types of love. He proposes that love consists of three parts: a *decision/commitment component*, encompassing the initial cognition that one loves someone and the longer-term feelings of commitment to maintain love; *an intimacy component*, encompassing feelings of closeness and connectedness; and a *passion component*, made up of the motivational drives relating to sex, physical closeness, and romance. These three components combine to produce the different types of love (Sternberg, Hojjat, & Barnes, 2001; Sternberg, 2004a; see Figure 2).

Is love a necessary ingredient in a good marriage? Yes, if you live in the United States. In contrast, it's considerably less important in other cultures. Although mutual attraction and love are the two most important characteristics desired in a mate by men and women in the United States, men in China rated good health as most important, and women there rated emotional stability and maturity as most important. Among the Zulu in South Africa, men rated emotional stability first and women rated dependable character first (Buss et al., 1990; see Figure 3).

Passionate (or romantic) love: A state of intense absorption in someone that includes intense physiological arousal, psychological interest, and caring for the needs of another.

Companionate love: The strong affection we have for those with whom our lives are deeply involved.

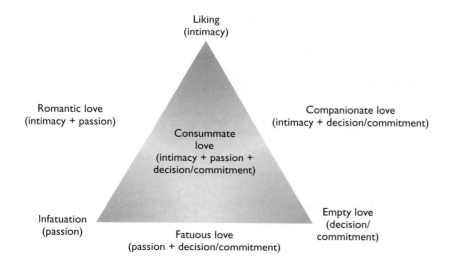

FIGURE 2 According to Sternberg, love has three main components: intimacy, passion, and decision/commitment. Different combinations of these components can create other types of love. Nonlove contains none of the three components.

Rank Ordering of Desired Characteristics in a Mate					
	United States		**China**		**South Africa Zulu**
	Females	**Males**	**Females**	**Males**	**Females**	**Males**
Mutual attraction—love	1	1	8	4	5	10
Emotional stability and maturity	2	2	1	5	2	1
Dependable character	3	3	7	6	1	3
Pleasing disposition	4	4	16	13	3	4
Education and intelligence	5	5	4	8	6	6
Good health	9	6	3	1	4	5
Good looks	13	7	15	11	16	14
Sociability	8	8	9	12	8	11
Desire for home and children	7	9	2	2	9	9
Refinement, neatness	12	10	10	7	10	7
Ambition and industriousness	6	11	5	10	7	8
Similar education	10	12	12	15	12	12
Good cook and housekeeper	16	13	11	9	15	2
Favorable social status or rating	14	14	13	14	14	17
Similar religious background	15	15	18	18	11	16
Good financial prospect	11	16	14	16	13	18
Chastity (no prior sexual intercourse)	18	17	6	3	18	13
Similar political background	17	18	17	17	17	15

FIGURE 3 Although love may be an important factor in choosing a marriage partner if you live in the United States, other cultures place less importance on it. (Source: Buss et al., 1990.)

Liking and loving clearly show a positive side of human social behavior. Now we turn to behaviors that are just as much a part of social behavior: aggression and helping behavior.

Aggression and Prosocial Behavior: Hurting and Helping Others

Drive-by shootings, carjackings, and abductions are just a few examples of the violence that seems all too common today. Yet we also find examples of generous, unselfish, thoughtful behavior that suggest a more optimistic view of humankind. Consider, for instance, people such as Mother Teresa, who ministered to the poor in India. Or contemplate the simple kindnesses of life: lending a valued compact disc, stopping to help a child who has fallen off her bicycle, or merely sharing a candy bar with a friend. Such instances of helping are no less characteristic of human behavior than are the distasteful examples of aggression (Miller, 1999).

HURTING OTHERS: AGGRESSION

We need look no further than the daily paper or the nightly news to be bombarded with examples of aggression, both on a societal level (war, invasion, assassination) and on an individual level (crime, child abuse, and the many petty cruelties humans are capable of inflicting on one another). Is such aggression an inevitable part of the human condition? Or is aggression primarily a product of particular circumstances that, if changed, could lead to its reduction?

The difficulty of answering such knotty questions becomes apparent as soon as we consider how best to define the term *aggression*. Depending on the way we define the word, many examples of inflicted pain or injury may or may not qualify as aggression (see Figure 4). For instance, a rapist is clearly acting with aggression toward his

Is This Aggression?

To see for yourself the difficulties involved in defining aggression, consider each of the following acts and determine whether it represents aggressive behavior—according to your own definition of aggression.

1. A spider eats a fly. Yes _____ No _____
2. Two wolves fight for the leadership of the pack. Yes _____ No _____
3. A soldier shoots an enemy at the front line. Yes _____ No _____
4. The warden of a prison executes a convicted criminal. Yes _____ No _____
5. A man viciously kicks a cat. Yes _____ No _____
6. A man, while cleaning a window, knocks over a flower pot, which, in falling, injures a pedestrian. Yes _____ No _____
7. Mr. X, a notorious gossip, speaks disparagingly of many people of his acquaintance. Yes _____ No _____
8. A man mentally rehearses a murder he is about to commit. Yes _____ No _____
9. An angry son purposely fails to write to his mother, who is expecting a letter and will be hurt if none arrives. Yes _____ No _____
10. An enraged boy tries with all his might to inflict injury on his antagonist, a bigger boy, but is not successful in doing so. His efforts simply amuse the bigger boy. Yes _____ No _____
11. A senator does not protest the escalation of bombing to which she is normally opposed. Yes _____ No _____
12. A farmer beheads a chicken and prepares it for supper. Yes _____ No _____
13. A hunter kills an animal and mounts it as a trophy. Yes _____ No _____
14. A physician gives a flu shot to a screaming child. Yes _____ No _____
15. A boxer gives his opponent a bloody nose. Yes _____ No _____
16. A Girl Scout tries to assist an elderly woman but trips her by accident. Yes _____ No _____
17. A bank robber is shot in the back while trying to escape. Yes _____ No _____
18. A tennis player smashes her racket after missing a volley. Yes _____ No _____
19. A person commits suicide. Yes _____ No _____
20. A cat kills a mouse, parades around with it, and then discards it. Yes _____ No _____

FIGURE 4 What is aggression? It depends on how the word is defined and in what context it is used. (Source: Adapted from Benjamin, 1985, p. 41.)

victim. On the other hand, it is less certain that a physician carrying out an emergency medical procedure without an anesthetic, thereby causing incredible pain to the patient, should be considered aggressive.

Most social psychologists define aggression in terms of the intent and the purpose behind the behavior. **Aggression** is intentional injury of or harm to another person (Berkowitz, 1993, 2001). By this definition, the rapist is clearly acting aggressively, whereas the physician causing pain during a medical procedure is not.

We turn now to several approaches to aggressive behavior developed by social psychologists (Berkowitz, 1993, 2001; Geen & Donnerstein, 1998).

Instinct Approaches: Aggression as a Release. If you have ever punched an adversary in the nose, you may have experienced a certain satisfaction, despite your better judgment. Instinct theories, noting the prevalence of aggression not only in humans but in animals as well, propose that aggression is primarily the outcome of innate—or inborn—urges.

Sigmund Freud was one of the first to suggest, as part of his theory of personality, that aggression is a primary instinctual drive. Konrad Lorenz, an ethologist (a scientist who studies animal behavior), expanded on Freud's notions by arguing that humans,

Aggression: The intentional injury of, or harm to, another person.

along with members of other species, have a fighting instinct, which in earlier times ensured protection of food supplies and weeded out the weaker of the species (Lorenz, 1966, 1974). Lorenz's instinct approach led to the controversial notion that aggressive energy constantly builds up within an individual until the person finally discharges it in a process called **catharsis.** The longer the energy builds up, says Lorenz, the greater will be the amount of the aggression displayed when it is discharged.

Probably the most controversial idea to come out of instinct theories of aggression is Lorenz's proposal that society should provide acceptable ways of permitting catharsis. For example, he suggested that participation in aggressive sports and games would prevent the discharge of aggression in less socially desirable ways. However, little research has found evidence for the existence of a pent-up reservoir of aggression that needs to be released. In fact, some studies flatly contradict the notion of catharsis, leading psychologists to look for other explanations for aggression (Bushman, Baumeister, & Phillips, 2001; Bushman & Anderson, 2002; Bushman, Wang, & Anderson, 2005).

Frustration-Aggression Approaches: Aggression as a Reaction to Frustration. Suppose you've been working on a paper that is due for a class early the next morning, and your computer printer runs out of ink just before you can print out the paper. You rush to the store to buy more ink, only to find the sales clerk locking the door for the day. Even though the clerk can see you gesturing and begging him to open the door, he refuses, shrugging his shoulders and pointing to a sign that indicates when the store will open the next day. At that moment, the feelings you experience toward the sales clerk probably place you on the verge of real aggression, and you are undoubtedly seething inside.

Frustration-aggression theory tries to explain aggression in terms of events like this one. When first put forward, the theory said flatly that frustration *always* leads to aggression of some sort, and that aggression is *always* the result of some frustration, where **frustration** is defined as the thwarting or blocking of some ongoing, goal-directed behavior (Dollard et al., 1939). More recent explanations have modified the original theory, suggesting instead that frustration produces anger, leading to a *readiness* to act aggressively. Whether actual aggression occurs depends on the presence of *aggressive cues*, stimuli that have been associated in the past with actual aggression or violence and that will trigger aggression again. In addition, frustration produces aggression to the degree to which it produces negative feelings (Berkowitz, 1989, 1990).

What kinds of stimuli act as aggressive cues? They can range from the most overt, such as the presence of weapons, to the subtlest, such as the mere mention of the name of an individual who behaved violently in the past. For example, in one experiment, angered participants behaved significantly more aggressively when in the presence of a rifle and a revolver than they did in a comparable situation in which no guns were present (Berkowitz & LePage, 1967). Similarly, frustrated participants in an experiment who had viewed a violent movie were more physically aggressive toward a confederate with the same name as the star of the movie than they were toward a confederate with a different name (Berkowitz & Geen, 1966). It appears, then, that frustration does lead to aggression, at least when aggressive cues are present (Marcus-Newhall, Pederson, & Carlson, 2000).

Observational Learning Approaches: Learning to Hurt Others. Do we learn to be aggressive? The *observational learning* (sometimes called *social learning*) approach to aggression says that we do. Taking an almost opposite view from instinct theories, which focus on innate explanations of aggression, observational learning theory emphasizes that social and environmental conditions can teach individuals to be aggressive. The

Catharsis: The process of discharging built-up aggressive energy.

Frustration: The thwarting or blocking of some ongoing, goal-directed behavior.

Is road rage a result of frustration? According to frustration-aggression approaches, frustration is a likely cause.

theory sees aggression not as inevitable, but rather as a learned response that can be understood in terms of rewards and punishments.

Observational learning theory pays particular attention not only to direct rewards and punishments that individuals themselves receive, but also to the rewards and punishments that models—individuals who provide a guide to appropriate behavior—receive for their aggressive behavior. According to observational learning theory, people observe the behavior of models and the subsequent consequences of that behavior. If the consequences are positive, the behavior is likely to be imitated when observers find themselves in a similar situation.

Suppose, for instance, a girl hits her younger brother when he damages one of her new toys. Whereas instinct theory would suggest that the aggression had been pent up and was now being discharged and frustration-aggression theory would examine the girl's frustration at no longer being able to use her new toy, observational learning theory would look to previous situations in which the girl had viewed others being rewarded for their aggression. For example, perhaps she had watched a friend get to play with a toy after he painfully twisted it out of the hand of another child.

Observational learning theory has received wide research support. For example, nursery-school-age children who have watched an adult model behave aggressively and then receive reinforcement for it later display similar behavior themselves if they have been angered, insulted, or frustrated after exposure. Furthermore, a significant amount of research links watching television shows containing violence with subsequent viewer aggression (Huesmann et al., 2003; Coyne & Archer, 2005; Winerman, 2005).

HELPING OTHERS: THE BRIGHTER SIDE OF HUMAN NATURE

Turning away from aggression, we move now to the opposite—and brighter—side of human nature: helping behavior. Helping behavior, or **prosocial behavior** as it is more formally known, has been considered under many different conditions. However, the question that psychologists have looked at most closely relates to bystander intervention in emergency situations. What are the factors that lead someone to help a person in need?

One critical factor is the number of others present. When more than one person witnesses an emergency situation, a sense of **diffusion of responsibility** can arise among the bystanders (as we discussed earlier in the book when we considered research methods). Diffusion of responsibility is the tendency for people to feel that responsibility for acting is shared, or diffused, among those present. The more people who are present in an emergency, the less personally responsible each individual feels—and therefore the less help he or she provides (Latané & Nida, 1981; Barron & Yechiam, 2002; Blair, Thompson, & Wuensch, 2005).

Although most research on helping behavior supports the diffusion-of-responsibility explanation, other factors are clearly involved in helping behavior. According to a model developed by Latané and Darley (1970), the process of helping involves four basic steps (see Figure 5):

- *Noticing a person, event, or situation that may require help.*
- *Interpreting the event as one that requires help.* Even if we notice an event, it may be sufficiently ambiguous for us to interpret it as a nonemergency situation (Shotland, 1985; Harrison & Wells, 1991). It is here that the presence of others first affects helping behavior. The presence of inactive others may indicate to us that a situation does not require help—a judgment we do not necessarily make if we are alone.
- *Assuming responsibility for helping.* It is at this point that diffusion of responsibility is likely to occur if others are present. Moreover, a bystander's particular expertise is likely to play a role in determining whether he or she helps. For instance, if people with training in medical aid or lifesaving techniques are present, untrained bystanders are less likely to intervene because they feel

Prosocial behavior: Helping behavior.

Diffusion of responsibility: The tendency for people to feel that responsibility for acting is shared, or diffused, among those present.

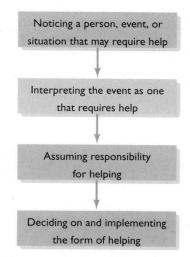

FIGURE 5 The basic steps of helping. (Source: Based on Latané & Darley, 1970).

they have less expertise. This point was well illustrated in a study by Jane and Irving Piliavin (1972), who conducted a field experiment in which an individual seemed to collapse in a subway car with blood trickling out of the corner of his mouth. The results of the experiment showed that bystanders were less likely to help when a person (actually a confederate) who appeared to be a medical intern was present than when the "intern" was not present.

- *Deciding on and implementing the form of helping.* After we assume responsibility for helping, we must decide how to provide assistance. Helping can range from very indirect forms of intervention, such as calling the police, to more direct forms, such as giving first aid or taking the victim to a hospital. Most social psychologists use a *rewards-costs approach* for helping to predict the nature of the assistance a bystander will choose to provide. The general notion is that the rewards for helping, as perceived by the bystander, must outweigh the costs if helping is to occur, and most research tends to support this notion (Bell et al., 1995).

Altruism: Helping behavior that is beneficial to others but clearly requires self-sacrifice.

After we determine the nature of the assistance needed, one step remains: the implementation of the assistance. A rewards-costs analysis suggests that we are most likely to use the least costly form of implementation. However, this is not always the case: In some situations, people behave altruistically. **Altruism** is helping behavior that is beneficial to others but clearly requires self-sacrifice. For example, people who helped strangers escape from the burning World Trade Center towers during the September 11, 2001, terrorist attack in New York City, putting themselves at mortal risk, would be considered altruistic (Shapiro & Gabbard, 1994; Krueger, Hicks, & McGue, 2001; Batson & Powell, 2003).

People who intervene in emergency situations tend to possess certain personality characteristics that differentiate them from nonhelpers. For example, helpers are more self-assured, sympathetic, emotionally understanding, and have greater *empathy* (a personality trait in which someone observing another person experiences the emotions of that person) than are nonhelpers (Batson et al., 2002; Dovidio & Penner, 2004).

Still, most social psychologists agree that no single set of attributes differentiates helpers from nonhelpers. For the most part, temporary situational factors (such as the mood we're in) determine whether we will intervene in a situation requiring aid (Knight et al., 1994; Bersoff, 1999; Eisenberg, Guthrie, & Cumberland, 2002).

Altruism is often the only bright side of a natural disaster.

At one time or another, almost everyone feels angry. The anger may result from a frustrating situation, or it may be due to the behavior of another individual. The way we deal with anger may determine the difference between a promotion and a lost job or a broken relationship and one that mends itself.

Social psychologists who have studied the topic suggest several good ways to deal with anger, strategies that maximize the potential for positive consequences (Deffenbacher, 1988, 1996; Bass, 1996; Nelson & Finch, 2000). Among the most useful strategies are the following:

BECOMING AN INFORMED CONSUMER
of Psychology
Dealing Effectively with Anger

- *Look again at the anger-provoking situation from the perspective of others.* By taking others' point of view, you may be able to understand the situation better, and with increased understanding you may become more tolerant of the apparent shortcomings of others.
- *Minimize the importance of the situation.* Does it really matter that someone is driving too slowly and that you'll be late to an appointment as a result? Reinterpret the situation in a way that is less bothersome.
- *Fantasize about getting even—but don't act on it.* Fantasy provides a safety valve. In your fantasies, you can yell at that unfair professor all you want and suffer no consequences at all. However, don't spend too much time brooding: Fantasize, but then move on.
- *Relax.* By teaching yourself the kinds of relaxation techniques used in systematic desensitization (see Figure 2 in Module 51), you can help reduce your reactions to anger. In turn, your anger may dissipate.

No matter which of these strategies you try, above all, don't ignore your anger. People who always try to suppress their anger may experience a variety of consequences, such as self-condemnation, frustration, and even physical illness (Sharma, Ghosh, & Spielberger, 1995; Finney, Stoney, & Engebretson , 2002).

RECAP/EVALUATE/RETHINK

RECAP

Why are we attracted to certain people, and what progression do social relationships follow?

- The primary determinants of liking include proximity, exposure, similarity, and physical attractiveness. (pp. 609–610)
- Loving is distinguished from liking by the presence of intense physiological arousal, an all-encompassing interest in another, fantasies about the other, rapid swings of emotion, fascination, sexual desire, exclusiveness, and strong feelings of caring. (p. 611)
- Love can be categorized as passionate or companionate. In addition, love has several components: intimacy, passion, and decision/commitment. (p. 611)

What factors underlie aggression and prosocial behavior?

- Aggression is intentional injury of or harm to another person. (p. 613)
- Explanations of aggression include instinct approaches, frustration-aggression theory, and observational learning. (pp. 613–615)

- Helping behavior in emergencies is determined in part by the phenomenon of diffusion of responsibility, which results in a lower likelihood of helping when more people are present. (p. 615)
- Deciding to help is the outcome of a four-stage process consisting of noticing a possible need for help, interpreting the situation as requiring aid, assuming responsibility for taking action, and deciding on and implementing a form of assistance. (pp. 615–616)

EVALUATE

1. We tend to like people who are similar to us. True or false?
2. Which of the following sets are the three components of love proposed by Sternberg?
   a. Passion, closeness, sexuality
   b. Attraction, desire, complementarity
   c. Passion, intimacy, decision/commitment
   d. Commitment, caring, sexuality

3. Based on research evidence, which of the following might be the best way to reduce the amount of fighting a young boy does?
   a. Take him to the gym and let him work out on the boxing equipment.
   b. Make him repeatedly watch violent scenes from the film *The Matrix Reloaded* in the hope that it will provide catharsis.
   c. Reward him if he doesn't fight during a certain period.
   d. Ignore it and let it die out naturally.
4. If a person in a crowd does not help in an apparent emergency situation because many other people are present, that person is falling victim to the phenomenon of _____ _____ _____.

RETHINK

1. Can love be studied scientifically? Is there an elusive quality to love that makes it at least partially unknow-

able? How would you define "falling in love"? How would you study it?

2. *From the perspective of a criminal justice worker:* How would the aggression of Eric Rudolph, who was convicted of exploding a bomb during the 1996 Summer Olympics in Atlanta and later attacking several women's clinics, be interpreted by proponents of the three main approaches to the study of aggression (instinct approaches, frustration-aggression approaches, and observational learning approaches)? Do you think any of these approaches fits the Rudolph case more closely than the others?

Answers to Evaluate Questions

1. true; 2. c; 3. c; 4. diffusion of responsibility

KEY TERMS

interpersonal attraction (or close relationship) p. 609
reciprocity-of-liking effect p. 610

passionate (or romantic) love p. 611
companionate love p. 611
aggression p. 613

catharsis p. 614
frustration p. 614
prosocial behavior p. 615

diffusion of responsibility p. 615
altruism p. 616

Psychology on the Web

1. Find examples on the Web of advertisements or other persuasive messages that use central route processing and peripheral route processing. What type of persuasion appears to be more prevalent on the Web? For what type of persuasion does the Web appear to be better suited? Is there a difference between Web-based advertising and other forms of advertising?

2. Is "hate crimes legislation" a good idea? Use the Web to find at least two discussions of hate crimes legislation—one in favor and one opposed—and summarize in writing the main issues and arguments presented. Using your knowledge of prejudice and aggression, evaluate the arguments for and against hate crimes legislation. State your opinion about whether this type of legislation is advisable.

3. After completing the PsychInteractive exercise on prejudice, use the Web to identify two recent incidents in the news in which prejudice played a role. Summarize the incidents and discuss the ways such prejudice might have been prevented.

Epilogue

We have touched on some of the major ideas, research topics, and experimental findings of social psychology in this chaper. We examined how people form, maintain, and change attitudes and how they form impressions of others and assign attributions to them. We also saw how groups, through conformity and tactics of compliance, can influence individuals' actions and attitudes. Finally, we discussed interpersonal relationships, including both liking and loving, and looked at the two sides of a coin that represent the extremes of social behavior: aggression and prosocial behavior.

Turn back to the prologue of this set of modules, which describes the heroic efforts of Kathleen Imel. Use your understanding of social psychology to consider the following questions.

1. What factors would a social psychologist consider in examining why Kathleen Imel stopped her van and helped Joshua escape from the dog attack?

2. Do you believe the fact that Imel was the only one driving by when Joshua was attacked made it more or less likely that she stopped to help? Why?

3. Given what social psychologists know about the factors that lead people to be helpful, do you believe that Imel's helpfulness was caused by situational factors or that it had more to do with her personality? Why?

4. What are some ways in which the incidence of helping behavior can be increased and the incidence of aggressive and antisocial behavior can be discouraged?

Persuasion can lead to attitude change in a variety of ways, including central and peripheral route processing. Use this visual guide to understand how attitude change occurs. Then answer the questions below to test your understanding of the concepts.

1 Attitude change starts with a message and a source. If the person delivering the message is perceived as attractive, trustworthy, and knowledgeable, and if different sides of an issue are presented, the message is more likely to be accepted. Additionally, the characteristics of the target audience affect their willingness to be persuaded.

Central route processing

2 In central route processing, we carefully consider the issues and arguments used to persuade us. People who are motivated, highly involved, and attentive are more receptive to central route processing. Central route processing can lead to commitment and more lasting attitude change.

EVALUATE

1 In the example above _____ evokes central route processing.
   a attending an expert's lecture on global warning
   b observing a student demonstration on global warming
   c watching a weather report
   d hearing a friend talk about how hot it was last summer

2 In this example, peripheral route processing might be occurring when
   a attending an expert's lecture on global warning
   b hearing a friend talk about how hot it was last summer
   c watching a weather report
   d observing a student demonstration on global warming

3 In peripheral route processing, we consider the source of the information and related information, rather than the message itself. Uninvolved, unmotivated, and inattentive individuals are more likely to use peripheral route processing. Although they might be persuaded initially, especially if the message comes from an attractive and famous person, their change in attitude is often weaker and less likely to last.

Peripheral route processing

3 Central route processing generally leads to more lasting attitude change than peripheral route processing. True or false?

RETHINK

I An advertising company wants to produce peripheral route processing when viewers watch a television commercial for clam chowder. Why would the advertiser want to do this, and what elements might the commercial include to evoke peripheral route processing?

Answers to Evaluate questions: 1. a; 2. d; 3. True

Going by the Numbers: Statistics in Psychology

Key Concepts for the Appendix

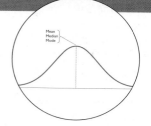
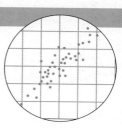

Prologue Selma Vorwerk

As the boat moved nearer to shore, the outline of the Statue of Liberty was plainly visible in the distance. Closer and closer it came, sending a chill down the spine of Selma Vorwerk. A symbol of America, the statue represented the hopes she carried from her native Europe in the early 1900s—hopes of liberty, of success, of a life free of economic and social strain.

Yet as the boat sailed closer to Ellis Island, the first point of arrival in the United States, Vorwerk did not realize that her very presence—and that of the other thousands of immigrants seeking their fortune in a land of opportunity—was threatened. A strong political movement was growing in the country on which she was pinning her hopes. That movement sought, by using information collected by psychologists, to stem the flow of immigrants through "scientific" analysis of data.

The major claim of the group was that a flood of "mentally deficient" immigrants was poisoning the intellectual capacity of the United States. To supporters of that view, unless drastic measures were taken, it would not be too many years before Western civilization collapsed from a lack of intelligence.

To support this assertion, Lathrop Stoddard, a member of the anti-immigration movement, reported the results of a study of intelligence in which tests were administered to a group of 82 children and 400 adults. On the basis of those test results, he concluded that the average mental age of people in the United States was only 14 years—proof to him that unlimited immigration had already produced a serious decline in the country's intelligence.

Looking Ahead

Fortunately for immigrants such as Selma Vorwerk, observers in favor of immigration pointed out the fallacy of using data from a relatively small sample—when a considerably larger set of intelligence test data was available. The U.S. Army had been collecting intelligence data for years and had the test scores of 1.7 million men available. When those scores were analyzed, it immediately became apparent that the claim that the average mental age of American adults was 14 years was completely without merit.

A debate reminiscent of this one rages today, as some observers suggest that an unrestrained flow of immigrants—this time from Latin America and Asia—will seriously damage the United States. This time, though, the debate is based more on analyses of social and economic statistics, with opponents of immigration suggesting that the social fabric of the country will be changed and that jobs are being taken away from longer-term residents because of the influx of immigrants. Equally vehement proponents of immigration suggest that the relevant statistics are being misinterpreted, and that their analyses of the situation result in a very different conclusion.

Statistics, the branch of mathematics concerned with collecting, organizing, analyzing, and drawing conclusions from numerical data, is a part of all of our lives. For instance, we are all familiar with the claims and counterclaims regarding the effects of smoking. The U.S. government requires that cigarette manufacturers include a warning that smoking is dangerous to people's health on every package of cigarettes and in their advertisements; the government's data show clear statistical links between smoking and disease. At the same time, the tobacco industry has long minimized the negative effects of smoking.

Statistics is also at the heart of a considerable number of debates in the field of psychology. How do we determine the nature and strength of the effects of heredity on behavior? What is the relationship between learning and schedules of reinforcement? How do we know if the double standard regarding male and female sexual practices has shifted over time? These questions, and most others of interest to psychologists, cannot be answered without a reliance on statistics (Leblanc, 2004).

In this set of modules, we consider the basic approaches to statistical measurement. We first discuss approaches to summarizing data that allow us to describe sets of observations. Next, we consider techniques for deciding how different one set of scores is from another. Finally, we examine approaches to measuring the relationship between two sets of scores.

Descriptive Statistics

Suppose, as an instructor of college psychology, you wanted to evaluate your class's performance on its initial exam. Where might you begin?

You would probably start by using **descriptive statistics,** the branch of statistics that provides a means of summarizing data, presenting the data in a usable and convenient form. For instance, you might first simply list the scores the pupils had received on the test:

> 72 78 78 92 69 73 85 49
> 86 86 72 59 58 85 89
> 80 83 69 78 90 90 96 83

Viewed in this way, the scores are a jumble of numbers of which it is difficult to make any sense. However, there are several methods by which you could begin to organize the scores in a more meaningful way. For example, you might sort them in order of highest score to lowest score, as is done in Figure 1. By indicating the number of people who obtained each score, you would have produced what is called a **frequency distribution,** an arrangement of scores from a sample that indicates how often a particular score is present.

Another way of summarizing the scores is to consider them visually. For example, you could construct the **histogram,** or bar graph, shown in Figure 2. In that histogram, the number of people obtaining a given score is represented pictorially. The scores are ordered along one dimension of the graph, and the number of people obtaining each score along the other dimension.

Arranging the scores from the highest to the lowest allows us to visually inspect the data. Most often, however, visual inspection is insufficient. For one thing, there may be so many scores in a sample that it is difficult to construct a meaningful visual representation. For another, our interpretations of patterns on a graph or table are often biased and inaccurate; more precise, mathematically based measures would seem to be preferable. In cases in which a precise means of summarizing the data is desirable, psychologists turn to measures of central tendency. **Central tendency** is an index of the central location within a distribution of scores. There are three major measures of central tendency: the mean, the median, and the mode.

Key Concept

What measures can we use to summarize sets of data?

Statistics: The branch of mathematics concerned with collecting, organizing, analyzing, and drawing conclusions from numerical data.

Descriptive statistics: The branch of statistics that provides a means of summarizing data.

Frequency distribution: An arrangement of scores from a sample that indicates how often a particular score is present.

Histogram: Bar graph.

Central tendency: An index of the central location within a distribution of scores; the most representative score in a distribution of scores (the mean, median, and mode are measures of central tendency).

Mean: The average of all scores, arrived at by adding scores together and dividing by the number of scores.

The Mean: Finding the Average

The most familiar measure of central tendency is the **mean.** A mean is the technical term for an average, which is simply the sum of all the scores in a set, divided by the number of scores making up the set. For example, to calculate the mean of the sample we have been using, begin by adding each of the numbers (96 + 92 + 90 + 90 + 89 + . . . and so forth). When you have the total, divide that sum by the number of scores, which is 23. This calculation, 1,800/23 = 78.26, produces a mean score, or average, for our sample.

In general, the mean is an accurate reflection of the central score in a set of scores; as you can see from the histogram in Figure 1, our mean of 78.26 falls roughly in the center of the distribution of scores. Yet the mean does not always provide the best measure

"*Meaningless statistics were up one-point-five percent this month over last month.*"

A Sample Frequency Distribution

Test Score	Number of Students Attaining That Score
96	1
92	1
90	2
89	1
86	2
85	2
83	2
80	1
78	3
73	1
72	2
69	2
59	1
58	1
49	1

FIGURE 1 Example of a frequency distribution, which arranges scores from a sample and indicates how often a particular score is present.

Median: The point in a distribution of scores that divides the distribution exactly in half when the scores are listed in numerical order.

of central tendency. For one thing, the mean is very sensitive to extreme scores. As an example, imagine that we added two scores of 20 and 22 to our sample scores. The mean would now become 1,842/25, or 73.68, a drop of almost five points. Because of its sensitivity to extreme scores, then, the mean can sometimes present a deceptive picture of a set of scores, especially in cases where the mean is based on a relatively small number of scores.

The Median: Finding the Middle

A measure of central tendency that is less sensitive to extreme scores than the mean is the median. The **median** is the point in a distribution of scores that divides the distribution exactly in half. If we arrange all the scores in order from the highest to the lowest, the median lies in the middle of the distribution.

For example, consider a distribution of five scores: 10, 8, 7, 4, and 3. The point that divides the distribution exactly in half is the score 7: Two scores in the distribution lie above the 7 score, and two scores lie below it. If there are an even number of scores in a distribution—in which case there will be no score lying in the middle—the two middle scores are averaged. If our distribution consisted of scores of 10, 8, 7, 6, 4, and 3, then, we would average the two middle scores of 7 and 6 to form a median of 7 + 6 divided by 2, or 13/2 = 6.5.

In our original sample test scores, there are twenty-three scores. The score that divides the distribution exactly in half will be the twelfth score in the frequency distribution of scores, because the twelfth score has eleven scores above it and eleven below it. If you count down to the twelfth score in the distribution depicted in Figure 1, you will see that the score is 80. Therefore, the median of the distribution is 80.

One feature of the median as a measure of central tendency is that it is insensitive to extreme scores. For example, adding the scores of 20 and 22 to our distribution would change the median no more than would adding scores of 48 and 47 to the distribution. The reason is clear: The median divides a set of scores in half, and the magnitude of the scores is of no consequence in this process.

The median is often used instead of the mean when extreme scores might be misleading. For example, government statistics on income are typically presented using

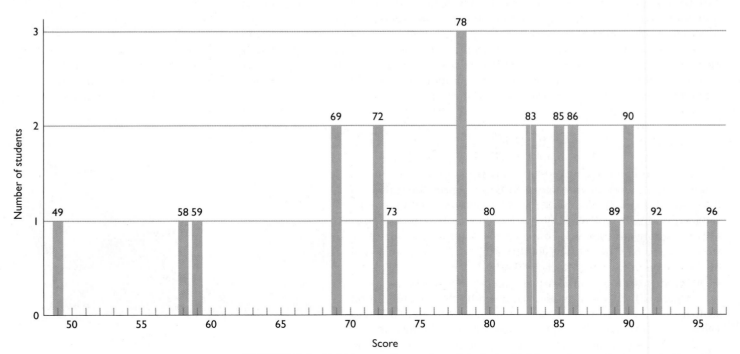

FIGURE 2 In this histogram, the number of students obtaining each score is represented by a bar.

the median as the measure of central tendency, because the median corrects for the small number of extreme cases of very wealthy individuals, whose high incomes might otherwise inflate the mean income.

The Mode: Finding What Is Most Frequent

The final measure of central tendency is the **mode.** The mode is the most frequently occurring score in a set of scores. If you return to the distribution in Figure 1, you can see that three people scored 78, and the frequency of all the other scores is either 2 or 1. The mode for the distribution, then, is 78.

Some distributions, of course, may have more than one score occurring most frequently. For instance, we could imagine that if the distribution had a score of 86 added to the two that are already there, there would be two most frequently occurring categories: 78 and now 86. In this instance, we would say there are two modes—a case known as a *bimodal distribution.*

The mode is often used as a measure of preference or popularity. For instance, if teachers wanted to know who was the most popular child in their elementary school classrooms, they might develop a questionnaire that asked the students to choose someone with whom they would like to participate in some activity. After the choices were tallied, the mode probably would provide the best indication of which child was the most popular.

Comparing the Three M's: Mean Versus Median Versus Mode

If a sample is sufficiently large, there is generally little difference between the mean, median, and mode. The reason is that with large samples, scores typically form what is called a normal distribution. A **normal distribution** is a distribution of scores that produces a symmetrical, bell-shaped curve, such as the one displayed in Figure 3, in which the right half mirrors the left half, and in which the mean, median, and mode all have the same value.

Most large distributions, those containing many scores, produce a normal curve. For instance, if you asked a large number of students how many hours a week they studied, you might expect to find that most studied within a similar range of hours, and there would be a few who studied many, many hours, and a very few who studied not at all. There would be many scores hovering around the center of the distribution of scores, then, and only a few at the extremes—producing a normal distribution. Many phenomena of interest to psychologists produce a normal curve when graphed. For example, the distribution of IQ scores among the general population falls into a normal distribution.

The mean, median, and mode fall at exactly the same point in a normal distribution. This means that in a normal distribution of scores, the mean score will divide the distribution exactly in half (making it the median), and it will be the most frequently occurring score in the distribution (making it the mode).

The mean, median, and mode differ, however, when distributions are not normal. In cases in which the distributions are *skewed,* or not symmetrical, there is a "hump" at one end or the other (see Figures 4 and 5). For instance, if we gave a calculus exam to a group of students enrolled in an elementary algebra class, we would expect that most of the students would fail the test, leading to low scores being overrepresented in the

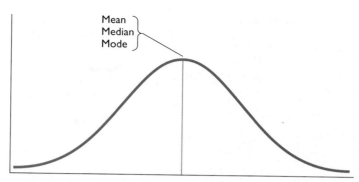

FIGURE 3 In a normal distribution, the mean, median, and mode are identical, falling at the center of the distribution.

Mode: The most frequently occurring score in a set of scores.

Normal distribution: A distribution of scores that produces a symmetrical, bell-shaped curve in which the right half mirrors the left half and in which the mean, median, and mode all have the same value.

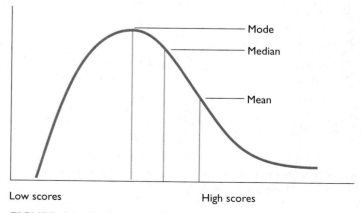

FIGURE 4 In this skewed distribution, most scores are low.

FIGURE 5 In this example of a skewed distribution, there tend to be more high scores than low scores.

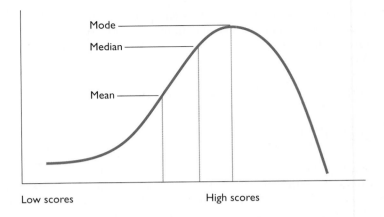

distribution, as in Figure 4. On the other hand, if we gave the same students a test of elementary addition problems, the scores would probably form a distribution in which high scores predominated, as in Figure 5. Both distributions are skewed, although in opposite directions, and the mean, median, and mode are different from one another.

RECAP/EVALUATE/RETHINK

RECAP

What measures can we use to summarize sets of data?

- Statistics is concerned with collecting, organizing, analyzing, and drawing conclusions from numerical data. (p. A-2)
- Descriptive statistics provides a means of summarizing data and presenting the data in a usable and convenient form. (p. A-3)
- A frequency distribution arranges scores from a sample by indicating how often a particular score is presented. A histogram, or bar graph, presents the same data pictorially. (p. A-3)
- Central tendency is the most representative score in a distribution of scores. The mean (or average) is generally the best measure of central tendency. The median is the point or score in a distribution that divides the distribution in half so that half the scores are higher and half are lower. The third measure of central tendency is the mode, the most frequently occurring score in a distribution of scores. (pp. A-3–A-5)

EVALUATE

1. A frequency distribution of numbers could be displayed pictorially by constructing a bar graph, or _____.

2. Match each item in the left-hand column with the corresponding item in the right-hand column.
   1. Mean = 10.0   a. 2, 8, 10, 12, 13, 18
   2. Median = 11   b. 4, 5, 10, 10, 15, 16
   3. Mode = 12   c. 4, 5, 12, 12, 12, 16
3. The mean, median, and mode are measures of
   _____.
4. Professor Garcia explains to the class that most of the forty exam scores fell within a B range, but there were two extremely high scores. Should she report the median or the mean as a measure of central tendency?
5. The mean, median, and mode will differ in a normal distribution. True or false?

RETHINK

1. Government statistics on family income are presented in a variety of ways. What would be the most useful way of providing a summary of family incomes across the country: the mean, median, or mode? Why might providing only the mean be misleading?

Answers to Evaluate Questions

1. histogram; 2. 1-b, 2-a, 3-c; 3. central tendency; 4. the median—the mean is too sensitive to extreme scores; 5. false; they will be equal

KEY TERMS

statistics p. A-3
descriptive statistics p. A-3
frequency distribution p. A-3

histogram p. A-3
central tendency p. A-3

mean p. A-3
median p. A-4

mode p. A-5
normal distribution p. A-5

Measures of Variability

Although measures of central tendency provide information about where the center of a distribution lies, often this information is insufficient. For example, suppose a psychologist was interested in determining the nature of people's eye movements while they were reading in order to perfect a new method to teach reading. It would not be enough to know how *most* people moved their eyes (information that a measure of central tendency would provide); it would also be important to know how much individual people's eye movements differed or varied from one another.

A second important characteristic of a set of scores provides this information: variability. **Variability** is a term that refers to the spread, or dispersion, of scores in a distribution. Figure 1 contains two distributions of scores that have identical means but differ in variability. Measures of variability provide a way to describe the spread of scores in a distribution.

The Range: Highest Minus Lowest

The simplest measure of variability is the **range.** The range is the difference between the highest score in a distribution and the lowest score. In the set of scores

96 92 90 90 89 86
86 85 85 83 83 80
78 78 78 73 72 72
69 69 59 58 49

the distribution has a range of 47 (96 − 49 = 47).

The fact that a range is simple to calculate is about its only virtue. The problem with this particular measure of variability is that it is based entirely on extreme scores, and a single score that is very different from the others in a distribution can distort the picture of the distribution as a whole. For example, the addition of a score

Key Concept

How can we assess the variability of a set of data?

Variability: The spread, or dispersion, of scores in a distribution.

Range: The difference between the highest score and the lowest score in a distribution.

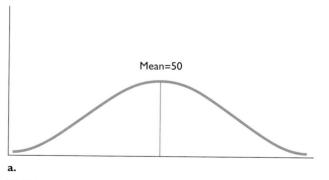
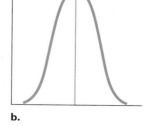

a.

b.

FIGURE 1 Although the mean is identical in these two distributions, the variability, or spread of scores, is very different. Specifically, the variability is considerably greater in (a) than in (b).

of 20 to the test score distribution we are considering would almost double the range, even though the variability of the remaining scores in the distribution would not have changed at all.

The Standard Deviation: Differences from the Mean

The most frequently used method of characterizing the variability of a distribution of scores is the standard deviation. The standard deviation bears a conceptual relationship to a mean. You will recall that the mean is the average score in a distribution of scores. A **standard deviation** is an index of the average deviation of a set of scores from the center of the distribution.

Standard deviation: An index of the average deviation of a set of scores from the center of the distribution.

Consider, for instance, the distributions in Figure 1. The distribution on the left is widely dispersed, and on the average an individual score in the distribution can be thought of as deviating quite a bit from the center of the distribution. Certainly the scores in the distribution on the left are going to deviate more from the center of the distribution than those in the distribution on the right.

In contrast, in the distribution on the right, the scores are closely packed together and there is little deviation of a typical score from the center of the distribution. On the basis of this analysis, then, it would be expected that a good measure of variability would yield a larger value for the distribution on the left than it would for the one on the right—and, in fact, a standard deviation would do exactly this by indicating how far away a typical score lies from the center of the distribution.

In a normal distribution, 68 percent of the scores fall within one standard deviation of the mean (34 percent on either side of it), 95 percent of the scores fall within two standard deviations, and 99.7 percent fall within three standard deviations. In the general population, IQ scores of intelligence fall into a normal distribution, and they have a mean of 100 and a standard deviation of 15. Consequently, an IQ score of 100 does not deviate from the mean, whereas an IQ score that is three standard deviations above the mean (or 145) is very unusual (higher than 99 percent of all IQ scores).

The calculation of the standard deviation follows the logic of calculating the difference of individual scores from the mean of the distribution (see Figure 2). Not only does the standard deviation provide an excellent indicator of the variability of a set of scores, it provides a means for converting initial scores on standardized tests such as the SAT (the college admissions exam) into the scales used to report results. In this way, it is possible to make a score of 585 on the verbal section of the SAT, for example, equivalent from one year to the next, even though the specific test items differ from year to year.

FIGURE 2 How to calculate a standard deviation.

Calculating a Standard Deviation

1. The calculation of a standard deviation begins with the calculation of the mean of distribution. In the following distribution of scores on a psychology student's weekly quizzes, the mean is 84.5: 82, 88, 71, 86, 96, 84. (As you recall, the mean is the sum of the scores divided by the number of scores in the distribution, or 507 ÷ 6 = 84.5.)

2. The next step is to produce a deviation score for each score in the distribution. A deviation score is simply an original score minus the mean of all the scores in a distribution. This has been done in the second column below:

Original Score	Deviation Score*	Deviation Score Squared
82	−2.5	6.25
88	3.5	12.25
71	−13.5	182.25
86	1.5	2.25
96	11.5	132.25
84	−.5	.25

3. In the third step, the deviation scores are squared (multiplied by themselves) to eliminate negative numbers. This has been carried out in the third column above.

4. The squared deviation scores are then added together, and this sum is divided by the number of scores. In the example above, the sum of the squared deviation scores is 6.25 + 12.25 + 182.25 + 2.25 + 132.25 + .25 = 335.50, and 335.50 ÷ 6 = 55.916.

5. The final step is to take the square root of the resulting number. The square root of 55.916 is 7.4777—which is the standard deviation of the distribution of scores.

6. To summarize, the standard deviation is calculated using the formula

$$\sqrt{\frac{\Sigma(\text{score} - \text{mean})^2}{N}}$$

*Original score minus the mean of 84.5

(Note: Because this formula provides the standard deviation for a sample, the sum of the deviation scores is divided by the number of scores. N. However, in some cases, in which we might wish to generalize beyond the specific sample to a larger population, the standard deviation is calculated by using the number of scores minus 1, or $N - 1$.)

RECAP/EVALUATE/RETHINK

RECAP

How can we assess the variability of a set of data?

- The range and standard deviation are two measures of variability, which is the spread, or dispersion, of scores in a distribution. The range is the distance between the largest score in a distribution and the smallest score. The standard deviation is an index of the extent to which the average score in a distribution deviates from the center of the distribution. (pp. A-7–A-8)

EVALUATE

1. A measure of variability based solely on the distance between the most extreme scores is the
   a. Spread
   b. Standard deviation
   c. Deviation score
   d. Range

2. By simply eyeing the following sets of numbers, predict which will have a higher standard deviation and why:
   a. 6, 8, 10, 10, 11, 12, 13
   b. 2, 5, 8, 11, 16, 17, 18

3. Calculate the mean and standard deviation for sets **a** and **b** in Question 2.

RETHINK

1. If you were interested in understanding the number of people living below the poverty line in the United States, why might the range and the standard deviation provide you with a better understanding of the extent of poverty than would measures of central tendency (the mean, median, and mode)?

Answers to Evaluate Questions

1. d; 2. b, because the numbers are more widely dispersed; 3a. mean = 10, standard deviation = 2.20; 3b. mean = 11, standard deviation = 5.80

KEY TERMS

variability p. A-7   range p. A-7   standard deviation p. A-8

Using Statistics to Answer Questions: Inferential Statistics and Correlation

Suppose you were a psychologist who was interested in whether there is a relationship between smoking and anxiety. Would it be reasonable to simply look at a group of smokers and measure their anxiety by using some rating scale? Probably not. It clearly would be more informative if you compared their anxiety with the anxiety exhibited by a group of nonsmokers.

Once you decided to observe anxiety in two groups of people, you would have to determine just who would be your subjects. In an ideal world with unlimited resources, you might contact *every* smoker and nonsmoker, because these are the two populations with which you are concerned. A **population** consists of all the members of a group of interest. Obviously, however, this would be impossible because of the all-encompassing size of the two groups; instead, you would limit your subjects to a sample of smokers and nonsmokers. A **sample,** in formal statistical terms, is a subgroup of a population of interest that is intended to be representative of the larger population. Once you had identified samples representative of the population of interest to you, it would be possible to carry out your study, yielding two distributions of scores—one from the smokers and one from the nonsmokers (Fowler, 2001).

The obvious question is whether the two samples differ in the degree of anxiety displayed by their members. The statistical procedures that we discussed earlier are helpful in answering this question, because each of the two samples can be examined in terms of central tendency and variability. The more important question, though, is whether the magnitude of difference between the two distributions is sufficient to conclude that the distributions truly differ from one another, or if, instead, the differences are attributable merely to chance.

To answer the question of whether samples are truly different from one another, psychologists use inferential statistics. **Inferential statistics** is the branch of statistics that uses data from samples to make predictions about a larger population, permitting generalizations to be drawn. To take a simple example, suppose you had two coins that both were flipped 100 times. Suppose further that one coin came up heads forty-one times and the other came up heads sixty-five times. Are both coins fair? We know that a fair coin should come up heads about fifty times in 100 flips. But a little thought would also suggest that it is unlikely that even a fair coin would come up heads exactly fifty times in 100 flips. The question is, then, how far a coin could deviate from fifty heads before that coin would be considered unfair.

Questions such as this—as well as whether the results found are due to chance or represent unexpected, nonchance findings—revolve around how "probable" certain events are. Using coin flipping as an example, fifty-three heads in 100 flips would be a highly probable outcome because it departs only slightly from the expected outcome of fifty heads. In contrast, if a coin was flipped 100 times and ninety of those times it came up heads, that would be a highly improbable outcome. In fact, ninety heads out of 100 flips should occur by chance only once in 2 million trials of 100 flips of a fair coin. Ninety heads in 100 flips, then, is an extremely improbable outcome; if ninety heads did appear, the odds would be that the coin or the flipping process was rigged.

Key Concepts

How do we generalize from data?

How can we determine the nature of a relationship, and the significance of differences, between two sets of scores?

Population: All the members of a group of interest.

Sample: A representative subgroup of a population of interest.

Inferential statistics: The branch of statistics that uses data from samples to make predictions about the larger population from which the sample is drawn.

Inferential statistics are used to mathematically determine the probability of observed events. By using inferential statistics to evaluate the result of an experiment, psychologists are able to calculate the likelihood that the difference is a reflection of a true difference between populations. For example, suppose we find that the mean on an anxiety scale is 68 for smokers and 48 for nonsmokers. Inferential statistical procedures allow us to determine whether this difference is really meaningful, or whether we might expect the same difference to occur merely because of chance factors (Cohen & Lea, 2003).

The results of inferential statistical procedures are described in terms of measures of significance. To a psychologist, a **significant outcome** is one in which the observed outcome would be expected to have occurred only by chance with a probability of .05 or less. Put another way, a significant difference between two means says that there are only five chances out of 100 (or less) that the difference an experimenter has found is due to chance, rather than to an actual difference between the means.

Obtaining a significant outcome in a study does not necessarily imply that the results of an experiment have real-world importance. An experiment may demonstrate that two groups differ significantly from one another, but the meaning of the differences in terms of what occurs outside the laboratory may be limited. Still, finding a significant outcome tells us something important: The differences a researcher has found are overwhelmingly likely to be true differences, not only due to chance (Lehmann & Romano, 2004).

Significant outcome: An outcome in which the observed outcome would be expected to have occurred by chance with a probability of .05 or less.

The Correlation Coefficient: Measuring Relationships

How do we know if television viewing is related to aggression, if reading romance novels is related to sexual behavior, or if mothers' IQs are related to their daughters' IQs?

Each of these questions revolves around the issue of the degree of relationship between two variables. One way of answering them is to draw a *scatterplot*, a means of graphically illustrating the relationship between two variables. We would first collect two sets of paired measures and assign one score to the horizontal axis (variable *x*) and the other score to the vertical axis (variable *y*). Then we would draw a dot at the place where the two scores meet on the graph. The first two scatterplots in Figure 1 present typical situations. In (a) and (b), there is a **positive relationship,** in which high values of variable *x* are associated with high values of variable *y* and low values of *x* are associated with low values of *y*. In (c) and (d), there is a **negative relationship:** As values of variable *x* increase, the values of variable *y* decrease. In (e), no clear relationship exists between variable *x* and variable *y*.

It is also possible to consider scores in terms of their mathematical relationship to one another, rather than simply the way they appear on a scatterplot. Suppose, for example, a psychologist was interested in the degree to which a daughter's IQ was related to her mother's IQ—specifically, if a mother with a high IQ tended to have a daughter who also had a high IQ, and whether a mother with a low IQ tended to have a daughter with a low IQ. To examine the issue, suppose the psychologist measured the IQs of ten mothers and daughters and arranged their IQs as presented in Figure 2.

Looking at the data in the table, it is obvious that mothers and daughters do not have identical IQs. Moreover, they do not even have IQs that are rank-ordered the same in the two columns. For example, the mother with the highest IQ does not have the daughter with the highest IQ, and the mother with the lowest IQ does not have the

Positive relationship: A relationship established by data that shows high values of one variable corresponding with high values of another, and low values of the first variable corresponding with low values of the other.

Negative relationship: A relationship established by data that shows high values of one variable corresponding with low values of the other.

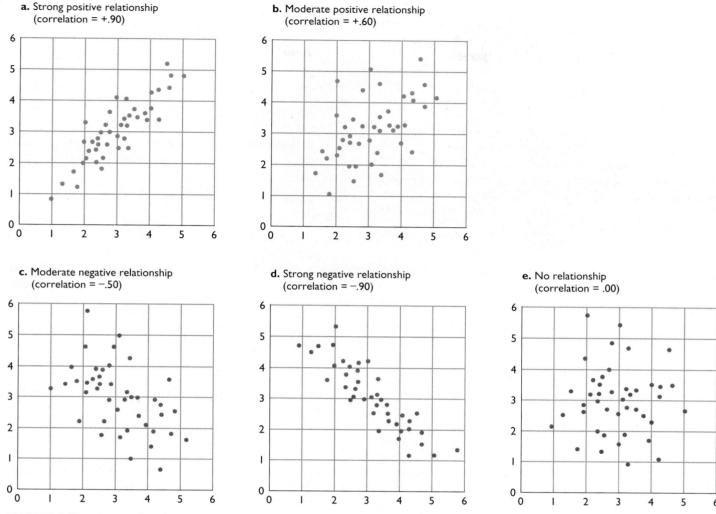

a. Strong positive relationship (correlation = +.90)

b. Moderate positive relationship (correlation = +.60)

c. Moderate negative relationship (correlation = −.50)

d. Strong negative relationship (correlation = −.90)

e. No relationship (correlation = .00)

FIGURE 1 These scatterplots show relationships of different strengths. In (a) and (b), the relationships are positive, although in (a) the relationship is considerably stronger than in (b). In contrast, the relationships in (c) and (d) are negative, with (d) representing a stronger negative relationship. Finally, (e) illustrates a case where no systematic relationship exists between the variables.

daughter with the lowest IQ. It is apparent, then, that there is not a *perfect* relationship between the IQ of a mother and the IQ of a daughter. However, it would be a mistake to conclude that there is a zero, or no, relationship between the IQs of the mothers and daughters, because it is clear that there is a tendency for mothers who have high IQs to have daughters with high IQs, and that mothers with low IQs tend to have daughters with low IQs.

The statistic that provides a precise mathematical index of the degree to which two variables are related is the correlation coefficient. A **correlation coefficient** is a numerical measure that indicates the extent of the relationship between two variables. It ranges in value from +1.00 to −1.00. A value of +1.00 would indicate that two variables had a perfect positive relationship with one another, meaning that the highest score on one variable would be associated with the highest score on the other variable, the second highest score on the first variable would be associated with

Correlation coefficient: A numerical measure that indicates the extent of the relationship between two variables.

IQ Scores of Mothers and Daughters

Mother's IQ	Daughter's IQ
135	122
128	130
125	110
120	132
114	100
110	116
102	108
96	89
90	84
86	92

FIGURE 2 In this distribution, each mother's IQ score is compared to her daughter's IQ score. Using a correlation coefficient, we can calculate the strength of the relationship between the set of pairs of scores.

the second highest score on the second variable, and so on. A value of –1.00 would indicate that there was a perfect negative relationship between the two variables; the highest score on the first variable would be associated with the lowest score on the second variable, the second highest score would be associated with the second lowest score, and so forth.

Correlation coefficients at or only slightly greater or slightly less than zero indicate that there is no relationship between the two variables. In such cases, there is no tendency for high values on one variable to be associated with either high or low values on the second variable.

Correlation coefficients that range between zero and ±1.00 reflect varying degrees of relationship between the two variables. For instance, a value of +.20 or –.20 would indicate that there was a slight relationship between the two variables, a value of around +.50 or –.50 would indicate a moderate relationship, and a value of +.80 or –.80 would indicate a relatively strong relationship. As an example, if we were to calculate the correlation of the two sets of variables in Figure 2 (most advanced calculators do the necessary calculations automatically), we would find a correlation that is quite strong: The coefficient is +.86.

It is important to note that finding a strong correlation between two variables does *not* in any way indicate that changes in one variable *cause* changes in another—only that the variables are associated with one another. Although it may seem plausible to us, for example, that it is the mother's intelligence that causes higher intelligence in a daughter, it is just as possible that a daughter's intelligence affects how the mother performs on an IQ test. (Perhaps the daughter's behavior affects the general home environment, influencing the mother's performance on IQ tests.) It is even plausible that some unmeasured—and previously unconsidered—third variable is causing both mother's and daughter's IQs to increase or decrease simultaneously. In a clear example of this possibility, even if we found that ice cream sales and rates of violent crime are positively correlated with one another (as they happen to be), we would not presume that they are causally related. In this case, it is likely that both are influenced by a third factor—the weather.

The crucial point is that even if we find a perfect correlation between two sets of variables, we will not be able to say that the two variables are linked causally—only that they are strongly related to one another (Good, 2003).

RECAP/EVALUATE/RETHINK

RECAP

How do we generalize from data?

- Inferential statistics—techniques that use data from samples to make predictions about a larger population—are useful in deciding whether differences between distributions of data are attributable to real differences or to chance variation. (p. A-11)

How can we determine the nature of a relationship, and the significance of differences, between two sets of scores?

- Measures of relationship provide a numerical index of the extent to which two variables are related. The correlation coefficient ranges in value from +1.00 to -1.00, with +1.00 indicating a perfect positive relationship and -1.00 indicating a perfect negative relationship. Correlations close to or at zero indicate there is little or no relationship between two variables. (pp. A-12–A-14)

EVALUATE

1. Researchers would like to estimate the level of stress for first-year college students for a given year at a large university. A stress index is given to a randomly assigned group of 500 first-year students. The class size is 6,000 for that year. In this example the group of 500 is known as a _____, and the entire class of first-year students is known as the _____.

2. Dr. Sanders states that the results of his experiment show a difference between the two groups, and that there is a 90 percent probability that the results are due to a true difference between the groups and not to chance. Are his results statistically significant in the way the term *significant* typically is used by psychologists?

3. A hypothetical set of data drawn from a sample of college sophomores at a university found that as the rate of caffeine consumption increases, the amount of sleep decreases. The scatterplot for these data is apt to show a _____ relationship.

4. What would the value of the correlation coefficient be for the following?
   a. A perfect negative relationship
   b. A perfect positive relationship
   c. No relationship

5. If we observed a correlation coefficient of -.90 in Question 3, we would probably be safe in saying that caffeine consumption causes lack of sleep in college students. True or false?

6. The researchers in Question 3 decide to extend the findings they obtain from their sample of college sophomores to all adults. Would you accept their generalization? Why or why not?

RETHINK

1. For many years, cigarette manufacturers argued that because the data linking smoking and disease was correlational, one could not infer that there was a causal connection between them and therefore no reason not to smoke. Did the manufacturers have a valid argument? How could you refute their argument?

KEY TERMS

population p. A-11

sample p. A-11

inferential statistics p. A-11

significant outcome p. A-12

positive relationship p. A-12

negative relationship p. A-12

correlation coefficient
    p. A-13

Looking Back

Psychology on the Web

1. Search the Web for the results of a recent survey, such as one conducted by the Gallup polling organization (www.gallup.com). Describe the results, summarizing the methodology and the sample size for the survey. How does the sample address the population to which the survey is being generalized?

Epilogue

In this Appendix, we've seen how statistical methods are used by psychologists to summarize data and support hypotheses. Return, for a moment, to the prologue about Selma Vorwerk, who immigrated to this country in the early 1900s, and use the statistical concepts that we covered to answer the following questions.

1. What was the sample size used by anti-immigrationist Lathrop Stoddard, and to what population was he generalizing?
2. What are the statistical flaws in the arguments made by critics of immigration in the early 1900s?
3. What statistical methods would you find useful in refuting Stoddard's conclusions about immigrants?

Glossary

abnormal behavior Behavior that causes people to experience distress and prevents them from functioning in their daily lives (Module 48)

absolute threshold The smallest intensity of a stimulus that must be present for the stimulus to be detected (Module 10)

achievement test A test designed to determine a person's level of knowledge in a given subject area (Module 26)

acquired immune deficiency syndrome (AIDS) A fatal, sexually transmitted infection caused by a virus that destroys the body's immune system (Module 36)

action potential An electric nerve impulse that travels through a neuron when it is set off by a "trigger," changing the neuron's charge from negative to positive (Module 7)

activation-synthesis theory J. Allan Hobson's theory that the brain produces random electrical energy during REM sleep that stimulates memories lodged in various portions of the brain (Module 14)

activity theory of aging A theory that suggests that the elderly who are more successful while aging are those who maintain the interests and activities they had during middle age (Module 41)

adaptation An adjustment in sensory capacity after prolonged exposure to unchanging stimuli (Module 10)

addictive drugs Drugs that produce a biological or psychological dependence in the user so that withdrawal from them leads to a craving for the drug that, in some cases, may be nearly irresistible (Module 16)

adolescence The developmental stage between childhood and adulthood (Module 40)

age of viability The point at which a fetus can survive if born prematurely (Module 38)

aggression The intentional injury of, or harm to, another person (Module 57)

algorithm A rule that, if applied appropriately, guarantees a solution to a problem (Module 23)

all-or-none law The rule that neurons are either on or off (Module 7)

altruism Helping behavior that is beneficial to others but clearly requires self-sacrifice (Module 57)

Alzheimer's disease A progressive brain disorder that leads to a gradual and irreversible decline in cognitive abilities (Module 22, Module 41)

amnesia Memory loss that occurs without other mental difficulties (Module 22)

anal stage According to Sigmund Freud, a stage from age 12 to 18 months to 3 years of age, in which a child's pleasure is centered on the anus (Module 42)

androgens Male sex hormones secreted by the testes (Module 34)

androgynous Characterized by gender roles that encompass psychological and behavioral traits thought typical of both sexes (Module 33)

anorexia nervosa A severe eating disorder in which people may refuse to eat while denying that their behavior and appearance—which can become skeleton-like—are unusual (Module 30)

anorgasmia (an-or-GAZ-mee-uh) A female's lack of orgasm (Module 36)

anterograde amnesia Amnesia in which memory is lost for events that follow an injury (Module 22)

antianxiety drugs Drugs that reduce the level of anxiety a person experiences, essentially by reducing excitability and increasing feelings of well-being (Module 53)

antidepressant drugs Medications that improve a severely depressed patient's mood and feeling of well-being (Module 53)

antipsychotic drugs Drugs that temporarily reduce psychotic symptoms such as agitation, hallucinations, and delusions (Module 53)

antisocial personality disorder A disorder in which individuals show no regard for the moral and ethical rules of society or the rights of others (Module 49)

anxiety disorder The occurrence of anxiety without an obvious external cause, affecting daily functioning (Module 49)

aptitude test A test designed to predict a person's ability in a particular area or line of work (Module 26)

archetypes According to Carl Jung, universal symbolic representations of a particular person, object, or experience (such as good and evil) (Module 42)

archival research Research in which existing data, such as census documents, college records, and newspaper clippings, are examined to test a hypothesis (Module 5)

arousal approaches to motivation The belief that we try to maintain certain levels of stimulation and activity, increasing or reducing them as necessary (Module 29)

association areas One of the major regions of the cerebral cortex; the site of the higher mental processes, such as thought, language, memory, and speech (Module 9)

assumed-similarity bias The tendency to think of people as being similar to oneself, even when meeting them for the first time (Module 54)

attachment The positive emotional bond that develops between a child and a particular individual (Module 39)

attention deficit hyperactivity disorder (ADHD) A disorder marked by inattention, impulsiveness, a low tolerance for frustration, and a great deal of inappropriate activity (Module 49)

attitudes Evaluations of a particular person, behavior, belief, or concept (Module 54)

attribution theory The theory of personality that seeks to explain how we decide, on the basis of samples of an individual's behavior, what the specific causes of that person's behavior are (Module 54)

authoritarian parents Parents who are rigid and punitive and value unquestioning obedience from their children (Module 39)

authoritative parents Parents who are firm, set clear limits, reason with their children, and explain things to them (Module 39)

autobiographical memories Our recollections of circumstances and episodes from our own lives (Module 20)

autonomic division The part of the peripheral nervous system that controls involuntary movement of the heart, glands, lungs, and other organs (Module 8)

autonomy-versus-shame-and-doubt stage The period which, according to Erik Erikson, toddlers (ages 1½ to 3 years) develop independence and autonomy if exploration and freedom are encouraged, or shame and self-doubt if they are restricted and overprotected (Module 39)

aversive conditioning A form of therapy that reduces the frequency of undesired behavior by pairing an aversive, unpleasant stimulus with undesired behavior (Module 51)

axon The part of the neuron that carries messages destined for other neurons (Module 7)

babble Meaningless speechlike sounds made by children from around the age of 3 months through 1 year (Module 25)

background stressors ("daily hassles") Everyday annoyances, such as being stuck in traffic, that cause minor irritations and may have long-term ill effects if they continue or are compounded by other stressful events (Module 45)

basilar membrane A vibrating structure that runs through the center of the cochlea, diving it into an upper chamber and a lower chamber and containing sense receptors for sound (Module 12)

behavior modification A formalized technique for promoting the frequency of desirable behaviors and decreasing the incidence of unwanted ones (Module 19)

behavioral assessment Direct measures of an individual's behavior used to describe personality characteristics (Module 44)

behavioral genetics The study of the effects of heredity on behavior (Module 8)

behavioral neuroscientists (or biopsychologists) Psychologists who specialize in considering the ways in which the biological structures and functions of the body affect behavior (Module 7)

behavioral perspective The approach that suggests that observable, measurable behavior should be the focus of study (Module 2)

behavioral perspective on psychological disorders The perspective that looks at the behavior itself as the problem (Module 48)

behavioral treatment approaches Treatment approaches that build on the basic processes of learning, such as reinforcement and extinction, and assume that normal and abnormal behavior are both learned (Module 51)

biofeedback A procedure in which a person learns to control through conscious thought internal physiological processes such as blood pressure, heart and respiration rate, skin temperature, sweating, and the constriction of particular muscles (Module 9)

biological and evolutionary approaches to personality Theories that suggest that important components of personality are inherited (Module 43)

biomedical therapy Therapy that relies on drugs and other medical procedures to improve psychological functioning (Module 51)

biopsychologists See behavioral neuroscientists (Module 7)

bipolar disorder A disorder in which a person alternates between periods of euphoric feelings of mania and periods of depression (Module 49)

bisexuals Persons who are sexually attracted to people of the same sex and the other sex (Module 35)

borderline personality disorder A disorder in which individuals have difficulty developing a secure sense of who they are (Module 49)

bottom-up processing Perception that consists of the progression of recognizing and processing information from individual components of a stimuli and moving to the perception of the whole (Module 13)

bulimia A eating disorder in which a person binges on incredibly large quantities of food (Module 30)

Cannon-Bard theory of emotion The belief that both physiological arousal and emotional experience are produced simultaneously by the same nerve stimulus (Module 31)

case study An in-depth, intensive investigation of an individual or small group of people (Module 5)

cataclysmic events Strong stressors that occur suddenly, affecting many people at once (e.g., natural disasters) (Module 45)

catharsis The process of discharging built-up aggressive energy (Module 57)

central core The "old brain," which controls basic functions such as eating and sleeping and is common to all vertebrates (Module 9)

central nervous system (CNS) The part of the nervous system that includes the brain and spinal cord (Module 8)

central route processing Message interpretation characterized by thoughtful consideration of the issues and arguments used to persuade (Module 54)

central tendency An index of the central location within a distribution of scores; the most representative score in a distribution of scores (the mean, median, and mode are measures of central tendency) (Module 58)

central traits The major traits considered in forming impressions of others (Module 54)

cerebellum (ser uh BELL um) The part of the brain that controls bodily balance (Module 9)

cerebral cortex The "new brain," responsible for the most sophisticated information processing in the brain; contains four lobes (Module 9)

chromosomes Rod-shaped structures that contain all basic hereditary information (Module 38)

chunk A meaningful grouping of stimuli that can be stored as a unit in short-term memory (Module 20)

circadian rhythms Biological processes that occur regularly on approximately a twenty-four-hour cycle (Module 14)

classical conditioning A type of learning in which a neutral stimulus comes to bring about a response after it is paired with a stimulus that naturally brings about that response (Module 17)

cochlea (KOKE lee uh) A coiled tube in the ear filled with fluid that vibrates in response to sound (Module 12)

cognitive approaches to motivation Theories suggesting that motivation is a product of people's thoughts and expectations—their cognitions (Module 29)

cognitive development The process by which a child's understanding of the world changes as a function of age and experience (Module 39)

cognitive dissonance The conflict that occurs when a person holds two contradictory attitudes or thoughts (referred to as *cognitions*) (Module 54)

cognitive learning theory An approach to the study of learning that focuses on the thought processes that underlie learning (Module 19)

cognitive perspective The approach that focuses on how people think, understand, and know about the world (Module 2)

cognitive perspective on psychological disorders The perspective that suggests that people's thoughts and beliefs are a central component of abnormal behavior (Module 48)

cognitive psychology The branch of psychology that focuses on the study of higher mental processes, including thinking, language, memory, problem solving, knowing, reasoning, judging, and decision making (Module 23)

cognitive treatment approaches Treatment approaches that teach people to think in more adaptive ways by changing their dysfunctional cognitions about the world and themselves (Module 51)

cognitive-behavioral approach A treatment approach that incorporates basic principles of learning to change the way people think (Module 51)

collective unconscious According to Carl Jung, a common set of ideas, feelings, images, and symbols that we inherit from our ancestors, the whole human race, and even nonhuman ancestors from the distant past (Module 42)

community psychology A branch of psychology that focuses on the prevention and minimization of psychological disorders in the community (Module 53)

companionate love The strong affection we have for those with whom our lives are deeply involved (Module 57)

compliance Behavior that occurs in response to direct social pressure (Module 55)

compulsion An irresistible urge to carry out some act that seems strange or unreasonable (Module 49)

concepts Categorizations of objects, events, or people that share common properties (Module 23)

concrete operational stage According to Jean Piaget, the period from 7 to 12 years of age that is characterized by logical thought and a loss of egocentrism (Module 39)

conditioned response (CR) A response that, after conditioning, follows a previously neutral stimulus (e.g., salivation at the ringing of a bell) (Module 17)

conditioned stimulus (CS) A once-neutral stimulus that has been paired with an unconditioned stimulus to bring about a response formerly caused only by the unconditioned stimulus (Module 17)

cones Cone-shaped, light-sensitive receptor cells in the retina that are responsible for sharp focus and color perception, particularly in bright light (Module 11)

confirmation bias The tendency to favor information that supports one's initial hypotheses and ignore contradictory information that supports alternative hypotheses or solutions (Module 24)

conformity A change in behavior or attitudes brought about by a desire to follow the beliefs or standards of other people (Module 55)

consciousness The awareness of sensations, thoughts, and feelings being experienced at a given moment (Module 14)

constructive processes Processes in which memories are influenced by the meaning we give to events (Module 21)

continuous reinforcement schedule Reinforcing of a behavior every time it occurs (Module 18)

control group A group participating in an experiment that receives no treatment (Module 5)

convergent thinking The ability to produce responses that are based primarily on knowledge and logic (Module 24)

conversion disorder A major somatoform disorder that involves an actual physical disturbance, such as the inability to use a sensory organ or the complete or partial inability to move an arm or a leg (Module 49)

coping The efforts to control, reduce, or learn to tolerate the threats that lead to stress (Module 45)

correlation coefficient A numerical measure that indicates the extent of the relationship between two variables (Module 60)

correlational research Research in which the relationship between two sets of variables is examined to determine whether they are associated, or "correlated" (Module 5)

creativity The ability to generate original ideas or solve problems in novel ways (Module 24)

cross-sectional research A research method that compares people of different ages at the same point in time (Module 37)

crystallized intelligence The accumulation of information, skills, and strategies that are learned through experience and can be applied in problem-solving situations (Module 26)

cue-dependent forgetting Forgetting that occurs when there are insufficient retrieval cues to rekindle information that is in memory (Module 22)

culture-fair IQ test A test that does not discriminate against the members of any minority group (Module 28)

daily hassles *See* background stressors (Module 45)

date rape Rape in which the rapist is either a date or a romantic acquaintance (Module 36)

daydreams Fantasies that people construct while awake (Module 14)

decay The loss of information in memory through its nonuse (Module 22)

declarative memory Memory for factual information, names, faces, dates, and the like (Module 20)

defense mechanisms In Freudian theory, unconscious strategies that people use to reduce anxiety by concealing the source of the anxiety from themselves and others (Module 42)

deinstitutionalization The transfer of former mental patients from institutions to the community (Module 53)

dendrite A cluster of fibers at one end of a neuron that receive messages from other neurons (Module 7)

dependent variable The variable that is measured and is expected to change as a result of changes caused by the experimenter's manipulation of the independent variable (Module 5)

depressants Drugs that slow down the nervous system (Module 16)

depth perception The ability to view the world in three dimensions and to perceive distance (Module 13)

descriptive research An approach to research designed to systematically investigate a person, group, or patterns of behavior (Module 5)

descriptive statistics The branch of statistics that provides a means of summarizing data (Module 58)

determinism The idea that people's behavior is produced primarily by factors outside of their willful control (Module 3)

developmental psychology The branch of psychology that studies the patterns of growth and change that occur throughout life (Module 37)

Diagnostic and Statistical Manual of Mental Disorders, Fourth Edition, Text Revision (DSM-IV-TR) A system, devised by the American Psychiatric Association, used by most professionals to diagnose and classify abnormal behavior (Module 48)

dialectical behavior therapy A form of treatment in which the focus is on getting people to accept who they are, regardless of whether it matches their ideal (Module 51)

difference threshold (just noticeable difference) The smallest level of added or reduced stimulation required to sense that a change in stimulation has occurred (Module 10)

diffusion of responsibility The tendency for people to feel that responsibility for acting is shared, or diffused, among those present (Module 57)

discrimination Behavior directed toward individuals on the basis of their membership in a particular group (Module 56)

disengagement theory of aging A theory that suggests that aging produces a gradual withdrawal from the world on physical, psychological, and social levels (Module 41)

display rules Guidelines that govern the appropriateness of showing emotion nonverbally (Module 32)

dispositional causes (of behavior) Perceived causes of behavior that are based on internal traits or personality factors (Module 54)

dissociative amnesia A disorder in which a significant, selective memory loss occurs (Module 49)

dissociative disorders Psychological dysfunctions characterized by the separation of critical personality facets that are normally integrated, allowing stress avoidance through escape (Module 49)

dissociative fugue A form of amnesia in which the individual leaves home and sometimes assumes a new identity (Module 49)

dissociative identity disorder (or multiple personality disorder) A disorder in which a person displays characteristics of two or more distinct personalities (Module 49)

divergent thinking The ability to generate unusual, yet nonetheless appropriate, responses to problems or questions (Module 24)

double standard The view that premarital sex is permissible for males but not for females (Module 35)

Down syndrome A cause of mental retardation resulting from the presence of an extra chromosome (Module 28)

dreams-for-survival theory The theory suggesting that dreams permit information that is critical for our daily survival to be reconsidered and reprocessed during sleep (Module 14)

drive Motivational tension, or arousal, that energizes behavior to fulfill a need (Module 29)

drive-reduction approaches to motivation Theories suggesting that a lack of a basic biological requirement such as water produces a drive to obtain that requirement (in this case, the thirst drive) (Module 29)

drug therapy Control of psychological disorders through the use of drugs (Module 53)

eardrum The part of the ear that vibrates when sound hits it (Module 12)

eclectic approach to therapy An approach to therapy that uses techniques taken from a variety of treatment methods, rather than just one (Module 52)

ego The part of the personality that provides a buffer between the id and the outside world (Module 42)

egocentric thought A way of thinking in which a child views the world entirely from his or her own perspective (Module 39)

ego-integrity-versus-despair stage According to Erik Erikson, a period from late adulthood until death during which we review life's accomplishments and failures (Module 40)

electroconvulsive therapy (ECT) A procedure in which an electric current of 70 to 150 volts is briefly administered to a patient's head, causing a loss of consciousness and often causing seizures (Module 53)

embryo A developed zygote that has a heart, a brain, and other organs (Module 38)

emotional intelligence The set of skills that underlie the accurate assessment, evaluation, expression, and regulation of emotions (Module 26)

emotions Feelings that generally have both physiological and cognitive elements and that influence behavior (Module 31)

endocrine system A chemical communication network that sends messages throughout the body via the bloodstream (Module 8)

episodic memory Memory for events that occur in a particular time, place, or context (Module 20)

erectile dysfunction The inability of a male to achieve or maintain an erection (Module 36)

erogenous zones Areas of the body that are particularly sensitive because of the presence of an unusually rich array of nerve receptors (Module 34)

estrogens Class of female sex hormones (Module 34)

evolutionary psychology The branch of psychology that seeks to identify behavior patterns that are a result of our genetic inheritance from our ancestors (Module 8)

excitatory message A chemical message that makes it more likely that a receiving neuron will fire and an action potential will travel down its axon (Module 7)

experiment The investigation of the relationship between two (or more) variables by deliberately producing a change in one variable in a situation and observing the effects of that change on other aspects of the situation (Module 5)

experimental bias Factors that distort how the independent variable affects the dependent variable in an experiment (Module 6)

experimental group Any group participating in an experiment that receives a treatment (Module 5)

experimental manipulation The change that an experimenter deliberately produces in a situation (Module 5)

explicit memory Intentional or conscious recollection of information (Module 20)

extinction A basic phenomenon of learning that occurs when a previously conditioned response decreases in frequency and eventually disappears (Module 17)

extramarital sex Sexual activity between a married person and someone who is not his or her spouse (Module 35)

facial-affect program Activation of a set of nerve impulses that make the face display the appropriate expression (Module 32)

facial-feedback hypothesis The hypothesis that facial expressions not only reflect emotional experience but also help determine how people experience and label emotions (Module 32)

familial retardation Mental retardation in which no apparent biological defect exists, but there is a history of retardation in the family (Module 28)

family therapy An approach that focuses on the family and its dynamics (Module 52)

feature analysis An approach to perception suggesting that we perceive a shape, pattern, object, or scene through the reaction of specific neurons to the individual elements that make up the stimulus (Module 13)

feature detection The activation of neurons in the cortex by visual stimuli of specific shapes or patterns (Module 11)

fetal alcohol syndrome The most common cause of mental retardation in newborns, occurring when the mother uses alcohol during pregnancy (Module 28)

fetus A developing individual, from eight weeks after conception until birth (Module 38)

fixations Conflicts or concerns that persist beyond the developmental period in which they first occur (Module 42)

fixed-interval schedule A schedule that provides reinforcement for a response only if a fixed time period has elapsed, making overall rates of response relatively low (Module 18)

fixed-ratio schedule A schedule by which reinforcement is given only after a specific number of responses are made (Module 18)

flashbulb memories Memories centered on a specific, important, or surprising event that are so vivid it is as if they represented a snapshot of the event (Module 21)

fluid intelligence Intelligence that reflects information-processing capabilities, reasoning, and memory (Module 26)

formal operational stage According to Jean Piaget, the period from age 12 to adulthood that is characterized by abstract thought (Module 39)

free will The idea that behavior is caused primarily by choices that are made freely by the individual (Module 3)

frequency distribution An arrangement of scores from a sample that indicates how often a particular score is present (Module 58)

frequency theory of hearing The theory that the entire basilar membrane acts like a microphone, vibrating as a whole in response to sound (Module 12)

frustration The thwarting or blocking of some ongoing, goal-directed behavior (Module 57)

functional fixedness The tendency to think of an object only in terms of its typical use (Module 24)

functionalism An early approach to psychology that concentrated on what the mind does—the functions of mental activity—and the role of behavior in allowing people to adapt to their environments (Module 2)

fundamental attribution error A tendency to overattribute others' behavior to dispositional causes and the corresponding minimization of the importance of situational causes (Module 54)

g or g-factor The single, general factor for mental ability assumed to underlie intelligence in some early theories of intelligence (Module 26)

gate-control theory of pain The theory that particular nerve receptors lead to specific areas of the brain related to pain (Module 12)

gender The perception of being male or female (Module 33)

gender roles The set of expectations, defined by a particular society, that indicate what is appropriate behavior for men and women (Module 33)

gender schema A mental framework that organizes and guides a child's understanding of information relevant to gender (Module 33)

general adaptation syndrome (GAS) A theory developed by Hans Selye that suggests that a person's response to a stressor consists of three stages: alarm and mobilization, resistance, and exhaustion (Module 45)

generalized anxiety disorder The experience of long-term, persistent anxiety and worry (Module 49)

generativity-versus-stagnation stage According to Erik Erikson, a period in middle adulthood during which we take stock of our contributions to family and society (Module 40)

genes The parts of the chromosomes through which genetic information is transmitted (Module 38)

genetic preprogramming theories of aging Theories that suggest that human cells have a built-in time limit to their reproduction, and that after a certain time they are no longer able to divide (Module 41)

genital stage According to Freud, the period from puberty until death, marked by mature sexual behavior (that is, sexual intercourse) (Module 42)

genitals The male and female sex organs (Module 34)

gestalt (geh SHTALLT) laws of organization A series of principles that describe how we organize bits and pieces of information into meaningful wholes (Module 13)

gestalt psychology An approach to psychology that focuses on the organization of perception and thinking in a "whole" sense rather than on the individual elements of perception (Module 2)

gestalt therapy A treatment approach in which people are led to examine their earlier experiences and complete any "unfinished business" from their past that may still affect and color present-day relationships (Module 52)

grammar The system of rules that determine how our thoughts can be expressed (Module 25)

group therapy Therapy in which people meet with a therapist to discuss problems with a group (Module 52)

groupthink A type of thinking in which group members share such a strong motivation to achieve consensus that they lose the ability to critically evaluate alternative points of view (Module 55)

habituation The decrease in response to a stimulus that occurs after repeated presentations of the same stimulus (Module 39)

hair cells Tiny cells covering the basilar membrane that, when bent by vibrations entering the cochlea, transmit neural messages to the brain (Module 12)

hallucinogen A drug that is capable of producing hallucinations, or changes in the perceptual process (Module 16)

halo effect A phenomenon in which an initial understanding that a person has positive traits is used to infer other uniformly positive characteristics (Module 54)

hardiness A personality characteristic associated with a lower rate of stress-related illness, consisting of three components: commitment, challenge, and control (Module 45)

health psychology The branch of psychology that investigates the psychological factors related to wellness and illness, including the prevention, diagnosis, and treatment of medical problems (Module 45)

hemispheres Symmetrical left and right halves of the brain that control the side of the body opposite to their location (Module 9)

heritability A measure of the degree to which a characteristic is related to genetic, inherited factors (Module 28)

heterosexuality Sexual attraction and behavior directed toward the other sex (Module 35)

heuristic A cognitive shortcut that may lead to a solution (Module 23)

histogram Bar graph (Module 58)

homeostasis The body's tendency to maintain a steady internal state (Module 29)

homosexuals Persons who are sexually attracted to members of their own sex (Module 35)

hormones Chemicals that circulate through the blood and regulate the functioning or growth of the body (Module 8)

humanistic approaches to personality Theories that emphasize people's innate goodness and desire to achieve higher levels of functioning (Module 43)

humanistic perspective The approach that suggests that all individuals naturally strive to grow, develop, and be in control of their lives and behavior (Module 2)

humanistic perspective on psychological disorders The perspective that emphasizes the responsibility people have for their own behavior, even when such behavior is abnormal (Module 48)

humanistic therapy Therapy in which the underlying rationale is that people have control of their behavior, can make choices about their lives, and are essentially responsible for solving their own problems (Module 52)

hypnosis A trancelike state of heightened susceptibility to the suggestions of others (Module 15)

hypochondriasis A disorder in which people have a constant fear of illness and a preoccupation with their health (Module 49)

hypothalamus A tiny part of the brain, located below the thalamus, that maintains homeostasis and produces and regulates vital behavior, such as eating, drinking, and sexual behavior (Module 9)

hypothesis A prediction, stemming from a theory, stated in way that allows it to be tested (Module 4)

id The raw, unorganized, inborn part of personality whose sole purpose is to reduce tension created by primitive drives related to hunger, sex, aggression, and irrational impulses (Module 42)

identical twins Twins who are genetically identical (Module 37)

identification The process of wanting to be like another person as much as possible, imitating that person's behavior and adopting similar beliefs and values (Module 42)

identity The distinguishing character of the individual: who each of us is, what our roles are, and what we are capable of (Module 40)

identity-versus-role-confusion stage According to Erik Erikson, a time in adolescence of major testing to determine one's unique qualities (Module 40)

implicit memory Memories of which people are not consciously aware, but which can affect subsequent performance and behavior (Module 20)

incentive approaches to motivation Theories suggesting that motivation stems from the desire to obtain valued external goals, or incentives (Module 29)

independent variable The variable that is manipulated by an experimenter (Module 5)

industrial-organizational (I/O) psychology The branch of psychology focusing on work and job-related issues, including worker motivation, satisfaction, safety, and productivity (Module 55)

industry-versus-inferiority stage According to Erik Erikson, the last stage of childhood, during which children age 6 to 12 years may develop positive social interactions with others or may feel inadequate and become less sociable (Module 39)

inferential statistics The branch of statistics that uses data from samples to make predictions about the larger population from which the sample is drawn (Module 60)

inferiority complex According to Alfred Adler, a problem affecting adults who have not been able to overcome the feelings of inferiority that they developed as children, when they were small and limited in their knowledge about the world (Module 42)

information processing The way in which people take in, use, and store information (Module 39)

informed consent A document signed by participants affirming that they have been told the basic outlines of the study and are aware of what their participation will involve (Module 6)

inhibited ejaculation The inability of a male to ejaculate when he wants to, if at all (Module 36)

inhibited sexual desire A sexual dysfunction in which the motivation for sexual activity is restrained or lacking entirely (Module 36)

inhibitory message A chemical message that prevents or decreases the likelihood that a receiving neuron will fire (Module 7)

initiative-versus-guilt stage According to Erik Erikson, the period during which children ages 3 to 6 years experience conflict between independence of action and the sometimes negative results of that action (Module 30)

insight A sudden awareness of the relationships among various elements that had previously appeared to be independent of one another (Module 24)

instincts Inborn patterns of behavior that are biologically determined rather than learned (Module 29)

intelligence The capacity to understand the world, think rationally, and use resources effectively when faced with challenges (Module 26)

intelligence quotient (IQ) A score that takes into account an individual's mental and chronological ages (Module 26)

intelligence tests Tests devised to quantify a person's level of intelligence (Module 26)

interference The phenomenon by which information in memory disrupts the recall of other information (Module 22)

interneurons Neurons that connect sensory and motor neurons, carrying messages between the two (Module 8)

interpersonal attraction (or close relationship) Positive feelings for others; liking and loving (Module 57)

interpersonal therapy (IPT) Short-term therapy that focuses on the context of current social relationships (Module 52)

intimacy-versus-isolation stage According to Erik Erikson, a period during early adulthood that focuses on developing close relationships (Module 40)

introspection A procedure used to study the structure of the mind in which subjects are asked to describe in detail what they are experiencing when they are exposed to a stimulus (Module 2)

James-Lange theory of emotion The belief that emotional experience is a reaction to bodily events occurring as a result of an external situation ("I feel sad because I am crying") (Module 31)

just noticeable difference *See* difference threshold (Module 10)

Korsakoff's syndrome A disease that afflicts long-term alcoholics, leaving some

abilities intact, but including hallucinations and a tendency to repeat the same story (Module 22)

language The communication of information through symbols arranged according to systematic rules (Module 25)

language-acquisition device A neural system of the brain hypothesized by Noam Chomsky to permit understanding of language (Module 25)

latency period According to Sigmund Freud, the period between the phallic stage and puberty during which children's sexual concerns are temporarily put aside (Module 42)

latent content of dreams According to Sigmund Freud, the "disguised" meaning of dreams, hidden by more obvious subjects (Module 14)

latent learning Learning in which a new behavior is acquired but is not demonstrated until some incentive is provided for displaying it (Module 19)

lateralization The dominance of one hemisphere of the brain in specific functions, such as language (Module 9)

learned helplessness A state in which people conclude that unpleasant or aversive stimuli cannot be controlled—a view of the world that becomes so ingrained that they cease trying to remedy the aversive circumstances, even if they actually can exert some influence (Module 45)

learning A relatively permanent change in behavior brought about by experience (Module 17)

learning-theory approach to language development The theory suggesting that language acquisition follows the principles of reinforcement and conditioning (Module 25)

levels-of-processing theory The theory of memory that emphasizes the degree to which new material is mentally analyzed (Module 21)

life review The process by which people examine and evaluate their lives (Module 41)

limbic system The part of the brain that controls eating, aggression, and reproduction (Module 9)

linguistic-relativity hypothesis The notion that language shapes and may determine the way people in a particular culture perceive and understand the world (Module 25)

lithium A drug made up of mineral salts that is used to treat and prevent manic episodes of bipolar disorder (Module 53)

lobes The four major sections of the cerebral cortex: frontal, parietal, temporal, and occipital (Module 9)

longitudinal research A research method that investigates behavior as participants age (Module 37)

long-term memory Memory that stores information on a relatively permanent basis, although it may be difficult to retrieve (Module 20)

major depression A severe form of depression that interferes with concentration, decision making, and sociability (Module 49)

mania An extended state of intense, wild elation (Module 49)

manifest content of dreams According to Sigmund Freud, the apparent story line of dreams (Module 14)

masturbation Sexual self-stimulation (Module 35)

mean The average of all scores, arrived at by adding scores together and dividing by the number of scores (Module 58)

means-ends analysis Repeated testing for differences between the desired outcome and what currently exists (Module 24)

median The point in a distribution of scores that divides the distribution exactly in half when the scores are listed in numerical order (Module 58)

medical perspective on psychological disorders The perspective that suggests that when an individual displays symptoms of abnormal behavior, the root cause will be found in a physical examination of the individual, which may reveal a hormonal imbalance, a chemical deficiency, or a brain injury (Module 48)

meditation A learned technique for refocusing attention that brings about an altered state of consciousness (Module 15)

memory The process by which we encode, store, and retrieve information (Module 20)

memory trace A physical change in the brain that occurs when new material is learned (Module 22)

menopause The period during which women stop menstruating and are no longer fertile (Module 41)

mental age The average age of individuals who achieve a particular level of performance on a test (Module 26)

mental images Representations in the mind that resemble the object or event being represented (Module 23)

mental retardation A condition characterized by significant limitations both in intellectual functioning and in conceptual, social, and practical adaptive skills (Module 27)

mental set The tendency for old patterns of problem solving to persist (Module 24)

metabolism The rate at which food is converted to energy and expended by the body (Module 30)

metacognition An awareness and understanding of one's own cognitive processes (Module 39)

Minnesota Multiphasic Personality Inventory-2 (MMPI-2) A widely used self-report test that identifies people with psychological difficulties and is employed to predict some everyday behaviors (Module 44)

mode The most frequently occurring score in a set of scores (Module 58)

mood disorder An emotional disturbance that is strong enough to intrude on everyday living (Module 49)

motivation The factors that direct and energize the behavior of humans and other organisms (Module 29)

motor area The part of the cortex that is largely responsible for the body's voluntary movement (Module 9)

motor (efferent) neurons Neurons that communicate information from the nervous system to muscles and glands (Module 8)

multiple personality disorder See dissociative identity disorder (Module 49)

myelin sheath A protective coat of fat and protein that wraps around the neuron (Module 7)

narcissistic personality disorder A personality disturbance characterized by an exaggerated sense of self-importance (Module 49)

narcotics Drugs that increase relaxation and relieve pain and anxiety (Module 16)

naturalistic observation Research in which an investigator simply observes some naturally occurring behavior and does not make a change in the situation (Module 5)

nature-nurture issue The issue of the degree to which environment and heredity influence behavior (Module 37)

need for achievement A stable, learned characteristic in which a person obtains satisfaction by striving for and attaining a level of excellence (Module 30)

need for affiliation An interest in establishing and maintaining relationships with other people (Module 30)

need for power A tendency to seek impact, control, or influence over others, and to be seen as a powerful individual (Module 30)

negative reinforcer An unpleasant stimulus whose *removal* leads to an increase in the probability that a preceding response will be repeated in the future (Module 18)

negative relationship A relationship established by data that shows high values of one variable corresponding with low values of the other (Module 60)

neo-Freudian psychoanalysts Psychoanalysts who were trained in traditional Freudian theory but who later rejected some of its major points (Module 42)

neonate A newborn child (Module 39)

neurons Nerve cells, the basic elements of the nervous system (Module 7)

neuroplasticity Changes in the brain that occur throughout the life span relating to the addition of new neurons, new interconnections between neurons, and the reorganization of information-processing areas (Module 9)

neuroscience perspective The approach that views behavior from the perspective of the brain, the nervous system, and other biological functions (Module 2)

neurotransmitters Chemicals that carry messages across the synapse to the dendrite (and sometimes the cell body) of a receiver neuron (Module 7)

neutral stimulus A stimulus that, before conditioning, does not naturally bring about the response of interest (Module 17)

normal distribution A distribution of scores that produces a symmetrical, bell-shaped curve in which the right half mirrors the left half and in which the mean, median, and mode all have the same value (Module 58)

norms Standards of test performance that permit the comparison of one person's score on a test with the scores

of other individuals who have taken the same test (Module 26)

obedience A change in behavior in response to the commands of others (Module 55)

obesity Body weight that is more than 20 percent above the average weight for a person of a particular height (Module 30)

object permanence The awareness that objects—and people—continue to exist even if they are out of sight (Module 39)

observational learning Learning by observing the behavior of another person, or model (Module 19)

obsession A persistent, unwanted thought or idea that keeps recurring (Module 49)

obsessive-compulsive disorder A disorder characterized by obsessions or compulsions (Module 49)

Oedipal conflict A child's sexual interest in his or her opposite-sex parent, typically resolved through identification with the same-sex parent (Module 42)

operant conditioning Learning in which a voluntary response is strengthened or weakened, depending on its favorable or unfavorable consequences (Module 18)

operational definition The translation of a hypothesis into specific, testable procedures that can be measured and observed (Module 5)

opponent-process theory of color vision The theory that receptor cells for color are linked in pairs, working in opposition to each other (Module 11)

optic nerve A bundle of ganglion axons that carry visual information to the brain (Module 11)

oral stage According to Sigmund Freud, a stage from birth to age 12 to 18 months, in which an infant's center of pleasure is the mouth (Module 42)

orgasm The peak of sexual excitement, during which rhythmic muscular contractions occur in the genitals (Module 34)

otoliths Tiny, motion-sensitive crystals within the semicircular canals that sense body acceleration (Module 12)

overgeneralization The phenomenon by which children apply language rules even when the application results in an error (Module 25)

ovulation The point at which an egg is released from the ovaries (Module 34)

panic disorder Anxiety disorder that takes the form of panic attacks lasting from a few seconds to as long as several hours (Module 49)

parasympathetic division The part of the autonomic division of the nervous system that acts to calm the body after an emergency [or a stressful situation] has ended (Module 8)

partial (or intermittent) reinforcement schedule Reinforcing of a behavior some but not all of the time (Module 18)

passionate (or romantic) love A state of intense absorption in someone that includes intense physiological arousal, psychological interest, and caring for the needs of another (Module 57)

perception The sorting out, interpretation, analysis, and integration of stimuli by the sense organs and brain (Module 10)

peripheral nervous system The part of the nervous system that includes the autonomic and somatic subdivisions; made up of neurons with long axons and dendrites, it branches out from the spinal cord and brain and reaches the extremities of the body (Module 8)

peripheral route processing Message interpretation characterized by consideration of the source and related general information rather than of the message itself (Module 54)

permissive parents Parents who give their children relaxed or inconsistent direction and, although warm, require little of them (Module 39)

personal stressors Major life events, such as the death of a family member, that have immediate consequences that generally fade with time (Module 45)

personality The pattern of enduring characteristics that produce consistency and individuality in a given person (Module 42)

personality disorder A disorder characterized by a set of inflexible, maladaptive behavior patterns that keep a person from functioning appropriately in society (Module 49)

person-centered therapy Therapy in which the goal is to reach one's potential for self-actualization (Module 52)

phallic stage According to Sigmund Freud, a period beginning around age 3 during which a child's pleasure focuses on the genitals (Module 42)

phobias Intense, irrational fears of specific objects or situations (Module 49)

phonemes The smallest units of speech that affect meaning (Module 25)

phonology The study of the smallest units of speech, called phonemes (Module 25)

pituitary gland The major component of the endocrine system, or "master gland," which secretes hormones that control growth and other parts of the endocrine system (Module 8)

place theory of hearing The theory that different areas of the basilar membrane respond to different frequencies (Module 12)

placebo A false treatment, such as a pill, "drug," or other substance, without any significant chemical properties or active ingredient (Module 6)

plateau phase The period in which the maximum level of arousal is attained, the penis and clitoris swell with blood, and the body prepares for orgasm (Module 34)

population All the members of a group of interest (Module 60)

positive reinforcer A stimulus added to the environment that brings about an increase in a preceding response (Module 18)

positive relationship A relationship established by data that shows high values of one variable corresponding with high values of another, and low values of the first variable corresponding with low values of the other (Module 60)

posttraumatic stress disorder (PTSD) A phenomenon in which victims of major catastrophes or strong personal stressors feel long-lasting effects that may include re-experiencing the event in vivid flashbacks or dreams (Module 45)

practical intelligence According to Robert Sternberg, intelligence related to overall success in living (Module 26)

prejudice A negative (or positive) evaluation of a particular group and its members (Module 56)

premature ejaculation The inability of a male to delay orgasm as long as he wishes (Module 36)

preoperational stage According to Jean Piaget, the period from 2 to 7 years of age that is characterized by language development (Module 39)

priming A phenomenon in which exposure to a word or concept (called a *prime*) later makes it easier to recall related information, even when there is no conscious memory of the word or concept (Module 20)

principle of conservation The knowledge that quantity is unrelated to the arrangement and physical appearance of objects (Module 39)

proactive interference Interference in which information learned earlier disrupts the recall of newer information (Module 22)

procedural memory Memory for skills and habits, such as riding a bike or hitting a baseball, sometimes referred to as *nondeclarative memory* (Module 20)

progesterone A female sex hormone secreted by the ovaries (Module 34)

projective personality tests A test in which a person is shown an ambiguous stimulus and asked to describe it or tell a story about it (Module 44)

prosocial behavior Helping behavior (Module 57)

prototypes Typical, highly representative samples of a concept (Module 23)

psychoactive drugs Drugs that influence a person's emotions, perceptions, and behavior (Module 16)

psychoanalysis Freudian psychotherapy in which the goal is to release hidden unconscious thoughts and feelings in order to reduce their power in controlling behavior (Module 51)

psychoanalytic perspective on psychological disorders The perspective that suggests that abnormal behavior stems from childhood conflicts over opposing wishes regarding sex and aggression (Module 48)

psychoanalytic theory Sigmund Freud's theory that unconscious forces act as determinants of personality (Module 43)

psychodynamic approaches to personality Approaches that assume that personality is motivated by inner forces and conflicts about which people have little awareness and over which they have no control (Module 42)

psychodynamic perspective The approach based on the view that behavior is motivated by unconscious inner forces over which the individual has little control (Module 2)

psychodynamic therapy Therapy that seeks to bring unresolved past conflicts and unacceptable impulses from the unconscious into the conscious, where patients may deal with the problems more effectively (Module 51)

psychological tests Standard measures devised to assess behavior objectively; used by psychologists to help people make decisions about their lives and understand more about themselves (Module 44)

psychology The scientific study of behavior and mental processes (Module 1)

psychoneuroimmunology (PNI) The study of the relationship among psychological factors, the immune system, and the brain (Module 45)

psychophysics The study of the relationship between the physical aspects of stimuli and our psychological experience of them (Module 10)

psychophysiological disorders Medical problems influenced by an interaction of psychological, emotional, and physical difficulties (Module 45)

psychosexual stages Developmental periods that children pass through during which they encounter conflicts between the demands of society and their own sexual urges (Module 42)

psychosocial development Development of individuals' interactions and understanding of each other and of their knowledge and understanding of themselves as members of society (Module 39)

psychosurgery Brain surgery once used to reduce the symptoms of mental disorder but rarely used today (Module 53)

psychotherapy Treatment in which a trained professional—a therapist—uses psychological techniques to help a person overcome psychological difficulties and disorders, resolve problems in living, or bring about personal growth (Module 51)

puberty The period at which maturation of the sexual organs occurs, beginning at about age 11 or 12 for girls and 13 or 14 for boys (Module 40)

punishment A stimulus that decreases the probability that a previous behavior will occur again (Module 18)

random assignment to condition A procedure in which participants are assigned to different experimental groups or "conditions" on the basis of chance and chance alone (Module 5)

range The difference between the highest score and the lowest score in a distribution (Module 59)

rape The act by which one person forces another person to submit to sexual activity (Module 36)

rapid eye movement (REM) sleep Sleep occupying 20 percent of an adult's sleeping time, characterized by increased heart rate, blood pressure, and breathing rate; erections (in males); eye movements; and the experience of dreaming (Module 14)

rational-emotive behavior therapy A form of therapy that attempts to restructure a person's belief system into a more realistic, rational, and logical set of views by challenging dysfunctional beliefs that maintain irrational behavior (Module 51)

reactance A disagreeable emotional and cognitive reaction that results from the restriction of one's freedom and that can be associated with medical regimens (Module 47)

recall Memory task in which specific information must be retrieved (Module 21)

reciprocity-of-liking effect A tendency to like those who like us (Module 57)

recognition Memory task in which individuals are presented with a stimulus and asked whether they have been exposed to it in the past or to identify it from a list of alternatives (Module 21)

reflex An automatic, involuntary response to an incoming stimulus (Module 8, Module 39)

refractory period A temporary period that follows the resolution stage and during which the male cannot develop an erection again (Module 34)

rehearsal The repetition of information that has entered short-term memory (Module 20)

reinforcement The process by which a stimulus increases the probability that a preceding behavior will be repeated (Module 18)

reinforcer Any stimulus that increases the probability that a preceding behavior will occur again (Module 18)

reliability The property by which tests measure consistently what they are trying to measure (Module 26)

replication The repetition of research, sometimes using other procedures, settings, and groups of participants, to increase confidence in prior findings (Module 5)

repression The primary defense mechanism in which unacceptable or unpleasant id impulses are pushed back into the unconscious (Module 42)

resolution phase The interval after orgasm in which the body returns to its unaroused state, reversing the changes brought about by arousal (Module 34)

resting state The state in which there is a negative electrical charge of about 270 millivolts within a neuron (Module 7)

reticular formation The part of the brain extending from the medulla through the pons and made up of groups of nerve cells that can immediately activate other parts of the brain to produce general bodily arousal (Module 9)

retina The part of the eye that converts the electromagnetic energy of light to electrical impulses for transmission to the brain (Module 11)

retroactive interference Interference in which there is difficulty in the recall of information learned earlier because of later exposure to different material (Module 22)

retrograde amnesia Amnesia in which memory is lost for occurrences prior to a certain event (Module 22)

reuptake The reabsorption of neurotransmitters by a terminal button (Module 7)

rods Thin, cylindrical receptor cells in the retina that are highly sensitive to light (Module 11)

Rorschach test A test that involves showing a series of symmetrical visual stimuli to people who then are asked what the figures represent to them (Module 44)

sample A representative subgroup of a population of interest (Module 60)

Schachter-Singer theory of emotion The belief that emotions are determined jointly by a nonspecific kind of physiological arousal and its interpretation, based on environmental cues (Module 31)

schedules of reinforcement Different patterns of frequency and timing of reinforcement following desired behavior (Module 18)

schemas Organized bodies of information stored in memory that bias the way new information is interpreted, stored, and recalled. In social cognition, sets of cognitions about people and social experiences (Module 21, Module 54)

schizophrenia A class of disorders in which severe distortion of reality occurs (Module 49)

scientific method The approach through which psychologists systematically acquire knowledge and understanding about behavior and other phenomena of interest (Module 4)

self-actualization A state of self-fulfillment in which people realize their highest potential, each in his or her own unique way (Modules 29, 43)

self-efficacy Belief in one's personal capabilities. Self-efficacy underlies people's faith in their ability to carry out a particular behavior or produce a desired outcome (Module 43)

self-esteem The component of personality that encompasses our positive and negative self-evaluations (Module 43)

self-report measures A method of gathering data about people by asking them questions about a sample of their behavior (Module 44)

self-serving bias The tendency to attribute personal success to personal factors (skill, ability, or effort) and to attribute failure to factors outside oneself (Module 54)

semantic memory Memory for general knowledge and facts about the world, as well as memory for the rules of logic that are used to deduce other facts (Module 20)

semantic networks Mental representations of clusters of interconnected information (Module 20)

semantics The rules governing the meaning of words and sentences (Module 25)

semicircular canals Three tubelike structures of the inner ear containing fluid that sloshes through them when the head moves, signaling rotational or angular movement to the brain (Module 12)

sensation The activation of the sense organs by a source of physical energy (Module 10)

sensorimotor stage According to Jean Piaget, the stage from birth to 2 years, during which a child has little competence in representing the environment by using images, language, or other symbols (Module 39)

sensory (afferent) neurons Neurons that transmit information from the perimeter of the body to the central nervous system (Module 8)

sensory area The site in the brain of the tissue that corresponds to each of the senses, with the degree of sensitivity related to the amount of the tissue allocated to that sense (Module 9)

sensory memory The initial, momentary storage of information, lasting only an instant (Module 20)

sequential research A research method that combines cross-sectional and longitudinal research by considering a number of different age groups and examining them at several points in time (Module 37)

sexism Negative attitudes and behavior toward a person based on that person's gender (Module 33)

sexually transmitted infection (STI) A disease transmitted through sexual contact (Module 36)

shaping The process of teaching a complex behavior by rewarding closer and closer approximations of the desired behavior (Module 18)

short-term memory Memory that holds information for fifteen to twenty-five seconds (Module 20)

significant outcome Meaningful results that make it possible for researchers to feel confident that they have confirmed their hypotheses. In statistics, an outcome in which the observed outcome would be expected to have occurred by chance with a probability of .05 or less (Module 5, Module 60)

situational causes (of behavior) Perceived causes of behavior that are based on environmental factors (Module 54)

skin senses The senses of touch, pressure, temperature, and pain (Module 12)

social cognition The cognitive processes by which people understand and make sense of others and themselves (Module 54)

social cognitive approaches to personality Theories that emphasize the influence of a person's cognitions—thoughts, feelings, expectations, and values—as well as observation of others' behavior, in determining personality (Module 43)

social influence The process by which the actions of an individual or group affect the behavior of others (Module 55)

social psychology The scientific study of how people's thoughts, feelings, and actions are affected by others (Module 54)

social support A mutual network of caring, interested others (Module 45)

social supporter A group member whose dissenting views make nonconformity to the group easier (Module 55)

sociocultural perspective The perspective that assumes that people's behavior—both normal and abnormal—is shaped by the kind of family group, society, and culture in which they live (Module 48)

somatic division The part of the peripheral nervous system that specializes in the control of voluntary movements and the communication of information to and from the sense organs (Module 8)

somatoform disorders Psychological difficulties that take on a physical (somatic) form, but for which there is no medical cause (Module 49)

sound The movement of air molecules brought about by a source of vibration (Module 12)

spinal cord A bundle of neurons that leaves the brain and runs down the length of the back and is the main means for transmitting messages between the brain and the body (Module 8)

spontaneous recovery The reemergence of an extinguished conditioned response after a period of rest and with no further conditioning (Module 17)

spontaneous remission Recovery without treatment (Module 52)

stage 1 sleep The state of transition between wakefulness and sleep, characterized by relatively rapid, low-amplitude brain waves (Module 14)

stage 2 sleep A sleep deeper than that of stage 1, characterized by a slower, more regular wave pattern, along with momentary interruptions of sleep spindles (Module 14)

stage 3 sleep A sleep characterized by slow brain waves, with greater peaks and valleys in the wave pattern than in stage 2 sleep (Module 14)

stage 4 sleep The deepest stage of sleep, during which we are least responsive to outside stimulation (Module 14)

standard deviation An index of the average deviation of a set of scores from the center of the distribution (Module 59)

statistics The branch of mathematics concerned with collecting, organizing, analyzing, and drawing conclusions from numerical data (Module 58)

status The social rank held within a group (Module 55)

stereotype A set of generalized beliefs and expectations about a particular group and its members (Module 56)

stimulants Drugs that have an arousal effect on the central nervous system, causing a rise in heart rate, blood pressure, and muscular tension (Module 16)

stimulus Energy that produces a response in a sense organ (Module 10)

stimulus discrimination The process that occurs if two stimuli are sufficiently distinct from one another that one evokes a conditioned response but the other does not; the ability to differentiate between stimuli (Module 17)

stimulus generalization Occurs when a conditioned response follows a stimulus that is similar to the original conditioned stimulus; the more similar the two stimuli are, the more likely generalization is to occur (Module 17)

stress A person's response to events that are threatening or challenging (Module 45)

structuralism Wilhelm Wundt's approach, which focuses on uncovering the fundamental mental components of consciousness, thinking, and other kinds of mental states and activities (Module 2)

subjective well-being People's own evaluation of their lives in terms of both their thoughts and their emotions (Module 47)

superego According to Sigmund Freud, the final personality structure to develop; it represents the rights and wrongs of society as handed down by a person's parents, teachers, and other important figures (Module 42)

survey research Research in which people chosen to represent a larger population are asked a series of questions about their behavior, thoughts, or attitudes (Module 5)

syllogistic reasoning Formal reasoning in which a person draws a conclusion from a set of assumptions (Module 23)

sympathetic division The part of the autonomic division of the nervous system that acts to prepare the body for action in stressful situations, engaging all the organism's resources to respond to a threat (Module 8)

synapse The space between two neurons where the axon of a sending neuron communicates with the dendrites of a receiving neuron by using chemical messages (Module 7)

syntax Ways in which words and phrases can be combined to form sentences (Module 25)

systematic desensitization A behavioral technique in which gradual exposure to an anxiety-producing stimulus is paired with relaxation to extinguish the response of anxiety (Module 51)

telegraphic speech Sentences in which words not critical to the message are left out (Module 25)

temperament Basic, innate disposition that emerges early in life (Modules 39, 43)

teratogens Environmental agents such as a drug, chemical, virus, or other factor that produce a birth defect (Module 38)

terminal buttons Small bulges at the end of axons that send messages to other neurons (Module 7)

test standardization A technique used to validate questions in personality tests by studying the responses of people with known diagnoses (Module 44)

thalamus The part of the brain located in the middle of the central core that acts primarily to relay information about the senses (Module 9)

Thematic Apperception Test (TAT) A test consisting of a series of pictures about which a person is asked to write a story (Module 44)

theories Broad explanations and predictions concerning phenomena of interest (Module 4)

theory of multiple intelligences Howard Gardner's theory that proposes that there are eight distinct spheres of intelligence (Module 26)

thinking The manipulation of mental representations of information (Module 23)

tip-of-the-tongue phenomenon The inability to recall information that one realizes one knows—a result of the difficulty of retrieving information from long-term memory (Module 21)

top-down processing Perception that is guided by higher-level knowledge, experience, expectations, and motivations (Module 13)

trait theory A model of personality that seeks to identify the basic traits necessary to describe personality (Module 43)

traits Consistent personality characteristics and behaviors displayed in different situations (Module 43)

transcranial magnetic stimulation (TMS) A depression treatment in which a precise magnetic pulse is directed to a specific area of the brain (Module 53)

transference The transfer of feelings to a psychoanalyst of love or anger that had been originally directed to a patient's parents or other authority figures (Module 51)

treatment The manipulation implemented by the experimenter (Module 5)

trichromatic theory of color vision The theory that there are three kinds of cones in the retina, each of which responds primarily to a specific range of wavelengths (Module 11)

trust-versus-mistrust stage According to Erik Erikson, the first stage of psychosocial development, occurring from birth to age 1½ years, during which time infants develop feelings of trust or lack of trust (Module 39)

Type A behavior pattern A cluster of behaviors involving hostility, competitiveness, time urgency, and feeling driven (Module 46)

Type B behavior pattern A cluster of behaviors characterized by a patient, cooperative, noncompetitive, and nonaggressive manner (Module 46)

unconditional positive regard An attitude of acceptance and respect on the part of an observer, no matter what a person says or does (Module 43)

unconditioned response (UCR) A response that is natural and needs no training (e.g., salivation at the smell of food) (Module 17)

unconditioned stimulus (UCS) A stimulus that naturally brings about a particular response without having been learned (Module 17)

unconscious A part of the personality that contains the memories, knowledge, beliefs, feelings, urges, drives, and instincts of which the individual is not aware (Module 42)

unconscious wish fulfillment theory Sigmund Freud's theory that dreams represent unconscious wishes that dreamers desire to see fulfilled (Module 14)

uninvolved parents Parents who show little interest in their children and are emotionally detached (Module 39)

universal grammar Noam Chomsky's theory that all the world's languages share a common underlying structure (Module 25)

validity The property by which tests actually measure what they are supposed to measure (Module 26)

variability The spread, or dispersion, of scores in a distribution (Module 59)

variable Behaviors, events, or other characteristics that can change, or vary, in some way (Module 5)

variable-interval schedule A schedule by which the time between reinforcements varies around some average rather than being fixed (Module 18)

variable-ratio schedule A schedule by which reinforcement occurs after a varying number of responses rather than a fixed number (Module 18)

visual illusions Physical stimuli that consistently produce errors in perception (Module 13)

wear-and-tear theories of aging Theories that suggest that the mechanical functions of the body simply stop working efficiently (Module 41)

Weber's law A basic law of psychophysics stating that a just noticeable difference is in constant proportion to the intensity of an initial stimulus (Module 10)

weight set point The particular level of weight that the body strives to maintain (Module 30)

working memory A set of active, temporary memory stores that actively manipulate and rehearse information (Module 20)

zone of proximal development (ZPD) According to Lev Vygotsky, the level at which a child can almost, but not fully, comprehend or perform a task on his or her own (Module 39)

zygote The new cell formed by the union of an egg and sperm (Module 38)

References

Aartsen, M. J., Martin, M., & Zimprich, D. (2002). Gender differences in level and change in cognitive functioning: Results from the longitudinal aging study Amsterdam. *Gerontology, 50,* 35–38.

Abboud, L. (2005, July 27). The next phase in psychiatry. *The Wall Street Journal,* pp. D1, D5.

Ablon, J. S., & Jones, E. E. (2002). Validity of controlled clinical trials of psychotherapy: Findings from the NIMH Treatment of Depression Collaborative Research Program. *American Journal of Psychiatry, 159,* 775–783.

Ablon, J. S., & Jones, E. E. (2005). On analytic process. *Journal of the American Psychoanalytic Association, 53,* 541–568.

Abramson, L. Y., Alloy, L. B., Hogan, M. E., Whitehouse, W. G., Donova, P., Rose, D. T., Panzarella, C., & Raniere, D. (2002). Cognitive vulnerability to depression: Theory and evidence. In R. L. Leahy & E. T. Dowd (Eds.), *Clinical advances in cognitive psychotherapy: Theory and Application* (pp. 75–92). New York: Springer.

Abt, S. (1999, July 26). Armstrong wins tour and journey. *The New York Times,* pp. D1, D4.

Accardo, P. J., & Capute, A. J. (1998). Mental retardations. *Mental Retardation & Developmental Disabilities Research Reviews, 4,* 2–5.

Ackard, D. M., & Neumark-Sztainer, D. (2002). Date violence and date rape among adolescents: Associations with disordered eating behaviors and psychological health. *Child Abuse and Neglect, 26,* 455–473.

Adams, B., & Parker, J. D. (1990). Maternal weight gain in women with good pregnancy outcome. *Obstetrics and Gynecology, 76,* 1–7.

Adams, K. B. (2004). Changing investment in activities and interests in elders' lives: Theory and measurement. *International Journal of Aging and Human Development, 58,* 87–108.

Adams-Byers, J., Squilkr Whitsell, S., & Moon, S. M. (2004). Gifted students' perceptions of the academic and social/emotional effects of homogeneous and heterogeneous grouping. *Gifted Child Quarterly, 48,* 7–20.

Addolorato, G., Leggio, L., Abenavoli, L., & Gasbarrini, G. (2005). Neurobiochemical and clinical aspects of craving in alcohol addiction: A review. *Addictive Behaviors, 30,* 1209–1224.

Adelson, R. (2005, May) Only the lonely. *Monitor on Psychology,* pp. 26–27.

Ader, R., Felten, D., & Cohen, N. (2001). *Psychoneuroimmunology* (3rd ed.). San Diego: Academic Press.

Adler, J. (1984, April 23). The fight to conquer fear. *Newsweek,* pp. 66–72.

Adolphs, R. (2002). Neural systems for recognizing emotion. *Current Opinion in Neurobiology, 12,* 169–177.

Advokat, C. (2005). Differential effects of clozapine versus other antipsychotics on clinical outcome and dopamine release in the brain. *Essential Psychopharmacology, 6,* 73–90.

Affleck, G., Tennen, H., Urrows, S., & Higgins, P. (1994). Person and contextual features of daily stress reactivity: Individual differences in relations of undesirable daily events with mood disturbance and chronic pain intensity. *Journal of Personality and Social Psychology, 66,* 329–340.

Aftanas, L., & Golosheykin, S. (2005). Impact of regular meditation practice on EEG activity at rest and during evoked negative emotions. *International Journal of Neuroscience, 115,* 893–909.

Aghajanian, G. K. (1994). Serotonin and the action of LSD in the brain. *Psychiatric Annals, 24,* 137–141.

Agras, W. S., & Berkowitz, R. I. (1996). Behavior therapy. In R. E. Hales & S. C. Yudofsky (Eds.), *The American Psychiatric Press synopsis of psychiatry.* Washington, DC: American Psychiatric Press.

Ahiima, R. S., & Osei, S. Y. (2004). Leptin signaling. *Physiology and Behavior, 81,* 223–241.

Ahissar, M., Ahissar, E., Bergman, H., & Vaadia, E. (1992). Encoding of sound-source location and movement: Activity of single neurons and interactions between adjacent neurons in the monkey auditory cortex. *Journal of Neurophysiology, 67,* 203–215.

Ahrons, C. (1995). *The good divorce: Keeping your family together when your marriage comes apart.* New York: HarperPerennial.

Aiken, L. (2000). *Dying, death, and bereavement* (4th ed.). Mahwah, NJ: Erlbaum.

Aiken, L. R. (1996). *Assessment of intellectual functioning* (2nd ed.). New York: Plenum.

Aiken, L. R. (1997). *Psychological testing and assessment* (9th ed.). Needham Heights, MA: Allyn & Bacon.

Aiken, L. R. (2000). *Personality: Theories, assessment, research, and applications.* Springfield, IL: Charles C. Thomas.

Ainsworth, M. D. S., Blehar, M. C., Waters, E., & Wall, S. (1978). *Patterns of attachment: A psychological study of the strange situation.* Hillsdale, NJ: Erlbaum.

Ajzen, I. (2002). Residual effects of past on later behavior: Habituation and reasoned action perspectives. *Personality and Social Psychology Review, 6,* 107–122.

Akil, H., & Morano, M. I. (1996). The biology of stress: From periphery to brain. In S. J. Watson (Ed.), *Biology of schizophrenia and affective disease.* Washington, DC: American Psychiatric Press.

Akman, I., Ozek, E., Bilgen, H., Ozdogan, T., & Cebeci, D. (2002). Sweet solutions and pacifiers for pain relief in newborn infants. *Journal of Pain, 3,* 199–202.

Akutsu, P. D., Sue, S., Zane, N. W. S., & Nakamura, C. Y. (1989). Ethnic differences in alcohol consumption among

Asians and Caucasians in the United States: An investigation of cultural and physiological factors. *Journal of Studies on Alcohol, 50,* 261–267.

Alford, B. A., & Beck, A. T. (1997) *The integrative power of cognitive therapy.* New York: Guilford Press.

Allhoff, F. (2005). Germ-line genetic enhancement and Rawlsian primary goods. *Kennedy Institute of Ethics Journal, 15,* 39–56.

Alloy, L. B., Jacobson, N. S., & Acocella, J. (1999). *Abnormal psychology* (8th ed.). New York: McGraw-Hill.

Allport, G. W. (1961). *Pattern and growth in personality.* New York: Holt, Rinehart and Winston.

Allport, G. W. (1966). Traits revisited. *American Psychologist, 21,* 1–10.

Allport, G. W., & Postman, L. J. (1958). The basic psychology of rumor. In E. D. Maccoby, T. M. Newcomb, & E. L. Hartley (Eds.), *Readings in social psychology* (3rd ed.). New York: Holt, Rinehart and Winston.

Alonso, A., Alonso, S., & Piper, W. (2003). Group psychotherapy. In G. Stricker & T. A. Widiger, et al. (Eds.), *Handbook of psychology: Clinical psychology* (Vol. 8). New York: Wiley.

Altman, N. (1996). The accommodation of diversity in psychoanalysis. In R. P. Foster, M. Moskowitz, & R. A. Javier (Eds.), *Reaching across boundaries of culture and class: Widening the scope of psychotherapy.* Northvale, NJ: Jason Aronson.

Amato, L., Davoili, M., Perucci, C. A., Ferri, M., Faggiano, F., & Mattick R. P. (2005). An overview of systematic reviews of the effectiveness of opiate maintenance therapies: Available evidence to inform clinical practice and research. *Journal of Substance Abuse Treatment, 28,* 321–329.

American Academy of Pediatrics. (1999, July 26). *Circumcision: Information for parents.* Retrieved from http://www.aap.org/family/circ.htm.

American Association of Mental Retardation (AAMR). (2002). *Mental retardation: Definition, classification, and systems of supports* (10th ed.). Washington, DC.: AAMR.

American Association of University Women (AAUW). (1992). *How schools shortchange women: The A.A.U.W. Report.* Washington, DC: AAUW Educational Foundation.

American Association of University Women (AAUW). (1993). *Hostile hallways: The AAUW survey on sexual harassment in American schools.* Washington, DC. AAUW Educational Foundation.

American Association of University Women (AAUW). (2001). *Hostile hallways: Bullying, teasing, and sexual harassment in school.* Washington, DC: American Association of University Women.

American Insomnia Association (2005). Causes of insomnia. In L. VandeCreek (Ed.), *Innovations in clinical practice: Focus on adults.* Sarasota, FL: Professional Resource Press/Professional Resource Exchange.

American Psychiatric Association. (2000). *Diagnostic and statistical manual of mental disorders DSM-IV-TR, 4th Edition.* Arlington, VA: American Psychiatric Association.

American Psychological Association (APA). (1988). *Behavioral research with animals.* Washington, DC: American Psychological Association.

American Psychological Association (APA). (1993a). *Employment survey.* Washington, DC: American Psychological Association.

American Psychological Association (APA). (1993b, January/February). Subgroup norming and the Civil Rights Act. *Psychological Science Agenda, 5,* 6.

American Psychological Association (APA). (1994). *Careers in psychology.* Washington, DC: American Psychological Association.

American Psychological Association (APA). (1999). *Talk to someone who can help.* Washington, DC: American Psychological Association.

American Psychological Association (APA). (2002, August 21). *APA Ethics Code, 2002.* Washington, DC: American Psychological Association.

American Psychological Association Task Force on Intelligence. (1996). *Intelligence: Knowns and unknowns.* Washington, DC: American Psychological Association.

Anand, G., & Burton, T. M. (2003, April 11). Drug debate: New antipsychotics pose a quandary for FDA, doctors. *The Wall Street Journal,* pp. A1, A8.

Anastasi, A., & Urbina, S. (1997). *Psychological Testing* (7th ed.). Englewood Cliffs, NJ: Prentice Hall.

Andersen, B. L., Kiecolt-Glaser, J. K., & Glaser, R. (1994). A biobehavioral model of cancer stress and disease course. *American Psychologist, 49,* 389–404.

Anderson, B. F. (1980). *The complete thinker: A handbook of techniques for creative and critical problem solving.* Englewood Cliffs, NJ: Prentice Hall.

Anderson, C. A., & Bushman, B. J. (2002, March 29). The effects of media violence on society. *Science, 295,* 2377–2378.

Anderson, C. A., & Dill, K. E. (2000). Video games and aggressive thoughts, feelings, and behavior in the laboratory and in life. *Journal of Personality and Social Psychology, 78,* 772–790.

Anderson, C. A., Carnagey, N. L., & Eubanks, J. (2003). Exposure to violent media: The effects of songs with violent lyrics on aggressive thoughts and feelings. *Journal of Personality and Social Psychology, 84,* 960–971.

Anderson, C. A., Carnagey, N. L., Flanagan, M., Benjamin, A. J., Jr., Eubanks, J., & Valentine, J. C. (2004). Violent video games: Specific effects of violent content on aggressive thoughts and behavior. In M. P. Zanna (Ed.), *Advances in experimental social psychology* (Vol. 36). San Diego, CA: Elsevier Academic Press.

Anderson, J. (1988). Cognitive styles and multicultural populations. *Journal of Teacher Education, 39,* 2–9.

Anderson, J. A., & Adams, M. (1992). Acknowledging the learning styles of diverse student populations: Implications for instructional design. *New Directions for Teaching and Learning, 49,* 19–33.

Anderson, J. R. (1981). Interference: The relationship between response latency and response accuracy. *Journal of Experimental Psychology: Human Learning and Memory, 7,* 311–325.

Anderson, J. R., & Bower, G. H. (1972). Recognition and retrieval processes in free recall. *Psychological Review, 79,* 97–123.

Anderson, K. B., Cooper, H., & Okamura, L. (1997). Individual differences and attitudes toward rape: A meta-analytic review. *Personality and Social Psychology Bulletin, 23,* 295–315.

Anderson, N. H. (1996). *A functional theory of cognition.* Mahwah, NJ: Erlbaum.

Anderson, R. N., & Smith, B. L. (2003). Deaths: leading causes for 2001. *National Vital Statistics Report 2003, 52,* 1–86.

Anderson, T., & Magnusson, D. (1990). Biological maturation in adolescence and the development of drinking habits and alcohol abuse among young males: A prospective longitudinal study. *Journal of Youth and Adolescence, 19,* 33–42.

Andreasen, N. C. (2005). *Research advances in genetics and genomics: Implications for psychiatry.* Washington, DC: American Psychiatric Publishing.

Andrews, F. M., & Withey, S. B. (1976). *Social indicators of well-being: Americans' perceptions of life quality* (pp. 207, 306). New York: Plenum.

Angier, N. (1991, January 22). A potent peptide prompts an urge to cuddle. *The New York Times,* p. C1.

Angier, N. (1996, November 1). Maybe gene isn't to blame for thrill-seeking manner. *The New York Times,* p. A12.

Angier, N., & Chang, K. (2005, January 24). Gray matter and the sexes: Still a scientific gray area. *The New York Times,* pp. A1, A15.

Angoff, W. H. (1988). The nature-nurture debate, aptitudes, and group differences. *American Psychologist, 43,* 713–720.

Ansaldo, A. I., Arguin, M., & Roch-Locours, L. A. (2002). The contribution of the right cerebral hemisphere to the recovery from aphasia: A single longitudinal case study. *Brain Languages, 82,* 206–222.

Antony, M. M., Brown, T. A., & Barlow, D. H. (1992). Current perspectives on panic and panic disorder. *Current Directions in Psychological Science, 1,* 79–82.

Apanovich, A. M., McCarthy, D., & Salovey, P. (2003). Using message framing to motivate HIV testing among low-income, ethnic minority women. *Health Psychology, 22,* 88–94.

Apkarian, A. V., Bushnell, M. C., Treede, R. D., & Zubeita, J. K. (2005). Human brain mechanisms of pain perception and regulation in health and disease. *European Journal of Pain, 9,* 463–484.

Aponte, J. F., & Wohl, J. (2000). *Psychological intervention and cultural diversity.* Needham Heights, MA: Allyn & Bacon.

Appelhans, B. M., & Schmeck, R. R. (2002). Learning styles and approach versus avoidant coping during academic exam preparation. *College Student Journal, 36,* 157–160.

Arafat, I., & Cotton, W. L. (1974). Masturbation practices of males and females. *Journal of Sex Research, 10,* 293–307.

Arambula, P., Peper, E., Kawakami, M., & Gibney, K. H. (2001). The physiological correlates of Kundalini yoga meditation: A study of a yoga master. *Applied Psychophysiology & Biofeedback, 26,* 147–153.

Arangure, J., Jr. (2005, August 2). Orioles Star Denied Use Before Congress. *Washington Post,* p. A01.

Arangure, J., Jr. (2005, August 2). Palmeiro Suspended For Steroid Violation. *Washington Post,* p. C2.

Archambault, D. L. (1992). Adolescence: A physiological, cultural, and psychological no man's land. In G. W. Lawson & A. W. Lawson (Eds.), *Adolescent substance abuse: Etiology, treatment, and prevention.* Gaithersburg, MD: Aspen.

Archer, J., & Lloyd, B. B. (2002). *Sex and gender* (2nd ed.). New York: Cambridge University Press.

Arena, J. M. (1984, April). A look at the opposite sex. *Newsweek on Campus,* p. 21.

Arlin, P. K. (1989). The problem of the problem. In J. D. Sinnott (Ed.), *Everyday problem solving: Theory and applications.* New York: Praeger.

Armstrong, T. (2000). *Multiple intelligences in the classroom* (2nd ed.). Washington, DC: Association for Supervision & Curriculum Development.

Armstrong, T. (2003). *The multiple intelligences of reading and writing: Making the words come alive* (2nd ed.). Washington, DC: Association for Supervision & Curriculum Development.

Aronow, E., Reznikoff, M., & Moreland, K. (1994). *The Rorschach technique: Perceptual basics, content interpretation, and applications.* Boston: Longwood.

Asch, S. E. (1946). Forming impressions of personality. *Journal of Abnormal and Social Psychology, 41,* 258–290.

Asch, S. E. (1951). Effects of group pressure upon the modification and distortion of judgments. In H. Guetzkow (Ed.), *Groups, leadership, and men.* Pittsburgh: Carnegie Press.

Aschcraft, M.H. (1994). *Human memory and cognition.* (2nd ed.) New York: Harper-Collins.

Asher, S. R., & Parker, J. G. (1991). Significance of peer relationship problems in childhood. In B. H. Schneider, G. Attili, J. Nadel, & R. P. Weissberg (Eds.), *Social competence in developmental perspective.* Amsterdam, Netherlands: Kluwer Academic.

Aspinwall, L. G., & Taylor, S. E. (1997). A stitch in time: Self-regulation and proactive coping. *Psychological Bulletin, 121,* 417–436.

Astbury-Ward, E. (2002). From Kama Sutra to dot.com: The history, myths and management of premature ejaculation. *Sexual and Relationship Therapy, 17,* 367–380.

Atkinson, H. (Ed.). (1997, January 21). Understanding your diagnosis. *HealthNews,* p. 3.

Atkinson, H. G. (2003, August). Are you a "good" patient? *HealthNews,* p. 5.

Atkinson, J. W., & Feather, N. T. (1966). *Theory of achievement motivation.* New York: Krieger.

Atkinson, R. C., & Shiffrin, R. M. (1968). Human memory: A proposed system and its control processes. In K. W. Spence & J. T. Spence (Eds.), *The psychology of learning and motivation: Advances in research and theory* (Vol. 2, pp. 80–195). New York: Academic Press.

Atran, S. (2003). Genesis of suicide terrorism. *Science, 299,* 1534–1539.

Attree, E., A., Brooks, B. M., & Rose, F. D. (2005). Use of virtual environments in training and rehabilitation: International perspectives [Special issue]. *CyberPyschology & Behavior, 8,* 185–186.

Auerbach, S. M., Kiesler, D. J., Strentz, T., Schmidt, J., & Serio, C. (1994). Interpersonal impacts and adjustment to the stress of simulated captivity: An empirical test of the Stockholm Syndrome. *Journal of Social and Clinical Psychology, 13,* 207–221.

Auld, F., Hyman, M., & Rudzinski, D. (2005). Theory and strategy of dream interpretation. In F. Auld & M. Hyman (Eds.), *Resolution of inner conflict: An introduction to psychoanalytic therapy* (2nd ed.). Washington, DC: American Psychological Association.

Austin, L. S. (2000). *What's holding you back? Eight critical choices for women's success.* New York: Basic Books.

Avenell, A. Brown, T. J., McGee, M. A., Campbell, M. K., Grant, A. M., Broom, J., Jung, R. T., & Smith, W. C. S. (2004). What are the long-term benefits of weight reducing diets in adults? A systematic review of randomized controlled trials. *Journal of Human Nutrition and Dietetics, 17,* 317–335.

Averill, J. R. (1975). A semantic atlas of emotional concepts. *Catalog of Selected Documents in Psychology, 5,* 330.

Averill, J. R. (1994). Emotions are many splendored things. In P. Ekman & R. J. Davidson (Eds.), *The nature of emotion: Fundamental questons.* New York: Oxford University Press.

Ayyash-Abdo, H. (2002). Adolescent suicide: An ecological approach. *Psychology in the Schools, 39,* 459–475.

Babkina, A. M., & Bondi, K. M. (Eds.). (2003). *Affirmative action: An annotated bibliography* (2nd ed.). New York: Nova Science.

Baddeley, A., & Wilson, B. (1985). Phonological coding and short-term memory in patients without speech. *Journal of Memory and Language, 24,* 490–502.

Baddeley, A., Gathercole, S., & Papagno, C. (1998). The phonological loop as a language learning device. *Psychological Review, 105,* 158–173.

Baddeley, A. D. (1990). *Human memory: Theory and practice.* Boston: Allyn & Bacon.

Baer, J. (1993). *Creativity and divergent thinking: A task-specific approach.* Hillsdale, NJ: Erlbaum.

Baer, J. S., Sampson, P. D., Barr, H. M., Connor, P. D., & Streissguth, A. P. (2003). A 21-year longitudinal analysis of the effects of prenatal alcohol exposure on young adult drinking. *Obstetrical and Gynecological Survey, 58,* 638–639.

Baer, L., Rauch, S. L., Callantine, T., Martuza, R., et al. (1995). Cingulotomy for intractable obsessive-compulsive disorder: Prospective long-term follow-up of 18 patients. *Archives of General Psychiatry, 52,* 384–392.

Bahrick, H. P. (1998). Loss and distortion of autobiographical memory content. In C. P. Thompson & D. J. Herrmann (Eds.), *Autobiographical memory: Theoretical and applied perspectives* (pp. 69–78). Mahwah, NJ: Lawrence Erlbaum.

Bai, L. (2005). Children at play: A childhood beyond the Confucian shadow. *Childhood: A Global Journal of Child Research, 12,* 9–32.

Bailey, J. M., Pillard, R. C., Kitzinger, C., & Wilkinson, S. (1997). Sexual orientation: Is it determined by biology? In M. R. Walsh (Ed.), *Women, men, and gender: Ongoing debates.* New Haven, CT: Yale University Press.

Bair, D. (2003). *Jung: A Biography.* New York: Little, Brown, and Company.

Baker, H. (2001). Hypnosis for anxiety reduction and ego-enhancement. *Australian Journal of Clinical and Experimental Hypnosis, 29,* 147–151.

Bakermans-Kranenburg, M. J., van Ijzendoorn, M. H., & Juffer, F. (2003). Less is more: Meta-analyses of sensitivity and attachment interventions in early childhood. *Psychological Bulletin, 129,* 195–215.

Balaban, C. D. (2002). Neural substrates linking balance control and anxiety [Special issue: The Pittsburgh special issue]. *Physiology and Behavior, 77,* 469–475.

Balbach, E. D., Gasior, R. J., & Barbeau, E. M. (2003). R. J. Reynolds' targeting of African Americans: 1988–2000. *American Journal of Public Health, 93,* 822–827.

Ball, D. (2004). Genetic approaches to alcohol dependence. *British Journal of Psychiatry, 185,* 449–451.

Baltes, P. B., & Kunzmann, U. (2003). Wisdom. *Psychologist, 16,* 131–133.

Bandura, A. (1977). *Social learning theory.* Englewood Cliffs, NJ: Prentice Hall.

Bandura, A. (1986). *Social foundations of thought and action: A social cognitive theory.* Englewood Cliffs, NJ: Prentice Hall.

Bandura, A. (1988). Self-regulation of motivation and action through goal systems. In V. Hamilton and H. Gordon (Eds.), *Cognitive perspectives on emotion and motivation.* Dordrecht, Netherlands: Kluwer Academic.

Bandura, A. (1994). Social cognitive theory of mass communication. In J. Bryant, & D. Zillmann (Eds.), *Media effects: Advances in theory and research: LEA's communication series.* Hillsdale, NJ: Erlbaum.

Bandura, A. (1997). *Self-efficacy: The exercise of control.* New York: W. H. Freeman.

Bandura, A. (1999). Social cognitive theory of personality. In D. Cervone & Y. Shod (Eds.), *The coherence of personality.* NY: Guilford.

Bandura, A. (2000). Self-efficacy: The foundation of agency. In W. J. Perrig and A. Grob (Eds.), *Control of human behavior, mental processes, and consciousness: Essays in honor of the 60th birthday of August Flammer.* Mahwah, NJ: Erlbaum.

Bandura, A. (2004). Swimming against the mainstream: The early years from chilly tributary to transformative mainstream. *Behaviour Research and Therapy, 42,* 613–630.

Bandura, A., Grusec, J. E., & Menlove, F. L. (1967). Vicarious extinction of avoidance behavior. *Journal of Personality and Social Psychology, 5,* 16–23.

Bandura, A., Ross, D., & Ross, S. (1963a). Imitation of film-mediated aggressive models. *Journal of Abnormal and Social Psychology, 66,* 3–11.

Bandura, A., Ross, D., & Ross, S. (1963b). Vicarious reinforcement and imitative learning. *Journal of Abnormal and Social Psychology, 67,* 601–607.

Banich, T., & Heller, W. (1998). Evolving perspectives on lateralization of function. *Current Directions in Psychological Science, 7,* 1–2.

Bannon, L. (2000, February 14). Why boys and girls get different toys. *The Wall Street Journal,* pp. B1, B4.

Barber, J. (2001). Freedom from smoking: Integrating hypnotic methods and rapid smoking to facilitate smoking cessation. *International Journal of Clinical & Experimental Hypnosis, 49,* 257–266.

Barber, S., & Lane, R. C. (1995). Efficacy research in psychodynamic therapy: A critical review of the literature. *Psychotherapy in Private Practice, 14,* 43–69.

Bargh, J. A., & Chartrand, T. L. (2000). The mind in the middle: A practical guide to priming and automaticity research. In H. T. Reis & C. M. Judd (Eds.), *Handbook of research methods in social and personality psychology.* New York: Cambridge University Press.

Barkley, R. (2000). *Taking charge of ADHD* (Rev. ed.). New York: Guilford Press.

Barkley, R. (2005). *ADHD and the nature of self-control.* New York: Guildford.

Barkow, J. H., Cosmides, L., & Tooby, J. (Eds.). (1992). *The adapted mind.* New York: Oxford University Press.

Barmeyer, C. I. (2004). Learning styles and their impact on cross-cultural training: An international comparison in France, Germany and Quebec. *International Journal of Intercultural Relations, 28,* 577–594.

Barnard, N. D. , & Kaufman, S. R. (1997, Febraury). Animal research is wasteful and misleading. *Scientific American, 276,* 80–82.

Barnes, V. A., Davis, H. C., Murzynowski, J., & Treiber, F. A. (2004). Impact of meditation on resting and ambulatory blood pressure and heart rate in youth. *Medicine, 66,* 909–914.

Barnett, R. C. (2004). Woman and work: Where are we, where did we come from, and where are we going? [Preface]. *Journal of Social Issues, 60,* 667–674.

Baron, R. S. (2005). So right it's wrong: Groupthink and the ubiquitous nature of polarized group decision making. In M. P. Zanna (Ed.), *Advances in experimental social psychology* (Vol. 37). San Diego, CA: Elsevier Academic Press.

Barrett, D. (2001). *The committee of sleep.* New York: Crown Publishers.

Barrett, L. F., & Salovey, P. (Eds). (2002). *The wisdom in feeling: Psychological processes in emotional intelligence.* New York: Guilford Press.

Barrett, M. (1999). *The development of language.* Philadelphia: Psychology Press.

Barringer, T. A., & Weaver, E. M. (2002). Does long-term bupropion (Zyban) use prevent smoking relapse after initial success at quitting smoking? *Journal of Family Practice, 51,* 172.

Barron, G., & Yechiam, E. (2002). Private e-mail requests and the diffusion of responsibility. *Computers in Human Behavior, 18,* 507–520.

Bartecchi, C. E., MacKenzie, T. D., & Schrier, R. W. (1995, May). The global tobacco epidemic. *Scientific American,* pp. 44–51.

Bartholow, B. D., & Anderson, C. A. (2002). Effects of violent video games on aggressive behavior: Potential sex differences. *Journal of Experimental Social Psychology, 38,* 283–290.

Bartlett, F. (1932). *Remembering: A study in experimental and social psychology.* Cambridge, England: Cambridge University Press.

Bartocci, G. (2004). Transcendence techniques and psychobiological mechanisms underlying religious experience. *Mental Health, Religion and Culture, 7,* 171–181.

Bartoshuk, L. (2000, July/August). The bitter with the sweet. *APS Observer, 11,* 33.

Bartoshuk, L., & Drewnowski, A. (1997, February). Symposium presented at the annual meeting of the American Association for the Advancement of Science, Seattle.

Bartoshuk, L., & Lucchina, L. (1997, January 13). Are you a supertaster? *U.S. News & World Report,* pp. 58–59.

Bartzokis, G., Nuechterlein, K. H., Lu, P. H., Gitlin, M., Rogers, S., & Mintz, J. (2003). Dysregulated brain development in adult men with schizophrenia: A magnetic resonance imaging study. *Biological Psychiatry, 53,* 412–421.

Basch, M. F. (1996). Affect and defense. In D. L. Nathanson (Ed.), *Knowing feeling: Affect, script, and psychotherapy.* New York: W. W. Norton.

Bass, A. (1996, April 21). Is anger good for you? *Boston Globe Magazine,* pp. 20–41.

Bates, E. (2005). Plasticity, localization, and language development. In S. T. Parker and J. Langer (Eds.), *Biology and knowledge revisited: From neurogenesis to psychogenesis.* Mahwah, NJ: Lawrence Erlbaum Associates.

Bates, P. E., Cuvo, T., Miner, C. A., & Korabek, C. A. (2001). Simulated and community-based instruction involving persons with mild and moderate mental retardation. *Research in Developmental Disabilities, 22,* 95–115.

Bates, R. (2002). Liking and similarity as predictors of multi-source ratings. *Personnel Review, 31,* 540–552.

Batson, C. D., & Powell, A. A. (2003). Altruism and prosocial behavior. In T. Millon & M. J. Lerner (Eds.), *Handbook of psychology: Personality and social psychology* (Vol. 5). New York: Wiley.

Batson, C. D., Ahmad, N., Lishner, D. A., & Tsang, J. A. (2002). Empathy and altruism. In C. R. Snyder & S. J. Lopez (Eds.), *Handbook of positive psychology,* pp. 485–498. London: Oxford University Press.

Bauer, P. J. (1996). What do infants recall of their lives? Memory for specific events by one- to two-year-olds. 102nd Annual Convention of the American Psychological Association. (1994, Los Angeles, California, U.S.). *American Psychologist, 51,* 29–41.

Baum, A. (1994). Behavioral, biological, and environmental interactions in disease processes. In S. Blumenthal, K. Matthews, & S. Weiss (Eds.), *New research frontiers in behavioral medicine: Proceedings of the National Conference.* Washington, DC: NIH Publications.

Baum, A. S., Revenson, R. A., & Singer, J. E. (Eds.). (2002). *Handbook of health psychology.* Mahwah, NJ: Erlbaum.

Baumeister, A. A., & Francis, J. L. (2002). Historical development of the dopamine hypothesis of schizophrenia. *Journal of the History of the Neurosciences, 11,* 265–277.

Baumeister, R. F. (1998). The self. In D. T. Gilbert & S. T. Fiske (Eds.), *The handbook of social psychology* (Vol. 1, 4th ed.). Boston: McGraw-Hill.

Baumeister, R. F., Campbell, J. D., & Krueger, J. I. (2003). Does high self-esteem cause better performance, interpersonal success, happiness, or healthier lifestyles? *Psychological Science in the Public Interest, 4,* 1–44.

Baumeister, R. F., DeWall, C. N., & Ciarocco, N. J. (2005) Social exclusion impairs self-regulation. *Journal of Personality and Social Psychology, 88,* 589–604.

Baumeister, R. F., & Twenge, J. M. (2002). Cultural suppression of female sexuality. *Review of General Psychology, 6,* 166–203.

Baumeister, R. F., Twenge, J. M., & Nuss, C. K. (2002). Effects of social exclusion on cognitive processes: Anticipated aloneness reduces intelligent thought. *Journal of Personality and Social Psychology, 83,* 817–827.

Baumgartner, F. (2002). The effect of hardiness in the choice of coping strategies in stressful situations. *Studia Psychologica, 44,* 69–75.

Baumrind, D. (1971). Current patterns of parental authority. *Developmental Psychology Monographs, 4* (1, pt. 2).

Baumrind, D. (1980). New directions in socialization research. *Psychological Bulletin, 35,* 639–652.

Baumrind, D., Larzelere, R. E., & Cowan, P. A. (2002). Ordinary physical punishment: Is it harmful? Comment on Gershoff (2002). *Psychological Bulletin, 32,* 42–51.

Bayer, D. L. (1996). Interaction in families with young adults with a psychiatric diagnosis. *American Journal of Family Therapy, 24,* 21–30.

Bayliss, D. M., Jarrold, C., Baddeley, A. D., & Gunn, D. M. (2005a). The relationship between short-term memory and working memory: Complex span made simple? *Memory, 13,* 414–421.

Bayliss, D. M., Jarrold, C., Baddeley, A. D., Gunn, D. M., & Leigh, E. (2005b). Mapping the developmental constraints on working memory span performance. *Developmental Psychology, 41,* 579–597.

Bayne, R. (2005). *Ideas and evidence: Critical reflections on MBTI® theory and practice.* Gainesville, FL: Center for Applications of Psychological Type, CAPT.

Baynes, K., Eliassenk J. C., Lutsep, H. L., & Gazzaniga, M. S. (1998, May 8). Modular organization of cognitive systems marked by interhemispheric integration. *Science, 280,* 902–905.

Bazell, B. (1998, August 25). Back pain goes high-tech. *Slate,* pp. 1–4.

Bearman, P. S., Moody, J., & Stovel, K. (2004). Chains of affection: The structure of adolescent romantic and sexual networks. *American Journal of Sociology, 110,* 44–91.

Beatty, J. (2000). *The human brain: Essentials of behavioral neuroscience.* Thousand Oaks, CA: Sage.

Beatty, W. W. (2002). Sex difference in geographical knowledge: Driving experience is not essential. *Journal of the International Neuropsychological Society, 8,* 804–810.

Beck, A. P., & Lewis, C. M. (Eds.). (2000). *The process of group psychotherapy: Systems for analyzing change.* Washington, DC: American Psychological Association.

Beck, A. T. (1991). Cognitive therapy: A 30-year perspective. *American Psychologist, 46,* 368–375.

Beck, A. T. (1995). Cognitive therapy: Past, present, and future. In M. J. Mahoney (Ed.), *Cognitive and constructive psychotherapies: Theory, research, and practice.* New York: Springer.

Beck, A. T. (2004). Cognitive therapy, behavior therapy, psychoanalysis, and pharmacotherapy: A cognitive continuum. In A. Freeman, M. J. Mahoney, P. Devito, & D. Martin (Eds.), *Cognition and Psychotherapy* (2nd ed.). New York: Springer Publishing Co.

Beck, A. T., & Emery, G., with Greenberg, R. L. (1985). *Anxiety disorders and phobias: A cognitive perspective.* New York: Basic Books.

Beck, A. T., Freeman, A., & Davis, D. D. (2004). *Cognitive therapy of personality disorders* (2nd edition). New York: Guilford Press.

Becker, T. (2003). Is emotional intelligence a viable concept? *Academy of Management Review, 28,* 192–195.

Beckham, E. E., & Leber, W. R. (Eds.). (1997). *Handbook of Depression* (2nd ed.). New York: Guilford Press.

Bedard, W. W., & Parsinger, M. A. (1995). Prednisolone blocks extreme intermale social aggression in seizure-induced, brain-damaged rats: Implications for the amygdaloid central nucleus, corticotrophin-releasing factor, and electrical seizures. *Psychological Reports, 77,* 3–9.

Begg, D., & Langley, J. (2001). Changes in risky driving behavior from age 21 to 26 years. *Journal of Safety Research, 32,* 491–499.

Begley, S. (2002, September 13). The memory of September 11 is seared in your mind; But is it really true? *The Wall Street Journal,* p. B1.

Begley, S. (2003, April 4). Likely suicide bombers include some profiles you'd never suspect. *The Wall Street Journal,* p. B1.

Begley, S. (2004, October 1). New ethical minefield: Drugs to boost memory and sharpen attention. *The Wall Street Journal,* p. B1.

Begley, S. (2005a, April 29). Evolution psychology may not help explain our behavior after all. *The Wall Street Journal,* p. D1.

Begley, S. (2005b, August 19). A spotless mind may ease suffering but erase identity. *The Wall Street Journal,* p. B1.

Beilin, H. (1996). Mind and meaning: Piaget and Vygotsky on causal explanation. *Human Development, 39,* 277–286.

Beilock, S. L., & Carr, T. H. (2005). When high-powered people fail: Working memory and "choking under pressure" in math. *Psychological Science, 16,* 101–105.

Bell, J., Grekul, J., Lamba, N., & Minas, C. (1995). The impact of cost on student helping behavior. *Journal of Social Psychology, 135,* 49–56.

Bellack, A. S., Hersen, M., & Kazdin, A. E. (1990). *International handbook of behavior modification and therapy.* New York: Plenum.

Bellezza, F. S. (2000). Mnemonic devices. In A. E. Kazdin (Ed.), *Encyclopedia of psychology: Vol. 5* (pp. 286–287). Washington, DC: American Psychological Association.

Bellezza, F. S., Six, L. S., & Phillips, D. S. (1992). A mnemonic for remembering long strings of digits. *Bulletin of the Psychonomic Society, 30,* 271–274.

Belli, R. F., & Loftus, E. F. (1996). The pliability of autobiographical memory: Misinformation and the false memory problem. In D. C. Rubin (Ed.), *Remembering our past: Studies in autobiographical memory* (pp. 157–179). New York: Cambridge University Press.

Belsky, J. (2002). Quantity counts: Amount of child care and children's socioemotional development. *Journal of Developmental and Behavioral Pediatarics, 23,* 167–170.

Belsky, J., & Rovine, M. (1988). Nonmaternal care in the first year of life and infant-parent attachment security. *Child Development, 59,* 157–167.

Bem, D. J. (1996). Exotic becomes erotic: A developmental theory of sexual orientation. *Psychological Review, 103,* 320–335.

Bem, D. J., & Honorton, C. (1994). Does psi exist? Replicable evidence for an anomalous process of information transfer. *Psychological Bulletin, 115,* 4–18.

Bem, S. L. (1993). *Lenses of gender.* New Haven, CT: Yale University Press.

Bem, S. L. (1998). *An unconventional family.* New Haven, CT: Yale University Press.

Benbow, C. P., Lubinski, D., & Hyde, J. S. (1997). Mathematics: Is biology the cause of gender differences in performance? In M. R. Walsh (Ed.), *Women, men, and gender: Ongoing debates.* New Haven, CT: Yale University Press.

Benca, R. M. (2005). Diagnosis and treatment of chronic insomnia: A review. *Psychiatric Services, 56,* 332–343.

Benderly, B. L. (2004). Looking beyond the SAT. *American Psychological Society, 17,* 12–18.

Benight, C. C. (2004). Collective efficacy following a series of natural disasters. *Stress and Coping: An International Journal, 17,* 401–420.

Benjamin, L. T., Jr. (1985, February). Defining aggression: An exercise for classroom discussion. *Teaching of Psychology, 12* (1), 40–42.

Bennett, M. R. (2000). The concept of long term potentiation of transmission of synapses. *Progress in Neurobiology, 60,* 109–137.

Benson, E. (2003, April). The science of sexual arousal. *Monitor on Psychology,* pp. 50–56.

Benson, H. (1993). The relaxation response. In D. Goleman & J. Guerin (Eds.), *Mind-body medicine: How to use your mind for better health.* Yonkers, NY: Consumer Reports Publications.

Benson, H., Kornhaber, A., Kornhaber, C., LeChanu, M. N., et al. (1994). Increases in positive psychological characteristics with a new relaxation-response curriculum in high school students. *Journal of Research and Development in Education, 27,* 226–231.

Bentall, R. P. (1992). The classification of schizophrenia. In D. J. Kavanagh (Ed.), *Schizophrenia: An overview and practical handbook.* London: Chapman & Hall.

Benton, S. A., Robertson, J. M., Tseng, W. C., Newton, F. B., & Benton, S. L. (2003). Changes in counseling center client problems across 13 years. *Professional Psychology: Research and Practice, 34,* 66–72.

Bergh, C., Sjostedt, S., Hellers, G., Zandian, M., & Sodersten, P. (2003). Meal size, satiety and cholecystokinin in gastrectomized humans. *Physiological Behavior, 78,* 143–147.

Bergin, A. E., & Garfield, S. L. (Eds.). (1994). *Handbook of psychotherapy and behavior change* (4th ed.). New York: Wiley.

Berguier, A., & Ashton, R. (1992). Characteristics of the frequent nightmare sufferer. *Journal of Abnormal Psychology, 101,* 246–250.

Berk, L. E. (2005). Why parenting matters. In S. Olfman (Ed.), *Childhood lost: How American culture is failing our kids* (pp. 19–53). Westport, CT: Praeger Publishers/Greenwood Publishing Group.

Berkowitz, C. D. (2000). The long-term medical consequences of sexual abuse. In R. M. Reece, et al. (Eds.), *Treatment of child abuse: Common ground for mental health, medical, and legal practitioners.* Baltimore: Johns Hopkins University Press.

Berkowitz, L. (1989). Frustration-aggression hypothesis. *Psychological Bulletin, 106,* 59–73.

Berkowitz, L. (1990). On the formation and regulation of anger and aggression: A cognitive-neoassociationistic analysis. *American Psychologist, 45,* 494–503.

Berkowitz, L. (1993). *Aggression: Its causes, consequences, and control.* New York: McGraw-Hill.

Berkowitz, L. (2001). On the formation and regulation of anger and aggression: A cognitive-neoassociationistic analysis. In W. G. Parrott (Ed.), *Emotions in social psychology: Essential readings.* New York: Psychology Press.

Berkowitz, L., & Geen, R. G. (1966). Film violence and the cue properties of available targets. *Journal of Personality and Social Psychology, 3,* 525–530.

Berkowitz, L., & LePage, A. (1967). Weapons as aggression-eliciting stimuli. *Journal of Personality and Social Psychology, 7,* 202–207.

Berliner, L., & Elliott, D. M. (2002). Sexual abuse of children. In J. E. B. Myers & L. Berliner, et al. (Eds.), *The APSAC handbook on child maltreatment* (2nd ed., pp. 55–78). Thousand Oaks, CA: Sage.

Berlyne, D. (1967). Arousal and reinforcement. In D. Levine (Ed.), *Nebraska symposium on motivation.* Lincoln: University of Nebraska Press.

Berman, R. M., Krystal, J. H., & Charney, D. S. (1996). Mechanism of action of antidepressants: Monoamine hypotheses and beyond. In S. J. Watson (Ed.), *Biology of schizophrenia and affective disease.* Washington, DC: American Psychiatric Press.

Bernal, G., Trimble, J. E., Burlew, A. K., & Leong, F. T. (Eds.) (2002). *Handbook of racial and ethnic minority psychology.* Thousand Oaks, CA: Sage.

Bernard, L. L. (1924). *Instinct: A study in social psychology.* New York: Holt.

Bernstein, D. M., Loftus, G. R., & Meltzoff, A. N. (2005). Object identification in preschool children and adults. *Developmental Science, 8,* 151–161.

Berntsen, D., & Rubin, D. C. (2004). Cultural life scripts structure recall from autobiographical memory. *Memory and Cognition, 32,* 427–442.

Berntsen, D., & Thomsen, D. K. (2005). Personal memories for remote historical events: Accuracy and clarity of flashbulb memories related to World War II. *Journal of Experimental Psychology: General, 134,* 242–257.

Berrettini, W. H. (2000). Are schizophrenic and bipolar disorders related? A review of family and molecular studies [Special issue: A special issue on bipolar disorder]. *Biological Psychiatry, 48,* 531–538.

Berridge, K. C. (2004). Motivation concepts in behavioral neuroscience. *Physiology and Behavior, 81,* 179–209.

Berrios, G. E. (1996). *The history of mental symptoms: Descriptive psychopathology since the nineteenth century.* Cambridge, England: Cambridge University Press.

Bersoff, D. M. (1999). Why good people sometimes do bad things: Motivated reasoning and unethical behavior. *Personality and Social Psychology Bulletin, 25,* 28–39.

Berthoud, H. R. (2002). Multiple neural systems controlling food intake and body weight. *Neuroscience and Biobehavioral Reviews, 26,* 393–428.

Betancourt, H., & Lopez, S. R. (1993). The study of culture, ethnicity, and race in American Psychology. *American Psychologist, 48,* 1586–1596.

Beutler, L. E., Brown, M. T., Crothers, L., Booker, K., et al. (1996). The dilemma of factitious demographic distinctions in psychological research. *Journal of Consulting and Clinical Psychology, 64,* 892–902.

Beyene, Y. (1989). *From menarche to menopause: Reproductive lives of peasant women in two cultures.* Albany, NY: State University of New York Press.

Beyene, Y. (1992). Menopause: A biocultural event. In A. J. Dan, & L. L. Lewis (Eds.), *Menstrual health in women's lives.* Chicago: University of Illinois Press.

Bialystok, E., & Martin, M. M. (2004). Attention and inhibition in bilingual children: Evidence from the dimensional change card sort task. *Developmental Science, 7,* 325–339.

Bianchi, S. M., & Casper, L. M. (2000). American Families. *Population Bulletin, 55*(4).

Biederman, I. (1987). Recognition-by-components: A theory of human image understanding. *Psychological Review, 94,* 115–147.

Biederman, I. (1990). Higher-level vision. In D. N. Osherson, S. Kosslyn, & J. Hollerbach (Eds.), *An invitation to cognitive science: Visual cognition and action.* Cambridge, MA: MIT.

Biernat, M. (2003). Toward a broader view of social stereotyping. *American Psychologist, 58,* 1019–1027.

Binet, A., & Simon, T. (1916). *The development of intelligence in children (The Binet-Simon Scale).* Baltimore: Williams & Wilkins.

Bingenheimer, J. B., Brennan, R. T., & Earls, F. J. (2005, May 27). Firearm violence exposure and serious violent behavior. *Science, 308,* 1323–1327.

Binstock, R., & George, L. K. (Eds.). (1996). *Handbook of aging and the social sciences* (4th ed.). San Diego, CA: Academic Press.

Birch, H. G. (1945). The role of motivation factors in insightful problem solving. *Journal of Comparative Psychology, 38,* 295–317.

Birren, J. E. (Ed.). (1996). *Encyclopedia of gerontology: Age, aging and the aged.* San Diego, CA: Academic Press.

Bishop, M. (2005). Quality of life and psychosocial adaptation to chronic illness and disability: Preliminary analysis of a conceptual and theoretical synthesis. *Rehabilitation Counseling Bulletin, 48,* 219–231.

Bjork, R. A., & Richardson-Klarehn, A. (1989). On the puzzling relationship between environmental context and human memory. In C. Izawa (Ed.), *Current issues in cognitive processes: The Tulane-Floweree symposium on cognition.* Hillsdale, NJ: Erlbaum.

Black, B. M., & Weisz, A. N. (2004). Dating violence: A qualitative analysis of Mexican American youths' views. *Journal of Ethnic and Cultural Diversity in Social Work, 13,* 69–90.

Black, P. H., & Barbutt, L. D. (2002). Stress, inflammation and cardiovascular disease. *Journal of Psychosomatic Research, 52,* 1–23.

Blagrove, M., Farmer, L., & Williams, E. (2004). The relationship of nightmare frequency and nightmare distress to well-being. *Journal of Sleep Research, 13,* 129–136.

Blair, C. A., Thompson, L. F., & Wuensch, K. L. (2005). Electronic helping behavior: The virtual presence of others makes a difference. *Basic and Applied Social Psychology, 27,* 171–178.

Blais, F. C., Morin, C. M., Boisclair, A., Grenier, V., & Guay, B. (2001). Insomnia: Prevalence and treatment of patients in general practice [Article in French]. *Canadian Family Physician, 47,* 759–767.

Blakeslee, S. (1991, August 7). Levels of caffeine in various foods. *The New York Times.*

Blakeslee, S. (1992, August 11). Finding a new messenger for the brain's signals to the body. *The New York Times,* p. C3.

Blakeslee, S. (2000, January 4). A decade of discovery yields a shock about the brain. *The New York Times,* p. D1.

Blass, T. (1996). Attribution of responsibility and trust in the Milgram obedience experiment. *Journal of Applied Social Psychology, 26,* 1529–1535.

Blass, T. (Ed.) (2000). *Obedience to authority: Current perspectives on the Milgram Paradigm.* Mahwah, NJ: Erlbaum.

Blau, Z. S. (1973). *Old age in a changing society.* New York: New Viewpoints.

Blewett, A. E. (2000). Help cards for patients. *Psychiatric Bulletin, 24,* 276.

Block, R. I., O'Leary, D. S., Ehrhardt, J. C., Augustinack, J. C., Ghoneim, M. M., Arndt, S., & Hall, J. A. (2000). Effects of frequent marijuana use on brain tissue volume and composition. *Neuroreport 11,* 491–496.

Blum, D. (2002). *Love at goon park: Harry Harlow and the science of affection.* Cambridge, MA: Perseus.

Blume, S. B. (1998, March). Alcoholism in women. *The Harvard Mental Health Letter,* pp. 5–7.

Boahen, K. (2005, May). Neuromorphic microchips. *Scientific American,* pp. 56–64.

Boehm, K. E., & Campbell, N. B. (1995). Suicide: A review of calls to an adolescent peer listening phone service. *Child Psychiatry and Human Development, 26,* 61–66.

Boles, D. B. (2005). A large-sample study of sex differences in functional cerebral lateralization. *Journal of Clinical and Experimental Neuropsychology, 27,* 759–768.

Bolger, N., Zuckerman, A., & Kessler, R. C. (2000). Invisible support and adjustment to stress. *Journal of Personality and Social Psychology, 79,* 953–961.

Bolla, K. I., Cadet, J. L., & London, E. D. (1998). The neuropsychiatry of chronic cocaine abuse. *Journal of Neuropsychiatry and Clinical Neurosciences, 10,* 280–289.

Boller, F. (2004). Rational basis of rehabilitation following cerebral lesions: A review of the concept of cerebral plasticity. *Functional Neurology: New Trends in Adaptive and Behavioral Disorders, 19,* 65–72.

Bolonna, A. A., & Kerwin, R. W. (2005). Partial agonism and schizophrenia. *British Journal of Psychiatry, 186,* 7–10.

Bonanno, G. A. (2004). Loss, trauma, and human resilience: Have we underestimated the human capacity to thrive after extremely aversive events? *American Psychologist, 59,* 20–28.

Bond, J. T., Thompson, C., Galinsky, E., & Prottas, D. (2003). *Highlights of the 2002 national survey of the changing workforce (No. 3).* New York: Families and Work Institute.

Borbely, A. (1986). *Secrets of sleep* (p. 43, graph). New York: Basic Books.

Bordnick, P. S., Elkins, R. L., Orr, T. E., Walters, P., & Thyer, B. A. (2004). Evaluating the relative effectiveness of three aversion therapies designed to reduce craving among cocaine abusers. *Behavioral Interventions, 19,* 1–24.

Bornstein, M. H., & Arterberry, M. (1999) Perceptual development. In M. Bornstein & M. Lamb (Eds.), *Developmental Psychology.* Mahwah, NJ: Erlbaum.

Bornstein, R. F. (2001). The impending death of psychoanalysis. *Psychoanalytic Psychology, 18,* 3–20.

Bornstein, R. F. (2003). Psychodynamic models of personality. In T. Millon & M. J. Lerner (Eds.), *Handbook of psychology: Personality and social psychology* (Vol. 5). New York: Wiley.

Bortfeld, H., & Whitehurst, G. J. (2001). Sensitive periods in first language acquisition. In D. B. Bailey, Jr., J. T. Bruer, et al. (Eds.), *Critical thinking about critical periods,* pp. 173–192. Baltimore, MD: Paul H. Brookes.

Bosma, H., van Boxtel, M. P. J., Ponds, R. W. H. M., Houx, P. J. H., Burdorf, A., & Jolles, J. (2002). Mental work demands protect against cognitive impairment: MAAS prospective cohort study. *Experimental Aging Research, 29,* 33–45.

Botting, J. H., & Morrison, A. R. (1997, February). Animal research is vital to medicine. *Scientific American, 276.* 83–86.

Botvinick, M. (2004, August 6). Probing the neural basis of body ownership. *Science, 305,* 782–783.

Bouchard, C., & Bray, G. A. (Eds.). (1996). *Regulation of body weight: Biological and behavioral mechanisms.* New York: Wiley.

Bouchard, T. J., Jr. (2004). Genetic influence on human psychological traits: A survey. *Current Directions in Psychological Science, 13,* 148–151.

Bouchard, T. J., Segal, N. L., & Tellegen, A. (2004). Genetic influence on social attitudes: Another challenge to psychology from behavior genetics. In L. F. DiLalla (Ed.), *Behavior genetics principles: Perspectives in development, personality, and psychopathology.* Washington, DC: American Psychological Association.

Bourke, P. A., & Duncan, J. (2005). Effect of template complexity on visual search and dual-task performance. *Psychological Science, 16,* 208–213.

Bourne, L. E., Dominowski, R. L., Loftus, E. F., & Healy, A. F. (1986). *Cognitive processes* (2nd ed.). Englewood Cliffs, NJ: Prentice Hall.

Bower, G. H., Thompson, S. S., & Tulving, E. (1994). Reducing retroactive interference: An interference analysis. *Journal of Experimental Psychology Learning, Memory, and Cognition, 20,* 51–66.

Bower, J. M., & Parsons, L. M. (2003, August). Rethinking the "lesser brain." *Scientific American,* pp. 51–57.

Boyce, W. T., & Ellis, B. J. (2005). Biological sensitivity to context: An evolutionary-developmental theory of the origins and functions of stress reactivity. *Development and Psychopathology, 17,* 271–301.

Boyd-Wilson, B. M., McClure, J., & Walkey, F. H. (2004). Are wellbeing and illusory perceptions linked? The answer may be yes, but. . . . *Australian Journal of Psychology, 56,* 1–9.

Boyle, G. J., Goldman, R., Svoboda, J. S., & Fernandez, E. (2002). Male circumcision: Pain, trauma and psychosexual sequelae. *Journal of Health Psychology, 7,* 329–343.

Boyle, S. H., Williams, R. B., Mark, D. B., Brummett, B. H., Siegler, I. C., & Barefoot, J. C. (2005). Hostility, age, and mortality in a sample of cardiac patients. *American Journal of Cardiology, 96*, 64–72.

Bozarth, J. D., Zimring, F. M., & Tausch, R. (2002). Client-centered therapy: The evolution of a revolution. In D. J. Cain (Ed.), *Humanistic psychotherapies: Handbook of research and practice* (pp. 147–188). Washington, DC: American Psychological Association.

Brady, N., Campbell, M., & Flaherty, M. (2005). Perceptual asymmetries are preserved in memory for highly familiar faces of self and friend. *Brain and Cognition, 58*, 334–342.

Brambilla, P., Cipriani, A., Hotopf, M., & Barbui, C. (2005). Side-effect profile of fluoxetine in comparison with other SSRIs, tricyclic and newer antidepressants: A meta-analysis of clinical trial data. *Pharmacopsychiatry, 38*, 69–77.

Brasic, J. R. (2002). Conversion disorder in childhood. *German Journal of Psychiatry, 5*, 54–61.

Brazelton, T. B. (1969). *Infants and mothers: Differences in development.* New York: Dell.

Breakwell, G. M., Hammond, S., & Fife-Schaw, C. (Eds.). (1995). *Research methods in psychology.* Newbury Park, CA: Sage.

Brehm, J. W., & Self, E. A. (1989). The intensity of motivation. *Annual Review of Psychology, 40*, 109–131.

Breland, K., & Breland, M. (1961). Misbehavior of organisms. *American Psychologist, 16*, 681–684.

Brendgen, M., Vitaro, F., & Bukowski, W. M. (2000). Stability and variability of adolescents' affiliation with delinquent friends: Predictors and consequences. *Social Development, 9*, 205–225.

Brewer, J. B., Zhao, Z., Desmond, J. E., Glover, G. H., & Gabrieli, J. D. E. (1998, August 21). Making memories: Brain activity that predicts how well visual experience will be remembered. *Science, 281*, 1185–1187.

Brewer, M. B., & Hewstone, M. (Eds.). (2003). *Social cognition.* Malden, MA: Blackwell Publishers.

Brislin, R. (1993). *Understanding culture's influence on behavior.* Fort Worth, TX: Harcourt Brace Jovanovich.

Brock, T. C., & Green, M. C. (Eds.). (2005). *Persuasion: Psychological insights and perspectives* (2nd ed.). Thousand Oaks, CA: Sage Publications.

Brody, A. L., Saxena, S., Stoessel, P., Gillies, L. A., Fairbanks, L. A.,

Alborzian, L., Phelps, M. E., Huang, S-C., Wu, H-M., Ho, M. L., Ho, M. K., Au, S. C., Maidment, K., & Baxter, L. R., Jr. (2001). Regional brain metabolic changes in patients with major depression treated with either paroxetine or interpersonal therapy. *Archives of General Psychiatry, 58*, 631–640.

Broidy, L. M., Nagin, D. S., & Tremblay, R. E. (2003). Developmental trajectories of childhood disruptive behaviors and adolescent delinquency: A six-site, cross-national study. *Developmental Psychology, 39*, 222–245.

Broman, C. L. (2005). Stress, race and substance use in college. *College Student Journal, 39*, 340–352.

Bronner, E. (1998, November 24). Study casts doubt on the benefits of S.A.T. coaching courses. *The New York Times,* p. A19.

Brookhiser, R. (1997, January 13). Lost in the weed. *U.S. News & World Report,* p. 9.

Brooks-Gunn, J., Han, W., & Waldfogel, J. (2002). Maternal employment and child cognitive outcomes in the first three years of life: The NICHD study of early child care. *Child Development, 73*, 1052–1072.

Brown, A. S., Susser, E. S., Butler, P. D., Andrews, R. R., et al. (1996). Neurobiological plausibility of prenatal nutritional deprivation as a risk factor for schizophrenia. *Journal of Nervous and Mental Disease, 184*, 71–85.

Brown, D. C. (1994). Subgroup norming: Legitimate testing practice or reverse discrimination? *American Psychologist, 49*, 927–928.

Brown, E. (2001, September 17). The World Health Organization takes on big tobacco (but don't hold your breath): Anti-smoking advocates are mounting a global campaign: It's going to be a long, hard fight. *Forbes,* pp. 37–41.

Brown, M. B., (2000). Diagnosis and treatment of children and adolescents with attention-deficit/hyperactivity disorder. *Journal of Counseling & Development, 78*, 195–203.

Brown, L. S., & Pope, K. S. (1996). *Recovered memories of abuse: Assessment, therapy, forensics.* Washington, DC: American Psychological Association.

Brown, P. K., & Wald, G. (1964). Visual pigments in single rod and cones of the human retina. *Science, 144*, 45–52.

Brown, R. (1958). How shall a thing be called? *Psychological Review, 65*, 14–21.

Brown, S. I., & Walter, M. I. (Eds.). (1993). *Problem posing: Reflections and applications.* Hillsdale, NJ: Erlbaum.

Bruce, B., & Wilfley, D. (1996). Binge eating among the overweight population: A serious and prevalent problem. *Journal of the American Dietetic Association, 96*, 58–61.

Bruce, V., Green, P. R., & Georgeson, M. (1997). *Visual perception: Physiology, psychology and ecology* (3rd ed.). Mahwah, NJ: Erlbaum.

Bruehl, S., & Chung, O. K. (2004). *Psychological interventions for acute pain.* Mahwah, NJ: Lawrence Erlbaum Associates.

Bruer, J. T. (2001). A critical and sensitive period primer. In D. B. Bailey, Jr., J. T. Bruer, et al. (Eds.), *Critical thinking about critical periods,* pp. 173–192. Baltimore, MD: Paul H. Brookes.

Bryant, R. M., Coker, A. D., Durodoye, B. A., McCollum, V. J., Pack-Brown, S. P., Constantine, M. G., & O'Bryant, B. J. (2005). Having our say: African American women, diversity, and counseling. *Journal of Counseling and Development, 83*, 313–319.

Brydon, L., Edwards, S., Mohamed-Ali, V., & Steptoe, A. (2004). Socioeconomic status and stress-induced increases in interleukin-6. *Brain, Behavior, and Immunity, 18*, 281–290.

Brzustowicz, L. M., Hodgkinson, K. A., Chow, E. W. C., Honer, W. G., & Bassett, A. S. (2000, April 28). Location of major susceptibility locus for familial schizophrenia on chromosome 1q21-q22. *Science, 288*, 678–682.

Buchanan, T. W., & Adolphs, R. (2004). The neuroanatomy of emotional memory in humans. In D. Reisberg & P. Hertel (Eds.), *Memory and emotion* (pp. 42–75). London: Oxford University Press.

Buchert, R., Thomasius, R., Wilke, F., Petersen, K., Nebeling, B., Obrocki, J., Schulze, O., Schmidt, U., & Clausen, M. (2004). A voxel-based PET investigation of the long-term effects of "ecstasy" consumption on brain serotonin transporters. *American Journal of Psychiatry, 161*, 1181–1189.

Buckout, R. (1974). Eyewitness testimony. *Scientific American, 231*, pp. 23–31.

Bukowski, W. M., Newcomb, A. F., & Hartup, W. W. (Eds.). (1996). *The company they keep: Friendship in childhood and adolescence.* New York: Cambridge University Press.

Bulik, C. M., Tozzi, F., Anderson, C., Mazzeo, S. E., Aggen, S., & Sullivan, P. F. (2003). The relation between eating disorders and components of perfectionism. *American Journal of Psychiatry, 160,* 366–368.

Burbach, M. E., Matkin, G. S., & Fritz, S. M. (2004). Teaching critical thinking in an introductory leadership course utilizing active learning strategies: A confirmatory study. *College Student Journal, 38,* 482–493.

Burchinal, M. R., Roberts, J. E., & Riggins, R., Jr. (2000). Relating quality of center-based child care to early cognitive and language development longitudinally. *Child Development, 71,* 338–357.

Burd, L., Cotsonas-Hassler, T. M., Martsolf, J. T., & Kerbeshian, J. (2003). Recognition and management of fetal alcohol syndrome. *Neurotoxicological Teratology, 25,* 681–688.

Burger, J. M. (1986). Increasing compliance by improving the deal: The that's-not-all technique. *Journal of Personality and Social Psychology, 51,* 277–283.

Burger, J. M., & Caldwell, D. F. (2003). The effects of monetary incentives and labeling on the foot-in-the-door effect: Evidence for a self-perception process. *Basic and Applied Social Psychology, 25,* 235–241.

Burgess, D., & Borgida, E. (1997). Sexual harassment: An experimental test of sex-role spillover theory. *Personality and Social Psychology Bulletin, 23,* 63–75.

Burgoon, J. K., & Bacue, A. E. (2003). Nonverbal communication skills. In J. O. Greene & B. R. Burleson (Eds.), *Handbook of communication and social interaction skills* (pp. 179–219). Mahwah, NJ: Lawrence Erlbaum.

Burgoon, J. K., Bonito, J. A., Ramirez, A. J. R., Dunbar, N. E., Kam, K., & Fischer, J. (2002). Testing the interactivity principle: Effects of mediation, propinquity, and verbal and nonverbal modalities in interpersonal interaction [Special Issue: Research on the relationship between verbal and nonverbal communication: Emerging integrations]. *Journal of Communication, 52,* 657–677.

Burke, D. M., & Shafto, M. A. (2004). Aging and language production. *Current Directions in Psychological Science, 13,* 21–25.

Bushman, B. J. (1993). Human aggression while under the influence of alcohol and other drugs: An integrative research review. *Current Directions in Psychological Science, 2,* 148–152.

Bushman, B. J., & Anderson, C. A. (2001). Media violence and the American public: Scientific facts versus media misinformation. *American Psychologist, 56,* 477–489.

Bushman, B. J., & Anderson, C. A. (2002). Violent video games and hostile expectations: A test of the general aggression model. *Personality and Social Psychology Bulletin, 28,* 1679–1686.

Bushman, B. J., Baumeister, R. F., Phillips, C. M. (2001). Do people aggress to improve their mood? Catharsis beliefs, affect regulation opportunity, and aggressive responding. *Journal of Personality and Social Psychology, 81,* 17–32.

Bushman, B. J., Wang, M. C., & Anderson, C. A. (2005). Is the curve relating temperature to aggression linear or curvilinear? Assaults and temperature in Minneapolis reexamined. *Journal of Personality and Social Psychology, 89,* 62–66.

Buss, D. (2003). *Evolutionary psychology.* Boston: Allyn & Bacon.

Buss, D. M. (2000). The evolution of happiness. *American Psychologist, 55,* 15–23.

Buss, D. M. (2001). Human nature and culture: An evolutionary psychological perspective. *Journal of Personality, 69,* 955–978.

Buss, D. M. (2003a) *The evolution of desire: Strategies of human mating.* New York: Basic Books.

Buss, D. M. (2003b). Sexual strategies: A journey into controversy. *Psychological Inquiry, 14,* 219–226.

Buss, D. M. (2004). Sex differences in human mate preferences: Evolutionary hypotheses tested in 37 cultures. In H. T. Reis & C. E. Rusbult (Eds.), *Close relationships: Key readings.* Philadelphia, PA: Taylor & Francis.

Buss, D. M., Abbott, M., & Angleitner, A. (1990). International preferences in selecting mates: A study of 37 cultures. *Journal of Cross-Cultural Psychology, 21,* 5–47.

Buss, D. M., & Kenrick, D. T. (1998). Evolutionary social psychology. In D. T. Gilbert, S. T. Fiske, & G. Lindzey (Eds.), *The handbook of social psychology.* (Vol. 2, 4th ed.). Boston: McGraw-Hill.

Buss, D. M., Larsen, R. J., Westen, D., & Semmelroth, J. (1992). Sex differences in jealousy: Evolution, physiology, and psychology. *Psychological Science, 3,* 251–255.

Butcher, J. N. (1995). Interpretation of the MMPI-2. In L. E. Beutler, & M. R. Berren (Eds.), *Integrative assessment of adult personality.* New York: Guilford Press.

Butcher, J. N. (2005). *A beginner's guide to the MMPI-2* (2nd ed.). Washington, DC: American Psychological Association.

Butcher, J. N., Graham, J. R., Dahlstrom, W. G., & Bowman, E. (1990). The MMPI-2 with college students. *Journal of Personality Assessment, 54,* 1–15.

Butler, L. T., & Berry, D. C. (2004). Understanding the relationship between repetition priming and mere exposure. *British Journal of Psychology, 95,* 467–487.

Byne, W. (1996). Biology and homosexuality: Implications of neuroendocrinological and neuroanatomical studies. In R. P. Cabaj & T. S. Stein (Eds.), *Textbook of homosexuality and mental health.* Washington, DC: American Psychiatric Press.

Byrne, B. M., & Watkins, D. (2003). The issue of measurement invariance revisited. *Journal of Cross-Cultural Psychology, 34,* 155–175.

Byrne, R. (2005, July 10). It's man vs. machine again, and man comes out limping. *The New York Times,* p. 29.

Cabanac, M., & Frankham, P. (2002). Evidence that transient nicotine lowers the body weight set point. *Physiology & Behavior, 76,* 539–542.

Cacioppo, J. T., & Berntson, G. G. (Eds.) (2004). *Essays in Social Neuroscience* Cambridge, MA: MIT.

Cacioppo, J. T., Berntson, G. G., & Crites, S. L., Jr. (1996). Social neuroscience: Principles of psychophysiological arousal and response. In E. T. Higgins & A. W. Kruglanski (Eds.), *Social psychology: Handbook of basic principles.* New York: Guilford.

Cadenhead, K., & Braff, D. L. Neurophysiology of schizophrenia: Attention, information processing, and inhibitory processes in schizophrenia. In J. A. Den Boer, H. G. M. Westenberg, & H. M. van Praag, *Advances in the neurobiology of schizophrenia.* Oxford, England: John Wiley & Sons.

Cadinu, M., Maass, A., & Rosabianca, A. (2005). Why do women underperform under stereotype threat? Evidence for the role of negative thinking. *Psychological Science, 16,* 572–578.

Cahill, L. (2005, May). His brain, her brain. *Scientific American,* pp. 40–47.

Cain, D. J. (Ed.). (2002). *Humanistic psychotherapies: Handbook of research and practice.* Washington, DC: American Psychological Association.

Calderon, M. E., & Minaya-Rowe, L. (2003). *Designing and implementing two-way bilingual programs: A step-by-step guide for administrators, teachers, and parents.* Thousand Oaks, CA: Corwin Press.

Calle, E. E., & Kaaks, R. (2004). Overweight, obesity and cancer: Epidemiological evidence and proposed mechanisms. *Nature Reviews Cancer 4,* 579–591.

Calmes, J. (1998, March 5). Americans retain puritan attitudes on matters of sex. *The Wall Street Journal,* p. A12.

Cameron, O. G. (2002). *Visceral sensory neuroscience: Interoception.* London: Oxford University Press.

Campfield, L. A., Smith, F. J., Rosenbaum, M., & Hirsch, J. (1996). Human eating: Evidence for a physiological basis using a modified paradigm [Special issue: Society for the Study of Ingestive Behavior, Second Independent Meeting]. *Neuroscience and Biobehavioral Reviews, 20,* 133–137.

Cannon, W. B. (1929). Organization for physiological homeostatics. *Physiological Review, 9,* 280–289.

Canteras, N. S. (2002). The medial hypothalamic defensive system: Hodological organization and functional implications [Special issue: Functional role of specific systems within the extended amygdala and hypothalamus]. *Pharmacology, Biochemistry and Behavior, 71,* 481–491.

Cantwell, R. H., & Andrews, B. (2002). Cognitive and psychological factors underlying secondary school students' feelings towards group work. *Educational Psychology, 22,* 75–91.

Capaldi, E. D. (Ed.). (1996). *Why we eat what we eat: The psychology of eating.* Washington, DC: American Psychological Association.

Cardemil, E. V., Pinedo, T. M., & Miller, I. W. (2005). Developing a culturally appropriate depression prevention program: The family coping skills program. *Cultural Diversity and Ethnic Minority Psychology, 11,* 99–112.

Carey, B. (2004, December 21). When pressure is on, good students suffer. *The New York Times,* p. D7.

Carli, L. L., & Bukatko, D. (2000). Gender, communication, and social influence: A developmental perspective. In T. Eckes & H. M. Thomas (Eds.), *Developmental social psychology of gender.* Mahwah, NJ: Lawrence Erlbaum.

Carmichael, M. (2004, December 6). Medicine's next level. *Newsweek,* pp. 45–49.

Carnegie Council on Adolescent Development. (1995). *Great transitions: Preparing adolescents for a new century.* New York: Carnegie Corporation of New York.

Carnegie Task Force on Meeting the Needs of Young Children. (1994). *Starting points: Meeting the needs of our youngest children.* New York: Carnegie Corporation.

Carney, R. N., & Levin, J. R. (1998). Coming to terms with the keyword method in introductory psychology: A "neuromnemonic" example. *Teaching of Psychology, 25,* 132–135.

Carney, R. N., & Levin, J. R. (2003). Promoting higher-order learning benefits by building lower-order mnemonic connections. *Applied Cognitive Psychology, 17,* 563–575.

Carpenter, S. (2001). Sleep deprivation may be undermining teen health. *APA Monitor, 32,* 42–45.

Carpenter, S. (2002, April). What can resolve the paradox of mental health disparities? *APA Monitor, 33,* 18.

Carpenter, J., & Maciel, O. (2004, July 6). Disabled man relies on monkey. *Orange County Register,* p. 1.

Carr, A. (2002). *Avoiding risky sex in adolescence.* New York: Blackwell.

Carroll, J. M., & Russell, J. A. (1997). Facial expressions in Hollywood's portrayal of emotion. *Journal of Personality and Social Psychology, 72,* 164–176.

Carter, A. S., O'Donnell, D. A., Schultz, R. T., Scahill, L., Leckman, J. F., & Pauls, D. (2000). Social and emotional adjustment in children affected with Gilles de la Tourette's Syndrome: Associations with ADHD and family functioning. *Journal of Child Psychology and Psychiatry, 41,* 215–223.

Carter, R. T. (2003). Becoming racially and culturally competent: The racial-cultural counseling laboratory. *Journal of Multicultural Counseling and Development, 31,* 20–30.

Carver, C., & Scheier, M. (2002). Coping processes and adjustment to chronic illness. In A. Christensen and M. Antoni (Eds.), *Chronic physical disorders: Behavioral medicine's perspective.* Malden: Blackwell Publishers.

Carver, C. S., Harris, S. D., Lehman, J. M., Durel, L. A., Antoni, M. H., Spencer, S. M., & Pozo-Kaderman, C. (2000). How important is the perception of personal control? Studies of early stage breast cancer patients. *Personality and Social Psychology Bulletin, 26,* 139–149.

Case, R., & Okamoto, Y. (1996). The role of central conceptual structures in the development of children's thought. *Monographs of the Society for Research in Child Development, 61,* v–265.

Casey, B. J. (2002, May 24). Windows into the human brain. *Science, 296,* 1408–1409.

Cashon, C. H., & Cohen, L. B. (2004). Beyond U-shaped development in infants' processing of faces: An information-processing account. *Journal of Cognition and Development, 5,* 59–80.

Caspi, A., Harrington, H., & Milne, B. (2003). Children's behavioral styles at age 3 are linked to their adult personality traits at age 26. *Journal of Personality, 71,* 495–513.

Cassidy, C., O'Connor, R. C., Howe, C., & Warden, D. (2004). Perceived discrimination and psychological distress: The role of personal and ethnic self-esteem. *Journal of Counseling Psychology, 51,* 329–339.

Cattell, R. B. (1965). *The scientific analysis of personality.* Chicago: Aldine.

Cattell, R. B. (1998). Where is intelligence? Some answers from the triadic theory. In J. J. McArdle & R. W. Woodcock (Eds.), *Human cognitive abilities in theory and practice* (pp. 29–38). Mahwah, NJ: Lawrence Erlbaum.

Cattell, R. B., Cattell, A. K., & Cattell, H. E. P. (1993). *Sixteen personality factor questionnaire (16PF)* (5th ed.). San Antonio, TX: Harcourt Brace.

Cattell, R. B., Cattell, A. K., & Cattell, H. E. P. (2000). *The sixteen personality factor™ (16PF®) questionnaire.* Champaign, IL: Institute for Personality and Ability Testing.

Cattell, R. B., Eber, L., & Tatsuoka, M. (1970, 1988, 1992). *Handbook for the 16PF.* Champaign, IL: Institute for Personality and Ability Testing.

Cavallini, E., Pagnin, A., and Vecchi, T. (2003). Aging and everyday memory:

The beneficial effect of memory training. *Archives of Gerontology & Geriatrics, 37,* 241–257.

Center on Addiction and Substance Abuse. (1994). *Report on college drinking.* New York: Columbia University Press.

Centers for Disease Control (CDC). (1992). *Most students sexually active: Survey of sexual activity.* Atlanta, GA: Centers for Disease Control.

Centers for Disease Control (CDC). (2000). *Suicide prevention fact sheet, National Center for Injury Prevention and Control.* Atlanta, GA: Centers for Disease Control and Prevention.

Centers for Disease Control (CDC). (2004a). *Chlamydia—CDC Fact Sheet.* Washington, DC: Centers for Disease Control and Prevention.

Centers for Disease Control (CDC). (2004b, June 11). Suicide and attempted suicide. *MMWR, 53,* 471.

Centers for Disease Control and Prevention (2003). *STD Surveillance Tables.* Atlanta, GA: Centers for Disease Control and Prevention.

Chamberlain, K., & Zika, S. (1990). The minor events approach to stress: Support for the use of daily hassles. *British Journal of Psychology, 81,* 469–481.

Chamberlin, J. (2000, February). Where are all these students coming from? *Monitor on Psychology,* pp. 32–34.

Chandler, M. J. (1976). Social cognition and life-span approaches to the study of child development. In H. W. Reese & L. P. Lipsitt (Eds.), *Advances in child development and behavior* (Vol 11). New York: Academic Press.

Chandran, S., & Menon, G. (2004). When a day means more than a year: Effects of temporal framing on judgments of health risk. *Journal of Consumer Research, 31,* 375–389.

Chang, S. W., & Ansley, T. N. (2003). A comparative study of item exposure control methods in computerized adaptive testing. *Journal of Educational Measurement, 40,* 71–103.

Chao, R. K. (2000). Cultural explanations for the role of parenting in the school success of Asian-American children. In R. D. Taylor & M. C. Wang (Eds.), *Resilience across contexts: Family, work, culture, and community* (pp. 333–363). Mahwah, NJ: Erlbaum.

Chapelot, D., Marmonier, C., Aubert, R., Gausseres, N., & Louis-Sylvestre, J. (2004). A role for glucose and insulin preprandial profiles to differentiate

meals and snacks. *Physiology and Behavior, 80,* 721–731.

Chapman, L. J., & Chapman, J. P. (1973). *Disordered thought in schizophrenia.* New York: Appleton-Century-Crofts.

Charles, N., Cheakalos, C., Hubbard, K., Miller, S., & Schindehette, S. (2001, December 10). Beyond the call. *People,* pp. 88–106.

Charles, S. T., Reynolds, C. A., & Gatz, M. (2001). Age-related differences and change in positive and negative affect over 23 years. *Journal of Personality and Social Psychology, 80,* 136–151.

Charman, D. P. (2004). *Core processes in brief psychodynamic psychotherapy: Advancing effective practice.* Mahwah, NJ: Lawrence Erlbaum Associates.

Chase, M. (1993, October 13). Inner music: Imagination may play role in how the brain learns muscle control. *Wall Street Journal,* pp. A1, A6.

Chastain, G., & Landrum, R. E. (Eds.). (1999). *Protecting human subjects: Departmental subject pools and institutional review boards.* Washington, DC: American Psychological Association.

Chatterjee, A. (2004). Cosmetic neurology: the controversy over enhancing movement, mentation, and mood. *Neurology, 28,* 968–974.

Cheakalos, C., & Heyn, E. (1998, November 2). Mercy mission. *People Weekly,* pp. 149–150.

Chen, A., Zhou, Y., & Gong, H. (2004). Firing rates and dynamic correlated activities of ganglion cells both contribute to retinal information processing. *Brain Research, 1017,* 13–20.

Chen, C., & Stevenson, H. W. (1995). Motivation and mathematics achievement: A comparative study of Asian-American, Caucasian-American, and East Asian high school students. *Child Development, 66,* 1215–1234.

Cheney, C. D. (1996). Medical nonadherence: A behavior analysis. In J. R. Cautela & W. Ishaq (Eds.), *Contemporary issues in behavior therapy: Improving the human condition: Applied Clinical Psychology.* New York: Plenum Press.

Cheng, C., & Cheung, M. L. (2005). Cognitive processes underlying coping flexibility: Differentiation and integration. *Journal of Personality, 73,* 859–886.

Cheng, H., Cao, Y., & Olson, L. (1996, July 26). Spinal cord repair in adult paraplegic rats: Partial restoration of hind limb function. *Science, 273,* 510–513.

Cherry, B. J., Buckwalter, J. G., & Henderson, V. W. (2002). Better pres-

ervation of memory span relative to supraspan immediate recall in Alzheimer's disease. *Neuropsychologia, 40,* 846–852.

Chess, S. (1997). Temperament: Theory and clinical practice. *Harvard Mental Health Letter.*

Cheston, S. E. (2002). A new paradigm for teaching counseling theory and practice. *Counselor Education & Supervision, 39,* 254–269.

Chi-Ching, Y., & Noi, L. S. (1994). Learning styles and their implications for cross-cultural management in Singapore. *Journal of Social Psychology, 134,* 593–600.

Chin, S. B., & Pisoni, D. B. (1997). *Alcohol and speech.* New York: Academic Press.

Cho, A. (2000, June 16). What's shakin' in the ear? *Science, 288,* 1954–1955.

Choi, Y. S. , Gray, H. , & Ambady, N. (2004). Glimpses of others: Unintended communication and unintended perception. In J. Bargh, J. Uleman, & R. Hassin (Eds.), *Unintended Thought* (2nd. ed.). New York: Oxford University Press.

Chomsky, N. (1968). *Language and mind.* New York: Harcourt Brace Jovanovich.

Chomsky, N. (1978). On the biological basis of language capacities. In G. A. Miller & E. Lennenberg (Eds.), *Psychology and biology of language and thought.* New York: Academic Press.

Chomsky, N. (1991). Linguistics and cognitive science: Problems and mysteries. In A. Kasher (Ed.), *The Chomskyan turn.* Cambridge, MA: Blackwell.

Chou, K. (2005). Everyday competence and depressive symptoms: Social support and sense of control as mediators or moderators? *Aging and Mental Health, 9,* 177–183.

Choudhary, M. I., Nawaz, S. A., Zaheer-ul-Haq, A., Azim, M. K., Ghayur, M. N., Lodhi, M. A., Jalil, S., Khalid, A., Ahmed, A., Rode, B. M., Atta-ur-Rahman, R., Gilani, A. U., & Ahmad, V. U. (2005, July 15). Juliflorine: A potent natural peripheral anionic-site-binding inhibitor of acetylcholinesterase with calcium-channel blocking potential, a leading candidate for Alzheimer's disease therapy. *Biochemical and Biophysical Research Communications, 15,* 1171–1177.

Chow, A. Y., Chow, V. Y., Packo, K. H., Pollack, J. S., Peyman, G. A., & Schuchard, R. (2004). The artificial silicon retina microchip for the treatment of vision loss from retinitis pigmentosa. *Archives of Ophthalmology, 122,* 460–469.

Christensen, A. J., & Johnson, J. A. (2002). Patient adherence with medical treatment regimens: An interactive approach. *Current Directions in Psychological Science, 11,* 94–101.

Christensen, T. C., Wood, J. V., & Barrett, L. F. (2003). Remembering everyday experience through the prism of self-esteem. *Personality and Social Psychology Bulletin, 29,* 51–62.

Chronicle, E. P., MacGregor, J. N., & Ormerod, T. C. (2004). What makes an insight problem? The roles of heuristics, goal conception, and solution recoding in knowledge-lean problems. *Journal of Experimental Psychology: Learning, Memory, and Cognition, 30,* 14–27.

Cialdini, R. B. (1988). *Influence: Science and practice* (2nd ed.). Glenview, IL: Scott, Foresman.

Cialdini, R. B., & Sagarin, B. J. (2005). Principles of interpersonal influence. In T. C. Brock & M. C. Green (Eds.), *Persuasion: Psychological insights and perspectives* (2nd ed.). Thousand Oaks, CA: Sage Publications.

Cialdini, R. B., Schaller, M., Houlihan, D., Arps, K., Fultz, J., & Beaman, A.L. (1975). Reciprocal concessions procedure for inducing compliance: The door-in-the-face technique. *Journal of Personality and Social Psychology, 31,* 206–215.

Cicero, F. R., & Pfadt, A. (2002). Investigation of a reinforcement-based toilet training procedure for children with autism. *Research in Developmental Disabilities, 23,* 319–331.

Cipolli, C., Fagioli, I., Mazzetti, M., & Tuozzi, G. (2005). Consolidation effect of the processing of declarative knowledge during human sleep: Evidence from long-term retention of interrelated contents of mental sleep experiences. *Brain Research Bulletin, 65,* 97–104.

Cisek, P., & Kalaska, J. F. (2004). Neural correlates of mental rehearsal in dorsal premotor cortex. *Nature, 431,* 993–996.

Clancy, S. A., Schacter, D. L., McNally, R. J., & Pitman, R. K. (2000). False recognition in women reporting recovered memories of sexual abuse. *Psychological Science, 2,* 26–33.

Clark, D. A. (2004). *Cognitive-behavioral therapy for OCD.* New York: Guilford.

Clark, L., & Watson, R. (1999). Temperament. In L.A. Pervin & O.P.

John (Eds.), *Handbook of personality: Theory and research* (2nd ed.). New York: Guilford.

Clark, R. E., & Squire, L. R. (1998, April 3). Classical conditioning and brain systems: The role of awareness. *Science, 280,* 77–81.

Clark, R., Anderson, N. B., Clark, V. R., & Williams, D. R. (1999). Racism as a stressor for African Americans: A biopsychosocial model. *American Psychologist, 54,* 805–816.

Clarke-Stewart, K. A., & Friedman, S. (1987). *Child development: Infancy through adolescence.* New York: Wiley.

Clarke-Stewart, K. A., Vandell, D. L., McCartney, K., Owen, M. T., & Booth, C. (2000). Effects of parental separation and divorce on very young children. *Journal of Family Psychology, 14,* 304–326.

Clarkin, J. F., & Lenzenweger, M. F. (Eds.) (2004). *Major theories of personality disorders* (2nd ed.). New York: Guilford.

Clay D. L. (2000). Commentary: Rethinking our interventions in pediatric chronic pain and treatment research. *Journal of Pediatric Psychology, 25,* 53–55.

Clements, M. (1994, August 7). Making love, how old, how often. *Parade,* p. 18.

Cloud, J. (2000, June 5). The lure of ecstasy. *Time,* pp. 60–68.

Coats, E. J., & Feldman, R. S. (1996). Gender differences in nonverbal correlates of social status. *Personality and Social Psychology Bulletin, 22,* 1014–1022.

Cobos, P., Sanchez, M., Garcia, C., Vera, M. N., & Vila, J. (2002). Revisiting the James versus Cannon debate on emotion: Startle and autonomic modulation in patients with spinal cord injuries. *Biological Psychology, 61,* 251–269.

Cochran, S. D. (2000). Emerging issues in research on lesbians' and gay men's mental health: Does sexual orientation really matter? *American Psychologist, 56,* 33–41.

Coffey, C. E., Saxton, J. A., & Ratcliff, G. (1999). Relation of education to brain size in normal aging: Implications for the reserve hypothesis. *Neurology, 53,* 189–196.

Cohen, B. H. (2002). *Explaining psychological statistics* (2nd ed.). New York: Wiley.

Cohen, B. H., & Lea, R. B. (2003). *Essentials of statistics for the social and behavioral sciences.* New York: Wiley.

Cohen, D. (1996). Law, social policy, and violence: The impact of regional cul-

tures. *Journal of Personality and Social Psychology, 70,* 961–978.

Cohen, J. (2003). Things I have learned (so far). In A. E. Kazdin (Ed.), *Methodological issues and strategies in clinical research* (3rd ed.). Washington, DC: American Psychological Association.

Cohen, L., & Cashon, C. (2003). Infant perception and cognition. In R. Lerner and M. Easterbrooks (Eds.), *Handbook of psychology: Developmental psychology* (Vol. 6). New York: Wiley.

Cohen, P., Slomkowski, C., & Robins, L. N. (Eds.). (1999). *Historical and geographical influences on psychopathology.* Mahwah, NJ: Erlbaum.

Cohen, S. (2004, November). Social relationships and health. *American Psychologist,* 676–684.

Cohen, S., Doyle, W. J., Turner, R., Alper, C. M., & Skoner, D. P. (2003). Sociability and susceptibility to the common cold. *Psychological Science, 14,* 389–395.

Cohen, S., Hamrick, N., & Rodriguez, M. (2002). Reactivity and vulnerability to stress-associated risk for upper respiratory illness. *Psychosomatic Medicine, 64,* 302–310.

Col, N., & Komaroff, A. L. (2004, May 10). How to think about HT. *Newsweek, 143,* 80–81.

Coleman, E. (2002). Masturbation as a means of achieving sexual health. *Journal of Psychology and Human Sexuality, 14,* 5–16.

Coles, C. D., Platzman, K. A., & Lynch, M. E. (2003). Auditory and visual sustained attention in adolescents parentally exposed to alcohol. *Clinical and Experimental Research, 26,* 263–271.

Coles, R. (1997). *The moral intelligence of children.* New York: Random House.

Coles, R., & Stokes, G. (1985). *Sex and the American teenager.* New York: Harper & Row.

Colland, V. T., Van Essen-Zandvliet, L. E. M., Lans, C., Denteneer, A., Westers, P., & Brackel, H. J. L. (2004). Poor adherence to self-medication instructions in children with asthma and their parents. *Patient Education and Counseling, 55,* 416–421.

Collins, A. M., & Loftus, E. F. (1975). A spreading-activation theory of semantic processing. *Psychological Review, 82,* 407–428.

Collins, A. M., & Quillian, M. R. (1969). Retrieval times from semantic memory. *Journal of Verbal Learning and Verbal Behavior, 8,* 240–247.

Collins, S. L., & Izenwasser, S. (2004). Chronic nicotine differentially alters cocaine-induced locomotor activity in adolescent vs. adult male and female rats. *Neuropharmacology, 46,* 349–362.

Coltraine, S., & Messineo, M. (2000). The perpetuation of subtle prejudice: Race and gender imagery in 1990s television advertising. *Sex Roles, 42,* 363–389.

Colwell, M. J., & Lindsey, E. W. (2005). Preschool children's pretend and physical play and sex of play partner: Connections to peer competence. *Sex Roles, 52,* 497–509.

Committee to Review the Scientific Evidence on the Polygraph. (2003). *The polygraph and lie detection.* Washington, DC: National Academies Press.

Comuzzie, A. G., & Allison, D. B. (1998, May 29). The search for human obesity genes. *Science, 280,* 1374–1377.

Conduit, R., Crewther, S. G., & Coleman, G. (2004). Spontaneous eyelid movements (ELMS) during sleep are related to dream recall on awakening. *Journal of Sleep Research, 13,* 137–144.

Conger, R. D., Wallace, L. E., Sun, Y., Simons, R. L., McLoyd, V. C., & Brody, G. H. (2002). Economic pressure in African American families: A replication and extension of the family stress model. *Developmental Psychology, 38,* 179–193.

Conner, M., Povey, R., Sparks, P., James, R., & Shepherd, R. (2003). Moderating role of attitudinal ambivalence within the theory of planned behaviour. *British Journal of Social Psychology, 42,* 75–94.

Consumer Reports (CR). (1993, June). Dieting and weight loss, p. 347.

Consumer Reports (CR). (1995, November). Mental health: Does therapy help? pp. 734–739.

Conway, M. A. (1997). *Cognitive models of memory.* Cambridge, MA: MIT.

Cooklin, A. (2000). Therapy, the family and others In H. Maxwell, *Clinical psychotherapy for health professionals.* Philadelphia: Whurr Publishers, Ltd.

Cookson, R. (2005, March 10). A noise for danger: Ten years ago, a Belgian rodent-lover decided that rats were smart. *The Independent* (London), p. F7.

Cooper, E. O. (2004). Candid camera: Computer-based facial recognition system spots terrorists entering the U.S. *Quest Summer, 7,* 33–39.

Cooper, J., Mirabile, R., & Scher, S. J. (2005). Actions and attitudes: The theory of cognitive dissonance. In T. C. Brock & M. C. Green (Eds.), *Persuasion:*

Psychological insights and perspectives (2nd ed.). Thousand Oaks, CA: Sage Publications.

Cooper, N. R., Kalaria, R. N., McGeer, P. L., & Rogers, J. (2000). Key issues in Alzheimer's disease inflammation. *Neurobiology of Aging, 21,* 451–453.

Cope, D. (2001). *Virtual music.* Cambridge, MA: MIT.

Cope, D. (2003). Computer analysis of musical allusions. *Computer Music Journal, 27,* 11–28.

Copolov, D. L., Seal, M. L., Maruff, P., Ulusoy, R., Wong, M. T. H., Tochon-Danguy, H. J., & Egan, G. F. (2003). Cortical activation associated with the human experience of auditory hallucinations and perception of human speech in schizophrenia: A PET correlation study. *Psychiatry Research: Neuroimaging, 123,* 139–152.

Corbetta, M., Kincade, J. M., & Shulman, G. L. (2002). Neural systems for visual orienting and their relationships to spatial working memory. *Journal of Cognitive Neuroscience, 14,* 508–523.

Corcoran, B. (2005, July 5). Large African rats being used to find landmines in Mozambique. *The Irish Times,* p. 10.

Coren, S. (1992). The moon illusion: A different view through the legs. *Perceptual and Motor Skills, 75,* 827–831.

Coren, S., & Ward, L. M. (1989). *Sensation and perception* (3rd ed.). San Diego, CA: Harcourt Brace Jovanovich.

Coren, S., Porac, C., & Ward, L. M. (1984). *Sensation and perception* (2nd ed.). New York: Academic Press.

Cornelius, M. D., Taylor, P. M., Geva, D., & Day, N. L. (1995). Prenatal tobacco and marijuana use among adolescents: Effects on offspring gestational age, growth, and morphology. *Pediatrics, 95,* 57–68.

Cosmides, L., & Tooby, J. (2004). Social exchange: The evolutionary design of a neurocognitive system. In M. S. Gazzaniga (Ed.), *Cognitive neurosciences* (3rd ed.). Cambridge, MA: MIT.

Cosser, C. (2002). Hypnosis in the treatment of chronic pain: An ecosystemic approach. *Australian Journal of Clinical and Experimental Hypnosis, 30,* 156–169.

Costa, P. T., Jr., & Widiger, T. A. (Eds.). (2002). *Personality disorders and the five-factor model of personality* (2nd ed.). Washington, DC: American Psychological Association.

Cothran, M. M., & White, J. P. (2002). Adolescent behavior and sexually

transmitted diseases: The dilemma of human papillomavirus [Special issue: Adolescent women's health]. *Health Care for Women International, 23,* 306–319.

Cotton, P. (1993, July 7). Psychiatrists set to approve DSM-IV. *Journal of the American Medical Association, 270,* 13–15.

Cottraux, J. (2005). Recent developments in research and treatment for social phobia (social anxiety disorder). *Current Opinion in Psychiatry, 18,* 51–54.

Council of National Psychological Associations for the Advancement of Ethnic Minority Interests (CNPAAEMI). (2000, January). *Guidelines for research in ethnic minority communities.* Washington, DC: American Psychological Association.

Coventry, K. R., Venn, S. F., Smith, G. D., & Morley, A. M. (2003). Spatial problem solving and functional relations. *European Journal of Cognitive Psychology, 15,* 71–99.

Cowan, N., Towse, J. N., Hamilton, Z., Saults, J. S., Elliott, E. M., Lacey, J. F., Moreno, M. V., & Hitch, G. J. (2003). Children's working-memory processes: A response-timing analysis. *Journal of Experimental Psychology: General, 132,* 113–132.

Cowley, G. (2000, January 31). Alzheimer's: Unlocking the mystery. *Time,* pp. 46–54.

Cox, J. (2003, May 6). How far would you go to save your life? *Denver Post,* p. F1.

Cox, R., Baker, S. E., Macdonald, D. W., & Berdoy, M. (2004). Protecting egg prey from carrion crows: The potential of aversive conditioning. *Applied Animal Behaviour Science, 87,* 325–342.

Coyle, D. (2005). *Lance Armstrong's war: One man's battle against fate, fame, love, death, scandal, and a few other rivals on the road to the Tour de France.* New York: HarperCollins.

Coyne, S. M., & Archer, J. (2005). The relationship between indirect and physical aggression on television and in real life. *Social Development, 14,* 324–338

Craig, R. J. (1999). *Interpreting personality tests: A clinical manual for the MMPI-2, MCMI-III, CPI-R, and 16PF.* New York: Wiley.

Craik, F. I. M. (1990). Levels of processing. In M. E. Eysenck (Ed.), *The Blackwell dictionary of cognitive psychology.* London: Blackwell.

Craik, F. I., & Lockhart, R. S. (1972). Levels of processing: A framework for memory research. *Journal of Verbal Behavior, 11,* 671–684.

Cramer, J. A. (1995). Optimizing long-term patient compliance. *Neurology, 45,* s25–s28.

Cramer, P. (2000a). Thematic apperception test. In A E. Kazdin (Ed.), *Encyclopedia of psychology* (Vol. 8). Washington, DC: American Psychological Association.

Cramer, P. (2000b). Defense mechanisms in psychology today: Further process for adaptation. *American Psychologist, 55,* 637–646.

Crawford, M., & Unger, R. (2004). *Women and gender: A feminist psychology* (4th ed.). New York: McGraw-Hill.

Crawford, N. (2002). Science-based program curbs violence in kids. *APA Monitor, 33,* 38–39.

Creasey, G. L. (2005). *Research methods in lifespan development* (6th ed.). Boston: Allyn & Bacon.

Crews, F. (1996). The verdict on Freud. *Psychological Science, 7,* 63–68.

Crits-Christoph, P. (1992). The efficacy of brief dynamic psychotherapy: A meta-analysis. *American Journal of Psychiatry, 149,* 151–158.

Crocker, J., & Park, L. E. (2004). The costly pursuit of self-esteem. *Psychological Bulletin, 130,* 392–414.

Crombag, H. S., & Robinson, R. E. (2004). Drugs, environment, brain, and behavior. *Current Directions in Psychological Science, 13,* 107–111.

Crosby, F. J., Williams, J. C., & Biernat, M. (2004). The maternal wall. *Journal of Social Issues, 60,* 675–682.

Crosnoe, R., & Elder, G. H., Jr. (2002). Successful adaptation in the later years: A life course approach to aging. *Social Psychology Quarterly, 65,* 309–328.

Csikszentmihalyi, M. (1997). *Creativity: Flow and the psychology of discovery and invention.* New York: BasicBooks/Mastermind Series.

Cuddy, A. J. C., Fiske, S. T., & Glick, P. (2004). When professionals become mothers, warmth doesn't cut the ice. *Journal of Social Issues, 60,* 701–718.

Cummings, E., & Henry, W. E. (1961). *Growing old.* New York: Basic Books.

Cummings, J., & Hall, C. (2002). Athletes' use of imagery in the off-season. *Sport Psychologist, 16,* 160–172.

Cutler, B., & Saporta, L. R. (2003). *Closing argument: Defending and befriending John Gotti, and other legal battles I have waged.* New York: Diane Publishing.

Cwikel, J., Behar, L., & Rabson-Hare, J. (2000). A comparison of a vote count and a meta-analysis review of intervention research with adult cancer patients. *Research on Social Work Practice, 10,* 139–158.

Czeisler, C. A., Duffy, J. F., Shanahan, T. L., Brown, E. N., Mitchell, J. F., Rimmer, D. W., Ronda, J. M., Silva, E. J., Allan, J. S., Emens, J. S., Dijk, D. J., & Kronauer, R. E. (1999, June 25). Stability, precision, and near-24-hour period of the human circadian pacemaker. *Science, 284,* 2177–2181.

Daftary, F., & Meri, J. W. (2002). *Culture and memory in medieval Islam.* London: I. B. Tauris.

Dalsgaro, O. J., Hansen, N. G., Soes-Petersen, U., Evald, T., Hoegholm, A., Barber, J., & Vestbo, J. (2004). A multicenter, randomized, double-blind, placebo-controlled, 6-month trial of bupropion hydrochloride sustained-release tablets as an aid to smoking cessation in hospital employees. *Nicotine and Tobacco Research, 6,* 55–61.

Damasio, A. (1999). *The feeling of what happens: Body and emotion in the making of consciousness.* New York: Harcourt Brace.

Damon, W. (1999, August). The moral development of children. *Scientific American,* pp. 72–78.

D'Argembeau, A., Comblain, C., & Van der Linden, M. (2003). Phenomenal characteristics of autobiographical memories for positive, negative, and neutral events. *Applied Cognitive Psychology, 17,* 281–294.

Darley, J. M. (1995). Constructive and destructive obedience: A taxonomy of principal-agent relationships. *Journal of Social Issues, 51,* 125–154.

Darwin, C. J., Turvey, M. T., & Crowder, R. G. (1972). An auditory analogue of the Sperling partial-report procedure: Evidence for brief auditory storage. *Cognitive Psychology, 3,* 255–267.

Davidson, J. E., Deuser, R., & Sternberg, R. J. (1994). The role of metacognition in problem solving. In J. Metcalfe & A. P. Shimamura (Eds.), *Metacognition: Knowing about knowing.* Cambridge, MA: MIT.

Davidson, P. S. R., & Glisky, E. L. (2002). Is flashbulb memory a special instance of source memory? Evidence from older adults. *Memory, 10,* 99–111.

Davidson, R. J., Gray, J. A., LeDoux, J. E., Levenson, R. W., Pankseep, J., & Ekman, P. (1994). Is there emotion-specific physiology? In P. Ekman & R. J.

Davidson (Eds.), *The nature of emotion.* New York: Oxford University Press.

Day, A. L., & Livingstone, H. A. (2003). Gender differences in perceptions of stressors and utilization of social support among university students. *Canadian Journal of Behavioural Science, 35,* 73–83.

Day, R. D., & Lamb, M. E. (2004). *Conceptualizing and measuring father involvement.* Mahwah, NJ: Lawrence Erlbaum Associates.

DeAngelis, T. (2002, March). Promising treatments for anorexia and bulimia. *Monitor on Psychology,* pp. 38–41.

de Araujo, I. E. T., Kringelbach, M. L., & Rolls, E. T. (2003). Representation of umami taste in the human brain. *Journal of Neurophysiology, 90,* 313–319.

Deary, I. J., & Der, G. (2005). Reaction time, age, and cognitive ability: Longitudinal findings from age 16 to 63 years in representative population samples. *Aging, Neuropsychology, & Cognition, 12,* 187–215.

Deater-Deckard, K., Ivy, L., & Smith, J. (2005). Resilience in gene-environment transactions. In S. Goldstein and R. B. Brooks (Eds.), *Handbook of resilience in children.* (pp. 49–63). New York: Kluwer Academic/Plenum Publishers.

Deaux, K. (1995). How basic can you be? The evolution of research on gender stereotypes. *Journal of Social Issues, 51,* 11–20.

deCharms, R. C., Blake, D. T., & Merzenich, M. M. (1998, May 29). Optimizing sound features for cortical neurons. *Science, 280,* 1439–1440.

Deci, E. L., Koestner, R., & Ryan, R. M. (2001). Extrinsic rewards and intrinsic motivation in education: Reconsidered once again. *Review of Educational Research, 71,* 1–27.

DeCoster, V. A. (2003). Predicting emotions in everyday social interactions: A test and comparison of affect control and social interactional theories. *Journal of Human Behavior in the Social Environment, 6,* 53–73.

Deffenbacher, J. L. (1988). Cognitive relaxation and social skills treatments of anger: A year later. *Journal of Consulting Psychology, 35,* 309–315.

Deffenbacher, J. L. (1996). Cognitive-behavioral approaches to anger reduction. In K. S. Dobson & K. D. Craig (Eds.), *Advances in cognitive-behavioral therapy* (Vol. 2). Thousand Oaks, CA: Sage Publications.

de Fockert, J. W., Rees, G., Frith, C. D., & Lavie, N. (2001, March 2). The role of working memory in visual selective attention. *Science, 291,* 1803–1806.

DeGaton, J. F., Weed, S., & Jensen, L. (1996). Understanding gender differences in adolescent sexuality. *Adolescence, 31,* 217–231.

deGroot, A. D. (1966). Perception and memory versus thought: Some old ideas and recent findings. In B. Kleinmuntz (Ed.), *Problem solving: Research, method, and theory.* New York: Wiley.

Delahanty, D., & Baum, A. (2000). Stress and breast cancer. In A. S. Baum, R. A. Revenson, & J. E. Singer (Eds.), *Handbook of health psychology.* Mahwah, NJ: Erlbaum.

DeLamater, J. D., & Sill, M. (2005). Sexual desire in later life. *Journal of Sex Research, 42,* 138–149.

Demaree, H. A., & Everhart, D. E. (2004). Healthy high-hostiles: Reduced parasympathetic activity and decreased sympathovagal flexibility during negative emotional processing. *Personality and Individual Differences, 36,* 457–469.

Demir, E., & Dickson, B. J. (2005). *Fruitless* splicing specifies male courtship behavior in *Drosophila. Cell 121,* 785–794.

De Mello, M. F., De Jesus Mari, J., Bacaltchuk, J., Verdeli, H., & Neugebauer, R. (2005). A systematic review of research findings on the efficacy of interpersonal therapy for depressive disorders. *European Archives of Psychiatry and Clinical Neuroscience, 255,* 75–82.

Dement, W. C. (1999). *The promise of sleep.* New York: Delacorte Press.

Dement, W. C., & Wolpert, E. A. (1958). The relation of eye movements, body mobility, and external stimuli to dream content. *Journal of Experimental Psychology, 55,* 543–553.

Dempster, F. N. (1981). Memory span: Sources for individual and developmental differences. *Psychological Bulletin, 89,* 63–100.

Denmark, G. L., & Fernandez, L. C. (1993). Historical development of the psychology of women. In F. L. Denmark & M. A. Paludi (Eds.), *A handbook of issues and theories.* Westport, CT: Greenwood Press.

Dennett, D. C. (2003). *Freedom evolves.* New York: Viking.

Dennis, T. A., Cole, P. M., Zahn-Waxler, C., & Mizuta, I. (2002). Self in context: Autonomy and relatedness in Japanese and U.S. mother-preschooler dyads. *Child Development, 73,* 1803–1817.

Denollet, J. (2005). DS14: standard assessment of negative affectivity, social inhibition, and Type D personality. *Psychosomatic Medicine, 67,* 89–97.

Denollet J., & Brutsaert, D. L. (1998). Personality, disease severity, and the risk of long-term cardiac events in patients with a decreased ejection fraction after myocardial infarction. *Circulation, 97,* 167–173.

Dentzer, S. (1986, May 5). Can you pass the job test? *Newsweek,* pp. 46–53.

DePaulo, B. M., & Morris, W. L. (2005). Discerning lies from truths: Behavioral cues to deception and the indirect pathway of intuition. In P. A. Granhag & L. A. Stromwall (Eds.), *Deception detection in forensic contexts.* Cambridge: Cambridge University Press.

DePaulo, B. M., Lindsay, J. J., Malone, B. E., Muhlenbruck, L., Charlton, K., & Cooper, H. (2003). Cues to deception. *Psychological Bulletin, 129,* 74–118.

Deregowski, J. B. (1973). Illusion and culture. In R. L. Gregory & G. H. Combrich (Eds.), *Illusion in nature and art,* pp. 161–192. New York: Scribner.

DeRubeis, R., Hollon, S., & Shelton, R. (2003, May 23). Presentation, American Psychiatric Association meeting, Philadelphia.

Deshields, T., Tibbs, T., Fan, M. Y., & Taylor, M. (2006). Differences in patterns of depression after treatment for breast cancer [Electronic article published August 12, 2005]. *Psycho-Oncology, 15(5),* 398–406.

Desimone, R. (1992, October 9). The physiology of memory: Recordings of things past. *Science, 258,* 245–255.

DeSouza, E., Fansler, A. G. (2003). Contrapower sexual harassment: A survey of students and faculty members. *Sex Roles, 48,* 519–542.

Dessing, J. C., Peper, C. E., Bullock, D., & Beek, P. J. (2005). How position, velocity, and temporal information combine in the prospective control of catching: Data and model. *Journal of Cognitive Neuroscience, 17,* 668–686.

DeSteno, D., Bartlett, M. Y., & Braverman, J. (2002). Sex differences in jealousy: Evolutionary mechanism or artifact of measurement? *Journal of Personality and Social Psychology, 83,* 1103–1116.

Detterman, D. K., Gabriel, L. T., & Ruthsatz, J. M. (2000). Intelligence and mental retardation. In R. J. Sternberg, et al. (Eds.), *Handbook of intelligence.* New York: Cambridge University Press.

de Valois, R. L., & de Valois, K. K. (1993). A multi-stage color model. *Vision Research, 33,* 1053–1065.

Devi, G. (2002). *Take a measure of your memory.* Dr. Gayatri Devi.

deVilliers, J. G., & deVilliers, P. A. (1999). Language development. In M. H. Bronstein & M. E. Lamb (Eds.), *Developmental psychology.* Mahwah, NJ: Erlbaum.

de Waal, F. B. M. (1999, December). The end of nature versus nurture. *Scientific American,* pp. 94–99.

Dey, E. L., Astin, A. W., Korn, W. S., & Berz, E. R. (1990). *The American freshman: National norms for fall, 1990.* Los Angeles: Higher Education Research Institute, Graduate School of Education, UCLA.

Diaz-Guerrero, R. (1979). Culture and personality revisited. *Annals of the New York Academy of Sciences, 285,* 119–130.

DiCano, P., & Everitt, B. J. (2002). Reinstatement and spontaneous recovery of cocaine-seeking following extinction and different durations of withdrawal. *Behavioural Pharmacology, 13,* 397–406.

Dickens, W. T., & Flynn, J. R. (2001). Heritability estimates versus large environmental effects: The IQ paradox resolved. *Psychological Review, 108,* 291–310.

Dickerson, S. S., Kemeny, M. E., Aziz, N., Kim, K. H., & Fahey, J. L. (2004). Immunological effects of induced shame and guilt. *Psychosomatic Medicine, 66,* 124–131.

Diefendorff, J. M., & Richard, E. M. (2003). Antecedents and consequences of emotional display rule perceptions. *Journal of Applied Psychology, 88,* 284–294.

Diener, E. (2000). Subjective well-being: The science of happiness and a proposal for a national index. *American Psychologist, 55,* 34–43.

Diener, E., & Biswas-Diener, R. (2002). Will money increase subjective well-being? *Social Indicators Research, 57,* 119–169.

Diener, E., & Clifton, D. (2002). Life satisfaction and religiosity in broad probability samples. *Psychological Inquiry, 13,* 206–209.

Diener, E., & Seligman, M. E. P. (2002). Very happy people. *Psychological Science, 18,* 81–84.

Diener, E., & Seligman, M.E.P. (2004). Beyond money: Toward an economy of well-being. *Psychological Science in the Public Interest, 5*, 1–31.

Diener, E., Lucas, R. E., & Oishi, S. (2002). Subjective well-being: The science of happiness and life satisfaction. In C. R. Snyder & S. J. Lopez (Eds.), *Handbook of positive psychology*, pp. 463–73. London: Oxford University Press.

Difede, J., & Hoffman, H. G. (2002). Virtual reality exposure therapy for World Trade Center post-traumatic stress disorder: A case report. *CyberPsychology and Behavior, 5*, 529–535.

DiGiovanna, A. G. (1994). *Human aging: Biological perspectives.* New York: McGraw-Hill.

Dillard, J. P., & Shen, L. (2004). On the nature of reactance and its role in persuasive health communication. *Communication Monographs, 72*, 144–168.

DiLorenzo, P. M., & Yougentob, S. L. (2003). Olfaction and taste. In M. Gallagher & R. J. Nelson, *Handbook of psychology: Biological psychology* (Vol 3). New York: Wiley.

DiMatteo, M. R. (1997). Health behaviors and care decisions: An overview of professional-patient communications. In D. S. Gochman (Ed.), *Handbook of health behavior research.* New York: Plenum.

Dinges, D. F., Pack, F., Wiliams, K., Gillen, K. A., Powell, J. W., Ott, G. E., Aptowicz, C., & Pack, A. I. (1997). Cumulative sleepiness, mood disturbance, and psychomotor vigilance performance decrements during a week of sleep restricted to 4–5 hours per night. *Sleep, 20*, 267–273.

Dixon, R. A., & Cohen, A. L. (2003). Cognitive development in adulthood. In R. M. Lerner, M. A. Easterbrooks, et al. (Eds.), *Handbook of psychology: Developmental psychology* (Vol. 6, pp. 443–461). New York: Wiley.

Dobbins, A. C., Jeo, R. M., Fiser, J., & Allman, J. M. (1998, July 24). Distance modulation of neural activity in the visual cortex. *Science, 281*, 552–555.

Dobelle, W. H. (2000). Artificial vision for the blind by connecting a television camera to the visual cortex. *ASAIO Journal, 46*, 3–9.

Dodge, K. A. (2004). The nature-nurture debate and public policy. *Merrill-Palmer Quarterly, 50*, 418–427.

Doi, T. (1990). The cultural assumptions of psychoanalysis. In J. W. Stigler, R. A. Shweder, & G. Herdt (Eds.), *Cultural psychology: Essays on comparative human development.* New York: Cambridge University Press.

Dolan, R. J. (2002, November 8). Emotion, cognition, and behavior. *Science, 298*, 1191–1194.

Dollard, J., Doob, L., Miller, N., Mower, O. H., & Sears, R. R. (1939). *Frustration and aggression.* New Haven, CT: Yale University Press.

Dollinger, S. J. (2003). Need for uniqueness, need for cognition and creativity. *Journal of Creative Behavior, 37*, 99–116.

Domhoff, G. W. (1996). *Finding meaning in dreams: A quantitative approach.* New York: Plenum Press.

Domhoff, G. W. (2001). A new neurocognitive theory of dreams. *Dreaming, 11*, 13–33.

Domhoff, G. W. (2003). *The scientific study of dreams: Neural networks, cognitive development, and content analysis.* Washington, DC: American Psychological Association.

Donahoe, J. W. (2003). Selectionism. In K. A. Lattal, & P. N. Chase (Eds.), *Behavior theory and philosophy.* New York: Kluwer Academic/Plenum Publishers.

Donahoe, J. W., & Vegas, R. (2004). Pavlovian Conditioning: The CS-UR Relation. *Journal of Experimental Psychology: Animal Behavior Processes, 30*, 17–33.

Dooren, J. C. (2005, March 29). Talking yourself to sleep. *The Wall Street Journal.* pp. D1–D2.

Dorion, A. A. (2000). Hemispheric asymmetry and corpus callosum morphometry: A magnetic resonance imaging study. *Neuroscience Research, 36*, 9–13.

Dortch, S. (1996, October). Our aching heads. *American Demographics*, pp. 4–8.

Doty, R. L., Green, P. A., Ram, C., & Yankell, S. L. (1982). Communication of gender from human breath odors: Relationship to perceived intensity and pleasantness. *Hormones and Behavior, 16*, 13–22.

Dougall, A. L., & Baum, A. (2004). Psychoneuroimmunology and trauma. In P. P. Schnurr and B. L. Green (Eds.), *Trauma and health: Physical health consequences of exposure to extreme stress* (pp. 129–155). Washington, DC: American Psychological Association.

Douglas Brown, R., Goldstein, E., & Bjorklund, D. F. (2000). The history and zeitgeist of the repressed-false-memory debate: Scientific and sociological perspectives on suggestibility and childhood memory. In D. F. Bjorklund (Ed.), *False-memory creation in children and adults: Theory, research, and implications* (pp. 1–30). Mahwah, NJ: Lawrence Erlbaum.

Doumas, M., Praamstra, P., & Wing, A. M. (2005). Low frequency rTMS effects on sensorimotor synchronization. *Experimental Brain Research, 88*, 1–8.

Dovidio, J. F. (2001). On the nature of contemporary prejudice: The third wave. *Journal of Social Issues, 57*, 829–849.

Dovidio, J. F., & Penner, L. A. (2004). Helping and altruism. In M. B. Brewer & M. Hewstone (Eds.), *Emotion and motivation.* Malden, MA: Blackwell Publishers.

Dovidio, J. F., Gaertner, S. L., & Kawakami, K. (2003). Intergroup contact: The past, present, and the future. *Group Processes and Intergroup Relations, 6*, 5–20.

Dovidio, J. F., Gaertner, S. L., & Pearson, A. R. (2005). On the nature of prejudice: The psychological foundations of hate. In R. J. Sternberg (Ed.), *Psychology of hate.* Washington, DC: American Psychological Association.

Dovidio, J. F., Kawakami, K., & Gaertner, S. L. (2000). Reducing contemporary prejudice: Combating explicit and implicit bias at the individual and intergroup level. In S. Oskamp (Ed.), *Reducing prejudice and discrimination: The Claremont Symposium on Applied Social Psychology* (pp. 137–163). Mahwah, NJ: Erlbaum.

Doyle, K. A. (2002). Rational Emotive Behavior Therapy and its application to women's groups. In W. Dryden, & M. Neenan (Eds.), *Rational emotive behaviour group therapy.* London: Whurr Publishers.

Dreman, S. (1997). *The family on the threshold of the 21st century.* Mahwah, NJ: Erlbaum.

Dressler, W. W., & Oths, K. S. (1997). Cultural determinants of health behavior. In D. S. Gochman (Ed.), *Handbook of health behavior research.* New York: Plenum.

Drewes, A. A. (2005). Play in selected cultures: Diversity and universality. In E. Gil and A. A. Drewes, *Cultural issues in play therapy* (pp. 26–71). New York: Guilford Press.

Drob, S. (2005). The mystical symbol: Some comments on Ankor, Giegerich, Scholem, and Jung. *Journal of Jungian Theory & Practice, 7*, 25–29.

Drogin, E. (2005). Civil and criminal trial matters. In E. Drogin, *Law & mental health professionals: Kentucky*. Washington, DC: American Psychological Association.

Druckman, D., & Bjork, R. A. (1991). *In the mind's eye: Enhancing human performance*. Washington, DC: National Academy Press.

Drummond, D. C., Tiffany, S. T., Glautier, S., & Remington, B. (Eds.). (1995). *Addictive behaviour: Cue exposure theory and practice*. Chichester, England: Wiley.

Dryden, W. (1999). *Rational emotive behavior therapy: A training manual*. New York: Springer.

Dryden, W. (2003). *Overcoming depression*. London: Sheldon Press.

DuBois, J. M. (2002). When is informed consent appropriate in educational research? *IRB: A Review of Human Subjects Research, 24*, 1–8.

Dubovsky, S. (1999, February 25). Tuning in to manic depression. *HealthNews, 5*, p. 8.

Duffy, M., Gillig, S. E., Tureen, R. M., & Ybarra, M. A. (2002). A critical look at the DSM-IV. *Journal of Individual Psychology, 58*, 363–373.

Dugger, C. W. (1996, December 28). Tug of taboos: African genital rite vs. U.S. law. *The New York Times*, pp. 1, 9.

Duke, M., & Nowicki, S., Jr. (1979). *Abnormal psychology: Perspectives on being different*. Monterey, CA: Brooks/Cole.

Duncan, J. (2005). Frontal lobe function and general intelligence: Why it matters. *Cortex, 41*, 215–217.

Duncan, J., Seitz, R. J., Kolodny, J., Bor, D., Herzog, H., Ahmed, A., Newell, F. N., & Emslie, H. (2000, July 21). A neural basis for general intelligence. *Science, 289*, 457–459.

Duncan, P. D., et al. (1985). The effects of pubertal timing on body image, school behavior, and deviance [Special Issue: Time of maturation and psychosocial functioning in adolescence: I]. *Journal of Youth and Adolescence, 14*, 227–235.

Duncker, K. (1945). On problem solving. *Psychological Monographs, 58* (5, whole no. 270).

Duncombe, J., Harrison, K., Allan, G., & Marsden, D. (2004). *The state of affairs: Explorations in infidelity and commitment*. Mahwah, NJ: Lawrence Erlbaum.

Dunham, R. M., Kidwell, J. S., & Wilson, S. M. (1986). Rites of passage at adolescence: A ritual process paradigm. *Journal of Adolescent Research, 1*, 139–153.

Dutton, D. G., & Aron, A. P. (1974). Some evidence for heightened sexual attraction under conditions of high anxiety. *Journal of Personality and Social Psychology, 30*, 510–517.

Dweck, C. S., Mangels, J., & Good, C. (2004). Motivational Effects on attention, cognition, and performance. In D.Y. Dai & R.J. Sternberg (Eds.), *Motivation, emotion, and cognition: Integrated perspectives on intellectual functioning*. Mahwah, NJ: Erlbaum. Annual Meeting of the American Psychological Society, May, 2004, Chicago.

Dworkin, J. B., Larson, R., & Hansen, D. (2003). Adolescents' accounts of growth experiences in youth activities. *Journal of Youth and Adolescence, 32*, 17–26.

Eagles, J. M. (2001). SAD—help arrives with the dawn? *Lancet, 358*, p. 2100.

Eagly, A., & Chaiken, S. (1998). Attitude structure and function. In D. T. Gilbert & S. T. Fiske (Eds.), *Handbook of social psychology* (Vol. 1, 4th ed.). New York: McGraw-Hill.

Eagly, A. H., & Wood, W. (2003). The origins of sex differences in human behavior: Evolved dispositions versus social roles. In C. B. Travis (Ed.), *Evolution, gender, and rape* (pp. 265–304). Cambridge, MA: MIT.

Eaker, E. D., Sullivan, L. M., Kelly-Hayes, M., D'Agostino, R. B., Sr., & Benjamin, E. J. (2004). Anger and hostility predict the development of atrial fibrillation in men in the Framingham Offspring Study. *Circulation, 109*, 1267–1271.

Earley, J. (1999). *Interactive group therapy: Integrating interpersonal, action-oriented and psychodynamic approaches*. New York: Brunner/Mazel.

Ebbinghaus, H. (1885/1913). *Memory: A contribution to experimental psychology* (H. A. Roger & C. E. Bussenius, Trans.). New York: Columbia University Press.

Eberhard, K. M., Cutting, J. C., & Bock, K. (2005). Making syntax of sense: Number agreement in sentence production. *Psychological Review, 112*, 531–559.

Eberhardt, J. L., Goff, P. A., Purdie, V. J., & Davies, P. G. (2004). Seeing Black: Race, crime, and visual processing. *Journal of Personality and Social Psychology, 87*, 876–893.

Ebstein, R. P., Benjamin, J., & Belmaker, R. H. (2003). Behavioral genetics, genomics, and personality. In R. Plomin & J. C. DeFries (Eds.), *Behavioral genetics in the postgenomic era* (pp. 365–388). Washington, DC: American Psychological Association.

Eccles, J. S., Lord, S. E., & Roeser, R. W. (1996). Round holes, square pegs, rocky roads, and sore feet: The impact of stage-environment fit on young adolescents' experiences in schools and families. In D. Cicchetti & S. L. Toth (Eds.), *Adolescence: Opportunities and challenges: Rochester symposium on developmental psychopathology* (Vol. 7). Rochester, NY: University of Rochester Press.

Ecenbarger, W. (1993, April 1). America's new merchants of death. *The Reader's Digest*, p. 50.

Eckardt, M. H. (2005). Karen Horney: A portrait: the 120th aniversay, Karen Horney, September 16, 1885. *American Journal of Psychoanalysis, 65*, 95–101.

Ecklund, A. (1999, July 12). Cochlear implant. *People Weekly*, p. 68.

Edinger, J. D., Wohlgemuth, W. K., Radtke, R. A., Marsh, G. R., & Quillian, R. E. (2001). Cognitive behavioral therapy for treatment of chronic primary insomnia A randomized controlled trial. *Journal of the American Medical Association, 285*, 1856–1864.

Egan, K. (2005). Students' development in theory and practice: The doubtful role of research. *Harvard Educational Review, 75*, 25–41.

Eichenbaum, H. (2004). Toward an information processing framework for memory representation by the hippocampus. In M. S. Gazzaniga (Ed.), *Cognitive neurosciences* (3rd ed., pp. 679–690). Cambridge, MA: MIT.

Einarsson, C., & Granstroem, K. (2002). Gender-biased interaction in the classroom: The influence of gender and age in the relationship between teacher and pupil. *Scandinavian Journal of Educational Research, 46*, 117–127.

Eisenberg, N., Guthrie, I. K., & Cumberland, A. (2002). Prosocial development in early adulthood: A longitudinal study. *Journal of Personality and Social Psychology, 82*, 993–1006.

Eizenberg, M. M., & Zaslavsky, O. (2004). Students' verification strategies for combinatorial problems. *Mathematical Thinking and Learning, 6*, 15–36.

Ekman, P. (1972). Universals and cultural differences in facial expressions of emotion. In J. Cole (Ed.), *Darwin and facial expression: A century of research in review* (pp. 169–222). New York: Academic Press.

Ekman, P. (1994a). All emotions are basic. In P. Ekman & R.J. Davidson (Eds.), *The nature of emotion: Fundamental questions.* New York: Oxford University Press.

Ekman, P. (1994b). Strong evidence for universals in facial expressions: A reply to Russell's mistaken critique. *Psychological Bulletin, 115,* 268–287.

Ekman, P. (2003). *Emotions revealed: Recognizing faces and feelings to improve communication and emotional life.* New York: Times Books.

Ekman, P., & O'Sullivan, M. (1991). Facial expression: Methods, means, and moues. In R. S. Feldman & B. Rimé (Eds.), *Fundamentals of nonverbal behavior.* Cambridge, England: Cambridge University Press.

Ekman, P., Davidson, R. J., & Friesen, W. V. (1990). Emotional expression and brain physiology: II. The Duchenne smile. *Journal of Personality and Social Psychology, 58,* 342–353.

Ekman, P., Levenson, R. W., & Friesen, W. V. (1983, September 16). Autonomic nervous system activity distinguishes among emotions. *Science, 223,* 1208–1210.

Ekstrom, S. R. (2004). The mind beyond our immediate awareness: Freudian, Jungian, and cognitive models of the unconscious. *Journal of Analytical Psychology, 49,* 657–682.

Elfenbein, H. A. (2005). It takes one to know one better: Controversy about the cultural in-group advantage in communicating emotion as a theoretical rather than methodological issue. In U. Hess & P. Philippot (Eds.), *Group dynamics and emotional expression.* Cambridge, England: Cambridge University Press.

Elfenbein, H. A., & Ambady, N. (2003). Universals and cultural differences in recognizing emotions. *Current Directions in Psychological Science, 12,* 159–164.

Elfenbein, H. A., Mandal, M., Ambady, N., Harizuka, S., & Kumar, S. (2004). Hemifacial differences in the in-group advantage in emotion recognition. *Cognition and Emotion, 18,* 613–629.

El-Hai, J. (2005). *The lobotomist: A maverick medical genius and his tragic quest to rid the world of mental illness.* New York: Wiley.

Elkind, D. (1985) Cognitive development and adolescent disabilities. *Journal of Adolescent Health Care, 6,* 84–89.

Elkins, G. R., & Rajab, M. H. (2004). Clinical hypnosis for smoking cessation: Preliminary results of a three-session intervention. *International Journal of Clinical and Experimental Hypnosis, 52,* 73–81.

Ellason, J. W., & Ross, C. A. (2004). SCL-90-R norms for dissociative identity disorder. *Journal of Trauma and Dissociation, 5,* 85–91.

Elliott, A. (2002). *Psychoanalytic theory: An introduction* (2nd ed.). Durham, NC: Duke University Press.

Elliott, J., Berman, H., & Kim, S. (2002). Critical ethnography of Korean Canadian women's menopause experience. *Health Care for Women International, 23,* 377–388.

Ellis, A. (1974). *Growth through reason.* Hollywood, CA: Wilshire Books.

Ellis, A. (2002). *Overcoming resistance: A rational emotive behavior therapy integrated approach* (2nd ed.). New York: Springer.

Ellis, A. (2004). Expanding the ABCs of rational emotive behavior therapy. In A. Freeman, M. J. Mahoney, P. Devito, & D. Martin (Eds.), *Cognition and psychotherapy* (2nd ed.). New York: Springer Publishing Co.

Ellis, B. J., & Bjorklund, D. F. (2005). *Origins of the social mind: Evolutionary psychology and child development.* New York, NY: Guilford.

Embretson, S. E. (2005). Measuring human intelligence with artificial intelligence: Adaptive item generation. In R. J. Sternberg & J. E. Pretz (Eds.), *Cognition and intelligence: Identifying the mechanisms of the mind* (pp. 251–267). New York: Cambridge University Press.

Emick, J., & Welsh, M. (2005). Association between formal operational thought and executive function as measured by the Tower of Hanoi-Revised. *Learning and Individual Differences, 15,* 177–188.

Enard, W., Przeworski, M., Fisher, S. E., Lai, C. S. L., Wiebe, V., Kitano, T., Monaco, A. P., & Pääbo, S. (2002, August 14). Molecular evolution of FOXP2, a gene involved in speech and language. *Nature, 388,* 14.

Engle-Friedman, M., Baker, A., & Bootzin, R. R. (1985). Reports of wakefulness during EEG identified stages of sleep. *Sleep Research, 14,* 152.

Engler, J., & Goleman, D. (1992). *The consumer's guide to psychotherapy.* New York: Simon & Schuster.

Enserink, M. (1999, April 9). Can the placebo be the cure? *Science, 284,* 238–240.

Enserink, M. (2000, April, 21). Are placebo-controlled drug trials ethical? *Science, 288,* 416.

Epstein, R. (1987). The spontaneous interconnection of four repertoires of behavior in a pigeon. *Journal of Comparative Psychology, 101,* 197–201.

Epstein, R. (1996). *Cognition, creativity, and behavior: Selected essays.* Westport, CT: Praeger/Greenwood.

Eranti, S. V., & McLoughlin, D. M. (2003). Electroconvulsive therapy: State of the art. *British Journal of Psychiatry, 182,* 8–9.

Erikson, E. H. (1963). *Childhood and society* (2nd ed.). New York: Norton.

Etchegary, H. (2004). Psychological aspects of predictive gentic-test decision: What do we know so far? *Analyses of Social Issues and Public Policy, 4,* 13–31.

Evans, J. B. T. (2004). Informal reasoning: Theory and method. *Canadian Journal of Experimental Psychology, 58,* 69–74.

Evans, J. B. T., & Feeney, A. (2004). The role of prior belief in reasoning. In J. P. Leighton (Ed.), *Nature of reasoning.* New York: Cambridge University Press.

Eysenck, H. J. (1990). Biological dimensions of personality. In L. A. Pervin (Ed.), *Handbook of personality: Theory and research,* p. 246. New York: Guilford Press.

Eysenck, H. J. (1994). The Big Five or giant three: Criteria for a paradigm. In C. F. Halverson, Jr., G. A. Kohnstamm, & R. P. Martin (Eds.), *The developing structure of temperament and personality from infancy to adulthood.* Hillsdale, NJ: Erlbaum.

Eysenck, H. J. (1995). *Eysenck on extraversion.* New York: Wiley.

Eysenck, H. J., Barrett, P., Wilson, G., & Jackson, C. (1992). Primary trait measurement of the 21 components of the P-E-N system. *European Journal of Psychological Assessment, 8,* 109–117.

Ezzell, C. (September 2002). Clocking cultures. *Scientific American,* pp. 74–75.

Fagan, J. F., & Holland, C. R. (2002). Equal opportunity and racial differences in IQ. *Intelligence, 30,* 361–387.

Falk, D., Forese, N., Sade, D. S., & Dudek, B. C. (1999). Sex differences in brain/body relationships of Rhesus monkeys and humans. *Journal of Human Evolution, 36,* 233–238.

Fallon, B. A., & Feinstein, S. (2001). Hypochondriasis. In K. A. Phillips (Ed.), *Somatoform and factitious disorders*. Washington, DC: American Psychiatric Association.

Fanselow, M. S., & Poulos, A. M. (2005). The neuroscience of mammalian associative learning. *Annual Review of Psychology, 56*, 207–234.

Farber, B. A., Brink, D. C., & Raskin, P. M. (Eds.). (1996). *The psychotherapy of Carl Rogers: Cases and commentary.* New York: Guilford Press.

Farkas, R. (2004, February 24). Ray Farkas stayed awake during brain surgery for Parkinson's—and filmed it. *People,* pp. 99–100.

Farley, F. (1986, May). The big T in personality. *Psychology Today,* pp. 44–52.

Farrell, E. F. (2005), July 15). To test or not to test? *The Chronicle of Higher Education,* pp. A39–A40.

Farver, J. M., & Lee-Shin, Y. (2000). Acculturation and Korean-American children's social and play behavior. *Social Development, 9,* 316–336.

Farver, J. M., Kim, Y. K., & Lee-Shin, Y. (1995). Cultural differences in Korean- and Anglo-American preschoolers' social interaction and play behaviors. *Child Development, 66,* 1088–1099.

Fearing, V. G., & Clark, J. (Eds.). (2000). *Individuals in context: A practical guide to client-centered practice.* Chicago: Slack Publishing.

Feeley, T. H. (2002). Comment on halo effects in rating and evaluation research [Special issue: Statistical and methodological issues in communication research]. *Human Communication Research, 28,* 578–586.

Feinberg, A. W. (2002, April). Homocysteine may raise Alzheimer's risk: A physician's perspective. *HealthNews,* p. 4.

Feingold, A. (1994). Gender differences in personality: A meta-analysis. *Psychological Bulletin, 116,* 429–456.

Feldman, D. H. (2003). Cognitive development in childhood. In R. M. Lerner, M. A. Easterbrooks, et al. (Eds.), *Handbook of psychology: Developmental psychology* (Vol. 6, pp. 195–210). New York: Wiley.

Feldman, D. H. (2004). Piaget's stages: The unfinished symphony of cognitive development. *New Ideas in Psychology, 22,* 175–231.

Feldman, R. S. (Ed.). (1982). *Development of nonverbal behavior in children.* New York: Springer-Verlag.

Feldman, R. S. (Ed.). (1993) *Applications of nonverbal behavioral theories and research.* Hillsdale, NJ: Erlbaum.

Feldman, R. S. (2003). *P.O.W.E.R. Learning* (2nd ed.). New York: McGraw-Hill.

Feldman, R. S., & Tyler, J. M. (2005) Lying to look good: Using deceptive behavior as a self-presentational strategy. Mahwah, NJ, Lawrence Erlbaum.

Feldman, R. S., Coats, E. J., & Schwartzberg, S. (1994). *Case studies and critical thinking about psychology.* New York: McGraw-Hill.

Feldman, R. S., Forrest, J. A., & Happ, B. R. (2002.) Self-presentation and verbal deception: Do self-presenters lie more? *Basic and Applied Social Psychology, 24,* 163–170.

Feldt, L. S. (2004). Estimating the reliability of a test battery composite or a test score based on weighted item scoring. *Measurement & Evaluation in Counseling & Development, 37,* 184–191.

Fellous, J. M., & Arbib, M. A. (2005). *Who needs emotions? The brain meets the robot.* New York: Oxford University Press, 2005.

Fenn, K. M., Nusbaum, H. C., & Margoliash, D. (2003, October 9). Consolidation during sleep of perceptual learning of spoken language. *Nature, 425,* 614–616.

Festinger, L. (1957). *A theory of cognitive dissonance.* Stanford, CA: Stanford University Press.

Festinger, L., & Carlsmith, J. M. (1959). Cognitive consequences of forced compliance. *Journal of Abnormal and Social Psychology, 58,* 203–210.

Festinger, L., Schachter, S., & Back, K. W. (1950). *Social pressure in informal groups.* New York: Harper.

Fields, R. D. (2004, April). The other half of the brain. *Scientific American,* pp. 55–61.

Fields, R. D. (2005, February). Making memories stick. *Scientific American,* 75–81.

Fields-Meyer, T. (1999, October 25). The whiz kids. *People,* pp. 59–63.

Fields-Meyer, T., & Haederle, M. (1996, June 24). Married to a stranger. *People,* pp. 48–51.

Fields-Meyer, T., & Lambert, P. (2004, November 15). Land of the Brave: These extraordinary Americans took on riptides, savage dogs—even an avalanche. *People Weekly,* p. 100.

Fields-Meyer, T., & Wihlborg, U. (2003, March 17). Gender jump. *People Magazine,* 109–111.

Fine, L. (1994). Personal communication.

Fine, R., & Fine, L. (2003). *Basic chess endings.* New York: Random House.

Fineran, S. (2002). Adolescents at work: Gender issues and sexual harassment. *Violence Against Women, 8,* 953–967.

Fink, G. (Ed.). (2000) *Encyclopedia of stress.* New York: Academic Press.

Fink, M. (1999). *Electroshock: Restoring the mind.* New York: Oxford University Press.

Fink, M. (2000). Electroshock revisited. *American Scientist, 88,* 162–167.

Finke, R. A. (1995). Creative insight and preinventive forms. In R. J. Sternberg & J. E. Davidson (Eds.), *The nature of insight.* Cambridge, MA: MIT.

Finkelhor, D., Ormrod, R., & Turner, H. (2005). The victimization of children and youth: A comprehensive, national survey. *Child Maltreatment: Journal of the American Professional Society on the Abuse of Children, 10,* 5–25.

Finkler, K. (2004). Traditional healers in Mexico: The effectiveness of spiritual practices. In U. P. Gielen, J. M. Fish, & J. G. Draguns (Eds.), *Handbook of culture, therapy, and healing.* Mahwah, NJ: Lawrence Erlbaum Associates.

Finlay, F. O., Jones, R., & Coleman, J. (2002). Is puberty getting earlier? The views of doctors and teachers. *Child: Care, Health and Development, 28,* 205–209.

Finley, C. L., & Cowley, B. J. (2005). The effects of a consistent sleep schedule on time taken to achieve sleep. *Clinical Case Studies, 4,* 304–311.

Finney, M. L., Stoney, C. M., & Engebretson, T. O. (2002). Hostility and anger expression in African American and European American men is associated with cardiovascular and lipid reactivity. *Psychophysiology, 39,* 340–349.

Firestein, B. A. (Ed.). (1996). *Bisexuality: The psychology and politics of an invisible minority.* Thousand Oaks, CA: Sage.

First, M. B., Frances, A., & Pincus, H. A. (2002). *DSM-IV-TR handbook of differential diagnosis.* Washington, DC: American Psychiatric Publishing.

Fischer, K. W., Shaver, P. R., & Carnochan, P. (1990). How emotions develop and how they organize development. *Cognition and Emotion, 4,* 81–127.

Fish, J. M. (Ed.) (2002). *Race and intelligence: Separating science from myth.* Mahwah, NJ: Erlbaum.

Fisher, C. B. (2003). *Decoding the ethics code: A practical guide for psychologists.* Thousand Oaks, CA: Sage.

Fisher, C. B., Hoagwood, K., Boyce, C., Duster, T., Frank, D. A., Grisso, T., Levine, R. J., Macklin, R., Spencer, M. B., Takanishi, R., Trimble, J. E., & Zayas, L. H. (2002). Research ethics for mental health science involving ethnic minority children and youths. *American Psychologist, 57,* 1024–1040.

Fisk, J. E., & Sharp, C. (2002). Syllogistic reasoning and cognitive ageing. *Quarterly Journal of Experimental Psychology: Human Experimental Psychology, 55A,* 1273–1293.

Fiske, S. T. (2002). What we know now about bias and intergroup conflict, the problem of the century. *Current Directions in Psychological Science, 11,* 123–128.

Fiske, S. T., & Taylor, S. E. (1991). *Social cognition* (2nd ed.). New York: McGraw-Hill.

Fitch, K. L., & Sanders, R. E. (2005). *Handbook of language and social interaction.* Mahwah, NJ: Lawrence Erlbaum Associates.

Fitzgerald, H., Mann, T., Cabrera, N., & Wong, M. M. (2003). Diversity in caregiving contexts. In R. M. Lerner, M. A. Easterbrooks, et al. (Eds.), *Handbook of psychology: Developmental psychology* (Vol. 6, pp. 135–167). New York: Wiley.

Fitzgerald, L. F. (2003). Sexual harassment and social justice: Reflections on the distance yet to go. *American Psychologist, 58,* 915–924.

Flam, F. (1991, June 14). Queasy riders. *Science, 252,* 1488.

Flavell, J. H. (2002). Development of children's knowledge about the mental world. In W. W. Hartup & R. K. Silbereisen (Eds.), *Growing points in developmental science: An introduction,* pp. 102–122. Philadelphia: Press.

Fleischman, D. A., Wilson, R. S., Gabrieli, J. D. E., Bienias, J. L., & Bennett, D. A. (2004). A longitudinal study of implicit and explicit memory in old persons. *Psychology and Aging, 19,* 617–625.

Fleming, J. (2000). Affirmative action and standardized test scores. *Journal of Negro Education, 69,* 27–37.

Flynn, J. R. (1999). Searching for justice: The discovery of IQ gains over time. *American Psychologist, 54,* 5–20.

Flynn, J. R. (2000). IQ gains and fluid g. *American Psychologist, 55,* 543.

Foderaro, L. W. (2006, February 16). Westchester lawyer, his memory lost, is found in Chicago Shelter after 6 months. *The New York Times,* p. B3.

Fogarty, J. S., & Young, G. A., Jr. (2000). Patient-physician communication. *Journal of the American Medical Association, 289,* 92.

Folkman, S., & Moskowitz, J. T. (2000). Stress, positive emotion, and coping. *Current Directions in Psychological Science, 9,* 115–118

Folkman, S., & Moskowitz, J. T. (2004). Coping: Pitfalls and promise. *Annual Review of Psychology, 55,* 745–774.

Follett, K., & Hess, T. M. (2002). Aging, cognitive complexity, and the fundamental attribution error. *Journal of Gerontology: Series B: Psychological Sciences and Social Sciences, 57B,* P312–P323.

Ford, C. S., & Beach, F. A. (1951). *Patterns of sexual behavior.* New York: Harper.

Forer, B. (1949). The fallacy of personal validation: A classroom demonstration of gullibility. *Journal of Abnormal and Social Psychology, 44,* 118–123.

Forgas, J. P., & Laham, S. M. (2005). The interaction between affect and motivation in social judgments and behavior. In J. P. Forgas, K. P. Williams, S. M. Laham (Eds.), *Social motivation: Conscious and unconscious processes.* New York: Cambridge University Press.

Forlenza, M. J., & Baum, A. (2004). Psychoneuroimmunology. In T. J. Boll & R. G. Frank (Eds.),. *Handbook of clinical health psychology: Volume 3. Models and perspectives in health psychology.* Washington, DC: American Psychological Association.

Fountoulakis, K. N., Vieta, E., Sanchez-Moreno, J., Kaprinis, S. G., Goikolea, J. M., & Kaprinis, G. S. (2005). Treatment guidelines for bipolar disorder: A critical review. *Journal of Affective Disorders, 86,* 1–10.

Fowler, F. J., Jr. (2001). *Survey research methods.* Thousand Oaks, CA: Sage.

Fowler, R. D. (February 2002). APA's directory tells us who we are. *Monitor on Psychology, 9.*

Fox, S., & Spector, P. E. (2000). Relations of emotional intelligence, practical intelligence, general intelligence, and trait affectivity with interview outcomes: It's not all just "G." *Journal of Organizational Behavior, 21,* 203–220.

Fraley, R. C., & Spieker, S. J. (2003). Are infant attachment patterns continuously or categorically distributed? A taxometric analysis of strange situation behavior. *Developmental Psychology, 39,* 387–404.

Frances, A., First, M. B., & Pincus, H. A. (1995). *DSM-IV guidebook.* Washington, DC: American Psychiatric Press.

Frank, L. R. (2002). Electroshock: A crime against the spirit. *Ethical Human Sciences and Services, 4,* 63–71.

Frankenberg, W. K., et al., 1992. *Denver II training manual.* Denver: Denver Developmental Materials.

Frankenberger, K. D. (2004). Adolescent egocentrism, risk perceptions, and sensation seeking among smoking and nonsmoking youth. *Journal of Adolescent Research, 19,* 576–590.

Franklin, A., Pilling, M., & Davies, I. (2005). The nature of infant color categorization: Evidence from eye movements on a target decision task. *Journal of Experimental Child Psychology, 91,* 227–248.

Franks, D. D., & Smith, T. S. (1999) (Eds.). *Mind, brain, and society: Toward a neurosociology of emotion.* Stamford, CT: JAI Press.

Franzek, E., & Beckmann, H. (1996). Gene-environment interaction in schizophrenia: Season-of-birth effect reveals etiologically different subgroups. *Psychopathology, 29,* 14–26.

Frasure-Smith, N., Lesperance, F., & Talajic, M. (2000). The prognostic importance of depression, anxiety, anger, and social support following myocardial infarction: Opportunities for improving survival. In P. M. McCabe, N. Schneiderman, T. M. Field, & A. R. Wellens (Eds.), *Stress, coping, and cardiovascular disease.* Mahwah, NJ: Erlbaum.

Fredrickson, B. L., Tugade, M. M., & Waugh, C. E. (2003). What good are positive emotions in crisis? A prospective study of resilience and emotions following the terrorist attacks on the United States on September 11th, 2001. *Journal of Personality & Social Psychology, 84,* 365–376.

Fredrickson, B. L., & Branigan, C. (2005). Positive emotions broaden the scope of attention and thought-action repertoires. *Cognition and Emotion, 19,* 313–332.

Free, M. L. (2000). *Cognitive therapy in groups: Guidelines and resources for practice.* New York: Wiley.

Freedman, D. S. (1995). The importance of body fat distribution in early life. *American Journal of the Medical Sciences, 310,* S72–S76.

Freedman, J. L., & Fraser, S. C. (1966). Compliance without pressure: The foot-in-the-door technique. *Journal of Personality and Social Psychology, 4,* 195–202.

Freeman, P. (1990, December 17) Silent no more. *People Weekly,* pp. 94–104.

French, H. W. (1997, February 2). Africa's culture war: Old customs, new values. *The New York Times,* pp. 1E, 4E.

Frensch, P. A., & Rünger, D. (2003). Implicit learning. *Current Directions in Psychological Science, 12,* 13–17.

Freud, S. (1900). *The interpretation of dreams.* New York: Basic Books.

Freud, S. (1922/1959). *Group psychology and the analysis of the ego.* London: Hogarth.

Friborg, O., Barlaug, D., Martinussen, M., Rosenvinge, J. H., & Hjemdal, O. (2005). Resilience in relation to personality and intelligence. *International Journal of Methods in Psychiatric Research, 14,* 29–42.

Friedman, A. F., Lewak, R., Nichols, D. S., & Webb, J. T. (2000). *Psychological assessment with the MMPI-2.* Mahwah, NJ: Erlbaum.

Friedman, D. E. (2004). *The new economics of preschool.* Washington, DC: Early Childhood Funders' Collaborative/NAEYC.

Friedman, J. M. (2003, February 7). A war on obesity, not the obese. *Science, 299,* 856–858.

Frijda, N. H. (2005). Emotion experience. *Cognition and Emotion, 19,* 473–497.

Frincke, J. L., & Pate, W. E, II. (2004, March). *Yesterday, today, and tomorrow. Careers in Psychology 2004, what students need to know.* Paper presented at the Annual Convention of the Southeastern Psychological Association, Atlanta, GA.

Fritsch, J. (1999, October 5). Scientists unmask diet myth: Willpower. *The New York Times,* pp. D1, D9.

Fromkin, V. A. (2000). On the uniqueness of language. In K. Emmorey, H. Lane, et al. (Eds.), *The signs of language revisited: An anthology to honor Ursula Bellugi and Edward Klima.* Mahwah, NJ: Erlbaum.

Fromm, E., & Nash, M. (Eds.) (1992). *Contemporary hypnosis research.* New York: Guilford.

Frost, L. E., & Bonnie, R. J. (Eds.). (2001). *The evolution of mental health law.* Washington, DC: American Psychological Association.

Frost, R. O., & Steketee, G. (Eds.). (2002). *Cognitive approaches to obsessions and compulsions: Theory, assessment, and treatment.* New York: Pergamon Press.

Frot, M., Feine, J. S., & Bushnel, M. C. (2004). Sex differences in pain perception and anxiety. A psychophysical study with topical capsaicin. *Pain, 108,* 230–236.

Frueh, B. C., Elhai, J. D., & Grubaugh, A. L. (2005). Documented combat exposure of US veterans seeking treatment for combat-related post-traumatic stress disorder. *British Journal of Psychiatry, 186,* 467–472.

Funder, D. C. (1991). Global traits: A neo-Allportian approach to personality. *Psychological Science, 2,* 31–39.

Funder, D. C. (1997). *The personality puzzle.* New York: W. W. Norton.

Funk, J. B. (2005). Children's exposure to violent video games and desensitization to violence. *Child and Adolescent Psychiatric Clinics of North America, 14,* 387–404.

Funk, M. S. (1996). Development of object permanence in the New Zealand parakeet (*Cyanoramphus auriceps*). *Animal Learning and Behavior, 24,* 375–383.

Furnham, A. (1995). The relationship of personality and intelligence to cognitive learning style and achievement. In D. H. Saklofske & M. Zeidner (Eds.), *International handbook of personality and intelligence. Perspectives on individual differences.* New York: Plenum.

Furnham, A., & Crump, J. (2005). Personality traits, types, and disorders: An examination of the relationship between three self-report measures. *European Journal of Personality, 19,* 167–184.

Furnham, A., Pallangyo, A. E., & Gunter, B. (2001). Gender-role stereotyping in Zimbabwean television advertisements. *South African Journal of Psychology, 31,* 21–29.

Furst, P. T. (1977). "High states" in culture-historical perspective. In N. E. Zinberg (Ed.), *Alternate states of consciousness.* New York: Free Press.

Furumoto, L., & Scarborough, E. (2002). Placing women in the history of psychology: The first American women psychologists. In W. E. Pickren (Ed.), *Evolving perspectives on the history of psychology* (pp. 527–543). Washington, DC: American Psychological Association.

Gaab, J., Rohleder, N., Nater, U. M., & Ehlert, U. (2005). Psychological determinants of the cortisol stress response: The role of anticipatory cognitive appraisal. *Psychoneuroendocrinology, 30,* 599–610.

Gagnon, G. H. (1977). *Human sexualities.* Glenview, IL: Scott, Foresman.

Galanter, E. (1962). Contemporary psychophysics. In R. Brown, E. Galanter, E. Hess, & G. Maroler (Eds.), *New directions in psychology* (pp. 87–157). New York: Holt.

Galanter, M., & Kleber, H. D. (Eds.). (1999). *The American Psychiatric Press textbook of substance abuse: Abuse treatment* (2nd ed.), Washington, DC: American Psychiatric Press.

Galatzer-Levy, R. M., & Cohler, B. J. (1997). *Essential psychoanalysis: A contemporary introduction.* New York: Basic Books.

Galavotti, C., Saltzman, L. E., Sauter, S. L., & Sumartojo, E. (1997, February). Behavioral science activities at the Center for Disease Control and Prevention: A selected overview of exemplary programs. *American Psychologist, 52,* 154–166.

Galef, D. (2001, April 27). The information you provide is anonymous, but what was your name again? *The Chronicle of Higher Education, 47,* p. B5.

Gallagher, A. M., & Kaufman, J. C. (2005). *Gender differences in mathematics: An integrated psychological approach.* Cambridge, England: Cambridge University Press.

Gallagher, D. J. (1996). Personality, coping, and objective outcomes: Extraversion, neuroticism, coping styles, and academic performance. *Personality & Individual Differences, 21,* 421–429.

Gallagher, J. J. (1994). Teaching and learning: New models. *Annual Review of Psychology, 45,* 171–195.

Gallagher, M., & Rapp, R. R. (1997). The use of animal models to study the effects of aging on cognition. *Annual Review of Psychology, 48,* 339–370.

Gallup News Service (1998). *Adults who find that premarital sex is not wrong.* Washington, DC: Gallup News Service.

Gallup Poll. (2001, June 8). *American's belief in psychic and paranormal phenomena is up over last decade.* Washington, DC: The Gallup Organization.

Gami, A. S., Howard, D. E., Olson, E. J., Somers, V. K. (2005). Day-night pattern of sudden death in obstructive sleep apnea. *New England Journal of Medicine, 353,* 1206–1214.

Gangestad, S. W., Simpson, J. A., Cousins, A. J., Garver-Apgar, C. E.,

& Christensen, P. N. (2004). Women's preferences for male behavioral displays change across the menstrual cycle. *Psychological Science, 15,* 203–207.

Ganong, L. H., & Coleman, M. (1999). *Changing families, changing responsibilities: Family obligations following divorce and remarriage.* Mahwah, NJ: Erlbaum.

Garb, H. N. (2002). Practicing psychological assessment. *American Psychologist, 57,* 990–991.

Garb, H. N. (2003). Observations on the validity of neuropsychological and personality assessment testing. *Australian Psychologist, 38,* 14–21.

Garb, H. N., Wood, J. M., Lilenfeld, S. O., & Nezworski, M. T. (2005). Roots of the Rorschach controversy. *Clinical Psychology Review, 25,* 97–118.

Garber, J., & Horowitz, J. L. (2002). Depression in children. In I. H. Gotlib & C. L. Hammen (Eds.), *Handbook of depression.* New York: Guilford Press.

Garcia, J. (1990). Learning without memory. *Journal of Cognitive Neuroscience, 2,* 287–305.

Garcia, J. (2003). Psychology is not an enclave. In R. J. Sternberg (Ed.), *Psychologists defying the crowd: Stories of those who battled the establishment and won.* Washington, DC: American Psychological Association.

Garcia, J., Hankins, W. G., & Rusiniak, K. W. (1974). Behavioral regulation of the milieu intern in man and rat. *Science, 185,* 824–831.

Garcia, S. M., Weaver, K., Moskowitz, G. B., & Darley, J. M. (2002). Crowded minds: The implicit bystander effect. *Journal of Personality and Social Psychology, 83,* 843–853.

Garcia-Andrade, C., Wall, T. L., & Ehlers, C. L. (1997). The firewater myth and response to alcohol in Mission Indians. *Journal of Psychiatry, 154,* 983–988.

Garcia-Palacios, A., Hoffman, H., & Carlin, A. (2002). Virtual reality in the treatment of spider phobia: A controlled study. *Behavior Research & Therapy, 40,* 983–993.

Gardner, E. P., & Kandel, E. R. (2000). Touch. In E. R. Kandel, J. H. Schwartz, & T. M. Jessell (Eds.), *Principles of neural science* (4th ed.). New York: McGraw-Hill.

Gardner, H. (1975). *The shattered mind: The person after brain damage.* New York: Knopf.

Gardner, H. (2000). *Intelligence reframed: Multiple intelligences for the 21st century.* New York: Basic Books.

Gardner, H. (2005). Scientific psychology: Should we bury it or praise it? In R. J. Sternberg (Ed.), *Unity in psychology: Possibility or pipe dream?* (pp. 77–90). Washington, DC: American Psychological Association.

Gardner, R. A., & Gardner, B. T. (1969). Teaching sign language to a chimpanzee. *Science, 165,* 664–672.

Garza-Guerrero, C. (2000). Idealization and mourning in love relationships: Normal and pathological spectra. *Psychoanalytic Quarterly, 69,* 121–150.

Gass, C. S., Luis, C. A., Meyers, T. L., & Kuljis, R. O. (2000). Familial Creutzfeldt-Jakob disease: A neuropsychological case study. *Archives of Clinical Neuropsychology, 15,* 165–175.

Gassio, R., Artuch, R., Vilaseca, M. A., Fuste, E., Boix, C., Sans, A., & Campistol, J. (2005). Cognitive functions in classic phenylketonuria and mild hyperphenylalaninaemia: experience in a paediatric population. *Developmental Medicine and Child Neurology, 47,* 443–448.

Gatchel, R. J., & Baum, A. (1983). *An introduction to health psychology.* Reading, MA: Addison-Wesley.

Gathchel, R. J., & Oordt, M. S. (2003). Obesity. In R. J. Gathchel & M. S. Oordt, *Clinical health psychology and primary care: Practical advice and clinical guidance for successful collaboration,* pp. 149–167. Washington, DC: American Psychological Association.

Gatchel, R. J., & Turk, D. C. (Eds.). (1996). *Psychological approaches to pain management: A practioner's handbook.* New York: Guilford.

Gatchel, R. J. & Weisberg, J. N. (2000). *Personality characteristics of patients with pain.* Washington, DC: APA Books.

Gathercole, S. E., & Baddeley, A.D. (1993). *Working memory and language processing.* Hillsdale, NJ: Erlbaum.

Gazzaniga, M. S. (1998, July). The split brain revisited. *Scientific American,* 50–55.

Gazzaniga, M. S., Ivry, R. B., & Mangun, G. R. (2002). *Cognitive neuroscience: The biology of the mind* (2nd ed.). New York: W. W. Norton.

Ge, X., Conger, R. D., & Elder, G. H., Jr. (1996). Coming of age too early: Pubertal influences on girls' vulnerability to psychological distress. *Child Development, 67,* 3386–3400.

Geen, R. G., & Donnerstein, E. (1983). *Aggression: Theoretical and empirical reviews.* New York: Academic Press.

Geen, R., & Donnerstein, E. (1998). *Human aggression: Theories, research, and implications for social policy.* San Diego, CA: Academic Press.

Gegenfurtner, K. R. (2003). Color vision. *Annual Review of Neuroscience, 26,* 181–206.

Geiselman, R. E., Fisher, R. P., MacKinnon, D. P., & Holland, H. L. (1985). Eyewitness memory enhancement in the police interview: Cognitive retrieval mnemonics versus hypnosis. *Journal of Applied Psychology, 70,* 401–412.

Gelfand, M. M. (2000). Sexuality among older women. *Journal of Women's Health and Gender Based Medicine, 9*(Suppl. 1), S15–S20.

Gelman, D. (1994, April 18). The mystery of suicide. *Newsweek,* pp. 44–49.

Gelman, R., & Baillargeon, R. (1983). A review of some Piagetian concepts. In J. H. Flavell & E. M. Markman (Eds.), *Handbook of child psychology, Vol. 3: Cognitive development* (4th ed.). New York: Wiley.

Gelman, R., & Kit-Fong Au, T. (Eds.). (1996). *Perceptual and cognitive development.* New York: Academic Press.

Gennaro, R. J. (2004). *Higher-order theories of consciousness: An anthology.* Amsterdam, Netherlands: John Benjamins.

Gentner, D., Goldin, S., & Goldin-Meadow, S. (Eds.). (2003). *Language in mind: Advances in the study of language and cognition.* Cambridge, MA: MIT.

Genuis, M., & Violato, C. (2000). Attachment security to mother, father, and the parental unit. In C. Violato, & E. Oddone-Paolucci (Eds.), *The changing family and child development.* Aldershot, England: Ashgate Publishing Ltd.

George, M. S. (2003, September). Stimulating the brain. *Scientific American,* pp. 66–73.

George, M. S., Wassermann, E. M., Williams, W. A., Callahan, A., et al. (1995). Daily repetitive transcranial magnetic stimulations (rTMS) improves mood in depression. *Neuroreport: An International Journal for the Rapid Communication of Research in Neuroscience, 6,* 1853–1856.

George, S., & Moselhy, H. (2005). Cocaine-induced trichotillomania. *Addiction, 100,* 255–256.

George, T. P. (1999) Design, measurement, and analysis in developmental research. In M. Bornstein & M. Lamb,

Developmental psychology. Mahwah, NJ: Erlbaum.

Georgiou, G. A., Bleakley, C., Hayward, J., Russo, R., Dutton, K., Eltiti, S., & Fox, E. (2005). Focusing on fear: Attentional disengagement from emotional faces. *Visual Cognition, 12,* 145–158.

Gershoff, E. T. (2002). Corporal punishment by parents and associated child behaviors and experiences: A meta-analytic and theoretical review. *Psychological Bulletin, 128,* 539–579.

Gerstel, N. (2005, April 8). In search of time. *Science, 308,* 204–205.

Getner, D., & Holyoak, K. J. (1997, January). Reasoning and learning by analogy. *American Psychologist, 52,* 32–34.

Gevirtz, R. (2000). The physiology of stress. In D. T. Kenny, J. G. Carlson, et al. (Eds.), *Stress and health: Research and clinical applications* (pp. 53–71). Amsterdam, Netherlands: Harwood Academic.

Ghaemi, S. N. (2003). *Mood disorders: A practical guide. Practical Guides in Psychiatry.* New York: Lippincott Williams & Wilkins.

Ghazvini, A., & Mullis, R. L. (2002). Center-based care for young children: Examining predictors of quality. *Journal of Genetic Psychology, 163,* 112–125.

Giacobbi, P. R., Jr., Lynn, T. K. Wetherington, J. M., Jenkins, J., Bodendorf, M., & Langley, B. (2004). Stress and coping during the transition to university for first-year female athletes. *Sports Psychologist, 18,* 1–20.

Gibbs, N. (2005, August 8). Being 13. *Time,* pp. 41–55.

Gibbs, W. W. (2002, August.) From mouth to mind. *Scientific American,* p. 26.

Gibson, B. (1997). Smoker-nonsmoker conflict: Using a social psychological framework to understand a current social controversy. *Journal of Social Issues, 53,* 97–112.

Gibson, H. B. (1995). A further case of the misuse of hypnosis in a police investigation. *Contemporary Hypnosis, 12,* 81–86.

Gilberson, T. A., Damak, S., & Margolskee, R. F. (2000). The molecular physiology of taste transduction. *Current Opinion in Neurobiology, 10,* 519–527.

Gilbert, B. (1996). New ideas in the air at the National Zoo. *Smithsonian,* pp. 32–43.

Gilbert, D. G. (1995). *Smoking: Individual differences, psychopathology, and emotion.* Philadelphia: Taylor & Francis.

Gilbert, D. T., Miller, A. G., & Ross, L. (1998). Speeding with Ned: A personal view of the correspondence bias. In J. M. Darley & J. Cooper (Eds.), *Attribution and social interaction: The legacy of Edward E. Jones.* Washington, DC: American Psychological Association.

Gilbert, D. T., McNulty, S. E., Guiliano, T. A., & Benson, J. E. (1992). Blurry words and fuzzy deeds: The attribution of obscure behavior. *Journal of Personality and Social Psychology, 62,* 18–25.

Gilligan, C. (1996). The centrality of relationships in psychological development: A puzzle, some evidence, and a theory. In G. G. Noam & K. W. Fischer (Eds.), *Development and vulnerability in close relationships.* Hillsdale, NJ: Erlbaum.

Gillyatt, P. (1997, February). When the nose doesn't know. *Harvard Health Letter,* pp. 6–7.

Gilovich, T., Griffin, D., & Kahneman, D. (Eds.). (2002). *Heuristics and biases: The psychology of intuitive judgment.* Cambridge, England: Cambridge University Press.

Gladwell, M. (2002, August 5). The naked face: Can you read people's thoughts just by looking at them? *The New Yorker,* pp. 38–49.

Gladwell, M. (2004, September 20). Annals of psychology: Personality, plus how corporations figure out who you are. *The New Yorker,* 42–45.

Gladwin, T. (1964). Culture and logical process. In N. Goodenough (Ed.), *Explorations in cultural anthropology: Essays in honor of George Peter Murdoch.* New York: McGraw-Hill.

Glassman, A. H., & Koob, G. F. (1996, February 22). Neuropharmacology: Psychoactive smoke. *Nature, 379,* 677–678.

Glenmullen, J. (2000). *Prozac backlash: Overcoming the dangers of Prozac, Zoloft, Paxil, and other antidepressants with safe, effective alternatives.* New York: Simon & Schuster.

Glenn, D. (2004, June 1). Students' performance on tests is tied to their views of their innate intelligence, researchers say. *The Chronicle of Higher Education,* p. 28.

Glick, P., & Fiske, S. T. (2001). An ambivalent alliance: Hostile and benevolent sexism as complementary justifications for gender inequality. *American Psychologist, 56,* 109–118.

Glick, P., Lameiras, M., Fiske, S. T., Eckes, T., Masser, B., Volpato, C., Huang, L. L., Sakalli-Ugurlu, N., Castro, Y. R., Pereira, M. L. D., Willemsen, T. M., Brunner, A., Six-Materna, I., & Wells, R. (2004). Bad but bold: Ambivalent attitudes toward men predict gender inequality in 16 nations. *Journal of Personality and Social Psychology, 86,* 713–728.

Goffin, R. D., Jelley, R. B., & Wagner, S. H. (2003). Is halo helpful? Effects of inducing halo on performance rating accuracy. *Social Behavior and Personality, 31,* 625–636.

Goin, M. K. (2005). A current perspective on the psychotherapies. *Psychiatric Services, 56,* 255–257.

Gold, P. E., Cahill, L., & Wenk, G. L. (2002). Ginkgo biloba: A cognitive enhancer? *Psychological Science in the Public Interest, 3,* 2–7.

Goldberg, C. (2003, May 1.) Some fear loss of privacy as science pries into brain. *The Boston Globe,* p. S1.

Golden, R. N., Gaynes, B. N., Ekstrom, R. D., Hamer, R. M., Jacobsen, F. M., Suppes, T., Wisner, K. L., & Nemeroff, C. B. (2005). The efficacy of light therapy in the treatment of mood disorders: A review and meta-analysis of the evidence. *American Journal of Psychiatry, 162,* 656–662.

Goldner, E. M., Cockell, S. J., & Srikameswaran, S. (2002). Perfectionism and eating disorders. In G. L. Flett & P. L. Hewitt (Eds.), *Perfectionism: Theory, research, and treatment,* pp. 319–340. Washington, DC: American Psychological Association.

Goldstein, E. B. (1984). *Sensation and perception* (2nd ed.). Pacific Grove, CA: Brooks/Cole.

Goldstein, G., Beers, S. R., Longmore, S., & McCue, M. (1996). Efficacy of memory training: A technological extension and replication. *Clinical Neuropsychologist, 10,* 66–72.

Goldstein, I. (2000). Female sexual arousal disorder: new insights. *International Journal of Impotence Research, 12*(Suppl. 4), S152–S157.

Goldston, D. B. (2003). *Measuring suicidal behavior and risk in children and adolescents.* Washington, DC: American Psychological Association.

Goldstone, R. L., & Kersten, A. (2003). Concepts and categorization. In A. F.

Healy & R. W. Proctor (Eds.), *Handbook of psychology: Experimental psychology* (Vol. 4, pp. 599–621). New York: Wiley.

Goleman, D. (1993, July 21). "Expert" babies found to teach others. *The New York Times*, p. C-10.

Goleman, D. (1995). *Emotional intelligence.* New York: Bantam.

Gontkovsky, S. T. (2005). Neurobiological bases and neuropsychological correlates of aggression and violence. In J. P. Morgan (Ed.), *Psychology of aggression.* Hauppauge, NY: Nova Science Publishers.

Good, C., Aronson, J., & Inzlicht, M. (2003). Improving adolescents' standardized test performance: An intervention to reduce the effects of stereotype threat. *Journal of Applied Developmental Psychology, 24,* 645–662.

Good, P. I. (2003). *Common errors in statistics and how to avoid them.* New York: Wiley.

Goode, E. (1999, April 13). If things taste bad, "phantoms" may be at work. *The New York Times*, pp. D1–D2.

Goode, E. (2001, September 12). Suicide attackers are sane, not suicidal in the normal sense, experts say. *The New York Times*, p. A13.

Goode, E. (2003, January 28). Even in the age of Prozac, some still prefer the couch. *The New York Times*, Section F, p. 1.

Goodman, G. S., Batterman-Faunce, J. M., Schaaf, J. M., & Kenney, R. (2002). Nearly 4 years after an event: Children's eyewitness memory and adults' perceptions of children's accuracy. *Child Abuse and Neglect, 26,* 849–884.

Goodman, G. S., Ghetti, S., Quas, J. A., Edelstein, R. S., Alexander K. W., Redlich, A. D., Cordon, I. M., & Jones, D. P. H. (2003). A prospective study of memory for child sexual abuse: New findings relevant to the repressed-memory controversy. *Psychological Science, 14,* 113–117.

Goodman, W., K., Rudorfer, M. V., & Maser, J. D. (2000). *Obsessive-compulsive disorder: Contemporary issues in treatment.* Mahwah, NJ: Lawrence Erlbaum Associates.

Goodwin, R. D., & Hamilton, S. P. (2003). Lifetime comorbidity of antisocial personality disorder and anxiety disorders among adults in the community. *Psychiatry Research, 117,* 159–166.

Goossens, L., Beyers, W., Emmen, M., & van Aken, M. (2002). The imaginary audience and personal fable: Factor analyses and concurrent validity of the "New Look" measures. *Journal of Research on Adolescence, 12,* 193–215.

Gordon, E. F. (2000). *Mockingbird years: A life in and out of therapy.* New York: Basic Books.

Gordon, P. (2004). Numerical cognition without words: Evidence from Amazonia. *Science, 306,* 496–499. First appeared in *Science Express*, online publication August 16th 2004.

Gotlib, I. H., Krasnoperova, E., Yue, D. N., & Joorman, J. (2004). Attentional biases for negative interpersonal stimuli in clinical depression. *Journal of Abnormal Psychology, 113,* 127–135.

Gottesman, I. I. (1991). *Schizophrenia genesis: The origins of madness.* New York: Freeman.

Gottesman, I. I. (1997, June 6). Twin: En route to QTLs for cogniton. *Science, 276,* 1522–1523.

Gottesman, I. I., & Hanson, D. R. (2005). Human development: Biological and genetic processes. *Annual Review of Psychology, 56,* 263–286.

Gottfredson, L. S. (2004). Schools and the *g* factor. *Wilson Quarterly*, pp. 35–45.

Gottfredson, L. S., & Deary, I. J. (2004). Intelligence predicts health and longevity, but why? *Current Directions in Psychological Science, 13,* 1–4.

Gottlieb, D. A. (2004). Acquisition with partial and continuous reinforcement in pigeon autoshaping. *Learning and Behavior, 32,* 321–334.

Gottlieb, G., & Lickliter, R. (2004). The various roles of animal models in understanding human development. *Social Development, 13,* 311–325.

Gould, E., Reeves, A. J., Graziano, M. S. A., & Gross, C. G. (1999, October 15). Neurogenesis in the neocortex of adult primates. *Science,* 548–552.

Gould, R. L. (1978). *Transformations.* New York: Simon & Schuster.

Gowaty, P. A. (2003). Power asymmetries between the sexes, mate preferences, and components of fitness. In C. B. Travis (Ed.), *Evolution, gender, and rape* (pp. 61–86). Cambridge, MA: MIT.

Gowing, L. R., Henry-Edwards, S. M., Irvine, R. J., & Ali, R. L. (2002). The health effects of ecstasy: A literature review. *Drug and Alcohol Review, 21,* 53–63.

Grady, D. (2002, November 26). Why we eat (and eat and eat). *The New York Times*, pp. D1, D4.

Grady, D., & Kolata, G. (2003, August, 29). Gene therapy used to treat patient with Parkinson's. *The New York Times*, pp. A1, A18.

Graf, P. (1990). Life-span changes in implicit and explicit memory. *Bulletin of the Psychonomic Society, 28,* 353–358.

Graffin, N. F., Ray, W. J., & Lundy, R. (1995). EEG concomitants of hypnosis and hypnotic susceptibility. *Journal of Abnormal Psychology, 104,* 123–131.

Graham, J. R. (1999). *MMPI-2: Assessing personality and psychopathology* (3rd ed.). New York: Oxford University Press.

Graham, S. (1992). "Most of the subjects were white and middle class": Trends in published research on African Americans in selected APA journals, 1970–1989. *American Psychologist, 47,* 629–639.

Graham, S. (2001, November 12). *9/11: The psychological aftermath.* Retrieved from the *Scientific American* Web site http://www.sciam.com/explorations/2001/111201anxiety/index.html

Granic, I., Hollenstein, T., & Dishion, T. (2003). Longitudinal analysis of flexibility and reorganization in early adolescence: A dynamic systems study of family interactions. *Developmental Psychology, 39,* 606–617.

Graswich, R. E. (2004, December 10). The bystander's dilemma: For light-rail attack victim, bystander apathy worse than thugs' blows. *The Sacramento Bee*, p. B1.

Graugaard, P. K., Eide, H., & Finset, A. (2003). Interaction analysis of physician-patient communication: The influence of trait anxiety on communication and outcome. *Patient Education and Counseling, 49,* 149–156.

Gray, J. R., Chabris, C. F., & Braver, T. S. (2003, February 18). Neural mechanisms of general fluid intelligence. *Nature: Neurosciences.* Retrieved from http://www.nature.com/cgitaf/DynaPage.taf? file=/neuro/journal/vaop/ ncurrent/abs/ nn1014.html

Graziano, M. S., Taylor, C. S., & Moore, T. (2002). Complex movements evolved by microstimulation of precentral cortex. *Neuron, 34,* 841–851.

Green, B. G., & Pravin, G. (2004). Thermal taste predicts higher responsiveness to chemical taste and flavor. *Chemical Senses, 29,* 617–628.

Green, J. S., Henderson, F. R., & Collinge, M. D. (2003). *Prevention and control of wildlife damage: Coyotes.* Lincoln:

University of Nebraska, Institute of Agriculture and Natural Resources. Retrieved from http://wildlifedam-age. unl.edu/handbook/handbook/carnivor/ ca_c51.pdf

Greenberg, R. L. (2000). The creative client in cognitive therapy [Special issue: Creativity in the context of cognitive therapy]. *Journal of Cognitive Psychotherapy, 14,* 163–174.

Greenberg, R. M., & Kellner, C. H. (2005). Electroconvulsive therapy: A selected review. *American Journal of Geriatric Psychiatry, 13,* 268–281.

Greene, B., & Herek, G. (1994). *Lesbian and gay psychology: Theory, research, and clinical applications.* Newbury Park, CA: Sage.

Greene, J. D., Sommerville, R. B., Nystrom, L. E., Darley, J. M., & Cohen, J. D. (2001, September 14). An fMRI investigation of emotional engagement in moral judgment. *Science, 293,* 2105–2108.

Greene, M., Scholl, K., Takahaski, S., Bateman-House, A., Beauchamp, T., Bok, H., Cheney, D., Coyle, J., Deacon, T., Dennett, D., Donovan, P., Flanagan, O., Goldman, S., Greely, H., Martin, L., Miller, E., Mueller, D., Siegel, A., Solter, D., Gearhart, McKhann, G., & Faden, R. (2005, July 15). Moral issues of human-non-human primate neural grafting. *Science, 309,* 385–386.

Greene, R. L., & Clopton, J. R. (2004). Minnesota Multiphasic Personality Inventory-2 (MMPI-2). In M. E. Maruish (Ed.), *Use of psychological testing for treatment planning and outcomes assessment: Instruments for adults* (Vol. 3, 3rd ed.). Mahwah, NJ: Lawrence Erlbaum Associates.

Greenfield, P. M. (1997). You can't take it with you: Why ability assessments don't cross cultures. *American Psychologist, 52,* 1115–1124.

Greenlaw, P. S., & Jensen, S. S. (1996). Race-norming and the Civil Rights Act of 1991. *Public Personnel Management, 25,* 13–24.

Greenwald, A. G., Banaji, M. R., Rudman, L. A., Farnham, S. D., Nosek, B. A., & Mellott, D. S. (2002). A unified theory of implicit attitudes, stereotypes, self-esteem, and self-concept. *Psychological Review, 109,* 3–25.

Greenwald, A. G., Draine S. C., & Abrams, R. L. (1996, September 20). Three cognitive markers of unconscious semantic activation. *Science, 272,* 1699–1702.

Greenwald, A.G., Nosek, B. A., & Banaji, M. R. (2003). Understanding and using the Implicit Association Test: 1. An improved scoring algorithm. *Journal of Personality and Social Psychology. 85,* 197–216.

Greenwald, A. G., Nosek, B. A., & Sririam, N. (2006). Consequential validity of the implicit association test: Comment on Blanton and Jaccard. *American Psychologist, 61,* 56–61.

Greenwald, A. G., Spangenberg, E. R., Pratkanis, A. R., & Eskenzai, J. (1991). Double-blind tests of subliminal self-help audiotapes. *Psychological Science, 2,* 119–122.

Greenwood, C. R., Carta, J. J., Hart, B., Kamps, D., Terry, B., Arreaga-Mayer, C., Atwater, J., Walker, D., Risley, T., & Delquadri, J. C. (1992). Out of the laboratory and into the community: 26 years of applied behavior analysis at the Juniper Gardens children's project. *American Psychologist, 47,* 1464–1474.

Gregory, R. L. (1978). *The psychology of seeing* (3rd ed.). New York: McGraw-Hill.

Gregory, S. (1856). *Facts for young women.* Boston.

Gregory, S. S. (1994, March 21). At risk of mutilation. *Time,* pp. 45–46.

Greist-Bousquet, S., & Schiffman, H. R. (1986). The basis of the Poggendorff effect: An additional clue for Day and Kasperczyk. *Perception and Psychophysics, 39,* 447–448.

Grezes, J., Frith, C., Passingham, R. E. (2004). Inferring false beliefs from the actions of oneself and others: An fMRI study. *Neuroimage, 21,* 744–750.

Grigorenko, E. L. (2000). Heritability and intelligence. In R. J. Sternberg, et al. (Eds.), *Handbook of intelligence.* New York: Cambridge University Press.

Grilo, C. M., Sanislow, C. A., Skodol, A. E., Gunderson, J. G., Stout, R. L., Shea, M. T., Zanarini, M. C., Bencer, D. S., Morey, L. C., Dyck, I. R., & McGlashan, T. H. (2003). Do eating disorders co-occur with personality disorders? Comparison groups matter. *International Journal of Eating Disorders, 33,* 155–164.

Gron, G., Kirstein, M., Thielscher, A., Riepe, M. W., & Spitzer, M. (2005, July). Cholinergic enhancement of episodic memory in healthy young adults. *Psychopharmacology (Berlin),* 1–10.

Gronholm, P., Rinne, J. O., Vorobyev, V., & Laine, M. (2005). Naming of newly learned objects: A PET activation study. *Brain Research and Cognitive Brain Research, 14,* 22–28.

Grossi, G., Semenza, C., Corazza, S., & Volterra, V. (1996). Hemispheric specialization for sign language. *Neuropsychologia, 34,* 737–740.

Groth-Marnat, G. (1996). *Handbook of psychological assessment* (3rd ed.). Somerset, NJ: Wiley.

Gruneberg, M. M., & Pascoe, K. (1996). The effectiveness of the keyword method for receptive and productive foreign vocabulary learning in the elderly. *Contemporary Educational Psychology, 21,* 102–109.

Grunwald, T., Boutros, N. N., Pezer, N., von Oertzen, J., Fernandez, G., Schaller, C., & Elger, C. E. (2003). Neuronal substrates of sensory gating within the human brain. *Biological Psychiatry, 15,* 511–519.

Guadagno, R. E., & Cialdini, R. B. (2002). Online persuasion: An examination of gender differences in computer-mediated interpersonal influence [Special issue: Groups and Internet]. *Group Dynamics:, 6,* 38–51.

Guadagno, R. E., Asher, T., Demaine, L. J., & Cialdini, R. B. (2001). When saying yes leads to saying no: Preference for consistency and the reverse foot-in-the-door effect. *Personality and Social and Social Psychology Bulletin, 27,* 859–867.

Gualtiere, C. T. (2003). Brain injury and mental retardation: Psycho-pharmacology and neuropsychiatry. *Human Psychopharmacology: Clinical and Experimental, 18,* 151.

Gueguen, N. (2002). Foot-in-the-door technique and computer-mediated communication. *Computers in Human Behavior, 18,* 11–15.

Guilford, J. P. (1982). Cognitive psychology's ambiguities: Some suggested remedies. *Psychological Review, 89,* 48–59.

Guilleminault, C., Kirisoglu, C., Bao, G., Arias, V., Chan, A., & Li, K. K. (2005). Adult chronic sleepwalking and its treatment based on polysomnography. *Brain, 128*(Pt. 5), 1062–1069.

Gullotta, T., Adams, G., & Markstrom, C. (1999). *The adolescent experience.* Orlando, FL: Academic Press.

Gur, R. C. (1996, March). Paper presented at the annual meeting of the American Association for the Advancement of Science, Baltimore, Maryland.

Gur, R. C., Gur, R. E., Obrist, W. D., Hungerbuhler, J. P., Younkin, D., Rosen, A. D., Skilnick, B. E., & Reivich,

M. (1982). Sex and handedness differences in cerebral blood flow during rest and cognitive activity. *Science, 217,* 659–661.

Gur, R. C., Mozley, L. H., Mozley, P. D., Resnick, S. M., Karp, J. S., Alavi, A., Arnold, S. E., & Gur, R. E. (1995, January 27). Sex differences in regional cerebral glucose metabolism during a resting state. *Science, 267,* 528–531.

Guralnick, M. J., Connor, R. T., Hammond, M., Gottman, J. M., et al. (1996). Immediate effects of mainstreamed settings on the social interactions and social integration of preschool children. *American Journal on Mental Retardation, 100,* 359–377.

Gutek, B. A., Cohen, A. G., & Tsui, A. (1996). Reactions to perceived sex discrimination. *Human Relations, 49,* 791–813.

Guterl, F. (2002, November 11). What Freud got right. *Newsweek,* pp. 50–51.

Guthrie, R. V. (1998). *Even the rat was white: A historical view of psychology* (2nd ed.). Needham Heights, MA: Allyn and Bacon.

Gutierrez, P. M., Muehlenkamp, J. L., Konick, L. C., & Osman, A. (2005). What role does race play in adolescent suicidal ideation? *Archives of Suicide Research, 9,* 177–192.

Guttman, M. (1995, March 3–5). She had electroshock therapy. *USA Weekend,* p. 16.

Gwynn, M. I., & Spanos, N. P. (1996). Hypnotic responsiveness, nonhypnotic suggestibility, and responsiveness to social influence. In R. G. Kunzendorf, N. P. Spahos, & B. Wallace (Eds.), *Hypnosis and imagination.* Amityville, NY: Baywood.

Haberstick, B. C., Schmitz, S., Young, S. E., & Hewitt, J. K. (2005). Contributions of genes and environments to stability and change in externalizing and internalizing problems during elementary and middle school. *Behavior Genetics, 35,* 381–396.

Hackett, T. A., & Kaas, J. H. (2003). Auditory processing in the primate brain. In M. Gallagher & R. J. Nelson (Eds.), *Handbook of psychology: Biological psychology* (Vol. 3). New York: Wiley.

Hadjistavropoulos, T., Craig, K. D., & Fuchs-Lacelle, S. (2004). *Social influences and the communication of pain.* Mahwah, NJ: Lawrence Erlbaum Associates.

Haier, R. J. (2003). Brain imaging studies of intelligence: Individual differences and neurobiology. In R. J. Sternberg & J. Lautrey (Eds.), *Models of intelligence: International perspectives* (pp. 185–193). Washington, DC: American Psychological Association.

Haley, W. E., Clair, J. M., & Saulsberry, K. (1992). Family caregiver satisfaction with medical care of their demented relatives. *Gerontologist, 32,* 219–226.

Halgin, R. P., & Whitbourne, S.K. (1994). *Abnormal psychology.* Fort Worth, TX: Harcourt Brace.

Hall, G. C. N. (1996). *Theory-based assessment, treatment, and prevention of sexual aggression.* New York: Oxford University Press.

Hall, J., & Bernieri, F. (Eds.). (2001). *Interpersonal sensitivity.* Mahwah, NJ: Lawrence Erlbaum Associates.

Hall, J. A., Roter, D. L., & Katz, N. R. (1988). Task versus socioemotional behaviors in physicians. *Medical Care, 25,* 399–412.

Hall, R. E. (2002). *The Bell Curve*: Implications for the performance of black/white athletes. *Social Science Journal, 39,* 113–118.

Hall, S. S. (2003, September). The quest for a smart pill. *Scientific American,* pp. 54–63.

Halling, S., & Goldfarb, M. (1996). The new generation of diagnostic manuals (DSM-III, DSM-III-R, and DSM-IV): An overview and a phenomenologically based critique. *Journal of Phenomenological Psychology, 27,* 49–71.

Hallschmid, M., Benedict, C., Born, J., Fehm, H., & Kern, W. (2004). Manipulating central nervous mechanisms of food intake and body weight regulation by intranasal administration of neuropeptides in man. *Physiology and Behavior, 83,* 55–64.

Halpern, D. F. (1998). Teaching critical thinking for transfer across domains. *American Psychologist, 53,* 449–455.

Halpern, D. F. (2000). *Sex differences in cognitive abilities* (3rd ed.). Mahwah, NJ: Erlbaum.

Halpern, D. F. (2005). Psychology at the intersection of work and family: Recommendations for employers, working families, and policymakers. *American Psychologist, 60,* 397–409.

Halpern, D., & Riggio, H. (2002). *Thinking critically about critical thinking.* Mahwah, NJ: Erlbaum.

Halpert, J. (2003, April 28). What do patients want? *Newsweek,* pp. 63–64.

Hamann, S. (2001). Cognitive and neural mechanisms of emotional memory. *Trends in Cognitive Sciences, 5,* 394–400.

Hamann, S. B., Ely, T. D., Hoffman, J. M., & Kilts, C. D. (2002). Ecstasy and agony: Activation of human amygdala in positive and negative emotion. *Psychological Science, 13,* 135–141.

Hamann, S., Herman, R. A., Nolan, C. L., & Wallen, K. (2004). Men and women differ in amygdala response to visual sexual stimuli. *Nature Neuroscience, 7,* 411–416.

Hamel, S., Leclerc, G., & Lefrancois, R. (2003). A psychological outlook on the concept of transcendent actualization. *International Journal of the Psychology of Religion, 13,* 3–15.

Hamer, D. H., Hu, S., Magnuson, V. L., Hu, N., & Pattatucci, A. M. L. (1993, July 16). A linkage between DNA markers on the X chromosome and male sexual orientation. *Science, 261,* 321–327.

Hamilton, C. E. (2000). Continuity and discontinuity of attachment from infancy through adolescence. *Child Development, 71,* 690–694.

Hanley, S. J., & Abell, S. C. (2002). Maslow and relatedness: Creating an interpersonal model of self-actualization. *Journal of Humanistic Psychology, 42,* 37–56.

Hanna, J. L. (1984). Black/white nonverbal differences, dance, and dissonance: Implications for desegregation. In A. Wolfgang (Ed.), *Nonverbal behavior: Perspectives, applications, intercultural insights.* Lewiston, NY: Hogrefe.

Hannon, E. E., & Johnson, S. P. (2005). Infants use meter to categorize rhythms and melodies: Implications for musical structure learning. *Cognitive Psychology, 50,* 354–377.

Harden, B. (2000, January 9). Very young, smart, and restless. *New York Times Education Life,* pp. 28–31.

Hardy, J., & Selkoe, D. J. (2002, July 19). The amyloid hypothesis of Alzheimer's disease: Progress and problems on the road to therapeutics. *Science, 297,* 353–356.

Harlaar, N., Spinath, F. M., Dale, P. S., & Plomin, R. (2005). Genetic influences on early word recognition abilities and disabilities: A study of 7-year-old twins. *Journal of Child Psychology and Psychiatry, 46,* 373–384.

Harlow, H. F., & Zimmerman, R. R. (1959). Affectional responses in the infant monkey. *Science, 130,* 421–432.

Harlow, J. M. (1869). Recovery from the passage of an iron bar through the head. *Massachusetts Medical Society Publication, 2,* 329–347.

Harmon-Jones, E., Peterson, H., & Vaughn, K. (2003). The dissonance-inducing effects of an inconsistency between experienced empathy and knowledge of past failures to help: Support for the action-based model of dissonance. *Basic and Applied Social Psychology, 25,* 69–78.

Harold, G. T., Fincham, F. D., Osborne, L. N., & Conger, R. D. (1997). Mom and dad are at it again: Adolescent perceptions of marital conflict and adolescent psychological distress. *Developmental Psychology, 33,* 333–350.

Harper, T. (1978, November 15). It's not true about people 65 or over. *Green Bay Press-Gazette* (Wisconsin), p. D-1.

Harris, C. R., & Christenfeld, N. (1996). Gender, jealousy, and reason. *Psychological Science, 7,* 364–366.

Harris, J. (2005). *On cloning.* New York: Routledge.

Harris Poll. (2000, February 2). *The power of tobacco addiction.* New York: Harris Interactive, Inc.

Harrison, J. A., & Wells, R. B. (1991). Bystander effects on male helping behavior: Social comparison and diffusion of responsibility. *Representative Research in Social Psychology, 19,* 53–63.

Hart, B., & Risley, T. R. (1997). Use of language by three-year-old children. Courtesy of Drs. Betty Hart and Todd Risley, University of Kansas.

Hartmann, E. (1967). *The biology of dreaming.* Springfield, IL: Thomas.

Harton, H. C., & Lyons, P. C. (2003). Gender, empathy, and the choice of the psychology major. *Teaching of Psychology, 30,* 19–24.

Hartung, C. M., & Widiger, T. A. (1998). Gender differences in the diagnosis of mental disorders: Conclusions and controversies of the DSM-IV. *Psychological Bulletin, 123,* 260–278.

Harvard Mental Health Letter (HMHL). (1994, March). Brief psychodynamic therapy—Part I. *Harvard Mental Health Letter,* p. 10.

Harvey, J. H., & Weber, A. L. (2002). *Odyssey of the heart: Close relationships in the 21st century* (2nd ed.). Mahwah, NJ: Erlbaum.

Harvey, J. H., & Wenzel, A. (2004). *The handbook of sexuality in close relationships.* Mahwah, NJ: Lawrence Erlbaum.

Hassold, T. J., & Patterson, D. (1999). *Down syndrome: A promising future, together.* New York, NY: Wiley-Liss.

Hasson, U., Nir, Y., Levy, I., Fuhrmann, G., & Malach, R. (2004, March 12). Intersubject synchronization of cortical activity during natural vision. *Science, 303,* 1634–1637.

Hastings, R. P., & Oakford, S. (2003). Student teachers' attitudes towards the inclusion of children with special needs. *Educational Psychology, 23,* 87–94.

Haugtvedt, C. P., Petty, R. E., & Cacioppo, J. T. (1992). Need for cognition and advertising: Understanding the role of personality variables in consumer behavior. *Journal of Consumer Psychology, 1,* 239–260.

Hauser, M. D. (2000). The sound and the fury: Primate vocalizations as reflections of emotion and thought. In N. L. Wallin & B. Merker (Eds.), *The origins of music.* Cambridge, MA: MIT.

Hauser, M. D., Chomsky, N., & Fitch, W. T. (2002, November, 22). The faculty for language: What is it, who has it, and how did it evolve? *Science, 298,* 1569–1579.

Haviland-Jones, J., & Chen, D. (1999, April 17). *Human olfactory perception.* Paper presented at the Association for Chemoreception Sciences, Sarasota, Florida.

Hawke, J. M., Jainchill, N., & De Leon, G. (2000). The prevalence of sexual abuse and its impact on the onset of drug use among adolescents in therapeutic community drug treatment. *Journal of Child & Adolescent Substance Abuse, 9,* 35–49.

Haxby, J. V., Gobini, M. I., Furey, M. L., Ishai, A., Schouten, J. L., & Pietrini, P. (2001, September 28). Distributed and overlapping representations of faces and objects in ventral temporal cortex. *Science, 293,* 2425–2430.

Hayes, J. R. (1966). Memory, goals, and problem solving. In B. Kleinmuntz (Ed.), *Problem solving: Research, method, and theory.* New York: Wiley.

Hayflick, L. (1994). *How and why we age.* New York: Ballatine.

Health Pages. (2003, March 13). Just what the doctor ordered. Retrieved from http://www.thehealthpages.com/articles/ar-drord.html

HealthNews. (1999, November 20). Losing weight: A little goes a long way. *HealthNews,* p. 1.

Heath, A. C., & Madden, P. A. F. (1995). Genetic influences on smoking behavior. In J. R. Turner, L. R. Cardon, & J. K. Hewitt (Eds.), *Behavior genetic approaches in behavioral medicine: Perspectives on individual differences.* New York: Plenum.

Hedgepeth, E. (2005). Different lenses, different vision. *School Administrator, 62,* 36–39.

Hedges, L. V., & Nowell, A. (July 7, 1995). Sex differences in mental test scores, variability, and numbers of high-scoring individuals. *Science, 269,* 41–45.

Heider, F. (1958). *The psychology of interpersonal relations.* New York: Wiley.

Heikkinen, H., Nutt, J. G., & LeWitt, P. A. (2001). The effects of different repeated doses of entacapone on the pharmacokinetics of L-dopa and on the clinical response to L-dopa in Parkinson's disease. *Clinical Neuropharmacology, 24,* 150–157.

Helgeson, V. S., Snyder, P., & Seltman, H. (2004). Psychological and physical adjustment to breast cancer over 4 years: Identifying distinct trajectories of change. *Health Psychology, 23,* 3–15.

Heller, S. (2005). *Freud A to Z.* New York: Wiley.

Helms, J. E. (1992). Why is there no study of cultural equivalence in standardized cognitive ability testing? *American Psychologist, 47,* 1083–1101.

Helmuth, L. (2000, August 25). Synapses shout to overcome distance. *Science, 289,* 1273.

Helmuth, L. (2003, October 31). In sickness or in health? *Science, 302,* 808–810.

Helps, S., Fuggle, P., Udwin, O., & Dick M. (2003). Psychosocial and neurocognitive aspects of sickle cell disease. *Child and Adolescent Mental Health, 8,* 11–17.

Henderlong, J., & Lepper, M. R. (2002). The effects of praise on children's intrinsic motivation: A review and synthesis. *Psychological Bulletin, 128,* 774–795.

Henderson, N. D. (1982). Correlations in IQ for pairs of people with varying degrees of genetic relatedness and shared environment. *Annual Review of Psychology, 33,* 219–243.

Hendrick, C., & Hendrick, S. S. (2003). Romantic love: Measuring cupid's arrow. In S. J. Lopez & C. R. Snyder (Eds.), *Positive psychological assessment: A handbook of models and measures.* Washington, DC: American Psychological Association.

Hentschel, U., Smith, G., Draguns, J. G., & Elhers, W. (2004). *Defense mechanisms: Theoretical, research and clinical perspectives.* Oxford, England: Elsevier Science Ltd.

Hermann, D., Raybeck, D., & Gruneberg, M. M. (2002). *Improving memory and study skills: Advances in theory and practice.* Cambridge, MA: Hogrefe & Huber.

Herrington, D. M., & Howard, T. D. (2003). From presumed benefit to potential harm—Hormone therapy and heart disease. *New England Journal of Medicine, 349,* 519–521.

Herrnstein, R. J., & Murray, D. (1994). *The bell curve.* New York: Free Press.

Herzog, H. A. (2005). Dealing with the animal research controversy. In C. K. Akins & S. Panicker (Eds.), *Laboratory animals in research and teaching: Ethics, care, and methods.* Washington, DC: American Psychological Association.

Heshka, S., Anderson, J. W., Atkinson, R. L., Greenway, F. L., Hill, J. O., Phinney, S. D., Kolotkin, R. L., Miller-Kovach, K., & Pi-Sunyer, F. X. (2003). Weight loss with self-help compared with a structured commercial program: A randomized trial. *Journal of the American Medical Association, 289,* 1792–1798.

Hess, T. M., Hinson, J. T., & Statham, J. A. (2004). Explicit and implicit stereotype activation effects on memory: Do age and awareness moderate the impact of priming? *Psychology and Aging, 19,* 495–505.

Hetherington, E. M. (Ed.). (1999). *Coping with divorce, single parenting, and remarriage: A risk and resiliency perspective.* Mahwah, NJ: Erlbaum.

Heward, W. L., & Orlansky, M. D. (1988). *Exceptional children* (3rd ed.). Columbus, OH: Merrill.

Hewitt, B., Gose, S. G., & Birkbeck, M. (2000, December 11). House divided. *People Weekly, 54,* 138–144.

Heyman, G. D., & Diesendruck, G. (2002). The Spanish *ser/estar* distinction in bilingual children's reasoning about human psychological characteristics. *Developmental Psychology, 38,* 407–417.

Hiby, E. F. Rooney, N. J., & Bradshaw, J. W. S. (2004). Dog training methods: Their use, effectiveness and interaction with behaviour and welfare. *Animal Welfare, 13,* 63–69.

Hicks, T. V., & Leitenberg, H. (2001). Sexual fantasies about one's partner versus someone else: Gender differ-ences in incidence and frequency. *Journal of Sex Research, 38,* 43–50.

Hilgard, E. (1992). Dissassociation and theories of hypnosis. In E. Fromm & M. E. Nash (Eds.), *Contemporary hypnosis research.* New York: Guilford.

Hilgard, E. R. (1975). Hypnosis. *Annual Review of Psychology, 26,* 19–44.

Hill, J. O., & Peters, J. C. (1998). Environmental contributions to the obesity epidemic. *Science, 280,* 1371–1374.

Hill, J. O., Catenacci, V., & Wyatt, H. R. (2005). Obesity: Overview of an epidemic. *Psychiatric Clinics of North America, 28,* 1–23.

Hill, J. O., Wyatt, H. R., Reed, G. W., & Peters, J. C. (2003, February 7). Obesity and the environment: Where do we go from here? *Science, 299,* 853–855.

Hines, M. (2004) *Brain gender.* New York: Oxford University Press.

Hines, M., Golombok, S., Rust, J., Johnston, K. J., Golding, J., & Avon Longitudinal Study of Parents and Children Study Team. (2002). Testosterone during pregnancy and gender role behavior of preschool children: A longitudinal, population study. *Child Development, 73,* 1678–1687.

Hinshaw, S. P., Zupan, B. A., Simmel, C., Nigg, J. T., & Melnick, S. (1997). Peer status in boys with and without attention-deficit hyperactivity disorder: Predictions from overt and covert antisocial behavior, social isolation, and authoritative parenting beliefs. *Child Development, 68,* 880–896.

Hinterberger, T., Birbaumer, N., & Flor, H. (2005). Assessment of cognitive function and communication ability in a completely locked-in patient. *Neurology, 64,* 1307.

Hipkiss, R. A. (1995). *Semantics: Defining the discipline.* Mahwah, NJ: Erlbaum.

Hirsh, I. J., & Watson, C. S. (1996). Auditory psychophysics and perception. *Annual Review of Psychology, 47,* 461–484.

Ho, S. M. Y., Saltel, P., Machavoine, J., Rapoport-Hubschman, N., & Spiegel, D. (2004). Cross-cultural aspects of cancer care. In National Institutes of Health and Stanford University School of Medicine, *Cancer, culture, and communication.* New York: Kluwer Academic/Plenum Publishers.

Ho, W. (2004). Using Kohonen neural network and principle component analysis to characterize divergent thinking. *Creativity Research Journal, 16,* 283–292.

Hobfoll, S. E., Freedy, J. R., Green B. L., & Solomon, S. D. (1996). Coping in reaction to extreme stress: The roles of resource loss and resource availability. In M. Zeidner & N. S. Endler (Eds.), *Handbook of coping: Theory, research, applications.* New York: Wiley.

Hobson, J. A. (1988). *The dreaming brain.* New York: Basic Books.

Hobson, J. A. (1996, February). How the brain goes out of its mind. *Harvard Mental Health Letter,* pp. 3–5.

Hobson, J. A. (2005). In bed with Mark Solms? What a nightmare! A reply to Domhoff (2005). *Dreaming, 15,* 21–29.

Hobson, J. A., & Silverstri, L. (1999, February). Parasomnias. *The Harvard Mental Health Letter,* pp. 3–5.

Hochschild, A. (2001, February). A generation without public passion. *Atlantic Monthly,* pp. 33–42.

Hochschild, A. R. (1990). The second shift: Employed women and putting in another day of work at home. *Utne Reader, 38,* 66–73.

Hochschild, A. R., & Machung, A. (2001). *The second shift: Working parents and the revolution at home.* New York: Viking.

Hoff, E. (2003). Language development in childhood. In R. M. Lerner, M. A. Easterbrooks, et al. (Eds.), *Handbook of psychology: Developmental psychology* (Vol. 6, pp. 171–193). New York: Wiley.

Hoffer, T. B., et al. (2005, March 8). *Doctorate recipients from United States universities: Summary report 2003.* Chicago: NORC at the University of Chicago.

Hoffman, E. (2001). *Psychological testing at work: How to use, interpret, and get the most out of the newest tests in personality, learning style, aptitudes, interests, and more!* New York: McGraw-Hill.

Hoffman, H. G. (2004, August). Virtual-reality therapy. *Scientific American,* pp. 58–65.

Hoffman, J. P., Baldwin, S. A., & Cerbone, F. G. (2003). Onset of major depressive disorder among adolescents. *Journal of the American Academy of Child and Adolescent Psychiatry, 42,* 217–224.

Hogan, R., Hogan, J., & Roberts, B. W. (1996). Personality measurement and employment decisions: Questions and answers. *American Psychologist, 51,* 469–477.

Hoge, C. W., Castro, C. A., Messer, S. C., McGurk, D., Cotting, D. I., & Koffman, R. L. (2004). Combat duty in Iraq and Afghanistan, mental health problems and barriers to care. *New England Journal of Medicine, 351,* 13–22.

Hogg, M. A., & Hains, S. C. (2001). Intergroup relations and group solidarity: Effects of group identification and social beliefs on depersonalized attraction. In M. A. Hogg & D. Abrams (Eds.), *Intergroup relations: Essential readings.* New York: Psychology Press.

Holden, C. (2003, January 17). Deconstructing schizophrenia. *Science, 299,* 333–335.

Holden, C. (2005, June 10). Sex and the suffering brain. *Science, 308,* 1574–1577.

Holden, G. W. (2002). Perspectives on the effects of corporal punishment: Comment on Gershoff (2002). *Psychological Bulletin, 128,* 590–595.

Holden, R. R. (2000). Are there promising MMPI substitutes for assessing psychopathology and personality? Review and prospect. In R. H. Dana, et al. (Eds.). *Handbook of cross-cultural and multicultural personality assessment. Personality and clinical psychology series.* Mahwah, NJ: Lawrence Erlbaum.

Holland, J. C., & Lewis, S. (2001). *The human side of cancer: Living with hope, coping with uncertainty.* New York: Quill.

Hollingworth, H. L. (1943/1990). *Leta Stetter Hollingworth: A biography.* Boston: Anker.

Hollis, K. L. (1997, September). Contemporary research on Pavlovian conditioning: A "new" functional analysis. *American Psychologist, 52,* 956–965.

Hollon, S. D., Thase, M. E., & Markowitz, J. C. (2002). Treatment and prevention of depression. *Psychological Science in the Public Interest, 3,* 39–77.

Holloway, L. (2000, December 16). Chief of New York City schools plans to revamp bilingual study. *The New York Times,* p. A1.

Holmes, A., Yang, R. J., Lesch, K. P., Crawley, J. N., & Murphy, D. L. (2003). Mice lacking the Serotonin Transporter Exhibit 5-HT-sub(1A) receptor-mediated abnormalities in tests for anxiety-like behavior. *Neuropsychopharmacology, 28,* 2077–2088.

Holmes, C. T., & Keffer, R. L. (1995). A computerized method to teach Latin and Greek root words: Effect on verbal SAT scores. *Journal of Educational Research, 89,* 47–50.

Holowka, S., & Pettito, L. A. (2002, August 30). Left hemisphere cerebral specialization for babies while babbling. *Science, 297,* 1515.

Holt, M., & Jahn, R. (2004, March, 26). Synaptic vesicles in the fast lane. *Science, 303,* 1986–1987.

Holy, T. E., Dulac, C., & Meister, M. (2000, September 1). Responses of vomeronasal neurons to natural stimuli. *Science, 289,* 1569–1572.

Hong, E., Milgram, R. M., & Gorsky, H. (1995). Original thinking as a predictor of creative performance in young children. *Roeper Review, 18,* 147–149.

Hong, S. (2000). Exercise and psychoneuroimmunology [Special issue: Exercise psychology]. *International Journal of Sport Psychology, 31,* 204–227.

Hong, Y., Morris, M., Chiu, C., & Benet-Martinez, V. (2000). Multicultural minds. *American Psychologist, 55,* 709–720.

Hoover, E. (2004). More college students report diagnoses of depression, survey finds. *The Chronicle of Higher Education.* Retrieved from http://chronicle.com/daily/2004/11/2004113004n.htm

Horgan, J. (1993, December). Fractured functions: Does the brain have a supreme integrator? *Scientific American,* pp. 36–37.

Horgan, J. (1995, November). Get smart, take a test. *Scientific American,* pp. 12–14.

Horgan, J. (1996, December). Why Freud isn't dead. *Scientific American,* pp. 106–111.

Horn, J. L. (2002). Selections of evidence, misleading assumptions, and over-simplifications: The political message of *The Bell Curve.* In J. M. Fish (Ed.), *Race and intelligence: Separating science from myth,* pp. 297–325. Mahwah, NJ: Erlbaum.

Horney, K. (1937). *Neurotic personality of our times.* New York: Norton.

Horton, K. D., Wilson, D. E., Vonk, J., Kirby, S. L., & Nielsen, T. (2005). Measuring automatic retrieval: A comparison of implicit memory, process dissociation, and speeded response procedures. *Acta Psychologica, 119,* 235–263.

Hovland, C., Janis, I., & Kelly, H. H. (1953). *Communication and persuasion.* New Haven, CT: Yale University Press.

Howatt, W. A. (2005). Cognitive-behavioral models. In R. H. Coombs (Ed.), *Addiction counseling review: Preparing for comprehensive, certification, and licensing examinations.* Mahwah, NJ: Lawrence Erlbaum Associates.

Howe, C. J. (2002). The countering of overgeneralization. *Journal of Child Language, 29,* 875–895.

Howells, J. G., & Osborn, M. L. (1984). *A reference companion to the history of abnormal psychology.* Westport, CT: Greenwood Press.

Howitt, D., & Cramer, D. (2000). *First steps in research and statistics: A practical workbook for psychology students.* Philadelphia: Psychology Press.

Hsu, B., Koing, A., Kessler, C., Knapke, K., et al (1994). Gender differences in sexual fantasy and behavior in a college population: A ten-year replication. *Journal of Sex and Marital Therapy, 20,* 103–118.

Hu, F. B., Li, T. Y., Colditz, G. A., Willett, W. C., & Manson, J. E. (2003). Television watching and other sedentary behaviors in relation to risk of obesity and type 2 diabetes mellitus in women. *Journal of the American Medical Association, 289,* 1785–1791.

Hubbard, K., O'Neill, A., & Cheakalos, C. (1999, April 12). Out of control. *People,* pp. 52–72.

Hubble, M. A., Duncan, B. L., & Miller, S. D. (Eds.). (1999). *The heart and soul of change: What works in therapy.* Washington, DC: American Psychological Association.

Hubel, D. H., & Wiesel, T. N. (2004). *Brain and visual perception: The story of a 25-year collaboration.* New York: Oxford University Press.

Huber, F., Beckmann, S. C., & Herrmann, A. (2004). Means-end analysis: Does the affective state influence information processing style? *Psychology and Marketing, 21,* 715–737.

Hudson, W. (1960). Pictorial depth perception in subcultural groups in Africa. *Journal of Social Psychology, 52,* 183–208.

Hudspeth, A. J. (2000). Hearing. In E. R. Kandel, J. H. Schwartz, & T. M. Jessell (Eds.), *Principles of neural science* (4th ed.). New York: McGraw-Hill.

Huesmann, L. R., Moise-Titus, J., Podolski, C. L., & Eron, L. D. (2003). Longitudinal relations between children's exposure to TV violence and their aggressive and violent behavior in young adulthood: 1977–1992 [Special issue: Violent children]. *Developmental Psychology, 39,* 201–221.

Huff, C. (2004, September). The baggage screener's brain scan. *Monitor on Psychology,* pp. 34–36.

Huffman, C. J., Matthews, T. D., & Gagne, P. E. (2001). The role of part-set cuing in the recall of chess positions: Influence of chunking in memory. *North American Journal of Psychology, 3,* 535–542.

Hughes, J. O., & Sandler, B. R. (1987). *In case of sexual harassment: A guide for women students.* Washington, D.C: Association of American Colleges.

Hull, C. L. (1943). *Principles of behavior.* New York: Appleton-Century-Crofts.

Humphreys, G. W., & Müller, H. (2000). A search asymmetry reversed by figure-ground assignment. *Psychological Science, 11,* 196–200.

Humphreys, J. (2003). Resilience in sheltered battered women. *Issues in Mental Health Nursing, 24,* 137–152.

Hunt, E. (1994). Problem solving. In R. J. Sternberg (Ed.), *Thinking and problem solving: Handbook of perception and cognition* (2nd ed.). San Diego, CA: Academic Press.

Hunt, E. (2005). Information processing and intelligence: Where we are and where we are going. In R. J. Sternberg & J. E. Pretz, *Cognition and intelligence: Identifying the mechanisms of the mind.* New York: Cambridge University Press.

Hunt, M. (1974). *Sexual behaviors in the 1970s.* New York: Dell.

Huston, A. C., Donnerstein, E., Fairchild, H. H., Feshback, N. D., Katz, P., Murray, J. P., Rubinstein, E. A., Wilcox, B. L., & Zuckerman, D. (1992). Big world, small screen: The role of television in American society. Omaha, NE: University of Nebraska Press.

Hyde, J. (2004). *Half the human experience: The psychology of women* (6th ed.). Boston: Houghton Mifflin.

Hyde, J. S. (1994). *Understanding human sexuality* (5th ed.). New York: McGraw-Hill.

Hyde, J. S., & Linn, M. C. (1988). Gender differences in verbal ability: A meta-analysis. *Psychological Bulletin, 104,* 53–69.

Hyde, J. S., DeLamater, J. D., & Byers, E. S. (2006). *Understanding human sexuality,* (3rd ed). New York: McGraw-Hill.

Hyde, J. S., Fennema, E., & Lamon, S.J. (1990). Gender differences in mathematics performance: A meta-analysis. *Psychological Bulletin, 107,* 139–155.

Hyman, R. (1994). Anomaly or artifact? Comments on Bem and Honorton. *Psychological Bulletin, 115,* 19–24.

Hyman, S..E. (2003, September). Diagnosing disorders. *Scientific American,* pp. 96–103.

Iachini, T., & Giusberti, F. (2004). Metric properties of spatial images generated from locomotion: The effect of absolute size on mental scanning. *European Journal of Cognitive Psychology, 16,* 573–596.

Ievers-Landis, C. E., Hoff, A. L., Brez, C., Cancilliere, M. K., McConnell, J., & Kerr, D. (2005). Situational analysis of dietary challenges of the treatment regimen for children and adolescents with phenylketonuria and their primary caregivers. *Journal of Developmental and Behavioral Pediatrics, 26,* 186–193.

Iglesias, A. (2005). Awake-alert hypnosis in the treatment of panic disorder: A case report. *American Journal of Clinical Hypnosis, 47,* 249–257.

Ihler, E. (2003). Patient-physician communication. *Journal of the American Medical Association, 289,* 92.

Ikonomidou, C., Bittigau, P., Ishimaru, M. J., Wozniak, D. F., Koch, C., Genz, K., Price, M. T., Stefovska, V., Hörster, F., Tenkova, T., Dikranian, K., & Olney, J. W. (2000, February 11). Ethanol-induced apoptotic neurodegeneration and fetal alcohol syndrome. *Science, 287,* 1056–1060.

Isay, R. A. (1994). *Being homosexual: Gay men and their development.* Lanham, MD: Jason Aronson.

Isbell, L. M., & Tyler, J. M. (2003). Teaching students about in-group favoritism and the minimal groups paradigm. *Teaching of Psychology, 30,* 127–130.

Ishikura, R., & Tashiro, N. (2002). Frustration and fulfillment of needs in dissociative and conversion disorders. *Psychiatry and Clinical Neurosciences, 56,* 381–390.

Iversen, L. L. (2000). *The science of marijuana.* Oxford, England: Oxford University Press.

Iverson, P., Kuhl, P. K., Reiko, A. Y., Diesch, E., Tohkura, Y., Ketterman, A., & Siebert, C. (2003). A perceptual interference account of acquisition difficulties for non-native phonemes. *Cognition, 87,* B47–B57.

Izard, C. E. (1990). Facial expressions and the regulation of emotions. *Journal of Personality and Social Psychology, 58,* 487–498.

Izard, C. E. (1994). Innate and universal facial expressions: Evidence from developmental and cross-cultural research. *Psychological Bulletin, 115,* 288–299.

Izard, C. E., & Abe, J. A. (2004). Developmental changes in facial expressions of emotions in the strange situation during the second year of life. *Emotion, 4,* 251–265.

Jackson, T. L. (Ed.). (1996). *Acquaintance rape: Assessment, treatment, and prevention.* Sarasota, FL: Professional Resource Press/Professional Resource Exchange.

Jacobs, J. A., & Gerson, K. (2004). *The time divide: Work, family, and gender inequality.* Cambridge, MA: Harvard University Press.

Jacobson, P. D., Wasserman, J., & Anderson, J. R. (1997). Historical overview of tobacco legislation and regulation. *Journal of Social Issues, 53,* 75–95.

Jaffe, S., & Hyde, J. S. (2000). Gender differences in moral orientation: A meta-analysis. *Psychological Bulletin, 126,* 703–726.

James, J. E. (1997). *Understanding caffeine: A biobehavioral analysis.* Newbury Park, CA: Sage.

James, H. S., Jr. (2005). Why did you do that? An economic examination of the effect of extrinsic compensation on intrinsic motivation and performance. *Journal of Economic Psychology, 26,* 549–566.

James, W. (1890). *The principles of psychology.* New York: Holt.

Jamison, K. R. (1993). *Touched with fire: Manic depressive illness and the artistic temperament.* New York: Free Press.

Jamison, K. R. (1995a). *An unquiet mind: A memoir of moods and madness.* New York: Knopf.

Jamison, K. R. (1995b, February). Manic-depressive illness and creativity. *Scientific American,* pp. 62–67.

Janis, I. L. (1989). *Crucial decisions: Leadership in policy-making management.* New York: Free Press.

Jaret, P. (1992, November/December). Mind over malady. *Health,* pp. 87–94.

Javitt, D. C., & Coyle, J. T. (January 2004). Decoding schizophrenia. *Scientific American,* pp. 46–55.

Jefferson, D. J. (2005, August 8). American's most dangerous drug. *Newsweek,* pp. 41–47.

Jenike, M. A. (1998). Neurosurgical treatment of obsessive-compulsive disorder. *British Journal of Psychiatry, 173*(Suppl. 35), 79–90.

Jenkins, C. D., Zyzanski, S. J., & Rosenman, R. H. (1978). Coronary-prone behavior: One pattern or several? *Psychosomatic Medicine, 40,* 25–43.

Jenkins, L. S., & Gortner, S. R. (1998). Correlates of self-efficacy expectation and prediction of walking behavior in cardiac surgery elders. *Annals of Behavioral Medicine, 20,* 99–103.

Jenkins, S. (2004, October 29). Mystics all-star cites depression for her absence. *The Washington Post,* p. A1.

Jenkins, S. R. (1994). Need for power and women's careers over 14 years: Structural power, job satisfaction, and motive change. *Journal of Personality and Social Psychology, 66,* 155–165.

Jensen, A. R. (2002). Galton's legacy to research on intelligence. *Journal of Biosocial Science, 34,* 145–172.

Jensen, A. R. (2003). Do age-group differences on mental tests imitate racial differences? *Intelligence, 31,* 107–121.

Jensen, A. R. (2005). Psychometric g and mental chronometry. *Cortex, 41,* 230–231.

Jequier, E. (2002). Pathways to obesity. *International Journal of Obesity and Related Metabolic Disorders, 26,* S12–S17.

Jhally, S., Goldman, R., Cassidy, M., Katula, R., Seiter, E., Pollay, R. W., Lee, J. S., Carter-Whitney, D., Steinem, G., et al. (1995). Advertising. In G. Dines & J. M. Humez (Eds.), *Gender, race, and class in media: A text-reader.* Thousand Oaks, CA: Sage.

Johns, M., Schmader, T., & Martens, A. (2005). Knowing is half the battle: Teaching stereotype threat as a means of improving women's math performance. *Psychological Science, 16,* 175–179.

Johnson, D. M., Parrott, G. R., & Stratton, R. P. (1968). Production and judgment of solutions to five problems. *Journal of Educational Psychology Monograph Supplement, 59* (6, pt. 2).

Johnson, G. B. (2000). *The Living World,* p. 600. Boston: McGraw-Hill.

Johnson, H. D. (2004). Gender, grade and relationship differences in emotional closeness within adolescent friendships. *Adolescence, 39,* 243–255.

Johnson, J. G., Cohen, P., Smailes, E. M., Kasen, S., & Brook, J. S. (2002, March 29). Television viewing and aggressive behavior during adolescence and adulthood. *Science, 295,* 2468–2471.

Johnson, S. P. (2004). Development of perceptual completion in infancy. *Psychological Science, 15,* 769–775.

Johnson, S. P., Bremner, J. G., Slater, A., Mason, U., Foster, K., & Cheshire, A. (2003). Infants' perception of object trajectories. *Child Development, 74,* 94–108.

John-Steiner, V., & Mahn, H. (2003). Sociocultural contexts for teaching and learning. In W. M. Reynolds & G. E. Miller (Eds.), *Handbook of psychology: Educational psychology* (Vol. 7, pp. 125–151). New York: Wiley.

Johnston, L. D., O'Malley, P. M., & Bachman, J. G. (2003). *Monitoring the future: National results on adolescent drug use: Overview of key findings, 2002.* Bethesda MD: National Institute on Drug Abuse.

Johnston, L. D., O'Malley, P. M., & Bachman. J. G. (2002, December 16). *Ecstasy use among American teens drops for the first time in recent years, and overall drug and alcohol use also decline in the year after 9/11.* Ann Arbor, MI: University of Michigan News and Information Services. www.monitoringthefuture.org; accessed December 26, 2002.

Johnston, L. D., O'Malley, P. M., Bachman, J. G., & Schulenberg, J. E. (2004, December 21). *Overall teen drug use continues gradual decline; but use of inhalants rises.* University of Michigan News and Information Services: Ann Arbor, MI. Retrieved August 23, 2005, from http://www.monitoringthefuture.org

Johnston, M. V. (2004). Clinical disorders of brain plasticity. *Brain and Development, 26,* 73–80.

Joiner, T. E., & Wagner, K. D. (1995). Attribution style and depression in children and adolescents: A meta-analytic review. *Clinical Psychology Review, 15,* 777–798.

Jones, A., & Crandall, R. (Eds.). (1991). Handbook of self-actualization. *Journal of Social Behavior and Personality, 6,* 1–362.

Jones, J. C., & Barlow, D. H. (1990). Self-reported frequency of sexual urges, fantasies, and masturbatory fantasies in heterosexual males and females. *Archives of Sexual Behavior, 19,* 269–279.

Jones, J. E., & Corp, E. S. (2003). Effect of naltrexone on food intake and body weight in Syrian hamsters depends on metabolic status. *Physiology and Behavior, 78,* 67–72.

Jones, K. M., & Friman, P. C. (1999). A case study of behavioral assessment and treatment of insect phobia. *Journal of Applied Behavior Analysis, 32,* 95–98.

Jones, R. K., Darroch, J. E., Singh, S. (2005). Religious differentials in the sexual and reproductive behaviors of young women in the United States. *Journal of Adolescent Health, 36,* 279–288.

Jorgenson, L. M., & Wahl, K. M. (2000). Psychiatrists as expert witnesses in sexual harassment cases under *Daubert* and *Kumho. Psychiatric Annals, 30,* 390–396.

Joyce, J. (1934). *Ulysses.* New York: Random House.

Julesz, B. (1986). Stereoscopic vision. *Vision Research, 26,* 1601–1612.

Juliano, L. M., & Griffiths, R. R. (2004). A critical review of caffeine withdrawal: Empirical validation of symptoms and signs, incidence, severity, and associated features. *Psychopharmacology, 176,* 1–29.

Julien, R. M (2001). *A primer of drug action* (9th ed.). New York: Freeman.

Jung, C. G. (1961). *Freud and psychoanalysis.* New York: Pantheon.

Jung, J. (2002). *Psychology of alcohol and other drugs: A research perspective.* Thousand Oaks, CA: Sage.

Juster, F. T., Ono, H., & Stafford, F. (2002). *Report on housework and division of labor.* Ann Arbor, MI: Institute for Social Research.

Jylha, M. (2004). Old age and loneliness: Cross-sectional and longitudinal analyses in the Tampere longitudinal study on aging. *Canadian Journal on Aging/La Revue canadienne du vieillissement, 23,* 157–168.

Kaasinen, V., & Rinne, J. O. (2002). Functional imaging studies of dopamine system and cognition in normal aging and Parkinson's disease. *Neuroscience & Biobehavioral Reviews, 26,* 785–793.

Kahn, J. P. (2004). Hostility, coronary risk, and alpha-adrenergic to beta-adrenergic receptor density ratio. *Psychosomatic Medicine, 66,* 289–297.

Kahn, R. S., Davidson, M., & Davis, K. L. (1996). Dopamine and schizophrenia revisited. In S. J. Watson (Ed.), *Biology of schizophrenia and affective disease.* Washington, DC: American Psychiatric Press.

Kahneman, D., Diener, E., & Schwarz, N. (1998). *Well-being: The foundations of hedonic psychology.* New York: Russell Sage Foundation.

Kahng, S. W., Iwata, B. A., & Lewin, A. B. (2002). Behavioral treatment of self-injury, 1964 to 2000. *American Journal on Mental Retardation, 107,* 212–221.

Kalb, C. (2001a, April 9). Playing with pain killers. *Newsweek,* pp. 45–48.

Kalb, C. (2001b, February 26). DARE checks into rehab. *Newsweek*, pp. 56.

Kaller, C. P., Unterrainer, J. M., Rahm, B., & Halsband, U. (2004). The impact of problem structure on planning: Insights from the Tower of London task. *Cognitive Brain Research, 20*, 462–472.

Kallio, S., & Revonsuo, A. (2003). Hypnotic phenomena and altered states of consciousness: A multilevel framework of description and explanation. *Contemporary Hypnosis, 20*, 111–164.

Kamieniecki, G. W., & Lynd-Stevenson, R. M. (2002). Is it appropriate to use United States norms to assess the "intelligence" of Australian children? *Australian Journal of Psychology, 54*, 67–78.

Kaminski, P., Chapman, B. P, Haynes, S. D., & Own, L. (2005). Body image, eating behaviors, and attitudes toward exercise among gay and straight men. *Eating Behaviors, 6*, 179–187.

Kandell, E. R., Schwartz, J. H., & Jessell, T. M. (Eds.) (2000). *Principles of neural science* (4th ed.). New York: McGraw-Hill

Kane, M. J., & Engle, R. W. (2002). The role of prefrontal cortex in working-memory capacity, executive attention, and general fluid intelligence: An individual-differences perspective. *Psychonomic Bulletin and Review, 9*, 637–671.

Kaniasty, K., & Norris, F. H. (1995, June). Mobilization and deterioration of social support following natural disasters. *Current Directions in Psychological Science, 4*, 94–98.

Kanner, A. D., Coyne, J. C., Schaefer, C., & Lazarus, R. (1981). Comparison of two modes of stress measurement: Daily hassles and uplifts versus major life events. *Journal of Behavioral Medicine, 4*, 14.

Kaplan, H. S. (1974). *The new sex therapy*. New York: Brunner-Mazel.

Kaplan, J. R., & Manuck, S. B. (1989). The effect of propranolol on behavioral interactions among adult male cynomolgus monkeys (Macaca fascicularis) housed in disrupted social groupings. *Psychosomatic Medicine*, 51, 449–462.

Kaplan, R. M., & Saccuzzo, D. P. (2001). *Psychological testing: Principles, applications, and issues* (5th ed.). Belmont, CA: Wadsworth/Thomson Learning.

Kapur, S., & Remington, G. (1996). Serotonin-dopamine interaction and its relevance to schizophrenia.

American Journal of Psychiatry, 153, 466–476.

Karni, A., Tanne, D., Rubenstein, B. S., Askenasy, J. J. M., & Sagi, D. (1994, July 29). Dependence on REM sleep of overnight improvement of a perceptual skill. *Science, 265*, 679–682.

Karni, A., Tanne, D., Rubenstein, B. S., Askenazy, J. J. M., & Sagi, D. (1992, October). No dreams—no memory: The effect of REM sleep deprivation on learning a new perceptual skill. *Society for Neuroscience Abstracts, 18*, 387.

Kassel, J. D., Stroud, L. R., & Paronis, C. A. (2003). Smoking, stress, and negative affect: Correlation, causation, and context across stages of smoking. *Psychological Bulletin, 129*, 270–304.

Kassin, S., M. (2005). On the psychology of confessions: Does innocence put innocents at risk? *American Psychologist, 60*, 215–228.

Katigbak, M. S., Church, A. T., Guanzon-Lapena, M. A., Carlota, A. J., & del Pilar, G. H. (2002). Are indigenous personality dimensions culture specific? Philippine inventories and the five-factor model. *Journal of Personality and Social Psychology, 82*, 89–101.

Kato, K., & Pedersen, N. L. (2005). Personality and coping: A study of twins reared apart and twins reared together. *Behavior Genetics, 35*, 147–158.

Katsiyannis, A., Zhang, D., & Archwamety, T. (2002). Place and exit patterns for students with mental retardation: An analysis of national trends. *Education and Training in Mental Retardation and Developmental Disabilities, 37*, 134–145.

Katsiyannis, A., Zhang, D., & Woodruff, N. (2005). Transition supports to students with mental retardation: An examination of data from the national longitudinal transition study 2. *Education and Training in Developmental Disabilities, 40*, 109–116.

Katz, A. N. (1989). Autobiographical memory as a reconstructive process: An extension of Ross's hypothesis. *Canadian Journal of Psychology, 43*, 512–517.

Katz, M. (2001). The implications of revising Freud's empiricism for drive theory. *Psychoanalysis and Contemporary Thought, 24*, 253–272.

Katz, P. A. (Ed.). (1976). *Towards the elimination of racism*. New York: Pergamon.

Kaufman, A. S., & Lichtenberger, E. O. (2000). *Essentials of WISC-III and WPPSI-R assessment*. New York: Wiley.

Kaufman, J. C. (2005). The door that leads into madness: Eastern European poets and mental illness. *Creativity Research Journal, 17*, 99–103.

Kaufman, J. C., & Baer, J. (2005). *Creativity across domains: Faces of the muse*. Mahwah, NJ: Lawrence Erlbaum Associates.

Kaufman, L., & Kaufman, J. H. (2000). From the cover: Explaining the moon illusion. *Proceedings of the National Academy of Science, 97*, 500–505.

Kausler, D. H. (1994). *Learning and memory in normal aging*. San Diego, CA: Academic Press.

Kavale, K. A. (2002). Mainstreaming to full inclusion: From orthogenesis to pathogenesis of an idea [Special issue: The slow learning child: 25 years on]. *International Journal of Disability, Development & Education, 49*, 201–214.

Kawasaki, C., Nugent, J. K., Miyashita, H., Miyahara, H., et al. (1994). The cultural organization of infants' sleep [Special issue: Environments of birth and infancy]. *Children's Environment, 11*, 135–141.

Kearns, K. P. (2005). Broca's aphasia. In L. L. LaPointe (Ed.), *Aphasia and related neurogenic language disorders* (3rd ed.). New York: Thieme New York.

Keating, D. P., & Clark, L. V. (1980). Development of physical and social reasoning in adolescence. *Developmental Psychology, 16*, 23–30.

Keillor, J. M., Barrett, A. M., Crucian, G. P., Kortenkamp, S., & Heilman, K. M. (2002). Emotional experience and perception in the absence of facial feedback. *Journal of the International Neuropsychological Society, 8*, 130–135.

Kelley, H. (1950). The warm-cold variable in first impressions of persons. *Journal of Personality and Social Psychology, 18*, 431–439.

Kelly, E. S. (1997, January 22). The latest in take-at-home tests: I.Q. *The New York Times*, p. B7.

Kelly, F. D. (1997). *The assessment of object relations phenomena in adolescents: TAT and Rorschach measures*. Mahwah, NJ: Erlbaum.

Keltikangas-Järvinen, L., Räikkönen, K., Ekelund, J., & Peltonen, L. (2004). Nature and nurture in novelty seeking. *Molecular Psychiatry, 9*, 308–311.

Kemeny, M. E. (2003). The psychobiology of stress. *Current Directions in Psychological Science, 12*, 124–129.

Kempermann, G., & Gage, F. H. (1999, May). New nerve cells for the adult brain. *Scientific American*, pp. 48–53.

Kenndy, Q., Mather, M., & Carstensen, L. L. (2004). The role of motivation in the age-related positivity effect in auto-biographical memory. *Psychological Science, 15,* 208–211.

Kennedy, J. E. (2004). A proposal and challenge for proponents and skeptics of psi. *Journal of Parapsychology, 68,* 157–167.

Kenshalo, D. R. (1968). *The skin senses.* Springfield, IL: Charles C. Thomas.

Kenway, L., & Wilson, M. A. (2001). Temporally structured replay of awake hippocampal ensemble activity during rapid eye movement sleep. *Neuron, 29,* 145–156.

Kersting, K. (2004, March). How do you test on the web? Responsibly. *Monitor on Psychology,* pp. 26–27.

Kess, J. F., & Miyamoto, T. (1994). *Japanese Psycholinguistics.* Amsterdam, Netherlands: John Benjamins.

Kessler, R. C., Berglund, P., & Demler, O. (2005). Lifetime prevalence and age-of-onset distributions of DSM-IV disorders in the National Comorbidity Survey replication. *Archives of General Psychiatry, 62,* 593–602.

Kettenmann, H., & Ransom, B. R. (2005). *Neuroglia* (2nd ed.). New York: Oxford University Press.

Ketterhargen, D., VandeVusse, L., & Berner, M. A. (2002). Self-hypnosis: Alternative anesthesia for childbirth. *American Journal of Maternal/Child Nursing, 27,* 335–341.

Kevenaar, T. A. M., Schrijen, G. J., van der Veen, M., Akkermans, A. H. M., & Zuo, F. (2005). Face recognition with renewable and privacy preserving binary templates. *Automatic Identification Advanced Technologies, 2005,* 21–26.

Key, W. B. (2003). Subliminal sexuality: The fountainhead for America's obsession. In T. Reichert & J. Lambaiase (Eds.), *Sex in advertising: Perspectives on the erotic appeal. LEA's communication series* (pp. 195–212). Mahwah, NJ: Lawrence Erlbaum.

Keyes, C. L., & Shapiro, A. D. (2004). Social well-being in the United States: A descriptive epidemiology. In O. G. Brim and C. D. Ryff, *How healthy are we? A national study of well-being at midlife.* Chicago: University of Chicago Press.

Kiecolt, J. K. (2003). Satisfaction with work and family life: No evidence of a cultural reversal. *Journal of Marriage and Family, 65,* 23–35.

Kiesler, C. A., & Simpkins, C. G. (1993). *The unnoticed majority in psychiatric inpatient care.* New York: Plenum.

Kiesler, D. J. (2000). *Beyond the disease model of mental disorders.* Westport, CT: Greenwood Publishing Group.

Kihlstrom, J. F. (2005). Is hypnosis an altered state of consciousness or what? Comment. *Contemporary Hypnosis, 22,* 34–38.

Kihlstrom, J. F., Schacter, D. L., Cork, R. C., Hurt, C. A., & Behr, S. E. (1990). Implicit and explicit memory following surgical anesthesia. *Psychological Science, 1,* 303–306.

Kilpatrick, D. G., Edmunds, C. S., & Seymour, A. K. (1992, November 13). *Rape in America: A report to the nation.* Arlington, VA: National Victims Center and Medical University of South Carolina.

Kim, H. S. (2002). We talk, therefore we think? A cultural analysis of the effect of talking on thinking. *Journal of Personality and Social Psychology, 83,* 828–842.

Kim, K. H., Relkin, N. R., Lee, K. M., & Hirsch, J. (1997, July 10). Distinct cortical areas associated with native and second languages. *Nature, 388,* 171–174.

Kim, S. Y. H., & Holloway, R. G. (2003). Burdens and benefits of placebos in antidepressant clinical trials: A decision and cost-effectiveness analysis. *American Journal of Psychiatry, 160,* 1272–1276.

Kim-Cohen, J., Caspi, A., & Moffitt, T. E. (2003). Prior juvenile diagnoses in adults with mental disorder: Developmental follow-back of a prospective-longitudinal cohort. *Archives of General Psychiatry, 60,* 709–717.

Kim-Cohen, J., Moffitt, T. E., Taylor, A., Pawlby, S. J., & Caspi, A. (2005). Maternal depression and children's antisocial behavior: Nature and nurture effects. *Archives of General Psychiatry, 62,* 173–181.

Kimura, D. (1992, September). Sex differences in the brain. *Scientific American,* pp. 119–125.

Kimura, D. (1999). *Sex and cognition.* Cambridge, MA: MIT.

Kinsey, A. C., Pomeroy, W. B., & Martin, C. E. (1948). *Sexual behavior in the human male.* Philadelphia: Saunders.

Kinsey, A. C., Pomeroy, W. B., Martin, C. E., & Gebhard, P. H. (1953). *Sexual behavior in the human female.* Philadelphia: Saunders.

Kirby, D. (1977). The methods and methodological problems of sex research. In J. S. DeLora & C. A. B. Warren (Eds.), *Understanding sexual interaction.* Boston: Houghton Mifflin.

Kirk, K. M., Bailey, J. M., & Martin, N. G. (2000). Etiology of male sexual orientation in an Australian twin sample. *Psychology, Evolution & Gender, 2,* 301–311.

Kirsch, I. (Ed.). (1999). *How expectancies shape experience.* Washington, DC: American Psychological Association.

Kirsch, I., & Braffman, W. (2001). Imaginative suggestibility and hypnotizability. *Current Directions in Psychological Science, 10,* 57–61.

Kirsch, I., & Lynn, S. J. (1995). The altered state of hypnosis: Changes in the theoretical landscape. *American Psychologist, 50,* 846–858.

Kirsch, I., & Lynn, S. J. (1998). Social-cognitive alternatives to dissociation theories of hypnotic involuntariness. *Review of General Psychology, 2,* 66–80.

Kirsch, I., Lynn, S. J., Vigorito, M., & Miller, R. R. (2004). The role of cognition in classical and operant conditioning. *Journal of Clinical Psychology, 60,* 369–392.

Kirschenbaum, H. (2004). Carl Rogers's life and work: An assessment on the 100th anniversary of his birth. *Journal of Counseling and Development, 82,* 116–124.

Kirschenbaum, H., & Jourdan, A. (2005). The current status of Carl Rogers and the person-centered approach. *Psychotherapy: Theory, Research, Practice, Training, 42,* 37–51.

Kish, S. J. (2002). Effects of dose, sex, and long-term abstention from use on toxic effects of MDMA (Ecstasy) on brain serotonin neurons: Comment. *Lancet, 359,* 1616.

Kiss, A. (2004). Does gender have an influence on the patient-physician communication? *Journal of Men's Health and Gender, 1,* 77–82.

Kitterle, F. L. (Ed.). (1991). *Cerebral laterality: Theory and research.* Hillsdale, NJ: Erlbaum.

Klein, M. (1998, February). Family chats. *American Demographics,* p. 37.

Kleinman, A. (1996). How is culture important for DSM-IV? In J. E Mezzich, A. Kleinman, H. Fabrega, Jr., & D. L. Parron (Eds.), *Culture and psychiatric diagnosis: A DSM-IV perspective.* Washington, DC: American Psychiatric Press.

Kleinman, A., & Cohen, A. (1997, March). Psychiatry's global challenge. *Scientific American,* pp. 86–89.

Kling, K. C., Ryff, C. D., Love, G. (2003). Exploring the influence of personality on depressive symptoms and self-esteem across a significant life transition. *Journal of Personality and Social Psychology, 85,* 922–932.

Kling, K. C., Ryff, C. D., Love, G. (2003). Exploring the influence of personality on depressive symptoms and self-esteem across a significant life transition. *Journal of Personality and Social Psychology, 85,* 922–932.

Klinke, R., Kral, A., Heid, S., Tillein, J., & Hartmann, R. (1999, September 10). Recruitment of the auditory cortex in congenitally deaf cats by long-term cochlear electrostimulation. *Science, 285,* 1729–1733.

Klinkenborg, V. (1997, January 5). Awakening to sleep. *The New York Times,* pp. 26–31, 41, 51, 55.

Kluft, R. P. (1999). An overview of the psychotherapy of dissociative identity disorder. *American Journal of Psychotherapy, 53,* 289–319.

Kluger, J. (2001, April 2). Fear not! *Time,* pp. 51–62.

Knight, G. P., Jonson, L. G., Carlo, G., & Eisenberg, N. (1994). A multiplicative model of the dispositional antecedents of a prosocial behavior: Predicting more of the people more of the time. *Journal of Personality and Social Psychology, 66,* 178–183.

Knops, A., Nuerk, H. C., Fimm, B., Vohn, R., & Willmes, K. (2005). A special role for numbers in working memory? An fMRI study. *Neuroimage, 22,* 125–132.

Kobasa, S. C. O., Maddi, S. R., Puccetti, M. C., & Zola, M. A. (1994). Effectiveness of hardiness, exercise and social support as resources against illness. In A. Steptoe & J. Wardle (Eds.), *Psychosocial processes and health: A reader.* Cambridge, England: Cambridge University Press.

Kobayashi, F., Schallert, D. L., & Ogren, H. A. (2003). Japanese and American folk vocabularies for emotions. *Journal of Social Psychology, 143,* 451–478.

Koch, J. (2003). Gender issues in the classroom. In W. M. Reynolds & G. E. Miller (Eds.), *Handbook of psychology: Educational psychology* (Vol. 7, pp. 259–281). New York: Wiley.

Koenig, A. M., & Eagly, A. H. (2005). Stereotype threat in men on a test of social sensitivity. *Sex Roles, 52,* 489–496.

Kohlberg, L. (1984). *The psychology of moral development: Essays on moral development* (Vol. 2). San Francisco: Harper & Row.

Kohlberg, L., & Ryncarz, R. A. (1990). Beyond justice reasoning: Moral development and consideration of a seventh stage. In C. N. Alexander & E. J. Langer (Eds.), *Higher stages of human development: Perspectives on adult growth.* New York: Oxford University Press.

Kohler, C. G., Turner, T., Stolar, N. M., Bilker, W. B., Brensinger, C. M., Gur, R. E., & Gur, R. C. (2004). Differences in facial expressions of four universal emotions. *Psychiatry Research, 128,* 235–244.

Köhler, W. (1927). *The mentality of apes.* London: Routledge & Kegan Paul.

Kolata, G. (2002, December 2). With no answers on risks, steroid users still say "yes." *The New York Times,* p. 1A.

Kolb, B., Gibb, R., & Robinson, T. E. (2003). Brain plasticity and behavior. *Current Directions in Psychological Science, 12,* 1–5.

Koocher, G. P., Norcross, J. C., & Hill, S. S. (2005). *Psychologists' Desk Reference* (2nd ed.). New York: Oxford University Press.

Kopelman, M. D., & Fleminger, S. (2002). Experience and perspectives on the classification of organic mental disorders. *Psychopathology, 35,* 76–81.

Koplewicz, H. (2002). *More than moody: Recognizing and treating adolescent depression.* New York: Putnam.

Kosfeld, M., Heinrich, M., Zak, P. J., Fischbacher, U., & Fehr, E. (2005, June 2). Oxytocin increases trust in humans. *Nature, 435,* 673–676.

Koss, M. P. (1993). Rape: Scope, impact, interventions, and public policy responses. *American Psychologist, 48,* 1062–1069.

Kosslyn, S. M. (2005). Mental images and the brain. *Cognitive Neuropsychology, 22,* 333–347.

Kosslyn, S. M., & Shin, L. M. (1994). Visual mental images in the brain: Current issues. In M. J. Farah & G. Ratcliff (Eds.), *The neuropsychology of high-level vision: Collected tutorial essays. Carnegie Mellon symposia on cognition.* Hillsdale, NJ: Erlbaum.

Kosslyn, S. M., Cacioppo, J. T., Davidson, R. J., Hugdahl, K., Lovallo, W. R., Spiegel, D., & Rose, R. (2002). Bridging psychology and biology. *American Psychologist, 57,* 341–351.

Kotre, J., & Hall, E. (1990). *Seasons of life.* Boston: Little, Brown.

Koval, J. J., Pederson, L. L., Mills, C. A., McGrady, G. A., & Carvajal, S. C. (2000). Models of the relationship of stress, depression, and other psychosocial factors to smoking behavior: A comparison of a cohort of students in grades 6 and 8. *Preventive Medicine: an International Devoted to Practice & Theory, 30,* 463–477.

Koveces, Z. (1987). *The container metaphor of emotion.* Paper presented at the University of Massachusetts, Amherst.

Kowert, P. A. (2002). *Groupthink or deadlock: When do leaders learn from their advisors? SUNY Series on the Presidency.* Albany: State University of New York Press.

Kozaric-Kovacic, D., & Borovecki, A. (2005). Prevalence of psychotic comorbidity in combat-related post-traumatic stress disorder. *Military Medicine, 170,* 223–226.

Kozulin, A., Gindis, B., Ageyev, V. S., & Miller, S. M. (2003). *Vygotsky's educational theory in cultural context.* New York: Cambridge University Press.

Kral, M. C., & Brown, R. T. (2004). Transcranial Doppler ultrasonography and executive dysfunction in children with sickle cell disease. *Journal of Pediatric Psychology, 29,* 185–195.

Kramer, P. (1993). *Listening to Prozac.* New York: Viking.

Kraus, S. J. (1995, January). Attitudes and the prediction of behavior: A meta-analysis of the empirical literature. *Personality and Social Psychology Bulletin, 21,* 58–75.

Krause, S. S. (2003). *Aircraft safety: Accident investigations, analyses, and applications* (2nd ed.). New York: McGraw-Hill.

Kremer, J. M. D., & Scully, D. M. (1994). *Psychology in sport.* London, England: Taylor & Francis.

Krijn, M., Emmelkamp, P. M. G., Olafsson, R. P., & Biemond, R. (2004). Virtual reality exposure therapy of anxiety disorders: A review. *Clinical Psychology Review, 24,* 259–281.

Krohne, H. W. (1996). Individual differences in coping. In M. Zeidner & N. S. Endler (Eds.), *Handbook of coping: Theory, research, applications.* New York: Wiley.

Krueger, R. G., Hicks, B. M., & McGue, M. (2001). Altruism and antisocial behavior: Independent tendencies, unique personality correlates, distinct etiologies. *Psychological Science, 12,* 397–402.

Krull, D. S., & Anderson, C. A. (1997). The process of explanation. *Current Directions in Psychological Science, 6,* 1–5.

Ku, L., St. Louis, M., Farshy, C., Aral, S., Turner, C. F., Lindberg, L. D., & Sonenstein, F. (2002). Risk behaviors, medical care, and chlamydial infection among young men in the United States. *American Journal of Public Health, 92,* 1140–1143.

Kübler-Ross, E. (1969). *On death and dying.* New York: Macmillan.

Kubovy, M., Epstein, W., & Gepshtein, S. (2003). Foundations of visual perception. In A. F. Healy, & R. W. Proctor (Eds.). *Handbook of psychology: Experimental psychology* (Vol. 4). New York: Wiley.

Kulynych, J. J., Vladar, K., Jones, D. W., & Weinberger, D. R. (1994). Gender differences in the normal lateralization of the supratemporal cortex: MRI surface-rendering morphometry of Heschl's gyrus and the planum temporale. *Cerebral Cortex, 4,* 107–118.

Kunda, Z. (2000). The case for motivated reasoning. In D. T. Higgins & A. W. Kruglanski (Eds.), *Motivational science: Social and personality perspectives. Key readings in social psychology* (pp. 313–335). Philadelphia: Psychology Press.

Kuriyama, K., Stickgold, R., & Walker, M. P. (2004). Sleep-dependent learning and motor-skill complexity. *Learning and Memory, 11,* 705–713.

Kuther, T. L. (2003). *Your career in psychology: Psychology and the law.* New York: Wadsworth.

Kwan, V. S. Y., Bond, M. H., & Singelis, T. M. (1997). Pancultural explanations for life satisfaction: Adding relationship harmony to self-esteem. *Journal of Personality & Social Psychology, 73,* 1038–1051.

Kwon, P., & Laurenceau, J. P. (2002). A longitudinal study of the hopelessness theory of depression: Testing the diathesis-stress model within a differential reactivity and exposure framework [Special issue: Reprioritizing the role of science in a realistic version of the scientist-practitioner model]. *Journal of Clinical Psychology, 50,* 1305–1321.

Lacerda, F., von Hofsten, C., & Heimann, M. (2001). *Emerging cognitive abilities in early infancy.* Mahwah, NJ: Lawrence Erlbaum Associates.

Lacey, M. (2002, January 6). In Kenyan family, ritual for girls still divides. *The New York Times,* p. 6.

LaFrance, M., & Harris, J. L. (2004). Gender and verbal and nonverbal communication. In M. A. Paludi (Ed.), *Praeger guide to the psychology of gender.* Westport, CT: Praeger Publishers/Greenwood Publishing Group.

LaFromboise, T., Coleman, H. L. K., & Gerton, J. (1995). Psychological impact of biculturalism: Evidence and theory. In N. R. Goldberger & J. B. Veroff (Eds.), *The culture and psychology reader.* New York: New York University Press.

Lahti, J., Räikkönen, K., Ekelund, J., Peltonen, L., Raitakari, O. T., & Keltikangas-Järvinen, L. (2005). Novelty seeking: Interaction between parental alcohol use and dopamine D4 receptor gene exon III polymorphism over 17 years. *Psychiatric Genetics, 15,* 133–139.

Laird, J. D., & Bressler, C. (1990). William James and the mechanisms of emotional experience. *Personality and Social Psychology Bulletin, 16,* 636–651.

Lal, S. (2002). Giving children security: Mamie Phipps Clark and the racialization of child psychology. *American Psychologist, 57,* 20–28.

Lamal, P. A. (1979). College students' common beliefs about psychology. *Teaching of Psychology, 6,* 155–158.

Lamb, H. R., & Weinberger, L. E. (2005). One-year follow-up of persons discharged from a locked intermediate care facility. *Psychiatric Services, 56,* 198–201.

Lamb, M. E. (1996). Effects of nonparental child care on child development: An update. *Canadian Journal of Psychiatry, 41,* 330–342.

Lamb, M. E., & Garretson, M. E. (2003), The effects of interviewer gender and child gender on the informativeness of alleged child sexual abuse victims in forensic interviews. *Law and Human Behavior, 27,* 157–171.

Lamb, R. J., Morral, A. R., Kirby, K. C., Iguchi, M. Y., & Galbicka, G. (2004). Shaping smoking cessation using percentile schedules. *Drug and Alcohol Dependence, 76,* 247–259.

Lambert, M. J., Shapiro, D. A., & Bergin, A. E. (1986). The effectiveness of psychotherapy. In S. L. Garfield & A. E. Bergin (Eds.), *Handbook of psychotherapy and behavior change* (3rd ed.). New York: Wiley.

Lana, R. E. (2002). The cognitive approach to language and thought [Special issue: Choice and chance in the formation of society: Behavior and cognition in social theory]. *Journal of Mind and Behavior, 23,* 51–57.

Landry, D. W. (1997, February). Immunotherapy for cocaine addiction. *Scientific American,* pp. 41–45.

Langdridge, D., & Butt, T. (2004). The fundamental attribution error: A phenomenological critique. *British Journal of Social Psychology, 43,* 357–369.

Langer, E., & Janis, I. (1979). *The psychology of control.* Beverly Hills, CA: Sage.

Langreth, R. (2000, May 1). Every little bit helps: How even moderate exercise can have a big impact on your health. *The Wall Street Journal,* p. R5.

Lankov, A. (2004). The dawn of modern Korea: Changes for better or worse. *The Korea Times,* p. A1.

Lanza, S. T., & Collins, L. M. (2002). Pubertal timing and the onset of substance use in females during early adolescence. *Prevention Science, 3,* 69–82.

Laqueur, T. W. (2003). *Solitary sex: A cultural history of masturbation.* New York: Zone.

Larsen, R. J., & Buss, D. M. (2006). *Personality psychology: Domains of knowledge about human nature with PowerWeb* (2nd ed.). New York: McGraw-Hill.

Larson, R. K. (1990). Semantics. In D. N. Osherson & H. Lasnik (Eds.), *Language.* Cambridge, MA: MIT.

Lasnik, H. (1990). Syntax. In D. N. Osherson & H. Lasnik (Eds.), *Language.* Cambridge, MA: MIT.

Latané, B., & Darley, J. M. (1970). *The unresponsive bystander: Why doesn't he help?* New York: Appleton-Century-Crofts.

Latané, B., & Nida, S. (1981). Ten years of research on group size and helping. *Psychological Bulletin, 89,* 308–324.

Laumann, E. O., Paik, A., & Rosen, R. C. (1999, February 10). Sexual dysfunction in the United States: Prevalence and predictors. *Journal of the American Medical Association, 281,* 537–544.

Lavelli, M., & Fogel, A. (2005). Developmental changes in the relationship between the infant's attention and emotion during early face-to-face communication. *Developmental Psychology, 41,* 265–280.

Lazarus, A. A. (1997). *Brief but comprehensive psychotherapy: The multimodal way.* New York: Springer.

Lazarus, R. S. (1991a). Cognition and motivation in emotion. *American Psychologist, 46,* 352–367.

Lazarus, R. S. (1991b). *Emotion and adaptation*. New York: Oxford University Press.

Lazarus, R. S. (1994). Appraisal: The long and short of it. In P. Ekman & R. J. Davidson (Eds.), *The nature of emotion: fundamental questions*. New York: Oxford University Press.

Lazarus, R. S. (1995). Emotions express a social relationship, but it is an individual mind that creates them. *Psychological Inquiry, 6*, 253–265.

Lazarus, R. S. (2000). Toward better research on stress and coping. *American Psychologist, 55*, 665–673.

Leavitt, F. (2002). The reality of repressed memories revisited and principles of science. *Journal of Trauma and Dissociation, 3*, 19–35.

Leblanc, D. C. (2004). *Statistics for science students: Concepts and applications for the sciences*. Boston: Jones and Bartlett.

Lee, A. Y., & Aaker, J. L. (2004). Bringing the frame into focus: The influence of regulatory fit on processing fluency and persuasion. *Journal of Personality and Social Psychology, 86*, 205–218.

Lee, F., Hallahan, M., & Herzog, T. (1996). Explaining real-life events: How culture and domain shape attributions. *Personality and Social Psychology Bulletin, 22*, 732–741.

Lee, H. J., & Kwon, S. M. (2003). Two different types of obsession: Autogenous obsessions and reactive obsessions. *Behaviour Research & Therapy, 41*, 11–29.

Lee, H. J., Kwon, S. M., Kwon, J. S., & Telch, M. J. (2005). Testing the autogenous-reactive model of obsessions. *Depress Anxiety, 21*, 118–129.

Lee, T. W., Wachtler, T., & Sejnowski, T. J. (2002). Color opponency is an efficient representation of spectral properties in natural scenes. *Vision Research, 42*, 2095–2103.

Lee-Chai, A. Y., Bargh, J. A. (Eds.). (2001). *The use and abuse of power: Multiple perspectives on the causes of corruption*. Philadelphia, PA: Psychology Press.

Lehar, S. (2003). *The world in your head: A gestalt view of the mechanism of conscious experience*. Mahwah, NJ: Erlbaum.

Lehman, D. R., & Taylor, S. E. (1988). Date with an earthquake: Coping with a probable, unpredictable disaster. *Personality and Social Psychology Bulletin, 13*, 546–555.

Lehman, D., Chiu, C., and Schaller, M. (2004). Psychology and culture. *Annual Review of Psychology, 55*, 689–714.

Lehmann, E. L., & Romano, J. P. (2004). *Testing statistical hypotheses*. New York: Springer-Verlag.

Lehrer, P. M. (1996). Recent research findings on stress management techniques. In Editorial Board of Hatherleigh Press, *The Hatherleigh guide to issues in modern therapy: The Hatherleigh guides series* (Vol. 4). New York: Hatherleigh Press.

Leib, J. R., Gollust, S. E., Hull, S. C., & Wilfond, B. S. (2005). Carrier screening panels for Ashkenazi Jews: is more better? *Genetic Medicine, 7*, 185–190.

Leibel, R. L., Rosenbaum, M., Hirsch, J. (1995, March 9). Changes in energy expenditure resulting from altered body. *New England Journal of Medicine, 332*, 621–628.

Leiter, S., & Leiter, W. M. (2003). *Affirmative action in antidiscrimination law and policy: An overview and synthesis. SUNY series in American constitutionalism*. Albany: State University of New York Press.

Lemonick, M. D. (2000, December 11). Downey's downfall. *Time*, p. 97.

Lengua, L. J., & Kovacs, E. A. (2005). Bidirectional associations between temperament and parenting and the prediction of adjustment problems in middle childhood. *Journal of Applied Developmental Psychology, 26*, 21–38.

Lengua, L. J., & Long, A. C. (2002). The role of emotionality and self-regulation in the appraisal-coping process: Tests of direct and moderating effects. *Journal of Applied Developmental Psychology, 23*, 471–493.

Lenzenweger, M. F., & Dworkin, R. H. (Eds.). (1998). *The origins and development of schizophrenia: Advances in experimental psychopathology*. Washington, DC: American Psychological Association.

Leonard, B. E. (2001). Changes in the immune system in depression and dementia: Causal or co-incidental effects? *International Journal of Developmental Neuroscience, 19*, 305–312.

Lepore, S. J., Ragan, J. D., & Jones, S. (2000). Talking facilities cognitive-emotional processes of adaptation to an acute stressor. *Journal of Personality and Social Psychology, 78*, 499–508.

Lepper, M. R., Corpus, J. H., & Iyengar, S. S. (2005). Intrinsic and extrinsic motivational orientations in the classroom: Age differences and academic correlates. *Journal of Educational Psychology, 97*, 184–196.

Lerner, R. M., Fisher, C. B., & Weinberg, R. A. (2000). Toward a science for and of the people: Promoting civil society through the application of developmental science. *Child Development, 71*, 11–20.

Lester, D. (1990). *Understanding and preventing suicide: New perspectives*. Springfield, IL: Thomas.

Leuchter, A. F., Cook, I. A., Witte, E. Z., Morgan, M., & Abrams, M. (2002). Changes in brain function of depressed subjects during treatment with placebo. *American Journal of Psychiatry, 159*, 122–129.

Leung, F. K. S. (2002). Behind the high achievement of East Asian students [Special issue: Achievements in mathematics and science in an international context]. *Education Research and Evaluation, 8*, 87–108.

LeVay, S. (1993). *The sexual brain*. Cambridge, MA: MIT.

Levenson, R. W. (1994). The search for autonomic specificity. In P. Ekman & R. J. Davidson (Eds.), *The nature of emotion: Fundamental questons*. New York: Oxford University Press.

Leventhal, H., & Cleary, P. D. (1980). The smoking problem: A review of the research and theory in behavioral risk modification. *Psychological Bulletin, 88*, 370–405.

Levick, S. E. (2004). *Clone being: Exploring the psychological and social dimensions*. Lanham, MD: Rowman and Littlefield.

Levine, J. M. (1989). Reaction to opinion deviance in small groups. In P. B. Paulus (Ed.), *Psychology of group influence* (2nd ed.). Hillsdale, NJ: Erlbaum.

Levine, S. C., Huttenlocher, J., Taylor, A., & Langrock, A. (1999). Early sex differences in spatial skill. *Developmental Psychology, 35*, 940–949.

Levinson, D. J. (1990). A theory of life structure development in adulthood. In C. N. Alexander & E. J. Langer, (Eds.), *Higher stages of human development: Perspectives on adult growth*. New York: Oxford University Press.

Levy, B. (1996). Improving memory in old age through implicit self-stereotyping. *Journal of Personality and Social Psychology, 71*, 1092–1107.

Levy, B., & Langer, E. (1994). Aging free from negative stereotypes: Successful memory in China and among the American deaf. *Journal of Personality and Social Psychology, 66*, 989–997.

Levy, B. R., & Myers, L. M. (2004). Preventive health behaviors influenced by self-perceptions of aging. *Preventive Medicine: An International Journal Devoted to Practice and Theory, 39,* 625–629.

Levy, B. R., Slade, M. D., Kunkel, S. R., & Kasl, S. V. (2002). Longevity increased by positive self-perceptions of aging. *Journal of Personality & Social Psychology, 83,* 261–270.

Levy, D. A. (1997). *Tools of critical thinking: Metathoughts for psychology.* Boston: Allyn & Bacon.

Levy, S. M., Lee, J., Bagley, C., & Lippman, M. (1988). Survival hazards analysis in first recurrent breast cancer patients: Seven-year follow-up. *Psychosomatic Medicine, 50,* 520–528.

Levy, Y. S., Stroomza, M., Melamed, E., & Offen, D. (2004). Embryonic and adult stem cells as a source for cell therapy in Parkinson's disease. *Journal of Molecular Neuroscience, 24,* 353–386.

Lewandowski, S., Stritzke, W. G. K., & Oberauer, K. (2005). Memory for fact, fiction and misinformation: The Iraq War 2003. *Psychological Science, 16,* 190–195.

Lewin, T. (2003, December 22). For more people in their 20s and 30s, going home is easier because they never left. *The New York Times,* A27.

Lewinsohn, P. M., & Essau, C. A. (2002). Depression in adolescents. In I. H. Gotlib & C. L. Hammen (Eds.), *Handbook of depression,* 541–559. New York: Guilford Press.

Lewinsohn, P. M., Petit, J. W., Joiner, T. E., Jr., & Seeley, J. R. (2003). The symptomatic expression of major depressive disorder in adolescents and young adults. *Journal of Abnormal Psychology, 112,* 244–252.

Lewis, M., & Haviland-Jones, J. M. (2000). *Handbook of emotions* (2nd ed.). New York: Guilford Press.

Li, J., Wang, L., & Fischer, K. W. (2004). The organization of Chinese shame concepts. *Cognition and Emotion, 18,* 767–797.

Li, M. D., Cheng, R., Ma, J. Z., & Swan, G. E. (2003). A meta-analysis of estimated genetic and environmental effects on smoking behavior in male and female adult twins. *Addiction, 98,* 23–31.

Li, S. C. (2005). Neurocomputational perspectives linking neuromodulation, processing noise, representational distinctiveness, and cognitive aging. In R. Cabeza, L. Nyberg, & D. Park (Eds.), *Cognitive neuroscience of aging: Linking cognitive and cerebral aging.* London: Oxford University Press.

Liben, L. S., & Bigler, R. S. (2002). The development course of gender differentiations: Conceptualizing, measuring, and evaluation constructs and pathways. *Monographs of the Society for Research in Child Development, 67,* 148–167.

Lichtenwalner, R. J., & Parent, J. M. (2005, June 15). Adult neurogenesis and the ischemic forebrain. *Journal of Cerebral Blood Flow & Metabolism,* advance online publication.

Lidz, J., & Gleitman, L. R. (2004). Argument structure and the child's contribution to language learning. *Trends in Cognitive Sciences, 8,* 157–161.

Lie, D. C., Song, H., Colamarino, S. A., Ming, G., & Gage, F. H. (2004). Neurogenesis in the adult brain: New strategies for central nervous system diseases. *Annual Review of Pharmacology and Toxicology, 44,* 399–421.

Lilienfeld, S. O., & Lynn, S. J. (2003). Dissociative identity disorder: Multiple personalities, multiple controversies. In S. O. Lilienfeld & S. J. Lynn (Eds.), *Science and pseudoscience in clinical psychology* (pp. 109–142). New York: Guilford Press.

Lilienfeld, S. O., Lynn, S. J., & Lohr, J. M. (Eds.). (2003). *Science and pseudoscience in clinical psychology.* New York: Guilford Press.

Lindorff, M. (2005). Determinants of received social support: Who gives what to managers? *Journal of Social and Personal Relationships, 22,* 323–337.

Lindsay, P. H., & Norman, D. A. (1977). *Human information processing* (2nd ed.). New York: Academic Press.

Lindsay, P., Maynard, I., & Thomas, O. (2005). Effects of hypnosis on flow states and cycling performance. *Sport Psychologist, 19,* 164–177.

Lindsey, E., & Colwell, M. (2003). Preschoolers' emotional competence: Links to pretend and physical play. *Child Study Journal, 33,* 39–52.

Linehan, M., Davison, G., Lynch, T., & Sanderson, C. (in press). Principles of therapeutic change in the treatment of personality disorders. In L. Beutler, & L. Castonguay (Eds.), *Identification of principles of therapeutic change.* New York: Oxford University Press.

Linehan, M.M. (2001). Dialectical behavior therapy. In N. J. Smelser, & P. B. Baltes, P.B. (Eds.), *International encyclopedia of the eocial and behavioral sciences.* Elmsford, NY: Pergamon, Oxford.

Linehan, M. M., Cochran, B., & Kehrer, C. A. (2001a). Borderline personality

disorder. In D.H. Barlow (Ed.), *Clinical handbook of psychological disorder* (3rd ed). New York: Guilford Press.

Linehan, M. M., Cochran, B. N., & Hehrer, C. A. (2001b). Dialectical behavior therapy for borderline personality disorder. In D. H. Barlow (Ed.), *Clinical handbook of psychological disorders: A step-by-step treatment manual* (3rd ed., pp. 470–522). New York: Guilford Press.

Linscheid, T. R., & Reichenbach, H. (2002). Multiple factors in the long-term effectiveness of contingent electric shock treatment for self-injurious behavior: A case example. *Research in Developmental Disabilities, 23,* 161–177.

Linszen, D. H., Dingemans, P. M., Nugter, M. A., Van der Does, A. J. W., et al. (1997). Patient attributes and expressed emotion as risk factors for psychotic relapse. *Schizophrenia Bulletin, 23,* 119–130.

Lippa, R. A. (2005). *Gender, nature, and nurture* (2nd ed.). Mahwah, NJ: Erlbaum.

Lips, H. M. (2003). *A new psychology of women: Gender, culture, and ethnicity.* New York: McGraw-Hill.

Lipsey, M. W., & Wilson, D. B. (1993). The efficacy of psychological, educational, and behavioral treatment: Confirmation from meta-analysis. *American Psychologist, 48,* 1181–1209.

Lockrane, B., Bhatia, P., & Gore, R. (2005). Successful treatment of narcolepsy and cataplexy: a review. *Canadian Respiratory Journal, 12,* 225–227.

Loehlin, J. C. (2002). The IQ paradox: Resolved? Still an open question. *Psychological Review, 109,* 754–758.

Loewenstein, G. (1994). The psychology of curiosity: A review and reinterpretation. *Psychological Bulletin, 116,* 75–98.

Lofholm, N. (2003, May 6). Climber's kin share relief: Ralston saw 4 options, they say; death wasn't one of them. *Denver Post,* p. A1.

Loftus, E. (1998, November). The memory police. *APA Observer, 3,* 14.

Loftus, E. F. (1993). Psychologists in the eyewitness world. *American Psychologist, 48,* 550–552.

Loftus, E. F. (1997). Memory for a past that never was. *Current Directions in Psychological Science, 6,* 60–65.

Loftus, E. F. (2003). The dangers of memory. In R. J. Sternberg (Ed.), *Psychologists defying the crowd: Stories of those who battled the establishment and won* (pp. 105–117). Washington, DC: American Psychological Association.

Loftus, E. F. (2004). Memories of things unseen. *Current Directions in Psychological Science, 13,* 145–147.

Loftus, E. F., & Palmer, J. C. (1974). Reconstruction of automobile destruction: An example of the interface between language and memory. *Journal of Verbal Learning and Verbal Behavior, 13,* 585–589.

Long, G. M., & Beaton, R. J. (1982). The case for peripheral persistence: Effects of target and background luminance on a partial-report task. *Journal of Experimental Psychology: Human Perception and Performance, 8,* 383–391.

López, S. R., & Guarnaccia, P. J. (2005). Cultural dimensions of psychopathology: The social world's impact on mental illness. In J. E. Maddux & B. A. Winstead (Eds.), *Foundations for a contemporary understanding.* Mahwah, NJ: Lawrence Erlbaum Associates.

López, S. R., & Guarnaccia, P. J. J. (2000). Cultural psychopathology: Uncovering the social world of mental illness. *Annual Review of Psychology, 51,* 571–598.

Lorenz, K. (1966). *On aggression.* New York: Harcourt Brace Jovanovich.

Lorenz, K. (1974). *Civilized man's eight deadly sins.* New York: Harcourt Brace Jovanovich.

Lothane, Z. (2005). Jung, A biography. *Journal of the American Psychoanalytic Association, 53,* 317–324.

Lowe, M. R. (1993). The effects of dieting on eating behavior: A three-factor model. *Psychological Bulletin, 114,* 100–121.

Lowery, D., Fillingim, R. B., & Wright, R. A. (2003). Sex differences and incentive effects on perceptual and cardiovascular responses to cold pressor pain. *Psychosomatic Medicine, 65,* 284–291.

Lubell, K. M., Swahn, M. H., Crosby, A. E., & Kegler, S. R. (2004). Methods of suicide among persons aged 10–19 years—United States, 1992–2001. *MMWR, 53,* 471–473. Retrieved from http://www.cdc.gov/mmwr/PDF/wk/mm5322.pdf

Lublin, H., Eberhard, J., & Levander, S. (2005). Current therapy issues and unmet clinical needs in the treatment of schizophrenia: A review of the new generation antipsychotics. *International Clinical Psychopharmacology, 20,* 183–198.

Luborsky, L. (1988). *Who will benefit from psychotherapy?* New York: Basic Books.

Luchins, A. S. (1946). Classroom experiments on mental set. *American Journal of Psychology, 59,* 295–298.

Lucki, I., & O'Leary, O. F. (2004). Distinguishing roles for norepinephrine and serotonin in the behavioral effects of antidepressant drugs. *Journal of Clinical Psychiatry, 65,* 11–24.

Ludwig, A. M. (1969). Altered states of consciousness. In C. T. Tart (Ed.), *Altered states of consciousness.* New York: Wiley.

Ludwig, A. M. (1996, March). Mental disturbances and creative achievement. *The Harvard Mental Health Letter,* pp. 4–6.

Luria, A. R. (1968). *The mind of a mnemonist.* Cambridge, MA: Basic Books.

Lurie, K., Robinson, A., & Pecsenye, M. (2005). *Cracking the GRE 2006.* New York: Random House.

Luthar, S. S., Cicchetti, D., & Becker, B. (2000). The construct of resilience: A critical evaluation and guidelines for future work. *Child Development, 71,* 543–562.

Ly, D. H., Lockhart, D. J., Lerner, R. A., & Schultz, P. G. (2000, March 31). Mitotic misregulation and human aging. *Science, 287,* 2486–2492.

Lykken, D. T. (1995). *The antisocial personalities.* Mahwah, NJ: Erlbaum.

Lykken, D., & Tellegen, A. (1996). Happiness is a stochastic phenomenon. *Psychological Science, 7,* 181–185.

Lymberis, S. C., Parhar, P. K., Katsoulakis, E., & Formenti, S. C. (2004). Pharmacogenomics and breast cancer. *Pharmacogenomics, 5,* 31–55.

Lynam, D. R., Milich, R., Zimmerman, R., Novak, S. P., Logan, T. K., Martin, C. Leukefeld, M. C., & Clayton, R. (1999). Project DARE: No effects at 10-year follow-up. *Journal of Consulting and Clinical Psychology, 67,* 590–593.

Lynn, S. J., & Rhue, J. W. (1988). Fantasy-proneness: Hypnosis, developmental antecedents, and psychopathology. *American Psychologist, 43,* 35–44.

Lynn, S. J., Fassler, O., & Knox, J. (2005). Hypnosis and the altered state debate: Something more or nothing more? Comment. *Contemporary Hypnosis, 22,* 39–45.

Lynn, S. J., Neufeld, V., Green, J. P., Sandberg, D., et al. (1996). Daydreaming, fantasy, and psychopathology. In R. G. Kunzendorf, N. P. Spanos, & B. Wallace (Eds.), *Hypnosis*

and imagination. Imagery and human development series. Amityville, NY: Baywood.

Macaluso, E., Frith, C. D., & Driver, J. (2000, August 18). Modulation of human visual cortex by crossmodal spatial attention. *Science, 289,* 1206–1208.

Maccoby, E. E., & Jacklin, C. N. (1974). *The psychology of sex differences.* Stanford, CA: Stanford University Press.

Machado, R. B., Suchecki, D., & Tufik, S. (2005). Sleep homeostasis in rats assessed by a long-term intermittent paradoxical sleep deprivation protocol. *Behavioural Brain Research, 160,* 356–364.

MacIntyre, T., Moran, A., & Jennings, D. J. (2002). Is controllability of imagery related to canoe-slalom performance? *Perceptual & Motor Skills, 94,* 1245–1250.

Mack, J. (2003). *The museum of the mind.* London: British Museum Publications.

Mackay, J., & Eriksen, M. (2002). *The tobacco atlas.* Geneva, Switzerland: World Health Organization.

MacKenzie, K. R., & Grabovac. A. D. (2001). Interpersonal psychotherapy group (IPT-G) for depression. *Journal of Psychotherapy Practice and Research, 10,* 46–51.

Macmillan, M. (1996). *Freud evaluated: The completed arc.* Cambridge, MA: MIT.

Macmillan, M. (2000). *An odd kind of fame: Stories of Phineas Gage.* Cambridge, MA: MIT.

MacPherson, K. (2002, March 17). Unfilled pink-collar jobs threaten service cuts. *Pittsburgh Post-Gazette,* p. 7.

Macrae, E. B., Monk, C. S., Nelson, E. E., Zarahn, E., Leibenluft, E., Bilder, R. M., Charney, D. S., Ernst, M., & Pine, D. S. (2004). A developmental examination of gender differences in brain engagement during evaluation of threat. *Biological Psychiatry, 55,* 1047–1055;.

Mader, S. S. (2000). *Biology,* p. 250. Boston: McGraw-Hill.

Madon, S., Guyll, M., Aboufadel, K., Montiel, E., Smith, A., Palumbo, P., & Jussim, L. (2001). Ethnic and national stereotypes: The Princeton Trilogy revisited and revised. *Personality and Social Psychology Bulletin, 27,* 996–1010.

Madon, S., Jussim, L., & Eccles, J. (1997). In search of the powerful self-fulfilling prophecy. *Journal of Personality and Social Psychology, 72,* 791–809.

Magley, V. J. (2002). Coping with sexual harassment: Reconceptualizing women's resistance. *Journal of Personality and Social Psychology, 83,* 930–946.

Magoni, M., Bassani, L., Okong, P., Kituuka, P., Germinario, E. P., Giuliano, M., & Vella, S. (2005). Mode of infant feeding and HIV infection in children in a program for prevention of mother-to-child transmission in Uganda. *AIDS, 19,* 433–437.

Mahmood, M., & Black, J. (2005). Narcolepsy-cataplexy: How does recent understanding help in evaluation and treatment. *Current Treatment Options in Neurology, 7,* 363–371.

Maidment, I. (2000). The use of St John's Wort in the treatment of depression. *Psychiatric Bulletin, 24,* 232–234.

Maier, S. F., & Watkins, L. R. (2000). Learned helplessness. In A. E. Kazdin, *Encyclopedia of psychology* (Vol. 4). Washington, DC: American Psychological Association.

Malamuth, N. M., Linz, D., Heavey, C. L., & Barnes, G. (1995). Using the confluence model of sexual aggression to predict men's conflict with women: A 10-year follow-up study. *Journal of Personality and Social Psychology, 69,* 353–369.

Maldonado, J. R., & Spiegel, D. (2003). Dissociative disorders. In R. E. Hales & S. C. Yudofsky, *The American Psychiatric Publishing textbook of clinical psychiatry, 4th edition.* Washington, DC: American Psychiatric Publishing.

Malle, B. F. (2004). *How the mind explains behavior: Folk explanations, meaning, and social interaction.* Cambridge, MA: MIT.

Mamassis, G., & Doganis, G. (2004). The effects of a mental training program on juniors pre-competitive anxiety, self-confidence, and tennis performance. *Journal of Applied Sport Psychology, 16,* 118–137.

Mangels, J. (2004). *The influence of intelligence beliefs on attention and learning a neurophysiological approach.* Presentation at the 16th Annual Convention of Social Cognitive Neuroscience. Washington, DC: American Psychological Society.

Mangels, J., Dweck, C., & Good, C. (2005, May). *Achievement motivation modulates the neural dynamics of error correction.* CASL Meeting, U.S. Department of Education.

Manly, J. J. (2005). Advantages and disadvantages of separate norms for African Americans. *Clinical Neuropsychologist, 19,* 270–275.

Mann, D. (1997). *Psychotherapy: An erotic relationship.* New York: Routledge.

Mann, K., Ackermann, K., Croissant, B., Mundle, G., Nakovics, H., Diehl, A. (2005). Neuroimaging of gender differences in alcohol dependence: are women more vulnerable? *Alcoholism: Clinical & Experimental Research, 29,* 896–901.

Manning, S. Y. (2005). Dialectical behavior therapy of severe and chronic problems. In L. VandeCreek (Ed.), *Innovations in clinical practice: Focus on adults.* Sarasota, FL: Professional Resource Press/ Professional Resource Exchange.

Manstead, A. S. R. (1991). Expressiveness as an individual difference. In R. S. Feldman & B. Rime (Eds.), *Fundamentals of nonverbal behavior.* Cambridge, England: Cambridge University Press.

Manstead, A. S. R., & Wagner, H. L. (2004). *Experience emotion.* Cambridge, England: Cambridge University Press.

Manstead, A. S. R., Frijda, N., & Fischer, A. H. (Eds.) (2003). *Feelings and emotions: The Amsterdam Symposium.* Cambridge, England: Cambridge University Press.

Marcaurelle, R., Bélanger, C., & Marchand, A. (2003). Marital relationship and the treatment of panic disorder with agoraphobia: A critical review. *Clinical Psychology Review, 23,* 247–276.

Marcaurelle, R., Bélanger, C., & Marchand, A. (2005). Marital predictors of symptom severity in panic disorder with agoraphobia. *Journal of Anxiety Disorders, 19,* 211–232.

Marcus, G. F. (1996). Why do children say "breaked"? *Current Directions in Psychological Science, 5,* 81–85.

Marcus-Newhall, A., Pedersen, W. C., & Carlson, M. (2000). Displaced aggression is alive and well: A meta-analytic review. *Journal of Personality and Social Psychology, 78,* 670–689.

Margoliash, D. (2005). Song learning and sleep. *Nature Neuroscience, 8,* 546–548.

Margolis, E., & Laurence, S. (Eds.). (1999). *Concepts: Core readings.* Cambridge, MA: MIT.

Markey, P. M. (2000). Bystander intervention in computer-mediated communication. *Computers in Human Behavior, 16,* 183–188.

Markowitz, J. C. (2003). Controlled trials of psychotherapy. *American Journal of Psychiatry, 160,* 186–187.

Markowsitsch, H. J. (2000). Memory and amnesia. In M. M. Mesulam (Ed.), *Principles of behavioral and cognitive neurology* (2nd ed.). London: Oxford University Press.

Marks, I. M. (2004). The Nobel prize award in physiology to Ivan Petrovich Pavlov-1904. *Australian and New Zealand Journal of Psychiatry, 38,* 674–677.

Markus, H. R., & Kitayama, S. (1991). Culture and the self: Implications for cognition, emotion, and motivation. *Psychological Review, 98,* 224–253.

Markus, H. R., & Kitayama, S. (2003). Models of agency: Sociocultural diversity in the construction of action. In V. Murphy-Berman & J. J. Berman (Eds.), *Cross-cultural differences in perspectives on the self.* Lincoln, NE: University of Nebraska Press.

Maroda, K. J. (2004). A relational perspective on women and power. *Psychoanalytic Psychology, 21,* 428–435.

Marrero, H., & Gamez, E. (2004). Content and strategy in syllogistic reasoning. *Canadian Journal of Experimental Psychology, 58,* 168–180.

Marsland, A. L., Bachen, E. A., Cohen, S., Rabin, B., & Manuck, S. B. (2002). Stress, immune reactivity and susceptibility to infectious disease [Special issue: The Pittsburgh special issue]. *Physiology and Behavior, 77,* 711–716.

Martelle, S., Hanley, C., & Yoshino K. (2003, January 28). "Sopranos" scenario in slaying? *Los Angeles Times,* p. B1.

Martin, A. J., & Marsh, H. W. (2002). Fear of failure: Friend or foe? *Australian Psychologist, 38,* 31–38.

Martin, C. L., Ruble, D. N., & Szkrybalo, J. (2002). Cognitive theories of early gender development. *Psychological Bulletin, 128,* 903–933.

Martin, L., & Pullum, G. K. (1991). *The great Eskimo vocabulary hoax.* Chicago: University of Chicago Press.

Martin, P. D., & Brantley, P. J. (2004). Stress, coping, and social support in health and behavior. In J. M. Raczynski & L. C. Leviton (Eds.), *Handbook of clinical health psychology: Vol. 2. Disorders of behavior and health.* Washington, DC: American Psychological Association.

Martin, S. (April 2002). Easing migraine pain. *Monitor on Psychology,* pp. 71–73.

Martindale, C. (1981). *Cognition and consciousness.* Homewood, IL: Dorsey.

Marx, J. (2004, July 16). Prolonging the agony. *Science, 305,* 326–328.

Maslow, A. H. (1987). *Motivation and personality* (3rd ed.). New York: Harper & Row.

Mason, M. (1995). *The making of Victorian sexuality.* New York: Oxford University Press.

Mast, F. W., & Kosslyn, S. M. (2002). Visual mental images can be ambiguous: Insights from individual differences in spatial transformation abilities. *Cognition, 86,* 57–70.

Masters, W. H., & Johnson, V. E. (1966). *Human sexual response.* Boston: Little, Brown.

Masters, W. H., & Johnson, V. E. (1979). *Homosexuality in perspective.* Boston: Little, Brown.

Masters, W., & Johnson, V. (1994). *Heterosexuality.* New York: Harper Collins.

Mastropieri, M. A., & Scruggs, T. E. (2000). *Teaching students ways to remember: Strategies for learning mnemonically.* Cambridge, MA: Brookline.

Masuda, M. (2003). Meta-analyses of love scales: Do various love scales measure the same psychological constructs? *Japanese Psychological Research, 45,* 25–37.

Mataix-Cols, D., & Bartres-Fax, D. (2002). Is the use of the wooden and computerized versions of the Tower of Hanoi Puzzle equivalent? *Applied Neuropsychology, 9,* 117–120.

Matlin, M. W. (2000). *The psychology of women* (4th ed.). Ft. Worth, TX: Harcourt.

Matsumoto, D. (2002). Methodological requirements to test a possible in-group advantage in judging emotions across cultures: Comment on Elfenbein and Ambady (2002) and evidence. *Psychological Bulletin, 128,* 236–242.

Matsumoto, D. (Ed.). (2001). *The handbook of culture and psychology.* New York: Oxford University Press.

Matsumoto, D. (2004). Reflections on culture and competence. In R. J. Sternberg & E. L. Grigorenko (Eds.), *Culture and competence: Contexts of life success.* Washington, DC: American Psychological Association.

Matsumoto, D., Yoo, S. H., Hirayama, S., & Petrova, G. (2005). Development and validation of a measure of display rule knowledge: The Display Rule Assessment Inventory. *Emotion, 5,* 23–40.

Matthews, G., Zeidner, M., & Roberts, R. D. (2003). *Emotional intelligence: Science and myth.* Cambridge, MA: MIT.

Maurer, D., Lewis, T. L., Brent, H. P., & Levin, A. V. (1999, October 1). Rapid improvement in the acuity of infants after visual input. *Science, 286,* 108–110.

Mayer, J. D., Salovey, P., & Caruso, D. R. (2004). Emotional intelligence: Theory, findings, and implications. *Psychological Inquiry, 15,* 197–215.

Mayer, J. D., Salovey, P., Caruso, D. R., & Sitarenios, G. (2003). Measuring emotional intelligence with the MSCEIT V2.0. *Emotion, 3,* 97–105.

Maynard, A. E., & Martini, M. I. (2005). *Learning in cultural context: Family, peers, and school.* New York: Kluwer Academic/Plenum Publishers.

Mayne, T. J., & Bonanno, G. A. (Eds.). (2001). *Emotions: Current issues and future directions.* New York: Guilford Press.

Mays, V. M., Rubin, J., Sabourin, M., & Walker, L. (1996). Moving toward a global psychology: Changing theories and practice to meet the needs of a changing world. *American Psychologist, 51,* 485–487.

Mazard, A., Laou, L., Joliot, M., & Mellet, E. (2005). Neural impact of the semantic content of visual mental images and visual percepts. *Brain Research and Cognitive Brain Research, 24,* 423–35.

McAdams, D. P., Diamond, A., de St. Aubin, E., & Mansfield, E. (1997). Stories of commitment: The psychosocial construction of generative lives. *Journal of Personality and Social Psychology, 72,* 678–694.

McAuillen, A., Nicastro, R., Guenot, F., Girard, M., Lissner, C., & Ferrero, F. (2005). Intensive dialectical behavior therapy for outpatients with borderline personality disorder who are in crisis. *Psychiatric Services, 56,* 193–197.

McCabe, P. M., Schneiderman, N., Field, T., & Wellens, A. R. (Eds.). (2000). *Stress, coping, and cardiovascular disease.* Mahwah, NJ: Lawrence Erlbaum.

McCarthy, J. (2005). Individualism and collectivism: What do they have to do with counseling? *Journal of Multicultural Counseling and Development, 33,* 108–117.

McCaul, K. D., Johnson, R. J., & Rothman, A. J. (2003). The effects of framing and action instructions on whether older adults obtain flu shots. *Health Psychology.*

McClelland, D. C. (1985). How motives, skills, and values determine what people do. *American Psychologist, 40,* 812–825.

McClelland, D. C. (1993). Intelligence is not the best predictor of job performance. *Current Directions in Psychological Research, 2,* 5–8.

McClelland, D. C., Atkinson, J. W., Clark, R. A., & Lowell, E. L. (1953). *The achievement motive.* New York: Appleton-Century-Crofts.

McClintock, M. K., & Herdt, G. (1996). Rethinking puberty: The development of sexual attraction. *Current Directions in Psychological Science, 5,* 178–183.

McClintock, M. K., Jacob, S., Zelano, B., & Hayreh, D. J. S. (2001). Pheromones and vasanas: The functions of social chemosignals. In J. A. French & A. C. Kamil (Eds.), *Evolutionary psychology and motivation.* Vol. 47 of the Nebraska symposium on motivation. Lincoln, NB: University of Nebraska Press.

McCormick, C. G. (2003). Metacognition and learning. In W. M. Reynolds & G. E. Miller (Eds.), *Handbook of psychology: Educational psychology* (Vol. 7. pp. 79–102). New York: Wiley.

McCoy, N.L., & Pitino, L. (2002). Pheromonal influences on socio-sexual behavior in young women. *Physiological Behavior 75,* 367-375.

McCrae R.R., Terracciano A., & 78 Members of the Personality Profiles of Cultures Project: Universal features of personality traits from the observer's perspective: Data from 50 cultures. *Journal of Personality and Social Psychology, 88:* 547–561, 2005.

McCrae, R. R., & Costa, P. T., Jr. (1986). A five-factor theory of personality. In L. A. Pervin & O. P. John (Eds.), *Handbook of personality: Theory and research* (2nd ed.). New York: Guilford.

McCullough, J. P., Jr. (1999). *Treatment for chronic depression: Cognitive behavioral analysis system of psychology (CBASP).* New York: Guilford Press.

McDaniel, M. A., Maier, S. F., & Einstein, G. O. (2002). "Brain specific" nutrients: A memory cure? *Psychological Science in the Public Interest, 3,* 12–18.

McDonald, C., & Murray, R. M. (2004). Can structural magnetic resonance imaging provide an alternative phenotype for genetic studies of schizophrenia? In M. S. Keshavan, J. L. Kennedy, & R. M. Murray (Eds.), *Neurodevelopment and schizophrenia.* New York: Cambridge University Press.

McDonald, H. E., & Hirt, E. R. (1997). When expectancy meets desire: Motivational effects in reconstructive memory. *Journal of Personality and Social Psychology, 72,* 5–23.

McDonald, J. W. (1999, September). Repairing the damaged spinal cord. *Scientific American,* pp. 65–73.

McDougall, W. (1908). *Introduction to social psychology.* London: Methuen.

McDowell, D. M., & Spitz, H. I. (1999). *Substance abuse.* New York: Brunner/Mazel.

McEwen, B. S. (1998, January 15). Protective and damaging effects of stress mediators [Review article]. *New England Journal of Medicine, 338,* 171–179.

McGaugh, J. L. (2003). *Memory and emotion: The making of lasting memories.* New York: Columbia University Press.

McGee, G., Caplan, A., & Malhotra, R. (Eds.). (2004). *The human cloning debate.* Berkeley, CA: Hills Books.

McGilvray, J. (Ed.). (2004). *The Cambridge companion to Chomsky.* Oxford, England: Cambridge University Press.

McGinn, D. (2003, June 9). Testing, testing: The new job search. *Time,* pp. 36–38.

McGlynn, F. D., Smitherman, T. A., & Gothard, K. D. (2004). Comment on the status of systematic desensitization. *Behavior Modification, 28,* 194–205.

McGregor, K. K., & Capone, N. C. (2004). Genetic and environmental interactions in determining the early lexicon: Evidence from a set of tri-zygotic quadruplets. *Journal of Child Language, 31,* 311–337.

McGue, M. (1999). The behavioral genetics of alcoholism. *Current Directions in Psychological Science, 8,* 109–115.

McGuire, S. (2003). The heritability of parenting. *Parenting: Science & Practice, 3,* 73–94.

McGuire, W. J. (1997). Creative hypothesis generating in psychology: Some useful heuristics. *Annual Review of Psychology, 48,* 1–30.

McHale, S. M., Crouter, A. C., & Tucker, C. J. (1999). Family context and gender role socialization in middle childhood: Comparing girls to boys and sisters to brothers. *Child Development, 70,* 990–1004.

McKeever, V. M., & Huff, M. E. (2003). A diathesis-stress model of post-traumatic stress disorder: Ecological, biological, and residual stress pathways. *Review of General Psychology, 7,* 237–250.

McKinley, M. J., Cairns, M. J., Denton, D. A., Egan, G., Mathai, M. L.,

Uschakov, A., Wade, J. D., Weisinger, R. S., & Oldfield, B. J. (2004). Physiological and pathophysiological influences on thirst. *Physiology and Behavior, 81,* 795–803.

McManus, C. (2004). *Right hand, left hand: The origins of asymmetry in brains, bodies, atoms and cultures.* Cambridge, MA: Harvard University Press.

McManus, F., & Waller, G. (1995). A functional analysis of binge-eating. *Clinical Psychology Review, 15,* 845–863.

McMillan, D. E., & Katz, J. L. (2002). Continuing implications of the early evidence against the drive-reduction hypothesis of the behavioral effects of drugs. *Psychopharmacology, 163,* 251–264.

McMullin, R. E. (2000). *The new handbook of cognitive therapy techniques.* New York: Norton.

McNally, R. J. (2003). Recovering memories of trauma: A view from the laboratory. *Current Directions in Psychological Science, 12,* 32–35.

McNamara, P. (2004). *An evolutionary psychology of sleep and dreams.* Westport, CT: Praeger Publishers/Greenwood Publishing Group.

McNeil, D. G., Jr. (2005, August 24). Obesity rate is nearly 25 percent, group says. *The New York Times,* p. A3.

McQuillan, A., Nicastro, R., Guenot, F., Girard, M., Lissner, C., & Ferrero, F. (2005). Intensive dialectical behavior therapy for outpatients with borderline personality disorder who are in crisis. *Psychiatric Services, 56,* 193–197.

Mead, M. (1949). *Male and female.* New York: Morrow.

Mealy, L. (2000). *Sex differences: Developmental and evolutionary strategies.* San Diego, CA: Academic Press.

Meeter, M., & Murre, J. M. J. (2004). Consolidation of long-term memory: Evidence and alternatives. *Psychological Bulletin, 130,* 843–857.

Mehl-Madrona, L. E. (2004). Hypnosis to facilitate uncomplicated birth. *American Journal of Clinical Hypnosis, 46,* 299–312.

Meier, R. P., & Willerman, R. (1995). Prelinguistic gesture in deaf and hearing infants. In K. Emmorey & J. S. Reilly (Eds.), *Language, gesture, and space.* Hillsdale, NJ: Erlbaum.

Mel, B. W. (2002, March 8). What the synapse tells the neuron. *Science, 295,* 1845–1846.

Mel'nikov, K. S. (1993, October–December). On some aspects of the

mechanistic approach to the study of processes of forgetting. *Vestnik Moskovskogo Universiteta Seriya 14 Psikhologiya,* pp. 64–67.

Melton, G. B., & Garrison, E. G. (1987). Fear, prejudice, and neglect: Discrimination against mentally disabled persons. *American Psychologist, 42,* 1007–1026.

Meltzer, H. Y. (2000). Genetics and etiology of schizophrenia and bipolar disorder. *Biological Psychiatry, 47,* 171–173.

Meltzoff, A. N. (1996). The human infant as imitative generalist: A 20-year progress report on infant imitation with implications for comparative psychology. In C. M. Heyes & B. G. Galef, Jr. (Eds.), *Social learning in animals: The roots of culture.* San Diego, CA: Academic Press.

Melzack, R., & Katz, J. (2004). *The gate control theory: Reaching for the brain.* Mahwah, NJ: Lawrence Erlbaum Associates.

Mendelsohn, J. (2003, November 7–9). What we know about sex. *USA Weekend,* pp. 6–9.

Mendelsohn, M. E., & Rosano, G. M. C. (2003). Hormonal regulation of normal vascular tone in males. *Circulation Research.* 93, 1142.

Merai, A. (Ed.). (1985). *On terrorism and combating terrorism.* College Park, MD: University Publications of America.

Merari, A. (2005). Israel facing terrorism. *Israel Affairs, 11,* 223–237.

Merari, A. (2005). Suicide terrorists. In R. I. Yufit & D. Lester, *Assessment, treatment and prevention of suicidal behavior.* New York: Wiley.

Merlin, D. (1993). Origins of the modern mind: Three stages in the evolution of culture and cognition. *Behavioral and Brain Sciences, 16,* 737–791.

Mesquita, B., & Frijda, N. H. (1992). Cultural variations in emotions: A review. *Psychological Bulletin, 112,* 179–204.

Messer, S. B., & McWilliams, N. (2003). The impact of Sigmund Freud and *The Interpretation of Dreams.* In R. J. Sternberg (Ed.), *The anatomy of impact: What makes the great works of psychology great* (pp. 71–88). Washington, DC: American Psychological Association.

Meston, C. M. (2003). Validation of the female sexual function index (FSFI) in women with female orgasmic disorder and in women with hypoactive sexual desire disorder. *Journal of Sex and Marital Therapy, 29,* 39–46.

Metcalfe, J. (1986). Premonitions of insight predict impending error. *Journal of Experimental Psychology: Learning, Memory, and Cognition, 12,* 623–634.

Metee, D. R., & Aronson, E. (1974). Affective reactions to appraisal from others. In T. L. Huston (Ed.), *Foundations of interpersonal attraction* (pp. 235–283). New York: Academic Press.

Meyer, G. J. (2000). Incremental validity of the Rorschach Prognostic Rating scale over the MMPI Ego Strength Scale and IQ. *Journal of Personality Assessment, 74,* 356–370.

Meyer, R. G., & Osborne, Y. V. H. (1987). *Case studies in abnormal behavior* (2nd ed.). Boston: Allyn & Bacon.

Meyer-Bahlburg, H. (1997). The role of prenatal estrogens in sexual orientation. In L. Ellis & L. Ebertz (Eds.), *Sexual orientation: Toward biological understanding.* Westport, CT: Praeger.

Meyerowitz, J. (2004). *How sex changed: A history of transsexuality in the United States.* Cambridge, MA: Harvard University Press.

Michael, R. T., Gagnon, J. H., Laumann, E. O., & Kolata, G. (1994). *Sex in America: A definitive survey.* Boston: Little, Brown.

Middlebrooks, J. C., Furukawa, S., Stecker, G. C., & Mickey, B. J. (2005). Distributed representation of sound-source location in the auditory cortex. In R. König, P. Heil, E. Budinger, & H. Scheich (Eds.), *Auditory cortex: A synthesis of human and animal research.* Mahwah, NJ: Lawrence Erlbaum Associates.

Miele, F. (2002). *Intelligence, race, and genetics: Conversations with Arthur R. Jensen.* Boulder, CO: Westview Press.

Mifflin, L. (1998, January 14). Study finds a decline in TV network violence. *The New York Times,* p. A14.

Mignon, A., & Mollaret, P. (2002). Applying the affordance conception of traits: A person perception study. *Personality and Social Psychology Bulletin, 28,* 1327–1334.

Miklowitz, D. J., & Thompson, M. C. (2003). Family variables and interventions in schizophrenia. In G. Sholevar & G. Pirooz (Eds.), *Textbook of family and couples therapy: Clinical applications* (pp. 585–617). Washington, DC: American Psychiatric Publishing.

Mikulincer, M., & Shaver, P. R. (2005). Attachment security, compassion, and altruism. *Current Directions in Psychological Science, 14,* 34–38.

Miletic, M. P. (2002). The introduction of a feminine psychology to psychoanalysis: Karen Horney's legacy [Special issue: Interpersonal psychoanalysis and feminism]. *Contemporary Psychoanalysis, 38,* 287–299.

Milgram, S. (1974). *Obedience to authority.* New York: Harper & Row.

Millar, M. (2002). Effects of guilt induction and guilt reduction on door-in-the-face. *Communication Research, 29,* 666–680.

Miller, A. G. (1999). Harming other people: Perspectives on evil and violence. *Personality and Social Psychology Review, 3,* 176–178.

Miller, A. G., Collins, B. E., & Brief, D. E. (1995). Perspectives on obedience to authority: The legacy of the Milgram experiments. *Journal of Social Issues, 51,* 1–19.

Miller, A. M., & Gross, R. (2005). Health and depression in women from the former Soviet Union living in the United States and Israel. *Journal of Immigrant Health, 6,* 187–196.

Miller, D. W. (2000, February 25). Looking askance at eyewitness testimony. *The Chronicle of Higher Education,* pp. A19–A20.

Miller, G. (2004, April 2). Learning to forget. *Science, 304,* 34–36.

Miller, G., & Cohen, S. (2001). Psychological interventions and the immune system: A meta-analytic review and critique. *Health Psychology, 20,* 47–63.

Miller, G. A. (1956). The magical number seven, plus or minus two: Some limits on our capacity for processing information. *Psychology Review, 63,* 81–97.

Miller, J. G. (1984). Culture and the development of everyday social explanation. *Journal of Personality and Social Psychology, 46,* 961–978.

Miller, L. A., Taber, K. H., Gabbard, G. O., Hurley, R. A. (2005). Neural underpinnings of fear and its modulation: Implications for anxiety disorders. *Journal of Neuropsychiatry and Clinical Neurosciences, 17,* 1–6.

Miller, L. T., & Vernon, P. A. (1997). Developmental changes in speed of information processing in young children. *Developmental Psychology, 33,* 549–554.

Miller, M. N., & Pumariega, A. J. (2001). Culture and eating disorders: A historical and cross-cultural review. *Psychiatry: Interpersonal and Biological Processes, 64,* 93–110.

Miller, M. W. (1994, December 1). Brain surgery is back in a limited way to treat mental ills. *The Wall Street Journal,* pp. A1, A12.

Miller, N. E., & Magruder, K. M. (Eds.). (1999). *Cost-effectiveness of psychotherapy: A guide for practitioners, researchers, and policymakers.* New York: Oxford University Press.

Miller-Jones, D. (1991). Informal reasoning in inner-city children. In J. F. Voss & D. N. Perkins (Eds.), *Informal reasoning and education.* Hillsdale, NJ: Lawrence Erlbaum.

Millon, T., & Davis, R. O. (1996). *Disorders of personality: DSM-IV and beyond* (2nd ed.). New York: Wiley.

Millon, T., Davis, R., & Millon, C. (2000). *Personality disorders in modern life.* New York: Wiley.

Mills, J. L. (1999). Cocaine, smoking, and spontaneous abortion. *New England Journal of Medicine, 340,* 380–381.

Mills, J. S., Polivy, J., Herman, C. P., & Tiggemann, M. (2002). Effects of exposure to thin media images: Evidence of self-enhancement among restrained eaters. *Personality and Social Psychology Bulletin, 28,* 1687–1699.

Milner, B. (1966). Amnesia following operation on temporal lobes. In C. W. M. Whitty & P. Zangwill (Eds.), *Amnesia.* London: Butterworth.

Milner, B. (2005). The medial temporal-lobe amnesic syndrome. *Psychiatric Clinics of North America, 28,* 599–611.

Milton, J., & Wiseman, R. (1999). Does psi exist? Lack of replication of an anomalous process of information transfer. *Psychological Bulletin, 125,* 387–391.

Miner-Rubino, K., Winter, D. G., & Stewart, A. J. (2004). Gender, social class, and the subjective experience of aging: Self-perceived personality change from early adulthood to late midlife. *Personality and Social Psychology Bulletin, 30,* 1599–1610.

Mingo, C., Herman C. J., & Jasperse, M. (2000). Women's stories: Ethnic variations in women's attitudes and experiences of menopause, hysterectomy, and hormone replacement therapy. *Journal of Women's Health and Gender Based Medicine, 9*(Suppl. 2), S27–S38.

Minuchin, S., & Nichols, M. P. (1992). *Family healing.* New York: Free Press.

Mischel, W. (2004). Toward an integrative science of the person. *Annual Review of Psychology, 55,* 1–22.

Mischoulon, D. (2000, June). Antidepressants: Choices and controversy. *HealthNews,* p. 4.

Miserando, M. (1991). Memory and the seven dwarfs. *Teaching of Psychology, 18,* 169–171.

Mitchell, T. (2000, November 3–5). Extinguish your habit for good. *USA Weekend,* p. 4.

Mitchener, B. (2001, March 14). Controlling a computer by the power of thought. *Wall Street Journal,* pp. B1, B4.

Mittleman, M. A., Maclure, M., Sherwood, J. B., Mulry, R. P., Tofler, G. H., Jacobs, S. C., Friedman, R., Benson, H., & Muller, J. E. (1995, October 1). Triggering of acute myocardial infarction onset by episodes of anger. *Circulation, 92,* 1720–1725.

Miyake, K., Chen, S., & Campos, J. J. (1985). Infant temperament, mother's mode of interaction, and attachment in Japan: An interim report. *Monographs of the Society for Research in Child Development, 50,* 276–297.

MLA (2005). MLA Language Map; All languages other than English combined. Retrieved from http://www. mla.org/census_map&source=county (based on 2000 U.S. Census Bureau figures)

Moghaddam, B., & Adams, B. W. (1998, August 28). Reversal of phencyclidine effects by a group II metabotropic glutamate receptor agonist in rats. *Science, 281,* 1349–1352.

Moghaddam, F. M. (2005). The staircase to terrorism: A psychological explanation. *American Psychologist, 60,* 161–169.

Mohapel, P., Leanza, G., Kokaia, M., & Lindvall, O. (2005). Forebrain acetylcholine regulates adult hippocampal neurogenesis and learning. *Neurobiology of Aging, 26,* 939–946.

Molfese, V. J., & Molfese, D. L. (2000). *Temperament and personality development across the life span.* Mahwah, NJ: Erlbaum.

Monaghan, P. (2004, October 14). Real fear, virtually overcome. *The Chronicle of Higher Education,* p. A12.

Monnier, J., Resnick, H. S., Kilpatrick, D. G., & Seals, B. (2002). The relationship between distress and resource loss following rape. *Violence and Victims, 17,* 85–92.

Montague, D. P. F., & Walker-Andrews, S. (2002). Mothers, fathers, and infants: The role of person familiarity and parental involvement in infants' perception of emotion expressions. *Child Development, 73,* 1339–1352.

Montgomery, C., Fisk, J. E., Newcombe, R., Wareing, M., & Murphy, P. N. (2005). Syllogistic reasoning performance in MDMA (Ecstasy) users. *Experimental and Clinical Psychopharmacology, 13,* 137–145.

Montgomery, G. M., & Bovbjerg, D. H. (2003). Expectations of chemotherapy-related nausea: Emotional and experimental predictors. *Annals of Behavioral Medicine, 25,* 48–54.

Monti, J. M. (2004). Primary and secondary insomnia: Prevalence, causes and current therapeutics. *Current Medicinal Chemistry—Central Nervous System Agents, 4,* 119–137.

Moody, H. R. (2000). *Aging: Concepts and controversies.* Thousand Oaks, CA: Sage.

Moore, M. M. (2002). Behavioral observation. In M. W. Wiederman & B. E. Whitley (Eds.), *Handbook for conducting research on human sexuality.* Mahwah, NJ: Lawrence Erlbaum.

Moore-Ede, M. (1993). *The twenty-four hour society.* Boston: Addison-Wesley.

Mora-Giral, M., Raich-Escursell, R. M., Segues, C. V., Torras-Clarasó, J., & Huon, G. (2004). Bulimia symptoms and risk factors in university students. *Eating and Weight Disorders, 9,* 163–169.

Moretti, M. M., & Higgins, E. T. (1990). The development of self-system vulnerabilities: Social and cognitive factors in developmental psychopathology. In R. J. Sternberg & J. Kolligian, Jr. (Eds.), *Competence considered.* New Haven, CT: Yale University Press.

Morgan, R. (2002, September 27). The men in the mirror. *The Chronicle of Higher Education,* pp. A53–A54.

Morin, C. M. (2004). Cognitive-behavioral approaches to the treatment of insomnia. *Journal of Clinical Psychiatry, 65,* 33–40.

Morris, J. F., Waldo, C. R., & Rothblum, E. D. (2001). A model of predictors and outcomes of outness among lesbian and bisexual women. *American Journal of Orthopsychiatry, 71,* 61–71.

Morrow, J., & Wolff, R. (1991, May). Wired for a miracle. *Health,* pp. 64–84.

Moskowitz, G. B. (2004). *Social cognition: Understanding self and others.* New York: Guilford Press.

Motley, M. T. (1987, February). What I meant to say. *Psychology Today,* pp. 25–28.

Muehlenhard, C. L., & Hollabaugh, L. C. (1988). Do women sometimes say no when they mean yes? The prevalence and correlates of women's token resistance to sex. *Journal of Personality and Social Psychology, 54,* 872–879.

Mukerjee, M. (1997, February). Trends in animal research. *Scientific American, 276,* pp. 86–93.

Mullen, B., & Rice, D. R. (2003). Ethnophaulisms and exclusion: The behavioral consequences of cognitive representation of ethnic immigrant groups. *Personality and Social Psychology Bulletin, 29,* 1056–1067.

Mulligan, C., Moreau, K., Brandolini, M., Livingstone, B., Beaufrere, B., & Boire, Y. (2002). Alterations of sensory perceptions in healthy elderly subjects during fasting and refeeding: A pilot study. *Gerontology, 48,* 39–43.

Mumenthaler, M. S. Yesavage, J. A., Taylor, J. L., O'Hara, R., Friedman, L., Lee, H., & Kraemer, H. C. (2003). Psychoactive drugs and pilot performance: a comparison of nicotine, donepezil, and alcohol effects. *Neuropsychopharmacology, 28,* 1366–1373.

Munroe, R. L., Hulefeld, R., Rodgers, J. M., Tomeo, D. L., & Yamazaki, S. K. (2000). Aggression among children in four cultures. *Cross-Cultural Research: The Journal of Comparative Social Science, 34,* 3–25.

Munson, L. J., Hulin, C., & Drasgow, F. (2000). Longitudinal analysis of dispositional influences and sexual harassment: Effects on job and psychological outcomes. *Personnel Psychology, 53,* 21–46.

Murphy, G. J., Glickfield, L. L., Balsen, Z., & Isaacson, J. S. (2004). Sensory neuron signaling to the brain: Properties of transmitter release from olfactory nerve terminals. *Journal of Neuroscience, 24,* 3023–3030.

Murphy, G. L. (2005). The study of concepts inside and outside the laboratory: Medin versus Medin. In W. Ahn, R. L. Goldstone, B. C. Love, A. B. Markman, & P. Wolff (Eds.), *Categorization inside and outside the laboratory: Essays in honor of Douglas L. Medin.* Washington, DC: American Psychological Association.

Murphy, R. T., Wismar, K., & Freeman, K. (2003). Stress symptoms among African-American college students after the September 11, 2001 terrorist attacks. *Journal of Nervous and Mental Disease, 191,* 108–114.

Murphy, S. T., & Zajonc, R. B. (1993). Affect, cognition, and awareness: Affective priming with optimal and suboptimal stimulus exposures. *Journal of Personality and Social Psychology, 64,* 723–739.

Murphy, S., et al. (1998). Interference under the influence. *Personality and Social Psychology Bulletin, 24,* 517–528.

Murray, B. (June 2002). Good news for bachelor's grads. *Monitor on Psychology,* pp. 30–32.

Murray, J. B. (1990). Nicotine as a psychoactive drug. *Journal of Psychology, 125,* 5–25.

Murray, S. L., Holmes, J. G., & Griffin, D. W. (2004). The benefits of positive illusions: Idealization and the construction of satisfaction in close relationships. In H. T. Reis & C. E. Rusbult (Eds.), *Close relationships: Key readings.* Philadelphia, PA: Taylor & Francis.

Murugasu, E. (2005). Recent advances in the treatment of sensorineural deafness. *Annals of the Academy of Medicine, Singapore, 34,* 313–9.

Myerhoff, B. (1982). Rites of passage: Process and paradox. In V. Turner (Ed.), *Celebration: Studies in festivity and ritual.* Washington, DC: Smithsonian Institution Press.

Myers, D. G., & Diener, E. (1996, May). The pursuit of happiness: New research uncovers some anti-intuitive insights into how many people are happy—and why. *Scientific American,* pp. 70–72.

Myers, D. G. (2000). The funds, friends, and faith of happy people. *American Psychologist, 55,* 56–67.

Myerson, J., Adams, D. R., Hale, S., & Jenkins, L. (2003). Analysis of group differences in processing speed: Brinley plots, Q-Q plots, and other conspiracies. *Psychonomic Bulletin and Review, 10,* 224–237.

Mytinger, C. (2001). *Headhunting in the Solomon Islands: Around the Coral Sea.* Santa Barbara, CA: Narrative Press.

Nadeem, E., & Graham, S. (2005). Early puberty, peer victimization, and internalizing symptoms in ethnic minority adolescents. *Journal of Early Adolescence, 25,* 197–222.

Nagai, Y., Goldstein, L. H., Fenwick, P. B. C., & Trimble, M. R. (2004). Clinical efficacy of galvanic skin response biofeedback training in reducing seizures in adult epilepsy: A preliminary randomized controlled study. *Epilepsy and Behavior, 5,* 216–223.

Naik, G. (2004, December 29). New obesity boom in Arab countries has old ancestry. *The Wall Street Journal,* p. A1.

Najman, J. M., Aird, R., Bor, W., O'Callaghan, M., Williams, G. M., & Shuttlewood, G. J. (2004). The generational transmission of socioeconomic inequalities in child cognitive development and emotional health. *Social Science and Medicine, 58,* 1147–1158.

Nakamura, Y., Ando, S., Nagahara, A., Sano, T., Ochiya, S., Maeda, T., Kawaji, M., Ogawa, A., Hirata, H., Terazaki, K., Haraoka, H., Tanihara, M., Ueda, M., Uchino, M., & Yamamura, K. (2004). Targeted conversion of the transthyretin gene *in vitro* and *in vivo. Gene Therapy, 11,* 838–846.

Nakamura, M., Kyo, S., Kanaya, T., Yatabe, N., Maida, Y., Tanaka, M., Ishida, Y., Fujii, C., Kondo, T., Inoue, M., & Mukaida, N. (2004). hTERT-promoter-based tumor-specific expression of MCP-1 effectively sensitizes cervical cancer cells to a low dose of cisplatin. *Cancer Gene Therapy, 2,* 1–7.

Narrow, W. E., Rae, D. S., Robins, L. N., & Regier, D. A. (2002). Revised prevalence estimates of mental disorders in the United States: Using a clinical significance criterion to reconcile 2 surveys' estimates. *Archives of General Psychiatry, 59,* 115–123.

Nash, M. R. (July 2001). The truth and hype of hypnosis. *Scientific American,* pp. 47–55.

Nathan, P. E., & Gorman, J. M. (Eds.). (1997). *A guide to treatments that work.* New York: Oxford University Press.

Nathan, P. E., Stuart, S. P., & Dolan, S. L. (2000). Research on psychotherapy efficacy and effectiveness: Between Scylla and Charybdis? *Psychological Bulletin, 126,* 964–981.

Nathans, J., Davenport, C. M., Maumenee, I. H., Lewis, R. A., Hejtmancik, J. F., Litt, M., Lovrien, E., Weleber, R., Bachynski, B., Zwas, F., Klingaman, R., & Fishman, G. (1989, August 25). Molecular genetics of human blue cone monochromacy. *Science, 245,* 831–838.

National Academy of Sciences (1999). *Marijuana and medicine: Assessing the science base.* Washington, DC: National Academy Press.

National Association for the Education of Young Children. (2005). *Position statements of the NAEYC.* http://www.naeyc.org/about/positions.asp#where.

National Depression Screening Day. (2003, March 26). Questionnaire on Web site. Retrieved from http://www.mentalhealthscreening.org/dep/dep-sample.htm#sampletest

National Institute of Child Health and Human Development (NICHD) Early Child Care Research Network. (1997). The effects of infant care on infant-mother attachment security: Results of the NICHD study of early child care. *Child Development, 68,* 860–879.

National Institute of Child Health and Human Development (NICHD). (2002). Child-care structure—process—outcome: Direct and indirect effects of child-care quality on young children's development. *Psychological Science, 13,* 199–206.

National Institute of Mental Health (NIMH). (2000). *Prevention of eating disorders: Challenges and opportunities.* Bethesda, MD: National Institute of Mental Health.

National Institute on Drug Abuse. (2000). *Principles of drug addiction treatment: A research-based guide.* Washington, DC: National Institute on Drug Abuse.

National Mental Health Information Center, U.S. Department of Health and Human Services. Reprinted in *Scientific American,* December 2002, p. 38.

Natvig, G. K., Albrektsen, G., & Ovarnstrom, U. (2003). Methods of teaching and class participation in relation to perceived social support and stress: Modifiable factors for improving health and well-being among students. *Educational Psychology, 23,* 261–274.

Navon, R., & Proia, R. L. (1989, March 17). The mutations in Ashkenazi Jews with adult G(M2) gangliosidosis, the adult form of Tay-Sachs disease. *Science, 243,* 1471–1474.

Neber, H., & Heller, K. A. (2002). Evaluation of a summer-school program for highly gifted secondary-school students: The German Pupils Academy. *European Journal of Psychological Assessment, 18,* 214–228.

Neisser, U. (1982). *Memory observed.* San Francisco: Freeman.

Neisser, U. (1996, April.) *Intelligence on the rise: Secular changes in IQ and related measures.* Conference at Emory University. Atlanta: Emory University Press.

Neisser, U., Boodoo, G., Bouchard, T. J., Jr., Boykin, A. W., Brody, N., Ceci, S. J., Halpern, D. F., Loehlin, J. C., Perloff, R., Sternberg, R. J., & Urbina, S. (1996). Intelligence: Knowns and unknowns. *American Psychologist, 51,* 77–101.

Neitz, J., Neitz, M., & Kainz, P. M. (1996, November 1). Visual pigment gene structure and the severity of color vision defects. *Science, 274,* 801–804.

Nelson, D. L., & Simmons, B. L. (2003). Health psychology and work stress: A more positive approach. In J. C. Quick & L. E. Tetrick (Eds.), *Handbook of occupational health psychology.* Washington, DC: American Psychological Association.

Nelson, W. M., III, & Finch, A. J., Jr. (2000). Managing anger in youth: A cognitive-behavioral intervention approach. In P. C. Kendall, *Child & adolescent therapy: Cognitive-behavioral procedures* (2nd ed.). New York: Guilford Press.

Nesdale, D., Maass, A., & Durkin, K. (2005). Group norms, threat, and children's racial prejudice. *Child Development, 76,* 652–663.

Nesheim, S., Henderson, S., Lindsay, M., Zuberi, J., Grimes, V., Buehler, J., Lindegren, M. L., & Bulterys, M. (2004). *Prenatal HIV testing and antiretroviral prophylasix at an urban hospital—Atlanta, Georgia, 1997–2000.* Atlanta, GA: Centers for Disease Control.

Ness, R. B., Grisso, J. A., Hirschinger, N., Markovic, N., Shaw, L. M., Day, N. L., & Kline, J. (1999). Cocaine and tobacco use and the risk of spontaneous abortion. *New England Journal of Medicine, 340,* 333–339.

Nesse, R. M. (2000). Is depression an adaptation? *Archives of General Psychiatry, 57,* 14–20.

Nestler, E. J. (2001, June 22). Total recall—the memory of addiction. *Science, 292,* 2266–2267.

Nestler, E. J., & Malenka, R. C. (2004, March). The addicted brain. *Scientific American,* pp. 78–83.

Neubauer, A. C., & Fink, A. (2005). Basic information processing and the psychophysiology of intelligence. In R. J. Sternberg & J. E. Pretz, *Cognition and intelligence: Identifying the mechanisms of the mind.* New York: Cambridge University Press, 2005.

Newby-Clark, I. R., & Ross, M. (2003). Conceiving the past and future. *Personality and Social Psychology Bulletin, 29,* 807–818.

Newcombe, N. S., Drummey, A. B., Fox, N. A., Lie, E., & Ottinger-Alberts, W. (2000). Remembering early childhood: How much, how, and why (or why not). *Current Directions in Psychological Science, 9,* 55–58.

Newell, A., & Simon, H. (1972). *Human problem solving.* Englewood Cliffs, NJ: Prentice Hall.

Newman, A. W., & Thompson, J. W., Jr. (2001). The rise and fall of forensic hypnosis in criminal investigation. *Journal of the American Academy of Psychiatry & the Law, 29,* 75–84.

Newman, C. F., Leahy, R. L., Beck, A. T., Reilly-Harrington, N. A., & Gyulai, L. (2002). *Bipolar disorder: A cognitive therapy approach.* Washington, DC: American Psychological Association.

Newport, E. L., Bavelier, D., & Neville, H. J. (2001). Critical thinking about critical periods: Perspectives on a critical period for language acquisition. In E. Dupoux (Ed.), *Language, brain, and cognitive development: Essays in honor of Jacques Mehler.* Cambridge, MA: MIT.

Newport, F., & Carroll, J. (2002, November 27). Battle of the bulge: Majority of Americans want to lose weight. *Gallup News Service,* pp. 1–9.

Nicholson, I. A. M. (2003). *Inventing personality: Gordon Allport and the science of selfhood.* Washington, DC: American Psychological Association.

Nickerson, R. S., & Adams, M. J. (1979). *Cognitive Psychology, 11,* 297.

Nielsen, S. L., Smart, D. W., Isakson, R. L., Worthen, V. E., Gregersen, A. T., & Lambert, M. J. (2004). The *Consumer Reports* effectiveness score: What did consumers report? *Journal of Counseling Psychology, 51,* 25–37.

Nierenberg, A. A. (1998, February 17). The physician's perspective. *HealthNews,* pp. 3–4.

Nigg, J. T., & Goldsmith, H. H. (1994). Genetics of personality disorders: Perspectives from personality and psychopathology research. *Psychological Bulletin, 115,* 346–380.

Nikles, C. D., II, Brecht, D. L., Klinger, E., & Bursell, A. L. (1998). The effects of current concern- and nonconcern-related waking suggestions on nocturnal dream content. *Journal of Personality and Social Psychology, 75,* 242–255.

Nisbett, R. (1994, October 31). Blue genes. *New Republic, 211,* 15.

Nisbett, R. (2003). *The geography of thought.* New York: Free Press.

Nissle, S., & Bschor, T. (2002). Winning the jackpot and depression: Money cannot buy happiness. *International Journal of Psychiatry in Clinical Practice, 6,* 183–186.

Niu, W., & Sternberg, R. J. (2003). Societal and school influences on student creativity: The case of China [Special issue: Psychoeducational and psychosocial functioning of Chinese children]. *Psychology in the Schools, 40,* 103–114.

Noble, H. B. (1999, March 12). New from the smoking wars: Success. *The New York Times,* pp. D1–D2.

Nolen-Hoeksema, S. (2004a). *Abnormal psychology* (3rd ed.). Boston: McGraw-Hill.

Nolen-Hoeksema, S. (2004b). Gender differences in risk factors and consequences for alcohol use and problems. *Clinical Psychology Review, 24,* 981–1010.

Noonan, D. (2005, June 6). A little bit louder, please. *Newsweek,* pp. 42–50.

Norcia, A. M., Pei, F., Bonneh, Y., Hou, C., Sampath, V., & Pettet, M. W. (2005). Development of sensitivity to texture and contour information in the human infant. *Journal of Cognitive Neuroscience, 17,* 569–579.

Norlander, T., Von Schedvin, H., & Archer, T. (2005). Thriving as a function of affective personality: Relation to personality factors, coping strategies and stress. *Anxiety, Stress & Coping: An International Journal, 18,* 105–116.

Nosek, B. A., Banaji, M. R., & Greenwald, A. G. (2002). Math=male, me=female, therefore math ≠ me. *Journal of Personality and Social Psychology, 83,* 44–59.

Novak, M. A., & Petto, A. J. (1991). *Through the looking glass: Issues of psychological well-being in captive nonhuman primates.* Washington, DC: American Psychological Association.

Noyes, R., Jr., Stuart, S. P., Langbehn, D. R., Happel, R. L., Longley, S. L., Muller, B. A., & Yagla, S. J. (2003). Test of an interpersonal model of hypochondriasis. *Psychosomatic Medicine, 65,* 292–300.

Noyes, R., Jr., Stuart, S., Longley, S. L., Langbehn, D. R., & Happel, R. L. (2002). Hypochondriasis and fear of death. *Journal of Nervous and Mental Disease, 190,* 503–509.

Noyes, R., Kathol, R. G., Fisher, M. M., Phillips, B. M., et al. (1993). The validity of DSM-III-R hypochondriasis. *Archives of General Psychiatry, 50,* 961–970.

Nucci, L. P. (2002). The development of moral reasoning. In U. Goswami (Ed.), *Blackwell handbook of childhood cognitive development. Blackwell Handbooks of developmental psychology* (pp. 303–325). Malden, MA: Blackwell.

Nyberg, L., & Tulving, E. (1996). Classifying human long-term memory: Evidence from converging dissociations. *European Journal of Cognitive Psychology, 8,* 163–183.

Oatley, K., & Jenkins, J. M. (1996). *Understanding emotions.* Oxford, England: Blackwell Publishers.

Obermeyer, C. M. (2001, May 18). Complexities of a controversial practice. *Science, 292,* 1305–1304.

O'Brien, C. P., Childress, A. R., McLellan, A. T., & Ehrman, R. (1992). Classical conditioning in drug-dependent humans. In P. W. Kalivas & H. H. Samson (Eds.), *The neurobiology of drug and alcohol addiction. Annals of the New York Academy of Sciences* (Vol. 654). New York: New York Academy of Sciences.

Occhionero, M. (2004). Mental processes and the brain during dreams. *Dreaming, 14,* 54–64.

O'Connor, D. B., & O'Connor, R. C. (2004). Perceived changes in food intake in response to stress: The role of conscientiousness. *Stress and Health: Journal of the International Society for the Investigation of Stress, 20,* 279–291.

O'Connor, S. C., & Rosenblood, L. K. (1996). Affiliation motivation in everyday experience: A theoretical comparison. *Journal of Personality and Social Psychology, 70,* 513–522.

O'Donohue, W. (Ed.). (1997). *Sexual harassment: Theory, research, and treatment.* Boston: Allyn & Bacon.

Oehman, A., & Mineka, S. (2003). The malicious serpent: Snakes as a prototypical stimulus for an evolved module of fear. *Current Directions in Psychological Science, 12,* 5–9.

Oezgen, E., & Davies I. R. L. (2002). Acquisition of categorical color perception: A perceptual learning approach to the linguistic relativity hypothesis. *Journal of Experimental Psychology: General, 131,* 477–493.

Offer, D., Kaiz, M., Howard, K. I., & Bennett, E. S. (2000). The altering of reported experiences. *Journal of the American Academy of Child & Adolescent Psychiatry, 39,* 735–742.

Ogbu, J. (1992). Understanding cultural diversity and learning. *Educational Researcher, 21,* 5–14.

Ogletree, S. M., Martinez, C. N., & Turner, T. R. (2004). Pokémon: Exploring the role of gender. *Sex Roles, 50,* 851–859.

O'Grady, W. D., & Dobrovolsky, M. (Eds.). (1996). *Contemporary linguistic analysis: An introduction* (3rd ed.). Toronto: Copp Clark Pitman.

Oishi, S., & Diener, E. (2001). Goals, culture, and subjective well-being. *Personality and Social Psychology Bulletin, 27,* 1674–1682.

O'Keefe, T., & Fox, K. (Eds.). (2003). *Finding the real me: True tales of sex and gender diversity.* San Francisco: Jossey-Bass.

Okun, B. F. (1996). *Understanding diverse families: What practitioners need to know.* New York: Guilford Press.

Olds, J., & Milner, P. (1954). Positive reinforcement produced by electrical stimulation of septal area and other regions of rat brain. *Journal of Comparative and Physiological Psychology, 47,* 411–427.

Olds, M. E., & Fobes, J. L. (1981). The central basis of motivation: Intracranial self-stimulation studies. *Annual Review of Psychology, 32,* 123–129.

Oliver, M. B., & Hyde, J. S. (1993). Gender differences in sexuality: A meta-analysis. *Psychological Bulletin, 114,* 29–51.

Olshansky, S. J., Carnes, B. A., & Cassel, C. (1990, November 2). In search of Methuselah: Estimating the upper limits to human longevity. *Science, 250,* 634–639.

Olson, D. H., & DeFrain, J. (2005). *Marriages and families: Intimacy, diversity, and strengths with PowerWeb.* New York: McGraw-Hill.

Olson, M. A., & Fazio, R. H. (2001). Implicit attitude formation through classical conditioning. *Psychological Science, 12,* 413–417.

Oppenheimer, D. M. (2004). Spontaneous discounting of availability in frequency judgment tasks. *Psychological Science, 15,* 100–105.

Oren, D. A., & Terman, M. (1998, January 16). Tweaking the human circadian clock with light. *Science, 279,* 333–334.

Orenstein, P. (2001). Unbalanced equations: Girls, math, and the confidence gap. In R. Satow (Ed.), *Gender and social life.* Needham Heights, MA: Allyn & Bacon.

Ornat, S. L., & Gallo, P. (2004). Acquisition, learning, or development of language? Skinner's "Verbal behavior" revisited. *Spanish Journal of Psychology, 7,* 161–170.

Orr, S. P., Metzger, L. J., & Pitman, R. K. (2002). Psychophysiology of post-traumatic stress disorder [Special issue: Recent advances in the study of bio-logical alterations in post-traumatic stress disorders]. *Psychiatric Clinics of North America, 25,* 271–293.

Orth-Gomér, K., Chesney, M. A., & Wenger, N. K. (Eds.). (1996). *Women, stress and heart disease.* Mahwah, NJ: Erlbaum.

Ortony, A., & Turner, T. J. (1990). What's basic about basic emotions? *Psychological Review, 97,* 315–331.

Orwin, R. G., & Condray, D. S. (1984). Smith and Glass' psychotherapy conclusions need further probing: On Landman and Dawes' re-analysis. *American Psychologist, 39,* 71–72.

Oskamp, S. (Ed.). (2000) *Reducing prejudice and discrimination.* Mahwah, NJ: Erlbaum.

Owens, R. E., Jr. (2001) *Language development: An introduction* (5th ed.). Boston: Allyn & Bacon.

Ozer, E. J., & Weiss, D. S. (2004). Who develops posttraumatic stress disorder? *Current Directions in Psychological Science, 13,* 169–172.

Ozer, E. J., Best, S. R., & Lipsey, T. L. (2003). Predictors of posttraumatic stress disorder and symptoms in adults: A meta-analysis. *Psychological Bulletin, 129,* 52–73.

Pääbo, S. (2001, February 16). The human genome and our view of ourselves. *Science, 291,* 1219–1220.

Paivio, A. (1971). *Imagery and verbal processes.* New York: Holt, Rinehart & Winston.

Paivio, A. (1975). Perceptual comparison through the mind's eye. *Memory and Cognition, 3,* 635–647.

Pajares, F. (2003). Self-efficacy beliefs, motivation, and achievement in writing: A review of the literature. *Reading and Writing Quarterly: Overcoming Learning Difficulties, 19,* 139–158.

Palanker, D., Vankov, A., Huie, P., & Baccus, S. (2005). Design of a high-resolution optoelectronic retinal prosthesis. *Journal of Neural Engineering, 2,* S105–120.

Paludi, M. A. (Ed.). (1996). *Sexual harassment on college campuses: Abusing the ivory power.* Albany: State University of New York Press.

Paniagua, F. A. (2000). *Diagnosis in a multicultural context: A casebook for mental health professionals.* Thousand Oaks, CA: Sage.

Papero, A. L. (2005). Is early, high-quality daycare an asset for the children of low-income, depressed mothers? *Developmental Review, 25,* 181–211.

Paquette, D., Carbonneau, R., & Dubeau, D. (2003). Prevalence of father-child rough-and-tumble play and physical aggression in preschool children. *European Journal of Psychology of Education, 18,* 171–189.

Paquier, P. F., & Mariën, P. (2005). A synthesis of the role of the cerebellum in cognition. *Aphasiology, 19,* 3–19.

Parasuraman, R., & Rizzo, M. (2005). *Neuroergonomics: The brain at work.* New York: Oxford University Press.

Park, C. L., & Grant, C. (2005). Determinants of positive and negative consequences of alcohol consumption in college students: Alcohol use, gender, and psychological characteristics. *Addictive Behaviors, 30,* 755–765.

Park, W. W. (2000). A comprehensive empirical investigation of the relationships among variables of the groupthink model. *Journal of Organizational Behavior, 21,* 873–887.

Parke, B. N. (2003). *Discovering programs for talent development.* Thousand Oaks, CA: Corwin Press.

Parke, R. D. (2002). Punishment revisited—Science, values, and the right question: Comment on Gershoff (2002). *Psychological Bulletin, 128,* 596–601.

Parke, R. D. (2004). Development in the family. *Annual Review of Psychology, 55,* 365–399.

Parke, R. S., Coltrane, S. Duffy, S., Buriel, R. Dennis, J., Powers, J. French, S., & Widaman, K. F. (2004). Economic stress, parenting, and child adjustment in Mexican American and European American children. *Child Development, 75,* 1632–1656.

Parker-Pope, T. (2003, April 22). The diet that works. *The Wall Street Journal,* pp. R1, R5.

Parlee, M. B. (1979, October). The friendship bond. *Psychology Today,* pp. 43–45.

Parrott, A. C. (2002). Recreational Ecstasy/ MDMA, the serotonin syndrome, and serotonergic neurotoxicity [Special issue: Serotonin]. *Pharmacology, Biochemistry & Behavior, 71,* 837–844.

Pascual, A., & Guéguen, N. (2005). Foot-in-the-door and door-in-the-face: A comparative meta-analytic study. *Psychological Reports, 96,* 122–128.

Pascual-Leone, A., et al. (1995). Modulation of muscle responses evoked by transcranial magnetic stimulation during the acquisition of new fine motor skills. *Journal of Neurophysiology 74,* 1037–1045.

Patel, D. R., Pratt, H. D., & Greydanus, D. E. (2003). Treatment of adolescents with anorexia nervosa [Special issue: Editing disorders in adolescents]. *Journal of Adolescent Research, 18,* 244–260.

Patterson, D. R. (2004). Treating pain with hypnosis. *Current Directions in Psychological Science, 13,* 252–255.

Paukert, A., Stagner, B., & Hope, K. (2004). The assessment of active listening skills in helpline volunteers. *Stress, Trauma, and Crisis: An International Journal, 7,* 61–76.

Paul, A. M. (2004). *Cult of personality: How personality tests are leading us to miseducate our children, mismanage our companies and misunderstand ourselves.* New York: Free Press.

Paunonen, S. V. (2003). Big Five factors of personality and replicated predictions of behavior. *Journal of Personality and Social Psychology, 84,* 411–422.

Pavlides, C., & Winson, J. (1989). Influences of hippocampal place cell firing in the awake state on the activity of these cells during subsequent sleep episodes. *Journal of Neuroscience, 9,* 2907–2918.

Pavlidis, I., Eberhardt, N. L., & Levine, J. A. (2002). Seeing through the face of deception. *Nature, 415,* 35.

Pavlov, I. P. (1927). *Conditioned reflexes.* London: Oxford University Press.

Pawlik, K., & d'Ydewalle, G. (1996). Psychology and the global commons: Perspectives of international psychology. *American Psychologist, 51,* 488–495.

Payne, D. G. (1986). Hyperamnesia for pictures and words: Testing the recall level hypothesis. *Journal of Experimental Psychology: Learning, Memory, and Cognition, 12,* 16–29.

Pearson, J., & Clifford, C. W. G. (2005). When your brain decides what you see: Grouping across monocular, binocular, and stimulus rivalry. *Psychological Science, 16,* 516–519.

Pedersen, D. M. (2002). Intrinsic-extrinsic factors in sport motivation. *Perceptual & Motor Skills, 95,* 459–476.

Pedersen, P. B., Draguns, J. G., Lonner, W. J., & Trimble, J. E. (Eds.). (2002). *Counseling across cultures* (5th ed.). Thousand Oaks, CA: Sage.

Pellegrini, S., Muzio, R. N., Mustaca, A. E., & Papini, M. R. (2004). Successive negative contrast after partial reinforcement in the consummatory behavior of rats. *Learning and Motivation, 35,* 303–321.

Penley, J. A., Tomaka, J., & Wiebe, J. S. (2002). The association of coping to physical and psychological health outcomes: A meta-analytic review. *Journal of Behavioral Medicine, 25,* 551–603.

Penn, D. L., Corrigan, P. W., Bentall, R. P., Racenstein, J. M., & Newman, L. (1997). Social cognition in schizophrenia. *Psychological Bulletin, 121,* 114–132.

Penney, J. B., Jr. (2000). Neurochemistry. In B. S. Fogel, R. B. Schiffer, et al. (Eds.), *Synopsis of neuropsychiatry.* New York: Lippincott Williams & Wilkins.

Pennington, B. F. (2002). *The development of psychopathology: Nature and nurture.* New York: Guilford Press.

Pennington, B., Moon, J., & Edgin, J. (2003). The neuropsychology of Down syndrome: Evidence for hippocampal dysfunction. *Child Development, 74,* 75–93.

Pennisi, E. (1997, October 24). Enzyme linked to alcohol sensitivity in mice. *Science, 278,* 573.

Pennisi, E., & Vogel, G. (2000, June 9). Animal cloning. Clones: A hard act to follow. *Science, 288,* 1722–1727.

Penzel, F. (2000). *Obsessive-compulsive disorders: A complete guide to getting well and staying well.* New York: Oxford University Press.

People Weekly. (2003, June 23). Kid Doc: He's no brain surgeon—yet. But Sho Yano, 12, is about to start med school. *People Weekly,* 125.

People Weekly. (2004, March 15). Who am I? And who are you? Amnesia victim John Prigg struggles to regain his memory, his family, his life [Interview]. *People Weekly, 61,* p. 136.

Peplau, L. A. (2003). Human sexuality: how do men and women differ? *Current Directions in Psychological Research, 12,* 37.

Peretz, I. (2001). Brain specialization for music: New evidence from congenital amusia. In R. J. Zatorre & I. Peretz (Eds.), *The biological foundations of music. Annals of the New York Academy of Sciences* (Vol. 930, pp. 153–165). New York: New York Academy of Sciences.

Perez, R. M., DeBord, K. A., & Bieschke, K. J. (Eds). (2000). *Handbook of counseling and psychotherapy with lesbian, gay, and bisexual clients.* Washington, DC: American Psychological Association.

Perkins, D. N. (1983). Why the human perceiver is a bad machine. In J. Beck, B. Hope, & A. Rosenfeld (Eds.),

Human and machine vision. New York: Academic Press.

Perloff, R. M. (2003). *The dynamics of persuasion: Communication and attitudes in the 21st century* (2nd ed.). Mahwah, NJ: Erlbaum.

Perls, F. S. (1970). *Gestalt therapy now: Therapy, techniques, applications.* Palo Alto, CA: Science and Behavior Books.

Perls, F., Hefferline, R., & Goodman, P. (1994). *Gestalt therapy: Excitement and growth in the human personality* (2nd ed.). New York: New York Journal Press.

Pert, C. B. (2002). The wisdom of the receptors: Neuropeptides, the emotions, and bodymind. *Advances in Mind-Body Medicine, 18,* 30–35.

Pervin, L. A. (2003). *The science of personality* (2nd ed.). London: Oxford University Press.

Petersen, S. E., & Fiez, J. A. (1993). The processing of single words studied with positron emission tomography. *Annual Review of Neuroscience, 16,* 509–530.

Peterson, A. (1985). Pubertal development as a cause of disturbance: Myths, realities, and unanswered questions. *Genetic, Social and General Psychology Monographs, 111,* 205–232.

Peterson, C. (2000). The future of optimism. *American Psychologist, 55,* 44–55.

Peterson, C., Maier, S. F., & Seligman, M. E. P. (1993). *Learned helplessness: A theory for the age of personal control.* New York: Oxford University Press.

Peterson, L. R., & Peterson, M. J. (1959). Short-term retention of individual items. *Journal of Experimental Psychology, 58,* 193–198.

Peterson, R. A., & Brown, S. P. (2005). On the use of beta coefficients in meta-analysis. *Journal of Applied Psychology, 90,* 175–181.

Peterson, S. E. (2001). *PET Scans.* Washington University.

Petri, H. L. (1996). *Motivation: Theory, research, and applications* (4th ed.). Pacific Grove, CA: Brooks/Cole.

Petrill, S. A. (2005). Introduction to this special issue: Genes, environment, and the development of reading skills. *Scientific Studies of Reading, 9,* 189–196.

Petrill, S. A., & Deater-Deckard, K. (2004). The heritability of general cognitive ability: A within-family adoption design. *Intelligence, 32,* 403–409.

Pettigrew, T. F. (2004). Justice deferred: A half century after *Brown v. Board of Education. American Psychologist, 59,* 521–529.

Pettigrew, T., & Tropp, L. (2000). *Reducing prejudice and discrimination.* Mahwah, NJ: Erlbaum.

Pettijohn, T. F., & Jungeberg, B. J. (2004). *Playboy* playmate curves: Changes in facial and body feature preferences across social and economic conditions. *Personality and Social Psychology Bulletin, 30,* 1186–1197.

Pettingale, K. W., Morris, T., Greer, S., & Haybittle, J. L. (1985). Mental attitudes to cancer: An additional prognostic factor. *Lancet,* p. 750.

Pettito, L. A. (1993). On the ontogenetic requirements for early language acquisition. In B. de Boysson-Bardies, S. de Schonen, P. W. Jusczyk, P. McNeilage, & J. Morton (Eds.), *Developmental neurocognition: Speech and face processing in the first year of life. NATO ASI series D: Behavioural and social sciences* (Vol. 69). Dordrecht, Netherlands: Kluwer Academic.

Pettito, L. A., & Marentette, P. F. (1991, March 22). Babbling in the manual mode: Evidence for the ontogeny of language. *Science, 251,* 1493–1496.

Petty, R. E., Cacioppo, J. T., Strathman, A. J., & Priester, J. R. (2005). To think or not to think: Exploring two routes to persuasion. In T. C. Brock & M. C. Green (Eds.), *Persuasion: Psychological insights and perspectives* (2nd ed.). Thousand Oaks, CA: Sage Publications.

Phelps, R. P. (2005). *Defending standardized testing.* Mahwah, NJ: Lawrence Erlbaum Associates.

Philip, P., Sagaspe, P., Moore, N., Taillard, J., Charles, A., Guilleminault, C., & Bioulac, B. (2005). Fatigue, sleep restriction and driving performance. *Accident Analysis and Prevention, 37,* 473–478.

Phillips, E. L., Greydanus, D. E., Pratt, H. D., & Patel, D. R. (2003). Treatment of bulimia nervosa: Psychological and psychopharmacologic considerations [Special issue: Eating disorders in adolescents]. *Journal of Adolescent Research, 18,* 261–279.

Phinney, J. S. (2003). Ethic identity and acculturation. In K. M. Chun, O. Balls, & P. Organista (Eds.), *Acculturation: Advances in theory, measurement, and applied research.* Washington, DC: American Psychological Association.

Piaget, J. (1970). Piaget's theory. In P. H. Mussen (Ed.), *Carmichael's manual of child psychology* (3rd ed., Vol. I). New York: Wiley.

Piaget, J., & Inhelder, B. (1958). *The growth of logical thinking from childhood to adolescence* (A. Parsons & S. Seagrin, Trans.). New York: Basic Books.

Piasecki, T. M., Kenford, S. L., Smith, S. S., Fiore, M. C., & Baker, T. B. (1997). Listening to nicotine: Negative affect and the smoking withdrawal conundrum. *Psychological Science, 8,* 184–189.

Picchioni, D., Goeltzenleucher, B., Green, D. N., Convento, M. J., Crittenden, R., Hallgren, M., & Hick, R. A. (2002). Nightmares as a coping mechanism for stress. *Dreaming: Journal of the Association for the Study of Dreams, 12,* 155–169.

Pich, E. M., Pagliusi, S. R., Tessari, M., Talabot-Ayer, D., Hooft van Huijsduijnen, R., & Chiamulera, C. (1997, January 3). Common neural substrates for the addictive properties of nicotine and cocaine. *Science, 275,* 83–86.

Piechowski, M. M. (2003). From William James to Maslow and Dabrowski: Excitability of character and self-actualization. In D. Ambrose, L. M. Cohen, et al. (Eds.), *Creative intelligence: Toward theoretic integration: Perspectives on creativity* (pp. 283–322). Cresskill, NJ: Hampton Press.

Pihlgren, E. M., Gidycz, C. A., & Lynn, S. J. (1993). Impact of adulthood and adolescent rape experiences on subsequent sexual fantasies. *Imagination, Cognition and Personality, 12,* 321–339.

Piliavin, J. A., & Piliavin, I. M. (1972). Effect of blood on reactions to a victim. *Journal of Personality and Social Psychology, 23,* 353–362.

Pilling, M., & Davies, I. R. L. (2004). Linguistic relativism and colour cognition. *British Journal of Psychology, 95,* 429–455.

Pincus, T., & Morley, S. (2001). Cognitive-processing bias in chronic pain: A review and integration. *Psychological Bulletin, 127,* 599–617.

Pinel, J. P. J., Assanand, S., & Lehman, D. R. (2000). Hunger, eating and ill health. *American Psychologist, 55,* 1105–1116.

Pinker, S. (1994). *The language instinct.* New York: William Morrow.

Pinker, S. (2002). *The blank slate: The modern denial of human nature.* New York: Viking.

Pinker, S. (2004). *How the mind works.* New York: Gardner Books.

Pinkerton, S. D., Bogart, L. M., Cecil, H., & Abramson, P. R. (2002). Factors associated with masturbation in a collegiate sample. *Journal of Psychology and Human Sexuality, 14,* 103–121.

Pinkerton, S. D., Cecil, H., Bogart, L. M., & Abramson, P. R. (2003). The pleasures of sex: An empirical investigation. *Cognition and Emotion, 17,* 341–353.

Pipe, M. E., Lamb, M. E., & Orbach, Y. (2004) Recent research on children's testimony about experienced and witnessed events. *Developmental Review, 24,* 440–468.

Pi-Sunyer, X. (2003). A clinical view of the obesity problem. *Science, 299,* 859–860.

Plomin, R. (2003a). 50 years of DNA: What it has meant to psychological science. *American Psychological Society, 16,* 7–8.

Plomin, R. (2003b). General cognitive ability. In R. Pomin, J. C. DeFries, et al. (Eds.), *Behavioral genetics in the postgenomic era.* Washington, DC: American Psychological Association.

Plomin, R., & Caspi, R. (1999). Behavioral genetics and personality. In L. A. Pervin & O. P. John (Eds.), *Handbook of personality: Theory and research.* (2nd ed.). New York: Guilford.

Plomin, R., & Kovas, Y. (2005). Generalist genes and learning disabilities. *Psychological Bulletin, 131,* 592–617.

Plomin, R., & McClearn, G. E. (Eds.) (1993). *Nature, nurture and psychology.* Washington, DC: American Psychological Association.

Plomin, R., & McGuffin, P. (2003). Psychopathology in the postgenomic era. *Annual Review of Psychology, 54,* 205–228.

Plomin, R., & Neiderhiser, J. M. (1992). Genetics and experience. *Current Directions in Psychological Science, 1,* 160–163.

Plomin, R., & Walker, S. O. (2003). Genetics and educational psychology. *British Journal of Educational Psychology, 73,* 3–14.

Plomin, R., DeFries, J. C., Craig, I. W., & McGuffin, P. (2003). *Behavioral genetics in the postgenomic era.* Washington, DC: American Psychological Association.

Plous, S. (1996a). Attitudes toward the use of animals in psychological research and education: Results from a national survey of psychologists. *American Psychologist, 51,* 1167–1180.

Plous, S. (1996b). Attitudes toward the use of animals in psychological research and education: Results from a national survey of psychology majors. *Psychological Science, 7,* 352–358.

Plous, S., & Herzog, H. A. (2000, October 27). Poll shows researchers favor lab animal protection. *Science, 290,* 711.

Plous, S. L., & Zimbardo, P. G. (2004, September 10). How social science can reduce terrorism. *The Chronicle of Higher Education,* pp. B9–B10.

Plunkett, K., & Wood, C. (2004). The development of children's understanding of grammar. In J. Oates and A. Grayson (Eds.), *Cognitive and language development in children* (pp. 163–204). Malden, MA: Blackwell Publishers Open University Press.

Plutchik, R. (1980). *Emotion, a psychorevolutionary synthesis.* New York: Harper & Row.

Pogarsky, G., & Piquero, A. R. (2003). Can punishment encourage offending? Investigating the "resetting" effect. *Journal of Research in Crime and Delinquency, 40,* 95–120.

Polivy, J., & Herman, C. P. (2002). Causes of eating disorders. *Annual Review of Psychology, 53,* 187–213.

Polivy, J., Herman, C. P., & Boivin, M. (2005). Eating disorders. In J. E. Maddux and B. A. Winstead, *Psychopathology: Foundations for a contemporary understanding* (pp. 229–254). Mahwah, NJ: Lawrence Erlbaum Associates.

Polk, N. (1997, March 30). The trouble with school testing systems. *The New York Times,* p. CN3.

Pollack, A. (2000, May 30). Neural cells, grown in labs, raise hopes on brain disease. *The New York Times,* pp. D1, D6.

Pollack, M. H., & Marzol, P. C. (2000). Panic: Course, complications and treatment of panic disorder. *Journal of Psychopharmacology, 14,* S25–S30.

Polyakov, A., & Pratt, H. (2003). Electrophysiologic correlates of direction and elevation cures for sound localization in the human brainstem. *International Journal of Audiology, 42,* 140–151.

Pomerlau, O. F. (1995). Individual differences in sensitivity to nicotine: Implications of genetic research on nicotine dependence [Special issue: Genetic, environmental, and situational factors mediating the effects of nicotine]. *Behavior Genetics, 25,* 161–177.

Pomponio, A. T. (2002). *Psychological consequences of terrorism.* New York: Wiley.

Poniewozik, James (2002, June 17). Hollywood, the mob and John Gotti. *Time,* p. 37.

Ponterotto, J. G., Gretchen, D., Chauhan, R. V. (2001). Cultural identity and multicultural assessment: Quantitative and qualitative tools for the clinician. In L. A. Suzuki, & J. G. Ponterotto (Eds.), *Handbook of multicultural assessment: Clinical, psychological, and educational applications* (2nd ed.). San Francisco: Jossey-Bass/Pfeiffer.

Popp, D., Donovan, R. A., & Crawford, M. (2003). Gender, race, and speech style stereotypes. *Sex Roles, 48,* 317–325.

Porkka-Heiskanen, T., Strecker, R. E., Thakkar, M., Bjorkum, A. A., Greene, R. W., & McCarley, R. W. (1997, May 23). Adensosine: A mediator of the sleep-inducing effects of prolonged wakefulness. *Science, 276,* 1265–1268.

Porte, H. S., & Hobson, J. A. (1996). Physical motion in dreams: One measure of three theories. *Journal of Abnormal Psychology, 105,* 329–335.

Porter, C. L., & Hsu, H. C. (2003). First-time mothers' perceptions of efficacy during the transition to motherhood: Links to infant temperament. *Journal of Family Psychology, 17,* 54–64.

Posner, M. I., & DiGirolamo, G. J. (2000). Cognitive neuroscience: Origins and promise. *Psychological Bulletin, 126,* 873–889.

Potheraju, A., & Soper, B. (1995). A comparison of self-reported dream themes for high school and college students. *College Student Journal, 29,* 417–420.

Poundstone, W. (2003). *How would you move Mount Fuji?: Microsoft's cult of the puzzle.* Boston: Little, Brown.

Povinelli, D. J., & Vonk, J. (2004). We don't need a microscope to explore the chimpanzee's mind. *Mind and Language, 19,* 1–28.

Praisner, C. L. (2003). Attitudes of elementary school principals toward the inclusion of students with disabilities. *Exceptional Children, 69,* 135–145.

Pratt, H. D., Phillips, E. L., Greydanus, D. E., & Patel, D. R. (2003). Eating disorders in the adolescent population: Future directions [Special issue: Eating disorders in adolescents]. *Journal of Adolescent Research, 18,* 297–317.

Pressley, M. (1987). Are keyword method effects limited to slow presentation rates? An empirically based reply to Hall and Fuson (1986). *Journal of Educational Psychology, 79,* 333–335.

Pressman, S. D., Cohen, S., Miller, G. E., Barkin, A., Rabin, B. S., & Treanor, J. J. (2005). Loneliness, social network size, and immune response to influenza vaccination in college freshman. *Health Psychology, 24*, 297–306.

Pretzer, J. L., & Beck, A. T. (2005). A cognitive theory of personality disorders. In M. F. Lenzenweger & J. F. Clarkin (Eds.), *Major theories of personality disorder* (2nd ed.). New York: Guilford Press.

Price, D. D. (2000, June 9). Psychological and neural mechanisms of the affective dimension of pain. *Science, 288,* 1769–1772.

Prince, C.V. (2005). Homosexuality, transvestism and transsexuality: Reflections on their etymology and differentiation. *International Journal of Transgenderism, 8,* 15 – 18.

Prislin, R., Brewer, M., & Wilson, D. J. (2002). Changing majority and minority positions within a group versus an aggregate. *Personality and Social Psychology Bulletin, 28,* 650–647.

Prohovnik, I., Skudlarski, P., Fulbright, R. K., Gore, J. C., & Wexler, B. E. (2004). Functional MRI changes before and after onset of reported emotions. *Psychiatry Research: Neuroimaging, 132,* 239–250.

Prokasy, W. F., Jr., & Hall, J. F. (1963). Primary stimulus generalization. *Psychological Review, 70,* 310–322.

Puca, R. M. (2005). The influence of the achievement motive on probability estimates in pre- and post-decisional action phases. *Journal of Research in Personality, 39,* 245–262.

Purves, D., Augustine, G. J., Fitzpatrick, D., Katz, L. C., LaMantia, A., & McNamara, J. O. (Eds.). (1997). *Neuroscience.* Sunderland, MA: Sinauer.

Putnam, F. W. (2000). Dissociative disorders. In A. J. Sameroff, M. Lewis (Eds.), *Handbook of developmental psychopathology* (2nd ed.). Dordrecht, Netherlands: Kluwer Academic Publishers.

Quenot, J. P., Boichot, C., Petit, A., Falcon-Eicher, S., d'Athis, P., Bonnet, C., Wolf, J. E., Louis, P., & Brunotte, F. (2005). Usefulness of MRI in the follow-up of patients with repaired aortic coarctation and bicuspid aortic valve. *International Journal of Cardiology, 103,* 312–6.

Quinn, D. M., Kahng, S. K., & Crocker, J. (2004). Discreditable: Stigma effects of revealing a mental illness history on test performance. *Personality and Social Psychology Bulletin, 30,* 803–815.

Quinn, T. C., & Overbaugh, J. (2005, June 10). HIV/AIDS in women: An expanding epidemic. *Science, 308,* 1582–1583.

Rabin, J. (2004). Quantification of color vision with cone contrast sensitivity. *Visual Neuroscience, 21,* 483–485.

Rachman, S., & deSilva, P. (2004). *Panic disorders: The facts.* Oxford, England: Oxford University Press.

Rahman, Q., Kumari, V., & Wilson, G. D. (2003). Sexual orientation-related differences in prepulse inhibition of the human startle response. *Behavioral Neuroscience, 117,* 1096–1102.

Rakoff, V. M. (1995). Trauma and adolescent rites of initiation. In R. C. Marohn & S. C. Feinstein (Eds.), *Adolescent psychiatry: Developmental and clinical studies* (Vol. 20). *Annals of the American Society for Adolescent Psychiatry.* Hillsdale, NJ: Analytic Press.

Ramachandran, V. S. (1995). Filling in gaps in logic: Reply to Durgin et al. *Perception, 24,* 841–845.

Ramachandran, V. S. (2004). *A brief tour of human consciousness: From impostor poodles to purple numbers.* New York: Pi Press.

Rambaud, C., & Guilleminault, C. (2004). "Back to sleep" and unexplained death in infants. *Journal of Sleep and Sleep Disorders, 27,* 1359–1366.

Rampon, C., Jiang, C. H., Dong, H., Tang, Y., Lockhart, D. J., Schultaz, P. G., et al. (2000). Effects of environmental enrichment on gene expression in the brain. *Proceedings of the National Academy of Sciences, 97,* 12880–12884.

Ramsay, M. C., Reynolds, C. R., & Kamphaus, R. W. (2002). *Essentials of behavioral assessment.* New York: Wiley.

Raskin, N. J., & Rogers, C. R. (1989). Person-centered therapy. In R. J. Corsini, & D. Wedding (Eds.), *Current psychotherapies* (4th ed.). Itasca, IL: F. E. Peacock.

Ratcliff, R., & McKoon, G. (1989). Memory models, text processing, and cue-dependent retrieval. In H. L. Roediger III & F. I. M. Craik (Eds.), *Varieties of memory and consciousness: Essays in honour of Endel Tulving.* Hillsdale, NJ: Erlbaum.

Rattazzi, M. C., LaFuci, G., & Brown, W. T. (2004). Prospects for gene therapy in the Fragile X Syndrome. *Mental Retardation and Developmental Disabilities Research Reviews, 10,* 75–81.

Rauschecker, J. P., & Shannon, R. V. (2005, February 8). Sending sound to the brain. *Science, 295,* 1025–9.

Ravindran, A. V., Matheson, K., Griffiths, J., Merali, Z., & Anisman, H. (2002). Stress, coping, uplifts, and quality of life in subtypes of depression: A conceptual framework and emerging data. *Journal of Affective Disorders, 71,* 121–130.

Rawsthorne, L. J., & Elliot, A. J. (1999). Achievement goals and intrinsic motivation: A meta-analytic review. *Personality and Social Psychology Review, 3,* 326–344.

Ray, W. J. (2000). *Methods: Toward a science of behavior and experience* (6th ed.). Belmont, CA: Wadsworth.

Raymond, J. (2003, March 24.). Now for a breath of fresh air. *Newsweek,* p. 67.

Redding, G. M. (2002). A test of size-scaling and relative-size hypotheses for the moon illusion. *Perception and Psychophysics, 64,* 1281–1289.

Redding, G. M., & Hawley, E. (1993). Length illusion in fractional Müller-Lyer stimuli: An object-perception approach. *Perception, 22,* 819–828.

Redish, A. D. (2004). Addiction as a computational process gone awry. *Science, 306,* 1944–1947.

Reed, S. K. (1996). *Cognition: Theory and applications* (4th ed.). Pacific Grove, CA: Brooks/Cole.

Reese, R. J., Conoley, C. W., & Brossart, D. F. (2002). Effectiveness of telephone counseling: A field-based investigation. *Journal of Counseling Psychology, 49,* 233–242.

Refinetti, R. (2005). *Circadian physiology.* New York: CRC Press.

Reichman, W. E., & Rabins, P. V. (1996). Schizophrenia and other psychotic disorders. In W. E. Reichman, & P. R. Katz (Eds.), *Psychiatric care in the nursing home.* New York: Oxford University Press.

Reif, A., & Lesch, K. P. (2003). Toward a molecular architecture of personality. *Behavioural Brain Research, 139,* 1–20.

Reijonen, J. H., Pratt, H. D., Patel, D. R., & Greydanus, D. E. (2003). Eating disorders in the adolescent population: An overview [Special issue: Eating disorders in adolescents]. *Journal of Adolescent Research, 18,* 209–222.

Reisberg, D. (1997). *Cognition: Exploring the science of the mind.* New York: W. W. Norton.

Reiss, S., & Havercamp, S. M. (2005). Motivation in developmental context: A new method for studying self-actualization. *Journal of Humanistic Psychology, 45,* 41–53.

Reitman, J. S. (1965). *Cognition and thought.* New York: Wiley.

Relier, J. P. (2001). Influence of maternal stress on fetal behavior and brain development. *Biology of the Neonate, 79,* 168–171.

Remington, G. (2003). Understanding antipsychotic 'atypicality': A clinical and pharmacological moving target. *Journal of Psychiatry & Neuroscience, 28,* 275–284.

Rescorla, R. A. (1988). Pavlovian conditioning: It's not what you think it is. *American Psychologist, 43,* 151–160.

Reyna, V. F. (1997). Conceptions of memory development with implications for reasoning and decision making. In R. Vasta (Ed.), *Annals of child development: A research annual* (Vol. 12, pp. 87–118). London: Jessica Kingsley.

Reynolds, C. R., & Ramsay, M. C. (2003). Bias in psychological assessment: An empirical review and recommendations. In J. R. Graham & J. A. Naglieri (Eds.), *Handbook of psychology: Assessment psychology* (Vol. 10, pp. 67–93). New York: Wiley.

Reynolds, R. I., & Takooshian, H. (1988, January). Where were you August 8, 1985? *Bulletin of the Psychonomic Society, 26,* 23–25.

Rhue, J. W., Lynn, S. J., & Kirsch, I. (Eds.). (1993). *Handbook of clinical hypnosis.* Washington, DC: American Psychological Association.

Ricciuti, H. N. (1993). Nutrition and mental development. *Current Directions in Psychological Science, 2,* 43–46.

Rice, M. L., Tomblin, J. B., Hoffman, L., Richman, W. A., & Marquis, J. (2004). Grammatical tense deficits in children with SLI and nonspecific language impairment: Relationships with nonverbal IQ over time. *Journal of Speech, Language, and Hearing Research, 47,* 816–834.

Rice, V. H. (Ed.). (2000). *Handbook of stress, coping and health.* Thousand Oaks, CA: Sage.

Richard, M. (2005). Effective treatment of eating disorders in Europe: Treatment outcome and its predictors. *European Eating Disorders Review, 13,* 169–179.

Richardson, A. S., Bergen, H. A., Martin, G., Roeger, L., & Allison, S. (2005). Perceived academic performance as an indicator of risk of attempted suicide in young adolescents. *Archives of Suicide Research, 9,* 163–176.

Richgels, D. J. (2004). Paying attention to language. *Reading Research Quarterly, 39,* 470–477.

Riedel, G., Platt, B., & Micheau, J. (2003). Glutamate receptor function in learning and memory. *Behavioural Brain Research, 140,* 1–47.

Rieder, R. O., Kaufmann, C. A., & Knowles, J. A. (1996). Genetics. In R. E. Hales & S. C. Yudofsky (Eds.), *The American Psychiatric Press synopsis of psychiatry.* Washington, DC: American Psychiatric Press.

Rierdan, J. (1996). *Adolescent suicide: One response to adversity.* In R. S. Feldman (Ed.)., *The psychology of adversity.* Amherst, MA: University of Massachusetts Press.

Ringold, D. J. (1996). Social criticisms of target marketing: Process or product? In R. P. Hill (Ed.), *Marketing and consumer research in the public interest.* Thousand Oaks, CA: Sage.

Riniolo, T. C., Koledin, M., Drakulic, G. M., & Payne, R. A. (2003). An archival study of eyewitness memory of the Titanic's final plunge. *Journal of General Psychology, 130,* 89–95.

Rinn, W. E. (1984). The neuropsychology of facial expression: A review of neurological and psychological mechanisms for producing facial expressions. *Psychological Bulletin, 95,* 52–77.

Rinn, W. E. (1991). Neuropsychology of facial expression. In R. S. Feldman & B. Rimé (Eds.), *Fundamentals of nonverbal behavior.* Cambridge, England: Cambridge University Press.

Rioult-Pedotti, M. S., Friedman, D., & Donoghue, J. P. (2000, October 20). Learning-induced LTP in neocortex. *Science, 290,* 533–536.

Ripley, A. (2005, March 7). Who says a woman can't be Einstein. *Time,* 51–60.

Rivera-Gaxiola, M., Klarman, L., Garcia-Sierra, A., & Kuhl, P. K. (2005). Neural patterns to speech and vocabulary growth in American infants. *Neuroreport: For Rapid Communication of Neuroscience Research, 16,* 495–498.

Rizley, R. C., & Rescorla, R. A. (1972). Associations in higher order conditioning and sensory pre-conditioning. *Journal of Comparative and Physiological Psychology, 81,* 1–11.

Rizza, M. G., & Morrison, W. F. (2003). Uncovering stereotypes and identifying characteristics of gifted students and students with emotional/behavioral disabilities. *Roeper Review, 25,* 73–77.

Robert-McComb, J. J. (2001). Physiology of stress. In J. J. Robert-McComb (Ed.), *Eating disorders in women and children: Prevention, stress management, and treatment,* pp. 119–146. Boca Raton, FL: CRC Press.

Roberts, S. M. (1995). Applicability of the goodness-of-fit hypothesis to coping with daily hassles. *Psychological Reports, 77,* 943–954.

Robinson, N. M. (2003). Two wrongs do not make a right: Sacrificing the needs of gifted students does not solve society's unsolved problems. *Journal for the Education of the Gifted, 26,* 251–273.

Rock, A. (1999, January). Quitting time for smokers. *Money,* pp. 139–141.

Rodd, Z. A., Bell, R. L., Sable, H. J. K., Murphy, J. M., & McBride, W. J. (2004). Recent advances in animal models of alcohol craving and relapse. *Pharmacology, Biochemistry and Behavior, 79,* 439–450.

Roediger, H. (1990). Implicit memory: Retention without remembering. *American Psychologist, 45,* 1043–1056.

Roediger, H. L., III, & McDermott, K. B. (2000). Tricks of memory. *Current Directions in Psychological Science, 9,* 123–127.

Roediger, H. L., & McDermott, K. B. (1995). Creating false memories: Remembering words not presented in lists. *Journal of Experimental Psychology: Learning, Memory, and Cognition, 21,* 803–814.

Roehricht, F., & Priebe, S. (2002). Do cenesthesias and body image aberration characterize a subgroup in schizophrenia? *Acta Psychiatrica Scandinavica, 105,* 276–282.

Roesch, S. C., Adams, L., Hines, A., Palmores, A., Vyas, P., Tran, C., Pekin, S., & Vaughn, A. A. (2005). Coping with prostate cancer: A meta-analytic review. *Journal of Behavioral Medicine, 28,* 281–293.

Rogers, C. R. (1951). *Client-centered therapy.* Boston: Houghton-Mifflin.

Rogers, C. R. (1971). A theory of personality. In S. Maddi (Ed.), *Perspectives on personality.* Boston: Little, Brown.

Rogers, C. R. (1995). *A way of being.* Boston: Houghton Mifflin.

Rogers, M. (1988, February 15). The return of 3-D movies—on TV. *Newsweek,* pp. 60–62.

Rogers, P. (2002, August 2). Too much, too soon. *People,* pp. 79–82.

Rogers, P., & Eftimiades, M. (1995, July 24). Bearing witness. *People Weekly,* pp. 42–43.

Rogler, L. H. (1999). Methodological sources of cultural insensitivity in mental health research. *American Psychologist, 54,* 424–433.

Rohm, W. G. (2003). Test-tube family reunion: Louise Brown turns 25. Happy birthday, IVF. *Wired.*

Roisman, G. I., Collins, W. A. Sroufe, L. A., & Egeland, B. (2005). Predictors of young adults' representations of and behavior in their current romantic relationship: Prospective tests of the prototype hypothesis. *Attachment and Human Development, 7,* 105–121.

Roizen, N. J., & Patterson, D. (2003). Down's syndrome. *Lancet, 361,* 1281–1289.

Rolland, J. S., & Walsh, F. (1996). Family therapy: Systems approaches to assessment and treatment. In R. E. Hales & S. C. Yudofsky (Eds.), *The American Psychiatric Press synopsis of psychiatry.* Washington, DC: American Psychiatric Press.

Rollman, G. B. (2004). *Ethnocultural variations in the experience of pain.* Mahwah, NJ: Lawrence Erlbaum Associates.

Romano, E., Tremblay, R. E, Vitaro, E., Zoccolillo, M., & Pagani, L. (2001.) Prevalence of psychiatric diagnoses and the role of perceived impairment: Findings from an adolescent community sample. *Journal of Child Psychology and Psychiatry and Allied Disciplines, 42,* 451–461.

Rorschach, H. (1924). *Psychodiagnosis: A diagnostic test based on perception.* New York: Grune & Stratton.

Rosch, E. & Mervis, C. B. (1975). Family resemblances: Studies in the internal structure of categories. *Cognitive-Psychology, 7,* 573–605.

Rose, N., & Blackmore, S. (2002). Horses for courses: Tests of a psychic claimant. *Journal of the Society for Psychical Research, 66,* 29–40.

Rose, S. A., Feldman, J. F., & Jankowski, J. J. (2002). Processing speed in the 1st year of life: A longitudinal study of preterm and full-term infants. *Developmental Psychology, 38,* 895–902.

Rosen, D. (1999, May 10). Dieting disorder: A physician's perspective. *Harvard Mental Health Newsletter,* p. 4.

Rosen, H. (2000). The creative evolution of the theoretical foundations for cognitive therapy. *Journal of Cognitive Psychotherapy, 14, Special issue: Creativity in the context of cognitive therapy,* 123–134.

Rosen, J. (2005, August 28.) The future v. Roberts. *The New York Times Magazine,* pp. 24–29, 44, 50–51.

Rosenberg, D., & Bai, M. (1997, October 13). Drinking and dying. *Newsweek,* p. 69.

Rosenberg, L., & Park, S. (2002). Verbal and spatial functions across the menstrual cycle in healthy young women. *Psychoneuroendocrinology, 27,* 834–841.

Rosenbloom, T., & Wolf, Y. (2002). Sensation seeking and detection of risky road signals: A developmental perspective. *Accident Analysis and Prevention, 34,* 569–580.

Rosenhan, D. L. (1973). On being sane in insane places. *Science, 179,* 250–258.

Rosenkranz, M. A., Jackson, D. C., Dalton, K. M., Dokski, I., Ryff, C. D., Singer, B. H., Muller, D., Kalin, N. H., Davidson, R. J. (2003). Affective style and in vivo immune response: neurobehavioral mechanisms. *Proceedings of the National Academy of Sciences, 100,* 48–52.

Rosenkranz, M. A., Jackson, D. C., Dalton, K. M., Dolski, I., Ryff, C. D., Singer, B. H., Muller, D., Kalin, N. H., & Davidson, R. J. (2003, September 16). Affective style and in vivo immune response: neurobehavioral mechanisms. *Proceedings of the National Academy of Sciences, USA, 100,* 11148–11152. Retrieved from http://www.pnas.org/cgi/reprint/100/19/11148?maxtoshow=&HITS=10&hits=10&RESULTFORMAT=&fulltext=davidson+2003&searchid=1125413201748_4140&stored_search=&FIRSTINDEX=0&journalcode=pnas

Rosenman, R. H., Brand, R.J., Sholtz, R.I., & Friedman, M. (1976). Multivariate prediction of coronary heart disease during 8.5 year follow-up in the Western collaborative group study. *American Journal of Cardiology, 37,* 903–910.

Rosenstein, D. S., & Horowitz, H. A. (1996). Adolescent attachment and psychopathology. *Journal of Consulting and Clinical Psychology, 64,* 244–253.

Rosenthal, E. (2005, June 3). For fruit flies, gene shift tilts sex orientation. *International Herald Tribune,* p. C1.

Rosenthal, J. (1997, March 9). The age boom. *The New York Times Magazine,* pp. 39–43.

Rosenthal, R. (2002). Covert communication in classrooms, clinics, courtrooms and cubicles. *American Psychologist, 57,* 838–849.

Rosenthal, R. (2003). Covert communication in laboratories, classrooms, and the truly real world. *Current Directions in Psychological Science, 12,* 151–154.

Rosner, H. (2001, April 30). The science of O. *New York,* pp. 25–31.

Ross, H. E. (2000). Sensation and perception. In D. S. Gupta, S. Deepa, & R. M. Gupta, et al. (Eds.), *Psychology for psychiatrists* (pp. 20–40). London: Whurr Publishers.

Ross, H. E., & Plug, C. (2002). *The mystery of the moon illusion: Exploring size perception.* Oxford: University Press.

Ross, L., & Nisbett, R. E. (1991). *The person and the situation.* New York: McGraw-Hill.

Ross, M., & Newby, I. R. (1996). Distinguishing memory from fantasy. *Psychological Inquiry, 7,* 173–177.

Ross, P. (2003, September). Mind readers. *Scientific American,* pp. 74–77.

Ross, P. E. (2004, April). Draining the language out of color. *Scientific American,* pp. 46–51.

Rossell, S. L., Bullmore, E. T., Williams, S. C. R., & David, A. S. (2002). Sex differences in functional brain activation during a lexical visual field task. *Brain and Language, 80,* 97–105.

Rossier J., Dahourou D., McCrae, R. R. (2005). Structural and mean level analyses of the Five-Factor Model and locus of control: Further evidence from Africa. *Journal of Cross-Cultural Psychology, 36,* 227–246.

Roter, D. L., Hall, J. A., & Aoki, Y. (2002). Physician gender effects in medical communication: A meta-analytic review. *Journal of the American Medical Association, 288,* 756–764.

Roth, A., & Fonagy, P. (1996). *What works for whom? A critical review of psychotherapy research.* New York: Guilford Press.

Rothblum, E. D. (1990). Women and weight: Fad and fiction. *Journal of Psychology, 124,* 5–24.

Rothman, A. J., & Salovey, P. (1997). Shaping perceptions to motivate healthy behavior: The role of message framing. *Psychological Bulletin, 121,* 3–19.

Roughton, R. E. (2002). Rethinking homosexuality: What it teaches us about psychoanalysis. *Journal of the American Psychoanalytic Association, 50,* 733–763.

Roush, W. (1995, September 1). Can "resetting" hormonal rhythms treat illness? *Science, 269,* 1220–1221.

Routtenberg, A., & Lindy, J. (1965). Effects of the availability of rewarding septal and hypothalamic stimulation on bar pressing for food under conditions of deprivation. *Journal of Comparative and Physiological Psychology, 60,* 158–161.

Rovee-Collier, C. (1993). The capacity for long-term memory in infancy. *Current Directions in Psychological Science, 2,* 130–135.

Rowe, J. B., Toni, I., Josephs, O., Frackowiak, R. S. J., & Passingham, R. E. (2000, June 2). The prefrontal cortex: Response selection or maintenance within working memory? *Science, 288,* 1656–1660.

Rowley, S. J., Sellers, R. M., Chavous, T. M., & Smith, M. A. (1998). The relationship between racial identity and self-esteem in African American college and high school students. *Journal of Personality and Social Psychology, 74,* 715–724.

Roysircar, G. (2005). Culturally sensitive assessment, diagnosis, and guidelines. In M. G. Constantine & D. W. Sue (Eds.), *Strategies for building multicultural competence in mental health and educational settings.* New York: Wiley.

Royzman, E. B., Cassidy, K. W., & Baron, J. (2003). "I know, you know": Epistemic egocentrism in children and adults. *Review of General Psychology, 7,* 38–65.

Rozencwajg, P., Cherfi, M., Ferrandez, A. M., Lautrey, J., Lemoine, C., & Loarer, E. (2005). Age-related differences in the strategies used by middle aged adults to solve a block design task. *International Journal of Aging and Human Development, 60,* 159–182.

Rozin, P. (1990). The importance of social factors in understanding the acquisition of food habits. In E. D. Capaldi & T. L. Powley (Eds.), *Taste, experience, and feeding.* Washington, DC: American Psychological Association.

Rozin, P., Kabnick, K., Pete, E., Fischler, C., & Shields, C. (2003). The ecology of eating: Smaller portion sizes in France than in the United States help explain the French paradox. *Psychological Science, 14,* 450–454.

Rubenstein, C. (1982, July). Psychology's fruit flies. *Psychology Today,* pp. 83–84.

Rubichi, S., Ricci, F., Padovani, R., & Scaglietti, L. (2005). Hypnotic susceptibility, baseline attentional functioning, and the Stroop task. *Consciousness and Cognition: An International Journal, 14,* 296–303.

Rubin, D. C. (1985, September). The subtle deceiver: Recalling our past. *Psychology Today,* pp. 39–46.

Rubin, D. C. (1995). *Memory in oral traditions.* New York: Oxford University Press.

Rubin, D. C. (1999). *Remembering our past: Studies in autobiographical memory.* New York: Cambridge University Press.

Rubin, B. D., & Katz, L. C. (1999). Optical imaging of odorant representations in the mammalian olfactory bulb. *Neuron 23,* 499–511.

Ruby, C. L. (2002). Are terrorists mentally deranged? *Analyses of Social Issues and Public Policy, 2,* 15–26.

Rudman, L. A., & Glick, P. (2001). Prescriptive gender stereotypes and backlash toward agentic women. *Journal of Social Issues, 57,* 743–762.

Runco, M. A., & Sakamoto, S. O. (1993). Reaching creatively gifted students through their learning styles. In R. M. Milgram, R. S. Dunn, & G. E. Price (Eds.), *Teaching and counseling gifted and talented adolescents: An international learning style perspective.* Westport, CT: Praeger/Greenwood.

Ruscher, J. B., Fiske, S. T., & Schnake, S. B. (2000). The motivated tactician's juggling act: Compatible vs. incompatible impression goals. *British Journal of Social Psychology, 39,* 241–256.

Russell, J. A. (1991). Culture and the categorization of emotion. *Psychological Bulletin, 110,* 426–450.

Russell, J. A., & Sato, K. (1995). Comparing emotion words between languages. *Journal of Cross Cultural Psychology, 26,* 384–391.

Russo, N. (1981).Women in psychology. In L. T. Benjamin, Jr. & K. D. Lowman (Eds.), *Activities handbook for the teaching of psychology.* Washington, DC: American Psychological Association.

Russo, R., & Parkin, A. J. (1993). Age differences in implicit memory: More apparent than real. *Memory & Cognition, 21,* 73–80.

Rutter, M. (2002). Nature, nurture, and development: From evangelism through science toward policy and practice. *Child Development, 73,* 1–21.

Ryan, R. M., & Deci, E. L. (2000). Intrinsic and extrinsic motivations: Classic definitions and new directions. *Contemporary Educational Psychology, 25,* 54–67.

Rychlak, J. (1997). *In defense of human consciousness.* Washington, DC: American Psychological Association.

Ryff, C. D., & Singer, B. (2003). Flourishing under fire: Resilience as a prototype of challenged thriving. In C. L. Keyes & J. Haidt (Eds.). *Flourishing: Positive psychology and the life well-lived,* pp. 15–36. Washington, DC: American Psychological Association.

Rymer, J., Wilson, R., & Ballard, K. (2003). Making decisions about hormone replacement therapy. *British Medical Journal, 326,* 322–326.

Rymer, R. (1994). *Genie: A scientific tragedy.* New York: Penguin.

Saab, C. Y., & Willis, W. D. (2003). The cerebellum: Organization, functions and its role in nociception. *Brain Research Reviews, 42,* 85–95.

Saariluoma, P., Karlsson, H., Lyytinen, H., Teräs, M., & Geisler, F. (2004). Visuospatial representations used by chess experts: A preliminary study. *European Journal of Cognitive Psychology, 16,* 753–766.

Saariluoma, P., & Laine, T. (2001). Novice construction of chess memory. *Scandinavian Journal of Psychology, 42,* 137–146.

Saarni, C. (1999). *Developing emotional competence.* New York: Guilford.

Sabater, J., & Sierra, C. (2005). Review on computational trust and reputation models. *Artificial Intelligence Review, 24,* 33–60.

Sachs-Ericsson, N., Joiner, T., Plant, E. A., & Blazer, D. G. (2005). The influence of depression on cognitive decline in community-dwelling elderly persons. *American Journal of Geriatric Psychiatry, 13,* 402–408.

Sackeim, H. A., Haskett, R. F., Mulsant, B. H., Thase, M. E., Mann, J. J., Pettinati, H. M., Greenberg, R. M., Crowe, R. R., Cooper, T. B., & Prudic, J. (2001). Continuation pharmacotherapy in the prevention of relapse following electroconvulsive therapy: A randomized controlled trial. *Journal of the American Medical Association, 285,* 1299–1307.

Sackheim, H. A., Luber, B., Katzman, G. P., et al. (1996, September). The effects of electroconvulsive therapy on quantitative electroencephalograms. *Archives of General Psychiatry, 53,* 814–824.

Sacks, O. (2003, July 28). The mind's eye. *The New Yorker,* pp. 48–59.

Saczynski, J., Willis, S., and Schaie, K. (2002). Strategy use in reasoning training with older adults. *Aging, Neuropsychology, & Cognition, 9,* 48–60.

Sadker, M., & Sadker, D. (1994). *Failing at fairness: How America's schools cheat girls*. New York: Scribners.

Saffran, E. M., & Schwartz, M. F. (2003). Language. In M. Gallagher & R. J. Nelson (Eds.), *Handbook of psychology: Biological psychology* (Vol. 3, pp. 595–636). New York: Wiley.

Sagi, A., Koren-Karie, N., Gini, M., Ziv, Y., & Joels, T. (2002). Shedding further light on the effects of various types and quality of early child care on infant-mother attachment relationship: The Haifa Study of Early Child Care. *Child Development, 73,* 1166–1186.

Saks, M. J., & Koehler, J. J. (2005, August 5). The coming paradigm shift in forensic identification science. *Science, 309,* 892–895.

Salovey, P., Rothman, A. J., Detweiler, J. B., & Steward, W. T. (2000). Emotional states and physical health. *American Psychologist, 55,* 110–121.

Salthouse, T. A. (1996, July). The processing-speed theory of adult age differences in cognition. *Psychological Review, 103,* 403–428.

Salvy, S. J., Mulick, J. A., & Butter, E. (2004). Contingent electric shock (SIBIS) and a conditioned punisher eliminate severe head banging in a preschool child. *Behavioral Interventions, 19,* 59–72.

Samantaray, S. K., Srivastava, M., & Mishra, P. K. (2002). Fostering self concept and self actualization as bases for empowering women in national development: A challenge for the new millennium. *Social Science International, 18,* 58–63.

Sams, M. Hari, R., Rif, J., & Knuutila, J. (1993). The human auditory memory trace persists about 10 sec: Neuromagnetic evidence. *Journal of Cognitive Neuroscience, 5,* 363–370.

Samuda, R. J. (1998). *Psychological testing of American minorities: Issues and consequences*. Thousand Oaks, CA: Sage.

Samuda, R. J., & Lewis, J. E. (1999). Multicultural assessment for the twenty-first century. In W. J. Lonner & D. L. Dinnel (Eds.), *Merging past, present, and future in cross-cultural psychology: Selected papers from the Fourteenth International Congress of the International Association for Cross-Cultural Psychology* (pp. 137–145). Lisse, Netherlands: Swets & Zeitlinger.

Sandoval, J., Frisby, C. L., Geisinger, K. F., Scheuneman, J. D., & Grenier, J. R. (Eds.). (1998). *Test interpretation and diversity: Achieving equity in assessment*. Washington, DC: American Psychological Association.

Sansone, C., & Harackiewicz, J. M. (Eds.). (2000). *Intrinsic and extrinsic motivation*. Orlando, FL: Academic Press.

Sanz, C. (2000). Implementing LIBRA for the design of experimental research in SLA. *Language Learning and Technology* Millennial issue *13,* 27–31.

Saper, C. B., Lu, J., Chou, T. C., & Gooley, J. (2005). The hypothalamic integrator for circadian rhythms. *Trends in Neuroscience, 28,* 152–157.

Sapolsky, R. M. (2003). Gene therapy for psychiatric disorders. *American Journal of Psychiatry, 160,* 208–220.

Saudino, K. J., & Plomin, R. (1996). Personality and behavioral genetics: Where have we been and where are we going? *Journal of Research in Personality, 30,* 335–347.

Savage-Rumbaugh, E. S., Murphy, J., Sevcik, R. A., Williams, S., Brakke, K., & Rumbaugh, D. M. (1993). Language comprehension in ape and child. *Monographs of the Society for Research in Child Development, 58*(3, 4).

Savage-Rumbaugh, S., & Brakke, K. E. (1996). Animal language: Methodological and interpretive issues. In M. Bekoff & D. Jamieson (Eds.), *Readings in animal cognition*. Cambridge, MA: MIT.

Sawa, A., & Snyder, S. H. (2002, April 26). Schizophrenia: Diverse approaches to a complex disease. *Science, 296,* 692–695.

Saxe, R., Carey, S., & Kanwisher, N. (2004). Understanding other minds: A linking developmental psychology and functional neuroimaging. *Annual Review of Psychology, 55,* 87–124.

Sayette, M. A. (1993). An appraisal disruption model of alcohol's effects on stress responses in social drinkers. *Psychological Bulletin, 114,* 459–476.

Saywitz, K., & Goodman, G. (1990). Unpublished study reported in Goleman, D. (1990, November 6). Doubts rise on children as witnesses. *The New York Times,* pp. C-1, C-6.

Scarr, S. (1993). Genes, experience, and development. In D. Magnusson, P. Jules, & M. Casaer (Eds.), *Longitudinal research on individual development: Present status and future perspectives. European network on longitudinal studies on individual development, 8.* Cambridge, England: Cambridge University Press.

Scarr, S. (1998). American child care today. *American Psychologist, 53,* 95–108.

Scarr, S., & Weinberg, R. A. (1976). I.Q. test performance of black children adopted by white families. *American Psychologist, 31,* 726–739.

Scaturo, D. J. (2004). Fundamental clinical dilemmas in contemporary group psychotherapy. *Group Analysis, 37,* 201–217.

Schaaf, J. M., Alexander, K. W., Goodman, G. S., Ghetti, S., Edelstein, R. S., & Castelli, P. (2002). Children's eyewitness memory: True disclosures and false reports. In B. L. Bottoms, M. Bull Kovera, et al. (Eds.), *Children, social science, and the law* (pp. 342–377). New York: Cambridge University Press.

Schab, F. R., & Crowder, R. G. (Eds.). (1995). *Memory for odors*. Mahwah, NJ: Erlbaum.

Schachter, S., & Singer, J. E. (1962). Cognitive, social, and physiological determinants of emotional state. *Psychological Review, 69,* 379–399.

Schacter, D. L., & Badgaiyan, R. D. (2001). Neuroimaging of priming: New perspectives on implicit and explicit memory. *Current Directions in Psychological Science, 10,* 1–4.

Schacter, D. L. & Scarry, E. (Eds.) (2000). *Memory, brain, and belief*. Cambridge, MA: Harvard University Press.

Schacter, D. L., Wagner, A. D., & Buckner, R. L. (2000). Memory systems of 1999. In E. Tulving, F. I. Craik, I. M. Fergus, et al. (Eds.), *The Oxford handbook of memory*. New York: Oxford University Press.

Schaefer, R. T. (2000). *Sociology: A brief introduction* (3rd ed.). Boston: McGraw-Hill.

Schafer, M., & Crichlow, S. (1996). Antecedents of groupthink: A quantitative study. *Journal of Conflict Resolution, 40,* 415–435.

Schaie, K. W. (1991). Developmental designs revisited. In S. H. Cohen & H. W. Reese (Eds.), *Life-span developmental psychology: Methodological innovations*. Hillsdale, NJ: Erlbaum.

Schaie, K. W. (1994). The course of adult intellectual development. *American Psychologist, 49,* 304–313.

Schaie, K. W. (1996). Intellectual development in adulthood. In J. E. Birren & K. W. Schaie (Eds.), *Handbook of the psychology of aging* (4th ed., pp. 266–286). San Diego, CA: Academic Press.

Schaller, M., & Crandall, C. S. (Eds.) (2004). *The Psychological foundations of culture*. Mahwah, NJ: Lawrence Erlbaum Associates.

Schaller, M., Asp, C. H., Rosell, M. C., & Heim, S. J. (1996). Training in statistical reasoning inhibits the formation of erroneous group stereotypes. *Personality and Social Psychology Bulletin, 22*, 829–844.

Schapira, A. H. V. (1999). Clinical review: Parkinson's disease. *British Medical Journal, 318*, 311–314.

Schechter, T., Finkelstein, Y., Koren, G. (2005). Pregnant "DES daughters" and their offspring. *Canadian Family Physician, 51*, 493–494.

Schedlowski, M., & Tewes, U. (Eds.) (1999). *Psychoneuroimmunology: An interdisciplinary introduction*. New York: Plenum.

Scheff, T. J. (1999). *Being mentally ill: A sociological theory* (3rd ed.). Hawthrone, NY: Aldine de Gruyter.

Scheier, M. F., Carver, C. S., & Bridges, M. W. (1994). Distinguishing optimism from neuroticism (and trait anxiety, self-mastery, and self-esteem): A revision of the Life Orientation Test. *Journal of Personality and Social Psychology, 67*, 1063–1078.

Schiffer, A. A., Pedersen, S. S., Widdershoven, J. W., Hendriks, E. H., Winter, J. B., & Denollet, J. (2005). The distressed (type D) personality is independently associated with impaired health status and increased depressive symptoms in chronic heart failure. *European Journal of Cardiovascular Prevention and Rehabilitation, 12*, 341–346.

Schiffman, S. S., Graham, B. G., Sattely-Miller, E. A., & Zervakis, J. (2002). Taste, smell and neuropsychological performance of individuals at familial risk for Alzheimer's disease. *Neurobiology of Aging, 23*, 397–404.

Schillinger, D., Bindman, A., Wang, F., Stewart, A., & Piette, J. (2004). Functional health literacy and the quality of physician-patient communication among diabetes patients. *Patient Education and Counseling, 52*, 315–323.

Schmidt, N. B., Kotov, R., & Joiner, T. E., Jr. (2004). *Taxometrics: Toward a new diagnostic scheme for psychopathology*. Washington, DC: American Psychological Association.

Schneider, D. J. (2003). *The psychology of stereotyping*. New York: Guilford Press.

Schnurr, P. P., & Cozza, S. J. (Eds.). (2004). *Iraq war clinician guide* (2nd ed.). Washington, DC: National Center for Post-Traumatic Stress Disorder.

Schoen, L. M. (1996). Mnemopoly: Board games and mnemonics. *Teaching of Psychology, 23*, 30–32.

Schoenpflug, U. (2003). The handbook of culture and psychology. *Journal of Cross-Cultural Psychology, 34*, 481–483.

Schofield, W., & Vaughan-Jackson, P. (1913). *What a boy should know*. New York: Cassell.

Schorr, A. (2001). Appraisal: The evolution of an idea. In K. R. Scherer, A. Schorr, et al. (Eds.), *Appraisal processes in emotion: Theory, methods, research. Series in affective science*, pp. 20–34. London: Oxford University Press.

Schredl, M., & Piel, E. (2005). Gender differences in dreaming: Are they stable over time? *Personality and Individual Differences, 39*, 309–316.

Schretlen, D., Pearlson, G. D., Anthony, J. C., Aylward, E. H., Augustine, A. M., Davis, A., & Barta, P. (2000). Elucidating the contributions of processing speed, executive ability, and frontal lobe volume to normal age-related differences in fluid intelligence. *Journal of the International Neuropsychological Society, 6*, 52–61.

Schupp, H. T., Öhman, A., Junghöfer, M., Weike, A., Stockburger, J., & Hamm, A. O. (2004). The facilitated processing of threatening faces: An ERP analysis. *Emotion, 4*, 189–200.

Schutt, R. K. (2001). *Investigating the social world: The process and practice of research*. Thousand Oaks, CA: Sage.

Schwartz, B. L. (2001). The relation of tip-of-the-tongue states and retrieval time. *Memory & Cognition, 29*, 117–126.

Schwartz, B. L. (2002). The phenomenology of naturally-occurring tip-of-the-tongue states: A diary study. In S. P. Shohov (Ed.), *Advances in psychology research* (Vol. 8, pp. 73–84). Huntington, NY: Nova.

Schwartz, B. L., Travis, D. M., Castro, A. M., & Smith, S. M. (2000). The phenomenology of real and illusory tip-of-the-tongue states. *Memory & Cognition, 28*, 18–27.

Schwartz, J., & Wald, M. L. (2003). NASA's curse?: "Groupthink" is 30 years old, and still going strong. *The New York Times*, p. C1.

Schwartz, S., & Maquet, P. (2002). Sleep imaging and the neuro-psychological assessment of dreams. *Trends in Cognitive Science, 6*, 23–30.

Schwarz, N., Bless, H., Strack, F., Klumpp, G., et al. (1991). Ease of retrieval as information: Another look at the avail-ability heuristic. *Journal of Personality and Social Psychology, 61*, 195–202.

Scullin, M. H., Kanaya, T., & Ceci, S. J. (2002). Measurement of individual differences in children's suggestibility across situations. *Journal of Experimental Psychology: Applied, 8*, 233–246.

Sears, D. O. (1986). College sophomores in the laboratory: Influences of a narrow data base on social psychology's view of human nature. *Journal of Personality and Social Psychology, 51*, 515–530.

Sears, R. R. (1977). Sources of life satisfaction of the Terman gifted men. *American Psychologist, 32*, 119–128.

Sebel, P. S., Bonke, B., & Winograd, E. (Eds.). (1993). *Memory and awareness in anesthesia*. Englewood Cliffs, NJ: Prentice-Hall.

Seeley, R., Stephens, T., & Tate, P. (2000). *Anatomy & Physiology* (5th ed., p. 384). Boston: McGraw-Hill.

Segal, N. L. (1993). Twin, sibling, and adoption methods: Tests of evolutionary hypotheses. *American Psychologist, 48*, 943–956.

Segall, M. H., Campbell, D. T., & Herskovits, M. J. (1966). *The influence of culture on visual perception*. New York: Bobbs-Merrill.

Segerstrom, S. C., & Miller, G. E. (2004). Psychological stress and the human immune system: A meta-analytic study of 30 years if inquiry. *Psychological Bulletin, 130*, 601–630.

Seibt, B., & Förster, J. (2005). Stereotype threat and performance: How self-stereotypes influence processing by inducing regulatory foci. *Journal of Personality and Social Psychology, 87*, 38–56.

Seidenberg, M. S., & Petitto, L. A. (1987). Communication, symbolic communication, and language: Comment on Savage-Rumbaugh, McDonald, Sevcik, Hopkins, & Rupert (1986). *Journal of Experimental Psychology: General, 116*, 279–287.

Seligman, M. E. P. (1975). *Helplessness: On depression, development, and death*. San Francisco: Freeman.

Seligman, M. E. P. (1988, October). Baby boomer blues. *Psychology Today*, p. 54.

Seligman, M. E. P. (1995, December). The effectiveness of psychotherapy: The *Consumer Reports* study. *American Psychologist, 50*, 965–974.

Seligman, M. E. P. (1996, October). Science as an ally of practice. *American Psychologist, 51*, 1072–1079.

Selikowitz, M. (2003). Down syndrome across the lifespan. *Journal of Intellectual and Developmental Disability, 28,* 312–313.

Selkoe, D. J. (1997, January 31). Alzheimer's disease: Genotypes, phenotype, and treatments. *Science, 275,* 630–631.

Selkoe, D. J. (2002). Alzheimer's disease is a synaptic failure. *Science, 298,* 789–791.

Sells, R. (1994, August). *Homosexuality study.* Paper presented at the annual meeting of the American Statistical Assocation, Toronto.

Selsky, A. (1997, February 16). African males face circumcision rite. *The Boston Globe,* p. C7.

Seltzer, L. (1986). *Paradoxical strategies in psychotherapy.* New York: Wiley.

Selye, H. (1976). *The stress of life.* New York: McGraw-Hill.

Selye, H. (1993). History of the stress concept. In L. Goldberger & S. Breznitz (Eds.), *Handbook of stress: Theoretical and clinical aspects* (2nd ed.). New York: Free Press.

Semler, C. N., & Harvey, A. G. (2005). Misperception of sleep can adversely affect daytime functioning in insomnia. *Behaviour Research and Therapy, 43,* 843–856.

Seroczynski, A. D., Jacquez, F. M., & Cole, D. A. (2003). Depression and suicide during adolescence. In G. R. Adams, M. D. Berzonsky (Eds.), *Blackwell handbook of adolescence.* Malden, MA: Blackwell Publishers.

Serok, S. (2000). *Innovative applications of gestalt therapy.* New York: Krieger.

Serpell, R. (2000). Intelligence and culture. In R. Sternberg (Ed.), *Handbook of intelligence.* Cambridge, England: Cambridge University Press.

Seventh U.S. Circuit Court of Appeals. (2001). *Chicago Firefighters Local 2, et al. v. City of Chicago, et al.* Nos. 00–1272, 00–1312, 00–1313, 00–1314, and 00–1330. Chicago, IL.

Seyfarth, R. M., & Cheney, D. L. (1992, December). Meaning and mind in monkeys (vocalizations and intent). *Scientific American, 267,* pp. 122–128.

Seyfarth, R., & Cheney, D. (1996). Inside the mind of a monkey. In M. Bekoff & D. Jamieson (Eds.), *Readings in animal cognition.* Cambridge, MA: MIT.

Shadish, W. R., Cook, T. D., & Campbell, D. T. (2002). *Experimental and quasi-experimental designs for generalized causal inference.* Boston: Houghton Mifflin.

Shapiro, A. P. (1996). *Hypertension and stress: A unified concept.* Mahwah, NJ: Erlbaum.

Shapiro, Y., & Gabbard, G. O. (1994). A reconsideration of altruism from an evolutionary and psychodynamic perspective. *Ethics & Behavior, 4,* 23–42.

Shappell, S., & Wiegmann, D. A. (2003). *A human error approach to aviation accident analysis: The human factors analysis and classification system.* Aldershot, England: Ashgate.

Sharma, J., Angelucci, A., & Sur, M. (2000). Induction of visual orientation modules in auditory cortex. *Nature, 404,* 841–847.

Sharma, S., Ghosh, S. N., & Spielberger, C. D. (1995). Anxiety, anger expression and chronic gastric ulcer. *Psychological Studies, 40,* 187–191.

Shaughnessy, J. J., Zechmeister, E. B., & Zechmeister, J. S. (2000). *Research methods in psychology* (5th ed.). New York: McGraw-Hill.

Shaywitz, B. A., Shaywitz, S. E., Pugh, K. R., Constable, R. T., Skudlarski, P., Fulbright, R. K., Bronen, R. A., Fletcher, J. M., Shankweller, D. P., Katz, L., & Gore, J. C. (1995, February 16). Sex differences in the functional organization of the brain for language. *Nature, 373,* 607–609.

Shelton, R. C., Keller, M. B., Gelenberg, A., Dunner, D. L., Hirschfeld, R. M. A., Thase, M. E., Russell, J., Lydiard, R. B., Crits-Cristoph, P., Gallop, R., Todd, L., Hellerstein, D., Goodnick, P., Keitner, G., Stahl, S. M., & Halbreich, R. U. (2002). The effectiveness of St. John's wort in major depression: A multi-center, randomized placebo-controlled trial. *Journal of the American Medical Association, 285,* 1978–1986.

Shepard, R., & Metzler, J. (1971). Mental rotation of three dimensional objects. *Science, 171,* 701–703.

Shepard, R. N., Metzler, J., Bisiach, E., Luzzati, C., Kosslyn, S. M., Thompson, W. L., Kim, I., & Alpert, N. M. (2000). Part IV: Imagery. In M. S. Gazzaniga et al. (Eds.), *Cognitive neuroscience: A reader.* Malden, MA: Blackwell.

Sheth, B. R., & Bhattacharya, D. W. (2004). On the neural track of eureka. *Program No. 138.4.* Washington, DC: Society for Neuroscience, 2004.

Shi, P., Huang, J. F., & Zhang, Y. P. (2005). Bitter and sweet/umami taste receptors with differently evolutionary pathways. *Yi Chuan Xue Bao, 32,* 346–353.

Shier, D., Butler, J., & Lewis, R. (2000). *Hole's essentials of human anatomy and physiology* (7th ed., p. 283). Boston: McGraw-Hill.

Shimono, K., & Wade N. J. (2002). Monocular alignment in different depth planes. *Vision Research, 42,* 1127–1135.

Shnek, Z. M., Foley, F. W., LaRocca, N. G., Smith, C. R., et al. (1995). Psychological predictors of depression in multiple sclerosis. *Journal of Neurologic Rehabilitation, 9,* 15–23.

Shotland, R. L. (1985, June). When bystanders just stand by. *Psychology Today,* pp. 50–55.

Shouler, K. (1992, August). The empire returns. *Sky,* pp. 40–44.

Shriqui, C. L., & Annable, L. (1995). Tardive dyskinesia. In C. L. Shriqui & H. A. Nasrallah (Eds.), *Contemporary issues in the treatment of schizophrenia.* Washington, DC: American Psychiatric Press.

Shuchter, S. R., Downs, N., & Zisook, S. (1996). *Biologically informed psychotherapy for depression.* New York: Guilford Press.

Shultz, S. K., Scherman, A., & Marshall, L. J. (2000). Evaluation of a university-based date rape prevention program: Effect on attitudes and behavior related to rape. *Journal of College Student Development, 41,* 193–201.

Shurkin, J. N. (1992). *Terman's kids: The groundbreaking study of how the gifted grow up.* Boston: Little, Brown.

Shweder, R. (2003). *Why do men barbecue? Recipes for cultural psychology.* Cambridge, MA: Harvard University Press.

Shweder, R. A. (1994). "You're not sick, you're just in love": Emotion as an interpretive system. In P. Ekman & R. J. Davidson (Eds.), *The nature of emotion: Fundamental questions.* New York: Oxford.

Siddle, R., Haddock, G., Tarrier, N., & Faragher, E. B. (2002). Religious delusions in patients admitted to hospital with schizophrenia. *Social Psychiatry and Psychiatric Epidemiology, 37,* 130–138.

Siderowf, A., & Stern, M. (2003). Update on Parkinson disease. *Annals of Internal Medicine, 138,* 651–658.

Siegel, J. M. (1990). Stressful life events and use of physician services among the elderly: The moderating role of pet ownership. *Journal of Personality and Social Psychology, 58,* 1081–1086.

Siegel, J. M. (1993). Companion animals: In sickness and in health. *Journal of Social Issues, 49,* 157–167.

Siegel, J. M. (2003, November). Why we sleep. *Scientific American,* pp. 92–97.

Siegert, R. J., & Ward, T. (2002). Clinical psychology and evolutionary psychology: Toward a dialogue. *Review of General Psychology, 6,* 235–259.

Siegler, R. S. (1998). *Children's thinking.* (3rd ed.). Upper Saddle River, NJ: Prentice Hall.

Sigman, M. (1995). Nutrition and child development: More food for thought. *Current Directions in Psychological Science, 4,* 52–55.

Silverman, J. (2001, August 1). Dating violence against adolescent girls linked with teen pregnancy, suicide attempts, and other health risk behaviors. *Journal of the American Medical Association, 286,* 15–20.

Silverman, K., Evans, S. M., Strain, E. C., & Griffiths, R. R. (1992, October 15). Withdrawal syndrome after the double-blind cessation of caffeine consumption. *New England Journal of Medicine, 327,* 1109–1114.

Simcock, G., & Hayne, H. (2002). Breaking the barrier? Children fail to translate their preverbal memories into language. *Psychological Science, 13,* 225–231.

Simmons, D. C., Kameenui, E. J., & Chard, D. J. (1998). General education teachers' assumptions about learning and students with learning disabilities: Design-of-instruction analysis. *Learning Disability Quarterly, 21,* 6–21.

Simmons, R., & Blyth, D. (1987). *Moving into adolescence.* New York: Aldine de Gruyter.

Simons, W., & Dierick, M. (2005). Transcranial magnetic stimulation as a therapeutic tool in psychiatry. *World Journal of Biological Psychiatry, 6,* 6–25.

Simonton, D. K. (2000a). Archival research. In A. E. Kazdin (Ed.), *Encyclopedia of psychology* (Vol. 1). Washington, DC: American Psychological Association.

Simonton, D. K. (2000b). Creativity: Cognitive, personal, developmental, and social aspects. *American Psychologist, 55,* 151–158.

Simonton, D. K. (2003). Scientific creativity as constrained stochastic behavior: the integration of product, person, and process perspectives. *Psychological Bulletin, 129,* 475–494.

Singer, J. L. (1975). *The inner world of daydreaming.* New York: Harper & Row.

Singh, S., Wulf, D., Samara, R, & Cuca, Y. P. (2000). Gender differences in the timeing of first intercourse: Data from 14 countries. *International Family Planning Perspectives, 26,* 21–28+43.

Sizemore, C. C. (1989). *A mind of my own: The woman who was known as Eve tells the story of her triumph over multiple personality disorder.* New York: Morrow.

Skinner, B. F. (1957). *Verbal behavior.* New York: Appleton-Century-Crofts.

Skinner, B. F. (1975). The steep and thorny road to a science of behavior. *American Psychologist, 30,* 42–49.

Slater, A. (1996). The organization of visual perception in early infancy. In F. Vital-Durand, J. Atkinson, & O. J. Braddick (Eds.), *Infant vision. The European brain and behaviour society publication series* (Vol. 2). Oxford, England: Oxford University Press.

Slater, E., & Meyer, A. (1959). Contributions to a pathography of the musicians. *Confinia Psychiatrica.* Reprinted in K. R. Jamison, *Touched with fire: Manic-depressive illness and the artistic temperament.* New York: Free Press.

Sleek, S. (1997 June). Can "emotional intelligence" be taught in today's schools? *APA Monitor,* p. 25.

Sloan, E. P., Hauri, P., Bootzin, R., Morin, C., et al. (1993). The nuts and bolts of behavioral therapy for insomnia. *Journal of Psychosomatic Research, 37* (Suppl.), 19–37.

Smetana, J. G. (2005). Adolescent-parent conflict: Resistance and subversion as developmental process. In L. Nucci (Ed.), *Conflict, contradiction, and contrarian elements in moral development and education.* (pp. 69–91). Mahwah, NJ: Lawrence Erlbaum Associates.

Smetana, J., Daddis, C., and Chuang, S. (2003). "Clean your room!" A longitudinal investigation of adolescent-parent conflict and conflict resolution in middle-class African American families. *Journal of Adolescent Research, 18,* 631–650.

Smith, C. A., & Lazarus, R. S. (2001). Appraisal components, core relational themes, and the emotions. In W. G. Parrott (Ed.), *Emotions in social psychology: Essential readings* (pp. 94–114). Philadelphia: Psychology Press.

Smith, D. (October 2001). Can't get your 40 winks? Here's what the sleep experts advise. *Monitor on Psychology, 37.*

Smith, D. V., & Margolskee, R. F. (March 2001). Making sense of taste. *Scientific American,* pp. 32–39.

Smith, E. (1988, May). Fighting cancerous feelings. *Psychology Today,* pp. 22–23.

Smith, E. E. (2000). Neural bases of human working memory. *Current Directions in Psychological Science, 9,* 45–49.

Smith, G. B. (2005, July 17). Secret mob cop tapes: Talk about deaths key to feds's case. "I've known John (Gotti) since I was a kid, how do I disrespect this guy?" accused cop says. *Daily News* (New York). p. 6.

Smith, K. A., Williams, C., & Cowen, P. J. (2000). Impaired regulation of brain serotonin function during dieting in women recovered from depression. *British Journal of Psychiatry, 176,* 72–75.

Smith, K. R. (2004). Gene therapy: The potential applicability of gene transfer technology to the human germline. *International Journal of Medical Science, 1,* 76–91.

Smith, L. C., Friedman, S., & Paradis, C. (2002). Panic disorder with agoraphobia: Women's issues. In F. Lewis-Hall & T. S. Williams (Eds.), *Psychiatric illness in women: Emerging treatments and research* (pp. 31–55). Washington, DC: American Psychiatric Publishing.

Smith, M., & Lin, K. M. (1996). Gender and ethnic differences in the pharmacogenetics of psychotropics. In M. F. Jensvold, U. Halbreich, & J. A. Hamilton (Eds.), *Psychopharmacology and women: Sex, gender, and hormones.* Washington, DC: American Psychiatric Press.

Smith, M. B. (2003). Moral foundations in research with human participants. In A. E. Kazdin (Ed.), *Methodological issues & strategies in clinical research* (3rd ed.). Washington, DC: American Psychological Association.

Smith, M. L., Glass, G. V., & Miller, T. J. (1980). *The benefits of psychotherapy.* Baltimore: Johns Hopkins University Press.

Smith, M. V. (1996). Linguistic relativity: On hypotheses and confusions. *Communication and Cognition, 29,* 65–90.

Snieder, H., Harshfield, G. A., Barbeau, P., Pollock, D. M., Pollock, J. S., & Treiber, F. A. (2002). Dissecting the genetic architecture of the cardiovascular and renal stress response. *Biological Psychology, 61,* 73–95.

Snyder, C. R. (1999). *Coping: The psychology of what works.* New York: Oxford University Press.

Snyder, D. J., Fast, K., & Bartoshuk, L. M. (2004). Valid comparisons of suprathreshold sensations. *Journal of Consciousness Studies, 11,* 96–112.

Snyder, J., Cramer, A., & Afrank, J. (2005). The contributions of ineffective discipline and parental hostile attributions of child misbehavior to the development of conduct problems at home and school. *Developmental Psychology, 41,* 30–41.

Snyder, M. (2002). Applications of Carl Rogers' theory and practice to couple and family therapy: A response to Harlene Anderson and David Bott. *Journal of Family Therapy, 24,* 317–325.

Sohn, D. (1996). Publication bias and the evaluation of psychotherapy efficacy in reviews of the research literature. *Clinical Psychology Review, 16,* 147–156.

Sokolove, M. (2003, November 16). Should John Hinckley go free? *The New York Times Magazine,* pp. 52–54, 92.

Solms, M. (2005). Neuroscience. In E. S. Person, A. M. Cooper, & G. O. Gabbard, *The American psychiatric publishing textbook of psychoanalysis.* Washington, DC: American Psychiatric Publishing.

Solso, R. L. (1991). *Cognitive psychology* (3rd ed.). Boston: Allyn & Bacon.

Sommer, R., & Sommer, B. (2001). *A practical guide to behavioral research: Tools and techniques* (5th ed.). New York: Oxford University Press.

Sommerhof, G. (2000). *Understanding consciousness: Its function and brain processes.* Thousand Oaks, CA: Sage.

Soussignan, R. (2002). Duchenne smile, emotional experience, and automatic reactivity: A test of the facial feedback hypothesis. *Emotion, 2,* 52–74.

Spangler, W. D. (1992). Validity of questionnaire and TAT measures of need for achievement: Two meta-analyses. *Psychological Bulletin, 112,* 140–154.

Spanos, N. P., Burgess, C. A., Roncon, V., Wallace-Capretta, S., et al. (1993). Surreptitiously observed hypnotic responding in simulators and in skill-trained and untrained high hypnotizables. *Journal of Personality and Social Psychology, 65,* 391–398.

Spearman, C. (1927). *The abilities of man.* London: Macmillan.

Spence, M. J., & DeCasper, A. J. (1982, March). *Human fetuses perceive maternal speech.* Paper presented at the meeting of the International Conference on Infant Studies, Austin, TX.

Spencer, S. J., Fein, S., Zanna, M. P., & Olson, J. M. (Eds.) (2003). *Motivated social perception: The Ontario Symposium* (Vol. 9). Mahwah, NJ: Erlbaum.

Spencer-Rodgers, J., Peng, K., Wang, L., & Hou, Y. (2004). Dialectical self-esteem and East-West differences in psychological well-being. *Personality and Social Psychology Bulletin, 30,* 1416–1432.

Sperry, R. (1982). Some effects of disconnecting the cerebral hemispheres. *Science, 217,* 1223–1226.

Spiegel, D. (1993). Social support: How friends, family, and groups can help. In D. Goleman & J. Gurin (Eds.), *Mind-body medicine.* Yonkers, NY: Consumer Reports Books.

Spiegel, D. (1996). Hypnosis. In R. E. Hales & S. C. Yudofsky (Eds.), *The American Psychiatric Press synopsis of psychiatry.* Washington, DC: American Psychiatric Press.

Spiegel, D. (Ed.). (1999). *Efficacy and cost-effectiveness of psychotherapy.* New York: American Psychiatric Press.

Spiegel, D., & Cardena, E. (1991). Disintegrated experience: The dissociative disorders revisited. *Journal of Abnormal Psychology, 100,* 366–378.

Spiller, L. D., & Wymer, W. W., Jr. (2001). Physicians' perceptions and use of commercial drug information sources: An examination of pharmaceutical marketing to physicians. *Health Marketing Quarterly, 19,* 91–106.

Spillmann, L., & Werner, J. (Eds.). (1990). *Visual perception: The neurophysiological foundations.* San Diego: Academic Press.

Spira, J. (Ed.). (1997). *Group therapy for medically ill patients.* New York: Guilford Press.

Spitz, H. H. (1987). Problem-solving processes in special populations. In J. G. Borkowski & J. D. Day (Eds.), *Cognition in special children: Comparative approaches to retardation, learning disabilities, and giftedness.* Norwood, NJ: Ablex.

Spitzer, R. L., Skodol, A. E., Gibbon, M., & Williams, J. B. W. (1983). *Psychopathology: A case book.* New York: McGraw-Hill.

Sprecher, S., & Hatfield, E. (1996). Premarital sexual standards among U.S. college students: Comparison with Russian and Japanese students. *Archives of Sexual Behavior, 25,* 261–288.

Sprenkle, D. H., & Moon, S. M. (Eds.). (1996). *Research methods in family therapy.* New York: Guilford Press.

Springen, K. (2004, August 9). Sweet, elusive sleep. *Newsweek,* p. 47.

Squire, L. R., Clark, R. E., & Bayley, P. J. (2004). Medial temporal lobe function

and memory. In M. S. Gazzaniga (Ed.), *Cognitive neurosciences* (3rd ed., pp. 691–708). Cambridge, MA: MIT.

Srivastava, A., Locke, E. A., & Bartol, K. M. (2001). Money and subjective well-being: It's not the money, it's the motives. *Journal of Personality and Social Psychology, 80,* 959–971.

St. Onge, S. (1995a). Modeling and role-playing. In M. Ballou (Ed.), *Psychological interventions: A guide to strategies.* Westport, CT: Praeger/ Greenwood.

St. Onge, S. (1995b). Systematic desensitization. In M. Ballou (Ed.), *Psychological interventions: A guide to strategies.* Westport, CT: Praeger/Greenwood.

Staddon, J. E. R., & Cerutti, D. T. (2003). Operant conditioning. *Annual Review of Psychology, 54,* 115–144.

Stankov, L. (2003). Complexity in human intelligence. In R. J. Sternberg, J. Lautrey, et al. (Eds.), *Models of intelligence: International perspectives* (pp. 27–42). Washington, DC: American Psychological Association.

Stanton, A. L., Danoff-Burg, S., Cameron, C. L., Bishop, M., Collins, C. A., Kirk, S. B., Sworowski, L. A., & Twillman, R. (2000). Emotionally expressive coping predicts psychological and physical adjustment to breast cancer. *Journal of Consulting and Clinical Psychology, 68,* 875–882.

Steblay, N., Dysart, J., Fulero, S., & Lindsay, R. C. L. (2003). Eyewitness accuracy rates in police showup and lineup presentations: A meta-analytic comparison. *Law & Human Behavior, 27,* 523–540.

Steele, C. M. (1992, April). Race and the schooling of black America. *Atlantic Monthly,* pp. 37–53.

Steele, C. M. (1997). A threat in the air: How stereotypes shape intellecutal identity and performance. *American Psychologist, 52,* 613–629.

Steele, C. M., & Aronson, J. (1995). Stereotype threat and the intellectual test performance of African Americans. *Journal of Personality and Social Psychology, 69,* 797–811.

Steele, C. M., & Josephs, R. A. (1990). Alcohol myopia: Its prized and dangerous effects. *American Psychologist, 45,* 921–933.

Steele, C. M., Spencer, S. J., & Aronson, J. (2002). Contending with group image. The psychology of stereotype and social identity threat. In M. P. Zanna (Ed.), *Advances in experimental social psychology* (Vol. 34, pp. 379–440). San Diego: Academic Press.

Steen, R. G. (1996). *DNA and destiny: Nature and nurture in human behavior.* New York: Plenum Press.

Stegerwald, F., & Janson, G. R. (2003). Conversion therapy: Ethical considerations in family counseling. *Family Journal—Counseling and Therapy for Couples and Families, 11,* 55–59.

Stein, L. A. R., & Graham, J. R. (2005). Ability of substance abusers to escape detection on the Minnesota Multiphasic Personality Inventory-Adolescent (MMPI-A) in a juvenile correctional facility. *Assessment, 12,* 28–39.

Stein, N. L., Ornstein, P. A., Tversky, B., & Brainerd, C. (Eds.). (1997). *Memory for everyday and emotional events.* Mahwah, NJ: Erlbaum.

Stein, R. (2004, October 19). Is every memory worth keeping? *The Washington Post,* p. A1.

Steinberg, L., & Dornbusch, S. (1991). Negative correlates of part-time employment during adolescence: Replication and elaboration. *Developmental Psychology, 27,* 304.

Steinhausen, H. C., & Spohr, H. L. (1998). Long-term outcome of children with fetal alcohol syndrome: Psychopathology, behavior, and intelligence. *Alcoholism: Clinical & Experimental Research, 22,* 44–51.

Steinmetz, J. E., Kim, J., & Thompson, R. F. (2003). Biological models of associative learning. In M. Gallagher & R. J. Nelson (Eds.), *Handbook of psychology: Biological psychology* (Vol. 3, pp. 499–541). New York: Wiley.

Stenklev, N. C., & Laukli, E. (2004). Cortical cognitive potentials in elderly persons. *Journal of the American Academy of Audiology, 15,* 401–413.

Stern, E., & Silbersweig, D. A. (2001). Advances in functional neuroimaging methodology for the study of brain systems underlying human neuropsychological function and dysfunction. In D.A. Silbersweig & E. Stern (Eds.), *Neuropsychology and functional neuroimaging: Convergence, advances and new directions.* Amsterdam, Netherlands: Swets and Zeitlinger.

Stern, P. (2001, November 2). Sweet dreams are made of this. *Science, 294,* 1047.

Stern, R. M., & Koch, K. L. (1996). Motion sickness and differential susceptibility. *Current Directions in Psychological Science, 5,* 115–120.

Sternberg, R. J. (1982). Reasoning, problem solving, and intelligence. In R. J. Sternberg (Ed.), *Handbook of human intelligence,* pp. 225–307. Cambridge, MA: Cambridge University Press.

Sternberg, R. J. (1990). *Metaphors of mind: Conceptions of the nature of intelligence.* New York: Cambridge University Press.

Sternberg, R. J. (1998). *Successful intelligence: How practical and creative intelligence determine success in life.* New York: Plume.

Sternberg, R. J. (2000). Intelligence and wisdom. In R. J. Sternberg et al. (Eds.), *Handbook of intelligence.* New York: Cambridge University Press.

Sternberg, R. J. (2001). What is the common thread of creativity? Its dialectical relation to intelligence and wisdom. *American Psychologist, 56,* 360–362.

Sternberg, R. J. (2002a). Individual differences in cognitive development. In U. Goswami (Ed.), *Blackwell handbook of childhood cognitive development. Blackwell handbooks of developmental psychology,* pp. 600–619 Malden, MA: Blackwell.

Sternberg, R. J. (Ed.). (2002b). *Why smart people can be so stupid.* New Haven, CT: Yale University Press.

Sternberg, R. J. (2004a). A triangular theory of love. In H. T. Reis & C. E. Rusbult (Eds.), *Close relationships: Key readings.* Philadelphia, PA: Taylor & Francis.

Sternberg, R. J. (2004b). Culture and intelligence. *American Psychologist, 59,* 325–338.

Sternberg, R. J. (2004c). Theory-based university admissions testing for a new millennium. *Educational Psychologist, 39,* 185–198.

Sternberg, R. J., & Beall, A. E. (1991). How can we know what love is? An epistemological analysis. In G. J. O. Fletcher & F. D. Fincham (Eds.), *Cognition in close relationships.* Hillsdale, NJ: Erlbaum.

Sternberg, R. J., & Grigorenko, E. (1997). Are cognitive styles still in style? *American Psychologist, 52,* 700–712.

Sternberg, R. J., & Grigorenko, E. L. (2005). Cultural explorations of the nature of intelligence. In A. F. Healy (Ed.), *Experimental cognitive psychology and its applications* (pp. 225–235). Washington, DC: American Psychological Association.

Sternberg, R. J., & Hedlund, J. (2002). Practical intelligence, "g", and work

psychology. *Human Performance, 15,* 143–160.

Sternberg, R. J., & Jarvin, L. (2003). Alfred Binet's contributions as a paradigm for impact in psychology. In R. J. Sternberg (Ed.), *The anatomy of impact: What makes the great works of psychology great* (pp. 89–107). Washington, DC: American Psychological Association.

Sternberg, R. J., & O'Hara, L. A. (2000). Intelligence and creativity. In R. Sternberg et al. (Eds.), *Handbook of intelligence.* New York: Cambridge University Press.

Sternberg, R. J., & Pretz, J. E. (2005). *Cognition and intelligence: Identifying the mechanisms of the mind.* New York: Cambridge University Press, 2005.

Sternberg, R., & The Rainbow Project Collaborators. (2005). Augmenting the SAT Through Assessments of Analytical, Practical, and Creative Skills. In W. J. Camara, & E. W. Kimmel, *Choosing students: Higher education admissions tools for the 21st century.* Mahwah, NJ: Lawrence Erlbaum Associates.

Sternberg, R. J., Hojjat, M., & Barnes, M. L. (2001). Empirical aspects of a theory of love as a story. *European Journal of Personality, 15,* 1–20.

Sternberg, R. J., Wagner, R. K., Williams, W. M., & Horvath, J. A. (1995). Testing common sense. *American Psychologist, 50,* 912–927.

Stetsenko, A., Little, T. D., Gordeeva, T., Grasshof, M., & Oettingen, G. (2000). Gender effects in children's beliefs about school performance: A cross cultural study. *Child Development, 71,* 517–527.

Stettler, N., Stallings, V. A., Troxel, A. B., Zhao. J., Z., Schinnar, R., Nelson, S. E., Ziegler, E. E., Strom, B. L. (2005). Weight gain in the first week of life and overweight in adulthood. *Circulation, 111,* 1897–1903.

Stevens, C. F. (1979, September). The neuron. *Scientific American,* p. 56.

Stevens, G., & Gardner, S. (1982). *The women of psychology: Pioneers and innovators* (Vol. 1). Cambridge, MA: Schenkman.

Stevenson, H. W., Lee, S., & Mu, X. (2000). Successful achievement in mathematics: China and the United States. In C. F. M. van Lieshout & P. G. Heymans (Eds.), *Developing talent across the life span.* New York: Psychology Press.

Stevenson, R. J., & Case, T. I. (2005). Olfactory imagery: A review.

Psychonomic Bulletin and Review, 12, 244–264.

Steward, E. P. (1995). *Beginning writers in the zone of proximal development.* Hillsdale, NJ: Erlbaum.

Stewart, D. W., & Kamins, M. A. (1993). *Secondary research: Information sources and methods.* (2nd ed.). Newbury Park, CA: Sage.

Stewart-Williams, S., & Podd, J. (2004). The placebo effect: Dissolving the expectancy versus conditioning debate. *Psychological Bulletin, 130,* 324–340.

Stickgold, R. A., Winkelman, J. W., & Wehrwein, P. (2004, January 19). You will start to feel very sleepy . . . . *Newsweek,* pp. 58–60.

Stickgold, R., Hobson, J. A., Fosse, R., & Fosse, M. (2001, November 2). Sleep, learning, and dreams: Off-line memory reprocessing. *Science, 294,* 1052–1057.

Stier, H., & Lewin-Epstein, N. (2000). Women's part-time employment and gender inequality in the family. *Journal of Family Issues, 21,* 390–410.

Stix, G. (1996, January). Listening to culture. *Scientific American,* pp. 16–17.

Stix, G. (2003, September). Ultimate self-improvement. *Scientific American,* pp. 44–45.

Stockton, R., Morran, D. K., & Krieger, K. M. (2004). An overview of current research and best practices for training beginning group leaders. In J. L. DeLucia-Waack, D. A. Gerrity, C. R. Kalodner, & M. T. Riva (Eds.), *Handbook of group counseling and psychotherapy.* Thousand Oaks, CA: Sage Publications.

Stompe, T., Ortwein-Swoboda, G., Ritter, K., & Schanda, H. (2003). Old wine in new bottles? Stability and plasticity of the contents of schizophrenic delusions. *Psychopathology, 36,* 6–12.

Stone, J. (2002). Battling doubt by avoiding practice: The effects of stereotype threat on self-handicapping in white athletes. *Personality and Social Psychology Bulletin, 28,* 1667–1678.

Storm, L., & Ertel, S. (2001). Does psi exist? Comments on Milton and Wiseman's (1999) meta-analysis of Ganzfeld's research. *Psychological Bulletin, 127,* 424–433.

Strathern, A., & Stewart, P. J. (2003). *Landscape, memory and history: Anthropological perspectives.* London: Pluto Press.

Strauss, E. (1998, May 8). Writing, speech separated in split brain. *Science, 280,* 287.

Streissguth, A. (1997). *Fetal alcohol spectrum disorder: A guide for families and communities.* Baltimore, MD: Brookes Publishing Co.

Streissguth, A. P., Barr, H. M., Bookstein, F. L., Sampson, P. D., & Olson, H. C. (1999). The long-term neurocognitive consequences of prenatal alcohol exposure: A 14-year study. *Psychological Science, 10,* 186–190.

Strickland, B. R. (1992). Women and depression. *Current Directions in Psychological Science, 1,* 132–135.

Striegel-Moore, R. H., & Smolak, L. (Eds.) (2001). *Eating disorders: Innovative directions in research and practice.* Washington, DC: American Psychological Association.

Stroebe, M. S., Stroebe, W., & Hansson, R. O. (Eds.). (1993). *Handbook of bereavement: Theory, research, and intervention.* Cambridge, England: Cambridge University Press.

Stronski, S. M., Ireland, M., & Michaud, P. (2000). Protective correlates of stages in adolescent substance use: A Swiss national study. *Journal of Adolescent Health, 26,* 420–427.

Strube, M. (Ed.). (1990). Type A behavior [Special issue]. *Journal of Social Behavior and Personality, 5.*

Strupp, H. H. (1996, October). The tripartite model and the *Consumer Reports* study. *American Psychologist, 51,* 1017–1024.

Strupp, H. H., & Binder, J. L. (1992). Current developments in psychotherapy. *The Independent Practitioner, 12,* 119–124.

Sue, D. (1979). Erotic fantasies of college students during coitus. *Journal of Sex Research, 15,* 299–305.

Sue, D. W., & Sue, D. (1999). *Counseling the culturally different: Theory and practice* (3rd ed.). New York: Wiley.

Sue, D. W., Sue, D., & Sue, S. (1990). *Understanding abnormal behavior* (3rd ed.). Boston: Houghton-Mifflin.

Suh, E. M. (2002). Culture, identity consistency, and subjective well-being. *Journal of Personality & Social Psychology, 83,* 1378–1391.

Suhail, K., & Chaudhry, H. R. (2004). Predictors of subjective well-being in an Eastern Muslim culture. *Journal of Social and Clinical Psychology, 23,* 359–376.

Sulzer-Azaroff, B., & Mayer, R. (1991). *Behavior analysis and lasting change.* New York: Holt.

Sun, T., Patoine, C., Abu-Khalil, A., Visvader, J., Sum, E., Cherry, T. J.,

Orkink, S. H., Geschwind, D. H., & Walsh, C. A. (2005, June 17). Early asymmetry of gene transcriptions in embryonic human left and right cerebral cortex. *Science, 308,* 1794–1796.

Super, C. M. (1980). Cognitive development: Looking across at growing up. In C. M. Super & S. Harakness (Eds.), *New directions for child development: Anthropological perspectives on child development* (pp. 59–69). San Francisco: Jossey-Bass.

Surette, R. (2002). Self-reported copycat crime among a population of serious and violent juvenile offenders. *Crime & Delinquency, 48,* 46–69.

Susser, E. S., Herman, D. B., & Aaron, B. (2002, August). Combating the terror of terrorism. *Scientific American,* pp. 70–77.

Suzuki, L., & Aronson, J. (2005). The cultural malleability of intelligence and its impact on the racial/ethnic hierarchy. *Psychology, Public Policy, and Law, 11,* 320–327.

Svarstad, B. (1976). Physician-patient communication and patient conformity with medical advice. In D. Mechanic (Ed.), *The growth of bureaucratic medicine.* New York: Wiley.

Svartdal, F. (2003). Extinction after partial reinforcement: Predicted vs. judged persistence. *Scandinavian Journal of Psychology, 44,* 55–64.

Swanson, H. L., Harris, K. R., & Graham, S. (Eds.). (2003). *Handbook of learning disabilities.* New York: Guilford Press.

Swets, J. A., & Bjork, R.A. (1990). Enhancing human performance: An evaluation of "new age" techniques considered by the U.S. Army. *Psychological Science, 1,* 85–96.

Szasz, T. (1982). The psychiatric will: A new mechanism for protecting persons against "psychosis" and psychiatry. *American Psychologist, 37,* 762–770.

Szasz, T. (2004). "Knowing what ain't so": R. D. Laing and Thomas Szasz. *Psychoanalytic Review, 91,* 331–346.

Szasz, T. S. (1994). *Cruel compassion: Psychiatric control of society's unwanted.* New York: Wiley.

Szegedy-Maszak, M. (2003, January 13). The sound of unsound minds. *U.S. News & World Report,* pp. 45–46.

Szurman, P., Warga, M., Roters, S., Grisanti, S., Heimann, U., Aisenbrey, S., Rohrbach, J. M., Sellhaus, B., Ziemssen, F., & Bartz-Schmidt, K. U. (2005). Experimental implantation and long-term testing of an intraocular vision aid in rabbits. *Archives of Ophthalmology, 123*, 964–969.

Tabakoff, B., & Hoffman, P. L. (1996). Effect of alcohol on neurotransmitters and their receptors and enzymes. In H. Begleiter, & B. Kissin (Eds.), *The pharmacology of alcohol and alcohol dependence. Alcohol and alcoholism, No. 2.* New York: Oxford University Press.

Tajfel, H., & Turner, J. C. (2004). The social identity theory of intergroup Behavior. In J. T. Jost & J. Sidanius (Eds.), *Political psychology: Key readings.* New York: Psychology Press.

Takahashi, M., Nakata, A., Haratani, T., Ogawa, Y., & Arito, H. (2004). Post-lunch nap as a worksite intervention to promote alertness on the job. *Ergonomics, 47*, 1003–1013.

Talarico, J. M., & Rubin, D. C. (2003). Confidence, not consistency, characterizes flashbulb memories. *Psychological Science, 14*, 455–461.

Tan, V. L., & Hicks, R. A. (1995). Type A-B behavior and nightmare types among college students. *Perceptual and Motor Skills, 81*, 15–19.

Tangney, J., & Dearing, R. (2002). Gender differences in morality. In R. Bornstein & J. Masling (Eds.), *The psychodynamics of gender and gender role.* Washington, DC: American Psychological Association.

Tanner, J. M. (1978). *Education and physical growth* (2nd ed.). New York: International Universities Press.

Tanner, J. M. (1990). *Foetus into man: Physical growth from conception to maturity* (Rev. ed.). Cambridge, MA: Harvard University Press.

Taras, H., & Potts-Datema, W. (2005). Chronic health conditions and student performance at school. *Journal of School Health, 75*, 255–266.

Tasker, F. (2005). Lesbian mothers, gay fathers, and their children: A review. *Journal of Developmental and Behavioral Pediatrics, 26*, 224–240.

Tattersall, I. (2002). *The monkey in the mirror: Essays on the science of what makes us human.* New York: Harcourt.

Tavris, C. (1992). *The mismeasure of woman.* New York: Simon & Schuster.

Taylor, C. (2004, November 29). The sky's the limit. *Time,* pp. 15–17.

Taylor, C. B., & Luce, K. H. (2003). Computer- and Internet-based psychotherapy interventions. *Current Directions in Psychological Science, 12*, 18–22.

Taylor, C. B., Jobson, K. O., Winzelberg, A., & Abascal, L. (2002). The use of the Internet to provide evidence-based integrated treatment programs for mental health. *Psychiatric Annals, 32*, 671–677.

Taylor, J., & Turner, R. J. (2002). Perceived discrimination, social stress and depression in the transition to adulthood: Racial contrasts. *Social Psychology Quarterly, 65*, 213–225.

Taylor, M. (1996). A theory of mind perspective on social cognitive development. In R. Gelman & T. K. F. Au (Eds.), *Perceptual and cognitive development: Handbook of perception and cognition* (2nd ed.). San Diego: Academic Press.

Taylor, S. E. (1995). Quandary at the crossroads: Paternalism versus advocacy surrounding end-of-treatment decisions. *American Journal of Hospital Palliatory Care, 12*, 43–46.

Taylor, S. E., & Aspinwall, L. G. (1996). Mediating and moderating processes in psychosocial stress: Appraisal, coping, resistance, and vulnerability. In H. B. Kaplan (Ed.), *Psychosocial stress: Perspectives on structure, theory, life-course, and methods.* San Diego: Academic Press.

Taylor, S. E., Kemeny, M. E., Reed, G. M., Bower, J. E., & Gruenewald, T. L. (2000). Psychological resources, positive illusions, and health. *American Psychologist, 55*, 99–109.

Tekcan, A. I. (2001). Flashbulb memories for a negative and a positive event: News of Desert Storm and acceptance to college. *Psychological Reports, 88*, 323–331.

Tellegen, A., Lykken, D. T., Bouchard, T. J., Jr., Wilcox, K. J., Segal, N. L., & Rich, S. (1988). Personality similarity in twins reared apart and together. *Journal of Personality and Social Psychology, 54*, 1031–1039.

Tenenbaum, H. R., & Leaper, C. (2002). Are parents' gender schemas related to their children's gender-related cognitios? A meta-analysis. *Developmental Psychology, 38*, 615–630.

Tenopyr, M. L. (2002). Theory versus reality: Evaluation of 'g' in the workplace. *Human Performance, 15*, 107–122.

Teodorov, E., Salzgerber, S. A., Felicio, L. F., Varolli, F. M. F., & Bernardi, M. M. (2002). Effects of perinatal picrotoxin and sexual experience on heterosexual and homosexual behavior in male rats. *Neurotoxicology and Teratology, 24*, 235–245.

Tepperman, L., & Curtis, J. (1995). A life satisfaction scale for use with national adult samples from the USA, Canada and Mexico. *Social Indicators Research, 35*, 255–270.

Terman, L. M., & Oden, M. H. (1947). *Genetic studies of genius: IV. The gifted child grows up.* Stanford, CA: Stanford University Press.

Terry, W. S. (2003). *Learning and memory: Basic principles, processes, and procedures* (2nd ed.). Boston: Allyn & Bacon.

Tetlock, P. E. (1997). Psychological perspectives on international conflict and cooperation. In D. F. Halpern & A. E. Voiskounsky (Eds.), *States of mind: American and post-Soviet perspectives on contemporary issues in psychology.* London: Oxford University Press.

Tharp, R. G. (1989). Psychocultural variables and constants: Effects on teaching and learning in schools [Special issue: Children and their development: Knowledge base, research agenda, and social policy application]. *American Psychologist, 44*, 349–359.

Thiffault, P., & Bergeron, J. (2003). Fatigue and individual differences in monotonous simulated driving. *Personality and Individual Differences, 34*, 159–176.

Thombs, D. L. (1999). *Introduction to addictive behaviors* (2nd ed.). New York: Guilford Press.

Thompson, B. (2002). *Score reliability: Contemporary thinking on reliability issues.* Thousand Oaks, CA: Sage.

Thompson, J. (2000, June 18). "I was certain, but I was wrong." *The New York Times,* p. E14.

Thompson, J. K., & Smolak, L. (Eds.). (2001). *Body image, eating disorders and obesity in youth: Assessment, prevention, and treatment.* Washington, DC: American Psychological Association.

Thompson, K. M., & Hanninger, K. (2001). Violence in e-rated video games. *Journal of the American Medical Association, 286*, 591–598.

Thompson, P. M., Hayaski, K. M., Simon, S. L., Geaga, J. A., Hong, M. S., Sui, Y., Lee, J. Y., Toga, A. W., Ling, W., & London, E. D. (2004, June 30). Structural abnormalities in the brains of human subjects who use methamphetamine. *The Journal of Neuroscience, 24(26)*, 6028–6036.

Thompson, R. A., & Nelson, C. A. (2001). Developmental science and the media. *American Psychologist, 56*, 5-15.

Thorndike, E. L. (1932). *The fundamentals of learning.* New York: Teachers College.

Thornton, A., & Young-DeMarco, L. (2001). Four decades of trends in attitudes toward family issues in the United States: The 1960s through the 1990s. *Journal of Marriage and the Family, 63,* 1009–1017.

Thrash, T. M., & Elliot, A. J. (2002). Implicit and self-attributed achievement motives: Concordance and predictive validity. *Journal of Personality, 70,* 729–755.

Thurstone, L. L. (1938). *Primary mental abilities.* Chicago : University of Chicago Press.

Time. (1982, October 4). "We're sorry: A case of mistaken identity." *Time,* p. 45.

Titone, D. A. (2002). Memories bound: The neuroscience of dreams. *Trends in Cognitive Science, 6,* 4–5.

Tkachuk, G. A., & Martin, G. L. (1999). Exercise therapy for patients with psychiatric disorders: Research and clinical implications. *Professional Psychology: Research and Practice, 33,* 275–282.

Tolman, E. C., & Honzik, C. H. (1930). Introduction and removal of reward and maze performance in rats. *University of California Publications in Psychology, 4,* 257–275.

Tomasello, M. (2000). Culture and cognitive development. *Current Directions in Psychological Science, 9,* 37–40.

Tomlinson-Keasey, C. (1985). *Child development: Psychological, sociological, and biological factors.* Homewood, IL: Dorsey.

Tonidandel, S., Quinones, M. A., & Adams, A. A. (2002). Computer-adaptive testing: The impact of test characteristics on perceived performance and test takers' reactions. *Journal of Applied Psychology, 87,* 320–332.

Toole, L. M., DeLeon, I. G., Kahng, S., Ruffin, G. E., Pletcher, C. A., & Bowman, L. G. (2004). Re-evaluation of constant versus varied punishers using empirically derived consequences. *Research in Developmental Disabilities, 25,* 577–586.

Torrey, E. F. (1997, June 13). The release of the mentally ill from institutions: A well-intentioned disaster. *The Chronicle of Higher Education,* pp. B4–B5.

Toth, J. P., & Daniels, K. A. (2002). Effects of prior experience on judgments of normative word frequency: Automatic bias and correction. *Journal of Memory and Language, 46,* 845–874.

Tracy, J. L., & Robins, R. W. (2004). Show your pride: Evidence for a discrete emotion expression. *Psychological Science, 15,* 194–197.

Trehub, S. E. (2001). Musical predispositions in infancy. In R. J. Zatorre & I. Peretz (Eds)., *The biological foundations of music. Annals of the New York Academy of Sciences* (Vol. 930, pp. 1–16). New York: New York Academy of Sciences.

Trehub, S. E., & Nakata, T. (2001–02). Emotion and music in infancy [Special issue: Musicae scientiae]. *Current Trends in the Study of Music and Emotion,* pp. 37–61.

Treisman, A. (1988). Features and objects: The fourteenth Bartlett memorial lecture. *Quarterly Journal of Experimental Psychology, 40,* 201–237.

Treisman, A. (1993). The perception of features and objects. In A. D. Baddeley & L. Weiskrantz (Eds.), *Attention: Selection, awareness, and control: A tribute to Donald Broadbent.* Oxford, England: Oxford University Press.

Treisman, A. (2004). Psychological issues in selective attention. In M. S. Gazzaniga (Ed.), *Cognitive neurosciences* (3rd ed.). Cambridge, MA: MIT.

Tremblay, A. (2004). Dietary fat and body weight set point. *Nutrition Review, 62(7 Pt 2),* S75–S77.

Trigo, M., Silva, D., & Rocha, E. (2005). Psychosocial risk factors in coronary heart disease: Beyond type A behavior. *Revista Portuguesa de Cardiologia, 24,* 261–281.

Tropp, L. R., & Pettigrew, T. F. (2005). Differential relationships between intergroup contact and affective and cognitive dimensions of prejudice. *Personality and Social Psychology Bulletin, 31,* 1145–1158.

Troxel, W. M., Matthews, K. A., Bromberger, J. T., & Sutton-Tyrell, K. (2003). Chronic stress burden, discrimination, and subclinical carotid artery disease in African American and Caucasian women. *Health Psychology, 22,* 300–309.

Trudel, G. (2002). Sexuality and marital life: Results of a survey. *Journal of Sex and Marital Therapy, 28,* 229–249.

Trull, T. J., & Widiger, T. A. (2003). Personality disorders. In. G. Stricker, T. A. Widiger, et al. (Eds.), *Handbook of psychology: Clinical psychology* (Vol. 8, pp. 149–172). New York: Wiley.

Trull, T. J., Stepp, S. D., & Durrett, C. A. (2003). Research on borderline personality disorder: An update. *Current Opinion in Psychiatry, 16,* 77–82.

Tryon, W. W. (2005). Possible mechanisms for why desensitization and exposure therapy work. *Clinical Psychology Review, 25,* 67–95.

Tryon, W. W., & Bernstein, D. (2003). Understanding measurement. In J. C. Thomas & M. Hersen (Eds.), *Understanding research in clinical and counseling psychology.* Mahwah, NJ: Erlbaum.

Tseng, W. S. (2003). *Clinician's guide to cultural psychiatry.* San Diego, CA: Elsevier Publishing.

Tsukasaki, T., & Ishii, K. (2004). Linguistic-cultural relativity of cognition: Rethinking the Sapir-Whorf hypothesis. *Japanese Psychological Review, 47,* 173–186.

Tsunoda, T. (1985). *The Japanese brain: Uniqueness and universality.* Tokyo: Taishukan Publishing.

Tucker, C. M., & Herman, K. C. (2002). Using culturally sensitive theories and research to meet the academic needs of low-income African American children. *American Psychologist, 57,* 762–773.

Tucker, J. A., Donovan, D. M., & Marlatt, G. A. (Eds.). (1999). *Changing addictive behavior: Bridging clinical and public health strategies.* New York: Guilford Press.

Tuerlinckx, F., De Boeck, P., & Lens, W. (2002). Measuring needs with the Thematic Apperception Test: A psychometric study. *Journal of Personality and Social Psychology, 82,* 448–461.

Tulving, E. (1993). What is episodic memory? *Current Directions in Psychological Science, 2,* 67–70.

Tulving, E. (2000). Concepts of memory. In E. Tulving, F. I. M. Craik, et al. (Eds.). *The Oxford handbook of memory.* New York: Oxford University Press.

Tulving, E. (2002). Episodic memory and common sense: How far apart? In A. Baddeley & J. P. Aggleton (Eds.), *Episodic memory: New directions in research* (pp. 269–287). London: Oxford University Press.

Tulving, E., & Psotka, J. (1971). Retroactive inhibition in free recall: Inaccessibility of information available in the memory store. *Journal of Experimental Psychology, 87,* 1–8.

Tulving, E., & Thompson, D. M. (1983). Encoding specificity and retrieval processes in episodic memory. *Psychological Review, 80,* 352–373.

Turati, C. (2004). Why faces are not special to newborns: An alternatiave account of the face preference. *Current Directions in Psychological Science, 13,* 5–8.

Turk, D. C. (1994). Perspectives on chronic pain: The role of psychological factors. *Current Directions in Psychological Science, 3,* 45–49.

Turkel, R. A. (2002). From victim to heroine: Children's stories revisited. *Journal of the American Academy of Psychoanalysis, 30,* 71–81.

Turkewitz, G. (1993). The origins of differential hemispheric strategies for information processing in the relationships between voice and face perception. In B. de Boysson-Bardies, S. de Schonen, P. W. Jusczyk, P. McNeilage, & J. Morton (Eds.), *Developmental neurocognition: Speech and face processing in the first year of life. NATO ASI series D: Behavioural and social sciences* (Vol. 69). Dordrecht, Netherlands: Kluwer Academic.

Turner, W. J. (1995). Homosexuality, Type 1: An Xq28 phenomenon. *Archives of Sexual Behavior, 24,* 109–134.

Tuvblad, C., Eley, T. C., & Lichtenstein, P. (2005). The development of antisocial behaviour from childhood to adolescence: A longitudinal twin study. *European Child & Adolescent Psychiatry, 14,* 216–225.

Tversky, A., & Kahneman, D. (1987). Rational choice and the framing of decisions. In R. Hogarth & M. Reder (Eds.), *Rational choice: The contrast between economics and psychology.* Chicago: University of Chicago Press.

Twenge, J. M., & Crocker, J. (2002). Race and self-esteem revisited: Reply to Hafdahl and Gray-Little. *Psychological Bulletin, 128,* 417–420.

Twenge, J. M., Catanese, K. R., & Baumeister, R. F. (2002). Social exclusion causes self-defeating behavior. *Journal of Personality and Social Psychology, 83,* 606–615.

Ubell, E. (1993, January 10). Could you use more sleep? *Parade,* pp. 16–18.

Ullman, S. (1996). *High-level vision: Object recognition and visual cognition.* Cambridge, MA: MIT.

UNAIDS. (2002). *AIDS epidemic update, 2002.* Geneva, Switzerland: World Health Organization.

Unsworth, N., & Engle, R. W. (2005). Individual differences in working memory capacity and learning: Evidence from the serial reaction time task. *Memory and Cognition, 33,* 213–220.

Updegraff, K. A., Helms, H. M., McHale, S. M., Crouter, A. C., Thayer, S. M., &

Sales, L. H. (2004). Who's the boss? Patterns of perceived control in adolescents' friendships. *Journal of Youth & Adolescence, 33,* 403–420.

U.S. Bureau of the Census. (2000). *Census 2000.* Retrieved from American Fact Finder http://factfinder.census.gov/servlet/BasicFactsServlet

U.S. Bureau of Labor Statistics. (2003). Women's weekly earnings as a percentage of men's earnings. Washington, DC: U.S. Bureau of Labor Statistics.

Uttl, B., Graf, P., & Cosentino, S. (2003). Implicit memory for new associations: Types of conceptual representations. In J. S. Bowers & C. J. Marsolek (Eds.), *Rethinking implicit memory* (pp. 302–323). London: Oxford University Press.

Uylings, H. B. M., & Vrije, U. (2002). About assumptions in estimation of density of neurons and glial cells. *Biological Psychiatry, 51,* 840–842.

Vaillant, G. E., & Vaillant, C. O. (1990). Natural history of male psychological health: XII. A 46-year study of predictors of successful aging at age 65. *American Journal of Psychiatry, 147,* 31–37.

Vaitl, D., Schienle, A., & Stark, R. (2005). Neurobiology of fear and disgust. *International Journal of Psychophysiology, 57,* 1–4.

Valencia, R. R., & Suzuki, L. A. (2003). *Intelligence testing and minority students: Foundations, performance factors, and assessment issues.* Thousand Oaks, CA: Sage.

Valente, S. M. (1991). Electroconvulsive therapy. *Archives of Psychiatric Nursing, 5,* 223–228.

Valsiner, J., Diriwächter, R., & Sauck, C. (2005). Diversity in unity: Standard questions and nonstandard interpretations. In *Science and medicine in dialogue: Thinking through particulars and universals* (pp. 289–307). Westport, CT: Praeger Publishers/Greenwood Publishing Group.

Van Beekum, S. (2005). The therapist as a new object. *Transactional Analysis Journal, 35,* 187–191.

Van De Graaff, K. (2000). *Human anatomy* (5th ed.). Boston: McGraw-Hill.

van den Bosch, L. M., Koeter, M. W., Stijnen, T., Verheul, R., & van den Brink, W. (2005). Sustained efficacy of dialectical behaviour therapy for borderline personality disorder. *Behavioral Research Therapy, 43,* 1231–1241.

Van den Wildenberg, W. P. M., & Van der Molen, M. W. (2004). Developmental

trends in simple and selective inhibition of compatible and incompatible responses. *Journal of Experimental Child Psychology, 87,* 201–220.

van Eck, M., Nicolson, N. A., & Berkhof, J. (1998). Effects of stressful daily events on mood states: Relationship to global perceived stress. *Journal of Personality and Social Psychology, 75,* 1572–1585.

Van Knippenberg, D. (1999). Social identity and persuasion: Reconsidering the role of group membership. In D. Abrams & M. A. Hogg (Eds.), *Social identity and social cognition.* Malden, MA: Blackwell.

van Leeuwen, M. L., & Macrae, C. N. (2004). Is beautiful always good? Implicit benefits of facial attractiveness. *Social Cognition, 22,* 637–649.

van Wel, F., Linssen, H., & Abma, R. (2000). The parental bond and the well-being of adolescents and young adults. *Journal of Youth & Adolescence, 29,* 307–318.

Vanasse, A., Niyonsenga, T., & Courteau, J. (2004). Smoking cessation within the context of family medicine: Which smokers take action? *Preventive Medicine: An International Journal Devoted to Practice and Theory, 38,* 330–337.

Vance, E. B., & Wagner, N. W. (1976). Written descriptions of orgasm: A study of sex differences. *Archives of Sexual Behavior, 5,* 87–98.

Vandell, D. L., Burchinal, M. R., Belsky, J., Owen, M. T., Friedman, S. L., Clarke-Stewart, A., McCartney, K., & Weinraub, M. (2005). *Early child care and children's development in the primary grades: Follow-up results from the NICHD Study of Early Child Care.* Paper presented at the biennial meeting of the Society for Research in Child Development, Atlanta, GA.

VanLehn, K. (1996). Cognitive skill acquisition. *Annual Review of Psychology, 47,* 513–539.

Varela, J. G., Boccaccini, M. T., Scogin, F., Stump, J., & Caputo, A. (2004). Personality testing in law enforcement employment settings: A meta-analytic review. *Criminal Justice and Behavior, 31,* 649–675.

Vargha-Khadem, F., Gadian, D. G., Copp, A., & Mishkin, M. (2005). FOXP2 and the neuroanatomy of speech and language. *Nature Reviews Neuroscience, 6,* 131–138.

Vaughn, L. A., & Weary, G. (2002). Roles of the availability of explanations, feelings of ease, and dysphoria in judgments about the future. *Journal of Science and Clinical Psychology, 21,* 686–704.

Veasey, S., Rosen, R., Barzansky, B., Rosen, I., & Owens, J. (2002). Sleep loss and fatigue in residency training: A reappraisal. *Journal of the American Medical Association, 288,* 1116–1124.

Vedantam, S. (2005, January 23). See no bias. *The Washington Post,* p. W12.

Veltman, M. W. M., & Browne, K. D. (2001). Three decades of child mal-treatment research: Implications for the school years. *Trauma Violence and Abuse, 2,* 215–239.

Veniegas, R. C. (2000). Biological research on women's sexual orientations: Evaluating the scientific evidence. *Journal of Social Issues, 56,* 267–282.

Verdejo, A., Toribio, I., & Orozco, C. (2005). Neuropsychological functioning in methadone maintenance patients versus abstinent heroin abusers. *Drug and Alcohol Dependence, 78,* 283–288.

Verfaellie, M., & Keane, M. M. (2002). Impaired and preserved memory processes in amnesia. In L. R. Squire & D. L. Schacter (Eds.), *Neuropsychology of memory* (3rd ed.). New York: Guilford Press.

Verhaeghen, P., Marcoen, A., & Goossens, L. (1992). Improving memory performance in the aged through mnemonic training: A meta-analytic study. *Psychology and Aging, 7,* 242–251.

Vernon, P. A., Jang, K. L., Harris, J. A., & McCarthy, J. M. (1997). Environmental predictors of personality differences: A twin and sibling study. *Journal of Personality and Social Psychology, 72,* 177–183.

Victor, S. B., & Fish, M. C. (1995). Lesbian mothers and the children: A review for school psychologists. *School Psychology Review, 24,* 456–479.

Viding, E., Blair, R. J., Moffitt, T. E., & Plomin, R. (2005). Evidence for substantial genetic risk for psychopathy in 7-year-olds. *Journal of Child Psychology and Psychiatry, 46,* 592–597.

Vihman, M. M. (1996). *Phonological development: The origins of language in the child.* London, England: Blackwell.

Villarosa, L. (2002, December 3). To prevent sexual abuse, abusers step forward. *The New York Times,* p. B1.

Villemure, C., Slotnick, B. M., & Bushnell, M. C. (2003). Effects of odors on pain perception: Deciphering the roles of emotion and attention. *Pain, 106,* 101–108.

Violani, C., & Lombardo, C. (2003). Peripheral temperature changes during rest and gender differences in thermal biofeedback. *Journal of Psychosomatic Research, 54,* 391–397.

Vital-Durand, F., Atkinson, J., & Braddick, O. J. (Eds.). (1996). *Infant vision. The European brain and behaviour society publication series* (Vol. 2). Oxford, England: Oxford University Press.

Vleioras, G., & Bosma, H. A. (2005). Are identity styles important for psychological well-being? *Journal of Adolescence, 28,* 397–409.

Vogel, G. W., Feng, P., & Kinney, G. G. (2000). Ontogeny of REM sleep in rats: Possible implications for endogenous depression. *Physiology & Behavior, 68,* 453–461.

Voicu, H., & Schmajuk, N. (2002). Latent learning, shortcuts and detours: A computational model. *Behavioural Processes, 59,* 67–86.

Volterra, V., Caselli, M. C., Capirci, O., Tonucci, F., & Vicari, S. (2003). Early linguistic abilities of Italian children with Williams syndrome [Special issue: Williams syndrome]. *Developmental Neuropsychology, 23,* 33–58.

von Restorff, H. (1933). Über die Wirking von Bereichsbildungen im Spurenfeld. In W. Kohler & H. von Restorff, *Analyse von Vorgangen in Spurenfeld: I. Psychologische forschung, 18,* 299–342.

Vrij, A. (2001). Detecting the liars. *Psychologist, 14,* 596–598.

Vygotsky, L. S. (1926/1997). *Educational psychology.* Delray Beach, FL: St. Lucie Press.

Wachs, T. D., Pollitt, E., Cueto, S., & Jacoby, E. (2004). Structure and cross-contextual stability of neonatal temperament. *Infant Behavior and Development, 27,* 382–396.

Wachtel, P. L., & Messer, S. B. (Eds.). (1997). *Theories of psychotherapy: Origins and evolution.* Washington, DC: American Psychological Association.

Wadden, T. A., Crerand, C. E., & Brock, J. (2005). Behavioral treatment of obesity. *Psychiatric Clinics of North America, 28,* 151–170.

Wagner, B. M. (1997). Family risk factors for child and adolescent suicidal behavior. *Psychological Bulletin, 121,* 246–298.

Wagner, E. F., & Atkins, J. H. (2000). Smoking among teenage girls. *Journal of Child & Adolescent Substance Abuse, 9,* 93–110.

Wagner, H. J., Bollard, C. M., Vigouroux, S., Huls, M. H., Anderson, R., Prentice, H. G., Brenner, M. K., Heslop, H. E., & Rooney, C. M. (2004). A strategy for treatment of Epstein Barr virus-positive Hodgkin's disease by targeting interleukin 12 to the tumor environment using tumor antigen-specific T cells. *Cancer Gene Therapy, 2,* 81–91.

Wagner, R. K. (2002). Smart people doing dumb things: The case of managerial incompetence. In R. J. Sternberg (Ed.), *Why smart people can be so stupid* (pp. 42–63). New Haven, CT: Yale University Press.

Wainer, H., Dorans, N. J., Eignor, D., Flaugher, R., Green, B. E., Mislevy, R. J., Steinberg, L., & Thissen D. (2000). *Computerized adaptive testing: A primer* (2nd ed.). Mahwah, NJ: Erlbaum.

Walcott, D. M. (2000). Repressed memory still lacks scientific reliability. *Journal of the American Academy of Psychiatry & the Law, 28,* 243–244.

Waldrep, D., & Waits, W. (2002). Returning to the Pentagon: The use of mass desensitization following the September 11, 2001 attack [Special issue: The mental health response to the 9–11 attack on the Pentagon]. *Military Medicine, 167,* 58–59.

Walker, M. P., & Stickgold, R. (2004). Sleep-dependent learning and memory consolidation. *Neuron, 44,* 121–133.

Walker, M. P., & Stickgold, R. (2005). It's practice, with sleep, that makes perfect: implications of sleep-dependent learning and plasticity for skill performance. *Clinical Sports Medicine, 24,* 301–311.

Walker, M. P., Brakefield, T., Morgan, A., Hobson, J. A., & Stickgold R. (2002). Practice with sleep makes perfect: Sleep-dependent motor skill learning. *Neuron, 35,* 205–211.

Walker, W. R., Skowronski, J. J., & Thompson, C. P. (2003). Consolidation of long-term memory: Evidence and alternatives. *Review of General Psychology, 7,* 203–210.

Wallerstein, J. S., Lewis, J., Blakeslee, S., & Lewis, J. (2000). *The unexpected legacy of divorce.* New York: Hyperion.

Wallis, C., & Willwerth, J. (1992, July 6). Schizophrenia: A new drug brings patients back to life. *Time,* pp. 52–57.

Walt, V. (2005, March 7). A land where girls rule in math. *Time*, pp. 56–57.

Walter, J. H., White F. J., Hall, S. K. MacDonald, A., Rylance, G., Boneh, A., Francis, D. E., Shortland, G. J., Schmidt, M., & Vail, A. (2002). How practical are recommendations for dietary control in phenylketonuria? *Lancet, 360*, 55–57.

Wang, A., & Clark, D. A. (2002). Haunting thoughts: The problem of obsessive mental intrusions [Special issue: Intrusions in cognitive behavioral therapy]. *Journal of Cognitive Psychotherapy, 16*, 193–208.

Wang, O. (2003). Infantile amnesia reconsidered: A cross-cultural analysis. *Memory, 11*, 65–80.

Wang, Q. (2004). The emergence of cultural self-constructs: autobiographical memory and self-description in European American and Chinese children. *Developmental Psychology, 40*, 3–15.

Wang, V. O., & Sue, S. (2005). In the eye of the storm: Race and genomics in research and practice. *American Psychologist, 60*, 37–45.

Wang, X., Lu, T., Snider, R. K., & Liang, L. (2005). Sustained firing in auditory cortex evoked by preferred stimuli. *Nature, 435*, 341–346.

Warburton, E. C., Glover, C. P., Massey, P. V., Wan, H., Johnson, B., Bienemann, A., Deuschle, U., Kew, J. N., Aggleton, J. P., Bashir, Z. I., Uney, J., & Brownj, M. W. (2005). cAMP responsive element-binding protein phosphorylation is necessary for perirhinal long-term potentiation and recognition memory. *Journal of Neuroscience, 25*, 6296–6303.

Ward, L. M. (2004). Wading through the stereotypes: Positive and negative associations between media use and Black adolescents' conceptions of self. *Developmental Psychology, 40*, 284–294.

Ward, W. C., Kogan, N., & Pankove, E. (1972). Incentive effects in children's creativity. *Child Development, 43*, 669–677.

Wark, G. R., & Krebs, D. L. (1996). Gender and dilemma differences in real-life moral judgement. *Developmental Psychology, 32*, 220–230.

Wass, T. S., Mattson, S. N., & Riley, E. P. (2004). Neuroanatomical and neurobehavioral effects of heavy prenatal alcohol exposure. In J. Brick (Ed.), *Handbook of the medical consequences of alcohol and drug abuse.* (pp. 139–169). New York: Haworth Press.

Wasserman, E. A., & Miller, R. R. (1997). What's elementary about associative learning? *Annual Review of Psychology, 48*, 573–607.

Waters, E., & Beauchaine, T. P. (2003). Are there really patterns of attachment? Comment on Fraley and Spieker (2003). *Developmental Psychology, 39*, 417–422.

Waters, E., Hamilton, C. E., & Weinfield, N. S. (2000). The stability of attachment security from infancy to adolescence and early adulthood: General introduction. *Child Development, 71*, 678–683.

Watson, D., Hubbard, B., & Wiese, D. (2000). Self-other agreement in personality and affectivity: The role of acquaintanceship, trait visibility, and assumed similarity. *Journal of Personality and Social Psychology, 78*, 546–558.

Watson, J. B. (1924). *Behaviorism.* New York: Norton.

Watson, J. B., & Rayner, R. (1920). Conditioned emotional reactions. *Journal of Experimental Psychology, 3*, 1–14.

Watson, J. M., Balota, D. A., & Roediger, H. L. (1995). Creating false memories with hybrid lists of semantic and phonological associates: Over-additive false memories produced by converging associative networks. *Journal of Memory and Language, 49*, 95–118.

Watson, J. M., Balota, D. A., & Roediger, H. L., (2003). Creating false memories with hybrid lists of semantic and phonological associates: Over-additive false memories produced by converging associative networks. *Journal of Memory and Language, 49*, 95–118.

Watson, M., Haviland, J. S., Greer, S., Davidson, J., & Bliss, J. M. (1999). Influence of psychological response on survival in breast cancer: a population-based cohort study. *Lancet, 354*, 1331–1336.

Waugh, C. E., & Larkin, G. R. (2003). What good are positive emotions in crises? A prospective study of resilience and emotions following the terrorist attacks on the United States on September 11th, 2001. *Journal of Personality and Social Psychology, 84*, 365–376.

Webb, W. B. (1992). *Sleep: The gentle tyrant* (2nd ed.). Boston: Anker.

Wechsler, H., Davenport, A., Dowdall, G., Moeykens, B., & Castillo, S. (1994). Health and behavioral consequences of binge drinking in college. A national survey of students at 140 campuses. *Journal of the American Medical Association, 272*, 1672–1677.

Wechsler, H., Kuo, M., Lee, H., & Dowdall, G. W. (2000). *Environmental correlates of underage alcohol use and related problems of college students.* Cambridge, MA: Harvard School of Public Health.

Wechsler, H., Lee, J. E., Nelson, T. F., & Kuo, M. (2002). Underage college students' drinking behavior, access to alcohol, and the influence of deterrence policies. *Journal of American College Health, 50*, 223–236.

Weeks, M., & Lupfer, M. B. (2004). Complicating race: The relationship between prejudice, race, and social class categorizations. *Personality and Social Psychology Bulletin, 30*, 972–984.

Wegener, D. T., Petty, R. E., Smoak, N. D., & Fabrigar, L. R. (2004). Multiple routes to resisting attitude change. In E. S. Knowles & J. A. Linn (Eds.), *Resistance and persuasion.* Mahwah, NJ: Lawrence Erlbaum Associates.

Wegner, D. M., Wenzlaff, R. M., & Kozak, M. (2004). Dream rebound: The return of suppressed thoughts in dreams. *Psychological Science, 15*, 232–236.

Weinberg, M. S., Williams, C. J., & Pryor, D. W. (1991, February 27). Personal communication. Indiana University, Bloomington.

Weiner, B. A., & Wettstein, R. (1993). *Legal issues in mental health care.* New York: Plenum Press.

Weiner, G. J. (2000). The immunobiology and clinical potential of immunostimulatory CpG oligodeoxynucleotides. *Journal of Leukocyte Biology, 68*, 455–463.

Weiner, I. B. (2004a). Monitoring psychotherapy with performance-based measures of personality functioning. *Journal of Personality Assessment, 83*, 323–331.

Weiner, I. B. (2004b). Rorschach Inkblot method. In M. E. Maruish (Ed.), *Use of psychological testing for treatment planning and outcomes assessment: Vol. 3: Instruments for adults* (3rd ed.). Mahwah, NJ: Lawrence Erlbaum Associates.

Weinstein, M., Glei, D. A., Yamazaki, A., & Ming-Cheng, C. (2004). The role of intergenerational relations in the association between life stressors and depressive symptoms. *Research on Aging, 26*, 511–530.

Weintraub, M. (1976). Intelligent noncompliance and capricious compliance. In L. Lasagna (Ed.), *Patient compliance.* Mt. Kisco, NY: Futura.

Weis, R., Crockett, T. E., & Vieth, S. (2004). Using MMPI-A profiles to predict success in a military-style residential treatment program for adolescents with academic and conduct problems. *Psychology in the Schools, 41,* 563–574.

Weissman, M. M., Bland, R. C., Canino, G. J., Faravelli, C., Greenwald, S., Hwu, H. G., Joyce, P. R., Karam, E. G., Lee, C. K., Lellouch, J., Lepine, J. P., Newman, S. C., Rubio-Stipec, M., Wells, J. E., Wickramarante, P. J., Wittchen, H., & Yeh, E. K. (1997, July 24–31). Cross-national emidemiology of major depression and bipolar disorder. *Journal of the American Medical Association, 276,* 293–299.

Weissman, M. W., & Olfson, M. (1995, August 11). Depression in women: Implications for health care research. *Science, 269,* 799–801.

Weisz, A., & Black, B. (2002). Gender and moral reasoning: African American youth respond to dating dilemmas. *Journal of Human Behavior in the Social Environment, 5,* 35–52.

Welch, K. C. (2002). *The Bell Curve* and the politics of Negrophobia. In J. M. Fish (Ed.), *Race and intelligence: Separating science from myth* (pp. 177–198). Mahwah, NJ: Erlbaum.

Welkowitz, L. A., Struening, E. L., Pittman, J., Guardino, M., & Welkowitz, J. (2000). Obsessive-compulsive disorder and comorbid anxiety problems in a national anxiety screening sample. *Journal of Anxiety Disorders, 14,* 471–482.

Wells, G. L., Olson, E. A., & Charman, S. D. (2002). The confidence of eyewitnesses in their identifications from lineups. *Current Directions in Psychological Science, 11,* 151–154.

Wenar, C. (1994). *Developmental psychopathology: From infancy through adolescence* (3rd ed.). New York: McGraw-Hill.

Werker, J. F., & Tees, R. C. (2005). Speech perception as a window for understanding plasticity and commitment in language systems of the brain. *Developmental Psychobiology, 46,* 233–234.

Werner, E. E. (1995). Resilience in development. *Current Directions in Psychological Science, 4,* 81–85.

Wertheimer, M. (1923). Untersuchungen zur Lehre von der Gestalt. II. *Psychol. Forsch., 5,* 301–350. In R. Beardsley and M. Wertheimer (Eds.). (1958), *Readings in perception.* New York: Van Nostrand.

West, D. S., Harvey-Berino, J., & Raczynski, J. M. (2004). Behavioral aspects of obesity, dietary intake, and chronic disease. In J. M. Raczynski and L. C. Leviton (Eds.), *Handbook of clinical health psychology: Vol. 2. Disorders of behavior and health.* (pp. 9–41). Washington, DC: American Psychological Association.

West, J. R., & Blake, C. A. (2005). Fetal alcohol syndrome: An assessment of the field. *Experimental Biological Medicine, 6,* 354–356.

West, R. L. (1995). Compensatory strategies for age-associated memory impairment. In A. D. Baddeley, B. A. Wilson, & F. N. Watts (Eds.), *Handbook of memory disorders.* Chichester, England: Wiley.

West, R. L., Thorn, R. M., Bagwell, D. K. (2003). Memory performance and beliefs as a function of goal setting and aging. *Psychology & Aging, 18,* 111–125.

Westen, D., & Gabbard, G. O. (1999). Psychoanalytic approaches to personality. In L. A. Pervin & O. P. John (Eds.), *Handbook of personality: Theory and research* (2nd ed.). New York: Guilford.

Westen, D., Novotny, C. M., & Thompson-Brenner, H. (2004). The empirical status of empirically supported psychotherapies: Assumptions, findings, and reporting in controlled clinical trials. *Psychological Bulletin, 130,* 631–663.

Wetter, D. W., Fiore, M. C., Gritz, E. R., Lando, H. A., Stitzer, M. L., Hasselblad, V., & Baker, T. B. (1998). The Agency for Health Care Policy and Research. Smoking cessation clinical practice guideline: Findings and implications for psychologists. *American Psychologist, 53,* 657–669.

Whaley, B. B. (Ed.). (2000). *Explaining illness: Research, theory, and strategies.* Mahwah, NJ: Erlbaum.

Wheeler, M. E., Petersen, S. E., & Buckner, R. L. (2000). Memory's echo: Vivid remembering reactivates sensory-specific cortex. *Proceedings of the National Academy of Sciences, 97,* 11125–11129.

Whisenant, W. A., Pedersen, P. M., & Obenour, B. L. (2002). Success and gender: Determining the rate of advancement for intercollegiate athletic directors. *Sex Roles, 47,* 485–491.

Whitbourne, S. K. (2000). The normal aging process. In S. K. Whitbourne & S. Krauss (Eds.), *Psychopathology in later adulthood.* New York: Wiley.

Whitbourne, S. K., & Wills, K. (1993). Psychological issues in institutional care of the aged. In S. B. Goldsmith (Ed.), *Long-term care.* Gaithersburg, MD: Aspen Press.

Whitbourne, S. K., Zuschlag, M. K., Elliot, L. B., & Waterman, A. S. (1992). Psychosocial development in adulthood: A 22-year sequential study. *Journal of Personality and Social Psychology, 63,* 260–271.

Whitehouse, W. G., Orne, E. C., Dinges, D. F., Bates, B. L., Nadon, R., & Orne, M. T. (2005). The cognitive interview: Does it successfully avoid the dangers of forensic hypnosis? *American Journal of Psychology, 118,* 213–234.

Whitfield, J. B., Zhu, G., Madden, P. A., Neale, M. C., Heath, A. C., & Martin, N. G. (2004). The genetics of alcohol intake and of alcohol dependence. *Alcoholism: Clinical and Experimental Research, 28,* 1153–1160.

WHO World Mental Health Survey Consortium. (2004). Prevalence, severity, and unmet need for treatment of mental disorders in the World Health Organization World Mental Health Surveys. *Journal of the American Medical Association, 291,* 2581–2590.

Whorf, B. L. (1956). *Language, thought, and reality.* New York: Wiley.

Wickelgren, E. A. (2004). Perspective distortion of trajectory forms and perceptual constancy in visual event identification. *Perception and Psychophysics, 66,* 629–641.

Wickelgren, I. (1998, June 26). Teaching the brain to take drugs. *Science, 280,* 2045–2047.

Wickelgren, I. (2001, March, 2). Working memory helps the mind focus. *Science, 291,* 1684–1685.

Wickens, C. D. (1984). *Engineering psychology and human performance.* Columbus, OH: Merrill.

Widiger, T. A., & Clark, L. A. (2000). Toward *DSM-V* and the classification of psychopathology. *Psychological Bulletin, 126,* 946–963.

Widmeyer, W. N., & Loy, J. W. (1988). When you're hot, you're hot! Warm-cold effects in first impressions of persons and teaching effectiveness. *Journal of Educational Psychology, 80,* 118–121.

Wiederhold, B. K., & Wiederhold, M. D. (2005a). Specific phobias and social phobia. In B. K. Wiederhold & M. D. Wiederhold (Eds.), *Virtual reality therapy for anxiety disorders: Advances in evaluation and treatment*. Washington, DC: American Psychological Association.

Wiederhold, B. K., & Wiederhold, M. D. (2005b). *Virtual reality therapy for anxiety disorders: Advances in evaluation and treatment*. Washington, DC: American Psychological Association.

Wiehe, V. R., & Richards, A. L. (1995). *Intimate betrayal: Understanding and responding to the trauma of acquaintance rape*. Thousand Oaks, CA: Sage Publications.

Wielgosz, A. T., & Nolan, R. P. (2000). Biobehavioral factors in the context of ischemic cardiovascular disease. *Journal of Psychosomatic Research, 48,* 339–345.

Wigfield, A., & Eccles, J. S. (2000). Expectancy-value theory of achievement motivation. *Contemporary Educational Psychology, 25,* 68–81.

Wiggins, J. S. (1997). In defense of traits. In R. Hogan, J. Johnson, & S. Briggs (Eds.), *Handbook of personality psychology*. Orlando, FL: Academic Press.

Wiggins, J. S. (2003). *Paradigms of personality assessment*. New York: Guilford Press.

Wildavsky, B. (2000, September 4). A blow to bilingual education. *U.S. News & World Report,* pp. 22–28.

Wilgoren, J. (1999, October 22). Quality day care, early, is tied to achievements as an adult. *The New York Times,* p. A16.

Williams, J. E., & Best, D. L. (1990). *Measuring sex stereotypes: A multinational study*. Newbury Park, CA: Sage.

Williams, J. E., Paton, C. C., Siegler, I. C., Eigenbrodt, M. L., Nieto, F. J., & Tyroler, H. A. (2000). Anger proneness predicts coronary heart disease risk: Prospective analysis from the Atherosclerosis Risk in Communities (ARIC) Study. *Circulation, 101,* 2034–2039.

Williams, J. W., Mulrow, C. D., Chiquette, E., Noel, P. H., Aguilar, C., & Cornell, J. (2000). A systematic review of newer pharmacotherapies for depression in adults: Evidence report summary. *Annals of Internal Medicine, 132,* 743–756.

Willis, G. L. (2005). The therapeutic effects of dopamine replacement therapy and its psychiatric side effects are mediated by pineal function. *Behavioural Brain Research, 160,* 148–160.

Willis, S. L., & Schaie, K. W. (1994). In C. B. Fisher & R. M. Lerner (Eds.), *Applied developmental psychology*. New York: McGraw-Hill.

Wilson, G. T., & Agras, W. S. (1992). The future of behavior therapy. *Psychotherapy, 29,* 39–43.

Wilson, G. T., & Fairburn, C. G. (2002). Treatments for eating disorders. In P. E. Nathan, & J. M. Gorman (Eds.), *A guide to treatments that work* (2nd ed.), pp. 559–592. London: Oxford University Press.

Wilson, J. P., & Keane, T. M. (Eds.). (1996). *Assessing psychological trauma and PTSD*. New York: Guilford.

Wilson, M. A. (2002). Hippocampal memory formation, plasticity and the role of sleep. *Neurobiology of Learning & Memory, 78,* 565–569.

Wilson, T. D. (2004). *Strangers to ourselves: Discovering the adaptive unconscious*. Cambridge, MA: Harvard University Press.

Windholz, G. (1997, September). Ivan P. Pavlov: An overview of his life and psychological work. *American Psychologist, 52,* 941–946.

Windholz, G., & Lamal, P. A. (2002). Koehler's insight revisited. In R. A. Griggs (Ed.), *Handbook for teaching introductory psychology, Vol. 3: With an emphasis on assessment,* pp. 80–81. Mahwah, NJ: Erlbaum.

Winerman, L. (2005, June). ACTing up. *Monitor on Psychology,* pp. 44–45.

Wines, M. (2004, March 18). For sniffing out land mines, a platoon of twitching noses. *The New York Times,* pp. A1, A4.

Winkler, K. J. (1997, July 11). Scholars explore the blurred lines of race, gender, and ethnicity. *The Chronicle of Higher Education,* pp. A11–A12.

Winner, E. (2000). The origins and ends of giftedness. *American Psychologist, 55,* 159–169.

Winner, E. (2003). Creativity and talent. In M. H. Bornstein & L. Davidson (Eds.), *Well-being: Positive development across the life course* (pp. 371–380). Mahwah, NJ: Lawrence Erlbaum.

Winningham, R. G., Hyman, I. E., Jr., & Dinnel, D. L. (2000). Flashbulb memories? The effects of when the initial memory report was obtained. *Memory, 8,* 209–216.

Winsler, A., Madigan, A. L., & Aquilino, S. A. (2005). Correspondence between maternal and paternal parenting styles in early childhood. *Early Childhood Research Quarterly, 20,* 1–12.

Winson, J. (1990, November). The meaning of dreams. *Scientific American,* pp. 86–96.

Winstead, B. A., & Sanchez, A. (2005). Gender and psychopathology. In J. E. Maddux & B. A. Winstead, *Psychopathology: Foundations for a contemporary understanding*. Mahwah, NJ: Lawrence Erlbaum Associates.

Winston, A. S. (2004). *Defining difference: Race and racism in the history of psychology*. Washington, DC: American Psychological Association.

Winter, D. G. (1973). *The power motive*. New York: Free Press.

Winter, D. G. (1987). Leader appeal, leader performance, and the motive profile of leaders and followers: A study of American presidents and elections. *Journal of Personality and Social Psychology, 52,* 196–202.

Winter, D. G. (1988). The power motive in women—and men. *Journal of Personality and Social Psychology, 54,* 510–519.

Winter, D. G. (1995). *Personality: Analysis and interpretation of lives*. New York: McGraw-Hill.

Winters, B. D., & Bussey, T. J. (2005). Glutamate receptors in perihinal cortex mediate encoding, retrieval, and consolidation of object recognition memory. *Journal of Neuroscience, 25,* 4243–4251.

Wiseman, R., & Greening, E. (2002). The mind machine: A mass participation experiment into the possible existence of extra-sensory perception. *British Journal of Psychology, 93,* 487–499.

Witelson, S. (1989, March). *Sex differences*. Paper presented at the annual meeting of the New York Academy of Sciences, New York.

Wixted, J. T., & Ebbesen, E. B. (1991). On the form of forgetting. *Psychological Science, 2,* 409–415.

Woldt, A. L., & Toman, S. M. (2005). *Gestalt therapy: History, theory, and practice*. Thousand Oaks, CA: Sage Publications.

Wolfe, D. A. (1999). *Child abuse: Implications for child development and psychopathology*. Thousand Oaks, CA: Sage.

Wolpe, J. (1990). *The practice of behavior therapy*. Boston: Allyn & Bacon.

Wong, M. M., & Csikszentmihalyi, M. (1991). Affiliation motivation and daily experience: Some issues on gender differences. *Journal of Personality and Social Psychology, 60,* 154–164.

Wood, E., Desmarais, S., & Gugula, S. (2002). The impact of parenting experience on gender stereotyped toy play of children. *Sex Roles, 47,* 39–49.

Wood, J. M., & Bootzin, R. (1990). The prevalence of nightmares and their independence from anxiety. *Journal of Abnormal Psychology, 99,* 64–68.

Wood, J. M., Nezworski, M. T., Lilienfeld, S. O., & Garb, H. N. (2003). *What's wrong with the Rorschach? Science confronts the controversial inkblot test.* New York: Wiley.

Wood, W. (2000). Attitude change: Persuasion and social influence. *Annual Review of Psychology, 51,* 539–570.

Wood, W., & Eagly, A. H. (2002). A cross-cultural analysis of the behavior of women and men: Implications for the origins of sex differences. *Psychological Bulletin, 128,* 699–727.

Wood, W., & Stagner, B. (1994). Why are some people easier to influence than others? In S. Savitt & T. C. Brock (Eds.), *Persuasion: Psychological insights and perspectives.* Boston: Allyn & Bacon.

Woodruff-Pak, D. S. (1999). New directions for a classical paradigm: Human eyeblink conditioning. *Psychological Science, 10,* 1–7.

Woods, S. C., & Seeley, R. J. (2002). Hunger and energy homeostasis. In H. Pashler & R. Gallistel (Eds.). *Steven's handbook of experimental psychology* (3rd ed.), *Vol. 3: Learning, motivation, and emotion,* pp. 633–668. New York: Wiley.

Woods, S. C., Schwartz, M. W., Baskin, D. G., & Seeley, R. J. (2000). Food intake and the regulation of body weight. *Annual Review of Psychology, 51,* 255–277.

Woods, S. C., Seeley, R. J., Porte, D., Jr., & Schwartz, M. W. (1998, May 29). Signals that regulate food intake and energy homeostasis. *Science, 280,* 1378–1383.

Wortman, C., Loftus, E., & Waver, C. (1999). *Psychology (5th ed.).* Boston: McGraw-Hill.

Wozniak, R. H., & Fischer, K. W. (Eds.). (1993). *Development in context: Acting and thinking in specific environments.* Hillsdale, NJ: Erlbaum.

Wright, K. (September 2002). Times of our lives. *Scientific American,* pp. 59–65.

Wuethrich, B. (2001, March 16). Does alcohol damage female brains more? *Science, 291,* 2077–2079.

Wurtz, R. H., & Kandel, E. R. (2000). Central visual pathways. In E. R. Kandel, J. H. Schwartz, & T. M. Jessell (Eds.), *Principles of neural science* (4th ed.). New York: McGraw-Hill.

Wyatt, E. (2005, July 22). Cycling world looks to life after Armstrong. *The New York Times,* p. C1.

Wyatt, G. E. (1992). The sociocultural context of African American and white American women's rape. *Journal of Social Issues, 48,* 77–92.

Wynn, K. (1995). Infants possess a system of numerical knowledge. *Current Directions in Psychological Science, 4,* 172–177.

Wynn, K. (2000). Findings of addition and subtraction in infants are robust and consistent: Reply to Wakeley, Rivera, and Langer. *Child Development, 71,* 1535–1536.

Wynn, K., Bloom, P., & Chiang, W. C. (2002). Enumeration of collective entities by 5-month-old infants. *Cognition, 83,* B55–B62.

Wynne, C. D. L. (2004). *Do animals think?* Princeton, NJ: Princeton University Press.

Yalom, I. D. (1997). *The Yalom reader: On writing, living, and practicing psychotherapy.* New York: Basic Books.

Yee, A. H., Fairchild, H. H., Weizmann, F., & Wyatt, G. E. (1993). Addressing psychology's problem with race. *American Psychologist, 48,* 1132–1140.

Yenerall, J. D. (1995). College socialization and attitudes of college students toward the elderly. *Gerontology and Geriatrics Education, 15,* 37–48.

Yost, W. A. (2000). *Fundamentals of hearing* (4th ed.). New York: Academic Press.

Young, M. W. (2000, March). The tick-tock of the biological clock. *Scientific American,* pp. 64–71.

Yuskauskas, A. (1992). Conflict in the developmental disabilities profession: Perspectives on treatment approaches, ethics, and paradigms. *Dissertation Abstracts International, 53,* 1870.

Zajonc, R. B. (1985). Emotion and facial efference: A theory reclaimed. *Science, 228,* 15–21.

Zajonc, R. B. (2001). Mere exposure: A gateway to the subliminal. *Current Directions in Psychological Science, 10,* 224–228.

Zajonc, R. B., & McIntosh, D. N. (1992). Emotions research: Some promising questions and some questionable promises. *Psychological Science, 3,* 70–74.

Zalsman, G., & Apter, A. (2002). Serotonergic metabolism and violence/aggression. In J. Glicksohn (Ed.), *The neurobiology of criminal behavior: Neurobiological foundation of aberrant behaviors* (pp. 231–250). Dordrecht, Netherlands: Kluwer Academic.

Zamarra, J. W., Schneider, R. H., Besseghini, I., Robinson, D. K., & Salerno, J. W. (1996). Usefulness of the transcendental meditation program in the treatment of patients with coronary artery disease. *American Journal of Cardiology, 77,* 867–870.

Zarren, J. I., & Eimer, B. N. (2002). *Brief cognitive hypnosis: Facilitating the change of dysfunctional behavior.* New York: Springer.

Zaslow, J. (2003, May 1). Going on after the unthinkable: A rape victim shares her story. *The Wall Street Journal,* p. A2.

Zatorre, R. J., Belin, P., & Penhune, V. B. (2002). Structure and function of auditory cortex: Music and speech. *Trends in Cognitive Sciences, 6,* 37–46.

Zautra, A. J., Reich, J. W., & Guarnaccia, C. A. (1990). Some everyday life consequences of disability and bereavement for older adults. *Journal of Personality and Social Psychology, 59,* 550–561.

Zebrowitz, L. A., & Montepare, J. M. (2005, June 10). Appearance DOES matter. *Science, 308,* 1565–1566.

Zebrowitz-McArthur, L. (1988). Person perception in cross-cultural perspective. In M. H. Bond (Ed.), *The cross-cultural challenge to social psychology.* Newbury Park, CA: Sage.

Zeidner, M., & Endler, N. S. (Eds.). (1996). *Handbook of coping: Theory, research, applications.* New York: Wiley.

Zeidner, M., Matthews, G., & Roberts, R. D. (2004). Emotional intelligence in the workplace: A critical review. *Applied Psychology: An International Review, 53,* 371–399.

Zeigler, D. W., Wang, C. C., Yoast, R. A., Dickinson, B. D., McCaffree, M. A., Robinowitz, C. B., & Sterling, M. L. (2005). The neurocognitive effects of alcohol on adolescents and college students. *Preventive Medicine: An International Journal Devoted to Practice and Theory, 40,* 23–32.

Zevon, M., & Corn, B. (1990). Paper presented at the annual meeting of the American Psychological Association, Boston, MA.

Zhang, F., Chen, Y., Heiman, M., & Dimarchi, R. (2005). Leptin: structure, function and biology. *Vitamins and*

Hormones: Advances in Research and Applications, 71, 345–372.

Zhou, Z., Liu, Q., & Davis, R. L. (2005). Complex regulation of spiral ganglion neuron firing patterns by neurotrophin-3. *Journal of Neuroscience, 25,* 7558–7566.

Ziegler, R., Diehl, M., & Ruther, A. (2002). Multiple source characteristics and persuasion: Source inconsistency as a determinant of message scrutiny. *Personality and Social Psychology Bulletin, 28,* 496–508.

Zigler, E., Bennett-Gates, D., Hodapp, R., & Henrich, C. (2002). Assessing personality traits of individuals with mental retardation. *American Journal on Mental Retardation, 107,* 181–193.

Zigler, E. F., Finn-Stevenson, M., & Hall, N. W. (2002). The first three years and beyond: Brain development and social policy. In E. F. Zigler, M. Finn-Stevenson, & N. W. Hall, *Current perspectives in psychology.* New Haven, CT: Yale University Press.

Zika, S., & Chamberlain, K. (1987). Relation of hassles and personality to subjective well-being. *Journal of Personality and Social Psychology, 53,* 155–162.

Zilbergeld, B., & Ellison, C. R. (1980). Desire discrepancies and arousal problems in sex therapy. In S. R. Leiblum & L. A. Pervin (Eds.), *Principles and practices of sex therapy.* New York: Guilford.

Zimbardo, P. G. (2004a). Does psychology make a significant difference in our lives? *American Psychologist, 59,* 339–351.

Zimbardo, P. G. (2004b). A situationist perspective on the psychology of evil: Understanding how good people are transformed into perpetrators. In A. G. Miller, *Social psychology of good and evil.* New York: Guilford Press.

Zimprich, D., & Martin, M. (2002). Can longitudinal changes in processing speed explain longitudinal age changes in fluid intelligence? *Psychology and Aging, 17,* 690–695.

Zito, J. M. (1993). *Psychotherapeutic drug manual* (3rd ed., rev.). New York: Wiley.

Zook, K. B. (2004, May 23). Analyze this. *Boston Globe,* B4.

Zubieta, J. K., Heitzeg, M. M., Smith, Y. R., Bueller, J. A., Xu, K., Xu, Y., Koeppe, R. A., Stohler, C. S., & Goldman, D. (2003). COMT val158met genotype affects mu-opioid neurotransmitter responses to a pain stressor. *Science, 21,* 1240–1243.

Zuckerman, M. (1978). The search for high sensation. *Psychology Today,* pp. 30–46.

Zuckerman, M. (1994). *Behavioral expression and biosocial expression of sensation seeking.* Cambridge, England: Cambridge University Press.

Zuckerman, M. (2002). Genetics of sensation seeking. In J. Benjamin, R. P. Ebstein, et al. (Eds.), *Molecular genetics and the human personality,* pp. 193–210. Washington, DC: American Psychiatric Publishing.

Zuckerman, M., & Kuhlman, D. M. (2000). Personality and risk-taking: Common biosocial factors [Special issue: Personality processes and problem behavior]. *Journal of Personality:, 68,* 999–1029.

Zuger, A. (1998, June 2). The "other" drug problem: Forgetting to take them. *The New York Times,* pp. C1, C5.

Zurbriggen, E. L. (2000). Social motives and cognitive power–sex associations: Predictors of aggressive sexual behavior. *Journal of Personality and Social Psychology, 78,* 559–581.

Credits

Chapter 1

Module 1: Figure 1: From Lamal, P. A. Students common beliefs about psychology. *Teaching of Psychology, 6,* Copyright © 1979 Lawrence Erlbaum Associates. **Figure 3:** From *Psychology, Careers for the Twenty-First Century.* Washington, DC: American Psychological Association. Copyright © 2000 by the American Psychological Association. Adapted with permission. **Figure 4:** From *Origin of Published Research.* Washington, DC: American Psychological Association. Copyright © 1991 American Psychological Association. Adapted with permission. **Figure 5:** From *The Psychology Major's Handbook,* 1st Edition by Kuther. © 2003 with permission of Wadsworth, a division of Thomson Learning: www.thomsonrights.com. Fax 800-730-2215.

Chapter 2

Module 5: Figure 4: Darley, J. M., & Latané, B. (1968). Bystanders intervention in emergencies: Diffusion of responsibility. *Journal of Personality and Social Psychology,* 8, 377–383. Copyright ©1968 American Psychological Association. Adapted with permission.

Chapter 3

Module 7: Figure 1: From *Human Anatomy,* 5th edition, by K. Van DeGraaff, p. 339. Copyright © 2000 by The McGraw-Hill Companies. **Figure 2:** From C. F. Stevens, "The Neuron" *Scientific American,* September 1979, page 56. Reprinted with permission of Carol Donner. **Figure 3:** From *Human Biology,* 6th edition, by S. Mader, page 250. Copyright © 2000 by The McGraw-Hill Companies. **Figure 4a:** From *Human Biology,* 6th edition, by S. Mader, page 250. Copyright © 2000 by The McGraw-Hill Companies. **Figure 4b:** From *The Living World,* 2nd edition, by G. B. Johnson, page 600. Copyright © 2000 by The McGraw-Hill Companies.

Module 8: Figure 2: From *Psychology,* 4th edition, by E. Loftus and C. Wortmann, pg. 63. Copyright © 1989 by The McGraw-Hill Companies. **Figure 4:** From *Human Biology,* 6th edition, by S. Mader, page 250. Copyright © 2000 by The McGraw-Hill Companies.

Module 9: Figure 2: From *Anatomy & Physiology,* 5th edition, by R. Seeley, T. Stephens, and P. Tate, p. 384. Copyright © 2000 by The McGraw-Hill Companies. **Figure 3:** From *The Living World,* 2nd edition, by G. B. Johnson, page 600. Copyright © 2000 by The McGraw-Hill Companies. **Figure 4:** From *Elements of Physiological Psychology,* by A. M. Schneider and B. Tarshis. Copyright © 1995 by The McGraw-Hill Companies. **Figure 5:** Courtesy of Dr. Robert B. Livingston, University of California-San Diego, and Philip J. Mercurio, Neurosciences Institute. **Figure 7:** Used with the permission of Dr. Edward G. Jones, University of California at Davis Center for Neuroscience.

Chapter 4

Module 11: Figure 1: From *Psychology,* 5th edition, by C. Wortman, E. Loftus, and C. Weaver, p. 113. Copyright © 1999 by The McGraw-Hill Companies. **Figure 3:** From *Hole's Essentials of Human Anatomy and Physiology, 7th edition,* by D. Sheir, J. Butler, and R. Lewis, p. 283. Copyright © 2000 by The McGraw-Hill Companies. **Figure 5:** From *Human Biology,* 6th edition, by S. Mader, page 250. Copyright © 2000 by The McGraw-Hill Companies.

Module 12: Figure 1: From *Anatomy & Physiology,* 5th edition, by R. Seeley, T. Stephens, and P. Tate, p. 384. Copyright © 2000 by The McGraw-Hill Companies. **Figure 2:** From *Anatomy & Physiology,* 5th edition, by R. Seeley, T. Stephens, and P. Tate, p. 384. Copyright © 2000 by The McGraw-Hill Companies. **Figure 3:** From Better Hearing Institute, 1998 Better Hearing Institute: Washington, DC. **Figure 4:** Adapted from S. Brownlee and T. Watson, "The Senses," *US News & World Report,* January 13, 1997, pp. 51–59. Reprinted with permission of Linda M. Bartoshuk. **Figure 5:** From Kensalo, *The Skin Senses,* 1968. Courtesy of Charles C. Thomas, Publisher, Ltd. Springfield, Illinois. **Figure 6:** From Ramachandran, V. S., & Hubbard, E. M. (2003, May). Hearing colors, tasting shapes. *Scientific American,* pp. 53–59. © 2003 by Scientific American, Inc. All rights reserved.

Module 13: Figure 1c: From *Mind Sights* by Roger N. Shepard © 1990 by Roger N. Shepard. Reprinted by permission of Henry Holt & Company. **Figure 4:** From *Sensation & Perception, 2nd edition,* by E. Goldstein © 1984. Reprinted with permission of Wadsworth, an imprint of the Wadsworth Group, a division of Thomson Learning. **Figure 5:** I. Biederman, Higher level vision. In D. N. Osherson, S. Kosslyn and J. Hollerback (eds.), *An Invitation to Cognitive Science: Visual Cognition and Action,* 1990. Reprinted with permission of MIT Press. **Figure 6:** Reprinted from *Vision Research, 26,* Julesz, B., Stereoscopic vision, pgs. 1601–1602. Copyright © 1986 with kind permission from Elsevier Science Ltd., The Boulevard, Langford Lane, Kidlington OX5 1GN, UK. **Figure 7:** Figure from *Sensation and Perception,* 3rd edition, by Stanley Coren and Lawrence M. Ward, copyright © 1989 by John Wiley & Sons reproduced by permission of the publisher. **Figure 8 a–d:** Figure from *Sensation and Perception,* 3rd edition, by Stanley Coren and Lawrence M. Ward, copyright © 1989 by John Wiley & Sons, reproduced by permission of the publisher. **Figure 9a:** Figure from *Sensation and Perception,* 3rd edition, by Stanley Coren and Lawrence M. Ward, copyright © 1989 by John Wiley & Sons, reproduced by permission of the publisher. **Figure 12:** From Gregory and Gombrich, *Illusion in Nature and Art,* Figure 5-16. Copyright © 1973, by permission of Gerald Duckworth & Co., Ltd.

Chapter 5

Module 14: Figure 1: From Palladino, J. J. & Carducci, B. J. Students knowledge of sleep and dreams. *Teaching of Psychology, 11,* 189–191. Copyright © 1984 Lawrence Erlbaum Associates. **Figure 2:** Fig 1 from *Sleep* by J. Allan Hobson © 1989 by J. Allan Hobson. Reprinted by permission of Henry Holt & Co. **Figure 3:** From E. Hartmann, *The Biology of Dreaming,* 1967. Courtesy of Charles C Thomas, Publisher, Ltd., Springfield, Illinois. **Figure 4:** From *Secrets of Sleep* by Alexander Borbely. English translation copyright © 1986 by Basic Books, Inc, copyright © 1984 by Deutsche Verlag-Anstalt GmbH, Stuttgart. Reprinted by permission of Basic Books, a member of Perseus Books, L.L.C. **Figure 5:** Reprinted with permission from H. P. Roffwarg, J. N. Munzio and W. C. Dement, "Ontogenic Development of the Human Sleep-Dream Cycle," *Science,* 152, p. 604–619. Copyright © 1996 American Association for the Advancement of Science. **Figure 6:** Used with the permission of G. William Domhof, Dreamresearch.net. **Figure 10:** Used with permission of Rockefeller University.

Module 15: Figure 1: From *The Relaxation Response* by Herbert Benson, M.D., with Miriam Z. Klipper. Copyright © 1975 by William Morrow & Company, Inc. Reprinted by permission of Harper-Collins Publishers.

Module 16: Figure 1: Monitoring the Future Study 2005. University of Michigan, Ann Arbor. **Figure 2:** From *Human Biology*, 6th edition, by S. Mader, page 250. Copyright © 2000 by The McGraw-Hill Companies. **Figure 3:** Copyright © 1991 by The New York Times Co. Reprinted by permission. **Figure 5:** Gawin, F. H., & Kleber, H. D. (Mar 29, 1991). Cocaine abstinence phases. *Science.* Copyright © 1991 American Association for the Advancement of Science. **Figure 6:** Adapted from Wechsler, H., et al. (2003). College binge drinking in the 1990s: a continuing problem: results of the Harvard School f Public Health 1999 College Health alcohol Study. Reprinted with permission of Henry Wechsler. **Figure 8:** Monitoring the Future Study 2005. University of Michigan, Ann Arbor.

Chapter 6

Module 19: Figure 1: E. C. Tolman & C.H. Honzik (1930). Introduction and removal of reward and maze performance in rats. *University of California Publications in Psychology, 4,* 257–275. **Figure 2:** From Anderson, J. A., & Adams, M. (1992). Acknowledging the learning styles of diverse student populations: Implications for instructional design. *New Directions for Teaching and Learning, 49,* 19–33. © Copyright 1992 Jossey Bass Publications.

Chapter 7

Module 20: Figure 2: Figure from "Human Memory: A Proposed System and Its Control Processes," by R. C. Atkinson and R. M. Shiffrin, from *The Psychology of Learning and Motivation: Advances in Research and Theory,* Volume 2, edited by K. W. Spence and J. T. Spence, copyright © 1968. Reprinted with permission from Elsevier. **Figure 3:** From "Perception and Memory Versus Thought: Some Old Ideas and Recent Findings," by A. D. deGroot in *Problem Solving: Research, Method & Theory,* by B. Kleinmuntz (ed.). Copyright © 1966 John Wiley & Sons, Inc. Reprinted by permission of John Wiley & Sons, Inc. **Figure 4:** From Gathercole, S. E., & Baddeley, A. D. (1993). *Working memory and language processing.* Hillsdale, NJ: Erlbaum. **Figure 6:** Adapted from Collins, A. M., & Loftus, E. F. (1975). A spreading-activation theory of semantic processing. *Psychological Review, 82,* 407-428. Copyright © 1975 American Psychological Association. Adapted with permission. **Figure 7:** From *Human Anatomy*, 5th edition, by K. Van De Graaff, p 339. Copyright © 2000 by The McGraw-Hill Companies.

Module 21: Figure 3: From D. C. Rubin "The subtle deceiver recalling," *Psychology Today,* September 1995. Reprinted with per-mission from *Psychology Today* Magazine. Copyright 1995 Sussex Publishers, Inc. **Figure 4:** From Loftus, E. F., & Palmer, J. C. (1974). Reconstruction of automobile destruction: An example of the interface between language and memory. *Journal of Verbal Learning and Verbal Behavior, 13,* 585–589, copyright © 1974 by Academic Press, reproduced by permission of the publisher. **Figure 5:** From H. P. Bahrick, L. K. Hall & S. A. Berger, "Accuracy and distortion in memory for high school grades," *Psychological Science,* Volume 7, 265–269. Reprinted with permission of Blackwell Publishers.

Module 22: Figure 1: From J. E. Williams and D. L. Best, Measuring sex stereotypes: A multinational study. Copyright © 1990 by Sage Publications. Reprinted by permission of Sage Publications. **Figure 3:** Figure from R. S. Nickerson, & M. J. Adams, *Cognitive Psychology,* Volume 11, pg. 297. Copyright © 1979 by Academic Press, used by permission of the publisher. **Figure 5:** Used with the permission of Dr. Paul Thompson, UCLA Laboratory of Neural Imaging.

Chapter 8

Module 23: Figure 1: Reprinted with permission from R. Shepard and J. Metzler, "Mental Rotation of Three Dimensional Objects," *Science,* 171 701–703. Copyright 1971 American Association for the Advancement of Science. **Figure 2:** Republished with permission of American Physiological Society, from *Journal of Neurophysiology,* by Alvaro Pascual-Leone, September 1995; permission conveyed through Copyright Clearance Center. **Figure 3:** From "Family Resemblances: Studies in the Internal Structure of Categories," by E. Rosch and C. Mervis in *Cognitive Psychology,* Volume 7, 573–605, copyright © 1975 by Academic Press, reproduced by permission of the publisher.

Module 24: Figure 3: From Bourne, L. E., Dominowski, E. F., & Healy, A. F. (1986). *Cognitive processes* (2nd ed.). Englewood Cliffs, NJ: Prentice-Hall. Adapted with permission. **Figure 5:** Reprinted with permission of Barry F. Anderson.

Module 25: Figure 1: Courtesy of Drs. Betty Hart and Todd Risley. **Figure 2:** Used with permission of the Modern Language Association, www.mla.org. **Figure 3:** Used with the permission of *Nature,* Copyright © 1997, http://www.nature.com/nature/.

Chapter 9

Module 26: Figure 1: From *Intelligence Reframed: Multiple perspectives for the 21st Century* by Howard Gardner. Copyright © 1999 by Howard Gardner. Reprinted by permission of Basic Books, a member of Perseus Books, L.L.C. **Figure 3:** Reprinted with permission from R. Sternberg, The Holy Grail of general intelligence. *Science, 289,* p. 389.

Copyright 2000 American Association for the Advancement of Science. **Figure 6:** Simulated items similar to those in Wechsler Intelligence scale for Children. Fourth Edition. Copyright © 2003, and Wechsler Intelligence Scale © 1997-Third Edition by Harcourt Assessment, Inc. Reproduced with permission. All rights reserved. **Figure 7:** Copyright © 1994 by The New York Times. Reprinted by permission.

Module 28: Figure 1: Adapted from Familial studies of intelligence: A review, by T. J. Bouchard and M. McGue, *Science,* 212, 1981, pp. 1055–1059. **Figure 2:** Reprinted with permission of Dmitry Schildovsky.

Module 29: Figure 2: From M. Zuckerman, The search for high sensation, *Psychology Today,* February 1978. Reprinted with permission of *Psychology Today* Magazine. Copyright © 1978, Sussex Publishers, Inc. **Figure 3:** *Motivation and Personality,* by A. Maslow, © 1998 Reprinted by Permission of Prentice Hall, Inc. Upper Saddle River, NJ.

Module 30: Figure 2: From *Anatomy & Physiology,* 5th edition, by R. Seeley, T. Stephens, and P. Tate, p. 384. Copyright © 2000 by The McGraw-Hill Companies. **Figure 3:** From *Time* Magazine, July 22, 1997. Copyright © 1997 Time Inc. Reprinted by permission.

Chapter 10

Module 31: Figure 1: K. W. Fischer, P. R. Shaver, and P. Carnochan, How emotions develop and how they organize development, *Cognition and Emotion,* 1990. Reprinted by permission of Psychology Press Limited, Hove, UK. **Figure 3:** M. S. George et al., Brain activity during transient sadness and happiness in healthy women. *American Journal of Psychiatry,* 152: 341–351, 1995 © 1995, The American Psychiatric Association.

Chapter 11

Module 33: Figure 2: U.S. Bureau of Labor Statistics. **Figure 3:** Hostile Hallways: The AAUW survey on sexual harassment in American Schools. 2001. Reprinted with permission of the American Association of University Women Educational Foundation. **Figure 4:** From Dey, E .L., Astin, A. W., Korn, W. S., & Berz, E. R. (2004). *The American Freshman: National Norms for Fall, 2004.* Reprinted with permission of Higher Education Research Institute. **Figure 5:** Republished with permission of *The Wall Street Journal* from February 14, 2000. Permission conveyed through the Copyright Clearance Center.

Module 34: Figure 2: Republished with permission of Society for the Scientific Study of Sexuality, from *Journal of Sex Research,* D. Sue, Erotic fantasies of college students during coitus, 1979. Permission conveyed through Copyright Clearance Center. **Figure 3:** E. E. Vance & N. W. Wagner, Written descriptions of orgasm: A study of sex differences, *Archives* *of Sexual Behavior, 6,* 1976, 87–98. Reprinted with permission of Kluwer Academic/Plenum Publishers. **Figure 4:** W. H. Masters & V. E. Johnson, 1966, *Human sexual response.* Boston: Little, Brown.

Module 35: Figure 1: Republished with permission of Society for the Scientific Study of Sexuality, from *Journal of Sex Research,* I. Arafat & W. L. Cotton, Masturbation practices of males and females, 1974. Permission conveyed through Copyright Clearance Center. **Figure 2:** Source: © 1972-1998 The Gallup Organization. All rights reserved. Reprinted with permission from www.gallup.com. **Figure 3:** From M. Clements, Making love, how old, how often. *Parade Magazine,* August 7, 1994. p. 5. **Figure 4:** From Kinsey, Pomeroy and Martin, *Sexual Behavior in the Male,* 1948. Reprinted with permission of W. B. Saunders Company.

Module 36: Figure 1: Used with permission of Dr. David Finkelhor, Director, Crimes Against Children Research Center, University of New Hampshire. **Figure 3:** Statistics from the United Nations Aids Program.

Chapter 12

Module 39: Figure 1: Reproduced with permission from *Pediatrics,* Vol. 89, Pages 91–97, 1992. **Figure 3:** National Center for Health Statistics, 2000. Boys and Girls stature for age and weight for age percentiles. Washington, DC. **Figure 4:** Figure adapted from W. J. Robbins, 1929, *Growth,* New Haven, CT: Yale University Press. Copyright Yale University Press. **Figure 6:** Used with the permission of Dr. Carol Tomlinson-Keasey. **Figure 10:** From Judith A. Schickendanz, et al. *Understanding Children and Adolescents,* 4th edition. © 2001 by Allyn & Bacon. Used with permission. **Figure 11:** Adapted from F. N. Dempster. Memory span: Sources for individual and developmental differences. *Psychological Bulletin, 89,* 63–100. Copyright © 1981 by the American Psychological Association. Adapted by permission.

Module 40: Figure 1: Reprinted from *Education and Physical Growth,* Tanner. Copyright © 1978 by International Universities Press. **Figure 2:** Used with the permission of David A. Goslin. **Figure 4:** K. E. Boehm and N. B. Campbell, Suicide: A review of calls to an adolescent peer listing phone service, *Child Psychiatry and Human Development,* 1996, 26, 61–66. Reprinted with permission of Kluwer Academic/Plenum Publishers.

Module 41: Figure 1: Statistical Office of the European Communities. **Figure 2:** U.S. Bureau of the Census. Census Population Survey, 2000. **Figure 3:** From K. W. Schaie, The course of adult intellectual development, *American Psychologist,* 49, 304–313. Copyright © 1994 by the American Psychological Association. Reprinted with permission.

Chapter 13

Module 43: Figure 1: Data derived from Cattell, Eber and Tatsuoka: *Handbook for the 16PF,* Copyright © 1970, 1988, 1992 by the Institute for Personality and Ability Testing, Inc., Champaign, Illinois, USA. All rights reserved. **Figure 2:** From H. J. Eysenck, Biological dimensions of personality. In L. A. Pervin (ed.), *Handbook of Personality: Theory & Research,* 1990, p. 246. Reprinted with permission of Guilford Press. **Figure 3:** From L. A. Pervin (ed.), *Handbook of Personality: Theory & Research,* 1990, Reprinted with permission of Guilford Press. **Figure 5:** From A. Tellegen, D. T. Lykken, T. J. Bouchard, Jr., K. J. Wilcox, N. L. Segal, & S. Rich. Personality similarity in twins reared apart and together, *Journal of Personality and Social Psychology, 54,* 1031–1039. Copyright © 1988 by the American Psychological Association. Reprinted with permission.

Module 44: Figure 1: From Scheier, M. F., Carver, C. S., & Bridges, M. W. (1994). Distinguishing optimism from neuroticism (and trait anxiety, self-mastery, and self-esteem): A revision of the Life Orientation Test. *Journal of Personality and Social Psychology, 67,* 1063–1078. Copyright © 1994 by the American Psychological Association. Adapted with permission. **Figure 2:** Based on R. P. Halgin & S. K. Whitbourne, 1994, *Abnormal Psychology,* Fort Worth, TX: Harcourt Brace, and *Minnesota Multiphasic Personality Inventory, 2,* University of Minnesota.

Chapter 14

Module 45: Figure 1: Source: Susser, E.S., Herman, D. B., & Aaron, B. (2002, August). Combating the terror of terrorism. Pg. 74. *Scientific American,* 70-77. Used with the permission of Cleo Vilett. **Figure 2 (Hassles):** Reprinted with permission form Chamberlain, K., & Zika, S. (1990). The minor events approach to stress: Support for the use of daily hassles. *British Journal of Psychology,* 81, 469-481. ©British Psychological Society. **Figure 2 (Uplifts):** From Comparison of two modes of stress measurement: Daily hassles and uplifts versus major life events. *Journal of Behavioral Medicine, 4,* 14, by A.D., Kanner, J. C. Coyne, C. Schaefer, & R. Lazarus. 1981, New York, Plenum. Copyright 1976 by Kluwer Academic/Plenum. **Figure 3:** Adapted from Cohen S., Kamarck, T., & Mermelstein, R. (1983). A global measure of perceived stress. *Journal of Health and Social Behavior,* 24, 385-396. **Figure 4:** From *The Stress of Life,* by H. Selye. Copyright © 1976 by The McGraw-Hill Companies.

Module 46: Figure 1: Adapted from Jenkins, C. D., Zyanski, S. J., & Rosenman, R.H. (1979). Coronary-prone behavior: One patter or several? *Psychosomatic Medicine,* 40, 25-43. **Figure 2:** Reprinted with permission from

Elsevier. Pettingale, K. W., Morris, T., Greer, S., & Haybittle, J. L. (1985). Mental attitudes to cancer: An additional prognostic factor. *Lancet,* 750. **Figure 4:** Monitoring the Future Study 2005. University of Michigan, Ann Arbor.

Module 47: Figure 1: Copyright © 1988 by The New York Times. Reprinted by Permission. **Figure 2:** Drawn from *Social Indicators of Well-Being: Americans' Perceptions of Life Quality* (p. 207 and p. 306), by F. M. Andrews and S. B. Withey, 1976, New York, Plenum. Copyright 1976 by Kluwer Academic/Plenum.

Chapter 15

Module 49: Figure 2: From *Anxiety Disorders and Phobias: A Cognitive Perspective* by Aaron T. Beck and Gary Emery, with Rith L. Greenberg. Copyright © by Aaron T. Beck, MD & Gary Emery, PhD. Reprinted with permission of Basic Books, a member of Perseus Books, L.L.C. **Figure 4:** Personal communication with W. Hill. 1992. Public Affairs Network Coordinator for the American Psychiatric Association. **Figure 5:** Copyright © 1993 By The New York Times Co. Reprinted by permission. **Figure 7:** Adapted with permission from Weissman, M.W., & Olfson, M. Depression in women: Implications for health care research. *Science,* 269. 799-801. Copyright 1995 AAAS. **Figure 10:** From *Schizophrenia Genesis* by Irving I. Gottesman © 1991 by Irving I. Gottesman. Used with permission of Henry Holt and Company. **Figure 11:** Reprinted with permission of Dr. Nancy C. Andreasen, University of Iowa Hospitals and Clinics.

Module 50: Figure 1: From Benton, S. A., et al. (2003). Changes in counseling center client problems across 13 years. *Professional Psychology: Research and Practice,* 34, 66–72. Copyright © 2003 by the American Psychological Association. Adapted with permission. **Figure 2:** The WHO World Mental Health Survey Consortium, 2004, Figure #3.

Chapter 16

Module 51: Figure 2: Reprinted by permission of Dr. Herbert Benson, Beth Israel Deaconess Medical Center, Boston, MA.

Module 52: Figure 1: Smith, Mary, Lee, Gene V. Glass, and Thomas I. Miller. *The Benefits of Psychotherapy,* pp. 89, Table 5-1. © 1980 (Copyright holder). Adapted with permission of The Johns Hopkins University Press. **Figure 2:** Mental Health: Does Therapy Help? © 1995 by Consumers Union of U.S., Inc., Yonkers, NY 10703–1057, a nonprofit organization. Reprinted with permission from the November 1995 issue of CONSUMER REPORTS® for educational purposes only. No commercial use or photocopying/transmitting permitted. To subscribe, call 1 800-234-1645 or log on to www.ConsumerReports.org.

Module 53: Figure 2: From Antidepressants: Choices and Controversy. Health News, June 2000. Content © 2000 Massachusetts Medical Society. Published by Englander Communications LLC, an affiliate of Belvoir Publications, Inc. **Figure 3:** From National Mental Health Information Center, U.S. Dept. of Health and Human Services, 2002. **Figure 4:** From Howard, A., Pion, G. M., Gottfredson, G. D., Flattau, P. E., Oskamp, S., Pfafflin, S. M., Bray, D. W., & Burstein, A.. D. (1986). The changing face of American psychology: A report from the committee on employment and human resources. *American Psychologist, 41,* 1311–1327. Copyright © 1986 by the American Psychological Association. Adapted with permission.

Chapter 17

Module 54: Figure 2: Adapted from Cacioppo, Bernston, & Crites, "Social Neurscience: Principles of psychophysiological arousal and response. In E. T. Higgins & A. W. Kruglanski (Eds.), *Social Psychology: Handbook of Basic Principles,* 1996 Guilford Press. **Figure 4:** Adapted from Anderson, C. A., Krull, D. S., & Weiner, B. (1996). Explanations: Processes and consequences. In E. T. Higgins & A. W. Kruglanski (Eds.), *Social Psychology: Handbook of basic principles* (pp. 271–296). NY: Guilford Press. (The figure is adapted from the one shown on pg. 274.)

Module 57: Figure 1: Reprinted with permission from *Psychology Today Magazine,* Copyright © (1985) Sussex Publishers, Inc. **Figure 2:** From Sternberg, R. J. (1986). Triangular theory of love. *Psychological Review, 93,* 119–135. Copyright © 1986 by the American Psychological Association. Adapted with permission. **Figure 3:** From D. M. Buss, International preferences in selecting mates: A study of 37 cultures, *Journal of Cross-Cultural Psychology, 21,* pp. 5–47. Copyright © 1990 by Sage Publications. Reprinted by permission of Sage Publications, Inc. **Figure 4:** From Benjamin, L. T., Jr. (1985, February). Defining aggression: An exercise for classroom discussion. *Teaching of Psychology, 12.* Copyright © 1985 Lawrence Erlbaum Associates. **Figure 5:** *The unresponsive bystander: Why doesn't he help?* By B. Latané & J.M. Darley ©1970 Reprinted by Permission of Pearson Education, Inc. Upper Saddle River, NJ.

Photos

Contents

Photos are credited as the first image of each chapter below.

Chapter 1

Opener: ©Jon Riley/Getty Images; **p. 3 (top):** ©Jeff Greenberg/Photo Researchers; **p. 3 (center):** ©Bettmann/Corbis Images; **p. 4 (top):** ©AP/Wide World Photos; **p. 4 (center):** ©Jon Riley/Getty Images; **p. 6:** ©Laura Dwight/Photo Edit; **p. 7 (bottom):** ©Zigy Kaluzny/Getty Images; **p. 7 (center):** ©Chuck Keeler/Getty Images; **p. 7 (top):** ©Jeff Greenberg/Photo Researchers; **p. 15:** ©Bettmann/Corbis Images; **p. 16 (center left):** ©Photo Researchers; **p. 16 (top left):** ©Corbis Images; **p. 16 (center):** ©The Granger Collection; **p. 16 (top right):** Courtesy, Wellesley College Archives. Photographed by Notman; **p. 16 (center right):** ©Bettmann/Corbis Images; **p. 17 (center right):** Courtesy, Elizabeth Loftus; **p. 17 (top left):** ©Culver Pictures; **p. 17 (top right, center):** ©The Granger Collection; **p. 19:** Bettmann/Corbis Images; **p. 21:** ©AP/Wide World Photos; **p. 25 (bottom left):** ©Richard T. Nowitz/National Geographic Image Collection; **p. 25 (bottom right):** ©Frank Herholdt/Getty Images; **p. 29:** ©Jon Riley/Getty Images

Chapter 2

Opener: ©Bob Daemmrich/Image Works; **p. 31 (top):** ©Spencer Grant/PhotoEdit; **p. 31 (center):** ©Tom Stewart/Corbis Images; **p. 31 (bottom):** ©Douglas Faulkner/Photo Researchers; **p. 32:** ©Bob Daemmrich/Image Works; **p. 38:** ©Robert I. M. Campbell/National Geographic Image Collection; **p. 42:** ©Bill Aron/Photo Edit; **p. 43:** ©James Wilson/Woodfin Camp; **p. 46 (top):** ©Spencer Grant/PhotoEdit; **p. 46 (center):** ©Jonathan Nourok/PhotoEdit; **p. 50:** ©Tom Stewart/Corbis Images; **p. 51:** ©Douglas Faulkner/Photo Researchers; **p. 55:** ©Bob Daemmrich/Image Works

Chapter 3

Opener: ©Alexander Tsiaras/Stock Boston; **p. 59 (top):** ©Dennis Kunkel/Visuals Unlimited; **p. 59 (bottom):** ©Martin Rotker/Photo Researchers; **p. 60 (top):** ©Sam Kittner; **p. 60 (center):** ©Alexander Tsiaras/Stock Boston; **p. 62:** ©Dennis Kunkel/Visuals Unlimited; **p. 67 (top, center):** ©Moonrunner Design Ltd.; **p. 67 (bottom):** ©AP/Wide World Photos; **p. 75:** ©Jonathan Ferrey/Getty Images; **p. 77:** ©Martin Rotker/Photo Researchers; **p. 78 (top left):** ©SPL/Photo Researchers; **p. 78 (center):** ©Bryan Christie Design; **p. 78 (center left):** ©Volker Steger/Peter Arnold; **p. 78 (center right):** ©Roger Ressmeyer/Corbis Images; **p. 79:** Photo courtesy of Dr. Raja Parasuraman, George Mason University; **p. 80:** ©AP/Wide World Photos; **p. 84:** Courtesy, Trustees of the British Museum, Natural History; **p. 85:** From: Damasio H., Grabowski, T., Frank R., Galaburda A.M., Damasio A.R.: The return of Phineas Gage: Clues about the brain from the skull of a famous patient. *Science,* 264:1102–1105, 1994. Department of Neurology and Image Analysis Facility, University of Iowa.; **p. 89:** Rossell S.L., Bullmore E.T., Williams S.C., David A.S. Sex differences in functional brain activation during a lexical visual field task. *Brain and Language,* 2002 Jan: 80(1):97–105. Fig. 1.; **p. 93:** ©Alexander Tsiaras/Stock Boston

Chapter 4

Opener: ©Martine Mouchy/Getty Images; **p. 97 (top):** ©Curtis Myers/Stock Connection/PictureQuest; **p. 97 (center):** ©Joe Epstein/Design Conceptions; **p. 97 (bottom):** ©Digital Vision; **p. 98:** ©Martine Mouchy/Getty Images; **p. 100:** ©Curtis Myers/Stock Connection/Picturequest; **p. 104 (both):** ©Biophoto Associates/Photo Researchers; **p. 109 (a–c):** ©Joe Epstein/Design Conceptions; **p. 114:** ©VideoSurgery/Photo Researchers; **p. 115:** ©John Clark; **p. 116:** ©NASA; **p. 117:** ©Kimberly Butler/Time & Life Pictures/Getty Images; **p. 119 (top):** ©NASA; **p. 119 (bottom):** ©Prof. P. Motta/Dept. of Anatomy/University "La Sapienza," Rome/SPL/Photo Researchers; **p. 120:** ©Omikron/Photo Researchers; **p. 123:** ©Lisa M. McGeady/Corbis Images; **p. 130 (both):** Courtesy, Bela Julesz; **p. 132:** ©Cary Wolinsky/Stock Boston; **p. 134:** ©Jeff Greenberg/Stock Boston; **p. 135:** ©John G. Ross/Photo Researchers; **p. 136 (both):** ©Innervisions; **p. 138:** ©AP/HO/Wide World Photos; **p. 141:** ©Martine Mouchy/Getty Images

Chapter 5

Opener: ©Nicholas Devore III/Network Aspen; **p. 145 (top):** ©Jose Carrillo/Stock Boston; **p. 145 (center):** ©AP, Midland Daily News/AP/Wide World Photos; **p. 145 (bottom):** ©Bob Daemmrich/Stock Boston; **p. 146:** ©Nicholas Devore III/Still Media; **p. 149 (all):** ©Ted Spagna/Photo Researchers; **p. 152:** ©PhotoDisc/Getty Images; **p. 157:** ©Jose Carrillo/Stock Boston; **p. 162:** ©AP, Midland Daily News/Wide World Photos; **p. 167:** ©Suzanne Opton; **p. 170:** Thompson, P.M.: Structural abnormalities in the brains of human subjects who use methamphetamine. J. Neurosci. 2004 Jun 30;24(26):6028–36. Fig. 1d, p. 6031. Photo courtesy, Paul Thompson, UCLA Laboratory of Neuroimaging; **p. 172 (left):** ©Bob Daemmrich/Stock Boston; **p. 172 (right):** ©IT Int'l/eStock Photography/PictureQuest; **p. 175:** ©Lawrence Migdale/Stock Boston; **p. 176:** ©Kal Muller/Woodfin Camp; **p. 179:** ©Nicholas Devore III/Still Media

Chapter 6

Opener: ©Joanna B. Penneo/Aurora Photos; **p. 181 (top):** ©PhotoDisc; **p. 181 (bottom):** ©Spencer Grant/Stock Boston; **p. 182:** ©Joanna B. Penneo/Aurora Photos; **p. 184:** ©Culver Pictures; **p. 186:** PhotoDisc/Getty Images; **p. 189 (both):** ©Stuart Ellins; **p. 192:** ©Nina Leen/Time Life Pictures/Getty Images; **p. 195 (top left):** ©PhotoDisc/Getty Images; **p. 195 (top right):** ©Corbis Images; **p. 195 (bottom left):** ©Banana Stock/Alamy; **p. 195 (bottom right):** ©Amy Etra/PhotoEdit; **p. 200:** Courtesy, Dr. Marian Bailey; **p. 201:** ©Sylvain Piraux; **p. 202 (left):** ©Michael Newman/PhotoEdit; **p. 202 (right):** ©Robin Nelson/PhotoEdit; **p. 209 (top):** Courtesy, Albert Bandura; **p. 209**

(bottom): ©Spencer Grant/Stock Boston; **p. 210 (both):** From Meltzhoff, A. N. (1988). Imitation of Televised Models by Infants. Child Development, 59, 1221–1229. Photo Courtesy of A. N. Meltzhoff & M. Hanak.; **p. 211:** ©Design Pics Inc./Alamy; **p. 213:** ©Joanna B. Penneo/Aurora/Aurora Photos

Chapter 7

Opener: ©Steve Raymer/Corbis Images; **p. 217 (top):** ©Dr. Steven E. Peterson/Washington University. From *Scientific American*, 12/93. **p. 217 (center):** ©Disney Enterprises, Inc; **p. 218 (top):** ©Nathanael Rehlander/LM Photography; **p. 218 (center):** ©Steve Raymer/Corbis Images; **p. 220:** ©Bob Wallace/Stock Boston; **p. 225 (top):** PhotoDisc/Getty Images; **p. 225 (bottom):** ©Susan Werner/PictureQuest; **p. 228:** ©Dr. Steven E. Peterson/Washington University. From *Scientific American*, 12/93; **p. 229:** ©Gary Conner/PhotoEdit; **p. 231:** ©Disney Enterprises, Inc; **p. 237:** ©Shahn Kermani; **p. 239:** ©Joseph Nettis/Photo Researchers; **p. 245:** Paul Thompson, UCLA Laboratory of Neuroimaging, 2003; **p. 249:** ©Steve Raymer/Corbis Images

Chapter 8

Opener: ©Dwayne Newton/Photo Edit; **p. 251 (top):** ©AP/Wide World Photos; **p. 251 (center):** ©Roberto Otero/Black Star; **p. 252 (top):** ©Getty Images; **p. 252 (center):** ©Dwayne Newton/PhotoEdit; **p. 254:** ©AP/Wide World Photos; **p. 255:** ©Pascual-Leone et al., 1995; **p. 256 (left):** ©Greg Girard/Contact Press Images/PictureQuest; **p. 256 (center):** ©Tom McHugh/Photo Researchers; **p. 256 (right):** ©Stephen Studd/Getty Images; **p. 265 (left):** PhotoDisc; **p. 265 (right):** Stockbyte; **p. 267 (all):** ©Superstock; **p. 271:** ©Roberto Otero/Black Star; **p. 273:** ©Bob Schatz/Stockschatz; **p. 276:** Courtesy, Dr. Laura Ann Petitto @1991/photo by Robert LaMarche; **p. 278:** ©AP/Wide World Photos; **p. 281:** Courtesy, The Language Research Center, Georgia State University; **p. 283:** From Kim, K.H., Relkin, N.R., Lee, K.M., Hirsch J. Distinct cortical areas associated with native and second languages. Nature 388, p. 171: Figs. 1, 5 (1997); **p. 285:** ©Dwayne Newton/PhotoEdit

Chapter 9

Opener: ©AP/Wide World Photos; **p. 287 (top):** ©Getty Images; **p. 287 (bottom):** ©Design Pics Inc./Alamy; **p. 288 (top left):** ©AP/The Citizens Voice/Wide World Photos; **p. 288 (center, right):** ©AP/Wide World Photos; **p. 289:** ©David Hiser/Network Aspen; **p. 290:** ©Bob Daemmrich/Image Works; **p. 293:** From Duncan, J., et al. July 21, 2000. "A neural basis for general intelligence." Science 289: 459. ©2000 American Association for the Advancement of Science. Photo courtesy John Duncan; **p. 297:** ©Roger Viollet/Getty Images; **p. 298:** ©M. Siluk/Image Works; **p. 302:** ©2001

Kaplan, Inc. Photo: eStock Photography/Leo de Wys; **p. 315:** ©Corbis; **p. 317:** ©AP/Wide World Photos; **p. 292 (1):** ©Getty Images; **p. 292 (2, 4, 6):** ©Bettmann/Corbis Images; **p. 292 (3):** ©Cold Spring Harbor Laboratory; **p. 292 (5):** ©David Hiser/Photographers/Aspen/Network Aspen; **p. 292 (7):** ©George C. Beresford/Getty Images; **p. 292 (8):** PhotoDisc/Getty Images

Chapter 10

Opener: ©Michael Schwarz; **p. 319 (top):** ©PhotoDisc; **p. 319 (center):** ©Donald G. Dutton; **p. 319 (bottom):** Matsumoto & Ekman, 1988; **p. 320 (top):** ©AP/Wide World Photos; **p. 320 (center):** ©Michael Schwarz; **p. 327 (top left, center):** ©Digital Vision; **p. 327 (top right, bottom left):** ©PhotoDisc/Getty Images; **p. 327 (bottom right):** ©Image 100; **p. 331:** ©PhotoDisc/Getty Images; **p. 333:** ©Ed Quinn/Corbis Images; **p. 336:** Reprinted by permission of the publishers from Henry A. Murray, THEMATIC APPERCEPTION TEST, Plate 12F, Cambridge, Mass.: Harvard University Press, Copyright ©1943 by the Presidents and Fellows of Harvard College, ©1971 by Henry A. Murray; **p. 343:** ©Eric Fowke/PhotoEdit; **p. 344 (top):** ©Donald G. Dutton; **p. 344 (bottom):** George, M.S., et al. "Brain activity during transient sadness and happiness in healthy women." American Journal of Psychiatry, 152:341-351, 1995. ©1995, The American Psychiatric Association. Reprinted by permission.; **p. 345:** ©Art Resource, NYC; **p. 350 (all):** Matsumoto & Ekman, 1988; **p. 351 (all):** From "Smiles when Lying." Ekman, Friesen, & O'Sullivan, 1988; **p. 353:** ©Michael Schwarz

Chapter 11

Opener: ©Esbin-Anderson/Photo Network/PictureQuest; **p. 355 (top):** ©Bob Daemmrich/Stock Boston/PictureQuest; **p. 355 (center):** ©Everett Collection; **p. 355 (bottom):** ©AP/Wide World Photos; **p. 356:** ©Esbin-Anderson/Photo Network/PictureQuest; **p. 357:** ©Pete Winkel/Focus Group/PictureQuest; **p. 360:** ©Bob Daemmrich/Stock Boston; **p. 362:** ©Ellis Herwig/Stock Boston/PictureQuest; **p. 365 (left):** ©Bob Daemmrich/Stock Boston/PictureQuest; **p. 365 (right):** ©David Young-Wolff/PhotoEdit; **p. 366:** ©David Young-Wolff/Photo Edit; **p. 367 (left):** ©Laura Dwight/Stock Connection/PictureQuest; **p. 367 (right):** ©Mark Gibson/Photo 20-20; **p. 373:** ©Everett Collection; **p. 374:** Hamann, S., Herman, R. A., Nolan, C. L., Wallen, K. Men and women differ in amygdala response to visual sexual stimuli. *Nature Neuroscience*, 7, 2004, p. 413, Figures 2E, 2F. Image courtesy of Stephan Hamann; **p. 377 (left):** ©Blue Lantern Studio/Corbis Images; **p. 377 (right):** ©Michael Newman/PhotoEdit; **p. 378:** ©AP/Wide World Photos; **p. 383:** ©Rachel Epstein/Image Works; **p. 395:** ©Esbin-Anderson/Photo Network/PictureQuest

Chapter 12

Opener: ©Look GMBH/eStock Photography/PictureQuest; **p. 397 (top):** ©Lennart Nilsson/Albert Bonniers Forlag AB/A Child is Born/Dell Publishing; **p. 397 (center left):** ©Laura Dwight/Peter Arnold; **p. 397 (center right):** ©Danny Lehman/Corbis Images; **p. 397 (bottom right):** ©Deborah Davis/PhotoEdit; **p. 398 (top):** ©AP/Wide World Photos; **p. 398 (center):** ©Look GMBH/eStock Photography/PictureQuest; **p. 399:** ©Peter Byron; **p. 403 (a):** ©D.W. Fawcett/Photo Researchers; **p. 403 (b):** ©L. Willatt, East Anglian Regional Genetics Service/SPL/Photo Researchers; **p. 403 (c):** ©Kenneth Eward/Photo Researchers; **p. 403 (d):** ©Biophoto Associates/Science Source/Photo Researchers; **p. 406 (left):** ©Lennart Nilsson/Albert Bonniers Forlag AB/A Child is Born/Dell Publishing; **p. 406 (right):** ©Petit Format/Science Source/Photo Researchers; **p. 411:** ©Charles Gupton/Stock Boston; **p. 413 (all):** From: A.N. Meltzoff & M.K. Moore. 1977. "Imitation of facial and manual gestures by human neonates." *Science*, 198: 75-78. ©1977 American Association for the Advancement of Science; **p. 416:** Harlow Primate Laboratory, University of Wisconsin; **p. 417:** ©Michael Philip Manheim/Photo Network/PictureQuest; **p. 419:** ©FotoKIA/Index Stock Imagery; **p. 422:** ©Farrell Grehan/Corbis Images; **p. 423:** ©Laura Dwight/Peter Arnold; **p. 430:** ©Danny Lehman/Corbis Images; **p. 432:** ©David Young Wolff/Getty Images; **p. 433:** ©Olive Pierce/Black Star; **p. 435:** ©AP/Wide World Photos; **p. 436:** ©Mary Kate Denny/PhotoEdit; **p. 440:** ©Don Mason/Corbis Images; **p. 445:** ©Deborah Davis/PhotoEdit; **p. 446:** ©Bob Daemmrich/Stock Boston/PictureQuest; **p. 449:** ©Look GMBH/eStock Photography/PictureQuest

Chapter 13

Opener: ©Jill Sabella/Getty Images; **p. 451 (top):** ©Guy Gillette/Photo Researchers; **p. 451 (center):** ©Meritt Vincent/Photo Edit; **p. 452:** ©Jill Sabella/Getty Images; **p. 455 (top):** ©SW Production/Index Stock Imagery; **p. 455 (bottom):** ©Bettmann/Corbis Images; **p. 456:** ©Guy Gillette/Photo Researchers; **p. 457:** ©Andy Sacks/Getty Images; **p. 459 (left):** ©20th Century Fox/The Kobal Collection/Hayes, Kerry 459 (right):** ©20th Century Fox/Everett Collection; **p. 460:** ©Bettmann/Corbis Images; **p. 467:** ©AP/Wide World Photos; **p. 469:** ©Ronnie Kaufman/Corbis Images; **p. 471:** ©Michael Newman/PhotoEdit; **p. 481:** ©Laura Dwight/Corbis Images; **p. 483:** ©Jill Sabella/Getty Images

Chapter 14

Opener: ©Orbit/Masterfile; **p. 485 (top):** ©James Schaffer/PhotoEdit; **p. 485 (center):** ©Reza/Webistan/Corbis Images; **p. 485 (bottom):** ©Jose Luis Pelaez/Corbis Images; **p. 486:** ©Orbit/Masterfile; **p. 488:** ©James Schaffer/PhotoEdit; **p. 491:** ©Corbis Digital Stock; **p. 494:** ©Dr. David Phillips/Visuals Unlimited;

Name Index

Subject Index